W9-BYD-475

The GALE ENCYCLOPEDIA *of* MENTAL DISORDERS

The GALE ENCYCLOPEDIA of MENTAL DISORDERS

VOLUME

2

M-Z

ELLEN THACKERY AND MADELINE HARRIS, EDITORS

Detroit • New York • San Diego • San Francisco • Cleveland • New Haven, Conn. • Waterville, Maine • London • Munich

The Gale Encyclopedia of Mental Disorders

Project Editor
Ellen Thackery

Editorial
Deirdre S. Blanchfield, Madeline Harris, Kate Kretschmann, Brigham Narins, Mark Springer

Editorial Systems Support
Andrea Lopeman

Permissions
Margaret Chamberlain

Imaging and Multimedia
Robert Duncan, Mary Grimes, Lezlie Light, Dan Newell, David Oblender, Christine O'Bryan, Kelly A. Quin

Product Design
Michelle DiMercurio, Tracey Rowens

Manufacturing
Evi Seoud

Indexing
Synapse, the Knowledge Link Corporation

©2003 by Gale. Gale is an imprint of the Gale Group, Inc., a division of Thomson Learning, Inc.

Gale and Design ™ and Thomson Learning™ are trademarks used herein under license.

For more information, contact
The Gale Group, Inc.
27500 Drake Road
Farmington Hills, MI 48331-3535
Or visit our Internet site at
http://www.gale.com

ALL RIGHTS RESERVED
No part of this work covered by the copyright hereon may be reproduced or used in any form or by any means—graphic, electronic, or mechanical, including photocopying, recording, taping, Web distribution, or information storage retrieval systems—without the written permission of the publisher.

For permission to use material from this product, submit your request via the Web at http://www.gale-edit.com/permissions, or you may download our Permissions Request form and submit your request by fax or mail to:

Permissions Department
The Gale Group, Inc.
27500 Drake Road
Farmington Hills, MI 48331-3535
Permissions hotline:
248-699-8006 or 800-877-4253, ext. 8006
Fax: 248-699-8074 or 800-762-4058

Since this page cannot legibly accommodate all copyright notices, the acknowledgments constitute an extension of the copyright notice.

While every effort has been made to ensure the reliability of the information presented in this publication, The Gale Group, Inc. does not guarantee the accuracy of the data contained herein. The Gale Group, Inc. accepts no payment for listing, and inclusion in the publication of any organization, agency, institution, publication, service, or individual does not imply endorsement of the editors or publisher. Errors brought to the attention of the publisher and verified to the satisfaction of the publisher will be corrected in future editions.

LIBRARY OF CONGRESS CATALOGING-IN-PUBLICATION DATA
Gale encyclopedia of mental disorders/ Ellen Thackery, editor.
v. < >p. ; cm.
Includes bibliographical references and index.
ISBN 0-7876-5768-9 (set) hc—ISBN 0-7876-5769-7 (vol. 1)—
ISBN 0-7876-5770-0 (vol. 2)
1. Psychiatry—Encyclopedias. 2. Mental illness—Encyclopedias.
I. Title: Encyclopedia of mental disorders. II. Thackery, Ellen, 1972-

RC437 .G35 2002
616.89'003—dc21 2002023257

Printed in the United States of America
10 9 8 7 6 5 4 3 2 1

CONTENTS

TOPIC LIST

A

B

C

D

E

F

G

H

I

K

L

M

N

O

P

Q

R

Reading disorder
Reinforcement
Relapse and relapse prevention
Respite
Rett's disorder
Risperidone
Rivastigmine
Rorschach technique
Rosemary
Rumination disorder

S

SAMe
Schizoaffective disorder
Schizoid personality disorder
Schizophrenia
Schizophreniform disorder
Schizotypal personality disorder
Seasonal affective disorder
Sedatives and related disorders
Seizures
Selective mutism
Self-control strategies
Self-help groups
Separation anxiety disorder
Sertraline
Sexual aversion disorder
Sexual dysfunctions
Sexual masochism
Sexual sadism
Sexual Violence Risk-20
Shared psychotic disorder
Single photon emission computed tomography
Sleep disorders
Sleep terror disorder
Sleepwalking disorder
Social phobia
Social skills training
Social workers
Somatization and somatoform disorders
Somatization disorder
Specific phobias
Speech-language pathology
St. John's wort
Stanford-Binet Intelligence Scale
Stereotypic movement disorder
Stigma
Stress
Stroke
Stuttering
Substance abuse and related disorders
Substance Abuse Subtle Screening Inventory
Substance-induced anxiety disorder
Substance-induced psychotic disorder
Suicide
Support groups
Systematic desensitization

T

Tacrine
Talk therapy
Tardive dyskinesia
Temazepam
Thematic Apperception Test
Thioridazine
Thiothixene
Tic disorders
Token economy system
Transvestic fetishism
Tranylcypromine
Trazodone
Triazolam
Trichotillomania
Trifluoperazine
Trihexyphenidyl
Trimipramine

U

Undifferentiated somatoform disorder
Urine drug screening

V

Vaginismus
Valerian
Valproic acid
Vascular dementia
Venlafaxine
Vocational rehabilitation
Voyeurism

W

Wechsler Adult Intelligence Scale
Wechsler Intelligence Scale for Children
Wernicke-Korsakoff syndrome
Wide Range Achievement Test

Y

Yoga

Z

Zaleplon
Ziprasidone
Zolpidem

PLEASE READ—IMPORTANT INFORMATION

The *Gale Encyclopedia of Mental Disorders* is a medical reference product designed to inform and educate readers about a wide variety of mental disorders, diagnostic techniques and tests, therapies, and psychiatric medications. The Gale Group believes the product to be comprehensive, but not necessarily definitive. It is intended to supplement, not replace, consultation with a physician or other health care practitioner. While the Gale Group has made substantial efforts to provide information that is accurate, comprehensive, and up-to-date, the Gale Group makes no representations or warranties of any kind, including without limitation, warranties of merchantability or fitness for a particular purpose, nor does it guarantee the accuracy, comprehensiveness, or timeliness of the information contained in this product. Readers should be aware that the universe of medical knowledge is constantly growing and changing, and that differences of medical opinion exist among authorities. Readers are also advised to seek professional diagnosis and treatment of any medical condition, and to discuss information obtained from this book with their health care provider.

INTRODUCTION

The *Gale Encyclopedia of Mental Disorders* is a valuable source of information for anyone who wants to learn more about mental disorders and their treatments. This collection of approximately 400 entries provides in-depth coverage of specific disorders recognized by the American Psychiatric Association (as well as some disorders not formally recognized as distinct disorders), diagnostic procedures and techniques, therapies, and psychiatric medications. In addition, entries have been included to facilitate understanding of related topics, such as Advance directives, Crisis housing, and Neurotransmitters.

This encyclopedia minimizes medical jargon and uses language that laypersons can understand, while still providing thorough coverage that will benefit health science students as well.

Entries follow a standardized format that provides information at a glance. Rubrics include:

Disorders	**Medications**
Definition	Definition
Description	Purpose
Causes and symptoms	Description
Demographics	Recommended dosage
Diagnosis	Precautions
Treatments	Side effects
Prognosis	Interactions
Prevention	Resources
Resources	

INCLUSION CRITERIA

A preliminary list of mental disorders and related topics was compiled from a wide variety of sources, including professional medical guides and textbooks, as well as consumer guides and encyclopedias. The advisory board, made up of professionals from a variety of health care fields including psychology, psychiatry, pharmacy, and social work, evaluated the topics and made suggestions for inclusion. Final selection of topics to include was made by the advisory board in conjunction with the Gale editor.

ABOUT THE CONTRIBUTORS

The essays were compiled by experienced medical writers, including physicians, pharmacists, and psychologists. The advisors reviewed the completed essays to ensure that they are appropriate, up-to-date, and accurate.

HOW TO USE THIS BOOK

The *Gale Encyclopedia of Mental Disorders* has been designed with ready reference in mind.

- Straight **alphabetical arrangement** of topics allows users to locate information quickly.
- **Bold-faced terms** within entries direct the reader to related articles.
- **Cross-references** placed throughout the encyclopedia direct readers from alternate names, drug brand names, and related topics to entries.
- A list of **key terms** is provided where appropriate to define unfamiliar terms or concepts. A **glossary** of key terms is also included at the back of Volume II.
- The **Resources** sections direct readers to additional sources of information on a topic.
- Valuable **contact information** for organizations and support groups is included with many of the disorder entries.
- A leaf graphic (❦) inserted next to the entry title denotes entries about herbals (such as Ginkgo biloba) or dietary supplements (such as SAMe). These entries have the same rubrics as the medication entries; however, the graphic is to draw attention to the fact that these entries are not about prescription medications.
- A **Symptoms list** at the back of Volume II has been included *not* for diagnosis but to reveal patterns in

symptoms and disorders and to provide a starting point for research or discussion with a health care provider.

- A comprehensive **general index** guides readers to all topics mentioned in the text.

GRAPHICS

The *Gale Encyclopedia of Mental Disorders* contains 100 illustrations, photos, and tables. A color insert in each volume has been included to enhance certain photos shown in the text in black and white.

ADVISORY BOARD

A number of experts in medicine, psychology, psychiatry, and pharmacy provided invaluable assistance in the formulation of this encyclopedia. The members of the advisory board performed a myriad of duties, from defining the scope of coverage to reviewing individual entries for accuracy and accessibility. The editor would like to express appreciation to them for their time and for their contributions.

Michael F. Cantwell, M.D., M.P.H.
Director, Health and Healing Clinic
California Pacific Medical Center
Member, National Advisory Council for Complementary and Alternative Medicine
San Francisco, California

Toby Benjamin DeWitt, M.D.
Children's Psychiatric Institute
John Umstead Hospital
Butner, North Carolina

Debra L. Franko, Ph.D.
Department of Counseling and Applied Educational Psychology
Northeastern University
Harvard Eating Disorders Center
Boston, Massachusetts

F. James Grogan, Pharm.D.
President
Grogan Communications, Inc.
Swansea, Illinois

Laith F. Gulli, MRS, M.D., M.Sc., M.Sc.(MedSci), M.Sc.(Admin.), M.Sc.Psych
DAPA, DABFC, DABCI
Attending Psychotherapist
Department of Outpatient Services
Insight Recovery Center
Flint, Michigan
Oxford Program in Evidence-Based Health Care
University of Oxford
Oxford, England

Irene S. Levine, Ph.D.
Clinical Professor
Psychiatry
New York University School of Medicine
New York, New York

Christopher Peterson, Ph.D.
Arthur F. Thurnau Professor
Department of Psychology
University of Michigan
Ann Arbor, Michigan

Jack Raber, Pharm.D.
Principal
Clinipharm Services
Seal Beach, California

George Stricker, Ph.D.
Distinguished Research Professor
Derner Institute of Advanced Psychological Studies
Adelphi University
Garden City, New York

Eric Zehr, M.S., CSADC, PCGC, MISA II
Vice President
Illinois Institute for Addiction Recovery
Proctor Hospital
Peoria, Illinois

CONTRIBUTORS

Bill Asenjo M.S., CRC
Medical Writer
Iowa City, Iowa

Danielle Barry, M.S.
Graduate Assistant
Center of Alcohol Studies
Rutgers University
Piscataway, New Jersey

Keith W. Beard, Psy.D.
Assistant Professor
Psychology
Marshall University
Huntington, West Virginia

Tanja C. Bekhuis, Ph.D.
Science Writer and Psychologist
TCB Research
Boalsburg, Pennsylvania

Kathleen Berrisford, M.S.W, CSW, CAC
Consultant Therapist
Macomb County Department of Health
Warren, Michigan

Tanya Bivins, B.S., B.S.N., RN
Ensign, Medical Service Corps
United States Navy
Virginia

Beth Bollinger, M.D.
Psychiatrist, Writer, Consultant
Huntingdon, Pennsylvania

Jack H. Booth, Psy.D.
Private Practice and Adjunct Professor
Counseling
Webster University
Charleston, South Carolina

Jody G. Bower, M.S.W
Medical Writer
Port Townsend, Washington

Rosalyn Carson-DeWitt, M.D.
Medical writer
Durham, North Carolina

Linda Chrisman
Science Writer
Oakland, California

Lisa Christenson
Science Writer
Hamden, Connecticut

Tish Davidson, A.M.
Davidson Editorial Services
Fremont, California

Robert Scott Dinsmoor
Medical Writer
South Hamilton, Massachusetts

Deborah Rosch Eifert Ph.D.
Assistant Clinical Professor
Psychiatry, School of Medicine
Case Western Reserve University
Cleveland, Ohio

Ali Fahmy, Ph.D.
Educational Research Analyst
Los Angeles, California

L. Fleming Fallon, Jr., M.D., Dr.P.H.
Associate Professor
Public Health
Bowling Green State University
Bowling Green, Ohio

Susan Fine, Psy.D.
Private Practice
New York, New York

Mary Finley
Supervisor of Science Curriculum (retired)
Pittsburgh Secondary Schools
Clairton, Pennsylvania

Jane A. Fitzgerald, Ph.D.
Psychologist and Writer
Hattiesburg, Mississippi

Paula Anne Ford-Martin, M.A.
Wordcrafts
Warwick, Rhode Island

Rebecca J. Frey, Ph.D.
Writer, Editor, and Editorial Consultant
New Haven, Connecticut

Sandra L. Friedrich, M.A.
Clinical Psychology
Science Writer
Chicago, Illinois

Rodney M. Gabel, Ph.D.
Assistant Professor
Department of Communication Disorders
Bowling Green State University
Bowling Green, Ohio

John Garrison, Ph.D., M.P.H.
Senior Psychologist
Psychiatry and Behavioral Medicine
Lahey Clinic
Burlington, Massachusetts

Gary Gilles, M.A., L.C.P.C.
Therapist, Private Practice, and Freelance Writer
Palatine, Illinois

Peter Gregutt
Science Writer
Asheville, North Carolina

Geoffrey G. Grimm, Ph.D.
Instructor
Department of Behavioral Medicine and Psychiatry
West Virginia University
Morgantown, West Virginia

Nancy J. Gustafson, M.S., R.D., F.A.D.A.
Medical Writer and Nutrition Consultant
Fargo, North Dakota

Jennifer Hahn, Ph.D.
Licensed Clinical Psychologist
Philadelphia, Pennsylvania

Ajna Hamidovic, Pharm.D.
Medical Writer and Consultant Pharmacist
Madison, Wisconsin

Dean A. Haycock, Ph.D.
Science and Medical Writer
Salem, New York

Linda Hesson, M.A., Psy.S., CAC
Program Manager
Insight Recovery Center
Flint, Michigan

Susan Hobbs, M.D.
Medical Writer and Consultant
Owings Mills, Maryland

Richard M. Kapit, M.D.
Medical and Science Writer
Garrett Park, Maryland

Kelly Dowhower Karpa, Ph.D., R.Ph.
Assistant Professor
Pharmacology
Pennsylvania State University College of Medicine
Hershey, Pennsylvania

Judy Koenigsberg, Ph.D.
Clinical Psychologist
Evanston, Illinois

Monique LaBerge, Ph.D.
Research Associate
Department of Biochemistry and Biophysics
University of Pennsylvania
Philadelphia, Pennsylvania

Judy Leaver, M.A.
Behavioral Health Writer and Consultant
Washington, D.C.

Nicole Mallory, M.S., PA-C
Physician Assistant
Detroit, Michigan

Jenifer P. Marom, Ph.D.
Scientific Writer and Consultant
New York, New York

Mark A. Mitchell, M.D.
Medical Writer
Seattle, Washington

Michael Mooney, M.A., CAC, CCS
Consultant Psychotherapist
Warren, Michigan

Alfredo Mori, M.D., FACEM, FFAEM
Emergency Physician
The Alfred Hospital
Victoria, Australia
Oxford's Program in Evidence-Based Health Care
University of Oxford
Oxford, England

Ralph M. Myerson, M.D.
Clinical Professor
Medicine
Medical College of Pennsylvania, Hahnemann University
Philadelphia, Pennsylvania

Bilal Nasser, M.D., M.S.
Professional Medical Writer
Dearborn, Michigan

Teresa G. Norris, R.N.
Medical Writer
Ute Park, New Mexico

Deanna S. Pledge, Ph.D.
Private Practitioner, Professor, Author, and Media Consultant
Columbia, Missouri

Michael Polgar, Ph.D.
Research Scientist
George Warren Brown School of Social Work
Washington University
St. Louis, Missouri

Robert Ramirez, B.S.
Medical Student
The University of Medicine and Dentistry of New Jersey
Newark, New Jersey

Elizabeth Reid, M.D.
Physician and Writer
Edina, Minnesota

Martha Sajatovic, M.D.
Associate Professor of Psychiatry
Case Western Reserve University
School of Medicine
Cleveland, Ohio

Holly Scherstuhl, M.Ed.
Marriage and Family Therapist
Duke University
Durham, North Carolina

Joan Schonbeck, R.N.
Medical Writer
Nursing
Massachusetts Department of Mental Health
Marlborough, Massachusetts

Catherine Seeley, CSW
Consultant Therapist
Probation Office
Eastpointe, Michigan

Barbara Sternberg, Ph.D.
Scientific Writer and Clinical Psychologist
Westchester, New York

Kurt Richard Sternlof
Science Writer
New Rochelle, New York

Jean Suvan, B.Sc., R.D.H.
Clinical Research Co-coordinator
Eastman Dental Institute
University of London
London, England
Oxford's Program in Evidence-Based Health Care
University of Oxford
Oxford, England

Joneis Thomas, Ph.D.
Licensed Clinical Psychologist
Charleston, South Carolina

Janice J. VanBuren, Ph.D.
Psychologist and Medical Writer
Princeton, New Jersey

Debra Wood, R.N.
Medical Writer
Orlando, Florida

Magnetic resonance imaging

Definition

Magnetic resonance imaging (MRI) is one of the newest diagnostic medical imaging technologies that uses strong magnets and pulses of radio waves to manipulate the natural magnetic properties in the body to generate a visible image. In the field of mental health, an MRI scan may be used when a patient seeks medical help for symptoms that could possibly be caused by a **brain** tumor. These symptoms may include headaches, emotional abnormalities, or intellectual or memory problems. In these cases, an MRI scan may be performed to "rule out" a tumor, so that other tests can be performed in order to establish an accurate **diagnosis**.

Purpose

MRI was developed in the 1980s. Its technology has been developed for use in magnetic resonance angiography (MRA), magnetic resonance spectroscopy (MRS), and, more recently, magnetic resonance cholangiopancreatography (MRCP). MRA was developed to study blood flow, whereas MRS can identify the chemical composition of diseased tissue and produce color images of brain function. MRCP is evolving into a non-invasive potential alternative for the diagnostic procedure endoscopic retrograde cholangiopancreatography (ERCP).

Advantages

DETAIL. MRI creates precise images of the body based on the varying proportions of magnetic elements in different tissues. Very minor fluctuations in chemical composition can be determined. MRI images have greater natural contrast than standard x rays, **computed tomography** scan (CT scan), or ultrasound, all of which depend on the differing physical properties of tissues. This sensitivity allows MRI to distinguish fine variations in tissues deep within the body. It is also particularly useful for spotting and distinguishing diseased tissues (tumors and other lesions) early in their development. Often, doctors prescribe an MRI scan to investigate more fully earlier findings of other imaging techniques.

SCOPE. The entire body can be scanned, from head to toe and from the skin to the deepest recesses of the brain. Moreover, MRI scans are not obstructed by bone, gas, or body waste, which can hinder other imaging techniques. (Although the scans can be degraded by motion such as breathing, heartbeat, and bowel activity.) The MRI process produces cross-sectional images of the body that are as sharp in the middle as on the edges, even of the brain through the skull. A close series of these two-dimensional images can provide a three-dimensional view of the targeted area. Along with images from the cross-sectional plane, the MRI can also provide images sagitally (from one side of the body to the other, from left to right for example), allowing for a better three-dimensional interpretation, which is sometimes very important for planning a surgical approach.

SAFETY. MRI does not depend on potentially harmful ionizing radiation, as do standard x ray and computed tomography scans. There are no known risks specific to the procedure, other than for people who might have metal objects in their bodies.

Despite its many advantages, MRI is not routinely used because it is a somewhat complex and costly procedure. MRI requires large, expensive, and complicated equipment, a highly trained operator, and a doctor specializing in radiology. Generally, MRI is prescribed only when serious symptoms or negative results from other tests indicate a need. Many times another test is appropriate for the type of diagnosis needed.

Uses

Doctors may prescribe an MRI scan of different areas of the body.

BRAIN AND HEAD. MRI technology was developed because of the need for brain imaging. It is one of the few

KEY TERMS

Angiography—A procedure in which a contrast medium is injected into the bloodstream (through an artery in the neck) and its progress through the brain is tracked. This illustrates where a blockage or hemorrhage has occurred.

Gadolinium—A very rare metallic element useful for its sensitivity to electromagnetic resonance, among other things. Traces of it can be injected into the body to enhance the MRI pictures.

Hydrogen—The simplest, most common element known in the universe. It is composed of a single electron (negatively charged particle). It is the nuclear proton of hydrogen that makes MRI possible by reacting resonantly to radio waves while aligned in a magnetic field.

Ionizing radiation—Electromagnetic radiation that can damage living tissue by disrupting and destroying individual cells. All types of nuclear decay radiation (including x rays) are potentially ionizing. Radio waves do not damage organic tissues they pass through.

Magnetic field—The three-dimensional area surrounding a magnet, in which its force is active. During MRI, the patient's body is permeated by the force field of a superconducting magnet.

Radio waves—Electromagnetic energy of the frequency range corresponding to that used in radio communications, usually 10,000 cycles per second to 300 billion cycles per second. Radio waves are the same as visible light, x rays, and all other types of electromagnetic radiation, but are of a higher frequency.

imaging tools that can see through bone (the skull) and deliver high-quality pictures of the brain's delicate soft tissue structures. MRI may be needed for patients with symptoms of a brain tumor, **stroke**, or infection (like meningitis). MRI may also be needed when cognitive or psychological symptoms suggest brain disease (like Alzheimer's or Huntington's diseases, or multiple sclerosis), or when developmental retardation suggests a birth defect. MRI can also provide pictures of the sinuses and other areas of the head beneath the face. In adult and pediatric patients, MRI may be better able to detect abnormalities than compared to computed tomography scanning.

SPINE. Spinal problems can create a host of seemingly unrelated symptoms. MRI is particularly useful for identifying and evaluating degenerated or herniated spinal discs. It can also be used to determine the condition of nerve tissue within the spinal cord.

JOINT. MRI scanning is most commonly used to diagnose and assess joint problems. MRI can provide clear images of the bone, cartilage, ligament, and tendon that comprise a joint. MRI can be used to diagnose joint injuries due to sports, advancing age, or arthritis. MRI can also be used to diagnose shoulder problems, such as a torn rotator cuff. MRI can also detect the presence of an otherwise hidden tumor or infection in a joint, and can be used to diagnose the nature of developmental joint abnormalities in children.

SKELETON. The properties of MRI that allow it to see through the skull also allow it to view the inside of bones. Accordingly, it can be used to detect bone cancer, inspect the marrow for leukemia and other diseases, assess bone loss (osteoporosis), and examine complex fractures.

HEART AND CIRCULATION. MRI technology can be used to evaluate the circulatory system. The heart and blood flow provides a good natural contrast medium that allows structures of the heart to be clearly distinguished.

THE REST OF THE BODY. Whereas computed tomography and ultrasound scans satisfy most chest, abdominal, and general body imaging needs, MRI may be needed in certain circumstances to provide better pictures or when repeated scanning is required. The progress of some therapies, like liver cancer therapy, needs to be monitored, and the effect of repeated x-ray exposure is a concern.

Precautions

MRI scans and metal

MRI scanning should not be used when there is the potential for an interaction between the strong MRI magnet and metal objects that might be embedded in a patient's body. The force of magnetic attraction on certain types of metal objects (including surgical steel) could move them within the body and cause serious injury. Metal may be embedded in a person's body for several reasons.

MEDICAL. People with implanted cardiac pacemakers, metal aneurysm clips, or who have broken bones repaired with metal pins, screws, rods, or plates must tell their radiologist prior to having an MRI scan. In some cases (like a metal rod in a reconstructed leg), the difficulty may be overcome.

INJURY. Patients must tell their doctor if they have bullet fragments or other metal pieces in their body from old wounds. The suspected presence of metal, whether from an old or recent wound, should be confirmed before scanning.

OCCUPATIONAL. People with significant work exposure to metal particles (working with a metal grinder, for example) should discuss this with their doctor and radiologist. The patient may need prescan testing—usually a single, regular x ray of the eyes to see if any metal is present.

Chemical agents

Chemical agents designed to improve the picture or allow for the imaging of blood or other fluid flow during MRA may be injected. In rare cases, patients may be allergic to, or intolerant of, these agents, and these patients should not receive them. If these chemical agents are to be used, patients should discuss any concerns they have with their doctor and radiologist.

General

The potential side effects of magnetic and electric fields on human health remain a source of debate. In particular, the possible effects on an unborn baby are not well known. Any woman who is, or may be, pregnant, should carefully discuss this issue with her doctor and radiologist before undergoing a scan.

As with all medical imaging techniques, **obesity** greatly interferes with the quality of MRI.

Description

In essence, MRI produces a map of hydrogen distribution in the body. Hydrogen is the simplest element known, the most abundant in biological tissue, and one that can be magnetized. It will align itself within a strong magnetic field, like the needle of a compass. The earth's magnetic field is not strong enough to keep a person's hydrogen atoms pointing in the same direction, but the superconducting magnet of an MRI machine can. This comprises the magnetic part of MRI.

Once a patient's hydrogen atoms have been aligned in the magnet, pulses of very specific radio wave frequencies are used to knock them back out of alignment. The hydrogen atoms alternately absorb and emit radio wave energy, vibrating back and forth between their resting (magnetized) state and their agitated (radio pulse) state. This comprises the resonance part of MRI.

The MRI equipment records the duration, strength, and source location of the signals emitted by the atoms as they relax and translates the data into an image on a television monitor. The state of hydrogen in diseased tissue differs from healthy tissue of the same type, making MRI particularly good at identifying tumors and other lesions.

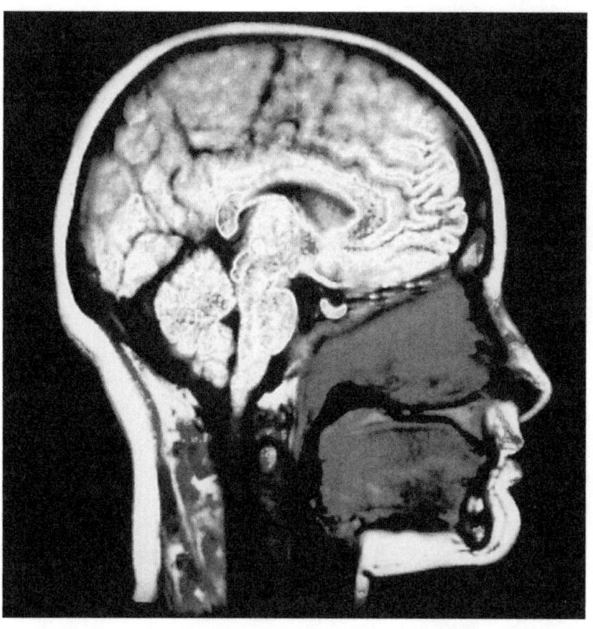

MRI scan of human brain. *(Scott Camazine and Sue Trainor. Photo Researchers, Inc. Reproduced by permission.) See color insert for color version of photo.*

In some cases, chemical agents such as gadolinium can be injected to improve the contrast between healthy and diseased tissue.

A single MRI exposure produces a two-dimensional image of a slice through the entire target area. A series of these image slices closely spaced (usually less than half an inch) makes a virtual three-dimensional view of the area.

Regardless of the exact type of MRI planned, or area of the body targeted, the procedure involved is basically the same. In a special MRI suite, the patient lies down on a narrow table and is made as comfortable as possible. Transmitters are positioned on the body and the table moves into a long tube that houses the magnet. The tube is as long as an average adult lying down, and is open at both ends. Once the area to be examined has been properly positioned, a radio pulse is applied. Then a two-dimensional image corresponding to one slice through the area is made. The table then moves a fraction of an inch and the next image is made. Each image exposure takes several seconds and the entire exam will last anywhere from 30 to 90 minutes. During this time, the patient must remain still as movement can distort the pictures produced.

Depending on the area to be imaged, the radio-wave transmitters will be positioned in different locations.

- For the head and neck, a helmet-like covering is worn on the head.

- For the spine, chest, and abdomen, the patient will be lying on the transmitters.
- For the knee, shoulder, or other joint, the transmitters will be applied directly to the joint.

Additional probes will monitor vital signs (like pulse, respiration, etc.) throughout the test.

The procedure is somewhat noisy and can feel confining to many patients. As the patient moves through the tube, the patient hears a thumping sound. Sometimes, music is supplied via earphones to drown out the noise. Some patients may become anxious or feel claustrophobic while in the small, enclosed tube. Patients may be reassured to know that throughout the study, they can communicate with medical personnel through an intercom-like system.

Recently, open MRIs have become available. Instead of a tube open only at the ends, an open MRI also has opening at the sides. Open MRIs are preferable for patients who have a fear of closed spaces and become anxious in traditional MRI machines. Open MRIs can also better accommodate obese patients, and allow parents to accompany their children during testing.

If the chest or abdomen is to be imaged, the patient will be asked to hold his to her breath as each exposure is made. Other instructions may be given to the patient as needed. In many cases, the entire examination will be performed by an MRI operator who is not a doctor. However, the supervising radiologist should be available to consult as necessary during the exam, and will view and interpret the results sometime later.

Magnetic resonance spectroscopy (MRS) is different from MRI because MRS uses a continuous band of radio wave frequencies to excite hydrogen atoms in a variety of chemical compounds other than water. These compounds absorb and emit radio energy at characteristic frequencies, or spectra, which can be used to identify them. Generally, a color image is created by assigning a color to each distinctive spectral emission. This comprises the spectroscopy part of MRS. MRS is still experimental and is available only in a few research centers.

Doctors primarily use MRS to study the brain and disorders like epilepsy, **Alzheimer's disease**, brain tumors, and the effects of drugs on brain growth and metabolism. The technique is also useful in evaluating metabolic disorders of the muscles and nervous system.

Magnetic resonance angiography (MRA) is another variation on standard MRI. MRA, like other types of angiography, looks specifically at fluid flow within the blood (vascular) system, but does so without the injection of dyes or radioactive tracers. Standard MRI cannot make a good picture of flowing blood, but MRA uses specific radio pulse sequences to capture usable signals. The technique is generally used in combination with MRI to obtain images that show both vascular structure and flow within the brain and head in cases of stroke, or when a blood clot or aneurysm is suspected.

MRI technology is also being applied in the evaluation of the pancreatic and biliary ducts in a new study called magnetic resonance cholangiopancreatography (MRCP). MRCP produces images similar to that of endoscopic retrograde cholangiopancreatography (ERCP), but in a non-invasive manner. Because MRCP is new and still very expensive, it is not readily available in most hospitals and imaging centers.

Preparation

In some cases (such as for MRI brain scanning or MRA), a chemical designed to increase image contrast may be given immediately before the exam. If a patient suffers from anxiety or claustrophobia, drugs may be given to help the patient relax.

The patient must remove all metal objects (watches, jewelry, eye glasses, hair clips, etc.). Any magnetized objects (like credit and bank machine cards, audio tapes, etc.) should be kept far away from the MRI equipment because they can be erased. The patient cannot bring any personal items such as a wallet or keys into the MRI machine. The patient may be asked to wear clothing without metal snaps, buckles, or zippers, unless a medical gown is worn during the procedure. The patient may be asked not to use hair spray, hair gel, or cosmetics that could interfere with the scan.

Aftercare

No aftercare is necessary, unless the patient received medication or had a reaction to a contrast agent. Normally, patients can immediately return to their daily activities. If the exam reveals a serious condition that requires more testing or treatment, appropriate information and counseling will be needed.

Risks

MRI poses no known health risks to the patient and produces no physical side effects. Again, the potential effects of MRI on an unborn baby are not well known. Any woman who is, or may be, pregnant, should carefully discuss this issue with her doctor and radiologist before undergoing a scan.

Normal results

A normal MRI, MRA, MRS, or MRCP result is one that shows the patient's physical condition to fall within normal ranges for the target area scanned.

Abnormal results

Generally, MRI is prescribed only when serious symptoms or negative results from other tests indicate a need. There often exists strong evidence of a condition that the scan is designed to detect and assess. Thus, the results will often be abnormal, confirming the earlier diagnosis. At that point, further testing and appropriate medical treatment is needed. For example, if the MRI indicates the presence of a brain tumor, an MRS may be prescribed to determine the type of tumor so that aggressive treatment can begin immediately without the need for a surgical biospy.

Resources

BOOKS

Faulkner, William H. *Tech's Guide to MRI: Basic Physics, Instrumentation and Quality Control.* Malden: Blackwell Science, 2001.

Fischbach, F. T. *A Manual of Laboratory and Diagnostic Tests.* 6th Edition. Philadelphia: Lippincott, 1999.

Goldman, L., and Claude Bennett, eds. *Cecil Textbook of Medicine.* 21st Edition. Philadelphia: W. B. Saunders, 2000: pp 977–970.

Kevles, Bettyann Holtzmann. *Naked to the Bone: Medical Imaging in the Twentieth Century.* New Brunswick, NJ: Rutgers University Press, 1997.

Roth, Carolyn K. *Tech's Guide to MRI: Imaging Procedures, Patient Care and Safety.* Malden: Blackwell Science, 2001.

Zaret, Barry L., and others, eds. *The Patient's Guide to Medical Tests.* Boston: Houghton Mifflin Company, 1997.

PERIODICALS

Carr-Locke, D., and others, "Technology Status Evaluation: Magnetic Resonance Cholangiopancreatography." *Gastrointestinal Endoscopy* (June 1999): 858–61.

ORGANIZATIONS

American College of Radiology. 1891 Preston White Drive, Reston, VA 22091. (800) ACR-LINE. <http://www.acr.org>.

American Society of Radiologic Technologists. 15000 Central Avenue SE, Albuquerque, NM 87123–3917. (505) 298–4500. <http://www.asrt.org>.

Kurt Richard Sternlof
Laith Farid Gulli, M.D.

Magnetocephalogram *see* **Electroencephalography**

Major depressive disorder

Definition

Major depressive disorder (MDD) is a condition characterized by a long-lasting depressed mood or marked loss of interest or pleasure (anhedonia) in all or nearly all activities. Children and adolescents with MDD may be irritable instead of sad. These symptoms, along with others described below, must be sufficiently severe to interfere significantly with the patient's daily functioning in order for a person to be diagnosed with MDD.

Description

Major depressive disorder is a serious mental disorder that profoundly affects an individual's quality of life. Unlike normal bereavement or an occasional episode of "the blues," MDD causes a lengthy period of gloom and hopelessness, and may rob the sufferer of the ability to take pleasure in activities or relationships that were previously enjoyable. In some cases, depressive episodes seem to be triggered by an obviously painful event, but MDD may also develop without a specific stressor. Research indicates that an initial episode of depression is likely to be a response to a specific stimulus, but later episodes are progressively more likely to start without a triggering event. A person suffering major depression finds job-related responsibilities and such other tasks as parenting burdensome and carried out only with great effort. Mental efficiency and memory are affected, causing even simple tasks to be tiring and irritating. Sexual interest dwindles; many people with MDD become withdrawn and avoid any type of social activity. Even the ability to enjoy a good meal or a sound night's sleep is frequently lost; many depressed people report a chronic sense of malaise (general discomfort or unease). For some, the pain and suffering accompanying MDD becomes so unendurable that **suicide** is viewed as the only option; MDD has the highest mortality rate of any mental disorder.

Major depressive disorder may be limited to a single episode of depression; more commonly, it may become a chronic condition with many episodes of depressed mood. Other symptoms that may develop include psychotic symptoms (bizarre thoughts, including delusional beliefs and **hallucinations**); **catatonia**; postpartum

KEY TERMS

Agitation—Excessive restlessness or emotional disturbance that is often associated with anxiety or psychosis. May be a symptom of major depressive disorder.

Anhedonia—Loss of the capacity to experience pleasure. Anhedonia is one of the so-called negative symptoms of schizophrenia, and is also a symptom of major depression.

Catatonia—Disturbance of motor behavior with either extreme stupor or random, purposeless activity.

Cortisol—A steroid hormone released by the cortex (outer portion) of the adrenal gland when a person is under stress.

Delusion—A false belief that is resistant to reason or contrary to actual fact. Women suffering from postpartum depression sometimes have delusions about their new baby.

Dysthymia—Depression of low intensity.

Dysthymic disorder—A mood disorder that is less severe than depression but usually more chronic.

Etiology—The cause or origin of a disease or disorder. The word is also used to refer to the study of the causes of disease.

Gingko—A shade tree native to China with fan-shaped leaves and fleshy seeds with edible kernels. Gingko extract has been approved in Europe as a complementary or adjunctive treatment for major depressive episodes.

Intrapsychic—Occurring inside a person's mind or psyche.

Labile—Subject to frequent change, particularly in reference to mood.

Limbic system—A group of structures in the brain that includes the amygdala, hippocampus, olfactory bulbs, and hypothalamus. The limbic system is associated with homeostasis and the regulation and arousal of emotions.

Malaise—The medical term for a general condition of unease, discomfort, or weakness.

Melancholia—A form of severe depression characterized by weight loss, insomnia, and an inability to experience pleasure.

Rumination—A tendency to dwell on certain thoughts, particularly negative ones, repeatedly or obsessively.

Serotonin—A widely distributed neurotransmitter that is found in blood platelets, the lining of the digestive tract, and the brain, and that works in combination with norepinephrine. It causes very powerful contractions of smooth muscle, and is associated with mood, attention, emotions, and sleep. Low levels of serotonin are associated with depression.

onset (sometimes accompanied by psychotic symptoms); and **seasonal affective disorder**, or SAD.

Such conditions as **postpartum depression** and seasonal affective disorder accompany MDD only under certain circumstances. Postpartum depression begins within four weeks of giving birth. Women with this disorder experience labile mood (frequent drastic mood changes). They may feel helpless and unable to care adequately for their infant, or they may be completely uninterested in the child. The symptoms of postpartum depression are much more severe than those of the relatively common "new baby blues," which affect up to 70% of new mothers. The presence of psychotic symptoms in the mother, too many ruminations (obsessive thoughts), or **delusions** about the infant are associated with a heightened risk of serious harm to the child. The symptoms of postpartum depression are usually attributed to fluctuations in the woman's hormone levels and the emotional impact of bearing a child. The condition is especially likely to occur in women who were highly anxious during pregnancy or had a previous history of mood disorder. Seasonal affective disorder (SAD) is also more common in women than in men; in this case, symptoms of MDD typically begin in fall and winter, especially in northern latitudes in the United States and Canada. Exposure to natural light is limited during the winter in these areas, but the symptoms of SAD typically improve during the spring and summer.

Causes and symptoms

Causes

Because MDD is a relatively common mental disorder, researchers have performed a range of different studies to identify possible underlying causes. Three types of causes are commonly identified: intrapsychic, environmental, and biological.

INTRAPSYCHIC. Since Sigmund Freud attributed the development of mental disorders to intrapsychic (occurring inside the mind) conflicts occurring during early childhood, a sizeable number of theorists have suggested that MDD results from a tendency to internalize negative events. Cognitive behavioral treatment models assume that a person's interpretation of situations is responsible for the development of depression rather than the events themselves. Some people blame themselves for negative experiences while attributing positive outcomes to external sources; they may tend to feel guilty, undeserving, and eventually depressed. For example, they may think of their present job as something they obtained by a chance stroke of good luck; at the same time, they may regard being laid off as something they brought on themselves. When these patterns of thought become habitual, they lead to a style of coping characterized by a view of oneself as worthless, ineffectual, and inferior. In some cases, people pick up these patterns of thinking from their parents or other family members.

Another theory regarding intrapsychic causes attributes depression to so-called "learned helplessness." This theory grew out of research studies on animal learning, comparing dogs that were able to escape from mild electric shocks to dogs that could not escape. The researchers discovered that the dogs who could not escape the mild shocks became passive; later, when they were put in a situation in which they could escape the shocks, they made no attempt to do so but simply lay on their stomachs and whimpered. The animals had, in short, learned to be helpless; they had learned during the first part of the experiment that nothing they had done had any effect on the shocks. Applied to human beings, this theory holds that people tend to become depressed when they have had long-term experiences of helplessness— as would be the case for abused children. Later, when the children have become adults, they do not see themselves as grownups with some control over their lives; they continue to react to setbacks or losses with the same feelings of helplessness that they had as children, and they become depressed.

ENVIRONMENTAL. Environmental theories of the etiology (causation) of MDD emphasize the role of external events in triggering depression. According to this perspective, people become depressed primarily due to unfortunate circumstances that are difficult to change. In some cases, these misfortunes may include environmental disasters or personal losses; but such other factors as low socioeconomic status, oppression associated with one's sex or race, or unpleasant or frustrating relationships are also thought to contribute to depression.

BIOLOGICAL. Ancient medicine alleged that one's state of mind was related to the presence of specific "humors," or fluids, in the body, and various theories have emerged since the eighteenth century regarding possible constitutional factors in humans that affect mood. In recent years, researchers have found numerous abnormalities in the neuroendocrine systems, **neurotransmitters**, and neuroanatomy of the brains of both children and adults with MDD, as well as strong evidence for genetic factors in MDD.

Levels of cortisol, a hormone associated with the human "fight-or-flight" response, have long been studied as possible biological markers for depression. In many adults, cortisol levels rise when the person is acutely depressed and return to normal when the depression passes. Research findings have been inconsistent regarding cortisol levels in children and adolescents, although there is some evidence that higher levels of cortisol secretion are associated with more severe depressive symptoms and with a higher likelihood of recurrence. As of 2002, however, cortisol levels are not considered to be reliable enough to be useful in diagnosing MDD.

Another biological factor that has been studied in humans are changes in the levels of neurotransmitters, which are chemicals that conduct nerve impulses across the tiny gaps between nerve cells. Variations in the levels of certain neurotransmitters have been researched for many years due to their importance in the brain's limbic system, which is the center of emotions and has many important pathways to other parts of the **brain**. In depression, the system that regulates a neurotransmitter called serotonin does not function properly. A group of medications known as serotonin specific reuptake inhibitors, or SSRIs, are assumed to be effective in relieving depression because they prevent serotonin from being taken back up too quickly by receptors in the brain.

Differences in the anatomical structure of the brains of children and adults with MDD have suggested several possible explanations for its development. In particular, the prefrontal cortex has been thought to play a role, on the basis of findings in stroke patients with damage to the prefrontal area of the brain, and in children and adults with MDD. Researchers found that stroke patients experienced more severe depression if their stroke occurred closer to the frontal lobe of the brain; similarly, people with MDD have been found to have decreased frontal lobe volume. Studies of depressed children and adults included subjects who were currently depressed as well as those with a history of depression who were in remission, which suggests that abnormalities in the frontal lobe may be a structural marker of depression. Other neurological studies have reported lower levels of electrical activity in the left frontal cortex among depressed subjects (including the infants of depressed mothers) compared to persons who are not depressed.

Researchers have also been interested in the relationship of genetic factors to depression. It has been known for many years that depression tends to run in families. Convincing evidence of the heritability of depression has been obtained by comparing identical twins (who have identical genetic inheritances) with fraternal twins; these studies have consistently found a higher likelihood of depression between identical than between fraternal twins. Other data indicate that people with a higher genetic risk of depression are more likely to become depressed following a stressful event than people with fewer genetic risk factors.

Symptoms

The core symptom of major depression is a sad mood that does not go away. While most people have occasional days when they feel out of sorts, persons with MDD experience low feelings that build gradually over a period of days or weeks. They are usually not able to "snap out of it" even when something positive happens. In some cases, the symptoms are preceded by an obvious loss or painful event, such as divorce or a death in the family, but the disorder may also appear to begin "out of the blue." People with MDD often appear sad, irritable, and easily moved to tears. They may sleep poorly and complain of vague physical aches and pains; experience sexual difficulties or loss of interest in sex; drop out of social activities; and come across to others as unhappy or lacking in energy. Some people with MDD may deny that they feel depressed, but they lose their enthusiasm for hobbies or work they once found enjoyable and rewarding. Children and adolescents present with many of these same characteristics, but they may often appear easily frustrated and cranky instead of sad. The symptoms of MDD can be summarized as follows:

- Disturbed mood (sad, hopeless, discouraged, "down in the dumps") during most of the day.
- Loss of interest or pleasure in activities.
- Change in appetite nearly every day, leading either to weight gain or to loss of 5% of body weight. In children, this symptom may appear as a failure to make normal weight gains related to growth.
- **Insomnia** (waking in the middle of the night and having difficulty returning to sleep, or waking too early in the morning) or **hypersomnia** (sleeping much more than normal).
- Psychomotor retardation (slowed thinking, speech, body movements) or agitation (inability to sit still, hand-wringing, pulling at clothing, skin, or other objects) that is apparent to others.
- Sense of worthlessness or unreasonable guilt over minor failings.
- Problems with clear thinking, concentration, and decision-making.
- Recurrent thoughts of death or suicide, or making a suicide attempt.

Demographics

Recent research indicates that 4.9% of the population of the United States meets the diagnostic criteria for MDD at any given time, but 17.1% will experience at least one episode of the disorder at some point during their lives. While the disorder may affect people at any age, it is most commonly diagnosed in young adults in their twenties. For reasons that are not well understood, women are twice as likely to develop MDD as are men; prior to puberty, however, MDD is about equally common in girls and boys. Adolescence is a high-risk period for MDD; while suicide may result from impulsive behavior under **stress** rather than from MDD, it is noteworthy that about 14% of all teenage deaths are due to suicide. The figures for gay and lesbian youth indicate that as many as 20%–35% make suicide attempts. Other risk factors include Hispanic ethnicity; younger age at onset; lower levels of education or income; and being separated or divorced.

Depression appears to have become a more common disorder over the past century. Epidemiologists studying the incidence of depression across time compared groups of people born between 1917 and 1936, between 1937 and 1952, and between 1953 and 1966; their results indicated that the rate of depression increased progressively from one generation to the next. While no single explanation for the rise in depressive disorders emerged, some researchers have suggested that the breakdown of social support networks caused by higher rates of family disruption and greater social mobility may be important contributing factors.

Diagnosis

Major depressive disorder may be diagnosed when a person visits his or her family doctor with concerns about mood, changes in appetite or sleeping patterns, and similar symptoms. Doctors in family practice, in fact, are more likely to be consulted by patients with depression than doctors in any other medical specialty. In addition, a large proportion of people discuss depressed feelings with their clergyperson, who, in the mainstream Christian and Jewish bodies, has typically been trained to recognize the signs of depression and to encourage the person to see their doctor. In some cases the patient may be brought to see the doctor by a concerned spouse or other family member.

The **diagnosis** of MDD involves a constellation of symptoms in addition to depressed mood. After taking a careful history, including asking the patient about his or her sleeping patterns, appetite, sex drive, and mood, the doctor will give the patient a physical examination to rule out other possible causes of the symptoms. Certain other disorders may resemble MDD, including cognitive dysfunction caused by the direct effects of a substance (drug of abuse, medication, or toxic chemical); various medical conditions (i.e., an underactive thyroid gland; strokes; or early stages of **dementia**), or other mental disorders. Such stressful life events as normal bereavement may also produce behaviors similar to those associated with MDD; while a bereaved person may appear to have many of the characteristics of MDD, the disorder would not be diagnosed unless the symptoms continued for more than two months or were extreme in some way. As part of the diagnostic interview, the doctor may give the patient a brief screening questionnaire, such as the **Beck Depression Inventory**, in order to obtain a clearer picture of the symptoms. In addition to interviewing the patient, the doctor may talk to family members or others who can provide information that the patient may forget, deny, or consider unimportant.

The diagnosis of MDD is complicated by the fact that people with MDD frequently suffer from other mental illnesses at the same time, including anxiety disorders, substance abuse problems, and **personality disorders**. Given that the patient's symptoms may vary according to age, sex, and stage of the illness, some clinicians have suggested that MDD may actually be a collection or group of disorders with a small number of underlying core symptoms rather than a single entity.

The diagnosis of a person with MDD may also include certain specifiers, including the severity and chronicity of the disorder; the presence of psychotic features (delusions or hallucinations) or catatonia (remaining motionless for long periods of time, and other peculiarities of posture, movement, or speech); melancholia (depressed mood that is worse in the morning; early morning wakening; psychomotor retardation or agitation; significant weight loss; or inappropriate guilt); and information regarding postpartum status. If the depression is currently in remission, this fact is also commonly listed as a diagnostic specifier.

Treatments

Because MDD can have a devastating impact on a person'slife, the importance of effective treatment cannot be overestimated. Treatment strategies have evolved over the years according to researchers' varying opinions of the underlying causes of depression, but the outpouring of interest in MDD allows treatment providers to select from a variety of tested approaches.

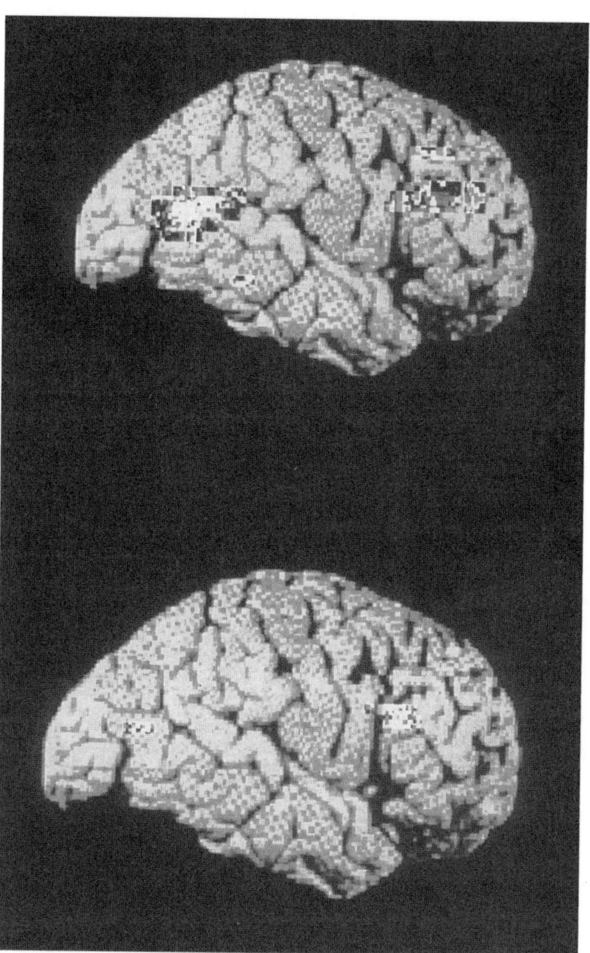

Colored positron emission tomography (PET) scans comparing the brain of a depressed person (top) with the brain of a healthy person. *(Photo Reasearchers, Inc. Reproduced by permission.) See color insert for color version of photo.*

Psychotherapy

Cognitive psychotherapies for depression are based on the belief that depressed people perceive themselves and the world in unrealistically negative ways. Considerable research has been done regarding the cognitive dimension of depression; for example, studies find that depressed people pay more attention to negative events than to positive ones, and that dwelling on unpleasant experiences prolongs and worsens depressive episodes. Cognitive therapists help patients identify the automatic thoughts that lead them to anticipate poor outcomes or to interpret neutral events in negative ways.

The patient is also encouraged to challenge negative thoughts by comparing his or her expectations of events with actual outcomes.

Evidence that poor interpersonal relationships may heighten vulnerability to depression, along with findings that depressed adults and depressed children tend to provoke negative reactions from other people, has prompted the use of **social skills training** as a form of treatment. In this type of therapy, patients are trained to recognize actions and attitudes that annoy or distance other people, and to replace these behaviors with more appropriate ones. Social skills training may be particularly helpful to depressed persons who tend to isolate themselves and have lost confidence in their ability to develop healthy relationships. This treatment model promotes the idea that depression is likely to lift when the patient becomes adept at making new friends and establishing rewarding social supports.

Psychodynamic psychotherapy is often effective in treating patients with MDD whose depression is related to unresolved issues from the past, particularly abuse or other painful childhood experiences. The growth of insight into one's emotional patterns, as well as the supportive aspects of this form of therapy, offers considerable relief from emotional pain to many patients.

Medications

The use of medications in the treatment of depression began in the late 1950s with the successful introduction of tricyclic antidepressants and MAO inhibitors. Treatment of depression with medications has greatly increased since the advent of selective serotonin reuptake inhibitors (SSRIs) such as **fluoxetine** (Prozac) and **sertraline** (Zoloft). While these medications are no more effective than their predecessors, they have fewer side effects and are much safer for patients who may be likely to overdose. Selecting the optimal antidepressant medication is not always a straightforward process, however, and the patient may have to try out various drugs for a period of weeks or months before finding one that is effective for him or her. In addition, while the SSRIs have comparatively few side effects, such complaints as loss of sexual interest or functioning, nervousness, headaches, gastrointestinal complaints, drowsiness, and insomnia can be significant obstacles to the patient's taking the medication as directed.

Other mainstream approaches

The use of **electroconvulsive therapy** (ECT), initially introduced in the 1930s, was virtually abandoned as a treatment for MDD for many years, largely as a result of the effectiveness and convenience of psychotropic (mind-altering) medications. Since the 1980s, however, interest in the procedure has renewed; in 1990 the American Psychiatric Association published new guidelines for the use of ECT. Despite media portrayals of ECT as an outdated and cruel form of treatment that causes considerable pain, in actuality the patient is given a sedative and the electrical stimulation is calibrated precisely to produce the maximum therapeutic effects. ECT may be the first line of treatment when a patient cannot tolerate the customary medications or is at high risk of harming themselves; it is more commonly used with patients who fail to respond to drug treatment. In terms of effectiveness, however, ECT actually outperforms medications even among patients who are helped by antidepressants, as well as those who are resistant to drug treatment.

The use of phototherapy (**light therapy**) has proven to be the treatment of choice for patients diagnosed with seasonal affective disorder. Although the reasons for the effectiveness of phototherapy are not yet clear, treatment involves exposing the eyes to bright (2,500 lux) light for several minutes a day. Currently, however, there is little evidence to suggest that phototherapy is useful in the treatment of other types of MDD.

Alternative and complementary treatments

The National Center for Complementary and Alternative Medicine (NCCAM) is conducting an ongoing series of clinical tests of alternative and complementary treatments for depression. Those that have been shown to reduce symptoms of depression and compare favorably with conventional treatments include **acupuncture**; Ayurvedic medicine; **meditation**; and a therapeutic diet designed to be free of caffeine and refined sugar.

Herbal preparations are common alternative treatments for depression; in fact an NCCAM study found that depression is the single most common reason for people in the United States to purchase herbal remedies. Some, such as St. John's wort, have been used in Europe for decades. The German Commission E, which regulates government approval of herbal preparations in German-speaking Europe, recently approved the use of ***Gingko biloba*** extract as a treatment for depression. The most important caution is that persons who are using herbal remedies, whether to treat depression or other conditions, *should always tell their doctor what they are taking, how much, and how often*. This warning is crucial because some herbal preparations that are safe in themselves can interact with prescription medications. In particular, St. John's wort has been reported to cause interactions with fluoxetine (Prozac).

Some complementary approaches appear to be helpful to persons with depression because they offer pleasurable experiences for the senses or lift the person's spirit. These include **aromatherapy**; music therapy; pet therapy; humor; therapeutic massage; and **yoga**.

Prognosis

Major depression is increasingly viewed as a chronic condition for many people. Left untreated, a depressive episode may last four months or longer, regardless of the age of onset. While most people recover fully from a given depressive episode, eventual recurrence is common. Long-term studies of people with MDD indicate that about 60% of patients who have one episode of depression will have a second episode; with each succeeding episode, the chances of a subsequent episode increase. For example, persons having a third episode stand a 90% chance of having a fourth. Between depressive episodes, the patient's mood may return to a nondepressed state (in about two-thirds of the cases) or continue to show some degree of impairment (one-third of cases). Patients who recover only partially between episodes appear to be at especially high risk of recurrence.

Community studies indicate that about 60% of the people diagnosed with MDD are greatly improved or fully recovered by one year after diagnosis. A very severe initial episode of depression, the presence of a coexisting **dysthymic disorder**, or the existence of a serious medical condition are associated with a poorer prognosis.

Prevention

While programs specifically aimed at preventing MDD are not widespread, early interventions with children to address some of the issues related to depression have met with success. In particular, social skills training has been found to reduce symptoms of depression, perhaps by enabling children to develop the kinds of social supports and friendships that promote good mental health. Cognitive behavioral techniques that teach people to challenge dysfunctional thought patterns, such as the tendency to deny responsibility for good outcomes and to feel overly responsible for negative events, has been found to successfully reduce the rates of depressive symptoms in children and college students. In addition, psychoeducational work with parents having mood disorders has been effective in improving the adjustment of their children. Long-term follow-up of such approaches is incomplete, but these studies support the possibility that improved individual and family functioning may help to lower rates of depression in the future.

As the factors that increase an individual's vulnerability to depression become better understood, effective strategies for early **intervention** and possible prevention become possible. Brief therapies that target such symptoms as maladaptive thought patterns or interpersonal problems may lower the risk of serious mood disturbances. Knowledge of the mental health implications of natural or humanly caused disasters has already resulted in much improved mental health services to communities in need. It is realistic to expect that appropriate treatment will become more available and accessible to people experiencing less dramatic setbacks to their ability to function in the future.

See also Adjustment disorder; Catatonic disorder; Children's Depression Inventory (CDI); Creative therapies; Family psychoeducation; Genetic factors and mental disorders; Grief

Resources

BOOKS

American Psychiatric Association. *Diagnostic and Statistical Manual of Mental Disorders.* 4th edition, text revised. Washington, DC: American Psychiatric Association, 2000.

Beck, Aaron T., M.D., and others. *Cognitive Therapy of Depression.* New York: Guilford Press, 1979.

Ingram, Rick E. and Joseph M. Price, eds. *Vulnerability to Psychopathology; Risk Across the Lifespan.* New York: Guilford Press, 2001.

Martell, Christopher, and others. *Depression in Context: Strategies for Guided Action.* New York: W. W. Norton, 2001.

McCullough, James P., Ph.D. *Treatment for Chronic Depression.* New York: Guilford Press, 2000.

Pelletier, Kenneth R., MD. "CAM Therapies for Specific Conditions: Depression." *The Best Alternative Medicine.* Part II. New York: Simon and Schuster, 2002.

Rush, John A., ed. *Mood and Anxiety Disorders.* Philadephia: Williams and Wilkins, 1998.

Seligman, Martin E. P., Ph.D. *Helplessness: On Depression, Development, and Death.* San Francisco: Freeman, 1975.

Simonds, Susan L. *Depression and Women: An Integrative Treatment Approach.* New York: Springer Publishing Company, 2001.

Steiner, Meir, M.D. and others, eds. *Mood Disorders in Women.* London: Martin Dunitz Limited, 2000.

PERIODICALS

Brodaty, H. and others. "A 25-year Longitudinal Comparison Study of the Outcome of Depression." *Psychological Medicine* 31 (2001): 1347-1358.

Nolan, Carla L., and others. "Prefrontal Cortical Volume in Childhood-Onset Major Depression." *Archives of General Psychiatry* 59 (2002): 173-175.

Nuland, Sherwin B., M.D. "The Uncertain Art: Lightning On My Mind." *The American Scholar* 71 (Spring 2002): 127-131.

ORGANIZATIONS

American Academy of Child and Adolescent Psychiatry. 3615 Wisconsin Avenue, NW, Washington, DC 20016. (202) 966-7300. <www.aacap.org>.

National Depressive and Manic-Depressive Association. 730 North Franklin Street, Suite 501, Chicago, IL 60610-3526. (800) 826-3632. <www.ndmda.org>.

OTHER

National Center for Complementary and Alternative Medicine (NCCAM) Clearinghouse. P.O. Box 7923, Gaithersburg, MD 20898. (888) 644-6226. TTY: (866) 464-3615. Fax: (866) 464-3616. <www.nccam.nih.gov>.

National Institute of Mental Health (NIMH). *Depression in Children and Adolescents: A Fact Sheet for Physicians.* <www.nimh.nih.gov/publicat/depchildresfact.cfm>.

Jane A. Fitzgerald, Ph.D.

Male erectile disorder *see* **Erectile dysfunction**

Male orgasmic disorder

Definition

Male orgasmic disorder may be defined as a persistent or recurrent inability to achieve orgasm despite lengthy sexual contact or while participating in sexual intercourse.

The mental health professional's handbook, the ***Diagnostic and Statistical Manual of Mental Disorders*** *(DSM-IV-TR)*, includes this disorder among the **sexual dysfunctions**, along with **premature ejaculation**, **dyspareunia**, and others.

Description

The individual affected by male orgasmic disorder is unable to experience an orgasm following a normal sexual excitement phase. The affected man may regularly experience delays in orgasm, or may be unable to experience orgasm altogether.

Normal orgasm

First, it is important to this discussion to understand the characteristics of a "normal" orgasm. The sensation of orgasm in the male includes emission followed by ejaculation. The term emission refers to a sensation of impending ejaculation produced by contractions of the prostate gland, seminal vesicles, and urethra accompanied by generalized muscular tension, perineal contractions, and involuntary pelvic thrusting. Orgasm is followed by a period of resolution characterized by feelings of well-being and generalized muscular relaxation. During this phase, men may be unable to respond to further sexual stimulation, erection, and orgasm for a variable period of time.

It is also important to distinguish orgasm from ejaculation, although in most instances they occur almost simultaneously. Orgasm is a peak emotional and physical experience, whereas ejaculation is simply a reflex action occurring at the lower portion of the spinal cord and resulting in ejection of semen. Some men have been able to recognize the separation of the two processes, enabling them to experience multiple orgasms without the occurrence of ejaculation. Once ejaculation takes place, a period of recovery time is required prior to a subsequent orgasm.

The sensation of orgasm differs between individuals, and individual orgasms may differ in the same person. All orgasms share certain characteristics in common including rhythmic body and pelvic contractions, elevation of the heart rate, systemic hypertension, hyperventilation, and muscle tension, followed by the sudden release of tension.

The physiological mechanism of normal orgasm

The cycle of sexual response is under the control of a balanced interplay between the two major nervous systems, the sympathetic and the parasympathetic. In general, the sympathetic nervous system prompts action whereas the parasympathetic system's main action is recovery and calming. In order for a penis to become erect, its smooth muscles are relaxed and it becomes congested with blood vessels. This process is mediated by a complex cascade of humoral, neurological and circulatory events in which the parasympathetic nervous system plays a key role. Orgasm and ejaculation and subsequent relaxation of the penis are predominantly functions of the sympathetic nervous system.

Thus, whereas emission is a balanced interplay between the parasympathetic and sympathetic nervous systems, orgasm and ejaculation are predominantly under the control of the sympathetic nervous system. The mechanisms of this system may be blocked by impaired function of the **brain** or of the hormonal, circulatory, and neurological systems. Additionally, certain medications may block these actions.

Abnormalities affecting the process of orgasm

Abnormalities in these processes may be "primary" or "secondary." Primary abnormalities are of lifelong duration with effective sexual performance never having been experienced. Secondary abnormalities are acquired after a period of normal function. If an orgasmic problem only occurs under a particular set of circumstances, or only with certain sexual partners, the condition is considered to be "situational" rather than "generalized" (occurring regardless of the circumstances or partner). The defect in sexual function may be total or partial.

The evidence strongly suggests that orgasm has more to do with the brain than with the body. Electrode stimulation of certain parts of the brain will produce sexual pleasure similar to that produced by physical stimulation. The fact that orgasm occurs during sleep is supportive of this concept.

Causes and symptoms

Causes

The cause of male orgasmic disorders may be organic (related to a condition in the body), but, in most cases, is of psychological origin. It is important for the physician to make every effort to find an underlying cause because the therapy and prognosis depend upon it. A detailed history (including an interview with the sexual partner, if feasible), a general physical examination, the performance of certain laboratory and, in some cases, special tests, are important in the investigation of the underlying cause of the male orgasmic disorder.

Organic causes of male orgasmic disorder include the following:

- Hypogonadism, in which the testes do not produce enough testosterone.
- Thyroid disorders (both hyperthyroidism—too much thyroid hormone— and hypothyroidism, or abnormally low levels of thyroid hormone).
- Pituitary conditions (Cushing's syndrome, excessive production of the hormone that induces lactation called prolactin).
- Diseases that affect the nervous system, such as strokes, multiple sclerosis, diabetic neuropathy, spinal cord injuries.
- Surgery affecting the prostate and other pelvic organs.
- Diseases of the penis.
- Substance abuse, including alcohol.

KEY TERMS

Antihypertensive—An agent used in the treatment of hypertension (high blood pressure).

Diabetes mellitus—A chronic disease affecting the metabolism of carbohydrates that is caused by insufficient production of insulin in the body.

Diabetic neuropathy—Condition existing in people with diabetes in which the nerves at the extremities, especially the feet, are less sensitive to touch and injury.

Humoral—A term describing a hormonal substance secreted by an endocrine gland (such as the thyroid).

Perineal—An anatomical area located between the external genitals and the anus.

Phenothiazine—A class of drugs widely used in the treatment of psychosis.

Prostate gland—The gland at the base of a male's urethra that produces a component of semen.

Retroperitoneal—The anatomical area between the peritoneum (lining of the abdominal cavity) and the muscular and connective tissues of the abdominal wall.

Seminal fluid—Fluid composed of semen from the testes and prostatic secretions.

Seminal vesicles—Sac-like structures bordering the male urethra and serving as storage depots for the seminal fluid.

Urethra—The tubular passage conducting urine from the bladder to the exterior. In the male, the urethra traverses the penis.

- Certain medications. Some of these medications include: the phenothiazines [antipsychotics such as **chlorpromazine** (Thorazine) or **trifluoperazine** (Stelazine)]; certain medications used to treat high blood pressure, including the thiazides [such as triamterene (Dyazide) or spironolactone (Aldactone)] and **beta blockers** [such as **propranolol** (Inderal)]; and the tricyclic antidepressants such as **doxepin** (Sinequan) and **protriptyline** (Vivactil).

The most common causes of the male orgasmic syndrome are psychological in nature. The responsible psychological mechanisms may be "intrinsic" (due to basic internal factors), or "extrinsic" (due to external or environmental factors).

Intrinsic psychological factors that may cause male orgasmic disorder include:

- depression
- feelings of guilt, anger, fear, low self-esteem, and anxiety
- fear of getting the partner pregnant or of contracting a sexually transmitted disease or HIV

Extrinsic psychological factors that may cause male orgasmic disorder include:

- living under conditions that cause undue **stress**
- unsatisfactory relationship with sexual partner
- past history of traumatic sexual encounters such as sexual abuse, rape or incest
- having been raised in an atmosphere of strict sexual taboos

Environmental factors may interfere with sexual functioning. There may be no safe, private place in which the patient can exercise sexual activity or he may be too fatigued from other activities to participate sexually. The difficulties in striving for "safe sex" and the psychological effects and stresses that may result from homosexuality may also interfere with sexual function.

Symptoms

In order to be diagnosed with male orgasmic disorder, the following symptoms must be present according to the *DSM-IV-TR*:

- Persistent or recurrent delay in, or absence of, orgasm following a normal sexual excitement phase during sexual activity that the clinician judges to be adequate. The affected man's age is considered, as well.
- As with all of the sexual dysfunctions, the manual states that the dysfunction must cause the affected man "distress or interpersonal difficulty." According to the *DSM-IV-TR,* the orgasmic dysfunction cannot be better accounted for by another disorder (except another sexual disorder), and cannot be due exclusively to the direct effects of substance abuse, a medication, or a general medical condition. This entry, however, discusses the full scope of male orgasmic difficulties, and so discusses general medical conditions and medications as well as psychological factors.

In addition to specific symptoms involving sexual function (inability or delay in reaching orgasm after sufficient stimulation), most patients complain of anxiety, guilt, shame and frustration, and many develop bodily complaints on a psychological basis. Although sexual dysfunction usually occurs during sexual activity with a partner, the clinician should inquire about sexual function during masturbation. If problems occur during masturbation, the problem probably has nothing to do with the sexual partner.

The physician should differentiate male orgasmic disorder from other sexual disorders such as retarded or delayed ejaculation and retrograde ejaculation. In both of these conditions, orgasm occurs but is delayed or, in the case of retrograde ejaculation, occurs in a retrograde direction (into the bladder).

Demographics

Male orgasmic disorder is found in all races and ethnic groups. In the case of the lifelong type of the disorder, manifestations will occur around the age of puberty. In certain genetic hypogonadism disorders, such as Klinefelter's syndrome, certain bodily signs and symptoms may alert the physician. Similarly, in associated thyroid, testicular and pituitary abnormalities, there may be other manifestations of the underlying disorder. In the acquired type of male orgasmic disorder, the patient will have had the previous experience of normal sexual function. In these cases, it is usually a situational factor that precipitates the disorder.

Diagnosis

The **diagnosis** is usually readily made on the basis of the patient's history and the presence of the *DSM-IV-TR* diagnostic criteria. Male orgasmic disorder may be part of a complex of sexual malfunctioning that may include **erectile dysfunction**, abnormalities in ejaculation (such as premature ejaculation or retrograde ejaculation), and **hypoactive sexual desire disorder**.

In order to differentiate between the various potential disorders, the physician may request laboratory tests and/or may perform further diagnostic evaluations. Blood plasma levels of testosterone are of help in diagnosing hypogonadism. A number of tests of thyroid, pituitary and adrenal function are available to diagnose hormonal abnormalities of those glands. A test for nocturnal penile erections may be performed to diagnose erectile dysfunction.

Treatments

If an extrinsic mechanism is discovered as the cause of the orgasmic disorder, steps should be taken to eliminate or ameliorate the problem. An example would be substance or alcohol abuse or the use of certain provocative medications. In the case of antihypertensives, for example, a number of equally effective agents are available if the one in current use is suspect. Therapy should be directed toward improvement of concurrent conditions such as diabetes that may be having an adverse effect on sexual function. Environmental factors that interfere with sexual activity should be corrected.

In the majority of cases, **psychotherapy** will be suggested even in those cases where psychological factors are secondary rather than the primary mechanism for the disorder. Such treatment should be rendered by therapists with special training in the disorders of sexual function and who can tactfully evaluate the sexual compatibility of the patient and his partner. Treatment usually requires the support of the sexual partner in improving both the psychological as well as the physical aspects of the problem. A step-wise program of partner stimulation of the patient to initially ejaculate outside the vagina, then at the vaginal labia, and finally inside the vagina may be helpful.

Prognosis

The prognosis of the patient with male orgasmic syndrome is dependent on whether the condition is lifelong or acquired and the condition's causes. Prognosis is best when it can be demonstrated that the condition is related to some extrinsic or environmental factor that can be corrected or ameliorated. The prognosis is also favorable in those cases that are due to a remedial organic condition such as a thyroid disorder or hypogonadism. The prognosis is guarded when the disorder is found to be secondary to a deep-seated and chronic psychological or actual psychiatric problem that, in itself, carries an unfavorable prognosis.

Prevention

There are no definitive steps that can be taken to prevent the onset of the male orgasmic disorder. Prompt recognition of the syndrome is important so that appropriate therapy can be attempted as early as possible. As with many chronic conditions, the longer the condition exists, the more difficult therapy becomes.

Resources

BOOKS

American Psychiatric Association. *Diagnostic and Statistical Manual of Mental Disorders.* 4th edition, text revised. Washington, DC: American Psychiatric Association, 2000.

Lue, Tom F., F. Goldstein. "Impotence and Infertility." In *Atlas of Clinical Urology.* Volume 1. New York: Current Medicine, 1999.

Masters, William and Virginia Johnson. *Masters and Johnson on Sex and Human Loving.* New York: Little, Brown, 1986.

Steidle, Christopher P., MD. *The Impotence Source Book.* Los Angeles: Howell House, 1998.

Ralph Myerson, M.D.

Malingering

Definition

The central theme to all definitions of malingering is that the term applies to persons who deliberately pretend to have an illness or disability in order to receive financial or other gain, or to avoid punishment or responsibility.

Description

Personal gain is always the motivation for malingering. Some external reward is sought and is the rationale for feigning an illness. For example, the criminal who does not want to pay for his/her crime, the soldier who does not want to fight, or the person who wishes to be paid for a nonexistent disability all may be tempted to feign an illness.

Malingering can take many forms. However, as specifically related to mental illness, the tendency is to fake more common disorders such as **major depressive disorder**, **post-traumatic stress disorder**, and **panic disorder** with **agoraphobia**. With very little coaching or research, even a beginner can simulate symptoms of these disorders. Generalized symptoms such as headaches, dizziness, low back pain, stomach pain, etc., are easily manufactured, and x rays, **magnetic resonance imaging** (MRIs), or CAT scans (computed axial tomography) are unable to determine a physical cause.

Malingerers tend to avoid symptoms such as those associated with more serious psychiatric disorders, because the pretense is very difficult to maintain and objective measures could detect the difference. For example, hearing voices and seeing demons, or living with the idea that others can hear unspoken thoughts, would become a difficult act to maintain over time. On the other hand, to feign a sad mood, loss of interest in formerly enjoyed activities, or a low energy level may not be so difficult to demonstrate. Likewise, responding positively to a series of questions about having heart palpitations, sweating, dizziness, or fear of impending death, could be done readily.

The concept that fakers use less severe symptoms to escape detection was validated in 2001 in a research study. Individuals were asked to fake mental illnesses in such a way as to avoid detection by sophisticated psychological tests. All or portions of the following tests were employed in the research: the Structured Inventory of Malingered Symptomatology, the Psychopathic Personality Inventory, the M-Test, and the Trauma Symptom Inventory. Slightly over 11% of the 540 research participants successfully avoided detection and were diagnosed with real disorders instead of with malingering. Questionnaires completed by those who successfully faked symptoms showed that they avoided detection by endorsing fewer actual symptoms, staying away from unduly strange or bizarre symptoms, and responding based upon personal experience.

Although ordinarily an intended fraud, malingering may serve an adaptive purpose under circumstances of duress, such as while being held captive. Faking an illness at such a time may allow a person to avoid cooperating with their captors or to avoid punishment.

Causes and symptoms

Lying for personal benefit has existed since the beginning of time. As previously stated, personal gain is the goal of the malingerer.

The symptoms may vary a great deal from person to person.

Demographics

Due to the difficulty of determining and exposing malingering, the incidence is unknown.

Diagnosis

When attempting to diagnose malingering, mental health professionals have three possibilities to consider. First, there is the possibility that the illness feigned by the malingerer is real. However, once it is determined that the disorder has no basis in fact, the professional is left with two viable diagnoses: **factitious disorder** and malingering. Factitious disorder is a legitimate malady, but malingering is not. Both have to do with feigned illnesses.

Unlike malingering, the individual with factitious disorder produces fake symptoms to fulfill the need to maintain the "sick role"—a sort of emotional gain. Being "sick" gives the person with factitious disorder attention from physicians and sympathy from friends and loved ones. Thus, this individual's goal is not the same as the malingerer's.

With malingering, motivation is always external and is designed to accomplish one of three things: (1) evade hard or dangerous situations, punishment, or responsibility; (2) gain rewards such as free income, source for drugs, sanctuary from police, or free hospital care; or (3) avenge a monetary loss, legal ruling, or job termination.

Mental health practitioners become alert to the possibility of malingering when circumstances exist that might help promote such a facade. Malingering is suspected when any combination of events such as the following occur:

- A person is referred by his/her attorney for an evaluation.
- There is a noticeable and distinct difference between the level of distress or disability claimed by the person when compared to information obtained by objective means. (Objective means could take the form of personal observation, task performance ability by the person, or a psychological test like those mentioned above.)
- There is a lack of cooperation from the individual.
- A **diagnosis** of **antisocial personality disorder** exists.

Resources

BOOKS

American Psychiatric Association. *Diagnostic and Statistical Manual of Mental Disorders.* 4th edition, text revised. Washington, DC: American Psychiatric Association, 2000.

Kaplan, Harold I., M.D., and Benjamin J. Sadock, M.D., "Malingering." In *Synopsis of Psychiatry: Behavioral Sciences, Clinical Psychiatry.* 8th edition. Lippincott, Williams and Wilkins, 1998.

PERIODICALS

Edens, John F., Laura S. Guy, Randy K. Otto, Jacqueline K. Buffington, Tara L. Tomicic, and Norman G. Poythress. "Factors differentiating successful versus unsuccessful malingerers." *Journal of Personality Assessment.* 77, no. 2 (2001): 333-338.

ORGANIZATIONS

American Psychiatric Association. 1400 K Street NW, Washington D.C. 20005. <http://www.psych.org>.

Jack H. Booth, Psy.D.

Managed care

Definition

Managed care is a generic term for various health care payment systems that attempt to contain costs by controlling the type and level of services provided. Health maintenance organization (HMO) is a term that is often used synonymously with managed care, but HMOs are actually a particular type of managed care organization.

Purpose

Health care reform has been an increasingly urgent concern in the United States over the past 40 years. Until recently, the primary source of health care coverage was indemnity insurance, which pays or reimburses the cost

KEY TERMS

Capitated payment system—A contract between managed care organizations and health care providers involving a prepaid amount for blocks of services.

Carve-out plans—Managed care plans that make provision for mental health services by creating subcontracts involving different terms of payment and utilization review from those used for general health care.

Case manager—A professional who designs and monitors implementation of comprehensive care plans (i.e., services addressing medical, financial, housing, psychiatric, vocational, social needs) for individuals seeking mental health or social services.

Case rate—A type of contract between managed care organizations and health care providers involving a prepaid amount for services on a case-by-case basis.

Deductible—The amount of money that must be paid out of pocket by health care consumers before the insurance provider will make payments.

Health maintenance organization (HMO)—A type of managed care system that involves payment contracts with a group or panel of health care providers.

Health Maintenance Organization Act of 1973—Federal legislation that provided aid to develop HMOs.

Indemnity insurance—Insurance plans that pay on a fee-for-service basis in the event of illness or injury.

Medicaid—A program jointly funded by state and federal governments that reimburses hospitals and physicians for the care of individuals who cannot pay for their own medical expenses. These individuals may be in low-income households or may have chronic disabilities.

Medicare—A federally funded health insurance program for individuals age 65 and older, and certain categories of younger persons with disabilities.

Preferred provider organization (PPO)—A type of managed care system involving payment contracts with a group or panel of health care providers.

Premium—The cost of enrollment in a health insurance plan. Premiums are usually paid on a monthly basis.

Utilization review—A process used by managed care organizations involving scrutiny of service care delivery to determine whether services are necessary.

of medical services in the event of a person's illness or injury. Indemnity insurance gives health care providers few reasons to use less expensive forms of treatment—the insurance companies generally pay for any treatment deemed necessary by a physician. Presumably, this type of system encourages providers to overuse expensive, unnecessary treatments and diagnostic procedures. Patient co-pays and deductibles attempt to limit excessive use of medical services. Yet costs continue to rise, resulting in insurance companies' frequently raising premium prices.

The primary intent of managed care is to reduce health care costs. Emphasis is placed on preventive care and early **intervention**, rather than care provided after an illness or injury has occurred. The responsibility of limiting services is placed on the service provider rather than the consumer. This limitation is achieved by (a) "gatekeeper" policies that require individuals to get referrals for specialized treatment from their primary physicians; (b) financial incentives (either bonuses or withholding money) for providers to restrict services and contain costs; (c) guidelines requiring adherence by providers at the cost of being dropped from the plan for noncompliance; (d) review of services by the managed care organization and **denial** of payment if services are considered unnecessary.

Description

Health maintenance organizations have been in existence in the United States since the late 1800s. It was not until the 1950s, however, that the government began to encourage the development of HMOs. In 1973, the Health Maintenance Organization Act was passed; and in 1978, a Congressional amendment increased federal aid for HMO development. From 1980 to 1989, enrollment in HMOs increased from 9 million to 36 million Americans. By 1990, 95% of private insurance companies used some form of managed care. In the 1990s, managed care was incorporated into Medicare and Medicaid plans as well.

Managed care organizations frequently contract with a group or panel of health care providers. HMOs and PPOs (preferred provider organizations) are examples of these types of contracts. Individuals insured under an HMO or PPO may receive care only from providers on the panel. These providers are expected to deliver services according to specific stipulations. Payment is often subject to utilization review, in which delivery of medical services is scrutinized to determine whether the services are necessary. The review may occur with each episode of treatment, or may be ongoing through the use of a case manager. If the managed care organization thinks that the services were unnecessary, payment is denied.

Payment arrangements between managed care organizations and care providers are often made in advance. Capitated payment systems are typically used with large health care facilities that serve many people. The health care provider receives a set amount of money each month based on the number of individuals covered by the plan. The provider may or may not serve that many people in one month. Capitation systems provide a steady, reliable cash flow, but involve some economic risk because the services provided may exceed the dollar amount allotted. Another type of payment system uses case rates. The provider receives a predetermined amount of money per individual on a case-by-case basis. The amount of money reflects the estimated service costs to treat the individual patient's condition. Again, the provider takes the risk that unanticipated services will be required.

In the past, mental health services (including substance abuse treatment) were routinely excluded from managed care plans. In the 1970s, some mental health care coverage was required in order to meet federal qualifications. Carve-out plans were developed in the 1990s. These plans essentially create a separate managed care plan for mental health services. Mental health services tend to be covered at a lower rate than general health services and have also been cut back more severely. From 1988 to 1997, mental health care spending decreased by 54%, which reflects cutbacks 670% higher than those for general health care benefits. Mental health care providers are also subjected to higher levels of utilization review than medical care providers.

Ethical concerns

Managed care has been successful in fulfilling its primary purpose of lowering health care costs in the United States. Statistics show drastic decreases in the use of inpatient care and accompanying overall reduction in costs. Many observers, however, would argue that the quality of care has suffered as a result. Individuals have fewer choices regarding the locations where they can receive treatment. If a managed care organization closes, individuals under that plan must switch to other care providers under a new plan, which disrupts ongoing treatment. Care providers often feel that their clients are denied essential care in favor of saving money. Employers have become disillusioned because of increasing disability claims due to employees having received inadequate treatment for illnesses or injuries. In addition to disability claims, inadequate treatment results in hidden costs to employers in terms of lost productivity.

Another factor in decreased quality of care involves conflicting loyalties for health care providers. On the one hand, providers want to ensure quality care for their clients. On the other hand, they are encouraged to provide the least amount of care possible in order to receive financial benefits. Just as dishonest practice was suspected in conjunction with indemnity insurance, managed care creates a powerful potential for inappropriately addressing patients' needs.

Future directions

Due to growing popular discontent with managed care organizations, many critics believe that the system will not continue in its current state. No one, however, expects managed care to disappear completely and indemnity plans to rise to their former prominence. Changes are expected to occur as managed care programs begin competing among themselves. Cost and efficiency will no longer be the main selling point; quality of services will take precedence. One researcher has suggested that along with new systems of managed care and continuing systems of indemnity plans, health care providers may even organize and offer services directly to employers, thus eliminating the middlemen. This development would be beneficial to all involved: employers would pay less; providers would be better compensated; and clients would receive better care.

See also Case management

Resources

BOOKS

Horwitz, Allan V. and Teresa L. Scheid, eds. *A Handbook for the Study of Mental Health.* New York: Cambridge University Press, 1999.

Sauber, S. Richard, ed. *Managed Mental Health Care: Major Diagnostic and Treatment Approaches.* Philadelphia: Brunner/Mazel, 1997.

Tuttle, Gayle McCracken and Diane Rush Woods. *The Managed Care Answer Book for Mental Health Professionals.* Bristol, Pennsylvania: Brunner/Mazel, 1997.

PERIODICALS

Gottlieb, Michael C. and Caren C. Cooper. "The Future of Mental Health Care Delivery: Ideals and Realities." *Counseling Psychologist* 28, no. 2 (2000): 263-266.

Reed, Geoffrey M., Ronald F. Levant, Chris E. Stout, Michael J. Murphey, and Randy Phelps. "Psychology in the Current Mental Health Marketplace." *Professional Psychology: Research and Practice* 32, no. 1 (2001): 65-70.

ORGANIZATIONS

American Association of Health Plans. 1129 20th Street NW, Suite 600, Washington, DC 20036-3421. <http://www.aahp.org>.

Department of Managed Health Care. California HMO Help Center, 980 Ninth Street, Suite 500, Sacramento, CA 95814-2725. <http://www.hmohelp.ca.gov>.

Medicare. 1-800-MEDICARE. <www.medicare.gov>.

Sandra L. Friedrich, M.A.

Mania *see* **Manic episode**

Manic episode

Definition

A discrete period lasting a week or more during which a person experiences mania, an abnormally elevated, cheerful, or euphoric mood.

Description

A person experiencing a manic episode shows persistent and often inappropriate enthusiasm which may involve taking on new projects for which he or she is ill suited. It might also involve engaging strangers in detailed conversations, acting without concern for consequences of one's actions, or increased sexual activities. Less commonly, a person may be abnormally irritable during a manic episode. On average, the episodes begin before age 25. This means that some individuals experience their first episode while in their teens and others during middle age.

Psychiatrists use five criteria to identify someone in the midst of this type of mood episode. First, the period of abnormal behavior must persist for at least one week unless the person is admitted to a hospital. Typically, the episodes last from a few weeks to a few months. Second, the **diagnosis** requires three additional symptoms if the mood change results in expansive behavior, or four if it results in unnatural irritability. These symptoms include an unwarranted sense of self-importance, a tendency to be easily distracted, a decreased need for sleep, a rapid flow of ideas with one replacing another before the first is acted upon, an inability to sit still or increased activity directed at achieving some goal, an irrepressible need to talk, and finally, a devotion to some activity the patient finds pleasurable but could be harmful. The third criterion is that the symptoms do not qualify the patient for a diagnosis of **mixed episode**. Fourth, the patient can not function normally at home or at work, or shows signs of **psychosis**. The fifth and last criterion is that the cause of the episode can not be attributed to side effects from any drug abuse, medication, medical treatment, or medical condition.

Many of these symptoms are also present in a hypomanic episode. A hypomanic episode is similar to a manic episode, but the symptoms may be experienced to a lesser extent. The main differences between a manic and hypomanic episode are the following:

- A hypomanic episode may only last four days, whereas a manic episode, by definition, lasts one week.
- In a manic episode, psychotic features (**hallucinations** and **delusions**) may be present, but in a hypomanic episode, they cannot be.
- A manic episode significantly impairs the affected person's functions, but a hypomanic episode does not.

Both of these kinds of episodes may be seen in patients with **bipolar disorder**.

Dean A. Haycock, Ph.D.

Maprotiline

Definition

Maprotiline is an oral antidepressant. It is a member of the tetracyclic antidepressant family of compounds. In the United States, it is sold under the trade name Ludiomil.

Purpose

Maprotiline is an antidepressant intended for use by persons with depressive **neurosis** and bipolar syndrome. It is also occasionally used for the relief of anxiety associated with depression.

Description

Maprotiline elevates mood. The precise pharmacological mode of action is not fully understood but it is

KEY TERMS

Barbiturates—A class of medications (including Seconal and Nembutal) that causes sedation and drowsiness. They may be prescribed legally, but may also be used as drugs of abuse.

Bipolar syndrome—An abnormal mental condition characterized by periods of intense elation, energy and activity followed by periods of inactivity and depression.

Guanethidine—An antihypertensive drug used to treat high blood pressure.

Hallucination—False sensory perceptions. A person experiencing a hallucination may "hear" sounds or "see" people or objects that are not really present. Hallucinations can also affect the senses of smell, touch, and taste.

Manic—Referring to mania, a state characterized by excessive activity, excitement or emotion.

Monoamine oxidase inhibitors—A group of antidepressant drugs that decrease the activity of monoamine oxidase, a neurotransmitter found in the brain that affects mood.

Norepinephrine—A neurotransmitter in the brain that acts to constrict blood vessels and raise blood pressure. It works in combination with serotonin.

Physostigmine—A short-acting drug that enhances levels of a substance (acetylcholine) between neurons in the brain.

Syncope—A brief lapse of consciousness caused by a temporarily insufficient flow of blood to the brain.

Tachycardia—A pulse rate above 100 beats per minute.

thought to inhibit the reuptake of the neurotransmitter norepinephrine at nerve endings in the **brain**. It is prescribed in 25-, 50-, and 75-mg tablets.

Recommended dosage

The recommended initial dosage of maprotiline is 75 mg, given by mouth in three 25-mg administrations. The initial dosage should be maintained for at least two weeks. Therapeutic results maybe observed in three to seven days. Typically, initial administration may have to be continued for two to three weeks before results are observed.

The recommended total dosage is 150 mg per day. Dosage should be increased 25 mg at a time. The maximum daily dosage in severely depressed persons is 225 mg. The elderly may require a total initial dosage of 25 mg per day.

Precautions

Maprotiline should be discontinued or reduced in dosage prior to surgery. This is due to the potential for interactions with anesthetic agents.

Maprotiline may promote seizure activity: of all the cyclic antidepressants it probably causes the highest incidence of **seizures** and has thus fallen out of favor with most psychiatrists. Also for this reason, it should not be combined with other neuroleptics (antipsychotics) that can also cause seizures. The drug increases the effect of alcohol and should not be taken with products containing alcohol or **barbiturates**. Persons taking monoamine oxidase inhibitors (MAOIs), such as Parnate (**tranylcypromine**) and Nardil (**phenelzine**), should not take maprotiline.

The possibility of **suicide** is a component of depression. A minimal number of doses should be dispensed at any one time to minimize the potential for use as a suicide agent. Because the drug may lower the threshold for a **manic episode** among persons with **bipolar disorders**, it should be used only with caution and under close supervision.

Side effects

The most commonly reported side effect of maprotiline is dry mouth. Slightly more than one person in five (22%) experiences this effect. Approximately 16% of users experience drowsiness, dizziness is reported by 8%, and nervousness and constipation by 6%. Other less common side effects include anxiety, agitation, **insomnia**, blurred vision, tremor, weakness, **fatigue**, nausea, and headache with blurred vision are also reported. Other rare side effects are similar to those experienced by users of tricyclic antidepressants. These include abnormally high or low blood pressure, tachycardia, and syncope. **Hallucinations**, disorientation, and mania have been reported, as have vomiting, diarrhea, and gastric distress.

Interactions

Cimetidine and **fluoxetine** reduce the elimination of maprotiline, thus increasing its plasma concentration. Barbiturates and phenytoin increase the elimination of maprotiline, thus decreasing its plasma concentration.

Cardiovascular toxicity has been reported when maprotiline is used simultaneously with thyroid-replacement medications such as levothyroxine, and maprotiline blocks the pharmacological effect of guanethidine.

An increased risk of seizures has been reported with the simultaneous use of physostigmine and maprotiline. A similar effect is observed when maprotiline is taken simultaneously with phenothiazine compounds.

See also Anxiety and anxiety disorders; Bipolar disorder; Bipolar disorders; Depression and depressive disorders

Resources

BOOKS

Adams, Michael and Norman Holland. *Core Concepts in Pharmacology.* Philadelphia: Lippincott-Raven, 1998.

Foreman, John C. and Torben Johansen. *Textbook of Receptor Pharmacology.* 2nd ed. Boca Raton, FL: CRC Press, 2002.

Page, Clive P., and Michael Murphy. *Integrated Pharmacology.* St. Louis: Mosby-Year Book, 2002.

Von Boxtel, Chris J., Budiono Santoso, and I. Ralph Edwards. *Drug Benefits and Risks: International Textbook of Clinical Pharmacology.* New York: John Wiley and Sons, 2001.

PERIODICALS

Martenyi F., M. Dossenbach, K. Mraz, and S. Metcalfe. "Gender differences in the efficacy of fluoxetine and maprotiline in depressed patients: a double-blind trial of antidepressants with serotonergic or norepinephrinergic reuptake inhibition profile." *European Journal of Neuropsychopharmacology* 11, no. 3 (2001): 227-232.

Normann C., K. Lieb, and J. Walden. "Increased plasma concentration of maprotiline by coadministration of risperidone." *Journal of Clinical Psychopharmacology* 22, no. 1 (2002): 92-93.

Pisani F., G. Oteri, C. Costa, G. Di Raimondo, and R. Di Perri. "Effects of psychotropic drugs on seizure threshold." *Drug Safety* 25, no. 2 (2002): 91-110.

ORGANIZATIONS

American Academy of Clinical Toxicology. 777 East Park Drive, PO Box 8820, Harrisburg, PA 17105-8820. Telephone: (717) 558-7750. Fax: (717) 558-7845. Web site: <http://www.clintox.org/index.html>.

American Academy of Family Physicians. 11400 Tomahawk Creek Parkway, Leawood, KS 66211-2672. Telephone: (913) 906-6000. Web site: <http://www.aafp.org/>.

American Medical Association. 515 N. State Street, Chicago, IL 60610. Telephone: (312) 464-5000. Web site: <http://www.ama-assn.org/>.

American Psychiatric Association. 1400 K Street NW, Washington, DC 20005. Telephone: (888) 357-7924. Fax (202) 682-6850. Web site: <http://www.psych.org/>.

American Society for Clinical Pharmacology and Therapeutics. 528 North Washington Street, Alexandria, VA 22314. Telephone: (703) 836-6981. Fax: 703-836-5223.

American Society for Pharmacology and Experimental Therapeutics. 9650 Rockville Pike, Bethesda, MD 20814-3995. Telephone: (301) 530-7060. Fax: (301) 530-7061. Web site: <http://www.aspet.org/>.

L. Fleming Fallon, Jr., M.D., Dr.P.H.

Marijuana *see* **Cannabis and related disorders**

Marital and family therapists

Definition

A marriage and family therapist is a person who has received advanced, specialized training and has practiced therapy for an extended period, typically a minimum of 3,000 hours, under the close supervision of a competent, licensed professional. A marital and family counselor must be licensed by passing both written and oral examinations as well as completing continuing education requirements. Licenses to practice are issued by individual states.

Description

A marital and family counselor concentrates on these two aspects of human behavior. While individuals may seek and receive individual counseling, complete families or marital pairs are more commonly seen together during counseling sessions.

Different theoretical models exist for marital and **family therapy**. However, these share a common thread of concentrating on interactions between and among members of a dysfunctional unit.

The goal of marital and family therapists is to improve relationships between marital partners or family members, or to help with the dissolution of a difficult relationship with minimum harm to all. Various techniques are employed. These include active listening, role-playing, **behavior modification**, and changing expectations concerning the behaviors of others. Persons receiving therapy are helped to understand the motivations and actions of others. They are taught techniques to modify their own behaviors, or how to accept more readily the behaviors of others.

Success in marital and family counseling requires patience, time, and a commitment to succeed. As dysfunctional behaviors are acquired over long periods of time, long periods are required to first unlearn troublesome habits and then replace them with more appropriate patterns of behavior. Patience and understanding facilitate this process. A commitment to succeed is mandatory for success. Therapists must be able to identify persons who enter therapy without a commitment to succeed.

Individual states regulate the activities in which marriage and family therapists may legally engage. This is done to protect consumers from incompetence and negligence of service providers who may potentially exploit them. Most state regulations closely delineate the minimum training and education requirements for marital and family therapists. Thus, the possession of a license to practice marital and family therapy certifies minimum competency and ensures that consumers receive safe and fair treatment. As of 2002, there are 42 states that license practitioners of marital and family therapy.

Marital and family therapists receive training in the following three areas to qualify for a license to practice the profession.

- Academic program. A person must earn a master's degree with an emphasis in marital and family therapy from an accredited academic institution. Most programs of study are 48 semester credit hours in length. The curriculum must include theoretical as well as practical training. Specific areas of competency such as human sexuality, assessing victims of child **abuse** and substance abuse must be embedded in the curriculum. Students must receive 30 hours of directly supervised counseling and an additional 150 hours of directed counseling practice.
- Supervised clinical experience. Prior to becoming eligible to sit for a licensure exam, candidates must complete a total of approximately 3,000 hours of supervised counseling experiences. The 3,000 hours may include activities related to personal **psychotherapy**, supervision, direct counseling experience, professional enrichment experiences, and maintaining records. Some (approximately one-quarter) of these hours may be included in the graduate degree training curriculum. All of the clinical experiences are closely supervised.
- Licensure examination. The examination has written and oral components. A license to practice is granted with the successful passage of both parts of the exam. A minimum of 36 hours of continuing education training must be completed every two years as a requirement for re-licensure.

See also Psychotherapy; Behavior modification; Play therapy

Resources

BOOKS

Bobes, Toby, and Barbara Rothman. *Doing Couple Therapy: Integrating Theory with Practice.* New York: W. W. Norton, W. W. 2002.

Carlson, Jon and Diane Kjos. *Theories and Strategies of Family Therapy.* Boston: Allyn and Bacon, 2001.

Walsh, William M., and James A. McGraw. *Essentials of Family Therapy: A Structured Summary of Nine Approaches.* 2nd ed. Denver: Love Publishing Co., 2002.

PERIODICALS

Helmeke, K. B., and A. M. Prouty. "Do We Really Understand? An Experiential Exercise for Training Family Therapists." *Journal of Marital and Family Therapy* 27, no. 4 (2001): 535–544.

Lebow, J. "What Does the Research Tell Us about Couple and Family Therapies?" *Journal of Clinical Psychology* 56, no. 8 (2000): 1083–1094.

Protinsky, H., and L. Coward. "Developmental Lessons of Seasoned Marital and Family Therapists: A Qualitative Investigation." *Journal of Marital and Family Therapy* 27, no. 3 (2001): 375–384.

OTHER

American Association for Marriage and Family Therapy. 1133 15th Street, NW Suite 300, Washington, DC 20005. Telephone: (202) 452-0109. Fax: (202) 223-2329. Web site: <http://www.aamft.org/index_nm.asp>.

American Family Therapy Academy. 2020 Pennsylvania Avenue, NW, #273, Washington, DC 20006. Telephone: (202) 333-3690. Fax: (202) 333-3692. Web site: <www.afta.org>.

American Psychiatric Association. 1400 K Street NW, Washington, DC 20005. Telephone: (888) 357-7924. Fax: (202) 682-6850. Web site: <http://www.psych.org/>.

American Psychological Association. 750 First Street NW, Washington, DC, 20002-4242. Telephone: (800) 374-2721 or (202) 336-5500. Web site: <http://www.apa.org/>.

National Mental Health Association. 1021 Prince Street, Alexandria, VA 22314-2971. Telephone: (800) 969-6942 or (703) 684-7722. Fax: (703) 684-5968. Web site: <http://www.nmha.org/>.

L. Fleming Fallon, Jr., M.D., Dr.P.H.

Marital therapy *see* **Couples therapy**

Masochism *see* **Sexual masochism**

Massage *see* **Bodywork therapies**

Mathematics disorder

Definition

Mathematics disorder, formerly called developmental arithmetic disorder, developmental acalculia, or dyscalculia, is a learning disorder in which a person's mathematical ability is substantially below the level normally expected based on his or her age, intelligence, life experiences, educational background, and physical impairments. This disability affects the ability to do calculations as well as the ability to understand word problems and mathematical concepts.

Description

Mathematics disorder was first described as a developmental disorder in 1937. Since then, it has come to encompass a number of distinct types of mathematical deficiencies. These include:

- difficulty reading and writing numbers
- difficulty aligning numbers in order to do calculations
- inability to perform calculations
- inability to comprehend word problems

The range and number of mathematical difficulties that have been documented suggests that there are several different causes for mathematics disorder. In addition, several known physical conditions cause mathematics disorder. Turner syndrome and fragile X syndrome, both genetic disorders that affect girls, are associated with difficulty in mathematics. Injury to certain parts of the **brain** can also cause inability to perform calculations. These conditions appear to be independent of other causes of mathematics disorder. Mathematics disorder is often associated with other **learning disorders** involving reading and language, although it may also exist independently in children whose reading and language skills are average or above average.

Causes and symptoms

The causes of mathematics disorder are not understood. Different manifestations of the disorder may have different causes. Symptoms of the disorder, however, can be grouped into four categories: language symptoms; recognition or perceptual symptoms; mathematical symptoms; and attention symptoms.

People with language symptoms have trouble naming mathematical terms; understanding word problems; or understanding such mathematical concepts as "greater than" or "less than." People with recognition symptoms have difficulty reading numbers and such operational signs as the plus or minus signs, or aligning numbers properly in order to perform accurate calculations. Mathematical symptoms include deficiencies in the ability to count; to memorize such basic arithmetical data as the multiplication tables; or to follow a sequence of steps in problem solving. Attention symptoms are related to failures in copying numbers and ignoring operational signs. Sometimes these failures are the result of a person's carelessness. At other times, however, they appear to result from a lack of understanding of the factors or operations involved in solving the problem.

In practical terms, parents and teachers may see the following signs of mathematics disorder in a child's schoolwork:

- problems counting
- difficulty memorizing multiplication tables
- inability to grasp the difference between such operations as addition and subtraction
- poor computational skills; many errors in simple arithmetic
- slowness in performing calculations
- difficulty arranging numbers in order (from smallest to largest, for example)
- inability to grasp information on graphs
- difficulty copying numbers or problems
- inability to grasp the concept of place value
- inability to align two or three digit numbers to do calculations
- difficulty understanding word problems
- inability to understand mathematical symbols

These symptoms must be evaluated in light of the person's age, intelligence, educational experience, exposure to mathematics learning activities, and general cultural and life experience. The person's mathematical ability must fall substantially below the level of others with similar characteristics. In most cases, several of these symptoms are present simultaneously.

KEY TERMS

Individual education plan (IEP)—A plan of instruction drawn up for an individual student who is having specific difficulties with mathematics, reading, or other skills necessary to progress beyond elementary school.

Demographics

The number of children with mathematics disorder is not entirely clear. The ***Diagnostic and Statistical Manual of Mental Disorders***, which is the basic manual consulted by mental health professionals in assessing the presence of mental disorders, indicates that about 1% of school age children have mathematics disorder. Other studies, however, have found higher rates of arithmetical dysfunction in children. Likewise, some studies find no gender difference in the prevalence of mathematics disorder, while others find that girls are more likely to be affected. Mathematics disorder, like other learning disabilities, however, appears to run in families, suggesting the existence of a genetic component to the disorder.

Diagnosis

Mathematics disorder is not usually diagnosed before a child is in the second or third grade because of the variability with which children acquire mathematical fluency. Many bright children manage to get through to fourth- or fifth-grade level in mathematics by using memorization and calculation tricks (such as counting on fingers or performing repeated addition as a substitute for multiplication) before their disability becomes apparent. Requests for testing usually originate with a teacher or parent who has observed several symptoms of the disorder.

To receive a **diagnosis** of mathematics disorder according to the criteria established by the American Psychiatric Association, a child must show substantially lower than expected ability in mathematics based on his or her age, intelligence, and background. In addition, the child's deficiencies must cause significant interference with academic progress or daily living skills.

In addition to an interview with a child **psychiatrist** or other mental health professional, the child's mathematical ability may be evaluated with such individually administered diagnostic tests as the Enright Diagnostic Test of Mathematics, or with curriculum-based assessments. If the results of testing suggest mathematics disorder, such other causes of difficulty as poor vision or hearing, **mental retardation**, or lack of fluency in the language of instruction, are ruled out. The child's educational history and exposure to opportunities for learning mathematics are also taken into account. On the basis of this information, a qualified examiner can make the diagnosis of mathematics disorder.

Treatments

Children who receive a diagnosis of mathematics disorder are eligible for an individual education plan (IEP) that details specific accommodations to learning. Because of the wide variety of problems found under the diagnosis of mathematics disorder, plans vary considerably. Generally, instruction emphasizes basic mathematical concepts, while teaching children problem-solving skills and ways to eliminate distractions and extraneous information. Concrete, hands-on instruction is more successful than abstract or theoretical instruction. IEPs also address other language or reading disabilities that affect a child's ability to learn mathematics.

Prognosis

Progress in overcoming mathematics disorder depends on the specific type of difficulties that the child has with mathematics, the learning resources available, and the child's determination to work on overcoming the disorder. Some children work through their disability, while others continue to have trouble with mathematics throughout life. Children who continue to suffer from mathematics disorder may develop low self-esteem and social problems related to their lack of academic achievement. Later in life they may be more likely to drop out of school and find themselves shut out of jobs or occupations that require the ability to perform basic mathematical calculations.

Prevention

There is no known way to prevent mathematics disorder.

See also Reading disorder; Disorder of written expression

Resources

BOOKS

American Psychiatric Association. *Diagnostic and Statistical Manual of Mental Disorders.* 4th ed., text revised. Washington DC: American Psychiatric Association, 2000.

Sadock, Benjamin J. and Virginia A. Sadock, eds. *Comprehensive Textbook of Psychiatry.* 7th ed. Vol. 2. Philadelphia: Lippincott Williams and Wilkins, 2000.

PERIODICALS

Jordan, Nancy, and Laurie B. Hanich. "Mathematical Thinking in Second-Grade Children with Different forms of LD." *Journal of Learning Disabilities* 33 (November 2000): 567-585.

ORGANIZATIONS

Learning Disabilities Association of America. 4156 Library Road Pittsburgh, PA 15234-1349. (412) 341-1515. <www.ldanatl.org>.

National Center for Learning Disabilities. 381 Park Avenue South, Suite 1401, New York, NY 10016. (888) 575-7373 (toll-free) or (212) 545-7510. <www.ncld.org>.

Tish Davidson, A.M.

Medication-induced movement disorders

Definition

Medication-induced movement disorder occurs due to treatment with antipsychotic medications. Most medication-induced movement disorders are caused by medications that block the action of dopamine, a neurotransmitter that allows communication between two neurons to take place and that is necessary for coordination of movements of different parts of the body. When the receptor where dopamine is supposed to bind is blocked, certain movement-related side effects occur. All of the medications that block dopamine receptors are called neuroleptics.

Neuroleptics include both conventional or typical antipsychotic agents, such as **chlorpromazine** (Thorazine), **haloperidol** (Haldol), and **fluphenazine** (Prolixin), as well as the newer, or atypical, antipsychotic agents such as **clozapine** (Clozaril), **risperidone** (Risperdal), **olanzapine** (Zyprexa), and **quetiapine** (Seroquel). In general, the newer, atypical antipsychotics appear to have a lower likelihood to cause movement disorders than the older, typical medications. Other neuroleptics include certain drugs used in the treatment of physical symptoms such as nausea, and include prochlorperazine, promethazine, and metoclopramide, as well as **amoxapine** (Asendin), which is marketed as an antidepressant.

There are other medications, however, that do not block dopamine action but still cause movement disorders. They are not referred to as neuroleptics, and they include **lithium carbonate**, **valproic acid** and a class of drugs called selective serotonin reuptake inhibitors (SSRIs). The disorder caused by these medications is called medication-induced postural tremor.

All of the disorders caused by neuroleptics, which include antipsychotics and other medications that block dopamine, as well as disorders caused by non-neuroleptic medications, are collectively referred to as medication-induced movement disorders.

Description

Neuroleptics

Medication-induced movement disorders caused by neuroleptics are divided into three time periods. The early-onset type, which usually occurs within the first seven days of treatment with neuroleptics, is known as neuroleptic-induced acute dystonia. Neuroleptic-induced acute dystonia is characterized by abnormal contractions of various muscle groups resulting in spasm and/or twisting of the head, neck, jaw, lips, tongue, and eye muscles as well as abnormal movements and postures of the limbs and the trunk.

The intermediate-onset types of movement disorders associated with the use of neuroleptics usually develop within the first three months of treatment. They are known as neuroleptic-induced Parkinsonism and neuroleptic-induced akathisia. Neuroleptic-induced Parkinsonism is associated with difficulty initiating movements. Once movements are initiated, they are very slow. Other characteristics of neuroleptic-induced Parkinsonism are tremor and rigidity in muscles. Neuroleptic-induced akathisia is associated with uncontrollable restlessness that may involve compulsive foot tapping, pacing, and a sense of inner tension.

The late-onset type of neuroleptic-related movement disorder is known as neuroleptic-induced **tardive dyskinesia** and the onset is usually seen many months to years after starting the neuroleptic treatment. Neuroleptic-induced tardive dyskinesia involves grotesque, repetitive, and involuntary movements. They are usually seen in the mouth and face.

A movement disorder that can occur at any time during the course of neuroleptic treatment is known as neuroleptic malignant syndrome. It is a serious condition and is characterized by changes in consciousness, ranging from agitation to coma. The patient may experience high fever, and increases in blood pressure and heart rate, as well as severe muscular rigidity.

Non-neuroleptics

All of the movement disorders mentioned above are related to the use of neuroleptic medications. However, other drugs, such as lithium, valproic acid, isoproterenol, amphetamine, theophylline, as well as a class of drugs known as tricyclic antidepressants, may also cause a movement disorder that is mainly characterized by postural tremor, a rhythmic alteration in movement. Lithium-induced tremor may take the form of twitching in the arms and legs.

KEY TERMS

Dystonia—A neurological disorder characterized by involuntary muscle spasms. The spasms can cause a painful twisting of the body and difficulty walking or moving.

Hyperthyroidism—Condition resulting from the thyroid glands secreting excessive thyroid hormone, causing increased basal metabolic rate, and causing an increased need for food to meet the demand of the metabolic activity; generally, however, weight loss results.

Neuroleptic—Another name for antipsychotic medications, such as haloperidol (Haldol) and chlorpromazine (Thorazine).

Neuroleptic malignant syndrome—An unusual but potentially serious complication that develops in some patients who have been treated with antipsychotic medications. NMS is characterized by changes in blood pressure, altered states of consciousness, rigid muscles, and fever. Untreated NMS can result in coma and death.

Neuroleptic-induced acute dystonia—A severe form of the neurological movement disorder caused by the use of neuroleptic drugs.

Neuroleptic-induced akathisia—Refers to the disorder characterized by a physical restlessness (the inability to sit still, for example), and manifested by excessive voluntary movements, as a result of the use of neuroleptic drugs; research indicates it is likely the most common of neuroleptic-induced movement disorders.

Neuroleptic-induced Parkinsonism—Symptoms similar to Parkinson's disease that may appear in people taking neuroleptic (antipsychotic) medications. These symptoms include tremors in muscles and a shuffling gait.

Neuroleptic-induced tardive dyskinesia—A potentially irreversible neurological disorder caused by the use of antipsychotic/neuroleptic medications, with symptoms involving uncontrollable movement of various body parts.

Postural tremor—A continuous quiver that affects body posture and movement.

SLE (Systemic Lupus Erythematosus)—An autoimmune disease that leads to inflammation and damage to various body tissues and parts, including joints, skin, kidneys, heart, lungs, blood vessels, and brain.

Sydenham's chorea—A serious manifestation of acute rheumatic fever that commonly occurs in children ages seven through 14, peaking at age eight. This disease of the central nervous system is characterized by emotional instability, purposeless movements, and muscular weakness. At its peak in the 1950s it occured in nearly 50% of the acute rheumatic fever cases, but by 2002 had subsided to a degree of less than 10% of the acute cases.

Causes and symptoms

Causes

Neuroleptic-induced movement disorders are caused because the actions of dopamine are blocked. Dopamine is a neurotransmitter necessary for coordination of movements of different parts of the body.

Other medications, which are not classified as neuroleptics, block the action of other **neurotransmitters** as well as dopamine. However, because they essentially block the action of dopamine, they cause similar unwanted effects associated with movements.

Symptoms

Neuroleptic-induced acute dystonia is associated with primarily abnormal postures and muscular spasms. They are usually characterized by abnormal positioning of the head and neck in relation to the body, spasms of the jaw muscles, impaired swallowing, speaking or breathing, thickened or slurred speech due to a slow movement of the tongue, tongue protrusion or tongue dysfunction, eyes deviated up, down, or sideways, and abnormal positioning of the limbs or trunk. Patients experience pain and cramps in the affected muscles. In addition, many patients experiencing dystonia due to the neuroleptic treatment also experience fear and anxiety. This is especially present in patients who are not aware of the possibility of developing dystonia and who mistakenly associate these side effects as part of their mental illness.

Neuroleptic-induced Parkinsonism includes rigidity, tremor, and bradykinesia (slow movements). The tremor is a rhythmic, three- to six-cycle-per-second motion that is present at rest. The tremor can affect the limbs, head, mouth, or lips. Rigidity signifies the degree of tension present in the muscle. It can be either continuous or intermittent in the affected limbs or joints. Bradykinesia includes decreased arm movements related to walking, as well as difficulty initiating movement. Drooling may occur due to a decrease in pharyngeal motor activity. People experiencing neuroleptic-induced akathisia usually feel anxious, agitated, and unable to relax. They also may pace, rock while sitting and standing, and often rapidly alternate between sitting and standing.

Neuroleptic-induced tardive dyskinesia manifests itself in involuntary movements of the tongue, jaw, trunk, or extremities. It occurs most commonly in patients who have taken older antipsychotic medications for many years, although the condition may appear earlier than that (after one year of treatment with neuroleptics, or even earlier than that, especially in elderly people). The movements can be rapid and jerky, slow and continual, or rhythmic in nature. Over three-fourths of the individuals with neuroleptic-induced tardive dyskinesia have abnormal movements of the face and the mouth. This may include licking, sucking or smacking of the lips, chewing movements, jaw deviations, grimacing, grunting and other peculiar sounds, or brow furrowing. About one-half of patients with tardive dyskinesia have abnormal limb movements, while about one-quarter have disposition of the trunk.

The basic features of neuroleptic malignant syndrome is the development of high fever and severe muscle rigidity. These can be accompanied by tremor, changes in level of consciousness ranging from confusion to coma, increased heart rate and blood pressure. The fever can be mildly elevated (99–100°F) or severe (106°F). Neuroleptic malignant syndrome can be fatal in some cases, while it is relatively benign in others. There are no known predictors of neuroleptic malignant syndrome. However, it usually develops four weeks after starting neuroleptics, and about two-thirds of cases develop within the first week of treatment. A very small number of patients develop neuroleptic malignant syndrome many months after taking the neuroleptic.

Medication-induced postural tremor is characterized by a regular, rhythmic oscillation of hands and fingers, head, mouth, or tongue. The frequency of the tremor ranges from eight to 12 cycles per second. These are most easily observed when the affected part is in a sustained position (for example if hands are outstretched or the mouth is held open).

Demographics

Neuroleptic-induced acute dystonia occurs most commonly in young males. It is far less likely to occur with the newer medications known as atypical neuroleptic medications, such as clozapine, risperidone, olanzapine, and quetiapine. The possibility of neuroleptic-induced acute dystonia occurring with these atypical medications is less than 5%. The possibility of this side effect occurring with the conventional or typical neuroleptics is about 15-20%. The incidence is inversely correlated with age, meaning that younger persons are more likely to experience dystonia.

Neuroleptic-induced Parkinsonism is directly correlated with age. This means that older patients are more likely to experience this effect. It occurs in about 30% of patients. Neuroleptic-induced acute akathisia is not related to age and occurs in about 20% of patients being treated with neuroleptics.

The incidence of neuroleptic-induced tardive dyskinesia is related to total lifetime of treatment with antipsychotics. The cumulative incidence is about 5% per year of therapy. This essentially means that there is a 50% chance of developing tardive dyskinesia with 10 years of treatment with neuroleptics.

The incidence of neuroleptic malignant syndrome is about 0.5%. This condition is fatal in about 20 to 30% of cases.

Most available information on medication-induced postural tremor is about lithium-induced tremor. The prevalence of this condition is about 40%.

Diagnosis

People taking antipsychotic medications and other medications that block dopamine action must be regularly evaluated by a physician to monitor for medication-induced movement disorders. In order for these conditions to be officially diagnosed, certain criteria must be met.

Neuroleptic-induced acute dystonia must have one or more of the following developed in association with the use of neuroleptic: abnormal positioning of the head and neck in relation to the body, spasms of the jaw muscles, impaired swallowing, thickened or slurred speech, tongue protrusion or dysfunction, eyes deviated up, down, or sideways, or abnormal positioning of limbs or trunk. These symptoms need to have developed within seven days of starting the neuroleptic medication. Moreover, the symptoms cannot be associated with an underlying mental disorder, and they can't be due to a medication other than a neuroleptic. Dystonia due to neuroleptics needs to be distinguished from dystonia due to neuroleptic malignant syndrome.

Neuroleptic-induced Parkinsonism needs to have the triad of symptoms described above which include tremor, rigidity, and bradykinesia (slow movements). These symptoms cannot be related to a non-neuroleptic medication, or a psychiatric condition, such as Parkinson's disease, Wilson's disease, neuroleptic malignant syndrome, or substance withdrawal. Neuroleptic-induced akathisia is due to the use of a neuroleptic and not to anxiety, substance withdrawal or psychotic agitation. At least one of the symptoms of fidgety movements or swinging the legs, rocking from foot to foot while standing, pacing to relieve restlessness, or inability to sit and stand needs to be present. These symptoms must have developed within four weeks of initiating the therapy with neuroleptics.

Neuroleptic-induced tardive dyskinesia needs to include involuntary movements over a period of at least four weeks that manifest themselves as rapid and jerky, slow and continual, or rhythmic movements. The exposure to neuroleptics needs to be for at least three months, and the symptoms cannot be due to a neurologic condition, such as Huntington's disease, Wilson's disease, Sydenham's (rheumatic) chorea, systemic lupus, or hyperthyroidism.

Neuroleptic malignant syndrome must include severe muscle rigidity and elevated temperature as well as at least two of the following symptoms: sweating, difficulty swallowing, tremor, incontinence, changes in level of consciousness, mutism, increased heart rate, elevated blood pressure, or laboratory evidence of muscle injury. These symptoms cannot be due to another substance or a medical condition, such as viral encephalitis, or mood disorder with catatonic features.

The criteria for diagnosing medication-induced postural tremor includes a development of tremor associated with the use of a medication other than a neuroleptic. The tremor cannot be due to a non-medication condition that was present prior to starting the medication and cannot continue to be present following discontinuation of the medication. These criteria are helpful in distinguishing the tremor due to medication use from the tremor due to anxiety, alcohol withdrawal, **stress**, or **fatigue**. The tremor must have a frequency between eight and 12 cycles per second, and the tremor must not be caused by neuroleptic-induced Parkinsonism.

Treatments

In an attempt to prevent acute dystonia from developing, physicians may prescribe a preventative medication along with the antipsychotic (see "Prevention," below). Once neuroleptic-induced acute dystonia has appeared, however, there are several treatment options. A medication called **benztropine** in doses ranging from 1 mg to 8 mg is effective in reducing symptoms associated with dystonia. Most patients take 2 mg twice daily for seven days for prevention of dystonia at the time they are starting neuroleptic treatment. When benztropine therapy is initiated, the dose is slowly increased. Moreover, when discontinuing the treatment with benztropine, the dose should be slowly decreased to prevent the nausea and vomiting associated with abrupt withdrawal. Another medication that may be useful in treating neuroleptic-induced acute dystonia is called **trihexyphenidyl**. The doses can vary from 10 mg to 45 mg daily. Younger patients may respond better to the treatment with trihexyphenidyl because they can tolerate higher doses. The third pharmacological option is **diphenhydramine** (Benadryl). This medication can be taken for the period dystonic symptoms last. Another option may include switching the patient to one of the newer antipsychotics, such as clozapine, risperidone, or olanzapine, since each of these has a low incidence of causing dystonia.

There are a couple of ways to treat intermediate-onset movement disorders due to neuroleptics. **Amantadine** is a medication that is approved by the United States Food and Drug Administration for the treatment of Parkinsonian symptoms. Another helpful medication called **propranolol** comes from a class of drugs called **beta blockers**. Propranolol has been reported effective in the treatment of akathisia. The doses that are effective range from 20 mg to 100 mg daily. The response to propranolol is usually seen within the 24 hours of administration. Switching the patient to a newer or atypical antipsychotic, such as clozapine, or decreasing the dose of the current antipsychotic sometimes helps the condition.

There are no effective treatments for tardive dyskinesia once it develops. Tardive dyskinesia is associated and strongly correlated with the cumulative dose of the antipsychotic during years of treatment. Hence, the key to tardive dyskinesia is prevention. If possible, a newer medication, such as clozapine or risperidone, which have only a few case reports of tardive dyskinesia, should be used whenever possible. In many cases, if tardive dyskinesia is noticed early in a regular check-up with the physician, and if the medication causing the condition is stopped, the symptoms of tardive dyskinesia will subside. If the symptoms continue after the antipsychotic has been discontinued, the situation becomes difficult. Treatment will most likely involve movement disorder specialists and may or may not be successful. The medications reserpine and levodopa may be helpful for some patients.

The most common medications used to treat neuroleptic malignant syndrome are dantrolene, (a muscle relaxant that helps with the fever), bromocriptine, and amantadine.

In order to reduce medication-induced postural tremor, the lowest possible dose of the psychiatric drug should be used. Moreover, a medication from the beta blockers, such as propranolol, can be used to help with the symptoms.

Prognosis

The prognoses for the early- and intermediate-onset of movement disorders are very good, especially with the option of switching the patient to a newer antipsychotic such as clozapine.

The prognosis for the late-onset disorder called tardive dyskinesia is very poor. Once the condition occurs, it is essentially irreversible and is very difficult to treat.

Neuroleptic malignant syndrome is a serious condition. It is deadly in about 20 to 30% of patients. Those who survive have a good chance of recovering.

Medication-induced postural tremor is very well-controlled with propranolol, and hence the prognosis is good while the patient is being treated with the medication causing the movement disorder.

Prevention

To prevent acute dystonia, some physicians prescribe benztropine, diphenhydramine, or other medications that treat dystonia, at the outset of treatment with an older antipsychotic.

The most important component of neuroleptic-induced tardive dyskinesia is prevention. If conventional antipsychotics are used, the drug use, drug dose, and the duration of use therefore should be minimized.

In order to avoid medication-induced postural tremor, patients should limit the amount of caffeine consumption. Also, in order to minimize the amount of daytime tremor they should take the psychiatric drug at bedtime.

Resources

BOOKS

American Psychiatric Association. *Diagnostic and Statistical Manual of Mental Disorders.* 4th edition, text revised. Washington, DC: American Psychiatric Association, 2000.

Gilman, Alfred G. *The Pharmacological Basis of Therapeutics.* McGraw-Hill, 1996.

Kaplan, Harold. *Comprehensive Textbook of Psychiatry.* Williams and Wilkins, 1995.

Lacy, Charles F. *Drug Information Handbook.* Lexi-Comp, Inc. 2002.

PERIODICALS

Heaton, Robert. "Stability and Course of Neuropsychological Deficits in Schizophrenia." *Archives of General Psychiatry* 58 (2001): 24–32.

Littrell, Kimberly. "Marked Reduction of Tardive Dyskinesia With Olanzapine." *Archives of General Psychiatry.* 55 (1998): 398–403.

ORGANIZATIONS

American Psychiatric Association. 1400 K Street NW, Washington D.C. 20005.<http://www.psych.org>.

American Thyroid Association. 6066 Leesburg Pike, Suite 650, Falls Church, VA 22041. <http://www.thyroid.org>.

Canadian Movement Disorder Group, affiliate of Canadian Congress of Neurological Sciences. 709 7015 Macleod Trail SW, Calgary, AB T2H 2K6 Canada. <http://www.cmdg.org>.

We Move, worldwide education and awareness of movement disorders. 204 West 84th St., New York, NY 10024. <http://www.wemove.org>.

Ajna Hamidovic, Pharm.D.

Meditation

Definition

Meditation or contemplation involves focusing the mind upon a sound, phrase, prayer, object, visualized image, the breath, ritualized movements, or consciousness in order to increase awareness of the present moment, promote relaxation, reduce **stress**, and enhance personal or spiritual growth.

Purpose

Meditation can benefit people who are ill or overwhelmed by stress. It also promotes well-being in healthy people. In general, people who meditate regularly experience less anxiety and depression. They also report more enjoyment and appreciation of life, as well as better social relationships. Meditation produces a state of deep relaxation and a sense of balance, or equanimity. According to Michael J. Baime in *Essentials of Complementary and Alternative Medicine*, meditation allows one to fully experience intense emotions without losing composure. The consequence of emotional balance is greater insight regarding one's thoughts, feelings, and actions. Insight, in turn, promotes confidence and awareness. Meditation also facilitates a greater sense of calmness, empathy, and acceptance of self and others.

Meditation is sometimes suggested as a complement to medical treatments of disease; in particular, it is an important complementary therapy for both the treatment and prevention of many stress-related conditions. Regular meditation may reduce the number of symptoms

KEY TERMS

Anxiety—A feeling of apprehension and fear characterized by physical symptoms (heart palpitations, sweating, and feelings of stress, for example).

Anxiety disorders—Chronic conditions that can be characterized by an excessive and regular sense of apprehension, with physical symptoms such as sweating, palpitations, and feelings of stress. Anxiety disorders can be caused by biological and environmental events.

Anxiety-reduction techniques—Skills taught by a therapist to help an individual overcome anxiety, stress, and tension, and can include relaxation, visualization and imagery, diaphragmatic breathing, stress inoculation, and meditation.

Biofeedback—Biofeedback is a technique that uses monitoring instruments to measure and feed back information about muscle tension, heart rate, sweat responses, skin temperature, or brain activity.

Bodywork—Any technique involving hands-on massage or manipulation of the body.

Dervish—A person who belongs to one of the various mystical and ascetic Muslim orders, such as the Sufis. A whirling dervish meditates by whirling or spinning an ecstatic dance.

Hypnotherapy—The use of an induced trance state, or hypnosis, as a therapy.

Mantra—Originally, a sacred word or phrase repeated over and over to help focus the mind during meditation; in the Western world, this may refer to any repeated syllable, word, or phrase used to meditate.

Pain disorder—One of several somatoform disorders described in the revised, fourth edition of the mental health professional's handbook, the *Diagnostic and Statistical Manual of Mental Disorders.* The term "somatoform" means that symptoms are physical but are not entirely understood as a consequence of a general medical condition or as a direct effect of a substance, such as a drug.

Progressive relaxation—A technique for managing stress in which the person relaxes major muscle groups in a fixed sequence, often beginning with the feet and moving towards the head.

Transcendental meditation (TM)—A meditation technique based on Hindu practices that involves the repetition of a mantra.

Yoga—A system of exercises for achieving bodily or mental control and well-being.

experienced by patients with a wide range of illnesses and disorders. Based upon clinical evidence, as well as theory, meditation is seen as an appropriate therapy for **panic disorder**, **generalized anxiety disorder**, substance dependence and abuse, ulcers, colitis, chronic pain, psoriasis, and dysthymic disorder—a disorder that involves a steady, depressed mood for at least two years. Moreover, meditation is a valuable adjunct therapy for moderate hypertension (high blood pressure), prevention of cardiac arrest (heart attack), prevention of atherosclerosis (hardening of the arteries), arthritis (including fibromyalgia), cancer, **insomnia**, migraine, and **stroke**. It is a complementary therapy for moderating allergies and asthma because it reduces stress, which is prevalent in these conditions. Additionally, meditation may improve function or reduce symptoms of patients with neurologic disorders such as Parkinson's disease, multiple sclerosis, and epilepsy.

In 1995, the authors of a report to the National Institutes of Health on complementary or alternative medicine reviewed 30 years of research and reports of individuals and health care providers. They concluded that meditation and related methods for the enhancement of relaxation are cost-effective ways to improve health and quality of life.

Precautions

Meditation appears to be safe for most people. There are, however, case reports and studies noting some adverse effects. For example, 33% to 50% of people who participated in long, silent meditation retreats (two weeks to three months) reported increased tension, anxiety, confusion, and depression. On the other hand, they also reported that meditation was associated with very positive effects. It has been noted, however, that these studies failed to differentiate between serious psychiatric disturbances and normal mood swings. Nevertheless, the evidence suggests that meditation may not be appropriate for people with psychotic disorders, major depression, or severe **personality disorders**. Some researchers point out that the relaxed, trance-like state that characterizes deep meditation is similar to a hypnotic trance. Hence, meditation, as well as hypnosis, may be contraindicated for people who have difficulty giving up control, such as people who are obsessive and compulsive.

Description

Background

Meditation has been practiced for millennia. Historically, meditation or contemplation was intended to develop spiritual understanding, awareness, or gratitude. It also was meant to help the person commune with God, or ultimate reality. The many different religious traditions in the world have given rise to a rich variety of meditative practices. These include the contemplative prayers and chants of Christian religious orders, the Buddhist practice of sitting meditation, and the whirling movements of the Sufi dervishes. Although meditation is an important spiritual practice in many traditions, it can be practiced by anyone to relieve stress and pain regardless of religious or cultural background.

In recent decades, a holistic approach to medicine has become increasingly popular. This approach developed in response to the ideas that health care providers treat whole persons, and that wellness and illness are better understood in terms of the body, mind, and soul. Some refer to this type of medicine as integrative, (that is, the Western biologic model of disease) and notions of appropriate treatment are modified by knowledge garnered from other cultures—especially those of China and India. When foreign ideas are tested in the U.S. both clinically and scientifically, if found to be valid, they are integrated into Western medicine.

With the increasing acceptance of holistic medicine, there has been more interest in the use of alternative or complementary therapies, such as meditation, hypnosis, and progressive relaxation. As a result, training in meditation and meditation sessions are offered in medical clinics and hospitals. Meditation has been used as primary therapy for treating certain diseases and as complementary therapy in a comprehensive treatment plan. Moreover, it has been employed as a means of improving the quality of life of people with debilitating, chronic, or terminal diseases.

When people are dying, they often cope with enduring pain, anxiety and fear, and end-of-life spiritual concerns. Meditation can be a way for the patient with terminal illness to self-manage pain and anxiety. This can partially reduce the amount of drugs required for effective pain control. People who are dying sometimes reject narcotics in an effort to preserve their consciousness and their communication with people who are important to them. Meditation is a means of preserving consciousness and life as the dying patient knows it. Also, meditation

This woman is sitting in the lotus position, practicing yoga. *(Duomo/Corbis. Reproduced by permission.)*

can be tailored to the religious or spiritual needs of the patient, and may be a means to spiritual solace.

In general, there are two main types of meditation: concentration, and mindful meditation. Concentration meditation involves focusing one's attention on the breath, an imagined or real image, ritualized movements (as in Tai chi, **yoga**, or qigong), or on a sound, word, or phrase that is repeated silently or aloud (mantra). In the Christian tradition, chanting and saying the rosary are forms of meditation. (A rosary is a string of beads used to keep track of the prayers recited.) One purpose of concentration meditation is to fully experience the present moment with serenity. The benefit of being fully present is that worries and anxieties fade, and a feeling of peace ensues. It is the feeling of peace that has physiological benefits, and has been referred to as the relaxation response. When thoughts or emotions arise, the person gently directs his or her mind back to the original focus of concentration.

In comparison, mindfulness meditation involves becoming aware of the entire field of attention. There is an awareness of all thoughts, feelings, perceptions or sensations as they arise from moment to moment. Mindfulness meditation is enhanced by the person's ability to quiet the mind and to accept all that is perceived with composure. Many approaches to meditation are a blend of concentration and mindfulness.

Meditation may involve a quiet, relatively motionless seated posture or it may involve ritualized movement. Sitting meditation is generally done in an upright position, either in a chair or cross-legged on a cushion or mat on the floor. The spine is straight, yet relaxed. The eyes may be closed or open and gazing softly into the distance or at an object. Depending on the tradition, the person may be concentrating on the sensation of the movement of the breath; counting breaths; silently repeating a mantra; chanting a prayer; visualizing a peaceful and meaningful place; focusing awareness on the center of the body; or increasing awareness of all sensory experiences.

Movement meditation may be spontaneous and free form or it may involve highly structured, choreographed, repetitive patterns, as in the practice of Tai chi or qigong. (Tai chi and qigong are ancient Chinese forms of meditation with movement; both are believed to promote health by preserving or restoring the life force, or qi.) Movement meditation is particularly helpful for those people who find it difficult to remain still.

Meditation in health care settings

The use of meditation in health care settings often involves one of the following: transcendental meditation (TM); methods developed by Dr. Herbert Benson to elicit the relaxation response; or adaptations of the program of mindfulness-based stress reduction (MBSR) developed by Jon Kabat-Zinn.

Transcendental meditation (TM) has its origins in the Vedic tradition of India and was introduced to the West by Maharishi Mahesh Yogi. TM has been taught to several million people and is one of the most widely practiced forms of meditation in the West. Much of what is known about the physiology of meditation is based on studies of TM. In transcendental meditation, the person sits with closed eyes and concentrates on a single syllable or word (mantra) for 20 minutes, twice a day. When thoughts or feelings arise, the attention is brought back to the mantra. According to Charles Alexander, a TM researcher, the experience of TM involves a calming of thoughts and ordinary wakefulness, which is transcended and replaced by fully aware consciousness.

Eliciting the relaxation response involves a similar form of mental focusing. Dr. Herbert Benson, one of the first Western doctors to conduct research on the effects of meditation, developed his approach after observing the profound health benefits of a state of bodily calm (the relaxation response). In order to elicit this response, he teaches patients to repeat a word, sound, prayer, phrase, or activity (including swimming, jogging, yoga, or even knitting) for 10 to 20 minutes, twice a day. Patients also are taught not to pay attention to distracting thoughts and to return their focus to the original repetition. What is repeated is up to the individual. For example, instead of Sanskrit terms, the person may choose something personally meaningful, such as a phrase from a Christian or Jewish prayer.

Mindfulness meditation stems from traditional Buddhist meditation practices. **Psychologist** Jon Kabat-Zinn has been instrumental in bringing this form of meditation into medical settings. In formal mindfulness practice, the person sits with eyes closed, focusing the attention on the sensations and movement of the breath for approximately 45 to 60 minutes, at least once a day. Informal mindfulness practice involves bringing awareness to every activity in daily life. Wandering thoughts or distracting feelings are simply noticed, without resistance or reaction. The essence of mindfulness meditation is not that on which the individual is focusing, but rather the quality of dispassionate awareness the person brings to each moment. According to Kabat-Zinn, the purpose of mindfulness meditation is to become aware of one's body and mind in the present moment. Discerning observation differentiates mindfulness from other types of meditation. The MBSR program consists of a series of classes involving meditation, movement, and group participation. There are over 240 MBSR programs offered in health care settings around the world.

Meditation is not considered a medical procedure or **intervention** by most insurers; therefore, if there is a cost associated with training, patients pay for it themselves. Frequently, religious groups or meditation centers offer meditation instruction free of charge or for a nominal donation. Hospitals may offer MBSR classes to their patients for a reduced fee, and to the general public for a somewhat higher fee.

Normal results

The scientific study of the physiological effects of meditation began in the early 1960s. These studies demonstrated that meditation affects metabolism, the endocrine system, the central nervous system, and the autonomic nervous system. In particular, there is a slowing of cardiac and respiratory rates, a decrease in blood pressure, and an increase in alpha **brain** waves. These effects are typical of reduced anxiety.

There is a growing body of evidence supporting the medical benefits of meditation. For example, meditation is particularly effective as a treatment for chronic pain. Researchers have found that meditation reduces symptoms of pain and reliance on drugs used to control pain. For example, in one four-year follow-up study, the majority of patients in an MBSR program reported improvement in the experience of pain as a result of participation in the program.

For many years, meditation has been recommended as a treatment for high blood pressure; however, there is a debate over the effectiveness of meditation compared with medical treatment. Although most studies show a reduction in blood pressure as a result of meditation, medication is relatively more effective.

Meditation may be an effective treatment for coronary artery disease (CAD). For example, a study of 21 patients practicing TM for eight months increased their tolerance of exercise and their capacity for work. Also, meditation is an important part of Dr. Dean Ornish's program for the prevention or reversal of CAD. His program involves a low-fat vegetarian diet, moderate exercise (for example, walking 30 minutes per day), and techniques for reducing stress, including meditation.

Researchers have found that meditation is effective in the treatment of chemical dependency. Gelderloos and others reviewed 24 studies and concluded that TM is helpful in programs that target smoking behavior and drug and alcohol abuse.

The scientific evidence also suggests that meditation is particularly helpful in treating anxiety-related disorders and in reducing symptoms of anxiety triggered by stress. For example, researchers conducted a study in 1998 of 37 patients with psoriasis—a chronic, stress-related skin condition. They found that patients who practiced mindfulness meditation and who received standard ultraviolet light treatment experienced a more rapid clearing of their skin condition than the control subjects. Another study found that meditation moderated the symptoms of fibromyalgia (a chronic condition where people suffer diffuse muscular pain at several sites on the body); over half of the patients reported significant improvement. Meditation was one of several stress management techniques used in a small study of HIV-positive men. The study showed improvements in immune function and psychological well-being.

In sum, holistic practitioners speak about the body's capacity for healing itself; since meditation leads to a peaceful, relaxed state with measurable physiological benefits. Healing is facilitated presumably by moderating the state of arousal generated by chronic stress. There is a variety of stress-reducing techniques available, such as hypnosis, progressive relaxation, **biofeedback**, guided imagery, and aerobic exercise. Health consumers are encouraged to investigate the various techniques and seek referrals to good physicians, therapists, or stress counselors who are willing to design a flexible program that meets their needs.

Resources

BOOKS

Astin, John A., and others. "Meditation." In *Clinician's Complete Reference to Complementary and Alternative Medicine,* edited by Donald Novey. St. Louis, MO: Mosby, 2000.

Baime, Michael J. "Meditation and Mindfulness." In *Essentials of Complementary and Alternative Medicine,* edited by Wayne B. Jonas and Jeffrey S. Levin. Baltimore, MD: Lippincott Williams and Wilkins, 1999.

Benson, Herbert, M.D. with Miram Z. Klipper. *The Relaxation Response.* New York: Avon Books, 1975.

Kaplan, Harold I., and Benjamin J. Sadock. "Alternative Medicine and Psychiatry." In *Kaplan and Sadock's Synopsis of Psychiatry: Behavioral Sciences / Clinical Psychiatry.* 8th ed. Baltimore, MD: Lippincott Williams and Wilkins, 1998.

Turpin, Graham C. H., and Michael Heap. "Arousal Reduction Methods: Relaxation, Biofeedback, Meditation, and Hypnosis." In *Comprehensive Clinical Psychology,* edited by Alan S. Bellack and Michel Hersen. Volume 6 edited by Paul Salkovskis. Oxford, UK: Elsevier Science, 1998.

PERIODICALS

Li, Ming, Kevin Chen, and Zhixian Mo. "Use of Qigong Therapy in the Detoxification of Heroin Addicts." *Alternative Therapies in Health and Medicine* 8, no. 1 (January/February 2002): 50-59.

ORGANIZATIONS

Insight Meditation Society. 1230 Pleasant, St. Barre, MA 01005. (978) 355-4378. <http://www.dharma.org>.

Mind/Body Medical Institute. 110 Francis Street, Boston, MA 02215. (617) 632-9530. <http://www.mbmi.org>.

National Center for Complementary and Alternative Medicine. NCCAM Clearinghouse, P.O. Box 7923, Gaithersburg, MD 20898. (888) 644-6226. <http://www.nccam.nih.gov>.

Linda Chrisman
Tanja Bekhuis, Ph.D.

Mellaril *see* **Thioridazine**

Mental retardation

Definition

Mental retardation (MR) is a developmental disability that first appears in children under the age of 18. It is defined as a level of intellectual functioning (as measured by standard **intelligence tests**) that is well below average and results in significant limitations in the person's daily living skills (adaptive functioning).

KEY TERMS

Amniocentesis—A test usually done between 16 and 20 weeks of pregnancy to detect any abnormalities in the development of the fetus. A small amount of the fluid surrounding the fetus (amniotic fluid) is drawn out through a needle inserted into the mother's womb. Laboratory analysis of this fluid can detect various genetic defects, such as Down syndrome, or neural tube defects.

Developmental delay—The failure to meet certain developmental milestones, such as sitting, walking, and talking, at the average age. Developmental delay may indicate a problem in development of the central nervous system.

Down syndrome—A genetic disorder characterized by an extra chromosome 21 (trisomy 21), mental retardation, and susceptibility to early-onset Alzheimer's disease.

Extensive support—Ongoing daily support required to assist an individual in a specific adaptive area, such as daily help with preparing meals.

Hib disease—An infection caused by *Haemophilus influenza*, type b (Hib). This disease mainly affects children under the age of five. In that age group, it is the leading cause of bacterial meningitis, pneumonia, joint and bone infections, and throat inflammations.

Inborn error of metabolism—A rare enzyme deficiency; children with inborn errors of metabolism do not have certain enzymes that the body requires to maintain organ functions. Inborn errors of metabolism can cause brain damage and mental retardation if left untreated. Phenylketonuria is an inborn error of metabolism.

Limited support—A predetermined period of assistance required to deal with a specific event, such as training for a new job.

Phenylketonuria—(PKU) An inherited disease in which the body cannot metabolize the amino acid phenylalanine properly. If untreated, phenylketonuria can cause mental retardation.

Trisomy—An abnormality in chromosomal development. Chromosomes are the structures within a cell that carry its genetic information. They are organized in pairs. Humans have 23 pairs of chromosomes. In a trisomy syndrome, an extra chromosome is present so that the individual has three of a particular chromosome instead of the normal pair. An extra chromosome 18 (trisomy 18) causes mental retardation.

Ultrasonography—A process that uses the reflection of high-frequency sound waves to make an image of structures deep within the body. Ultrasonography is routinely used to detect fetal abnormalities.

Description

Mental retardation begins in childhood or adolescence before the age of 18. In most cases, it persists throughout adult life. A **diagnosis** of mental retardation is made if an individual has an intellectual functioning level well below average, as well as significant limitations in two or more adaptive skill areas. Intellectual functioning level is defined by standardized tests that measure the ability to reason in terms of mental age (intelligence quotient or IQ). Mental retardation is defined as an IQ score below 70–75. Adaptive skills is a term that refers to skills needed for daily life. Such skills include the ability to produce and understand language (communication); home-living skills; use of community resources; health, safety, leisure, self-care, and social skills; self-direction; functional academic skills (reading, writing, and arithmetic); and job-related skills.

In general, mentally retarded children reach such developmental milestones as walking and talking much later than children in the general population. Symptoms of mental retardation may appear at birth or later in childhood. The child's age at onset depends on the suspected cause of the disability. Some cases of mild mental retardation are not diagnosed before the child enters preschool or kindergarten. These children typically have difficulties with social, communication, and functional academic skills. Children who have a neurological disorder or illness such as encephalitis or meningitis may suddenly show signs of cognitive impairment and adaptive difficulties.

Mental retardation varies in severity. The ***Diagnostic and Statistical Manual of Mental Disorders***, fourth edition, text revision (*DSM-IV-TR*), which is the diagnostic standard for mental health care professionals in the United States, classifies four different degrees of mental retardation: *mild, moderate, severe*, and *profound*. These categories are based on the person's level of functioning.

Mild mental retardation

Approximately 85% of the mentally retarded population is in the mildly retarded category. Their IQ score ranges from 50–70, and they can often acquire academic skills up to about the sixth-grade level. They can become fairly self-sufficient and in some cases live independently, with community and social support.

Moderate mental retardation

About 10% of the mentally retarded population is considered moderately retarded. Moderately retarded persons have IQ scores ranging from 35–55. They can carry out work and self-care tasks with moderate supervision. They typically acquire communication skills in childhood and are able to live and function successfully within the community in such supervised environments as **group homes**.

Severe mental retardation

About 3–4% of the mentally retarded population is severely retarded. Severely retarded persons have IQ scores of 20–40. They may master very basic self-care skills and some communication skills. Many severely retarded individuals are able to live in a group home.

Profound mental retardation

Only 1–2% of the mentally retarded population is classified as profoundly retarded. Profoundly retarded individuals have IQ scores under 20–25. They may be able to develop basic self-care and communication skills with appropriate support and training. Their retardation is often caused by an accompanying neurological disorder. Profoundly retarded people need a high level of structure and supervision.

The American Association on Mental Retardation (AAMR) has developed another widely accepted diagnostic classification system for mental retardation. The AAMR classification system focuses on the capabilities of the retarded individual rather than on his or her limitations. The categories describe the level of support required. They are: *intermittent support; limited support; extensive support*, and *pervasive support*. To some extent, the AAMR classification mirrors the *DSM-IV-TR* classification. Intermittent support, for example, is support that is needed only occasionally, perhaps during times of **stress** or crisis for the retarded person. It is the type of support typically required for most mildly retarded people. At the other end of the spectrum, pervasive support, or life-long, daily support for most adaptive areas, would be required for profoundly retarded persons. The AAMR classification system refers to the "below-average intellectual function" as an IQ of 70–75 or below.

Demographics

The prevalence of mental retardation in North America is a subject of heated debate. It is thought to be between 1%–3% depending upon the population, methods of assessment, and criteria of assessment that are used. Many people believe that the actual prevalence is probably closer to 1%, and that the 3% figure is based on misleading mortality rates; cases that are diagnosed in early infancy; and the instability of the diagnosis across the age span. If the 1% figure is accepted, however, it means that 2.5 million mentally retarded people reside in the United States. The three most common causes of mental retardation, accounting for about 30% of cases, are Down syndrome, fragile X, and fetal alcohol syndrome. Males are more likely than females to have MR in a 1.5:1 ratio.

Causes and symptoms

Low IQ scores and limitations in adaptive skills are the hallmarks of mental retardation. Aggression, self-injury, and mood disorders are sometimes associated with the disability. The severity of the symptoms and the age at which they first appear depend on the cause. Children who are mentally retarded reach developmental milestones significantly later than expected, if at all. If retardation is caused by chromosomal or other genetic disorders, it is often apparent from infancy. If retardation is caused by childhood illnesses or injuries, learning and adaptive skills that were once easy may suddenly become difficult or impossible to master.

In about 40% of cases, the cause of mental retardation cannot be found. Biological and environmental factors that can cause mental retardation include:

Genetic factors

About 30% of cases of mental retardation is caused by hereditary factors. Mental retardation may be caused by an inherited genetic abnormality, such as fragile X syndrome. Fragile X, a defect in the chromosome that determines sex, is the most common inherited cause of mental retardation. Single-gene defects such as phenylketonuria (PKU) and other inborn errors of metabolism may also cause mental retardation if they are not discovered and treated early. An accident or mutation in genetic development may also cause retardation. Examples of such accidents are development of an extra

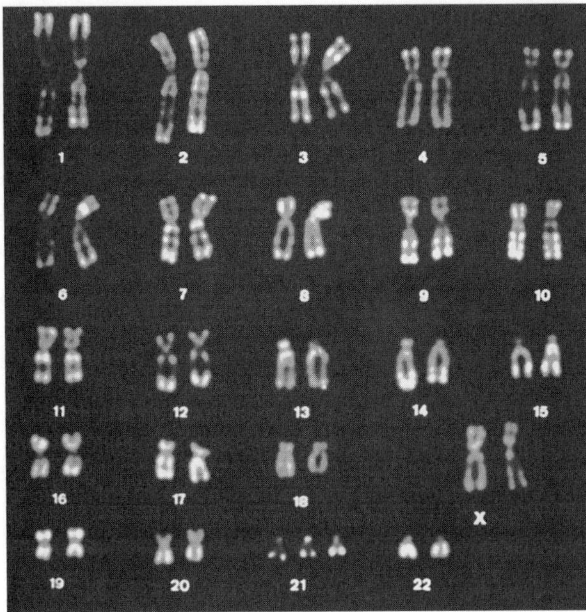

An accident or mutation in genetic development may cause retardation. An example of such a mutation is the development of an extra chromosome 21 that causes Down syndrome. Shown here is a chart (karyotype) showing the 22 chromosome pairs, and in pair 21, three chromosomes (instead of two) are shown. *(Phototake/NYC. Reproduced by permission.) See color insert for color version of photo.*

chromosome 18 (trisomy 18) and Down syndrome. Down syndrome, also called mongolism or trisomy 21, is caused by an abnormality in the development of chromosome 21. It is the most common genetic cause of mental retardation.

Prenatal illnesses and issues

Fetal alcohol syndrome (FAS) affects one in 3,000 children in Western countries. It is caused by the mother's heavy drinking during the first twelve weeks (trimester) of pregnancy. Some studies have shown that even moderate alcohol use during pregnancy may cause learning disabilities in children. Drug abuse and cigarette smoking during pregnancy have also been linked to mental retardation.

Maternal infections and such illnesses as glandular disorders, rubella, toxoplasmosis, and cytomegalovirus (CMV) infection may cause mental retardation. When the mother has high blood pressure (hypertension) or blood poisoning (toxemia), the flow of oxygen to the fetus may be reduced, causing **brain** damage and mental retardation.

Birth defects that cause physical deformities of the head, brain, and central nervous system frequently cause mental retardation. Neural tube defect, for example, is a birth defect in which the neural tube that forms the spinal cord does not close completely. This defect may cause children to develop an accumulation of cerebrospinal fluid inside the skull (hydrocephalus). Hydrocephalus can cause learning impairment by putting pressure on the brain.

Childhood illnesses and injuries

Hyperthyroidism, whooping cough, chickenpox, measles, and Hib disease (a bacterial infection) may cause mental retardation if they are not treated adequately. An infection of the membrane covering the brain (meningitis) or an inflammation of the brain itself (encephalitis) can cause swelling that in turn may cause brain damage and mental retardation. Traumatic brain injury caused by a blow to the head or by violent shaking of the upper body may also cause brain damage and mental retardation in children.

Environmental factors

Ignored or neglected infants who are not provided with the mental and physical stimulation required for normal development may suffer irreversible learning impairment. Children who live in poverty and suffer from malnutrition, unhealthy living conditions, **abuse,** and improper or inadequate medical care are at a higher risk. Exposure to lead or mercury can also cause mental retardation. Many children have developed lead poisoning from eating the flaking lead-based paint often found in older buildings.

Diagnosis

If mental retardation is suspected, a comprehensive physical examination and medical history should be done immediately to discover any organic cause of symptoms. Such conditions as hyperthyroidism and PKU are treatable. If these conditions are discovered early, the progression of retardation can be stopped and, in some cases, partially reversed. If a neurological cause such as brain injury is suspected, the child may be referred to a neurologist or neuropsychologist for testing.

A complete medical, family, social, and educational history is compiled from existing medical and school records (if applicable) and from interviews with parents. Children are given intelligence tests to measure their learning abilities and intellectual functioning. Such tests include the **Stanford-Binet Intelligence Scale**, the Wechsler Intelligence Scales, the Wechsler Preschool and Primary Scale of Intelligence, and the **Kaufman Assessment Battery for Children**. For infants, the Bayley Scales of Infant Development may be used to assess motor, language, and problem-solving skills. Interviews with parents or other caregivers are used to assess the child's daily living, muscle control, communication, and social skills. The Woodcock-Johnson Scales of Independent Behavior and the Vineland Adaptive Behavior Scale (VABS) are frequently used to evaluate these skills.

Treatment

Federal legislation entitles mentally retarded children to free testing and appropriate, individualized education and skills training within the school system from ages three to 21. For children under the age of three, many states have established early **intervention** programs that assess children, make recommendations, and begin treatment programs. Many day schools are available to help train retarded children in such basic skills as bathing and feeding themselves. Extracurricular activities and social programs are also important in helping retarded children and adolescents gain self-esteem.

Training in independent living and job skills is often begun in early adulthood. The level of training depends on the degree of retardation. Mildly retarded people can often acquire the skills needed to live independently and hold an outside job. Moderate to profoundly retarded persons usually require supervised community living in a group home or other residential setting.

Family therapy can help relatives of the mentally retarded develop coping skills. It can also help parents deal with feelings of guilt or anger. A supportive, warm home environment is essential to help the mentally retarded reach their full potential.

Prognosis

People with mild to moderate mental retardation are frequently able to achieve some self-sufficiency and to lead happy and fulfilling lives. To reach these goals, they need appropriate and consistent educational, community, social, family, and vocational supports. The outlook is less promising for those with severe to profound retardation. Studies have shown that these persons have a shortened life expectancy. The diseases that are usually associated with severe retardation may cause the shorter life span. People with Down syndrome will develop the brain changes that characterize **Alzheimer's disease** in later life and may develop the clinical symptoms of this disease as well.

Prevention

Immunization against diseases such as measles and Hib prevents many of the illnesses that can cause mental retardation. In addition, all children should undergo routine developmental screening as part of their pediatric care. Screening is particularly critical for those children who may be neglected or undernourished or may live in disease-producing conditions. Newborn screening and immediate treatment for PKU and hyperthyroidism can usually catch these disorders early enough to prevent retardation.

Good prenatal care can also help prevent retardation. Pregnant women should be educated about the risks of alcohol consumption and the need to maintain good nutrition during pregnancy. Such tests as amniocentesis and ultrasonography can determine whether a fetus is developing normally in the womb.

See also Childhood disintegrative disorder; Pica

Resources

BOOKS

American Psychiatric Association. "Mental Retardation." In *Diagnostic and Statistical Manual of Mental Disorders.* 4th ed., text revision. Washington, DC: American Psychiatric Press, Inc., 2000.

Jaffe, Jerome H., M.D. "Mental Retardation." In *Comprehensive Textbook of Psychiatry,* edited by Benjamin J. Sadock, M.D. and Virginia A. Sadock, M.D. 7th edition. Philadelphia, PA: Lippincott Williams and Wilkins, 2000.

Julian, John N. "Mental Retardation." In *Psychiatry Update and Board Preparation,* edited by Thomas A. Stern, M.D., and John B. Herman, M.D. New York: McGraw Hill, 2000.

PERIODICALS

Bozikas,Vasilis, M.D., and others. "Gabapentin for Behavioral Dyscontrol with Mental Retardation." *American Journal Psychiatry* June 2001: 965-966.

Margolese, Howard C., M.D., and others. "Olanzapine-Induced Neuroleptic Malignant Syndrome with Mental Retardation." *American Journal Psychiatry* July 1999: 1115A-1116.

ORGANIZATIONS

American Association on Mental Retardation (AAMR) [The organization voted to change its name to American Association on Intellectual Disabilities on March 25, 2002.]. 444 North Capitol Street, NW, Washington, D.C. 20001. (800) 424-3688. <http://www.aamr.org>.

The Arc of the United States (formerly Association of Retarded Citizens of the United States). 1010 Wayne Avenue, Silver Spring, M.D. 20910. (301) 565-3842. <http://thearc.org>.

OTHER

National Information Center for Children and Youth and Disabilities. P.O. Box 1492,Washington, D.C. 20013. (800) 695-0285. <http://www.nichcy.org>.

Paula Anne Ford-Martin, M.A.

Mesoridazine

Definition

Mesoridazine is a member of the phenothiazine family of drugs (drugs that reduce the action of the neurotransmitter, dopamine, in the **brain**) and sold under the brand name Serentil in the United States.

Purpose

Mesoridazine is effective in the treatment of **schizophrenia**, alcoholism, psychoneuroses (disorders of the brain), and organic brain disorders (disorders caused by temporary brain dysfunction or permanent brain damage).

Description

When used for the treatment of schizophrenia, mesoridazine reduces symptoms of emotional withdrawal, anxiety, tension, **hallucinations**, reduced **affect**, and **paranoia** (suspiciousness). It is often useful in persons for whom other tranquilizers are ineffective. In treating organic brain syndrome, mesoridazine effectively manages hyperactivity and difficult behaviors associated with mental deficiency. Mesoridazine relieves anxiety, nausea, vomiting, tension, and depression when used to treat alcoholism. It does not have side effects that affect liver function. It relieves similar symptoms when used to treat persons with psychoneurotic disorders.

Mesoridazine can be taken by mouth or given by intramuscular injection. It is supplied as 25 mg/mL in injection form, and in 10-, 25-, 50-, and 100-mg tablets.

Recommended dosage

The usual dosage used for treating schizophrenia is 50–400 mg per day and is usually administered three times per day. It is begun at a low level and slowly increased until an adequate therapeutic effect is achieved. For persons with organic brain syndrome, an optimum dosage is 75–300 mg per day, administered in three equal amounts. The optimum dosage for persons being treated for alcoholism is 50–300 mg per day, administered in three doses. The usual dosage range for persons with psychoneuroses is 30–150 mg per day, administered in three equal amounts.

KEY TERMS

Akathisia—Agitated or restless movement, usually affecting the legs. Movement is accompanied by a sense of discomfort and an inability to sit, stand still, or remain inactive for periods of time. Akathisia is a common side effect of some neuroleptic (antipsychotic) medications.

Dopamine—A chemical in brain tissue that serves to transmit nerve impulses (is a neurotransmitter) and helps to regulate movement and emotions.

Dystonia—A neurological disorder characterized by involuntary muscle spasms. The spasms can cause a painful twisting of the body and difficulty walking or moving.

Neurotransmitter—A chemical in the brain that transmits messages between neurons, or nerve cells.

Organic brain syndrome—A class of disorders characterized by progressive deterioration of mental processes caused by temporary brain dysfunction or permanent brain damage. Symptoms include delusions, dementia, amnesia, and delirium that are not caused by drugs, alcohol, or as a side effect of medication.

Psychoneurotic—Pertaining to a neurosis or disorder of the brain. Informally, refers to a person with unstable emotions.

Schizophrenia—A severe mental illness in which a person has difficulty distinguishing what is real from what is not real. It is often characterized by hallucinations, delusions, language and communication disturbances, and withdrawal from people and social activities.

Tachycardia—A pulse rate above 100 beats per minute.

Tardive dyskinesia—A condition that involves involuntary movements of the tongue, jaw, mouth or face or other groups of skeletal muscles that usually occurs either late in antipsychotic therapy or even after the therapy is discontinued. It may be irreversible.

Precautions

Mesoridazine has the potential to produce a serious syndrome called **tardive dyskinesia**. This syndrome consists of involuntary, uncoordinated movements (especially of the tongue, jaw, mouth, or face). It usually develops either late in the course of treatment or after medication has been discontinued and is potentially irreversible. Symptoms similar to those experienced by people with Parkinson's disease have been linked with the administration of mesoridazine. Mesoridazine is inappropriate for use with central nervous system depression, nor should it be administered to persons in a coma.

Side effects

A serious and relatively common side effect of mesoridazine is tardive dyskinesia, a potentially irreversible syndrome for which there is no known effective treatment. An important feature of tardive dyskinesia is that it typically develops either late into treatment or after treatment has ceased. Tardive dyskinesia consists of involuntary, uncoordinated movements of the tongue, jaw, mouth, or face that also may be accompanied by involuntary movements of the arms, legs, and trunk. The chances of developing tardive dyskinesia increase with both increasing dosage and increasing patient age.

The most common side effects of mesoridazine are drowsiness and low blood pressure and are most frequently reported in persons given relatively high dosages. Side effects also tend to appear relatively early in treatment. Mesoridazine tends to have a remarkably low incidence of side effects compared to other phenothiazine compounds. However, as mentioned, Parkinson-like symptoms have been linked with the administration of mesoridazine. These include restlessness and agitation (akathisia) and difficulty walking or moving (dystonia). These are generally controlled with **benztropine** mesylate or **trihexyphenidyl** hydrochloride.

Other known side effects include anxiety, restlessness, agitation, **insomnia**, headache, euphoria, drowsiness, depression, confusion, and dizziness. Unwanted or unexpected effects associated with the use of mesoridazine have been reported for virtually all organ systems in the body. Although numerous, such side effects are relatively uncommon. An occasionally reported side effect is neuroleptic malignant syndrome, a complicated and potentially fatal condition characterized by muscle rigidity, high fever, alterations in mental status, and cardiac symptoms such as irregular pulse or blood pressure, sweating, tachycardia and arrhythmias.

Interactions

Mesoridazine increases the effect of drugs and substances that depress the central nervous system. This class of drugs includes anesthetics, opiates, **barbiturates**, atropine, and alcohol.

See also Alcohol and related disorders

Resources

BOOKS

Adams, Michael and Norman Holland. *Core Concepts in Pharmacology.* Philadelphia: Lippincott-Raven, 1998.

Foreman, John C. and Torben Johansen. *Textbook of Receptor Pharmacology.* 2nd ed. Boca Raton, FL: CRC Press, 2002.

Page, Clive P., and Michael Murphy. *Integrated Pharmacology.* St. Louis: Mosby-Year Book, 2002.

Von Boxtel, Chris J., Budiono Santoso, and I. Ralph Edwards. *Drug Benefits and Risks: International Textbook of Clinical Pharmacology.* New York: John Wiley and Sons, 2001.

PERIODICALS

Dallaire, S. "Thioridazine (Mellaril) and mesoridazine (Serentil): prolongation of the QTc interval." *Canadian Medical Association Journal* 164, no 1 (2001): 91-95.

Nelson, J. C. "Diagnosing and treating depression in the elderly." *Journal of Clinical Psychiatry* 62, Supplement 24 (2001): 18-22.

Ray, W. A., S. Meredith, P. B. Thapa, K. G. Meador, K. Hall, and K. T. Murray. "Antipsychotics and the risk of sudden cardiac death." *Archives of General Psychiatry* 58, no. 12 (2001): 1161-1167.

Varvel A., E. Vann, E. Wise, D. Philibin, and H. Porter. "Effects of antipsychotic drugs on operant responding after acute and repeated administration." *Psychopharmacology (Berlin)* 160, no. 2 (2002): 182-191.

ORGANIZATIONS

American Academy of Clinical Toxicology. 777 East Park Drive, PO Box 8820, Harrisburg, PA 17105-8820. Telephone: (717) 558-7750. Fax: (717) 558-7845. Web site: <http://www.clintox.org/index.html>.

American Academy of Family Physicians. 11400 Tomahawk Creek Parkway, Leawood, KS 66211-2672. Telephone: (913) 906-6000. Web site: <http://www.aafp.org/>.

American Medical Association. 515 N. State Street, Chicago, IL 60610. Telephone: (312) 464-5000. Web site: <http://www.ama-assn.org/>.

American Psychiatric Association. 1400 K Street NW, Washington, DC 20005. Telephone: (888) 357-7924. Fax (202) 682-6850. Web site: <http://www.psych.org/>.

American Society for Clinical Pharmacology and Therapeutics. 528 North Washington Street, Alexandria, VA 22314. Telephone: (703) 836-6981 Fax: (703) 836-5223.

American Society for Pharmacology and Experimental Therapeutics. 9650 Rockville Pike, Bethesda, MD 20814-3995. Telephone: (301) 530-7060. Fax: (301) 530-7061. Web site: <http://www.aspet.org/>.

L. Fleming Fallon, Jr., M.D., Dr.P.H.

Methadone

Definition

Methadone is classified as an opioid (an analgesic that is used for severe pain). In the United States, methadone is also known as dolophine, methenex and methadose.

Purpose

Methadone is used in the long-term maintenance treatment of narcotic **addiction**. Both heroin and methadone are opioids; as such, methadone and heroin bind to the same places in the **brain**. Methadone, however, is the opioid of choice for the treatment of narcotic addiction since it is longer lasting and patients don't experience the "high" associated with the drug of abuse. In opioid maintenance therapy, a person addicted to heroin receives methadone instead of heroin. Essentially, the person is switched from an opioid that gives a "high" to an opioid that does not. The dose of methadone may then be decreased over time so that the person can overcome his or her opioid addiction without experiencing withdrawal symptoms, or, after a person has received methadone for a period of time, he or she may choose to go through **detoxification** with **clonidine**. In the United States, methadone treatment is associated with a significant reduction in predatory crime, improvement in socially acceptable behavior, and psychological well-being.

Methadone may also be prescribed for pain relief, but in these cases, the physician must note this use on the prescription.

Description

Methadone has been used successfully to treat narcotic addiction for over twenty years in the United States. Methadone is the only FDA-approved agent in its class for the maintenance treatment of narcotic addiction.

Methadone for maintenance treatment is dispensed in methadone clinics. The program needs to be registered with the Drug Enforcement Agency. For admission to methadone treatment in clinical programs, federal standards mandate a minimum of one year of opiate addiction as well as current evidence of addiction. Pregnant, opiate-addicted females can be admitted with less than a one-year history and AIDS patients are routinely accepted. New patients must report daily, take medication under observation, and participate in recommended psychosocial treatments.

Some studies have shown that over 50% of patients in methadone clinics do not abuse drugs in the first month of treatment. After ten months, however, the success rate drops to approximately 20%. Moreover, major depression is a powerful predictor of relapse in methadone treatment. If the patient has dual addictions (alcoholism along with the heroin addiction, for example), management of the other addiction increases the success rate of the methadone therapy. Proper psychiatric and psychological treatment can considerably improve methadone treatment outcome.

In the cases of pregnant women who are addicted to heroin, detoxification (discontinuing the opioid altogether) is associated with a high rate of spontaneous abortions in the first trimester and premature delivery in the third trimester. Therefore, pregnant women can be in methadone maintenance programs if they are at risk of returning to drug dependence. These women should receive the lowest effective dose, receive appropriate prenatal care, and be warned about risks of returning to drug abuse, as well as the dangers associated with withdrawal effects of methadone. Methadone is associated with lower birth weights and smaller head circumference,

KEY TERMS

Benzodiazepines—A group of central nervous system depressants used to relieve anxiety or to induce sleep.

Glaucoma—A group of eye diseases characterized by increased pressure within the eye significant enough to damage eye tissue and structures. If untreated, glaucoma results in blindness.

Maintenance treatment—The period of treatment beginning after the initial introduction of the treatment medication. During this period, the dose of medication can be either increased or decreased, depending on the program and needs of the patient.

MAO inhibitors—A group of antidepressant drugs that decrease the activity of monoamine oxidase, a neurotransmitter found in the brain that affects mood.

Naloxone—A drug that combines competitively with opiate receptors on the nerve cells and blocks or reverses the action of narcotic analgesics.

Neurotransmitter—A chemical in the brain that transmits messages between neurons, or nerve cells.

Relapse—When a person returns to a habit (such as drug use) that he or she was trying to overcome.

but it has never been shown that this has any impact on the infants' further development.

Methadone is available in 5-, 10-, and 40-mg tablets and a solution.

Recommended dosage

The initial dose of methadone is 40 mg daily administered in single or divided doses. After achieving initial dosing of about 40 mg daily, the dose should be increased since there is evidence that the relapse rate is significantly lower in patients on 80-100 mg daily rather than 40-50 mg daily. The stabilization to maintenance dosing requires one to three months.

The minimum effective dose is 60 mg daily taken at once or in divided doses. Patients on lower maintenance doses have recently been studied and have shown shorter treatment retention and have continued heroin use. If patients are stable on methadone for six months or longer, their methadone dose should not be increased by 33% or over, as this sudden increase in dose is associated with an increase in craving for the drugs that were previously abused. Some heroin patients need to be on doses up to 180 mg daily to provide adequate maintenance and to prevent relapse.

Precautions

Methadone should not be used in patients who have had hypersensitivity to methadone. Patients who experience an allergic reaction to other opioids, which may include a generalized rash or shortness of breath, such as morphine, hydromorphone, oxymorphone, or codeine may try methadone. They are less likely to develop the same reaction since methadone has a different chemical structure. Methadone should be administered carefully in patients with pre-existing respiratory problems, history of bowel obstruction, glaucoma, renal problems, and hyperthyroidism.

As stated, pregnant women can be in methadone maintenance programs if they are at risk of returning to drug dependence. Methadone is associated with smaller birth weights and smaller head circumference.

Side effects

Most adverse effects of methadone are mild and seen only in the beginning of therapy. Initially, patients may develop sedation and analgesia. It takes about four to six weeks for tolerance to these effects to develop. Tolerance to constipation and sweating may take longer to develop.

A few patients who are on larger doses of methadone may experience respiratory problems. These patients also may experience unwanted cardiac effects.

A small number of patients report a decrease in libido, impotence, and premature, delayed, or failed ejaculation. There are a few reports of occasional menstrual irregularities in female patients on methadone.

Interactions

Life-threatening interactions with other drugs have not been identified. One of the initial side effects of methadone could include dizziness and sedation, and these effects are worsened if the patient is also taking other narcotics, benzodiazepines, or is consuming alcohol.

Monoamine oxidase inhibitors (MAOIs), such as Parnate (**tranylcypromine**) and Nardil (**phenelzine**), should be avoided by people taking methadone. Medications such as **naltrexone** and naloxone should never be used concurrently with methadone. People must stop taking methadone for seven to 10 days before starting naltrexone or naloxone.

See also Alcohol and related disorders; Disease concept of chemical dependency; Opioids and related disorders

Resources

BOOKS

Albers, Lawrence J., M.D., Rhoda K. Hahn, M.D., and Christopher Reist, M.D. *Handbook of Psychiatric Drugs. 2001–2002.* Laguna Hills, CA: Current Clinical Strategies Publishing, 2001.

Kay, Jerald. *Psychiatry: Behavioral Science and Clinical Essentials.* Philadelphia: W. B. Saunders Company, 2000.

PERIODICALS

Curran, Valarie H. "Additional Methadone Increases Craving for Heroin: A Double-Blind, Placebo-Controlled Study of Chronic Opiate Users Receiving Methadone Substitution Treatment." *Addiction* 94 (1999):665-74.

Strain, Eric. "Moderate-vs High-Dose Methadone in the Treatment of Opioid Dependence." *Journal of the American Medical Association* 281 (1999):1000-5.

Ajna Hamidovic, Pharm.D.

Methylphenidate

Definition

Methylphenidate is a mild, central nervous system stimulant. In the United States, the drug is sold under the brand name Ritalin.

KEY TERMS

Anticoagulant—A medication (such as warfarin, Coumadin, or Heparin) that decreases the blood's clotting ability preventing the formation of new clots. Although anticoagulants will not dissolve existing clots, they can stop them from getting larger. These drugs are commonly called blood thinners.

Glaucoma—A group of eye diseases characterized by increased pressure within the eye significant enough to damage eye tissue and structures. If untreated, glaucoma results in blindness.

Opiate—A drug derived from opium.

Tachycardia—A pulse rate above 100 beats per minute.

Tourette syndrome—Neurological disorder characterized by multiple involuntary movements and uncontrollable vocalizations called tics that come and go over years, usually beginning in childhood and becoming chronic. Sometimes the tics include inappropriate language.

Purpose

Methylphenidate is used primarily in the treatment of **attention-deficit/hyperactivity disorder** (ADHD) in children and adults. It also may be used to treat the sleep disorder, **narcolepsy**. In rare cases, it is used to decrease sedation and lethargy from opioid pain medications and to help improve the mood of a terminally ill person suffering from depression.

Description

The mode of action for methylphenidate is not fully understood. It presumably activates the **brain** stem arousal system and cortex to produce a stimulant effect. The brain stem arousal system increases levels of electrical activity in the brain. The effect of methylphenidate is to produce increased alertness and, although children with ADHD are overactive and have decreased attention spans, in these children, methylphenidate actually decreases motor restlessness and increases attention span. Tablets are available in 5-, 10-, and 20-mg strengths, as well as in an extended release, 20-mg tablet.

Recommended dosage

The recommended dosage of methylphenidate is determined by trial and error based on individual responses. Methylphenidate is usually administered in two or three separate doses each day, preferably 45 minutes before a meal. For children suffering from ADHD, the initial recommended dosage is 5 mg twice daily before breakfast and lunch, increased by 5–10 mg per week to a maximum of 60 mg per day. The average total dosage is 20–30 mg per day, although 10–60 mg is not uncommon. For narcolepsy in adults, the recommended dose is 5–20 mg two to three times a day, 30–45 minutes before meals.

The drug should be taken exactly as directed. Methylphenidate can become habit forming if taken in greater amounts or for longer periods than necessary. Individuals should take the last dose of the day before 6 P.M. to decrease sleep difficulties. The tablet should not be broken or crushed, as this changes the time for absorption. If the normal time of administration is missed, people should take the drug as soon as possible. However, two tablets should *not* be taken at the same time.

Precautions

Methylphenidate has a great potential to produce physical and mental dependence. Administration should not be stopped abruptly. Such action can cause withdrawal symptoms including depression, paranoid feelings, thoughts of **suicide**, anxiety, agitation, and sleep disturbances. Methylphenidate should not be given to people with extreme anxiety, tension, agitation, severe depression, mental or emotional instability, or a history of alcohol or drug abuse. It is not indicated for use by those with Tourette's syndrome, people with **tic disorders**, glaucoma, or certain mental health conditions. The drug should be used cautiously by those with high blood pressure, those with a history of **seizures**, and women who are breast-feeding. Methylphenidate is not typically ordered for women during their childbearing years, unless the physician determines that the benefits outweigh the risks.

Methylphenidate should not be ordered for children younger than six years of age as its safety has not been determined in this age group. People should not drive or operate machinery or appliances until they understand how this drug affects them. They should not drive if they become lightheaded or dizzy. Methylphenidate may cause irregularities in the composition of the blood and produce changes in liver function. People taking methylphenidate should receive regular blood tests.

Side effects

The most common side effects are nervousness, difficulties with sleep, tachycardia, and increased blood pressure. Reducing the dose or changing the time the drug is taken may reduce some side effects. Affected persons should discuss any adverse reactions with their health care professional. Individuals taking methylphenidate should receive regular blood pressure and pulse checks. Methylphenidate also may cause dizziness, irritability, vision changes, drowsiness, and a poor appetite. Less common side effects include chest pain, palpitations, joint pain, skin rash, and uncontrolled movements or speech. Side effects may also include a rapid or irregular heartbeat, stomach upset, nausea, headache, blood in the urine or stools, muscle cramps, red dots on the skin, or bruises. At higher dosages or with long-term use, people may experience weight loss or mental changes such as confusion, false beliefs, mood changes, **hallucinations**, or feelings that they or their environment are not real.

Interactions

Several drugs may interact adversely with methylphenidate, including anticoagulants and drugs to prevent seizures, combat depression, and treat high blood pressure. The dosages of these drugs may be reduced when taken simultaneously with methylphenidate.

Resources

BOOKS

Adams, Michael and Norman Holland. *Core Concepts in Pharmacology.* Philadelphia: Lippincott-Raven, 1998.

Breggin, Peter R. and Dick Scruggs. *Talking Back to Ritalin: What Doctors Aren't Telling You About Stimulants and ADHD.* Boulder, CO: Perseus Book Group, 2001.

Foreman, John C. and Torben Johansen. *Textbook of Receptor Pharmacology.* 2nd Ed. Boca Raton, FL: CRC Press, 2002.

Markowitz, John S., and C. Lindsay DeVane. *The Ritalin Handbook.* Kearney, NJ: Morris Publishing, 2000.

Page, Clive P. and Michael Murphy. *Integrated Pharmacology.* St. Louis: Mosby-Year Book, 2002.

Von Boxtel, Chris, Budiono Santoso, and I. Ralph Edwards. *Drug Benefits and Risks: International Textbook of Clinical Pharmacology.* New York: John Wiley and Sons, 2001.

PERIODICALS

Miller, A. R., C. E. Lalonde, K. M. McGrail, and R. W. Armstrong. "Prescription of methylphenidate to children and youth, 1990-1996." *Canadian Medical Journal* (2001) 165, no. 11: 1489-1494.

Perring C. "Medicating children: the case of Ritalin." *Bioethics* (1997) 11, no. 3-4: 228-240.

Sund, A. M., and P. Zeiner. "Does extended medication with amphetamine or methylphenidate reduce growth in hyperactive children?" *Norwegian Journal of Psychiatry* (2002) 56, no. 1: 53-57.

ORGANIZATIONS

American Academy of Family Physicians. 11400 Tomahawk Creek Parkway, Leawood, KS 66211-2672. Telephone: (913) 906-6000. Web site: <http://www.aafp.org>.

American College of Physicians. 190 N Independence Mall West, Philadelphia, PA 19106-1572. Telephone: (800) 523-1546, x2600 or (215) 351-2600. Web site: <http://www.acponline.org>.

American Medical Association. 515 N. State Street, Chicago, IL 60610. Telephone: (312) 464-5000. Web site: <http://www.ama-assn.org>.

American Psychiatric Association. 1400 K Street NW, Washington, DC 20005. Telephone: (888) 357-7924. Fax (202) 682-6850.

American Society for Clinical Pharmacology and Therapeutics; 528 North Washington Street, Alexandria, VA 22314; Phone: (703) 836-6981. Fax: (703) 836-5223.

American Society for Pharmacology and Experimental Therapeutics. 9650 Rockville Pike, Bethesda, MD 20814-3995. Telephone: (301) 530-7060.

National Institute on Drug Abuse: <http://www.nida.nih.gov/Infofax/ritalin.html>.

Nurse's PDR Resource Center. <http://www.nursespdr.com/members/database/>.

L. Fleming Fallon, Jr., M.D., Dr.P.H.

Mini-mental state examination

Definition

The mini-mental state examination, which is also known as the MMSE, standardized MMSE, SMMSE, or the Folstein, is a brief examination consisting of eleven questions intended to evaluate an adult patient's level of cognitive functioning. It was introduced in 1975 and designed for use with elderly patients who are able to cooperate at an optimum level with an examiner for only a brief period of time—no more than a few minutes.

Purpose

The MMSE concentrates on the cognitive aspects of mental functioning, excluding questions about the patient's mood or such abnormal experiences as dissociation. It is used most often to evaluate older adults for **delirium** or **dementia**. The MMSE can be used to detect a decline in cognitive function; to follow the course of

KEY TERMS

Cognition—The act or process of knowing or perceiving.

Delirium—A disturbance of consciousness marked by confusion, difficulty paying attention, delusions, hallucinations, or restlessness. It can be distinguished from dementia by its relatively sudden onset and variation in the severity of the symptoms.

Dementia—A group of symptoms (syndrome) associated with a progressive loss of memory and other intellectual functions that is serious enough to interfere with a person's ability to perform the tasks of daily life. Dementia impairs memory, alters personality, leads to deterioration in personal grooming, impairs reasoning ability, and causes disorientation.

Dissociation—A reaction to trauma in which the mind splits off certain aspects of the traumatic event from conscious awareness. Dissociation can affect the patient's memory, sense of reality, and sense of identity.

Orientation—In psychiatry, the ability to locate oneself in one's environment with respect to time, place and people.

the patient's illness, and to monitor responses to treatment. Recently, it has been professionally approved as a measurement of a patient's ability to complete an advance directive, or so-called living will.

The test has also been used in research as a screener in epidemiological studies for disorders that affect cognition, and to monitor changes in subjects' cognition during clinical trials. In 2001 the MMSE was recommended by a special panel of experts for use as a screener in evaluating cognitive function in depressed patients. It has also been used recently to measure the effects of **acupuncture** in improving mood and some cognitive skills in patients with Alzheimer's.

The MMSE evaluates six areas of cognitive function: orientation, attention, immediate recall, short-term recall, language, and the ability to follow simple verbal and written commands. In addition, it provides a total score allowing the examiner to place the patient on a scale of cognitive function. It correlates well with a standard measure of cognition in adults, the **Wechsler Adult Intelligence Scale** (WAIS). In contrast to the Wechsler, which takes about an hour or more to administer, the MMSE can be completed in ten minutes or less.

Precautions

The MMSE should not be used as the sole criterion for assessment during differential **diagnosis** of psychiatric disorders, as there are many disorders and conditions that affect cognitive functioning. The results of the MMSE should be interpreted in the context of the patient's history, a full mental status examination, a physical examination, and laboratory findings, if any.

A patient's score on the MMSE must be interpreted according to his or her age and educational level. Whereas the median score is 29 for persons 18–24 years of age, it is 25 for those who are 80 or older. The median score is 22 for persons with a fourth-grade education or less; 26 for those who completed the eighth grade; and 29 for those who completed high school or college. There is a complete table available for interpreting MMSE scores according to the patient's reference groups for age and education level.

The MMSE should be administered and scored only by a qualified health care professional, such as a **psychologist**, physician, or nurse.

Description

The mini-mental state examination is divided into two sections. The first part requires vocal responses to the examiner's questions. The patient is asked to repeat a short phrase after the examiner; to count backward from 100 by 7s; to name the current President of the United States (in Great Britain, the names of the Queen and her four children); and similar brief items. It tests the patient's orientation, memory, and attention. The maximum score on this section is 21.

In the second part of the examination, the patient is asked to follow verbal and written instructions, write a sentence spontaneously, and copy a complex geometric figure similar to a Bender-Gestalt figure—a series of nine designs each on separate cards given the test taker who is asked to reproduce them on blank paper. The sentence item usually asks the patient to explain the meaning of a simple proverb such as "People who live in glass houses shouldn't throw stones." The maximum score for the second section is 9. Patients with vision problems can be assisted with large writing. The MMSE is not timed.

There is little information available on allowances made in scoring the MMSE for patients whose first language is not English or who have difficulty with standard spoken English.

Results

The maximum total score on the MMSE is 30. As a rule, scores of 20 or lower indicate delirium, dementia, **schizophrenia**, or a mood disorder. Normal subjects and those with a primary diagnosis of personality disorder score close to the median for their age and education level.

Resources

BOOKS

Eisendrath, Stuart J., MD, and Jonathan E. Lichtmacher, MD. "Psychiatric Disorders: Psychiatric Assessment." In *Current Medical Diagnosis & Treatment 2001.* 40th edition. Edited by L. M. Tierney, Jr., MD, and others. New York: Lange Medical Books/McGraw-Hill, 2001.

PERIODICALS

Crum, R. M., and others. "Population-Based Norms for the Mini-Mental State Examination by Age and Educational Level." *Journal of the American Medical Association* 18 (1993): 2386–2391.

Folstein, Marshal F., Susan E. Folstein, and Paul R. McHugh. "Mini-mental state: A practical method for grading the cognitive state of patients for the clinician." *Journal of Psychiatric Research* 12 (1975): 189–198.

Lombardo, Emerson, L. Vehvilainen, W. L. Ooi, and others. "Acupuncture to Treat Anxiety and Depression in Alzheimer's." *The Gerontologist* (October 15, 2001): 391.

Mor, Vincent. "SMMSE Measures Capacity for Advance Directives." *Brown University Long-Term Care Quality Letter* 8 (July 1996): 6.

ORGANIZATIONS

American Psychiatric Association. 1400 K Street, NW. Washington, DC 20005. (202) 682-6220. <www.psych.org>.

Department of Psychiatry, Tufts University School of Medicine/Tufts-New England Medical Center. <www.nemc.org>.

National Institute of Neurological Disorders and Stroke (NINDS). Building 31, Room 8A06, 9000 Rockville Pike, Bethesda, MD 20892. (301) 496-5751. <www.ninds.nih.gov>.

Rebecca J. Frey, Ph.D.

Minnesota Multiphasic Personality Inventory

Definition

The Minnesota Multiphasic Personality Inventory, known as the MMPI, and its revised second edition (MMPI-2) are psychological assessment instruments completed by the person being evaluated, and scored and interpreted by the examiner. The clinician evaluates the test taker's personal characteristics by comparing the test taker's answers to those given by various psychiatric and nonpsychiatric comparison groups. By analyzing the test taker's patterns of response to the test items, the examiner is able to draw some tentative conclusions about the client's level of adaptation, behavioral characteristics, and personality traits. The MMPI-2 is preferred to the older MMPI because of its larger and more representative community comparison group (also referred to as the "normative" group). The original version of the MMPI is no longer available from the publisher, although some institutions continue to use old copies of it.

Purpose

The results of the MMPI-2 allow the test administrator to make inferences about the client's typical behaviors and way of thinking. The test outcomes help the examiner to determine the test taker's severity of impairment, outlook on life, approaches to problem solving, typical mood states, likely diagnoses, and potential problems in treatment. The MMPI-2 is used in a wide range of settings for a variety of procedures. The inventory is often used as part of inpatient psychiatric assessments, differential **diagnosis**, and outpatient evaluations. In addition, the instrument is often used by expert witnesses in forensic settings as part of an evaluation of a defendant's mental health, particularly in criminal cases. The MMPI has also been used to evaluate candidates for employment in some fields, and in educational counseling.

Precautions

Although the MMPI-2 may be administered by trained clerical staff or by computer, for best results the examiner should meet the test taker before giving the test in order to establish the context and reassure the client. Most importantly, the test responses should be interpreted only by a qualified mental health professional with postgraduate education in psychological assessment and specialized training in the use of the MMPI-2. While computer-generated narrative reports are available and can be a useful tool, they should be evaluated (and edited if needed) by the on-site professional to individualize the reported results. Computer scoring and hypothesis generation is complex, and only reputable software programs should be used.

Although the MMPI-2 may yield extensive information about the client, it is not a replacement for a clinical

KEY TERMS

Battery—A number of separate items (such as tests) used together. In psychology, a group or series of tests given with a common purpose, such as personality assessment or measurement of intelligence.

Biopsychosocial history—A history of significant past and current experiences that influence client behaviors, including medical, educational, employment, and interpersonal experiences. Alcohol or drug use and involvement with the legal system are also assessed in a biopsychosocial history.

Empirical—Verified by actual experience or by scientific experimentation.

Forensic—Pertaining to courtroom procedure or evidence used in courts of law.

Hypothesis—An assumption, proposition, or educated guess that can be tested empirically.

Personality inventory—A type of psychological test that is designed to assess a client's major personality traits, behavioral patterns, coping styles, and similar characteristics. The MMPI-2 is an example of a personality inventory.

Psychological assessment—A process of gathering and synthesizing information about a person's psychological makeup and history for a specific purpose, which may be educational, diagnostic, or forensic.

Scale—A subset of test items from a multi-item test.

interview. The clinical interview helps the test administrator to develop conclusions that best apply to the client from the many hypotheses generated from test results. Furthermore, important aspects of the client's behaviors may emerge in an interview that were not reflected in the test results. For similar reasons, the test results should not be interpreted until the clinician has obtained a biopsychosocial history from the client.

The MMPI-2 should be administered as part of a battery, or group, of tests rather than as an isolated assessment measure. A comprehensive assessment of a person will typically include the **Rorschach technique**, the **Thematic Apperception Test** (TAT) or the Sentence Completion Test, and the **Wechsler Adult Intelligence Scale**, Revised (WAIS-R) or similar test of cognitive functioning as well as the MMPI-2.

Description

The MMPI-2 is composed of 567 true/false items. It can be administered using a printed test booklet and an answer sheet filled in by hand, or by responding to the items on a computer. For the person with limited reading skills or the visually impaired respondent, the MMPI-2 items are available on audiotape. Although the MMPI-2 is frequently referred to as a test, it is not an academic test with "right" and "wrong" answers. Personality inventories like the MMPI-2 are intended to discover what the respondent is like as a person. A number of areas are "tapped into" by the MMPI-2 to answer such questions as: "Who is this person and how would he or she typically feel, think and behave? What psychological problems and issues are relevant to this person?" Associations between patterns of answers to test items and particular traits or behaviors have been discovered through personality research conducted with the MMPI-2. The inventory items are not arranged into topics or areas on the test. The areas of personality that are measured are interspersed in a somewhat random fashion throughout the MMPI-2 booklet. Some examples of true-or-false statements similar to those on the MMPI-2 are: "I wake up with a headache almost every day"; "I certainly feel worthless sometimes"; "I have had peculiar and disturbing experiences that most other people have not had"; "I would like to do the work of a choir director."

The MMPI-2 is intended for use with adults over age 18; a similar test, the MMPI-A, is designed for use with adolescents. The publisher produces the MMPI-2 in English and Spanish versions. The test has also been translated into Dutch-Flemish, two French dialects (France and Canada), German, Hebrew, Hmong, Italian, and three Spanish dialects (for Spain, Mexico or United States).

From the 1940s to the 1980s, the original MMPI was the most widely used and most intensely researched psychological assessment instrument in the United States and worldwide. The test was originally developed in 1943 using a process called empirical keying, which was an innovation. Most assessment tools prior to the MMPI used questions or tasks that were merely assumed by the test designer to realistically assess the behaviors under question. The empirical keying process was radically different. To develop empirical keying, the creators of the original MMPI wrote a wide range of true-or-false statements, many of which did not directly target typical psychiatric topics. Research was then conducted with groups of psychiatric inpatients, hospital visitors, college students and medical inpatients, who took the MMPI in order to determine which test items reliably differentiated the psychiatric patients from the others. The test developers also evaluated the items that reliably distinguished groups of patients with a particular diagnosis from the remaining pool of psychiatric patient respondents; these items were grouped into subsets referred to as clinical scales.

An additional innovation in the original MMPI was the presence of validity scales embedded in the test questions. These sets of items, scattered randomly throughout the MMPI-2, allow the examiner to assess whether the respondent answered questions in an open and honest manner, or tried to exaggerate or conceal information. One means of checking for distortions in responding to the instrument is asking whether the test taker refused to admit to some less-than-ideal actions that most people probably engage in and will admit to doing. An example of this type of question would be (true or false) "If I could sneak into the county fair or an amusement park without paying, I would." Another type of validity check that assesses honesty in responses is whether the client admits to participating in far more unusual behaviors and actions than were admitted to by both the psychiatric comparison group and the general community sample. The validity scales also identify whether the test taker responded inconsistently or randomly.

The MMPI-2, which has demonstrated continuity and comparability with its predecessor, was published in 1989. The revised version was based on a much larger and more racially and culturally diverse normative community comparison group than the original version. Also, more in-depth and stringent research on the qualities and behaviors associated with different patterns of scores allows improved accuracy in predicting test-respondents' traits and behaviors from their test results.

Results

The true/false items are organized after scoring into validity, clinical, and content scales. The inventory may be scored manually or by computer. After scoring, the configuration of the test taker's scale scores is marked on a profile form that contrasts each client's responses to results obtained by the representative community comparison group. The clinician is able to compare a respondent's choices to those of a large normative comparison group as well as to the results derived from earlier MMPI and MMPI-2 studies. The clinician forms inferences about the client by analyzing his or her response patterns on the validity, clinical and content scales, using published guidebooks to the MMPI-2. These texts are based on results obtained from over 10,000 MMPI/MMPI-2 research studies.

In addition to the standard validity, clinical, and content scales, numerous additional scales for the MMPI have been created for special purposes over the years by researchers. These special supplementary scale scores are often incorporated into the examiner's interpretation of the test results. Commonly used supplementary scales include the MacAndrews Revised Alcoholism Scale, the **Addiction** Potential Scale, and the Anxiety Scale. The clinician may also choose to obtain computerized reporting, which yields behavioral hypotheses about the respondent, using scoring and interpretation algorithms applied to a commercial database.

Resources

BOOKS

Butcher, J. N., W. G. Dahlstrom, J. R. Graham, A. Tellegen, and B. Kaemmer. *MMPI-2: Manual for Administration, Scoring and Interpretation.* Revised. Minneapolis: University of Minnesota Press, 1989.

Butcher, J. N. and C. L. Williams. *Essentials of MMPI-2 and MMPI-A Interpretation.* Revised. Minneapolis: University of Minnesota Press, 1999.

Graham, John R. *MMPI-2: Assessing Personality and Psychopathology.* 3rd edition, revised. New York: Oxford University Press, 2000.

Graham, John R., Yossef S. Ben-Porath, and John L. McNulty. *MMPI-2: Correlates for Outpatient Community Mental Health Settings.* Minneapolis: University of Minnesota Press, 1999.

PERIODICALS

McNulty, J. L., J. R. Graham, and Y. Ben-Porath. "An empirical examination of the correlates of well-defined and not defined MMPI-2 codetypes." *Journal of Personality Assessment* 71 (1998): 393-410.

Deborah Rosch Eifert, Ph.D.

Mirtazapine

Definition

Mirtazapine is most commonly used to treat depression. Mirtazapine is available in the United States under the trade names of Remeron and Remeron SolTab.

Mirtazapine, sold under the trade name Remeron, is taken by mouth and swallowed whole. Remeron SolTabs should be allowed to dissolve in the mouth. No water is needed when taking the SolTabs, since these tablets disintegrate in saliva and are not swallowed whole.

KEY TERMS

Anti-anxiety agent—A medication that is used to treat symptoms of generalized fear that dominates a person's life.

Antihistamine—A medication used to alleviate allergy or cold symptoms such as runny nose, itching, hives, watering eyes, or sneezing.

Antipsychotic—A medication used to treat psychotic symptoms of schizophrenia such as hallucinations, delusions and delirium. May be used to treat symptoms in other disorders, as well.

Depression—A mental state characterized by excessive sadness. Other symptoms include altered sleep patterns, thoughts of suicide, difficulty concentrating, agitation, lack of energy, and loss of enjoyment in activities that are usually pleasurable.

Mania—An elevated or euphoric mood or irritable state that is characteristic of bipolar I disorder. This state is characterized by mental and physical hyperactivity, disorganization of behavior, and inappropriate elevation of mood.

Purpose

Mirtazapine is best known for treating depression. However, it may also be used for treating anxiety or to make people drowsy just before surgery.

Description

Mirtazapine is usually thought of as an antidepressant, or a drug that alleviates symptoms of depression. Approved by the Federal Drug Administration (FDA) in 1996, it is believed to alter the activities of some chemicals in the **brain** and, in this way, reduce chemical imbalances responsible for causing depression and anxiety. As with all antidepressants, it may take several weeks of treatment before full beneficial effects are seen. Mirtazapine is broken down by the liver and eliminated from the body mostly by the kidneys. It is supplied in 15-, 30-, and 45-mg tablets.

Recommended dosage

The recommended initial dose of mirtazapine in 15 mg taken at bedtime. The dose may be increased in 15-mg increments every one or two weeks as needed until symptoms of depression or anxiety resolve. Typical doses range between 15 and 45 mg. Dosages above 45 mg per day are not recommended. Elderly people or those with liver or kidney disease should use mirtazapine carefully, since they may be more sensitive to some of the drug's side effects.

Precautions

Mirtazapine may cause weight gain and may increase cholesterol levels and should be used carefully in overweight individuals and those with high cholesterol levels. If symptoms of fever, sore throat, or irritation in the mouth occur, a health care provider should be notified. Rarely, mirtazapine may lower blood counts, causing people to be at an increased risk of serious complications, including infections. Mirtazapine may increase the tendency for **seizures**. As a result, it should be used carefully in people with epilepsy or other seizure disorders. Mirtazapine may alter moods or cause mania. It should be used carefully in people with a history of mania. Mirtazapine may alter liver function and should be used cautiously by those with a history of liver disease. If abdominal pain, yellowing of the skin or eyes, darkening of urine, or itching occurs, a health care provider should be notified immediately.

More than 50% of individuals using mirtazapine report feeling sleepier than normal and 7% feel dizzy. As a result, people taking mirtazapine should not participate in activities that require mental alertness—like driving—until they know how the drug will affect them. Because there is an increased likelihood of **suicide** in depressed individuals, close supervision of those at high risk for suicide attempts using this drug is recommended. Mirtazapine is not recommended in pregnant or breast-feeding women.

Side effects

The most common side effects that cause people to stop taking mirtazapine are sleepiness and nausea. Other common side effects are dizziness, increased appetite and weight gain. Less common adverse effects include weakness and muscle aches, flu-like symptoms, low blood-cell counts, high cholesterol, back pain, chest pain, rapid heartbeats, dry mouth, constipation, water retention, difficulty sleeping, nightmares, abnormal thoughts, vision disturbances, ringing in the ears, abnormal taste in the mouth, tremor, confusion, upset stomach, and increased urination.

Interactions

Use of mirtazapine with antidepressants referred to as monoamine oxidase inhibitors (MAOIs) such as Parnate (**tranylcypromine**) and Nardil (**phenelzine**), is strongly prohibited due to the potential for high fever, muscle stiffness, sudden muscle spasms, rapid changes in heart rate and blood pressure, and the possibility of death. In fact, there should be a lapse of at least 14 days between taking an MAOI and mirtazapine.

Because mirtazapine may cause drowsiness, it should be used carefully with other medications that also make people prone to sleepiness, such as antidepressants, antipsychotics, antihistamines, anti-anxiety agents, and alcohol. Increased sleepiness has been reported when mirtazapine was used with both alcohol and the anti-anxiety drug **diazepam**.

See also Depression and depressive disorders

Resources

BOOKS

Ellsworth, Allan J., and others. *Mosby's Medical Drug Reference.* St. Louis, MO: Mosby, Inc, 1999.

Facts and Comparisons Staff. *Drug Facts and Comparisons.* 6th Edition. St. Louis, MO: Facts and Comparisons; Philadelphia: Lippincott Williams and Wilkins, 2002.

Organon Staff. *Remeron Package Insert.* West Orange, NJ: Organon Inc, 2001.

Kelly Karpa, RPh, Ph.D.

Mixed episode

Definition

A mixed episode is a discrete period during which a person experiences nearly daily fluctuations in mood that qualify for diagnoses of **manic episode** and major depressive episode. Over the course of at least one week, the mood of a person experiencing a mixed episode will rapidly change between abnormal happiness or euphoria and sadness or irritability.

Description

To qualify for a **diagnosis** of mixed episode, symptoms must be severe enough to interfere with an individual's ability to carry out daily routines at work or home, or to require **hospitalization**. Males may be more susceptible to this condition than females. Young people and those more than 60 years of age with **bipolar disorder** may be more prone to mixed episodes than others. A manic episode or a major depressive episode is more likely to turn into a mixed episode than vice versa. Manic episodes can also appear in an individual who does not suffer from these or other disturbances. If the episode can be attributed to side effects related to any medical treatment, medical condition, medication, or drugs of abuse, it is not classified as a mixed episode.

See also Bipolar disorder ; Depression and depressive disorders; Major depressive disorder

Dean A. Haycock, Ph.D.

Mixed receptive-expressive language disorder

Definition

Mixed receptive-expressive language disorder is diagnosed when a child has problems expressing him- or herself using spoken language, and also has problems understanding what people say to him or her.

Description

Mixed receptive-expressive language disorder is generally a disorder of childhood. There are two types of mixed receptive-expressive language disorder: developmental and acquired. Developmental mixed receptive-expressive language disorder does not have a known cause and normally appears at the time that a child is learning to talk. Acquired mixed receptive-expressive language disorder is caused by direct damage to the **brain**. It occurs suddenly after such events as a **stroke** or traumatic head injury. The acquired type can occur at any age.

Causes and symptoms

Causes

There is no known cause of developmental mixed receptive-expressive language disorder. Researchers are conducting ongoing studies to determine whether biological or environmental factors may be involved. The acquired form of the disorder results from direct damage to the brain. Damage can be sustained during a stroke, or as the result of traumatic head injury, **seizures**, or other medical conditions. The specific symptoms of the acquired form of the disorder generally depend on the parts of the patient's brain that have been injured and the severity of the damage.

Symptoms

The signs and symptoms of mixed receptive-expressive language disorder are for the most part the same as

KEY TERMS

Phonological disorder—A developmental disorder of childhood in which the child fails to use speech sounds that are appropriate for his or her age level and native language or dialect.

the symptoms of **expressive language disorder**. The disorder has signs and symptoms that vary considerably from child to child. In general, mixed receptive-expressive language disorder is characterized by a child's difficulty with spoken communication. The child does not have problems with the pronunciation of words, which is found in **phonological disorder**. The child does, however, have problems constructing coherent sentences, using proper grammar, recalling words, or similar communication problems. A child with mixed receptive-expressive language disorder is not able to communicate thoughts, needs, or wants at the same level or with the same complexity as his or her peers. In addition, the child often has a smaller vocabulary than his or her peers.

Children with mixed receptive-expressive language disorder also have significant problems understanding what other people are saying to them. This lack of comprehension may result in inappropriate responses or failure to follow directions. Some people think these children are being deliberately stubborn or obnoxious, but this is not the case. They simply do not understand what is being said. Some children with this disorder have problems understanding such specific types of terms as abstract nouns, complex sentences, or spatial terms.

Diagnosis

The ***Diagnostic and Statistical Manual of Mental Disorders***, fourth edition, text revised (*DSM-IV-TR*), which is the standard reference work consulted by mental health professionals, specifies four general criteria for diagnosing mixed receptive-expressive language disorder. The first criterion states that the child communicates using speech and appears to understand spoken language at a level that is lower than expected for the child's general level of intelligence. Second, the child's problems with self-expression and comprehension must create difficulties for him or her in everyday life or in achieving his or her academic goals. If the child understands what is being said at a level that is normal for his or her age or stage of development, then the **diagnosis** would be expressive language disorder. If the child is mentally retarded, hard of hearing, or has other physical problems, the difficulties with speech must be greater than generally occurs with the other handicaps the child may have in order for the child to be diagnosed with this disorder.

The disorder is usually diagnosed in children because a parent or teacher expresses concern about the child's problems with spoken communication. The child's pediatrician may give the child a physical examination to rule out such medical problems as hearing loss. Specific testing for mixed expressive-receptive language disorder requires the examiner to demonstrate that the child not only communicates less well than expected, but also understands speech less well. It can be hard, however, to determine what a child understands. As a result, most examiners will use non-verbal tests in addition to tests that require spoken questions and answers in order to assess the child's condition as accurately as possible. In children who are mildly hearing-impaired, the problem can often be corrected by using hearing aids. Children who speak a language other than English (or the dominant language of their society) at home should be tested in that language if possible. In some cases, the child's ability to understand and communicate in English is the problem, not his or her competence with spoken language in general.

Demographics

Mixed receptive-expressive language disorder is diagnosed in about 5% of preschool-age children, and 3% of children in school. It is less common than expressive language disorder. Children who have mixed receptive-expressive language disorder are more likely to have other disorders as well. Between 40%–60% of preschoolers who have this disorder may also have phonological disorder (difficulty forming sounds). **Reading disorder** is linked to as many as half the children with mixed receptive-expressive language disorder who are of school age. Children with mixed receptive-expressive language disorder are also more likely to have psychiatric disorders, especially attention-deficit disorder (ADD); it is estimated that 30–60 percent of children with mixed receptive-expressive language disorder also have ADD. Children from families with a history of language disorders are more likely to have this or other language disorders.

Treatment

Mixed receptive-expressive language disorder should be treated as soon as it is identified. Early **intervention** is the key to a successful outcome. Treatment involves teachers, siblings, parents, and anyone else who interacts regularly with the child. Regularly scheduled one-on-one treatment that focuses on specific language skills can also be effective, especially when combined with a more general approach involving family members and caregivers. Teaching children with this disorder specific communication skills so that they can interact with their peers is important, as problems in this area may lead to later social isolation, depression, or behavioral problems. Children who are diagnosed early and taught reading skills may benefit especially, because problems with reading are often associated with mixed receptive-expressive language disorder and can cause serious long-term academic problems. There is little information comparing different treatment methods; often several are tried in combination.

Prognosis

The developmental form of mixed receptive-expressive language disorder is less likely to resolve well than the developmental form of expressive language disorder. Most children with the disorder continue to have problems with language skills. They develop them at a much slower rate than their peers, which puts them at a growing disadvantage throughout their educational career. Some persons diagnosed with the disorder as children have significant problems with expressing themselves and understanding others in adult life.

The prognosis of the acquired type of mixed receptive-expressive language disorder depends on the nature and location of the brain injury. Some people get their language skills back over days or months. For others it takes years, and some people never fully recover expressive language function or the ability to understand speech.

Prevention

Because the causes of developmental mixed receptive-expressive language disorder are unclear, there are no specific ways to prevent it. A healthy diet during pregnancy and regular prenatal care are always recommended. Because the acquired form of the disorder is caused by damage to the brain, anything that helps to prevent brain damage may offer protection against that form of the disorder. Preventive measures include such precautions as lowering blood cholesterol levels, which may help to prevent stroke; or wearing bicycle helmets or automobile seat belts to prevent traumatic head injury.

Resources

BOOKS

American Psychiatric Association. *Diagnostic and Statistical Manual of Mental Disorders.* 4th ed., text revised. Washington DC: American Psychiatric Association, 2000.

Sadock, Benjamin J. and Virginia A. Sadock, eds. *Comprehensive Textbook of Psychiatry.* 7th ed. Philadelphia: Lippincott Williams and Wilkins, 2000.

PERIODICALS

Stein, Martin T., Steven Parker, James Coplan, Heidi Feldman. "Expressive Language Delay in a Toddler." *Journal of Developmental & Behavioral Pediatrics* 22 no. 2 (April 2001): 99.

ORGANIZATIONS

American Academy of Pediatrics. 141 Northwest Point Boulevard, Elk Grove Village, IL 60007-1098. (847) 434-4000. <www.aap.org>.

American Psychological Association. 750 First Street NE, Washington, DC 20002-4242. Telephone: (800) 374-2721. <www.apa.org>.

American Speech-Language-Hearing Association. 10801 Rockville Pike, Rockville, MD 20852. (800) 638-8355. <http://www.asha.org>.

See also Attention-deficit/hyperactivity disorder

Tish Davidson, A.M.

MMPI *see* **Minnesota Multiphasic Personality Inventory**

Moban *see* **Molindone**

Modeling

Definition

Modeling, which is also called observational learning or imitation, is a behaviorally based procedure that involves the use of live or symbolic models to demonstrate a particular behavior, thought, or attitude that a client may want to acquire or change. Modeling is sometimes called vicarious learning, because the client need not actually perform the behavior in order to learn it.

Purpose

Modeling therapy is based on social learning theory. This theory emphasizes the importance of learning from observing and imitating role models, and learning about rewards and punishments that follow behavior. The technique has been used to eliminate unwanted behaviors, reduce excessive fears, facilitate learning of social behaviors, and many more. Modeling may be used either to strengthen or to weaken previously learned behaviors.

Modeling has been used effectively to treat individuals with anxiety disorders, **post-traumatic stress disorder**, **specific phobias**, **obsessive-compulsive disorder**, eating disorders, **attention-deficit/hyperactivity disorder**, and **conduct disorder**. It has also been used

KEY TERMS

Generalization—A person's ongoing use of new behaviors that were previously modeled for him or her. Generalization is also called transfer of training or maintenance.

In vivo—A Latin phrase that means "in life." In modeling and exposure therapies, it refers to practicing new behaviors in a real setting, as distinct from using imagery or imagined settings.

Reinforcement—In behavioral therapy, the ability of a behavior to produce effects that will make the user want to perform the behavior again. In modeling, reinforcement refers to rewarding the model's demonstration of a skill or the client's performance of the newly acquired skill in practice or in real-life situations.

Role-playing—A technique used in therapy in which participants act out roles relevant to real-life situations in order to change their attitudes and behaviors.

Vicarious—Acquired through imagined participation in the experience of others. Modeling is a form of vicarious learning.

successfully in helping individuals acquire such social skills as public speaking or assertiveness. The effectiveness of modeling has led to its use in behavioral treatment of persons with substance abuse disorders, who frequently lack important behavioral skills. These persons may lack assertiveness, including the ability to say "no"; in addition, they may have thought patterns that make them more susceptible to substance abuse.

Modeling when used alone has been shown to be effective for short-term learning. It is, however, insufficient for long-lasting behavior change if the target behavior does not produce rewards that sustain it. Modeling works well when it is combined with role-play and **reinforcement**. These three components are used in a sequence of modeling, role-play, and reinforcement. Role-play is defined as practice or behavioral rehearsal of a skill to be used later in real-life situations. Reinforcement is defined as rewarding the model's performance or the client's performance of the newly acquired skill in practice or in real-life situations.

Several factors increase the effectiveness of modeling therapy in changing behaviors. Modeling effects have been shown to be more powerful when:

- The model is highly skilled in enacting the behavior; is likable or admirable; is friendly; is the same sex and age; and is rewarded immediately for the performance of the particular behavior.
- The target behavior is clearly demonstrated with very few unnecessary details; is presented from the least to the most difficult level of behavior; and several different models are used to perform the same behavior(s).

Description

Types of modeling

Therapy begins with an assessment of the client's presenting problem(s). The assessment usually covers several areas of life, including developmental history (the client's family background, education, employment, social relationships); past traumatic experiences; medical and psychiatric history; and an outline of the client's goals. The client works with the therapist to list specific treatment goals; to determine the target behavior(s) to be learned or changed; and to develop a clear picture of what the behavior(s) will look like. The therapist then explains the rationale and concepts of the treatment. He or she also considers any negative consequences that may arise as the client makes changes in his or her behavior.

The client then observes the model enacting the desired behavior. Some models may demonstrate poor or inadequate behaviors as well as those that are effective. This contrast helps the client to identify ineffective behaviors as well as desired ones. Modeling can be done in several different ways, including live modeling, symbolic modeling, participant modeling, or covert modeling.

Live modeling refers to watching a real person, usually the therapist, perform the desired behavior the client has chosen to learn. For example, the therapist might model good telephone manners for a client who wants a job in a field that requires frequent telephone contact with customers.

Symbolic modeling includes filmed or videotaped models demonstrating the desired behavior. Other examples of symbolic models include photographs, picture books, and plays. A common example of symbolic modeling is a book for children about going to the hospital, intended to reduce a child's anxiety about hospitals and operations. With child clients, cartoon figures or puppets can be used as the models. Self-modeling is another form of symbolic modeling in which clients are videotaped performing the target behavior. The video is than replayed and clients can observe their behaviors and how they appear to others. For example, public speaking is one of the most common feared situations in the general adult population. A law student who is afraid of having to present arguments

Young girls in a ballet dancing class. The instructors are serving as live models, showing the girls a behavior that they are to imitate and practice. This is an example of learning through modeling. *(Bob Krist/CORBIS. Photo reproduced by permission.)*

in a courtroom might be videotaped speaking to classmates who are role-playing the judge and members of the jury. The student can then review the videotape and work on his or her speech problems or other aspects of the performance that he or she would like to change.

In participant modeling, the therapist models anxiety-evoking behaviors for the client, and then prompts the client to engage in the behavior. The client first watches as the therapist approaches the feared object, and then approaches the object in steps or stages with the therapist'sencouragement and support. This type of modeling is often used in the treatment of specific phobias. For example, a person who is afraid of dogs might be asked to watch the therapist touch or pet a dog, or perhaps accompany the therapist on a brief walk with a dog. Then, with the therapist's encouragement, the client might begin by touching or holding a stuffed dog, then watching a live dog from a distance, then perhaps walking a small dog on a leash, and eventually by degrees touching and petting a live dog.

In covert modeling, clients are asked to use their imagination, visualizing a particular behavior as the therapist describes the imaginary situation in detail. For example, a child may be asked to imagine one of his or her favorite cartoon characters interacting appropriately with other characters. An adult client is asked to imagine an admired person in his or her life performing a behavior that the client wishes to learn. For example, a person may greatly admire his or her mother for the way she handled the challenges of coming to the United States from another country. If the client is worried about the challenge of a new situation (changing careers, having their first child, etc.), the therapist may ask him or her to imagine how their mother would approach the new situation, and then imagine themselves acting with her courage and wisdom.

Models in any of these forms may be presented as either a coping or a mastery model. The coping model is shown as initially fearful or incompetent and then is shown as gradually becoming comfortable and competent performing the feared behavior. A coping model might show a small child who is afraid of swimming in the ocean, for example. The little boy or girl watches smaller children having fun playing in the waves along the edge of the shore. Gradually the child moves closer and closer to the water and finally follows a child his or her age into the surf. The mastery model shows no fear and is competent from the beginning of the demonstration. Coping models are considered more appropriate for reducing fear because they look more like the client, who will probably make mistakes and have some setbacks when trying the new behavior.

Having the model speak his or her thoughts aloud is more effective than having a model who does not verbalize. As the models speak, they show the client how to think through a particular problem or situation. A common example of this type of modeling is sports or cooking instruction. A golf or tennis pro who is trying to teach a beginner how to hold and swing the club or racquet will often talk as they demonstrate the correct stance and body movements. Similarly, a master chef will often talk to students in a cooking class while he or she is cutting up the ingredients for a dish, preparing a sauce, kneading dough, or doing other necessary tasks. The model's talking while performing an action also engages the client's sense of hearing, taste, or smell as well as sight. Multisensory involvement enhances the client's learning.

Role-playing

Role-playing is a technique that allows the client opportunities to imitate the modeled behaviors, which strengthens what has been learned. Role-play can be defined as practice or behavior rehearsal; it allows the client to receive feedback about the practice as well as encouraging the use of the newly learned skill in real-life situations. For example, a group of people who are trying to learn social skills might practice the skills needed for a job interview or for dealing with a minor problem (returning a defective item to a store, asking someone for directions, etc.). Role-play can also be used for modeling, in that the therapist may role-play certain situations with clients. During practice, the therapist frequently coaches, prompts, and shapes the client's enactment of the behavior so that the rehearsals can come increasingly close to the desired behavior.

Feedback and social reinforcement of the client's performance in the practice phase is an important motivator for behavior change. Feedback may take the form of praise, approval, or encouragement; or it may be corrective, with concrete suggestions for improving the performance. Suggestions are followed by additional practice. Such tangible reinforcements as money, food, candy, or tokens have been used with young children and chronic psychiatric patients. The therapist may teach the client how to use self-reinforcement; that is, using self-praise after performing the desired behavior. The purpose of reinforcement is to shift the client's performance concerns from external evaluation by others to internal evaluation of their own efforts.

Modeling in group settings

Modeling has been shown to be effective in such group programs as **social skills training** and **assertiveness training** as well as in individual therapy. The general approach to both social skills training and assertiveness training is the incorporation of the modeling, role-play, and reinforcement sequence. After assessment of each group member's presenting problem, each member is asked to keep a diary of what happened when the situation occurred during the week. Group members develop goals for dealing with their individual situations, and each person determines how he or she can meet these goals. Modeling is done with either the therapist or other group members role-playing how to deal effectively with a particular problem situation.

Length of treatment

While modeling therapy is a relatively short-term approach to behavioral change, some therapeutic techniques take longer than others. Imagery, for example, requires more sessions than in vivo (real-life) treatments. In vivo work that takes place outside the therapist's office would require longer time periods for each session. Other considerations include the nature of the client's problem; the client's willingness to do homework; the client's financial resources; and the presence and extent of the client's support network. The therapist's length of experience and personal style also affect the length of therapy.

There are, however, guidelines of treatment length for some disorders. Treatment of obsessive-compulsive disorder may require five weekly sessions for approximately three weeks, with weekly follow-up sessions for several months. Depressive disorders may require three to six months, with the client experiencing short-term relief after three to four weeks of treatment. General anxiety disorder may also take several months of weekly sessions. The length of treatment depends on the ability to define and assess the target behaviors. Clients may meet with the therapist several times a week at the beginning of treatment; then weekly for several months; then monthly for follow-up sessions that may become fewer in number or spaced more widely until therapy is terminated.

Normal results

Modeling or observational learning is effective as a method of learning such behaviors as self-assertion, self-disclosure, helping others, empathic behaviors, moral judgment, and many other interpersonal skills. Modeling is also effective in eliminating or reducing such undesirable behaviors as uncontrolled aggression, smoking, weight problems, and single phobias.

The expected outcome is that clients will be able to use their new behaviors outside the treatment setting in real-life situations. This result is called transfer of training, generalization, or maintenance. Homework is the most frequently used technique for transfer of training. Homework may represent a contractual agreement between the therapist and the client in which the client gives a report on his or her progress at each meeting.

To ensure that generalization occurs and that clients will use their new skills, several "tranfer enhancers" are used to increase the likelihood of successful transfer of training. Transfer enhancers include:

- Giving clients appropriate rationales and concepts, rules, or strategies for using skills properly.
- Giving clients ample opportunity to practice new skills correctly and successfully.
- Making the treatment setting as much like the real-life situation as possible.
- Giving clients opportunities to practice their new skills in a variety of physical and interpersonal settings.
- Giving clients adequate external social reinforcement and encouraging internal self-reinforcement as they use their skills successfully in real life.

See also Behavior modification

Resources

BOOKS

Braswell, Lauren and Philip C. Kendall. "Cognitive-Behavioral Therapy with Youth." In *Handbook of Cognitive Behavioral Therapies,* edited by Keith S. Dobson. 2nd ed. New York: The Guilford Press. 2001.

Jinks, Gordon. "Specific Strategies and Techniques." In *Handbook of Counselling and Psychotherapy,* edited by Colin Feltham and Ian Horton. London: Sage Publications, 2000.

Sharf, Richard S. "Behavior Therapy." In *Theories of Psychotherapy and Counseling: Concepts and Cases.* 2nd ed. Stamford: Thomson Learning, 2000.

ORGANIZATIONS

American Psychological Association. 750 First St. N.E., Washington, D.C. 20002. (202) 336-5800. <http://helping.apa.org>.

Association for Advancement of Behavior Therapy. 305 Seventh Ave., 16th Floor, New York, NY 10001. (212) 647-1890. <http://www.aabt,org>.

National Institute of Mental Health. 6001 Executive Boulevard, RM8184, MSC 9663, Bethesda, MD 20892-9663. (301) 443-4513. <http://www.nimh.nih.gov>.

National Mental Health Association. 1021 Prince Street, Alexander, VA 22314-2971. (703) 684-7722. <http://www.nmha.org>.

Janice VanBuren, Ph.D.

Molindone

Definition

Molindone is an antipsychotic. It is sold in the United States under the trade name of Moban.

Purpose

Molindone is used to treat psychotic symptoms that may appear in depression, mania, or **schizophrenia**.

Description

Molindone is taken orally, and is rapidly absorbed and metabolized. Peak levels are reached within 90 minutes of taking the medication, and its effect lasts 24 to 36 hours. Molindone is available in 5-, 10-, 25-, and 100-mg tablets.

Recommended dosage

The dosage of molindone should be adjusted to the lowest level needed to control symptoms. The usual initial dosage is 50 to 75 mg per day. This may be increased to 100 mg per day three to four days after beginning treatment. A maximal dosage of up to 225 mg per day may be required.

Precautions

Prolonged or chronic administration of molindone increases the probability of developing **tardive dyskinesia**, a cluster of involuntary, uncoordinated movements that is potentially irreversible. These movements involve the head, neck, trunk, feet, and hands. Some of the movements involving the face and head include worm-like movement of the tongue, grimacing, chewing, and lip smacking. Tardive dyskinesia usually disappears once the affected person stops taking the medication, but it may not.

KEY TERMS

Akathisia—Agitated or restless movement, usually affecting the legs. Movement is accompanied by a sense of discomfort and an inability to sit, stand still, or remain inactive for periods of time. Akathisia is a common side effect of some neuroleptic (antipsychotic) medications.

Dystonia—A neurological disorder characterized by involuntary muscle spasms. The spasms can cause a painful twisting of the body and difficulty walking or moving.

Orthostatic hypotension—A sudden decrease in blood pressure due to a change in body position, as when moving from a sitting to standing position.

Schizophrenia—A severe mental illness in which a person has difficulty distinguishing what is real from what is not real. It is often characterized by hallucinations, delusions, language and communication disturbances, and withdrawal from people and social activities.

Tardive dyskinesia—A condition that involves involuntary movements of the tongue, jaw, mouth or face or other groups of skeletal muscles that usually occurs either late in antipsychotic therapy or even after the therapy is discontinued. It may be irreversible.

Tranquilizer—A medication that induces a feeling of calm and relaxation.

People who are comatose or are experiencing central nervous system depression from alcohol, **barbiturates** or narcotics are not prescribed this medication.

Drowsiness is often reported by people using molindone. For that reason, people using molindone should not operate machinery or drive automobiles.

Molindone administration causes the level of prolactin (a hormone that initiates lactation) in the blood to rise. This is a potential problem for people with a personal or family history of breast cancer. The drug may lead to the initiation of breast cancer. For this reason, the benefits of the drug must be carefully evaluated before it is administered.

Side effects

As stated, molindone has the potential to produce tardive dyskinesia. This is a syndrome consisting of involuntary, uncoordinated movements that is potentially irreversible. The incidence of tardive dyskinesia increases with increasing age and with increasing dosage of molindone. Tardive dyskinesia is more likely to occur after a long period of taking antipsychotic drugs, like molindone, but it may also appear after molindone use has been discontinued. Females are at greater risk than males for developing tardive dyskinesia. Involuntary movements of the tongue, jaw, mouth or face characterize tardive dyskinesia. These may be accompanied by involuntary movements of the arms, legs and trunk. There is no known effective treatment for tardive dyskinesia.

Parkinson-like symptoms have been linked with the administration of molindone. These include restlessness and agitation (akathisia) and difficulty walking or moving (dystonia). These are generally controlled with **benztropine** mesylate or **trihexyphenidyl** hydrochloride.

An occasionally reported side effect of molindone is neuroleptic malignant syndrome. This is a complicated and potentially fatal condition characterized by muscle rigidity, high fever, alterations in mental status, and cardiac symptoms such as irregular pulse or blood pressure, sweating, tachycardia and arrhythmias. This condition is considered a medical emergency.

Interactions

Molindone increases the effect of drugs and substances that depress the central nervous system. This class of drugs includes anesthetics, opiates, barbiturates, atropine and alcohol.

Molindone interferes with the absorption of phenytoin and tetracyclines.

Resources

BOOKS

Adams, Michael and Norman Holland. *Core Concepts in Pharmacology.* Philadelphia: Lippincott-Raven, 1998.

Foreman, John C. and Torben Johansen. *Textbook of Receptor Pharmacology.* 2nd Ed. Boca Raton, FL: CRC Press, 2002.

Page, Clive P., and Michael Murphy. *Integrated Pharmacology.* St. Louis: Mosby-Year Book, 2002.

Von Boxtel, Chris J., Budiono Santoso, and I. Ralph Edwards. *Drug Benefits and Risks: International Textbook of Clinical Pharmacology.* New York: John Wiley and Sons, 2001.

PERIODICALS

Bagnall A., M. Fenton, R. Lewis, M. L. Leitner, and J. Kleijnen. "Molindone for schizophrenia and severe mental illness." *Cochrane Database Systematic Review* no. 2 (2000), CD002083.

Dhaware, B. S., J. J. Balsara, N. V. Nandal and A. G. Chandorkar. "Effects of amantadine on modification of dopamine-dependent behaviours by molindone." *Indian Journal of Medical Science* 54, no. 8 (2000): 321-324.

W. M. Glazer. "Expected incidence of tardive dyskinesia associated with atypical antipsychotics." *Journal of Clinical Psychiatry.* 61, Supplement 4 (2000): 21-26.

OTHER

American Academy of Clinical Toxicology. 777 East Park Drive, PO Box 8820, Harrisburg, PA 17105-8820. Telephone: (717) 558-7750. Fax: (717) 558-7845. Web site: <http://www.clintox.org/index.html>.

American Academy of Family Physicians. 11400 Tomahawk Creek Parkway, Leawood, KS 66211-2672. Telephone: (913) 906-6000. Web site: <http://www.aafp.org/>.

American Medical Association, 515 N. State Street, Chicago, IL 60610. Telephone: (312) 464-5000. Web site: <http://www.ama-assn.org/>.

American Psychiatric Association. 1400 K Street NW, Washington, DC 20005. Telephone: (888) 357-7924. Fax: (202) 682-6850. Web site: <http://www.psych.org/>.

American Society for Clinical Pharmacology and Therapeutics. 528 North Washington Street, Alexandria, VA 22314. Telephone: (703) 836-6981. Fax: (703) 836-5223.

American Society for Pharmacology and Experimental Therapeutics. 9650 Rockville Pike, Bethesda, MD 20814-3995. Telephone: (301) 530-7060. Fax: (301) 530-7061. Web site: <http://www.aspet.org/>.

L. Fleming Fallon, Jr., M.D., Dr.P.H.

Mood disorders *see* **Depression and depressive disorders and Bipolar disorders**

Movement disorders

Definition

Movement disorders describe a variety of abnormal movements of the body that have a neurological basis. These abnormal movements are characterized by changes in the coordination and speed of voluntary movement. They may also involve the presence of additional movements that are not voluntary.

Description

Movement disorders are sometimes referred to by medical professionals as extrapyramidal diseases because this class of disorders is distinct from the disorders caused by disorders of the pyramidal region of the **brain**. Researchers have determined that movement disorders are caused by diseases in various parts of the brain, including the substantia nigra, the subthalamic nucleus, the globus pallidus, the striatum, and the basal ganglia.

Movement disorders are usually broken down into two types of movement: hyperkinetic movement and hypokinetic movement. Hyperkinetic movement disorders are characterized by a significant and excessive amount of motor activity. This type also includes cases in which there is a significant amount of abnormal involuntary movement. Hypokinetic movement disorders are those in which there is an abnormally reduced amount of intentional motor activity.

Hyperkinetic movement disorders are characterized by two types of behavior: rhythmical and irregular. Tremor is a rhythmic movement that is further divided into three forms: rest, postural, and intention. Rest tremor is most prominent when an individual is at rest and decreases with voluntary activity. Postural tremor occurs when an individual attempts to support a position against gravity (such as holding an arm outstretched). Intention tremor occurs during voluntary movement toward a specific target.

Irregular involuntary movements are classified by their speed and site of occurrence. Tics are rapid irregular movements that are controlled with voluntary effort. The types of rapid irregular movements that cannot be controlled voluntarily are called chorea, hemiballismus, and myoclonus. Chorea is a rapid, jerking movement that most

KEY TERMS

Basal ganglia—A group of masses of gray matter located in the cerebral hemispheres of the brain that control movement as well as some aspects of emotion and cognition.

Dementia—A group of symptoms (syndrome) associated with a progressive loss of memory and other intellectual functions that is serious enough to interfere with a person's ability to perform the tasks of daily life. Dementia impairs memory, alters personality, leads to deterioration in personal grooming, impairs reasoning ability, and causes disorientation.

Dopamine—A chemical in brain tissue that serves to transmit nerve impulses (is a neurotransmitter) and helps to regulate movement and emotions.

Extrapyramidal—Brain structures located outside the pyramidal tracts of the central nervous system.

Substantia nigra—Dark-colored matter located in a section of the crus cerebri area of the brain.

often affects the face or limbs. Hemiballismus is the sudden and extreme swinging of a limb. Myoclonus is a rapid, irregular movement that usually occurs for a short period of time. It usually occurs when the person is at rest, and it often affects more than one area of the body at a time.

One of the most well-known hyperkinetic movement disorders is called Huntington's disease, characterized by chorea-type movements. This disease is inherited and usually develops between 30 and 50 years of age. Persons with this condition have progressive **dementia**, and the condition eventually causes death. Children of persons with Huntington's disease have a 50% chance of developing the condition. **Stereotypic movement disorder** is characterized by repetitive behaviors that meet no functional need such as hand waving; rocking; head banging; mouthing of objects; or biting, picking, or hitting oneself. These behaviors interfere with normal activities and are not caused by substance abuse or a general medical condition.

The symptoms of hypokinetic movement disorders include a rigid, stone-like face; decreased limb motion during walking; and stiff turning movements. These features are classified as bradykinesia, while akinesia is the absence of purposeful movement. The most common type of hypokinetic movement disorder is Parkinson's disease, caused by the loss of neurons containing dopamine in the area of the brain called the substantia nigra pars compacta. The loss of these neurons is a part of the alteration of vital motor circuits in the brain that leads to a slowing of intentional movements.

Resources

BOOKS

Braunwald, Eugene, Anthony S. Fauci, Dennis L. Kasper, and others. *Harrison's Principles of Internal Medicine.* New York: McGraw-Hill, 2001.

Weisiger, Richard A. *Cecil Textbook of Medicine.* Philadelphia, PA: W. B. Saunders, 2000.

ORGANIZATIONS

NIH Neurological Institute. P.O. Box 5801. Bethesda, MD 20824. (800) 352-9424. <http://www.ninds.nih.gov>.

Mark Mitchell, M.D.

Movement therapies *see* **Bodywork therapies**

MRI *see* **Magnetic resonance imaging**

Multiple personality disorder *see* **Dissociative identity disorder**

Multisystemic therapy

Definition

Multisystemic therapy (MST) is an intensive family- and community-based treatment program designed to make positive changes in the various social systems (home, school, community, peer relations) that contribute to the serious antisocial behaviors of children and adolescents who are at risk for out-of-home placement. These out-of-home placements might include foster care, **group homes**, residential care, correctional facilities, or **hospitalization**.

Purpose

MST is licensed by MST Services, Inc., through the Medical University of South Carolina and operates with the fundamental assumption that parents (defined as guardians), or those who have primary caregiving responsibilities to children, have the most important influence in changing problem behaviors in children and adolescents.

The primary goals of MST are to:

- develop in parents or caregivers the capacity to manage future difficulties
- reduce juvenile criminal activity
- reduce other types of antisocial behaviors, such as drug abuse
- achieve these outcomes at a cost savings by decreasing rates of incarceration and other out-of-home placements

MST was created approximately 25 years ago as an intensive family- and community-based treatment program to focus on juvenile offenders presenting with serious antisocial behaviors and who were at-risk for out-of-home placement. The program has been shown to be effective with targeted populations that include inner-city delinquents, violent and chronic juvenile offenders, juvenile offenders who abuse or are dependent on substances and also have psychiatric disorders, adolescent sex offenders, and abusive and neglectful parents. A more recent focus (1994–1999) of MST has been to treat youths with psychiatric emergencies such as suicidal ideation, homicidal ideation, **psychosis**, or threat of harm to self or others due to mental illness. The results are promising and indicate that MST is an effective alternative to psychiatric hospitalization. Some treatment conditions and interventions were modified to take care of this population, including developing a crisis plan during the initial family assessment and adding child and adolescent psychiatrists, psychiatric residents, and crisis caseworkers to the MST treatment team. Supervision of the treatment team was initially increased from weekly to daily meetings. Caseloads of MST therapists were reduced from five to three families, increasing the intensity of the **intervention**. When some adolescents were hospitalized for safety, the MST staff maintained clinical responsibility for the adolescent who was insulated from the usual activities due to inpatient care.

Description

MST programs are usually housed in community-based mental health organizations considered to have a culture more rehabilitative than punitive. The program staff creates strong working relationships with referral sources such as juvenile justice and the family court. They work closely with deputy juvenile officers, social welfare workers, teachers, and guidance counselors, for example, to obtain the perspectives of multiple systems or "stake-holders" who have the common goal of improving children, adolescent and family treatment goals. Each youth referred to the program is assigned to an MST therapist who designs individualized interventions in accordance with the nine MST treatment principles, thereby addressing specific needs of the youth and his or her specific environment.

MST is a time-limited (four to six months) intensive therapeutic program that provides services in the family's home, at other locations (school, neighborhoods), or wherever the family feels most comfortable. After the initial sessions, family members who attend family sessions with the therapist will vary depending on the nature of the particular problem being discussed. For example, children are not included in sessions addressing intimate marital issues between parents or dealing with poor parental discipline, so as not to undermine parental authority.

Characteristics of the MST model—such as availability of the MST staff (24 hours a day, seven days per week), flexible scheduling, and delivery of services in the home—all provide safety for the family, prevent violence, develop a joint working relationship between therapist and family, provide the family with easier access to needed services, increase the likelihood that the family will stay in treatment, and help the family maintain changes in behaviors. The MST staff are full-time practitioners, wear pagers, carry cellular telephones, and work in teams of three. They can provide intensive services because of small caseloads and have multiple contacts with the family during the week (sometimes daily). They stay as long as required and at times most convenient to the family, including weekends, evenings, and holidays. Services provided by staff at unusual times (10 P.M. to 8 A.M.) are discouraged, except in emergencies. The development of an informal support system in which the family can call on a friend or family member at crucial times is part of the treatment goals. Families have less contact with the therapist as they get closer to being discharged from treatment.

KEY TERMS

Psychotropic medication—Medication that has an effect on the mind, brain, behavior, perceptions, or emotions. Psychotropic medications are used to treat mental illnesses because they affect a patient's moods and perceptions.

Punitive—Concerned with, or directed toward, punishment.

Rehabilitative—To restore; to put back into good condition.

MST is designed to be a flexible intervention to provide highly individualized treatment to families. Specific treatment techniques or therapies are used as a part of MST interventions. These include behavior parent training, structural **family therapy**, and strategic family and **cognitive-behavioral therapy**. In addition, some biological influences such as **depression and depressive disorders** may be identified, and psychotropic medications are integrated into treatment. This model does not support one method for obtaining successful changes in behaviors; however, there are nine guiding principles of treatment:

- The primary purpose of assessment is to understand the fit between the identified problems and their broader systemic context. At the initial visit with the family, the staff begins to assess the family's strengths; capabilities; needs; problems; environmental support systems; and transactions with social systems such as peers, extended family, friends, teachers, parental workplace, referral resources, and neighbors. The therapist and family work together to identify and prioritize problems to be targeted for change, determine interventions, and develop a treatment plan. The assessment is conducted in a manner that empowers family members by encouraging them to define their problems, needs, strengths, and—except in matters of imminent safety—set their priorities. The assessment is gradually updated until the family has reached its goals and is functioning independently.
- Therapeutic contacts emphasize the positive and should use systemic strengths as levers for change. MST is a strength-based treatment program and adherence to this principle decreases negativity among family members,

builds positive expectations and hope, identifies strengths, and decreases therapist and family frustrations by emphasizing problem-solving. It also builds the caregiver's confidence. The therapist develops and maintains the focus on the strength of families and positive thinking through the use of positive language, teaching, and the technique of reframing negative thoughts and beliefs; the liberal use of positive rewards for appropriate behaviors; using a problem-solving stance rather than one of failure and seeing barriers as challenges; and identifying and using what the family does well.

- Interventions are designed to promote responsible behavior and decrease irresponsible behavior among family members. The therapist assists parents and youths in behaving in a responsible manner across a variety of domains. Parental responsibilities include providing support, guidance, and discipline; expressing love and nurturance; protection; advocacy; and meeting basic physical needs. The child and adolescent's primary responsibilities include complying with family and societal rules, attending school and putting forth reasonable effort, helping around the house, and not harming self or others. Therapists will spend a great deal of time throughout the treatment process enhancing, developing, and maintaining the responsible behaviors of parents through praise and support. Other family members who become engaged in the treatment process are also encouraged by the therapist to reinforce responsible parental behaviors that will help maintain these behaviors when treatment ends. It has been noted that when parents increase their responsibilities, there is almost always improvement in the child's behavior. Parental abdication of responsibilities may be caused by factors such as mental illness or the lack of necessary parenting skills. Interventions would be designed to address these influences. For children and adolescents, positive **reinforcement** and discipline are used to increase responsible behaviors and decrease irresponsible behaviors. Parents are encouraged to spell out clearly expectations and punishment for **compliance** and noncompliance before putting them into action. For example, the child should know ahead of time that missing curfew will result in being grounded for a week. Parents are also taught to praise often for compliant behaviors.
- Interventions are focused on the present and are action oriented, targeting specific and well-defined problems. Due to time limitations of the MST model, family members are required to work intensely to solve often long-standing problems. Once information has been gathered and assessed, therapist and family jointly formalize problem and goals into a treatment plan. The plan specifies which changes in what behavior or skill will be achieved by whom, by what method or action, and in what period of time within the limits of the program. The treatment plan contains the family's overarching goals or ultimate aims that are to be accomplished by the end of the treatment period, and intermediate goals or incremental steps needed to reach the overarching goal. These intermediate goals are measurable and time limited and the interventions chosen are those that have been determined to have the most immediate and powerful impact on the problem behavior. The therapist assists families in meeting their specific goals by helping them focus their time, energy, and resources on their assignments. Also, the expected outcome of each intervention is described in observable and measurable terms before the treatment plan is put into action. This aids the MST staff and the family to determine whether the interventions are effective or if alternatives are needed.
- Interventions should target sequences of behavior within and between multiple systems that maintain the identified problem. As an example, an ineffective parenting style (permissive, authoritarian, neglectful) may be identified as a factor in influencing the problem behavior and is, therefore, targeted for an intervention. However, the parents are having marital difficulties that lead to disagreements in child rearing practices; these difficulties are maintaining the poor parenting style and will be the focus of an intervention as well. In addition, the family may have some practical or concrete needs (housing, heat, transportation) that are, in turn, having an impact on parental discipline and require interventions across the family—community support system that is also a factor in maintaining the identified problem.
- Interventions are developmentally appropriate and fit the developmental needs of the youth. The nature of the intervention should take into account the age and maturity of the child or adolescent and the caregiver. It is noted that, for children and young adolescents, interventions aimed at increasing parental control are the most appropriate. Such interventions might include introducing systematic monitoring, reward, and discipline systems. For an older adolescent, interventions would most likely focus on preparing the youth for entry into the adult world, such as increasing his or her social maturity. Other interventions may be needed to overcome obstacles to independent living, such as having the teenager participate in GED classes or enter a vocational training school. The developmental stage of the caregiver is also important to consider. For example, grandparents may not have the physical or emotional health to become primary caregivers but may be able to assist parents in other ways, such as helping with homework or sitting with the youth after school for a few hours.

- Interventions are designed to require daily or weekly effort by family members. This leads to a more rapid decrease in the problem behavior, and current and continuous evaluation of whether the intervention is working and producing the expected results. For example, if a parent sits near the child while he or she is doing homework, progress toward the anticipated goal of better school performance is gauged. This design also allows family members to experience immediate success and obtain positive feedback.
- Intervention effectiveness is evaluated continuously from multiple perspectives with providers assuming accountability for overcoming barriers to successful outcomes. To assess the impact of an intervention, before intervention is implemented the therapist is required to document anticipated outcomes for each intervention by describing the observable and measurable outcome that he or she is aiming for. This information is used to assess the successes made or barriers encountered during treatment. The MST staff may also be in daily contact with teachers and administrators, deputy juvenile officers, and welfare professionals who provide feedback regarding whether the interventions across systems are successful in changing behaviors.
- Interventions are designed to promote treatment generalization and long-term maintenance of therapeutic change by empowering caregivers to address family members' needs across multiple systemic contexts. The MST therapist, the MST team, and the provider agency are responsible for engaging the family in treatment, making services for the family easier to obtain, and achieving positive outcomes for the child or adolescent and the family in every case. The program's achievement of successful goals and maintenance of behavior change is due to staff adherence to the treatment model. Research has demonstrated that strong adherence correlates to strong case outcomes. The key to the success of the model is intensive and ongoing staff training. Clinical staff training includes five days of orientation training, weekly supervision with an MST expert, and quarterly booster training. On-site supervisors are also intensively trained to ensure that the MST staff adhere to the MST model.

Normal results

At the end of MST treatment, parents have been provided with the resources needed to parent effectively and maintain better family structure and cohesion. Specifically, parents:

- are able to monitor their child(ren) or adolescent's behaviors systematically
- have learned to use appropriate reward and discipline measures to maintain new behavioral changes
- can communicate more effectively with each other and their children
- can advocate for their children and themselves across social systems (school, social services)
- can problem-solve daily conflicts
- can maintain positive relations with natural social supports such as extended family, friends, and church members
- are able to maintain a positive working relationship with school personnel
- have learned strategies to monitor and promote the child's or adolescent's school performance and/or vocational functioning

Other outcomes to be expected have to do with the youth's relationships with peers and his or her performance in school. Specifically, it is expected that the child or adolescent has decreased his or her association with delinquent and/or drug-using peers; has increased his or her relationships with positive peers and engages in positive activities through after-school activities, organized athletics, or volunteer or paid activities; has better school performance; and has had no, or has decreased, days requiring out-of-home placement.

See also Antisocial personality disorder; Cognitive-behavioral therapy; Community mental health; Family education; Family psychoeducation; Family therapy

Resources

BOOKS

Brown, Tamara L., and others. "Treating Juvenile Offenders in Community Settings." In *Treating Adult and Juvenile Offenders With Special Needs,* edited by J. B. Ashford and others. Washington, DC: American Psychological Association, 2001.

Henggeler, Scott W., and others. *Multisystemic Treatment of Antisocial Behavior in children and Adolescents.* New York: The Guilford Press, 1998.

ORGANIZATIONS

National Institute of Mental Health. 6001 Executive Bloulevard, RM.8184, MSC 9663, Bethesda, MD 20892-9663. (301) 443-4513. Fax: (301) 443-4279. TTY: (301) 443-8431. <http://www.nimh.nih.gov>.

Office of Juvenile Justice and Delinquency Prevention. 810 Seventh Street NW, Washington, D.C. 20531. (202) 307-5911. Fax: (202) 307-2093. <http://www.ojjdp.ncjrs.org>.

OTHER

Scott W. Henggeler, Ph.D., Director, Department of Psychiatry and Behavioral Sciences, Family Services Research

Center, Medical University of South Carolina, 67 President Street, Suite CPP, Charleston, SC 29425, Box 250861. (843) 876-1800.

Janice VanBuren, Ph.D.

Munchausen syndrome *see* **Factitious disorder**

Music therapy *see* **Creative therapies**

Mutual support *see* **Support groups**

Naltrexone

Definition

Naltrexone is classified as a pure opiate antagonist. It is sold in the United States under the brand names ReVia and Depade, but is also manufactured and sold under its generic name.

Purpose

Naltrexone is used as part of medically supervised **behavior modification** programs in order to maintain a patient previously addicted to opiates in an opiate-free state following successful opiate **detoxification**. Naltrexone is also used in the management of alcohol dependence and abstinence in combination with medically supervised behavior modification programs.

Description

Opiates are a group of drugs that are either derived from opium (i.e. morphine, hydromorphone, oxymorphone, heroin, codeine, hydrocodone, oxycodone) or chemically resemble these opium derivatives (such as meperidine). They are commonly referred to as narcotics. Some opiates have medically valid uses, while others are recreational drugs of abuse. All are physically addictive.

The drug naltrexone is an opiate antagonist. This means that it blocks and reverses the physical effects of drugs such as morphine, hydromorphone, oxymorphone, heroin, meperidine, codeine, hydrocodone, oxycodone and other drugs classified as narcotics. When given to patients who have been successfully treated for opiate **addiction**, it not only decreases craving for these types of drugs, it also prevents patients who use opiates while taking naltrexone from experiencing the euphoria associated with their use. In these two ways, naltrexone helps prevent re-addiction to opiates.

Chemically, naltrexone is not an alcohol antagonist. However, when it is used in combination with behavior modification in the recovering alcoholic, naltrexone decreases the craving for alcohol. This helps to prevent a return to alcohol use, or it decreases the severity of relapse by reducing the amount of alcohol consumed during the relapse or decreasing the length of the relapse.

Naltrexone is available in 50-mg oral tablets.

Recommended dosage

After a person has been successfully detoxified from opiates, he or she will receive a test dose of 25 mg of naltrexone, then be observed for one hour for symptoms of opiate withdrawal. If no problems occur after this test dose, another 25 mg test dose is administered.

Getting a person to comply with treatment for opiate addiction is the single most important aspect in maintaining an opiate-free state. Different schedules for taking naltrexone have been developed to help meet the needs of individuals in order to make taking the drug easier. Following successful initiation of therapy, naltrexone may be administered in one of the following ways:

- 50 mg daily Monday through Friday and 100 mg Saturday
- 100 mg every other day
- 150 mg every third day
- 100 mg on Monday and Wednesday and 150 mg on Friday
- 150 mg on Monday and 200 mg on Thursday

The duration of treatment with naltrexone for opiate dependence varies with patient need, although most patients will require at least six months of treatment.

The usual dose of naltrexone for alcohol dependence is 50 mg daily, although a few patients may require only 25 mg daily. The proper duration of therapy is not known, as studies of the use of naltrexone in alcohol dependence did not go beyond 12 weeks.

KEY TERMS

Antagonist—A substance whose actions counteract the effects of or work in the opposite way from another chemical or drug.

Opiates—A class of drugs that is either derived from opium (i.e. morphine, hydromorphone, oxymorphone, heroin, codeine, hydrocodone, oxycodone) or resembles these opium derivatives (such as meperidine) and is commonly referred to as narcotics.

Precautions

In a very small number of patients, naltrexone may be toxic and cause damage to the liver. Before starting naltrexone and throughout treatment, patients should receive monthly liver function tests to assess the drug's effect on the liver.

Patients should be free of all opiates for seven to 10 days before starting naltrexone. Naltrexone may cause opiate withdrawal symptoms in people whose bodies are not free from opiates. Patients should be observed for opiate withdrawal immediately following the first dose of the drug.

Patients may have a false sense of security that the presence of naltrexone in their system makes them immune from the effects of opiates. In fact, the opiate antagonism caused by naltrexone is not absolute and patients can still experience both analgesia (suppression of pain) and euphoria by administration of larger-than-normal amounts of opiates. Consequently, patients receiving naltrexone who continue to use or receive opiates may take larger doses and should be monitored for signs and symptoms of opiate overdose.

Side effects

The following represents the most common side effects associated with naltrexone:

- nausea, vomiting, diarrhea, cramps
- headache, **insomnia**, anxiety, irritability, depression, dizziness
- joint and muscle pain
- rash

Interactions

Because naltrexone is an opiate antagonist, opiate derivatives that are used for medicinally in treating cough, diarrhea, and pain may no longer be effective.

The combination of naltrexone and **disulfiram**, a drug that is also used for alcohol abuse, may cause increased liver toxicity and liver damage when taken together. This combination should be avoided unless in consultation with a physician, it is decided that the potential benefits of this combination outweigh the risks.

Resources

BOOKS

American Society of Health-System Pharmacists. *AHFS Drug Information 2002.* Bethesda: American Society of Health-System Pharmacists, 2002.

O'Brien, Charles P. "Drug Addiction and Drug Abuse." In *Goodman & Gillman's The Pharmacological Basis of Therapeutics Tenth Edition* edited by Joel G. Hardman, Ph.D. and Lee E. Limbird, Ph.D. New York: McGraw-Hill, 2001.

Jack Raber, Pharm.D.

Narcissistic personality disorder

Definition

Narcissistic personality disorder (NPD) is defined by the Fourth Edition Text Revision of the ***Diagnostic and Statistical Manual of Mental Disorders*** (*DSM-IV-TR*, a handbook that mental health professionals use to diagnose mental disorders) as one of ten **personality disorders**. As a group, these disorders are described by *DSM-IV-TR* as "enduring pattern[s] of inner experience and behavior" that are sufficiently rigid and deep-seated to bring a person into repeated conflicts with his or her social and occupational environment. *DSM-IV-TR* specifies that these dysfunctional patterns must be regarded as nonconforming or deviant by the person's culture, and cause significant emotional pain and/or difficulties in relationships and occupational performance.

To meet the **diagnosis** of a personality disorder, the patient's problematic behaviors must appear in two or more of the following areas:

- perception and interpretation of the self and other people
- intensity and duration of feelings and their appropriateness to situations
- relationships with others
- ability to control impulses

It is important to note that all the personality disorders are considered to have their onset in late adolescence or early adulthood. Doctors rarely give a diagnosis of personality disorder to children on the grounds that children's personalities are still in process of formation and may change considerably by the time they are in their late teens.

NPD is defined more specifically as a pattern of grandiosity (exaggerated claims to talents, importance, or specialness) in the patient's private fantasies or outward behavior; a need for constant admiration from others; and a lack of empathy for others. The term *narcissistic* is derived from an ancient Greek legend, the story of Echo and Narcissus. According to the legend, Echo was a woodland nymph who fell in love with Narcissus, who was an uncommonly handsome but also uncommonly vain young man. He contemptuously rejected her expressions of love. She pined away and died. The god Apollo was angered by Narcissus' pride and self-satisfaction, and condemned him to die without ever knowing human love. One day, Narcissus was feeling thirsty, saw a pool of clear water nearby, and knelt beside it in order to dip his hands in the water and drink. He saw his face reflected on the surface of the water and fell in love with the reflection. Unable to win a response from the image in the water, Narcissus eventually died beside the pool.

Havelock Ellis, a British **psychologist**, first used the story of Echo and Narcissus in 1898 as a capsule summary of pathological self-absorption. The words *narcissist* and *narcissistic* have been part of the vocabulary of psychology and psychiatry ever since. They have, however, been the subjects of several controversies. In order to understand NPD, the reader may find it helpful to have an outline of the different theories about narcissism in human beings, its relation to other psychiatric disorders, and its connections to the wider culture. NPD is unique among the *DSM-IV-TR* personality disorders in that it has been made into a symbol of the problems and discontents of contemporary Western culture as a whole.

KEY TERMS

Grandiosity—Exaggerated and unrealistic self-importance; inflated self-assessment. Grandiosity is considered one of the core characteristics of persons diagnosed with NPD.

Macrosocial—Pertaining to the wider society, as distinct from such smaller social groupings as families, neighborhoods, etc.

Narcissistic Personality Inventory (NPI)—The most widely used English-language diagnostic instrument for narcissistic personality disorder. Based on the *DSM-III* criteria for NPD, the NPI is frequently used in research studies as well as patient assessment.

Primary narcissism—Sigmund Freud's term for a normal phase in early childhood development in which the infant has not yet learned to distinguish between itself and its world, and sees other people and things in its environment as extensions of itself.

Projection—A psychological process in which a person unconsciously attributes unacceptable feelings to someone else. Narcissists often project their envy onto other people, claiming that the person in question is envious of them.

Splitting—A psychological process that occurs during the childhood of a person with NPD, in which the child separates aspects of him- or herself that the parents value from those that they disregard.

Superego—According to Freud, the part of the mind that represents traditional parental and societal values. The superego is the source of guilt feelings.

Description

A good place to begin a discussion of the different theories about narcissism is with the observation that NPD exists as a diagnostic category only in *DSM-IV-TR*, which is an American diagnostic manual. The *International Statistical Classification of Diseases and Related Health Problems, Tenth Revision* (*ICD-10*, the European equivalent of *DSM*) lists only eight personality disorders. What *DSM-IV-TR* defines as narcissistic personality disorder, *ICD-10* lumps together with "eccentric, impulsive-type, immature, passive-aggressive, and psychoneurotic personality disorders."

DSM-IV-TR specifies nine diagnostic criteria for NPD. For the clinician to make the diagnosis, an individual must fit five or more of the following descriptions:

- He or she has a grandiose sense of self-importance (exaggerates accomplishments and demands to be considered superior without real evidence of achievement).
- He or she lives in a dream world of exceptional success, power, beauty, genius, or "perfect" love.
- He or she thinks of him- or herself as "special" or privileged, and that he or she can only be understood by other special or high-status people.

- He or she demands excessive amounts of praise or admiration from others.
- He or she feels entitled to automatic deference, **compliance**, or favorable treatment from others.
- He or she is exploitative towards others and takes advantage of them.
- He or she lacks empathy and does not recognize or identify with others' feelings.
- He or she is frequently envious of others or thinks that they are envious of him or her.
- He or she "has an attitude" or frequently acts in haughty or arrogant ways.

In addition to these criteria, *DSM-IV-TR* groups NPD together with three other personality disorders in its so-called Cluster B. These four disorders are grouped together on the basis of symptom similarities, insofar as patients with these disorders appear to others as overly emotional, unstable, or self-dramatizing. The other three disorders in Cluster B are antisocial, borderline, and histrionic personality disorders.

The *DSM-IV-TR* clustering system does not mean that all patients can be fitted neatly into one of the three clusters. It is possible for patients to have symptoms of more than one personality disorder or to have symptoms from different clusters. In addition, patients diagnosed with any personality disorder may also meet the criteria for mood, substance abuse, or other disorders.

Subtypes of NPD

AGE GROUP SUBTYPES. Ever since the 1950s, when psychiatrists began to notice an increase in the number of their patients that had narcissistic disorders, they have made attempts to define these disorders more precisely. NPD was introduced as a new diagnostic category in *DSM-III*, which was published in 1980. Prior to *DSM-III*, narcissism was a recognized phenomenon but not an official diagnosis. At that time, NPD was considered virtually untreatable because people who suffer from it rarely enter or remain in treatment; typically, they regard themselves as superior to their therapist, and they see their problems as caused by other people's "stupidity" or "lack of appreciation." More recently, however, some psychiatrists have proposed dividing narcissistic patients into two subcategories based roughly on age: those who suffer from the stable form of NPD described by *DSM-IV-TR*, and younger adults whose narcissism is often corrected by life experiences.

This age group distinction represents an ongoing controversy about the nature of NPD—whether it is fundamentally a character disorder, or whether it is a matter of learned behavior that can be unlearned. Therapists who incline toward the first viewpoint are usually pessimistic about the results of treatment for patients with NPD.

PERSONALITY SUBTYPES. Other psychiatrists have noted that patients who meet the *DSM-IV-TR* criteria for NPD reflect different clusters of traits within the *DSM-IV-TR* list. One expert in the field of NPD has suggested the following subcategories of narcissistic personalities:

- Craving narcissists. These are people who feel emotionally needy and undernourished, and may well appear clingy or demanding to those around them.
- Paranoid narcissists. This type of narcissist feels intense contempt for him- or herself, but projects it outward onto others. Paranoid narcissists frequently drive other people away from them by hypercritical and jealous comments and behaviors.
- Manipulative narcissists. These people enjoy "putting something over" on others, obtaining their feelings of superiority by lying to and manipulating them.
- Phallic narcissists. Almost all narcissists in this subgroup are male. They tend to be aggressive, athletic, and exhibitionistic; they enjoy showing off their bodies, clothes, and overall "manliness."

Causes and symptoms

Causes

At present there are two major theories about the origin and nature of NPD. One theory regards NPD as a form of arrested psychological development while the other regards it as a young child's defense against psychological pain. The two perspectives have been identified with two major figures in psychoanalytic thought, Heinz Kohut and Otto Kernberg respectively.

Both theories about NPD go back to Sigmund Freud's pioneering work *On Narcissism,* published in 1914. In this essay, Freud introduced a distinction which has been retained by almost all later writers—namely, the distinction between primary and secondary narcissism. Freud thought that all human infants pass through a phase of primary narcissism, in which they assume they are the center of their universe. This phase ends when the baby is forced by the realities of life to recognize that it does not control its parents (or other caregivers) but is in fact entirely dependent on them. In normal circumstances, the baby gives up its fantasy of being all-powerful and becomes emotionally attached to its parents rather than itself. What Freud defined as secondary narcissism is a pathological condition in which the infant does not invest its emotions in its parents but rather redirects them back to itself. He thought that secondary narcissism developed in what he termed the pre-Oedipal phase of childhood; that is, before the age of three. From a Freudian perspective, then, narcissistic disorders originate in very early childhood development, and this early origin is thought to explain why they are so difficult to treat in later life.

CAUSES IN THE FAMILY OF ORIGIN. Kohut and Kernberg agree with Freud in tracing the roots of NPD to disturbances in the patient's family of origin—specifically, to problems in the parent-child relationship before the child turned three. Where they disagree is in their accounts of the nature of these problems. According to Kohut, the child grows out of primary narcissism through opportunities to be mirrored by (i.e., gain approval from) his or her parents and to idealize them, acquiring a more realistic sense of self and a set of personal ideals and values through these two processes. On the other hand, if the parents fail to provide appropriate opportunities for idealization and mirroring, the child remains "stuck" at a developmental stage in which his or her sense of self remains grandiose and unrealistic while at the same time he or she remains dependent on approval from others for self-esteem.

In contrast, Kernberg views NPD as rooted in the child's defense against a cold and unempathetic parent, usually the mother. Emotionally hungry and angry at the depriving parents, the child withdraws into a part of the self that the parents value, whether looks, intellectual ability, or some other skill or talent. This part of the self becomes hyperinflated and grandiose. Any perceived weaknesses are "split off" into a hidden part of the self. Splitting gives rise to a lifelong tendency to swing between extremes of grandiosity and feelings of emptiness and worthlessness.

In both accounts, the child emerges into adult life with a history of unsatisfactory relationships with others. The adult narcissist possesses a grandiose view of the self but has a conflict-ridden psychological dependence on others. At present, however, psychiatrists do not agree in their description of the central defect in NPD; some think that the problem is primarily emotional while others regard it as the result of distorted cognition, or knowing. Some maintain that the person with NPD has an "empty" or hungry sense of self while others argue that the narcissist has a "disorganized" self. Still others regard the core problem as the narcissist's inability to test reality and construct an accurate view of him- or herself.

MACROSOCIAL CAUSES. One dimension of NPD that must be taken into account is its social and historical context. Psychiatrists became interested in narcissism shortly after World War II (1939–45), when the older practitioners in the field noticed that their patient population had changed. Instead of seeing patients who suffered from obsessions and compulsions related to a harsh and punishing superego (the part of the psyche that internalizes the standards and moral demands of one's parents and culture), the psychiatrists were treating more patients with character disorders related to a weak sense of self. Instead of having a judgmental and overactive conscience, these patients had a weak or nonexistent code of morals. They were very different from the patients that Freud had treated, described, and analyzed. The younger generation of psychiatrists then began to interpret their patients' character disorders in terms of narcissism.

in the 1960s historians and social critics drew the attention of the general public to narcissism as a metaphorical description of Western culture in general. These writers saw several parallels between trends in the larger society and the personality traits of people diagnosed with narcissistic disorders. In short, they argued that the advanced industrial societies of Europe and the United States were contributing to the development of narcissistic disorders in individuals in a number of respects. Some of the trends they noted include the following:

- The mass media's preoccupation with "lifestyles of the rich and famous" rather than with ordinary or average people.
- Social approval of open displays of money, status, or accomplishments ("if you've got it, flaunt it") rather than modesty and self-restraint.
- Preference for a leadership style that emphasizes the leader's outward appearance and personality rather than his or her inner beliefs and values.
- The growth of large corporations and government bureaucracies that favor a managerial style based on "impression management" rather than objective measurements of performance.
- Social trends that encourage parents to be self-centered and to resent their children's legitimate needs.
- The weakening of churches, synagogues, and other religious or social institutions that traditionally helped children to see themselves as members of a community rather than as isolated individuals.

Although discussion continues about the location and forms of narcissism in the larger society, no one now denies that personality disorders both reflect and influence the culture in which they arise. Family therapists are now reporting on the treatment of families in which the children are replicating the narcissistic disorders of their parents.

Symptoms

Most observers regard grandiosity as the most important single trait of a narcissistic personality. It is note that grandiosity implies more than ...ideful display as such—it signifies self-...ment that is not borne out by reality. For exam-ple, a person who claims that he or she was the most valuable player on a college athletic team may be telling the truth about their undergraduate sports record. Their claim may be bad manners but is not grandiosity. On the other hand, someone who makes the same claim but had an undistinguished record or never even made the team is being grandiose. Grandiosity in NPD is related to some of the diagnostic criteria listed by *DSM-IV-TR*, such as demanding special favors from others or choosing friends and associates on the basis of prestige and high status rather than personal qualities. In addition, grandiosity complicates diagnostic assessment of narcissists because it frequently leads to lying and misrepresentation of one's past history and present accomplishments.

Other symptoms of NPD include:

- a history of intense but short-term relationships with others; inability to make or sustain genuinely intimate relationships
- a tendency to be attracted to leadership or high-profile positions or occupations
- a pattern of alternating between unrealistic idealization of others and equally unrealistic devaluation of them
- assessment of others in terms of usefulness
- a need to be the center of attention or admiration in a working group or social situation
- hypersensitivity to criticism, however mild, or rejection from others
- an unstable view of the self that fluctuates between extremes of self-praise and self-contempt
- preoccupation with outward appearance, "image," or public opinion rather than inner reality
- painful emotions based on shame (dislike of who one is) rather than guilt (regret for what one has done)

People diagnosed with NPD represent a range of levels of functioning. Otto Kernberg has described three levels of narcissistic impairment. At the top are those who are talented or gifted enough to attract all the admiration and attention that they want; these people may never enter therapy because they don't feel the need. On the second level are those who function satisfactorily in their jobs but seek professional help because they cannot form healthy relationships or because they feel generally bored and aimless. Narcissists on the lowest level have frequently been diagnosed with another mental disorder and/or have gotten into trouble with the law. They often have severe difficulties with anxiety and with controlling their impulses.

Demographics

DSM-IV-TR states that 2% to 16% of the clinical population and slightly less than 1% of the general population of the United States suffers from NPD. Between 50% and 75% of those diagnosed with NPD are males. Little is known about the prevalence of NPD across racial and ethnic groups.

Gender issues

The high preponderance of male patients in studies of narcissism has prompted researchers to explore the effects of gender roles on this particular personality disorder. Some have speculated that the gender imbalance in NPD results from society's disapproval of self-centered and exploitative behavior in women, who are typically socialized to nurture, please, and generally focus their attention on others. Others have remarked that the imbalance is more apparent than real, and that it reflects a basically sexist definition of narcissism. These researchers suggest that definitions of the disorder should be rewritten in future editions of *DSM* to account for ways in which narcissistic personality traits manifest differently in men and in women.

Professional and leadership positions

One important aspect of NPD that should be noted is that it does not prevent people from occupying, as well as aspiring to, positions of power, wealth, and prestige. Many people with NPD, as Kernberg's classification makes clear, are sufficiently talented to secure the credentials of success. In addition, narcissists' preoccupation with a well-packaged exterior means that they often develop an attractive and persuasive social manner. Many high-functioning narcissists are well liked by casual acquaintances and business associates who never get close enough to notice the emptiness or anger underneath the polished surface.

Unfortunately, narcissists in positions of high visibility or power—particularly in the so-called helping professions (medicine, education, and the ministry)—often do great harm to others. In recent years a number of books and articles have been published within the religious, medical, and business communities regarding the problems caused by professionals with NPD. One **psychiatrist** noted in a lecture on substance abuse among physicians that NPD is one of the three most common psychiatric diagnoses among physicians in court-mandated substance abuse programs. A psychologist who serves as a consultant in the evaluation of seminary students and ordained clergy has remarked that the proportion of narcissists in the clergy has risen dramatically since the 1960s. Researchers in the field of business organization and management styles have compiled data on the human and economic costs of executives with undiagnosed NPD.

Diagnosis

The diagnosis of NPD is complicated by a number of factors.

Complications of diagnosis

NPD is difficult to diagnose for several reasons. First, some people with NPD function sufficiently well that they do not come to the attention of therapists. Second, narcissists are prone to lie about themselves; thus it may take a long time for a therapist to notice discrepancies between a patient's version of his or her life and information gained from others or from public records. Third, many traits and behaviors associated with NPD may be attributed to other mental disorders. Low-functioning narcissists are often diagnosed as having **borderline personality disorder** (BPD), particularly if they are female; if they are male, they may be diagnosed as having **antisocial personality disorder** (ASPD). If the person with NPD has a substance abuse disorder, some of their narcissistic behaviors may be written off to the mood-altering substance. More recently, some psychiatrists have pointed to a tendency to confuse narcissistic behaviors in people with NPD who have had a traumatic experience with full-blown **post-traumatic stress disorder** (PTSD). Given the lack of clarity in the differential diagnosis of NPD, some therapists are calling for a fundamental revision of *DSM-IV-TR* definitions of the personality disorders.

An additional complication is posed by economic considerations. The coming of **managed care** has meant that third-party payers (insurance companies) prefer short-term **psychotherapy** that concentrates on a patient's acute problems rather than on underlying chronic issues. Since narcissists are reluctant to trust others or form genuine interpersonal bonds, there is a strong possibility that many therapists do not recognize NPD in patients that they are treating for only a few weeks or months.

Diagnostic interviews

Diagnosis of NPD is usually made on the basis of several sources of information: the patient's history and self-description, information from family members and others, and the results of diagnostic questionnaires. One questionnaire that is often used in the process of differential diagnosis is the Structured Clinical Interview for *DSM-III-R* Disorders, known as the SCID-II.

The most common diagnostic instrument used for narcissistic NPD is the Narcissistic Personality Inventory (NPI). First published by Robert R. Raskin and Calvin S. Hall in 1979, the NPI consists of 223 items consisting of paired statements, one reflecting narcissistic traits and the other nonnarcissistic. Subjects are required to choose one of the two items. The NPI is widely used in research as well as diagnostic assessment.

Treatments

Treatments for NPD include a variety of pharmacologic, individual, and group approaches; none, however, have been shown to be particularly effective as of 2002.

Medication

As of 2002, there are no medications that have been developed specifically for the treatment of NPD. Patients with NPD who are also depressed or anxious may be given drugs for relief of those symptoms. There are anecdotal reports in the medical literature that the selective serotonin reuptake inhibitors, or SSRIs, which are frequently prescribed for depression, reinforce narcissistic grandiosity and lack of empathy with others.

Psychotherapy

Several different approaches to individual therapy have been tried with NPD patients, ranging from classical **psychoanalysis** and Adlerian therapy to rational-emotive approaches and **Gestalt therapy**. The consensus that has emerged is that therapists should set modest goals for treatment with NPD patients. Most of them cannot form a sufficiently deep bond with a therapist to allow healing of early-childhood injuries. In addition, the tendency of these patients to criticize and devalue their therapists (as well as other authority figures) makes it difficult for therapists to work with them.

An additional factor that complicates psychotherapy with NPD patients is the lack of agreement among psychiatrists about the causes and course of the disorder. One researcher has commented that much more research is necessary to validate *DSM-IV-TR*'s description of NPD before outcome studies can be done comparing different techniques of treatment.

Hospitalization

Low-functioning patients with NPD may require inpatient treatment, particularly those with severe self-harming behaviors or lack of impulse control. Hospital treatment, however, appears to be most helpful when it is focused on the immediate crisis and its symptoms rather than the patient's underlying long-term difficulties.

Prognosis

The prognosis for younger persons with narcissistic disorders is hopeful to the extent that the disturbances reflect a simple lack of life experience. The outlook for long-standing NPD, however, is largely negative. Some narcissists are able, particularly as they approach their midlife years, to accept their own limitations and those of others, to resolve their problems with envy, and to accept their own mortality. Most patients with NPD, on the other hand, become increasingly depressed as they grow older within a youth-oriented culture and lose their looks and overall vitality. The retirement years are especially painful for patients with NPD because they must yield their positions in the working world to the next generation. In addition, they do not have the network of intimate family ties and friendships that sustain most older people.

Prevention

The best hope for prevention of NPD lies with parents and other caregivers who are close to children during the early preschool years. Parents must be able to demonstrate empathy in their interactions with the child and with each other. They must also be able to show that they love their children for who they are, not for their appearance or their achievements. And they must focus their parenting efforts on meeting the child's changing needs as he or she matures, rather than demanding that the child meet their needs for status, comfort, or convenience.

Resources

BOOKS

American Psychiatric Association.*Diagnostic and Statistical Manual of Mental Disorders.* 4th edition, text revised. Washington, DC: American Psychiatric Association, 2000.

Capps, Donald. *The Depleted Self: Sin in a Narcissistic Age.* Minneapolis: Fortress Press, 1993.

Donaldson-Pressman, Stephanie, and Robert M. Pressman. *The Narcissistic Family: Diagnosis and Treatment.* San Francisco, CA: Jossey-Bass Publishers, 1994.

Lowen, Alexander. *Narcissism: Denial of the True Self.* New York and London: Collier Macmillan, 1983.

Weiser, Conrad W. *Healers— Harmed & Harmful.* Minneapolis: Fortress Press, 1994.

World Health Organization (WHO). *The ICD-10 Classification of Mental and Behavioural Disorders.* Geneva: WHO, 1992.

PERIODICALS

Billingham, Robert E. "Narcissistic Injury and Sexual Victimization Among Women College Students." *College Student Journal* 33: 62-70.

Coid, J. W. "Aetiological Risk Factors for Personality Disorders." *British Journal of Psychiatry* 174 (June 1999): 530-538.

Gunderson, J. G., and E. Ronningstam. "Differentiating Narcissistic and Antisocial Personality Disorders." *Journal of Personality Disorders* 15 (April 2001): 103-109.

Imperio, Winnie Anne. "Don't Ignore Colleagues' Psychiatric Disorders." *OB/GYN News (March 1, 2001): 36.*

Raskin, R., and C. S. Hall. "A Narcissistic Personality Inventory.". *Psychological Reports* 45 (1979): 590.

Simon, R. I. "Distinguishing Trauma-Associated Narcissistic Symptoms from Post-Traumatic Stress Disorder: A Diagnostic Challenge." *Harvard Review of Psychiatry* 10 (February 2002): 28-36.

Tschanz, Brian T. "Gender Differences in the Study of Narcissism: A Multi-Sample Analysis of the Narcissistic Personality Inventory." *Sex Roles: A Journal of Research* 38 (May, 1998): 209-216.

ORGANIZATIONS

American Psychiatric Association. 1400 K Street, NW, Washington, DC 20005. (202) 682-6220. <www.psych.org>.

National Institute of Mental Health. 6001 Executive Boulevard, Room 8184, MSC 9663, Bethesda, MD 20892-9663. (301) 443-4513. <www.nimh.nih.gov>.

OTHER

Rhodewalt, Frederick. "Interpersonal Self-Construction: Lessons from the Study of Narcissism." Lecture given at the Second Annual Sydney Symposium on Social Psychology, March 1999.

Rebecca J. Frey, Ph.D.

Narcolepsy

Definition

Narcolepsy is a disorder marked by excessive daytime sleepiness, uncontrollable sleep attacks, and cataplexy (a sudden loss of muscle tone, usually lasting up to half an hour).

Description

Narcolepsy is the second-leading cause of excessive daytime sleepiness (after obstructive sleep apnea). Persistent sleepiness and sleep attacks are the hallmarks of this condition. The sleepiness has been compared to the feeling of trying to stay awake after not sleeping for two or three days.

People with narcolepsy fall asleep suddenly—anywhere, at any time, even in the middle of a conversation. These sleep attacks can last from a few seconds to more than an hour. Depending on where the sleep attacks occur, they may be mildly inconvenient or even dangerous to the person, particularly if they occur while he or she is driving. Some people continue to function outwardly during the sleep episodes, such as continuing a conversation or putting things away. But when they wake up, they have no memory of the event.

Sleep researchers have identified several different types of sleep in humans. One type of sleep is called rapid eye movement (REM) sleep, because the person's eyes move rapidly back and forth underneath the closed eyelids. REM sleep is associated with dreaming. Normally, when people fall asleep, they experience 90 minutes of non-REM sleep, which is then followed by a phase of REM sleep. People with narcolepsy, however, enter REM sleep immediately. In addition, REM sleep occurs inappropriately in patients with narcolepsy throughout the day.

Causes and symptoms

Causes

One of the causes of narcolepsy is a genetic mutation. In 1999 researchers identified the gene that causes the disorder. The narcolepsy gene allows cells in the hypothalamus (the part of the **brain** that regulates sleep behavior) to receive messages from other cells. As a result of the mutation, the cells cannot communicate properly, and abnormal sleeping patterns develop.

Other researchers are also looking into the possibility that narcolepsy may be caused by some kind of autoimmune disorder. This theory suggests that the person's immune system accidentally turns against the specific area of the brain that controls alertness and sleep, injuring or destroying it.

The disorder sometimes runs in families, but most people with narcolepsy have no relatives with the disorder. Researchers believe that the inheritance of narcolepsy is similar to that of heart disease. In heart disease, several genes play a role in being susceptible to the disorder, but it does not usually develop without an environmental trigger of some sort.

Symptoms

While the symptoms of narcolepsy usually appear during a person's late teens or early 20s, the disease may not be diagnosed for many years. Most often, the first symptom is an overwhelming feeling of **fatigue**. After several months or years, cataplexy and other symptoms of the disorder appear.

Cataplexy is the most dramatic symptom of narcolepsy, affecting 75% of people with the disorder. During attacks, the knees buckle and the neck muscles go slack. In extreme cases, the person may become paralyzed and fall to the floor. This loss of muscle tone is temporary, lasting from a few seconds to half an hour, but it is frightening. The attacks can occur at any time but are often triggered by such strong emotions as anger, joy, or surprise.

Other symptoms of narcolepsy include:

- sleep attacks: short, uncontrollable sleep episodes throughout the day
- sleep paralysis: a frightening inability to move shortly after awakening or dozing off

KEY TERMS

Cataplexy—A symptom of narcolepsy marked by a sudden episode of muscle weakness triggered by strong emotions. The muscle weakness may cause the person's knees to buckle, or the head to drop. In severe cases, the patient may become paralyzed for a few seconds to minutes.

Hypnagogic hallucinations—Dream-like auditory or visual hallucinations that occur while a person is falling asleep.

Hypothalamus—A part of the forebrain that controls heartbeat, body temperature, thirst, hunger, blood pressure, blood sugar levels, and other functions.

Polysomnogram—A machine that is used to diagnose sleep disorders by measuring and recording a variety of body functions related to sleep, including heart rate, eye movements, brain waves, muscle activity, breathing, changes in blood oxygen concentration, and body position.

Rapid eye movement (REM) sleep—A type of sleep during which the person's eyes move back and forth rapidly underneath their closed eyelids. REM sleep is associated with dreaming.

Sleep paralysis—An abnormal episode of sleep in which the patient cannot move for a few minutes, usually occurring while falling asleep or waking up. Sleep paralysis is often found in patients with narcolepsy.

- auditory or visual **hallucinations**: intense, sometimes terrifying experiences at the beginning or end of a sleep period
- disturbed nighttime sleep: tossing and turning, nightmares, and frequent awakenings during the night

Demographics

There has been debate over the incidence of narcolepsy. It is thought to affect between one in every 1,000 to 2,000 Americans. The known prevalence in other countries varies, from one in 600 in Japan to one in 500,000 in Israel. The reasons for these demographic differences are not clear. In about 8–12% of cases, people diagnosed with narcolepsy know of other family members with similar symptoms.

Diagnosis

The **diagnosis** of narcolepsy can be made by a general practitioner familiar with the disorder as well as by a **psychiatrist**. If a person comes to the doctor with reports of both excessive daytime sleepiness and cataplexy, a diagnosis may be made on the patient's history alone. Laboratory tests, however, can confirm a diagnosis of narcolepsy. These tests may include an overnight polysomnogram— a test in which sleep is monitored with a variety of electrodes that record information about heart rate, eye movements, brain waves, muscle activity, breathing, changes in blood oxygen concentration, and body position. A Multiple Sleep Latency Test, which measures sleep latency (onset) and how quickly REM sleep occurs, may also be used. People who have narcolepsy usually fall asleep in less than five minutes.

If the diagnosis is still open to question, a genetic blood test can reveal the existence of certain substances in people who have a tendency to develop narcolepsy. Positive test results suggest, but do not prove, that the patient has narcolepsy.

Narcolepsy is a complex disorder, and it is often misdiagnosed. Many people with the disorder struggle with symptoms for an average of 14 years before being correctly diagnosed.

Treatment

There is no cure for narcolepsy. It is not progressive, and it is not fatal, but it is a chronic disorder. The symptoms can be managed with lifestyle adjustments and/or medication.

People with narcolepsy must plan their days carefully. Scheduling regular naps (either several short, fifteen-minute naps or one long nap in the afternoon) can help boost alertness and awakeness. A full eight hours of nighttime sleep should also be a goal. Exercise can often help people with narcolepsy feel more alert and energetic, although they should avoid exercising within a few hours of bedtime. Substances that contain alcohol, nicotine, and caffeine should be avoided because they can interfere with refreshing sleep and with daytime alertness.

Medications for narcolepsy may include the use of antidepressants (tricyclic antidepressants or selective serotonin-reuptake inhibitors) to treat such symptoms of the disorder as cataplexy, hypnagogic hallucinations, and/or sleep paralysis.

Stimulants (**amphetamines**) may also be used to help individuals with narcolepsy stay awake and alert.

With the recent discovery of the gene that causes narcolepsy, researchers are hopeful that other treatments can be designed to relieve the symptoms of the disorder.

Prognosis

Narcolepsy is not a degenerative disease, and patients do not develop other neurologic symptoms. Narcolepsy can, however, interfere with a person's ability to work, play, drive, socialize, and perform other daily activities. In severe cases, the disorder prevents people from living a normal life, leading to depression and a loss of independence.

Prevention

As of 2002, narcolepsy is not a preventable disorder.

Resources

PERIODICALS

Mignot, E. "Genetics of Narcolepsy and Other Sleep Disorders." *American Journal of Human Genetics* 60 (1997): 1289-1302.

Siegel, Jeremy M. "Narcolepsy." *Scientific American* (January 2000). Available at: <http://www.sciam.com/2000/0100issue/0100siegel.html>.

ORGANIZATIONS

American Academy of Sleep Medicine. 6301 Bandel Rd. NW, Suite 101 Rochester, MN 55901. (507) 287-6008. www.aasmnet.org.

American Sleep Disorders Association. 1610 14th St. NW, Suite 300, Rochester, MN 55901. (507) 287-6006.

Narcolepsy Network. PO Box 42460, Cincinnati, OH 45242. (973) 276- 0115.

National Center on Sleep Disorders Research. Two Rockledge Centre, 6701 Rockledge Dr., Bethesda, MD 20892. (301) 435-0199.

National Sleep Foundation. 1522 K St., NW, Suite 500, Washington, DC 20005. (202) 785-2300. <http://www.sleepfoundation.org>.

Stanford Center for Narcolepsy. 1201 Welch Rd-Rm P-112, Stanford, CA 94305. (415) 725-6517.

University of Illinois Center for Narcolepsy Research. 845 S. Damen Ave., Chicago, IL 60612. (312) 996-5176.

OTHER

"Stanford Researchers Nab Narcolepsy Gene For Sleep Disorders." *Stanford University Medical Center*. [August 5, 1999]. <http://www.stanford.edu/%7Edement/ngene.html>.

Rosalyn Carson-DeWitt, M.D.

Nardil *see* **Phenelzine**

Navane *see* **Thiothixene**

Nefazodone

Definition

Nefazodone is a prescription antidepressant. Nefazodone is available in the United States under the trade name of Serzone.

Purpose

Nefazodone is used to treat depression. It may be used to treat **major depressive disorder**, **dysthymic disorder**, and the depressed phase of **bipolar disorder**. As with all antidepressants, it may take several weeks before full beneficial effects are seen.

Description

Nefazodone was approved by the FDA in 1994. It is believed to increase the activities of some chemicals in the **brain**. By altering the activities of specific brain chemicals, nefazodone may reduce the chemical imbalances responsible for causing depression.

The drug is available as tablets in several different strengths, including 50-, 100-, 150-, 200-, and 250-mg tablets.

Nefazodone is broken down by the liver.

Recommended dosage

For most people, the recommended initial dose of nefazodone is 100 mg taken by mouth twice daily. The dose may be increased in 100 or 200 mg increments once a week. Most commonly, final dosages range between 300-600 mg taken by mouth each day.

It is recommended that the initial dose of nefazodone be lowered to 50 mg twice daily for elderly or debilitated individuals, because these individuals may be more sensitive to some of the drug's side effects.

KEY TERMS

Antihistamine—A medication used to alleviate allergy or cold symptoms such as runny nose, itching, hives, watering eyes, or sneezing.

Antipsychotic—A medication used to treat psychotic symptoms of schizophrenia such as hallucinations, delusions and delirium. May be used to treat symptoms in other disorders, as well.

Depression—A mental state characterized by excessive sadness. Other symptoms include altered sleep patterns, thoughts of suicide, difficulty concentrating, agitation, lack of energy, and loss of enjoyment in activities that are usually pleasurable.

Mania—An elevated or euphoric mood or irritable state that is characteristic of bipolar I disorder. This state is characterized by mental and physical hyperactivity, disorganization of behavior, and inappropriate elevation of mood.

Milligram (mg)—One-thousandth of a gram. A gram is the metric measure that equals about 0.035 ounces.

Precautions

People who have a history of epilepsy or other seizure disorders, heart attack, **stroke**, high blood pressure, or mania may require close physician supervision while taking nefazodone. Nefazodone may increase the tendency to have **seizures**, and should be used carefully by people with epilepsy or other seizure disorders. Nefazodone may lower blood pressure. This effect may be most noticeable when rising suddenly from a lying or sitting position. People with a history of heart attack or stroke, those taking medications for high blood pressure, or people who are dehydrated may be most sensitive to this effect and may feel dizzy or faint when standing up suddenly. Nefazodone may alter moods or cause mania, so patients with a history of mania should use nefazodone with caution.

In rare situations, men taking nefazodone may experience long, painful erections. If this occurs, a health care provider should be notified immediately.

Because there is an increased likelihood of **suicide** in depressed individuals, close supervision of those at high risk for suicide attempts is recommended. Nefazodone is not recommended for pregnant or breast-feeding women.

Side effects

The most common side effects that cause people to stop taking nefazodone are dizziness, difficulty sleeping, weakness, or agitation. Other common adverse effects are sleepiness, dry mouth, nausea, constipation, blurred vision, and confusion.

Other, less common adverse effects associated with nefazodone are headache, flu-like symptoms, low blood pressure, itching, rash, upset stomach, fluid retention, muscle aches, thirst, memory impairment, nerve pain, nightmares, difficulty walking, ringing in the ears, urinary difficulties, breast pain, or vaginal irritation.

It has recently been discovered that in rare situations, nefazodone causes liver failure. If nausea, stomach pains, yellowing of the skin or eyes, itching, or darkening of urine occurs while taking nefazodone, a health care professional should be consulted immediately.

Interactions

Use of nefazodone with antidepressants referred to as monoamine oxidase inhibitors (MAOIs) is strongly discouraged due to the potential for high fever, muscle stiffness, sudden muscle spasms, rapid changes in heart rate and blood pressure, and the possibility of death. In fact, there should be a lapse of at least 14 days between taking a monoamine oxidase inhibitor and nefazodone or at least seven days should pass if switching from nefazodone to a monoamine oxidase inhibitor. Some examples of MAOIs include **phenelzine** (Nardil) and **tranylcypromine** (Parnate).

Some other drugs such as **trazodone** (Desyrel) and sibutramine may also interact with nefazodone and cause a syndrome characterized by irritability, muscle stiffness, shivering, muscle spasms, and altered consciousness. If nefazodone is used with **buspirone** (BuSpar), the dosage of buspirone should be lowered to prevent adverse effects. Additionally, when nefazodone is used in combination with digoxin (Lanoxin), frequent monitoring of blood levels of digoxin is recommended to prevent toxicity.

Nefazodone should not be used with the drugs **triazolam** (Halcion) and **alprazolam** (Xanax) because the side effects of these drugs are likely to increase. Use of nefazodone should also be avoided with **carbamazepine** (Tegretol), because nefazodone is likely to lose its effectiveness.

It is best to avoid using nefazodone with **pimozide** (Orap) due to an increased tendency for severe and potentially life-threatening irregular heartbeats.

When used with gemfibrozil or other drugs that lower cholesterol levels, the risk of muscle pain and weakness may be increased.

Because nefazodone may cause drowsiness, it should be used carefully with other medications that also make people prone to sleepiness such as antidepressants, antipsychotics, antihistamines, and alcohol.

Resources

BOOKS

Bristol-Meyers Squibb Staff. *Serzone Package Insert.* Princeton, NJ: Bristol-Meyers Squibb Company, 2001.

Facts and Comparisons Staff. *Drug Facts and Comparisons.* 6th Edition. St. Louis, MO: A Wolter Kluwer Company, 2002.

Mosby Staff. *Mosby's Medical Drug Reference.* St. Louis, MO: Mosby, Inc, 1999.

Kelly Karpa, RPh, Ph.D.

Negative symptoms

Definition

Negative symptoms are thoughts, feelings, or behaviors normally present that are absent or diminished in a person with a mental disorder.

Description

Examples of negative symptoms are social withdrawal, **apathy** (decreased motivation), poverty of speech (brief replies), inability to experience pleasure (anhedonia), limited emotional expression, or defects in attention control. The term "negative symptoms" is specifically used for describing **schizophrenia**, but sometimes used more generally in reference to disorders such as depression or **dementia**. These symptoms may be associated with altered brainwave activity or **brain** damage. They can be more difficult to diagnose than **positive symptoms** (**hallucinations**, **delusions**, bizarre behavior, or formal thought disorder) because they represent a lesser degree of normal, desirable activity rather than the presence of undesirable or bizarre behavior. Side effects of certain medications, demoralization (loss of positive emotions like hope or confidence usually as the result of situations in which one feels powerless), or a lack of stimulation in one's environment can also cause negative symptoms, so these possibilities must be ruled out before attributing the symptoms to a disorder.

Sandra L. Friedrich, M.A.

Neglect

Definition

Neglect occurs when a parent or other primary caretaker chooses not to fulfill their obligations to care for, provide for, or adequately supervise and monitor the activities of their child. Parental and caregiving obligations include the physical, emotional, and educational well-being of the child. Thus, neglect can also occur when the parent or caretaker does not seek adequate medical or dental care for the child. Another definition of neglect is when the parental figure does not provide sufficient food, clothing, or shelter.

Parents are also expected to provide for the emotional needs of the child. Thus, neglect can occur when parents abandon the child, or simply have no time to spend with the child, in essence leaving the child to raise himself. If the child is actually left without supervision, this certainly constitutes neglect as well.

The final feature of neglect includes educational neglect, which often occurs when one child is responsible for other children in the family. Shifting the responsibility of caring for younger children to another child in the family prevents the caregiving child from participating in age-appropriate activities for themselves, such as attending school. This is a relatively common situation that makes it difficult for the oldest—and perhaps all of the children—to attend school. Parental responsibility includes providing adequate guidance and supervision for the children to regularly attend school. Truancy is not only a problem for children, but may be part of the picture of neglect as well.

Effects of neglect

Consequences of neglect are generally cumulative, and often negatively affect the child's development. For example, poor nutrition has negative consequences on the child's physical and psychological development. If proper nutrients are not available at critical growth periods, the child's development will not follow the normal and usual pattern. Common physical and psychological reactions to neglect include stunted growth, chronic medical problems, inadequate bone and muscle growth, and lack of neurological development that negatively affects normal **brain** functioning and information processing. Processing problems may often make it difficult for children to understand directions, may negatively impact the child's ability to understand social relationships, or may make completion of some academic tasks impossible without assistance or **intervention** from others. Lack of adequate medical care may result in long-term health problems or impairments such as hearing loss from untreated ear infections.

Long-term mental health effects of neglect are inconsistent. Effects of neglect can range from chronic depression to difficulty with relationships; however, not all adults neglected as children will suffer from these results. Some individuals are more resilient than others and are able to move beyond the emotional neglect they may have experienced. Characteristics of resilient individuals include an optimistic or hopeful outlook on life, and feeling challenged rather than defeated by problems.

Factors associated with neglect

Although each family's situation is unique with regard to stressors and characteristics that might precipitate neglect, there are some general factors that have been associated with neglect of a child. These factors include characteristics of the parental figure, and socioeconomic status.

Parental figures who neglect may have been neglected or abused themselves. There is a tendency for parental figures that neglect their children to have low self-esteem, poor impulse control, and to experience anxiety or depression. Other factors associated with neglect often include inadequate information about child development, including age-appropriate expectations of what children may be able to do. The parents may also feel overwhelmed by parenting responsibilities, and feel negatively about the child's demands on them. Such parents may never have fully adopted the role of parent or the caregiving the parental role requires. Internal pressures often push the caregivers to take care of their own needs (perhaps inappropriately), while ignoring the needs of the child. Substance abuse is often associated with neglect, particularly for those parents who are more self-absorbed and focused on their needs rather than their child's. This characteristic is also consistent with the findings of other studies indicating that some neglectful parents have an inability to be empathic, or to understand the feelings and needs of others.

Although **abuse** may occur across all levels of income and education, neglect is more often associated with severe levels of poverty and lower educational level. The external stressors may feel more extreme in single parent families as well, leading to neglectful behavior. Even in families where the parent is attempting to provide for the children, absence due to multiple work demands may lead to a neglectful situation. Families that are disorganized and socially isolated are more likely to neglect the children in their care.

Unlike victims of abuse, there are few consistent characteristics associated with victims of neglect. Retrospective studies of adults neglected as children indicate that females are slightly less resilient to neglect than men.

Prevalence

The number of children nationwide who are harmed or endangered by neglect is greater than any type of abuse. Neglect is consistently reported in more than half of the substantiated reports of mistreatment handled by the authorities.

Prevention and treatment

Interventions are usually aimed at two levels: community prevention efforts and individual parenting skills. A community-based program that actually combines the two facets of intervention is the "Parents as Teachers" program, which is available through many local school districts throughout the nation and is free of charge. Benefits of the program include its accessibility—parents simply need to call for the free service—and the in-home interventions provided by the program. Although the program is not part of the social service network of agencies, the fact that workers go into the home replicates that aspect of caseworker interventions. The simple act of having a paraprofessional in one's home can reduce the likelihood of neglect. Specific interventions that further reduce the likelihood of neglect include focusing on the parent-child relationship, reviewing appropriate expectations for the child's behavior (based on child development principles), and teaching basic parenting skills.

Other treatment options are generally more formal, and may be initiated by a call from a mandated reporter with concerns about neglect. Mandated reporters include physicians, teachers, and counselors. Any of these professionals may make the initial call if neglect is suspected. Concerned individuals may also call social services to report suspected neglect. In these cases of forced treatment, parents may be less willing participants in treatment efforts aimed at behavioral change for themselves and their families. In other instances, the parent or child may already be in treatment, and the focus on reducing neglectful behaviors may be incorporated into the existing treatment relationship. Factors to focus on in formal treatment aimed at reducing the likelihood of neglect may include specific parenting skills, home visits to allow monitoring of the relationship, as well as other individual needs such as substance abuse treatment, or empathy skill training.

Treatment efforts for the child should include family counseling aimed at communication skills and appropriate expression of affection and emotion within the family. Assertiveness skills training may be helpful for older adolescents in asking for their perceived needs.

See also Assertiveness skills training; Family therapy

Resources

BOOKS

McKenry, P. C., and S. J. Price, eds. *Families & Change.* Thousand Oaks, CA: Sage Publications, 2000.

PERIODICALS

English, D. J. "The extent and consequences of child maltreatment." *The Future of Children* 8, no. 1 (Spring 1998): 39-53.

Horwitz, A. V., C. S. Widom, J. McLaughlin, H. R. White. "The impact of childhood abuse and neglect on adult mental health: A prospective study." *Journal of Health & Social Behavior* 42, no. 2 (Jun 2001): 184-201.

Deanna Pledge, Ph.D.

Neurolinguistic programming *see* **Hypnotherapy**

Neurontin *see* **Gabapentin**

Neuropsychological testing

Definition

Clinical neuropsychology is a field with historical origins in both psychology and neurology. The primary activity of neuropsychologists is assessment of **brain** functioning through structured and systematic behavioral observation. Neuropsychological tests are designed to examine a variety of cognitive abilities, including speed of information processing, attention, memory, language, and executive functions, which are necessary for goal-directed behavior. By testing a range of cognitive abilities and examining patterns of performance in different cognitive areas, neuropsychologists can make inferences about underlying brain function. Neuropsychological testing is an important component of the assessment and treatment of traumatic brain injury, **dementia**, neurological conditions, and psychiatric disorders. Neuropsychological testing is also an important tool for examining the effects of toxic substances and medical conditions on brain functioning.

Description

As early as the seventeenth century, scientists theorized about associations between regions of the brain and specific functions. The French philosopher, Descartes, believed the human soul could be localized to a specific brain structure, the pineal gland. In the eighteenth century, Franz Gall advocated the theory that specific mental qualities such as spirituality or aggression were governed by discrete parts of the brain. In contrast, Pierre Flourens contended that the brain was an integrated system that governed cognitive functioning in a holistic manner. Later discoveries indicated that brain function is both localized and integrated. Paul Broca and Karl Wernicke furthered understanding of localization and integration of function when they reported the loss of language abilities in patients with lesions to two regions in the left hemisphere of the brain.

The modern field of neuropsychology emerged in the twentieth century, combining theories based on anatomical observations of neurology with the techniques of psychology, including objective observation of behavior and the use of statistical analysis to differentiate functional abilities and define impairment. The famous Soviet neuropsychologist Alexander Luria played a major role in defining neuropsychology as it is practiced today. Luria formulated two principle goals of neuropsychology: to localize brain lesions and analyze psychological activities arising from brain function through behavioral observation. American neuropsychologist Ralph Reitan emphasized the importance of using standardized psychometric tests to guide systematic observations of brain-behavior relationships.

Before the introduction of neuroimaging techniques like the **computed tomography** (CAT scan) and **magnetic resonance imaging** (MRI), the primary focus of neuropsychology was **diagnosis**. Since clinicians lacked non-surgical methods for directly observing brain lesions or structural abnormalities in living patients, neuropsychological testing was the only way to determine which part of the brain was affected in a given patient. Neuropsychological tests can identify syndromes associated with problems in a particular area of the brain. For instance, a patient who performs well on tests of attention, memory, and language, but poorly on tests that require visual spatial skills such as copying a complex geometric figure or making designs with colored blocks, may have dysfunction in the right parietal lobe, the region of the brain involved in complex processing of visual information. When a patient complains of problems with verbal communication after a **stroke**, separate tests that examine production and comprehension of language help neuropsychologists identify the location of the stroke in the left hemisphere. Neuropsychological tests can also be used as screening tests to see if more extensive diagnostic evaluation is appropriate. Neuropsychological screening of elderly people complaining of memory problems can help identify those at risk for dementia versus those experiencing normal age-related memory loss.

As neuropsychological testing came to play a less vital role in localization of brain dysfunction, clinical neuropsychologists found new uses for their skills and knowledge. By clarifying which cognitive abilities are impaired or preserved in patients with brain injury or illness, neuropsychologists can predict how well individuals will respond to different forms of treatment or rehabilitation. Although patterns of test scores illustrate profiles of cognitive strength and weakness, neuropsychologists can also learn a great deal about patients by

KEY TERMS

Abstraction—Ability to think about concepts or ideas separate from specific examples.

Battery—A number of separate items (such as tests) used together. In psychology, a group or series of tests given with a common purpose, such as personality assessment or measurement of intelligence.

Executive functions—A set of cognitive abilities that control and regulate other abilities and behaviors. Necessary for goal-directed behavior, they include the ability to initiate and stop actions, to monitor and change behavior as needed, and to plan future behavior when faced with novel tasks and situations.

Hemisphere—One side of the brain, right or left.

Psychometric—Pertaining to testing and measurement of mental or psychological abilities. Psychometric tests convert an individual's psychological traits and attributes into a numerical estimation or evaluation.

Syndrome—A group of symptoms that together characterize a disease or disorder.

observing how they approach a particular test. For example, two patients can complete a test in very different ways yet obtain similar scores. One patient may work slowly and methodically, making no errors, while another rushes through the test, making several errors but quickly correcting them. Some individuals persevere despite repeated failure on a series of test items, while others refuse to continue after a few failures. These differences might not be apparent in test scores, but can help clinicians choose among rehabilitation and treatment approaches.

Performance on neuropsychological tests is usually evaluated through comparison to the average performance of large samples of normal individuals. Most tests include tables of these normal scores, often divided into groups based on demographic variables like age and education that appear to affect cognitive functioning. This allows individuals to be compared to appropriate peers.

The typical neuropsychological examination evaluates sensation and perception, gross and fine motor skills, basic and complex attention, visual spatial skills, receptive and productive language abilities, recall and recognition memory, and executive functions such as cognitive flexibility and abstraction. Motivation and personality are often assessed as well, particularly when clients are seeking financial compensation for injuries, or cognitive complaints are not typical of the associated injury or illness.

Some neuropsychologists prefer to use fixed test batteries like the **Halstead-Reitan Battery** or the Luria-Nebraska Battery for all patients. These batteries include tests of a wide range of cognitive functions, and those who advocate their use believe that all functions must be assessed in each patient in order to avoid diagnostic bias or failure to detect subtle problems. The more common approach today, however, is to use a flexible battery based on hypotheses generated through a clinical interview, observation of the patient, and review of medical records. While this approach is more prone to bias, it has the advantage of preventing unnecessary testing. Since patients often find neuropsychological testing stressful and fatiguing, and these factors can negatively influence performance, advocates of the flexible battery approach argue that tailoring test batteries to particular patients can provide more accurate information.

Resources

BOOKS

Lezak, Muriel Deutsh. *Neuropsychological Assessment.* 3rd edition. New York: Oxford University Press, 1995.

Mitrushina, Maura N., Kyle B. Boone, and Louis F. D'Elia. *Handbook of Normative Data for Neuropsychological Assessment.* New York: Oxford University Press, 1999.

Spreen, Otfried and Esther Strauss. *A Compendium of Neuropsychological Tests: Administration, Norms, and Commentary.* 2nd Edition. New York: Oxford University Press, 1998.

Walsh, Kevin and David Darby. *Neuropsychology: A Clinical Approach.* 4th edition. Edinburgh: Churchill Livingstone, 1999.

ORGANIZATIONS

American Psychological Association. Division 40, 750 First Street, N.E., Washington, DC 20002-4242. <http://www.div40.org/>.

International Neuropsychological Society. 700 Ackerman Road, Suite 550, Columbus, OH 43202. <http://www.acs.ohio-state.edu/ins/>.

National Academy of Neuropsychology. 2121 South Oneida Street, Suite 550, Denver, CO 80224-2594. <http://nanonline.org/>.

Danielle Barry, M.S.

Neurosis

Definition

Neurosis is a term generally used to describe a nonpsychotic mental illness which triggers feelings of distress and anxiety and impairs functioning.

Description

Origins

The word *neurosis* means "nerve disorder," and was first coined in the late eighteenth century by William Cullen, a Scottish physician. Cullen's concept of neurosis encompassed those nervous disorders and symptoms that do not have a clear organic cause. Sigmund Freud later used the term *anxiety neurosis* to describe mental illness or distress with extreme anxiety as a defining feature.

There is a difference of opinion over the clinical use of the term neurosis today. It is not generally used as a diagnostic category by American psychologists and psychiatrists any longer, and was removed from the American Psychiatric Association's ***Diagnostic and Statistical Manual of Mental Disorders*** in 1980 with the publication of the third edition (it last appeared as a diagnostic category in *DSM-II*). Some professionals use the term to describe anxious symptoms and associated behavior, or to describe the range of mental illnesses outside of the psychotic disorders (such as **schizophrenia**, **delusional disorder**). Others, particularly psychoanalysts (psychiatrists and psychologists who follow a psychoanalytical model of treatment, as popularized by Freud and Carl Jung), use the term neurosis to describe the internal process itself (called an unconscious conflict) that triggers the anxiety characteristic.

Categories

The neurotic disorders are distinct from psychotic disorders in that the individual with neurotic symptoms has a firm grip on reality, and the psychotic patient does not. Before their reclassification, there were several major traditional categories of psychological neuroses, including: anxiety neurosis, depressive neurosis, obsessive-compulsive neurosis, somatization, **post-traumatic stress disorder**, and compensation neurosis—not a true neurosis, but a form of **malingering**, or feigning psychological symptoms for monetary or other personal gain.

Resources

BOOKS

American Psychiatric Association. *Diagnostic and Statistical Manual of Mental Disorders.* 4th edition, text revised. Washington, DC: American Psychiatric Press, Inc., 2000.

Fenichel, Otto M. *The Psychoanalytic Theory of Neurosis: 50th Anniversary Edition.* New York: W.W. Norton and Son. 1995.

Paula Ford-Martin, M.A.

Neurotransmitters

Definition

Neurotransmitters are chemicals located and released in the **brain** to allow an impulse from one nerve cell to pass to another nerve cell.

Description

There are approximately 50 neurotransmitters identified. There are billions of nerve cells located in the brain, which do not directly touch each other. Nerve cells communicate messages by secreting neurotransmitters. Neurotransmitters can excite or inhibit neurons (nerve cells). Some common neurotransmitters are acetylcholine, norepinephrine, dopamine, serotonin and gamma aminobutyric acid (GABA). Acetylcholine and norepinephrine are excitatory neurotransmitters while dopamine, serotonin, and GABA are inhibitory. Each neurotransmitter can directly or indirectly influence neurons in a specific portion of the brain, thereby affecting behavior.

KEY TERMS

Acetylcholine—A naturally occurring chemical in the body that transmits nerve impulses from cell to cell. Generally, it has opposite effects from dopamine and norepinephrine; it causes blood vessels to dilate, lowers blood pressure, and slows the heartbeat. Central nervous system well-being is dependent on a balance among acetylcholine, dopamine, serotonin, and norepinephrine.

Catecholamine—A group of neurotransmitters synthesized from the amino acid tyrosine and released by the hypothalamic-pituitary-adrenal system in the brain in response to acute stress. The catecholamines include dopamine, serotonin, norepinephrine, and epinephrine.

Dopamine—A chemical in brain tissue that serves to transmit nerve impulses (is a neurotransmitter) and helps to regulate movement and emotions.

GABA—Gamma-aminobutyric acid, an inhibitory neurotransmitter in the brain.

Norepinephrine—A neurotransmitter in the brain that acts to constrict blood vessels and raise blood pressure. It works in combination with serotonin.

Serotonin—A widely distributed neurotransmitter that is found in blood platelets, the lining of the digestive tract, and the brain, and that works in combination with norepinephrine. It causes very powerful contractions of smooth muscle, and is associated with mood, attention, emotions, and sleep. Low levels of serotonin are associated with depression.

Synaptic cleft—An area between nerve cells which can contain neurotransmitters.

Mechanism of impulse transmission

A nerve impulse travels through a nerve in a long, slender cellular structure called an axon, and it eventually reaches a structure called the presynaptic membrane, which contains neurotransmitters to be released in a free space called the synaptic cleft. Freely flowing neurotransmitter molecules are picked up by receptors (structures that appear on cellular surfaces that pick up molecules that fit into them like a "lock and key") locat-

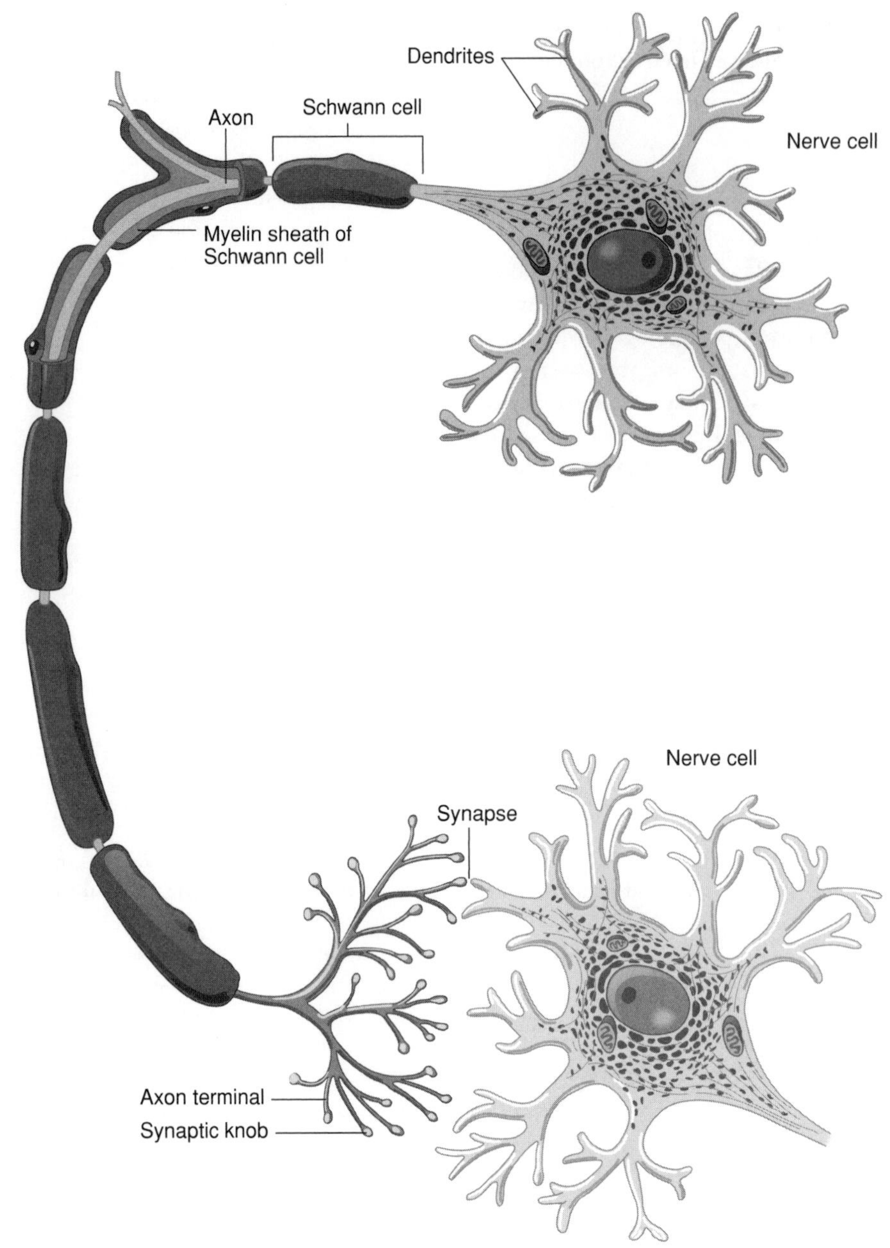

Neurotransmitters are chemicals that transmit messages from one nerve cell (neuron) to another. The nerve impulse travels from the first nerve cell through the axon—a single smooth body arising from the nerve cell— to the axon terminal and the synaptic knobs. Each synaptic knob communicates with a dendrite or cell body of another neuron, and the synaptic knobs contain neurovesicles that store and release neurotransmitters. The synapse lies between the synaptic knob and the next cell. For the impulse to continue traveling across the synapse to reach the next cell, the synaptic knobs release the neurotransmitter into that space, and the next nerve cell is stimulated to pick up the impulse and continue it.

ed in a structure called the postsynaptic membrane of another nearby neuron. Once the neurotransmitter is picked up by receptors in the postsynaptic membrane, the molecule is internalized in the neuron and the impulse continues. This process of nerve cell communication is extremely rapid.

Once the neurotransmitter is released from the neurotransmitter vesicles of the presynaptic membrane, the normal movement of molecules should be directed to receptor sites located on the postsynaptic membrane. However, in certain disease states, the flow of the neurotransmitter is defective. For example, in depression, the flow of the inhibitory neurotransmitter serotonin is defective, and molecules flow back to their originating site (the presynaptic membrane) instead of to receptors on the postsynaptic membrane that will transmit the impulse to a nearby neuron.

The mechanism of action and localization of neurotransmitters in the brain has provided valuable information concerning the cause of many mental disorders, including clinical depression and chemical dependency, and in researching medications that allow normal flow and movement of neurotransmitter molecules.

Neurotransmitters, mental disorders, and medications

Schizophrenia

Impairment of dopamine-containing neurons in the brain is implicated in **schizophrenia**, a mental disease marked by disturbances in thinking and emotional reactions. Medications that block dopamine receptors in the brain, such as **chlorpromazine** and **clozapine**, have been used to alleviate the symptoms and help patients return to a normal social setting.

Depression

In depression, which afflicts about 3.5% of the population, there appears to be abnormal excess or inhibition of signals that control mood, thoughts, pain, and other sensations. Depression is treated with antidepressants that affect norepinephrine and serotonin in the brain. The antidepressants help correct the abnormal neurotransmitter activity. A newer drug, **fluoxetine** (Prozac), is a selective serotonin reuptake inhibitor (SSRI) that appears to establish the level of serotonin required to function at a normal level. As the name implies, the drug inhibits the re-uptake of serotonin neurotransmitter from synaptic gaps, thus increasing neurotransmitter action. In the brain, then, the increased serotonin activity alleviates depressive symptoms.

Alzheimer's disease

Alzheimer's disease, which affects an estimated four million Americans, is characterized by memory loss and the eventual inability for self-care. The disease seems to be caused by a loss of cells that secrete acetylcholine in the basal forebrain (region of brain that is the control center for sensory and associative information processing and motor activities). Some medications to alleviate the symptoms have been developed, but presently there is no known treatment for the disease.

Generalized anxiety disorder

People with **generalized anxiety disorder** (GAD) experience excessive worry that causes problems at work and in the maintenance of daily responsibilities. Evidence suggests that GAD involves several neurotransmitter systems in the brain, including norepinephrine and serotonin.

Attention-deficit/hyperactivity disorder

People affected by **attention-deficit/hyperactivity disorder** (ADHD) experience difficulties in the areas of attention, overactivity, impulse control, and distractibility. Research shows that dopamine and norepinephrine imbalances are strongly implicated in causing ADHD.

Others

Substantial research evidence also suggests a correlation of neurotransmitter imbalance with disorders such as borderline **personality disorders**, **schizotypal personality disorder**, **avoidant personality disorder**, **social phobia**, **histrionic personality disorder**, and **somatization disorder**.

Drug addictions

Cocaine and crack cocaine are psychostimulants that affect neurons containing dopamine in the areas of the brain known as the limbic and frontal cortex. When cocaine is used, it generates a feeling of confidence and power. However, when large amounts are taken, people "crash" and suffer from physical and emotional exhaustion as well as depression.

Opiates, such as heroin and morphine, appear to mimic naturally occurring peptide substances in the brain that act as neurotransmitters with opiate activity called endorphins. Natural endorphins of the brain act to kill pain, cause sensations of pleasure, and cause sleepiness. Endorphins released with extensive aerobic exercise, for example, are responsible for the "rush" that long-distance runners experience. It is believed that morphine and heroin combine with the endorphin receptors in the brain, resulting in reduced natural endorphin production. As a result, the drugs are needed to replace the naturally produced endorphins and **addiction** occurs. Attempts to counteract the effects of the drugs involve using medications that mimic them, such as nalorphine, naloxone, and **naltrexone**.

Alcohol is one of the depressant drugs in widest use, and is believed to cause its effects by interacting with the GABA receptor. Initially anxiety is controlled, but greater amounts reduce muscle control and delay reaction time due to impaired thinking.

Resources

BOOKS

Tasman, Allan, Kay Jerald, MD, Jeffrey A. Lieberman, MD, eds. *Psychiatry.* 1st ed. Philadelphia: W. B. Saunders Company, 1997.

Laith Farid Gulli, M.D.
Mary Finley

Nicotine and related disorders

Definition

Nicotine disorders are caused by the main psychoactive ingredient in tobacco. Nicotine is a physically and psychologically addictive drug. It is the most influential dependence-producing drug in the United States and worldwide, and its use is associated with many serious health risks.

Description

Nicotine is the most addictive and psychoactive chemical in tobacco, a plant native to the New World. Early European explorers learned to smoke its leaves from indigenous peoples who had been using tobacco for hundreds of years. They took tobacco back to Europe, where it became immensely popular. Tobacco became a major source of income for the American colonies and later for the United States. Advances in cigarette-making technology caused a boom in cigarette smoking in the early 1900s. Before the early twentieth century, most people who smoked had used pipes, cigars, or chewing tobacco.

In the 1950s researchers began to link cigarette smoking to certain respiratory diseases and cancers. In 1964 the Surgeon General of the United States issued the first health report on smoking. Cigarette smoking peaked in the United States in the 1970s, then began to decline as health concerns about tobacco increased. In 1971 cigarette advertising was banned from television, although tobacco products continue to be heavily advertised in other media even today. By 1998, it was estimated that 25% of Americans (about 60 million people) were active smokers, 25% were former smokers, and the remaining half have never smoked. About 85% of active smokers are addicted to nicotine.

Pure nicotine is a colorless liquid that turns brown and smells like tobacco when exposed to air. Nicotine can be absorbed through the skin, the lining of the mouth and nose, and the moist tissues lining the lungs. Cigarettes are the most efficient nicotine delivery system. Once tobacco smoke is inhaled, nicotine reaches the **brain** in less than 15 seconds. Since people who smoke pipes and cigars do not inhale, they absorb nicotine more slowly. Nicotine in chewing tobacco and snuff is absorbed through the mucous membranes lining the mouth and nasal passages. In 2002 a new smokeless tobacco product was test-marketed in the United States. Called Ariva, it is compressed tobacco powder about the size of a vitamin pill that is placed between the cheek and gum until it dissolves completely. The nicotine it contains is also absorbed through the mucous membranes of the mouth.

Causes and symptoms

How nicotine works

Nicotine is the main addictive drug among the 4,000 compounds found in tobacco smoke. Such other substances in smoke as tar and carbon monoxide present documented health hazards, but they are not addictive and do not cause cravings or withdrawal symptoms to the extent that nicotine does.

Nicotine is both a stimulant and a sedative. It is a psychoactive drug, meaning that it works in the brain, alters brain chemistry, and changes mood. Once tobacco smoke is inhaled, nicotine passes rapidly through the linings of the lungs and into the blood. It quickly circulates to the brain where it indirectly increases the supply of dopamine, a chemical in the brain that affects mood. Dopamine is normally released in response to pleasurable sensations. Nicotine, like cocaine or heroin, artificially stimulates the release of dopamine. This release accounts for the pleasurable sensation that most smokers feel almost as soon as they light up a cigarette. Nicotine also decreases anger and increases the efficiency of a person's performance on long, dull tasks.

At the same time nicotine is affecting the brain, it also stimulates the adrenal glands. The adrenal glands are small, pea-sized pieces of tissue located above each kidney. They produce several hormones, one of which is epinephrine, also called adrenaline. Under normal circumstances, adrenaline is released in response to **stress** or a perceived threat. It is sometimes called the "fight or flight" hormone, because it prepares the body for action. When adrenaline is released, blood pressure, heart rate, blood flow, and oxygen use increase. Glucose, a simple form of sugar used by the body, floods the body to provide extra energy to muscles. The overall effect of the release of these hormones is strain on the cardiovascular (heart and blood vessels) system. Stressed this way many times a day for many years, the body responds by increasing the buildup of plaque, a sticky substance, in the blood vessels. These deposits of plaque significantly increase a person's risk of **stroke** or heart attack.

Most people begin smoking between the ages of 12 and 20. Surprisingly few people start smoking as adults over 21. Adolescents who smoke tend to begin as casual smokers, out of rebelliousness or a need for social acceptance. Dependence on nicotine develops rapidly, however; one study suggests that 85–90% of adolescents who smoke four or more cigarettes become regular smokers. Nicotine is so addictive that being tobacco-free soon feels uncomfortable. In addition, smokers quickly develop tolerance to nicotine. Tolerance is a condition that occurs when the body needs a larger and larger dose of a substance to produce the same effect. For smokers, tolerance to nicotine means more frequent and more rapid smoking. Soon most smokers develop physical withdrawal symptoms when they try to stop smoking. Users of other forms of tobacco experience the same effects; however, the delivery of nicotine is slower and the effects may not be as pronounced.

Nicotine dependence

In addition to the physical dependence caused by the actions of nicotine on the brain, there is a strong psychological component to the dependency of most users of tobacco products, especially cigarette smokers. Most people who start smoking or using smokeless tobacco products do so because of social factors. These include:

- the desire to fit in with peers
- acceptance by family members who use tobacco
- rebelliousness
- the association of tobacco products with maturity and sophistication
- positive response to tobacco advertising

Such personal factors as mental illness (depression, anxiety, **schizophrenia**, or alcoholism); the need to reduce stress and anxiety; or a desire to avoid weight gain also influence people to start smoking. Once smoking has become a habit, whether physical **addiction** occurs or not, psychological factors play a significant role in continuing to smoke. People who want to stop smoking may be discouraged from doing so because:

- They live or work with people who smoke and who are not supportive of their quitting.
- They believe they are incapable of quitting.
- They perceive no health benefits to quitting.
- They have tried to quit before and failed.

KEY TERMS

Adrenaline—Another name for epinephrine, the hormone released by the adrenal glands in response to stress. It is the principal blood-pressure raising hormone and a bronchial and intestinal smooth muscles relaxant.

Cold turkey—A slang term for stopping the use of nicotine (or any other addictive drug) suddenly and completely.

Dopamine—A chemical in brain tissue that serves to transmit nerve impulses (is a neurotransmitter) and helps to regulate movement and emotions.

Epinephrine—A hormone secreted by the adrenal glands in response to stress.

Plaque—A sticky cholesterol-containing substance that builds up on the walls of blood vessels, reducing or blocking blood flow.

Supportive—An approach to smoking cessation that seeks to encourage the patient or offer emotional support to him or her, as distinct from insight-oriented or exploratory approaches to treatment.

Tolerance—Progressive decrease in the effectiveness of a drug with long-term use.

Withdrawal—Symptoms experienced by a person who has become physically dependent on a drug, experienced when the drug use is discontinued.

- They associate cigarettes with specific pleasurable activities or social situations that they are not willing to give up.
- They fear gaining weight. Successful smoking cessation programs must treat both the physical and psychological aspects of nicotine addiction.

Nicotine withdrawal

The American Psychiatric Association first recognized nicotine dependence and nicotine withdrawal as serious psychological problems in 1980. Today nicotine is considered an addictive drug, although a common and legalized one.

Studies show that three-quarters of smokers try to quit, but only about 5–10% are eventually successful. Even those who succeed often make between five and ten attempts to quit before finally succeeding. Symptoms of nicotine withdrawal occur in about half the smokers try-

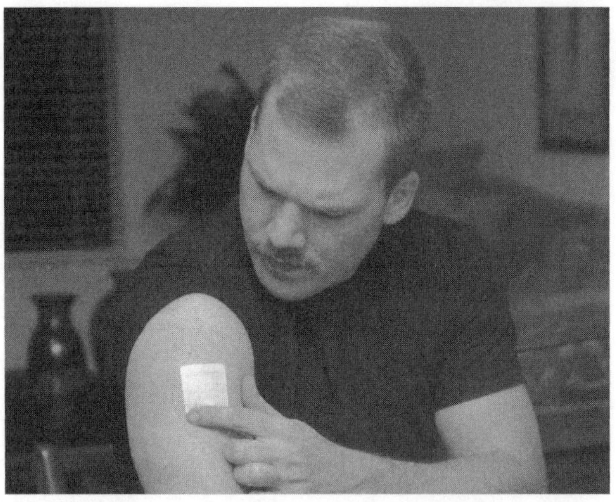

Transdermal patches are worn on the skin between the neck and the waist, and provide a steady delivery of nicotine through the skin. Patches come in varying strengths, and after several weeks, users can move down to a patch that delivers a lower dose. *(Robert J. Huffman/ Field Mark Publications. Reproduced by permission.)*

ing to quit who do not use nicotine replacement therapy (nicotine patches, inhalers, or gum).

As former smokers can attest, the combination of physiological and psychological factors make withdrawal from nicotine very difficult. Symptoms of nicotine withdrawal include:

- irritability
- restlessness
- increased anger or frustration
- sleep disturbances
- inability to concentrate
- increased appetite or desire for sweets
- depression
- anxiety
- constant thoughts about smoking
- cravings for cigarettes
- decreased heart rate
- coughing

Withdrawal symptoms are usually more pronounced in smokers than in those who use smokeless tobacco products, and heavy smokers tend to have more symptoms than light smokers when they try to stop smoking. People with depression, schizophrenia, alcoholism, or mood disorders find it especially difficult to quit, as nicotine offers temporary relief for some of the symptoms of these disorders.

Symptoms of nicotine withdrawal begin rapidly and peak within one to three days. Because of this rapid onset of withdrawal symptoms, only about 30% of people who try to quit smoking remain tobacco-free for even two days. Withdrawal symptoms generally last three to four weeks, but a significant number of smokers have withdrawal symptoms lasting longer than one month. Some people have strong cravings for tobacco that last for months, even though the physical addiction to nicotine is gone. These cravings often occur in social settings in which the person formerly smoked, such as at a bar or party, or after sex. Researchers believe that much of this extended craving is psychological.

Demographics

About 60 million Americans smoke cigarettes, cigars, and pipes; and about six million more use smokeless tobacco. Worldwide, there are more than a billion smokers. Although the prevalence of smoking has gradually decreased in the United States and many other industrialized countries since the 1970s, the use of tobacco products is rapidly increasing in the developing nations of Africa and Asia. Use of tobacco products in developing countries is of particular concern, because these countries often lack adequate health care resources to treat smoking-related diseases, let alone support smoking cessation programs.

In the past, the number of American men who smoked outnumbered women, but by 2000, the rate of smoking was almost the same for these two groups—about 35% of the population. Men in the United States greatly outnumber women, however, in the use of smokeless tobacco (14% to 1%). In developing countries, male smokers outnumber women smokers by a margin of eight to one. People who smoke tend to have lower levels of income and formal education than those who don't. About half the patients diagnosed with psychiatric problems are smokers, while more than three-quarters of those who abuse other substances also smoke.

In 2001, the most recent year for which statistics are available, smoking among high school students decreased. Daily use of cigarettes among eighth graders decreased from 7.4% to 5.5% and among tenth graders from 14% to 12.2%—both significant declines. The rate of smokeless tobacco usage stayed constant at about 4% of eighth graders and 7% of tenth graders, almost all of whom were boys. Smoking among women with less than a high school education increased, however. Although African American men overall have the highest rate of smoking in the United States population, smoking among African American high school students has decreased significantly. Only about 19% of African American high school students smoke, compared to about 38% of Caucasian high school students. The change in rates of smoking among different subgroups in the population may reflect to some extent changes in the target groups of the billion-dollar advertising campaigns of cigarette manufacturers.

Recent research suggests that there may be a genetic component to nicotine dependence, just as there is for alcohol dependence. Studies show that girls (but not boys) whose mothers smoked during pregnancy are four times more likely to smoke than those whose mothers were tobacco-free during pregnancy. Other research suggests that the absence of a certain enzyme in the body protects the body against nicotine dependence.

Diagnosis

Smokers usually self-diagnose their nicotine dependence and nicotine withdrawal. Such questionnaires as the Fagerstrom Test for Nicotine Dependence (FTND), a short six-item assessment of cigarette use, help to determine the level of tobacco dependence. Physicians and mental health professionals are less concerned with **diagnosis**, which is usually straightforward, than with determining the physical and psychological factors in each patient that must be addressed for successful smoking cessation.

Treatments

Most smokers want to quit; over 75% have tried to stop at least once. Each year, over 40% of smokers make at least one attempt to quit. Many people try a dozen times before they are successful in finding the right combination of medications, therapies, and support to achieve success. Even with repeated attempts, however, only half of all smokers are able to stop smoking completely and eliminate their dependence on nicotine.

Most people do not suddenly wake up one morning and decide to stop smoking. Instead, they go through several preparatory stages before taking action. First is the precontemplation stage, in which the smoker doesn¸t even think about quitting. Precontemplation is followed by the contemplation stage, in which the smoker thinks about quitting, but takes no action. Contemplation eventually turns to preparation, often when counselors or family members encourage or urge the smoker to quit. Now the smoker starts making plans to quit in the near future. Finally the smoker arrives at the point of taking action.

Having decided to stop smoking, a person has many choices of programs and approaches. When mental health professionals are involved in smoking cessation efforts, one of their first jobs is to identify the physical and psychological factors that keep the person smoking. This identification helps to direct the smoker to the most appropriate type of program. Assessment examines the frequency of the person's smoking, his or her social and emotional attachment to cigarettes, commitment to change, available support system, and barriers to change. These conditions vary from person to person, which is why some smoking cessation programs work for one person and not another.

Medications

Before 1984, there were no medications to help smokers quit. In that year, a nicotine chewing gum (Nicorette) was approved by the United States Food and Drug Administration (FDA) as a prescription drug for smoking cessation. In 1996 it became available without prescription. Nicorette was the first of several medications that are used for nicotine replacement therapy, intended to gradually reduce nicotine dependence in order to prevent or reduce withdrawal symptoms. This approach, called tapering, is used in withdrawal of other addictive drugs.

About 15% of people using nicotine gum are able to stop smoking permanently. This rate is about three times higher than for people who simply go "cold turkey" and stop smoking without any assistance. Nicotine gum comes in two strengths. As it is chewed, nicotine is released and absorbed through the lining of the mouth. Over a six- to 12-week period, the amount and strength of gum chewed is decreased, until the smoker is weaned away from his or her dependence on nicotine. Chewing gum may not be pleasant or socially acceptable to some people, and cannot be used by people who have diseases of the jaw. In addition, some people report that the gum makes them feel queasy.

The nicotine transdermal patches have been available without prescription since 1996. They are marketed under several brand names, including Habitrol, Nicoderm, NicoDerm CQ, Prostep and Nicotrol. All but Nicotrol are 24-hour patches. Nicotrol is a 16-hour patch designed to be removed at night. The patches are worn on the skin between the neck and the waist, and provide a steady delivery of nicotine through the skin. Patches come in varying strengths. After several weeks, users can move down to a patch that delivers a lower dose. Some people using the 24-hour patches experience sleep disturbances, and a few develop mild skin irritations, but generally side effects are few.

Two other nicotine delivery devices are available by prescription only. One is a nicotine nasal spray. It has the advantage of delivering nicotine rapidly, just as a cigarette does. Treatment with nasal spray usually lasts four

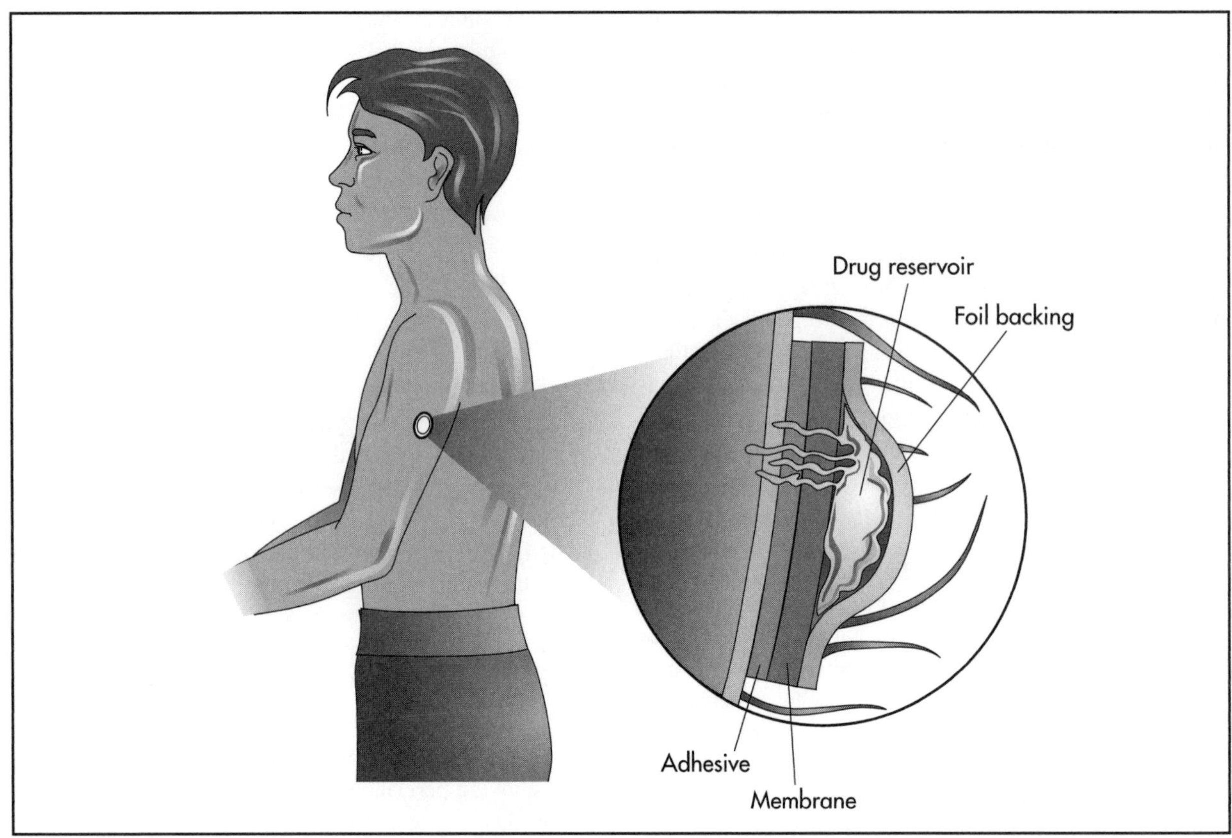

The nicotine patch is a transepidermal patch designed to deliver nicotine, the addictive substance in cigarettes, directly through the skin into the bloodstream. The patch contains a drug reservoir sandwiched between a nonpermeable back layer and a permeable adhesive layer that attaches to the skin. The drug leaches slowly out of the reservoir, releasing small amounts of the drug at a constant rate for up to 24 hours. *(Illustration by Electronic Illustrators Group.)*

to six weeks. Side effects include cold-like symptoms (runny nose, sneezing, etc.). A nicotine inhaler is also available that delivers nicotine through the tissues of the throat. A major advantage of the inhaler is that it provides an alternative to having a cigarette in one's hands while it delivers nicotine.

One prescription drug that is not nicotine replacement therapy has also been approved for treatment of nicotine dependence. **Bupropion** (Zyban) was originally developed as antidepressant medication that appears to increase dopamine levels in the brain. Bupropion has been shown to be effective in smoking cessation. It has the advantage of being a pill taken twice a day. Its side effects include dry mouth and **insomnia**; in addition, it may not be suitable for people with certain medical conditions.

Behavioral treatments

Behavioral treatments are used to help smokers learn to recognize and avoid specific situations that trigger desire for a cigarette. They also help the smoker learn to substitute other activities for smoking. Behavioral treatments are almost always combined with smoker education, and usually involve forming a support network of other smokers who are trying to quit.

Behavioral treatments often take place in **support groups** either in person or online. They are most effective when combined with nicotine reduction therapy. Other supportive techniques include the use of rewards for achieving certain goals and contracts to clarify and reinforce the goals. Aversive techniques include asking the smoker to inhale the tobacco smoke deeply and repeatedly to the point of nausea, so that smoking is no longer associated with pleasurable sensations. Overall, quit rates are highest (about 30%) when **behavior modification** is combined with nicotine replacement therapy and tapering.

Alternative treatments

Many alternative therapies have been tried to help smokers withdraw from nicotine. Hypnosis has proved helpful in some cases, but has not been tested in controlled clinical trials. **Acupuncture**, relaxation techniques, restricted environmental stimulation therapy (REST, a combination of relaxation and hypnosis techniques), special **diets**, and herbal supplements have all been used to help people stop smoking. Of these alternative techniques, clinical studies of REST showed substantial promise in helping people stop smoking permanently.

Prognosis

Smoking is a major health risk associated with nicotine dependence. About half of all smokers die of a smoking-related illness, often cancer. About 90% of lung cancers are linked to smoking. Smoking also causes such other lung problems as chronic bronchitis and emphysema, as well as worsening the symptoms of asthma. Other cancers associated with smoking include cancers of the mouth, esophagus, stomach, kidney, and bladder. Smoking accounts for 20% of cardiovascular deaths. It significantly increases the risk of heart disease, heart attack, stroke, and aneurysm. Women who smoke during pregnancy have more miscarriages, premature babies, and low-birth-weight babies. In addition, secondhand smoke endangers the health of nonsmokers in the smoker's family or workplace. Although most of these effects are not caused directly by nicotine, it is dependence on nicotine that keeps people smoking.

Even though it is difficult for smokers to break their chemical and psychological dependence on nicotine, they should remember that most of the negative health effects of smoking are reduced or reversed after quitting. Therefore, it is worth trying to quit smoking at any age, regardless of the length of time a person has had the habit.

Prevention

The best way to avoid nicotine dependence and withdrawal is to avoid the use of tobacco products.

See also Stress; Substance abuse and related disorders

Resources

BOOKS

American Psychiatric Association. *Diagnostic and Statistical Manual of Mental Disorders.* 4th edition, text revised. Washington DC: American Psychiatric Association, 2000.

Brigham, Janet. *Dying to Quit: Why we Smoke and How we Stop.* Washington DC: John Henry Press, 1998.

Galanter, Marc and Herbert D. Kleber, eds. *Textbook of Substance Abuse Treatment.* 2nd ed. Washington DC: American Psychiatric Press, Inc., 1999.

O'Brien, Charles P. "Drug Addiction and Drug Abuse." Chapter 24. In *Goodman & Gilman's The Pharmacological Basis of Therapeutics,* edited by J. G. Hardman and L. E. Limbird. 9th edition. New York and St. Louis, MO: McGraw-Hill, 1996.

Sadock, Benjamin J. and Virginia A. Sadock, eds. *Comprehensive Textbook of Psychiatry.* 7th ed. Vol. 1. Philadelphia: Lippincott Williams & Wilkins, 2000.

PERIODICALS

Mathias, Robert. "Daughters of Mothers Who Smoked During Pregnancy Are More Likely to Smoke, Study Says." *NIDA Notes* 10, no. 5 (September/October 1995).

National Institute on Drug Abuse. "Nicotine Addiction." *National Institute on drug Abuse Research Report Series* 21 (February 2001).

United States Department of Health and Human Services. "2001 Monitoring the Future Survey Released" *HHS News* 10 December 2001.

ORGANIZATIONS

American Cancer Society. National Headquarters, 1599 Clifton Road NE, Atlanta, GA 30329. (800) (ACS)-2345. <http://www.cancer.org>.

American Lung Association. 1740 Broadway, New York, NY 10019. (212) 315-8700. <http://www.lungusa.org>.

Cancer Information Service. National Cancer Institute, Building 31, Room 10A19, 9000 Rockville Pike, Bethesda, MD 20892. (800) 4-CANCER. <http://www.nci.nih.gov/cancerinfo/index.html>.

OTHER

Campaign for Tobacco-Free Kids. "Public Health Groups File Petition Urging FDA to Regulate New 'Reduced Risk' Products Being Marketed to Smokers as Healthier Alternatives." <http://tobaccofreekids.org/Script/DisplayPressRelease.php3?Display=429>.

Tish Davidson, A.M.

Nightmare disorder

Definition

Nightmare disorder, which is also called dream anxiety disorder, is characterized by the occurrence of repeated dreams during which the sleeper feels threatened and frightened. The sense of fear causes the person to awake.

Description

Nightmares are dreams that cause intense fear. These dreams are often complex and fairly long. During the dream, the sleeper usually encounters or experiences a threat to their life or safety. Nightmares are also reported that do not involve physical danger.

As the dream progresses, the threat to the person usually increases, as does their sense of fear. Waking usu-

KEY TERMS

Dream anxiety disorder—Another name for nightmare disorder.

Sleep terror disorder—A sleep disorder that is distinguished from nightmare disorder by the intensity of associated anxiety symptoms, the absence of complete wakefulness, and the person's difficulty recalling the episode.

ally occurs just as the threat or danger reaches its climax. It is often difficult for a person to return to sleep after waking from a nightmare. Nightmares usually occur during the second half of the night's sleep.

Causes and symptoms

During the course of a nightmare the sleeper may moan, talk, or move slightly, although these signs do not always appear. The person wakes from the nightmare with a profound sense of fear. Waking is complete, and usually accompanied by increased heart rate, sweating, and other symptoms of anxiety or fear. Once fully awake, the person usually has a good recall of the dream and what was so frightening about it. Because of the physical symptoms of anxiety and because clarity is achieved immediately upon waking, returning to sleep after a nightmare is often difficult. The vividness of the recall and the prominence of the dream images in the person's mind can also make it difficult to calm down and return to sleep.

Sometimes people may avoid going to sleep after a particularly intense nightmare because of the fear of having another bad dream. In addition, people may have problems falling asleep if they are experiencing anxiety caused by the fear of having nightmares. As a result, these people may have the signs and symptoms associated with mild sleep deprivation, such as decreased mental clarity, problems paying attention, excessive daytime sleepiness, irritability, or mild depression.

The causes of nightmares are not known for certain. Adults who have nightmares on a regular basis are a small minority of the American population. About half of these people are thought to suffer from psychiatric disorders that cause the nightmares. Nightmares may also be triggered by major psychological traumas, such as those experienced by patients with **post-traumatic stress disorder**. For most patients who do not have an underlying mental disorder, the nightmares are attributed to stress. Nightmares that occur on an irregular and occasional basis are usually attributed to life stressors and associated anxiety.

Some researchers think that artistic or creative people are at greater risk for nightmares, as are people who are generally sensitive. These people are considered to have well-developed imaginations and are very sensitive to environmental and social factors.

Nightmares can be a side effect of some medications or drugs of abuse, including drugs given for high blood pressure; levodopa and other drugs given to treat Parkinson's disease; **amphetamines**, cocaine, and other stimulants; and some antidepressants. Withdrawal from alcohol and other medications can also sometimes cause nightmares.

Demographics

The actual percentage of people that suffer from nightmare disorder is not known, as many people do not seek treatment for it. There are, however, estimates of the proportion of the population that experience occasional nightmares. Many children suffer from nightmares that concern their parents. Estimates on the number of children who have recurrent nightmares range from 10–50%. In children, however, nightmares are not usually associated with psychiatric illness.

The number of children experiencing nightmares decreases as they get older. More than 3% of young adults have frequent nightmares, but only about 1% of mature adults experience nightmares once or twice a week. Half of the adults in the United States who experience regular nightmares have diagnosable psychiatric illnesses. Women are estimated to have nightmares two to four times more frequently than men. There is some uncertainty as to whether this figure reflects an actual difference between the sexes in the frequency of nightmares, or whether women are simply more likely than men to report nightmares. Nightmares typically decrease in frequency as people grow older.

Diagnosis

A **diagnosis** of nightmare disorder is usually made because the person reports the problem to their family physician or a **psychiatrist**. There are no laboratory tests for nightmare disorder, although the doctor may give the patient a physical examination to rule out any medical conditions that may be causing anxiety or stress.

Nightmares are characterized by awakening with a sense of fear, a clear recollection of the dream, and physical symptoms of anxiety. Nightmares can occur during nighttime sleep or daytime naps. A patient experiencing nightmares must meet the criteria listed in the ***Diagnostic and Statistical Manual of Mental Disorders*** to be diagnosed with nightmare disorder. The manual, which provides guidelines used by the American Psychiatric Association for diagnosing psychiatric disturbances, gives four distinct criteria:

- The patient must experience repeated awakenings from frightening dreams.
- When the patient awakes, he or she must wake fully and be aware of his or her surroundings.
- The nightmares must cause the patient distress in important areas of his or her life.
- The nightmares cannot be directly attributed to another disorder, or be the direct effects of medications, substance abuse, or a medical condition.

Nightmare disorder can be confused with **sleep terror disorder**. Both disorders are characterized by an arousal during sleep when the patient shows symptoms of anxiety or fear. Sleep terror, however, is characterized by a partial arousal from sleep during which the patient is generally nonresponsive. After a nightmare, the patient becomes fully awake and is aware of his or her surroundings. During an episode of sleep terror, a patient often gets out of bed and is active, and often screams or cries. During a nightmare, the patient may move slightly or moan but does not display such dramatic or active symptoms. Patients do not remember either the sleep terror episode or what caused the fear, but patients who have nightmares remember them with great clarity and often in considerable detail. Such symptoms of fear or anxiety as increased heart rate, dilated pupils, and sweating are not as dramatic in patients with nightmare disorder as they are in patients experiencing sleep terrors.

Treatments

Nightmares that are associated with a psychiatric disorder are managed by treating the underlying disorder. For patients without psychiatric disorders, psychological counseling to deal with any recurring themes in the nightmares may be helpful. Children may not require treatment for nightmares unless the dreams are causing significant distress, as nightmares generally resolve as children mature.

Because stress is thought to be the most common cause of nightmares, stress reduction techniques may prove to be effective complementary treatments. Typical relaxation techniques such as **yoga**, **meditation**, or exercise may be helpful. **Psychotherapy** can be an effective way to identify major stressors in the person's life, and to explore ways in which they may be reduced or eliminated.

Prognosis

Nightmare disorder can be a lifelong disorder. A general improvement in symptoms often takes place, however, as the patient gets older. Treatment for any underlying psychological disorders can be very successful.

Resources

BOOKS

Aldrich, Michael S. *Sleep Medicine.* New York: Oxford University Press, 1999.

American Psychiatric Association. *Diagnostic and Statistical Manual of Mental Disorders.* 4th edition, text revised. Washington DC: American Psychiatric Association, 2000.

Chokroverty, Susan, ed. *Sleep Disorders Medicine: Basic Science, Technical Considerations, and Clinical Aspects.* 2nd ed. Boston: Butterworth-Heinemann, 1999.

Sadock, Benjamin J., and Virginia A. Sadock, eds. *Comprehensive Textbook of Psychiatry.* 7th ed. Vol. 2. Philadelphia: Lippincott Williams and Wilkins, 2000.

PERIODICALS

Krakow, Barry, and others. "Imagery Rehearsal Therapy for Chronic Nightmares in Sexual Assault Survivors with Posttraumatic Stress Disorder." *Journal of the American Medical Association* 286, no. 5 (August 1 2001).

ORGANIZATIONS

American Academy of Sleep Medicine. 6301 Bandel Road NW, Suite 101, Rochester, MN 55901. (507) 287-6006. <www.asda.org>.

Tish Davidson, A.M.

NLP *see* **Hypnotherapy**

Norpramin *see* **Desipramine**

Nortriptyline

Definition

Nortriptyline is a tricyclic antidepressant. It is sold in the United States under the brand names Aventyl and Pamelor, and is also available under its generic name.

Purpose

Nortriptyline is used to relieve symptoms of depression. The drug is more effective for endogenous depression than for other forms of depression. Endogenous depression is depression arising from metabolic changes within a person, such as chemical or hormonal imbalances. Nortriptyline is also used occasionally to treat

KEY TERMS

Acetylcholine—A naturally occurring chemical in the body that transmits nerve impulses from cell to cell. Generally, it has opposite effects from dopamine and norepinephrine; it causes blood vessels to dilate, lowers blood pressure, and slows the heartbeat. Central nervous system well-being is dependent on a balance among acetylcholine, dopamine, serotonin, and norepinephrine.

Benign prostate hypertrophy—Enlargement of the prostate gland.

Bipolar syndrome—An abnormal mental condition characterized by periods of intense elation, energy and activity followed by periods of inactivity and depression.

Catecholamine—A group of neurotransmitters synthesized from the amino acid tyrosine and released by the hypothalamic-pituitary-adrenal system in the brain in response to acute stress. The catecholamines include dopamine, serotonin, norepinephrine, and epinephrine.

Endogenous depression—Depression arising from causes within a person, such as chemical or hormonal imbalances.

Manic—Referring to mania, a state characterized by excessive activity, excitement or emotion.

Neurotransmitter—A chemical in the brain that transmits messages between neurons, or nerve cells.

premenstrual depression, **attention-deficit/hyperactivity disorder** in children, and bed-wetting (**enuresis**).

Description

Tricyclic antidepressants act to change the balance of naturally occurring chemicals in the **brain** that regulate the transmission of nerve impulses between cells. The precise way in which nortriptyline elevates mood is not fully understood. The drug inhibits the activity of **neurotransmitters** such as acetylcholine, histamine, and 5-hydroxytryptamine. Studies have indicated that nortriptyline interferes with the release, transport, and storage of catecholamines, another group of chemicals involved in nerve impulse transmission.

Recommended dosage

As with any antidepressant, the dose of nortriptyline must be carefully adjusted by the physician to produce the desired therapeutic effect. Nortriptyline is available in 10-, 25-, 50-, and 75-mg capsules as well as in a 10 mg/5mL solution. The usual dosage for nortriptyline is 25 mg given three or four times each day. The optimum total dose of the drug is 50 to 150 mg daily. Total dosage in excess of 150 mg is not recommended. The recommended dose for older adults (over age 60) and adolescents is 30 to 50 mg per day. Nortriptyline is not recommended for use by children.

The therapeutic effects of nortriptyline, like other tricyclic antidepressants, appear slowly. Maximum benefit is often not evident for two to three weeks after starting the drug. People taking nortriptyline should be aware of this and continue taking the drug as directed even if they do not see immediate improvement.

Once symptoms of depression have been controlled, the lowest dosage that maintains the effect should be taken. People who take 100 mg or more of nortriptyline per day should have their blood tested periodically for nortriptyline concentrations. The results of these tests will show whether the dose is appropriate, too high, or too low.

Precautions

Like all tricyclic antidepressants, nortriptyline should be used cautiously and with close physician supervision in people, especially the elderly, who have benign prostatic hypertrophy, urinary retention, and glaucoma, especially angle-closure glaucoma (the most severe form). Before starting treatment, people with these conditions should discuss the relative risks and benefits of treatment with their doctors to help determine if nortriptyline is the right antidepressant for them.

A common problem with tricyclic antidepressants such as nortriptyline, is sedation (drowsiness, lack of physical and mental alertness). This side effect is especially noticeable early in therapy. In most patients, sedation decreases or disappears entirely with time, but until then, patients taking nortriptyline should not perform hazardous activities requiring mental alertness or coordination. The sedative effect is increased when nortriptyline is taken with other central nervous system depressants, such as alcoholic beverages, sleeping medications, other sedatives, or antihistamines. It may be dangerous to take nortriptyline in combination with these substances.

Nortriptyline may increase the possibility of having **seizures**. Patients should tell their physician if they have a history of seizures, including seizures brought on by the abuse of drugs or alcohol. These people should use nortriptyline only with caution and be closely monitored by their physician. Nortriptyline can also cause ringing in the ears, tingling in the extremities, and numbness in the extremities, although none of these side effects are common when the drug is used as directed.

When used by people with **schizophrenia**, nortriptyline may worsen psychotic, increase hostility in some patients, or activate other symptoms that had not previously been expressed. When used by people with **bipolar disorder** (manic-depressive illness), symptoms of mania may be magnified. Patients with a history of **suicide** attempts, thoughts of suicide, or drug overdose should be monitored carefully when using nortriptyline. Nortriptyline can either increase or decrease blood sugar levels, depending on the patient and his or her medical condition. Nortriptyline should be used with great caution when a patient is receiving **electroconvulsive therapy**.

Nortriptyline may increase heart rate and cause irregular heartbeat. It may also raise or lower blood pressure. It may be dangerous for people with cardiovascular disease, especially those who have recently had a heart attack, to take this drug or other antidepressants in the same pharmacological class. In rare cases in which patients with cardiovascular disease must receive nortriptyline, they should be monitored closely for cardiac rhythm disturbances and signs of cardiac stress or damage.

Side effects

Nortriptyline shares side effects common to all tricyclic antidepressants. The most frequent of these are dry mouth, constipation, urinary retention, increased heart rate, sedation, irritability, dizziness, and decreased coordination. As with most side effects associated with tricyclic antidepressants, the intensity is highest at the beginning of therapy and tends to decrease with continued use.

Dry mouth, if severe to the point of causing difficulty speaking or swallowing, may be managed by dosage reduction or temporary discontinuation of the drug. Patients may also chew sugarless gum or suck on sugarless candy in order to increase the flow of saliva. Some artificial saliva products may give temporary relief.

Men with prostate enlargement who take nortriptyline may be especially likely to have problems with urinary retention. Symptoms include having difficulty starting a urine flow and more difficulty than usual passing urine. In most cases, urinary retention is managed with dose reduction or by switching to another type of antidepressant.

Problems associated with the skin (loss of sensation, numbness and tingling, rashes, spots, itching and puffiness), seizures and ringing in the ears have also been reported. Nausea, vomiting, loss of appetite, diarrhea and abdominal cramping are associated with nortriptyline usage. Skin rash, sensitivity to sunlight and itching have been linked to nortriptyline use. People who think they may be experiencing any side effects from this or any other medication should talk to their physicians.

Interactions

Dangerously high blood pressure has resulted from the combination of tricyclic antidepressants, such as nortriptyline, and members of another class of antidepressants known as monoamine oxidase (MAO) inhibitors. Because of this, nortriptyline should never be taken in combination with MAO inhibitors. Patient taking any MAO inhibitors, for example Nardil (**phenelzine** sulfate) or Parmate (**tranylcypromine** sulfate), should stop the MAO inhibitor then wait at least 14 days before starting nortriptyline or any other tricyclic antidepressant. The same holds true when discontinuing nortriptyline and starting an MAO inhibitor.

Cimetidine (Tagamet) may slow the elimination of nortriptyline, thus effectively increasing the dosage of nortriptyline. Quinidine also raises the circulating levels of the drug, requiring a decrease in the dosage of nortriptyline.

The sedative effects of nortriptyline are increased by other central nervous system depressants such as alcohol, sedatives, sleeping medications, or medications used for other mental disorders such as schizophrenia. The symptoms of increased heart rate, blurred vision, and difficulty urinating are additive with other drugs such as **benztropine**, **biperiden**, **trihexyphenidyl**, and antihistamines.

See also Neurotransmitters

Resources

BOOKS

Adams, Michael, and Norman Holland. *Core Concepts in Pharmacology.* Philadelphia: Lippincott-Raven, 1998.

Foreman, John C. and Torben Johansen. *Textbook of Receptor Pharmacology.* 2nd ed. Boca Raton, FL: CRC Press, 2002.

Page, Clive P., and Michael Murphy. *Integrated Pharmacology.* St. Louis: Mosby-Year Book, 2002.

Von Boxtel, Chris J., Budiono Santoso, and I. Ralph Edwards. *Drug Benefits and Risks: International Textbook of Clinical Pharmacology.* New York: John Wiley and Sons, 2001.

PERIODICALS

Mulsant B. H., and others. "A twelve-week, double-blind, randomized comparison of nortriptyline and paroxetine in older depressed inpatients and outpatients."*American Journal of Geriatric Psychiatry* 9, no. 4 (2001): 406-414.

Nelson J. C. "Diagnosing and treating depression in the elderly." *Journal of Clinical Psychiatry* 62, Supplement 24 (2001): 18-22.

Stolar A. G., and J. T. Stewart. "Nortriptyline for depression and vulvodynia." *American Journal of Psychiatry* 159, no. 2 (2002): 316-317.

ORGANIZATIONS

American Medical Association. 515 N. State Street, Chicago, IL 60610. Telephone: (312) 464-5000. Web site: <http://www.ama-assn.org/>.

American Psychiatric Association. 1400 K Street NW, Washington, DC 20005. Telephone: (888) 357-7924. Fax (202) 682-6850. Web site: <http://www.psych.org/>.

American Society for Clinical Pharmacology and Therapeutics. 528 North Washington Street, Alexandria, VA 22314. Telephone: (703) 836-6981. Fax: (703) 836-5223.

American Society for Pharmacology and Experimental Therapeutics. 9650 Rockville Pike, Bethesda, MD 20814-3995. Telephone: (301) 530-7060. Fax: (301) 530-7061. Web site: <http://www.aspet.org/>.

L. Fleming Fallon, Jr., M.D., Dr.P.H.

Nutrition and mental health

Nutrition and the brain

A person's food intake affects mood, behavior, and **brain** function. A hungry person may feel irritable and restless, whereas a person who has just eaten a meal may feel calm and satisfied. A sleepy person may feel more productive after a cup of coffee and a light snack. A person who has consistently eaten less food or energy than needed over a long period of time may be apathetic and moody.

The human brain has high energy and nutrient needs. Changes in energy or nutrient intake can alter both brain chemistry and the functioning of nerves in the brain. Intake of energy and several different nutrients affect levels of chemicals in the brain called **neurotransmitters**. Neurotransmitters transmit nerve impulses from one nerve cell to another, and they influence mood, sleep patterns, and thinking. Deficiencies or excesses of certain vitamins or minerals can damage nerves in the brain, causing changes in memory, limiting problem-solving ability, and impairing brain function.

Several nutritional factors can influence mental health, including: overall energy intake, intake of the energy-containing nutrients (proteins, carbohydrates, and fats), alcohol intake, and intake of vitamins and minerals. Often deficiencies of multiple nutrients rather than a single nutrient are responsible for changes in brain functioning.

In the United States and other developed countries, alcoholism is often responsible for nutritional deficiencies that affect mental functioning. Diseases can also cause nutritional deficiencies by affecting absorption of nutrients into the body or increasing nutritional requirements. Poverty, ignorance, and fad **diets** also contribute to nutritional deficiencies.

Energy intake and mental health

Energy, often referred to as the calorie content of a food, is derived from the carbohydrate, protein, fat, and alcohol found in foods and beverages. Although vitamins and minerals are essential to the body, they provide no energy. The human brain is metabolically very active and uses about 20 to 30% of a person's energy intake at rest. Individuals who do not eat adequate calories from food to meet their energy requirements will experience changes in mental functioning. Simply skipping breakfast is associated with lower fluency and problem-solving ability, especially in individuals who are already slightly malnourished. A hungry person may also experience lack of energy or motivation.

Chronic hunger and energy deprivation profoundly affects mood and responsiveness. The body responds to energy deprivation by shutting or slowing down nonessential functions, altering activity levels, hormonal levels, oxygen and nutrient transport, the body's ability to fight infection, and many other bodily functions that directly or indirectly affect brain function. People with a consistently low energy intake often feel apathetic, sad, or hopeless.

Developing fetuses and young infants are particularly susceptible to brain damage from malnutrition. The extent of the damage depends on the timing of the energy deprivation in relation to stage of development. Malnutrition early in life has been associated with below-normal intelligence, and functional and cognitive defects.

Carbohydrates and mental health

Carbohydrates include starches, naturally occurring and refined sugars, and dietary fiber. Foods rich in starches and dietary fiber include grain products like breads, rice, pasta and cereals, especially whole-grain products; fruits; and vegetables, especially starchy vegetables like potatoes. Foods rich in refined sugars include cakes, cookies, desserts, candy, and soft drinks.

Carbohydrates significantly affect mood and behavior. Eating a meal high in carbohydrates triggers release of a hormone called insulin in the body. Insulin helps let blood sugar into cells where it can be used for energy, but insulin also has other effects in the body. As insulin levels rise, more tryptophan enters the brain. Tryptophan is an amino acid, or a building block of protein, that affects levels of neurotransmitters in the brain. As more tryptophan enters the brain, more of the neurotransmitter serotonin is produced. Higher serotonin levels in the brain enhance mood and have a sedating effect, promoting sleepiness. This effect is partly responsible for the drowsiness some people experience after a large meal.

Some researchers claim that a high sugar intake causes hyperactivity in children. Although carefully controlled studies do not support this conclusion, high sugar intake is associated with dental problems. Further, foods high in refined sugars are often low in other nutrients, making it prudent to limit their use.

Proteins and mental health

Proteins are made up of amino acids linked together in various sequences and amounts. The human body can manufacture some of the amino acids, but there are eight essential amino acids that must be supplied in the diet. A complete or high-quality protein contains all eight of the essential amino acids in the amounts needed by the body. Foods rich in high-quality protein include meats, milk and other dairy products, and eggs. Dried beans and peas, grains, and nuts and seeds also contain protein, although the protein in these plant foods may be low in one or more essential amino acid. Generally, combining any two types of plant protein foods together will yield a complete, high-quality protein. For example, a peanut butter and jelly sandwich combines grain protein from the bread with nut protein from the peanut butter to yield a complete protein. A bean-rice hot dish combines bean and grain protein for another complete protein combination.

Protein intake and intake of individual amino acids can affect brain functioning and mental health. Many of the neurotransmitters in the brain are made from amino acids. The neurotransmitter dopamine is made from the amino acid tyrosine. The neurotransmitter serotonin is made from the amino acid tryptophan. If the needed amino acid is not available, levels of that particular neurotransmitter in the brain will fall, and brain functioning and mood will be affected. For example, if there is a lack of tryptophan in the body, not enough serotonin will be produced, and low brain levels of serotonin are associated with low mood and even aggression in some individuals. Likewise, some diseases can cause a buildup of certain amino acids in the blood, leading to brain damage and mental defects. For example, a buildup of the amino acid phenylalanine in individuals with a disease called pheylketonuria can cause brain damage and **mental retardation**.

KEY TERMS

Amino acid—A building block of protein.

Anemia—Condition that results when there is a deficiency of oxygen in the blood. Can cause fatigue and impair mental functions.

Antioxidant—Substance that protects the body from damaging reactive oxygen molecules in the body. These reactive oxygen molecules can come from inside the body or from environmental pollution and are thought to play a role in the aging process and the development of degenerative disease.

Atherosclerosis—Clogging of the arteries, creating a risk factor for stroke.

Homocysteine—A chemical that builds up in the blood when methionine is not properly processed. High blood levels of homocysteine increase risk of heart disease and stroke.

Methionine—An amino acid that, when not metabolized properly, allows homocysteine to build up in the blood. Folic acid aids methionine metabolism.

Neurotransmitter—A chemical in the brain that transmits messages between neurons, or nerve cells.

Phenylketonuria—(PKU) An inherited disease in which the body cannot metabolize the amino acid phenylalanine properly. If untreated, phenylketonuria can cause mental retardation.

Serotonin—A widely distributed neurotransmitter that is found in blood platelets, the lining of the digestive tract, and the brain, and that works in combination with norepinephrine. It causes very powerful contractions of smooth muscle, and is associated with mood, attention, emotions, and sleep. Low levels of serotonin are associated with depression.

Trace mineral—An element essential to nutrition or bodily processes that is found in minute quantities.

Tryptophan—An essential amino acid released from proteins during the process of digestion. Tryptophan is an important ingredient in the body's production of serotonin.

Fats and mental health

Dietary intake of fats may also play a role in regulating mood and brain function. Dietary fats are found in both animal and plant foods. Meats, regular-fat dairy products, butter, margarine, and plant oils are high in fats.

Although numerous studies clearly document the benefits of a cholesterol-lowering diet for the reduction of heart disease risk, some studies suggest that reducing fat and cholesterol in the diet may deplete brain serotonin levels, causing mood changes, anger, and aggressive behavior.

Other studies have looked at the effects of a particular kind of fat, the omega-3 fatty acids found in fish oils, and brain functioning. Although a few studies suggest omega-3 fatty acids are helpful with bipolar affective disorder and **stress**, results are inconclusive.

High levels of fat and cholesterol in the diet contribute to atherosclerosis, or clogging of the arteries. Atherosclerosis can decrease blood flow to the brain, impairing brain functioning. If blood flow to the brain is blocked, a **stroke** occurs.

Alcohol and mental health

A high alcohol intake can interfere with normal sleep patterns, and thus can affect mood. Alcoholism is one of the most common causes of nutritional deficiencies in developed countries. Alcoholic beverages provide energy but virtually no vitamins or minerals. A person who consumes large amounts of alcohol will meet their energy needs but not their vitamin and mineral needs. In addition, extra amounts of certain vitamins are needed to break down alcohol in the body, further contributing to nutrient deficiencies.

Vitamins and mental health

Thiamin

Thiamin is a B vitamin found in enriched grain products, pork, legumes, nuts, seeds, and organ meats. Thiamin is intricately involved with metabolizing glucose, or blood sugar, in the body. Glucose is the brain's primary energy source. Thiamin is also needed to make several neurotransmitters.

Alcoholism is often associated with thiamin deficiency. Alcohol interferes with thiamin metabolism in the body, and diets high in alcohol are often deficient in vitamins and minerals. Individuals with a thiamin deficiency can develop **Wernicke-Korsakoff syndrome**, which is characterized by confusion, mental changes, abnormal eye movements, and unsteadiness that can progress to severe memory loss.

Vitamin B-12

Vitamin B-12 is found only in foods of animal origin like milk, meat, or eggs. Strict vegans who consume no animal-based foods need to supplement their diet with vitamin B-12 to meet the body's need for this nutrient.

Vitamin B-12 is needed to maintain the outer coating, called the myelin sheath, on nerve cells. Inadequate myelin results in nerve damage and impaired brain function. Vitamin B-12 deficiency can go undetected in individuals for years, but it eventually causes low blood iron, irreversible nerve damage, **dementia**, and brain atrophy.

Folic acid

Folic acid is another B vitamin found in foods such as liver, yeast, asparagus, fried beans and peas, wheat, broccoli, and some nuts. Many grain products are also fortified with folic acid. In the United States, alcoholism is a common cause of folic acid deficiency.

Folic acid is involved in protein metabolism in the body and in the metabolism of some amino acids, particularly the amino acid methionine. When folic acid levels in the body are low, methionine cannot be metabolized properly and levels of another chemical, homocysteine, build up in the blood. High blood homocysteine levels increase risk of heart disease and stroke.

Even modest folic acid deficiency in women causes an increased risk of neural tube defects, such as spina bifida, in developing fetuses. Folic acid deficiency also increases risk of stroke. Some studies suggest that folic acid deficiency leads to a range of mental disorders, including depression, but this concept remains controversial. Folic acid deficiency can lower levels of serotonin in the brain.

Niacin

The B vitamin niacin is found in enriched grains, meat, fish, wheat bran, asparagus, and peanuts. The body can also make niacin from the essential amino acid tryptophan, which is found in high-quality animal protein foods like meat and milk. Niacin deficiency used to be common in the southern United States but is now common only in developing countries such as India and China.

Niacin is involved in releasing energy in the body from carbohydrates, proteins, and fats. A deficiency of niacin produces many mental symptoms such as irritability, headaches, loss of memory, inability to sleep, and emotional instability. Severe niacin deficiency progresses to a condition called pellagra, which is characterized by the four D's: dermatitis (a rash resembling a sunburn), diarrhea, dementia, and ultimately, death. The mental

ESSENTIAL VITAMINS	
Vitamin	***What It Does For The Body***
Vitamin A (Beta Carotene)	Promotes growth and repair of body tissues; reduces susceptibility to infections; aids in bone and teeth formation; maintains smooth skin
Vitamin B-1 (Thiamin)	Promotes growth and muscle tone; aids in the proper functioning of the muscles, heart, and nervous system; assists in digestion of carbohydrates
Vitamin B-2 (Riboflavin)	Maintains good vision and healthy skin, hair, and nails; assists in formation of antibodies and red blood cells; aids in carbohydrate, fat, and protein metabolism
Vitamin B-3 (Niacinamide)	Reduces cholesterol levels in the blood; maintains healthy skin, tongue, and digestive system; improves blood circulation; increases energy
Vitamin B-5	Fortifies white blood cells; helps the body's resistance to stress; builds cells
Vitamin B-6 (Pyridoxine)	Aids in the synthesis and breakdown of amino acids and the metabolism of fats and carbohydrates; supports the central nervous system; maintains healthy skin
Vitamin B-12 (Cobalamin)	Promotes growth in children; prevents anemia by regenerating red blood cells; aids in the metabolism of carbohydrates, fats, and proteins; maintains healthy nervous system
Biotin	Aids in the metabolism of proteins and fats; promotes healthy skin
Choline	Helps the liver eliminate toxins
Folic Acid (Folate, Folacin)	Promotes the growth and reproduction of body cells; aids in the formation of red blood cells and bone marrow
Vitamin C (Ascorbic Acid)	One of the major antioxidants; essential for healthy teeth, gums, and bones; helps to heal wounds, fractures, and scar tissue; builds resistance to infections; assists in the prevention and treatment of the common cold; prevents scurvy
Vitamin D	Improves the absorption of calcium and phosphorous (essential in the formation of healthy bones and teeth) maintains nervous system
Vitamin E	A major antioxidant; supplies oxygen to blood; provides nourishment to cells; prevents blood clots; slows cellular aging
Vitamin K (Menadione)	Prevents internal bleeding; reduces heavy menstrual flow

Essential vitamins and their effects. *(Stanley Publishing.)*

symptoms in pellagra can progress to **psychosis**, **delirium**, coma, and death.

Vitamin B-6

Vitamin B-6, also known as pyridoxine, is found in many plant and animal foods, including chicken, fish, pork, whole wheat products, brown rice, and some fruits and vegetables. In healthy individuals, deficiency of vitamin B-6 is rare, but certain drugs, including some antidepressant drugs, can induce vitamin B-6 deficiency.

Vitamin B-6 is needed by the body to produce most of the brain's neurotransmitters. It is also involved in hormone production. Although rare, vitamin B-6 deficiency is characterized by mental changes such as **fatigue**, nervousness, irritability, depression, **insomnia**, dizziness, and nerve changes. These mental changes are related to the body's decreased ability to manufacture neurotransmitters with vitamin B-6 deficiency.

Just as vitamin B-6 deficiency causes mental changes, so does excess of vitamin B-6. Vitamin B-6 supplements are used by many individuals for a variety of conditions, including carpal tunnel syndrome, premenstrual syndrome, and fibrocystic breast disease. Doses of 500 mg per day or more can cause nerve damage, dizziness, sensory loss, and numbness.

Vitamin E

Vitamin E is a fat-soluble vitamin that is plentiful in the diet, particularly in plant oils, green leafy vegetables, and fortified breakfast cereals. Vitamin E deficiency is very rare, except in disorders that impair absorption of fat-soluble vitamins into the body, such as cystic fibrosis, and liver diseases.

Vitamin E deficiency causes changes in red blood cells and nerve tissues. It progresses to dizziness, vision changes, muscle weakness, and sensory changes. If left untreated, the nerve damage from vitamin E deficiency can be irreversible. Because it is an antioxidant, vitamin E has also been studied for treatment of neurological conditions such as Parkinson's and **Alzheimer's disease**. Although results are inconclusive, vitamin E shows some promise in slowing the progression of Parkinson's disease.

Vitamin A

Vitamin A is a fat-soluble vitamin found in meats, fish and eggs. A form of vitamin A, beta-carotene, is found in orange and green leafy vegetables such as carrots, yellow squash, and spinach. Headache and increased pressure in the head is associated with both deficient and excess vitamin A intake. Among other effects, excess vitamin A intake can cause fatigue, irritability, and loss of appetite. Generally, doses must exceed 25,000 international units of vitamin A over several months to develop such symptoms.

Minerals and mental health

Iron

Iron is a trace mineral that is essential for formation of hemoglobin, the substance that carries oxygen to cells throughout the body. Iron is found in meat, poultry, and fish. Another form of iron that is not as well absorbed as the form in animal foods is found in whole or enriched grains, green leafy vegetables, dried beans and peas, and dried fruits. Consuming a food rich in vitamin C, such as orange juice, at the same time as an iron-containing plant food will enhance iron absorption from the food.

Iron deficiency eventually leads to anemia, with insufficient oxygen reaching the brain. The anemia can cause fatigue and impair mental functioning. Iron deficiency during the first two years of life can lead to permanent brain damage.

Magnesium

The mineral magnesium is found in green leafy vegetables, whole grains, nuts, seeds, and bananas. In areas with hard water, the water may provide a significant amount of magnesium. In addition to its involvement in bone structure, magnesium aids in the transmission of nerve impulses.

Magnesium deficiency can cause restlessness, nervousness, muscular twitching, and unsteadiness. Acute magnesium deficiency can progress to **apathy**, delirium, convulsions, coma, and death.

Manganese

Manganese is a trace mineral found in whole grains and nuts, and to a lesser extent, fruits and vegetables. Manganese is involved in carbohydrate metabolism and brain functioning. Although very rare, manganese deficiency can cause abnormalities in brain function. Miners of manganese in South America have developed manganese toxicity called manganese madness, with neurological symptoms similar to Parkinson's disease.

Copper

The richest sources of the trace mineral copper in the diet are organ meats, seafood, nuts, seeds, whole grain breads and cereals, and chocolate. In addition to other functions, copper is involved in iron metabolism in the body and in brain function. Deficiency of copper causes anemia, with inadequate oxygen delivery to the brain and other organs. Copper deficiency also impairs brain functioning and immune system response, including changes in certain chemical receptors in the brain and lowered levels of neurotransmitters.

Zinc

The trace mineral zinc is found in red meats, liver, eggs, dairy products, vegetables, and some seafoods. Among other functions, zinc is involved in maintaining cell membranes and protecting cells from damage. Zinc deficiency can cause neurological impairment, influencing appetite, taste, smell, and vision. It has also been associated with apathy, irritability, jitteriness, and fatigue.

Selenium

Good sources of the trace mineral selenium include seafood, liver, and eggs. Grains and seeds can also be good sources of selenium depending on the selenium content of the soil they are grown in. Selenium is needed for the synthesis of some hormones and helps protect cell membranes from damage.

Although selenium deficiency is very rare, selenium toxicity has occurred in regions of the world with high selenium soil content, such as China. Selenium toxicity causes nervous system changes, fatigue, and irritability.

See also Diets; Nutrition counseling

Resources

BOOKS

Jeffery, Douglas R., M.D., Ph.D. "Nutrition and Diseases of the Nervous System." In *Modern Nutrition in Health and Disease.* 9th edition. Edited by Maurice E. Shils, M.D., Sc.D., James A. Olson, Ph.D., Moshe Shike, M.D., and A. Catharine Ross, Ph.D. Baltimore: Williams and Wilkins, 1999.

Katz, David L., M.D., M.P.H. *Nutrition in Clinical Practice.* New York: Lippincott, Williams, and Wilkins, 2001.

Shiveley, LeeAnn R., M.P.H, R.D. and Patrick J. Connolly, M.D. "Medical Nutrition Therapy for Neurologic Disorders." In *Krause's Food, Nutrition, & Diet Therapy.* 10th edition. Edited by L. Kathleen Mahan, M.S., R.D., C.D.E., and Sylvia Escott-Stump, M.A., R.D., L.D.N. New York: W. B. Saunders Company, 2000.

Westermarck T., M.D., D.Sc. and E. Antila, M.D., Ph.D. "Diet in Relation to the Nervous System." In *Human Nutrition and Dietetics.* 10th edition. Edited by J. S. Garrow, M.D., Ph.D., W. P. T. James, M.D., S.Sc., and A. Ralph, Ph.D. New York: Churchill Livingstone, 2000.

PERIODICALS

Young, Simon N. "Clinical Nutrition: 3. The Fuzzy Boundary Between Nutrition and Psychopharmacology." *Canadian Medical Association Journal* 166 (2002): 205-209.

ORGANIZATIONS

American Dietetic Association. 216 West Jackson Boulevard, Chicago, Illinois, 60606-6995.<http://www.eatright.org>.

Nancy Gustafson, M.S., R.D., F.A.D.A., E.L.S.

Nutrition counseling

Definition

Nutrition counseling is an ongoing process in which a health professional, usually a registered dietitian, works with an individual to assess his or her usual dietary intake and identify areas where change is needed. The nutrition counselor provides information, educational materials, support, and follow-up to help the individual make and maintain the needed dietary changes.

KEY TERMS

Body mass index, or BMI—A measure of body fat, calculated as weight in kilograms over the square of height in meters.

Food frequency questionnaire—A listing of how often a person consumes foods from certain food groups in a given period of time.

Registered dietitian—A person who has met certain education and experience standards and is well-qualified to provide nutrition counseling.

Twenty-four-hour recall—A listing of the type and amount of all foods and beverages consumed by a person in a 24-hour period.

Purpose

The goal of nutrition counseling is to help a person make and maintain dietary changes. For a person with a mental disorder, dietary change may be needed to promote healthier eating, to adopt a therapeutic diet, or to avoid nutrient-drug interactions. Nutrition counseling is an integral part of treatment for persons with eating disorders or chemical dependencies. Persons taking certain drugs, such as monoamine oxidase inhibitors, used to treat depression and anxiety disorders, need to follow a tyramine-controlled diet to avoid dietary interference with their medication. Many drugs used to treat mental disorders can cause weight gain or loss, so persons taking these medications may also benefit from nutrition counseling.

The nutrition counselor and individual work together to assess current eating patterns and identify areas where change is needed. Registered dietitians have met certain education and experience standards and are well qualified to provide nutrition counseling, but nurses, physicians, and health educators also provide nutrition counseling.

Description

Assessing dietary habits

Nutrition counseling usually begins with an interview in which the counselor asks questions about a person's typical food intake. Nutrition counselors use different methods to assess typical food intake.

The 24-hour recall method is a listing of all the foods and beverages a person consumed within the previous 24-hour period. The nutrition counselor may ask a person to recall the first thing he or she ate or drank the previous morning. The counselor then records the estimated amounts of all the foods and beverages the person consumed the rest of the day. The 24-hour food recall can be used to provide an estimate of energy and nutrient intake. However, people tend to over- or underestimate intake of certain foods, and food intake on one day may not accurately represent typical food intake.

A food frequency questionnaire can sometimes provide a more accurate picture of a person's typical eating patterns. The nutrition counselor may ask the client how often he or she consumes certain food groups. For example, the counselor may ask a person how many servings of dairy products, fruits, vegetables, grains and cereals, meats, or fats he or she consumes in a typical day, week, or month.

Daily food records are also useful in assessing food intake. An individual keeps a written record of the amounts of all foods and beverages consumed over a given period of time. The nutrition counselor can then use the food records to analyze actual energy and nutrient intake. Three-day food records kept over two weekdays and one weekend day are often used.

Assessing body weight

Nutrition counselors may assess an individual's body weight by comparing his or her weight to various weight-for-height tables. A rough rule of thumb for determining a woman's ideal body weight is to allow 100 lb (45 kg) for the first 5 ft (1.5 m) of height plus 5 lb (2.3 kg) for every additional inch. A man is allowed 106 lb (48 kg) for the first 5 ft (1.5 m) of height plus 6 lb (2.7 kg) for every additional inch. However, this guide does not take into account a person's frame size.

Body mass index, or BMI, is another indicator used to assess body weight. BMI is calculated as weight in kilograms divided by height in meters squared. A BMI of 20 to 25 is considered normal weight, a BMI of less than 20 is considered underweight, and a BMI of greater than 25 is considered overweight.

Identifying changes needed

The initial dietary assessment and interview provide the basis for identifying behaviors that need to be changed. Sometimes a person already has a good idea of what dietary changes are needed, but may require help making the changes. Other times the nutrition counselor can help educate a person on the health effects of different dietary choices. The nutrition counselor and client work together to identify areas where change is needed, prioritize changes, and problem-solve as to how to make the changes.

Making dietary change is a gradual process. An individual may start with one or two easier dietary changes the first few weeks and gradually make additional or more difficult changes over several weeks or months. For example, an easy change for a person might be switching from 2% to skim milk, or taking time for a quick yogurt or granola bar in the morning instead of skipping breakfast. More difficult changes might be learning to replace high-fat meat choices with leaner ones, or including more servings of vegetables daily.

In making dietary changes, each individual's situation and background must be carefully considered. Factors that affect food decisions include an individual's ethnic background, religion, group affiliation, socioeconomic status, and world view.

Identifying barriers to change

Once the needed changes have been identified, the client and nutrition counselor think through potential problems that may arise. For example, changing eating behaviors may mean involving others, purchasing different foods, planning ahead for social events, or bringing special foods to work. Some common barriers to changing eating habits include:

- inconvenience
- social gatherings
- food preferences
- lack of knowledge or time
- cost

Setting goals

The nutrition counselor and client set behavior-oriented goals together. Goals should focus on the behaviors needed to achieve the desired dietary change, not on an absolute value, such as achieving a certain body weight. For a person working to prevent weight gain associated with certain medications, for example, his or her goals might be to increase the amount of fruits, vegetables, and whole grains consumed each day. Such changes would help prevent weight gain while placing the emphasis on needed behaviors rather than on actual weight.

Finding support

Family members are encouraged to attend nutrition counseling sessions with the client, especially if they share responsibility for food selection and preparation. Although the individual must make food choices and take responsibility for dietary changes, having the support and understanding of family and friends makes success more likely.

Maintaining changes

The challenge for the nutrition client lies not in making the initial dietary changes, but in maintaining them over the long term. Self-monitoring, realistic expectations, and continued follow-up can help a person maintain dietary changes.

Self-monitoring involves regularly checking eating habits against desired goals and keeping track of eating behaviors. Keeping a food diary on a daily or periodic basis helps the individual be more aware of his or her eating behaviors and provides a ready tool to analyze eating habits. Sometimes a simplified checklist to assure adequate intake of different food groups may be used.

Individuals and nutrition counselors should not expect perfect dietary compliance—slips inevitably occur. The goal is to keep small slips, such as eating a few extra cookies, from becoming big slips, like total abandonment of dietary change. The counselor can help the client identify situations that may lead to relapse and plan ways to handle the situations ahead of time.

Nutrition counseling is an ongoing process that can take months or years. In follow-up nutrition counseling sessions, the individual and counselor analyze food records together and problem-solve behaviors that are especially difficult to change. Follow-up counseling also allows the opportunity to reevaluate goals and strategies for achieving those goals.

See also Diets; Nutrition and mental health

Resources

BOOKS

American Dietetic Association and Dietitians of Canada. *Manual of Clinical Dietetics.* 6th edition. Chicago, Illinois: American Dietetic Association, 2000.

Hammond, Kathleen A., M.S., R.D. "Dietary and Clinical Assessment." In *Krause's Food Nutrition, and Diet Therapy,* written by L. Kathleen Mahan, M.S., R.D. and Sylvia Escott-Stump, M.A., R.D. Philadelphia: W.B. Saunders Company, 2000.

Mitchell, Mary Kay, Ph.D. *Nutrition Across the Life Span.* Philadelphia: W. B. Saunders Company, 1997.

Scarlet, Sue. "Dietary Counseling."In *Essentials of Human Nutrition.* Written by Jim Mann, Ph.D. and A. Stewart Truswell, Ph.D. Oxford: Oxford University Press, 1998.

PERIODICALS

Harris-Davis, E., and B. Haughton. "Model for Multicultural Nutrition Counseling Competencies." *Journal of the American Dietetic Association* 100 (2000):1178-85.

ORGANIZATIONS

American Dietetic Association. 216 West Jackson Boulevard, Chicago, IL 60606-6995. <http://www.eatright.org>.

Nancy Gustafson, M.S., R.D., F.A.D.A., E.L.S.

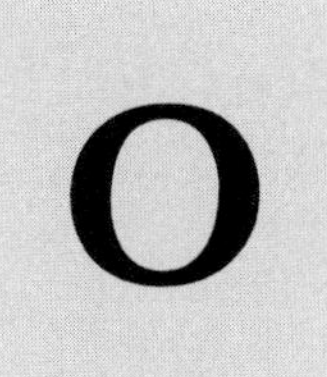

Obesity

Definition

Obesity is the condition of having an excessive accumulation of fat in the body, resulting in a body weight more than 20% above the average for height, age, sex, and body type, and in elevated risk of disability, illness, and death.

Description

The human body is composed of bone, muscle, specialized organ tissues, and fat. Together, all of these tissues comprise the total body mass, which is measured in pounds. Fat, or adipose tissue, is a combination of essential fat (an energy source for the normal physiologic function of cells and organs) and storage fat (a reserve supply of energy for future needs). When the amount of energy consumed as food exceeds the amount of energy expended in the normal maintenance of life processes and in physical activity, storage fat accumulates in excessive amounts. Essential fat is tucked in and around internal organs, and is an important building block of all cells in the body. Storage fat accumulates in the chest and abdomen, and, in much greater volume, under the skin.

Causes and symptoms

The human body was designed for life forty thousand years ago, when the ability to store energy in times of plenty meant the difference between life and death during famine. This protective mechanism is a source of trouble when food, in unlimited quantities, is readily available,. This is evident in the increasing prevalence of obesity in modern times, particularly in Western cultures. While obesity is just an exaggeration of a normal body, the storage of energy for future is properly classified as a health problem. This is because excessive amounts of storage fat may interfere with the normal physiology of the body. Obesity is directly related to the increasing prevalence of Type II diabetes in American society and for the appearance of Type II diabetes in children, previously a rarity. Because obesity promotes degenerative disease of joints and heart and blood vessels, it increases the need for some surgical procedures. At the same time, surgical complication rates are higher in obese patients. Obesity contributes to **fatigue**, high blood pressure, menstrual disorders, infertility, digestive complaints, low levels of physical fitness, and to the development of some cancers. The social costs of obesity that include decreased productivity, discrimination, depression, and low self-esteem, are less easily described and measured. Worldwide, obesity has reached epidemic proportions in the last thirty years, affecting both sexes and all ethnic, age, and socioeconomic groups. More than 50% of adults in the United States currently fall into overweight or obese classifications, and 22% of preschool children are classified as overweight. The increasing prevalence of obesity and diabetes in children and young adults heralds spiraling health care costs in the near future.

Because obesity reflects an imbalance between the amount of energy taken into the body in the form of food and the amount of energy expended in metabolism and physical activity, and because eating is an activity that involves choice and volition, obesity is classified by the Health Care Financing Administration (HCFA) as a "behavior" rather than as a disease. In recent years, following a pattern established in other behavioral problems such as alcoholism, researchers have attempted to establish a biologic basis for the development of obesity. They have succeeded in identifying many markers of the biochemical mechanisms that appear to be involved in feedback loops that control energy balance. However, much of the information is extrapolated from experimental work in rodents. Leptin, a hormone produced in fat cells is an example of such a marker. Leptin excited a great deal of hope as a potential treatment of obesity, but, as with many other laboratory discoveries, the hormone has proved far more complex and less easily understood in humans. Research to date indicates that

KEY TERMS

Behavior—A stereotyped motor response to an internal or external stimulus.

Biochemical—Chemical reactions occurring in living systems.

Body mass—The quantity of matter in the body (measured by dividing weight by acceleration due to gravity).

Calorie—The quantity of heat necessary to raise the temperature of 1kg of water 1°C.

Energy—The capability of producing force, performing work, or generating heat.

Feedback loops—Chains of biochemical reactions in which the products of reactions limit or enhance the subsequent reactions, and in which the chain ends up back at the first reaction, either limiting or enhancing it.

Genetic pool—The genetic material of an entire population.

Ideal weight—A range of body weights recommended for generally healthy adults.

Physiology—The branch of medicine concerned with biological processes or functions in the human body or any of its parts.

Prevalence—Occurence in a population.

Type II diabetes—Resistance to the effects of insulin in the presence of normal or elevated insulin levels, resulting in failure of glucose to enter cells and in a cascade of other abnormal physiologic reactions.

obesity is the end product of numerous contributing factors, including genetics, hormonal influences, behavioral tendencies, medication effects, and the surrounding society. But the rapid and widespread increase in obesity in the last thirty years reflects changes in activity patterns and in eating habits, not a change in the human genetic pool or in physiology.

Diagnosis

There are two methods of diagnosing obesity. The first method is inspection—whereby an excessive amount of storage fat is usually noticeable upon visual inspection. The second method is inference of body fat content, obtained from body measurements such as weight or skinfold thickness, and comparison with charts of similar measurements in broad populations. The determination of obesity is based on the amount of variance from "normal," a value that comes from statistics on death rates in people with similar measurements. Calculations such as the body mass index (BMI) use a height-weight relationship to calculate an individual's ideal weight and personal risk of developing obesity-related health problems. An individual with a BMI of 25.9–29, for example, is considered overweight; a person with a BMI over 30 is classified as obese.

The problem with using weight as a measure of obesity is the fact that weight does not accurately represent body composition. A heavily-muscled football player may weigh far more than a sedentary man of similar height, but have significantly less body fat. Chronic dieters, who have lost significant muscle mass during periods of caloric deprivation, may look slim and weigh little, but have elevated body fat percentages. The most accurate means of estimating body fat content involves weighing a person two ways: First, the person is weighed under water. The difference between dry and underwater weight is calculated to obtain the volume of water displaced by the mass of the body. While this method is impractical, it has the advantage of determining body composition most accurately, and is the truest reflection of the actual percentage of body mass that is fat. Women whose body fat exceeds 30% of total body mass and men whose body fat exceeds 25% are generally considered obese.

The pattern of fat distribution on the body may indicate whether an individual has a predisposition to develop certain diseases or conditions that may accompany obesity. "Apple-shaped" individuals who store most of their weight around the waist and abdomen are at greater risk for cancer, heart disease, **stroke**, and diabetes than "pear-shaped" people, whose extra pounds settle primarily on their hips and thighs.

Treatment

Since obesity develops when intake of the food required to produce energy exceeds the amount of energy used in metabolism and in physical activity, the treatment of obesity must alter one or both aspects of the energy stream. The options are to decrease energy intake or to increase energy output, or both. However, the problem does not yield rapidly to either method. Storage fat is meant to protect its bearer from starvation when food is unavailable, and before fat is tapped for energy. In the face of decreased intake of food, the body breaks down muscle to construct the sugar it needs to feed the **brain**. Much of the early weight loss on a very low calorie diet represents loss of muscle tissue rather than loss of fat. Similarly, fat

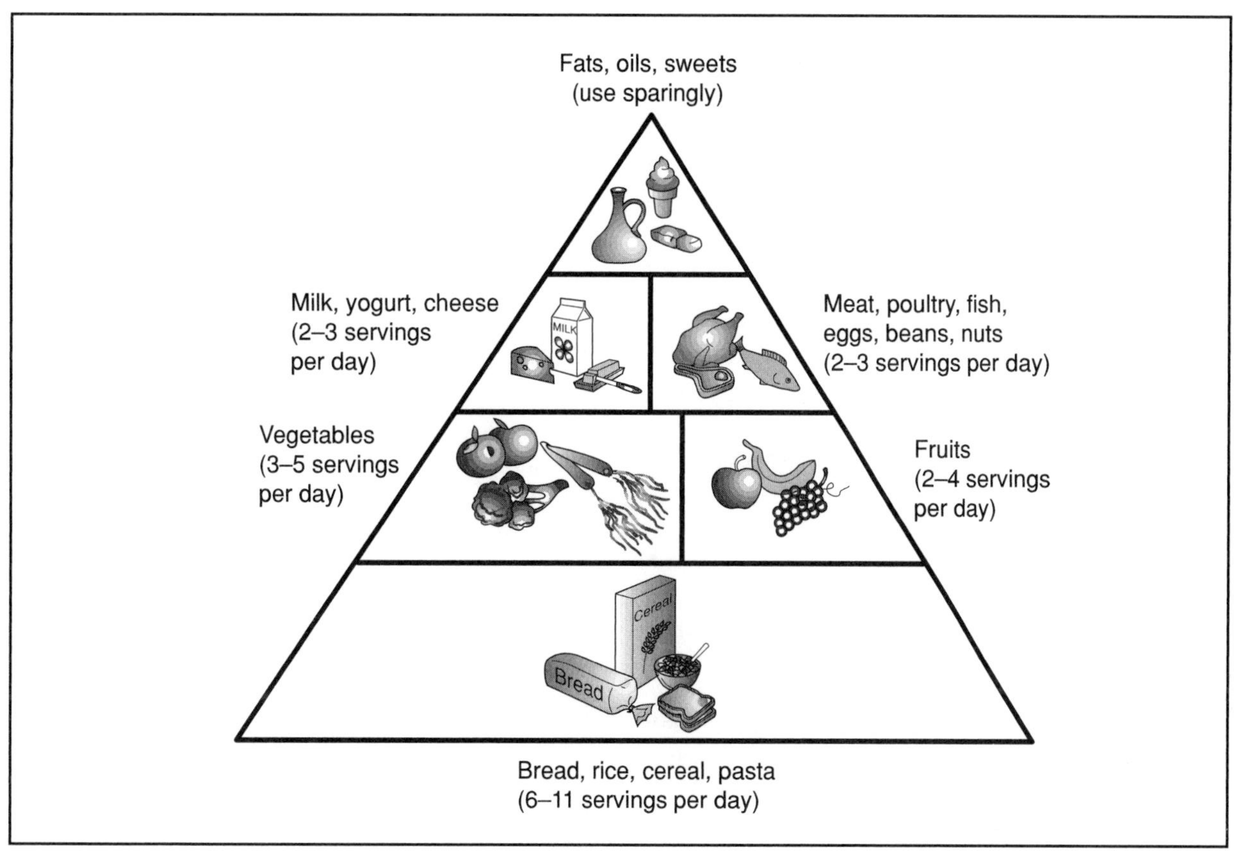

Suggested daily food servings. *(Illustration by Electronic Illustrators Group.)*

is not easy to access as fuel for exercise. A person of normal weight (according to one of the charts as described above) has enough body fat to fuel the muscles for days of continuous running, but will collapse long before burning any significant amount fat stored by the body.

When obesity develops in childhood, the total number of fat cells increases (hyperplastic obesity), whereas in adulthood, it is the total amount of fat in each cell that increases (hypertrophic obesity). Decreasing the amount of energy (food) consumed or increasing the amount of energy expended cannot change the number of fat cells already present. These actions can only reduce the amount of fat in each cell, and only if the process is slow and steady—as it was in reverse, when the excess fat accumulated. Prevention, as in so many problems, is far superior to any available treatment of obesity.

The strategy for weight loss in obese patients is first to change behavior; then, it is to decrease the expectation of rapid change. Behavioral treatment is goal-directed, process-oriented, and relies heavily on self-monitoring. Emphasis is on:

- Food intake: The potential energy provided by food is measured in calories, and the capacity of a certain type and amount of food to provide energy is called its caloric content. Keeping a food diary and developing a better understanding of the nutritional value and fat content of foods, changing grocery-shopping habits, paying attention to timing and appearance of meals, and slowing the speed of eating all help to modify food intake.
- Response to food: The body is capable of matching energy intake and output perfectly, but, in obese individuals, food intake is often unrelated from physiologic cues. Eating occurs for many reasons other than hunger. What psychological issues underlie the eating habits? Does **stress** cause **binge eating**? Is food seen as a reward? Recognition of psychological triggers is necessary for the development of alternate coping mechanisms that do not focus on food.
- Time usage: The body is suited for an ancient world in which physical activity was a necessity. In the modern world, physical activity must be a conscious choice. Making activity and exercise an integrated part of everyday life is a key to achieving and maintaining weight loss. Sedentary and overweight individuals have to reclaim slowly the endurance that is natural by managing their time to allow for gradual increases in both programmed and conscious lifestyle activity.

Behavior modification

For most individuals who are mildly obese, behavior modifications entail life-style changes they can make independently if they have access to accurate information and have reached the point of readiness to make a serious commitment to losing weight. A family physician's evaluation is helpful, particularly in regard to exercise capacity and nutritional requirements. Commercial weight-loss programs may be helpful for some mildly obese individuals, but they are of varying quality. A good program emphasizes realistic goals, gradual progress, sensible and balanced eating, and increased physical activity; it is often recommended by physicians. Programs that promise instant weight loss or feature severe restrictions in types and amounts of food are not effective, and, in some cases, can be dangerous.

For individuals who are moderately obese, medically supervised **behavior modification** and weight loss are more likely to be effective than an independent program. A realistic goal is loss of 10% of current weight over a six-month period. While doctors put most moderately obese patients on balanced, low-calorie **diets** (1,200–1,500 calories a day), occasionally they recommend a very low calorie liquid protein diet (400–700 calories), with supplementation of vitamins and minerals, for as long as three months. Professional help with behavior modification is of paramount importance in such cases; without changing eating habits and exercise patterns, weight lost will be regained quickly.

Surgery

For individuals who are morbidly obese, surgery to bypass portions of the stomach and small intestine may at times be the only effective means of producing sustained and significant weight loss. Such obesity surgery, however, can be risky, and it is performed only on patients for whom other strategies have failed and whose obesity seriously threatens health. Liposuction is a purely cosmetic procedure in which a suction device is used to remove fat from beneath the skin, and has no place in the treatment of obesity.

Medications

Most of the current research on obesity is aimed at identifying biochemical pathways that will be amenable to **intervention** with drug treatments. These medications would be specifically tailored to interfere with the energy cycles to facilitate weight loss. As of 2002, there are two major classes of drugs that are approved for the treatment of obesity by the U.S. Food and Drug Administration (FDA). History of the field is littered with drugs that have failed or that have caused serious side effects. Appetite suppressant drugs such as Dexatrim and Meridia (sibutramine) change the amounts of some **neurotransmitters** in the brain. These chemical changes result in decreased appetite, but only in the presence of the drug. Digestive inhibitors such as Orlistat (Xenical) are drugs that interfere with the breakdown and absorption of dietary fat in the intestines; they are, however, poorly tolerated by the person who is obese because the effects of fat malabsorption are unpleasant.

These drugs also interfere with the absorption of some necessary vitamins. Fat substitutes such as Olestra, while technically not drugs, attempt to recreate the pleasant taste that fat adds to food, but create the same negative side effects as digestive inhibitors. Unless an obese individual has also made necessary behavioral changes, excess weight returns quickly when **appetite suppressants** or malabsorptive agents are stopped.

The use of any drug is associated with unwanted side effects, so that the decision to take a drug must come after the potential side effects are weighed against the potential benefits. No drug, current or past, has had such dramatic effects on obesity that it warrants its casual use. While most of the immediate side effects that may occur are reversible, the long-term effects, in many cases, are unknown. Even after a new drug successfully negotiates the stringent FDA approval process, its widespread use over a longer time frame may lead to the side effects that were not initially observable in the test population. Two popular obesity drugs of the early 1990s have already been withdrawn from the market because of unanticipated and severe cardiac problems. Meridia, just released in 1997, is already under scrutiny by a consumer group for its relationship to several deaths. Nevertheless, studies show that when obesity drugs are combined with behavioral changes—and especially with a portion controlled diet—weight loss is significantly greater than in a control group treated with behavior modification alone, at least after six months. It remains to be proved whether drug-assisted weight loss is long lasting.

Alternative treatment

The Chinese herb, ephedra (*Ephedra sinica*), combined with caffeine, exercise, and a low-fat diet, can cause a temporary increase in weight loss, at best. However, ephedra and caffeine are both central nervous system (CNS) stimulants, and the large doses of ephedra required to achieve the weight loss can also cause anxiety, irritability, and **insomnia**. Further, ephedra has been implicated in more serious conditions, such as seizure and stroke. Ephedra should not be used by anyone with a history of diabetes, heart disease, or thyroid problems.

HEIGHT AND WEIGHT GOALS			
Men			
Height	**Small Frame**	**Medium Frame**	**Large Frame**
5'2"	128-134 lbs.	131-141 lbs.	138-150 lbs.
5'3"	130-136	133-143	140-153
5'4"	132-138	135-145	142-153
5'5"	134-140	137-148	144-160
5'6"	136-142	139-151	146-164
5'7"	138-145	142-154	149-168
5'8"	140-148	145-157	152-172
5'9"	142-151	148-160	155-176
5'10"	144-154	151-163	158-180
5'11"	146-157	154-166	161-184
6'0"	149-160	157-170	164-188
6'1"	152-164	160-174	168-192
6'2"	155-168	164-178	172-197
6'3"	158-172	167-182	176-202
6'4"	162-176	171-187	181-207
Women			
Height	**Small Frame**	**Medium Frame**	**Large Frame**
4'10"	102-111 lbs.	109-121 lbs.	118-131 lbs.
4'11"	103-113	111-123	120-134
5'0"	104-115	113-126	112-137
5'1"	106-118	115-129	125-140
5'2"	108-121	118-132	128-143
5'3"	111-124	121-135	131-147
5'4"	114-127	124-141	137-151
5'5"	117-130	127-141	137-155
5'6"	120-133	130-144	140-159
5'7"	123-136	133-147	143-163
5'8"	126-139	136-150	146-167
5'9"	129-142	139-153	149-170
5'10"	132-145	142-156	152-176
5'11"	135-148	145-159	155-176
6'0"	138-151	148-162	158-179

Height and weight goals as determined by the Metropolitan Life Insurance Company. *(Source: Based on the height and weight charts by Heart Screen, Inc. Available at <http://heartscreen.com/hw_info.html>.)*

Diuretic herbs, which increase urine production, can cause short-term weight loss, but cannot help patients achieve lasting weight control. The body responds to heightened urine output by increasing thirst to replace lost fluids, and patients who use diuretics for an extended period of time retain water even in the presence of the diuretic. In moderate doses, psyllium, a mucilaginous herb available in bulk-forming laxatives like Metamucil, absorbs fluid and makes patients feel as if they have eaten enough. Red peppers, mustard, and dandelion are said to generate weight loss by accelerating the metabolic rate. Dandelion also counteracts the desire for sweet foods. Walnuts contain serotonin, the brain chemical that signals satiety.

Acupressure and **acupuncture** can also suppress food cravings. Visualization and **meditation** can create and reinforce a positive self-image that enhances determination to lose weight. By improving physical strength, mental concentration and emotional serenity, **yoga** can provide the same benefits.

The correct balance of the basic food groups is also important, and believed by some experts to enhance the metabolic rate.

Prognosis

As many as 85% of dieters who do not exercise on a regular basis regain their lost weight within two years. In five years, the figure rises to 90%. Repeatedly losing and regaining weight (yo-yo dieting) encourages the body to store fat and may increase a patient's risk of developing heart disease. The primary factor in achieving and maintaining weight loss is a lifelong commitment to regular exercise and sensible eating habits.

Prevention

Obesity experts suggest that a key to preventing excess weight gain is monitoring fat consumption rather than counting calories; in fact, the National Cholesterol Education Program maintains that only 30% of calories should be derived from fat. Only one-third of those calories should come from saturated fats (the kind of fat found in high concentrations in meat, poultry, and dairy products). However, total caloric intake cannot be ignored, since it usually the slow accumulation of excess caloric intake, regardless of its source, that results in obesity. Erring on the side of 25 excess calories a day, a single cookie will result in a five-pound weight gain by the end of a year. Without recognition of the problem, weight balloons up another 45 pounds by the end of 10 years, and the return to normal weight is an arduous process. Because most people eat more than they think they do, keeping a detailed and honest food diary is a useful way to recognize eating habits. Eating three balanced, moderate-portion meals a day—with the main meal at mid-day—is a more effective way to prevent obesity than fasting or crash diets, which convince the body that there is an ongoing famine. After 12 hours without food, the body has depleted its stores of readily available energy, and hunkers down to begin protecting itself for the long term. Metabolic rate starts to slow, and breakdown of muscle tissue for the raw materials needed for energy maintenance begins. Until more food appears, famine mode persists and deepens; when the fast is lifted, the body is in a state of slowed metabolism, has a bit less muscle, and requires less food than before the fast. Exercise increases the metabolic rate by creating muscle, which burns more calories than fat. When regular exercise is combined with consistent, healthful meals, calories continue to burn at an accelerated rate for several hours.

Finally, encouraging healthful habits in children is a key to preventing childhood obesity and the health problems that follow in adulthood.

Resources

BOOKS

Aronne, Louis J. "Obesity and Weight Management." In *Textbook of Primary Care Medicine. 3rd ed.* Edited by John Noble, M.D. St. Louis, MO: Mosby, 2001.

The Editors of Time-Life Books. *The Medical Advisor: The Complete Guide to Alternative & Conventional Treatments.* Alexandria, VA: Time Life, Inc. 1996.

Harris, Dan R., ed. *Diet and Nutrition Sourcebook.* Detroit, MI: Omnigraphics, 1996.

Wilmore, Jack H. and David L. Costill. "Obesity, Diabetes, and Physical Activity." In *Physiology of Sport and Health.* 2nd ed. Champaign, IL: Human Kinetics, 1999.

PERIODICALS

Jensen, Michael D., ed. "Obesity." *Medical Clinics of North America* 84, no.2 (March 2000): 305–518.

Lustig, Robert H. "The Neuroendocrinology of Obesity." *Endocrinology and Metabolism Clinics* 30, no. 3 (September 2001): 765–785.

Patel, Manesh R. and Darren K. McGuire. "Pounds of Prevention." *American Heart Journal* 142, no.3 (September 2001): 388–90.

Rocchini, Albert P. "Childhood Obesity and A Diabetes Epidemic." *New England Journal of Medicine* 346, no. 11 (March 14, 2002): 854–855.

ORGANIZATIONS

American Dietetic Association. 216 West Jackson Blvd., Chicago, IL 60606-6995. <http://www.eatright.org>.

American Obesity Association. 1250 24th St. NW, Washington D.C. 20037. <http://www.obesity.org>.

Shape Up America. 6707 Democracy Blvd., Suite 306, Bethesda, MD 20817. <http://www.shapeup.org/general/index.html>.

Weight-Control Information Network. 1 Win Way, Bethesda, MD 20892-3665. <http://www.niddk.nih.gov/health/nutrit/win.html>.

Elizabeth Reid, M.D.

Obsession

Definition

An obsession is an unwelcome, uncontrollable, and persistent idea, thought, image, or emotion that a person cannot help thinking even though it creates significant distress or anxiety.

Description

Obsessive ideas seem unnatural or alien to those who have them, but are nevertheless recognized as originating from the person's own thoughts—they are not seen as **delusions** sent or controlled by an outside party.

Typical obsessions include fear of contamination as from doorknobs or handshakes, worry about leaving things in their proper order, persistent doubts about one's responsible behavior, scary images involving violent acts, and images of sexual acts. People with obsessions may find themselves acting in compulsive ways in largely futile attempts to relieve the anxiety associated with their persistent, unpleasant thoughts. Others suffering from obsessions may try very hard to control or ignore them. It is important to note that legitimate worries about daily concerns—paying bills, studying for exams, keeping a job, interpersonal relationships—are not obsessions. Although they can occasionally be carried to obsessive lengths, these concerns can change with circumstances and, in most cases be controlled, with planning, effort, and action. Obsessions relate to problems that most people would consider far removed from normal, daily events and concerns.

See also Compulsion; Obsessive-compulsive disorder

Dean A. Haycock, Ph.D.

Obsessive-compulsive disorder

Definition

Obsessive-compulsive disorder (OCD) is currently classified as an anxiety disorder marked by the recurrence of intrusive or disturbing thoughts, impulses, images or ideas (obsessions) accompanied by repeated attempts to suppress these thoughts through the performance of certain irrational and ritualistic behaviors or mental acts (compulsions). The obsessions and compulsions take up large amounts of the patient's time (an hour or longer every day) and usually cause significant emotional distress for the patient and difficulties in his or her relationships with others.

Some researchers have questioned whether OCD really belongs with the other anxiety disorders. They think that it should be grouped with the spectrum of such obsessive-compulsive disorders as Tourette's syndrome, which are known to have biological causes.

OCD should not be confused with **obsessive-compulsive personality disorder** even though the two disorders have similar names. Obsessive-compulsive personality disorder is not characterized by the presence of obsessions and compulsions; rather, it is a lifelong pattern of insistence on control, orderliness, and perfection that begins no later than the early adult years. It is possible, however, for a person to have both disorders.

Description

Obsessive-compulsive disorder is a mental disorder with two components: obsessions, which consist of thoughts, impulses, or mental images; and compulsions, which are repetitive behaviors that the person feels driven to perform in response to the obsessions. In some cases, the **compulsion** may represent a strict rule that the patient must apply rigidly in every situation (tying one's shoes a certain number of times, for example) in order to feel "right." The exact content of obsessions varies from person to person, although certain themes are common. People with OCD experience their disturbing thoughts and images as intrusive and troublesome, but they recognize that their thoughts are products of their own minds. Obsessive thoughts are different from worries about such real-life problems as losing one's job or bad grades in school. In addition, obsessive thoughts are not usually related to any real-life problems.

The most common types of obsessions in persons with OCD in Western countries are:

- fear of contamination (impurity, pollution, badness)
- doubts (worrying about whether one has omitted to do something)
- an intense need to have or put things in a particular order
- aggressive or frightening impulses
- recurrent sexual thoughts or images

It is important to understand that patients diagnosed with OCD do not perform their compulsions for pleasure or satisfaction. A compulsive behavior becomes linked to an obsessional thought because the behavior lowers the level of anxiety produced by the obsession(s).

The most common compulsions in Western countries are:

- washing/cleaning
- counting

KEY TERMS

Basal ganglia—A group of masses of gray matter located in the cerebral hemispheres of the brain that control movement as well as some aspects of emotion and cognition.

Behavioral therapy—An approach to treatment that focuses on extinguishing undesirable behavior and replacing it with desired behavior.

Cognitive-behavioral therapy—An approach to psychotherapy that emphasizes the correction of distorted thinking patterns and changing one's behaviors accordingly.

Compulsion—A strong impulse to perform an act, particularly one that is irrational or contrary to one's will.

Epidemiology—The study of the causes, incidence, transmission, and control of diseases.

Neurotransmitter—A chemical in the brain that transmits messages between neurons, or nerve cells.

Obsession—A persistent image, idea, or desire that dominates a person's thoughts or feelings.

Onset—The point in time at which the symptoms of a disorder first became apparent.

Serotonin—A widely distributed neurotransmitter that is found in blood platelets, the lining of the digestive tract, and the brain, and that works in combination with norepinephrine. It causes very powerful contractions of smooth muscle, and is associated with mood, attention, emotions, and sleep. Low levels of serotonin are associated with depression.

Streptococcus (plural, streptococci)—A type of bacterium that is spherical in shape and occurs in chains or pairs. Some diseases that are caused by streptococci appear to be related to OCD.

Sydenham's chorea—A serious manifestation of actue rheumatic fever that commonly occurs in children ages seven through 14, peaking at age eight. This disease of the central nervous system is characterized by emotional instability, purposeless movements, and muscular weakness. At its peak in the 1950s it occured in nearly 50% of the acute rheumatic fever cases, but by 2002 had subsided to a degree of less than 10% of the acute cases.

Tic—A sudden involuntary behavior that is difficult or impossible for the person to suppress. Tics may be either motor (related to movement) or vocal, and may become more pronounced under stress.

Trichotillomania—A disorder marked by repeated pulling and tugging of one's hair, usually resulting in noticeable hair loss on the scalp or elsewhere on the body.

- hoarding
- checking
- putting objects in a certain order
- repeated "confessing" or asking others for assurance
- repeated actions
- making lists

Although descriptions of patients with OCD have been reported since the fifteenth century in religious and psychiatric literature, the condition was widely assumed to be rare until very recently. Epidemiological research since 1980 has now identified OCD as the fourth most common psychiatric illness, after phobias, substance use disorders, and major depressive disorders. OCD is presently classified as a form of anxiety disorder, but current studies indicate that it results from a combination of psychological, neurobiological, genetic, and environmental causes.

Causes and symptoms

Causes

PSYCHOSOCIAL. In the early part of the century, Sigmund Freud theorized that OCD symptoms were caused by punitive, rigid toilet-training practices that led to internalized conflicts. Other theorists thought that OCD was influenced by such wider cultural attitudes as insistence on cleanliness and neatness, as well as by the attitudes and parenting style of the patient's parents. Cross-cultural studies of OCD indicate that, while the incidence of OCD seems to be about the same in most countries around the world, the symptoms are often shaped by the patient's culture of origin. For example, a patient from a Western country may have a contamination **obsession** that is focused on germs, whereas a patient from India may fear contamination by touching a person from a lower social caste.

Studies of families with OCD members indicate that the particular expression of OCD symptoms may be affected by the responses of other people. Families with a high tolerance for the symptoms are more likely to have members with more extreme or elaborate symptoms. Problems often occur when the OCD member's obsessions and rituals begin to control the entire family.

BIOLOGICAL. There is considerable evidence that OCD has a biological component. Some researchers have noted that OCD is more common in patients who have suffered head trauma or have been diagnosed with Tourette's syndrome. Recent studies using **positron emission tomography** (PET) scanning indicate that OCD patients have patterns of **brain** activity that differ from those of people without mental illness or with some other mental illness. Other studies using **magnetic resonance imaging** (MRI) found that patients diagnosed with OCD had significantly less white matter in their brains than did normal control subjects. This finding suggests that there is a widely distributed brain abnormality in OCD. Some researchers have reported abnormalities in the metabolism of serotonin, an important neurotransmitter, in patients diagnosed with OCD. Serotonin affects the efficiency of communication between the front part of the brain (the cortex) and structures that lie deeper in the brain known as the basal ganglia. Dysfunction in the serotonergic system occurs in certain other mental illnesses, including major depression. OCD appears to have a number of features in common with the so-called obsessive-compulsive spectrum disorders, which include Tourette's syndrome; Sydenham's chorea; eating disorders; **trichotillomania**; and delusional disorders.

There appear to be genetic factors involved in OCD. The families of persons who are diagnosed with the disorder have a greater risk of OCD and **tic disorders** than does the general population. Childhood-onset OCD appears to run in families more than adult-onset OCD, and is more likely to be associated with tic disorders. Twin studies indicate that monozygotic, or identical twins, are more likely to share the disorder than dizygotic, or fraternal twins. The concordance (match) rate between identical twins is not 100%, however, which suggests that the occurrence of OCD is affected by environmental as well as genetic factors. In addition, it is the general nature of OCD that seems to run in families rather than the specific symptoms; thus, one family member who is affected by the disorder may have a compulsion about washing and cleaning while another is a compulsive counter.

Large epidemiological studies have found a connection between streptococcal infections in childhood and the abrupt onset or worsening of OCD symptoms. The observation that there are two age-related peaks in the onset of the disorder increases the possibility that there is a common causal factor. Patients with childhood-onset OCD often have had one of two diseases caused by a group of bacteria called Group A beta-hemolytic streptococci ("strep" throat and Sydenham's chorea) prior to the onset of the OCD symptoms. The disorders are sometimes referred to as pediatric autoimmune neuropsychiatric disorders associated with streptococcal infections, or PANDAS. It is thought that antibodies in the child's blood cross-react with structures in the basal ganglia, producing or worsening the symptoms of OCD or tic disorders.

Symptoms

The symptoms of OCD should not be confused with the ability to focus on detail or to check one's work that is sometimes labeled "compulsive" in everyday life. This type of attentiveness is an important factor in academic achievement and in doing well in fields that require close attention to detail, such as accounting or engineering. By contrast, the symptoms of OCD are serious enough to interfere with the person's day-to-day functioning. Historical examples of OCD include a medieval Englishman named William of Oseney, who spent twelve hours per day reading religious books in order to be at peace with God; and Freud's Rat Man, a patient who had repeated dreams of cursing Freud and covering him with dung. While the Rat Man was ashamed of these impulses and had no explanation for them, he could not control them.

More recent accounts of OCD symptoms include those of a young man who compulsively touched every electrical outlet as he passed, washed his hands several times an hour, and returned home repeatedly to check that the doors and windows were locked. Another account describes a firefighter who was worried that he had throat cancer. He spent three hours a day examining his throat in the mirror, feeling his lymph nodes, and asking his wife if his throat appeared normal.

Brief descriptions of the more common obsessions and compulsions follow.

CONTAMINATION. People with contamination obsessions are usually preoccupied with a fear of dirt or germs. They may avoid leaving home or allowing visitors to come inside in order to prevent contact with dirt or germs. Some people with contamination obsessions may wear gloves, coats, or even masks if they are forced to leave their house for some reason. Obsessions with contamination may also include abnormal fears of such environmental toxins as lead, asbestos, or radon.

Washing compulsions are commonly associated with contamination obsessions. For example, a person concerned about contamination from the outside may shower and launder all clothing immediately upon coming home. The compulsion may be triggered by direct contact with the feared object, but in many cases, even being in its general vicinity may stir up intense anxiety and a strong need to engage in a washing compulsion. One man who was afraid of contamination could not even take a short walk down the street without experiencing a compulsion to disinfect the soles of his shoes, launder all his clothing, and wash his hands until they were raw after he returned to his apartment.

Washing compulsions may not always be caused by a fear of germs. That is, a need for perfection or for symmetry may also lead to unnecessary washing. In such cases, the individual may be concerned about being "perfectly" clean, or feel that he cannot leave the shower until his left foot has been washed exactly as many times as his right foot. Other people with washing compulsions may be unable to tolerate feeling sweaty or otherwise not clean.

OBSESSIONAL DOUBTING. Obsessional doubting refers to the fear of having failed to perform some task adequately, and that dire consequences will follow as a result. Although the person may try to suppress the worrisome thoughts or images, he or she usually experiences a rising anxiety which then leads to a compulsion to check the task. For example, someone may worry about forgetting to lock the door or turn off the gas burner on the stove and spend hours checking these things before leaving home. In one instance, a man was unable to throw away old grocery bags because he feared he might have left something valuable inside one of them. Immediately after looking into an empty bag, he would again have the thought, "What if I missed something in there?" In many cases, no amount of checking is sufficient to dispel the maddening sense of doubt.

NEED FOR SYMMETRY. Persons suffering from an obsession about symmetry often report feeling acutely uncomfortable unless they perform certain tasks in a symmetrical or balanced manner. Thus, crossing one's legs to the right must be followed by crossing legs to the left; scratching one side of the head must be followed by scratching the other; tapping the wall with a knuckle on the right hand must be followed by tapping with one on the left, etc. Sometimes the person may have a thought or idea associated with the compulsion, such as a fear that a loved one will be harmed if the action is not balanced, but often there is no clearly defined fear, only a strong sense of uneasiness.

AGGRESSIVE AND SEXUAL OBSESSIONS. Aggressive and sexual obsessions are often particularly horrifying to those who experience them. For some people, obsessive fears of committing a terrible act in the future compete with fears that they may already have done something awful in the past. Compulsions to constantly check and confess cause such individuals to admit to evildoing they had no part in, a phenomenon familiar to law enforcement following highly publicized crimes. These obsessions often involve violent or graphic imagery that is upsetting and disgusting to the person, such as rape, physical assault, or even murder. One case study concerned a young woman who constantly checked the news to reassure herself that she had not murdered anyone that day; she felt deeply upset by unsolved murder cases. A middle-aged man repeatedly confessed to having molested a woman at work, despite no evidence of such an action ever occurring in his workplace.

SYMPTOMS IN CHILDREN. Obsessions and compulsions in children are often focused on germs and fears of contamination. Other common obsessions include fears of harm coming to self or others; fears of causing harm to another person; obsessions about symmetry; and excessive moralization or religiosity. Childhood compulsions frequently include washing, repeating, checking, touching, counting, ordering and arranging. Younger children are less likely to have full-blown anxiety-producing obsessions, but they often report a sense of relief or strong satisfaction (a "just right" feeling) from completing certain ritualized behaviors. Since children are particularly skillful in disguising their OCD symptoms from adults, they may effectively hide their disorder from parents and teachers for years.

Unusual behaviors in children that may be signs of OCD include:

- Avoidance of scissors or other sharp objects. A child may be obsessed with fears of hurting herself or others.
- Chronic lateness or dawdling. The child may be performing checking rituals (repeatedly making sure all her school supplies are in her bookbag, for example).
- Daydreaming or preoccupation. The child may be counting or performing balancing rituals mentally.
- Spending long periods of time in the bathroom. The child may have a handwashing compulsion.
- Schoolwork handed in late or papers with holes erased in them. The child may be repeatedly checking and correcting her work.

For both children and adults, the symptoms of OCD wax and wane in severity; and the specific content of obsessions and compulsions may change over time. The disorder, however, very seldom goes away by itself without treatment. People with OCD in all age groups typically find that their symptoms worsen during major life changes or following highly stressful events.

Demographics

As noted above, OCD is a relatively common mental disorder, with about 2.3% of the population of the United States being diagnosed with the condition at some point in their lives. As of 2000, the annual social and economic costs of OCD in the United States are estimated at $9 billion. Although the disorder may begin at any age, the typical age of onset is late adolescence to young adulthood, with slightly more women than men being diagnosed with OCD. Interestingly, childhood OCD is more common in males, and the sex ratio does not favor females until adulthood. People with OCD appear to be less likely to marry than persons diagnosed with other types of mental disorders.

Diagnosis

OCD is a disorder that may not be diagnosed for years. People who suffer from its symptoms are often deeply ashamed, and go to great lengths to hide their ritualistic behaviors. The disorder may be diagnosed when family members get tired of the impact of the patient's behaviors on their lives, and force the patient to consult a doctor. In other cases, the disorder may be self-reported. The patient may have come to resent the amount of time wasted by the compulsions; or he or she may have taken a screening questionnaire such as the brief screener available on the NIMH website (listed in the Resources section below).

The **diagnosis** of OCD may be complicated because of the number of other conditions that resemble it. For example, major depression may be associated with self-perceptions of being guilty, bad, or worthless that are excessive and unreasonable. Similarly, eating disorders often include bizarre thoughts about size and weight, ritualized eating habits, or the hoarding of food. Delusional disorders may entail unusual beliefs or behaviors, as do such other mental disorders as trichotillomania, **hypochondriasis**, the **paraphilias**, and substance use disorders. Thus, accurate diagnosis of OCD depends on the careful analysis of many variables to determine whether the apparent obsessions and compulsions might be better accounted for by some other disorder, or to the direct effects of a substance or a medical condition.

In addition, OCD may coexist with other mental disorders, most commonly depression. It has been estimated that about 34% of patients diagnosed with OCD are depressed at the time of diagnosis, and that 65% will develop depression at some point in their lives.

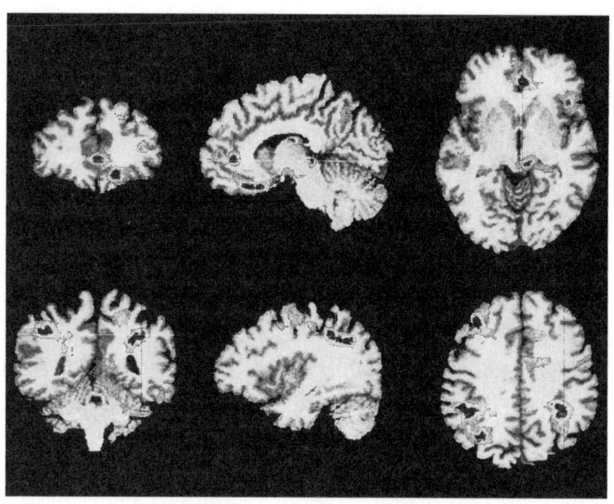

Colored positron emission tomography scans (PET scans) of a human brain, showing active areas in obsessive-compulsive disorder. In this patient, some parts of the brain show increased activity as the symptoms strengthen (areas shown in the top row), while other brain areas show decreased activity as symptoms strengthen (bottom row). *(Wellcome Dept of Cognitive Neurology. Photo Researchers, Inc./ Science Photo Library. Reproduced by permission.) See color insert for color version of photo.*

Treatments

As of 2002, a combination of behavioral therapy and medications appears to be the most effective treatment for OCD. The goal of treatment is to reduce the frequency and severity of the obsessions and compulsions so that the patient can work more efficiently and have more time for social activities. Few OCD patients become completely symptom-free, but most benefit considerably from treatment.

Psychotherapy

Behavioral treatments using the technique of exposure and response prevention are particularly effective in treating OCD. In this form of therapy, the patient and therapist draw up a list, or hierarchy, of the patient's obsessive and compulsive symptoms. The symptoms are arranged in order from least to most upsetting. The patient is then systematically exposed to the anxiety-producing thoughts or behaviors, beginning with the least upsetting. The patient is asked to endure the feared event or image without engaging in the compulsion normally used to lower anxiety. For example, a person with a contamination obsession might be asked to touch a series of increasingly dirty objects without washing their hands. In this way, the patient learns to tolerate the feared object, reducing both worrisome obsessions and anxiety-reducing compulsions. About 75%–80% of patients respond well to exposure and response prevention, with very significant reductions in symptoms.

Other types of **psychotherapy** have met with mixed results. **Psychodynamic psychotherapy** is helpful to some patients who are concerned about the relationships between their upbringing and the specific features of their OCD symptoms. Cognitive-behavioral psychotherapy may be valuable in helping the patient to become more comfortable with the prospect of exposure and prevention treatments, as well as helping to identify the role that the patient's particular symptoms may play in his or her own life and what effects family members may have on the maintenance and continuation of OCD symptoms. Cognitive-behavioral psychotherapy is not intended to replace exposure and response prevention, but may be a helpful addition to it.

Medications

The most useful medications for the treatment of OCD are the selective serotonin reuptake inhibitors (SSRIs), which affect the body's reabsorption of serotonin, a chemical in the brain that helps to transmit nerve impulses across the very small gaps between nerve cells. These drugs, specifically **clomipramine** (Anafranil), **fluoxetine** (Prozac), **fluvoxamine** (Luvox), **sertraline** (Zoloft), and **paroxetine** (Paxil) have been found to relieve OCD symptoms in over half of the patients studied. It is not always possible for the doctor to predict which of the SSRIs will work best for a specific patient. Lack of response to one SSRI does not mean that other drugs within the same family will not work. Treatment of OCD often proceeds slowly, with various medications being tried before the most effective one is found. While studies report that about half of those treated with SSRIs show definite improvement, relapse rates may be as high as 90% when medications are discontinued.

Other mainstream approaches

Some treatments that have been used for OCD include **electroconvulsive therapy** (ECT) and, as a technique of last resort, **psychosurgery** for truly intractable OCD. Some patients have benefited from ECT; however, the National Institute of Mental Health (NIMH) recommends reserving ECT for OCD patients who have not responded to psychotherapy or medication.

Prognosis

While most patients with OCD benefit from a combination of medications and psychotherapy, the disorder is usually a lifelong condition. In addition, the presence of **personality disorders** or additional mental disorders is associated with less favorable results from treatment. The total elimination of OCD symptoms is very rare, even with extended treatment.

The onset of OCD in childhood is the single strongest predictor of a poor prognosis. Treatment in children is also complicated by the fact that children may find the response and exposure techniques very stressful. It is also hard for children to understand the potential value of such treatments; however, creative therapists have learned to use anxiety reduction strategies, education, and behavioral rewards to help their young patients with the treatment tasks. Concern about the long-term use of medications in children with OCD has further encouraged the use of cognitive-behavioral techniques whenever possible.

See also: Exposure treatment; Tic disorders

Resources

BOOKS

Kay, Jerald, M.D., and Allan Tasman, M.D. eds. "Obsessive-Compulsive Disorder." In *Psychiatry:Behavioral Science and Clincial Essentials.* Philadelphia: W.B. Saunders Company, 2000.

Millon, Theodore, M.D. *Personality-Guided Therapy.* New York:Wiley and Sons,1999.

Pato, Michele T., and others. " Obsessive-Compulsive Disorder." In *Psychiatry* Volume 2. Philadelphia: W.B. Saunders Company, 1997.

Piacentini, John, Ph.D., and Lindsey Bergman, Ph.D. "Anxiety Disorders in Children." In *Kaplan and Sadock's Comprehensive Textbook of Psychiatry.* Volume II. Edited by Benjamin Sadock, M.D. and Virginia Sadock, M.D. Philadelphia: Lippincott, Williams and Wilkins, 2000.

Sadock, Benjamin, M.D. and Sadock, Virginia, M.D. eds. *Kaplan and Sadock's Comprehensive Textbook of Psychiatry.* Volume I. 7th edition. Philadelphia: Lippincott, Williams, and Wilkins, 2000.

PERIODICALS

Abramowitz, J. S. "Effectiveness of Psychological and Pharmacological Treatments for Obsessive-Compulsive Disorder: A Quantitative Review." *Journal of Consulting and Clinical Psychology* 65 (1997): 44-52.

McLean, Peter D. and others. "Cognitive Versus Behavioral Therapy in the Group Treatment of Obsessive-Compulsive Disorder." *Journal of Consulting and Clinical Psychology* 69, no.2 (2001): 205-214.

ORGANIZATIONS

Anxiety Disorders Association of America (ADAA). 11900 Parklawn Drive, Suite 100, Rockville, MD 20852-2624. (301) 231-9350. <www.adaa.org>.

Freedom From Fear. 308 Seaview Avenue, Staten Island, NY 10305 (718) 351-1717. <www.freedomfromfear.com>.

Obsessive-Compulsive Foundation, Inc. 337 Notch Hill Road, North Branford, CT 06471. (203) 315-2196. <www.ocfoundation.org>.

OTHER

National Institute of Mental Health (NIMH). *Obsessive-Compulsive Disorder,* 3rd revised edition, 1999. NIH Publication No. 99-3755. <www.nimh.nih.gov/publicat/ocd.cfm>.

National Institute of Mental Health (NIMH). *A Screening Test for Obsessive-Compulsive Disorder.* <www.nimh.nih.gov/publicat/ocdtrt1.htm.>.

Jane A. Fitzgerald, Ph.D.

Obsessive-compulsive personality disorder

Definition

Obsessive-compulsive personality disorder (OCPD) is a type of personality disorder marked by rigidity, control, perfectionism, and an overconcern with work at the expense of close interpersonal relationships. Persons with this disorder often have trouble relaxing because they are preoccupied with details, rules, and productivity. They are often perceived by others as stubborn, stingy, self-righteous, and uncooperative.

The mental health professional's handbook, the ***Diagnostic and Statistical Manual of Mental Disorders***, fourth edition, text revision (2000), which is also called *DSM-IV-TR*, groups obsessive-compulsive personality disorder together with the avoidant and dependent **personality disorders** in Cluster C. The disorders in this cluster are considered to have anxiety and fearfulness as common characteristics. The ICD-10, which is the European counterpart of *DSM-IV-TR*, refers to OCPD as "anankastic personality disorder."

It is important to distinguish between OCPD and **obsessive-compulsive disorder** (OCD), which is an anxiety disorder characterized by the presence of intrusive or disturbing thoughts, impulses, images or ideas (obsessions), accompanied by repeated attempts to suppress these thoughts through the performance of irrational and ritualistic behaviors or mental acts (compulsions). It is unusual but possible, however, for a patient to suffer from both disorders, especially in extreme cases of hoarding behavior. In some reported cases of animal hoarding, the people involved appear to have symptoms of both OCD and OCPD.

KEY TERMS

Anankastic personality disorder—The European term for obsessive-compulsive personality disorder.

Compulsion—A strong impulse to perform an act, particularly one that is irrational or contrary to one's will.

Obsession—A persistent image, idea, or desire that dominates a person's thoughts or feelings.

Therapeutic alliance—The technical term for the cooperative relationship between therapist and patient that is considered essential for successful psychotherapy.

Description

People suffering from OCPD have careful rules and procedures for conducting many aspects of their everyday lives. While their goal is to accomplish things in a careful, orderly manner, their desire for perfection and insistence on going "by the book" often overrides their ability to complete a task. For example, one patient with OCPD was so preoccupied with finding a mislaid shopping list that he took much more time searching for it than it would have taken him to rewrite the list from memory. This type of inflexibility typically extends to interpersonal relationships. People with OCPD are known for being highly controlling and bossy toward other people, especially subordinates. They will often insist that there is one and only one right way (their way) to fold laundry, cut grass, drive a car, or write a report. In addition, they are so insistent on following rules that they cannot allow for what most people would consider legitimate exceptions. Their attitudes toward their own superiors or supervisors depend on whether they respect these authorities. People with OCPD are often unusually courteous to superiors that they respect, but resistant to or contemptuous of those they do not respect.

While work environments may reward their conscientiousness and attention to detail, people with OCPD do not show much spontaneity or imagination. They may feel paralyzed when immediate action is necessary; they feel overwhelmed by trying to make decisions without concrete guidelines. They expect colleagues to stick to detailed rules and procedures, and often perform poorly in jobs that require flexibility and the ability to compromise. Even when people with OCPD are behind schedule, they are uncomfortable delegating work to others because the others may not do the job "properly." People with OCPD often get so lost in the finer points of a task that they cannot see the larger picture; they are frequently described as "unable to see the forest for the trees." They are often highly anxious in situations without clearly defined rules because such situations arouse their fears of making a mistake and being punished for it. An additional feature of this personality disorder is stinginess or miserliness, frequently combined with an inability to throw out worn-out or useless items. This characteristic has sometimes been described as "pack rat" behavior.

People diagnosed with OCPD come across to others as difficult and demanding. Their rigid expectations of others are also applied to themselves, however; they tend to be intolerant of their own shortcomings. Such persons feel bound to present a consistent facade of propriety and control. They feel uncomfortable with expressions of tender feelings and tend to avoid relatives or colleagues who are more emotionally expressive. This strict and ungenerous approach to life limits their ability to relax; they are seldom if ever able to release their needs for control. Even recreational activities frequently become another form of work. A person with OCPD, for example, may turn a tennis game into an opportunity to perfect his or her backhand rather than simply enjoying the exercise, the weather, or the companionship of the other players. Many OCPD sufferers bring office work along on vacations in order to avoid "wasting time," and feel a sense of relief upon returning to the structure of their work environment. Not surprisingly, this combination of traits strains their interpersonal relationships and can lead to a lonely existence.

Causes and symptoms

Causes

No single specific cause of OCPD has been identified. Since the early days of Freudian **psychoanalysis**, however, faulty parenting has been viewed as a major factor in the development of personality disorders. Current studies have tended to support the importance of early life experiences, finding that healthy emotional development largely depends on two important variables: parental warmth and appropriate responsiveness to the child's needs. When these qualities are present, the child feels secure and appropriately valued. By contrast, many people with personality disorders did not have parents who were emotionally warm toward them. Patients with OCPD often recall their parents as being emotionally withholding and either overprotective or overcontrolling. One researcher has noted that people with OCPD appear to have been punished by their parents for every transgression of a rule, no matter how minor, and rewarded for almost nothing. As a result, the child is unable to safely develop or express a sense of joy, spontaneity, or independent thought, and begins to develop the symptoms of OCPD as a strategy for avoiding punishment. Children with this type of upbringing are also likely to choke down the anger they feel toward their parents; they may be outwardly obedient and polite to authority figures, but at the same time treat younger children or those they regard as their inferiors harshly.

Genetic contributions to OCPD have not been well documented. Cultural influences may, however, play a part in the development of OCPD. That is, cultures that are highly authoritarian and rule-bound may encourage child-rearing practices that contribute to the development of OCPD. On the other hand, simply because a culture is comparatively strict or has a strong work ethic does not mean it is necessarily unhealthful. In Japanese societies, for example, excessive devotion to work, restricted emotional expression, and moral scrupulosity are highly valued characteristics that are rewarded within that culture. Similarly, certain religions and professions require exactness and careful attention to rules in their members; the military is one example. OCPD is not diagnosed in persons who are simply behaving in accordance with such outside expectations as military regulations or the rule of a religious order. Appropriate evaluation of persons from other cultures requires close examination in order to differentiate people who are merely following culturally prescribed patterns from people whose behaviors are excessive even by the standards of their own culture.

Symptoms

The symptoms of OCPD include a pervasive overconcern with mental, emotional, and behavioral control of the self and others. Excessive conscientiousness means that people with this disorder are generally poor problem-solvers and have trouble making decisions; as a result, they are frequently highly inefficient. Their need for control is easily upset by schedule changes or minor unexpected events. While many people have some of the following characteristics, a person who meets the *DSM-IV-TR* criteria for OCPD must display at least four of them:

- Preoccupation with details, rules, lists, order, organization, or schedules to the point at which the major goal of the activity is lost.
- Excessive concern for perfection in small details that interferes with the completion of projects.
- Dedication to work and productivity that shuts out friendships and leisure-time activities, when the long hours of work cannot be explained by financial necessity.

- Excessive moral rigidity and inflexibility in matters of ethics and values that cannot be accounted for by the standards of the person's religion or culture.
- Hoarding things, or saving worn-out or useless objects even when they have no sentimental or likely monetary value.
- Insistence that tasks be completed according to one's personal preferences.
- Stinginess with the self and others.
- Excessive rigidity and obstinacy.

Demographics

Obsessive-compulsive personality disorder is estimated to occur in about 1% of the population, although rates of 3%–10% are reported among psychiatric outpatients. The disorder is usually diagnosed in late adolescence or young adulthood. In the United States, OCPD occurs almost twice as often in men as in women. Some researchers attribute this disproportion to gender stereotyping, in that men have greater permission from general Western culture to act in stubborn, withholding, and controlling ways.

Diagnosis

It is relatively unusual for OCPD to be diagnosed as the patient's primary reason for making an appointment with their doctor. In many cases the person with OCPD is unaware of the discomfort that his or her stubbornness and rigidity cause other people, precisely because these traits usually enable them to get their way with others. They are more likely to enter therapy because of such other issues as anxiety disorders, serious relationship difficulties, or stress-related medical problems. **Diagnosis** of OCPD depends on careful observation and appropriate assessment of the individual's behavior; the person must not only give evidence of the attitudes and behaviors associated with OCPD, but these must be severe enough to interfere with their occupational and interpersonal functioning.

The differential diagnosis will include distinguishing between obsessive-compulsive disorder (OCD) and OCPD. A person who has obsessions and compulsions that they experience as alien and irrational is more likely to be suffering from OCD, whereas the person who feels perfectly comfortable with self-imposed systems of extensive rules and procedures for mopping the kitchen floor probably has OCPD. In addition, the thoughts and behaviors that are found in OCD are seldom relevant to real-life problems; by contrast, people with OCPD are preoccupied primarily with managing (however inefficiently) the various tasks they encounter in their daily lives.

Some features of OCPD may occur in other personality disorders. For example, a person with a **narcissistic personality disorder** may be preoccupied with perfection and be critical and stingy toward others; narcissists are usually generous with themselves, however, while people with OCPD are self-critical and reluctant to spend money even on themselves. Likewise, a person with **schizoid personality disorder**, who lacks a fundamental capacity for intimacy, may resemble someone with OCPD in being formal and detached in dealing with others. The difference here is that a person with OCPD, while awkward in emotional situations, is able to experience caring and may long for close relationships. Certain medical conditions may also mimic OCPD, but are distinct in that the onset of the symptoms is directly related to the illness. Certain behaviors related to substance abuse may also be mistaken for symptoms of OCPD, especially if the substance problem is unrecognized.

As described earlier, diagnosis may also be complicated by the fact that behaviors similar to OCPD may be normal variants within a given culture, occupation, or religion; however, in order to fulfill criteria for the personality disorder, the behaviors must be sufficiently severe as to impair the patient's functioning.

Treatments

Psychotherapy

Psychotherapeutic approaches to the treatment of OCPD have found insight-oriented psychodynamic techniques and cognitive behavioral therapy to be helpful for many patients. This choice of effective approaches stands in contrast to the limitations of traditional forms of **psychotherapy** with most patients diagnosed with OCD. Learning to find satisfaction in life through close relationships and recreational outlets, instead of only through work-related activities, can greatly enrich the OCPD patient's quality of life. Specific training in relaxation techniques may help patients diagnosed with OCPD who have the so-called "Type A" characteristics of competitiveness and time urgency as well as preoccupation with work.

It is difficult, however, for a psychotherapist to develop a therapeutic alliance with a person with OCPD. The patient comes into therapy with a powerful need to control the situation and the therapist; a reluctance to trust others; and a tendency to doubt or question almost everything about the therapy situation. The therapist must be alert to the patient's defenses against genuine change and work to gain a level of commitment to the therapeutic process. Without this commitment, the therapist may be fooled into thinking that therapy has been successful when, in fact, the patient is simply being superficially compliant.

Medications

For many years, medications for OCPD and other personality disorders were thought to be ineffective since they did not affect the underlying causes of the disorder. More recent studies, however, indicate that treatment with specific drugs may be a useful adjunct (help) to psychotherapy. In particular, the medications known as selective serotonin reuptake inhibitors (SSRIs) appear to help the OCPD patient with his or her rigidity and compulsiveness, even when the patient did not show signs of pre-existing depression. Medication can also help the patient to think more clearly and make decisions better and faster without being so distracted by minor details. While symptom control may not "cure" the underlying personality disorder, medication does enable some OCPD patients to function with less distress.

Prognosis

Individuals with OCPD often experience a moderate level of professional success, but relationships with a spouse or children may be strained due to their combination of emotional detachment and controlling behaviors. In addition, people with OCPD often do not attain the level of professional achievement that might be predicted for their talents and abilities because their rigidity and stubbornness make them poor "team players" or supervisors. Although there are few large-scale outcome studies of treatments for OCPD, existing reports suggest that these patients do benefit from psychotherapy to help them understand the emotional issues underlying their controlling behaviors and to teach them how to relax. Since OCPD sufferers, unlike people with OCD, usually view their compulsive behaviors as voluntary, they are better able to consider change, especially as they come to fully recognize the personal and interpersonal costs of their disorder.

Prevention

Most theories attribute the development of OCPD to early life experiences, including a lack of parental warmth; parental overcontrol and rigidity, and few rewards for spontaneous emotional expression. Little work has been done, however, in identifying preventive strategies.

See also Gender issues in mental health

Resources

BOOKS

Alarcon, Renato D., Edward F. Foulks, and Mark Vakkur. *Personality Disorders and Culture.* New York: John Wiley and Sons, 1998.

Baer, Lee. "Personality Disorders in Obsessive-Compulsive Disorder." In *Obsessive-Compulsive Disorders: Practical Management.* 3rd edition. Edited by Michael Jenike and others. St. Louis: Mosby, 1998.

Jenike, Michael. "Psychotherapy of Obsessive-Compulsive Personality." In *Obsessive-Compulsive Personality Disorders: Practical Management.* 3rd edition. Edited by Michael Jenike and others. St. Louis: Mosby, 1998.

Kay, Jerald, Allen Tasman, and Jeffery Liberman. "Obsessive-Compulsive Disorder." In *Psychiatry: Behavioral Science and Clinical Essentials,* edited by Michael Jenike, Lee Baer, and William Minichiello. Philadelphia: W. B. Saunders, 2000.

Millon, Theodore. *Personality-Guided Therapy.* New York: John Wiley and Sons, 1999.

World Health Organization (WHO). *The ICD-10 Classification of Mental and Behavioural Disorders.* Geneva: WHO, 1992.

PERIODICALS

Barber, Jacques P., Connolly, Mary B., Crits-Christoph, Lynn G., and Siqueland, Lynne. "Alliance Predicts Patients' Outcome Beyond In-Treatment change in Symptoms." *Journal of Consulting and Clinical Psychology* 68 (2000); 1027-1032.

Nordahl, Hans M. and Tore C. Stiles. "Perceptions of Parental Bonding in Patients with Various Personality Disorders, Lifetime Depressive Disorders, and Healthy Controls." *Journal of Personality Disorders* 11 (1997): 457-462.

Samuels, Jack, and others. "Personality Disorders and Normal Personality Dimensions in Obsessive-Compulsive Disorder." *British Journal of Psychiatry* 177 (2000) 457-462.

Zaider, Talia, Jeffrey G. Johnson, Sarah J. Cockell. "Psychiatric Comorbidity Associated with Eating Disorder Symptomatology Among Adolescents in the Community." *International Journal of Eating Disorders* 28 (2000): 58-67.

ORGANIZATIONS

Anxiety Disorders Association of America (ADAA). 11900 Parklawn Drive, Suite 100, Rockville, MD 20852-2624. (301) 231-9350. <www.adaa.org>.

Freedom From Fear. 308 Seaview Avenue, Staten Island, NY 10305. (718) 351-1717. <www.freedomfromfear.com>.

Jane A. Fitzgerald, Ph.D.

Olanzapine

Definition

Olanzapine is classified as an atypical antipsychotic drug. It is available in the United States under the brand names Zyprexa and Zyprexa Zydis.

Purpose

Olanzapine is used to treat **schizophrenia**, to control manic episodes of **bipolar disorder** (manic-depressive disorder), or to treat **dementia** related to **Alzheimer's disease**.

Description

Olanzapine is thought to modify the actions of several chemicals in the **brain**. Onlanzapine is chemically related to another atypical antipsychotic agent, **clozapine**, but differs both chemically and pharmacologically from the earlier phenothiazine antipsychotics.

Olanzapine is available as 2.5-mg, 5-mg, 7.5-mg, 10-mg, 15-mg, and 20-mg tablets that can be swallowed (Zyprexa) and 5-mg, 10-mg, 15-mg, and 20-mg tablets that disintegrate when placed under the tongue (Zyprexa Zydis). Olanzapine is broken down by the liver.

Recommended dosage

The dosage of olanzapine varies depending upon the reason for its use. When used to treat schizophrenia, 5–10 mg is the typical starting dosage. If dosage adjustments are needed, increases are made in 5-mg increments once a week. When treating schizophrenia, a total daily dosage of 10–15 mg is usually effective. When olanzapine is used to treat acute manic episodes, initial doses of olanzapine are often 10–15 mg; 20 mg per day may be needed for maximum effect. The safety of doses greater than 20 mg per day has not been determined.

Olanzapine is eliminated from the body more quickly in young people than in older (over age 60) individuals, in men than in women, and in smokers faster than in non-smokers. Dosage adjustments may be needed based upon individual patient characteristics.

Precautions

Caution should be used in patients with heart disease because the drug may cause blood pressure to fall too low resulting in dizziness, rapid heartbeats, or fainting. Olanzapine should be used carefully in people with known seizure disorders since olanzapine may alter properties of the brain making **seizures** occur more easily. People with liver disease should have their liver function monitored regularly while taking olanzapine. Women who are pregnant or breast-feeding should not take olanzapine. People with phenylketonuria, a disorder in which the body is unable to metabolize a protein called phenylalanine, should avoid olanzapine disintegrating tablets, because this form of the drug contains phenylalanine.

KEY TERMS

Antipsychotic—A medication used to treat psychotic symptoms of schizophrenia such as hallucinations, delusions and delirium. May be used to treat symptoms in other disorders, as well.

Bipolar disorder (formerly manic-depressive disorder)—A mental disorder characterized by dramatic, and sometimes rapid mood swings, resulting in both manic and depressive episodes.

Mania—An elevated or euphoric mood or irritable state that is characteristic of bipolar I disorder. This state is characterized by mental and physical hyperactivity, disorganization of behavior, and inappropriate elevation of mood.

Neuroleptic malignant syndrome—An unusual but potentially serious complication that develops in some patients who have been treated with antipsychotic medications. NMS is characterized by changes in blood pressure, altered states of consciousness, rigid muscles, and fever. Untreated NMS can result in coma and death.

Psychosis—Severe state that is characterized by loss of contact with reality and deterioration in normal social functioning; examples are schizophrenia and paranoia. Psychosis is usually one feature of an over-arching disorder, not a disorder in itself. (Plural: psychoses)

Schizophrenia—A severe mental illness in which a person has difficulty distinguishing what is real from what is not real. It is often characterized by hallucinations, delusions, language and communication disturbances, and withdrawal from people and social activities.

Tardive dyskinesia—A condition that involves involuntary movements of the tongue, jaw, mouth or face or other groups of skeletal muscles that usually occurs either late in antipsychotic therapy or even after the therapy is discontinued. It may be irreversible.

Side effects

Side effects that occur in more than 5% of patients taking olanzapine include involuntary movements, weakness, dizziness, extreme drowsiness, nonviolent objectionable behavior, constipation, weight gain, dry mouth, low blood pressure, stomach upset, increased appetite, cold-such as symptoms, or fever.

Other side effects that are possible include rash, body aches and pains, elevated liver enzymes, vision abnormalities, chest pain, or rapid heartbeats.

Olanzapine has the potential to produce a serious side effect called **tardive dyskinesia**. This syndrome consists of involuntary, uncoordinated movements that may appear late in therapy and not disappear even after the drug is stopped. Tardive dyskinesia involves involuntary movements of the tongue, jaw, mouth or face or other groups of skeletal muscles. The incidence of tardive dyskinesia increases with increasing age and with increasing dosage of olanzapine. Women are at greater risk than men for developing tardive dyskinesia. There is no known effective treatment for tardive dyskinesia, although gradual (but rarely complete) improvement may occur over a long period.

An occasionally reported side effect of olanzapine is neuroleptic malignant syndrome. This is a complicated and potentially fatal condition characterized by muscle rigidity, high fever, alterations in mental status, and cardiac symptoms such as irregular pulse or blood pressure, sweating, tachycardia (fast heartbeat), and arrhythmias (irregular heartbeat).

Interactions

Any drug that causes drowsiness may lead to decreased mental alertness and impaired motor skills when taken with olanzapine. Some examples include alcohol, antidepressants such as **imipramine** (Tofranil) or **paroxetine** (Paxil), antipsychotics such as **thioridazine** (Mellaril), and some antihistamines. Because olanzapine may lower blood pressure, it may reduce blood pressure to dangerously low levels if taken with drugs that are used to treat high blood pressure. **Carbamazepine** (Tegretol), a drug commonly used to treat seizures, may decrease the effectiveness of olanzapine.

Resources

BOOKS

Medical Economics Co. Staff. *Physician's Desk Reference.* 56th edition. Montvale, NJ: Medical Economics Company, 2002.

Facts and Comparisons Staff. *Drug Facts and Comparisons.* 6th Edition. St. Louis, MO: A Wolter Kluwer Company, 2002.

Mosby Staff. *Mosby's Medical Drug Reference.* St. Louis, MO: Mosby, Inc, 1999.

Kelly Karpa, RPh, Ph.D.

Opioids and related disorders

Definition

Opioids are a class of drugs that include both natural and synthetic substances. The natural opioids (referred to as opiates) include opium and morphine. Heroin, the most abused opioid, is synthesized from opium. Other synthetics (only made in laboratories) and commonly prescribed for pain, such as cough suppressants, or as anti-diarrhea agents, include codeine, oxycodone (OxyContin), meperidine (Demerol), fentanyl (Sublimaze), hydromorphone (Dilaudid), **methadone**, and propoxyphene (Darvon). Heroin is usually injected, either intravenously (into a vein) or subcutaneously (under the skin), but can be smoked or used intranasally (i.e., "snorted"). Other opioids are either injected or taken orally.

The manual that is used by mental health professionals to diagnose mental disorders is the ***Diagnostic and Statistical Manual of Mental Disorders***. The latest edition of this manual was published in 2000, and is also known as the *DSM-IV-TR*. *DSM-IV-TR* lists opioid dependence and opioid abuse as substance use disorders. In addition, the opioid-induced disorders of opioid intoxication and opioid withdrawal are listed in the substance-related disorders section as well.

Opioid dependence

Opioid dependence, or **addiction**, is essentially a syndrome in which a person continues to use opioids in spite of significant problems caused by or made worse by the use of opioids. Typically individuals with opioid dependence are physically dependent on the drug as evidenced by tolerance and/or withdrawal.

Opioid abuse

Opioid abuse is less severe than opioid dependence and typically does not involve physical dependence on the drug. Opioid abuse is essentially repeated significant negative consequences of using opioids recurrently.

Opioid intoxication

When an individual uses a sufficient amount of an opioid, they will get "high" from the drug. Some people, however, have negative experiences when they use an opioid. When too much of an opioid is taken, an individual can overdose.

Opioid withdrawal

Individuals who use opioids on a regular basis, even if only for a few days, may develop a tolerance to the drug and experience physiological and psychological symptoms when they stop using the drug. The "abstinence syndrome" related to opioids is very similar to a bad case of influenza (or the "flu").

Description

Opioid dependence

Dependence on opioids involves significant physiological and psychological changes, which make it extremely difficult for an individual to stop using the opioids. Recurrent use of opioids causes actual changes in how the **brain** functions. An individual who is addicted to opioids cannot simply just stop using, despite significant negative consequences related to their use. Marital difficulties, including divorce, unemployment, and drug-related legal problems are often associated with opioid dependence. People dependent on opioids often plan their day around obtaining and using opioids.

Opioid abuse

People who abuse opioids typically use them less frequently than those who are dependent on opioids. However, despite less frequent use, an individual with opioid abuse suffers negative consequences. For example, while intoxicated on opioids, an individual may get arrested for their behavior.

Opioid intoxication

An individual who uses opioids typically experiences drowsiness ("nodding off"), mood changes, a feeling of heaviness, dry mouth, itching, and slurred speech. Individuals who use heroin intravenously describe an intense euphoria (or "rush"), a floating feeling, and total indifference to pain. Symptoms of intoxication usually last several hours. Severe intoxication from an overdose of opioids is life-threatening because breathing may stop.

Opioid withdrawal

Tolerance to opioids occurs quickly. Regular users of opioids take doses that would kill someone who has never used before. After regular use, the human body adapts to the regular presence of the drug and the person only feels "normal" when they have opioids in their system. Therefore, when an opioid-dependent individual stops using opioids abruptly, he or she will experience withdrawal symptoms. Withdrawal symptoms from heroin usually begin six to eight hours after last use and peak after two days. Acute withdrawal typically lasts no more than seven to ten days, but some symptoms of withdrawal (such as craving, **insomnia**, anxiety, lack of interest) can last six months or longer. Although withdrawal is very uncomfortable, it is not life-threatening unless there is an underlying medical condition, such as heart disease. In addition to physical withdrawal, "psychological withdrawal" often occurs. The individual who is dependent on opioids has difficulty imagining living without the drug, since they were dependent on it to function. This is similar to how someone addicted to nicotine may feel after giving up cigarettes.

KEY TERMS

Tolerance—Progressive decrease in the effectiveness of a drug with long-term use.

Causes and symptoms

Causes

There are no clear-cut causes of drug use other than the initial choice to use the drug. This decision to use may be highly influenced by peer group. Typically, the age of first use of heroin is about 16 years old, but this age has been dropping in recent years.

Certain social and behavioral characteristics, however, are more commonly seen among individuals who become dependent on opioids than those who do not. For instance, many heroin users come from families in which one or more family members use alcohol or drugs excessively or have mental disorders (such as **antisocial personality disorder**). Often heroin users have had health problems early in life, behavioral problems beginning in childhood, low self-confidence, and anti-authoritarian views.

Among opioid-dependent adolescents, a "heroin behavior syndrome" has sometimes been described. This syndrome consists of depression (often with anxiety symptoms), impulsiveness, fear of failure, low self-esteem, low frustration tolerance, limited coping skills, and relationships based primarily on mutual drug use.

Symptoms

OPIOID DEPENDENCE. The *DSM-IV-TR* specifies that three or more of the following symptoms must occur at any time during a 12-month period (and cause significant impairment or distress) in order to meet diagnostic criteria for opioid dependence:

- Tolerance: The individual either has to use increasingly higher amounts of the drug over time in order to achieve the same drug effect or finds that the same amount of the drug has much less of an effect over time than before.
- Withdrawal: The individual either experiences the characteristic abstinence syndrome (i.e., opioid-specific withdrawal) or the individual uses opioids or similar-acting drugs in order to avoid or relieve withdrawal symptoms.
- Loss of control: The individual either repeatedly uses more opioids than planned or uses the opioids over longer periods of time than planned.
- Inability to stop using: The individual has either unsuccessfully attempted to cut down or stop using the opioids or has a persistent desire to stop using.
- Time: The individual spends a lot of time obtaining opioids, getting money to buy opioids, using opioids, being under the influence of opioids, and recovering from the effects of opioids.
- Interference with activities: The individual either gives up or reduces the amount of time involved in recreational activities, social activities, and/or occupational activities.
- Harm to self: The individual continues to use opioids despite having either a physical or psychological problem (depression, for example) that is caused or made worse by the opioid use.

OPIOID ABUSE. The *DSM-IV-TR* specifies that one or more of the following symptoms must occur at any time during a 12-month period (and cause significant impairment or distress) in order to meet diagnostic criteria for opioid abuse:

- Interference with role fulfillment: The individual's use of opioids repeatedly interferes with the ability to fulfill obligations at work, home, or school.
- Danger to self: The individual repeatedly uses opioids in situations in which it may be physically hazardous (while driving a car, for example).
- Legal problems: The individual has recurrent opioid-related legal problems (such as arrests for possession of narcotics).
- Social problems: The individual continues to use opioids despite repeated interpersonal or relationship problems caused by or made worse by the use of opioids.

OPIOID INTOXICATION. The *DSM-IV-TR* specifies that the following symptoms must be present in order to meet diagnostic criteria for opioid intoxication:

- Use: The individual recently used an opioid.
- Changes: The individual experiences significant behavioral or psychological changes during, or shortly after, use of an opioid. These changes may include euphoria initially, followed by slowed movements or agitation, impaired judgment, **apathy** ("don't care attitude"), dysphoric mood (depression, for example), or impaired functioning socially or at work.
- Opioid-specific intoxication syndrome: The pupils in the eyes get smaller. In addition, drowsiness or coma, slurred speech, and/or impaired memory or attention during, or shortly after, opioid use occur.

OPIOID WITHDRAWAL. The *DSM-IV-TR* specifies that the following symptoms must be present in order to meet diagnostic criteria for opioid withdrawal:

- Abstinence: Either the individual has stopped using (or has reduced the amount of) opioids, or an opioid antagonist (i.e., a drug, such as naloxone, that blocks the action of opioids) has been administered.
- Opioid-specific withdrawal syndrome: Three or more symptoms develop after abstinence. These symptoms include dysphoric (negative) mood, nausea or vomiting, muscle aches, runny nose or watery eyes, dilated pupils, goosebumps, or sweating, diarrhea, yawning, fever, and insomnia.
- Impairment or distress: The withdrawal symptoms must cause significant distress to the individual or impairment in functioning (socially, at work, or any other important area).
- Not due to other disorder: The withdrawal symptoms cannot be due to a medical condition or other mental disorder.

Demographics

There are at least 600,000 individuals with opioid dependence living in the United States. It has been estimated that almost 1% of the population has met criteria for opioid dependence or abuse at some time in their lives.

In the late 1800s and early 1900s, individuals who were dependent on opioids were primarily white and from middle socioeconomic groups. However, since the 1920s, minorities and those from lower socioeconomic groups have been overrepresented among those with opioid dependence. It appears that availability of opioids and subcultural factors are key in opioid use. Therefore, medical professionals (who have access to opioids) are at higher risk for developing opioid-related disorders.

Males are more commonly affected by opioid disorders than females—males are three to four times more likely to be dependent on opioids than females. Age also is a factor in opioid dependence. There is a tendency for rates of dependence to decrease beginning at 40 years of age. Problems associated with opioid use are usually first seen in the teens and 20s.

Diagnosis

Diagnosis of opioid-related disorders are based on patient interview and observations of symptoms, including signs of withdrawal such as dilated pupils, watery eyes, frequent yawning, and anxiety, among others.

Opioid dependence

Other mental disorders are common among individuals with opioid dependence. It has been estimated that 90% of those with opioid dependence have one or more other mental disorders. Depression (usually either major depression or substance-induced mood disorder) is the most common disorder. Opioid-dependent individuals frequently report suicidal ideation (thoughts) and insomnia. Other substance use disorders (such as alcoholism), anxiety disorders, antisocial personality disorder, **post-traumatic stress disorder**, and a history of **conduct disorder** are also fairly common.

Opioid intoxication

Intoxication on other substances, such as alcohol, sedatives, hypnotics, and anxiolytics, can resemble intoxication on opioids. Furthermore, dilated pupils can be seen in hallucinogen intoxication, amphetamine intoxication, and cocaine intoxication.

Opioid withdrawal

The restlessness and anxiety seen in opioid withdrawal is also seen in withdrawal from sedatives, hypnotics, and anxiolytics.

Treatments

Opioid dependence

Because opioid-related disorders are complex, multiple treatment approaches are often necessary. Generally, the more treatment (a combination of medication, individual therapy, and **self-help groups**, for example) and longer the treatment (i.e., at least three months), the better the outcomes. There are a wide variety of treatment options, both inpatient or residential and outpatient:

- Methadone maintenance treatment. Methadone is a long-acting opioid that is generally administered in an outpatient setting (a methadone maintenance clinic). The methadone prevents the individual from experiencing opioid withdrawal, reduces opioid craving, and enables the individual to have access to other services (such as individual counseling, medical services, and HIV-prevention education). A proper dose of methadone also prevents the individual from getting "high" from heroin. Methadone maintenance therapy can decrease criminal activity, decrease HIV-risk behaviors, and increase stability of employment. Low-dose methadone maintenance treatment is preferable for pregnant individuals who would otherwise use illicit opioids. A longer-acting alternative to methadone is LAAM (levo-alphacetylmethadol). Individuals receiving the proper doses of LAAM only need to take it three times per week, instead of every day as with methadone.
- Opioid antagonist treatment. An opioid antagonist is a medication that blocks the effects of opioids. Treatment with an antagonist, usually **naltrexone** (Trexan), typically takes place on an outpatient basis following an inpatient medical **detoxification** from opioids. The effects of taking any opioids are blocked by the naltrexone and prevent the individual from getting "high," thereby discouraging individuals from seeking opioids. By itself, this treatment is suitable for individuals highly motivated to discontinue opioid use. However, antagonists can be used in addition to other treatment modalities or with individuals who have been abstinent for some time but fear a relapse.
- Opioid agonist-antagonist treatment. An opioid agonist is a drug that has a similar action to morphine. Buprenorphine (Buprenex) is an example of an opioid agonist-antagonist, which means it acts as both an agonist (having some morphine-like action) and antagonist (it blocks the effects of additional opioids). Buprenorphine has been shown to effectively reduce opioid use. It is also being studied for opioid detoxification.
- Outpatient drug-free treatment. These are outpatient treatment approaches that do not include medications. There are a number of different types of programs ranging from simple drug education to intensive outpatient programs that offer most of the services of an inpatient setting. Some programs may specialize in treating specific groups of people who are opioid-dependent (those with co-occurring mental disorders, for example).

- Residential or inpatient treatment. These include inpatient rehabilitation programs (usually seven to 30 days in length) and long-term residential programs (such as therapeutic communities). Rehabilitation programs provide an inpatient atmosphere following detoxification and usually offer individual and group counseling as well as medical services. Therapeutic communities are designed to be more than six months long and are highly structured. The primary focus is on resocializing the individual to a drug-free and crime-free lifestyle.
- Individualized drug counseling. Individual counseling is often a part of a methadone maintenance program or inpatient rehabilitation program. The primary focus is on helping the individual learn strategies to reduce or stop their opioid use and learn coping mechanisms to maintain abstinence. Twelve-step participation is encouraged and referrals for medical, psychiatric, employment, or other services are made as necessary.
- Supportive-expressive **psychotherapy**. This type of individual psychotherapy may be a part of a methadone maintenance program or offered alone. The focus of this type of therapy is to help individuals feel comfortable talking about themselves, work on relationship issues, and solve problems without resorting to opioids or other drugs.
- **Self-help groups.** Narcotics Anonymous (NA) is a twelve-step group based on the same model as Alcoholics Anonymous. This self-help group can provide social support to an individual in the process of reducing or stopping opioid use. Participation in NA is often encouraged or is a required component of other types of treatment for opioid dependence. Nar-Anon is a group for family members and friends of opioid-dependent individuals.
- Alternative therapies. Hypnosis, guided imagery, **biofeedback**, massage, and **acupuncture** have all been studied as adjunctive treatments for opioid dependence, but none have been proven to be effective.

Opioid abuse

Most of the treatments for opioid dependence would be appropriate for opioid abuse except methadone maintenance and opioid antagonist treatment.

Opioid intoxication

An opioid antagonist, naloxone (Narcan), can be administered to reverse the effects of acute intoxication or overdose on most opioids.

Opioid withdrawal

Opioid withdrawal can be treated either on an inpatient basis (detoxification) or on an outpatient basis (methadone detoxification):

- Inpatient detoxification program. Typically, this would be from three to seven days. The withdrawal can be medically managed. **Clonidine** may be administered to help reduce some symptoms of withdrawal.
- Outpatient methadone detoxification. Methadone would be substituted for the illicit opioid and the dose would be gradually reduced. Detoxification from methadone is easier (i.e., the symptoms are less severe) than from heroin. However, the withdrawal or abstinence syndrome also lasts longer. Clonidine may also be administered during the methadone detoxification to help reduce withdrawal symptoms.

Prognosis

Opioid dependence

Recovering from opioid dependence is a long, difficult process. Typically, multiple treatment attempts are required. Relapsing, or returning to opioids, is not uncommon even after many years of abstinence. Brief periods of abstinence are common.

Inpatient detoxification from opioids alone, without additional treatment, does not appear to have any effect on opioid use. However, other treatments have been shown to reduce opioid use, decrease illegal activity, decrease rates of HIV-infection, reduce rates of death, and increase rates of employment. Benefits are greatest for those who remain in treatment longer and participate in many different types of treatment (individual and group counseling in addition to methadone maintenance, for example).

Opioid abuse

Very little is known about the course of opioid abuse.

Prevention

The best single thing an individual can do to prevent opioid-related disorders is never to use illicit opioids such as heroin. Opioids are powerfully addicting, especially if used intravenously. The risk of becoming dependent on appropriately prescribed opioids, however, is generally low except for individuals who already have a substance use disorder.

On a larger scale, comprehensive prevention programs that utilize family, schools, communities, and the media can be effective in reducing substance abuse. The recurring theme in these programs is not to use drugs in the first place.

Resources

BOOKS

American Psychiatric Association. *Diagnostic and Statistical Manual of Mental Disorders.* 4th edition, text revised. Washington, DC: American Psychiatric Association, 2000.

Jenkins, Susan C., Joyce A. Tinsley, and Jon A. van Loon. *A Pocket Reference for Psychiatrists.* 3rd edition. Washington, DC: American Psychiatric Press, 2001.

Kaplan, Harold I., M.D., and Benjamin J. Sadock, M.D. *Kaplan and Sadock's Synopsis of Psychiatry: Behavioral Sciences, Clinical Psychiatry.* 8th edition. Baltimore: Williams and Wilkins.

ORGANIZATIONS

American Psychiatric Association. 1400 K Street, Washington, DC 20005. (202) 682-6000. <http://www.psych.org>.

American Psychological Association. 750 First Street, NE, Washington, DC 20002-4242. (800) 374-2721. <http://www.apa.org>.

National Institute of Mental Health, 6001 Executive Boulevard, Room 8184, MSC 9663, Bethesda, MD 20892-9663. (301) 443-4513. <http://www.nimh.nih.gov>.

National Institute on Drug Abuse. 5600 Fishers Lane, Room 10-05, Rockville, MD 20857. Nationwide Helpline: (800) 662-HELP. <http://www.nida.nih.gov>.

National Library of Medicine. 8600 Rockville Pike, Bethesda, MD 20894. <http://www.nlm.nih.gov/medlineplus/drugabuse.html>.

Jennifer Hahn, Ph.D.

Oppositional defiant disorder

Definition

Oppositional defiant disorder (ODD) is a disorder found primarily in children and adolescents. It is characterized by negative, disobedient, or defiant behavior that is worse than the normal "testing" behavior most children display from time to time. Most children go through periods of being difficult, particularly during the period from 18 months to three years, and later during adolescence. These difficult periods are part of the normal developmental process of gaining a stronger sense of individuality and separating from parents. ODD, however, is defiant behavior that lasts longer and is more severe than normal individuation behavior, but is not so extreme that it involves violation of social rules or the rights of others.

The mental health professional's handbook, ***Diagnostic and Statistical Manual of Mental Disorders***, fourth edition, text revision (*DSM-IV-TR*), classifies ODD as a disruptive behavior disorder.

KEY TERMS

Attention-deficit/hyperactivity disorder—A learning and behavioral disorder characterized by difficulty in sustaining attention, impulsive behavior, and excessive activity.

Behavioral therapy—An approach to treatment that focuses on extinguishing undesirable behavior and replacing it with desired behavior.

Cognitive therapy—Psychological treatment aimed at changing a person's way of thinking in order to change his or her behavior and emotional state.

Conduct disorder—A behavioral and emotional disorder of childhood and adolescence in which children display physical aggression and infringe on or violate the rights of others. Youths diagnosed with conduct disorder may set fires, exhibit cruelty toward animals or other children, sexually assault others, or lie and steal for personal gain.

Oppositional defiant disorder—An emotional and behavioral problem of children and adolescents characterized by defiant, hostile, or disobedient behavior that has lasted for longer than six months.

Passive-aggressive behaviors—Behaviors that represent covert expressions of hostile or negative feelings that the person is unable or unwilling to express directly.

Description

Children who have ODD are often disobedient. They are easily angered and may seem to be angry much of the time. Very young children with the disorder will throw temper tantrums that last for 30 minutes or longer, over seemingly trivial matters.

In addition, the child with ODD often starts arguments and will not give up. Winning the argument seems to be very important to a child with this disorder. Even if the youth knows that he or she will lose a privilege or otherwise be punished for continuing the tantrum or argument, he or she is unable to stop. Attempting to reason with such a child often backfires because the child perceives rational discussion as a continuation of the argument.

Most children with ODD, however, do not perceive themselves as being argumentative or difficult. It is usual for such children to blame all their problems on others. Such children can also be perfectionists and have a strong sense of justice regarding violations of what they consider correct behavior. They are impatient and intolerant of others. They are more likely to argue verbally with other children than to get into physical fights.

Older children or adolescents with ODD may try to provoke others by being deliberately annoying or critical. For example, a teenager may criticize an adult's way or speaking or dressing. This oppositional behavior is usually directed at an authority figure such as a parent, coach, or teacher. Youths diagnosed with ODD, however, can also be bullies who use their language skills to taunt and **abuse** other children.

Causes and symptoms

Causes

ODD has been called a problem of families, not of individuals. It occurs in families in which some or all of the following factors are present:

- Limits set by parents are too harsh or too lax, or an inconsistent mix of both.
- Family life lacks clear structure; rules, limits, and discipline are uncertain or inconsistently applied.
- At least one parent models oppositional behavior in his or her own interactions with others. For example, mother or father may get into frequent disputes with neighbors, store clerks, other family members, etc., in front of the child.
- At least one parent is emotionally or physically unavailable to the child due to emotional problems of the parent (such as depression), separation or divorce, or work hours.

The defiant behavior may be an attempt by the child to feel safe or gain control. It may also represent an attempt to get attention from an unresponsive parent.

There may be a genetic factor involved in ODD; the disorder often seems to run in families. This pattern may, however, reflect behavior learned from previous generations rather than the effects of a gene or genes for the disorder.

Symptoms

According to *DSM-IV-TR*, a **diagnosis** of ODD may be given to children who meet the following criteria, provided that the behavior occurs more frequently than usual compared to children of the same age and developmental level.

A pattern of negativistic, hostile, and defiant behavior lasting at least six months, during which four (or more) of the following are present. The child:

- often loses his or her temper
- frequently argues with adults
- often disregards adults' requests or rules
- deliberately tries to provoke people
- frequently blames others for his or her mistakes or misbehavior
- is often easily irritated by others
- is often angry and resentful
- is often spiteful

In order to make the diagnosis of oppositional defiant disorder, the behavioral disturbances must cause significant impairment in the child's social, academic or occupational functioning, and the behaviors must not occur exclusively during the course of a psychotic or mood disorder. In addition, the child must not meet criteria for **conduct disorder**, which is a more serious behavioral disorder. If the youth is 18 years or older, he or she must not meet criteria for **antisocial personality disorder**.

Demographics

Oppositional defiant disorder is thought to occur in about 6% of all children in the United States. It is more common in families of lower socioeconomic status. In one study, 8% of children from low-income families were diagnosed with ODD. The disorder is often apparent by the time a child is about six years old. Boys tend to be diagnosed with this disorder more often than girls in the preteen years, but it is equally common in males and females by adolescence.

It is estimated that about one-third of children who have **attention-deficit/hyperactivity disorder** (ADHD) also have ODD. Children who have ODD are also often diagnosed with anxiety or depression.

Diagnosis

Oppositional defiant disorder is diagnosed when the child's difficult behavior lasts longer than six months. There is no standard test for diagnosing ODD. A full medical checkup may be done to make sure that there is no medical problem causing the child's behavior. The medical examination is followed by a psychological evaluation of the child, which involves an interview with a mental health professional. The mental health professional may also interview the child's parents and teachers. Psychological tests are sometimes given to the child to rule out other disorders.

Evaluation for ODD includes ruling out a more disruptive behavioral disorder known as conduct disorder (CD). CD is similar to ODD but also includes physical aggression toward others, such as fighting or deliberately trying to hurt another person. Children with CD also frequently break laws or violate the rights of others, for example by stealing. They tend to be more covert than children with ODD, lying and keeping some of their unacceptable behavior secret.

The diagnosis of ODD may specify its degree of severity as mild, moderate, or severe.

Treatments

Treatment of ODD focuses on both the child and on the parents. The goals of treatment include helping the child to feel protected and safe and to teach him or her appropriate behavior. Parents may need to learn how to set appropriate limits with a child and how to deal with a child who acts out. They may also need to learn how to teach and reinforce desired behavior.

Parents may also need help with problems that may be distancing them from the child. Such problems can include alcoholism or drug dependency, depression, or financial difficulties. In some cases, legal or economic assistance may be necessary. For example, a single mother may need legal help to obtain child support from the child's father so that she won't need to work two jobs, and can stay at home in the evenings with the child.

Behavioral therapy is usually effective in treating ODD. Behavioral therapy focuses on changing specific behaviors, not on analyzing the history of the behaviors or the very early years of the child's life. The theory behind behavioral therapy is that a person can learn a different set of behaviors to replace those that are causing problems. As the person obtains better results from the new behavior, he or she will want to continue that behavior instead of reverting to the old one. To give an example, the child's parents may be asked to identify behaviors that usually start an argument. They are then shown ways to stop or change those behaviors in order to prevent arguments.

Contingency management techniques may be included in behavioral therapy. The child and the parents may be helped to draw up contracts that identify unwanted behaviors and spell out consequences. For example, the child may lose a privilege or part of his or her allowance every time he or she throws a temper tantrum. These contracts can include steps or stages—for example, lowering the punishment if the child begins an argument but manages to stop arguing within a set period of time. The same contract may also specify rewards for desired behavior. For example, if the child has gone for a full week without acting out, he or she may get to choose which movie the family sees that weekend. These contracts may be shared with the child's teachers.

The parents are encouraged to acknowledge good or nonproblematic behavior as much as possible. Attention or praise from the parent when the child is behaving well can reinforce his or her sense that the parent is aware of the child even when he or she is not acting out.

Cognitive therapy may be helpful for older children, adolescents, and parents. In cognitive therapy, the person is guided to greater awareness of problematic thoughts and feelings in certain situations. The therapist can then suggest a way of thinking about the problem that would lead to behaviors that are more likely to bring the person what they want or need. For example, a girl may be helped to see that much of her anger derives from feeling that no one cares about her, but that her angry behavior is the source of her problem because it pushes people away.

Although **psychotherapy** is the cornerstone of treatment for ODD, medicine may also be helpful in some cases. Children who have concurrent ADHD may need medical treatment to control their impulsivity and extend their attention span. Children who are anxious or depressed may also be helped by appropriate medications.

Prognosis

Treatment for ODD is usually a long-term commitment. It may take a year or more of treatment to see noticeable improvement. It is important for families to continue with treatment even if immediate results are not apparent.

If ODD is not treated or if treatment is abandoned, the child has a higher likelihood of developing conduct disorder. The risk of developing conduct disorder is lower in children who are only mildly defiant. It is higher in children who are more defiant and in children who also have ADHD. In adults, conduct disorder is called antisocial personality disorder, or ASD.

Children who have untreated ODD are also at risk for developing passive-aggressive behaviors as adults. Persons with passive-aggressive characteristics tend to see themselves as victims and blame others for their problems.

Prevention

Prevention of ODD begins with good parenting. If at all possible, families and the caregivers they encounter should be on the lookout for any problem that may prevent parents from giving children the structure and attention they need.

Early identification of ODD and ADHD is necessary to obtain help for the child and family as soon as possible. The earlier ODD is identified and treated, the more likely it is that the child will be able to develop healthy patterns of relating to others.

Resources

BOOKS

Hales, R. E., S. C. Yudofsky, J. A. Talbott, eds. *Textbook of Psychiatry.* 3rd ed. Washington DC: American Psychiatric Press, 1999.

Sadock, B. J., and V. A. Sadock. *Kaplan & Sadock's Comprehensive Textbook of Psychology,* 7th ed. Philadelphia: Lippincott Williams and Wilkins, 1999.

PERIODICALS

Loeber, Rolf. "Oppositional defiant and conduct disorder: a review of the past 10 years, part I." *Journal of the American Academy of Child and Adolescent Psychiatry* Dec. 2000.

ORGANIZATIONS

American Academy of Child and Adolescent Psychiatry. 3615 Wisconsin Avenue, NW, Washington, DC 20016-3007. (202) 966-7300. Fax: (202) 966-2891. <www.aacap.org>.

Jody Bower, M.S.W.

Orap *see* **Pimozide**

Origin of mental illnesses

History of theories about mental illness

Mental illness in the ancient world

Over the history of the healing arts, there has been an evolution of theories regarding the root causes of mental illness. Early writings from such ancient civilizations as those of Greece, Rome, India, and Egypt focused on demonic possession as the cause. This concept eventually disappeared only to resurface again in the Middle Ages in Europe, along with inadequate treatment of the mentally ill. Demons or "foul spirits" were believed to attach themselves to individuals and make them depressed ("poor-spirited") or "mad." The word *mad* became an early synonym for **psychosis**. Unfortunately, the "possessed" included people with seizure disorders as well as others suffering from what are now known to be medical disorders. Few genuinely helpful treatments were available to relieve the suffering of the mentally ill.

The Hippocratic tradition

Hippocrates, a Greek physician who lived around 400 B.C. and is regarded as the source of the Hippocratic Oath taken by modern physicians, first introduced the concept of disturbed physiology (organic processes or functions) as the basis for all illnesses, mental or otherwise. Hippocrates did not describe disturbances of the nervous system as we do today, in terms of a chemical imbalance or a low level of **neurotransmitters** (neurotransmitters are the chemical messengers sent between **brain** cells). Instead, he used the notion of an imbalance of "humors." Humors were defined as bodily fluids, and were believed to be influenced by the environment, the weather, foods, and so on, producing various imbalances in a person's state of health. Hippocrates' theory was an early version of the idea that physiological disturbances or body chemistry might play a role in the development of mental illness. Most importantly, perhaps, Hippocrates' concept placed mental illness on the same footing as other medical disorders by highlighting the belief that the mentally ill are genuinely suffering, and therefore to be treated like other sick persons rather than as moral degenerates. Sadly, modern society has not fully overcome the tendency to stigmatize persons with mental disorders. Hippocrates' more "enlightened" perspective, however, meant that someone with depression or **schizophrenia** could be viewed as being in a state of "dis-ease," just like a diabetic or someone with high blood pressure.

The nineteenth century

Toward the end of the nineteenth century, several European neurologists began actively investigating the causes of mental illness. Chief among them, and destined to change forever the understanding of mental illness, was Sigmund Freud. Although psychology and psychiatry have advanced considerably since Freud (as have other fields of medicine), his explorations were revolutionary. Freud introduced the concepts of the unconscious and the ego to modern thought, and reintroduced the ancient art of dream interpretation, but from a psychological standpoint. Freud also regarded human psychological states as an energy system in which blockages in the flow of thought (repression or suppression, for

KEY TERMS

Acetylcholine—A naturally occurring chemical in the body that transmits nerve impulses from cell to cell. Generally, it has opposite effects from dopamine and norepinephrine; it causes blood vessels to dilate, lowers blood pressure, and slows the heartbeat. Central nervous system well-being is dependent on a balance among acetylcholine, dopamine, serotonin, and norepinephrine.

Delirium—A disturbance of consciousness marked by confusion, difficulty paying attention, delusions, hallucinations, or restlessness.

Delirium tremens—Serious alcohol withdrawal symptoms that must be treated in a hospital and that may include shaking, delirium, and hallucinations.

Delusion—A false belief that is resistant to reason or contrary to actual fact.

Dementia—A group of symptoms (syndrome) associated with a progressive loss of memory and other intellectual functions that is serious enough to interfere with a person's ability to perform the tasks of daily life. Dementia impairs memory, alters personality, leads to deterioration in personal grooming, impairs reasoning ability, and causes disorientation.

Dissociation—A reaction to trauma in which the mind splits off certain aspects of the traumatic event from conscious awareness. Dissociation can affect the patient's memory, sense of reality, and sense of identity.

Dopamine—A chemical in brain tissue that serves to transmit nerve impulses (is a neurotransmitter) and helps to regulate movement and emotions.

Electrolytes—Substances or elements that dissociate into electrically charged particles (ions) when dissolved in the blood. The electrolytes in human blood include potassium, magnesium, and chloride.

Etiology—The cause or origin of a disease or disorder. The word is also used to refer to the study of the causes of disease.

Flashback—The re-emergence of a traumatic memory as a vivid recollection of sounds, images, and sensations associated with the trauma. The person having the flashback typically feels as if he or she is reliving the event.

Fugue state—A form of amnesia in which the person appears to be conscious and to make rational decisions, but upon recovery, the period is not remembered. Fugue states represent one type of reaction to traumatic experiences.

Hallucination—False sensory perceptions. A person experiencing a hallucination may "hear" sounds or "see" people or objects that are not really present. Hallucinations can also affect the senses of smell, touch, and taste.

Humor—In ancient medicine, one of four body fluids (blood, phlegm, yellow bile, and black bile) that were thought to determine a person's basic constitution and personality.

Insult—In medicine, an injury or trauma to the brain or other part of the body.

Metabolism—The group of biochemical processes within the body that release energy in support of life.

Neurotransmitter—A chemical in the brain that transmits messages between neurons, or nerve cells.

Norepinephrine—A neurotransmitter in the brain that acts to constrict blood vessels and raise blood pressure. It works in combination with serotonin.

Physiology—The branch of medicine concerned with biological processes or functions in the human body or any of its parts.

Psychosis—Severe state that is characterized by loss of contact with reality and deterioration in normal social functioning; examples are schizophrenia and paranoia. Psychosis is usually one feature of an over-arching disorder, not a disorder in itself. (Plural: psychoses)

Serotonin—A widely distributed neurotransmitter that is found in blood platelets, the lining of the digestive tract, and the brain, and that works in combination with norepinephrine. It causes very powerful contractions of smooth muscle, and is associated with mood, attention, emotions, and sleep. Low levels of serotonin are associated with depression.

Thyrotoxicosis—A disease characterized by an enlarged thyroid gland and speeded-up body metabolism caused by excessive thyroid secretion. It is also known as Graves' disease.

Tryptophan—An essential amino acid released from proteins during the process of digestion. Tryptophan is an important ingredient in the body's production of serotonin.

example) would result in disease or illness, expressed as mental or emotional loss of balance. He introduced the notion of a "talking cure"; through the use of **talk therapy** alone, many patients would improve. This method of treatment is still used today, although the technique of talk therapy itself has undergone further development. Freud's early advances in understanding the mind, however, awaited further anatomical and biochemical discoveries of the structures and functions of the human brain. As a result, early psychiatry (from two Greek words, *psyche*, meaning "soul" or "mind," and *iatros*, meaning "physician") split into two competing traditions, one that followed Freud in emphasizing thoughts, emotions and dreams as keys to the healing of mental disorders, and another that looked for clues to these disorders in the tissues of the brain.

In the first half of the twentieth century, psychiatry was advanced by the discovery of medications that helped to alleviate depression, mania, and psychosis. As often occurs in the history of medicine, physicians stumbled upon solutions before they understood the mechanisms that made the treatment work. Later studies began to reveal that certain patients responded to medications that increased certain neurotransmitters. Drugs that increased the levels of the neurotransmitters norepinephrine and serotonin seemed to help depressed patients. Similarly, medications that blocked the transmission of dopamine, another neurotransmitter, provided relief for patients suffering from **hallucinations** and **paranoia**. These insights have led to the present emphasis on the biochemistry of the human brain. If, however, the biochemical model becomes the only view of mental health, modern psychiatry risks becoming "mindless." Clearly, a unified theory is needed to understand all the factors that contribute to mental disorders, and to do justice to the complexity of each human being. Understanding all the factors that lead to a disease state has much to do with an adequate treatment response.

Nature and nurture

One attempt to unify the varied theories regarding the origin of mental illness is called simply the "nature versus nurture" theory. It is really the "nature *and* nurture" theory, however, as it establishes the importance of two forces in the development of mental illness. For example, "nature" refers to biological factors that produce a tendency or predisposition to develop certain diseases. For instance, parents who have high blood pressure have offspring who have a higher probability of developing the same condition. If, on the other hand, these offspring learn to eat properly, exercise, and live in a relatively peaceful home, for instance, they may be able to avoid the expression of high blood pressure that runs in their family. This example illustrates the impact that a person's environment may have on the development of physical disease. Researchers believe the same holds true for mental illnesses. For example, researchers know that patients with schizophrenia who return to a family environment in which there is a high level of expressed emotion, such as critical and angry remarks, have more frequent psychotic episodes that require **hospitalization**. Thus, it appears that the interaction between the biological and psychological dimensions of a person and his or her environment determines the likelihood of expressing a mental illness, or perhaps any illness whatsoever. There is, however, no accurate prediction or test that will determine whether or not a specific person will develop a certain mental illness, even if many members of his or her are positive for that disease.

Conversely, a child with minimal genetic predisposition to mental illness may develop mental illness if he or she is traumatized in any number of ways, such as being raised in a non-nurturing or a physically, mentally, or emotionally abusive household. As of 2002, scientists do not know why some people become mentally ill while others do not. Much research remains to be done; although theories abound, the precise etiology or origin of all mental illnesses remains uncertain.

Current theories about the origin of mental disorders

Biological theories

GENETICS. Genetics is at this time an important area of research for psychiatric disorders. For example, a specific gene has been associated with **bipolar disorder** (also known as manic-depressive disorder), but unfortunately, the "switch" that controls the expression of the disorder is still unknown. It is presently thought that many genes go into the expression or nonexpression of any human characteristic, such as a facial feature or a certain aspect of mental health. Research done on identical twins has provided strong support for a genetic component in the development of schizophrenia. For instance, the average person in the United States has a 1% chance of developing schizophrenia, while the identical twin of a person diagnosed with schizophrenia has a 50% chance, even if he or she has been reared by adoptive parents. Other researchers who are studying schizophrenia have found that during embryonic development, there are nerve cells that do not migrate to their proper position in the brain. On the other hand, none of the genetic or embryological findings can account for the rare but occasional recoveries from schizophrenia, indicating that biology alone does not determine the occurrence of mental disorders.

Dementias are also noted to run in families, but most of these disorders cannot be predicted with any certainty for the following generation. Only one disorder, Huntington's chorea, which is really a movement disorder with a psychiatric component, appears to be determined by a single gene. **Dementia** of the Alzheimer's type does seem to have familial pattern, but again, the expression of the disease in any specific individual is not predictable at this time. Scientists believe that similar statements can be made for many mental disorders that run in families, such as **obsessive-compulsive disorder** (OCD), depression, anxiety, and **panic disorder**. The roles of the environment and learning behavior in the ultimate expression of genetically predisposed individuals are, however, undisputed.

NEUROTRANSMITTER-RELATED CHEMICAL IMBALANCES. This theory regarding the origin of mental disorders has become the foundation of most psychiatric treatment today. It has legitimized psychiatry by returning it to the world of biological medicine. Diabetes may offer a helpful analogy. In diabetes, a chemical necessary to health (insulin) is missing and can be replaced, essentially restoring the patient's health. In mental illness, the neurotransmitters in the brain may be present in insufficient amounts. These chemicals or transmitters allow communication between nerve cells; as a result, they coordinate information processing throughout the brain. As a person reads, for example, chemical levels rise and fall in response to the letters; the meaning they have; the reader's eye movements, thoughts, reflections and associations; and to the feelings the reader may have while reading. Thus, a person's brain chemistry is changed by everything that influences him or her, whether internally or externally. While the discovery of certain neurotransmitters and their roles in mental disorders has led in turn to the discovery of effective medications to treat these disorders, it has also resulted in the unfortunate notion that medication is the only method of treatment that is helpful.

Major neurotransmitters identified thus far include acetylcholine, dopamine, epinephrine, norepinephrine, histamine, and serotonin. Serotonin and norepinephrine are most highly implicated in depression, panic disorder and anxiety, as well as OCD. Most of the medications found effective for these disorders are drugs that increase the availability of serotonin and norepinephrine (such as selective serotonin re-uptake inhibitors, or SSRIs). In particular, depression, panic disorder, anxiety disorders, and OCD have responded strongly to medications that increase serotonin levels. On the other hand, medications that block the effects of dopamine in certain parts of the brain are effective in controlling auditory and visual hallucinations as well as paranoia in patients with psychotic disorders.

STRESS-RELATED FACTORS. **Stress** is something everyone in modern society seems to understand. There are two basic kinds of stress: inner stress from previous traumas or wounds that affect one's present life; and outer stress, or the environmental issues that complicate life on a daily basis, such as work or family problems. The interplay of these two forms of stress affects brain chemistry just as it can affect physical health. Numerous studies have shown that when people are chronically stressed in life, they are vulnerable to depression, anxiety, and other disorders. Interestingly, 70% of the adults in one recent European war situation were found to have depression, which is a normal human response to relentless stress. Researchers presently think that the mechanism that triggers this depression is the depletion of certain neurotransmitters, particularly serotonin and norepinephrine, which may lead to other biochemical imbalances. For instance, most people diagnosed with schizophrenia have their first psychotic episode during such stressful situations as leaving home for college or military service.

Genetic factors may add to a person's susceptibility to mental illness by lowering the body's production of neurotransmitters during difficult life transitions. The same combination of circumstances might affect the development of high blood pressure, diabetes, or ulcers in some families.

MEDICAL CONDITIONS. It is important to note that bacterial and viral infections, metabolic illnesses, medications and street drugs can all affect a person's mental status. Insults (injuries) to the brain can cause a person to be disoriented, speak incoherently, have difficulty concentrating, hallucinate, or even act out violently. When clinicians see disorientation and an abrupt change in a person's level of alertness, they refer to the altered mental state as **delirium**. Delirium is considered a medical emergency because the underlying cause must be identified and treated as quickly as possible. The exact way in which infectious disease and chemical agents change human mental function is unclear, and thus may not be visible on **imaging studies**.

The elderly are particularly vulnerable to changes in mental status resulting from apparently minor changes in body chemistry. Fever, dehydration, electrolyte imbalances, and even aspirin or antibiotics can all have an abrupt effect on the mental status of the elderly. Older people are susceptible simply because older brain tissue is more sensitive to the slightest change in metabolism or the presence of toxins.

Certain diseases have severe effects on the brain. An example is HIV/AIDS, in which approximately 70% of patients suffering from full-blown AIDS develop dementia, depression, or delirium. Similarly, at least 50% of patients with multiple sclerosis develop depression from the effects of the disease on brain tissues—not simply as a reaction to knowing that they have MS. Any infectious disease that causes inflammation inside the skull, such as meningitis or encephalitis, will usually result in some change in mental status; fortunately, these changes are usually completely reversible.

Recently, there has been an exciting development involving infectious disease and OCD as exemplified by "PANDAS," the acronym for Pediatric Autoimmune Neuropsychiatric Disorder Associated with Group A Streptococcus. Group A Streptococcus is an autoimmune disorder thought to cause OCD symptoms (neuropsychiatric symptoms) in children with streptococcal infection of the tonsils and pharynx (more commonly known as strep throat). The OCD symptoms resolve when the infection is treated with antibiotics. The neuropsychiatric symptoms are believed to result from an autoimmune reaction, meaning that antibodies made to fight the bacteria mistakenly attack part of the brain, resulting in symptoms of OCD. The discovery of this connection between a streptococcal infection and an autoimmune reaction may have great importance for treating certain mental illnesses in the future, since links between the onset of psychiatric disorders and physical infections have been observed from time to time.

Disorders of metabolism can certainly mimic depression, anxiety and sometimes, even psychosis. Overproduction of thyroid hormone (thyrotoxicosis) can cause agitation, anxiety, mania and even psychosis; while a lack of thyroid hormone produces symptoms of depression and is routinely checked in patients with depression of recent onset. Imbalances in glucose (sugar) management can result in mood swings and should always be evaluated. Less commonly, malfunctions of the adrenal glands can profoundly affect a person's energy level and mental activity. The role of estrogen in postmenopausal depression has been intensively studied in recent years, but the findings remain inconclusive.

NEUROPATHOLOGY. Neuropathology refers to damage to the brain tissue itself that results in mental illness. Dementias are placed in this category, since the brains of persons diagnosed with dementia exhibit microscopic changes in tissue structure when viewed under a microscope. These changes may ultimately appear on tests such as a CAT scan of the brain. Larger changes are seen with strokes, which result when the blood supply is cut off to a specific area of the brain and causes localized damage. In these instances, a person may have altered speech patterns but retain the ability to think clearly, or vice versa. The losses are somewhat predictable and specific, based on the area of the brain that was affected and the extent of oxygen starvation of the tissue in that region.

Brain tumors and accidental injuries are random in their effects, and the deficits are usually less predictable. Each case must be examined individually. As with strokes, however, the location of the injury or tumor will determine the resulting mental status changes or deficits.

Pancreatic and certain colon cancers are particularly interesting for psychiatrists. For reasons that are unknown as of 2002, these tumors are frequently accompanied by depression even though they are located in organs that are far removed from the brain. More research is needed on the relationship between mood disorders and certain illnesses; it is possible that the tumor releases compounds into the bloodstream that have depressive effects.

NUTRITIONAL FACTORS. There is no doubt that poor nutrition leads to mental imbalances. While few people in the United States are truly starving or completely depleted nutritionally, instances of mental disorders related to malnutrition still occur in this country. The B vitamins are essential for mental clarity and stability. Insufficient amounts of the B vitamins, which include thiamin, nicotinamide, pyridoxine, and B, can result in confusion, irritability, **insomnia**, depression, and in extreme cases, psychosis. The body does not store these vitamins, so one should monitor one's daily intake to ensure a sufficient supply. Tryptophan is an amino acid and supplement that is a building block for serotonin, the neurotransmitter that has been found to be essential in treating depression, anxiety, panic, and OCD, among others. Tryptophan is so important nutritionally that studies have shown that its absence in the diet will result in depression even when the person is taking a prescription antidepressant to increase the availability of serotonin.

Psychological/interpersonal theories

PSYCHODYNAMIC THEORIES. Freud certainly opened the doors for humans to understand themselves in terms of psychology, or the notion that how one thinks and feels affects one's view of the world. Freud also found that simple conversation could help some very sick people out of depressions and other mental disorders. His work essentially demonstrated that extreme inner conflicts can become a source of mental illness. These extreme internal conflicts can occur, for instance, when one loves another deeply but also feels that that person is hurting them or limiting their development in some way. If the person who is causing pain or hindering growth is a parent or other powerful figure, these intense feelings can be hidden away or repressed. Also, a lack of honesty about reality can lead to any number of illnesses. For instance, feelings of anger and powerlessness, if unrecognized, may place the person at risk for developing aggressive behaviors or depression if insights and appropriate coping skills are not gained. These psychological dis-harmonies, if ignored, can lead to dis-ease if they are sufficiently intense or associated with central relationships in the person's life.

Freud's view of psychological conflicts as rooted in sexual repression was questioned by Jung, a **psychiatrist** and protégé of Freud, who felt that people's lives were affected by deep spiritual forces. Jung's work centered on psychological imbalances stemming from spiritual distress. There were other theorists after Freud, such as Adler, who regarded power as the central motivating force of human personality, or Melanie Klein, who emphasized the significance of envy.

Since the Second World War, behavioral and cognitive theories have emphasized the role of learning in the development of mental disorders. Children growing up in an abusive home, for example, may be "rewarded" by not getting beaten if they learn to be quiet and internalize everything. This internalized state may be a precursor of full-blown depression in later years. Unconscious assumptions based on early experiences may spill over into other situations later in life. As another example, children may learn to be "good" for their parents or society by taking on careers they don't like or belief systems that don't fit them, all for approval by the perceived higher authority.

Cognitive approaches to therapy maintain that people construct their view of the world from beliefs and feelings based on deeper assumptions about their own competencies. Depression, for instance, would be seen as a spiral downward into negative "self-talk" and feelings of inadequacy. Re-examining these negative assumptions then breaks the cycle based on erroneous thinking (cognition) which is causing the depression, anxiety, or aberrant behavior. Studies have shown that three months of cognitive therapy is as effective as medication in the treatment of depression. This finding shows clearly that talk therapy does change the chemistry of the brain.

TRAUMA-RELATED FACTORS. Psychological traumas refer to events that are outside the experience of everyday life, although the exact definition of a traumatic experience may vary from person to person, country to country, and century to century. Traumas in early life, such as sexual or physical **abuse**, can lead to mood disorders and contribute to the development of **personality disorders**. Horrendous early traumas involving torture of a child, other people, or animals, may result in **dissociative identity disorder**, formerly called multiple personality disorder. Dissociation is a self-protective mechanism for separating conscious awareness from repeated traumas. It has sometimes been described as self-hypnosis, but most clinicians believe that it is not under the patient's control, at least initially.

In later life, such severe traumas as war, rape, natural disasters, or any similar event, can lead to psychiatric difficulties. **Post-traumatic stress disorder** (PTSD) is a well-known disorder that affects war veterans. Extreme trauma causes the brain to record impressions in a way that is different from ordinary formation of memories. These disjointed impressions may re-emerge as flashbacks months or years after the traumatic experience. Chronic and repetitive trauma, exemplified by intermittent abuse or hostage situations, can lead to a chronic form of PTSD as well.

A subcategory of psychiatric disorders that occur in response to traumatic shock are termed fugue states. Fugue states are poorly understood, but can be described as conditions of total memory loss after witnessing an overwhelmingly horrible accident or atrocity. These states of memory loss can last from minutes to years.

SOCIOCULTURAL FACTORS. Some mental disorders are influenced by social values and social interactions shaped by those values. **Anorexia nervosa**, **bulimia nervosa**, and **body dysmorphic disorder** are the most commonly used examples of mental illnesses in this category. With the increased visibility of unnaturally slender women in modern society (as seen everywhere in advertising, television shows, movies, and celebrity fan magazines) doctors have seen a tremendous rise in the occurrence eating disorders. "You can never be too thin or too rich," a saying attributed to the Duchess of Windsor, is a phrase that has many women, and some men, monitoring their every ounce of food intake. The core of the illness is a lack of self-esteem combined with feelings that one's world is out of control. Some clinicians add fear of sexual maturation to this list of psychological causes of eating disorders. The common denominator is that these patients apparently believe they can control their world by controlling their food intake. Although neurotransmitter deficits have been found in patients with bulimia, whose vomiting may actually change their body chemistry, the desire to be thin is the conscious motivating force.

Modern society also values activity over rest, doing over being, thinking over feeling, resulting in many people becoming slaves to work and productivity, and having little respect for their inner life. Many cases of mild stress-related disorders run the risk of developing into full-blown generalized anxiety, panic, and depressive disorders. Mental health requires a reasonable balance between work and activity on the one hand and periods of rest and relaxation on the other.

ALCOHOL AND SUBSTANCE ABUSE. Alcohol is a central nervous system depressant. It plays a prominent role in the development of at least depression and is often involved in other mental disorders. In addition, people who abuse alcohol are at increased risk of mental disorders related to nutritional deficiencies. A lack of thiamin, a B-vitamin, can result in permanent brain damage in the form of severe dementia even at an early age. People in withdrawal from alcohol are also at risk for delirium tremens, a serious condition that can result in cardiovascular shock and death.

Street drugs are well known for their effects on young people's mood and behavior. Permanent brain damage may result from the use of some "designer" drugs. One example is "Ecstasy," which can cause permanent memory loss and severe depression that responds only slowly to treatment. Street drugs must always be considered as a possible factor in the sudden onset of a mental illness in a young person. Moreover, drugs may precipitate a first psychotic episode in a person with a genetic predisposition to schizophrenia. In this case, the drug is the stressor that reveals the person's dormant susceptibility to the disorder.

Current theory and future directions

The biopsychosocial model of mental illness

All of the above factors are most succinctly summarized in terms of the biopsychosocial model of mental illness. Biological contributions, thoughts and perceptions, social pressures, and environmental stressors, the presence or absence of nurturing and consistency of love, core values, and self-worth are just a few of the things that contribute to making up the psychological uniqueness of every human being on the planet. In addition to the above, researchers are actively examining the role of spirituality in mental health and recovery. No one factor can be said to be the sole cause of mental illness; rather, disorders result from a complex set of forces that act upon each person as an individual. Finding the various elements that contributed to the onset of an illness requires considerable patience from the patient, his or her family, and health workers. Identifying all factors, if possible, provides the best road map for the healing process.

New directions

In the future, scientists will certainly modify and expand our thought-models about the mind and brain. For example, a new treatment called transcranial magnetic stimulation (TMS) is being evaluated as an alternative to electric shock therapy. TMS uses powerful magnets instead of electricity, and is delivered to specific areas of the brain. Hence, in the future scientists must integrate some of the electromagnetic aspects of nature into the mind-brain puzzle. In addition, the National Institute of Mental Health (NIMH) is researching alternative healing modalities. Prominent among them is **acupuncture**, which has been used to treat depression, anxiety and panic disorder. Other alternative treatments being studied include the effects of prayer, **meditation**, creative writing, and **yoga**.

Deeper exploration of the human condition is both inevitable and desirable. Perhaps researchers will find better answers by asking the question, "What makes people healthy?" instead of simply looking at what makes us sick. In the end, researchers may find proof of some of the ancient truths taught by spiritual teachers from all traditions; and that the physical changes seen with human eyes or under a microscope are really just the symptoms of and not the causes of imbalances.

See also Genetic factors and mental disorders; Psychoanalysis

Resources

BOOKS

American Psychiatric Association. *Diagnostic and Statistical Manual of Mental Disorders.* 4th edition, text revised. Washington DC: American Psychiatric Association, 2000.

Kaplan, Harold I., and Benjamin J. Sadock. *Kaplan and Sadock's Synopsis of Psychiatry: Behavioral Sciences–Clinical Psychiatry.* Eighth edition. Philadelphia: Lippincott Williams and Wilkins, 1998.

Beth A. Bollinger, M.D.

Oxazepam

Definition

Oxazepam is a member of a family of tranquilizers known as benzodiazepines. It is sold in the United States under the brand name Serax and in Canada under the brand name Ox-Pam. Generic forms of oxazepam are also available.

Purpose

Oxazepam is prescribed to treat feelings of tension and anxiety. It is also used to calm patients who are suffering from the symptoms of alcohol withdrawal.

Description

Oxazepam is one of several drugs in the class called benzodiazepines. Oxazepam slows down certain **brain** functions by blocking specific chemicals that transmit messages among the nerve cells in the brain.

Recommended dosage

The typical starting dose for adults ranges from 5–15 mg per day. The dosage is sometimes increased by the doctor, but 80 mg is usually the maximum amount prescribed per day. The amount used each day is typically divided into at least two doses. Oxazepam is taken by mouth, and is available in tablets and capsules. It can be taken with food if the patient is having side effects in the digestive tract.

Oxazepam is not FDA-approved for use in children under six years. However, often in clinical practice, the medication is used with close physician supervision. The typical starting dose for children aged two to 16 years is 5 mg. The doctor may increase this dose if necessary. Typically, the dose does not exceed 40 mg per day, and is given in divided doses. Children under two years of age may receive a dose based on body weight. The doctor must determine whether the child needs the drug as well as the dosage.

Precautions

The doctor should monitor the patient at regular intervals to ensure that the medicine is not causing troublesome side effects. Monitoring the patient is particularly important if the drug is being taken over a long period of time. Patients should not stop taking oxazepam suddenly, especially if they are taking large doses. The dose should be tapered (gradually decreased), and then stopped. Suddenly discontinuing oxazepam may cause a rebound effect. In a few cases patients have reported serious withdrawal symptoms when they stopped taking oxazepam, including nausea, vomiting, muscle cramps, and unusual irritability.

Oxazepam should be given with great care to elderly patients; to people who are significantly disabled; and to people with a history of liver or kidney disease, drug abuse, or breathing problems. Pregnant women should not take oxazepam because of the risk of birth defects in the baby. Likewise, nursing mothers should not use oxazepam while they breast-feed. Oxazepam and other benzodiazepines should never be combined with alcohol or other drugs that depress (lower the activity of) the central nervous system. Oxazepam and other benzodiazepines should be prescribed and used very carefully if they are given for long-term treatment because they are habit-forming. Patients who have been diagnosed with glaucoma or serious psychological disorders should not receive oxazepam. Patients who have a history of alcohol abuse, drug abuse, brain disease, mental depression, mental illness, sleep apnea, or myasthenia gravis should tell their doctor about their condition. Similarly, a woman who becomes pregnant while she is taking the drug should tell her doctor at once.

KEY TERMS

Glaucoma—A group of eye diseases characterized by increased pressure within the eye significant enough to damage eye tissue and structures. If untreated, glaucoma results in blindness.

Hallucination—False sensory perceptions. A person experiencing a hallucination may "hear" sounds or "see" people or objects that are not really present. Hallucinations can also affect the senses of smell, touch, and taste.

Myasthenia gravis—A disease characterized by weakness of the muscles caused by an autoimmune reaction.

Paranoid—A mental attitude characterized by unjustified or excessive distrust of other people, usually combined with anger.

Rebound effect—A physical reaction to stopping a medication characterized by the reappearance of the symptom(s) that the medication was given to suppress. For example, people who stop taking oxazepam may experience rebound excitability and sleeping problems.

Sleep apnea—Temporary stoppage of breathing during sleep that occurs often enough to significantly disrupt the patient's sleeping pattern.

Withdrawal—Symptoms experienced by a person who has become physically dependent on a drug, experienced when the drug use is discontinued.

Side effects

Rare but serious side effects associated with the use of oxazepam include: anxiety, mental depression, reduced memory, and confusion. Even more rare are disorientation, **delusions**, **seizures**, unusually low blood pressure, sleeping difficulties, muscle weakness, and changes in behavior.

Less serious but more common side effects include: difficulty talking, dizziness, clumsiness, and drowsiness. Less common but not particularly serious side effects include dry mouth, general weakness, headache, mild abdominal pain, constipation, diarrhea, nausea, and vomiting.

When the patient stops taking oxazepam, nervousness, irritability, and sleeping problems are common withdrawal side effects. Less common withdrawal side effects can include confusion, hearing problems, stomach cramps, increased sweating, mental depression, nausea, and vomiting. Rare withdrawal side effects can include seizures, **hallucinations**, and paranoid ideas.

Interactions

Patients should always inform every health professional that they deal with— doctors, pharmacists, nurses, dentists, and others— about every medication they take. Oxazepam, alcohol, and other medications that cause drowsiness can intensify one another's effects. Some medications that are used to treat viral infections, fungal infections, high blood pressure, and some heart rhythm problems can increase the effects of oxazepam.

Heavy smoking decreases the effectiveness of oxazepam.

See also: Alcohol and related disorders

Resources

BOOKS

Consumer Reports Staff, eds. *Consumer Reports Complete Drug Reference.* 2002 ed. Denver, CO: Micromedex Thomson Healthcare, 2001.

Ellsworth, Allan J. and others. *Mosby's Medical Drug Reference.* 2001-2002. St. Louis, MO: Mosby, 2001.

Hardman, Joel G., Lee E. Limbird, ed. *Goodman & Gilman's The Pharmacological Basis of Therapeutics.* 10th ed. New York, NY: McGraw-Hill, 2001.

Mosby's GenRx Staff. *Mosby's GenRx.* 9th ed. St. Louis, MO: Mosby, 1999.

Venes, Donald, and others, eds. *Taber's Cyclopedic Medical Dictionary.* 19th ed. Philadelphia, PA: F. A. Davis, 2001.

Mark Mitchell, M.D.

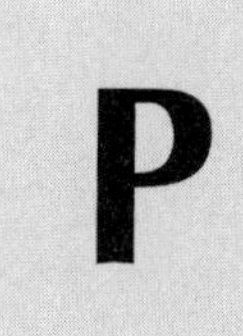

Pain disorder

Definition

Pain disorder is one of several somatoform disorders described in the revised, fourth edition of the mental health professional's handbook, the ***Diagnostic and Statistical Manual of Mental Disorders*** *(known as* DSM-IV-TR). The term "somatoform" means that symptoms are physical but are not entirely understood as a consequence of a general medical condition or as a direct effects of a substance, such as a drug. Pain in one or more anatomical sites is the predominant complaint and is severe enough to require medical or therapeutic **intervention**. Pain disorder is classified as a mental disorder because psychological factors play an important role in the onset, severity, worsening, or maintenance of pain.

Earlier names for this disorder include psychogenic pain disorder and somatoform pain disorder. There is some overlap in the meaning of these terms, but views regarding the nature of pain have been changing and they are, therefore, not equivalent diagnostic categories. Sometimes pain disorder is referred to as somatization, but this is an imprecise term and is easily confused with **somatization disorder**.

Description

In 1994, the International Association for the Study of Pain (IASP) defined pain as an unpleasant sensory or emotional experience arising from real or probable tissue damage. In other words, the perception of pain is, in part, a psychological response to noxious stimuli. This definition addresses the complex nature of pain and moves away from the earlier dualistic idea that pain is either psychogenic (of mental origin) or somatogenic (of physical origin). The contemporary view characterizes pain as multidimensional; the central nervous system, emotions, cognitions (thoughts), and beliefs are simultaneously involved.

When a patient's primary complaint is the experience of pain and when impairment at home, work, or school causes significant distress, a **diagnosis** of pain disorder may be warranted. The diagnosis is further differentiated by subtype; subtype is assigned depending on whether or not pain primarily is accounted for by psychological factors or in combination with a general medical condition, and whether the pain is acute (less than six months) or chronic (six months or more). The classification of pain states is important since the effectiveness of treatment depends on the aptness of the diagnosis of pain disorder and its type.

Causes and symptoms

Causes

Common sites of pain include the back (especially lower back), the head, abdomen, and chest. Causes of pain vary depending on the site; however, in pain disorder, the severity or duration of pain or the degree of associated disability is unexplained by observed medical or psychological problems.

The prevailing biopsychosocial model of mental disorders suggests that multiple causes of varying kinds may explain pain disorder, especially when the pain is chronic. There are four domains of interest:

- The underlying organic problem or medical condition, if there is one. For example, fibromyalgia (a pain syndrome involving fibromuscular tissue), skeletal damage, pathology of an internal organ, migraine headache, and peptic ulcer all have characteristic patterns of pain and a particular set of causes.
- The experience of pain. The severity, duration, and pattern of pain are important determinants of distress. Uncontrolled or inadequately managed pain is a significant stressor.
- Functional impairment and disability. Pain is exacerbated by loss of meaningful activities or social rela-

KEY TERMS

Biopsychosocial model—A hypothetical explanation for why something occurs that includes biological, psychological, and social causes or correlates.

Inter-rater reliability—The degree to which judgments about a person are consistent among raters or diagnosticians.

Multiaxial—Refers to a type of classification system that involves numeric measurement along more than one dimension and is not based on assignment to mutually exclusive categories.

Multimodal—Involving several types of therapeutic interventions such as heat or ice packs, electrical stimulation, ultrasound; sometimes refers to a mix of physical and psychological therapies.

Neuropathic—Relating to neural damage.

Painstates—Refers to the four-way classification of pain disorder as being (1) acute with psychological factors, (2) acute with psychological factors and a general medical condition, (3) chronic with psychological factors, and (4) chronic with psychological factors and a general medical condition.

Somatization—When mental or emotional distress is expressed physically in a way that disrupts body function.

tionships. Disruption or loss may lead to isolation and resentment or anger, which further increases pain.

- Emotional distress. Depression and anxiety are the most common correlates of pain, especially when the person suffering feels that the pain is unmanageable, or that the future only holds more severe pain and more losses.

In sum, there are multiple causes of pain disorder. A therapist or team of health professionals will weigh the relative causal contributions, assign priorities for therapeutic intervention, and address the several domains in a multimodal fashion. For example, the design of a treatment plan in a pain clinic may involve a physician, psychotherapist, occupational therapist, physical therapist, anesthesiologist, **psychologist**, and nutritionist.

Symptoms

Symptoms vary depending on the site of pain and are treated medically. However, there are common symptoms associated with pain disorder regardless of the site:

- negative or distorted cognition, such as feeling helpless or hopeless with respect to pain and its management
- inactivity, passivity, and/or disability
- increased pain requiring clinical intervention
- **insomnia** and **fatigue**
- disrupted social relationships at home, work, or school
- depression and/or anxiety

Demographics

There is very little information regarding rates of pain disorder. A major difficulty is that the diagnostic categories for psychogenic pain disorder in *DSM-III*, somatoform pain disorder in *DSM-III-R*, and pain disorder in *DSM-IV* and *DSM-IV-TR* are not equivalent. Furthermore, many criticize the somatoform disorder group (which includes pain disorder) as being an aggregate of disorders that are not truly distinct from one another. This lack of distinctiveness suggests to some researchers that a more appropriate system of classification should be dimensional rather than categorical. In other words, if shared dimensions or characteristics of the several somatoform disorders exist, differences among disorders should be a matter of degree along the possible dimensions. The critics of the *DSM* categorical approach would prefer a dimensional or multiaxial system because when classification systems are improved, the reliability and validity of measures assessing disorder improve, and better estimates of rates are possible.

Nevertheless, some researchers find the *DSM-IV* category for pain disorder useful. For example, in one study of psychiatric pain clinic outpatients, 79% met the criteria for pain disorder of the subtype where psychological factors and a general medical condition co-exist; 9% of the outpatients met the criteria for pain disorder with psychological factors and no medical condition. In another study of patients at a psychiatric clinic, 38% of the patients at admission and 18% of the outpatients reported significant pain. In comparison, 51% in a study of general medical and surgical inpatients met the criteria for pain disorder.

Currently, there are no good estimates for rates of pain disorder in the general population.

Diagnosis

A **psychiatrist** or mental health professional arrives at the diagnosis of pain disorder after considering several questions. An important preliminary question is whether the pain is entirely accounted for by a general medical condition. If so, the diagnosis of pain disorder is ruled out; and if not, the psychiatrist considers whether the pain is feigned. If the psychiatrist believes the patient is pretending to be in pain, the patient is diagnosed as **malingering** for external rewards, such as seeking mood-altering drugs, or as having a **factitious disorder** that reflects the patient's need to adopt a sick role. Neither malingering nor factitious disorder is in the somatoform group.

The psychiatrist may employ a variety of methods to assess the severity of pain and the contribution of psychological factors to the experience of pain. These include structured interviews (where the questions asked are standardized), open or unstructured interviews, numerical rating scales, visual analog scales (where the patient makes a mark along a line to indicate severity of pain, or if the patient is a child, or is illiterate, selects a face to represent the degree of pain), and instruments such as the McGill Pain Questionnaire or the West Haven-Yale Multidimensional Pain Inventory.

There are several conditions that rule out a diagnosis of pain disorder:

- Dyspareunia. (The patient's primary complaint relates to the experience of painful sexual intercourse.)
- Somatization disorder. (The patient has a long history of pain that began prior to age 30 and involves the gastrointestinal, reproductive, and nervous systems.)
- Conversion disorder. (In addition to pain, there are other symptoms associated with motor or sensory dysfunction.)
- Mood, anxiety, or psychotic disorder. (Any one of these more fully accounts for the pain. This last exclusion rests upon a very subjective opinion. Subjectivity reduces inter-rater reliability and is one of the points raised by critics of the *DSM* category for pain disorder.)

A final consideration is whether the pain is acute or chronic.

Treatments

Depending on whether the pain is acute or chronic, management may involve one or more of the following: pharmacological treatment (medication); **psychotherapy** (individual or group); family, behavioral, physical, hypnosis, and/or occupational therapy. If the pain is acute, the primary goal is to relieve the pain. Customary agents are acetaminophen or nonsteroidal anti-inflammatory drugs (NSAIDs); if opioid analgesics are prescribed, they often are combined with NSAIDs so that the dosage of opioids may be reduced. Psychotherapy is less important for the treatment of acute pain as compared to chronic pain disorder. In comparison, treatment of chronic pain disorder usually requires some sort of psychotherapy in combination with medication.

Antidepressants

Tricyclic antidepressants (TCAs) reduce pain, improve sleep, and strengthen the effects of opioids (such as codeine and oxycodone), as well as moderate depression. Relief of pain may occur in a few days while lessening of depression may take several weeks. Usually, TCAs for pain are prescribed at doses 33% to 50% lower than when prescribed for depression. TCAs are particularly effective for neuropathic pain, headache, facial pain, fibromyalgia, and arthritis.

Treatment of sleep dysfunction

Pain and depression diminish the restorative quality of sleep. When the cycle of pain, depression, insomnia, and fatigue is established, it tends to be self-perpetuating. Treatment may include antidepressants, relaxation training, and education regarding good sleep hygiene.

Cognitive-behavioral therapy

Many people who suffer chronic pain experience isolation, distress, frustration, and a loss of confidence regarding their ability to cope; subsequently, they may adopt a passive, helpless style of problem solving. The goal of **cognitive-behavioral therapy** (CBT) is to restore a sense of self-efficacy by educating patients about the pain-and-tension cycle, by teaching them how to actively manage pain and distress, and by informing them about the therapeutic effects of their medications. CBT is time-limited, structured, and goal-oriented.

Some tension-reducing techniques include progressive muscle relaxation, visual imagery, hypnosis, and **biofeedback**. Pain diaries are useful for describing daily patterns of pain and for helping the patient identify activities, emotions, and thoughts that alleviate or worsen pain. Diaries also are useful in evaluating the effectiveness of medication. Patients may be taught pacing techniques or scheduling strategies to restore and maintain meaningful activities.

The cognitive aspect of CBT is based on cognitive-social learning theory. The focus is on helping the patient to restructure his or her ideas about the nature of pain and the possibility of effective self-management. In particular, the patient is taught to identify and then modify negative or distorted thought patterns of helplessness and hopelessness.

Operant conditioning

The principles of operant conditioning are taught to the patient and family members so that activity and non-pain behaviors are reinforced or encouraged. The goal is to eliminate pain behaviors, such as passivity, inactivity, and over-reliance on medication.

Other Treatments

Other treatments effective in the management of pain include **acupuncture**, transcutaneous electrical nerve stimulation (TENS), trigger point injections, massage, nerve blocks, surgical ablation (removal of a part or pathway), **meditation**, exercise, **yoga**, music and art therapy.

Prognosis

The prognosis for total remission of symptoms is good for acute pain disorder and not as promising for chronic pain disorder. The typical pattern for chronic pain entails occasional flare-ups alternating with periods of low to moderate pain. The prognosis for remission of symptoms is better when patients are able to continue working; conversely, unemployment and the attendant isolation, resentment, and inactivity are correlates of a continuing pain disorder. Additionally, if **reinforcement** of pain behavior is in place (for example, financial compensation for continuing disability, an overly solicitous spouse, abuse of addictive drugs), remission is less likely.

The results of outcome studies comparing pain disorder treatments point to cognitive-behavioral therapy in conjunction with antidepressants as the most continually effective regimen. However, people in chronic pain may respond better to other treatments and it is in keeping with the goal of active self-management for the patient and health professional(s) to find an individualized mix of effective coping strategies.

Prevention

Pain disorder may be prevented by early intervention i.e., at the onset of pain or in the early stages of recurring pain. When pain becomes chronic, it is especially important to find help or learn about and implement strategies to manage the distress before inactivity and hopelessness develop. Most patients in pain first contact their primary care physician who may make a referral to a mental health professional or pain clinic. Many physicians will reassure the patient that a referral for psychological help is not stigmatizing, does not in any way minimize the experience of pain or the medical condition, and does not imply that the physician believes the pain is imaginary. On the contrary, the accepted IASP definition of pain fully recognizes that all pain is, in part, an emotional response to actual damage or to the threat of damage.

See also: Abuse; Assessment and diagnosis; Creative therapies; Personality disorders

Resources

BOOKS

American Psychiatric Association. *Diagnostic and Statistical Manual of Mental Disorders.* 4th edition, text revised. Washington, DC: American Psychiatric Association, 2000.

Martin, Ronald L., and Sean H. Yutzy. "Somatoform Disorders." In *Psychiatry.* 2 vols. Edited by Allan Tasman, Jerald Kay, and Jeffrey A. Lieberman. Philadelphia: W. B. Saunders Company, 1997.

Masheb, Robin M., and Robert D. Kerns. "Pain Disorder." In *Effective Brief Therapies: A Clinician's Guide,* edited by Michael Hersen and Maryka Biaggio. San Diego: Academic Press, 2000.

Simon, Gregory E. "Management of Somatoform and Factitious Disorders." In *A Guide to Treatments that Work,* edited by Peter E. Nathan and Jack M. Gorman. New York: Oxford University Press, 1998.

PERIODICALS

King, Steven. "The Classification and Assessment of Pain." *International Review of Psychiatry* 12, no. 2 (2000): 86–90.

Merskey, Harold. "Pain, Psychogenesis, and Psychiatric Diagnosis." *International Review of Psychiatry* 12, no. 2 (2000): 99–102.

Sunil, Verma, and Rollin M. Gallagher. "Evaluating and Treating Co-morbid Pain and Depression." *International Review of Psychiatry* 12, no. 2 (2000): 103–114.

ORGANIZATIONS

American Academy of Pain Medicine. 4700 W. Lake, Glenview, IL 60025. (847) 375-4731. <http://www.painmed.org>.

The American Chronic Pain Association. PO Box 850, Rocklin, CA 95677. (916) 632-3208. <http://www.theacpa.org>.

Tanja Bekhuis, Ph.D.

Pamelor *see* **Nortriptyline**

Panic attack

Definition

Panic attacks, the hallmark of **panic disorder**, are discrete episodes of intense anxiety. Panic attacks can also be experienced by people with specific phobia, **social phobia**, or by people who have used or consumed certain substances, such as cocaine.

Description

Panic attacks are intense anxiety experiences that are usually accompanied by symptoms in the affected person's body and thinking. The panic attack can occur unexpectedly during early stages of panic disorder illness. As panic disorder progresses, panic attacks may become associated with certain situations that trigger attacks. Panic attacks triggered by a specific experience are called situational panic attacks, since a certain situation initiates the intense anxiety.

Persons affected with panic attacks usually exhibit a broad range of clinical signs and symptoms that include:

- heart palpitations (accelerated heart rate)
- shaking or trembling
- sweating
- shortness of breath or sensation of feeling smothered or choked
- feeling of tingling
- chest discomfort or pain
- nausea or abdominal distress
- feeling dizzy, light headed, unsteady or faint
- perceptions of being detached from oneself (**depersonalization**), or a feeling out of touch with reality (derealization)
- chills or hot flashes
- fear of dying
- fear of going crazy or losing control

A person meets the criteria for a panic attack if the symptoms start abruptly, reach a quick peak (usually within 10 minutes), and if the affected individual has at least four symptoms as listed above. In persons who have less than four symptoms during an attack, the disorder is called a limited symptom attack.

It is typical that affected persons who seek treatment usually have one to two attacks a week and in worse periods may have one daily attacks or several within a week.

As stated, panic attacks can be experienced as a result of stimulant chemical usage, such as cocaine usage. There is evidence to suggest that persons with panic attacks are sensitive to certain chemicals such as caffeine, carbon dioxide, antihistamines, and, in women, progesterone replacement. Exposure to these substances may precipitate an attack.

Resources

BOOKS

Rakel, Robert E. *Conn's Current Therapy.* 54th ed. Philadelphia: W. B. Saunders Company, 2002.

Tasman, Allan. *Psychiatry.* 1st ed. Philadelphia: W. B. Saunders Company, 1997.

Laith Farid Gulli, M.D.
Jean Suvan, B.S., RDH

Panic disorder

Definition

Panic disorder is a condition in which the person with the disorder suffers recurrent panic attacks. Panic attacks are sudden attacks that are not caused by a substance (like caffeine), medication, or by a medical condition (like high blood pressure), and during the attack, the sufferer may experience sensations such as accelerated or irregular heartbeats, shortness of breath, dizziness, or a fear of losing control or "going crazy." The sudden attack builds quickly (usually within 10 minutes) and is almost paralyzing in its severity. When a **diagnosis** of panic disorder is given, the disorder can be considered one of two different types—panic disorder with or without **agoraphobia**.

The handbook for mental health professionals (called the ***Diagnostic and Statistical Manual of Mental Disorders****, or the* DSM-IV-TR) classifies both types of panic disorder as anxiety disorders.

Panic disorder without agoraphobia

Panic disorder without agoraphobia is defined by the *DSM-IV-TR* as a disorder in which patients are plagued by panic attacks that occur repeatedly and without warning. After these attacks, the affected individual worries for one month or more about having more embarrassing attacks, and may change his or her behavior with regard to these attacks. For example, a patient may fear that he or she has a cardiac condition, and may quit a job or quit exercising because of the fear. Patients may also worry that they are going to lose control or appear insane to other people. Panic disorder without agoraphobia has a less severe set of symptoms than panic disorder with agoraphobia. Patients without agoraphobia do not become housebound—they suffer panic attacks but do not have significant interference in their level of function and are still able to accomplish their daily activities.

Panic disorder with agoraphobia

People who suffer from this kind of panic disorder may experience their agoraphobia in one of two ways. They may experience sudden, unexpected panic attacks

KEY TERMS

Agoraphobia—People with this condition worry that they will not be able to get help or flee a place if they have a panic attack; they may refuse to go to places that might trigger a panic attack.

Amygdala—An almond-shaped brain structure in the brain's limbic system that is activated in acute stress situations to trigger the emotion of fear.

Cognitive-behavioral therapy (CBT)—An approach to psychotherapy that emphasizes the correction of distorted thinking patterns and changing one's behaviors accordingly.

GABA—Gamma-aminobutyric acid, an inhibitory neurotransmitter in the brain.

Hypersensitive internal suffocation alarm—A sensitive alarm goes off and the affected person's brain sends the body false signals that not enough oxygen is being received, causing an increase in their breathing rate.

Locus ceruleus—A part of the brain where the neurotransmitter causes excitation.

Panic attack—Specific periods of time when a person has a feeling that s/he is dying or having a heart attack with chest pain, a feeling as though s/he could pass out, and fear that s/he is going insane.

Panic disorder with agoraphobia—Repeated panic attacks in which the patient is worried about the attacks enough that the worry restricts their activity.

Panic disorder without agoraphobia—Repeated panic attacks without symptoms of agoraphobia.

that cause them to fear being in a place where help might not be available; or, they may experience sudden panic attacks in specific, known situations, and fear those situations or places that may trigger attacks. In either case, the fear of further panic attacks restricts the affected person's activities. For example, people whose attacks are triggered by being in crowds may avoid shopping malls for fear that they will be in a crowd and have a **panic attack**. Or, a person may experience sudden, debilitating panic attacks without a particular trigger, and, as a result, he or she is afraid to go to a supermarket (or similar place) for fear that a panic attack could occur while there and no one could help.

Description

Panic disorder can be very difficult to distinguish from other mental illnesses such as major depression, other anxiety disorders, or medical conditions such as heart attacks. Panic attacks differ from general anxiety in that they are episodes that last for discrete periods of time and the symptoms that people suffer are more intense. Panic attacks have three types: unexpected, situationally bound, and situationally predisposed. The unexpected attacks occur without warning and without a trigger. The situationally bound attacks happen repeatedly when the person is performing some activity, about to do that activity, or even when the person thinks about doing that activity. For example, a person whose panic attacks are triggered by being in crowds can have an attack just by thinking about going to a shopping mall. Situationally predisposed attacks are similar to the situationally bound attacks, except that they do not always occur when the trigger stimulus is encountered. For example, someone who experiences panic attacks while in crowds may sometimes be in crowds and not experience attacks, or may experience attacks in other, non-crowded situations, as well.

Patients who suffer from panic disorder without treatment usually have a diminished quality of life and end up spending excessive money on health care because of frequent visits to emergency rooms and to other medical doctors. However, very effective treatments for panic disorder exist.

Agoraphobia is a fear of being in a place or situation from which escape might be difficult or embarrassing, or in which help may not be available in the case of a panic attack. It is not clear why some people develop agoraphobia and other people do not. Many people may develop their agoraphobia symptoms right after their first attack, but others do not develop agoraphobia until sometimes years after their attacks began.

Causes and symptoms

Causes

BIOCHEMICAL/PHYSIOLOGICAL CAUSES. It is extremely difficult to study the **brain** and the underlying causes of psychiatric illness; and understanding the chemistry of the brain is the key to unlocking the mystery of panic disorder. The amygdala is the part of the brain that causes fear and the response to **stress**. It has been implicated as a vital part of anxiety disorders. Sodium lactate, a chemical that the body produces when muscles are fatigued, and carbon dioxide are known to induce panic attacks. These substances are thought to inhibit the release of **neurotransmitters** in the brain, which leads to the panic attacks. One hypothesis is that sodium lactate stimulates the amygdala and causes panic attacks. Another hypothesis is that patients with panic disorder have a hypersensitive internal suffocation alarm. This means that the patient's brain sends the body false signals that not enough oxygen is being received, causing the affected person to increase his or her breathing rate. Panic disorder patients have attacks when their overly sensitive alarm goes off unpredictably. Yohimbine, a drug used to treat male sexual dysfunction, stimulates a part of the brain called the locus ceruleus and induces panic symptoms thus pointing to this area of the brain's involvement in panic disorder. Brain neurotransmitters serotonin and GABA are suspected to be involved in causing the disorder, as well.

GENETICS. Genetics also plays a pivotal role in the development of panic disorder. Twin studies have demonstrated that there is a higher concordance in identical versus fraternal twins thus supporting the idea that panic disorders are inherited. Family studies have also demonstrated that panic attacks run in families. Relatives of patients with panic disorder are four to 10 times more likely to develop panic disorder. People who develop early onset of panic attacks in their mid-20s are more likely to have relatives who have panic disorder. When relatives of patients with panic disorder are exposed to high levels of carbon dioxide, they have panic attacks. Another hypothesis is that patients with panic disorder who develop agoraphobia have a more severe form of the disease. Current efforts to identify a gene for panic disorder have not been successful.

PERSONAL VARIABLES. There are several themes in the psychology of panic disorder. Research has shown that patients who develop panic disorder have difficulty with anger. They also have difficulty when their job responsibilities are increased (as in the case of a promotion), and are sensitive to loss and separation. People with this disorder often have difficulty getting along with their parents, whom they see as controlling, critical, and demanding, causing the patients to feel inadequate. Early maternal separation is thought to be an underlying cause of panic disorder.

Panic disorder patients also have a pattern of dependency in their interpersonal relationships. As children, people with panic disorder relied on parents to protect them from fear. As a result, they develop an angry dependence on their parents and fear detaching from them. They constantly feel as though they are trapped.

There is also an association between sexual **abuse** and patients who have panic attacks. Sixty percent of female patients with panic disorder were sexually abused as children. This explains their difficulty with developing trusting relationships.

Symptoms

PANIC ATTACK SYMPTOMS. The *DSM-IV-TR* lists thirteen symptoms to meet the criteria for a diagnosis of panic attack. The affected person must have four or more of these symptoms within ten minutes of the beginning of an attack in order to meet the panic attack criteria:

- bounding or pounding heartbeat or fast heart rate
- sweating
- shaking
- shortness of breath
- feeling of choking
- pains in the chest; many people they feel as though they are having a heart attack
- nausea or stomach ache
- feeling dizzy or lightheaded as if he or she is going to pass out
- feeling of being outside of one's body or being detached from reality
- fear that he or she is out of control or crazy
- fear that he or she is going to die
- feeling of tingling or numbness
- chills or hot flashes

Symptoms of panic disorder without agoraphobia

The *DSM-IV-TR* criteria for panic disorder without agoraphobia include:

- recurrent panic attacks (see above) that occur without warning for one month
- persistent worry that panic attacks will recur
- possible change in behavior because of that fear
- no agoraphobia
- not due to a medical condition or substance abuse
- not due other mental illness like specific phobia, **social phobia**, **obsessive-compulsive disorder**, **separation anxiety disorder**, or **post-traumatic stress disorder**

Symptoms of panic disorder with agoraphobia

The *DSM-IV-TR* criteria for panic disorder with agoraphobia are the same as above, but agoraphobia is present. The symptoms of agoraphobia include fear of being in situations that can trigger panic attacks, and avoiding places where attacks have occurred because of the affected person's fear that he or she will not be able to leave, or will not be able to get help. People with this condition may need to have another person accompany them when going to a place that may trigger anxiety attacks.

Sometimes this fear can be so severe that the person becomes housebound. This fact is important to consider because 15% of the general population can have one spontaneous panic attack without the recurrence of symptoms.

Demographics

Factors such as race, gender and socioeconomic status are important factors in the development of panic disorder. An individual has a chance of between one and two percent of developing panic disorder with or without agoraphobia. The symptoms usually begin when the person is in his or her early to mid-twenties. Women are twice as likely as men to develop panic attacks regardless of age. The National Institute of Mental Health Epidemiologic Catchment Area Study (ECA) shows no real significant differences between the races or ethnic groups, although it appears that African American and Hispanic men between the ages of 40 and 50 have lower rates of panic disorder than white men. Panic disorder patients are at increased risk for major depression and the development of agoraphobia. According to ECA studies, an individual with panic disorder has a 33% chance of developing agoraphobia. People without panic disorder only have a 5.5% chance of developing agoraphobia. Again, women were more likely to develop agoraphobia than men. Over the course of their lifetime, African Americans were more likely to develop agoraphobia than whites or Hispanics. Agoraphobia is more prevalent among people with less education and lower economic class.

Diagnosis

Differential diagnosis

Differential diagnosis is the process of distinguishing one diagnosis from other, similar diagnoses. Panic disorder can be difficult to distinguish from other anxiety disorders such as specific phobia and social phobia. However, in general, specific phobia is cued by a specific trigger or stimulus and social phobia by specific social situations, while the panic attacks of panic disorder are completely uncued and unexpected. In certain cases, it may be difficult to distinguish between certain, situational phobias and panic disorder with agoraphobia, and the mental health professional must use the *DSM* and professional judgment in these cases. Panic attacks that occur during sleep and wake the person up are more characteristic of panic disorder, than are the other disorders that include panic attacks. It can be distinguished from post-traumatic stress disorder (PTSD), obsessive-compulsive disorder (OCD), and **generalized anxiety disorder** (GAD) again by what cues the attacks. In PTSD, thinking about the traumatic event can trigger attacks. In obsessive-compulsive disorder, worries about getting dirty can fuel an attack of anxiety. In generalized anxiety disorder, general worries or concerns can lead to the symptoms of panic. However, in panic disorder, a main component is that the affected individual fears recurrent panic attacks.

Panic attacks can often be difficult to distinguish from other physical problems such as hyperthyroidism, hyperparathyroidism, seizure disorder, and cardiac disease. If patients are middle aged or older and have other complaints, including dizziness and headaches, their attacks are more likely to be another medical problem and not panic attacks. Panic attacks can also be difficult to distinguish from drug abuse since any drug that stimulates the brain can cause the symptoms. For example, cocaine, caffeine, and **amphetamines** can all cause panic attacks. Therefore, a person must be free of all drugs before a diagnosis of panic disorder can be made. Many patients may attempt to self-medicate with alcohol to try to calm down. Withdrawal from alcohol can lead to worse panic symptoms. The patient may believe that he or she is reducing symptoms while actually exacerbatng their panic attacks.

Dual diagnosis

Individuals with panic disorders have a high rate of coexisting depression. Patients who have panic disorder have about a 40–80% chance of developing major depression. In most situations, the panic disorder happens first and the depression comes later. Patients are also at risk for substance abuse difficulties as a result of attempts to stop attacks. These attempts may involve the use of alcohol, illicit or unprescribed sedatives, or benzodiazepines (medications that slow down the central nervous system, having a calming effect). Patients with panic disorder are not at high risk for **suicide** attempts. A recent Harvard-Brown study showed that people with panic disorder with or without agoraphobia are not at risk for suicide unless they have other conditions such as depression or substance abuse.

Psychological measures and diagnostic testing

Currently there is no diagnostic test for panic disorder. Any patient who has panic attacks should receive a thorough medical examination to rule out any medical condition. Patients should have baseline blood counts and glucose should be measured. Patients with cardiac symptoms need a cardiac workup and should see their primary medical doctor. Patients who have complaints of dizziness should receive a thorough neurological evaluation. There are several psychological inventories that can help the clinician diagnose panic disorder including the **Beck**

Depression Inventory (BDI), Beck Anxiety Inventory (BAI), Specific Fear Inventory, Clinical Anxiety Scale (CAS), and the Clinical Global Inventory (CGI).

Treatments

Psychological and social interventions

A psychotherapeutic technique that is critical to the treatment of panic disorder is **cognitive-behavioral therapy** (CBT). Patients are panic-free within six months in about 80–90% of cases. Some people even experience long-term effects after the treatments have been stopped. About half of the patients say that they have rare attacks even two years after treatment has ended.

New studies reveal that the approach to treating panic disorder should have three aspects: the cognitive, the physiological, and the behavioral. The cognitive techniques try to focus on changing the patient's negative thoughts—for example, "I will die if I don't get help." Patient education about symptoms is also critical to the treatment of panic attacks. In one physiological approach, patients are taught breathing techniques in an effort to try to help them lower their heart rate and decrease their anxiety. Repeated exposure to physical symptoms associated with the panic disorder is also a part of treatment. The patients cause themselves to hyperventilate in effort to reproduce the panic symptoms. In behavioral approaches, the individual who experiences panic attacks also needs to be exposed to situations that he or she may have previously feared. A patient can also be taken to places associated with agoraphobia with the therapist.

Some patients may benefit from **psychodynamic psychotherapy** and **group therapy**. Psychodynamic **psychotherapy** explores thoughts and ideas of the person's subconscious. It takes a longer time to achieve efficacy than cognitive-behavioral therapy, but it can be just as effective for patients with panic disorder. Group therapy is also just as helpful to some patients as CBT. **Support groups** can also be helpful to some patients. It can be very therapeutic and healing to the individual to discuss their problems with someone who has actually experienced the same symptoms. Patients can learn from each other's coping styles.

Medical treatments

Panic disorder patients have a 50–80% chance of responding to treatment, which attempts to block the symptoms of panic attacks. Treating the agoraphobia symptoms is more challenging. Developing some anti-panic regimens that address all symptoms is important. The Food and Drug Administration (FDA) to treat panic disorder approves only five classes of drugs. They are:

- benzodiazepines
- Selective serotonin reuptake inhibitors (SSRIs), which cause a buildup of serotonin. This buildup is thought to cause the antidepressant effect.
- Tricylic antidepressants (TCAs).
- Monoamine oxidase inhibitors (MAOIs) and reversible MAOIs, which inhibit the breakdown of neurotransmitters in the brain, including dopamine and serotonin.
- Atypical antidepressants, including **bupropion** (Wellbutrin), **mirtazapine** (Remeron), **trazodone** (Desyrel), and others.

Patients should first be started on a low-dose SSRI and then the dose should be increased slowly. Patients with panic disorder are extremely sensitive to the side effects that many patients experience in the first weeks of antidepressant therapy. Patients should also have a benzodiazepine, such as **clonazepam** (Klonopin) or **alprazolam** (Xanax), in the first weeks of treatment until the antidepressant becomes therapeutic. Most people need the same dose of antidepressant as patients with major depression. About 60% of patients will have improvement in their symptoms while taking an antidepressant and a benzodiazepine. Patients with mitral valve prolapse may benefit from a beta blocker. Patients who have tried an SSRI, and after six weeks, show no improvement can be switched to another SSRI, benzodiazepine, TCA, MAOI, or **venlafaxine** (Effexor). An SSRI should be stopped if the patient has intolerable side effects such as loss of sexual libido, weight gain, or mild form of manic depression. When SSRIs are stopped, it is important that the dosage is gradually tapered because patients can suffer symptoms when it is abruptly withdrawn. These symptoms may include confusion, anxiety and poor sleep.

Alternative therapies

Some alternative therapies for panic disorder are hypnosis, **meditation**, **yoga**, proper nutrition, exercise, and abdominal breathing techniques that foster relaxation and visualization. Visualization is imagining oneself in the stressful situation while relaxed so that coping strategies can be discovered. The herb **kava kava** has been studied in trials to treat anxiety attacks and has been found to be effective in some clinical trials; but has not been studied intensely enough to determine its benefits and side effects, and has been associated liver toxicity. The National Center for Complementary and Alternative Medicine was going to conduct two research studies of kava kava but as of 2002 it has suspended the trials until the FDA has determined whether or not the herbal supplement is safe.

Prognosis

Patients with panic disorder have a poor prognosis particularly if untreated. Patients often relapse when they attempt to discontinue treatment. However, if patients are compliant and willing to stay in treatment, then the long-term prognosis is good. According to one study, eight years after treatment has been done, 30–40% of patient are doing better. Only 10–20% of patients do poorly. The patient with panic attacks has a relapsing and remitting course that can be worsened by significant stressors such as the death of the spouse or divorce. Cognitive-behavioral therapy has an 80–90% chance that the patient will benefit six months after treatment. Medications have a 50–80% efficacy. If patients are committed to staying in treatment, their prognosis is very favorable.

Prevention

Although panic disorder is not totally preventable, individuals with a strong family history of them who are susceptible to panic atacks are encouraged to be aware of the symptoms and get treatment early. **Compliance** with treatment is important to the recovery from panic disorder.

Resources

BOOKS

American Psychiatric Association. *Diagnostic and Statistical Manual of Mental Disorders.* 4th edition, text revised. Washington DC: American Psychiatric Association, 2000.

Cox, Brian J. and Stephen Taylor. "Anxiety Disorders Panic and Phobias." In *Oxford Textbook of Psychopathology,* edited by Theodore Millon, Paul H. Blaney, and Roger D. Davis. New York: Oxford University Press, 1999.

Sadock, Benjamin J., M.D., and Virginia A. Sadock,M.D., eds. "Anxiety Disorders." In *Comprehensive Textbook of Psychiatry.* Volume I, 7th edition. Written by Jack Gorman M.D., Laszlo A. Papp, M.D., Glen O. Gabbard, M.D., and others. Philadelphia, PA: Lippincott Williams and Wilkins, 2000.

Swede, Shirley and Seymour Sheppard Jaffe, M.D. *The Panic Attack Recovery Book: Revised and Updated.* 2nd edition, revised. New York: Penguin Putnam Inc, 2000.

PERIODICALS

Frank, Ellen, Ph.D. and others. "Influence of Panic Agoraphobic Spectrum Symptoms on Treatment Response in Patients With Recurrent Major Depression." *American Journal of Psychiatry* July 2000: 1101–1107.

Kessler, Ronald C., Ph.D. and others. "The Use of Complementary and Alternatives Therapies to Treat Anxiety and Depression in the United States." *American Journal of Psychiatry* February 2001: 289–294.

Milrod, Barbara, M.D., and others. "Open Trial of Psychodynamic Psychotherapy for Panic Disorder: A Pilot Study." *The American Journal of Psychiatry* November 2000: 1878–1880.

Sheikh, Javaid I.,M.D., M.B.A., Gregory A. Leskin, Ph.D. and Donald F. Klein, M.D. "Gender Differences in Panic Disorder: Findings From the National Comorbidity Survey." *American Journal of Psychiatry* January 2002: 55–58.

Warsaw, Meredith G., M.S.S. and others. "Suicidal Behavior in Patients With Current or Past Panic Disorder: Five Years of Prospective Data From the Harvard /Brown Anxiety Research Program." *American Journal of Psychiatry* November 2000,1876–1878.

ORGANIZATIONS

American Psychiatric Association. 1400 K Street NW,Washington, D.C. 20005. <http://www.psych.org/public_info/panic.html>.

Anxiety Disorders Association of America. 11900 Parklawn Drive, Suite 100, Rockville, MD 20852. (301) 231-9350. <www.adaa.org>.

National Center for Complementary and Alternative Medicine. P.O. Box 7923, Gaithersburg, MD 20898. (888) 644-6226. <http://nccam.nih.gov>.

National Institute of Mental Health. 6001 Executive Boulvevard, Rm.8184, MSC9663,Bethesda, MD 20892-9663. (301) 443-4513. <http://www.nimh.nih.gov/anxiety/panicmenu.cfm>.

Open Mind, <http://open-mind.org/SP>.

Susan Hobbs, M.D.

Paranoia

Definition

Paranoia is a symptom in which an individual feels as if the world is "out to get" him or her. When people are paranoid, they feel as if others are always talking about them behind their backs. Paranoia causes intense feelings of distrust, and can sometimes lead to overt or covert hostility.

Description

An individual suffering from paranoia feels suspicious, and has a sense that other people want to do him or her harm. As a result, the paranoid individual changes his or her actions in response to a world that is perceived as personally threatening. Objective observers may be quite clear on the fact that no one's words or actions are actually threatening the paranoid individual. The hallmark of paranoia is a feeling of intense distrust and suspiciousness that is not in response to input from anybody or anything in the paranoid individual's environment.

Other symptoms of paranoia may include

- Self-referential thinking: The sense that other people in the world (even complete strangers on the street) are always talking about the paranoid individual.
- Thought broadcasting: The sense that other people can read the paranoid individual's mind.
- Magical thinking: The sense that the paranoid individual can use his or her thoughts to influence other people's thoughts and actions.
- Thought withdrawal: The sense that people are stealing the paranoid individual's thoughts.
- Thought insertion: The sense that people are putting thoughts into the paranoid individual's mind.
- Ideas of reference: The sense that the television and/or radio are specifically addressing the paranoid individual.

Demographics

Paranoia is a very human feeling. Nearly everyone has experienced it at some or another time, to varying degrees. Paranoia exists on a continuum, ranging from a feeling of distrust due to an occasional misinterpretation of cues that can be appropriately dealt with and reinterpreted, to an overarching pattern of actual paranoia that affects every interpersonal interaction.

Some research studies have suggested that 6% of all women and 13% of all men have some chronic level of mistrust towards the motivations of others towards them. Only about 0.5% to 0.25% of men and women can actually be diagnosed with **paranoid personality disorder**, however. It remains interesting to researchers that men are more prone to paranoid traits and mental disorders with paranoid features than are women.

Causes of paranoia

Researchers do not understand fully what chemical or physical changes in the **brain** cause paranoia. Paranoia is a prominent symptom that occurs in a variety of different mental disorders, as well as a symptom of certain physical diseases. Furthermore, use of certain drugs or chemicals may cause symptoms of paranoia in an otherwise normal individual.

Paranoia is often manifested as part of the symptom complex of **schizophrenia**. In fact, one of the subtypes of schizophrenia is termed "paranoid schizophrenia," which actually refers to a type of schizophrenia in which the individual is particularly preoccupied with **delusions** in which the world seems to be pitted against him or her. As with other forms of schizophrenia, sufferers often lack contact with reality, and display **hallucinations**, flat or emotionless **affect**, and disorganized thinking and behavior.

Paranoid personality disorder is diagnosed when an individual does not have other symptoms of schizophrenia, but a personality that is driven by chronic manifestations of paranoia. These individuals are mistrustful, suspicious, and convinced that the world is out to get them.

In order for an individual to be diagnosed with paranoid personality disorder, he or she must display at least four of the following traits:

- chronically suspicious that people are lying or cheating him or her in some way
- frequently preoccupied with whether people are loyal or trustworthy
- cannot confide in others for fear of being betrayed
- misinterprets benign comments or events as being personally threatening
- harbors long-term grudges against others who are perceived as having been threatening or insulting in some way
- sees others' actions and/or words attacking him or her in some way, and therefore goes on the counterattack
- repeatedly assumes that partner or spouse is unfaithful

Paranoia can also occur as a symptom of other neurological diseases. Individuals suffering from the aftereffects of strokes, brain injuries, various types of **dementia** (including **Alzheimer's disease**), Huntington's disease, and Parkinson's disease may manifest paranoia as part of their symptom complex. The paranoia may decrease in intensity when the underlying disease is effectively treated, although since many of these diseases are progressive, the paranoia may worsen over time along with the progression of the disease's other symptoms.

A number of different medications and drugs can cause paranoia. These include corticosteroid medications, H-2 blockers (cimetidine, ranitidine, famotidine), some muscle relaxants (Baclofen), antiviral/anti-Parkinson drugs (**amantadine**), some **amphetamines** (including methylphenidate, or Ritalin), anti-HIV medications, antidepressants (Nardil). Abused drugs that can prompt paranoia include alcohol, cocaine, marijuana, ecstasy (MDMA), amphetamines (including Ritalin), LSD, and PCP (angel dust). Withdrawal from addictive drugs may also cause symptoms of paranoia.

·atments

It can be quite challenging to get an individual who is suffering from paranoia to accept treatment. Their paranoid condition makes them distrustful of people's motivations towards them, so that even a medical doctor appears to be a suspicious party. Medications that may be offered are usually looked at with great distrust, and efforts at **psychotherapy** are considered "mind control" by a profoundly paranoid individual.

The first step to be taken when someone is suffering from paranoia is that of determining whether an easily reversible situation (such as an adverse reaction to a medication) might be causing the paranoia. If so, discontinuing the drug (either immediately or by gradually weaning the dose) might end the symptoms of paranoia.

Patients who have other diseases, such as Alzheimer's disease or other forms of dementia, Huntington's disease, or Parkinson's disease may notice that their paranoid symptoms improve when their general medical condition is treated. The circumstance that can occur as their underlying disease progresses, is that the paranoia may return or worsen over time.

People who are suffering from diagnosable mental conditions such as schizophrenia or paranoid personality disorder may benefit from the use of typical antipsychotic medications, such as **chlorpromazine** or **haloperidol**, or from the newer, atypical antipsychotic medications, such as **clozapine**, **olanzapine**, or **risperidone**.

Cognitive-behavioral therapy (CBT) or other forms of psychotherapy may be helpful for certain people who have paranoia. CBT attempts to make a person more aware of his or her actions and motivations, and tries to help the individual learn to more accurately interpret cues around him or her, in an effort to help the individual change dysfunctional behaviors. Difficulty can enter into a therapeutic relationship with a paranoid individual, due to the level of mistrust and suspicion that is likely to interfere with their ability to participate in this form of treatment.

Support groups can be helpful for some paranoid individuals—particularly helpful in assisting family members and friends who must learn to live with, and care for paranoid individuals.

Prognosis

It is difficult to predict the prognosis of an individual who has paranoia. If there is an underlying mental illness, such as schizophrenia or paranoid personality disorder, then the paranoia is likely to be a lifelong condition. It may improve with some treatments (remission), only to become exacerbated under other more stressful conditions, or with changes in medication.

Individuals who have symptoms of paranoia as part of another medical condition may also have a waxing-and-waning-course.

When paranoia is caused by the use of a particular drug or medication, it is possible that discontinuing that substance may completely reverse the symptoms of paranoia.

Resources

BOOKS

Tasman, Allan, and others. *Psychiatry.* Philadelphia: W. B. Saunders, 1997.

ORGANIZATIONS

National Alliance for the Mentally Ill. Colonial Place Three, 2107 Wilson Blvd., Suite 300, Arlington, VA 22201. (703) 524-7600. <http://www.nami.org>.

National Institute for Mental Health. 6001 Executive Blvd., Room 8184, MSC 9663, Bethesda, MD 20892. (301)443-4513. <http://www.nimh.nih.gov>.

Rosalyn Carson-DeWitt, M.D.

Paranoid personality disorder

Definition

People with paranoid personality disorder (PPD) have long-term, widespread and unwarranted suspicions that other people are hostile, threatening or demeaning. These beliefs are steadfastly maintained in the absence of any real supporting evidence. The disorder, whose name comes from the Greek word for "madness," is one of ten **personality disorders** described in the 2000 edition of the ***Diagnostic and Statistical Manual of Mental Disorders***, (the fourth edition, text revision or *DSM-IV-TR*), the standard guidebook used by mental health professionals to diagnose mental disorders.

Despite the pervasive suspicions they have of others, patients with PPD are not delusional (except in rare, brief instances brought on by **stress**). Most of the time, they are in touch with reality, except for their misinterpretation of others' motives and intentions. PPD patients are not psychotic but their conviction that others are trying to "get them" or humiliate them in some way often leads to hostility and social isolation.

Description

People with PPD do not trust other people. In fact, the central characteristic of people with PPD is a high degree of mistrustfulness and suspicion when interacting with others. Even friendly gestures are often interpreted as being manipulative or malevolent. Whether the patterns of distrust and suspicion begin in childhood or in early adulthood, they quickly come to dominate the lives of those suffering from PPD. Such people are unable or afraid to form close relationships with others.

They suspect strangers, and even people they know, of planning to harm or exploit them when there is no good evidence to support this belief. As a result of their constant concern about the lack of trustworthiness of others, patients with this disorder often have few intimate friends or close human contacts. They do not fit in and they do not make good "team players." Interactions with others are characterized by wariness and not infrequently by hostility. If they marry or become otherwise attached to someone, the relationship is often characterized by pathological jealousy and attempts to control their partner. They often assume their sexual partner is "cheating" on them.

People suffering from PPD are very difficult to deal with. They never seem to let down their defenses. They are always looking for and finding evidence that others are against them. Their fear, and the threats they perceive in the innocent statements and actions of others, often contributes to frequent complaining or unfriendly withdrawal or aloofness. They can be confrontational, aggressive and disputatious. It is not unusual for them to sue people they feel have wronged them. In addition, patients with this disorder are known for their tendency to become violent.

Despite all the unpleasant aspects of a paranoid lifestyle, however, it is still not sufficient to drive many people with PPD to seek therapy. They do not usually walk into a therapist's office on their own. They distrust mental health care providers just as they distrust nearly everyone else. If a life crisis, a family member or the judicial system succeeds in getting a patient with PPD to seek help, therapy is often a challenge. Individual counseling seems to work best but it requires a great deal of patience and skill on the part of the therapist. It is not unusual for patients to leave therapy when they perceive some malicious intent on the therapist's part. If the patient can be persuaded to cooperate— something that is not easy to achieve— low-dose medications are recommended for treating such specific problems as anxiety, but only for limited periods of time.

If a mental health care provider is able to gain the trust of a patient with PPD, it may be possible to help the patient deal with the threats that they perceive. The disorder, however, usually lasts a lifetime.

KEY TERMS

Delusion—A false belief that is resistant to reason or contrary to actual fact.

Delusional disorder of the persecutory type—A psychotic disorder characterized by a patient's belief that others are conspiring against him or her.

Hallucination—False sensory perceptions. A person experiencing a hallucination may "hear" sounds or "see" people or objects that are not really present. Hallucinations can also affect the senses of smell, touch, and taste.

Neuroleptic—Another name for the older antipsychotic medications, such as haloperidol (Haldol) and chlorpromazine (Thorazine).

Paranoia—A mental disorder characterized by baseless suspicions or distrust of others, often delusional in intensity.

Paranoid personality—A personality disorder characterized by unwarranted suspicion, jealousy, hypersensitivity, social isolation and a tendency to detect malicious intent in the words and actions of others.

Psychosis—Severe state that is characterized by loss of contact with reality and deterioration in normal social functioning; examples are schizophrenia and paranoia. Psychosis is usually one feature of an over-arching disorder, not a disorder in itself. (Plural: psychoses)

Rapport—A relation of empathy and trust between a therapist and patient.

Schizophrenia—A severe mental illness in which a person has difficulty distinguishing what is real from what is not real. It is often characterized by hallucinations, delusions, language and communication disturbances, and withdrawal from people and social activities.

Supportive—An approach to psychotherapy that seeks to encourage the patient or offer emotional support to him or her, as distinct from insight-oriented or exploratory approaches to treatment.

Causes and symptoms

Causes

No one knows what causes paranoid personality disorder, although there are hints that familial factors may influence the development of the disorder in some cases. There seem to be more cases of PPD in families that have one or more members who suffer from such psychotic disorders as **schizophrenia** or **delusional disorder**.

Other possible interpersonal causes have been proposed. For example, some therapists believe that the behavior that characterizes PPD might be learned. They suggest that such behavior might be traced back to childhood experiences. According to this view, children who are exposed to adult anger and rage with no way to predict the outbursts and no way to escape or control them develop paranoid ways of thinking in an effort to cope with the stress. PPD would emerge when this type of thinking becomes part of the individual's personality as adulthood approaches.

Studies of identical (or monozygotic) and fraternal (or dizygotic) twins suggest that genetic factors may also play an important role in causing the disorder. Twin studies indicate that genes contribute to the development of childhood personality disorders, including PPD. Furthermore, estimates of the degree of genetic contribution to the development of childhood personality disorders are similar to estimates of the genetic contribution to adult versions of the disorders.

Symptoms

A core symptom of PPD is a generalized distrust of other people. Comments and actions that healthy people would not notice come across as full of insults and threats to someone with the disorder. Yet, generally, patients with PPD remain in touch with reality; they don't have any of the **hallucinations** or **delusions** seen in patients with psychoses. Nevertheless, their suspicions that others are intent on harming or exploiting them are so pervasive and intense that people with PPD often become very isolated. They avoid normal social interactions. And because they feel so insecure in what is a very threatening world for them, patients with PPD are capable of becoming violent. Innocuous comments, harmless jokes and other day-to-day communications are often perceived as insults.

Paranoid suspicions carry over into all realms of life. Those burdened with PPD are frequently convinced that their sexual partners are unfaithful. They may misinterpret compliments offered by employers or coworkers as hidden criticisms or attempts to get them to work harder. Complimenting a person with PPD on their clothing or car, for example, could easily be taken as an attack on their materialism or selfishness.

Because they persistently question the motivations and trustworthiness of others, patients with PPD are not inclined to share intimacies. They fear such information might be used against them. As a result, they become hostile and unfriendly, argumentative or aloof. Their unpleasantness often draws negative responses from those around them. These rebuffs become "proof" in the patient's mind that others are, indeed, hostile to them. They have little insight into the effects of their attitude and behavior on their generally unsuccessful interactions with others. Asked if they might be responsible for negative interactions that fill their lives, people with PPD are likely to place all the blame on others.

A brief summary of the typical symptoms of PPD includes:

- suspiciousness and distrust of others
- questioning hidden motives in others
- feelings of certainty, without justification or proof, that others are intent on harming or exploiting them
- social isolation
- aggressiveness and hostility
- little or no sense of humor

Demographics

As of 2002, it has not been possible to determine the number of people with PPD with any accuracy. This lack of data might be expected for a disorder that is characterized by extreme suspiciousness. Such patients in many cases avoid voluntary contact with such people as mental health workers who have a certain amount of power over them. There are, nonetheless, some estimates of the prevalence of PPD. According to the *DSM-IV-TR*, between 0.5% and 2.5% of the general population of the United States may have PPD, while 2%–10% of outpatients receiving psychiatric care may be affected. A significant percentage of institutionalized psychiatric patients, between 10% and 30%, might have symptoms that qualify for a **diagnosis** of PPD. Finally, the disorder appears to be more common in men than in women.

There are indications in the scientific literature that relatives of patients with chronic schizophrenia may have a greater chance of developing PPD than people in the general population. Also, the incidence of the disorder may be higher among relatives of patients suffering from another psychotic disorder known as delusional disorder of the persecutory type.

Diagnosis

There are no laboratory tests or **imaging studies** as of 2002 that can be used to confirm a diagnosis of PPD. The diagnosis is usually made on the basis of the doctor's interview with the patient, although the doctor may also give the patient a diagnostic questionnaire. In addition, input from people who know the patient may be requested.

Diagnostic criteria

Mental health care providers look for at least five distinguishing symptoms in patients who they think might suffer from PPD. The first is a pattern of suspiciousness about, and distrust of, other people when there is no good reason for either. This pattern should be present from at least the time of the patient's early adulthood.

In addition to this symptom that is required in order to make the PPD diagnosis, the patient should have at least four of the following seven symptoms as listed in the *DSM-IV-TR*:

- The unfounded suspicion that people want to deceive, exploit or harm the patient.
- The pervasive belief that others are not worthy of trust or that they are not inclined to or capable of offering loyalty.
- A fear that others will use information against the patient with the intention of harming him or her. This fear is demonstrated by a reluctance to share even harmless personal information with others.
- The interpretation of others' innocent remarks as insulting or demeaning; or the interpretation of neutral events as presenting or conveying a threat.
- A strong tendency not to forgive real or imagined slights and insults. People with PPD nurture grudges for a long time.
- An angry and aggressive response in reply to imagined attacks by others. The counterattack for a perceived insult is often rapid.
- Suspicions, in the absence of any real evidence, that a spouse or sexual partner is not sexually faithful, resulting in such repeated questions as "Where have you been?" "Whom did you see?" etc., and other types of jealous behavior.

Differential diagnosis

Psychiatrists and clinical psychologists should be careful not to confuse PPD with other mental disorders or behaviors that have some symptoms in common with the paranoid personality. For example, it is important to make sure that the patient is not a long-term user of amphetamine or cocaine. Chronic abuse of these stimulants can produce paranoid behavior. Also, some prescription medications might produce **paranoia** as a side effect; so it is important to find out what drugs, if any, the patient is taking.

There are other conditions that, if present, would mean a patient with paranoid traits does not have PPD. For example, if the patient has symptoms of schizophrenia, hallucinations or a formal thought disorder, a diagnosis of PPD can't be made. The same is true of delusions, which are not a feature of PPD.

Also, the suspiciousness and other characteristic features of PPD must have been present in the patient for a long time, at least since early adulthood. If the symptoms appeared more recently than that, a person can't be given a diagnosis of this disorder.

There are at least a dozen disorders or other mental health conditions listed in the *DSM-IV-TR* that could be confused with PPD after a superficial interview because they share similar or identical symptoms with PPD. It is important, therefore, to eliminate the following entities before settling on a diagnosis of PPD: paranoid schizophrenia; **schizotypal personality disorder**; **schizoid personality disorder**; persecutory delusional disorder; mood disorder with psychotic features; symptoms and/or personality changes produced by disease, medical conditions, medication or drugs of abuse; paranoia linked to the development of physical handicaps; and borderline, histrionic, avoidant, antisocial or narcissistic personality disorders.

In some individuals, symptoms of PPD may precede the development of schizophrenia. Should a patient who as been correctly diagnosed with PPD later develop schizophrenia, the *DSM-IV-TR* suggests that the diagnosis on the patient's medical record be changed from "Paranoid Personality Disorder" to "Paranoid Personality Disorder (Premorbid)."

Treatments

Because they are suspicious and untrusting, patients with PPD are not likely to seek therapy on their own. A particularly disturbing development or life crisis may prompt them to get help. More often, however, the legal system or the patient's relatives order or encourage him or her to seek professional treatment. But even after a patient finally agrees or is forced to seek treatment, the nature of the disorder poses very serious challenges to therapists.

Psychotherapy

The primary approach to treatment for such personality disorders as PPD is **psychotherapy**. The problem is that patients with PPD do not readily offer therapists the trust that is needed for successful treatment. As a result, it has been difficult to gather data that would indicate what kind of psychotherapy would work best. Therapists face the challenge of developing rapport with someone who is, by the nature of his personality disorder, distrustful and suspicious; someone who often sees malicious intent in the innocuous actions and statements of others. The patient may actively resist or refuse to cooperate with others who are trying to help.

Mental health workers treating patients with PPD must guard against any show of hostility on their part in response to hostility from the patient, which is a common occurrence in people with this disorder. Instead, clinicians are advised to develop trust by persistently demonstrating a nonjudgmental attitude and a professional desire to assist the patient.

It is usually up to the therapist alone to overcome a patient's resistance. **Group therapy** that includes family members or other psychiatric patients, not surprisingly, isn't useful in the treatment of PPD due to the mistrust people with PPD feel towards others. This characteristic also explains why there are no significant **self-help groups** dedicated to recovery from this disorder. It has been suggested, however, that some people with PPD might join cults or extremist groups whose members might share their suspicions.

To gain the trust of PPD patients, therapists must be careful to hide as little as possible from their patients. This transparency should include note taking; details of administrative tasks concerning the patient; correspondence; and medications. Any indication of what the patient would consider "deception" or covert operation can, and often does, lead the patient to drop out of treatment. Patients with paranoid tendencies often don't have a well-developed sense of humor; those who must interact with people with PPD probably should not make jokes in their presence. Attempts at humor may seem like ridicule to people who feel so easily threatened.

With some patients, the most attainable goal may be to help them to learn to analyze their problems in dealing with other people. This approach amounts to supportive therapy and is preferable to psychotherapeutic approaches that attempt to analyze the patient's motivations and possible sources of paranoid traits. Asking about a patient's past can undermine the treatment of PPD patients. Concentrating on the specific issues that are troubling the patient with PPD is usually the wisest course.

With time and a skilled therapist, the patient with PPD who remains in therapy may develop a measure of trust. But as the patient reveals more of his paranoid thoughts, the clinician will continue to face the difficult task of balancing the need for objectivity about the paranoid ideas and the maintenance of a good rapport with the patient. The therapist thus walks a tightrope with this type of patient. If the therapist is not straightforward enough, the patient may feel deceived. If the therapist challenges paranoid thoughts too directly, the patient will be threatened and probably drop out of treatment.

Medications

While individual supportive psychotherapy is the treatment of choice for PPD, medications are sometimes used on a limited basis to treat related symptoms. If, for example, the patient is very anxious, anti-anxiety drugs may be prescribed. In addition, during periods of extreme agitation and high stress that produce delusional states, the patient may be given low doses of antipsychotic medications.

Some clinicians have suggested that low doses of neuroleptics should be used in this group of patients; however, medications are not normally part of long-term treatment for PPD. One reason is that no medication has been proven to relieve effectively the long-term symptoms of the disorder, although the selective serotonin reuptake inhibitors such as **fluoxetine** (Prozac) have been reported to make patients less angry, irritable and suspicious. Antidepressants may even make symptoms worse. A second reason is that people with PPD are suspicious of medications. They fear that others might try to control them through the use of drugs. It can therefore be very difficult to persuade them to take medications unless the potential for relief from another threat, such as extreme anxiety, makes the medications seem relatively appealing. The best use of medication may be for specific complaints, when the patient trusts the therapist enough to ask for relief from particular symptoms.

Prognosis

Paranoid personality disorder is often a chronic, lifelong condition; the long-term prognosis is usually not encouraging. Feelings of paranoia, however, can be controlled to a degree with successful therapy. Unfortunately, many patients suffer the major symptoms of the disorder throughout their lives.

Prevention

With little or no understanding of the cause of PPD, it is not possible to prevent the disorder.

See also Paranoia

Resources

BOOKS

Allen, Thomas E., Mayer C. Liebman, Lee Crandall Park, and William C. Wimmer. *A Primer on Mental Disorders: A Guide for Educators, Families, and Students.* Lantham, MD: Scarecrow Press, 2001.

American Psychiatric Association. *Diagnostic and Statistical Manual of Mental Disorders.* 4th edition, text revised.

Washington, DC: American Psychiatric Association, 2000.

Beers, Mark H., and Robert Berkow, eds. "Personality disorders." In *The Merck Manual of Diagnosis and Therapy.* 17th edition. Whitehouse Station, NJ: Merck Research Laboratories, 1999.

Frances, Allen. *Your Mental Health: A Layman's Guide to the Psychiatrist's Bible.* New York, NY: Scribner, 1999.

Kernberg, Paulina F., Alan S. Weiner and Karen K. Bardenstein. *Personality Disorders in Children and Adolescents.* 1st edition. New York, NY: Basic Books, 2000.

PERIODICALS

Coolidge, F. L., L. L. Thede and K. L. Jang. "Heritability of personality disorders in childhood: A preliminary investigation." *Journal of Personality Disorders* 15, no. 1 (Feb. 2001): 33-40.

Webb, C. T. and D. F. Levinson. "Schizotypal and paranoid personality disorder in the relatives of patients with schizophrenia and affective disorders: A review." *Schizophrenia Research* 11, no. 1 (Dec. 1993): 81-92.

ORGANIZATIONS

American Psychiatric Association. 1400 K Street NW, Washington D.C. 20005. <http://www.psych.org>.

International Society for the Study of Personality Disorders. 115 Mill Street, Belmont, MA 02478. <http://www.isspd.com/>.

National Mental Health Association. 1021 Prince Street, Alexandria, Virginia 22314-2971. <http://www.nmha.org/>.

OTHER

Beers, Mark H., and Robert Berkow, eds. The Merck Manual of Diagnosis and Therapy. 1995-2002. (cited March 12, 2002).< http://www.merck.com/pubs/mmanual/section15/chapter191/191a.htm>.

Ekleberry, Sharon, C., Dual Diagnosis and the Paranoid Personality Disorder. The Dual Diagnosis Pages. 25 March 2000. (cited 19 March 2002). <http://www.toad.net/~arcturus/dd/paranoid.htm>.

Grohol, John M. "Paranoid Personality Disorder." Psych Central. 1 March 2002. (cited 16 March 2002). <http://psychcentral.com/disorders/sx37t.htm>.

Dean A. Haycock, Ph.D.

Paraphilias

Definition

Paraphilias are sexual feelings or behaviors that may involve sexual partners that are not human, not consenting, or that involve suffering by one or both partners.

Description

According to the ***Diagnostic and Statistical Manual of Mental Disorders*** *(known as the* DSM) fourth edition text revised (*DSM-IV-TR*), the manual used by mental health professionals to diagnose mental disorders, it is not uncommon for an individual to have more than one paraphilia. The *DSM-IV-TR* lists the following paraphilias: **exhibitionism**, **fetishism**, **frotteurism**, **pedophilia**, **sexual masochism**, **sexual sadism**, **transvestic fetishism**, and **voyeurism**. The *DSM-IV-TR* also includes a category for paraphilia not otherwise specified, which is the category for the less common paraphilias, including necrophilia, zoophilia, and others.

Exhibitionism

Exhibitionism is the exposure of genitals to a non-consenting stranger. In some cases, the individual may also engage in autoeroticism while exposing himself. Generally, no additional contact with the observer is sought; the individual is stimulated sexually by gaining the attention of and startling the observer.

Fetishism

People with this disorder achieve sexual gratification with the use of objects, most commonly women's undergarments, shoes, stockings, or other clothing items.

Frotteurism

Individuals with this disorder are gratified by touching or rubbing a non-consenting person. This behavior often occurs in busy, crowded places, such as on busy streets or on crowded buses or subways.

Pedophilia

Pedophilia involves sexual activity with a child, generally under age 13. The *DSM-IV-TR* describes a criterion that the individual with pedophilia be over 16 years of age and be at least five years older than the child. Individuals with this disorder may be attracted to either males or females or both, although incidents of pedophilic activity are almost twice as likely to be repeated by those individuals attracted to males. Individuals with this disorder develop procedures and strategies for gaining access to and trust of children.

Sexual masochism

Masochism is a term applied to a specific sexual disorder but which also has a broader usage. The sexual disorder involves pleasure and excitement produced by pain, either inflicted by others or by oneself. It usually begins in childhood or adolescence and is chronic. An individual with this disorder achieves gratification by experiencing pain. Masochism is the only paraphilia in which any noticeable number of women participate—about 5% of masochists are female. The term comes from the name of a nineteenth-century Austrian writer, Leopold von Sacher-Masoch, whose novels often included characters who were obsessed with the combination of sex and pain.

In the broader sense, masochism refers to any experience of receiving pleasure or satisfaction from suffering pain. The psychoanalytic view is that masochism is aggression turned inward, onto the self, when a person feels too guilty or is afraid to express it outwardly.

Sexual sadism

A sadistic individual achieves sexual gratification by inflicting pain on another person.

In psychoanalytic theory, sadism is related to the fear of castration, while the behaviorist explanation of sadomasochism (the deviant sexual practice combining sadism and masochism) is that its constituent feelings are physiologically similar to sexual arousal. Separate but parallel descriptions are given for sexual sadism and sexual masochism in the *DSM-IV-TR*. The clinical diagnostic criteria for both are recurrence of the behavior over a period of at least six months, and significant distress or impairment of the ability to function as a result of the behavior or associated urges or fantasies. Either type of behavior may be limited to fantasies (sometimes while one is engaged in outwardly nondeviant sex) or acted out with a consenting partner, a non-consenting partner, or in the case of masochism, alone. Sadomasochism occurs in both males and females, and in both heterosexual and homosexual relationships.

Transvestic fetishism

This disorder is characterized by heterosexual males who dress in women's clothing to achieve a sexual response. The activity may begin in adolescence, and in secret; later, as an adult, the man may dress as a woman completely and in public. Not all men who cross-dress are unhappy with their gender, but some are. In a small minority of men with transvestic fetishism, gender dysphoria (unhappiness with original gender) may emerge, and those men may eventually seek hormonal treatments or surgical sex reassignment to enable them to live permanently as women.

Voyeurism

Voyeurism is a paraphilia in which a person finds sexual excitement in watching unsuspecting people who are nude, undressing, or having sex. Voyeurs are almost always male, and the victims are usually strangers. A voyeur may fantasize about having sex with the victim but almost never actually pursues this. The voyeur may return to watch the same stranger repeatedly, but there is rarely any physical contact.

Voyeurs are popularly known as "peeping Toms," based on the eleventh-century legend of Lady Godiva. According to the story, Tom was a tailor who "peeped" at Lady Godiva as she rode naked through the streets of Coventry, England, in a sacrificial act to get her husband to lower taxes. Tom was struck with blindness for not looking away like everyone else.

Uncommon paraphilias

BESTIALITY. Bestiality is a term that describes sexual feelings or behaviors involving animals. Termed zoophilia by *DSM-IV* this is an uncommon disorder. The disorder does not specify an animal or category of animals; the person with zoophilia may focus sexual feelings on domesticated animals, such as dogs, or farm animals, such as sheep or goats.

NECROPHILIA. Necrophilia is a term that describes sexual feelings or behaviors involving corpses.

Resources

BOOKS

American Psychiatric Association. *Diagnostic and Statsistical Manual of Mental Disorders.* Fourth edition, text revised. Washington DC: American Psychiatric Association, 2000.

Baumeister, Roy F. *Escaping the Self: Alcoholism, Spirituality, Masochism, and Other Flights from the Burden of Selfhood.* New York: Basic Books, 1993.

Caplan, Paula J. *The Myth of Women's Masochism.* Toronto: University of Toronto Press, 1993.

Carnes, Patrick. *Out of the Shadows: Understanding Sexual Addiction.* 3rd ed. Center City, MN: Hazelden Educational Materials, 2001.

Parent management training

Definition

Parent management training (PMT) is an adjunct to treatment that involves educating and coaching parents to change their child's problem behaviors using principles of learning theory and **behavior modification**.

Purpose

The aim of PMT is to decrease or eliminate a child's disruptive or inappropriate behaviors at home or school and to replace problematic ways of acting with positive interactions with peers, parents and such authority figures as teachers. In order to accomplish this goal, PMT focuses on enhancing parenting skills. The PMT therapist coaches parents in applying such strategies as rewarding positive behavior, and responding to negative behavior by removing rewards or enforcing undesirable consequences (punishments). Although PMT focuses on specific targeted behaviors rather than on the child's **diagnosis** as such, it has come to be associated with the treatment of certain disorders. PMT is used in treating **oppositional defiant disorder**, **conduct disorder**, **intermittent explosive disorder** (age-inappropriate tantrums), and attention deficit disorder with hyperactivity (**attention-deficit/hyperactivity disorder**). Such antisocial behaviors as firesetting and truancy can also be addressed through PMT.

KEY TERMS

Behavior modification—An approach to therapy based on the principles of operant conditioning. Behavior modification seeks to replace undesirable behaviors with preferable behaviors through the use of positive or negative reinforcement.

Positive reinforcement—A procedure or response that rewards a desired behavior.

Response-contingent—An approach to treatment in which rewards or punishments are given in response to a particular behavior to be encouraged or corrected.

Social learning theory—A subset of learning theories based on the concept that human behavior originates in and is affected by the interplay among the person's learned experiences, previous behaviors, and environmental influences.

Description

In PMT, the therapist conducts initial teaching sessions with the parent(s), giving a short summary of foundational concepts in behavior modification; demonstrating interventions for the parents; and coaching parents in carrying out the techniques of PMT. Early meetings with the therapist focus on training in the principles of behavior modification, response-contingent learning, and ways to apply the techniques. Parents are instructed to define the behavior(s) to be changed concretely and specifically. In addition, they learn how to observe and identify relevant behavior and situational factors, and how to chart or otherwise record the child's behavior. Defining, observing and recording behavior are essential to the success of this method, because when such behaviors as fighting or tantrums are highlighted in concrete, specific ways, techniques of **reinforcement** and punishment can be put to use. Progress or its absence is easier to identify when the description of the behavior is defined with enough clarity to be measurable, and when responses to the PMT interventions are tracked on a chart. After the child's parents grasp the basic interventions as well as when and how to apply them, the techniques that the parents practiced with the therapist can be carried out at home.

Learning theory, which is the conceptual foundation of PMT, deals with the ways in which organisms learn to respond to their environment, and the factors that affect the frequency of a specific behavior. The core of learning theory is the notion that actions increase or decrease in frequency in response to the consequences that occur immediately after the action. Research in parent-child interactions in families with disruptive, difficult or defiant children shows that parental responses are unintentionally reinforcing the unwanted behavior. PMT trains parents to become more careful in their reactions to a child's behavior. The parents learn to be more discerning: to provide attention, praise and increased affection in reaction to the child's behaving in desired ways; and to withdraw attention, to suspend displays of affection, or to withdraw privileges in instances of less desirable behavior.

The most critical element of PMT is offering positive reinforcement for socially appropriate (or at least nondeviant) behaviors. An additional component involves responding to any undesired behaviors by removing rewards or applying punishment. These two types of response to the child must be carried out with great consistency. Consistent responding is important because erratic responses to unwanted behavior can actually cause the behavior to increase in frequency. For instance, if a child consistently throws tantrums in stores, hoping to be given something to end the tantrum, inconsistent parent responses can worsen the situation. If a parent is occasionally determined not to give in, but provides a candy bar or a toy to end the tantrum on other occasions, the child learns either to have more tantrums, or to have more dramatic tantrums. The rise in the number or intensity of tantrums occurs because the child is trying to increase the number of opportunities to obtain that infrequent parental reward for the behavior. Planning responses ahead of time to predefined target behaviors by rewarding desired actions and by withdrawing rewards or applying punishment for undesirable behavior is a fundamental principle of PMT. Consistent consequences, which are contingent on (in response to) the child's behavior, result in behavior change. Parents practice therapeutic ways of responding to their child's behavior in the PMT sessions with the therapist.

Through PMT, parents learn that positive rewards for appropriate behaviors can be offered in a variety of ways. Giving praise, providing extra attention, earning points toward obtaining a reward desired by the child, earning stickers or other small indicators of positive behavior, earning additional privileges, hugging (and other affectionate gestures) are all forms of reward. The technical term for the rewarding of desired behavior is *positive reinforcement*. Positive reinforcement refers to consequences that cause the desired target behavior to increase.

PMT instructs parents to cancel rewards or give punishments when the child behaves in undesirable ways. The removal of rewards usually entails time away from the circumstances and situations in which the child can do desired activities or receive attention. The concept of a "time out" is based on this notion of removal of rewards. Time out from rewards customarily means that the child is removed from people and stimulation for a certain period of time; it can also include deprivation of privileges.

Punishment in PMT is not necessarily what parents typically refer to as punishment; it most emphatically is *not* the use of physical punishment. A punishment in PMT involves a response to the child's negative behavior by exposing the child to something he or she regards as unpleasant. Examples of punishments might include having to redo the correct behavior so many times that it becomes annoying; verbal reproaches; or the military standby—"drop and give me fifty"—having to do pushups or situps or laps around a playing field to the point of discomfort.

The least challenging problems, which have the greatest likelihood of successful change, are tackled first, in hope of giving the family a "success experience." The success experience is a positive reinforcement for the family, increasing the likelihood that they will continue using PMT in efforts to bring about change. In addition, lower-level behavioral problems provide opportunities for parents to become skilled in intervening and to learn consistency in their responses. After the parents have practiced using the skills learned in PMT on the less important problems, more severe issues can be tackled.

In addition to face-to-face sessions with the parents, some PMT therapists make frequent telephone calls to the parents between sessions. The purposes of the calls are to remind parents to continue to be consistent in applying the techniques; to answer questions about the work at home; and to praise the parents' attempts to correct the child's behavior. In addition, ongoing support in sessions and on the telephone helps parents feel less isolated and thus more likely to continue trying to use learning principles in managing their child. Troubleshooting any problems that arise regarding the application of the behavioral techniques is handled over the telephone and in the office sessions.

An additional aspect of learning theory is that rewarding subunits of the ultimately desired behavior can lead to developing more complex new actions. The subunits are finally linked together by changing the ways in which the rewards are given. This process is called "chaining." Sometimes, if the child shows no elements of the desired response, then the desired behavior is demonstrated for the child and subsequent "near hits" or approximations are rewarded. To refine "close but not quite" into the targeted response, rewards are given in a slightly "pickier" manner. Rewarding successive approximations of the desired behavior is also called "shaping."

Risks

The best way to learn to alter parental responses to child behaviors is with the support and assistance of a behavioral health professional (**psychologist**, **psychiatrist**, clinical social worker). As noted earlier, parents often inadvertently reinforce the problem behaviors, and it is difficult for a parent to see objectively the ways in which he or she is unintentionally supporting the defiant or difficult behavior. Furthermore, inappropriate application of such behavioral techniques as those used in PMT can actually make the problem situation worse. Families should seek therapists with valid credentials, skills, training and experience in PMT.

Normal results

Typically, the parents should notice a decrease in the unwanted behaviors after they implement the techniques learned in PMT at home. Of the various therapies used to treat childhood disorders, PMT is among those most frequently researched. PMT has shown effectiveness in changing children's behavior in very well-designed and rigorous studies. PMT has a greater effect on behavior than many other treatments, including **family therapy** or **play therapy**. Furthermore, the results— improved child behavior and reduction or elimination of undesirable behavior— are sustained over the long term. When a group of children whose families had used PMT were examined one to fourteen years later, they had maintained higher rates of positive behavior and lower levels of problem behavior.

See also: Pyromania

Resources

BOOKS

Hendren, R. L. *Disruptive behavior disorders in children and adolescents.* Review of Psychiatry Series, vol. 18, no. 2. Washington, DC: American Psychiatric Press, 1999.

Webster-Stratton, C., and M. Herbert. *Troubled families—problem children: Working with parents, a collaborative process.* Chichester, England: Wiley, 1995.

PERIODICALS

Feldman, Julie and Alan E. Kazdin. "Parent management training for oppositional and conduct problem children." *The Clinical Psychologist* 48, no. 4 (1995): 3-5.

Golding, Kim. "Parent management training as an intervention to promote adequate parenting." *Clinical Child Psychology and Psychiatry* 5, no. 3 (2000): 357-372.

Kazdin, A. E. "Parent management training: Evidence, outcome and issues." *Journal of American Academic Child and Adolescent Psychiatry* 36, no. 10 (October, 1997): 1349-1356.

ORGANIZATIONS

American Academy of Child and Adolescent Psychiatry. 3615 Wisconsin Ave., NW, Washington, D.C. 20016-3007. Telephone: (202) 966-7300. Web site: <www.aacap.org/>.

Association for the Advancement of Behavior Therapy. 305 Seventh Avenue, 16th Floor, New York, NY 10001-60008. Telephone: (212) 647-1890. Web site: <www.aabt.org>.

North American Family Institute. 10 Harbor Street, Danvers, MA 01923. Telephone: (978) 774-0774. Web site: <www.nafi.com>.

OTHER

The Explosive Child <www.explosivechild.com>.

Parents & Teachers of Explosive Kids. <www.explosivekids.org>.

Deborah Rosch Eifert, Ph.D

Parnate *see* **Tranylcypromine**

Paroxetine

Definition

Paroxetine is an antidepressant of the type known as selective serotonin reuptake inhibitors (SSRI). It is sold in the United States under the brand name Paxil.

KEY TERMS

Bioavailability—Medication that is available in the body. If the bioavailability of a drug is increased, more is available to the body for use, and if it is decreased, less is available for use.

Bipolar syndrome—An abnormal mental condition characterized by periods of intense elation, energy and activity followed by periods of inactivity and depression; formerly called manic-depression.

Hyponatremia—A condition characterized by an abnormally low concentration of sodium in the blood.

Manic—Referring to mania, a state characterized by excessive activity, excitement or emotion.

Neurotransmitter—A chemical in the brain that transmits messages between neurons, or nerve cells.

Tryptophan—An essential amino acid released from proteins during the process of digestion. Tryptophan is an important ingredient in the body's production of serotonin.

Purpose

Paroxetine is approved by the United States Food and Drug Administration (FDA) for treatment of depression and for the following anxiety disorders: **obsessive-compulsive disorder**, **panic disorder**, **generalized anxiety disorder**, **post-traumatic stress disorder**, and social anxiety disorder.

Description

Paroxetine increases the amount of serotonin (also called 5-HT) available in the **brain**. Serotonin is a neurotransmitter, or chemical in the brain that carries nerve impulses from a sending neuron (nerve cell) to a receiving neuron. The sending neuron releases serotonin into a little gap between neurons, called the synapse. The receiving neuron picks up the serotonin from the synapse, allowing the nerve impulse to continue on its way.

Researchers think that depression and certain other disorders may be caused, in part, because there is not enough available serotonin in the brain. Normally, once a nerve impulse has crossed the synapse, serotonin is reabsorbed by the sending neuron that released it. Once reabsorbed, this serotonin is no longer available and cannot interact with a receiving neuron. Paroxetine blocks the reabsorption, or re-uptake, of serotonin, leaving it available to stimulate receiving neurons. Therefore, paroxetine facilitates the transmission of nerve impulses by increasing available serotonin in the brain and thus increasing its effectiveness.

Paroxetine is an antidepressant that is virtually completely absorbed via oral administration. Food does not reduce its absorption.

The benefits of paroxetine develop slowly over a period of up to four weeks. Patients should be aware of this and continue to take the drug as directed, even if they feel no immediate improvement.

Recommended dosage

The recommended dosage of paroxetine is 20–50 mg per day. The drug should be taken only once per day. An appropriate initial dosage is 20 mg. Dosage changes should not be made more frequently than once per week.

The recommended dosage for older persons or individuals with liver or kidney disease is 10 mg per day. The total dosage for such persons should not exceed 40 mg per day.

Precautions

Paroxetine should never be taken with monoamine oxidase inhibitors (MAOIs)(see interactions below).

Paroxetine may lower the threshold for a **manic episode** among people with bipolar (manic-depressive) disorders. For this reason, the drug should be used only with caution and under close supervision in these patients. It may also increase the change of having a seizure in people with a history of seizure disorders.

The possibility of **suicide** is a component of depression. The minimum number of doses of paroxetine should be dispensed at any one time to minimize the potential for use as a suicide agent.

Hyponatremia (abnormally low concentration of sodium in the blood) has been associated with the use of paroxetine. In all cases, this condition resolved when the drug was discontinued. Most of these instances occurred among older individuals who were also taking diuretics (water pills).

Side effects

Common side effects associated with paroxetine include headache, weakness, chills, malaise, nausea, and sleepiness. Other complaints included dry mouth, dizziness, tremors, constipation, diarrhea, and problems with ejaculation. Adverse reactions to paroxetine have been reported for all organ systems of the body, but all of these side effects are uncommon.

In general, the incidence of side effects increases as the dosage of paroxetine increases.

Interactions

There is the potential for a fatal interaction with another class of antidepressant drugs called monoamine-oxidase (MAO) inhibitors. There have been reports of dangerously elevated body temperature, muscle rigidity, and rapid changes in vital signs such as heart rate and blood pressure. Mental changes ranging from extreme agitation to **delirium** and coma have also been reported. Because of this, paroxetine should never be taken in combination with MAO inhibitors. Patient taking any MAO inhibitors, for example Nardil (**phenelzine** sulfate) or Parmate (**tranylcypromine** sulfate), should stop the MAO inhibitor then wait at least 14 days before starting paroxetine or any other antidepressant. The same holds true when discontinuing paroxetine and starting an MAO inhibitor.

The combination of paroxetine with the antipsychotic drug **thioridazine** has the potential to cause fatal cardiac arrhythmias (irregular heartbeat). The use of paroxetine in combination with tryptophan may result in unwanted reactions including agitation, restlessness, and gastrointestinal distress. Paroxetine may also increase the change of having a seizure in people with a history of seizure disorders. People taking anticonvulsants to control **seizures** should be closely monitored and a physician may need to adjust the dosage of their seizure medication.

People with **bipolar disorder** are commonly treated with lithium. No interactions between paroxetine and lithium have been reported, nor have are there any reported interactions with the common anti-anxiety drug **diazepam** (Valium).

Phenobarbital at dosages greater than 100 mg per day decreases the bioavailability of paroxetine in some persons. Paroxetine has been reported to increase the systemic bioavailability of procyclidine.

Resources

BOOKS

Adams, Michael and Norman Holland. *Core Concepts in Pharmacology.* Philadelphia: Lippincott-Raven, 1998.

Foreman, John C. and Torben Johansen. *Textbook of Receptor Pharmacology.* 2nd ed. Boca Raton, FL: CRC Press, 2002.

Page, Clive P., and Michael Murphy. *Integrated Pharmacology.* St. Louis: Mosby-Year Book, 2002.

Von Boxtel, Chris J., Budiono Santoso, and I. Ralph Edwards. *Drug Benefits and Risks: International Textbook of Clinical Pharmacology.* New York: John Wiley and Sons, 2001.

PERIODICALS

Cherek D. R., S. D. Lane, C. J. Pietras, and J. L. Steinberg. "Effects of chronic paroxetine administration on measures of aggressive and impulsive responses of adult males with a history of conduct disorder." *Psychopharmacology (Berlin)* 159, no. 3 (2002): 266-274.

Mulsant B. H. and others. "A twelve-week, double-blind, randomized comparison of nortriptyline and paroxetine in older depressed inpatients and outpatients." *American Journal of Geriatric Psychiatry* 9, no. 4 (2001): 406-414.

Pisani F., G. Oteri, C. Costa, G. Di Raimondo, and R. Di Perri. "Effects of psychotropic drugs on seizure threshold." *Drug Safety* 25, no. 2 (2002): 91-110.

ORGANIZATIONS

American Academy of Clinical Toxicology. 777 East Park Drive, PO Box 8820, Harrisburg, PA 17105-8820. Telephone: (717) 558-7750. Fax: (717) 558-7845. Web site: <http://www.clintox.org/index.html>.

American Academy of Family Physicians. 11400 Tomahawk Creek Parkway, Leawood, KS 66211-2672. Telephone: (913) 906-6000. Web site: <http://www.aafp.org/>.

American Medical Association. 515 N. State Street, Chicago, IL 60610. Telephone: (312) 464-5000. Web site: <http://www.ama-assn.org/>.

American Psychiatric Association. 1400 K Street NW, Washington, DC 20005. Telephone: (888) 357-7924. Fax: (202) 682-6850. Web site: <http://www.psych.org/>.

American Society for Clinical Pharmacology and Therapeutics. 528 North Washington Street, Alexandria, VA 22314. Telephone: (703) 836-6981 Fax: (703) 836-5223.

American Society for Pharmacology and Experimental Therapeutics. 9650 Rockville Pike, Bethesda, MD 20814-3995. Telephone: (301) 530-7060. Fax: (301) 530-7061. Web site: <http://www.aspet.org/>.

L. Fleming Fallon, Jr., M.D., Dr.P.H.

Passionflower

Definition

Passionflower (*Passiflora incarnata*) is a vine whose leaves and flowers are widely used in Europe to make a herbal remedy for anxiety and **insomnia**. The plant, which is native to the tropical regions of North America, was first used by the Aztecs of Mexico as a folk remedy for these conditions. Passionflower is also known as maypop, apricot vine, passion vine, and granadilla. It grows as much as 30 ft (10 m) tall, with a thick, woody stem.

KEY TERMS

Antispasmodic—A medication or preparation given to relieve muscle or digestive cramps.

Anxiolytic—A preparation or substance given to relieve anxiety; a tranquilizer.

Chrysin—A flavonoid found in passionflower that may be the source of its anxiolytic properties.

Flavonoids—Plant pigments that have a variety of effects on human physiology. Some of these pigments have anti-inflammatory, anti-carcinogenic, and antioxidant effects, for example.

Gastritis—Inflammation of the lining of the stomach.

Infusion—The most potent form of extraction of a herb into water. Infusions are steeped for a longer period of time than teas.

Tincture—An alcohol-based herbal extract prepared by soaking parts of the plant in a mixture of alcohol and water. Established ratios and dilutions are followed.

Topical—A type of medication or preparation intended for use on the skin or external suface of the body.

Passionflower received its name from the sixteenth-century conquistadors who claimed Mexico for the Spanish Empire. The priests and soldiers who accompanied Hernando Cortez thought that the whitish-purple flowers of the vine symbolized certain features of the passion of Christ. The corona in the center of the flower reminded them of Christ's crown of thorns, the five stamens of the number of Christ's wounds, and the tendrils of the whips that were used to scourge Christ.

Purpose

Passionflower is still used as a sedative and anxiolytic, although far more frequently in Great Britain and Europe than in the United States. In Britain, passionflower is the single most common ingredient in herbal sedatives, and the German Commission E approved it for use as a tranquilizer. It is also used in homeopathic remedies. In addition to its long-standing uses as a remedy for anxiety and insomnia, passionflower has also been recommended for the treatment of gastrointestinal disorders related to anxiety; asthma; tachycardia (an abnormally rapid heartbeat); menstrual cramps; **seizures**; **attention-deficit/hyperactivity disorder**; and hysteria. A topical preparation made from passionflower has been used to treat hemorrhoids.

The parts of the plant that grow above the ground are gathered to make passionflower preparations. They may be used either fresh or dried. The most common sources of the passionflower that is used today are India, the West Indies, and the southern United States, even though the vine can also be grown in Mexico and Latin America.

Description

Passionflower preparations may be made from the flowers, leaves, or shoots of the plant. After the first fruits of the plant have matured, younger shoots growing 12.7–17.8 cm. above the ground are harvested and air-dried. The plant material is then used to prepare infusions, teas, liquid extracts, and tinctures of passionflower. In Europe, passionflower is often combined with lemon balm or **valerian** to make a sedative tea. The standardized formula approved by the German Commission E contains 30% passionflower, 40% valerian root, and 30% lemon balm. Passionflower is also used to make a special sedative tea for children, which typically includes 30% passionflower, 30% lemon balm, 30% **lavender** flower, and 10% **St. John's wort**. Passionflower is sometimes combined with hawthorn to make a remedy for stomach cramps associated with gastritis.

Although passionflower has been shown in animal studies to have sedative and antispasmodic effects, researchers are not yet certain which compounds in the plant have these properties. Passionflower is known to contain flavonoids and a group of alkaloid compounds that include harman, harmine, harmaline, and harmalol. Some researchers have hypothesized that the medicinal effects of passionflower derive from a combination of these substances rather than from any of them in isolation. A recent Swiss study, however, appears to indicate that a flavonoid called chrysin may be the source of passionflower's anxiolytic properties.

Recommended dosage

As the German recipe indicates, passionflower is considered safe for children. Dosages for children should be calculated on the basis of the child's weight. Since most adult dosages of herbal remedies assume an average adult weight of 150 lb (70 kg), a child weighing 50 lb (23 kg) can be given 1/3 of the adult dose.

Recommended adult doses of passionflower are as follows:

- Infusion: 2–5 g of dried herb, up to three times daily
- Fluid extract (1:1 ratio in a solution of 25% alcohol): 0.5–1.0 mL up to three times daily
- Tincture (1:5 ratio in a solution of 45% alcohol): 0.5–2.0 mL up to three times daily.

Precautions

Passionflower should not be used in doses higher than the recommended levels. Because it has a sedative effect, it should not be combined with alcoholic beverages or prescription sedatives. Passionflower should not be used by pregnant or lactating women, or for children under six months old.

Side effects

As of 2002, passionflower has not been reported to cause any significant side effects when taken at recommended dosage levels.

Interactions

The alkaloids found in passionflower, especially harman and harmaline, may increase the effects of a class of prescription antidepressants called monoamine oxidase inhibitors (MAOIs). These drugs are most often prescribed for depression, panic attacks, and eating disorders. Passionflower may also increase the effects of over-the-counter sedatives as well as prescription sedatives.

Resources

BOOKS

Pelletier, Kenneth R., MD. "Western Herbal Medicine: Nature's Green Pharmacy." Chapter 6 in *The Best Alternative Medicine*. New York: Simon and Schuster, 2000.

Tyler, Varro E. *Herbs of Choice*. New York: Pharmaceutical Products Press, 1994.

PERIODICALS

Capasso, A., and A. Pinto. "Experimental Investigations of the Synergistic-Sedative Effect of Passiflora and Kava." *Acta Therapeutica* 21 (1995): 127–140.

Soulimani, R., C. Younos, S. Jarmouni, and others. "Behavioural Effects of *Passiflora incarnata L.* and its Indole Alkaloid and Flavonoid Derivatives and Maltol in the Mouse." *Journal of Ethnopharmacology* 57 (1997): 11–20.

Zanoli, P., R. Avallone, and M. Baraldi. "Behavioral Characterisation of the Flavonoids Apigenin and Chrysin." *Fitoterapia* 71 (2000): S117–S123.

OTHER

American Botanical Council. PO Box 144345. Austin, TX 78714-4345. <www.herbalgram.org>.

Herb Research Foundation. 1007 Pearl Street. Suite 200. Boulder, CO 80302. <www.herbs.org>.

Rebecca J. Frey, Ph.D.

Pathological gambling disorder

Definition

Pathological gambling disorder occurs when a person gambles compulsively to such an extent that the wagering has a severe negative effect on his or her job, relationships, mental health, or other important aspects of life. The person may continue to gamble even after they have developed social, economic, interpersonal, or legal problems as a result of the gambling.

Description

Pathological gambling disorder is characterized by uncontrollable gambling well beyond the point of a social or recreational activity, such that the gambling has a major disruptive effect on the gambler's life. People who are pathological gamblers may lose their life savings, and may even commit crimes (stealing, embezzling, or forging checks) to get money for their "habit." Relationships and jobs may also be lost as a result of the disorder.

Pathological gambling disorder is an example of a process, or behavioral, **addiction**, as distinct from an addiction to such substances as food, drugs, tobacco, or alcohol. In process addictions, the characteristic "rush" or "high" comes from the series of steps or actions that are involved in the addictive behavior. With gambling, the "high" may be stimulated by the social atmosphere or group setting of the casino, race track, or bingo hall as well as by the excitement of risk-taking. Some gamblers have a "lucky" outfit, item of clothing, or accessory that they wear or take along when gambling; sometimes putting on the outfit or item in question is enough to start the "rush."

People with pathological gambling disorder may engage in many different types of gambling activities. These may include games of chance that are found in casinos, such as slot machines, card games, and roulette. Many of these games are now available on the Internet, the chief difference being that the bettor uses a credit card instead of cash or chips. Other gambling activities may include the state lottery, horse or dog racing, or even bingo. The person may place bets on the outcome of an election, baseball or football games, or even the weather on a particular day. Pathological gambling usually develops slowly over time; people tend to begin with acceptable levels of social or recreational gambling and slowly progress to pathological gambling. In most cases the disorder develops slowly over a period of years; however, there are cases of patients who gambled socially for decades and then began to gamble compulsively under the impact of a major life stressor, such as divorce or being laid off from work.

KEY TERMS

Aversion therapy—An approach to treatment in which an unpleasant or painful stimulus is linked to an undesirable behavior in order to condition the patient to dislike or avoid the behavior.

Chasing—Betting larger and larger sums of money, or taking greater risks, in order to make up for money previously lost in gambling.

Denial—A psychological defense mechanism that reduces anxiety by excluding recognition of an addiction or similar problem from the conscious mind.

Process addiction—An addiction to a mood-altering behavior or series of behaviors rather than a substance.

Reinforcement—A term that refers to the ability of a drug, substance, or behavior to produce effects that will make the user want to take the substance or perform the behavior again.

Rush—The initial intensely pleasurable sensation experienced from injecting a narcotic or stimulant drug. The term has also been applied to the feeling of excitement experienced from the behaviors involved in process addictions.

Causes and symptoms

Causes

There are no known biological causes of pathological gambling disorder. Some studies have found interesting differences between compulsive gamblers and the general population on the biological level, but none that are thought to be an actual cause of pathological gambling. Many people, however, have significant psychological causes for excessive gambling. They may use gambling as an emotional escape from depression; this pattern appears more often in females with the disorder than in males. Some people who are pathologic gamblers are seeking the mood alteration associated with gambling— specifically the excitement and energy that they find in the activity— more than the money involved. In other words, the person with the disorder is reinforced by an emotional "high" rather than by the money itself. Some researchers have found that males diagnosed with pathological gambling disorder were more likely to have

Pathological gambling disorder is characterized by uncontrollable gambling well beyond the point of a social or recreational activity, such that the gambling has a major disruptive effect on the gambler's life. People who are pathological gamblers may lose their life savings, and may even commit crimes to get money for their "habit." *(AP/Wide World Photos, Inc. Reproduced by permission.)*

been diagnosed with **attention-deficit/hyperactivity disorder** as children than males in the general population. Other researchers have described compulsive gamblers in general as highly competitive people who are restless and easily bored.

Other theories about the causes of pathological gambling emphasize cognitive distortions rather than mood problems. Pathological gambling has been associated with dysfunctional thinking patterns; many people with this disorder are highly superstitious or believe that they can control the outcome of events when they are gambling. Many people diagnosed with the disorder also have distorted beliefs about money, tending to see it at the same time as the source of all their problems and the answer to all their problems. Patients diagnosed with pathological gambling disorder have an increased risk of either having or developing histrionic, narcissistic, or **borderline personality disorder**.

One social change that has been linked with the rise in the number of adults diagnosed with pathological gambling disorder in the United States is the increased availability of legalized gambling.

Symptoms

The symptoms of pathological gambling include preoccupation with gambling activity, often to the extent of interfering with the person's occupational or social functioning. The person is often unable to control the gambling behavior, continuing to place bets or go to casinos in spite of attempts to cut back or stop. A common behavior in persons with pathological gambling disorder is "chasing," which refers to betting larger sums of money or taking greater risks in order to undo or make up for previous losses. The person may also lie about their gambling or engage in such antisocial behaviors as stealing, credit card fraud, check forgery, embezzling from an employer, or similar dishonest behaviors in order to obtain more money for gambling.

Demographics

More males than females in the United States are diagnosed with pathological gambling disorder; the sex ratio is thought to be about 2:1. Relatively few women, however, are in treatment programs for the disorder, most probably because of the greater social **stigma** attached to women who gamble. As a rule, men diagnosed with pathological gambling disorder began gambling as teenagers, whereas women tend to start compulsive gambling at a later age. Pathological gambling disorder tends to be more common in minority groups and in people with lower socioeconomic status. About 25% of people diagnosed as pathological gamblers had a parent with the disorder. People who smoke tobacco or abuse alcohol are more likely to have pathological gambling disorder than people who do not use these substances.

As many as 4% of the general population in the United States may meet criteria for pathological gambling disorder at some point in their lives. In some countries such as Australia the number is thought to be as high as 7%.

Diagnosis

Pathological gambling disorder is more likely to be diagnosed when the affected person's spouse or family becomes concerned than to be self-reported. **Denial** is common among persons with the disorder. The professional handbook, the ***Diagnostic and Statistical Manual of Mental Disorders,*** *fourth edition, text revision, or* DSM-IV-TR, specifies that the patient must have at least five of the following symptoms to meet criteria for the disorder:

- thinks about gambling all the time
- uses larger and larger amounts of money when gambling
- has tried to stop gambling but failed
- is moody or cranky when trying to stop gambling
- uses gambling as a way to escape problems
- keeps gambling to try to make back money that had previously been lost ("chasing")
- lies about the extent of gambling

- has tried to make money for gambling by engaging in illegal or immoral behavior
- has problems at work or home caused by the gambling
- relies on other people to get him or her out of financial problems caused by the gambling

Pathological gambling disorder is distinguished from social gambling, in which the person is typically socializing with friends, gambling for a limited period of time, and gambling with a limited sum of money that they can afford to lose. Pathological gambling disorder is also distinguished from professional gambling, in which participants limit their risks and discipline their behavior. Lastly, pathological gambling disorder must be distinguished from a **manic episode**; in most cases, the distinguishing feature of the disorder is that the manic-like behavior disappears after the person leaves the gambling setting.

Treatments

There are a number of different treatments for pathological gambling disorder. **Psychodynamic psychotherapy** attempts to uncover any underlying psychological factors that trigger the gambling. For people who are gambling to escape, such as those who are depressed, this approach may be very successful. Treating any substance abuse problems that may coexist with the pathological gambling can also be helpful. Other types of treatments involve behavioral techniques used to teach relaxation and avoidance of stimuli associated with gambling. **Aversion therapy** appears to be successful in treating pathological gambling disorder in highly motivated patients with some insight into the problem, but is not helpful for patients who are less educated or resistant to behavioral methods of treatment.

Gamblers Anonymous, or GA, is a Twelve-Step program patterned on the model of Alcoholics Anonymous (AA). The gambler's admission that she or he does have a gambling problem and a willingness to go to meetings are considered the first steps in treating pathological gambling disorder. Looking realistically at what gambling has done to a person's life, and a willingness to work hard to stop gambling are also important parts of the GA program. People involved in this program are expected to attend meetings regularly, try to make amends for wrongs that their gambling has caused, and find a sponsor (usually of the same sex) to help them through the program. Gamblers Anonymous also expects that people who stop gambling to understand that they probably will never be able to gamble again socially, just as recovering alcoholics cannot drink socially.

Prognosis

There are very few statistics on the number of people successfully treated for pathological gambling disorder. Treatment for any underlying psychological disorders or substance abuses can be very helpful. Sometimes **family therapy** is recommended. Some types of relaxation or behavioral therapy can also be helpful. Gamblers Anonymous can help in many cases, although the program has a high dropout and recurrence rate. For many people, a combination of more than one of these approaches is probably the most effective. Even when a person has successfully stopped compulsive gambling, it is unlikely that he or she will ever be able to gamble socially again, or even spend time in places where he or she once gambled.

Prevention

Prevention of pathological gambling disorder is very difficult because it is impossible to predict when someone will react to gambling in a way that leads to compulsive gambling. If a person begins to feel, however, that he or she may have a problem, immediate treatment can prevent the development of a disorder that affects all areas of life and may have legal as well as economic consequences.

See also Internet addiction disorder; Self-help groups

Resources

BOOKS

American Psychiatric Association. *Diagnostic and Statistical Manual of Mental Disorders.* 4th ed., text revised. Washington D.C.: American Psychiatric Association, 2000.

Forward, Susan, Ph.D., and Craig Buck. "Compulsive Gambling." Chapter 5 in *Money Demons.* New York and Toronto: Bantam Books, 1994.

Sadock, Benjamin J. and Virginia A. Sadock, eds. *Comprehensive Textbook of Psychiatry.* 7th ed. Vol. 2. Philadelphia: Lippincott Williams and Wilkins, 2000.

PERIODICALS

Emerson, Jim. "Gamblers." *Direct* 12, no. 8 (June 2000): 83.

Manisses Communications Group Inc. "Study Finds Other Psychiatric Ills Accompany Pathological Gambling." *The Brown University Digest of Addiction Theory and Application* 18, no. 7 (July 1999): 4.

Nicol, John. "Gambling It All Away: The Spread of Casinos in Canada is Posing a Threat to the Country's Growing Population of Seniors." *Maclean's* February 7, 2000:16.

ORGANIZATIONS

Gamblers Anonymous. P. O. Box 17173, Los Angeles, CA 90017. (219) 386-8789. <www.gamblersanonymous.org>.

Tish Davidson, A.M.

Paxil *see* **Paroxetine**

Paxipam *see* **Galantamine**

PCP *see* **Phencyclidine and related disorders**

Pedophilia

Definition

Pedophilia is a paraphilia that involves an abnormal interest in children. A paraphilia is a disorder that is characterized by recurrent intense sexual urges and sexually arousing fantasies generally involving: nonhuman objects; the suffering or humiliation of oneself or one's partner (not merely simulated); or animals, children, or other nonconsenting persons. Pedophilia is also a psychosexual disorder in which the fantasy or actual act of engaging in sexual activity with prepubertal children is the preferred or exclusive means of achieving sexual excitement and gratification. It may be directed toward children of the same sex or children of the other sex. Some pedophiles are attracted to both boys and girls. Some are attracted only to children, while others are attracted to adults as well as to children.

Pedophilia is defined by mental health professionals as a mental disorder, but the American legal system defines acting on a pedophilic urge as a criminal act.

Description

The focus of pedophilia is sexual activity with a child. Many courts interpret this reference to age to mean children under the age of 18. Most mental health professionals, however, confine the definition of pedophilia to sexual activity with prepubescent children, who are generally age 13 or younger. The term *ephebophilia*, derived from the Greek word for "youth," is sometimes used to describe sexual interest in young people in the first stages of puberty.

The sexual behaviors involved in pedophilia cover a range of activities and may or may not involve the use of force. Some pedophiles limit their behaviors to exposing themselves or masturbating in front of the child, or fondling or undressing the child, but without genital contact. Others, however, compel the child to participate in oral sex or full genital intercourse.

The most common overt aspect of pedophilia is an intense interest in children. There is no typical pedophile. Pedophiles may be young or old, male or female, although the great majority are males. Unfortunately, some pedophiles are professionals who are entrusted with educating or maintaining the health and well-being of young persons, while others are entrusted with children to whom they are related by blood or marriage.

Causes and symptoms

Causes

A variety of different theories exist as to the causes of pedophilia. A few researchers attribute pedophilia along with the other **paraphilias** to biology. They hold that testosterone, one of the male sex hormones, predisposes men to develop deviant sexual behaviors. As far as genetic factors are concerned, as of 2002 no researchers have claimed to have discovered or mapped a gene for pedophilia.

Most experts regard pedophilia as resulting from psychosocial factors rather than biological characteristics. Some think that pedophilia is the result of having been sexually abused as a child. Still others think that it derives from the person's interactions with parents during their early years of life. Some researchers attribute pedophilia to arrested emotional development; that is, the pedophile is attracted to children because he or she has never matured psychologically. Some regard pedophilia as the result of a distorted need to dominate a sexual partner. Since children are smaller and usually weaker than adults, they may be regarded as nonthreatening potential partners. This drive for domination is sometimes thought to explain why most pedophiles are males.

Symptoms

A pedophile is often very attractive to the children who are potential victims. Potential pedophiles may volunteer their services to athletic teams, Scout troops, or religious or civic organizations that serve youth. In some cases, pedophiles who are attracted to children within their extended family may offer to baby-sit for their relatives. They often have good interpersonal skills with children and can easily gain the children's trust.

Some pedophiles offer rationalizations or excuses that enable them to avoid assuming responsibility for their actions. They may blame the children for being too attractive or sexually provocative. They may also maintain that they are "teaching" the child about "the facts of life" or "love"; this rationalization is frequently offered by pedophiles who have molested children related to them. All these rationalizations may be found in pornography with pedophilic themes.

Demographics

Pedophilia is one of the more common paraphilias; the large worldwide market for child pornography suggests that it is more frequent in the general population than prison statistics would indicate. Together with **voyeurism** and **exhibitionism**, pedophilia is one of the three paraphilias most commonly leading to arrest by the police.

The onset of pedophilia usually occurs during adolescence. Occasional pedophiles begin their activities during middle age but this late onset is uncommon. In the United States, about 50% of men arrested for pedophilia are married.

The frequency of behavior associated with pedophilia varies with psychosocial **stress**. As the pedophile's stress levels increase, the frequency of his or her acting out generally rises also.

Pedophilia is more common among males than among females. In addition, the rate of recidivism for persons with a pedophilic preference for males is approximately twice that of pedophiles who prefer females.

Little is known about the incidence of pedophilia in different racial or ethnic groups.

Diagnosis

According to the ***Diagnostic and Statistical Manual of Mental Disorders***, fourth edition text revised, the following criteria must be met to establish a **diagnosis** of pedophilia.

- Over a period of at least six months, the affected person experiences recurrent, intense and sexually arousing fantasies, sexual urges or actual behaviors involving sexual activity with a prepubescent child or children aged 13 or younger.
- The fantasies, sexual urges or behaviors cause clinically significant distress or impairment in social, occupational or other important areas of daily functioning.
- The affected person must be at least age sixteen and be at least five years older than the child or children who are the objects or targets of attention or sexual activity.

A diagnosis of pedophilia cannot be assigned to an individual in late adolescence (age 17 to 19) who is involved in an ongoing sexual relationship with a 12- or 13-year-old person.

In establishing a diagnosis of pedophilia, it is important for a mental health professional to determine if the patient is attracted to males, females or both. It is also important to determine whether incest is a factor in the relationship. Finally, the doctor must determine whether the pedophilia is exclusive or nonexclusive; that is, whether the patient is attracted only to children (exclusive pedophilia) or to adults as well as to children (nonexclusive pedophilia).

KEY TERMS

Aversion therapy—An approach to treatment in which an unpleasant or painful stimulus is linked to an undesirable behavior in order to condition the patient to dislike or avoid the behavior.

Castration—Desexing a person or animal by surgical removal of the testes (in males) or ovaries (in females). Castration is sometimes offered as a treatment option to pedophiles who are violent rapists and/or repeat offenders.

Comorbidity—Association or presence of two or more mental disorders in the same patient. A disorder that is said to have a high degree of comorbidity is likely to occur in patients diagnosed with other disorders that may share or reinforce some of its symptoms.

Ephebophilia—Sexual desire on the part of an adult for youths in the early stages of puberty, as distinct from prepubertal children.

Incest—Unlawful sexual contact between persons who are biologically related. Many therapists, however, use the term to refer to inappropriate sexual contact between any members of a family, including stepparents and stepsiblings.

Paraphilia—A disorder that is characterized by recurrent intense sexual urges and sexually arousing fantasies generally involving (1) non-human objects, (2) the suffering or humiliation of oneself or one's partner (not merely simulated), or (3) children or other non-consenting persons.

Recidivism—A tendency to return to a previously treated activity, or repeated relapse into criminal or deviant behavior.

Voyeurism—A paraphilia that involves watching unsuspecting people, usually strangers, undress or engage in sexual activity.

One difficulty with the diagnosis of the disorder is that persons with pedophilia rarely seek help voluntarily from mental health professionals. Instead, counseling and treatment is often the result of a court order. An interview that establishes the criteria for diagnosis listed above may be enough to diagnose the condition, or surveillance or Internet records obtained through the criminal investigation may also be used.

An additional complication in diagnosis is that the paraphilias as a group have a high rate of comorbidity with one another and an equally high rate of comorbidity with major depression, anxiety disorders, and substance abuse disorders. A person diagnosed with pedophilia may also meet the criteria for exhibitionism or for a substance abuse or mood disorder.

Treatments

In the earliest stages of **behavior modification** therapy, pedophiles may be narrowly viewed as being attracted to inappropriate persons. Such aversive stimuli as electric shocks have been administered to persons undergoing therapy for pedophilia. This approach has not been very successful.

In 2002, the most common form of treatment for pedophilia is **psychotherapy**, often of many years' duration. It does not have a high rate of success in inducing pedophiles to change their behavior.

Pedophilia may also be treated with medications. The three classes of medications most often used to treat pedophilia (and other paraphilias) are: female hormones, particularly medroxyprogesterone acetate, or MPA; luteinizing hormone-releasing hormone (LHRH) agonists, which include such drugs as triptorelin (Trelstar), leuprolide acetate, and goserelin acetate; and anti-androgens, which block the uptake and metabolism of testosterone as well as reducing blood levels of this hormone. Most clinical studies of these drugs have been done in Germany, where the legal system has allowed their use in treating repeat sexual offenders since the 1970s. The anti-androgens in particular have been shown to be effective in reducing the rate of recidivism.

Surgical castration is sometimes offered as a treatment to pedophiles who are repeat offenders or who have pleaded guilty to violent rape.

Increasingly, pedophiles are being prosecuted under criminal statutes and being sentenced to prison terms. Imprisonment removes them from society for a period of time but does not usually remove their pedophilic tendencies. In 2002, many states have begun to publish the names of persons being released from prison after serving time for pedophilia. Legal challenges to this practice are pending in various jurisdictions.

Prognosis

The prognosis of successfully ending pedophilic habits among persons who practice pedophilia is not favorable. Pedophiles have a high rate of recidivism; that is, they tend to repeat their acts often over time.

The rate of prosecution for pedophiles through the criminal justice system has increased in recent years. Pedophiles are at high risk of being beaten or killed by other prison inmates. For this reason, they must often be kept isolated from other members of a prison population. Knowledge of the likelihood of abuse by prison personnel and inmates is not, however, an effective deterrent for most pedophiles.

Prevention

The main method for preventing pedophilia is avoiding situations that may promote pedophilic acts. Children should never be allowed to in one-on-one situations with any adult other than their parents or trustworthy family members. Having another youth or adult as an observer provides some security for all concerned. Conferences and other activities can be conducted so as to provide privacy while still within sight of others.

Children should be taught to yell or run if they are faced with an uncomfortable situation. They should also be taught that it is acceptable to scream or call for help in such situations.

Another basis of preventing pedophilia is education. Children must be taught to avoid situations that make them vulnerable to pedophiles. Adults who work with youth must be taught to avoid situations that may be construed as promoting pedophilia.

Many states have adopted legislation that requires periodic background investigations of any adult who works with children. These persons may be paid, such as teachers, or they may be volunteers in a youth-serving organization.

The Boy Scouts of America has tried to address the problem of pedophilia by creating a training program that is required for all adults in the organization. All applications for volunteers are reviewed and approved by several persons. Adults and youth are required to use separate facilities on all activities. Secret meetings and one-on-one interactions between adults and youth are prohibited. This program has received several national awards.

See also Abuse; Aversion therapy

Resources

BOOKS

American Psychiatric Association. *Diagnostic and Statistical Manual of Mental Disorders.* Fourth edition, text revised. Washington DC: American Psychiatric Association, 2000.

Gelder, Michael, Richard Mayou, and Philip Cowen. *Shorter Oxford Textbook of Psychiatry.* 4th ed. New York: Oxford University Press, 2001.

Wilson, Josephine F. *Biological Foundations of Human Behavior.* New York: Harcourt, 2002.

PERIODICALS

Berlin, F. S. "Treatments to change sexual orientation." *American Journal of Psychiatry* 157, no. 5 (2000): 838-839.

Cohen, L. J., and others. "Impulsive personality traits in male pedophiles versus healthy controls: Is pedophilia an impulsive-aggressive disorder?" *Comprehensive Psychiatry* 43, no. 2 (2002): 127-134.

Hill, S. A. "The man who claimed to be a paedophile." *Journal of Medical Ethics* 26, no. 2 (2000): 137-138.

O'Donohue, W., L. G. Regev, and A. Hagstrom. "Problems with the DSM-IV diagnosis of pedophilia. " *Sexual Abuse* 12, no. 2 (2000): 95-105.

ORGANIZATIONS

American Academy of Family Physicians. 11400 Tomahawk Creek Parkway, Leawood, KS 66211-2672. Phone: (913) 906-6000. Web site: <http://www.aafp.org>.

American Academy of Pediatrics. 141 Northwest Point Boulevard, Elk Grove Village, IL 60007-1098. Telephone: (847) 434-4000. Fax: (847) 434-8000. Web site: <http://www.aap.org/default.htm>.

American Medical Association. 515 N. State Street, Chicago, IL 60610. Telephone: (312) 464-5000. Web site: <http://www.ama-assn.org>.

American Psychiatric Association. 1400 K Street NW, Washington, DC 20005. Telephone: (888) 357-7924. Fax: (202) 682-6850.

American Psychological Association. 750 First Street NW, Washington, DC, 20002-4242. Phone: (800) 374-2721 or (202) 336-5500. Web site: <http://www.apa.org>.

L. Fleming Fallon, Jr., M.D., Dr.P.H.

Peer groups

Definition

Peer groups are an important influence throughout one's life, but they are more critical during the developmental years of childhood and adolescence. There is often controversy about the influence of a peer group versus parental influence, particularly during adolescence. Recent studies show that parents continue to have significant influence, even during adolescence, a reassuring finding for many parents. It appears that the power of the peer group becomes more important when the family relationships are not close or supportive. For example, if the parents work extra jobs and are largely unavailable, their children may turn to their peer group for emotional support. This also occurs when the conflict between parents and children during adolescence, or at any time during a child's development, becomes so great that the child feels pushed away and seeks closeness elsewhere. Most children and adolescents in this situation are not discriminating about the kind of group they join. They will often turn to a group simply because that group accepts them, even if the group is involved in illegal or negative activities. Gang involvement, for example, is a common form of organized—often antisocial—peer interaction. Gangs may be based on ethnicity, sex, and/or common activity. Most youths who join gangs come from families where drug and alcohol use, financial burdens, and broken relationships are common. The need for affiliation or closeness is often greater than the need to "do the right thing" for some adolescents who feel isolated and abandoned by members of their own family. Being part of a gang provides such individuals with acceptance and security not available at home or in other peer groups.

KEY TERMS

Cluster suicide—Refers to the phenomenon of additional suicides being attempted or completed after one suicide has occurred within a small community, such as a group of high school students.

Membership in peer groups

Despite significant gains in diversity training, current studies continue to show that children are less likely to accept those who are different from themselves. The differences can be as obvious as physical impairments, or as subtle as differences in academic motivation. These rigid standards may create an atmosphere of exclusion for some children and adolescents that pushes them toward peer acceptance of any type.

Peer groups offer children and adults alike the opportunity to develop various social skills, such as leadership, sharing or teamwork, and empathy. Peer groups also offer the opportunity to experiment with new roles and interactions, similar to treatment groups, although they are less structured. It is for this reason that many children and adolescents drift from one group to another as they "find themselves," or work toward formation of their relatively permanent identity.

Aggression in peer groups

Although bullying and teasing have long been part of peer group interactions, these negative behaviors have increased over the last decade, resulting in school violence in many instances. As children and adolescents feel

Peer groups offer children and adults alike the opportunity to develop various social skills, such as leadership, sharing or teamwork, and empathy. Peer groups also offer the opportunity to experiment with new roles and interactions, and can have positive or negative influences on an individual. *(Bill Varie/ CORBIS. Reproduced by permission.)*

marginalized from their peers, anger builds to a point of rage at times. It is at those times that violence erupts within the school or community setting.

Negative peer interactions also occur more frequently following friendships or romantic relationships that have gone sour. The level of harassment that many of these children—often young women—experience is great enough for parents to become involved. In some cases, it may be necessary to move the child to another school district. A potential remediation for these negative interactions includes more active teacher involvement when negative social interactions are observed.

Influence of peer groups

Peer groups can also have a positive influence—a fact many parents have known for years. Studies support parent's perceptions that the influence of friends can have a positive effect on academic motivation and performance. Conversely, experimentation with drugs, drinking, vandalism, and stealing may also be increased by interaction with the peer group.

Interventions

Since schools are often the site of negative peer interactions, school personnel have a unique opportunity for effective **intervention**. Many schools have peer-mediation programs, in which students are encouraged to resolve conflicts on their own without the use of violence or aggression. School counselors also organize groups within the school to handle various problems, including providing **social skills training** and empathy training.

Risks

Peer groups often provide an example for negative and harmful behaviors. Cluster **suicide** is one such example. When a teen realizes that someone he or she knew has attempted or has committed suicide, the teen may see suicide as a viable option for him- or herself as well. For this reason, schools and local media should exercise caution when reporting such tragedies. Care must be taken not to portray the suicide glamorously or mythically.

When parents try to protect their children by telling them to stay away from certain friends, they should realize that sometimes this only encourages them to seek out negative role models. Parents should be supportive of their child and redirect their child's activities to more positive and prosocial peers and events. A trusted adult friend, such as a scout leader or a respected coach, may be an important part of the redirection effort.

As noted, children and adolescents without strong family connections, or at least a positive connection with other adults in their life, face a higher risk of negative influence from peer groups. If the child or adolescent has not been able to form bonds with positive peer groups, it is more likely they will be perceived as distant and different from their peers, making them feel more like outsiders. Lower standards of acceptance often exist in less positive peer groups, making it easier for people to join. Unfortunately, many such groups often engage in self-destructive and anti-social activities.

See also: Family therapy

Resources

BOOKS

Juvonen, J. and S. Graham, eds. *Peer harassment in school: The plight of the vulnerable and victimized.* New York: The Guilford Press, 2001.

PERIODICALS

Pearl, R., T. W. Farmer, R. Van Acker, P. C. Rodkin, K. K. Bost, M. Coe, and W. Henley. "The social integration of students with mild disabilities in general education classrooms: Peer group membership and peer-assessed social behavior." *Elementary School Journal* 99, no. 2 (Nov 1998): 167-185.

Ryan, A. M. "The peer group as a context for the development of young adolescent motivation and achievement." *Child Development* 72, no. 4 (Jul-Aug 2001): 1135-1150.

Schwartz, D. "Subtypes of victims and aggressors in children's peer groups." *Journal of Abnormal Child Psychology* 28, no. 2 (Apr 2000): 181-192.

Deanna Pledge, Ph.D.

Pemoline

Definition

Pemoline is classified as a central nervous system (CNS) stimulant. It is sold in the United States under the brand names Cylert and PemADD and is also available under its generic name.

Purpose

Pemoline is used in combination with psychological, educational, and social support for the treatment of **attention-deficit/hyperactivity disorder** (ADHD).

Description

Pemoline is a central nervous system stimulant that derives at least some of its effects by increasing levels of dopamine in the **brain**. Dopamine is one of several **neurotransmitters** in the brain. Neurotransmitters are naturally occurring chemicals that regulate the transmission of nerve impulses from one cell to another. Mental and physical well-being are partially dependent on maintaining the proper balance among the various neurotransmitters in the brain.

Pemoline is similar in its effects to dextroamphetamine and **methylphenidate**, two other drugs used to treat ADHD, although it is not chemically related to these drugs. The mechanism of action of CNS stimulants in the treatment of ADHD is not totally clear, but probably includes increased mental alertness, decreased mental **fatigue**, and an increased sense of well-being.

Pemoline should not be used as a substitute for psychological, educational, and social support in treating ADHD. Because pemoline may be associated with liver toxicity (poisoning causing liver damage), it should be used only after other drugs to treat ADHD have been tried. Patients should try dextroamphetamine or methylphenidate first.

Pemoline is available in 18.75-mg, 37.5-mg, and 75-mg oral tablets and in 37.5-mg chewable tablets.

KEY TERMS

Attention-deficit/hyperactivity disorder (ADHD)—A learning and behavioral disorder characterized by difficulty in sustaining attention, impulsive behavior, and excessive activity.

Dopamine—A chemical in brain tissue that serves to transmit nerve impulses (is a neurotransmitter) and helps to regulate movement and emotions.

Neurotransmitter—A chemical in the brain that transmits messages between neurons, or nerve cells.

Recommended dosage

The dose of pemoline should be carefully adjusted to patient need. The initial dose of pemoline in children six years of age or older is 37.5 mg each morning. The dose may be increased by 18.75 mg each week to as much as 75 mg daily. Most people respond to doses ranging from 56.25 mg to 75 mg daily, although some people may require as much as 112.5 mg daily.

There is no need to continue pemoline indefinitely. Rather, patients should be evaluated both during therapy and during periods in which the medication is voluntarily stopped. In many situations, the drug may be safely discontinued altogether when the child reaches adolescence.

Precautions

Pemoline is associated with liver toxicity. Symptoms range from mild reversible changes in liver function tests to acute liver failure. The risk of liver damage should be weighed against any therapeutic benefit derived from treatment with pemoline. Therefore, if no therapeutic benefit is observed within three to four weeks of starting the drug, pemoline should be discontinued. In order to detect the early signs of liver damage, liver function tests should be performed before starting the drug and every two weeks while taking pemoline.

Because pemoline is a central nervous stimulant, physical or psychological **addiction** is possible in people who are emotionally unstable.

Side effects

Loss of appetite accompanied by weight loss generally occurs during the first few weeks after starting pemoline. With continued treatment, appetite and body weight usually stabilize.

Because it is a central nervous system stimulant, **insomnia** is a common side effect of pemoline.

The most serious side effect is liver toxicity. Liver toxicity is usually characterized by changes in liver function tests without obvious liver damage, but in rare cases, liver failure resulting in death or requiring a liver transplant has occurred.

Interactions

There are no scientific data concerning drugs that negatively interact with pemoline. However, because pemoline is considered a stimulant, other drugs with stimulant properties (caffeine, over-the-counter decongestants, **amphetamines**, antidepressants) may theoretically and inappropriately increase CNS stimulation.

Resources

BOOKS

American Society of Health-System Pharmacists. *AHFS Drug Information 2002.* Bethesda: American Society of Health-System Pharmacists, 2002.

O'Brien, Charles P. "Drug Addiction and Drug Abuse." In *Goodman & Gillman's The Pharmacological Basis of Therapeutics,* edited by Joel G. Hardman, Ph.D. and Lee E. Limbird, Ph.D. Tenth Edition. New York: McGraw-Hill, 2001.

Jack Raber, Pharm.D.

Pentobarbitol *see* **Barbiturates**

Permitil *see* **Fluphenazine**

Perphenazine

Definition

Perphenazine is a phenothiazine antipsychotic used to treat serious mental disorders. It has also been used to treat severe nausea and vomiting. It is sold in the United States under the brand name Trilafon and is also available under its generic name.

Purpose

Perphenazine is used to treat psychotic disorders and severe nausea and vomiting.

Description

Perphenazine is one of many drugs in the class called phenothiazine derivatives. Phenothiazines work by inhibiting the actions of the **brain** chemicals, dopamine and norepinephrine, which are overproduced in individuals with **psychosis**.

Recommended dosage

For the treatment of psychosis, adults usually receive a total of 4 mg to 16 mg taken as tablets in three or four doses daily, up to a maximum of 64 mg each day. Injections of perphenazine are also available and are typically given in 5 mg doses every six hours, up to 15 mg per day. Hospitalized patients can receive up to 30 mg per day in the injectable form of perphenazine.

Adult patients with serious nausea and vomiting receive 8 mg to 16 mg per day as tablets in divided into several doses up to a maximum of 24 mg per day. Injections are typically given in 5 mg to 10 mg doses every six hours, up to 15 mg per day in patients who are not confined to bed. Hospitalized patients can receive up to a maximum of 30 mg per day. Intravenous perphenazine can be given to nausea and vomiting patients up to 1 mg every one to two minutes to a maximum of 5 mg.

The correct dosage of perphenazine must be carefully determined for each patient. Physicians try to find a dose that controls symptoms of the disease without causing intolerable side effects. Dosage guidelines for the treatment of psychosis have not been established for children under the age of 12 years. In children over age 12, the lowest adult dosage is generally used to treat psychosis. Children with severe nausea and vomiting are usually given 5 mg injections every six hours.

Precautions

Persons who take perphenazine should not stop taking the drug abruptly. Instead, the dose should be decreased gradually, then stopped. People who take perphenazine often have develop sunburn more easily than Sunscreen should be used by people, especially fair-skinned individuals, taking perphenazine.

People who are known to have severe central nervous system depression should not take perphenazine or any other drug in its class. In addition, those with a prior history of brain damage, coma, or bone marrow depression should not receive perphenazine without a thorough evaluation by a doctor.

Children under the age of 12 years, the elderly (over age 65), those with a history of epilepsy, glaucoma, prostate problems, severe asthma, and other severe breathing problems should receive perphenazine only with great caution and under close supervision of a physician. In addition, persons with a history of heart or blood vessel disease and those with a history of liver or kidney disease should take perphenazine only after a thorough evaluation. Perphenazine should also be used cautiously when taken over a long period. Rarely should perphenazine be taken by pregnant or nursing women.

Side effects

Serious or life-threatening side effects due to perphenazine are rare. However, if any of these occur, patients should contact their doctors or get immediate medical attention: **seizures**, irregular heartbeat, significant changes in blood pressure, muscle stiffness, weakness, pale skin color, and increased sweating. The treating doctor should be contacted immediately if any of these common side effects develop: rapid movements of the tongue, uncontrolled chewing movement, unusual amounts of lip smacking, and frequent movement of the arms or legs. The treating doctor should be contacted relatively soon if any of the following common side effects develop: reduced balance control, muscle spasms, restlessness, trembling, weakness in the limbs, blurred vision, and decreased night vision.

Less common side effects that need to be reported to the doctor include severe sunburn, skin rashes, and urination problems. Rare side effects that should be reported to the doctor include abdominal pain, muscle aches, joint aches, fever, chills, muscle weakness, and vomiting. Common and not serious side effects include constipation, drowsiness, decreased sweating, mouth dryness, and nasal congestion. Uncommon and not typically serious side effects include decreased sexual desire, increased susceptibility to sunburn, menstrual cycle changes, swelling or pain in the breasts, and weight gain.

Interactions

Combining perphenazine with drugs such as the anti-mallarials amodiaquine, chloroquine, and sulfadoxine-pyrimethamine (Fansidar) can increase the concentrations within the body of these three latter drugs.

Perphenazine combined with **barbiturates** tends to lower the concentrations of perphenazine in the body. Combining perphenazine with **clonidine** (Catapres), guanadrel (Hylorel), and guanethidine (Ismelin) can produce dangerously low blood pressure.

Perphenazine should not be combined with alcohol, because alcohol increases the drug's depressive effect on the central nervous system. Perphenazine inhibits the effects of levodopa in Parkinson patients when the two are combined. Lithium combined with perphenazine lowers the levels of both drugs.

Perphenazine should not be combined with analgesics (pain killers) containing narcotics because of the combination increases depressive effects on the central nervous system. Orphenadrine (Norflex) combined with perphenazine can reduce the beneficial effects of perphenazine.

KEY TERMS

Glaucoma—A group of eye diseases characterized by increased pressure within the eye significant enough to damage eye tissue and structures. If untreated, glaucoma results in blindness.

Psychosis—Severe state that is characterized by loss of contact with reality and deterioration in normal social functioning; examples are schizophrenia and paranoia. Psychosis is usually one feature of an over-arching disorder, not a disorder in itself. (Plural: psychoses)

Resources

BOOKS

Consumer Reports Staff, eds. *Consumer Reports Complete Drug Reference*. 2002 ed. Denver: Micromedex Thomson Healthcare, 2001.

Ellsworth, Allan J. and others. *Mosby's Medical Drug Reference*. 2001-2002. St. Louis: Mosby, 2001.

Hardman, Joel G., Lee E. Limbird, eds. *Goodman & Gilman's The Pharmacological Basis of Therapeutics*. 10th ed. New York: McGraw-Hill, 2001.

Mosby's GenRx Staff. *Mosby's GenRx*. 9th ed. St. Louis: Mosby, 1999.

Venes, Donald, and others, eds. *Taber's Cyclopedic Medical Dictionary*. 19th ed. Philadelphia: F. A. Davis, 2001.

Mark Mitchell, M.D.

Personality disorders

Definition

Long-standing, deeply ingrained patterns of social behavior that are detrimental to those who display them or to others.

...tion

...ality disorders constitute a separate diagnostic ... (Axis II) in the American Psychiatric ...on's ***Diagnostic and Statistical Manual of Me... Disorders*** (DSM). Unlike the major mental disorders (Axis I), which are characterized by periods of illness and remission, personality disorders are generally ongoing. Often, they first appear in childhood or adolescence and persist throughout a person's lifetime. Aside from their persistence, the other major characteristic of personality disorders is inflexibility. Persons affected by these disorders have rigid personality traits and coping styles, are unable to adapt to changing situations, and experience impaired social and/or occupational functioning. A further difference between personality disorders and the major clinical syndromes listed in Axis I of *DSM-IV-TR (DSM*, fourth edition, text revised) is that people with personality disorders may not perceive that there is anything wrong with their behavior and are not motivated to change it. Although the *DSM-IV-TR* lists specific descriptions of 10 personality disorders, these conditions are often difficult to diagnose. Some characteristics of the various disorders overlap. In other cases, the complexity of human behavior makes it difficult to pinpoint a clear dividing line between pathology and normality in the assessment of personality. In still other cases, persons may have more than one personality disorder, complicating the **diagnosis**. There also has been relatively little research done on some of the personality disorders listed in *DSM-IV-TR*.

The 10 personality disorders listed in *DSM-IV-TR* include:

- **Paranoid personality disorder**. The individual affected with this disorder believes in general that people will exploit, harm, or deceive him or her, even if there is no evidence to support this belief.
- **Schizoid personality disorder**. The individual with this disorder seems to lack desire for intimacy or belonging in a social group, and often chooses being alone to being with others. This individual also tends not to show a full range of emotions.
- **Schizotypal personality disorder**. With this disorder, the affected person is uncomfortable with (and may be unable to sustain) close relationships, and also has odd behaviors and thoughts that would typically be viewed by others as eccentric, erratic, and bizarre.
- **Antisocial personality disorder**. Individuals with this disorder have no regard for the rights of others. Other, recent names associated with this personality type are psychopath and sociopath. Unable to base their actions on anything except their own immediate desires, persons with this disorder demonstrate a pattern of impulsive, irresponsible, thoughtless, and sometimes criminal behavior. They are often intelligent, articulate individuals with an ability to charm and manipulate others; at their most dangerous, they can become violent criminals who are particularly dangerous to society because of their ability to gain the trust of others combined with their lack of conscience or remorse.
- **Borderline personality disorder**. People with this disorder are unstable in their relationships, decisions, moods, and self-perceptions. These individuals are often impulsive and insecure.
- **Histrionic personality disorder**. The behavior of individuals of this personality type is characterized by persistent attention-seeking, exaggerated emotional displays (such as tantrums), and overreaction to trivial problems and events.
- **Narcissistic personality disorder**. This disorder consists primarily of an inflated sense of self-importance coupled with a lack of empathy for others. Individuals with this disorder display an exaggerated sense of their own importance and abilities and tend to fantasize about them. Such persons also have a sense of entitlement, expecting (and taking for granted) special treatment and concessions from others. Paradoxically, individuals with narcissistic personality disorder are generally very insecure and suffer from low self-esteem.
- **Avoidant personality disorder**. This disorder has characteristics that resemble those of **social phobia**, including hypersensitivity to possible rejection and the resulting social withdrawal in spite of a strong need for love and acceptance. Individuals with this disorder are inhibited and feel inadequate in social situations.
- **Dependent personality disorder**. Persons with dependent personality disorder are extremely passive and tend to subordinate their own needs to those of others. Due to their lack of self-confidence, they avoid asserting themselves and allow others to take responsibility for their lives.
- **Obsessive-compulsive personality disorder**. This disorder is characterized by a preoccupation with orderliness, perfectionism, and control.

An additional category for personality disorders exists—personality disorder not otherwise specified. This category is reserved for clinicians' use when they encounter a patient with symptoms similar to one of the above disorders, but the exact criteria for a specific disorder are not met.

Resources

BOOKS

American Psychiatric Association. *Diagnostic and Statistical Manual of mental Disorders.* Fourth edition, text revised. Washington DC: American Psychiatric Association, 2000.

Davidson, Kate. *Cognitive Therapy for Personality Disorders.* Cary: Edward Arnold, 2000.

Millon, T. *Disorders of Personality: DSM-IV and Beyond.* New York: Wiley-Interscience, 1995.

Millon, T. *Personality Disorders in Modern Life: Character Disorders.* New York: John Wiley and Sons, 1999.

Person-centered therapy

Definition

Person-centered therapy, which is also known as client-centered, non-directive, or Rogerian therapy, is an approach to counseling and **psychotherapy** that places much of the responsibility for the treatment process on the client, with the therapist taking a nondirective role.

Purpose

Two primary goals of person-centered therapy are increased self-esteem and greater openness to experience. Some of the related changes that this form of therapy seeks to foster in clients include closer agreement between the client's idealized and actual selves; better self-understanding; lower levels of defensiveness, guilt, and insecurity; more positive and comfortable relationships with others; and an increased capacity to experience and express feelings at the moment they occur.

Description

Background

Developed in the 1930s by the American **psychologist** Carl Rogers, client-centered therapy departed from the typically formal, detached role of the therapist emphasized in **psychoanalysis** and other forms of treatment. Rogers believed that therapy should take place in a supportive environment created by a close personal relationship between client and therapist. Rogers's introduction of the term "client" rather than "patient" expresses his rejection of the traditionally hierarchical relationship between therapist and client and his view of them as equals. In person-centered therapy, the client determines the general direction of therapy, while the therapist seeks to increase the client's insight and self-understanding through informal clarifying questions.

Beginning in the 1960s, person-centered therapy became associated with the human potential movement. This movement, dating back to the beginning of the 1900s, reflected an altered perspective of human nature. Previous psychological theories viewed human beings as inherently selfish and corrupt. For example, Freud's theory focused on sexual and aggressive tendencies as the primary forces driving human behavior. The human potential movement, by contrast, defined human nature as inherently good. From its perspective, human behavior is motivated by a drive to achieve one's fullest potential.

Self-actualization, a term derived from the human potential movement, is an important concept underlying person-centered therapy. It refers to the tendency of all human beings to move forward, grow, and reach their fullest potential. When humans move toward self-actualization, they are also pro-social; that is, they tend to be concerned for others and behave in honest, dependable, and constructive ways. The concept of self-actualization focuses on human strengths rather than human deficiencies. According to Rogers, self-actualization can be blocked by an unhealthy self-concept (negative or unrealistic attitudes about oneself).

Rogers adopted terms such as "person-centered approach" and "way of being" and began to focus on personal growth and self-actualization. He also pioneered the use of encounter groups, adapting the sensitivity training (T-group) methods developed by Kurt Lewin (1890-1947) and other researchers at the National Training Laboratories in the 1950s. More recently, two major variations of person-centered therapy have developed: experiential therapy, developed by Eugene Gendlin in 1979; and process-experiential therapy, developed by Leslie Greenberg and colleagues in 1993.

While person-centered therapy is considered one of the major therapeutic approaches, along with psychoanalytic and **cognitive-behavioral therapy**, Rogers's influence is felt in schools of therapy other than his own. The concepts and methods he developed are used in an eclectic fashion by many different types of counselors and therapists.

Process

Rogers believed that the most important factor in successful therapy was not the therapist's skill or training, but rather his or her attitude. Three interrelated attitudes on the part of the therapist are central to the success of person-centered therapy: congruence; unconditional positive regard; and empathy. Congruence refers to the therapist's openness and genuineness—the willingness to relate to clients without hiding behind a professional facade. Therapists who function in this way have all their

KEY TERMS

Congruence—A quality of the client-centered therapist, consisting of openness to the client.

Empathy—A quality of the client-centered therapist, characterized by the therapist's conveying appreciation and understanding of the client's point of view.

Encounter groups—A term coined by Carl Rogers for therapist-run groups that focus on personal exploration, experiencing in the here-and-now (that is, feelings and interpersonal exchanges occurring in the group setting), and genuine concern and honesty among the members.

Experiential therapy—An approach to therapy that focuses on experiencing inner feelings, rather than talking about problems in a disconnected, intellectual way. Although it is based on person-centered therapy, experiential therapy is more directive because it uses techniques from a variety of therapeutic approaches to draw out a person's inner experiences.

Human potential movement—A movement dating back to the beginning of the 1900s that reflected an altered perspective of human nature from inherently corrupt to inherently good.

Nondirective therapy—An approach to therapy in which the therapist actively attempts to avoid giving advice, making interpretations, or otherwise influencing the focus of the individual's thoughts or statements.

Play therapy—A type of psychotherapy for young children involving the use of toys and games to build a therapeutic relationship and encourage the child's self-expression.

Process-experiential therapies—A group of therapies based on a person-centered approach that incorporate elements of cognitive and Gestalt therapies.

Self-actualization—The belief that all human beings have an inborn tendency toward growth and self-improvement.

Self-concept—Attitudes about oneself.

Sensitivity training—Training conducted in T-groups to reduce tensions and racial prejudice among the public.

T-groups—Short for "basic skills training groups" that were focused on education and discussion regarding social issues, personal problems experienced outside the group setting, and problems from one's past.

Unconditional positive regard—A quality of the client-centered therapist, characterized by the therapist's acceptance of the client without judgment.

feelings available to them in therapy sessions and may share significant emotional reactions with their clients. Congruence does *not* mean, however, that therapists disclose their own personal problems to clients in therapy sessions or shift the focus of therapy to themselves in any other way.

Unconditional positive regard means that the therapist accepts the client totally for who he or she is without evaluating or censoring, and without disapproving of particular feelings, actions, or characteristics. The therapist communicates this attitude to the client by a willingness to listen without interrupting, judging, or giving advice. This attitude of positive regard creates a nonthreatening context in which the client feels free to explore and share painful, hostile, defensive, or abnormal feelings without worrying about personal rejection by the therapist.

The third necessary component of a therapist's attitude is empathy ("accurate empathetic understanding"). The therapist tries to appreciate the client's situation from the client's point of view, showing an emotional understanding of and sensitivity to the client's feelings throughout the therapy session. In other systems of therapy, empathy with the client would be considered a preliminary step to enabling the therapeutic work to proceed; but in person-centered therapy, it actually constitutes a major portion of the therapeutic work itself. A primary way of conveying this empathy is by active listening that shows careful and perceptive attention to what the client is saying. In addition to standard techniques, such as eye contact, that are common to any good listener, person-centered therapists employ a special method called reflection, which consists of paraphrasing and/or summarizing what a client has just said. This technique shows that the therapist is listening carefully and accurately, and gives clients an added opportunity to examine their own thoughts and feelings as they hear them repeated by another person. Generally, clients respond by elaborating further on the thoughts they have just expressed.

According to Rogers, when these three attitudes (congruence, unconditional positive regard, and empathy) are conveyed by a therapist, clients can freely express themselves without having to worry about what the therapist thinks of them. The therapist does not attempt to change the client's thinking in any way. Even negative expressions are validated as legitimate experiences. Because of this nondirective approach, clients can explore the issues that are most important to them—not those considered important by the therapist. Based on the principle of self-actualization, this undirected, uncensored self-exploration allows clients to eventually recognize alternative ways of thinking that will promote personal growth. The therapist merely facilitates self-actualization by providing a climate in which clients can freely engage in focused, in-depth self-exploration.

Applications

Rogers originally developed person-centered therapy in a children's clinic while he was working there; however, person-centered therapy was not intended for a specific age group or subpopulation but has been used to treat a broad range of people. Rogers worked extensively with people with **schizophrenia** later in his career. His therapy has also been applied to persons suffering from depression, anxiety, alcohol disorders, cognitive dysfunction, and **personality disorders**. Some therapists argue that person-centered therapy is not effective with nonverbal or poorly educated individuals; others maintain that it can be successfully adapted to any type of person. The person-centered approach can be used in individual, group, or **family therapy**. With young children, it is frequently employed as **play therapy**.

There are no strict guidelines regarding the length or frequency of person-centered therapy. Generally, therapists adhere to a one-hour session once per week. True to the spirit of person-centered therapy, however, scheduling may be adjusted according to the client's expressed needs. The client also decides when to terminate therapy. Termination usually occurs when he or she feels able to better cope with life's difficulties.

Normal results

The expected results of person-centered therapy include improved self-esteem; trust in one's inner feelings and experiences as valuable sources of information for making decisions; increased ability to learn from (rather than repeating) mistakes; decreased defensiveness, guilt, and insecurity; more positive and comfortable relationships with others; an increased capacity to experience and express feelings at the moment they occur; and openness to new experiences and new ways of thinking about life.

Outcome studies of humanistic therapies in general and person-centered therapy in particular indicate that people who have been treated with these approaches maintain stable changes over extended periods of time; that they change substantially compared to untreated persons; and that the changes are roughly comparable to the changes in clients who have been treated by other types of therapy. Humanistic therapies appear to be particularly effective in clients with depression or relationship issues. Person-centered therapy, however, appears to be slightly less effective than other forms of humanistic therapy in which therapists offer more advice to clients and suggest topics to explore.

Abnormal results

If therapy has been unsuccessful, the client will not move in the direction of self-growth and self-acceptance. Instead, he or she may continue to display behaviors that reflect self-defeating attitudes or rigid patterns of thinking.

Several factors may affect the success of person-centered therapy. If an individual is not interested in therapy (for example, if he or she was forced to attend therapy), that person may not work well together with the therapist. The skill of the therapist may be another factor. In general, clients tend to overlook occasional therapist failures if a satisfactory relationship has been established. A therapist who continually fails to demonstrate unconditional positive regard, congruence, or empathy cannot effectively use this type of therapy. A third factor is the client's comfort level with nondirective therapy. Some studies have suggested that certain clients may get bored, frustrated, or annoyed with a Rogerian style of therapeutic interaction.

Resources

BOOKS

Cain, David J., ed. *Humanistic Psychotherapies: Handbook of Research and Practice*. Washington, DC: American Psychological Association, 2001.

Greenberg, Leslie S., Jeanne C. Watson, and Germain Lietauer, eds. *Handbook of Experiential Psychotherapy*. New York: Guilford Press, 1998.

Rogers, Carl. *Client-Centered Therapy*. Boston: Houghton Mifflin, 1951.

———. *On Becoming a Person*. Boston: Houghton Mifflin, 1961.

———. *A Way of Being*. Boston: Houghton Mifflin, 1980.

Sachse, Rainer, and Robert Elliott. "Process-Outcome Research on Humanistic Therapy Variables." In *Humanistic Psychotherapies: Handbook of Research and*

Practice, edited by David J. Cain. Washington, DC: American Psychological Association, 2001.

Thorne, Brian, and Elke Lambers, eds. *Person-Centered Therapy: A European Perspective.* London, UK: Sage Publications, 1999.

PERIODICALS

Kahn, Edwin. "A Critique of Nondirectivity in the Person-Centered Approach." *Journal of Humanistic Psychology* 39, no. 4 (1999): 94-110.

Kensit, Denise A. "Rogerian Theory: A Critique of the Effectiveness of Pure Client-Centred Therapy." *Counselling Psychology Quarterly* 13, no. 4 (2000): 345-351.

Myers, Sharon. "Empathic Listening: Reports on the Experience of Being Heard." *Journal of Humanistic Psychology* 40, no. 2 (2000): 148-173.

Walker, Michael T. "Practical Applications of the Rogerian Perspective in Postmodern Psychotherapy." *Journal of Systemic Therapies* 20, no. 2 (2001): 41-57.

Ward, Elaine, Michael King, Margaret Lloyd, Peter Bower, Bonnie Sibbald, Sharon Farrelly, Mark Gabbay, Nicholas Tarrier, and Julia Addington-Hall. "Randomised Controlled Trial of Non-Directive Counselling, Cognitive-Behaviour Therapy, and Usual General Practitioner Care for Patients with Depression. I: Clinical Effectiveness." *British Medical Journal* 321, no. 7273 (2000): 1383-1388.

ORGANIZATIONS

Association for the Development of the Person-Centered Approach. <http://www.adpca.org>.

Center for Studies of the Person. 1150 Silverado, Suite 112, La Jolla, California 92037. (858) 459-3861. <http://www.centerfor theperson.org>.

World Association for Person-Centered and Experiential Psychotherapy and Counseling (WAPCEPC). c/o SGGT Office, Josefstrasse 79, CH-8005 Zürich, Switzerland. +41 1 2717170. <http://pce-world.org>.

Sandra L. Friedrich, M.A.

Pervasive developmental disorders

Definition

Pervasive developmental disorders are a group of conditions originating in childhood that involve serious impairment in several areas, including physical, behavioral, cognitive, social, and language development.

Description

Pervasive developmental disorders (PDDs) are thought to be genetically based, with no evidence linking them to environmental factors; their incidence in the general population is estimated at 1%. The most serious PDD is **autism**, a condition characterized by severely impaired social interaction, communication, and abstract thought, and often manifested by stereotyped and repetitive behavior patterns. Many children who are diagnosed with PDDs today would have been labeled psychotic or schizophrenic in the past.

The handbook used by mental health professionals to diagnose mental disorders such as PDDs is the ***Diagnostic and Statistical Manual of Mental Disorders***. The 2000 edition of this manual (fourth edition, text revised) is known as the *DSM-IV-TR*. Published by the American Psychiatric Association, the *DSM* contains diagnostic criteria, research findings, and treatment information for mental disorders. It is the primary reference for mental health professionals in the United States.

Besides autism, the *DSM* lists several other conditions as PDDs:

Rett's disorder

Characterized by physical, mental, and social impairment, this syndrome appears between the ages of five months and four years in children whose development has been normal up to that point. Occurring only in girls, it involves impairment of coordination, repetitive movements, a slowing of head growth, and severe or profound **mental retardation**, as well as impaired social and communication skills.

Childhood disintegrative disorder

This disorder is marked by the deterioration of previously acquired physical, social, and communication skills after at least two years of normal development. More common in males than females, it first appears between the ages of two and 10 (usually at three or four years of age), and many of its symptoms resemble those of autism. Other names for this disorder are Heller's syndrome, **dementia** infantilis, and disintegrative **psychosis**. It sometimes appears in conjunction with a medical condition such as Schilder's disease, but usually no organic cause can be found.

Asperger's disorder

Children with this disorder have many of the same social and behavioral impairments as autism, except for difficulties with language. They lack normal tools of social interaction, such as the ability to meet someone else's gaze, use appropriate body language and gestures, or react to another person's thoughts and feelings. Behavioral impairments include the repetitive, stereotyped motions and rigid adherence to routines that are characteristic of autism. Like **childhood disintegrative disorder**, **Asperger's disorder** is more common in males than females.

Prognosis

In general, the prognosis in each of these conditions is tied to the severity of the illness.

The prognosis for Asperger's syndrome is more hopeful than the others in this cluster. These children are likely to become functional, independent adults, but will always have problems with social relationships. They are also at greater risk for developing serious mental illness than the general population.

The prognosis for autistic disorder is not as good, although great strides have been made in recent years in its treatment. The higher the patient's intelligence quotient (IQ) and ability to communicate, the better the prognosis. However, many patients will always need some level of custodial care. In the past, most of these individuals were confined to institutions, but many are now able to live in **group homes** or supervised apartments. The prognosis for childhood disintegrative disorder is the least favorable. These children will require intensive and long-term care.

Resources

BOOKS

American Psychiatric Association. *Diagnostic and Statistical Manual of Mental Disorders.* Fourth edition, text revised. Washington DC: American Psychiatric Association, 2000.

Volkmar, Fred R., ed. *Autism and Pervasive Developmental Disorders.* New York: Cambridge University Press, 1998.

Waltz, Mitzi, and Linda Lamb. *Pervasive Developmental Disorders: Finding a Diagnosis & Getting Help.* Cambridge: O'Reilly & Associates, Incorporated, 1999.

ORGANIZATIONS

Autism National Committee (AUTCOM). P.O. Box 6175, North Plymouth, MA 02362-6175. Web site: <http://www.autcom.org/>.

Autism Research Institute. 4182 Adams Avenue, San Diego, CA 92116. Telephone: (619) 281-7165. Web site: <http://www.autism.com/ari>.

New Jersey Center for Outreach and Services for the Autism Community (COSAC). 1450 Parkside Avenue Suite 22, Ewing, NJ 08638. Telephone: (609) 883-8100 or (800) 4-AUTISM (428-8476). Web site: <http://www.njcosac.org>.

PET *see* **Positron emission tomography**

Phencyclidine and related disorders

Definition

Phencyclidine (PCP) is a street drug known as "angel dust" that causes physiological changes to the nervous and circulatory system, disturbances in thinking and behavior, and can cause **hallucinations**, psychotic disorder, mood disorder, and anxiety disorder.

Description

Phencyclidine (PCP) is the best known of several related drugs including ketamine, cyclohexamine, and dizocilpine. PCP was first synthesized by a pharmaceutical company in the 1950s and sold under the brand names Sernyl and Sernylan until 1967. It was hoped that PCP could be used as a dissociative anesthetic, because it produced a catatonic state in which patients were dissociated from their environment and from pain, but not unconscious. Problems with side effects as the drug wore off, including agitated behavior and hallucinations made PCP unsuitable for medical use. Ketamine (Ketlar, Ketaject) is less potent, has fewer side effects and is approved for use as a human anesthetic.

PCP became an illicit street drug in the mid-1960s. It was most commonly found in large cities such as New York and San Francisco, and even today, most users tend to live in urban areas. Into the 1970s, PCP appeared mainly as a contaminant of other illict drugs, especially marijuana and cocaine. This complicated **diagnosis** of PCP use, as many people did not know that they had ingested the drug.

PCP is easy to manufacture and is inexpensive. By the late 1970s, in some urban areas its use equaled that of crack cocaine. Use of PCP peaked between 1973 and 1979. Since 1980, PCP use has declined, although as with most illicit drugs, its popularity increases and decreases in cycles.

People who use PCP exhibit both behavioral and physiological signs. The effects of PCP are erratic, and serious complications can occur at relatively low doses. It is often difficult to distinguish PCP use from the use of other illicit drugs, and many people who use PCP also abuse other substances. According to the ***Diagnostic and Statistical Manual of Mental Disorders*** (*DSM-IV-TR*), which presents guidelines used by the American Psychiatric Association for diagnosis of mental disorders, phencyclidine can induce mood disorder, psychotic disorder, and anxiety disorder—but these classifications are somewhat controversial and not all are recognized by

Phencyclidine, also known as "angel dust." *(Custom Medical Stock Photo, Inc. Reproduced by permission.)*

international psychiatric organizations. No human studies have been done on PCP tolerance and withdrawal. Animal studies suggest that both conditions occur, just as they do with many other abused drugs.

PCP is a Schedule II drug under the Controlled Substances Act. In its pure form, it is a white powder that dissolves easily in water. Once dissolved, the solution can be sprayed on tobacco or marijuana cigarettes. Less pure forms range from yellowish-tan to brown and can be a sticky mass. On the street PCP has many names including angel dust, devil dust, tranq, hog, crazy Eddie, rocket fuel, embalming fluid, wack, and ozone. Ketamine, which is legal and not regulated as a Schedule III controlled substance, also used illicitly, is known on the street as K, special K, and cat valium. Crack cocaine combined with PCP is sometimes called tragic magic. Marijuana laced with PCP is called love boat, killer weed, or crystal supergrass.

Causes and symptoms

Causes

PCP is easy to manufacture and is inexpensively available on the street in most cities, especially East Coast cities. It can be eaten, smoked, injected, snorted, and is readily soluble and will cross the skin barrier if liquid PCP is spilled on skin or clothing. The most common methods of ingestion are eating and smoking marijuana or tobacco on which liquid PCP has been sprayed. PCP is long acting. It accumulates in body fat, and flashbacks can occur as it is released from fat during exercise.

PCP binds to receptors in the **brain** and interferes with the chemical reactions that mediate the transmission of nerve impulses. It is deactivated slowly by the liver and excreted in urine. Although there are no controlled human studies on PCP intoxication, monkeys allowed free use of PCP will dose themselves repeatedly and maintain an almost continuous state of intoxication. They exhibit withdrawal symptoms if their supply of the drug is restricted. PCP is considered to be psychologically and possibly physically addictive in humans.

Symptoms

PCP produces both physiological and psychological symptoms. Effects of the drug are erratic and not always dose-dependent. Physical symptoms include:

- involuntary rapid movements of the eyes vertically or horizontally
- high blood pressure
- racing heartbeat
- dizziness and shakiness
- drooling
- increased body temperature
- reduced response to pain
- slurred speech
- excessive sensitivity to sound
- lack of muscle coordination
- muscle rigidity or frozen posture
- **seizures**
- breakdown of muscle and excretion of muscle proteins in urine
- coma
- death

Psychiatric and social symptoms include:

- disordered thinking and confusion
- impaired judgment
- belligerence
- aggressiveness
- agitation
- impulsiveness and unpredictability
- schizophrenic-like psychoses
- hallucinations of sight, sound, or touch
- memory impairment
- difficulty in social-emotional relationships
- chaotic lifestyle including difficulty functioning at work or school, legal and financial problems

PCP is known for its variability of symptoms, which change both from person to person and from exposure to exposure. In addition, symptoms come and go throughout a period of intoxication that can last from one to two hours for low dose exposure to one to four days for high dose exposure. Severity of symptoms is not always related to the size of the dose as measured by blood levels of the drug.

Three rough phases of intoxication have been established: behavioral toxicity, stuperous stage, and comatose stage. Many patients fluctuate between phases, and some present symptoms that do not fit neatly into any phase. In the behavioral toxicity stage, people tend to gaze blankly while their eyes dart horizontally or vertically. Muscle control is poor, and the person may make repetitive movements, grind the teeth, or grimace. Body temperature, heart rate, and respiration are mildly elevated. Vomiting and drooling may occur.

In the stuperous phase the eyes are wide open, and the person appears wide awake, but in a stupor. Seizures may occur if the person is stimulated. The eyes may dart in any direction while the gaze remains fixed. Body temperature is increased substantially. Heart and respiration rate are increased by about 25%. Muscles are rigid with twitching.

In the comatose stage, which may last from one to four days, the person is in a deep coma. The pupils are dilated and the eyes drift. Body temperature is elevated to the point of being life-threatening. The heart rate is dangerously high, increasing to about twice the normal level and blood pressure is dangerously low. Breathing may stop for brief periods (apnea). There is no response to pain, and the person sweats heavily. Death is possible, although most deaths with PCP occur in earlier stages through accidents or **suicide**.

Demographics

In the 1970s, PCP was used mainly by adolescents. Today the largest regular users are between the ages of 26 and 35. Men outnumber women users two to one, and men account for about three-quarters of PCP-related emergency room visits. Most users live in cities. About 90% of people who use PCP use other drugs as well, usually marijuana and alcohol. About 3% of substance abuse deaths are caused by PCP. Studies by the National Institute of Drug Abuse show that PCP use by high school students has declined steadily from about 13% in 1979 to about 4% in 1997.

Diagnosis

Diagnosis of PCP abuse or dependence is often complicated by the fact that symptoms are variable. Most people who use PCP use other drugs; and PCP can be a contaminant in other street drugs or can itself be contaminated with other chemicals. PCP use is also found among people with psychiatric disorders. In many ways, PCP mimics the symptoms of **schizophrenia**.

The American Psychiatric Association recognizes two levels of PCP disorders: PCP dependence and PCP abuse. In addition, it recognizes seven other PCP-induced psychiatric disorders.

PCP dependence is characterized by a psychological dependence or craving for the drug, as well as withdrawal symptoms if it is discontinued. Although physical dependence has been shown in animal studies with suggestions that physical dependence is present in heavy human users, no human studies have confirmed this. Heavy users may take the drug several times a day. They continue to use it despite experiencing psychological or physical problems. People with psychiatric disorders are more likely to have bad side effects from PCP than those without psychiatric problems. Adverse effects of PCP dependence can continue for weeks after the drug is discontinued.

Individuals with PCP abuse use the drug less regularly than those with PCP dependence. They experience both physical and psychological symptoms of PCP intoxication and often are unable to meet the normal demands of society (work, school, family responsibilities). Because PCP use impairs judgment and increases aggressiveness, they often are involved in accidents while under the drug's influence.

Phencyclidine-induced disorders include:

- PCP intoxication with or without perceptual disturbances
- PCP intoxication **delirium**
- PCP-induced psychotic disorder
- PCP-induced mood disorder
- PCP-induced anxiety disorder
- PCP-induced disorders not otherwise specified

PCP intoxication and delirium are diagnosed by a history of recent PCP use, behavioral changes and physical changes that are not accounted for by any other substance use, medical condition, or psychiatric condition. PCP is present in the blood and urine. With PCP intoxication, a patient may have hallucinations but be aware that these are caused by PCP use.

PCP delirium is diagnosed when a patient exhibits muddled thinking, hostility, bouts of hyperactivity and aggressiveness, and schizophrenic-like symptoms, as well as the more severe physical symptoms listed above. PCP delirium can last for hours or days.

It may be difficult initially to separate PCP intoxication or delirium from other mental disorders, as symptoms may mimic depression, schizophrenia, mood disorders, **conduct disorder**, and **antisocial personality disorder**. People with PCP intoxication also have physical and psychological symptoms similar to those that occur with the use of other illicit drugs, complicating diagnosis. A complete physical and psychological history helps rule out these other conditions.

Treatments

People experiencing PCP intoxication or delirium often hurt themselves or others. They are generally kept in an environment where there is as little stimulation as possible. They are restrained only as much as is necessary to keep them from hurting themselves or others until the level of PCP in their bodies can be reduced. Antipsychotic medications may be used to calm patients in cases of PCP delirium.

There are no quick ways to rid the body of PCP. If the PCP has been eaten, stomach pumping or feeding activated charcoal may help keep the drug from being absorbed into the bloodstream. Physical symptoms such as high body temperature are treated as needed.

Most people recover from PCP intoxication or delirium without major medical complications. Many are habitual users who return to use almost immediately. There are no specific behavioral therapies to treat PCP use. Antidepressants are sometimes prescribed. Long-term residential treatment or intensive outpatient treatment along with urine monitoring offers some chance of success. Narcotics Anonymous, a self-help group, may be helpful for some patients.

Prognosis

Relapse and return to PCP use is common, even among people who have experienced severe medical and psychiatric complications from the drug. Since many users also abuse other drugs, their success in renouncing PCP is tied to their successful treatment for other addictions. Successful treatment takes persistence, patience, and a functional support system, all of which many users lack.

Prevention

PCP intoxication and related disorders can be prevented by not using the drug.

Resources

BOOKS

American Psychiatric Association. *Diagnostic and Statistical Manual of Mental Disorders*. 4th ed. text revised. Washington DC: American Psychiatric Association, 2000.

Galanter, Marc and Herbert D. Kleber, eds. *Textbook of Substance Abuse Treatment*. 2nd ed. Washington DC: American Psychiatric Press, Inc., 1999.

Giannini, James. *Drug Abuse: A Family Guide to Detection, Treatment and Education*. Los Angeles: Health Information Press, 1999.

Sadock, Benjamin J. and Virginia A. Sadock, eds. *Comprehensive Textbook of Psychiatry*. 7th ed. Vol.1. Philadelphia: Lippincott Williams and Wilkins, 2000.

ORGANIZATIONS

National Clearinghouse for Alcohol and Drug Information. P. O. Box 2345, Rockville, MD 20852. (800) 729-6686. <http://www.health.org>.

National Institute on Drug Abuse. 5600 Fishers Lane, Room 10 A-39, Rockville, MD 20857. (888) 644-6432. <http://niad.nih.gov>.

Tish Davidson, A.M.

Phenelzine

Definition

Phenelzine is classified as a monoamine oxidase (MAO) inhibitor. In the United States, phenelzine is sold under the brand name Nardil.

Purpose

Phenelzine is used to treat certain types of serious depression and severe depression complicated by severe anxiety that do not respond to other antidepressant drugs.

Description

Phenelzine is a member of a class of drugs called monoamine oxidase inhibitors. Monoamine oxidase, or MAO, is an enzyme found throughout the body. In the **brain**, MAO breaks down norepinephrine and serotonin, two naturally occurring chemicals that are important in maintaining mental well-being and preventing depression. Monoamine oxidase inhibitors, such as phenelzine, reduce the activity of MAO. Less norepinephrine and serotonin are broken down, so their levels rise. This helps to lift depression.

Phenelzine is effective for treating depression, especially complicated types of depression that have not responded to more traditional antidepressants. However, phenelzine also affects the MAO enzyme in many other areas of the body. This accounts for the large number of serious side effects and drug interactions it causes.

Recommended dosage

Adults are usually started on 15 mg of phenelzine three times per day. This dosage can be increased to a maximum of 90 mg per day if lower doses are not effective, and the patient can tolerate the higher dose without excessive side effects. After the maximum benefits are achieved, the dosage is usually lowered over several weeks to the lowest level that is effective. This could be as little as 15 mg daily or every other day.

In general, phenelzine is not recommended for people over the age of 60. When it is used by the elderly, the starting dosage is usually 15 mg taken in the morning. This dose may be gradually increased over time to a maximum of 60 mg. Phenelzine is not frequently given to children under the age of 16, and recommended dosage in such cases has not been established.

Phenelzine can be taken with food or on an empty stomach. It should not be taken close to bedtime, because it can interfere with sleep. The benefits of this drug may not become apparent for as long as four to eight weeks. Patients should be aware of this and continue taking the drug as directed even if they do not see an immediate improvement.

Precautions

People with a history of congestive heart failure, high blood pressure, cardiovascular disease, headache, kidney disease, or liver disease should not take phenelzine or, if they do take it, they should be under careful medical supervision and monitoring. Children under the age of 16 and people with a history of low blood pressure, **bipolar disorders**, angina, hyperactivity, diabetes mellitus, **seizures**, suicidal thoughts, and overactive thyroid should discuss the risks and benefits of this drug with their physician, and a decision to treat should be made on an individual basis. If these patients receive phenelzine, it should be taken only under the careful supervision of a doctor. Evidence suggests that phenelzine should not be used during pregnancy or while nursing.

People taking phenelzine should get up slowly from a reclining position to prevent dizziness. Those who use phenelzine should use caution when operating heavy machinery or performing hazardous activities that require alertness.

It is very important for the doctor to determine the lowest dosage of phenelzine that produces benefits. When this dosage is exceeded, side effects and interactions increase substantially. Over-the-counter medications that contain decongestants or dextromethorphan (for example, some cough syrups and cold remedies) should not be taken while using phenelzine (see "Interactions," below). In addition, foods and beverages that contain tyramine should not be eaten while using this medication. These foods include yeast or meat extracts, fermented sausage, overripe fruit, sauerkraut, cheese, and fava beans. Phenelzine should not be used within two weeks of undergoing surgery that requires anesthesia.

KEY TERMS

Amphetamines—A group of powerful and highly addictive substances that stimulate the central nervous system. May be prescribed for various medical conditions, but are often purchased illicitly and abused.

Angina—Severe pain and a feeling of constriction around the heart.

Bipolar affective disorder—A disorder in which a person alternates manic and depressive episodes.

Hepatitis—An inflammation of the liver that can be caused by a variety of factors.

Jaundice—A yellowing of the skin caused by excess bilirubin in the blood; a liver disorder.

Nonendogenous—A factor that arises or is produced outside of the organism.

Tyramine—Intermediate product between the chemicals tyrosine and epinephrine in the body and a substance normally found in many foods. Found especially in protein-rich foods that have been aged or fermented, pickled, or bacterially contaminated, such as cheese, beer, yeast, wine, and chicken liver.

Side effects

The enzyme monoamine oxidase regulates functions throughout the body. Phenelzine decreases the activity of monoamine oxidase in all the areas of the body where it exists, not just in the brain. This is why phenelzine is capable of causing a wide variety of side effects in many different organ systems.

The most common and unavoidable side effects associated with phenelzine use are swelling of the feet and ankles, low blood pressure upon arising from a reclining position, and **insomnia** if taken near bedtime. Mild side effects and ones that are not frequent include skin rash, headache, dizziness, confusion, memory impairment, drowsiness, weakness, shakiness, muscle twitching, constipation, indigestion, appetite changes, and dry mouth. Although these side effects are considered mild, they should be reported to the treating doctor.

More serious side effects include hepatitis coupled with jaundice, high blood pressure crisis, excessive nervousness, and changes in heart rate. The high blood pressure crisis involves significantly increased blood pressure, severe headache, heart palpitations, nausea, vomiting, and sweating. These symptoms need immediate medical attention. Sexual function can be affected in both men and women.

Interactions

Phenelzine interacts with a long list of drugs. Some of these interactions can cause death. This section is not a complete list of interactions, but it includes the most serious ones. Patients must make sure that every health care professional who takes care of them (for example, doctors, dentists, podiatrists, optometrists, pharmacists, nurses) knows that they take phenelzine, as well as all of the other prescription, nonprescription, and herbal drugs they take.

All foods and beverages containing tyramine need to be avoided while taking this medication. Coffee, tea, and cola beverages should be restricted to one serving per day. Alcohol should not be used while taking phenelzine, because it can significantly increase blood pressure.

Any type of amphetamine and other stimulant should not be used, because this combination can increase blood pressure to dangerously high levels. Phenelzine should not be combined with other antidepressants, because of increased risk of dangerously high blood pressure and manic episodes. Patients taking phenelzine should stop the drug, then wait at least 14 days before starting any other antidepressant. The same holds true when discontinuing another antidepressant and starting phenelzine. Phenelzine combined with **barbiturates** can prolong the effects of barbiturates.

Phenelzine combined with **clomipramine** (Anafranil) can cause death. Diet drugs and decongestants containing compounds such as dextromethorphan should not be combined with phenelzine because of an increased risk of seizures and agitation. Phenelzine can decrease the effectiveness of high blood pressure drugs, such as guanadrel (Hylorel) and guanethidine (Ismelin). Phenelzine combined with the Parkinson disease drug levodopa (Dopar, Larodopa) can produce severely high blood pressure. Lithium should not be used with phenelzine because of the risk of developing extremely high fever. Phenelzine can prolong the effects of muscle relaxants when the two are combined.

Resources

BOOKS

Consumer Reports Staff. *Consumer Reports Complete Drug Reference.* 2002 ed. Denver: Micromedex Thomson Healthcare, 2001.

Ellsworth, Allan J. and others. *Mosby's Medical Drug Reference.* 2001-2002. St. Louis: Mosby, Inc., 2001.

Hardman, Joel G., Lee E. Limbird,ed. *Goodman & Gilman's The Pharmacological Basis of Therapeutics.* 10th ed. New York: McGraw-Hill, 2001.

Mosby's GenRx Staff. *Mosby's GenRx.* 9th ed. St. Louis: Mosby, 1999.

Venes, Donald, and others. *Taber's Cyclopedic Medical Dictionary.* 19th ed. Philadelphia: F. A. Davis, 2001.

Mark Mitchell, M.D.

Phobias *see* **Agoraphobia, Social phobias, and Specific phobias**

Phonological disorder

Definition

Phonological disorder occurs when a child does not develop the ability to produce some or all sounds necessary for speech that are normally used at his or her age.

Description

Phonological disorder is sometimes referred to as articulation disorder, developmental articulation disorder, or speech sound production disorder. If there is no known cause, it is sometimes called "developmental phonological disorder." If the cause is known to be of neurological origin, the names "dysarthria" or "dyspraxia" are often used. Phonological disorder is characterized by a child's inability to create speech at a level expected of his or her age group because of an inability to form the necessary sounds.

There are many different levels of severity of phonological disorder. These range from speech that is completely incomprehensible, even to a child's immediate family members, to speech that can be understood by everyone but in which some sounds are slightly mispronounced. Treatment for phonological disorder is important not only for the child's development to be able to form speech sounds, but for other reasons, as well. Children who have problems creating speech sounds may have academic problems in subject areas such as spelling or reading. Also, children who sound different than their peers may find themselves frustrated and ridiculed, and may become less willing to participate in play or classroom activities.

Causes

Phonological disorder is often divided into three categories, based on the cause of the disorder. One cause is structural problems, or abnormalities in the areas necessary for speech sound production, such as the tongue or the roof of the mouth. These abnormalities make it difficult for children to produce certain sounds, and in some cases make it impossible for a child to produce the sounds at all. The structural problem causing the phonological disorder generally needs to be treated before the child goes into language therapy. This therapy is especially useful, because, in many of these cases, correction of the structural problem results in correction of the speech sound problem.

The second category of phonological disorder is problems caused by neurological problems or abnormalities. This category includes problems with the muscles of the mouth that do not allow the child sufficient fine motor control over the muscles to produce all speech sounds. The third category of phonological disorder is phonological disorder of an unknown cause. This is sometimes called "developmental phonological disorder." Although the cause is not known, there is much speculation. Possible causes include slight **brain** abnormalities, causes rooted in the child's environment, and immature development of the neurological system. As of 2002, there is research pointing to all of these factors, but no definitive cause has been found.

Symptoms

The symptoms of phonological disorder differ significantly depending on the age of the child. It is often difficult to detect this disorder, as the child with phonological disorder develops speech sounds more slowly than his or her peers; generally, however, he or she develops them in the same sequence. Therefore, speech that may be normal for a four-year-old child may be a sign of phonological disorder in a six-year-old.

Nearly all children develop speech sounds in the same sequence. The consonant sounds are grouped into three main groups of eight sounds each: the early eight, the middle eight, and the late eight. The early eight include consonant sounds such as "m," "b,", and "p." The middle eight include sounds such as "t," "g", and "chi," and the late eight include more complicated sounds such as "sh," "th," "z," and "zh." Many children do not normally finish mastering the late eight until they are seven or eight years old. As children normally develop speech sound skills, there are some very common mistakes that are made. These include the omission of sounds, (i.e., frequently at the end of words), the distortion of sounds, or the substitution of one sound for another. Often the substitution is of a sound that the child can more easily produce for one that he or she cannot.

KEY TERMS

Dysarthria—A group of speech disorders caused by disturbances in the strength or coordination of the muscles of the speech mechanism as a result of damage to the brain or nerves. Difficulty talking and speaking.

Dyspraxia—Developmental dyspraxia is an impairment or immaturity of the organization of movement. It is a defect in the way the brain processes information, resulting in messages not being correctly or fully transmitted. The term dyspraxia comes from the word "praxis", meaning "doing" or "acting". Dyspraxia is associated with problems of perception, language, and thought.

Diagnosis

The **diagnosis** for phonologic disorder depends greatly on the age of the child in question. Children who are four years old may have speech production difficulties that show normal development for their age, while children who are eight years old and making the same mistakes may have phonological disorder. In children with phonological disorder, the pattern and order of speech sound acquisition is usually similar to that of normally developing children. However, the speech sound skills develop more slowly, so age is an important factor in determining a diagnosis of phonological disorder. Children with phonological disorder may make the same speech sound mistakes as younger, normally developing children. In some cases, however, children with phonological disorder have demonstrated more instances of omissions, substitutions, and distortions in their speech.

When exploring a diagnosis of phonological disorder, it is generally recommended that a physician check for other possible causes of the signs and symptoms. A child's hearing should be checked, because speech sounds that are not heard well by a child cannot be imitated and learned well. In school-age children, reading comprehension should be checked to discover any other language disorders, which are sometimes present in addition to phonological disorder. Any general developmental delays should also be checked by the physician. It is important to remember that for some children whose native language is one other than English, the problems with speech sounds may result from poor crossover of sounds between the child's languages. Therefore, when diagnosing a child with a different native language, it is recommended that tests involve the child's first language, as well as English. Also, it must be remembered that in some parts of the country, normal pronunciation of some words is different from pronunciation in other parts of the country. Therefore a child's background and history can be very important in making a diagnosis.

The ***Diagnostic and Statistical Manual of Mental Disorders*** (*DSM-IV-TR*) states that for a diagnosis of phonological disorder to be made, three general criteria must be met. The first criterion is that the child is not developing speech sounds skills considered to be appropriate for his or her age group. Also, this lack of speech sound acquisition must be causing problems for the child at home, at school, or in other important aspects of the child's life. If the child is mentally retarded, has problems with his or her speech muscles or hearing, or if there is environmental deprivation, a diagnosis of phonological disorder may still be appropriate. The diagnosis can only be made, however, if the lack of speech sounds skill is considered greater than the child's other problems.

Demographics

Phonological disorder of unknown cause is considered significantly more common than phonological disorder that is caused by neurological or structural abnormalities. It has been estimated that 7–8% children who are five years old have phonological disorder with any cause (developmental phonological disorder). About 7.5% of children between the ages of three and eleven are thought to have development phonological disorder. Phonological disorder is more common in boys than it is in girls. Estimates suggest that two to four times as many boys as girls have the disorder. Children who have phonological disorder are more likely to have other language problems and disorders. Children with one or more family members who have this or similar language disorders are also considered to be more likely to have phonological disorders.

Treatment

Treatment by a speech-language pathologist is generally recommended for children with phonological disorders. The therapy will differ depending on an individual child's needs, but generally takes the form of practicing sounds. Sometimes the child is shown the physical ways that the sound is made, such as where to place the tongue and how to form the lips. Repetition of the difficult sounds with the therapist is an integral part of treatment. There is debate, however, over the way that children with more severe forms of the disorder should be treated. Some therapists believe that the sounds that are learned later in development should be addressed first, even if the child has not developed the more simple sound skills. Other therapists believe that simple sounds should be treated first, as it is easier for children with phonological disorder to master them. One other school of thought is that when the child develops a sense of accomplishment when these sounds are mastered, and he or she will more willingly continue with treatment. There is ongoing research on this debate, and the results as of 2002 are still mixed.

Children who have phonological disorder because of neurological or structural problems that do not allow them to produce some sounds are often helped to find approximate alternatives for the sounds within the range of sounds that they are able to produce.

Prognosis

The prognosis for children with phonological disorder is generally good. For many children, the problem resolves spontaneously. It is reported that in 75% of children with mild-or-moderate forms of the disorder, and whose problems do not stem from a medical condition, the symptoms resolve before age six. In many other cases, children who receive treatment eventually develop normal or close to normal speech. In some cases, there may be mild effects that last until adulthood, but speech is completely understandable. For children with phonological disorder due to a neurological or structural cause, the outcome generally rests on how well the cause of the problem is treated.

Prevention

There is no known way to prevent phonological disorder. A healthy diet during pregnancy and regular prenatal care may help to prevent some of the neurological or structural problems that can result in the disorder.

Resources

BOOKS

American Psychiatric Association. *Diagnostic and Statistical Manual of Mental Disorders*. 4th ed. text revised. Washington DC: American Psychiatric Association, 2000.

Sadock, Benjamin J. and Virginia A. Sadock, eds. *Comprehensive Textbook of Psychiatry.* 7th edition. Philadelphia: Lippincott Williams and Wilkins, 2000.

PERIODICALS

Rvachew, Susan, and Michele Nowak. "The Effect of Target-Selection Strategy on Phonological Learning." *Journal of Speech, Language, and Hearing Research* 44, no. 3 (June 2001): 610.

Weismer, Susan Ellis, and others. "Nonword Repetition Performance in School-age Children with and without Language Impairment." *Journal of Speech, Language, and Hearing Research* 43, no. 4 (August 2000).

ORGANIZATIONS

American Academy of Child and Adolescent Psychiatry. 3615 Wisconsin Ave. NW, Washington, DC 20016-3007. (202) 966- 7300. <www.aacap.org>.

The American Academy of Pediatrics. 141 Northwest Point Boulevard, Elk Grove Village, IL 60007-1098. (847) 434-4000 <www.aap.org>.

American Speech-Language-Hearing Association. 10801 Rockville Pike, Rockville, MD 20852. (800) 638-8355. <http://www.asha.org>.

Tish Davidson, A.M.

Pica

Definition

Pica is a term that refers to cravings for substances that are not foods. Materials consumed by patients with pica include dirt, ice, clay, glue, sand, chalk, beeswax, chewing gum, laundry starch, and hair.

Description

Pica is the craving or ingestion of nonfood items. The cravings found in patients diagnosed with pica may be associated with a nutritional deficiency state, such as iron-deficiency anemia; with pregnancy; or with **mental retardation** or mental illness. The word *pica* is derived from the Latin word for magpie, a species of bird that feeds on whatever it encounters.

The mental health professional's handbook, the ***Diagnostic and Statistical Manual of Mental Disorders****, fourth edition, text revision (2000), which is abbreviated as* DSM-IV-TR, classifies pica under the heading of "Feeding and Eating Disorders of Infancy or Early Childhood." A **diagnosis** of pica requires that the patient must persist in eating nonfood substances for at least one month. This behavior must be inappropriate for the child's stage of development. Further, it must not be approved or encouraged by the child's culture.

KEY TERMS

Behavior modification—An approach to therapy based on the principles of operant conditioning. Behavior modification seeks to replace undesirable behaviors with preferable behaviors through the use of positive or negative reinforcement.

Bezoar—A hard ball of hair or vegetable fiber that may develop in the stomach of humans as the result of ingesting nonfood items.

Chelation—A method of treating lead or mercury poisoning by giving medications that remove heavy metals from the bloodstream. The medications that are used are called chelating agents.

Dopamine—A chemical in brain tissue that serves to transmit nerve impulses (is a neurotransmitter) and helps to regulate movement and emotions.

Neurotransmitter—A chemical in the brain that transmits messages between neurons, or nerve cells.

Toxocariasis—Infection with roundworm larvae, commonly transmitted by the feces of dogs and cats.

Toxoplasmosis—A parasitic infection caused by the intracellular protozoan *Toxoplasmosis gondii.* Humans are most commonly infected by swallowing the oocyte form of the parasite in soil (or kitty litter) contaminated by feces from an infected cat; or by swallowing the cyst form of the parasite in raw or undercooked meat.

Trichuriasis—Infection with the larvae of roundworms. These parasites may live for 10–20 years in humans.

Causes and symptoms

Causes

The cause of pica is not known. Many hypotheses have been developed to explain the behavior. These have included a variety of such factors as cultural influences; low socioeconomic status; deficiency diseases; and psychological disorders.

Malnutrition is often diagnosed at the same time as pica. A causal link has not been established. Eating clay has been associated with iron deficiency; however, whether decreased iron absorption is caused by eating clay or whether iron deficiency prompts people to eat clay is not known. Some cultural groups are said to teach youngsters to eat clay. Persons with iron deficiency anemia have also been reported to chew on ice cubes. Again, the mechanism or causal link is not known.

Eating paint is most common among children from families of low socioeconomic status. It is often associated with lack of parental supervision. Hunger also may result in pica.

Among persons with mental retardation, pica has been explained as the result of an inability to tell the difference between food and nonfood items. This explanation, however, is not supported by examples of nonfood items that were deliberately selected and eaten by persons with limited mental faculties.

Pica, iron deficiency, and a number of other physiological disturbances in humans have been associated with decreased activity of the dopamine system in the **brain**. Dopamine is a neurotransmitter, or chemical that helps to relay the transmission of nerve impulses from one nerve cell to another. This association has led some researchers to think that there may be a connection between abnormally low levels of dopamine in the brain and the development of pica. No specific underlying biochemical disorders have been identified, however.

Risk factors for pica include the following:

- parental/child psychopathology
- family disorganization
- environmental deprivation
- pregnancy
- epilepsy
- brain damage
- mental retardation
- pervasive developmental disorders

Symptoms

Infants and children diagnosed with pica commonly eat paint, plaster, string, hair, and cloth. Older children may eat animal droppings, sand, insects, leaves, pebbles and cigarette butts. Adolescents and adults most often ingest clay or soil.

The symptoms of pica vary with the item ingested.

- Sand or soil is associated with gastric pain and occasional bleeding.
- Chewing ice may cause abnormal wear on teeth.
- Eating clay may cause constipation.
- Swallowing metal objects may lead to bowel perforation.
- Eating fecal material often leads to such infectious diseases as toxocariasis, toxoplasmosis, and trichuriasis.
- Consuming lead can lead to kidney damage and mental retardation.

Demographics

Pica tends to taper off as children grow older. The disorder occasionally continues into adolescence but is rarely observed in adults who are not disabled.

Pica is observed more commonly during the second and third years of life and is considered to be developmentally inappropriate in children older than 18–24 months. Research findings indicate that the disorder occurs in 25%–33% of young children and 20% of children in mental health clinics. Among individuals with mental retardation, pica occurs most often in those between the ages of 10–20 years. Among young pregnant women, the onset of pica is frequently associated with a first pregnancy in late adolescence or early adulthood. Although pica usually stops at the end of the pregnancy, it may continue intermittently for years.

Pica usually occurs with equal frequency among males and females. It is relatively uncommon, however, among adolescent and adult males of average intelligence who live in developed countries.

Diagnosis

Pica is often diagnosed in a hospital emergency room, when the child or adolescent develops symptoms of lead poisoning, bowel perforation, or other medical complications caused by the nonfood items that have been swallowed. Laboratory studies may be used to assess these complications. The choice of imaging or laboratory studies depends on the characteristics of the ingested materials and the resultant medical problems.

The examining doctor may order a variety of **imaging studies** in order to identify the ingested materials and treat the gastrointestinal complications of pica. These imaging studies may include the following:

- abdominal x rays
- barium examinations of the upper and lower gastrointestinal (GI) tracts
- upper GI endoscopy to diagnose the formation of bezoars (solid masses formed in the stomach) or to identify associated injuries to the digestive tract

Films and studies may be repeated at regular intervals to track changes in the location of ingested materials.

Treatments

As of 2002, there is no standard treatment for pica. Currently, the most effective strategies are based on **behavior modification**, but even these treatments have achieved limited success. Pica associated with a nutritional deficiency often clears up when the missing nutrient is added to the patient's diet.

Few studies have examined the efficacy of drug treatments for pica. Ongoing research, however, is exploring the relationship between pica and abnormally low levels of the neurotransmitter dopamine. This line of research may help to identify new medications for the treatment of pica. There is some evidence that medications used to manage severe behavioral problems in children may be useful in treating coexisting pica.

Lead poisoning resulting from pica may be treated by chelating medications, which are drugs that remove lead or other heavy metals from the bloodstream. The two medications most often given for lead poisoning are dimercaprol, which is also known as BAL or British Anti-Lewisite; and edetate calcium disodium (EDTA). A medical toxicologist (a doctor who specializes in treating poisoning cases) may be consulted regarding children's dosages of these drugs.

In some cases, surgery may be required to remove metal objects from the patient's digestive tract or to repair tissue injuries. It is particularly important to remove any objects made of lead (fishing weights, lead shot, pieces of printer's type, etc.) as quickly as possible because of the danger of lead poisoning.

Prognosis

Pica frequently ends spontaneously in young children and pregnant women. Untreated pica, however, may persist for years, especially in persons with mental retardation and developmental disabilities.

Prevention

There is no known way to prevent pica at the present time. Educating people, particularly young couples with children, about healthy nutritional practices is the best preventive strategy.

Resources

BOOKS

American Psychiatric Association. "Pica." In *Diagnostic and Statistical of Mental Disorders*. 4th edition, text revised. Washington, DC: American Psychiatric Association, 2000.

Herrin, Marcia, and Nancy Matsumoto. *The Parent's Guide to Childhood Eating Disorders*. New York: Henry Holt and Company, 2002.

Palmer, Robert L. *Helping People With Eating Disorders: A Clinical Guide to Assessment and Treatment*. New York: John Wiley and Sons, 2002.

Woolsey, Monika M. *Eating Disorders: A Clinical Guide to Counseling and Treatment*. Chicago: American Dietetic Association, 2002.

PERIODICALS

Grewal P. and B. Fitzgerald. "Pica with learning disability." *Journal of the Royal Society of Medicine* 95, no. 1 (2002): 39-40.

Hamilton S., S. J. Rothenberg, F. A. Khan, M. Manalo, and K. C. Norris. "Neonatal lead poisoning from maternal pica behavior during pregnancy." *Journal of the National Medical Association* 93, no. 9 (2001): 317-319.

Roberts-Harewood M. and S. C. Davies. "Pica in sickle cell disease: 'She ate the headboard.'" *Archives of Diseases of Children* 85, no. 6 (2001): 510.

ORGANIZATIONS

American Academy of Family Physicians. 11400 Tomahawk Creek Parkway, Leawood, KS 66211-2672. Telephone: (913) 906-6000. Web site: <http://www.aafp.org>.

American Academy of Pediatrics. 141 Northwest Point Boulevard, Elk Grove Village, IL 60007-1098. Telephone: (847) 434-4000. Fax: (847) 434-8000. Web site: <http://www.aap.org/default.htm>.

American College of Physicians, 190 N Independence Mall West, Philadelphia, PA 19106-1572, Phone: (800) 523-1546, x2600 or (215) 351-2600, Web site: <http://www.acponline.org>.

American Medical Association. 515 N. State Street, Chicago, IL 60610. Telephone: (312) 464-5000. Web site: <http://www.ama-assn.org>.

OTHER

Anorexia Nervosa and Related Eating Disorders, Inc.: <http://www.anred.com/pica.html>.

Support, Concern and Resources For Eating Disorders: <http://www.eating-disorder.org/pica.html>.

L. Fleming Fallon, Jr., M.D., Dr.P.H.

Pimozide

Definition

Pimozide is an atypical antipsychotic drug used to treat serious motor and verbal tics associated with Tourette's syndrome. It is sold under the brand name Orap.

KEY TERMS

Parkinsonian—Related to symptoms associated with Parkinson's disease, a nervous system disorder characterized by abnormal muscle movement of the tongue, face, and neck, inability to walk or move quickly, walking in a shuffling manner, restlessness, and/or tremors.

Schizophrenia—A severe mental illness in which a person has difficulty distinguishing what is real from what is not real. It is often characterized by hallucinations, delusions, language and communication disturbances, and withdrawal from people and social activities.

Tic—A sudden involuntary behavior that is difficult or impossible for the person to suppress. Tics may be either motor (related to movement) or vocal, and may become more pronounced under stress.

Tourette syndrome—Neurological disorder characterized by multiple involuntary movements and uncontrollable vocalizations called tics that come and go over years, usually beginning in childhood and becoming chronic. Sometimes the tics include inappropriate language.

Purpose

Pimozide is classified as an atypical antipsychotic drug. It is structurally similar to another drug, **haloperidol**, which was the first drug to be used in Tourette's syndrome. Pimozide is most often used to treat symptoms of Tourette's syndrome, although it has also been used for treating **schizophrenia** mania, and other behavioral disorders.

Description

Excess dopamine activity in the **brain** is associated with the verbal and physical tics observed in Tourette's syndrome. Like haloperidol, pimozide is believed to inhibit the actions of the brain chemical, dopamine.

Pimozide is broken down by the liver and eliminated from the body by the kidneys. Because pimozide is associated with health risks, it should not be used for tics that are simply annoying or cosmetic. Pimozide should be used only in patients with severe symptoms after other drug therapy has been tried and failed.

Pimozide is available in 1-mg and 2-mg tablets.

Recommended dosage

The common starting dose of pimozide in adults is 1-2 mg per day. The dose may be increased every other day until 0.2 mg per kg (or 0.9 mg per pound) of body weight per day or 10 mg per day is reached, whichever is less. Doses that exceed 0.2 mg per kg per day or 10 mg daily are not recommended.

In children, the usual initial dose is 0.05 mg per kg daily, and increased every three days to a maximum dose of 0.2 mg per kg (or 10 mg) per day.

Periodically, the dosage of pimozide should be reduced to determine if tics are still present. Patients should be maintained on the lowest dose that is effective in treating their disorder.

Precautions

Pimozide may alter the rhythm of the heart. As a result, it should be used with caution in people with heart disease, and these patients should be observed carefully while receiving the drug.

Pimozide should not be taken with grapefruit juice.

Pimozide should be used with close physician supervision by people who have a history of seizure disorders, because it may increase the tendency to have **seizures**.

Pimozide may cause extreme drowsiness and should be used carefully by people who need to be mentally alert.

Patients should not take pimozide while pregnant or breast-feeding.

Pimozide should not be used by people with mild tics, by individuals taking stimulants such as **methylphenidate** (Ritalin), **pemoline** (Cylert), or dextroamphetamine (Dexedrine) since these drugs may cause tics.

Side effects

The most common side effects associated with pimozide are sleepiness, headache, stomach upset, muscle tightness, muscle weakness, difficulty moving, tremor, abnormal behavior, visual disturbances, and impotence.

Other side effects that might also occur with pimozide involve rapid heart rates or irregular heart rhythms, low blood pressure, constipation, dry mouth and eyes, rash, breast pain, breast milk production, loss of bladder control, or low blood cell counts.

Pimozide use may lead to the development of symptoms that resemble Parkinson's disease. These symptoms may include a tight or mask-like expression on the face, drooling, tremors, pill-rolling motions in the hands, cogwheel rigidity (abnormal rigidity in muscles characterized by jerky movements when the muscle is passively stretched), and a shuffling gait. Taking anti-Parkinson drugs **benztropine** mesylate or **trihexyphenidyl** hydrochloride along with the pimozide usually controls these symptoms.

Pimozide has the potential to produce a serious side effect called **tardive dyskinesia**. This syndrome consists of involuntary, uncoordinated movements that may appear late in therapy and not disappear even after the drug is stopped. Tardive dyskinesia involves involuntary movements of the tongue, jaw, mouth or face or other groups of skeletal muscles. The incidence of tardive dyskinesia increases with increasing age and with increasing dosage of pimozide. Women are at greater risk than men for developing tardive dyskinesia. There is no known effective treatment for tardive dyskinesia, although gradual (but rarely complete) improvement may occur over a long period.

An occasionally reported side effect of pimozide is neuroleptic malignant syndrome. This is a complicated and potentially fatal condition characterized by muscle rigidity, high fever, alterations in mental status, and cardiac symptoms such as irregular pulse or blood pressure, sweating, tachycardia (fast heartbeat), and arrhythmias (irregular heartbeat). People who think they may be experiencing any side effects from this or any other medication should talk to their physician promptly.

Interactions

If pimozide is used with bethanechol (Urecholine), **clonidine** (Catapres), **fluoxetine** (Prozac), indomethacin (Indocin), meperidine (Demerol), **paroxetine** (Paxil), quinidine, or **trazodone** (Desyrel), the side effects associated with pimozide may be increased.

There is an increased risk of irregular heart rhythms if pimozide is used with other antipsychotics, certain antidepressants, some heart drugs, and antibiotics like erythromycin.

The beneficial effects of pimozide may be reduced if used with bromocriptine (Parlodel), **carbamazepine** (Tegretol), levodopa (Larodopa, Sinemet), lithium, or phenobarbital.

Some antibiotics, antifungals, antidepressants, and drugs used for AIDS may prevent the breakdown of pimozide by the liver and thus, increase the amount of pimozide in the body. The combination of pimozide and the above classes of drugs should be used cautiously if at all.

Pimozide may interact with other central nervous system depressants such as alcohol, sleeping pills, antihistamines, and antidepressants.

Resources

BOOKS

Ellsworth, Allan J., and others. *Mosby's Medical Drug Reference*. St. Louis, MO: Mosby, Inc, 1999.

Facts and Comparisons Staff. *Drug Facts and Comparisons*. 6th Edition. St. Louis, MO: A Wolter Kluwer Company, 2002.

Medical Economics Co. Staff. *Physician's Desk Reference*. 56th edition Montvale, NJ: Medical Economics Company, 2002.

Kelly Karpa, RPh, Ph.D.

Play therapy

Definition

Play therapy refers to a method of **psychotherapy** with children in which a therapist uses a child's fantasies and the symbolic meanings of his or her play as a medium for understanding and communication with the child.

Purpose

The aim of play therapy is to decrease those behavioral and emotional difficulties that interfere significantly with a child's normal functioning. Inherent in this aim is improved communication and understanding between the child and his parents. Less obvious goals include improved verbal expression, ability for self-observation, improved impulse control, more adaptive ways of coping with anxiety and frustration, and improved capacity to trust and to relate to others. In this type of treatment, the therapist uses an understanding of cognitive development and of the different stages of emotional development as well as the conflicts common to these stages when treating the child.

Play therapy is used to treat problems that are interfering with the child's normal development. Such difficulties would be extreme in degree and have been occurring for many months without resolution. Reasons for treatment include, but are not limited to, temper tantrums, aggressive behavior, non-medical problems with bowel or bladder control, difficulties with sleeping or having nightmares, and experiencing worries or fears. This type of treatment is also used with children who have experienced sexual or physical **abuse**, **neglect**, the loss of a family

Children communicate their thoughts and feelings through play more naturally than they do through verbal communication. As the child plays, the therapist begins to recognize themes and patterns or ways of using the materials that are important to the child. Over time, the clinician helps the child begin to make meaning out of the play. *(S. Villeger/Explorer. Photo Researchers, Inc. Reproduced by permission.)*

member, medical illness, physical injury, or any experience that is traumatic.

At times, children in play therapy will also receive other types of treatment. For instance, youngsters who are unable to control their attention, impulses, tendency to react with violence, or who experience severe anxiety may take medication for these symptoms while participating in play therapy. The play therapy would address the child's psychological symptoms. Other situations of dual treatment include children with **learning disorders**. These youngsters may receive play therapy to alleviate feelings of low self-esteem, excessive worry, helplessness, and incompetency that are related to their learning problems and academic struggles. In addition, they should receive a special type of tutoring called **cognitive remediation**, which addresses the specific learning issues.

Precautions

Play therapy addresses psychological issues and would not be used to alleviate medical or biological problems. Children who are experiencing physical problems should see a physician for a medical evaluation to clarify the nature of the problem and, if necessary, receive the appropriate medical treatment. Likewise, children who experience academic difficulties need to receive a neuropsychological or in-depth psychological evaluation in order to clarify the presence of a biologically based learning disability. In both of these cases, psychological problems may be present in addition to medical ailments and learning disabilities, but they may not be the primary problem and it would not be sufficient to treat only the psychological issues. Alternatively, evaluations may show that medical or biological causes are not evident, and this would be important information for the parents and therapist to know.

Description

In play therapy, the clinician meets with the child alone for the majority of the sessions and arranges times to meet with parents separately or with the child, depending on the situation. The structure of the sessions is maintained in a consistent manner in order to provide a feeling of safety and stability for the child and parents. Sessions are scheduled for the same day and time each week and occur for the same duration. The frequency of sessions is typically one or two times per week, and meetings with parents occur about two times per month, with some variation. The session length will vary depending on the environment. For example, in private settings, sessions usually last 45 to 50 minutes while in hospitals and mental health clinics the duration is typically 30 minutes. The number of sessions and duration of treatment varies according to treatment objectives of the child.

During the initial meeting with parents, the therapist will want to learn as much as possible about the nature of the child's problems. Parents will be asked for information about the child's developmental, medical, social and school history, whether or not previous evaluations and interventions were attempted and the nature of the results. Background information about parents is also important since it provides the therapist with a larger context from which to understand the child. This process of gathering information may take one to three sessions, depending on the style of the therapist. Some clinicians gather the important aspects of the child's history during the first meeting with parents and will continue to ask relevant questions during subsequent meetings. The clinician also learns important information during the initial sessions with the child.

Sessions with parents are important opportunities to keep the therapist informed about the child's current functioning at home and at school and for the therapist to offer some insight and guidance to parents. At times, the clinician will provide suggestions about parenting techniques, about alternative ways to communicate with their child, and will also serve as a resource for information about child development. Details of child sessions are not routinely discussed with parents. If the child's privacy is maintained, it promotes free expression in the therapist's office and engenders a sense of trust in the therapist. Therapists will, instead, communicate to the parents their understanding of the child's psychological needs or conflicts.

For the purposes of explanation, treatment can be described as occurring in a series of initial, middle and final stages. The initial phase includes evaluation of the problem and teaching both child and parents about the process of therapy. The middle phase is the period in which the child has become familiar with the treatment process and comfortable with the therapist. The therapist is continuing to evaluate and learn about the child, but has a clearer sense of the youngster's issues and has developed, with the child, a means for the two to communicate. The final phase includes the process of ending treatment and saying goodbye to the therapist.

During the early sessions, the therapist talks with the child about the reason the youngster was brought in for treatment and explains that the therapist helps make children's problems go away. Youngsters often deny experiencing any problems. It is not necessary for them to acknowledge having any since they may be unable to do so due to normal cognitive and emotional factors or because they are simply not experiencing any problems. The child is informed about the nature of the sessions. Specifically, the child is informed that he or she can say or play or do anything desired while in the office as long as no one gets hurt, and that what is said and done in the office will be kept private unless the child is in danger of harming himself.

Children communicate their thoughts and feelings through play more naturally than they do through verbal communication. As the child plays, the therapist begins to recognize themes and patterns or ways of using the materials that are important to the child. Over time, the clinician helps the child begin to make meaning out of the play. This is important because the play reflects issues which are important to the child and typically relevant to their difficulties.

When the child's symptoms have subsided for a stable period of time and when functioning is adequate with peers and adults at home, in school, and in extracurricular activities, the focus of treatment will shift away from problems and onto the process of saying goodbye. This last stage is known as the termination phase of treatment and it is reflective of the ongoing change and loss that human beings experience throughout their lives. Since this type of therapy relies heavily on the therapist's relationship with the child and also with parents, ending therapy will signify a change and a loss for all involved, but for the child in particular. In keeping with the therapeutic process of communicating thoughts and feelings, this stage is an opportunity for the child to work through how they feel about ending therapy and about leaving the therapist. In addition to allowing for a sense of closure, it also makes it less likely that the youngster will misconstrue the ending of treatment as a rejection by the therapist, which would taint the larger experience of therapy for the child. Parents also need a sense of closure and are usually encouraged to process the treatment experience with the therapist. The therapist also appreciates the opportunity to say goodbye to the parents and child after having become involved in their lives in this important way, and it is often beneficial for parents and children to hear the clinician's thoughts and feelings with regards to ending treatment.

Preparation

It is recommended that parents explain to the child that they will be going to see a therapist, that they discuss, if possible, the particular problem that is interfering with the child's growth and that a therapist is going to teach both parents and child how to make things better. As described earlier, the child may deny even obvious problems, but mainly just needs to agree to meet the therapist and to see what therapy is like.

Aftercare

Children sometimes return to therapy for additional sessions when they experience a setback that cannot be easily resolved.

Normal results

Normal results include the significant reduction or disappearance of the main problems for which the child was initially seen. The child should also be functioning adequately at home, in school, with peers and should be able to participate in and enjoy extracurricular activities.

Abnormal results

Sometimes play therapy does not alleviate the child's symptoms. This situation can occur if the child is extremely resistant and refuses to participate in treatment or if the child's ways of coping are so rigidly held that it is not possible for them to learn more adaptive ones.

Resources

BOOKS

Chethik, Morton. *Techniques of Child Therapy.* 2nd edition. New York: The Guilford Press, 2000.

Lovinger, Sophie L. *Child Psychotherapy: From Initial Therapeutic Contact to Termination.* New Jersey: Jason Aronson, Inc., 1998.

Webb, Nancy Boyd, ed. *Play Therapy with Children in Crisis.* 2nd edition. New York: The Guilford Press, 1999.

ORGANIZATIONS

American Psychological Association. 750 First Street, NE, Washington D.C. 20002. < http://www.apa.org>.

Susan Fine, Psy.D.

Polysomnography

Definition

Polysomnography is a series of tests performed on patients while they sleep. Polysomnography is a comprehensive overnight procedure that evaluates **sleep disorders**. It generally includes monitoring of the patient's airflow through the nose and mouth, blood pressure, heartbeat as measured by an electrocardiograph, blood oxygen level, **brain** wave patterns, eye movements, and the movements of respiratory muscles and limbs. The word *polysomnography* is derived from the Greek root *poly* meaning "many," the Latin noun *somnus* meaning "sleep," and the Greek verb *graphein* meaning "to write."

Purpose

Polysomnography is used to help diagnose and evaluate a number of sleep disorders. For instance, it can help diagnose sleep apnea, a common disorder in middle-aged and elderly obese men, in which the muscles of the soft palate in the back of the throat relax and close off the airway during sleep. Sleep apnea may cause the person to snore loudly and gasp for air at night. It may also cause the person to be excessively drowsy and likely to fall asleep during the day. Another syndrome often uncovered by polysomnography is **narcolepsy**. Persons with narcolepsy have sudden attacks of sleep and/or cataplexy (temporary loss of muscle tone caused by moments of emotion, such as fear, anger, or surprise, which causes people to slump or fall over), sleep paralysis or **hallucinations** while they are falling asleep.

Polysomnography is often used to evaluate such parasomnias (abnormal behaviors or movements during sleep) as sleepwalking; talking in one's sleep; nightmares; and bed-wetting (**enuresis**). It can also be used to detect or evaluate **seizures** that occur in the middle of the night, when the patient and his or her family are unlikely to be aware of them.

Other problems uncovered by polysomnography include sleep-related psychiatric depression, asthma, and **panic disorder**. Polysomnography is generally not used if the sleep disorder has been clearly identified by the treating physician. It is also not used in cases of **insomnia** that have simple and obvious causes.

KEY TERMS

Apnea—A brief suspension or interruption of breathing.

Arrhythmia—Any disturbance in the normal rhythm of the heartbeat.

Bruxism—Habitual, often unconscious, grinding of the teeth.

Hypopnea—Breathing that is too shallow to maintain adequate levels of oxygen in the blood.

Narcolepsy—A disorder characterized by frequent and uncontrollable attacks of deep sleep.

Oximetry—The measurement of blood oxygen levels.

Parameter—A characteristic or factor that is measured during a test of a complex process or activity like sleep.

Parasomnia—A type of sleep disorder characterized by abnormal changes in behavior or body functions during sleep, specific stages of sleep, or the transition between sleeping and waking.

Thermistor—An electrical device whose resistance decreases with rises in temperature.

Precautions

Polysomnography is extremely safe, and no special precautions need to be taken.

Description

Polysomnography requires an overnight stay in a sleep laboratory. While the patient sleeps, he or she is monitored in a number of ways that can provide useful information.

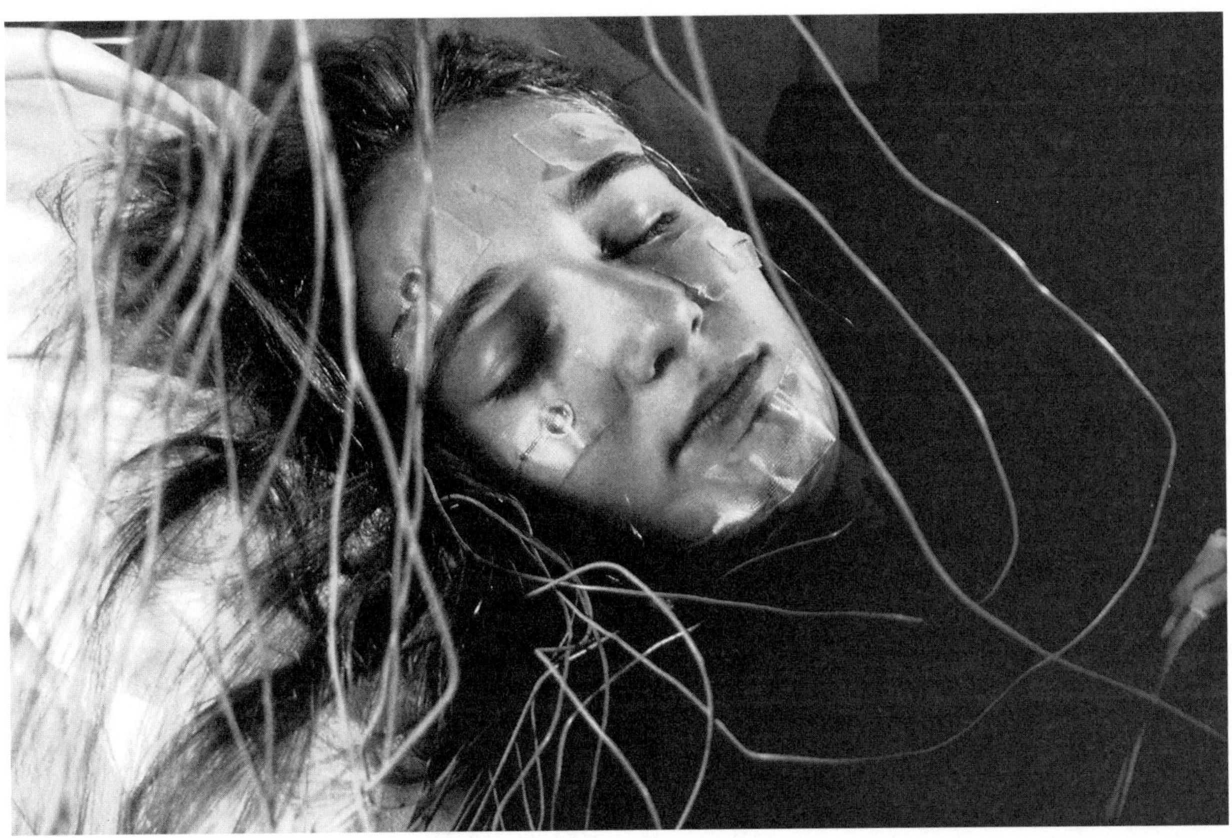

A polysomnograph collects data on the electrical activity of the heart and brain, and muscle activity in the face and neck of a sleeping subject. *(Photograph by Philippe Plailly. Science Source/ Photo Researchers, Inc. Reproduced by permission.)*

One form of monitoring is **electroencephalography** (EEG), which involves the attachment of electrodes to the patient's scalp to record his or her brain wave activity. The electroencephalograph records brain wave activity from different parts of the brain and charts them on a graph. The EEG not only helps doctors establish what stage of sleep the patient is in, but may also detect seizures.

Another form of monitoring is continuous electrooculography (EOG), which records eye movements. EOG is used to determine the time periods during which the patient is going through a stage of sleep called rapid-eye-movement (REM) sleep. Both EEG and EOG can be helpful in determining sleep latency (the time period between getting into bed and the onset of sleep); total sleep time; the time spent in each sleep stage; and the number of arousals from sleep.

The airflow through the patient's nose and mouth are measured by heat-sensitive devices called thermistors. The thermistors can help detect episodes of apnea (stopped breathing), or hypopnea (inadequate or too-shallow breathing). Another test called pulse oximetry measures the amount of oxygen in the patient's blood. Pulse oximetry can be used to assess the degree of oxygen starvation during episodes of hypopnea or apnea.

The electrical activity of the patient's heart is also measured on an electrocardiogram, or EKG. Electrodes are attached to the patient's chest. The electrodes pick up electrical activity from various areas of the heart. They help to detect cardiac arrythmias (abnormal heart rhythms), which may occur during periods of sleep apnea. The patient's blood pressure is also measured, because some episodes of sleep apnea can raise blood pressure to dangerously high levels.

In some cases, sleep laboratories monitor the movement of the patient's arms and legs during sleep. This measurement can be helpful in detecting such sleep disorders as periodic limb movements. Some sleep laboratories perform an additional test called multiple sleep latency testing (MSLT), which records several naps throughout the day. In addition, many sleep researchers prefer to evaluate the patient over a period of a few days rather than just one night. This approach is based on the recognition that the patient may need more than one night to adjust to the unfamiliar surroundings of the sleep laboratory.

Preparation

The patient may be asked to discontinue taking any medications, and avoid alcohol and strenuous exercise the day before the sleep analysis is performed. Before the patient goes to sleep, the technician hooks him or her up to all of the monitors being used.

Aftercare

After the test is completed, the monitors are detached from the patient. No special measures need to be taken after polysomnography. On occasion, skin irritation from the adhesive can develop in the areas where the electrodes have been attached to the patient.

Normal results

A normal result in polysomnography shows normal results for all parameters (EEG, EKG, blood pressure, eye movement, air flow, pulse oximetry, etc.) that were monitored throughout all stages of sleep.

Abnormal results

Polysomnography may yield a number of abnormal results, indicating one or more potential sleep disorders. For instance, abnormal transitions into and out of various stages of sleep, as documented by the EEG and the EOG, may be signs of narcolepsy. Reduced air flow through the nose and mouth, along with a fall in blood oxygen levels, may indicate apnea or hypopnea. If apnea is accompanied by abnormal patterns on the EKG or elevations in blood pressure, then the sleep apnea may be producing harmful effects. Frequent movements of the patient's arms and legs may suggest a sleep disorder called periodic limb movement. A related condition that affects sleep as well as daytime movement is called restless legs syndrome. Polysomnography can also be used to diagnose bruxism, which is the chronic grinding of the teeth during sleep.

See also Breathing-related sleep disorder

Resources

BOOKS

Czeisler, C. A. and others, eds. *Harrison's Principles of Internal Medicine.* 15th Ed. New York: McGraw-Hill, 2001.

PERIODICALS

"Practice parameters for the indications for polysomnography and related procedures." *Sleep* 1997 (Reviewed 2000); 20: 406-22.

ORGANIZATIONS

American Sleep Disorders Association. 6301 Bandel Road NW, Suite 101, Rochester, MN 55901. <http://www.asda.org>.

National Heart, Lung and Blood Institute. P.O. Box 30105, Bethesda, MD 20824-0105. (301) 251-1222. <http://www.nhlbi.nih.gov>.

Robert Scott Dinsmoor

Polysubstance dependence

Definition

Polysubstance dependence refers to a type of substance dependence disorder in which an individual uses at least three different classes of substances indiscriminately and does not have a favorite drug that qualifies for dependence on its own.

Description

Polysubstance dependence is listed as a substance disorder in the ***Diagnostic and Statistical Manual of Mental Disorders*** published in 2000 (also known as the *DSM-IV-TR*). The *DSM-IV-TR* is the latest revision of the manual that it is used by mental health professionals to diagnose mental disorders. When an individual meets criteria for dependence on a group of substances (at least three different types used in the same 12-month period) he or she is given the **diagnosis** of polysubstance dependence. For example, an individual may use cocaine, sedatives, and hallucinogens indiscriminately (i.e., no single drug predominated; there was no "drug of choice") for a year or more. The individual may not meet criteria for cocaine dependence, sedative dependence, or hallucinogen dependence, but may meet criteria for substance dependence when all three drugs are considered as a group.

Causes and symptoms

Causes

There is very little documented regarding the causes of polysubstance dependence.

Symptoms

The *DSM-IV-TR* specifies that three or more of the following symptoms must occur at any time during a 12-month period (and cause significant impairment or distress) in order to meet diagnostic criteria for substance dependence:

- Tolerance: The individual either has to use increasingly higher amounts of the drugs over time in order to achieve the same drug effect or finds that the same amount of the drug has much less of an effect over time than before. After using several different drugs regularly for a while, an individual may find that he or she needs to use at least 50% more of the amount they began using in order to get the same effect.
- Withdrawal: The individual either experiences the withdrawal symptoms when he or she stops using the drugs or the individual uses drugs in order to avoid or relieve withdrawal symptoms.
- Loss of control: The individual either repeatedly uses more drugs than planned or uses the drugs over longer periods of time than planned. For instance, an individual may begin using drugs (any combination of three or more types of drugs) on weekdays in addition to weekends.
- Inability to stop using: The individual has either unsuccessfully attempted to cut down or stop using the drugs or has a persistent desire to stop using. An individual may find that, despite efforts to stop using drugs on weekdays, he or she is unable to do so.
- Time: The individual spends a lot of time obtaining drugs, using drugs, being under the influence of drugs, and recovering from the effects of drugs.
- Interference with activities: The individual either gives up or reduces the amount of time involved in recreational activities, social activities, and/or occupational activities because of the use of drugs. An individual may use drugs instead of engaging in hobbies, spending time with friends, or going to work.
- Harm to self: The individual continues to use drugs despite having either a physical or psychological problem that is caused by or made worse by the use of drugs.

Demographics

Young adults (i.e., between the ages of 18 and 24) have the highest rates of use for all substances. Generally, males tend to be diagnosed with more substance use disorders.

Diagnosis

Individuals who abuse alcohol and other drugs usually meet criteria for substance abuse and/or dependence for each individual substance used. Multiple diagnoses are given in this situation (cocaine dependence, hallucinogen dependence, and sedative dependence, for example). Polysubstance dependence is reserved only for those situations when an individual uses multiple substances indiscriminately and meets criteria for dependence on these substances, taken as a whole.

Treatments

There is very little documented regarding the treatment of polysubstance dependence. However, several treatments have been tried. Psychological evaluation and tests may be used to assess the affected individual. The person may be admitted into a hospital or treatment center as an inpatient, and/or he or she may receive **cognitive-behavioral therapy**.

Prognosis

The course of substance dependence varies from short-lived episodes to chronic episodes lasting years. The individual with substance dependence may alternate between periods of heavy use with severe problems, periods of no use at all, and periods of use with few problems.

Prevention

The best single thing an individual can do to prevent polysubstance dependence is to avoid using drugs including alcohol altogether. On a larger scale, comprehensive prevention programs that utilize family, schools, communities, and the media (such as television) can be effective in reducing substance abuse.

Resources

BOOKS

American Psychiatric Association. *Diagnostic and Statistical Manual of Mental Disorders.* 4th edition, text revised. Washington, DC: American Psychiatric Association, 2000.

Kaplan, Harold I., M.D., and Benjamin J. Sadock, M.D. *Kaplan and Sadock's Synopsis of Psychiatry: Behavioral Sciences, Clinical Psychiatry.* 8th edition. Baltimore: Williams and Wilkins.

Jennifer Hahn, Ph.D.

Positive symptoms

Definition

Positive symptoms are thoughts, behaviors, or sensory perceptions present in a person with a mental disorder, but not present in people in the normal population.

Description

Examples of positive symptoms are **hallucinations** (seeing, hearing, or smelling things not really there), **delusions** (belief in ideas not based on reality), disorganized speech (loose association between ideas, derailment of sentences, incoherence, illogical statements, excessive detail, and rhyming of words), or bizarre behavior. In other disorders, positive symptoms are primarily associated with **schizophrenia** or **psychosis**.

See also Negative symptoms

Sandra L. Friedrich, M.A.

Positron emission tomography

Definition

Positron emission tomography (PET) is a highly specialized imaging technique using short-lived radiolabeled substances to produce extremely high resolution images of the body's biological function.

Purpose

Besides being used to investigate the metabolism of normal organs, PET has also become the technique of choice to investigate various neurological diseases, including **stroke**, epilepsy, **Alzheimer's disease**, Parkinson's disease, and Huntington's disease. Various psychiatric disorders, such as **schizophrenia**, depression, **obsessive-compulsive disorder**, **attention-deficit/hyperactivity disorder**, and Tourette syndrome, are also imaged by PET, because these disorders have changes in specific areas of the **brain**. Additionally, PET scanning is a powerful research tool to detect changes or abnormalities in areas that may be difficult to visualize using other radiological procedures. In the field of mental health, a PET scan may be used when a patient seeks medical help for symptoms that could possibly be caused by a brain tumor. These symptoms may include headaches, emotional abnormalities, or intellectual or memory problems. In these cases, a PET scan may be performed to "rule out" a tumor, so that other tests can be performed in order to establish an accurate **diagnosis**.

PET is especially utilized in persons affected by cancer because it can detect metastatic tumors that may not be visualized by other imaging techniques. It is also being increasingly used not only as a cancer diagnostic tool, but also to help researchers design the most beneficial therapies. For example, it may be used to assess response to chemotherapy. PET imaging is very accurate in differentiating malignant from benign cell growths, and in assessing the spread of malignant tumors. PET is also used to detect recurrent brain tumors and cancers of the lung, colon, breast, lymph nodes, skin, and other organs.

KEY TERMS

Benign growth—A noncancerous cell growth that does not metastasize and does not recur after treatment or removal.

Cancer screening—A procedure designed to detect cancer even though a person has no symptoms, usually performed using an imaging technique.

CT scan—An imaging technique that uses a computer to combine multiple x-ray images into a two-dimensional cross-sectional image.

Electron—One of the small particles that make up an atom. An electron has the same mass and amount of charge as a positron, but the electron has a negative charge.

Gamma ray—A high-energy photon, emitted by radioactive substances.

Half-life—The time required for half of the atoms in a radioactive substance to disintegrate.

Malignant growth—A cell growth or tumor that becomes progressively worse and that can metastasize elsewhere in the body.

Metabolism—The group of biochemical processes within the body that release energy in support of life.

MRI—Magnetic resonance imaging. A special imaging technique used to image internal parts of the body, especially soft tissues.

Photon—A light particle.

Positron—One of the small particles that make up an atom. A positron has the same mass and amount of charge as an electron, but the positron has a positive charge.

Precautions

In some cases, patients may be allergic to the radioactive agents used for PET. A patient with known allergies should discuss this with their specialist before undergoing the PET scan.

Description

PET is used in conjunction with compounds that closely resemble a natural substance used by the body, such as a simple sugar (glucose, for example), labeled with a radioactive atom and injected into the patient. These compounds (radionuclides or radiopharmaceuticals) emit particles called positrons. As positrons emitted from the radionuclides encounter electrons in the body, they produce high-energy photons (gamma rays) that can be recorded as a signal by detectors surrounding the body. The radionuclides move through the body and accumulate in the organs targeted for examination. A computer collects the distribution of radioactivity and reassembles them into actual images.

By further defining a lesion seen on other imaging modalities, PET may enhance assessment of tumors exceedingly well. This is because of its operating principle. The radiolabeled sugars injected into the patient will be used by all body cells, but more sugar will be used by cells that have an increased metabolism. Cancer cells are highly metabolic, meaning that they use more sugar than healthy nearby cells, and they are easily seen on the PET scan. PET images thus show the chemical functioning of an organ or tissue, unlike x ray, **computed tomography**, or **magnetic resonance imaging**, which show only body structure.

Preparation

The radiopharmaceutical is given by intravenous injection or inhaled as a gas a few minutes before the PET procedure. How it is administered depends on the radiopharmaceutical used and which one is selected depends on what organ or body part is being scanned. During the scan, the patient lies comfortably; the only discomfort involved may be the pinprick of a needle used to inject the radiopharmaceutical.

Aftercare

No special aftercare measures are indicated for PET.

Risks

Some of radioactive compounds used for PET scanning can persist for a long time in the body. Even though only a small amount is injected each time, the long half-lives of these compounds can limit the number of times a patient can be scanned. However, PET is a relatively safe procedure. PET scans using radioactive fluorine result in patients receiving exposures comparable to (or less than) those from other medical procedures, such as the taking of x rays. Other scanning radiopharmaceuticals—for instance, 6-F-dopa or radioactive water—normally cause even less exposure.

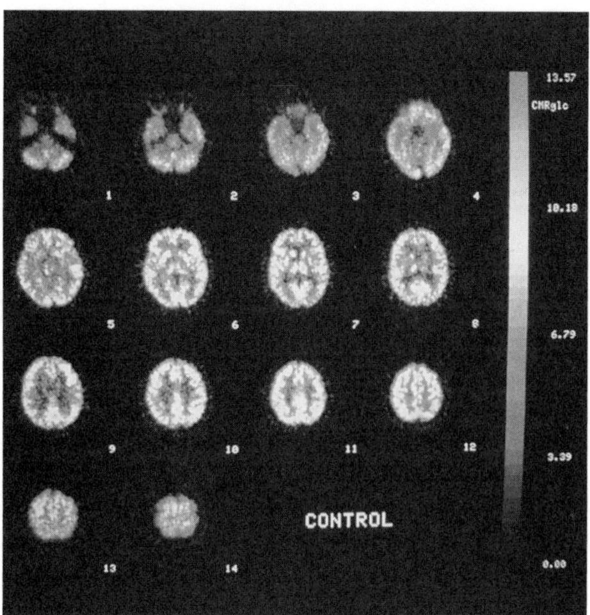

A positron emission tomography (PET) scan of the human brain. *(Jon Meyer. Cutom Medical Stock Photo. Reproduced by permission.) See color insert for color version of photo.*

Normal results

The PET scan of a healthy organ or body part will yield images without contrasting regions, because the radiolabeled sugar will have been metabolized at the same rate.

Abnormal results

The PET scan of a diseased organ or body part, however, will yield images showing contrasting regions, because the radiolabeled sugar will not have been metabolized (breaking down a large molecule to a smaller molecule that can be used by the body) at the same rate by the healthy and diseased cells.

Resources

BOOKS

Balazs, G., ed. *Positron Emission Tomography: A Critical Assessment of Recent Trends.* Norwell, MA: Kluwer Academic Publishers, 1998.

von Schulthess, G. K., ed. *Clinical Positron Emission Tomography.* Philadelphia: Lippincott, Williams and Wilkins, 1999.

PERIODICALS

Anderson, H., and P. Price. "What Does Positron Emission Tomography Offer Oncology?" *European Journal of Cancer* 36 (October 2000):2028–35.

Arulampalam, T. H., D. C. Costa, M. Loizidou, D. Visvikis, P. J. Ell, and I. Taylor. "Positron Emission Tomography and Colorectal Cancer." *British Journal of Surgery* 88 (February 2001): 176–89.

Roelcke, U., and K. L. Leenders. "PET in Neuro-oncology." *Journal of Cancer Research and Clinical Oncology* 127 (January 2001): 2–8.

Lisa Christenson
Monique LaBerge, Ph.D.

Postpartum depression

Definition

Postpartum depression is a depression that can range from mild to suicidal and can occur anytime after delivery up to one year later.

Description

Postpartum depression is an affective disorder (any mental disorder characterized by a consistent change in mood that affects thoughts and behaviors) that can occur after pregnancies of all duration, from spontaneous (not induced) abortions, also called miscarriages, to full-term deliveries. The depression can take a mild clinical course or it can range to suicidal ideations (thoughts). The depression can occur anytime post-delivery to one year after delivery. Symptoms commonly start within four to six weeks after delivery. Differentiating postpartum depression from "maternity blues" or the **stress** from the pregnancy and delivery can be difficult. Postpartum depression can be differentiated from other types of depression if the mother exhibits signs of ambivalence to the infant and **neglect** of other family members.

Causes and symptoms

Causes

The cause of postpartum depression has been extensively studied. Alterations of hormone levels for prolactin, progesterone, estrogen, and cortisol are not significantly different from those of patients who do not suffer from postpartum depression. However, some research indicates a change in a **brain** chemical that controls the release of cortisol.

Research seems to indicate that postpartum depression is unlikely to occur in a patient with an otherwise psychologically uncomplicated pregnancy and past history. There is no association of postpartum depression with marital status, social class, or the number of live children born to the mother. However, there seems to be an increased chance to develop this disorder after pregnancy loss.

Certain characteristics have been associated with increased risk of developing postpartum depression. These risk factors include:

- medical indigence— being in need of health care and not being able to receive it, possibly due to lack of medical insurance
- being younger than 20 years old at time of delivery
- being unmarried
- having been separated from one or both parents in childhood or adolescence
- receiving poor parental support and attention in childhood
- having had limited parental support in adulthood
- poor relationship with husband or boyfriend
- economic problem with housing or income
- dissatisfaction with amount of education
- low self-esteem
- past or current emotional problem(s)
- family history of depression

Symptoms

The symptoms can range from mild depression to a severe depression with thoughts of ending one's life (**suicide**). The disorder should be suspected during its peak (four to six weeks after delivery) in a patient who demonstrates signs and symptoms of clinical depression (feelings of worthlessness and hopelessness, changes in eating and sleeping patterns, irritability, difficulty with motivation, and difficulty getting out of bed in the morning). Additionally, patients may be emotionally detached from the infant and unable to display loving affection towards family members. Physical and emotional stress during delivery in conjunction with great demands for infant care may cause the patient to neglect other family members, increasing the woman's feelings of self-worthlessness, isolation, and being trapped. Patients may also feel as if they are inadequate mothers, causing them guilt and embarrassment.

Demographics

There is a 20% to 30% risk of postpartum depression for women who had a previous depressive episode that was not associated with pregnancy. Additionally, there is an increased risk of recurrence in subsequent pregnancies since 50–100% of patients will have more than one episode.

Diagnosis

Patients should undergo careful clinical assessment from a **psychologist** or **psychiatrist**, who can determine the risk factors and diagnose the condition. A careful, comprehensive psychological assessment interview could reveal a previous depressive cycle or a family history of depression—important risk factors. The most widely used standard for **diagnosis** is the Edinburgh Postnatal Depression Scale (EPDS). This is a simple and short 10-question scale. A score of 12 or greater on the EPDS is considered high risk for postpartum depression.

Treatments

Treatment should begin as soon as the diagnosis is established. A typical treatment plan includes **psychotherapy** and medications. Recent studies have found that a group of medications known as the selective serotonin reuptake inhibitors (SSRIs) are effective in treating postpartum depression. These antidepressants have fewer side effects than other antidepressants and can be taken by breast-feeding mothers. SSRIs are secreted into breast milk, however, in varying amounts. Some studies indicate that **paroxetine** secretes the least amount of medication into breast milk. Breast-feeding women considering taking an antidepressant should discuss medication choices with their doctor. SSRIs can be given two to three weeks before delivery to patients who had a previous episode to avoid recurrence. Some SSRIs include: **fluoxetine** (Prozac), paroxetine (Paxil), **sertraline** (Zoloft), and **citalopram** (Celexa).

When medications are combined with psychological therapy, the rates for successful treatment are increased. **Interpersonal therapy** and **cognitive-behavioral therapy** have been found to be effective.

Prognosis

The prognosis for postpartum depression varies because this disorder is usually implicated with difficult social factors, a personal history of emotional problems, and adverse pregnancy outcomes, such as miscarriage. The prognosis is better if depression is detected early during its clinical course and a combination of SSRIs and psychotherapy is available and inititated.

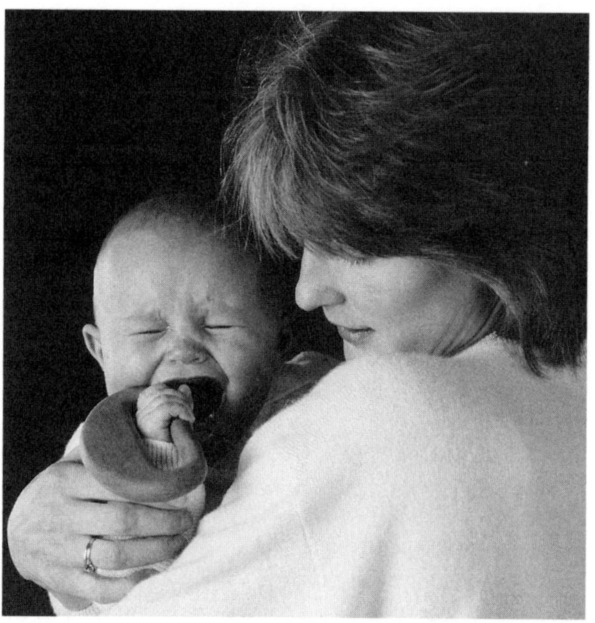

Care for a newborn can be overwhelming, and some women experience postpartum depression shortly after birth. *(Layne Kennedy/CORBIS. Photo reproduced by permission.)*

Prevention

The best method to prevent the disorder is through education. Mothers should be advised prior to hospital discharge that if the "maternity blues" last longer than two weeks or pose tough difficulties with family interactions, they should call the hospital where their baby was delivered and pursue a referral for a psychological evaluation. Education concerning risk factors and reduction of these is important. Prophylactic (preventive) use of SSRIs is indicated two to three weeks before delivery to prevent the disorder in a patient with a past history of depression, since recurrence rates are high if the mother had a previous depressive episode.

Resources

BOOKS

Gabbe, Steven, Jennifer R. Niebyl, Joe Leigh Simpson. *Obstetrics: Normal & Problem Pregnancies.* 4th ed. Philadelphia : W. B. Saunders Company, 2002.

Ryan, Kenneth J., Ross S. Berkowitz, Robert L. Barbieri, and others. *Kistner's Gynecology & Women's Health.* 7th ed. Saint Louis: Mosby, Incorporated, 1999.

PERIODICALS

Evins, G. G., J. P. Theofrastous, and S. L. Galvin. "Postpartum Depression: a comparison of screening and routine clinical evaluation." *American Journal of Obstetrics and Gynecology* 182, no. 5 (May 2000).

ORGANIZATIONS

Online PPD Support Group. <http://www.ppdsupportpage.com>.

Laith Farid Gulli, M.D.
Nicole Mallory, M.S., PA-C

Post-traumatic stress disorder

Definition

Post-traumatic stress disorder, often abbreviated as PTSD, is a complex disorder in which the affected person's memory, emotional responses, intellectual processes, and nervous system have all been disrupted by one or more traumatic experiences. It is sometimes summarized as "a normal reaction to abnormal events." The *DSM-IV-TR* (the professional's diagnostic manual) classifies PSTD as an anxiety disorder.

Description

PTSD has a unique position as the only psychiatric **diagnosis** (along with **acute stress disorder**) that depends on a factor outside the individual, namely, a traumatic stressor. A patient cannot be given a diagnosis of PTSD unless he or she has been exposed to an event that is considered traumatic. These events include such obvious traumas as rape, military combat, torture, genocide, natural disasters, and transportation or workplace disasters. In addition, it is now recognized that repeated traumas or such traumas of long duration as child **abuse**, domestic violence, stalking, cult membership, and hostage situations may also produce the symptoms of PTSD in survivors.

A person suffering from PTSD experiences flashbacks, nightmares, or daydreams in which the traumatic event is experienced again. The person may also experience abnormally intense startle responses, **insomnia**, and may have difficulty concentrating. Trauma survivors with PTSD have been effectively treated with **group therapy** or individual psychological therapy, and other therapies have helped individuals, as well. Some affected individuals have found **support groups** or peer counseling groups helpful. Treatment may require several years, and in some cases, PTSD may affect a person for the rest of his or her life.

Demographics

General United States population

PTSD is much more widespread in the general population than was thought when it was first introduced as a diagnostic category. The National Comorbidity Survey, a major epidemiological study conducted between 1990 and 1992, estimates that the lifetime prevalence among adult Americans is 7.8%, with women (10.4%) twice as likely as men (5%) to be diagnosed with PTSD at some point in their lives. These figures represent only a small proportion of adults who have experienced at least one traumatic event—60.7% of men and 51.2% of women respectively. More than 10% of the men and 6% of the women reported experiencing four or more types of trauma in their lives. The most frequently mentioned traumas are:

- witnessing someone being badly hurt or killed
- involvement in a fire, flood, earthquake, severe hurricane, or other natural disaster
- involvement in a life-threatening accident (workplace explosion or transportation accident)
- military combat

The traumatic events most frequently mentioned by men diagnosed with PTSD are rape, combat exposure, childhood **neglect**, and childhood physical abuse. For women diagnosed with PTSD, the most common traumas are rape, sexual molestation, physical attack, being threatened with a weapon, and childhood physical abuse.

High-risk populations

Some subpopulations in the United States are at greater risk of developing PTSD. The lifetime prevalence of PTSD among persons living in depressed urban areas or on Native American reservations is estimated at 23%. For victims of violent crimes, the estimated rate is 58%.

Military veterans

Information about PTSD in veterans of the Vietnam era is derived from the National Vietnam Veterans Readjustment Survey (NVVRS), conducted between 1986 and 1988. The estimated lifetime prevalence of PTSD among American veterans of this war is 30.9% for men and 26.9% for women. An additional 22.5% of the men and 21.2% of the women have been diagnosed with partial PTSD at some point in their lives. The lifetime prevalence of PTSD among veterans of World War II and the Korean War is estimated at 20%.

Cross-cultural issues

Further research needs to be done on the effects of ethnicity and culture on post-traumatic symptoms. As of 2001, most PTSD research has been done by Western clinicians working with patients from a similar background. Researchers do not yet know whether persons from non-Western societies have the same psychological reactions to specific traumas or whether they develop the same symptom patterns.

Causes and symptoms

Causes

When PTSD was first suggested as a diagnostic category for *DSM-III* in 1980, it was controversial precisely because of the central role of outside stressors as causes of the disorder. Psychiatry has generally emphasized the internal weaknesses or deficiencies of individuals as the source of mental disorders; prior to the 1970s, war veterans, rape victims, and other trauma survivors were often blamed for their symptoms and regarded as cowards, moral weaklings, or masochists. The high rate of psychiatric casualties among Vietnam veterans, however, led to studies conducted by the Veterans Administration. These studies helped to establish PTSD as a legitimate diagnostic entity with a complex set of causes.

BIOCHEMICAL/PHYSIOLOGICAL CAUSES. Present neurobiological research indicates that traumatic events cause lasting changes in the human nervous system, including abnormal secretions of stress hormones. In addition, in PTSD patients, researchers have found changes in the amygdala and the hippocampus—the parts of the **brain** that form links between fear and memory. Experiments with ketamine, a drug that inactivates one of the neurotransmitter chemicals in the central nervous system, suggest that trauma works in a similar way to damage associative pathways in the brain. **Positron emission tomography** (PET) scans of PTSD patients suggest that trauma affects the parts of the brain that govern speech and language.

SOCIOCULTURAL CAUSES. Studies of specific populations of PTSD patients (combat veterans, survivors of rape or genocide, former political hostages or prisoners, etc.) have shed light on the social and cultural causes of PTSD. In general, societies that are highly authoritarian, glorify violence, or sexualize violence have high rates of PTSD even among civilians.

OCCUPATIONAL FACTORS. Persons whose work exposes them to traumatic events or who treat trauma survivors may develop secondary PTSD (also known as compassion **fatigue** or burnout). These occupations include specialists in emergency medicine, police officers, firefighters, search-and-rescue personnel, psychotherapists, disaster investigators, etc. The degree of risk for PTSD is related to three factors: the amount and intensity of exposure to the suffering of trauma victims; the worker's degree of empathy and sensitivity; and unresolved issues from the worker's personal history.

PERSONAL VARIABLES. Although the most important causal factor in PTSD is the traumatic event itself, individuals differ in the intensity of their cognitive and emotional responses to trauma; some persons appear to be more vulnerable than others. In some cases, this greater vulnerability is related to temperament or natural disposition, with shy or introverted people being at greater risk. In other cases, the person's vulnerability results from chronic illness, a physical disability, or previous traumatization—particularly abuse in childhood. As of 2001, researchers have not found any correlation between race and biological vulnerability to PTSD.

KEY TERMS

Acute stress disorder—Symptoms occuring in an individual following a traumatic event to oneself or surrounding environment. Symptoms include a continued response of intense fear, helplessness, or terror within four weeks of the event, extreme nervousness, sleep disorders, increased anxiety, poor concentration, absence of emotional response to surroundings, and sometimes a dissociative amnesia—not recalling the significance of the trauma. Symptoms last a minimum of two days and maximum of four weeks. Can become post-traumatic stress disorder.

Adjustment disorder—A disorder defined by the development of significant emotional or behavioral symptoms in response to a stressful event or series of events. Symptoms may include depressed mood, anxiety, and impairment of social and occupational functioning.

Borderline personality disorder—A severe and usually life-long mental disorder characterized by violent mood swings and severe difficulties in sustaining interpersonal relationships.

Somatoform—Referring to physical symptoms with a psychological origin.

Substance abuse disorder—Disorder that is characterized by: an individual's need for more of a drug or alcohol than intended, an inability to stop using by choice, and an ongoing difficulty in recovering from the effects of the substance.

Symptoms

DSM-IV-TR specifies six diagnostic criteria for PTSD:

- Traumatic stressor: The patient has been exposed to a catastrophic event involving actual or threatened death or injury, or a threat to the physical integrity of the self or others. During exposure to the trauma, the person's emotional response was marked by intense fear, feelings of helplessness, or horror. In general, stressors caused intentionally by human beings (genocide, rape, torture, abuse, etc.) are experienced as more traumatic than accidents, natural disasters, or "acts of God."
- Intrusive symptoms: The patient experiences flashbacks, traumatic daydreams, or nightmares, in which he or she relives the trauma as if it were recurring in the present. Intrusive symptoms result from an abnormal process of memory formation. Traumatic memories have two distinctive characteristics: 1) they can be triggered by stimuli that remind the patient of the traumatic event; 2) they have a "frozen" or wordless quality, consisting of images and sensations rather than verbal descriptions.
- Avoidant symptoms: The patient attempts to reduce the possibility of exposure to anything that might trigger memories of the trauma, and to minimize his or her reactions to such memories. This cluster of symptoms includes feeling disconnected from other people, psychic numbing, and avoidance of places, persons, or things associated with the trauma. Patients with PTSD are at increased risk of substance abuse as a form of self-medication to numb painful memories.
- Hyperarousal: Hyperarousal is a condition in which the patient's nervous system is always on "red alert" for the return of danger. This symptom cluster includes hypervigilance, insomnia, difficulty concentrating, general irritability, and an extreme startle response. Some clinicians think that this abnormally intense startle response may be the most characteristic symptom of PTSD.
- Duration of symptoms: The symptoms must persist for at least one month.
- Significance: The patient suffers from significant social, interpersonal, or work-related problems as a result of the PTSD symptoms. A common social symptom of PTSD is a feeling of disconnection from other people (including loved ones), from the larger society, and from spiritual or other significant sources of meaning.

Diagnosis

The diagnosis of PTSD is complicated by several factors.

Time of onset/symptom duration

In the case of a known trauma of recent occurrence—most often a civilian disaster or war—the diagnosis of PTSD is relatively straightforward, based on the criteria listed above.

DSM-IV introduced a new diagnostic category, acute stress disorder, to differentiate between time-limited and longer-term stress reactions. In acute stress disorder, the hyperarousal and intrusive symptoms last between two days and four weeks. If the symptoms last beyond four weeks, and all of the above criteria are met, the diagnosis is changed to PTSD.

The diagnosis of PTSD is more difficult in cases of delayed reaction to trauma. Some individuals do not develop symptoms of PTSD until months or even years after the traumatic event. *DSM-IV-TR* specifies an interval of at least six months between the event and the development of symptoms for a diagnosis of PTSD with delayed onset. Delayed symptoms are often triggered by a situation that resembles the original trauma, as when a person raped in childhood experiences workplace sexual harassment.

Individual variations in response to stressors

DSM-III and its successors included the category of **adjustment disorder** to differentiate abnormal reactions to such painful but relatively common life events ("ordinary stressors") as divorce, job loss, or bereavement from symptoms resulting from overwhelming trauma. The differential diagnosis (the process of determining that the diagnosis is one disorder although it may resemble another) is complicated, however, by the fact that "ordinary stressors" sometimes reawaken unresolved childhood trauma, producing the delayed-reaction variant of PTSD.

Dual diagnoses

Most patients with PTSD (as many as 80%) have been diagnosed with one of the anxiety (30–60%), dissociative, mood (26–85%), or somatoform disorders as well as with PTSD. Between 40–60% of persons with delayed-reaction PTSD are diagnosed with a personality disorder, most often **borderline personality disorder**. Another common **dual diagnosis** is PTSD/substance abuse disorder. Between 60%–80% of patients who develop PTSD turn to alcohol or narcotics in order to avoid or numb painful memories. According to the NVVRS, the estimated lifetime prevalence of alcohol abuse among male Vietnam veterans is 39.2%, and the estimated lifetime prevalence of drug abuse is 5.7%. Dual diagnoses complicate treatment because the thera-

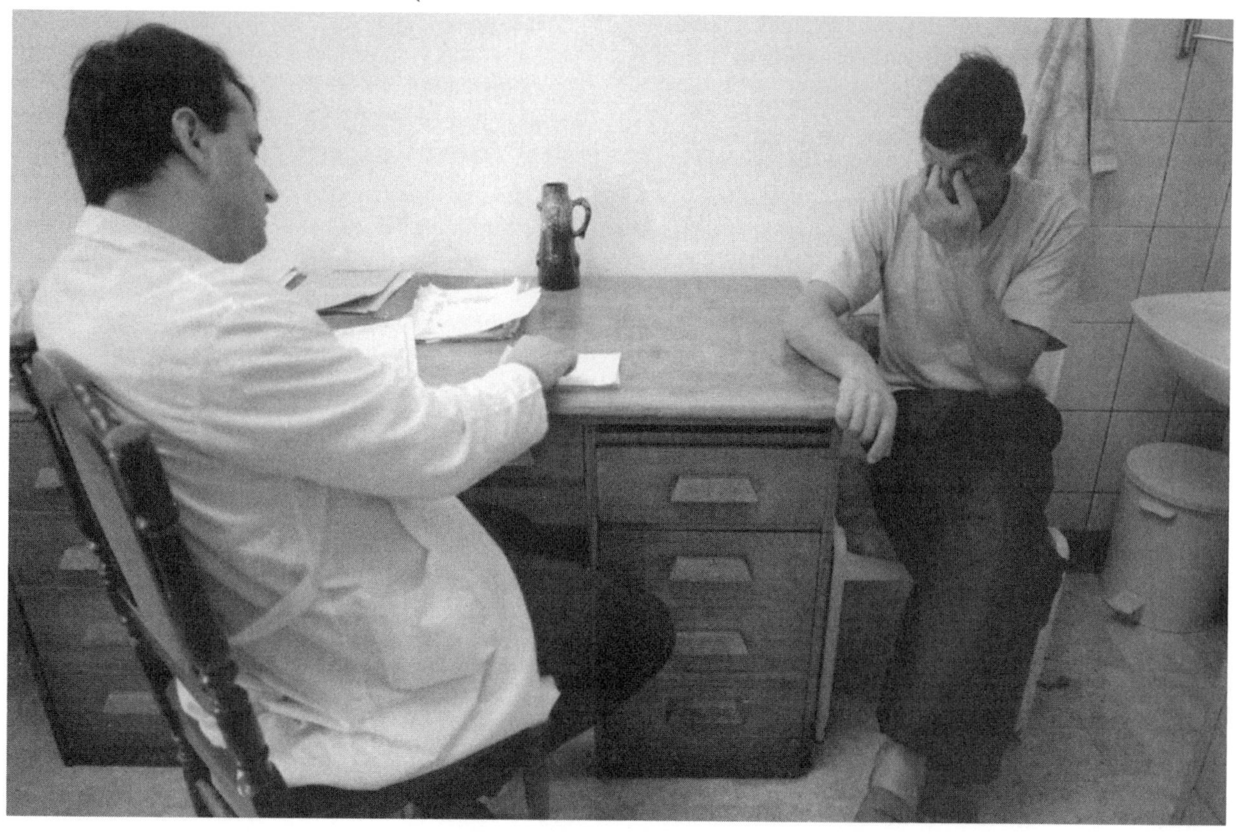

A Bosnian man with post-traumatic stress disorder talks with a therapist. *(AP/Wide World Photos. Reproduced by permission.)*

pist must decide whether to treat the disorders in sequence or concurrently. PTSD patients diagnosed with **personality disorders** are regarded as the most difficult to treat.

Psychological measures

As of 2002, there are no physical tests to establish a diagnosis of PTSD. The diagnosis is usually made on the basis of the patient's history and results from one or more short-answer interviews or symptom inventories. The instruments most often used to evaluate patients for PTSD include the Anxiety Disorders Interview Scale (ADIS), the **Beck Depression Inventory**, the Clinician-Administered PTSD Scale (CAPS), the Disorders of Extreme Stress Inventory (DESI), the Dissociative Experiences Scale (DES), the **Hamilton Anxiety Scale**, and the Impact of Event Scale (IES).

Treatments

Psychological and social interventions

In general, there have been few well-controlled clinical trials of treatment options for PTSD, particularly for severely affected patients.

Critical incident stress debriefing (CISD) is a treatment offered to patients within 48 hours following a civilian disaster or war zone trauma. It is intended to weaken the acute symptoms of the trauma and to forestall the development of full-blown PTSD. CISD usually consists of four phases:

- description of the traumatic event
- sharing of survivors' emotional reactions to the event
- open discussion of symptoms caused by the event
- reassurance that the symptoms are normal responses to trauma, followed by discussion of coping strategies

Critical incident stress management is a system of interventions designed to help emergency/disaster response workers, public safety personnel, and therapists deal with stress reactions before they develop secondary PTSD.

Other mainstream treatment methods used with patients who have already developed PTSD include:

- **Cognitive-behavioral therapy**. There are two treatment approaches to PTSD included under this heading: exposure therapy, which seeks to desensitize the patient to reminders of the trauma; and anxiety management training, which teaches the patient strategies for reducing anxiety. These strategies may include relaxation training, **biofeedback**, **social skills training**, distraction techniques, or cognitive restructuring.

- **Psychodynamic psychotherapy**. This method helps the patient recover a sense of self and learn new coping strategies and ways to deal with intense emotions related to the trauma. Typically, it consists of three phases: 1) establishing a sense of safety for the patient; 2) exploring the trauma itself in depth; 3) helping the patient re-establish connections with family, friends, the wider society, and other sources of meaning.
- Discussion groups or peer-counseling groups. These groups are usually formed for survivors of specific traumas, such as combat, rape/incest, and natural disasters. They help patients to recognize that other survivors of the shared experience have had the same emotions and reacted to the trauma in similar ways. They appear to be especially beneficial for patients with guilt issues about their behavior during the trauma (such as submitting to rape to save one's life, or surviving the event when others did not).
- **Family therapy**. This form of treatment is recommended for PTSD patients whose family life has been affected by the PTSD symptoms.

Medications

In general, medications are used most often in patients with severe PTSD to treat the intrusive symptoms of the disorder as well as feelings of anxiety and depression. These drugs are usually given as one part of a treatment plan that includes **psychotherapy** or **group therapy**. As of 2002, there is no single medication that appears to be a "magic bullet" for PTSD. The selective serotonin reuptake inhibitors (SSRIs) appear to help the core symptoms when given in higher doses for five to eight weeks, while the tricyclic antidepressants (TCAs) or the monoamine oxidase inhibitors (MAOIs) are most useful in treating anxiety and depression.

Alternative therapies

Some alternative therapies for PTSD include:

- Spiritual/religious counseling. Because traumatic experiences often affect patients' spiritual views and beliefs, counseling with a trusted religious or spiritual advisor may be part of a treatment plan. A growing number of pastoral counselors in the major Christian and Jewish bodies have advanced credentials in trauma therapy.
- **Yoga** and various forms of bodywork are often recommended as ways of releasing physical tension or muscle soreness caused by anxiety or hypervigilance.
- Martial arts training can be helpful in restoring the patient's sense of personal effectiveness and safety. Some martial arts programs, such as Model Mugging, are designed especially for survivors of rape and other violent crimes.
- Art therapy, journaling, dance therapy, and creative writing groups offer safe outlets for the strong emotions that follow traumatic experiences.

Recent controversial therapies

Since the mid-1980s, several controversial methods of treatment for PTSD have been introduced. Some have been developed by mainstream medical researchers while others are derived from various forms of alternative medicine. They include:

- Eye Movement Desensitization and Reprocessing. This is a technique in which the patient reimagines the trauma while focusing visually on movements of the therapist's finger. It is claimed that the movements of the patient's eyes reprogram the brain and allow emotional healing.
- Tapas Acupressure Technique (TAT). TAT was derived from traditional Chinese medicine (TCM), and its practitioners maintain that a large number of **acupuncture** meridians enter the brain at certain points on the face, especially around the eyes. Pressure on these points is thought to release traumatic stress.
- Thought Field Therapy. This therapy combines the acupuncture meridians of TCM with analysis of the patient's voice over the telephone. The therapist then provides an individualized treatment for the patient.
- Traumatic Incident Reduction. This is a technique in which the patient treats the trauma like a videotape and "runs through" it repeatedly with the therapist until all negative emotions have been discharged.
- Emotional Freedom Techniques (EFT). EFT is similar to TAT in that it uses the body's acupuncture meridians, but it emphasizes the body's entire "energy field" rather than just the face.
- Counting Technique. Developed by a physician, this treatment consists of a preparation phase, a counting phase in which the therapist counts from 1 to 100 while the patient reimagines the trauma, and a review phase. Like Traumatic Incident Reduction, it is intended to reduce the patient's hyperarousal.

Prognosis

Trauma survivors who receive critical incident stress debriefing as soon as possible after the event have the best prognosis for full recovery. For patients who develop full-blown PTSD, a combination of peer-group meetings and individual psychotherapy are often effective. Treatment may require several years, however, and the patient is likely to experience relapses.

There are no studies of untreated PTSD, but long-term studies of patients with delayed-reaction PTSD or delayed diagnosis of the disorder indicate that treatment of patients in these groups is much more difficult and complicated.

In some patients, PTSD becomes a chronic mental disorder that can persist for decades, or the remainder of the patient's life. Patients with chronic PTSD often have a cyclical history of symptom remissions and relapses. This group has the poorest prognosis for recovery; some patients do not respond to any of the currently available treatments for PTSD.

Prevention

Some forms of trauma, such as natural disasters and accidents, can never be completely eliminated from human life. Traumas caused by human intention would require major social changes to reduce their frequency and severity, but given the increasing prevalence of PTSD around the world, these long-term changes are worth the effort. In the short term, educating people—particularly those in the helping professions—about the signs of critical incident stress may prevent some cases of exposure to trauma from developing into full-blown PTSD.

See also Anxiety reduction techniques; Bodywork therapies; Creative therapies; Exposure treatment; Somatization and Somatoform disorders

Resources

BOOKS

American Psychiatric Association. *Diagnostic and Statistical Manual of Mental Disorders.* 4th edition, text revised. Washington, DC: American Psychiatric Association, 2000.

Beers, Mark H., M.D., and Robert Berkow, M.D., eds. "Post-traumatic Stress Disorder." In *The Merck Manual of Diagnosis and Therapy,* 17th edition. Whitehouse Station, NJ: Merck Research Laboratories, 1999.

Herman, Judith, M.D. *Trauma and Recovery.* 2nd ed., revised. New York: Basic Books, 1997.

Laub, Dori, M.D. "An Event Without A Witness: Truth, Testimony and Survival." In *Testimony: Crises of Witnessing in Literature, Psychoanalysis, and History,* written by Dori Laub, M.D. and Shoshana Felman. New York: Routledge, 1992.

ORGANIZATIONS

American Psychiatric Association. 1400 K Street NW, Washington D.C. 20005. <http://www.psych.org>.

Anxiety Disorders Association of America, Inc. 11900 Parklawn Drive, Suite 100, Rockville, MD 20852. (301) 231-9350. <http://www.adaa.org>.

International Critical Incident Stress Foundation, Inc. 10176 Baltimore National Pike, Unit 201, Ellicott City, MD 21042. (410) 750-9600. Emergency: (410) 313-2473. <http://www.icisf.org>.

International Society for Traumatic Stress Studies. 60 Revere Drive, Suite 500, Northbrook, IL 60062. (847) 480-9028. <http://www.istss.org>.

National Center for PTSD. 1116D V.A. Medical Center, 215 N. Main Street, White River Junction, VT 05009-0001. (802) 296-5132. <http://www.ncptsd.org>.

National Institute of Mental Health. 6001 Executive Boulevard, Rm. 8184, MSC 9663, Bethesda, MD 20892-9663. (301) 443-4513. <http://www.nimh.nih.gov>.

Rebecca J. Frey, Ph.D.

Premature ejaculation

Definition

Premature ejaculation (PE) refers to the persistent or recurrent discharge of semen with minimal sexual stimulation before, on, or shortly after penetration, before the person wishes it, and earlier than he expects it. In making the **diagnosis** of PE, the clinician must take into account factors that affect the length of time that the man feels sexually excited. These factors include the age of the patient and his partner, the newness of the sexual partner, and the location and recent frequency of sexual activity.

Causes

Premature ejaculation (PE) is a common complaint. The available evidence supports the notion that control and modulation of sexual excitement is learned behavior. If someone has learned it incorrectly or inadequately, they can relearn it. PE is only rarely caused by a physical or structural problem; in these cases it is usually associated with other physical symptoms, usually pain. In rare cases, PE may be associated with a neurological condition; infection of the prostate gland; or urethritis (inflammation of the duct that carries urine and semen to the outside of the body). With the rising prevalence of substance abuse, an increasing number of cases of PE are being diagnosed in patients withdrawing from drugs, especially opioids.

PE may be of lifelong duration or develop in later life, especially if a difficult interpersonal relationship is

KEY TERMS

Abstinence—Refraining from sexual intercourse for a period of time.

Ejaculation—The discharge of semen by the male reproductive organs.

Glans—The tip of the penis.

Orgasm—Another word for sexual climax. In the male, orgasm is usually accompanied by ejaculation but may be experienced as distinct from ejaculation.

Prostate—A muscular gland surrounding the urethra in males at the base of the urinary bladder. The prostate gland secretes the fluid that combines with the male sperm cells to form semen.

Semen—A thick whitish fluid containing sperm, produced by the male reproductive organs.

Urethritis—Inflammation of the urethra, which is the duct that carries urine and (in males) semen to the outside of the body.

one of its causes. Although PE is commonly associated with psychological symptoms, especially performance anxiety and guilt, these symptoms are its consequences rather than its causes. Once PE is firmly established, however, the accompanying psychological factors, especially in combination with sexual overstimulation, may form a self-perpetuating cycle that makes the disorder worse.

Premature ejaculation is common in adolescents where it may be made worse by feelings of sinfulness concerning sexual activity, fear of discovery, fear of making the partner pregnant, or fear of contracting a sexually transmitted disease (STD). All of these may be made worse by performance anxiety. Adults may have similar concerns as well as interpersonal factors related to the sexual partner.

Symptoms

In PE, ejaculation occurs earlier than the patient and/or the couple would like, thus preventing full satisfaction from intercourse, especially on the part of the sexual partner, who frequently fails to attain orgasm. PE is almost invariably accompanied by marked emotional upset and interpersonal difficulties that may add frustration to an already tense situation, which makes the loss of sexual fulfillment even worse. It is also important to differentiate male orgasm from ejaculation. Some men are able to distinguish between the two events and enjoy the pleasurable sensations associated with orgasm apart from the emission of semen, which usually ends the moment of orgasm. In these cases, the partner is capable of achieving orgasm and sexual satisfaction.

Diagnosis

The physical examination of a patient who is having problems with PE usually results in normal findings. Abnormal findings are unusual. The best source of information for diagnosing the nature of the problem is the patient's sexual history. On taking the patient's history, the clinician should concentrate on the sexual history, making sure that both partners have adequate and accurate sexual information. Ideally, the sexual partner should participate in the history and is often able to contribute valuable information that the patient himself may be unaware of or unwilling to relate. The female partner should also be examined by a gynecologist in order to ascertain her sexual capabilities and to eliminate the possibility that the size or structure of her genitals is part of the reason for the male's premature ejaculation.

Treatment

Preferably, therapy for PE should be conducted under the supervision of a health professional trained in sexual dysfunction. Both partners must participate responsibly in the therapeutic program. Treatment of PE requires patience, dedication and commitment by both partners, and the therapist must convey this message to both. The first part of therapy requires both partners to avoid intercourse for a period of several weeks. This period of abstinence is helpful in relieving any troublesome performance anxiety on the part of the man that may interfere with therapy.

Behavioral techniques, taught either individually, conjointly, or in groups, are effective in the therapy of PE. A preliminary stage of all treatment is termed "sensate focus" and involves the man's concentration on the process of sexual arousal and orgasm. He should learn each step in the process, most particularly the moment prior to the "point of no return." The sexual partner participates in the process, maintaining an awareness of the patient's sensations and how close he is to ejaculating. At this point, two techniques are commonly used:

- The "stop and start" technique. This approach involves sexual stimulation until the man recognizes that he is about to ejaculate. At this time, the stimulation is discontinued for about thirty seconds and then resumed. This sequence of events is repeated until ejaculation is desired by both partners, with stimulation continuing until ejaculation occurs.

- The "squeeze" technique. This approach involves sexual stimulation, usually by the sexual partner, until the man recognizes that he is about to ejaculate. At this time stimulation ceases. The patient or his partner gently squeezes the end of the penis at the junction of the glans penis (tip of the penis) with the shaft. The squeezing is continued for several seconds. Sexual stimulation is withheld for about 30 seconds and then resumed. This sequence of events is repeated by the patient alone or with the assistance of his partner until ejaculation is desired. At this point stimulation is continued until the man ejaculates.

The patient and his partner should be advised against trying any of the many unproven remedies that are available either over the counter or popularized on the Internet. Certain prescription medications, especially antidepressants that produce delayed ejaculation as a side effect, may be useful as therapeutic adjuncts. Recently, the use of a class of drugs known as selective serotonin receptor inhibitors (SSRIs) has shown promise in the treatment of premature ejaculation. The SSRIs prolong the time it takes the man to ejaculate by as much as 30 minutes. The SSRIs most commonly used to treat PE are **sertraline** (Zoloft) and **fluoxetine** (Prozac), which are currently approved by the Food and Drug Administration (FDA) for use in treating depression and panic attacks. It is important to emphasize that the use of these drugs to treat premature ejaculation is still considered experimental, as the FDA has not approved them for this specific use as of 2002.

Potential complications

Premature ejaculation that takes place before the man's penis enters the woman's vagina will interfere with conception, if the couple is planning a pregnancy. Continued lack of ejaculatory control may lead to sexual dissatisfaction for either or both members of the couple. It may become a source of marital tension, disturbed interpersonal relationships, and eventual separation or divorce.

Failure to respond to treatment for PE and the complications that may result from it should encourage the patient to seek further help from a health provider trained and experienced in treating the problem.

Prognosis

In most cases (some observers claim a 95% success rate), the patient is able to control ejaculation through education and practice of the techniques outlined. In chronic cases that do not respond to treatment, the PE may be related to a serious psychological or psychiatric condition, including depression or anxiety. Patients in this category may benefit from **psychotherapy**.

See also Male orgasmic disorder

Resources

BOOKS

Lue, Tom F., F. Goldstein. "Impotence and Infertility." In *Atlas of Clinical Urology.* Volume 1. New York: Current Medicine, 1999.

Masters. William, and Virginia Johnson. *Masters and Johnson on Sex and Human Loving.* New York: Little, Brown, 1986.

Steidle, Christopher P., M.D. *The Impotence Source Book.* Los Angeles: Howell House, 1998.

Ralph Myerson, M.D.

Primary hypersomnia *see* **Hypersomnia**

Primary insomnia *see* **Insomnia**

Prolixin *see* **Fluphenazine**

Propranolol

Definition

Propranolol is classified as a beta blocker. It is sold in the United States under the brand name Inderal. When combined with the diuretic, hydrochlorothiazide, it is sold under the brand name Inderide. Propranolol also is produced as a generic product by a number of generic manufacturers.

Purpose

Propranolol is approved by the Food and Drug Administration (FDA) for the treatment of hypertension (high blood pressure), angina, certain types of cardiac arrhythmias, certain types of cardiac output diseases, a sympathetic nervous system disorder known as pheochromocytoma, hyperthyroid conditions, migraine, heart attack, and tremors of a variety of origins. It is also used on occasion for the treatment of **medication-induced movement disorders** caused by antipsychotic drugs and certain anxiety states in people suffering from a specific form of **social phobia**. **Beta blockers**, such as propanolol, are not useful for people with general social phobia who are anxious in most social situations; instead, propanolol may be useful for people who are anxious about specific performance situations, such as presenting a speech before an audience.

KEY TERMS

Beta blocker—Drugs that block beta-adrenergic receptors on neurons in the central nervous system. When these sites are blocked, heart rate, blood pressure, and anxiety levels decrease.

Brachycardia—Slow heartbeat, defined as a rate of less than 60 beats per minute.

Diuretic—An agent that increases the amount of urine; often used to decrease fluid retention in bodily tissues.

Epinephrine (adrenaline)—The principal blood pressure-raising hormone and a bronchial and intestinal smooth muscles relaxant; prescribed to (among other things) stimulate the heart and as a muscle relaxant in bronchial asthma.

Glaucoma—A group of eye diseases characterized by increased pressure within the eye significant enough to damage eye tissue and structures. If untreated, glaucoma results in blindness.

Hypotension—Low blood pressure.

Ischemia—Localized anemia of tissues due to obstructed inflow of blood.

Laryngospasm—Spasms that close the vocal apparatus of the larynx (the organ of voice production).

Norepinephrine (noradrenaline)—A hormone with similar stimulatory effects to epinephrine but, in contrast to epinephrine, has little effect on cardiac (heart) output and in relaxing smooth muscles.

Raynaud's syndrome—A disorder of the circulatory or vascular system characterized by abnormally cold hands and feet because of constricted blood vessels in these areas.

Thrombocytopenia—A condition involving abnormally low numbers of platelets (blood-clotting agents) in the blood; usually associated with hemorrhaging (bleeding).

Description

Propranolol falls into the broad pharmacologic category known as beta blockers. Beta blockers block specific sites in the central nervous system known as beta-adrenergic receptor sites. When these sites are blocked, heart rate and blood pressure are reduced and patients become less anxious. Because of this, propranolol is useful in treating chest pain, high blood pressure, and excessive nervousness. Unfortunately, propranolol often makes breathing disorders, such as asthma, worse because it tends to constrict breathing passages and sometimes causes fluid to build up in the lungs if it excessively depresses the heart.

In the treatment of anxiety, propranolol is usually not administered on a chronic basis but, rather, prior to stressful events such as public speaking or acting. In the treatment of certain types of tremors, especially tremors secondary to a drug, and movement disorders secondary to antipsychotic therapy, propranolol is administered throughout the day in divided doses. Propranolol is available in 10-, 20-, 40-, 60-, and 80-mg tablets; in long-acting capsules; and an injectable form containing 1 mg per mL. It is also combined with the diuretic hydrochlorothiazide in tablets and extended-release capsules.

Recommended dosage

For the treatment of performance anxiety or stage fright, a single dose of 10–40 mg may be administered 20–30 minutes before the event. For the treatment of tremors, especially tremors secondary to lithium, doses range from 20 to 160 mg per day administered in two or three divided doses. For the treatment of movement disorders secondary to antipsychotic drug therapy, doses range from 10 to 30 mg three times daily.

Precautions

Precautions should be taken when administering propranolol in the following situations:

- liver or renal (kidney) failure
- prior to screening tests for glaucoma
- a history of immediate allergic reaction (known as anaphylaxis) to a beta blocker of any kind

Side effects

The following side effects have been observed with propranolol. Most have been mild and transient (temporary) and rarely require the withdrawal of therapy:

- Cardiovascular: bradycardia, congestive heart failure, hypotension, Raynaud's syndrome.
- Central nervous system: light-headedness, mental depression, **insomnia**, vivid dreams, disorientation, memory loss.
- Gastrointestinal: nausea, vomiting, abdominal pain, cramping, diarrhea, constipation, bowel ischemia.
- Allergic: fever, rash, laryngospasm, thrombocytopenia.

- Respiratory: bronchospasm.
- Hematologic: bone marrow suppression, bleeding under the skin.

Interactions

- When drugs that deplete the body of epinephrine and norepinephrine (such as reserpine and guanethidine) are taken with propranolol, interactions have been reported. Some of these interactions include: fainting, hypotension, dizziness, and slow heart rate.
- Drugs known as calcium channel blockers may decrease the pumping ability of the heart and lead to the development of cardiac arrhythmias.
- Nonsteroidal anti-inflammatory agents (i.e., ibuprofen and naproxen) may blunt the blood pressure-lowering effects of propranolol.
- Aluminum hydroxide antacids greatly reduce the rate of intestinal absorption of propranolol.
- Alcohol slows the rate of propranolol absorption.
- Interactions have also been reported with phenytoin, rifampin, phenobarbital, **chlorpromazine**, lidocaine, thyroxin, cimetidine, and theophylline.

See also Alcohol and related disorders; Anxiety and related disorders

Resources

BOOKS

Medical Economics Staff. *Physicians' Desk Reference.* 56th edition, Montvale, N.J., 2002.

Springhouse Publishers Staff. *Nursing 2002 Drug Handbook.* Springhouse, PA: Lippincott, Williams and Wilkins, 2001.

Thomas, Clayton, MD, editor. *Taber's Cyclopedic Medical Dictionary.* 19th edition; Philadelphia: F. A. Davis Publishers, 2001.

Ralph Myerson, M.D.

Prosom *see* **Estazolam**

Protriptyline

Definition

Protriptyline is an oral tricyclic antidepressant. It is sold in the United States under the brand name Vivactil and is also available under its generic name.

KEY TERMS

Acetylcholine—A naturally occurring chemical in the body that generally produces effects that are the opposite of those produced by dopamine and norepinephrine. Central nervous system well-being is dependent on a balance among acetylcholine, dopamine, serotonin, and norepinephrine.

Anticholinergic—Related to the ability of a drug to block the nervous system chemical acetylcholine. When acetylcholine is blocked, patients often experience dry mouth and skin, increased heart rate, blurred vision, and difficulty urinating. In severe cases, blocking acetylcholine may cloud thinking and cause delirium.

Benign prostate hypertrophy—Enlargement of the prostate gland.

Norepinephrine—A neurotransmitter in the brain that acts to constrict blood vessels and raise blood pressure. It works in combination with serotonin.

Serotonin—A widely distributed neurotransmitter that is found in blood platelets, the lining of the digestive tract, and the brain, and that works in combination with norepinephrine. It causes very powerful contractions of smooth muscle, and is associated with mood, attention, emotions, and sleep. Low levels of serotonin are associated with depression.

Purpose

Protriptyline is used primarily to treat depression and to treat the combination of symptoms of anxiety and depression. Like most antidepressants of this chemical and pharmacological class, protriptyline has also been used in limited numbers of patients to treat **panic disorder**, **obsessive-compulsive disorder**, **attention-deficit/hyperactivity disorder**, **enuresis** (bed-wetting), eating disorders such as **bulimia nervosa**, cocaine dependency, and the depressive phase of **bipolar disorder** (manic-depressive) disorder. It has also been used to support smoking cessation programs.

Description

Tricyclic antidepressants act to change the balance of naturally occurring chemicals in the **brain** that regulate the transmission of nerve impulses between cells. Protriptyline acts primarily to increase the concentration of norepinephrine and serotonin (both chemicals that stimulate nerve cells) and, to a lesser extent, to block the action of another brain chemical, acetylcholine. Protriptyline shares most of the properties of other tricyclic antidepressants, such as **amitriptyline**, **clomipramine**, **desipramine**, **imipramine**, **nortriptyline**, and **trimipramine**. Studies comparing protriptyline with these other drugs have shown that protriptyline is no more or less effective than other antidepressants of its type. Its choice for treatment is as much a function of physician preference as any other factor.

The therapeutic effects of protriptyline, like other antidepressants, appear slowly. Maximum benefit is often not evident for at least two weeks after starting the drug. People taking protriptyline should be aware of this and continue taking the drug as directed even if they do not see immediate improvement.

Recommended dosage

As with any antidepressant, protriptyline must be carefully adjusted by the physician to produce the desired therapeutic effect. Protriptyline is available as 5-mg and 10-mg tablets. Doses range from 15 to 40 mg per day and can be taken in one daily dose or divided into up to four doses daily. Some people with severe depression may require up to 60 mg per day.

In adolescents and people over age 60, therapy should be initiated at a dose of 5 mg three times a day and increased under supervision of a physician as needed. Patients over age 60 who are taking daily doses of 20 mg or more should be closely monitored for side effects such as rapid heart rate and urinary retention.

Precautions

Like all tricyclic antidepressants, protriptyline should be used cautiously and with close physician supervision in people, especially the elderly, who have benign prostatic hypertrophy (enlarged prostate gland), urinary retention, and glaucoma, especially angle-closure glaucoma (the most severe form). Before starting treatment, people with these conditions should discuss the relative risks and benefits of treatment with their doctors to help determine if protriptyline is the right antidepressant for them.

A common problem with tricyclic antidepressants is sedation (drowsiness, lack of physical and mental alertness). This side effect is especially noticeable early in therapy. In most people, sedation decreases or disappears entirely with time, but, until then, patients taking protriptyline should not perform hazardous activities requiring mental alertness or coordination. The sedative effect is increased when protriptyline is taken with other central nervous system depressants, such as alcoholic beverages, sleeping medications, other sedatives, or antihistamines. It may be dangerous to take protriptyline in combination with these substances. Protriptyline may increase the possibility of having **seizures**. Patients should tell their physician if they have a history of seizures, including seizures brought on by the abuse of drugs or alcohol. These people should use protriptyline only with caution and should be closely monitored by their physician.

Protriptyline may increase heart rate and stress on the heart. It may be dangerous for people with cardiovascular disease, especially those who have recently had a heart attack, to take this drug or other antidepressants in the same pharmacological class. In rare cases in which patients with cardiovascular disease must take protriptyline, they should be monitored closely for cardiac rhythm disturbances and signs of cardiac stress or damage.

Side effects

Protriptyline shares side effects common to all tricyclic antidepressants. The most frequent of these are dry mouth, constipation, urinary retention, increased heart rate, sedation, irritability, dizziness, and decreased coordination. As with most side effects associated with tricyclic antidepressants, the intensity is highest at the beginning of therapy and tends to decrease with continued use.

Dry mouth, if severe to the point of causing difficulty speaking or swallowing, may be managed by dosage reduction or temporary discontinuation of the drug. Patients may also chew sugarless gum or suck on sugarless candy in order to increase the flow of saliva. Some artificial saliva products may give temporary relief.

Men with prostate enlargement who take protriptyline may be especially likely to have problems with urinary retention. Symptoms include having difficulty starting a urine flow and more difficulty than usual passing urine. In most cases, urinary retention is managed with dose reduction or by switching to another type of antidepressant. In extreme cases, patients may require treatment with bethanechol, a drug that reverses this particular side effect. People who think they may be experiencing any side effects from this or any other medication should tell their physicians.

Interactions

Dangerously high blood pressure has resulted from the combination of tricyclic antidepressants, such as protriptyline, and members of another class of antidepressants known as monoamine oxidase (MAO) inhibitors.

Because of this, protriptyline should never be taken in combination with MAO inhibitors. Patient taking any MAO inhibitors, for example Nardil (**phenelzine** sulfate) or Parmate (**tranylcypromine** sulfate), should stop the MAO inhibitor then wait at least 14 days before starting protriptyline or any other tricyclic antidepressant. The same holds true when discontinuing protriptyline and starting an MAO inhibitor.

Protriptyline may decrease the blood pressure–lowering effects of **clonidine**. Patients who take both drugs should be monitored for loss of blood-pressure control and the dose of clonidine increased as needed.

The sedative effects of protriptyline are increased by other central nervous system depressants such as alcohol, sedatives, sleeping medications, or medications used for other mental disorders such as **schizophrenia**. The anticholinergic effects of protriptyline are additive with other anticholinergic drugs such as **benztropine**, **biperiden**, **trihexyphenidyl**, and antihistamines.

See also Neruotransmitters

Resources

BOOKS

American Society of Health-System Pharmacists. *AHFS Drug Information 2002*. Bethesda: American Society of Health-System Pharmacists, 2002.

DeVane, C. Lindsay, Pharm.D. "Drug Therapy for Mood Disorders." In *Fundamentals of Monitoring Psychoactive Drug Therapy*. Baltimore: Williams and Wilkins, 1990.

Jack Raber, Pharm.D.

Prozac *see* **Fluoxetine**

Pseudocyesis

Definition

Pseudocyesis is the medical term for a false pregnancy. Pseudocyesis can cause many of the signs and symptoms of pregnancy, and often resembles the condition in every way except for the presence of a fetus.

Description

Pseudocyesis has been observed and written about since antiquity. Hippocrates set down the first written account around 300 B.C., and recorded 12 different cases of women with the disorder. One of the most famous historical examples is Mary Tudor (1516-1558), Queen of England, who believed on more than one occasion that she was pregnant when she was not. Some even attribute the violence that gave her the nickname "Bloody Mary" as a reaction to the disappointment of finding out that she was not carrying a child. Other historians believe that the queen's physicians mistook fibroid tumors in her uterus for a pregnancy, as fibroids can enlarge a nonpregnant uterus.

Pseudocyesis has become increasingly rare in many parts of the world in which accurate pregnancy tests have become widely available. Cultures that place high value on pregnancy, or that make close associations between fertility and a person's worth, still have high rates of the disorder.

KEY TERMS

Cervix—The neck or narrow lower end of the uterus. Softening of the cervix is one of the signs of pregnancy.

Distension—The condition of being stretched or expanded, as the abdomen of a pregnant woman.

Quickening—A term that refers to the movements or other signs of life of a fetus in the womb.

Signs and symptoms

The symptoms of pseudocyesis are similar to the symptoms of true pregnancy and are often hard to distinguish from such natural signs of pregnancy as morning sickness, tender breasts, and weight gain. Many health care professionals can be deceived by the symptoms associated with pseudocyesis. Eighteen percent of women with pseudocyesis were at one time diagnosed as pregnant by a medical professional. In some cases, the only difference between pregnancy and pseudocyesis is the presence of a fetus.

The sign of pseudocyesis that is common to all cases is that the affected patient is convinced that she is pregnant. Abdominal distension is the most common physical symptom of pseudocyesis (63– 97% of women are found to experience this). The abdomen expands in the same manner as it does during pregnancy, so that the affected woman looks pregnant. This phenomenon is thought to be caused by buildup of gas, fat, feces, or urine. These symptoms often resolve under general anesthesia and the woman's abdomen returns to its normal size.

The second most common physical sign of pseudocyesis is menstrual irregularity (56–98% of women experience this). Between 48% and 75% of women are also reported to experience the sensation of fetal movements known as quickening, even though there is no fetus present. Some of the other common signs and symptoms include: gastrointestinal symptoms, breast changes or secretions, labor pains, uterine enlargement, and softening of the cervix. One percent of women eventually experience false labor.

Causes

No single theory about the causes of pseudocyesis is universally accepted by mental health professionals. The first theory attributes the false pregnancy to emotional conflict. It is thought that an intense desire to become pregnant, or an intense fear of becoming pregnant, can create internal conflicts and changes in the endocrine system, which may explain some of the symptoms of pseudocyesis. The second theory concerns wish-fulfillment. It holds that if a women desires pregnancy badly enough she may interpret minor changes in her body as signs of pregnancy. The third leading theory is the depression theory, which maintains that chemical changes in the nervous system associated with some depressive disorders could trigger the symptoms of pseudocyesis.

Demographics

The rate of pseudocyesis in the United States has declined significantly in the past century. In the 1940s there was one occurrence for approximately every 250 pregnancies. This rate has since dropped to between one and six occurrences for every 22,000 births. The average age of the affected woman is 33, though cases have been reported for women as young as 6-1/2 and as old as 79. More than two-thirds of women who experience pseudocyesis are married, and about one-third have been pregnant at least once. Women who have been victims of incest may be at greater risk for developing pseudocyesis. Pseudocyesis is found in some mammals other than humans—most often cats, dogs, and rabbits.

Treatment

Because pseudocyesis is not known to have a direct underlying physical cause, there are no general recommendations regarding treatment with medications. In some cases, however, the patient may be given medications for such symptoms as the cessation of menstruation. Because most patients with pseudocyesis have underlying psychological problems, they should be referred to a psychotherapist for the treatment of these problems. It is important at the same time, however, for the treating professional not to minimize the reality of the patient's physical symptoms.

The treatment that has had the most success is demonstrating to the patient that she is not really pregnant by the use of ultrasound or other imaging techniques.

Alternative therapies

There have been reports of patients being cured of pseudocyesis by hypnosis, purgatives, massage, opioids, or after nine months of symptoms, by experiencing "hysterical childbirth," but there are few data available on the effectiveness of these or similar procedures.

Prognosis

Symptoms of pseudocyesis generally last from a few months to a few years. In most cases, symptoms last for a full nine months. There is a high success rate for treatments involving **psychotherapy**, as it treats the underlying psychological causes of the disorder.

Resources

BOOKS

Knobil, Ernst, and Jimmy D. Neill, eds. *Encyclopedia of Reproduction.* New York: Academic Press, 1998.

Sadock, Benjamin J. and Virginia A. Sadock, eds. *Comprehensive Textbook of Psychiatry.* 7th ed. Vol. 2. Philadelphia: Lippincott Williams and Wilkins, 2000.

PERIODICALS

Hendricks-Matthews, Marybeth K., Douglas M. Hoy. "Pseudocyesis in an Adolescent Incest Survivor." *Journal of Family Practice* 36 no. 1 (January 1993): 97-104.

Paulman, Paul M., and Abdul Sadat. "Pseudocyesis." *Journal of Family Practice* 30 no. 5 (May 1990): 575-582.

OTHER

Aldrich, Knight, M.D. "Sixteenth-Century Psychosomatics." *Psychiatric News.* April 16 1999 (cited 15 March 2002). <www.psych.org/pnews/99-04-16/history.html>.

Tish Davidson, A.M.

Psychiatric assessment *see* **Assessment and diagnosis**

Psychiatrist

Definition

A psychiatrist is a physician who specializes in the **diagnosis** and treatment of mental disorders.

Description

Psychiatrists treat patients privately and in hospital settings through a combination of **psychotherapy** and medication. Their training consists of four years of medical school, followed by one year of internship and at least three years of psychiatric residency. Psychiatrists may receive certification from the American Board of Psychiatry and Neurology (ABPN), which requires two years of clinical experience beyond residency and the successful completion of a written and an oral test. Unlike a medical license, board certification is not legally required in order to practice psychiatry.

Psychiatrists may practice general psychiatry or choose a specialty, such as child psychiatry, geriatric psychiatry, treatment of substance abuse, forensic (legal) psychiatry, emergency psychiatry, **mental retardation**, community psychiatry, or public health. Some focus their research and clinical work primarily on psychoactive medication, in which case they are referred to as psychopharmacologists. Psychiatrists may be called upon to address numerous social issues, including juvenile delinquency, family and marital dysfunction, legal competency in criminal and financial matters, and treatment of mental and emotional problems among prison inmates and in the military.

Psychiatrists treat the biological, psychological, and social components of mental illness simultaneously. They can investigate whether symptoms of mental disorders have physical causes, such as a hormone imbalance or an adverse reaction to medication, or whether psychological symptoms are contributing to physical conditions, such as cardiovascular problems and high blood pressure. Because they are licensed physicians, psychiatrists—unlike psychologists and psychiatric social workers—can prescribe medication; they are also able to admit patients to the hospital. Other mental health professionals who cannot prescribe medication themselves often establish a professional relationship with a psychiatrist.

Psychiatrists may work in private offices, private psychiatric hospitals, community hospitals, state and federal hospitals, or community mental centers. Often, they combine work in several settings. In addition to their clinical work, psychiatrists often engage in related professional activities, including teaching, research, and administration. The American Psychiatric Association, the oldest medical specialty organization in the United States, supports the profession by offering continuing education and research opportunities, keeping members informed about new research and public policy issues, helping to educate the public about mental health issues, and serving as an advocate for people affected by mental illness.

Psychoanalysis

Definition

Psychoanalysis, as a form of therapy, is based on the understanding that human beings are largely unaware of the mental processes that determine their thoughts, feelings, and behavior, and that psychological suffering can be alleviated by making those processes known to the individual.

Sigmund Freud originally developed the theory and technique of psychoanalysis in the 1890s. Freud's ideas are still used in comptemporary practice; however, many have been further developed or refined and some even abandoned. The theory and technique of psychoanalyis contnues to integrate new insights about human development and behavior based on psychoanalytic research and discoveries from related fields. Different schools of psychoanalytic theory have evolved out of the original Freudian one, reflecting a variety of ideas and perspectives. Psychoanalysis is practiced by a trained psychoanalyst, also referred to as an analyst.

Purpose

Primary goals of psychoanalysis include symptom relief, increased self-awareness, and a more objective capacity for self-observation. Other aims might include improved relationships with others and the capacity to live a more deeply satisfying life. Typically, an individual seeks treatment in order to alleviate some difficulty, such as unhappiness in work or love, disturbances in mood or self-esteem, or troubling personality traits. With the exception of those that are physically based, psychoanalysis views such symptoms as related to unconscious mental processes, and because these mental forces are not within the individual's awareness, symptoms cannot be relieved with perseverance or with the help of friends or family. Through a slowly unfolding process, psychoanalysis demonstrates to the individual how unconscious mental processes affect current modes of thinking, feeling and interacting with others. It also demonstrates that these processes can be traced back to early experiences and relationships with caregivers and family members. This kind of insight enables the person to identify the sources of their sometimes troubling thoughts, feelings and behavior and, as a result, gives new meaning to current modes of functioning. This kind of transformation of character takes several years to accomplish due to the intense nature of the process. It requires a sacrifice of time, money, and mental energy. The resulting transformation offers the means for adaptive, enduring changes in

Patients often seek psychoanalysis to help them achieve a greater sense of self-understanding and personal satisfaction. *(Laurent/Meeus/BSIP/Science Source. Photo Researchers, Inc. Reproduced by permission.)*

personality. These are changes that enable the individual to live a more productive, satisfying and pleasurable life.

Precautions

The term "psychoanalyst" can be used by anyone, so it is important to know the credentials of an analyst prior to beginning treatment.

Credentials

In addition to having received advanced degrees in mental health (psychiatry, psychology, social work), trained psychoanalysts have also graduated from psychoanalytic training institutes. Institute training consists of three parts: course work on psychoanalytic theory and technique; supervised analyses (meaning that the candidate conducts analyses while being supervised by a seasoned psychoanalyst); and, third, candidates undergo a personal psychoanalysis. A personal analysis is considered a vital part of the training, as it enables candidates to learn about their own psychological processes. In turn, the knowledge enhances their capacity to treat others. This type of training program takes a minimum of four years to complete. Psychoanalysts also practice psychoanalytic **psychotherapy**, a less intensive form of treatment. It relies on the same theory of human development and a similar technique.

Description

In psychoanalysis, an individual in treatment is seen four to five times per week for 45- to 50-minute sessions. The individual lies comfortably on a couch while the analyst sits in a chair behind the person, out of view. The person is then asked to say whatever comes into his or her mind. Although this structure varies depending on the theory and style of the analyst, this is the most typical and traditional manner in which sessions are conducted. These conditions are maintained consistently, making it possible for thoughts and feelings to emerge that had once been outside of the person's awareness. The process of free associating, or saying whatever comes to mind, is challenging because people are taught at a young age to keep many ideas and feelings to themselves. When the analyst is out of view, it removes the possibility for eye contact, making it easier to speak spontaneously. Free association is also made easier by the analyst's nonjudgmental attitude—in listening to the individual, in the attention and interest given to seemingly unimportant details, and the objective and caring attitude with which the analyst understands the individual.

As the person speaks, unconscious sources of present-day difficulties gradually appear. Specifically, the analyst begins to notice repetitive aspects of behavior. Some of them may include particular subjects about which the person finds it hard to speak, as well as habitual ways in which the person relates to the psychoanalyst. The analyst begins to reveal these to the person in a gradual and thoughtful manner. Sometimes these revelations are accepted as correct and helpful. At other times they are rejected, corrected, or refined.

During the years of an analysis, the individual will grapple with new insights repeatedly, each time comprehending them in new ways. There will be an enhanced emotional and intellectual understanding, in addition to seeing matters from the perspective of different periods of life. As in all worthwhile learning processes, this one includes times of deep satisfaction and great frustration, periods of growth and regression. Overall, the analyst and individual work together to modify debilitating life patterns, to ameliorate troubling symptoms, and to release emotional and intellectual resources bound up in unconscious psychological processes. A transformation will occur eventually, and be one in which the person's understanding of themselves and of others, along with their productivity in work and capacity to love, changes in profound and enduring ways.

Who can benefit from psychoanalysis?

Anyone interested should seek a consultation with a psychoanalyst in order to determine if this treatment is appropriate. People often begin psychoanalysis also after having participated in psychoanalytic psychotherapy, which is a less intense form of treatment.

Individuals who are the most suited for psychoanalysis are those who have experienced satisfactions in work, with friends, in marriage, but who nonetheless experience a general dissatisfaction with their life—suffering from long-standing depression, anxiety, sexual difficulties, physical symptoms without physical basis, or typically feel isolated or alone. Some people need analysis because their habitual ways of living interfere with experiencing greater pleasure or productivity in life. Individuals need to be psychologically minded with an interest in becoming more self-aware, and a determination to forgo quick symptom relief in favor of a more gradual therapeutic process.

Psychoanalysis is also practiced with children and adolescents, with some variation in technique. Specifically, fantasy play and drawings are used with children in addition to verbal communication. During the treatment of children and young adolescents, parents are consulted on a regular basis so that the analyst can develop a more holistic understanding of the youngster's world. The goal of child and adolescent psychoanalysis is to alleviate symptoms and to remove any obstacles that interfere with normal development.

With other treatments

Psychoanalysis is used at times with other forms of treatment. Medication may be warranted in selected situations—if an individual suffers from a severe mood disturbance which interferes with his or her capacity to participate in treatment, for example. In general, medication is used as a tool that allows the individual to benefit from the psychoanalytic process; it is an adjunct therapy, while psychoanalysis is the primary curative one. There are also occasions in which psychoanalysis is provided concurrently with **couples therapy** or **family therapy** or with **group therapy**. Treatment recommendations, whether for psychoanalysis alone or in combination with couples, family, or group therapy, are based both on the individual's particular needs and the practice of the treating psychoanalyst.

Finally, psychoanalysis is not only a type of therapy. It is also a theory of human development from infancy to old age, a method for understanding thought processes. It offers a way of thinking about aspects of society and culture such as religion, prejudice, and war.

Normal results

Normal results include symptom relief and an enduring, adaptive change in personality.

Abnormal results

Some individuals do not benefit from this in-depth form of treatment. They instead experience increased distress, or do not progress after a sufficient amount of treatment sessions have elapsed. In these cases, people are typically transitioned to a less intensive form of treatment such as psychoanalytic psychotherapy.

Resources

BOOKS

Galatzer-Levy, Robert, M.D. *Does Psychoanalysis Work?* New Haven: Yale University Press, 2000.

Mitchell, Stephen A. and Margaret J. Black. *Freud and Beyond.* New York: Basic Books, 1995.

Oldham, John M., M.D. "Combining Treatment Modalities." In *Textbook of Psychoanalysis,* edited by Edward Nersessian, M.D. and Richard G. Kopff Jr., M.D. Washington, DC: American Psychiatric Press, Inc.,1996.

Weinshel, Edward M., M.D. and Owen Renik, M.D. "Psychoanalytic Technique." In *Textbook of Psychoanalysis* edited by Edward Nersessian, M.D and Richard G. Kopff, Jr., M.D. Washington, DC:American Psychiatric Press, Inc., 1996.

ORGANIZATIONS

American Psychoanalytic Association. 309 East 49th Street, New York, NY 10017. (212) 752-0450. <http://www.apsa.org>.

International Psychoanalytical Association. Broomhills, Woodside Lane, London N128UD.<http//www.ipa.org.uk>.

Susan Fine, Psy.D

Psychodynamic psychotherapy

Definition

Psychodynamic **psychotherapy** is a method of verbal communication used to help a person find relief from emotional pain. It is based on the theories and techniques of **psychoanalysis**. Psychodynamic psychotherapy is similar to psychoanalysis in that it attributes emotional problems to the patient's unconscious motives and conflicts. It differs from classical psychoanalysis, however, in that psychodynamic psychotherapists do not necessarily accept Freud's view that these unconscious motives and conflicts are ultimately sexual in nature.

Purpose

The goals of psychodynamic psychotherapy vary depending on the method of treatment, which can be broadly described as either expressive or supportive. Expressive therapy seeks to relieve symptoms through the development of insight, or the slowly developing awareness of feelings and thoughts that were once outside of the person's awareness. Expressive therapy is based on the rationale that difficulties experienced in adult life originate in childhood; that children do not possess the maturity for making effective choices nor the independence to do so; and that methods of adapting that were developed in childhood may no longer be effective for adapting to the world as an adult. Through guidance from a therapist, the adult becomes aware of present ways of coping that are ineffective and how they served a purpose in childhood that is no longer relevant. The person learns that he or she now has a range of new options for solving problems, and for living in general that are now based on his or her maturity and independence.

In contrast to expressive therapy which is exploratory, supportive therapy remains closer to the surface of the patient's issues. Supportive therapy is an approach that is used to relieve immediate distress; to return the person to his or her previous level of functioning; and to strengthen adaptive ways of coping that the individual already possesses in order to prevent further discomfort. Expressive and supportive methods of treatment are not completely separate categories because elements of supportive therapy are used in expressive treatment and vice versa, depending on the therapeutic need. For instance, if a person in exploratory treatment is experiencing distress, a supportive approach may be used for a period of time in order to help the person feel more stable.

While many patients benefit from individual psychotherapy alone, some instances call for such additional therapies as **family therapy**, **couples therapy**, or **group therapy** in combination with individual treatment. A second treatment modality might be recommended when the patient's progress in individual treatment is highly dependent on relationships with significant others or with interpersonal relationships in general. Psychotropic (mood- or behavior-altering) medication may also be prescribed as an adjunct (help) to treatment in order to manage disturbances in anxiety level, mood or thinking. Whether additional treatments are recommended is based on the needs of the individual.

People seek psychodynamic psychotherapy for a variety of reasons that include but are not limited to the following: prolonged sadness, anxiety, sexual difficulties, physical symptoms without physical basis, persistent feelings of isolation and loneliness, and the desire to be more successful in work or love. People seek therapy because they have not been able to develop a stable resolution for their difficulties on their own or with the help of friends and family members.

Description

Sessions of psychodynamic psychotherapy may be scheduled from one to three days per week, with greater frequency allowing for more in-depth treatment. The duration of individual sessions varies, but typically lasts for 45–50 minutes. It is not usually possible at the outset of treatment to estimate the number of sessions that will be necessary in order to achieve the person's goals. It is possible, however, for the person to make arrangements for a specific number of sessions.

Psychodynamic psychotherapy begins with a period of evaluation during which the client discusses with the therapist the reasons for seeking treatment. This process gives the therapist the opportunity to learn about the person, to develop an understanding of his or her troubles, and to formulate ideas about how treatment should proceed. This phase of interviewing and learning may take place in one session or over a series of sessions; or it may be done in a less structured manner, depending on the therapist's style. During the initial sessions, such factors as the frequency and length of sessions and the policy for payment will also be discussed. At some point within the first few sessions, the therapist and the individual will come to a mutual understanding of the goals for treatment. After this point, the sessions will become less like an interview; the person is asked to say whatever is on his or her mind. It is the therapist's job to listen and to help identify patterns of thinking, feeling and interacting that may be contributing to the patient's current struggles. Consequently, the person becomes more aware of his or her thoughts and feelings; learns how some present ways of coping are no longer adaptive even though they may have been necessary in childhood; and discovers that he or she as an adult has a greatly expanded repertoire of resources and can use far more effective ways of dealing with problems. Deeper awareness and new insights stimulate psychological growth and change.

Psychodynamic psychotherapy places great importance on the therapeutic dyad, which is a medical term for the relationship between the therapist and the patient. It is within the context of the therapeutic dyad that positive changes in the patient's outlook and behaviors are able to unfold. This relationship is unique because the therapist maintains a uniform, neutral and accepting stance. Unlike other well-intentioned people in the person's life, the therapist has been trained to listen objectively and without criticism. This therapeutic attitude makes it easier for the person seeking treatment to speak freely and to therefore provide as much information for the therapist to work with as is possible.

Treatment continues until the troubling symptoms have been reduced or alleviated and the person is consistently making use of more adaptive methods of coping with greater insight. For some people, this positive experience inspires them to proceed with further treatment in order to bring about additional adaptive changes. For others, meeting the initial goals will be sufficient. If so, the focus of sessions turns to issues related to the end of treatment. This final phase of treatment is as important as the beginning and middle stages because it allows the individual to develop insight about his or her therapeutic experience. People need time to clarify how they feel about leaving the therapeutic relationship, and this termination involves identifying and understanding feelings about separation, maturation, loss and change. The length of time allotted to the termination phase varies with the type of treatment and with the needs of the individual.

KEY TERMS

Adjunct—A form of treatment that is not strictly necessary to a therapy regimen but is helpful.

Expressive therapy—An approach to psychotherapy that seeks to relieve the patient's symptoms through exploration of previously unconscious material, leading to greater insight and more adaptive behaviors.

Modality—A term used in medicine for a method of treatment. For example, multimodal treatment plans make use of more than one treatment or therapeutic modality.

Psychotropic—Having an effect on the mind, brain, behavior, perceptions, or emotions. Psychotropic medications are used to treat mental illnesses because they affect a patient's moods and perceptions.

Supportive therapy—An approach to psychotherapy that seeks to encourage the patient or offer emotional support to him or her, and to return the patient to previous levels of functioning, as distinct from insight-oriented or educational approaches to treatment.

Therapeutic dyad—A term that refers to the two people involved in a psychotherapeutic relationship, namely the therapist and the person seeking treatment.

Normal results

After a course of psychodynamic psychotherapy has ended, the person should, overall, continue to handle difficulties in a more adaptive manner; experience improved interpersonal relationships and productivity at work; and continue to develop new insights into his or her thoughts, feelings and behavior. In supportive treatment, insight and personality change are not the primary goals of treatment; the therapist and patient work toward a continuation of general stability in the person's life.

Resources

BOOKS

Balsam, Rosemary Marshall, M.D., and Alan Balsam, M.D. *Becoming a Psychotherapist.* Chicago: The University of Chicago Press, 1984.

Dewald, Paul, M.D. "The Psychoanalytic Psychotherapies." In *Textbook of Psychoanalysis,* edited by Edward Nersessian, M.D. and Richard G. Kopff, M.D. Washington, DC: American Psychiatric Press, 1996.

Prochaska, James O., and John C. Norcross. *Systems of Psychotherapy: A Transtheoretical Analysis.* 4th edition. Pacific Grove: Brooks/Cole Publishing Company, 1999.

ORGANIZATIONS

American Psychoanalytic Association. 309 East 49th Street, New York, NY 10017. (212) 752-0450. <http://www.apsa.org>.

American Psychological Association. 750 First Street, NE, Washington D.C. 20002. (800) 374-2721. <http://www.apa.org>.

Susan Fine, Psy.D.

Psychologist

Definition

A psychologist is a social scientist who studies behavior and mental processes, generally in a research or clinical setting.

Description

As psychology has grown and changed throughout history, it has been defined in numerous ways. As early as 400 B.C., the ancient Greeks philosophized about the relationship of personality characteristics to physiological traits. Since then, philosophers have proposed theories to explain human behavior. In the late nineteenth century, the emergence of scientific method gave the study of psychology a new focus. In 1879, the first psychological laboratory was opened in Leipzig, Germany by Wilhelm Wundt, and soon afterwards the first experimental studies of memory were published. Wundt was instrumental in establishing psychology as the study of conscious experience, which he viewed as made up of elemental sensations. In addition to the type of psychology practiced by Wundt—which became known as structuralism—other early schools of psychology were functionalism, which led to the development of behaviorism, and Gestalt psychology. The American Psychological Association was founded in 1892 with the goals of encouraging research, enhancing professional competence, and disseminating knowledge about the field.

With the ascendance of the Viennese neurologist Sigmund Freud and his method of **psychoanalysis** early in the twentieth century, emphasis shifted from conscious experience to unconscious processes investigated by means of free association and other techniques. According to Freud, behavior and mental processes were the result of mostly unconscious struggles within each person between the drive to satisfy basic instincts, such as sex or aggression, and the limits imposed by society. At the same time that Freud's views were gaining popularity in Europe, an American psychology professor, John B. Watson, was pioneering the behavioral approach, which focuses on observing and measuring external behaviors rather than the internal workings of the mind. B. F. Skinner, who spent decades studying the effects of reward and punishment on behavior, helped maintain the predominance of behaviorism in the United States through the 1950s and 1960s. Since the 1970s, many psychologists have been influenced by the cognitive approach, which is concerned with the relationship of mental processes to behavior. Cognitive psychology focuses on how people take in, perceive, and store information, and how they process and act on that information.

Additional psychological perspectives include the neurobiological approach, focusing on relating behavior to internal processes within the **brain** and nervous system, and the phenomenological approach, which is most concerned with the individual's subjective experience of the world rather than the application of psychological theory to behavior. While all these approaches differ in their explanations of individual behavior, each contributes an important perspective to the overall psychological understanding of the total human being. Most psychologists apply the principles of various approaches in studying and understanding human nature.

Along with several approaches to psychology there are also numerous, overlapping subfields in which these approaches may be applied. Most subfields can be categorized under one of two major areas of psychology referred to as basic and applied psychology. Basic psychology encompasses the subfields concerned with the advancement of psychological theory and research. Experimental psychology employs laboratory experiments to study basic behavioral processes shared by different species, including sensation, perception, learning, memory, communication, and motivation. Physiological psychology is concerned with the ways in which biology shapes behavior and mental processes, and developmental psychology is concerned with behavioral development over the entire life span. Other subfields include social psychology, quantitative psychology, and the psychology of personality.

Applied psychology is the area of psychology concerned with applying psychological research and theory to problems posed by everyday life. It includes clinical psychology, the largest single field in psychology.

Clinical psychologists—accounting for 40% of all psychologists—are involved in **psychotherapy** and psychological testing. Clinical psychologists are trained in research and often work in university or research settings, studying carious aspects of psychology. Like clinical psychologists, counseling psychologists apply psychological principles to diagnose and treat individual emotional and behavioral problems. Other subfields of applied psychology include school psychology, which involves the evaluation and placement of students; educational psychology, which investigates the psychological aspects of the learning process; and industrial and organizational psychology, which study the relationship between people and their jobs. Community psychologists investigate environmental factors that contribute to mental and emotional disorders; health psychologists deal with the psychological aspects of physical illness, investigating the connections between the mind and a person's physical condition; and consumer psychologists study the preferences and buying habits of consumers as well as their reactions to certain advertising.

In response to society's changing needs, new fields of psychology are constantly emerging. One new type of specialization, called environmental psychology, focuses on the relationship between people and their physical surroundings. Its areas of inquiry include such issues as the effects of overcrowding and noise on urban dwellers and the effects of building design. Another relatively new specialty is forensic psychology, involving the application of psychology to law enforcement and the judicial system. Forensic psychologists may help create personality profiles of criminals, formulate principles for jury selection, or study the problems involved in eyewitness testimony. Yet another emerging area is program evaluation, whose practitioners evaluate the effectiveness and cost efficiency of the programs.

Depending on the nature of their work, psychologists may practice in a variety of settings, including colleges and universities, hospitals and **community mental health** centers, schools, and businesses. A growing number of psychologists work in private practice and may also specialize in multiple subfields. Most psychologists earn a Ph.D. degree in the field, which requires completion of a four- to six-year post-bachelors' degree program offered by a university psychology department. The course of study includes a broad overview of the field, as well as specialization in a particular subfield, and completion of a dissertation and an internship (usually needed only for applied psychology, such as clinical, counseling, and school psychology). Students who intend to practice only applied psychology rather than conduct research have the option of obtaining a Psy.D. degree, which differs in the limited emphasis that is put on research and a dissertation that does not have to be based on an empirical research study.

Psychosis

Definition

Psychosis is a symptom of mental illness characterized by a radical change in personality and a distorted or diminished sense of objective reality.

Description

Psychosis appears as a symptom of a number of mental disorders, including mood and **personality disorders**, **schizophrenia**, **delusional disorder**, and substance abuse. It is also the defining feature of the psychotic disorders (i.e., **brief psychotic disorder**, **shared psychotic disorder**, psychotic disorder due to a general medical condition, and **substance-induced psychotic disorder**).

Patients suffering from psychosis are unable to distinguish the real from the unreal. They experience **hallucinations** and/or **delusions** that they believe are real, and they typically behave in an inappropriate and confused manner.

A mental illness can exhibited through various forms of psychosis, such as:

- *Delusions.* An unshakable and irrational belief in something untrue. Delusions defy normal reasoning, and remain firm even when overwhelming proof is presented to disprove them.
- *Hallucinations.* Psychosis causes false or distorted sensory experience that appear to be real. Psychotic patients often see, hear, smell, taste, or feel things that aren't there.
- *Disorganized speech.* Psychotic patients often speak incoherently, using noises instead of words and "talking" in unintelligible speech patterns.
- *Disorganized or catatonic behavior.* Behavior that is completely inappropriate to the situation or environment. Catatonic patients have either a complete lack of or inappropriate excess of motor activity. They can be completely rigid and unable to move (vegetative), or in constant motion. Disorganized behavior is unpredictable and inappropriate for a situation (such as screaming obscenities in the middle of class).

Paula Ford-Martin, M.A.

Psychosurgery

Definition

Psychosurgery is the treatment of a psychiatric disorder using surgical techniques to destroy **brain** tissue and is now rarely used.

Purpose

It is a last-resort treatment for extreme, debilitating, psychiatric disorders.

Description

Early psychosurgery—historical perspective

Ironically, brain surgery, a medical practice requiring extraordinary levels of skill and care, may be one of the oldest of all medical procedures. This surprising observation is supported by physical evidence dating back 40,000 years ago to Neolithic times. Archeologists have found numerous human skulls showing signs of a procedure called trepanation or trepanning—an operation in which a hole is cut through the bone that covers the brain (skull) in order to access the brain. A key feature of the wounds found in these ancient skulls is the smoothness and shininess around the edges of the holes. This is a clear sign of new bone growth and evidence that the person whose skull was opened not only survived the operation but lived months or even years afterwards while the bone regrew.

Having one's skull opened in a modern surgical setting is not taken lightly, even with the most modern surgical techniques. The prospect of undergoing the operation in the late Stone Age may appear to us to imply certain death. However, the survival rate of the operation was quite high. Close examination of archeological findings suggests that 75% of those who underwent the procedure lived long enough for new bone to grow around the opening. That number is actually higher than the survival rate for brain surgery during the nineteenth century, when Stone Age trepanned skulls were first identified. Brain surgery during the mid-1860s frequently resulted in infections that killed up to 75% of patients.

Trepanned skulls have been found all over the world, including sites in Peru, China, India, and France, and parts of the Middle East and Africa. While trepanning is an effective surgical technique for relieving pressure on the brain caused by bleeding, most archeologists suspect the operation was carried out in the Stone Age to achieve a different goal. Trepanning, they suspect, was performed to release evil spirits or demons, which the shamans or witch doctors of the time believed produced symptoms of what we know as mental disorders and, perhaps, diseases of the brain. The instruments used in trepanning were likely to have been made of obsidian, a very hard, glasslike, volcanic rock that can hold a very sharp cutting edge. There is also evidence that the end of a wooden stick, hardened by fire and turned back-and-forth rapidly while pressed against the skull may have served as a primitive, but effective, surgical drill.

Neuroscientist and author Elliot Valenstein believes that trepanning did not amount to intentional brain surgery. He quotes from the Latin text by the twelfth-century surgeon Roger of Salerno, who wrote: "For mania and melancholy, the skin of the top of the head should be incised in a cruciate fashion and the skull perforated to allow matter to escape."

A curious example of what might be called pseudo-psychosurgery occurred during the Middle Ages. Some unscrupulous individuals wandered across Europe convincing gullible people that mental disorders were caused by a "stone of madness." To fool others, these quacks faked operating on the brains of mentally ill individuals and, using sleight-of-hand, appeared to produce a real stone from the victim's head, thus "proving" their claim and effecting a "cure." No doubt, these frauds quickly moved on to other towns before their patients showed signs of continuing psychiatric symptoms.

The impetus for developing a radical treatment

Unfortunately, effective treatments for mental illnesses remained unavailable until the second half of the twentieth century. Before then, psychiatric "care" consisted mostly of imprisonment, **neglect**, restraint, and/or punishment. During the eighteenth century, more humane conditions of confinement were introduced, but effective treatments remained unavailable. Physicians were desperate for treatments that might make it easier to control violent and deranged patients.

By the end of the nineteenth century, researchers became aware of the role played by the frontal cortex—a part of the brain located behind the forehead—in behavior control. They discovered from the results of animal experiments and observing humans who suffered damage to this part of the brain that the frontal lobes affect emotions and behavior. This bit of knowledge, combined with the development of effective anesthesia, led to the first modern instances of psychosurgery during the 1890s. A Swiss surgeon named Gottlieb Burkhardt deliberately damaged the frontal lobes of six psychiatric patients in hopes of relieving psychiatric symptoms; at least one of his subjects died and the experimental surgery was discontinued amid criticism from other physicians.

Psychosurgery in the twentieth century

PREFRONTAL LEUCOTOMY. In 1900, an Estonian surgeon, Lodivicus Pussepp, picked up where Burkhardt left off. He cut nerve tracks leading from the frontal lobes to other parts of the brain in psychiatric patients, with unimpressive results. A decade later, he injected tissue-destroying chemicals into the frontal lobes of mentally ill patients through holes drilled over the frontal lobes. Although the procedure accomplished little or nothing in the way of therapy, Pussepp remained optimistic about the ability of this procedure to improve the condition of psychiatric patients. Interest in the frontal lobes as a target for treating mental disorders continued on a small scale until the heyday of psychosurgery began in the 1930s.

In 1935, researchers in the United States reported that damaging the frontal lobes and a nearby region of the brain called the prefrontal cortex could pacify a previously aggressive chimpanzee. A Portuguese **psychiatrist**, Antonio Egas Moniz, learned of these results and recruited neurosurgeon Almeida Lima to operate on some humans suffering from severe psychoses. Moniz's aim was to disconnect nerve pathways running from the frontal lobes to a part of the brain called the thalamus, which is located closer to the center of the brain. By cutting these connections, Moniz hypothesized that he could disconnect a neural circuit that ran from the frontal cortex to the thalamus and then to other parts of the brain's surface. He hoped that interrupting this pathway would disrupt the repetitive thoughts that Moniz believed were responsible for psychotic symptoms.

But as Elliot Valenstein writes in his book *Great and Desperate Cures, The Rise and Decline of Psychosurgery and Other Radical Treatments for Mental Illness*, "Although Moniz' rationale for prefrontal leucotomy was so vague as to constitute no theory at all, his explanation was repeated so often that it—like the emperor's new clothes in Hans Christian Andersen's famous story—acquired a veneer of truth and was accepted (or at least repeated) by many other people." Psychiatrists were so desperate for a treatment for severe cases of mental illness that they allowed themselves to support the use of a procedure that was unproven and increasingly subject to abuse.

Moniz and Lima called their procedure leucotomy. It involved trepanning the skull, one hole on each side of the head, inserting a wire knife and cutting the targeted nerve fibers. Results were mixed enough for Moniz to recommend that the procedure be reserved only for the most seriously mentally ill patients for whom no other course of care or treatment worked. Nevertheless, after 1936, use of the technique spread rapidly, with equally unimpressive results overall. With little evidence of effectiveness and facing opposition from many psychiatrists, particularly psychotherapists, the technique would probably have been abandoned were it not for a pair of American physicians who revived the questionable procedure.

THE PREFRONTAL LOBOTOMY. American neurologist Walter Freeman and neurosurgeon James Watts began operating on patients in 1936 and soon began aggressively promoting its effectiveness. Eventually, they overcame doubts expressed by their colleagues who somewhat reluctantly accepted the procedure now referred to as prefrontal lobotomy. In 1946, Freeman simplified Moniz's leucotomy procedure, reducing it to a less complicated, less messy, and less time-consuming operation known as the "ice-pick lobotomy." This allowed Freeman to line up patients and, under local anesthesia, tap an ice pick through the thin bone on the roof of their eye sockets. With the ice pick in the brain, Freeman would sweep it back and forth to cut the frontal lobe's connections to the rest of the brain. This in-and-out procedure required no **hospitalization** but many physicians viewed it with alarm. Watts himself refused to cooperate with Freeman after this technique was developed.

Still, in the 1940s, U.S. physicians performed an estimated 18,000 lobotomies. It was equally popular in other countries where more than 50,000 operations were conducted during the same period. Sadly, Moniz's warning was forgotten. The procedure was not reserved for the most hopeless cases but instead applied to "difficult" patients and became a way to control behavior rather than to relieve symptoms of mental disorder. The abuse often bordered on the criminal. Yet, Moniz received the 1949 Nobel Prize for Medicine and Physiology for pioneering the procedure.

KEY TERMS

Frontal lobes—A region of the brain that influences higher mental functions often associated with intelligence, such as the ability to foresee the consequences of actions, planning, comprehension, and mood.

Leucotomy or leukotomy—White matter cutting; severing the white matter of the frontal lobe of the brain.

Lobotomy—A surgical procedure involving the cutting of nerve fiber bundles in the brain.

Trepanation or trepanning—Surgical removal of a piece of the skull to expose the brain.

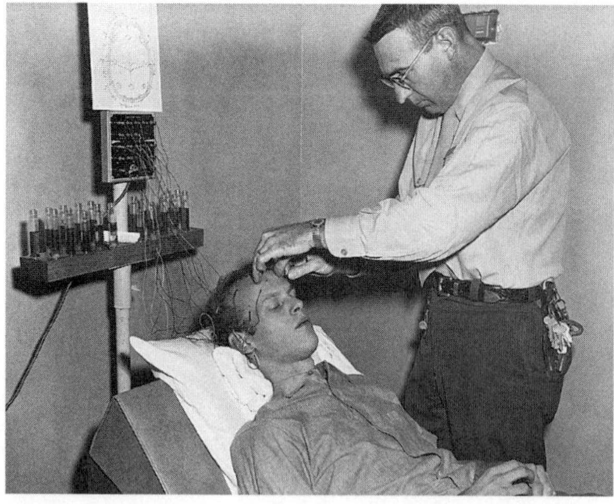

Prisoner at Vacaville Penitentiary in California being prepared for a lobotomy in 1961. At the time, many psychiatrists believed that "criminal" behavior was lodged in certain parts of the brain, and lobotomies were frequently practiced on prisoners. *(Ted Streshinsky/ CORBIS. Reproduced by permission.)*

Fortunately, but still too late, critics of the operation began to convince others that there was no scientific proof that lobotomies helped mentally ill patients. It could certainly calm violent patients but it did so at a terrible cost. As one nurse who recently treated an aged patient who had been lobotomized years before said, "You look in her eyes and you see there is no one there." Victims of the procedure lack emotions, ambition, social skills, and the ability to plan. The operation was used to control the mentally ill and others, such as uncontrollable children and political dissidents, whose behavior did not conform to society's standards. Arguments against the procedure were powerful: it permanently and severely damaged the brain and often produced unreactive, lifeless individuals whose personalities were forever destroyed. With the introduction of psychotherapeutic drugs—especially **chlorpromazine** (Thorazine)—in the mid-1950s, lobotomies fell out of fashion.

Psychosurgery today

No one advocates the use of classical lobotomies today as a treatment for mental disorders. However, a small minority of neurologists advocates the use of very precise surgical techniques to produce small lesions in defined areas of the brain to treat rare cases of severe mental illness such as life-threatening depression or incapacitating anxiety or obsessions. However, there is little need for such procedures today. Antipsychotic and antidepressant medications are the treatments of choice for treating mental disorders. Mainstream medicine now classifies psychosurgery as an experimental procedure, and many rules exist to protect patients who might be subjected to it. The majority of mental health professionals believe that psychosurgery is either never justified or should only be considered as a last resort, to be reserved for the most extreme cases of untreatable mental disease when all other therapies have failed.

Resources

BOOKS

Pressman, Jack D. *Last Resort: Psychosurgery and the Limits of Medicine.* New York, NY: Cambridge University Press, 1998.

Valenstein, Elliot S. *Great and Desperate Cures, The Rise and Decline of Psychosurgery and Other Radical Treatments for Mental Illness.* New York: Basic Books, 1986.

Valenstein, Elliot S., ed. *The Psychosurgery Debate.* San Francisco: W.H. Freeman, 1980.

Woods, Michael and Mary B. Woods. *Ancient Medicine, From Sorcery to Surgery.* Minneapolis: MN: Runestone Press, 2000.

ORGANIZATIONS

American Psychiatric Association. 1400 K Street NW, Washington D.C. 20005. <http://www.psych.org>.

Dean A. Haycock, Ph.D.

Psychotherapy

Definition

The treatment of mental or emotional disorders and adjustment problems through the use of psychological techniques rather than through physical or biological means.

Description

Psychoanalysis, the first modern form of psychotherapy, was called the "talking cure," and the many varieties of therapy practiced today are still characterized by their common dependence on a verbal exchange between the counselor or therapist and the person seeking help. The therapeutic interaction is characterized by mutual trust, with the goal of helping individuals change destructive or unhealthy behaviors, thoughts, and emotions. It is common for experienced therapists to combine several different approaches or techniques.

Psychodynamic approach

Freudian psychoanalysis places emphasis on uncovering unconscious motivations and breaking down defenses. Therapy sessions may be scheduled once or even twice a week for a year or more. This type of therapy is appropriate when internal conflicts contribute significantly to a person's problems.

Behavioral techniques

In contrast to the psychodynamic approach, behavior-oriented therapy is geared toward helping people see their problems as learned behaviors that can be modified, without looking for unconscious motivations or hidden meanings. According to the theory behind this approach, once behavior is changed, feelings will change as well. Probably the best-known type of behavioral therapy is **behavior modification**, which focuses on eliminating undesirable habits by providing positive **reinforcement** for the more desirable behaviors.

Another behavioral technique is **systematic desensitization**, in which people are deliberately and gradually exposed to a feared object or experience to help them overcome their fears. A person who is afraid of dogs may first be told to visualize a dog, then is given a stuffed toy dog, then exposed to a real dog seen at a distance, and eventually forced to interact with a dog at close range. Relaxation training is another popular form of behavior therapy. Through such techniques as deep breathing, visualization, and progressive muscle relaxation, clients learn to control fear and anxiety.

Cognitive methods

Some behavior-oriented therapy methods are used to alter not only overt behavior, but also the thought patterns that drive it. This type of treatment is known as **cognitive-behavioral therapy** (or just cognitive therapy). Its goal is to help people break out of distorted, harmful patterns of thinking and replace them with healthier ones. Common examples of negative thought patterns include magnifying or minimizing the extent of a problem; "all or nothing" thinking (i.e., a person regards himself as either perfect or worthless); overgeneralization (arriving at broad conclusions based on one incident, for example); and personalization (continually seeing oneself as the cause or focus of events).

In cognitive-behavioral therapy, a therapist may talk to the client, pointing out illogical thought patterns, or use a variety of techniques, such as thought substitution, in which a frightening or otherwise negative thought is driven out by substituting a pleasant thought in its place. Clients may also be taught to use positive self-talk, a repetition of positive affirmations. Cognitive therapy usually takes a longer amount of time as it treats more serious problems.

Couples therapy

Couples therapy focuses on the relationship between two people, typically who have a romantic or sexual connection. The therapy aims to concentrate on the problems of the relationship and make each partner feel that they have an equal role. The therapy can be administered by either a male or female therapist, but many couples feel that having both a male and female therapist in the session is beneficial.

Family and group therapy

Family therapy has proven effective in treating a number of emotional and adjustment problems. While the client's immediate complaint is the initial focus of attention, the ultimate goal of family therapy is to improve the interaction between all family members and enhance communication and coping skills on a long-term basis (although therapy itself need not cover an extended time period). **Group therapy**, which is often combined with individual therapy, offers the support and companionship of other people experiencing the same or similar problems and issues.

Therapy is terminated when the treatment goals have been met or if the client and/or therapist conclude that it is not working. It can be effective to phase out treatment by gradually reducing the frequency of therapy sessions. Even after regular therapy has ended, the client may return for periodic follow-up and reassessment sessions.

Psychotherapy integration

Definition

Psychotherapy integration is defined as an approach to **psychotherapy** that includes a variety of attempts to look beyond the confines of single-school approaches in order to see what can be learned from other perspectives. It is characterized by an openness to various ways of integrating diverse theories and techniques. Psychotherapy integration can be differentiated from an eclectic approach in that an eclectic approach is one in which a therapist chooses interventions because they work (the therapist relies solely on supposed efficacy) without looking for a theoretical basis for using the technique. The rationale of efficacy is reasonable, but it often is based on imprecise memories of past experience without any reference to theory or research data. In contrast, psychotherapy integration attends to the relationship between theory and technique.

Description

The term psychotherapy integration has been used in several different ways. The term has been applied to a Common Factors approach to understanding psychotherapy, to Assimilative Integration, to Technical Integration, and to Theoretical Integration.

Common Factors

Common Factors refers to aspects of psychotherapy that are present in most, if not all, approaches to therapy. These techniques cut across all theoretical lines and are present in all psychotherapeutic activities. Because the techniques are common to all approaches to psychotherapy, the name Common Factors has been given to this variety of psychotherapy integration. There is no standard list of common factors, but if a list were to be constructed, it surely would include:

- a therapeutic alliance established between the patient and the therapist
- exposure of the patient to prior difficulties, either in imagination or in reality
- a new corrective emotional experience that allows the patient to experience past problems in new and more benign ways
- expectations by both the therapist and the patient that positive change will result from the treatment
- therapist qualities, such as attention, empathy, and positive regard, that are facilitative of change in treatment
- the provision by the therapist to the patient of a reason for the problems that are being experienced

No matter what kind of therapy is practiced, each of these common factors is present. It is difficult to imagine a treatment that does not begin with the establishment of a constructive and positive therapeutic alliance. The therapist and the patient agree to work together and they both feel committed to a process of change occurring in the patient. Within every approach to treatment, the second of the common factors, the exposure of the patient to prior difficulties, is present. In some instances the exposure is in vivo (occurs in real life), and the patient will be asked directly to confront the source of the difficulties. In many cases, the exposure is verbal and in imagination. However, in every case, the patient must express those difficulties in some manner and, by doing so, re-experiences those difficulties through this exposure. In successful treatment, the exposure usually is followed by a new corrective emotional experience. The corrective emotional experience refers to a situation in which an old difficulty is re-experienced in a new and more positive way. As the patient re-experiences the problem in a new way, that problem can be mastered and the patient can move on to a more successful adjustment.

Having established a therapeutic alliance, and being exposed to the problem in a new and more positive context, both the therapist and the patient always expect positive change to occur. This faith and hope is a common factor that is an integral part of successful therapy. Without this hope and expectation of change, it is unlikely that the therapist can do anything that will be useful, and if the patient does not expect to change, it is unlikely that he or she will experience any positive benefit from the treatment. The therapist must possess some essential qualities, such as paying attention to the patient, being empathic with the patient, and making his positive regard for the patient clear in the relationship. Finally, the patient must be provided with a credible reason for the problems that he or she is undergoing. This reason is based in the therapist's theory of personality and change. The same patient going to different therapists may be given different reasons for the same problem. It is interesting to speculate as to whether the reason must be an accurate one or whether it is sufficient that it be credible to the patient and not remarkably at variance with reality. As long as the reason is credible and the patient has a way of understanding what previously had been incomprehensible, that may be sufficient for change to occur.

Assimilative Integration

The second major approach to psychotherapy integration is Assimilative Integration. Assimilative Integration is an approach in which the therapist has a commitment to one theoretical approach but also is willing to use techniques from other therapeutic approaches.

As an example, a therapist may try to understand patients in terms of psychodynamic theory, because he or she finds this most helpful in understanding what is going on in the course of the treatment. However, the therapist may also recognize that there are techniques that are not suggested by psychodynamic theory that work very well, and these may then be used in the treatment plan. The psychodynamic therapist can occasionally use cognitive-behavioral techniques such as homework, and may occasionally use humanistic approaches, such as a two-chair technique, but always retains a consistent psychodynamic understanding. The treatment can take place in a way that is beneficial to the patient and is not bound by the restrictions of the therapist's favorite way of intervening. The patient may not be aware that integration is taking place, but he or she does feel that a consistent approach is being maintained. Most patients are not familiar with theory, don't realize that different techniques are generated by different theoretical understandings, and only are concerned with whether or not the treatment is helpful.

Inherent in psychotherapy integration is the conviction that there is no one approach to therapy that is suitable to every patient. Both in single-school approaches and in psychotherapy integration, the treatment must be suitable for the individual patient. In making the treatment suitable for the individual patient, the therapist must understand the patient, and that establishes a place for theory. Assimilative Integration is particularly useful in that theory helps in the understanding of the needs of the patient, but then several different approaches to technique can help to design a treatment that fits that particular understanding. The treatment plan then must undergo continuous revision as the understanding of the patient gets fuller and deeper over the course of the treatment.

Technical Eclecticism

Technical Eclecticism is a variation of Assimilative Integration and is most common among those practitioners who refer to themselves as eclectic. In Technical Eclecticism, the same diversity of techniques is displayed as in Assimilative Integration, but there is no unifying theoretical understanding that underlies the approach. Rather, the therapist relies on previous experience and on knowledge of the theoretical and research literature to choose interventions that are appropriate for the patient.

The obvious similarity between Assimilative Integration and Technical Eclecticism is that both rely on a wide variety of therapeutic techniques, focusing on the welfare of the patient rather than on allegiance to any particular school of psychotherapy. The major difference between the two is that Assimilative Integration is bound by a unifying theoretical understanding whereas Technical Eclecticism is free of theory and relies on the experience of the therapist to determine the appropriate interventions.

Theoretical Integration

The fourth approach to psychotherapy integration is called Theoretical Integration. This is the most difficult level at which to achieve integration because it requires integrating theoretical concepts from different approaches, and these approaches may differ in their fundamental philosophy about human behavior. Whereas Assimilative Integration begins with a single theory and brings together techniques from different approaches, Theoretical Integration tries to bring together those theoretical approaches themselves and then to develop what in physics is referred to as a "Grand Unified Theory." Neither psychotherapists nor physicists have been successful to date in producing a Grand Unified Theory. It is difficult to imagine a theory that really can combine an approach that has one philosophical understanding with another approach that has a different philosophical understanding. For example, a psychodynamic approach believes that an early difficulty leads to a pattern of behavior that is repetitive, destructive, and nearly impossible to resolve. In contrast, behavior therapy sees problems as much more amenable to change. This difference may represent a basic incompatibility between the two theories. Therefore, theoretical integration would be faced with the task of integrating a theory about the stability of behavior with a theory about the ready changeability of behavior, and unless this obstacle can be overcome, Theoretical Integration will not be achieved.

Conclusions

In any case, the general point in three of these approaches, Common Factors, Assimilative Integration, and Theoretical Integration, is that there is a clear value to the role of theory in psychotherapy integration, whether the theory deals with the way integration works (Theoretical Integration), the framework that governs the choice of interventions (Assimilative Integration), or the organizing principle for understanding the Common Factors that are present in all psychotherapy. The fourth approach, Technical Eclecticism, is not concerned with theory, but does view the benefit of the patient to be of more significance than the adherence to any single theory.

Resources

BOOKS

Messer, S. B. "A critical examination of belief structures in interpretive and eclectic psychotherapy." In *Handbook of Psychotherapy Integration,* edited by J. C. Norcross and M. R. Goldfried. New York: Basic Books, 1992: 130-165.

Stricker, G., and J. Gold. (Eds.) *Comprehensive handbook of psychotherapy integration.* New York: Plenum, 1993.

PERIODICALS

Stricker, G. "Reflections on psychotherapy integration." *Clinical Psychology: Science and Practice* 1 (1994): 3-12.

Stricker, G., and J. R. Gold. "Psychotherapy integration: An assimilative, psychodynamic approach." *Clinical Psychology: Science and Practice* 3 (1996): 47-58.

Weinberger, J. "Common factors aren't so common: The common factors dilemma." *Clinical Psychology: Science and Practice* 2 (1995): 45-69.

George Stricker, Ph.D.

Pyromania

Definition

Pyromania is defined as a pattern of deliberate setting of fires for pleasure or satisfaction derived from the relief of tension experienced before the fire-setting. The name of the disorder comes from two Greek words that mean "fire" and "loss of reason" or "madness." The clinician's handbook, the ***Diagnostic and Statistical Manual of Mental Disorders**, also known as the* DSM, classifies pyromania as a disorder of impulse control, meaning that a person diagnosed with pyromania fails to resist the impulsive desire to set fires—as opposed to the organized planning of an arsonist or terrorist.

The position of the **impulse-control disorders** as a group within the *DSM-IV-TR* (*DSM,* fourth edition, text revised) diagnostic framework, however, has been questioned by some psychiatrists. The differential **diagnosis** of pyromania and the other five disorders listed under the heading of impulse-control problems (**intermittent explosive disorder**, **kleptomania**, pathological gambling, **trichotillomania**, and impulse-control disorder not otherwise specified) includes **antisocial personality disorder** (ASPD), mood disorders, conduct disorders (among younger patients), and temporal lobe epilepsy. It is not clear whether the impulse-control disorders derive from the same set of causes as ASPD and mood disorders, or whether "impulse-control disorder" is simply an all-inclusive category for disorders that are otherwise difficult to classify. Some American researchers would prefer to categorize pyromania and the other disorders of impulsivity as a subset of the obsessive-compulsive spectrum.

In addition, the relationship between pyromania in adults and firesetting among children and adolescents is not well defined as of 2002. Although pyromania is considered to be a rare disorder in adults, repeated firesetting at the adolescent level is a growing social and economic problem that poses major risks to the health and safety of other people and the protection of their property. In the United States, fires set by children and adolescents are more likely to result in someone's death than any other type of household disaster. The National Fire Protection Association stated that for 1998, fires set by juveniles caused 6,215 deaths, 30,800 injuries, and $11 billion in property damage. It is significant that some European psychiatrists question the *DSM-IV-TR* definition of pyromania as a disorder of impulse control precisely because of the connection they find between adolescent firesetting and similar behavior in adults. One team of German researchers remarked, "Repeated firesetting, resulting from being fascinated by fire, etc., may be less a disturbance of impulse control but rather the manifestation of a psychoinfantilism, which, supported by alcohol abuse, extends into older age." Pyromania is considered a relatively rare impulse-control disorder in the adult population in North America.

Description

Firesetting in children and adolescents

Although most cases of firesetting in the United States involve children or adolescents rather than adults, the *DSM-IV-TR* criteria for pyromania are difficult to apply to this population. Most younger firesetters are diagnosed as having conduct disorders rather than pyromania as *DSM-IV-TR* defines it; significantly, most of the psychiatric literature dealing with this age group speaks of "firesetting" rather than using the term "pyromania" itself.

Some observers have attempted to classify children and adolescents who set fires as either pathological or nonpathological. Youngsters in the former group are motivated primarily by curiosity and the desire to experiment with fire; some are teenagers playing "scientist." Most are between five and 10 years of age, and do not understand the dangers of playing with fire. Few of them have major psychological problems.

Those who are considered to be pathological firesetters have been further subdivided into five categories, which are not mutually exclusive:

- Firesetting as a cry for help. Youngsters in this category set fires as a way of calling attention to an intrapsychic problem such as depression, or an interpersonal problem, including parental separation and divorce or physical and sexual abuse.
- Delinquent firesetters. Firesetters in this category are most likely to be between the ages of 11 and 15. Their firesetting is part of a larger pattern of aggression, and may include vandalism and hate crimes. They are, however, more likely to damage property with their firesetting than to injure people.
- Severely disturbed firesetters. These youths are often diagnosed as either psychotic or paranoid, and appear to be reinforced by the sensory aspects of fire setting. Some set fires as part of **suicide** attempts.
- Cognitively impaired firesetters. This group includes youngsters whose impulse control is damaged by a neurological or medical condition such as fetal alcohol syndrome.
- Sociocultural firesetters. Youngsters in this group are influenced by antisocial adults in their community, and set fires in order to win their approval.

Pyromania in adults

Pyromania in adults resembles the other disorders of impulse control in having a high rate of comorbidity with other disorders, including substance abuse disorders, **obsessive-compulsive disorder** (OCD), anxiety disorders, and mood disorders. As of 2002, however, few rigorously controlled studies using strict diagnostic criteria have been done on adult patients diagnosed with pyromania or other impulse-control disorders.

Causes and symptoms

Causes

Most studies of causation regarding pyromania have focused on children and adolescents who set fires. Early studies in the field used the categories of Freudian **psychoanalysis** to explain this behavior. Freud had hypothesized that firesetting represented a regression to a primitive desire to demonstrate power over nature. In addition, some researchers have tried to explain the fact that pyromania is predominantly a male disorder with reference to Freud's notion that fire has a special symbolic relationship to the male sexual urge. A study done in 1940 attributed firesetting to fears of castration in young males, and speculated that adolescents who set fires do so to gain power over adults. The 1940 study is important also because it introduced the notion of an "ego triad" of firesetting, **enuresis** (bed-wetting), and cruelty to animals as a predictor of violent behavior in adult life. Subsequent studies have found that a combination of firesetting and cruelty to animals is a significant predictor of violent behavior in adult life, but that the third member of the triad (bed-wetting) is not.

INDIVIDUAL. The causes of firesetting among children and teenagers are complex and not well understood as of 2002. They can, however, be described in outline as either individual or environmental. Individual factors that contribute to firesetting include:

- Antisocial behaviors and attitudes. Adolescent firesetters have often committed other crimes, including forcible rape (11%), nonviolent sexual offenses (18%), and vandalism of property (19%).
- Sensation seeking. Some youths are attracted to firesetting out of boredom and a lack of other forms of recreation.
- Attention seeking. Firesetting becomes a way of provoking reactions from parents and other authorities.
- Lack of social skills. Many youths arrested for firesetting are described by others as "loners" and rarely have significant friendships.

KEY TERMS

Arson—The deliberate setting of fires for criminal purposes, usually to collect insurance money or to cover up evidence of another crime. It is distinguished from pyromania by its connection with planning and forethought rather than failure of impulse control.

Comorbidity—Association or presence of two or more mental disorders in the same patient. A disorder that is said to have a high degree of comorbidity is likely to occur in patients diagnosed with other disorders that may share or reinforce some of its symptoms.

Delusion—A false belief that is resistant to reason or contrary to actual fact. Common delusions include delusions of persecution, delusions about one's importance (sometimes called delusions of grandeur), or delusions of being controlled by others. Pyromania is excluded as a diagnosis if the patient is setting fires on the basis of a delusion.

Kleptomania—A disorder of impulse control characterized by repeated stealing or shoplifting of items that the person does not need.

Spontaneous remission—Recovery from a disease or disorder that cannot be attributed to medical or psychiatric treatments.

Trichotillomania—A disorder marked by repeated pulling and tugging of one's hair, usually resulting in noticeable hair loss on the scalp or elsewhere on the body.

- Lack of fire-safety skills and ignorance of the dangers associated with firesetting.

There are discrepancies between adult researchers' understanding of individual factors in firesetting and reports from adolescents themselves. One study of 17 teenaged firesetters, 14 males and three females, found six different self-reported reasons for firesetting: revenge, crime concealment, peer group pressure, accidental firesetting, **denial** of intention, and fascination with fire. The motivations of revenge and crime concealment would exclude these teenagers from being diagnosed with pyromania according to *DSM-IV-TR* criteria.

ENVIRONMENTAL. Environmental factors in adolescent firesetting include:

- Poor supervision on the part of parents and other significant adults.

- Early learning experiences of watching adults use fire carelessly or inapproriately.
- Parental **neglect** or emotional uninvolvement.
- Parental psychopathology. Firesetters are significantly more likely to have been physically or sexually abused than children of similar economic or geographic backgrounds. They are also more likely to have witnessed their parents abusing drugs or acting violently.
- Peer pressure. Having peers who smoke or play with fire is a risk factor for a child's setting fires himself.
- Stressful life events. Some children and adolescents resort to firesetting as a way of coping with crises in their lives and/or limited family support for dealing with crises.

Symptoms

Firesetting among children and adolescents and pyromania in adults may be either chronic or episodic; some persons may set fires frequently as a way of relieving tension, others apparently do so only during periods of unusual **stress** in their lives.

In addition to the outward behavior of firesetting, pyromania in adults has been associated with symptoms that include depressed mood, thoughts of suicide, repeated conflicts in interpersonal relationships, and poor ability to cope with stress.

Demographics

The true incidence of pyromania in the general American population remains unknown. Of the six impulse-control disorders listed in *DSM-IV-TR,* only trichotillomania and pathological gambling appear to be common in the general population (4% and 3% respectively). Pyromania, like intermittent explosive disorder and pathological gambling, is diagnosed more frequently in men than in women.

Repeated firesetting appears to be more common in children and adolescents than in adult males. In addition, the incidence appears to be rising in these younger age groups: in 1992, males 18 and younger accounted for 40% of arrests for firesetting; in 2001, they accounted for 55%. As of 1999, 89% of juvenile arrests for firesetting involved males; 79% involved Caucasian juveniles. Within the group of male juveniles, 67% were younger than age 15, and 35% younger than age 12.

Less is known about the incidence of pyromania among adults. Some researchers have theorized that children and adolescents attracted to firesetting when they are younger "graduate" in adult life to more serious crimes with a "macho" image, including serial rape and murder. A number of serial killers, including David Berkowitz, the "Son of Sam" killer, and David Carpenter, the so-called Trailside Killer of the San Francisco Bay area, turned out to have been firesetters in their adolescence. David Berkowitz admitted having started more than 2,000 fires in Brooklyn-Queens in the early 1970s.

Another hypothesis regarding pyromania in adults is that it is more likely to emerge in the form of workplace violence. The recent rapid increase in the number of workplace killings and other violent incidents— a 55% rise between 1992 and 1996— is a source of great concern to employers. One of the complications in the situation is that the Americans with Disabilities Act (ADA), passed by Congress in 1990, forbids employers to discriminate against workers with mental or physical disabilities as long as they are qualified to perform their job. Since 1996, the Equal Employment Opportunities Commission (EEOC) reports that the third-largest category of civil rights claims alleging employer discrimination concerns psychiatric disabilities. In 1997, the EEOC issued a set of guidelines on the ADA and psychiatric disabilities. Significantly, the EEOC excluded pyromania (along with kleptomania, compulsive gambling, disorders of sexual behavior, and the use of illegal drugs) from the list of psychiatric conditions for which employers are expected to make "reasonable accommodation." The EEOC's exclusion of pyromania indicates that workers with this disorder are considered a sufficiently "direct threat" to other people and property that employers are allowed to screen them out during the hiring process.

Diagnosis

DSM-IV-TR specifies six criteria that must be met for a patient to be diagnosed with pyromania:

- The patient must have set fires deliberately and purposefully on more than one occasion.
- The patient must have experienced feelings of tension or emotional arousal before setting the fires.
- The patient must indicate that he or she is fascinated with, attracted to, or curious about fire and situations surrounding fire (for example, the equipment associated with fire, the uses of fire, or the aftermath of firesetting).
- The patient must experience relief, pleasure, or satisfaction from setting the fire or from witnessing or participating in the aftermath.
- The patient does not have other motives for setting fires, such as financial motives; ideological convictions (such as terrorist or anarchist political beliefs); anger or revenge; a desire to cover up another crime; **delusions** or **hallucinations**; or impaired judgment resulting

from substance abuse, **dementia**, **mental retardation**, or traumatic **brain** damage.

- The fire setting cannot be better accounted for by antisocial personality disorder, a **conduct disorder**, or a manic episode.

Diagnosis of pyromania is complicated by a number of factors; one important factor is the adequacy of the diagnostic category itself. As was mentioned earlier, some psychiatrists are not convinced that the impulse-control disorders should be identified as a separate group, in that problems with self-control are part of the picture in many psychiatric disorders. **Bulimia nervosa**, **borderline personality disorder**, and antisocial personality disorder are all defined in part by low levels of self-control.

Another complication in diagnosis is the lack of experience on the part of mental health professionals in dealing with firesetting. In many cases they are either unaware that the patient is repeatedly setting fires, or they regard the pattern as part of a cluster of antisocial or dysfunctional behaviors.

Treatments

Children and adolescents

Treatment of children and adolescents involved with repeated firesetting appears to be more effective when it follows a case-management approach rather than a medical model, because many young firesetters come from chaotic households. Treatment should begin with a structured interview with the parents as well as the child, in order to evaluate stresses on the family, patterns of supervision and discipline, and similar factors. The next stage in treatment should be tailored to the individual child and his or her home situation. A variety of treatment approaches, including problem-solving skills, anger management, communication skills, aggression replacement training, and cognitive restructuring may be necessary to address all the emotional and cognitive issues involved in each case.

Adults

Pyromania in adults is considered difficult to treat because of the lack of insight and cooperation on the part of most patients diagnosed with the disorder. Treatment usually consists of a combination of medication— usually one of the selective serotonin reuptake inhibitors— and long-term insight-oriented **psychotherapy**.

Prognosis

The prognosis for recovery from firesetting among children and adolescents depends on the mix of individual and environmental factors involved. Current understanding indicates that children and adolescents who set fires as a cry for help, or who fall into the cognitively impaired or sociocultural categories, benefit the most from therapy and have fairly positive prognoses. The severely disturbed and delinquent types of firesetters have a more guarded outlook.

The prognosis for adults diagnosed wih pyromania is generally poor. There are some cases of spontaneous remission among adults, but the rate of spontaneous recovery is not known.

Prevention

Prevention of pyromania requires a broad-based and flexible approach to treatment of children and adolescents who set fires. In addition to better assessments of young people and their families, fire-safety education is an important preventive strategy that is often overlooked.

In addition to preventive measures directed specifically at firesetting, recent research into self-control as a general character trait offers hope that it can be taught and practiced like many other human skills. If programs could be developed to improve people's capacity for self-control, they could potentially prevent a wide range of psychiatric disorders.

Resources

BOOKS

American Psychiatric Association. *Diagnostic and Statistical Manual of Mental Disorders.* 4th edition, text revised. Washington, DC: American Psychiatric Association, 2000.

Baumeister, Roy F., PhD. "Crossing the Line: How Evil Starts." In *Evil: Inside Human Violence and Cruelty.* New York: W. H. Freeman and Company, 1999.

Douglas, John, and Mark Olshaker. *Mindhunter: Inside the FBI's Elite Serial Crime Unit.* New York: Simon and Schuster, 1995.

Lion, J. R., and A. W. Schienberg. "Disorders of Impulse Control." *Treatments of Psychiaric Disorders.* 2nd edition, edited by Glen O. Gabbard. Washington, DC: American Psychiatric Press, 1995.

PERIODICALS

Everall, Ian Paul, and Ann Leconteur. "Firesetting in an Adolescent Boy with Asperger's Syndrome. " *British Journal of Psychiatry* 157 (August 1990): 284–288.

Hollander, E., and J. Rosen. "Impulsivity." *Journal of Psychopharmacology* 14 (2000): S39–S44.

Laubichler W., A. Kuhberger, P. Sedlmeier. "'Pyromania' and Arson. A Psychiatric and Criminologic Data Analysis." [in German] *Nervenarzt* 67 (September 1996): 774–780.

Slavkin, Michael L. "Enuresis, Firesetting, and Cruelty to Animals: Does the Ego Triad Show Predictive Ability?" *Adolescence* 36 (Fall 2001): 535–540.

Slavkin, Michael L., and Kenneth Fineman. "What Every Professional Who Works with Adolescents Needs to Know About Firesetters. " *Adolescence* 35 (Winter 2000): 759-764.

Strayhorn, Joseph M., Jr. "Self-Control: Theory and Research." *Journal of the American Academy of Child and Adolescent Psychiatry* 41 (January 2002): 7–16.

Swaffer, Tracey, and Clive R. Hollin. "Adolescent Firesetting: Why Do They Say They Do It?" *Journal of Adolescence* 18 (October 1995): 619–624.

Zugelder, Michael T. "Dangerous Directives? Liability and the Unstable Worker." *Business Horizons* 42 (January-February 1999): 40–48.

ORGANIZATIONS

American Academy of Child and Adolescent Psychiatry. 3615 Wisconsin Avenue, NW, Washington, DC 20016-3007. (202) 966-7300. Fax: (202) 966-2891. <www.aacap.org>.

OTHER

Federal Emergency Management Agency. *Socioeconomic Factors and the Incidence of Fire.* Washington, DC: United States Fire Administration and National Fire Data Center, 1995.

Rebecca J. Frey, Ph.D.

Quazepam

Definition

Quazepam belongs to a class of drugs called benzodiazepines. These drugs ease anxiety and slow the central nervous system. In the United States quazepam is sold under brand name Doral.

Purpose

Quazepam is approved by the United States Food and Drug Administration for the treatment of **insomnia**.

Description

Quazepam is unique in its drug properties in two ways. Several medications from the same class of drugs have an effect called rebound insomnia. This means that the insomnia becomes worse than the original insomnia when the drug is used for extended periods. Quazepam has a minimal tendency to cause rebound insomnia. Secondly, quazepam is eliminated from the body slowly. This gives quazepam advantage over certain other medications in the benzodiazepine class, such as **alprazolam** or halazepam, in that patients do not experience early-morning insomnia, since there is still enough medication to induce sleep in the very early morning hours.

Quazepam's sedating effect that reduces insomnia lasts only for about four weeks of continuous use. The medication is most effective for an intermediate-term treatment of insomnia (two weeks), rather than a long duration of treatment of over four weeks. Hence, long-term treatment for insomnia with quazepam should be avoided.

Quazepam comes in 7.5-mg and 15-mg tablets.

Recommended dosage

Effective doses of quazepam for the treatment of insomnia range from 7.5 mg to 30 mg at bedtime. Most patients start by taking 15 mg at bedtime. Adjustments from this dosage can be made as determined by individual. In some patients, a dosage as low as 7.5 mg is sufficient to reduce insomnia.

Elderly patients (over age 65) should receive a reduced dosage of 7.5 mg, because it takes a longer time to eliminate the drug from their bodies. Because quazepam is eliminated by the liver, dosage reduction may be necessary in patients with liver problems.

Precautions

Patients who have a condition known as sleep apnea should not use quazepam. This condition involves episodes of breathing difficulty and oxygen deficiency that occur throughout the night. Patients who are pregnant or who had an allergic reaction to quazepam should not take quazepam

People who need to remain mentally alert such as those who are driving or operating dangerous machinery, need to take quazepam with caution as it may cause drowsiness. This effect is intensified when quazepam is taken with alcohol. It is best not to drink alcoholic beverages while taking quazepam. Patients with compromised respiratory function (breathing problems), as well as patients with a history of drug or alcohol abuse, should closely be monitored during the short-term treatment with quazepam.

Side effects

The effects of quazepam taken at bedtime may last, or hang over, into the next day. This is the most common side effect of quazepam. The symptoms of this condition include drowsiness, daytime sleepiness, slurred speech, and mental sluggishness. This effect is dose related, and seems to occur most frequently in patients taking 30-mg doses. These effects are experienced less commonly with the 15-mg dose, but this dose may not be effective in

KEY TERMS

Benzodiazepines—A group of central nervous system depressants used to relieve anxiety or to induce sleep.

eliminating insomnia some patients. Some people experience headache and dizziness when taking quazepam.

A small number of patients experience dry mouth, weight loss, abnormal taste perception, abdominal pain, nausea, vomiting, and either diarrhea or constipation due to quazepam. These effects occur in about 1% to 10% of people taking the drug.

Side effects that occur in less than 1% of patients include skin problems, such as rash or skin inflammation, muscle cramps, rigidity, and blurred vision.

Interactions

Cimetidine (Tagamet) and ketoconazole increase the levels of quazepam in the body, potentially causing toxicity or increased side effects.

Theophylline decreases the effectiveness of quazepam. **Valerian**, **kava kava**, and alcohol cause increased central nervous depression, which may increase sedation, drowsiness, and slowed reflexes if used while taking quazepam.

Resources

BOOKS

Gilman, Alfred G. *The Pharmacological Basis of Therapeutics*. McGraw-Hill, 1996.

Kaplan, Harold. *Comprehensive Textbook of Psychiatry*. Williams and Wilkins, 1995.

Lacy, Charles F. *Drug Information Handbook*. Lexi-Comp, Inc. 2002.

Ajna Hamidovic, Pharm.D.

Quetiapine

Definition

Quetiapine is an atypical antipsychotic drug used to treat symptoms of **schizophrenia**. It is available with a prescription under the trade name Seroquel.

Purpose

Quetiapine is classified as an atypical antipsychotic. It is used to treat psychotic disorders such as schizophrenia.

Description

Quetiapine is thought to modify the actions of several chemicals in the **brain**. It is chemically related to another atypical antipsychotic agent, **clozapine**, but differs both chemically and pharmacologically from the earlier phenothiazine antipsychotics.

It is available 25-mg, 100-mg, and 200-mg tablets.

Recommended dosage

Initially, a dosage of 25 mg should be taken twice a day. Each dose should be increased by 25-50 mg increments every three to four days until a target dose of 300-400 mg per day, administered in two or three divided doses, is achieved. It is not known whether doses higher than 800 mg per day are safe.

Precautions

Caution should be used in patients with heart disease because the drug may cause blood pressure to fall too low resulting in dizziness, rapid heartbeat, or fainting.

Quetiapine may cause liver damage. As a result, patients should notify their health care provider if they experience flu-like symptoms, notice yellowing of their skin or eyes, or experience abdominal pain. Liver function should be assessed periodically. The drug should be used cautiously in people with a history of liver disease or alcoholic cirrhosis.

Quetiapine may alter the function of the thyroid gland. Those taking supplements for low thyroid function may require dosage adjustments in their thyroid medication.

Quetiapine may increase cholesterol levels and contribute to the formation of cataracts. Because of this possibility, cholesterol levels should be checked periodically and yearly eye exams should be performed.

Quetiapine should be used carefully in those with a history of seizure disorders because it may increase the tendency to have **seizures**.

Quetiapine may cause extreme drowsiness and should be used carefully by people who need to be mentally alert.

Quetiapine should not be taken while pregnant or breast-feeding.

Side effects

Relatively common side effects that accompany quetiapine include drowsiness, dizziness, rash, dry mouth, **insomnia**, **fatigue**, muscular weakness, anorexia, blurred vision, some loss of muscular control, and amenorrhea (lack of menstruation) in women.

Dystonia (difficulty walking or moving) may occur with quetiapine use. This condition may subside in 24 to 48 hours even when the person continues taking the drug and usually disappears when quetiapine is discontinued.

Quetiapine use may lead to the development of symptoms that resemble Parkinson's disease. These symptoms may include a tight or mask-like expression on the face, drooling, tremors, pill-rolling motions in the hands, cogwheel rigidity (abnormal rigidity in muscles characterized by jerky movements when the muscle is passively stretched), and a shuffling gait. Taking anti-Parkinson drugs **benztropine** mesylate or **trihexyphenidyl** hydrochloride along with the quetiapine usually controls these symptoms.

Quetiapine has the potential to produce a serious side effect called **tardive dyskinesia**. This syndrome consists of involuntary, uncoordinated movements that may appear late in therapy and may not disappear even after the drug is stopped. Tardive dyskinesia involves involuntary movements of the tongue, jaw, mouth or face or other groups of skeletal muscles. The incidence of tardive dyskinesia increases with increasing age and with increasing dosage of quetiapine. Women are at greater risk than men for developing tardive dyskinesia. There is no known effective treatment for tardive dyskinesia, although gradual (but rarely complete) improvement may occur over a long period.

An occasionally reported side effect of quetiapine is neuroleptic malignant syndrome. This is a complicated and potentially fatal condition characterized by muscle rigidity, high fever, alterations in mental status, and cardiac symptoms such as irregular pulse or blood pressure, sweating, tachycardia (fast heartbeat), and arrhythmias (irregular heartbeat). People who think they may be experiencing any side effects from this or any other medication should talk to their physician promptly.

Interactions

Quetiapine may be less effective when it is taken with drugs like **carbamazepine** (Tegretol), phenytoin (Dilantin), rifampin (Rifadin), **barbiturates**, **thioridazine** (Mellaril), or corticosteroids such as prednisolone, methlylprednisolone, prednisone, and dexamethasone because these drugs increase the breakdown of quetiapine in the liver causing lower-than-normal levels of the drug.

Antifungal drugs such as fluconazole (Diflucan) or ketoconazole (Nizerol), antibiotics such as erythromycin or clarithromycin (Biaxin), and cimetidine (Tagamet), because these drugs may decrease the breakdown of quetiapine in the liver causing higher-than-normal levels of the drug.

Any drug that causes drowsiness may lead to decreased mental alertness and impaired motor skills when taken with Quetiapine. Some examples include alcohol, antidepressants such as **imipramine** (Tofranil) or **paroxetine** (Paxil), antipsychotics such as thioridazine (Mellaril), and some antihistamines.

KEY TERMS

Neuroleptic malignant syndrome—An unusual but potentially serious complication that develops in some patients who have been treated with antipsychotic medications. NMS is characterized by changes in blood pressure, altered states of consciousness, rigid muscles, and fever. Untreated NMS can result in coma and death.

Parkinsonian—Related to symptoms associated with Parkinson's disease, a nervous system disorder characterized by abnormal muscle movement of the tongue, face, and neck, inability to walk or move quickly, walking in a shuffling manner, restlessness, and/or tremors.

Schizophrenia—A severe mental illness in which a person has difficulty distinguishing what is real from what is not real. It is often characterized by hallucinations, delusions, language and communication disturbances, and withdrawal from people and social activities.

Tardive dyskinesia—A condition that involves involuntary movements of the tongue, jaw, mouth or face or other groups of skeletal muscles that usually occurs either late in antipsychotic therapy or even after the therapy is discontinued. It may be irreversible.

Resources

BOOKS

AstraZeneca Staff. *Seroquel Package Insert.* Wilmington, DE: AstraZeneca Pharmaceuticals LP, 2001.

Ellsworth, Allan J., and others, eds. *Mosby's Medical Drug Reference*. St. Louis, MO: Mosby, Inc, 1999.

Facts and Comparisons Staff. *Drug Facts and Comparisons*. 6th Edition. St. Louis, MO: Facts and Comparisons, 2002.

Kelly Karpa, RPh, Ph.D.

Rational behavior therapy *see* **Rational emotive therapy**

Rational emotive therapy

Definition

Rational emotive therapy (RET) is a psychotherapeutic approach which proposes that unrealistic and irrational beliefs cause many emotional problems.

Purpose

RET is a form of **cognitive-behavioral therapy** (CBT). The primary focus of this treatment approach is to suggest changes in thinking that will lead to changes in behavior, thereby alleviating or improving symptoms. The therapy emphasizes changing irrational thinking patterns that cause emotional distress into thoughts that are more reasonable and rational. RET can be used to treat people affected from disorders such as anxiety, depression and stess.

Precautions

There are no major precautions, except that persons entering treatment must be willing to change behaviors that promote symptoms.

Description

Rational emotive therapy was developed by Albert Ellis in the mid-1950s. Ellis proposed that people become unhappy and develop self-defeating habits because of unrealistic or faulty beliefs. In research reports from Ellis in 1979 and 1987 he introduced the model that most irrational beliefs originate from three core ideas, each one of which is unrealistic. These three core and unrealistic views include: 1) I must perform well to be approved of by others who are perceived significant; 2) you must treat me fairly—if not, then it is horrible and I cannot bear it; 3) conditions must be my way and if not I cannot stand to live in such a terrible and awful world. These irrational thoughts can lead to **grief** and needless suffering.

As a therapy, RET is active. The RET therapist strives to change irrational beliefs, challenge thinking, and promote rational self-talk, and various strategies are used to achieve these goals. These strategies may include: disputing irrational beliefs (the therapist points out how irrational it would be for a client to believe he or she had to be good at everything to be considered a worthwhile person), reframing (situations are viewed from a more positive angle), problem solving, role-playing, **modeling**, and the use of humor. The client may also be requested to complete certain exercises at home, and **bibliotherapy** (reading about the disorder) may also be used as components of RET.

Preparation

Before a client begins RET, he or she may undergo an assessment with the therapist. This assessment is called a biopsychosocial assessment, consisting of a structured interview. The questions and information-gathering during this assessment typically cover areas such as past medical and psychological history, family and social history, sex and drug history, employment and education history and criminal history. The interview provides information for a **diagnosis** or a tentative diagnosis that requires further testing or consultation.

Aftercare

Aftercare may or may not be indicated. This is usually decided on between the patient and mental health practitioner. Aftercare follow-up may be recommended if the affected person is at risk of relapse behaviors (returning to old behaviors that the client had sought to change).

Risks

There are no real risks associated with RET. There is a possibility that treatment may not benefit the affected person. This possibility becomes more likely for patients who have multiple psychological disorders.

Normal results

The person undergoing RET will begin to understand the repetitive patterns of irrational thoughts and disruption caused by symptoms. The individual in therapy will develop skills to improve his or her specific problems, and usual results include improved self-esteem and the development of a sense that life events change and that outcomes may not always be favorable.

Abnormal results

There are no abnormal results per se, but persons who are unwilling to change and adhere to treatment recommendations may not gain any new beneficial behaviors.

Resources

BOOKS

Coon, D. *Essentials of Psychology.* 7th ed. Pacific Grove: Brooks/Cole Publishing Company, 1997.

ORGANIZATIONS

The Albert Ellis Institute. 45 East 65th Street, New York, NY 10021. Telephone: (800) 323-4738.

Laith Farid Gulli, M.D.
Nicole Mallory, M.S., PA-C

Reactive attachment disorder of infancy or early childhood

Definition

In reactive attachment disorder, the normal bond between infant and parent is not established or is broken. Infants normally "bond" or form an emotional attachment, to a parent or other caregiver by the eighth month of life. From about the second through the eighth month, most infants will respond to attention from a variety of caregivers, if the caregivers are familiar. By the eighth month, however, normal infants have established a strong emotional preference for one or two primary caregivers. They are distressed if separated from these caregivers for even a few hours, even if another familiar person is present. If this bonding process is interfered with, it can have severe emotional and physical consequences for the child.

Reactive attachment disorder is sometimes called a post-traumatic disorder.

Description

In reactive attachment disorder, an infant or young child has not formed an emotional bond with a parent or other caregiver. This affects the child's ability to interact normally with others. The child may have severe emotional and social problems that extend into adulthood. There may be learning problems and physical problems such as slow growth and failure to develop as expected.

Causes and symptoms

Causes

An infant does not know how to form an emotional attachment to another person, any more than it knows how to feed or clean itself. Bonding is a necessary developmental step in a baby's growth. It occurs as the infant is cared for, talked to, played with, and comforted consistently. This helps the infant feel like it knows what will happen every time it sees a certain person. When this process is interfered with, the infant may never learn how to trust or love.

Many things can interfere with the bonding process:

- Loss of parents. The most common cause of reactive attachment disorder is being orphaned or put in foster care at a very early age. The infant may receive care from many people or be moved from place to place often. A bond to a single consistent caregiver cannot be formed.
- **Neglect** or impaired caregiving. If the infant is not cared for consistently, it will not learn to trust. This includes emotional neglect, where the caregivers may keep the baby clean and fed, but do not allow time for play and bonding. Very often this occurs when the parent or caregiver has a problem that prevents him or her from giving adequate, consistent attention to the infant. Such problems include major depression, **psychosis**, drug or alcohol abuse, **mental retardation**, physical illness, and poverty. The parent may also have been a neglected child or may be very young themselves and simply not know how to parent adequately.
- **Abuse** or pain. Even if an infant is getting love and attention some of the time, it may not learn to attach if it comes to expect pain on occasion from the caregiver.

Illness or pain that the caregiver cannot ease can have the same effect.

In disrupted families with more than one child, one child may have reactive attachment disorder while others do not. It is not clear what role personality plays in this problem.

Symptoms

Infants with this problem often resist being held or touched. They may seem sleepy or "slow." They may not seem aware of what's going on around them. They may be slow to gain weight. On the other hand, some appear to be overly aware and nervous.

Young children may seem withdrawn and passive. They may ignore others or respond to others in odd ways. Some may seem overly familiar with strangers and touch or cling to people they've just met. However, they lack empathy for others. Their behavior comes across to others as needy and strange, unlike the normal friendliness of children.

Other symptoms of reactive attachment disorder in children can include the following:

- inability to learn from mistakes (poor cause-and-effect thinking)
- learning problems or delays in learning
- impulsive behavior
- abnormal speech patterns
- destructive or cruel behavior

Demographics

The prevalence of reactive attachment disorder has been estimated at 1% of all children under the age of five. Children orphaned at a young age have a much higher likelihood of this problem.

Diagnosis

The standard manual for mental health professionals in the United States is the ***Diagnostic and Statistical Manual of Mental Disorders.*** This manual lists criteria for diagnosing various mental disorders. The most recent edition, the fourth edition text revised, is also known as the *DSM-IV-TR*. According to the *DSM-IV-TR,* reactive attachment disorder is diagnosed when the following criteria are met:

- Presence of strange and developmentally inappropriate social interactions, beginning before age five years. The child does not respond to or initiate social interactions in a way that would be developmentally appropriate; instead, the child is either inhibited or is disinhibited in his or her interactions. Inhibited reactions may be excessively vigilant, restrained or ambivalent. (The child may respond to caregivers with a mixtures of approach, avoidance, and resistance to comforting, as an example from the manual.) Disinhibited reactions occur in a variety of social interactions and the child does not discriminate among people he or she chooses as attachment figures. This child will treat near strangers with inappropriate familiarity.
- The child's inappropriate social skills are not due exclusively to developmental delay (as in mental retardation) and the child's symptoms do not meet criteria for a **pervasive developmental disorder**.
- The child has received care in which his or her basic needs—either emotional or physical— are often unmet, or in which stable attachments have not been able to form (such as when primary caregivers change often).

An infant is diagnosed as having reactive attachment disorder when he or she fails to show signs of bonding to a parent or caregiver by the age of eight months. Infants normally start to follow the parent or caregiver with their eyes and smile in response to attention by about two months. By about five months, the child should reach out to be picked up and obviously enjoy simple interactive games like "peekaboo."

Treatments

First, the child's safety and physical health must be attended to. A child that is being abused or has been physically neglected may need to be hospitalized. This is done to separate the child from the harmful situation and

KEY TERMS

Behavioral therapy—An approach to treatment that focuses on extinguishing undesirable behavior and replacing it with desired behavior.

Cognitive therapy—Psychological treatment aimed at changing a person's way of thinking in order to change his or her behavior and emotional state.

Holding therapy—A controversial treatment for autism, reactive attachment disorder, and other problems of children in which an adult holds a child despite any resistance from the child until the child submits and experiences an emotional release.

take care of any medical problems resulting from neglect or abuse.

The next step is to either make the child's home environment stable, or place the child in a more stable home. Child protective services may be brought in at this point. The home situation must be evaluated, and the parents or caregivers assessed for emotional fitness to care for the child. The parents or caregivers may be given training in proper childcare and emotional nurturing. **Family therapy** may be needed in some cases to help the parents or caregivers and other children in the family.

With a young infant, the parents or caregivers will be encouraged to have a regular schedule for the infant and to spend time each day simply holding and playing with the infant.

Treatment of children who are past infancy is difficult. It is important to find a therapist experienced in the treatment of children with reactive attachment disorder. Most therapists use a mix of techniques. The therapist may seek to help the child relive and work through **grief** and anger from a prior trauma or loss. Cognitive therapy may be used to help an older child understand and reframe negative thoughts about himself or herself, or about parents or caregivers. If the child is too young to verbalize or think rationally, techniques such as **play therapy** or art therapy may be used to help bring out and work through feelings. Behavioral therapy may be used to help guide development of wanted behaviors.

Prognosis

There has not been much research to date on the course of this problem. It appears that children who are identified and treated early have a better chance of learning how to form appropriate bonds with other people.

Children who are not treated or who are treated later in life have a greater chance of having permanent problems relating to other people.

Prevention

Prevention of reactive attachment disorder begins with good parenting. As far as possible, health care providers and families should be on the lookout for any problem that may prevent parents from giving children the structure and attention they need. If a child loses its primary caregivers, a stable environment with consistent attention from one or two caregivers should be provided as soon as possible.

Early identification of reactive attachment disorder is necessary to get help to the child and family as soon as possible. The earlier this problem is identified and treated, the more likely it is that the child will be able to develop healthy patterns of relating to others.

See also Cognitive-behavioral therapy; Creative therapies; Post-traumatic stress disorder

Resources

BOOKS

Hales Robert E., Stuart C.Yudofsky, and John A. Talbott, eds. *Textbook of Psychiatry.* 3rd ed. Washington DC: American Psychiatric Press, 1999.

Sadock, Benjamin J. and Viginia A. Sadock, eds. *Kaplan & Sadock's Comprehensive Textbook of Psychology.* 7th ed. Philadelphia: Lippincott Williams and Wilkins, 1999.

ORGANIZATIONS

Association for Treatment and Training in the Attachment of Children (ATTACh). <http://www.attach.org>.

Jody Bower, M.S.W.

Reading disorder

Definition

Reading disorder is a learning disorder that involves significant impairment of reading accuracy, speed, or comprehension to the extent that the impairment interferes with academic achievement or activities of daily life. People with reading disorder perform reading tasks well below the level one would expect on the basis of their general intelligence, educational opportunities, and physical health. Reading disorder is most commonly called dyslexia. Dyslexia, however, usually includes deficits in spelling and writing as well as reading.

Description

Reading disorder is a learning disorder characterized by a significant disparity between an individual's general intelligence and his or her reading skills. **Learning disorders**, formerly called academic skills disorders, are disorders that account for difficulty learning and poor academic performance when low performance cannot be attributed to **mental retardation**, low intelligence, lack of learning opportunities, or such specific physical problems as vision or hearing deficits. Common learning disabilities include reading disorder (often called dyslexia), **mathematics disorder**, **disorder of written expression**, and some language processing disorders.

Reading disorder can cause severe problems in reading, and consequently in academic work, even in people with normal intelligence, educational opportunities, motivation to learn to read, and emotional self-control. Reading disorder is different from slowness in learning or mental retardation. In reading disorder, there is a significant gap between the expected level of performance and actual achievement. Difficulties in reading can occur on many levels, and reading disorder may have several causes that manifest in different ways. Common problems in people with reading disorder include:

- slow reading speed
- poor comprehension when reading material either aloud or silently
- omission of words while reading
- reversal of words or letters while reading
- difficulty decoding syllables or single words and associating them with specific sounds (phonics)
- limited sight word vocabulary

Causes and symptoms

Causes

Reading disorder was first recognized in the late nineteenth century, when it was called pure word blindness, then developmental alexia. Starting in the 1960s, educators commonly referred to reading disorder as dyslexia, from the Greek word *dys*, meaning poor or inadequate, and the word *lexis* meaning words or language. Despite the long history of reading disorder, its cause is not known.

Learning to read is a complex task. It requires coordination of the eye muscles to follow a line of print, spatial orientation to interpret letters and words, visual memory to retain the meaning of letters and sight words, sequencing ability, a grasp of sentence structure and grammar, and the ability to categorize and analyze. In addition, the **brain** must integrate visual cues with memory and associate them with specific sounds. The sounds must then be associated with specific meanings. For comprehension, the meanings must be retained while a sentence or passage is read. Reading disorder occurs when any of these processes are disrupted. For that reason, the roots of reading disorder have proved difficult to isolate, and may be different in different individuals.

Despite the complexity of reading disorder, researchers have found that the condition is at least partially inherited. In 1999, the Centre for Reading Research in Norway studied a large family with reading problems. By evaluating the reading and writing abilities of about 80 family members across four generations, the researchers were able to pinpoint mutations in specific genes that are associated with reading and writing deficits.

KEY TERMS

Digraph—A pair of letters that represents a single speech sound. In English, the *th* in "thumb" and the *ei* in "vein" are examples of digraphs.

Dyslexia—Another term for reading disorder.

Phonics—A method of teaching reading and spelling based on the phonetic interpretation of ordinary spelling.

It appears that reading disorder may also have causes other than genetic inheritance, as about half the people with this learning disability do not come from families with a history of the problem. Many theories suggest that functional problems in specific areas of the brain underlie reading disorder. Given the complicated demands on the human nervous system involved in reading, it is entirely possible that there are several different problems in brain function related to difficulty in learning to read. What is known is that 90% of children diagnosed with reading disorder have other language deficits. Still other research suggests a possible link with a subtle visual problem that affects the speed with which affected people can read.

Symptoms

Common characteristics of children with reading disorder include:

- difficulty identifying single words
- problems understanding the sounds in words, sound order, or rhymes
- problems with spelling
- transposing letters in words
- omitting or substituting words
- poor reading comprehension
- slow reading speed (oral or silent)

In addition to these symptoms, children with reading disorder often have other delays or learning problems. These include:

- delays in spoken language
- confusion with directions, or right/left-handedness
- confusion with opposites (up/down, early/late)
- mathematics disorder
- disorder of written expression

Reading disorder is most commonly called dyslexia. Dyslexia, however, usually includes deficits in spelling and writing as well as reading. Symptoms of reading disorder include poor comprehension, reversal of words or letters while reading, and difficulty decoding syllables or single words and associating them with specific sounds (phonics). Here, a child with dyslexia attempts to reproduce a teacher's sentence. *(Will and Deni McIntyre/Science Source, National Audubon Society Collection/ Photo Researchers, Inc. Reproduced with permission.)*

Diagnosis

Evaluation of children's reading ability must be done on an individual basis in order to make a **diagnosis** of reading disorder and distinguish it from slow learning or low intelligence. The examiner must take into account the child's age, intelligence, educational opportunities, and such cultural factors as whether the language spoken at home is different from the language taught and used at school. Reading disorder is diagnosed when a child's reading achievement is substantially below what would be expected after taking these factors into account.

In addition, the reading problems must interfere in significant ways with the person's schoolwork or daily life. If a physical condition is present (for example, mental retardation, poor eyesight, or hearing loss), the reading deficit must be in excess of what one would normally associate with the physical handicap.

Diagnosis is complicated by the fact that 20%–55% of children with reading disorder have **attention-deficit/hyperactivity disorder** (ADHD), a behavioral disorder that aggravates learning difficulties. In addition, about one-quarter of children with reading disorder have **conduct disorder**. **Oppositional defiant disorder** and depression also occur in higher-than-average rates in children with reading disorder. Almost all people with reading disorder have difficulties spelling, and about 80% of them have other language problems.

Anyone who is suspected of having reading disorder or any other learning disability should have a comprehensive evaluation, including hearing, vision, and intelligence testing. The test should include all areas of learning and learning processes, not just reading. In school-age children, this evaluation often involves a team of educators, educational psychologists, and child psychiatrists.

Demographics

Estimates by the National Institutes of Health of the number of people with learning disorders range from 5%–15% of the general population. About 80% of people with a learning disorder have reading disorder. Other studies suggest that about 4% of school-age children have reading disorder. People with reading disorder are more likely to have a parent or sibling with the disorder.

Between 60% and 80% of children diagnosed with reading disorder are boys. For various reasons often related to behavior, boys tend to be referred more frequently to special education classes, which suggests that girls with reading disorder may be underdiagnosed. Some experts think that this disparity comes about because boys are more often disruptive in class.

Treatments

Reading disorder, like other learning disorders, falls under the federal Individuals with Disabilities Education Act (IDEA). Definitions of learning disabilities vary among the states, and some school districts are more willing than others to recognize specific learning disabilities. Any child, however, who has a diagnosed learning disability, including reading disorder or dyslexia, should be eligible for an Individual Education Program (IEP) that provides customized instruction at school designed to address the disability.

Treatment approaches vary from visual stimulation to special **diets** to enhanced reading instruction. However, it is generally agreed that customized education is the only successful remedy. The American Academy of Ophthalmology, the American Academy of Pediatrics, and the American Association for Pediatric Ophthalmology and Strabismus have issued a policy statement warning against visual treatments and recommending a cross-disciplinary educational approach.

The first researcher to identify and study dyslexia, Samuel Torrey Orton, developed the core principles of such an approach in the 1920s. The work of three of his followers—teachers Bessie Stillman, Anna Gillingham, and Beth Slingerland—underlies many of the programs in use today, including Project READ, the Wilson Reading System, and programs based on the Herman method. There are many successful programs to address individual reading needs. In general, all good programs are:

- Sound/symbol (phonics)-based. They break words down into their smallest visual components: letters and the sounds associated with them.
- Multisensory. Good programs attempt to form and strengthen mental associations among visual, auditory, and kinesthetic channels of stimulation. The student simultaneously sees, feels, and says the sound-symbol association. For example, a student may trace the letter or letter combination with his or her finger while pronouncing a word out loud.
- Highly structured. Remediation begins at the level of the single letter-sound; works up to digraphs (a pair of letters representing a single speech sound); then syllables; then into words and sentences in a systematic fashion. Repetitive drill and practice serve to form necessary associations between sounds and written symbols.

Prognosis

Many famous and successful people have suffered from reading disorders, including at least two Presidents of the United States. How well a person compensates for this disorder depends on the severity of the impairment and the type of educational remediation that he or she receives. Generally, people who are identified as having a reading disorder before grade three and who receive intensive reading education can do well. There is, however, a great deal of variation among people in intelligence, educational opportunities, and the will to overcome a reading disorder, as well as in the type and severity of the problem. All these factors combine to determine the ultimate outcome of this disorder. The prognosis is usually good if the condition is diagnosed early and the person is enrolled in a good remedial program. Strong self-esteem, together with supportive family, friends, and teachers also improve a person's chances of overcoming this disorder.

Prevention

There is no known way to prevent reading disorder. Early **intervention** is the key to preventing the associated symptoms of low self-esteem, lack of interest in school, and poor behavior that often accompany low academic achievement.

Resources

BOOKS

American Psychiatric Association. *Diagnostic and Statistical Manual of Mental Disorders.* 4th ed. text revised. Washington DC: American Psychiatric Association, 2000.

Hales, Robert E., Stuart C. Yudofsky, and John A. Talbot. *The American Psychiatric Press Textbook of Psychiatry.* 3rd ed. Washington, DC: American Psychiatric Press, 2000.

Sadock, Benjamin J. and Virginia A. Sadock, eds. *Comprehensive Textbook of Psychiatry.* 7th ed. Vol. 2. Philadelphia: Lippincott Williams and Wilkins, 2000.

PERIODICALS

Bower, Bruce. "Dyslexia Tied to Disrupted Brain Network." *Science News* 153 (7 March 1998): 150.

Matvy, Mike. "A Silicon Bullet for Dyslexia: A new Solution for an Old Problem." *The Exceptional Parent* 30 (November 2000) 52-56.

ORGANIZATIONS

Learning Disabilities Association. 4156 Library Rd., Pittsburgh, PA 15234. (412) 341-1515. <http://www.ladnatl.org>.

National Center for Learning Disabilities. 381 Park Avenue South, Suite 1401, New York, NY 10016. (212) 545-7510. <http://www.ncld.org>.

OTHER

Dyslexia Resources on the Web. <http://home.clara.net/ghrow/subjects/dyslexia.html>. Extensive links to dyslexia resources; updated frequently.

Tish Davidson, A.M.

Reinforcement

Definition

A reinforcer is a stimulus that follows some behavior and increases the probability that the behavior will occur. For example, when a dog's owner is trying to teach the dog to sit on command, the owner may give the dog a treat every time the dog sits when commanded to do so. The treat reinforces the desired behavior.

Description

In operant conditioning (as developed by B. F. Skinner), positive reinforcers are rewards that strengthen a conditioned response after it has occurred, such as feeding a hungry pigeon after it has pecked a key. Negative reinforcers are stimuli that are removed when the desired response has been obtained. For example, when a rat is receiving an electric shock and presses a bar that stops the shock, the shock is a negative reinforcer— it is an aversive stimulus that reinforces the bar-pressing behavior. The application of negative reinforcement may be divided into two types: escape and avoidance conditioning. In escape conditioning, the subject learns to escape an unpleasant or aversive stimulus (a dog jumps over a barrier to escape electric shock). In avoidance conditioning, the subject is presented with a warning stimulus, such as a buzzer, just before the aversive stimulus occurs and learns to act on it in order to avoid the stimulus altogether.

Punishment can be used to decrease unwanted behaviors. Punishment is the application of an aversive stimulus in reaction to a particular behavior. For children, a punishment could be the removal of television privileges when they disobey their parents or teacher. The removal of the privileges follows the undesired behavior and decreases its likelihood of occurring again.

Reinforcement may be administered according to various schedules. A particular behavior may be reinforced every time it occurs, which is referred to as continuous reinforcement. In many cases, however, behaviors are reinforced only some of the time, which is termed partial or intermittent reinforcement. Reinforcement may also be based on the number of responses or scheduled at particular time intervals. In addition, it may be delivered in regularly or irregularly. These variables combine to produce four basic types of partial reinforcement. In fixed-ratio (FR) schedules, reinforcement is provided following a set number of responses (a factory worker is paid for every garment he assembles). With variable-ratio (VR) schedules, reinforcement is provided after a variable number of responses (a slot machine pays off after varying numbers of attempts). Fixed-interval (FI) schedules provide for reinforcement of the first response made within a given interval since the previous one (contest entrants are not eligible for a prize if they have won one within the past 30 days). Finally, with variable-interval (VI) schedules, first responses are rewarded at varying intervals from the previous one.

See also Behavior modification

Relapse and relapse prevention

Definition

In the course of illness, relapse is a return of symptoms after a period of time when no symptoms are present. Any strategies or treatments applied in advance to prevent future symptoms are known as relapse prevention.

Purpose

When people seek help for mental disorders, they receive treatment that, hopefully, reduces or eliminates symptoms. However, once they leave treatment, they may gradually revert to old habits and ways of living. This results in a return of symptoms known as relapse. Relapse prevention aims to teach people strategies that will maintain the wellness skills they learned while in treatment.

Prevention of relapse in mental disorders is crucial—not only because symptoms are detrimental to quality of life but also because the occurrence of relapse increases chances for future relapses. In addition, with each relapse, symptoms tend to be more severe and have more serious consequences.

Description

Relapse is a concern with any disorder, whether physical or psychological. Cancer is a prime example of a physical condition where relapse is common, either after a short period or many years of remission (being symptom-free). Psychological disorders can follow a similar pattern, and certain psychological disorders tend to have a higher rate of relapse than others. Addictive disorders, such as alcohol and drug abuse, smoking, overeating, and **pathological gambling**, are well known for high levels of relapse. Many addictions involve a lifestyle centered around the addictive behavior. In such cases, individuals must not only discontinue the addictive habit, they must also restructure their entire lives in order for changes to last. Such vast changes are difficult at best, approaching impossible in the worst scenarios. For example, an individual with a drug **addiction** may live in a neighborhood where drugs are prevalent but may lack the resources to move. According to recent statistics, relapse rates are approximately 33% for people who gamble pathologically (within three months of treatment), 90% for people who quit smoking, and 50% for people who abuse alcohol. Within one year of treatment, people struggling with **obesity** typically regain 30% to 50% of the weight they lost.

Affective disorders, such as depression and anxiety, also have high rates of relapse. People with affective disorders are thought to engage in self-defeating, negative thought patterns that occur more or less automatically. These thought patterns affect behavior, resulting in unproductive or negative consequences. Negative consequences are regarded by such individuals as proof that their original self-defeating thoughts must be correct. The thought-behavior pattern becomes a repetitive cycle, with negative thoughts resulting in negative behavioral outcomes, and consequences of negative behavior encouraging more self-defeating thoughts. This cycle is extremely difficult to break because it becomes a habitual way of responding to the world that occurs almost without awareness. Relapse rates for depression are reportedly as high as 80%.

Relapse among people who commit sex offenses is a constant safety concern for those in the community. However, some statistics show that this population has a very low rate of relapse. A recent report by Robin J. Wilson and colleagues indicated rates as low as 3.7% to 6.3%. This same report stated that, among various criminal offenses, those who commit sex offenses relapse at lower rates than those who commit general offenses. Other professionals may not necessarily agree with this study, however. Those who commit sex offenses are considered at a higher risk for relapse if they display little insight into the impact of their crime. Those at high risk of committing a sex offense are not typically released back into the community.

For many types of disorders, initial treatment is often effective at eliminating the unwanted behavior. However, these effects are rarely maintained long-term without

KEY TERMS

Addictive disorder—A disorder involving repetitive participation in a certain activity, in spite of negative consequences and despite attempts to stop the behavior. Alcohol abuse is an example.

Affective disorder—A disorder involving extreme emotional experience that is not congruent with the environmental circumstances (for example, feeling sad when there is no easily identifiable reason, as in depression).

Cognitive restructuring—An approach to psychotherapy that focuses on helping the patient examine distorted patterns of perceiving and thinking in order to change their emotional responses to people and situations.

Guided imagery—Techniques in which individuals actively imagine themselves in a scene (usually a different location, such as a relaxing beach, or a trigger situation where one handles the situation successfully), typically guided by another person describing the scene.

Lapse—A single, isolated occurrence of a symptom or negative behavior.

Positive affirmation statements—Statements repeated to oneself, either aloud or mentally, that reflect attitudes of self-worth.

Progressive muscle relaxation—Relaxation exercises where one slowly tenses and then relaxes each muscle group separately in a systematic order.

Refocusing techniques—Techniques that direct one's attention away from overwhelming, negative thoughts and emotions by focusing on inner peace and managing one issue at a time.

Remission—In the course of an illness or disorder, a period of time when symptoms are absent.

Trigger—Any situation (people, places, times, events, etc.) that causes one to experience a negative emotional reaction, which is often accompanied by a display of symptoms or problematic behavior.

some type of preventive planning. Results of medications are similar; symptoms are alleviated, but once the medication is discontinued, symptoms return unless the individual has had some type of training in coping with his or her disorder and that training has been effective. There are various forms of relapse prevention training. Most follow a similar pattern with and employ the following common elements:

- Identifying high-risk situations: Symptoms are often initiated by particular times, places, people, or events. For example, a person with **agoraphobia** is more likely to experience symptoms of panic in a crowded building. An essential key to preventing relapse is to be aware of the specific situations where one feels vulnerable. These situations are called "triggers," because they trigger the onset of symptoms. While people with the same mental disorder may share similar triggers, triggers can also be highly individual. People tend to react—sometimes unknowingly—to negative experiences in their past. For example, a woman who was sexually abused as a child may have negative emotions when in the presence of men who resemble her abuser. Because some triggers occur without conscious awareness, individuals may not know all their triggers. Many prevention programs encourage individuals to monitor their behavior closely, reflecting on situations where symptoms occurred and determining what was happening immediately before the onset of symptoms. With this kind of analysis, a pattern often emerges that gives clues about the trigger.
- Learning alternate ways to respond to high-risk situations: Once triggers have been identified, one must find new ways of coping with those situations. The easiest coping mechanism for high-risk situations is to avoid them altogether. This may include avoiding certain people who have a negative influence or avoiding locations where the symptom is likely to occur. In some instances, avoidance is a good strategy. For example, individuals who abuse alcohol may successfully reduce their risk by avoiding bars or parties. In other instances, avoidance is not possible or advisable. For example, individuals attempting to lose weight may notice that they are more likely to binge at certain times during the day. One cannot avoid a time of day. Rather, by being aware of this trigger, one can purposely engage in alternate activities during that time. Strategies for coping with unavoidable triggers are generally skills that need to be learned and practiced in order to be effective. Strategies include—but are not limited to—discussion of feelings, whether with a friend, counselor, or via a hotline; distraction, such as music, exercise, or engaging in a hobby; refocusing techniques, such as **meditation**, deep-breathing exercises, progressive muscle relaxation (focusing on each muscle group separately, and routinely tensing then relaxing that muscle), prayer, or journaling; and cognitive restructuring, such as positive affirmation statements (such as, "I am worthwhile"), active problem solving (defining the problem, generating possible solutions, identifying the consequences of those solutions, choosing the best solution), challenging the validity of negative thoughts, or guided imagery (imagining oneself in a different place or handling a situation appropriately).
- Creating a plan for healthy living: Besides being prepared for high-risk situations, relapse prevention also focuses on general principles of mental health that, if followed, greatly reduce the likelihood of symptoms. These include factors such as balanced nutrition, regular exercise, sufficient sleep, health education, reciprocally caring relationships, productive and recreational interests, and spiritual development.
- Developing a support system: Many research studies have demonstrated the importance of social support in maintaining a healthy lifestyle. Individuals who are socially isolated tend to display more symptoms of mental disorders. Conversely, individuals with mental disorders tend to have more difficultly initiating and maintaining relationships due to inappropriate social behavior. For such people, a support system may be nonexistent. Research suggests that support systems are most effective when they are naturally occurring—in other words, when a circle of family and friends who genuinely care about the individual is already in place. However, artificially created support systems are certainly better than none at all. For this reason, relapse prevention programs strive to involve family members and other significant persons in the treatment program. Everyone in the support system should be knowledgeable about the person's goals, what that person is like when he or she is doing well, and warning signs that the person may be on a path toward relapse. The support system agrees on who will take what role in encouraging, confronting, or otherwise caring for that person. **Self-help groups** such as Alcoholics Anonymous or Moderation Management are often examples of artificially created support systems.
- Preparing for possible relapse: Although the ultimate goal of relapse prevention is to avoid relapse altogether, statistics demonstrate that relapse potential is very real. Individuals need to be aware that, even when exerting their best efforts, they may occasionally experience lapses (one occurrence of a symptom or behavior) or relapses (return to a previous, undesirable level of symptoms or behavior). Acknowledging the potential for relapse is important, because many people consider a lapse or relapse as evidence of personal failure

and give up completely. In their widely acclaimed book for professionals, *Motivational Interviewing*, William R. Miller and Stephen Rollnick cite a study by Prochaska and DiClemente that found that smokers typically relapse between three and seven times before quitting for good. From the perspective of Miller and Rollnick, each relapse can be a step closer to full recovery if relapse is used as a learning experience to improve prevention strategies. Although some argue that such a tolerant attitude invites relapse, general consensus is that individuals need to forgive themselves if relapse occurs and then move on. Some prevention programs include designing a crisis plan to be put into effect if a relapse occurs. The crisis plan involves specific actions to be taken by the individual or members of the support system.

These elements are common to all relapse prevention programs, but programs can be further customized to meet the particular characteristics of a disorder. For example, prevention of depression or anxiety may focus on becoming aware of thoughts as passing mental events rather than facts about self or reality. Learning to identify bodily sensations that accompany maladaptive thoughts is also important for preventing depression and anxiety. Addictive disorders concentrate on reactions to social pressure, interpersonal conflicts, and negative emotional states as part of a relapse prevention plan.

Preparation

As with any type of therapeutic treatment, success of relapse prevention programs depend heavily on motivation. If an individual is not interested in making life changes, he or she is not likely to follow a prevention plan. Individuals low in motivation may need to participate in group or individual **psychotherapy** before deciding whether to enter a relapse prevention program.

Aftercare

Aftercare typically consists of participation in **support groups**. For addictions, 12-step groups (such as Alcoholics Anonymous) are most commonly recommended. These types of groups can be attended daily. Support groups exist for other types of mental disorders, and may be run by peers or a professional facilitator. Aftercare groups, usually run in treatment facilities by professional staff, may be used to continue practicing skills and to trouble-shoot problems individuals are experiencing with their prevention plans in everyday life. Aftercare groups usually meet less frequently (once a week or month) and may gradually taper off. Some relapse-prevention programs may use telephone contacts or individual therapy sessions to help individuals continue to use prevention skills effectively.

Normal results

Successful relapse prevention programs will empower individuals to make choices about how they respond in stressful, high-risk situations (triggers) rather than responding in habitual, unhealthy ways. Individuals should be aware of their personal triggers, use positive strategies for coping with **stress**, practice healthy lifestyle choices, involve others in their efforts, and have a realistic attitude regarding relapse. Use of these prevention skills should reduce symptoms and increase the time span between occurrences of lapses or relapses.

Abnormal results

If an individual is unmotivated to make life changes, or a relapse prevention program has been ineffective, that individual will demonstrate few (if any) of the prevention skills learned. The individual will show little improvement in symptomatic or problematic behavior. Periods of remission (symptom-free behavior) will be short and relapses will occur frequently.

See also Alcohol and related disorders; Anxiety-reduction techniques; Cognitive-behavioral therapy; Cognitive problem-solving skills training; Substance abuse and related disorders

Resources

BOOKS

Copeland, Mary Ellen. *Winning Against Relapse: A Workbook of Action Plans for Recurring Health and Emotional Problems.* Oakland, CA: New Harbinger Publications, 1999.

Miller, William R. and Stephen Rollnick. *Motivational Interviewing: Preparing People to Change Addictive Behavior.* New York: Guilford Press, 1991.

PERIODICALS

Brandon, Thomas H., Bradley N. Collins, Laura M. Juliano, and Amy B. Lazev. "Preventing Relapse Among Former Smokers: A Comparison of Minimal Interventions Through Telephone and Mail." *Journal of Consulting and Clinical Psychology* 68, no. 1 (2000): 103-113.

Carich, Mark S., and Mark H. Stone. "Using Relapse Intervention Strategies to Treat Sexual Offenders." *Journal of Individual Psychology* 57, no. 1 (2001): 26-36.

Echeburua, Enrique, Javier Fernandez-Montalvo, and Concepcion Baez. "Relapse Prevention in the Treatment of Slot-Machine Pathological Gambling: Long-Term Outcome." *Behavior Therapy* 31, no. 2 (2000): 351-364.

Hartzler, Bryan, and Chris Brownson. "The Utility of Change Models in the Design and Delivery of Thematic Group Interventions: Applications to a Self-Defeating Behaviors Group." *Group Dynamics: Theory, Research, and Practice* 5, no. 3 (2001): 191-199.

Monti, Peter M. and Damaris J. Rohsenow. "Coping Skills Training and Cue-Exposure Therapy in the Treatment of Alcoholism." *Alcohol Research and Health* 23, no. 2 (1999): 107-115.

Perri, Michael G., Arthur M. Nezu, Wendy F. McKelvey, Rebecca L. Shermer, David A. Renjilian, and Barbara J. Viegener. "Relapse Prevention Training and Problem-Solving Therapy in the Long-Term Management of Obesity." *Journal of Consulting and Clinical Psychology* 69, no. 4 (2000): 722-726.

Teasdale, John D., Zindel V. Segal, J. Mark G. Williams, Valerie A. Ridgeway, Judith M. Soulsby, and Mark A. Lau. "Prevention of Relapse/Recurrence in Major Depression by Mindfulness-Based Cognitive Therapy." *Journal of Consulting and Clinical Psychology* 68, no. 4 (2000): 615-623.

Wilson, Robin J., Lynn Stewart, Tania Stirpe, Marianne Barrett, and Janice E. Cripps. "Community-Based Sex Offender Management: Combining Parole Supervision and Treatment to Reduce Recidivism." *Canadian Journal of Criminology* 42, no. 2 (2000): 177-188.

ORGANIZATIONS

National Institute on Alcohol Abuse and Alcoholism.6000 Executive Boulevard, Willco Building, Bethesda, Maryland 20892-7003. <http://www.niaaa.nih.gov>.

National Institute on Drug Abuse, National Institutes of Health. 6001 Executive Boulevard, Room 5213, Bethesda, Maryland 20892-9561. (301) 443-1124. <http://www.nida.nih.gov>.

National Institute of Mental Health. 6001 Executive Boulevard, Room 8194, MSC 9663, Bethesda, Maryland 20892-9663. (301) 443-4513. <http://www.nimh.nih.gov>.

Sandra L. Friedrich, M.A.

Remeron *see* **Mirtazapine**

Respite

Definition

Respite literally means a period of rest or relief. Respite care provides a caregiver temporary relief from the responsibilities of caring for individuals with chronic physical or mental disabilities. Respite care is often referred to as a gift of time.

Purpose

Respite was developed in response to the **deinstitutionalization** movement of the 1960s and 1970s. Maintaining individuals in their natural homes rather than placing them in long-term care facilities was viewed as beneficial to the individual, the involved family, and society (in terms of lowered health care costs). The primary purpose of respite care is to relieve caregiver **stress**, thereby enabling them to continue caring for the individual with a disability.

Respite care is typically provided for individuals with disorders related to aging (**dementia**, frail health), terminal illnesses, chronic health issues, or developmental disabilities. More recently, children with behavior disorders have also been eligible for respite care. Respite care is usually recreational and does not include therapy or treatment for the individual with the disability.

Caregivers frequently experience stress in the forms of physical **fatigue**, psychological distress (resentment, frustration, anxiety, guilt, depression), and disruption in relations with other family members. The emotional aspects of caring for a family member are often more taxing than the physical demands. Increased caregiver stress may result in health problems such as ulcers, high blood pressure, difficulty sleeping, weight loss or gain, or breathing difficulties.

Types of respite

Length of respite care can be anywhere from a few hours to several weeks. Services may be used frequently or infrequently, such as for emergencies, vacations, one day per week or month, weekends, or everyday.

A variety of facilities provide respite care services. The type of service available is often closely related to the characteristics of the facility, including:

- In-home respite services consist of a worker who comes to the family home while the caregiver is away. These services are usually provided by agencies that recruit, screen, and train workers. This type of respite is usually less disruptive to the individual with the disability, provided there is a good match between the worker and the individual. However, issues of reliability and trustworthiness of the worker can be an additional source of stress for the caregiver.
- Respite centers are residential facilities specifically designed for respite care. Adult day care programs and respite camps also fall into this category. This type of respite offers more peace of mind to the caregiver, and may provide a stimulating environment for the individual with the disability. However, centers usually restrict

length of stay and may exclude individuals based on severity of disability.

- Institutional settings sometimes reserve spaces to be used for respite purposes. These include skilled nursing facilities, intermediate care facilities, **group homes**, senior housing, regular day care or after-school programs for children, and hospitals. Some of these facilities provide higher levels of care, but are less home-like. The individual with the disability may oppose staying in an institutional setting or may fear abandonment.
- Licensed foster care providers can also provide respite services in their homes.

Funding

Costs of respite care present a financial burden to many families. **Community mental health** centers often fund respite services if the individual meets certain criteria, including eligibility for Medicaid. Wraparound programs (also accessed through community mental health centers) for children with emotional or behavioral disorders also pay for respite services. Veteran's Administration hospitals provide respite care at little or no charge if the individual receiving the care is a veteran (but not if the caregiver is a veteran). Private insurance companies rarely pay for respite, and many respite providers do not accept this form of payment. Some respite facilities have sliding-scale fees. Other facilities operate as a co-op, where caregivers work at the facility in exchange for respite services.

In addition, respite agencies may have difficulty recruiting and retaining qualified employees, because limited funding prevents agencies from offering desirable salaries. The high turnover and unavailability of employees may result in delays in service delivery or family dissatisfaction with services. Advocacy for policy changes regarding funding is needed.

Barriers to using respite services

Recent research suggests that families who use respite tend to have higher levels of perceived stress, lower levels of support from others, and fewer resources. In many of these families, the individuals in need of care have more severe disabilities, problem behaviors such as aggression or self-injury, and communication difficulties; are school-aged; and are more dependent for basic needs such as eating, toileting, and dressing.

It has been well documented that many families eligible for respite care never utilize these services. Research regarding the use, availability, and effectiveness of respite care is still in the preliminary stages. Various reasons for non-utilization of respite include:

KEY TERMS

Behavior disorders—Disorders characterized by disruptive behaviors such as conduct disorder, oppositional defiant disorder, and attention-deficit/hyperactivity disorder.

Community mental health centers—Organizations that manage and deliver a comprehensive range of mental health services, education, and outreach to residents of a given community.

Deinstitutionalization—The process of moving people out of mental hospitals into treatment programs or halfway houses in local communities. With this movement, the responsibility for care shifted from large (often governmental) agencies to families and community organizations.

Developmental disabilities—Disabilities that are present from birth and delay or prevent normal development, such as mental retardation or autism.

Intermediate care facility—An inpatient facility that provides periodic nursing care.

Medicaid—A program jointly funded by state and federal governments that reimburses hospitals and physicians for the care of individuals who cannot pay for their own medical expenses. These individuals may be in low-income households or may have chronic disabilities.

Skilled nursing facility—An inpatient facility that provides 24-hour nursing services to individuals in need of extended care.

Veteran's Administration hospitals—Medical facilities operated by the federal government explicitly for veterans of the United States military.

Wraparound—A relatively new form of mental health service delivery that strives to accommodate all family members based on self-defined needs, flexibly incorporating both formal and informal community services

- Unfamiliarity: Some families are unaware that such services exist, or may be uncertain about how to access services. This implies a need for improved referral services.
- Funding: Limited funding may prevent some families from receiving services.
- Caregiver qualities: Some caregivers experience guilt or anxiety over allowing someone else to care for their loved one. Being able to maintain one's family independently may be tied to gender roles or cultural cus-

An adolescent swings on the playground at a respite care facility that provides short-term care for families who have children with developmental disabilities. *(AP Photo/ Fort Collins Coloradoan, Sherry Barber. Photo reproduced by permission.)*

toms. Relatives and friends may assist in caregiving, making formal respite unnecessary.

- Care recipient qualities: Occasionally the individual with the disability is opposed to respite care. He or she may not trust strangers or may refuse to leave home. In other instances, the individual may have behaviors, or require physical care, that is too challenging for the respite provider.
- Program qualities: Many researchers believe that respite programs are not adequately meeting the needs of families. In some cases, times that services are offered are inconvenient. Individuals with severe disabilities who pose the most need for services are sometimes excluded.

Many caregivers obtain respite in informal ways not offered by respite services. Some researchers have suggested that respite care should be just one form of service available to caregivers. Other services that may alleviate caregiver stress could include home-delivered meals, transportation assistance, recreational resources, or care skills training.

See also Case management

Resources

BOOKS

Ownby, Lisa L. *Partners Plus: Families and Caregivers in Partnerships: A Family-Centered Guide to Respite Care.* Washington, DC: Child Development Resources, U.S. Department of Education, Office of Educational Research and Improvement, Educational Resources Information Center, 1999.

Tepper, Lynn M. and John A. Toner, eds. *Respite Care: Programs, Problems, and Solutions.*Philadelphia: The Charles Press, 1993.

PERIODICALS

Chan, Jeffrey B., and Jeff Sigafoos. "A Review of Child and Family Characteristics Related to the Use of Respite Care in Developmental Disability Services." *Child and Youth Care Forum* 29, no. 1 (2000): 27-37.

Chappell, Neena L., R. Colin Reid, and Elizabeth Dow. "Respite Reconsidered: A Typology of Meanings Based on the Caregiver's Point of View." *Journal of Aging Studies* 15, no. 2 (2001): 201-216.

ORGANIZATIONS

The Arc National Headquarters, P.O. Box 1047, Arlington, Texas 76004. (817) 261-6003; (817) 277-0553 TDD. thearc@metronet.com.<http://www.thearc.org>.

ARCH National Respite Network and Resource Center. Chapel Hill Training-Outreach Project, 800 Eastowne Drive, Suite 105, Chapel Hill, North Carolina 27514. (888) 671-2594; (919) 490-5577. <http://www.chtop.com>.

National Aging Information Center. Administration on Aging, 330 Independence Avenue, SW, Room 4656, Washington, DC 20201. (202) 619-7501. <http://www.aoa.gov/naic>.

National Information Center for Children and Youth with Disabilities. P.O. Box 1492, Washington, DC 20013. (800)-695-0285. <http://www.nichcy.org>.

OTHER

Senior Care Web. <http://www.seniorcareweb.com>.

Sandra L. Friedrich, M.A.

Response prevention *see* **Exposure treatment**

Restoril *see* **Temazepam**

Rett's disorder

Definition

Rett's disorder, which is also known as Rett's syndrome or RS, belongs to a group of childhood disorders known as **pervasive developmental disorders** (PDDs) or autistic spectrum disorders. It is classified by the mental health professional's handbook (the ***Diagnostic and Statistical Manual of Mental Disorders*** or the *DSM-IV-TR*) as a developmental disorder of childhood. Rett's disorder is characterized by an early-onset slowing of the infant's head growth and a reduction in **brain** size, as much as 30%.

Description

RS was first described by an Austrian physician, Andreas Rett, in 1966; prior to 1983, however, little was known about the syndrome because its occurrence is quite rare. Although RS was thought at first to result from the destruction or degeneration of brain tissue, genetic research has indicated that it is caused by the failure of the infant's brain to develop normally. This developmental failure is in turn caused by a genetic mutation affecting production of a key protein that regulates brain development.

Rett's disorder has a distinctive onset and course. The child— almost always a girl— develops normally during the first five months of life. After the fifth month, head growth slows down and the child loses whatever purposeful hand movements she had developed during her first five months. After 30 months, the child frequently develops repetitive hand-washing or hand-wringing gestures; 50%–80% of children with the disorder will eventually develop epilepsy. Rett's disorder is also associated with severe or profound **mental retardation**.

Causes and symptoms

Causes

The cause of Rett's disorder is a genetic mutation on the long arm of the X chromosome (Xq28) at a locus known as MECP2. The gene was discovered in 1999, and it produces a protein known as MeCP2, which is essential to life and crucial to the normal development of the human brain. The mutation that causes Rett's disorder allows other genes to become or remain active at inappropriate points in the brain's development. These activated genes interfere with the normal pattern of development and maturation of the brain's functions. Although Rett's disorder was previously thought to result from degeneration or deterioration of brain tissue, the discovery of the Rett's gene provides evidence that the disorder may be due to a failure of normal brain development. The sensory, motor, and emotional functions of the brain are not integrated in Rett's patients as they are in persons without the mutation. Certain regions of the brain in Rett's patients essentially remain at an infantile stage of development.

RS is classified by geneticists as an X-linked dominant disorder with a high rate of new mutations. Most of these mutations (99.5%) occur while the fetus is developing in the mother's womb; only 0.5% of cases of Rett's disorder are recurrences within families. One of the most important aspects of the discovery of the Rett gene is that RS is the first disorder in humans to be traced to defects in a protein (MeCP2) that controls the expression of other genes through its interaction with methylated DNA. The discovery uncovered a new class of genetic disease that might extend far beyond RS in its applications to other disorders related to developmental failures of the nervous system.

Symptoms

The symptoms of Rett's disorder have been described in terms of four stages in the child's development.

KEY TERMS

Hyperventilation—A pattern of rapid, shallow breathing that is frequently found in patients with Rett's disorder.

Mosaicism—A genetic condition in which some cells in an organism have one set of chromosomes and other cells have a different set.

Mutation—A spontaneous change in the sequence of nucleotides in a chromosome or gene. Mutations may affect the number and structure of chromosomes or cause deletions of part of a chromosome. Rett's disorder is caused by a mutation on the long arm of the X chromosome.

Pervasive developmental disorders (PDDs)—A category of childhood disorders that includes Asperger's syndrome and Rett's disorder. The PDDs are sometimes referred to collectively as autistic spectrum disorders.

Scoliosis—An abnormal lateral (sidewise) curvature of the spine. Many patients with RS develop scoliosis after puberty.

STAGE ONE, EARLY-ONSET (SIX–18 MONTHS OF AGE). The early symptoms of RS are not always noticeable in Stage 1. The infant may not make eye contact with family members and may not show much interest in toys. She may be considered a "good baby" because she is so calm and quiet. On the other hand, there may be noticeable hand-wringing and slowing of head growth.

STAGE TWO, RAPID DETERIORATION (ONE–FOUR YEARS). This stage may be either rapid or gradual in onset. The child loses her ability to speak and to make purposeful hand movements. Hand-to-mouth movements may appear, as well as hand-wringing or hand-clapping gestures. These movements may be nearly constant while the child is awake but disappear during sleep. There may be noticeable episodes of breath holding and hyperventilating (rapid shallow breathing). The child may have trouble sleeping, and may become irritable. If she is able to walk, she will start to look unsteady on her feet and may have periods of trembling or shaking. Slowed growth of the head is usually most noticeable during this stage.

STAGE THREE, PLATEAU (TWO–10 YEARS). Motor problems and **seizures** often appear during this stage. The child's behavior, however, often shows some improvement, with less irritability and crying. She may show greater interest in her surroundings, and her attention span and communication skills often improve. Many patients with RS remain in stage 3 for most of their lives.

STAGE FOUR, LATE DETERIORATION OF MOTOR SKILLS (USUALLY AFTER 10 YEARS OF AGE). In stage 4, patients with RS gradually lose their mobility; some stop walking while others have never learned to walk. There is, however, no loss of cognitive or communication skills, and the repetitive hand movements may decrease. The spine begins to develop an abnormal sideways curvature (scoliosis), and the patient may develop muscle rigidity. Puberty begins at the same age as in most girls.

Demographics

RS is less common than the other PDDs. Recent estimates of its prevalence range between 1:10,000 births and 1:15,000 births. As of 2002, little is known about its prevalence across different racial and ethnic groups.

Until 2000, Rett's disorder was thought to occur only in girls, but at least two cases have been reported in boys as well. Since RS is caused by a mutation on the X chromosome that affects the production of a protein essential to life, and the Y chromosome that determines male sex cannot compensate for a damaged X chromosome, a male fetus with a defective X chromosome does not usually survive. The two known cases of RS in boys involve one child who has two X chromosomes as well as a Y, and a child whose X chromosome is faulty in some of the cells in his body but not all. This condition is known as mosaicism.

Diagnosis

The **diagnosis** of Rett's disorder is made on the basis of observation of the child—usually over a period of several hours or days—and interviews with the parents. There are no laboratory or diagnostic imaging tests for RS. The diagnosis can be made by a pediatrician or primary care physician, but should be confirmed by a pediatric neurologist (specialist in disorders of the nervous system in children) or developmental pediatrician. After the examiner has excluded the possibility of other developmental disorders, there are six criteria that must be met for a diagnosis of Rett's disorder, and a secondary group of supportive criteria that are frequently observed in RS patients but are not necessary to make the diagnosis.

Diagnostic criteria

The diagnostic criteria for RS include the following:

- a period of apparently normal development before six–18 months of age
- a normal-sized head at birth followed by slowing of head growth between five months and four years
- severe impairment in the use of language and loss of purposeful hand motion
- repetitive hand movements that include one or more of the following: hand washing, hand wringing, or hand clapping
- shaking of the chest or torso, particularly when the child is agitated or upset
- in children able to walk, an unsteady, stiff-legged, wide-based gait

Supportive criteria

Supportive criteria are criteria that are not essential to the diagnosis of a particular disorder (because some people with the disorder do not have them). Supportive criteria are nonetheless strong evidence that a person who exhibits these criteria does in fact have the disorder. Supportive criteria for Rett's disorder include:

- dysfunctional breathing, which may include hyperventilation, breath holding, and air swallowing
- abnormal electroencephalogram (EEG) patterns
- seizures
- difficulties in chewing and swallowing
- constipation

- muscle rigidity and contracting of the joints that increase with age
- scoliosis (curvature of the spine from side to side)
- teeth grinding
- small feet in relation to overall height
- slow overall growth
- loss of body fat and muscle mass
- abnormal sleeping patterns combined with irritability or agitation
- poor circulation in the feet and legs

These supportive criteria do not always appear in young children with RS but are often observed as the child grows older.

Treatments

There is no single treatment regimen that is applicable to all patients with Rett's disorder. Some patients benefit from medications for muscular rigidity or for specific mood or behavioral problems, such as anxiety or irritability. A child **psychiatrist** should be consulted in regard to medications.

The degree of mental retardation associated with RS means that patients with this disorder will not benefit from **psychotherapy**. Parents of children with RS, however, are often helped by supportive therapy groups for parents of children with PDDs. Another type of program that is helpful for parents is learning skills for coping with the behaviors of RS children. These programs are usually led by a behavioral **psychologist**.

The U. S. National Institute of Mental Health (NIMH) is presently conducting research studies of psychosocial approaches to treatment of Rett's and other PDDs as well as studies of medications given for these disorders. Readers who would like more information about this research may contact NIMH Public Inquiries at 6001 Executive Boulevard, Rm. 8184, MSC 9663, Bethesda, MD 20892-9663. (301) 443-4513; Fax (301) 443-4279; TTY (301) 443-8431.

Prognosis

It is important to note that current information about the prognoses of children with Rett's syndrome is derived from treatments given to patients in the 1970s or 1980s. As knowledge of effective treatments continues to accumulate, children with RS are receiving treatment earlier than they did two decades ago. It is likely that future prognoses for the disorder will reflect these improvements.

As of 2002, the prognosis for RS patients is poor. In most cases, there is a steady loss of cognition, movement-related, social, and behavioral skills throughout the patient's lifetime. Some patients, however, make modest developmental gains in adolescence. The average life expectancy of patients with RS has not yet been determined, although some are presently middle-aged.

Prevention

As of 2002, there are no effective strategies for preventing Rett's disorder, since most cases result from new mutations of the MECP2 gene rather than transmission of a defective gene from the parents.

Resources

BOOKS

American Psychiatric Association. *Diagnostic and Statistical Manual of Mental Disorders.* 4th edition, text revised. Washington, DC: American Psychiatric Association, 2000.

"Psychiatric Conditions in Childhood and Adolescence." Section 19, Chapter 274. In *The Merck Manual of Diagnosis and Therapy*, edited by Mark H. Beers, MD, and Robert Berkow, MD. Whitehouse Station, NJ: Merck Research Laboratories, 1999.

Thoene, Jess G., editor. *Physicians' Guide to Rare Diseases.* Montvale, NJ: Dowden Publishing Company, 1995.

PERIODICALS

Gura, T. "Gene Defect Linked to Rett Syndrome." *Science* 286 (October 1, 1999): 27.

Jan, M., J. M. Dooley, and K. E. Gordon. "A Male Rett Syndrome Variant: Application of Diagnostic Criteria." *Pediatric Neurology* 20 (1999): 238-240.

Rett Syndrome Diagnostic Criteria Work Group. "Diagnostic Criteria for Rett Syndrome." *Annals of Neurology* 23 (1988): 425-428.

Smith, Jill C., MD. "Rett Syndrome in Boys." *The Rett Gazette* (Winter 2001): 1-2.

ORGANIZATIONS

Institute for Community Inclusion/UAP. 300 Longwood Avenue, Boston, MA 02115. (617) 355-6506. TTY (617) 355-6956. E-mail: ici@a1.tch.harvard.edu.

International Rett Syndrome Association (IRSA). 9121 Piscataway Road, Suite 2-B, Clinton, MD 20735. (301) 856-3334 or (800) 818-RETT. Fax: (301) 856-3336. <www.rettsyndrome.org>.

National Association of Rare Disorders (NORD). P.O. Box 8923, New Fairfield, CT 06812-8923. (800) 999-NORD or (203) 746-6518.

OTHER

"Gene Today, Gone Tomorrow." Baylor College of Medicine press release, September 30, 1999.

Willard, Huntington F., and Brian D. Hendrich. "Breaking the Silence in Rett Syndrome." Manuscript circulated by the Department of Genetics, Center for Human Genetics, Case Western Reserve University and University Hospitals of Cleveland, OH, January 2002.

Rebecca J. Frey, Ph.D.

Revia *see* **Naltrexone**

Risperdal *see* **Risperidone**

Risperidone

Definition

Risperidone is classified as an atypical antipsychotic drug. It is sold in the United States under the brand name of Risperdal.

Purpose

Risperidone is used for the management of symptoms of psychotic disorders such as **schizophrenia**.

Description

Risperidone is an atypical antipsychotic agent for two reasons. First, it is chemically unrelated to the older antipsychotic drugs. Second, unlike older antipsychotic drugs that primarily inhibit the actions of dopamine, a chemical in the **brain**, risperidone may also have some action against another brain chemical, serotonin. The proper level of both dopamine and serotonin are influential in maintaining mental well-being.

An advantage of using risperidone over one of the older antipsychotic drugs is a lower incidence of parkinsonian-like side effects. These side effects may be sufficiently troublesome to cause patients to discontinue treatment for their schizophrenia. For this reason, patients who have had negative experiences with older antipsychotics may benefit from risperidone. Also, some patients who showed little improvement with older antipsychotic drugs respond better to risperidone.

Risperidone is available in 0.25-mg, 0.5-mg, 1-mg, 2-mg, 3-mg, and 4-mg tablets and a solution containing 1 mg of drug in each milliliter of solution.

KEY TERMS

Dopamine—A chemical in brain tissue that serves to transmit nerve impulses (is a neurotransmitter) and helps to regulate movement and emotions.

Parkinsonian—Related to symptoms associated with Parkinson's disease, a nervous system disorder characterized by abnormal muscle movement of the tongue, face, and neck, inability to walk or move quickly, walking in a shuffling manner, restlessness, and/or tremors.

Serotonin—A widely distributed neurotransmitter that is found in blood platelets, the lining of the digestive tract, and the brain, and that works in combination with norepinephrine. It causes very powerful contractions of smooth muscle, and is associated with mood, attention, emotions, and sleep. Low levels of serotonin are associated with depression.

Recommended dosage

For treating psychotic disorders in adults, the usual starting dose of risperidone is 1 mg twice daily. Dosage is increased gradually until a target dose of 3 mg twice daily is reached. Some patients do just as well with a single daily dose (6 mg once a day, for example). There is little clinical evidence to indicate that increasing the daily dose beyond 8 mg offers additional benefit. However, higher doses may contribute to additional side effects. If the dose needs to be adjusted, the changes should made no more often than once per week.

In older patients (over age 60), starting dosage should not exceed 1 mg daily. Most patients should not take more than 3 mg daily. People with low blood pressure and those who have kidney disease should take a similarly reduced dose.

Precautions

Patients with a history of cardiovascular disease or low blood pressure should take risperidone only after discussing the risks and benefits with their physician, and then with close physician monitoring.

Risperidone has occasionally been associated with **seizures**. People with a past history of seizures should discuss with their doctor whether risperidone is the right antipsychotic for them to use.

People taking risperidone should avoid operating a motor vehicle or other dangerous machinery until they see how risperidone affects them.

Some people have trouble regulating their body temperature while taking risperidone. Patients receiving this drug should be aware of this and avoid extremes in outdoor temperatures.

Side effects

The most common and bothersome side effect associated with risperidone is decreased blood pressure while standing up (known as orthostatic hypotension). This can cause dizziness or fainting. A decrease in blood pressure usually occurs early in therapy, while the proper dose is being established. It is more common in older patients than in younger ones. Usually, this side effect disappears entirely with time. If it continues, the physician may decrease the dose. Meanwhile, people taking risperidone should be aware of this side effect and get up slowly if they have been sitting for an extended time.

The most common nervous system side effects of risperidone include **insomnia**, agitation, anxiety, and headache. Early in therapy, patients may experience an inability to think clearly or perform certain tasks that require mental alertness. High doses of risperidone can cause unwanted sleepiness in about 40% of patients.

Antipsychotic drugs, including risperidone, can cause side effects that are similar to the symptoms of Parkinson's disease. The patient does not have Parkinson's disease, but may have shaking in muscles at rest, difficulty with voluntary movements, and poor muscle tone. These symptoms normally disappear if the drug is stopped.

The most common gastrointestinal side effects include nausea, vomiting, constipation, and difficulty digesting food.

Up to 10% of patients taking risperidone experience rhinitis (runny nose).

Interactions

There is very little information about how risperidone interacts with other drugs. However, because some patients receiving risperidone experience lowered blood pressure while standing, it is expected that other drugs that lower blood pressure may increase the incidence and severity of this side effect when taken with risperidone.

Resources

BOOKS

American Society of Health-System Pharmacists. *AHFS Drug Information 2002.* Bethesda: American Society of Health-System Pharmacists, 2002.

O'Brien, Charles P. "Drug Addiction and Drug Abuse." In *Goodman & Gillman's The Pharmacological Basis of Therapeutics,* edited by Joel G. Hardman, Ph.D. and Lee E. Limbird, Ph.D. Tenth Edition. New York: McGraw-Hill, 2001.

Jack Raber, Pharm.D.

Ritalin *see* **Methylphenidate**

Rivastigmine

Definition

Rivastigmine is a drug used to treat symptoms of **Alzheimer's disease**. In the United States, rivastigmine is sold as the brand name drug Exelon.

Purpose

Rivastigmine is used to treat symptoms of Alzeheimer's disease in individuals with mild to moderate illness. It has also been used to treat **dementia** caused by other conditions such as Lewy-body disease or following strokes. The drug may produce mild improvements in symptoms of thinking for a short period of time, but rivastigmine does not cure or stop progression of underlying diseases.

Description

The Food and Drug Administration approved rivastigmine in 2000 specifically for treating Alzheimer's disease. In Alzheimer's disease, some cells in specific regions of the **brain** die. Because of this cell death, these brain cells lose their ability to transmit nerve impulses. Brain cells normally transmit nerve impulses another by secreting various chemicals known as **neurotransmitters**.

Brain cells that make and secrete a neurotransmitter called acetylcholine are affected early in the course of Alzheimer's disease. Rivastigmine prevents the breakdown of acetylcholine in the brain, thus temporarily increasing its concentration. In doing so, rivastigmine may improve the thinking process by facilitating nerve impulse transmission within the brain.

KEY TERMS

Acetylcholine—A naturally occurring chemical in the body that transmits nerve impulses from cell to cell. Generally, it has opposite effects from dopamine and norepinephrine; it causes blood vessels to dilate, lowers blood pressure, and slows the heartbeat. Central nervous system well-being is dependent on a balance among acetylcholine, dopamine, serotonin, and norepinephrine.

Dementia—A group of symptoms (syndrome) associated with a progressive loss of memory and other intellectual functions that is serious enough to interfere with a person's ability to perform the tasks of daily life. Dementia impairs memory, alters personality, leads to deterioration in personal grooming, impairs reasoning ability, and causes disorientation.

Lewy-body disease—A type of dementia that resembles Alzheimer's disease, but progresses more rapidly. Common symptoms include fluctuations in confusion and recurring visual hallucinations. In this disease, abnormal brain cells are distributed throughout the brain.

Milligram (mg)—One-thousandth of a gram. A gram is the metric measure that equals about 0.035 ounces.

Neurotransmitter—A chemical in the brain that transmits messages between neurons, or nerve cells.

Placebo—An inactive substance or preparation used as a control in experiments with human subjects to test the effectiveness of a drug or herbal preparation. Some patients may experience a medicinal response or experience side effects to a placebo simply because they have faith in its powers even though it contains no medicine.

Rivastigmine is available as capsules in four different strengths and as an oral solution for use by people who have difficulty swallowing. Unlike some other drugs used to treat Alzheimer's disease, the liver does not break down rivastigmine. As a result, it may be preferred in the treatment of people with Alzeheimer's disease who have liver disease.

Recommended dosage

The initial dosage of rivastigmine is 1.5 mg taken two times per day. If this dose is tolerated without difficulty, the dosage may be increased to 3 mg twice a day after at least two weeks at the lower dosage. Some people are unable to tolerate nausea, vomiting, anorexia, and weight loss that occur with higher dosages. If the drug does not cause significant adverse effects, the dose may be increased to 4.5 mg two times per day, followed by 6 mg two times per day. The dosage should be increased slowly, at two-week intervals. If side effects occur and cannot be tolerated, the drug may be stopped for several doses. When the drug is started again, the same dosage or the next lower dosage may be tried. The maximum daily dosage is 6 mg two times per day.

Precautions

Rivastigmine may slow heart rates, increase acid in the stomach, make urination difficult, cause breathing difficulties, and may possibly contribute to **seizures**. As a result, it should be used with close physician supervision and monitoring in people with certain heart conditions, those who are prone to stomach ulcers, people with bladder obstruction, individuals with asthma or chronic obstructive pulmonary disease, and people with a history of seizures disorders.

Individuals taking rivastigmine should be reassessed periodically to determine whether the drug is providing any benefits. If caregivers feel the drug is no longer beneficial, it may be stopped.

Side effects

The most frequent side effects associated with rivastigmine involve stomach upset. Nausea, vomiting, anorexia, heartburn, and weakness occur in more than 5% of people and at twice the rate of placebo pills. Dizziness and headaches also occur in more than 10% of people taking rivastigmine.

Other, less common, side effects are difficulty sleeping, confusion, depression, anxiety, sleepiness, **hallucinations**, tremors, fainting, aggression, constipation, gas, overwhelming **fatigue**, weight loss, increased sweating, and infections.

Interactions

Drugs such as dicyclomine may inhibit the effects of rivastigmine. Other drugs like bethanechol may possibly increase some of the side effects of rivastigmine. Rivastigmine may interact with some of the drugs used to relax muscles during surgery. The interaction increases the effects of both drugs.

Resources

BOOKS

Ellsworth, Allan J. *Mosby's Medical Drug Reference*. St. Louis, MO: Mosby, Inc, 1999.

Facts and Comparisons Staff. *Drug Facts and Comparisons*. 6th Edition. St. Louis, MO: Facts and Comparisons, 2002.

Novartis Staff. *Exelon Package Insert*. Basle, Switzerland: Novartis Pharma AG, 2001.

Kelly Karpa, RPh, Ph.D.

Rorschach technique

Definition

The Rorschach technique, sometimes known as the Rorschach test or the inkblot test, is a projective personality assessment based on the test taker's reactions to a series of 10 inkblot pictures.

The Rorschach technique is the most widely used projective psychological test. The Rorschach is used to help assess personality structure and identify emotional problems and mental disorders. Like other projective techniques, it is based on the principle that subjects viewing neutral, ambiguous stimuli will project their own personalities onto them, thereby revealing a variety of unconscious conflicts and motivations. Administered to both adolescents and adults, the Rorschach can also be used with children as young as three years old, although the commonly used Exner scoring system (discussed below) is appropriate only for test taker five years or older.

Purpose

The Rorschach technique is used to elicit information about the structure and dynamics of an individual's personality functioning. The test provides information about a person's thought processes, perceptions, motivations, and attitude toward his or her environment, and it can detect internal and external pressures and conflicts as well as illogical or psychotic thought patterns.

The Rorschach technique can also be used for specific diagnostic purposes. Some scoring methods for the Rorschach elicit information on symptoms related to depression, **schizophrenia**, and anxiety disorders. Also, the test can be used to screen for coping deficits related to developmental problems in children and adolescents.

KEY TERMS

Projective test—A psychological test in which the test taker responds to or provides ambiguous, abstract, or unstructured stimuli, often in the form of pictures or drawings.

Reliability—The ability of a test to yield consistent, repeatable results.

Standardization—The administration of a test to a sample group of people for the purpose of establishing test norms.

Validity—The ability of a test to measure accurately what it claims to measure.

Precautions

The Rorschach is generally used as part of a battery of tests and must be administered by a trained **psychologist**. Also, scoring the Rorschach test requires training in and knowledge of a comprehensive scoring system.

There is some disagreement concerning the reliability, validity, and clinical utility of the test and its scoring systems. Diagnoses for clinical disorders should not generally be based solely on the Rorschach test.

Description

The Rorschach technique is named for its developer, Swiss **psychiatrist** Hermann Rorschach (1884-1922). Rorschach, whose primary interest was in the psychoanalytic work of Carl Jung, began experimenting with inkblots as early as 1911 as a means of assessing introversion and extroversion.

The Rorschach technique is administered using 10 cards, each containing a complicated inkblot pattern, five in black and gray, two in black and red, and three in various pastel colors. Subjects look at the cards one at a time and describe what each inkblot resembles. They are instructed to look at the shape, shading, and color of the inkblots. After the subject has viewed all 10 cards, the examiner usually goes back over the responses for additional information. The subject may be asked to clarify some responses or to describe which features of each inkblot prompted the responses. Actually, there is no one correct response to any inkblot card, although there are certain common responses to some cards.

The test taker is given a lot of flexibility with how to respond to the inkblots. If a test taker asks if he or she is allowed to turn the card upside-down, the test adminis-

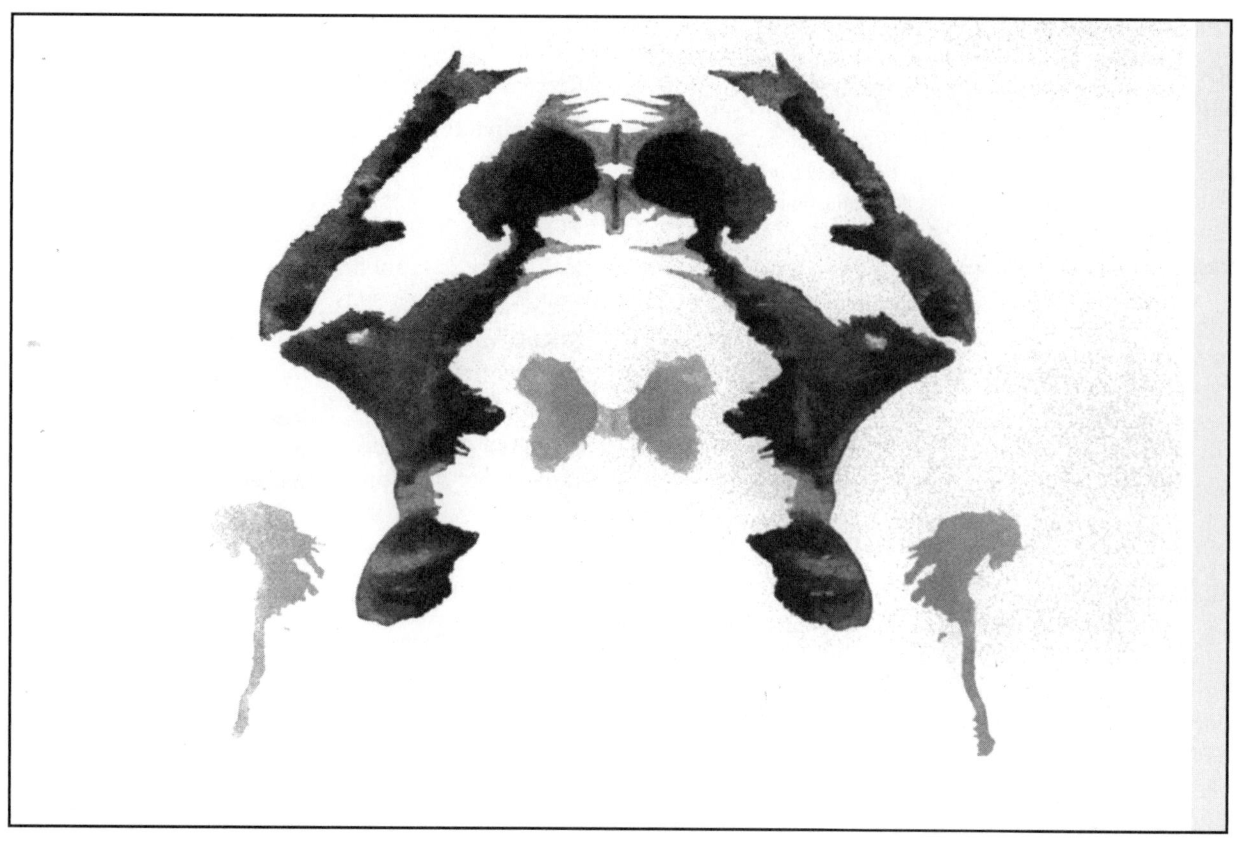

Example of a Rorschach inkblot test. *(Stan Goldblatt. Photo Researchers, Inc. Reproduced by permission.)*

trator will be non-directive, indicating it is the test taker's choice. A response like this from the test administrator is consistent with the projective nature of the Rorschach technique in that the test taker is projecting his or her personality onto the test stimuli.

Results

Rorschach, who pioneered the test in 1921, did not provide a comprehensive scoring system. In response to complaints about validity, scoring methods have been devised that aim at providing greater objectivity by clearly specifying certain personality variables and relating them to clinical diagnoses. Originally published in the 1960s, the Exner Comprehensive Rorschach System used today (the 1987 updated version) is a computer-based scoring system that provides score summaries and lists likely personality and adjustment descriptions for each test taker. Specifically, this scoring system considers aspects of a test taker's response such as the content of the response, the reasons for the events present on the card, the location of events on the card, and elaboration on cooperative and aggressive behavior. Exner also recorded certain popular and common responses to the cards and the degree to which test takers chose these responses. It should be noted, however, that many examiners still interpret the scores without benefit of a computer.

Test scores, whether based on Rorschach's original formulation, Exner's comprehensive scoring system, or other scoring systems, are based on several factors. One is location, or what part of the blot a person focuses on: the whole blot, sections of it, or only specific details within a particular section. Another is whether the response is based on factors such as form, color, movement, or shading. These factors are referred to as determinants. For example, people who tend to see movement in Rorschach blots are thought to be intellectual and introspective; those who see mostly stationary objects or patterns are described as practical and action-oriented. Finally, content refers to which objects, persons, or situations the person sees in the blot. Content categories include humans, animals, clothing, and nature.

Most examiners also assess responses based on the frequency of certain responses as given by previous test takers. Many psychologists interpret the test freely according to their subjective impressions, including their impression of the subject's demeanor while taking the test (cooperative, anxious, defensive, etc.). Such interpretations, especially when combined with clinical observation and knowledge of a client's personal history, can help a therapist arrive at a more expansive, in-depth understanding of the client's personality.

While the Rorschach technique is still widely used, its popularity has decreased somewhat in recent decades. Unlike objective personality inventories, which can be administered to a group, the Rorschach test must be given individually. A skilled examiner is required, and the test can take several hours to complete and interpret. Like other projective tests, it has been criticized for lack of validity and reliability. Interpretation of responses is highly dependent on an examiner's individual judgment: two different testers may interpret the same responses quite differently. In addition, treatment procedures at mental health facilities often require more specific, objective types of personality description than those provided by the Rorschach technique.

There have, however, been studies that support the validity of the Rorschach test. When trained psychologists use a comprehensive scoring system, agreement between administrators on certain variables ranges between 80% and 100%. Also, Exner's comprehensive system is based on a standardization sample of more than 2,000 children, adolescents, and adults. This sample included a large number of schizophrenic and depressed individuals.

See also Figure drawings; House-Tree-Person

Resources

BOOKS

Exner, John E. *The Rorschach—A Comprehensive System. Basic Foundations, Volume One*. New York: John Wiley and Sons, 1993.

Groth-Marnat, Gary. *Handbook of Psychological Assessment*. 3rd edition. New York: John Wiley and Sons, 1997.

Kline, Paul. *The Handbook of Psychological Testing*. New York: Routledge, 1999.

Reynolds, Cecil R. *Comprehensive Clinical Psychology. Volume 4: Assessment*. Amsterdam: Elsevier, 1998.

Ali Fahmy, Ph.D.

KEY TERMS

Antioxidant—Substance that protects the body from damaging reactive oxygen molecules in the body. These reactive oxygen molecules can come from inside the body or from environmental pollution and are thought to play a role in the aging process and the development of degenerative disease. The phenolic compounds in essential oil of rosemary have been shown to be effective antioxidants.

Astringent—A substance or compound that causes contraction or constriction of soft tissue. Rosemary's astringent qualities have made it a popular ingredient in treatments for oily skin.

Essential oil—The product of special ducts or cells in the tissues of aromatic plants (or the sap of certain trees) that gives the plant its characteristic aroma and therapeutic properties. Essential oils are sometimes called volatile oils because they evaporate readily at room temperature.

Flavonoids—Plant pigments that have a variety of effects on human physiology. Some of these pigments have anti-inflammatory, anti-carcinogenic, and antioxidant effects, for example. The diosmin contained in rosemary is a flavonoid.

Middle note—A term used in perfumery and aromatherapy to designate essential oils whose odors emerge later than "top notes" but evaporate more rapidly than "bottom notes." Rosemary is considered a middle note in aromatherapy.

Phenol—A white crystalline water-soluble substance used chiefly as an antiseptic and disinfectant.

Topical—A type of medication or preparation intended for use on the skin or external suface of the body. Rosemary is a common ingredient in astringent cleansers and in hand lotions or similar preparations intended to warm the skin or increase blood circulation.

Rosemary

Definition

Rosemary is an herb derived from an evergreen shrub, *Rosmarinus officinalis*, related to the mint or Lamiaceae family of plants. Rosemary is a native of the Mediterranean regions of Europe and the Near East; Tunisia is a major modern-day source of the plant. Rosemary can grow as tall as 5 ft, producing strongly scented, leathery leaves used in perfumes and seasonings. Its Latin name, *Rosmarinus*, means "ocean dew." Other names for rosemary include compass weed, compass plant, or polar plant. An interesting tradition about rosemary is that it grows best in gardens tended by forceful or strong-willed women; a Spanish folk saying has it that "where rosemary thrives the mistress is master."

The major chemical compounds found in essential oil of rosemary include eugenol, borneol, camphene, camphor, cineol, lineol, pinene, and terpineol. Compounds found in rosemary that are considered to be highly effective antioxidants include monoterpenoid ketone compounds, such as thujone, camphor, verbenone and carvone, as well as such phenols as methylchavicol, carvacrol, eugenol and thymole. Rosemary extract also contains numerous polyphenolic compounds that possess high antioxidant activity, including rosmanol, rosmaridiphenol, rosmarinic acid, carnosol, carnosic acid, and ursolic acid.

Purpose

Although rosemary is most familiar to contemporary Westerners as a kitchen herb used to add a spicy or slightly medicinal flavor to some foods, it was traditionally used as an antiseptic, astringent, and food preservative before the invention of refrigeration. It was burned in sickrooms to disinfect the air. Rosemary's antioxidant properties are still used to extend the shelf life of prepared foods.

Rosemary is also a well known "middle note" in the making of perfumes and **aromatherapy** products. The aroma of its essential oil lasts about two to three days, and is regarded as having energizing and invigorating qualities. It is thought to improve memory and the ability to concentrate, and has been used to relieve migraine headaches. Its astringent qualities make it appropriate for use in facial cleansers for oily skin. Rosemary is frequently added to compresses to heal bruises and sprains, and in topical salves, lotions, or creams to relieve muscle cramps or improve circulation. It is a favorite ingredient in hand creams for gardeners or for use in cold weather. The herb contains a flavonoid called diosmin, which has been shown to strengthen capillaries in the circulatory system. Some research studies are investigating the usefulness of rosemary in the treatment of varicose veins and hemorrhoids. The German Commission E has approved the use of rosemary for low blood pressure, and for painful joints or muscles. In addition, rosemary is still listed as a medicinal herb in the official *United States Pharmacopoeia*.

Several of the compounds in rosemary have been shown to have anti-inflammatory effects. As a result, some cancer researchers are studying rosemary as a natural non-steroidal anti-inflammatory drug, or NSAID. Since the use of NSAIDs is associated with a lowered risk of certain types of cancer in the general population, these researchers are investigating the possibility that rosemary may act as a cancer preventive.

Description

Essential oil and extract of rosemary are prepared for use in aromatherapy by steam distillation from the leaves and flowers of the plant during its second year of growth. The leaves can also be stripped from the stems of the second-year plant and dried for internal use. Although rosemary is more commonly used to flavor dishes rather than as a separate item in the diet, it can be taken as a tea.

Recommended dosages

Rosemary tea is made by pouring 1 cup of boiling water into a cup containing 1 teaspoon of the dried leaves. Tea made from fresh rosemary leaves require .35 ounces–.52 ounces of the herb. The tea may be taken up to three times daily.

Essential oil of rosemary should not be used full-strength on the skin, as it has been reported to cause skin irritation. When it is diluted, as in a carrier oil for massage or in a salve, hand cream, or facial cleanser, it is safe for use as often as desired. In aromatherapy rosemary oil can be used in burners, potpouri, or in sachets.

Precautions

Rosemary tea should not be taken by pregnant or lactating women, although they may safely use it in cooking to season food. Children under six months of age also should not be given rosemary tea. Rosemary should not be taken by persons with epilepsy, ulcerative colitis, or high blood pressure.

Side effects

When rosemary is harvested appropriately and used within recommended guidelines, side effects are minimal. A few instances of allergic skin reactions to topical preparations containing rosemary have been reported.

Recent European research has shown that rosemary interferes with the absorption of iron in the diet, which indicates that it should not be used internally by persons with iron deficiency anemia.

Interactions

Rosemary is not known to interact with any current Western prescription medications.

Resources

BOOKS

Medical Economics Staff. *PDR for Herbal Medicines.* Montvale, NJ: Medical Economics Company, 1998.

Pelletier, Kenneth R., MD. "Western Herbal Medicine: Nature's Green Pharmacy." Chapter 6 in *The Best Alternative Medicine.* New York: Simon and Schuster, 2002.

Price, Shirley. *Practical Aromatherapy.* Second edition, revised. London, UK: Thorsons, 1994.

PERIODICALS

Fahim, Fawzia A., and others. "Allied Studies on the Effect of *Rosmarinus officinalis L.* on Experimental Hepatotoxicity and Mutagenesis." *International Journal of Food Sciences and Nutrition* 50 (November 1999): 413.

Samman, Samir, Brittmarie Sandstrom, Maja Bjorndal Toft, and others. "Green Tea or Rosemary Extract Added to Foods Reduces Nonheme Iron Absorption." *American Journal of Clinical Nutrition* 73 (March 2001): 607.

Tyler, Varro E. "Nature's Surprising Antioxidants." *Prevention* 51 (December 1999): 105.

Wargovich, Michael J., and others. "Herbals, Cancer Prevention, and Health." *Journal of Nutrition* 131 (November 2001): 3034S-3036S.

OTHER

American Botanical Council. PO Box 144345. Austin, TX 78714-4345.

National Association for Holistic Aromatherapy (NAHA). 4509 Interlake Avenue North, #233, Seattle, WA 98103-6773. (888) ASK-NAHA or (206) 547-2164. <www.naha.org>.

Rebecca J. Frey, Ph.D.

Rumination disorder

Definition

Rumination disorder may be diagnosed when a person deliberately brings food back up into the mouth and either rechews and reswallows it or spits it out.

Description

Rumination disorder is sometimes called merycism. It is a disorder most commonly found in infants, and associated with **mental retardation**. During rumination, previously eaten food is intentionally brought back into the mouth. Sometimes the child spits it out, but in other cases, the food is rechewed and reswallowed. The regurgitation is not caused by a medical condition. In many cases, the child has had an illness associated with vomiting that occurs before the onset of rumination disorder. Rumination has also been observed in severe cases of eating disorders among teenagers as well as adults.

KEY TERMS

Merycism—Another name for rumination disorder.

Regurgitation—The return of partly digested food from the stomach to the mouth. Regurgitation may be either an intentional act or an involuntary physical reaction.

Ruminate—To chew or rechew regurgitated food.

Causes and symptoms

Causes

There is no general agreement on the causes of rumination disorder. In infants, it is thought to be caused by a lack of nurturing or physical contact. The child's rumination may represent an attempt to stimulate or soothe him- or herself. Biological factors are also being explored as possible causes of rumination disorder.

Symptoms

The symptoms of rumination include both the regurgitation of food and, in infants, the effort made to regurgitate that food. In infants, the attempts to bring up food can include putting fingers in the mouth, sucking on the tongue, and arching the back. When food is brought up, the cheeks expand and appear puffed. Sometimes an observer can detect the rechewing; the person often appears to take pleasure in the act. The person's breath may have a foul or sour odor. Some infants, especially those who have just begun ruminating, will expel most or all of the regurgitated food from their mouths. When this expulsion occurs, it is often mistaken for normal infant vomiting. As an infant continues to ruminate, he or she often learns to keep more and more of the regurgitated food in the mouth.

Demographics

Rumination disorder occurs primarily in infants. The onset usually occurs before the infant's first birthday. The disorder is also more common in people with mental retardation. The onset of rumination disorder is typically later in mentally retarded patients, however; it may not appear until puberty or even the early adult years. Rumination disorder is rare and thought to occur more often in males than in females. People who have **anorexia nervosa** or **bulimia nervosa** may begin to ruminate only in adult life. One report found that up to 20% of people with bulimia may ruminate.

Diagnosis

The ***Diagnostic and Statistical Manual of Mental Disorders***, fourth edition, text revision (*DSM-IV-TR*), which is the standard reference work for mental health professionals, gives only three general criteria for diagnosing rumination disorder. The first is that the person's behavior of deliberately bringing up and rechewing food must have lasted for at least a month. The regurgitation and rechewing must happen after a period of time in which the person did not ruminate. In addition, the rumination cannot result from a medical condition such as esophageal reflux. In addition, the manual specifies that the rumination cannot be associated with anorexia or bulimia.

Rumination disorder may be difficult to diagnose. One reason for this difficulty is that infants or adults who do not expel any of their regurgitated food can often be identified only by a puffing of the cheeks when the food is in the mouth or by an unpleasant breath odor. In addition, because many people and infants who ruminate find the experience a positive and pleasurable one, there are no physical signs of discomfort to bring the disorder to the attention of caretakers or others.

Some experts disagree with the statement of the *Diagnostic and Statistical Manual* that a **diagnosis** of rumination disorder cannot be made if the rumination is associated with anorexia or bulimia. These experts maintain that diagnosing and treating rumination disorder in patients who have other eating disorders is important for the sake of the patient's health.

Treatment

Treatment for rumination disorder depends on the cause of the behavior. Infants who are thought to ruminate because of a lack of affection may be fed by someone other than their mother or father. This person can be a replacement while their parents receive treatment themselves. Other approaches involve therapy and parenting education to create a stronger bond between the parents and the child.

The treatment of adult patients includes giving them chewing gum to use when rumination might normally occur. Other researchers have found that giving mentally retarded adults filling meals may reduce rumination. Often, treating such eating disorders as anorexia or bulimia helps to resolve the rumination that may be associated with those disorders. **Behavior modification** techniques that help a patient to unlearn the ruminating behavior have also been used.

Prognosis

In many cases, rumination that begins in infancy stops on its own. The disorder should be treated, however, because infants with untreated rumination disorder are at risk of malnutrition and death caused by dehydration. Treatments for rumination disorder are generally very effective. Treatment of associated eating disorders in adults is generally regarded as successful.

Prevention

There is no known way to prevent rumination disorder. It is possible, however, that a strong parent-child bond may reduce the possibility of the disorder occurring in infants.

Resources

BOOKS

American Psychiatric Association *Diagnostic and Statistical Manual of Mental Disorders*. 4th ed. text revised. Washington DC: American Psychiatric Association, 2000.

Sadock, Benjamin J. and Virginia A. Sadock, eds. *Comprehensive Textbook of Psychiatry.* 7th edition. Philadelphia: Lippincott Williams and Wilkins, 2000.

PERIODICALS

Weakley, Melinda M., Theodore A. Petti, George Karwisch. "Case Study: Chewing Gum Treatment of Rumination in an Adolescent with an Eating Disorder." *Journal of the American Academy of Child and Adolescent Psychiatry* 36, no. 8 (August 1997):1124-1128.

ORGANIZATIONS

American Academy of Pediatrics. 141 Northwest Point Boulevard, Elk Grove Village, IL 60007-1098. (847) 434-4000. <www.aap.org>.

Tish Davidson, A.M.

S

SAD *see* **Seasonal affective disorder**

Sadism *see* **Sexual sadism**

SAMe

Definition

SAMe (or S-adenosyl-L-methionine) is a naturally occurring chemical that is found throughout the entire body. It is involved in many chemical reactions that are necessary for life. SAMe is available as a natural dietary supplement that can be found at some pharmacies or health food stores, and can be purchased without a prescription.

Purpose

People take supplements of SAMe for many reasons including its possible antidepressant effects. Some evidence suggests that taking SAMe can improve symptoms of depression within two weeks, which is considerably faster than the time it takes for oral antidepressant prescription drugs to work. (Prescription antidepressants often take a minimum of two weeks for patients to begin noticing any effect, and many take four to six weeks.)

Description

SAMe is a specific form of the amino acid methionine, a substance that, when not metabolized properly, allows homocysteine to build up in the blood. SAMe is also an antioxidant, a substance that protects the body from damaging reactive oxygen molecules in the body. These reactive oxygen molecules can come from inside the body or from environmental pollution and are thought to play a role in the aging process and the development of degenerative disease. In general, SAMe is thought to raise the level of functioning of other amino acids in the body.

Although people use SAMe for many reasons including osteoarthritis, depression, heart disease, fibromyalgia, bursitis, tendonitis, chronic low back pain, **dementia**, **Alzheimer's disease**, improving **brain** function, multiple sclerosis, spinal cord injuries, migraine headaches, lead poisoning, liver disease, and to slow aging, the best evidence to date indicates that SAMe may be effective in relieving symptoms of osteoarthritis and for treating depression.

Several studies have indicated that oral SAMe and intravenous SAMe are effective treatments for depression. The studies researching the oral SAMe were small studies, and often were of short duration. However, the studies indicate that SAMe is effective in treating depression, and that it may be almost as effective as tricyclic antidepressants. Larger studies of SAMe are necessary.

Recommended dosage

SAMe can be taken orally or intravenously. Oral administration is more common. When taken by mouth, doses of 400–1,600 mg have been suggested. For osteoarthritis, 200–600 mg daily is a typical dose. For depression, 400–1,600 mg daily is a typical dose.

200 mg of SAMe have been administered intravenously or intramuscularly for 14 days while the patient simultaneously begins therapy with prescription antidepressant medication. If SAMe is used without prescription antidepressants, 200-400 mg per day by intravenous or intramuscular injections has been used. When treating other medical conditions, doses as high as 800 mg daily by injection have been used. Again, however, intravenous administration is rare in the United States.

Precautions

As a natural supplement, SAMe has not been evaluated by the Food and Drug Administration. Claims of safety or effectiveness for treating any medical disorder have not been thoroughly studied by any governmental

KEY TERMS

Antidepressant—A medication used to treat the symptoms of depression.

Bipolar disorder—A mental disorder characterized by dramatic, and sometimes rapid mood swings, resulting in both manic and depressive episodes; formerly called manic-depressive disorder.

Depression—A mental state characterized by excessive sadness. Other symptoms include altered sleep patterns, thoughts of suicide, difficulty concentrating, agitation, lack of energy, and loss of enjoyment in activities that are usually pleasurable.

Homocysteine—A chemical that builds up in the blood when methionine is not properly processed. High blood levels of homocysteine increase the risk of heart disease and stroke.

Mania—An elevated or euphoric mood or irritable state that is characteristic of bipolar I disorder. This state is characterized by mental and physical hyperactivity, disorganization of behavior, and inappropriate elevation of mood.

Milligram (mg)—One-thousandth of a gram. A gram is the metric measure that equals about 0.035 ounces.

agency and there is no regulation of natural supplements. This means that potencies may vary between lots or among different manufacturers. It is also possible that supplements may not contain the ingredients that are listed on product labels.

SAMe should be used carefully by individuals with a history of **bipolar disorder** since it may aggravate symptoms of mania. When used with prescription antidepressant medications, life-threatening symptoms may occur. It should be used with prescription antidepressant drugs only under close medical supervision.

Side effects

When taken by mouth, SAMe may cause stomach upset including gas, vomiting, diarrhea, headache, and nausea. These symptoms are more common at high doses.

Anxiety has also occurred in people with depression, and mania has been reported in those with a history of bipolar disorder.

Interactions

As stated, use of SAMe with antidepressants (especially selective serotonin reuptake inhibitors, or SSRIs) may cause life-threatening symptoms including agitation, tremors, anxiety, rapid heartbeats, difficulty breathing, diarrhea, shivering, muscle stiffness, and excessive sweating. The combination can also cause **insomnia**. If SAMe is used at the same time that prescription antidepressants are taken, close medical supervision is required.

SAMe may offer beneficial drug interactions when used with some medications. More research is necessary to determine whether SAMe does indeed protect the liver, but some scientists think that SAMe may protect the liver from damage caused by some drugs, including acetaminophen, alcohol, estrogens, steroids, and several other prescription drugs.

People interested in taking SAMe for depression should discuss its use with their doctor to weigh the potential benefits and risks.

Resources

BOOKS

Therapeutic Research Faculty. *Natural Medicines Comprehensive Database*. Stockton, CA: Natural Medicines Database, 2000.

PERIODICALS

Fetrow, C. W., Pharm.D. and J. R. Avila, Pharm.D. "Efficacy of the dietary supplement S-adenosyl-L-methionine." *Annals of Pharmacotherapy* 35, no. 11 (November 2001): 1414-1425.

Kelly Karpa, RPh, Ph.D.

Schizoaffective disorder

Definition

One of the most challenging mental disorders to identify accurately and treat appropriately is schizoaffective disorder. This condition involves both psychotic symptoms and conspicuous, long-enduring, severe symptoms of mood disorder. The cluster of symptoms experienced by persons with schizoaffective disorder can resemble—at various times in its course—bipolar disorder, major depressive episode with psychotic features, or **schizophrenia**.

The schizoaffective disorder classification is applied when a mental health client meets diagnostic criteria for both schizophrenia and an "affective" (mood) disorder—depression or **bipolar disorder**. In schizoaffective disorder, the experiencing of mood and psychotic symptoms occurs predominantly simultaneously and the mood disturbance is long lasting. However, periods of experiencing serious psychotic symptoms without serious mood disturbance are also a definitive feature. In bipolar disorder and depression with psychotic features, psychotic symptoms *only* occur during an active episode of mania or severe clinical depression. Schizoaffective disorder is characterized by periods during which psychotic symptoms are experienced *without* simultaneous severe mood changes. If the patient is encountered for the first time during such a period of psychotic symptoms in the absence of mood changes, it can appear that the individual has schizophrenia. However, in a person who has psychotic symptoms, the presence of long-standing severe mood disturbance suggests possible schizoaffective disorder if there are also periods of psychotic symptoms *without* concurrent mood fluctuations.

Schizoaffective disorder is typically identified by a process of lengthy observation and elimination of another diagnostic alternative over a long course of care. Because of the need for longitudinal observation and collection of a wealth of information before an accurate **diagnosis** is possible, most people with schizoaffective disorder have borne other diagnostic labels prior to the schizoaffective diagnosis (usually, bipolar disorder).

Description

Psychotic symptoms

Both psychotic symptoms and mood disorder symptoms are experienced by the individual with schizoaffective disorder. In schizoaffective disorder, at least two of the major symptoms of **psychosis** are evident in the client. Classic psychotic symptoms can occur during mood disturbances as well as in periods without extreme mood changes. **Hallucinations**, **delusions**, and strange bodily movements or lack of movements (catatonic behavior) are all psychotic symptoms that may be observed. Additionally, minimal or peculiar speech, lack of drive to act on one's own behalf, bizarre or primitive (socially inappropriate or immature) behavior, a wooden quality to one's emotions, or near-absent emotionality are also typical psychotic symptoms that may occur. Of course, not all of the possible psychotic symptoms will occur concurrently in a single person with schizoaffective disorder. Importantly, to meet the criteria for the schizoaffective disorder diagnosis, delusions or hallucinations (the most "prototypical" of the psychotic symptoms) must be observed within a fairly lengthy period of time during which there is no form of mood disturbance.

Mood disturbance

An extremely important and challenging aspect of schizoaffective disorder is that mood problems are prominent. During mood episodes, psychotic features are simultaneously evident. The disruption of mood may be depressive, manic, or take the form of a **mixed episode** (which includes both depressive and manic features). If only depressed mood occurs, the individual is described as having the depressive subtype of schizoaffective disorder. If mixed episodes or manic episodes are noted, the client is identified as having the bipolar form of schizoaffective disorder.

Causes and symptoms

Causes

Because clear identification of schizoaffective disorder has traditionally been challenging, scientists have conducted far less research relating to the disorder than studies relating to schizophrenia or mood disorders. However, there are indications that there is a genetic component to the disorder. Close relatives of persons with schizoaffective disorder have higher rates of both schizophrenia and mood disorder. The disorder most typically strikes in early adulthood; in some cases, there appears to be a major trigger—some form of life **stress** initiating the occurrence of the symptoms. In cases where there is an identifiable stressor involved, the person tends to have a better outcome than when such is not the case. Some evidence suggests that the bipolar form of schizoaffective disorder is more treatable and yields better outcomes than the depressive form.

RELATIONSHIP TO PERSONALITY DISORDER. Persons with **personality disorders** appear to be more susceptible to developing psychotic reactions in response to stress. One aspect of personality disorder is that, when life becomes more demanding and difficult than can be tolerated, the individual with personality disorder may lapse into a brief psychotic episode. For some individuals, personality disorder may be a predecessor to the development of schizoaffective disorder. Apparently, a chronic problem of lacking effective adult mechanisms for coping with life becomes an ongoing schizoaffective disorder in some predisposed persons. Persons with preexisting schizotypal, paranoid, schizoid, and borderline personality disorders may be more vulnerable to develop a schizoaffective disorder than the general population.

Symptoms

The ***Diagnostic and Statistical Manual of Mental Disorders***, *DSM-IV-TR*, produced by the American

KEY TERMS

Catatonic behavior or catatonia—Catatonic behavior or catatonia is a descriptive term that describes both possible extremes related to movement. Catalepsy is the motionless aspect of catatonia—a person with catalepsy may remain fixed in the same position for hours on end. Rapid or persistently repeated movements, frequent grimacing and strange facial expressions, and unusual gestures are the opposite end of the catatonia phenomenon, involving an excess or distorted extreme of movement.

Delusion—A false belief that is resistant to reason or contrary to actual fact.

Hallucinations—False sensory perceptions. A person experiencing a hallucination may "hear" sounds or "see" people or objects that are not really present. Hallucinations can also affect the senses of smell, touch, and taste.

Psychosis or psychotic symptoms—Disruptions in perceiving reality, thinking logically, and speaking or behaving in normal fashion. Hallucinations, delusions, catatonic behavior, and peculiar speech are all symptoms of psychosis. In *DSM-IV-TR,* psychosis is usually one feature of an overarching disorder, not a disorder in itself (with the exception of the diagnosis *psychosis not otherwise specified.*

Psychiatric Association, is used by most mental health professionals in North America and Europe to diagnose mental disorders. The *DSM-IV-TR* provides these major criteria for schizoaffective disorder:

- At least two symptoms of psychosis from among the following, present for at least one month: Delusions; hallucinations; disorganized speech (strange, peculiar, difficult to comprehend); disorganized (bizarre or child-like) behavior; catatonic behavior; minimal speech (approaching mutism); lack of drive to act on one's own behalf; a wooden quality to one's emotions, or near-absent emotionality.
- Delusions or hallucinations have occurred for at least two weeks in the absence of prominent mood symptoms.
- During a "substantial portion" of the period of active illness, the individual meets criteria for one of the following mood disturbances: Major depressive episode, **manic episode**, mixed episode.
- The symptoms are not caused by a biologically active entity such as drugs, alcohol, adverse reaction to a medication, physical injury, or medical illness.

Demographics

Because of the imprecise nature of the diagnosis, the actual rate of brief schizoaffective disorder in adults is unknown. The proportion of schizoaffective disorder identified in persons undergoing treatment for psychiatric disorders has ranged from 2% to almost 30%, depending on the study cited. More females than males (overall) suffer from schizoaffective disorder. However, similar to gender ratios in clinical depression and bipolar disorder, it seems that there is a much higher ratio of women to men *in the depressive subtype* whereas the bipolar subtype has a more even gender distribution. Thus, the higher ratio of women overall is primarily caused by the concentration of women within the depressive subtype of schizoaffective disorder.

Diagnosis

Even using the *DSM-IV-TR* criteria, identification of schizoaffective disorder remains difficult and relatively subjective. An unusual condition in this set of diagnostic criteria is the need to weigh the relative prominence of the mood symptoms and to identify a period of psychotic symptoms that occurred without significant mood disturbance. In the various other psychotic disorders, there is frequently a low level of depression accompanying the symptoms. When depressive symptoms are the sole form of mood disturbance, only subjective clinical judgment determines whether there has been sufficient severity or duration of that disturbance to merit the possibility of schizoaffective disorder. An additional complication is the cultural relativity of "psychotic symptoms." If the psychotic-like behaviors shown are expected and valued in the person's culture or religion, and these behaviors occur in a traditionally affirming context such as religious services or **meditation**, then schizoaffective disorder would not be diagnosed.

As stated, schizoaffective disorder is typically identified by a process of lengthy observation and elimination of another diagnostic alternative over a long course of care. A very thorough history of the client's entire past experiences of psychiatric symptoms, mental health treatments, and response to different kinds of medications that have been taken, helps in determining whether that individual is suffering from schizoaffective disorder. Information about current and past experiences is collected in interviews with the client and possibly in discussion with the client's immediate family. Data also may be gathered from earlier medical records with the client's consent. In order to examine the sufferer's ability to concentrate, to remember, to understand his or her situation realistically, and to think logically, the clinician may use a semi-structured interview called a mental status examination. The mental status examination is designed to uncover psychotic or demented thought processes. Psychological assessment instruments, such as the MMPI-2, The Rorschach Inkblot Test, various mood disorder questionnaires, or structured diagnostic interviews, are sometimes used as well to aid in diagnosis. The criteria used by the clinician to classify this constellation of symptoms as schizoaffective disorder are presented in the *DSM-IV-TR*.

Treatments

Atypical, novel, or newer-generation antipsychotic medications are very effective in schizoaffective disorder treatment. Examples of atypical or novel antipsychotic medications include **risperidone** (Risperdal), **quetiapine** (Seroquel), and **olanzapine** (Zyprexa). If the patient's psychotic symptoms are acute and accompanied by agitation, a number of different antipsychotics can be used to terminate the flare-up of acute agitated psychosis. Agitation is a state of frantic activity that is often accompanied by anger or marked fearfulness; when in an agitated state, the client is more likely to cause harm to self or others. In agitated psychotic states, the antipsychotic agent **haloperidol** (Haldol) is often given as an injection, accompanied by other medications that decrease anxiety and slow behavior (often **lorazepam**, also known as Ativan). At this time, there are no atypical antipsychotics available in an injectable formulation. If the client is not extremely agitated, usually a novel antipsychotic is used, given orally daily, for a lengthier period of time.

In some cases, the antipsychotic medication is not sufficient to overcome the mood disturbance component of the disorder, even though some antipsychotics have thymoleptic (mood-affecting) qualities. Some of the atypical antipsychotic medications are thought to have antidepressant properties, while olanzapine has an FDA approval for the management of acute manic psychosis.

If there is little response to novel antipsychotic monotherapy (treatment with only one medication) an additional compound may be given to target the mood disorder aspect of the illness. The choice of which drug should be added to the medication regimen to decrease mood disorder problems is determined by the subtype of schizoaffective disorder shown by the client. If the client experiences the bipolar form, a mood stabilizer is added, often **valproic acid** (Depakote), **carbamazepine** (Tegretol), or lithium (Eskalith or Lithabid). In schizoaffective disorder of the bipolar type, if little response occurs to the usual antipsychotic/mood stabilizer combinations, the mental health consumer may be prescribed **clozapine** (Clozaril or other generic formulations) which appears to be both anti-psychotic and mood-stabilizing. However, because clozapine has the potential (in a very minute number of cases) to cause lethal alterations in the composition of blood, and because its use requires regular monitoring with recurrent blood testing, it is reserved as a "last-resort" therapy. In cases of the depressive subtype, psychiatrists may prescribe an antidepressant such as **citalopram** (Celexa), **venlafaxine** (Effexor), **paroxetine** (Paxil), or **fluoxetine** (Prozac) as an adjunct to the antipsychotic. In certain cases of depressive subtypes, where medications have been ineffective in resolving the extreme mood or where psychosis is so severe as to be life-threatening, **electroconvulsive therapy** may be utilized. Electroconvulsive therapy has also been shown to be effective in major depressive episode with psychotic features.

Medication is not the only treatment avenue. Supportive **psychotherapy** and psychoeducation is helpful to decrease the client's fears and to inform the client about the psychiatric illness. **Cognitive-behavioral therapy** aims to modify the thoughts and behaviors that provoke mood disturbance or prevent full involvement and collaboration in therapy for the mental illness. Psychoeducation and cognitive-behavioral therapy are not effective in lieu of biological therapy, but are enhancing, meaningful components of a "whole-person" approach used in concert with medications for the best possible outcomes.

Prognosis

The prognosis for clients with schizoaffective disorder is largely dependent on the form of the disorder and the presence or absence of a trigger. If there is a major life event as a prompting stressor, or an unusual traumatic experience preceded the occurrence of the disorder, chances for improvement are higher. If there is not a particular triggering event, or if the schizoaffective disorder occurred in an individual with a premorbid personality disorder, the outcome is less likely to be positive. The bipolar form of the disorder may respond better to treatment than the depressive form. Generally, the earlier the disorder is identified and treated, and the fewer lapses from medications, the more positive the outcome.

Prevention

Given that this disorder appears to have a strong genetic or biologic aspect, society-wide prevention approaches are not likely to be fruitful. However, a promising strategy is to educate physicians, psychologists, and workers, as well as persons at higher risk for the ...er, about the characteristics and treatability of ...oaffective disorder. Such education of care providers and high-risk individuals would foster early identification and treatment. In schizoaffective disorder, similar to schizophrenia and bipolar disorder, better response is predicted the earlier treatment begins. Because theoretically, severe stressors can be a trigger for this disorder (in some cases), strong social support and immediate post-crisis counseling for severe stress could possibly prevent the development of the disorder in some susceptible persons.

See also Compliance

Resources

BOOKS

American Psychiatric Association. *Diagnostic and Statistical Manual of Mental Disorders.* 4th edition, text revised. Washington, DC: American Psychiatric Association, 2000.

Fuller, Mark and M. Sajatovic. *Drug Information for Mental Health.* Hudson, Ohio: Lexi-comp, 2000.

PERIODICALS

Ferfel D. "Rationale and guidelines for the inpatient treatment of acute psychosis." *Journal of Clinical Psychiatry* 61, Supplement 14, (2000): 27-32.

Keck, Paul E., S. L. McElroy and Stephan M. Strakowski. "Schizoaffective disorder: role of atypical antipsychotics." *Schizophrenia Research* 35 (1999): S5-S12.

Levinson, Douglas, C. Umapathy and M. Musthaq. "Treatment of schizoaffective disorder and schizophrenia with mood symptoms." *American Journal of Psychiatry* 156 (1999): 1138-1148.

Norman, Ross and Laurel A. Townsend. "Cognitive-behavioural therapy for psychosis: A status report." *Canadian Journal of Psychiatry* 44 (1999): 245-252.

Sajatovic, Martha, Sue Kim Giovanni, Bijan Bastani, Helen Hattab, and Luis F. Ramirez. "Risperidone therapy in treatment refractory acute bipolar and schizoaffective mania." *Psychopharmacology Bulletin* 32, no. 1 (1996): 55-81.

ORGANIZATIONS

National Alliance for the Mentally Ill. Colonial Place Three, 2107 Wilson Blvd., Suite 300, Arlington, VA 22201. Telephone: (703) 524-7600. NAMI HelpLine: (800) 950-NAMI (6264). Web site: <www.nami.org>.

National Association for Research on Schizophrenia and Affective Disorders (NARSAD). 60 Cutter Mill Road, Suite 404, Great Neck, NY 11021. Main Line: (516) 829-0091. Infoline: (800) 829-8289. Web site: <www.narsad.org>.

Deborah Rosch Eifert, Ph.D.
Martha Sajatovic, M.D.

Schizoid personality disorder

Definition

Schizoid personality disorder is characterized by a persistent withdrawal from social relationships and lack of emotional responsiveness in most situations. It is sometimes referred to as a "pleasure deficiency" because of the seeming inability of the person affected to experience joyful or pleasurable responses to life situations.

Description

A person with schizoid personality disorder has little or no interest in developing close interpersonal relationships. They appear aloof, introverted and prefer being alone. Those who know them often label them as shy or a "loner." They turn inward in an effort to shut out social relationships. It is common for a person with schizoid personality disorder to avoid groups of people or appear disinterested in social situations even when they involve family. They are often perceived by others as socially inept.

A closely related trait is the absence of emotional expression. This apparent void of emotion is routinely interpreted by others as disinterested, lacking concern and insensitive to the needs of others. The person with schizoid personality disorder has particular difficulty expressing anger or hostility. In the absence of any recognizable emotion, the person portrays a dull demeanor and is easily overlooked by others. The typical person with schizoid personality disorder prefers to be viewed as "invisible" since it aids their quest to avoid social contact with others.

The person with schizoid personality disorder may be able to hold a job and meet the expectations of an employer if the responsibilities do not require more than minimal interpersonal involvement. People with this disorder may be married, but do not develop close intimate relationships with their spouse and typically show no interest in sexual relations. Their speech is typically slow and monotonous with a lethargic demeanor. Because their tendency is to turn inward, they can easily become preoccupied with their own thoughts to the exclusion of what is happening in their environment. Attempts to communicate may drift into tangents or confusing associations. They are also prone to being absent-minded.

Causes and symptoms

Causes

The schizoid personality disorder has its roots in the family of the affected person. These families are typically emotionally reserved, have a high degree of formality, and have a communication style that is aloof and impersonal. Parents usually express inadequate amounts of affection to the child and provide insufficient amounts of emotional stimulus. This lack of stimulus during the first year of life is thought to be largely responsible for the person's disinterest in forming close, meaningful relationships later in life.

People with schizoid personality disorder have learned to imitate the style of interpersonal relationships modeled in their families. In this environment, affected people fail to learn basic communication skills that would enable them to develop relationships and interact effectively with others. Their communication is often vague and fragmented, which others find confusing. Many individuals with schizoid personality disorder feel misunderstood by others.

Symptoms

DSM-IV-TR specifies seven diagnostic criteria for schizoid personality disorder:

- Avoids close relationships: People with this disorder show no interest or enjoyment in developing interpersonal relationships; this may also include family members. They perceive themselves as social misfits and believe they can function best when not dependent on anyone except themselves. They rarely date, often do not marry, and have few, if any, friends.
- Prefers solitude: They prefer and choose activities that they can do by themselves without dependence upon or involvement by others. Examples of activities they might choose include mechanical or abstract tasks such as computer or mathematical games.
- Avoids sex: There is typically little or no interest in having a sexual experience with another person. This would include a spouse if the affected person is married.
- Lacks pleasure: There is an absence of pleasure in most activities. A person with schizoid personality disorder seems unable to experience the full range of emotion accessible to most people.
- Lacks close friends: People affected with this disorder typically do not have the social skills necessary to develop meaningful interpersonal relationships. This results in few ongoing social relationships outside of immediate family members.

KEY TERMS

Asperger's disorder—A condition in which young children experience impaired social interactions and develop limited repetitive patterns of behavior.

Autistic disorder—A developmental disability that appears early in life, in which normal brain development is disrupted and social and communication skills are retarded, sometimes severely.

Millon Clinical Multiaxial Inventory (MCMI-II)—A self-report instrument designed to help the clinician assess DSM-IV-related personality disorders and clinical syndromes. It provides insight into 14 personality disorders and 10 clinical syndromes.

Minnesota Multiphasic Personality Inventory (MMPI-2)—A comprehensive assessment tool widely used to diagnose personality disorders.

Rorschach Psychodiagnostic Test—This series of 10 "ink blot" images allows the patient to project their interpretations which can be used to diagnose particular disorders.

Thematic Apperception Test (TAT)—A projective test using stories and descriptions of pictures to reveal some of the dominant drives, emotions, sentiments, conflicts, and complexes of a personality.

- Indifferent to praise or criticism: Neither positive nor negative comments made by others elicit an emotionally expressive reaction. They don't appear concerned about what others might think of them. Despite their tendency to turn inward to escape social contact, they practice little introspection.
- Emotional detachment: Their emotional style is aloof and perceived by others as distant or "cold." They seem unable or uninterested in expressing empathy and concern for others. Emotions are significantly restricted and most social contacts would describe their personality as very bland, dull or humorless. The person with schizoid personality disorder rarely picks up on or reciprocates normal communicational cues such as facial expressions, head nods, or smiles.

Demographics

Of all **personality disorders**, schizoid personality disorder is the least commonly diagnosed personality disorder in the general population. The prevalence is approximately one percent. It is diagnosed slightly more often in males.

Diagnosis

The symptoms of schizoid personality disorder may begin in childhood or adolescence showing as poor peer relationships, a tendency toward self-isolation, and underachievement in school. Children with these tendencies appear socially out-of-step with peers and often become the object of malicious teasing by their peers, which increases the feelings of isolation and social ineptness they feel.

For a **diagnosis** of schizoid personality disorder to be accurately made, there must be an ongoing avoidance of social relationships and a restricted range of emotion in interpersonal relationships that begin by early adulthood. There must also be the presence of at least four of the above-mentioned symptoms.

A common difficulty in diagnosing schizoid personality disorder is distinguishing it from Autistic Disorder and **Asperger's Disorder**, which are characterized by more severe deficits in social skills. Other individuals who would display social habits that might be viewed as "isolating" should not be given the diagnosis of schizoid personality disorder unless the personality traits are inflexible and cause significant obstacles to adequate functioning.

The diagnosis is based on a clinical interview to assess symptomatic behavior. Other assessment tools helpful in diagnosing schizoid personality disorder include:

- Minnesota Multiphasic Personality Inventory (MMPI-2)
- Millon Clinical Multiaxial Inventory (MCMI-II)
- Rorschach Psychodiagnostic Test
- **Thematic Apperception Test** (TAT)

Treatments

A major goal of treating a patient diagnosed with schizoid personality disorder is to combat the tendencies toward social withdrawal. Strategies should focus on enhancing self-awareness and sensitivity to their relational contacts and environment.

Psychodynamically oriented therapies

A psychodynamic approach would typically not be the first choice of treatment due to the patient's poor ability to explore his or her thoughts, emotions, and behavior. When this treatment is used, it usually centers around building a therapeutic relationship with the patient that can act as a model for use in other relationships.

Cognitive-behavioral therapy

Attempting to cognitively restructure the patient's thoughts can enhance self-insight. Constructive ways of accomplishing this would include concrete assignments such as keeping daily records of problematic behaviors or thoughts. Another helpful method can be teaching social skills through role-playing. This might enable individuals to become more conscious of communication cues given by others and sensitize them to others' needs.

Group therapy

Group therapy may provide the patient with a socializing experience that exposes them to feedback from others in a safe, controlled environment. It can also provide a means of learning and practicing social skills in which they are deficient. Since the patient usually avoids social contact, timing of group therapy is of particular importance. It is best to develop first a therapeutic relationship between therapist and patient before starting a group therapy treatment.

Family and marital therapy

It is unlikely that a person with schizoid personality disorder will seek **family therapy** or marital therapy. If pursued, it is usually on the initiative of the spouse or other family member. Many people with this disorder do not marry and end up living with and are dependent upon first-degree family members. In this case, therapy may be recommended for family members to educate them on aspects of change or ways to facilitate communication. Marital therapy (also called **couples therapy**) may focus on helping the couple to become more involved in each other's lives or improve communication patterns.

Medications

Some patients with this disorder show signs of anxiety and depression which may prompt the use of medication to counteract these symptoms. In general, there is to date no definitive medication that is used to treat schizoid symptoms.

Prognosis

Since a person with schizoid personality disorder seeks to be isolated from others, which includes those who might provide treatment, there is only a slight chance that most patients will seek help on their own initiative. Those who do may stop treatment prematurely because of their difficulty maintaining a relationship with the professional or their lack of motivation for change.

If the degree of social impairment is mild, treatment might succeed if its focus is on maintenance of relationships related to the patient's employment. The patient's need to support him- or herself financially can act as a higher incentive for pursuit of treatment outcomes.

Once treatment ends, it is highly likely the patient will relapse into a lifestyle of social isolation similar to that before treatment.

Prevention

Since schizoid personality disorder originates in the patient's family of origin, the only known preventative measure is a nurturing, emotionally stimulating and expressive caretaking environment.

See also Cognitive-behavioral therapy; Rorschach technique

Resources

BOOKS

American Psychiatric Association. *Diagnostic and Statistical Manual of Mental Disorders.* 4th edition, text revised. Washington, DC:American Psychiatric Association, 2000.

Beers, Mark H., M.D., and Robert Berkow, M.D., eds. *The Merck Manual of Diagnosis and Therapy.* 17th edition. Whitehouse Station, NJ: Merck Research Laboratories, 1999.

Millon, Theodore, Ph.D., D.Sc. *Disorders of Personality: DSM IV and Beyond.* New York: John Wiley and Sons, Inc., 1996.

Sperry, Len, M.D., Ph.D. *Handbook of Diagnosis and Treatment of DSM-IV Personality Disorders.* New York: Brunner/Mazel, Inc., 1995.

ORGANIZATIONS

American Psychiatric Association. 1400 K Street NW, Washington D.C. 20005 <http://www.psych.org>.

Gary Gilles, M.A.

Schizophrenia

Definition

Schizophrenia is the most chronic and disabling of the severe mental disorders, associated with abnormalities of **brain** structure and function, disorganized speech and behavior, **delusions**, and **hallucinations**. It is sometimes called a psychotic disorder or a **psychosis**.

Description

People diagnosed with schizophrenia do not always have the same set of symptoms; in addition, a given patient's symptoms may change over time. Since the nineteenth century, doctors have recognized different subtypes of the disorder, but no single classification system has gained universal acceptance. Some psychiatrists prefer to speak of schizophrenia as a group or family of disorders ("the schizophrenias") rather than as a single entity. A standard professional reference, **The Diagnostic and Statistical Manual of Mental Disorders** (also known as the *DSM-IV-TR)* acknowledges that its present classification of subtypes is not fully satisfactory for either clinical or research purposes, and states that "alternative subtyping schemes are being actively investigated."

The symptoms of schizophrenia can appear at any time after age six or seven, although onset during adolescence and early adult life is the most common pattern. There are a few case studies in the medical literature of schizophrenia in children younger than five, but they are extremely rare. Schizophrenia that appears after age 45 is considered late-onset schizophrenia. About 1%–2% of cases are diagnosed in patients over 80.

The onset of symptoms in schizophrenia may be either abrupt (sudden) or insidious (gradual). Often, however, it goes undetected for about two to three years after the onset of diagnosable symptoms, because the symptoms occur in the context of a previous history of cognitive and behavioral problems. The patient may have had panic attacks, **social phobia**, or substance abuse problems, any of which can complicate the process of **diagnosis**. In most cases, however, the patient's first psychotic episode is preceded by a prodromal (warning) phase, with a variety of behaviors that may include angry outbursts, withdrawal from social activities, loss of attention to personal hygiene and grooming, anhedonia (loss of one's capacity for enjoyment), and other unusual behaviors. The psychotic episode itself is typically characterized by delusions, which are false but strongly held beliefs that result from the patient's inability to separate real from unreal events; and hallucinations, which are disturbances of sense perception. Hallucinations can affect any of the senses, although the most common form of hallucination in schizophrenia is auditory ("hearing voices"). Autobiographical accounts by people who have recovered from schizophrenia indicate that these hallucinations are experienced as frightening and confusing. Patients often find it difficult to concentrate on work, studies, or formerly pleasurable activities because of the constant "static" or "buzz" of hallucinated voices.

There is no "typical" pattern or course of the disorder following the first acute episode. The patient may never have a second psychotic episode; others have occasional episodes over the course of their lives but can lead fairly normal lives otherwise. About 70% of patients diagnosed with schizophrenia have a second psychotic breakdown within five to seven years after the first one.

KEY TERMS

Affect—The expression of emotion displayed to others through facial expressions, hand gestures, tone of voice, etc. Types of affect include: flat (inanimate, no expression), blunted (minimally responsive), inappropriate (incongruous expressions of emotion relative to the content of a conversation), and labile (sudden and abrupt changes in type and intensity of emotion).

Agranulocytosis—A blood disorder characterized by a reduction in the number of circulating white blood cells (granulocytes). White blood cells defend the body against infections. Agranulocytosis is a potential side effect of some of the newer antipsychotic medications used to treat schizophrenia.

Akathisia—Agitated or restless movement, usually affecting the legs. Movement is accompanied by a sense of discomfort and an inability to sit, stand still, or remain inactive for periods of time. Akathisia is a common side effect of some neuroleptic (antipsychotic) medications.

Anhedonia—Loss of the capacity to experience pleasure. Anhedonia is one of the so-called negative symptoms of schizophrenia, and is also a symptom of major depression.

Anosognosia—Lack of awareness of the nature of one's illness. The term is usually applied to stroke patients, but is sometimes used to refer to lack of insight on the part of patients with schizophrenia. Anosognosia appears to be caused by the illness itself; it does not appear to be a form of denial or inappropriate coping mechanism. It is, however, a factor in nonadherence to treatment regimens and the increased risk of relapse.

Atypical antipsychotics—A group of newer medications for the treatment of psychotic symptoms that were introduced in the 1990s. The atypical antipsychotics include clozapine, risperidone, quetiapine, ziprasidone, and olanzapine. They are sometimes called serotonin dopamine antagonists, or SDAs.

Blunted affect—A term that refers to the loss of emotional expressiveness sometimes found in patients with schizophrenia. It is sometimes called flattened affect.

Catatonia—Disturbance of motor behavior with either extreme stupor or random, purposeless activity.

Delusion—A false belief that is resistant to reason or contrary to actual fact. Common delusions in schizophrenia include delusions of persecution, delusions about one's importance (sometimes called delusions of grandeur), or delusions of being controlled by others.

Dementia praecox—A late nineteenth-century term for schizophrenia.

Dopamine—A neurotransmitter that acts within certain brain cells to help regulate emotions and movement. Some of the symptoms of schizophrenia are related to excessive levels of dopamine activity in a part of the brain called the striatum.

Dystonia—A neurological disorder characterized by involuntary muscle spasms. The spasms can cause a painful twisting of the body and difficulty walking or moving.

First-rank symptoms—A list of symptoms that have been considered to be diagnostic of schizophrenia. They include delusions; somatic hallucinations; hearing voices commenting on one's behavior; and thought insertion or withdrawal. First-rank symptoms are sometimes called Schneiderian symptoms, after the name of Kurt Schneider, the German psychiatrist who listed them in 1959.

Gingko—A shade tree native to China with fan-shaped leaves and fleshy seeds with edible kernels. Gingko extract is being studied as a possible

Some patients remain chronically ill; of these, some remain at a fairly stable level while others grow steadily worse and become severely disabled.

About 20% of patients with schizophrenia recover the full level of functioning that they had before the onset of the disorder, according to NIMH statistics; but the remaining 80% have problems reintegrating into mainstream society. These patients are often underachievers in school and in the workplace, and they usually have difficulty forming healthy relationships with others. The majority (60%–70%) of patients with schizophrenia do not marry or have children, and most have very few friends or social contacts. The impact of these social difficulties as well as the **stress** caused by the symptoms themselves is reflected in the high **suicide** rate among patients with schizophrenia. About 10% commit suicide

KEY TERMS CONTINUED

complementary or adjunctive treatment for schizophrenia.

Hallucination—False sensory perceptions. A person experiencing a hallucination may "hear" sounds or "see" people or objects that are not really present. Hallucinations can also affect the senses of smell, touch, and taste.

Hebephrenic schizophrenia—An older term for what is now known as the disorganized subtype of schizophrenia.

Insidious—Proceeding gradually and inconspicuously but with serious effect. Schizophrenia sometimes has an insidious rather than an acute onset.

Morbidity—The unhealthiness or disease characteristics associated with a mental disorder.

Negative symptoms—Symptoms of schizophrenia that represent a loss or reduction of normal functioning.

Neuroleptic—Another name for the older antipsychotic medications, such as haloperidol (Haldol) and chlorpromazine (Thorazine).

Polygenic—A trait or disorder that is determined by a group of genes acting together. Most human characteristics, including height, weight, and general body build, are polygenic. Schizophrenia and late-onset Alzheimer's disease are considered polygenic disorders.

Positive symptoms—Symptoms of schizophrenia that represent excesses or distortions of normal mental functions.

Prodromal—Premonitory; having the character of a warning. The first psychotic episode in schizophrenia is often preceded by a prodromal phase.

Psychosis—Severe state that is characterized by loss of contact with reality and deterioration in normal social functioning; examples are schizophrenia and paranoia. Psychosis is usually one feature of an over-arching disorder, not a disorder in itself. (Plural: psychoses)

Reality testing—A phrase that refers to a person's ability to distinguish between subjective feelings and objective reality. A person who knows that their body is real even though they may be experiencing it as unreal, for example, is said to have intact reality testing.

Referential—A type of delusion in which the person misinterprets items, minor occurrences, or other people's behavior as referring to them. Misinterpretations of this sort that are not as resistant to reality as a delusion are sometimes called ideas of reference.

Schneiderian symptoms—Another name for first-rank symptoms of schizophrenia.

Striatum—A part of the basal ganglia, a deep structure in the cerebral hemisphere of the brain. Abnormally high levels of dopamine in the striatum are thought to be related to the delusions and hallucinations of schizophrenia.

Supportive—An approach to psychotherapy that seeks to encourage the patient or offer emotional support to him or her, as distinct from insight-oriented or educational approaches to treatment.

Tardive dyskinesia—A condition that involves involuntary movements of the tongue, jaw, mouth or face or other groups of skeletal muscles that usually occurs either late in antipsychotic therapy or even after the therapy is discontinued. It may be irreversible.

Thought insertion/withdrawal—The notion that an outside force (space aliens, evil people, etc.) can put thoughts or ideas into one's mind or remove them. It is considered one of the first-rank symptoms of schizophrenia.

within the first 10 years after their diagnosis— a rate 20 times higher than that of the general population.

Subtypes of schizophrenia

DSM-IV-TR specifies five subtypes of schizophrenia:

- Paranoid type. The central feature of this subtype is the presence of auditory hallucinations or delusions alongside relatively unaffected mood and cognitive functions. The patient's delusions usually involve persecution, grandiosity, or both. About a third of patients diagnosed with schizophrenia in the United States belong to this subtype.
- Disorganized type. The core features of this subtype include disorganized speech, disorganized behavior, and flat or inappropriate affect. The person may lose

the ability to perform most activities of daily living, and may also make faces or display other oddities of behavior. This type of schizophrenia was formerly called hebephrenic (derived from the Greek word for puberty), because some of the patients' behaviors resemble adolescent silliness.

- Catatonic type. **Catatonia** refers to disturbances of movement, whether remaining motionless for long periods of time or excessive and purposeless movement. The absence of movement may take the form of catalepsy, which is a condition in which the patient's body has a kind of waxy flexibility and can be repositioned by others; or negativism, a form of postural rigidity in which the patient resists being moved by others. A catatonic patient may assume bizarre postures or imitate the movements of other people.
- Undifferentiated type. Patients in this subtype have some of the characteristic symptoms of schizophrenia but do not meet the full criteria for the paranoid, disorganized, or catatonic subtypes.
- Residual type. Patients in this category have had at least one psychotic episode, continue to have some **negative symptoms** of schizophrenia, but do not have current psychotic symptoms.

Cultural variables

There appear to be some differences across cultures in the symptoms associated with schizophrenia. The catatonic subtype appears to be more common in non-Western countries than in Europe or North America. Other studies indicate that persons diagnosed with schizophrenia in developing countries have a more acute onset of the disorder but better outcomes than patients in the developed countries.

Causes and symptoms

Causes

As of 2002, schizophrenia is considered the end result of a combination of genetic, biochemical, developmental, and environmental factors, some of which are still not completely understood. There is no known single cause of the disorder.

GENETIC. Researchers have known for many years that first-degree biological relatives of patients with schizophrenia have a 10% risk of developing the disorder, as compared with 1% in the general population. The monozygotic (identical) twin of a person with schizophrenia has a 40%–50% risk. The fact that this risk is not higher, however, indicates that environmental as well as genetic factors are implicated in the development of schizophrenia.

Some specific regions on certain human chromosomes have been linked to schizophrenia. In late 2001, a multidisciplinary team of researchers reported positive associations for schizophrenia on chromosomes 15 and 13. Chromosome 15 is linked to schizophrenia in European-American families as well as some Taiwanese and Portuguese families. A recent study of the biological pedigrees found among the inhabitants of Palau (an isolated territory in Micronesia) points to chromosomes 2 and 13. Still another team of researchers has suggested that a disorder known as 22q deletion syndrome may actually represent a subtype of schizophrenia, insofar as people with this syndrome have a 25% risk of developing schizophrenia. At present scientists are inclined to think that the genetic factors underlying schizophrenia vary across different ethnic groups, so that it is highly unlikely that susceptibility to the disorder is determined by only one gene. As of 2002, schizophrenia is considered a polygenic disorder.

There appears to be a connection between aging and genetic mutations that increases susceptibility to schizophrenia. A recent Israeli study found that the age of a person's father is a risk factor for schizophrenia; the older the father, the higher the rate of mutations in sperm cells. The child of a father older than 50 is three times more likely to develop schizophrenia than children born to younger men. The researchers suggest that mutations in the sperm cells of older men help to explain why schizophrenia has persisted in the human population even though few schizophrenics marry and have children.

DEVELOPMENTAL. As of 2002, there is some evidence that schizophrenia may be a type of developmental disorder related to the formation of faulty connections between nerve cells during fetal development. The changes in the brain that normally occur during puberty then interact with these connections to trigger the symptoms of the disorder. Other researchers have suggested that a difficult childbirth may result in developmental vulnerabilities that eventually lead to schizophrenia.

NEUROBIOLOGICAL. In early 2002, researchers at the NIMH demonstrated the existence of a connection between two abnormalities of brain functioning in patients with schizophrenia. The researchers used radioactive tracers and **positron emission tomography** (PET) to show that reduced activity in a part of the brain called the prefrontal cortex was associated in the patients, but not in the control subjects, with abnormally elevated levels of dopamine in the striatum. High levels of dopamine are related to the delusions and hallucinations of psychotic episodes in schizophrenia. The findings suggest that treatment directed at the prefrontal cortex might be more effective than present antipsychotic medications,

PHOTO GALLERY

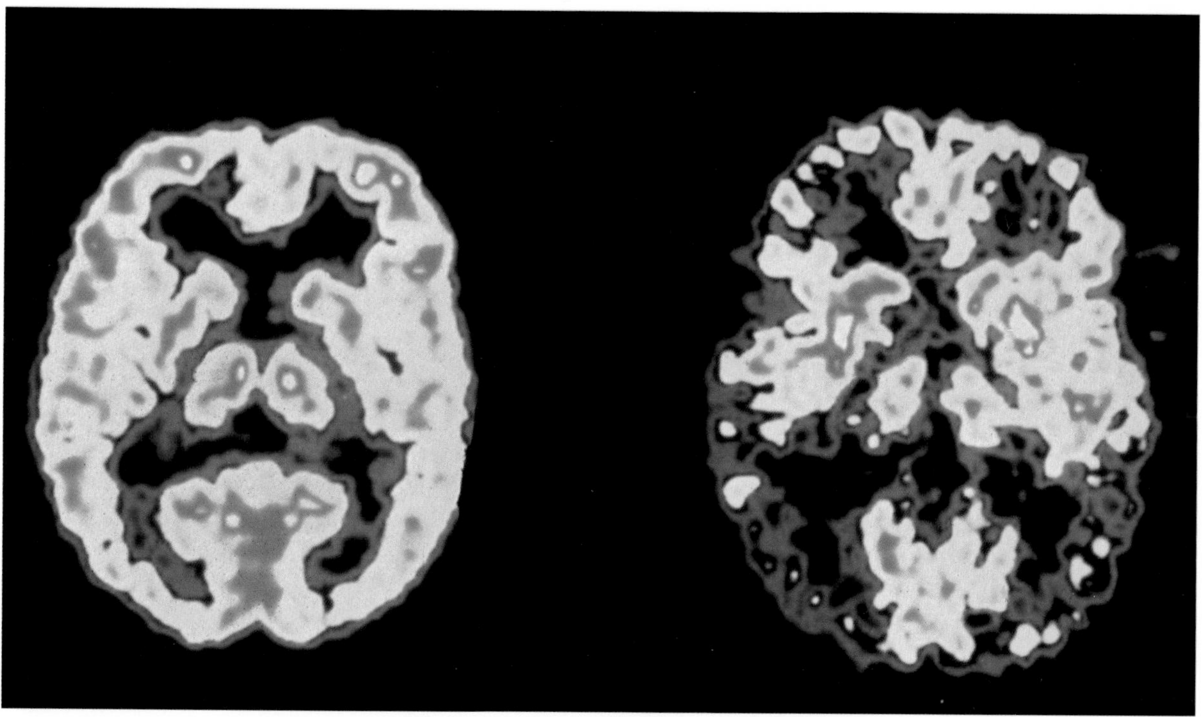

Colored positron emission tomography (PET) brain scans comparing a normal brain (left) with the brain of a person with Alzheimer's disease. See entry, "Alzheimer's disease," page 36. *(Photo Researchers, Inc. Reproduced by permission.)*

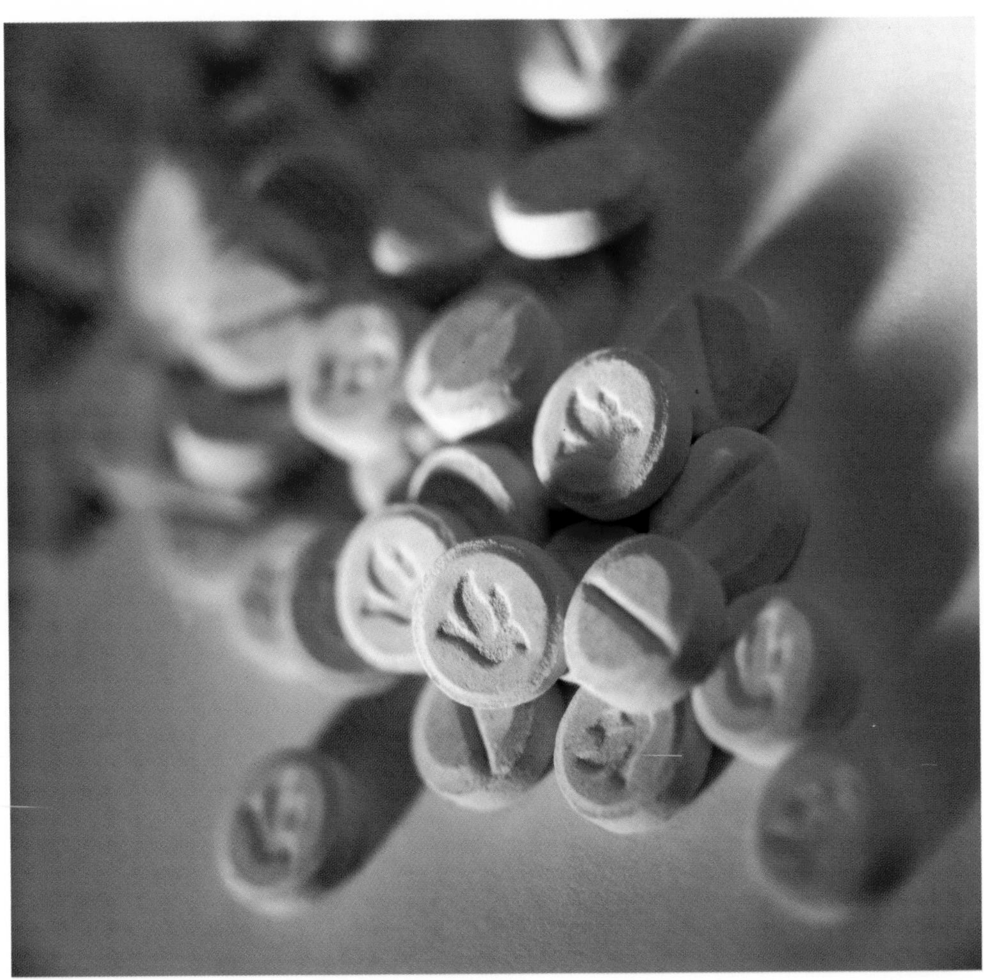

Amphetamines are a group of powerful and highly addictive substances that dramatically affect the central nervous system. Closely related are the so-called "designer amphetamines," the most well-known of which is the "club drug" MDMA, or "ecstasy" (pictured). Use of MDMA produces increased blood pressure, heart rate, and heart oxygen consumption, and may lead to harmful reactions such as dehydration, hyperthermia, and seizures. See entry, "Amphetamines and related disorders," page 56. *(Andrew Brookes/ CORBIS. Photo reproduced by permission.)*

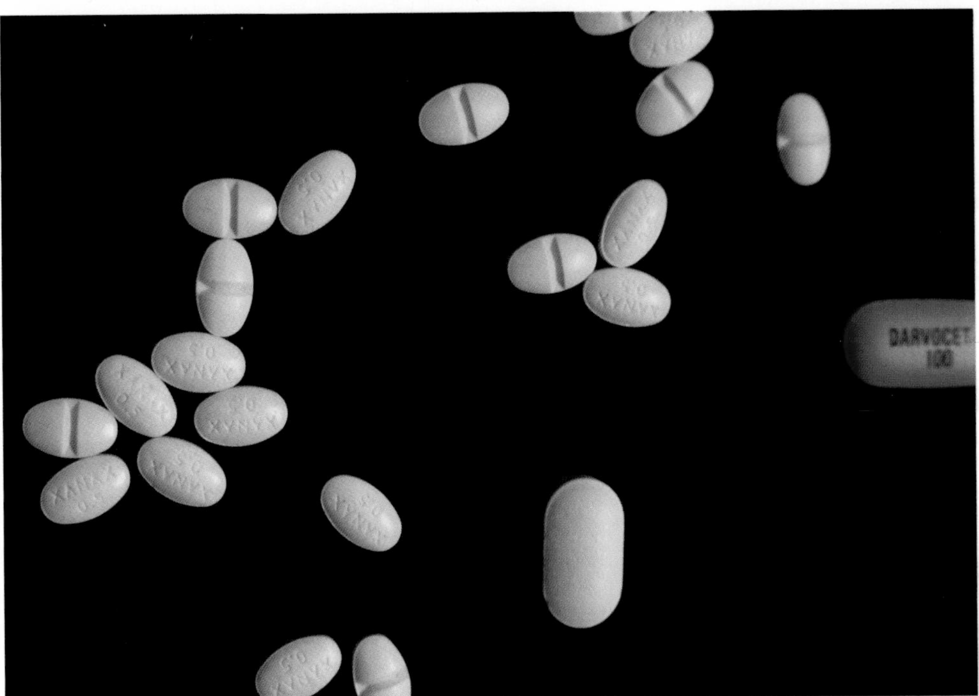

Anti-anxiety drugs are powerful central nervous system depressants. They are often prescribed to reduce feelings of tension and anxiety, and/or to induce sleep. Anti-anxiety medications are among the most abused drugs in the United States. See entry, "Anti-anxiety drugs and abuse," page 64. *(Thomas Craig/FPG International Corp. Reproduced by permission.)*

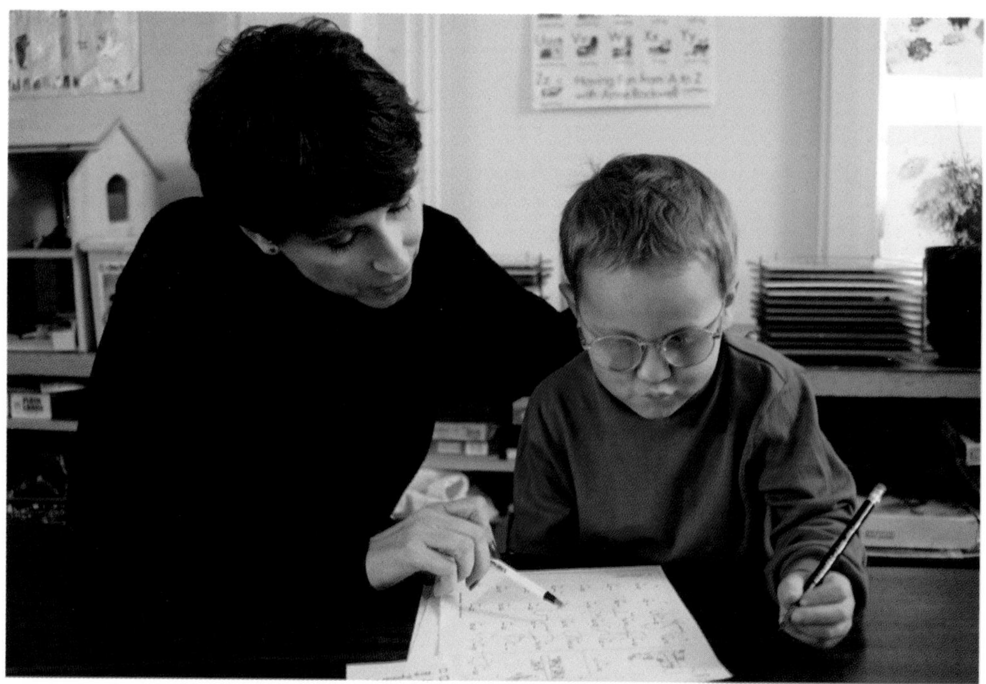

A special education teacher helps a student with attention-deficit/hyperactivity disorder with his math assignment. See entry, "Attention-deficit/hyperactivity disorder," page 93. *(Ellen B. Senisi. Photo Researchers, Inc. Reproduced by permission.)*

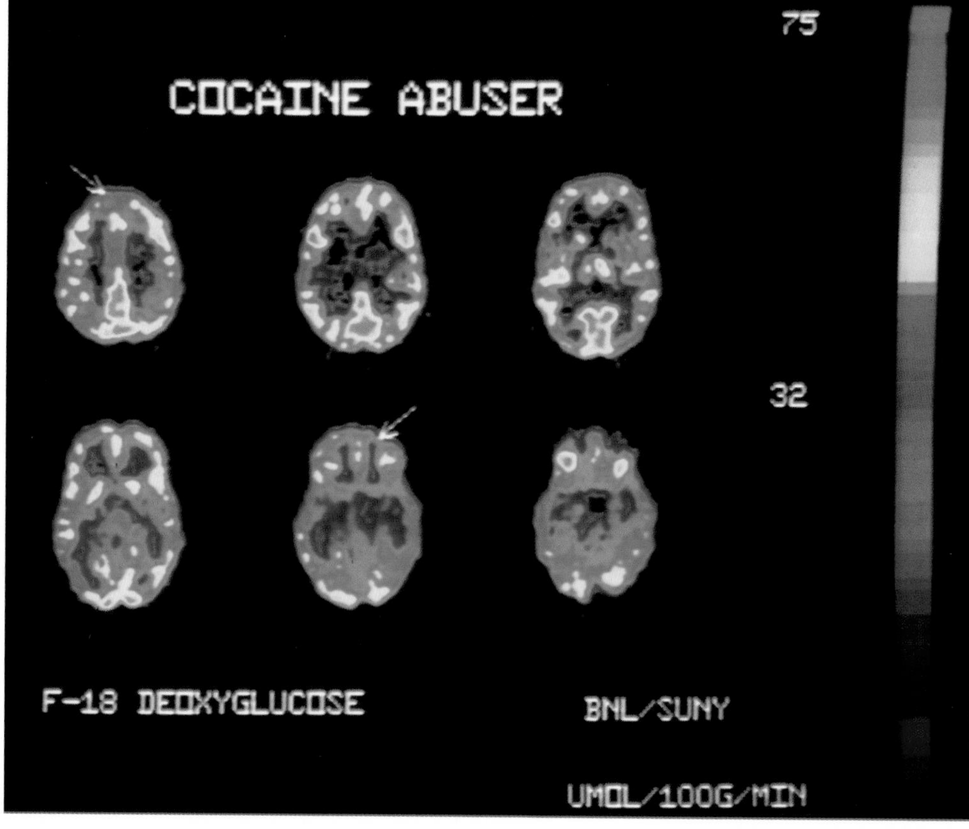

Colored positron emission tomography (PET) brain scans of a cocaine user. See entry, "Cocaine and related disorders," page 212. *(Photo Researchers, Inc. Reproduced by permission.)*

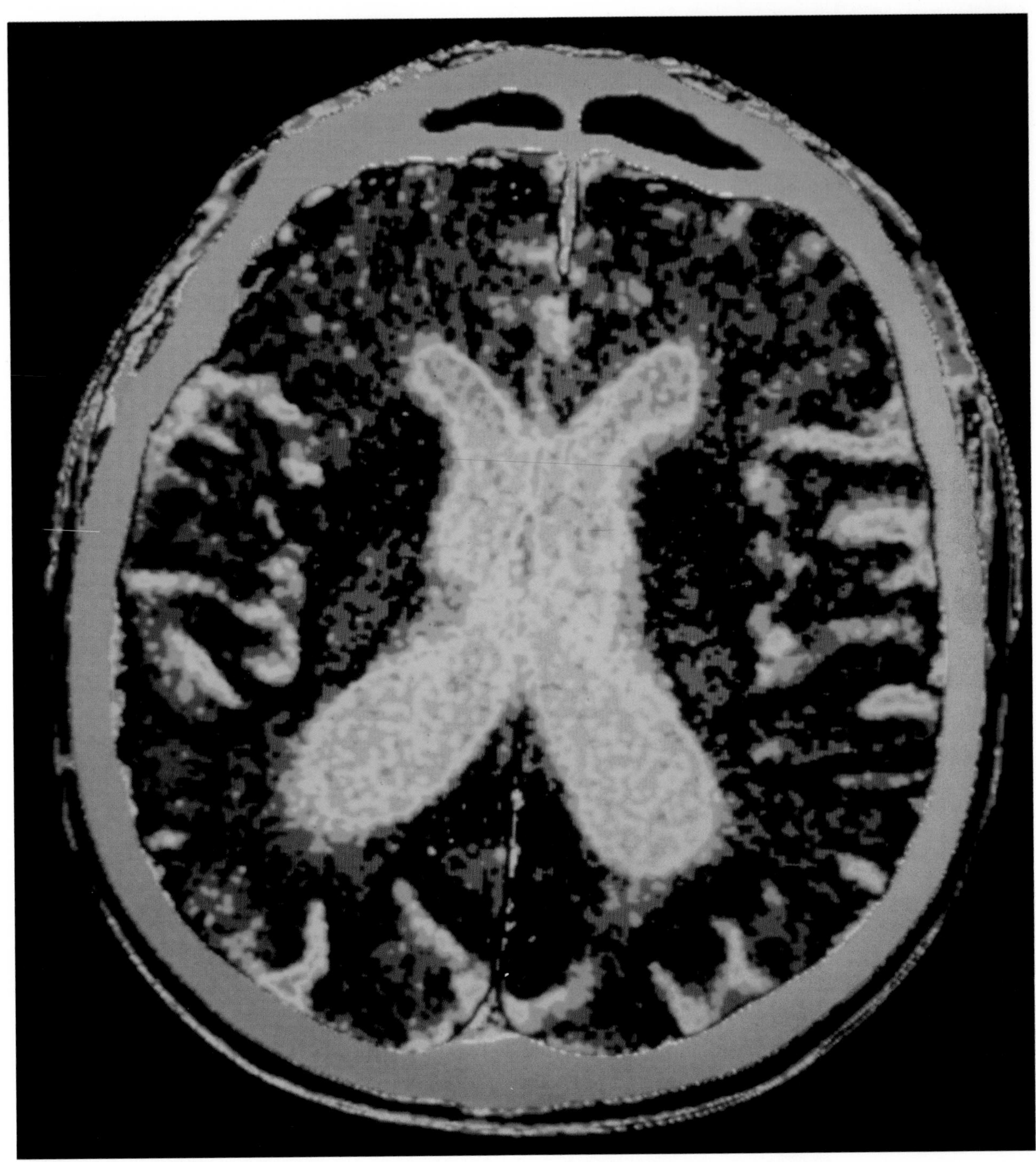

Computerized axial tomography (CAT) scan of a human brain with Parkinson's disease showing atrophy. See entry, "Computed tomography," page 233. *(GJLP/CNRI/Phototake. Reproduced by permission.)*

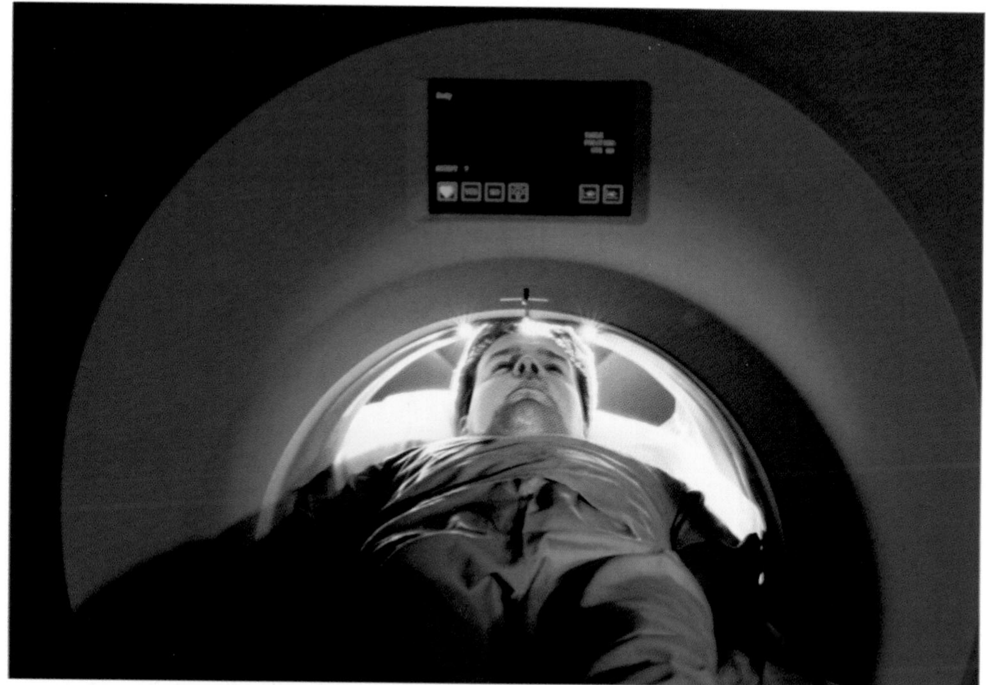

Patient lying on mobile table, entering a CT (computed tomography or CAT) scanner. See entry, "Computed tomography," page 233. *(Volker Steger/Science Photo Library, Science Source/Photo Researchers, Inc. Reproduced by permission.)*

Self-portrait done by a girl while in treatment for anorexia nervosa. See entry, "Creative therapies," page 251. *(Susan Rosenberg, Science Photo Library/Photo Researchers, Inc. Reproduced by permission.)*

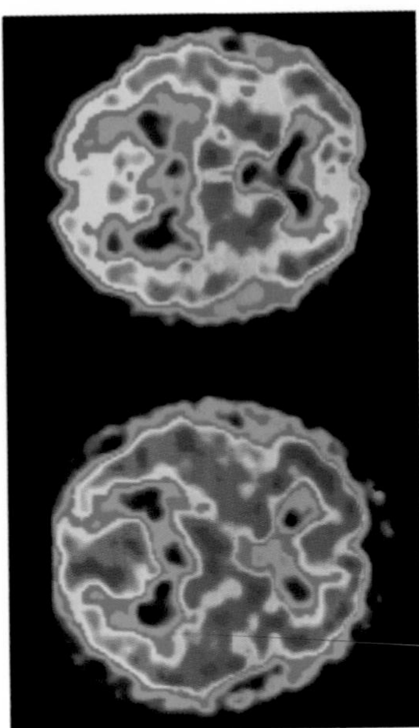

Colored positron emission tomography scan of an AIDS patient with dementia. See entry, "Dementia," page 275. *(Photo Researchers, Inc. Reproduced by permission.)*

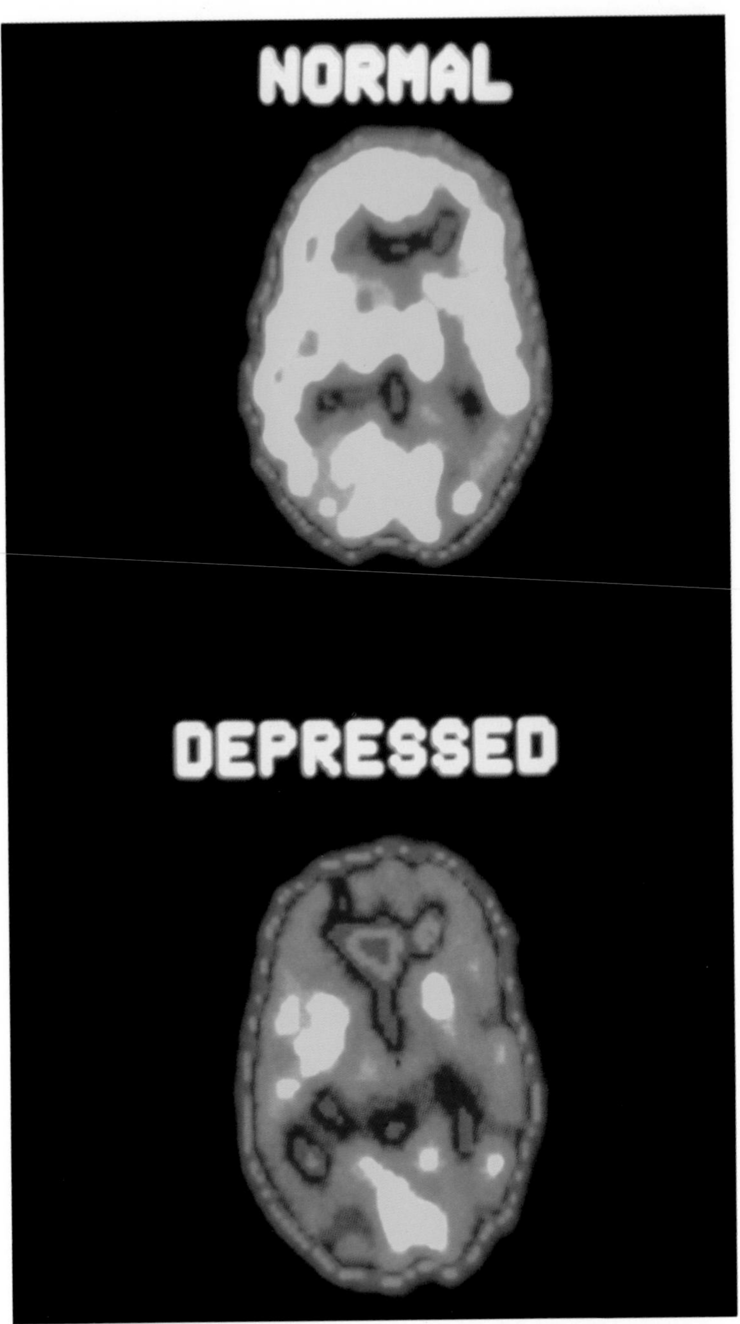

Two false-colored positron emission tomography (PET) scans of human brains. At the top is the brain of a healthy person, and below that is the brain of a depressed person. See entry, "Depression and depressive disorders," page 291. *(NIH/Science Source, National Audubon Society Collection/ Photo Researchers, Inc. Reproduced by permission.)*

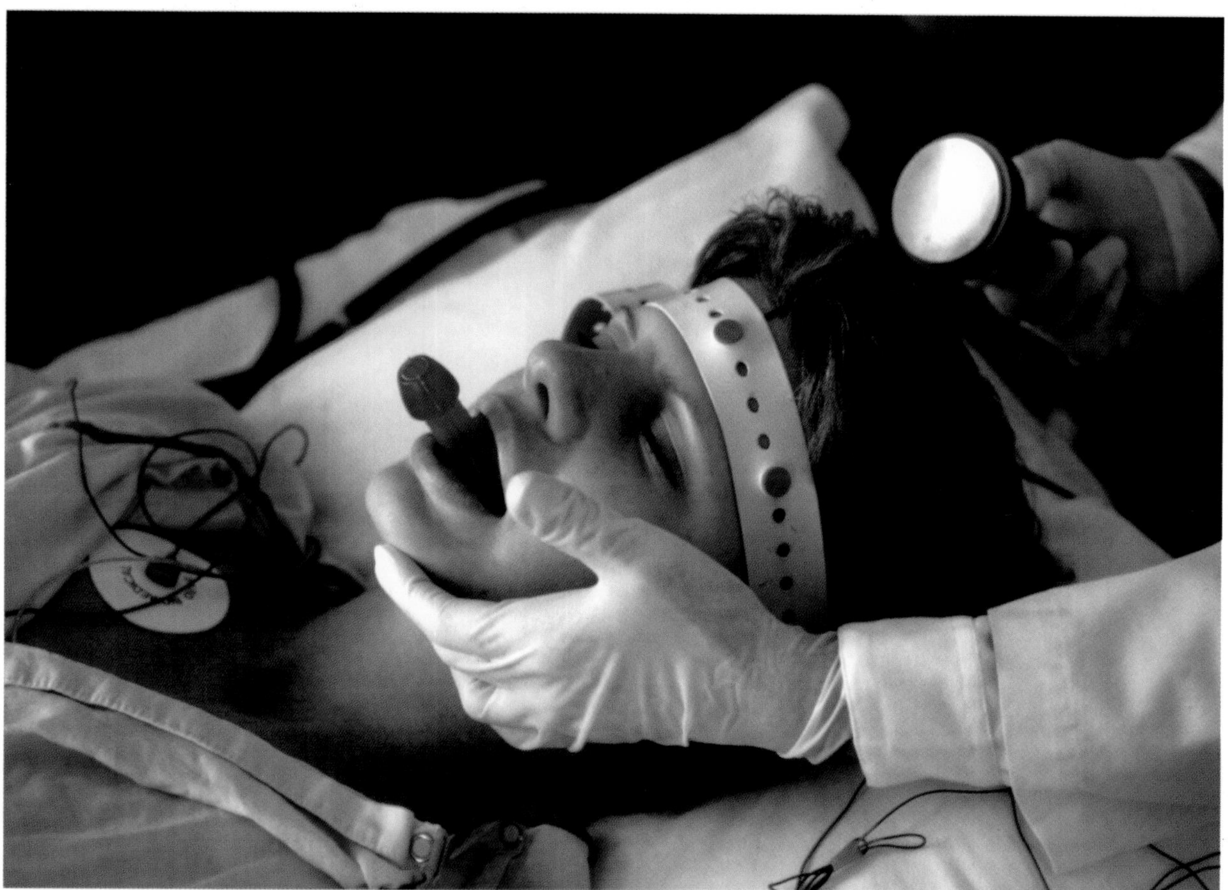

This woman has been prepared to receive electroconvulsive therapy—an effective treatment for depression. This patient has been given a short-acting medication that induces unconsciousness, and another medication was given that relaxes her muscles so that the induced seizures will not produce any violent contractions. Instead, the patient lies quietly on the operating table. The rubber mouthpiece keeps her from biting down on teeth or her tongue during the seizure. **See entry, "Electroconvulsive therapy," page 347.** *(Photo Researchers, Inc. Reproduced by permission.)*

Leaves of the ginkgo tree. See entry, "Ginkgo biloba," page 455. *(Robert J. Huffman. Field Mark Publications. Reproduced by permission.)*

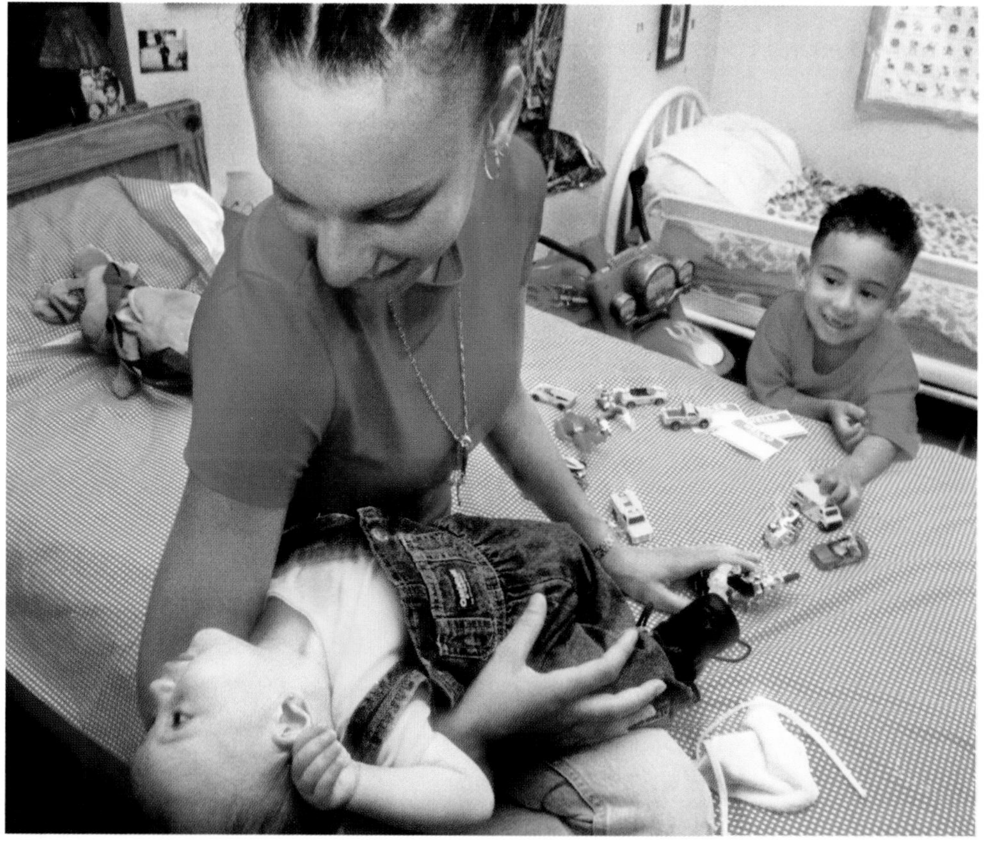

Group homes are facilities in residential communities that house people with physical or mental disabilities or other challenges. The group home residents pictured live in a teen group home in Massachusetts for low-income mothers and their children. See entry, "Group homes," page 463. *(Lisa Poole. AP/Wide World Photos. Reproduced by permission.)*

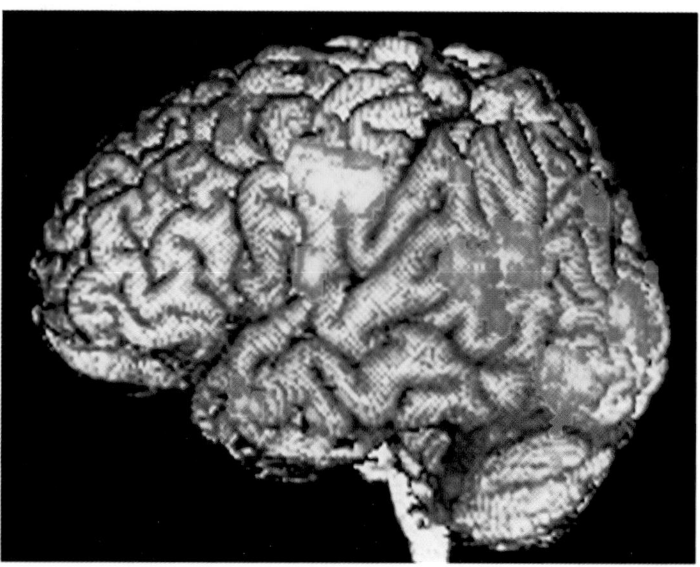

Colored positron emission tomography scan (PET scan) of the brain of a patient with schizophrenia who is experiencing a hallucination. Highlighted areas show brain activity. The patient's hallucination consisted of heads that spoke to him. The active areas of the brain seen here (the auditory and visual areas) confirm that the patient "saw" and "heard" the heads in the hallucination. See entry, "Hallucinations," page 475. *(Wellcome Department of Cognitive Neurology. Photo Researchers, Inc./Science Source. Reproduced by permission.)*

People who develop problems with their Internet use may start off using the Internet on a casual basis and then progress to using the technology in dysfunctional ways. Use of the Internet may interfere with the person's social life, school work, or job-related tasks at work. See entry, "Internet addiction disorder," page 537. *(Oleg Nikishin/Getty Images. Reproduced by permission.)*

This eight-year-old boy has a learning disability that causes him to write some of these numbers backwards. See entry, "Learning disorders," page 565. *(Ellen B. Senisi. Photo Researchers, Inc. Reproduced by permission.)*

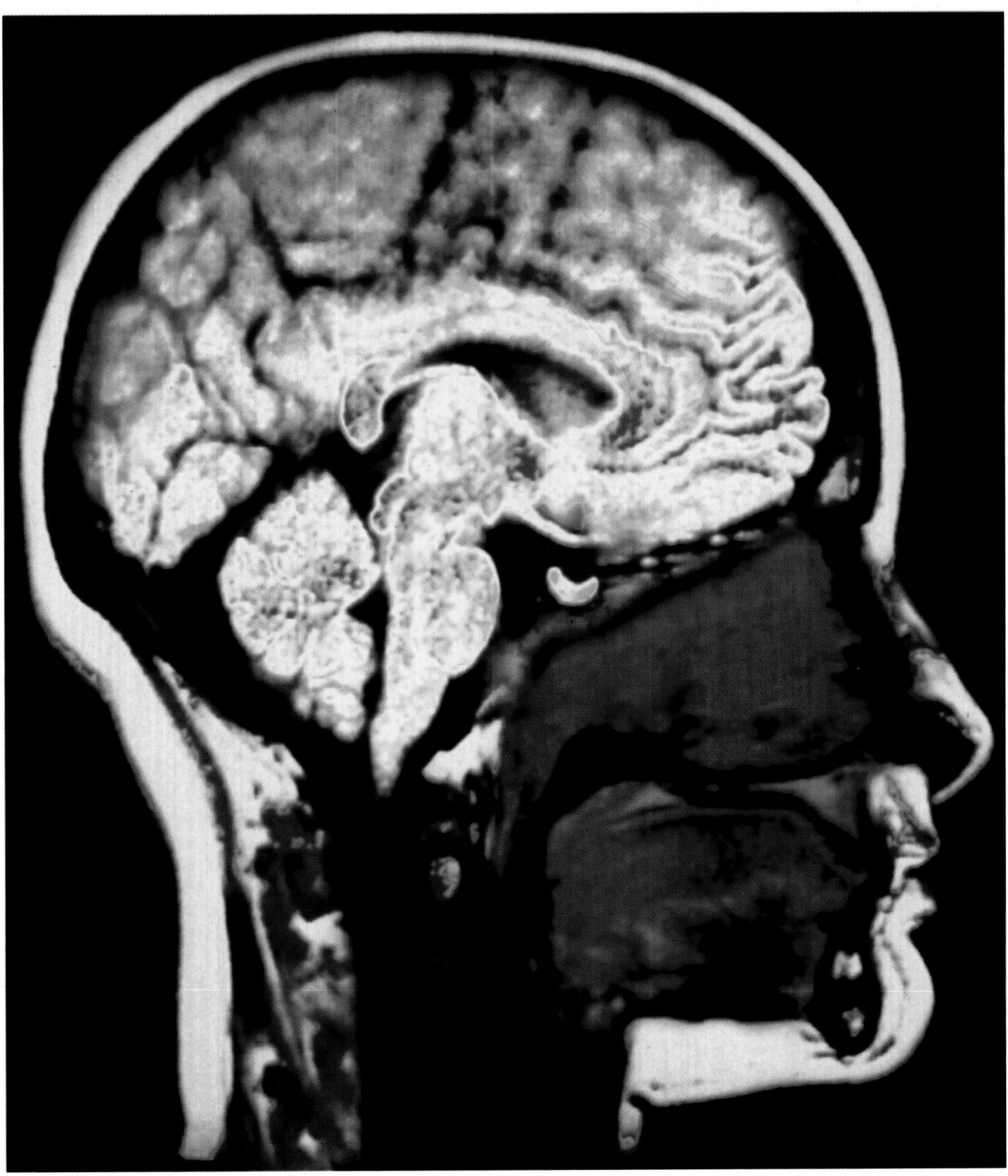

MRI scan of human brain with hypothalamus highlighted (green dot). See entry, "Magnetic resonance imaging," page 579. *(Scott Camazine and Sue Trainor. Photo Researchers, Inc. Reproduced by permission.)*

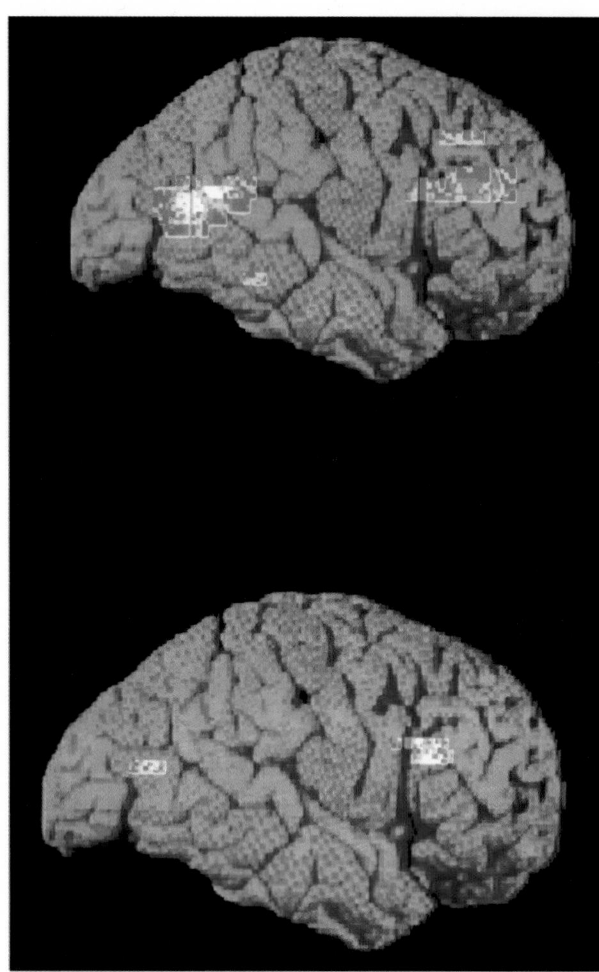

Colored positron emission tomography (PET) scans comparing the brain of a depressed person (top) with the brain of a healthy person. **See entry, "Major depressive disorder," page 583.** *(Photo Researchers, Inc. Reproduced by permission.)*

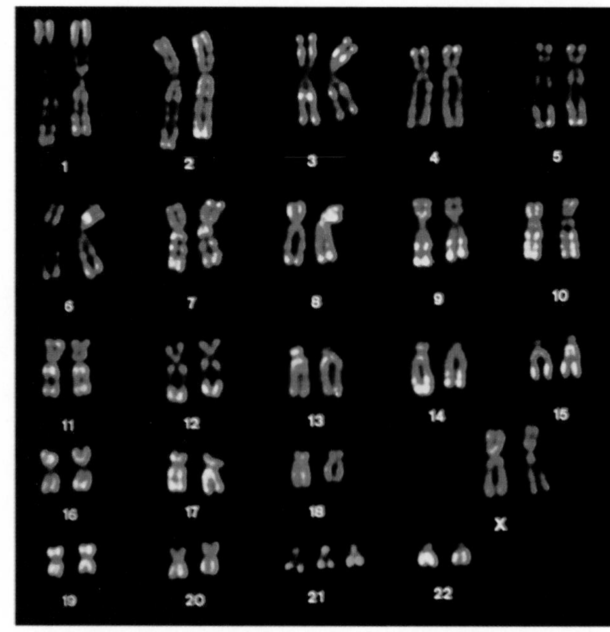

An accident or mutation in genetic development may cause retardation. An example of such a mutation is the development of an extra chromosome 21 that causes Down syndrome. Shown here is a chart (karyotype) showing the 22 chromosome pairs, and in pair 21, three chromosomes (instead of two) are shown. **See entry, "Mental retardation," page 611.** *(Phototake/NYC. Reproduced by permission.)*

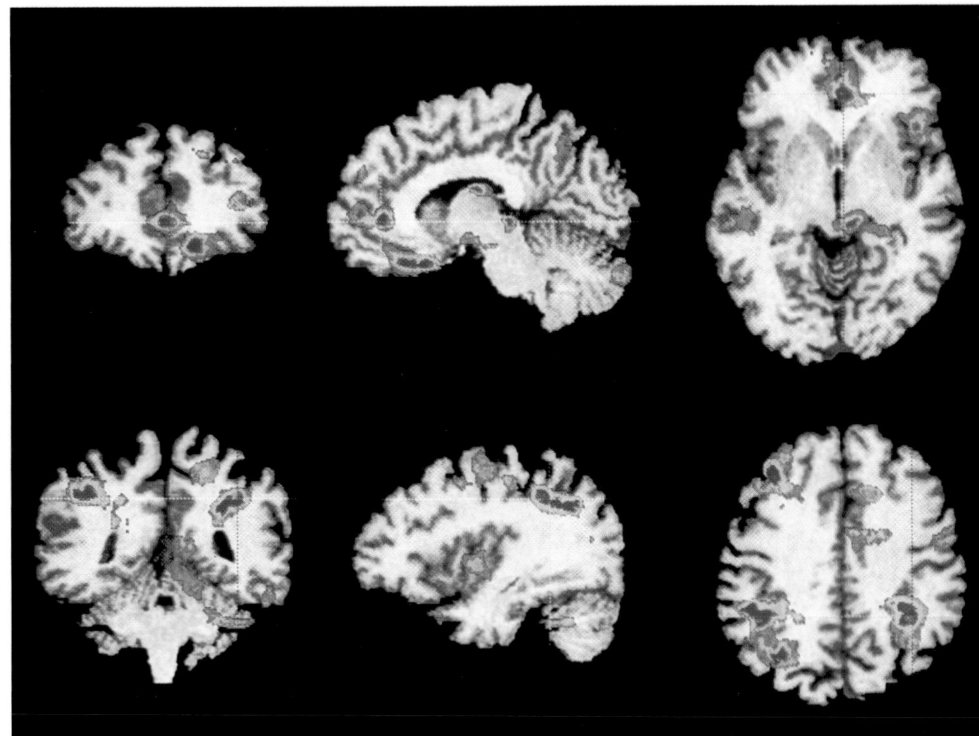

Colored positron emission tomography scans (PET scans) of a human brain, showing active areas in obsessive-compulsive disorder. In this patient, some parts of the brain show increased activity as the symptoms strengthen (areas shown in the top row), while other brain areas show decreased activity as symptoms strengthen (bottom row). See entry, "Obsessive-compulsive disorder," page 685. *(Wellcome Department of Cognitive Neurology. Photo Researchers, Inc./ Science Photo Library. Reproduced by permission.)*

A polysomnograph collects data on the electrical activity of the heart and brain, and muscle activity in the face and neck of a sleeping subject. See entry, "Polysomnography," page 768. *(Photograph by Philippe Plailly. Science Source/Photo Researchers, Inc. Reproduced by permission.)*

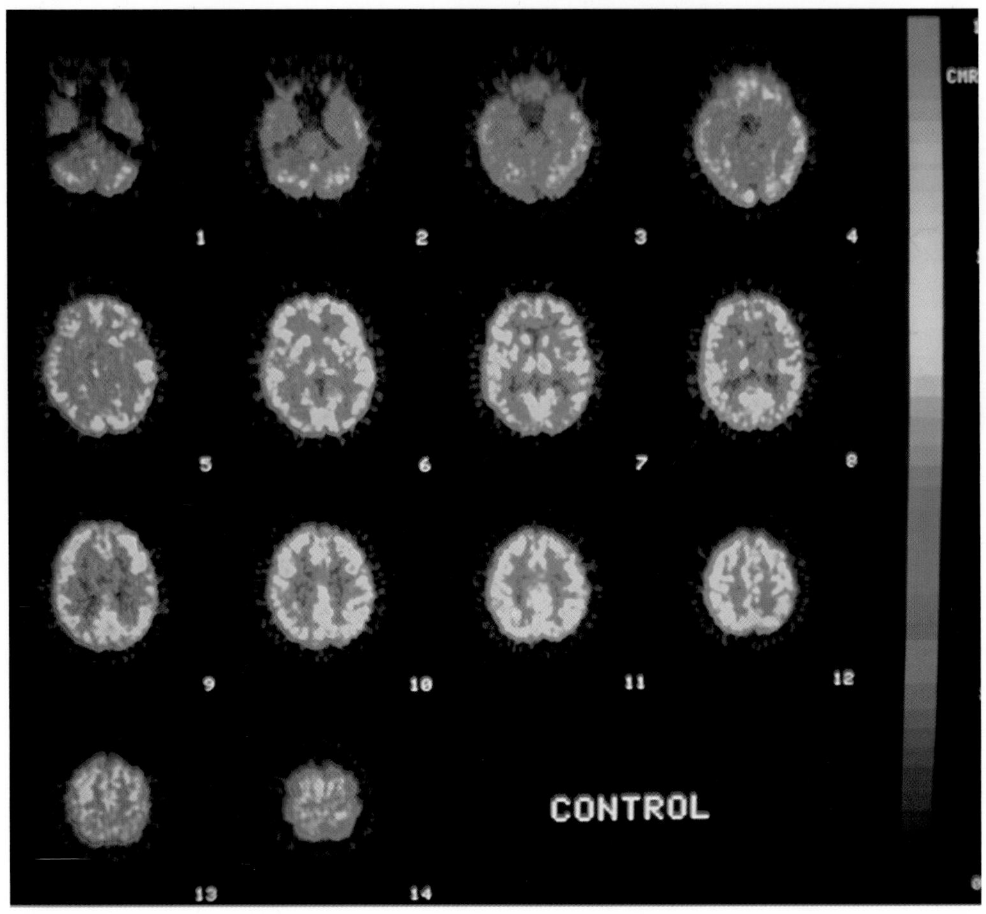

A positron emission tomography (PET) scan of the human brain. See entry, "Positron emission tomography," page 772. *(Jon Meyer. Custom Medical Stock Photo. Reproduced by permission.)*

Reading disorder is most commonly called dyslexia. Dyslexia, however, usually includes deficits in spelling and writing as well as reading. Symptoms of reading disorder include poor comprehension, reversal of words or letters while reading, and difficulty decoding syllables or single words and associating them with specific sounds (phonics). Here, a child with dyslexia attempts to reproduce a teacher's sentence. See entry, "Reading disorder," page 814. *(Will and Deni McIntyre/Science Source, National Audubon Society Collection/ Photo Researchers, Inc. Reproduced by permission.)*

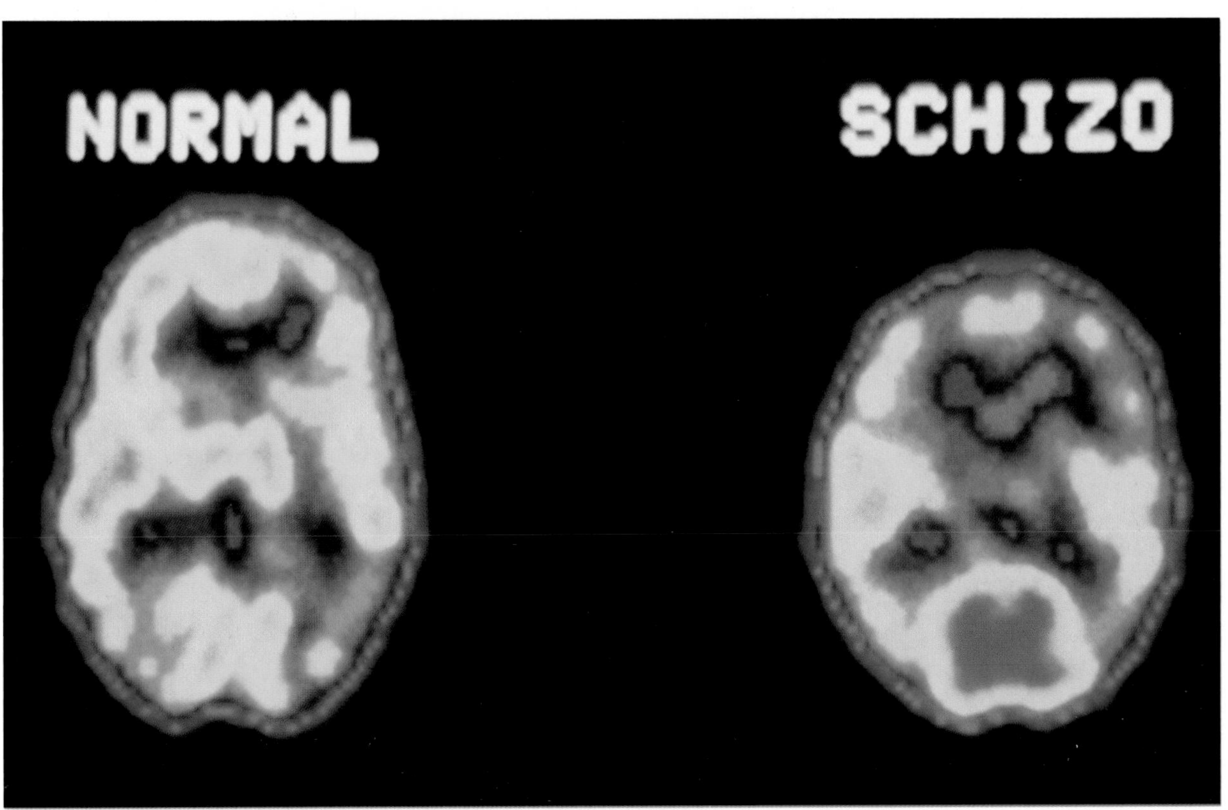

Colored positron emission tomography (PET) scans comparing normal brain (left) with the brain of a person with schizophrenia (right). See entry, "Schizophrenia," page 845. *(Photo Researchers, Inc. Reproduced by permission.)*

St. John's wort flowers. See entry, "St. John's wort," page 927. *(Photo Researchers, Inc. Reproduced by permission.)*

Woman in child's pose, a hatha yoga position. See entry, "Yoga," page 1041. *(Photo Researchers, Inc. Reproduced by permission.)*

which essentially target dopamine levels without regard to specific areas of the brain.

Another area of investigation concerns abnormalities in brain structure that are found in some patients with schizophrenia. One of these abnormalities is the increased size of the ventricles, which are cavities in the interior of the brain filled with cerebrospinal fluid. Another is a decrease in size of some areas of the brain. A California study of MRI scans of teenagers with early-onset schizophrenia found that they lost over 10% of the gray matter of the brain over the course of five years. The frontal eye fields showed the most rapid rate of tissue loss—about 5% per year. A major difficulty in interpreting these findings is that these abnormalities are not found in the brains of all patients with schizophrenia. In addition, they sometimes occur in the brains of people who do not have the disorder.

ENVIRONMENTAL. Certain environmental factors during pregnancy are associated with an increased risk of schizophrenia in the offspring. These include the mother's exposure to starvation or famine; influenza during the second trimester of pregnancy; and Rh incompatibility in a second or third pregnancy.

Some researchers are investigating a possible connection between schizophrenia and viral infections of the hippocampus, a structure in the brain that is associated with memory formation and the human stress response. It is thought that damage to the hippocampus might account for the sensory disturbances found in schizophrenia. Another line of research related to viral causes of schizophrenia concerns a protein deficiency in the brain. Researchers at the University of Kiel in Germany think that the deficiency is the result of viral infections.

Environmental stressors related to home and family life (parental death or divorce, family dysfunction) or to separation from the family of origin in late adolescence (going away to college or military training; marriage) may trigger the onset of schizophrenia in individuals with genetic or psychological vulnerabilities.

Symptoms

The symptoms of schizophrenia are divided into two major categories: **positive symptoms**, which are defined by *DSM-IV-TR* as excesses or distortions of normal mental functions; and **negative symptoms**, which represent a loss or reduction of normal functioning. Of the two types, the negative symptoms are more difficult to evaluate because they may be influenced by a concurrent depression or a dull and unstimulating environment, but they account for much of the morbidity (unhealthiness) associated with schizophrenia.

POSITIVE SYMPTOMS. The positive symptoms of schizophrenia include four so-called "first-rank" or Schneiderian symptoms, named for a German **psychiatrist** who identified them in 1959:

- Delusions. A delusion is a false belief that is resistant to reason or to confrontation with actual facts. The most common form of delusion in patients with schizophrenia is persecutory; the person believes that others—family members, clinical staff, terrorists, etc.—are "out to get" them. Another common delusion is referential, which means that the person interprets objects or occurrences in the environment (a picture on the wall, a song played on the radio, laughter in the corridor, etc.) as being directed at or referring to them.
- Somatic hallucinations. Somatic hallucinations refer to sensations or perceptions about one's body organs that have no known medical cause, such as feeling that snakes are crawling around in one's intestines or that one's eyes are emitting radioactive rays.
- Hearing voices commenting on one's behavior or talking to each other. Auditory hallucinations are the most common form of hallucination in schizophrenia, although visual, tactile, olfactory, and gustatory hallucinations may also occur. Personal accounts of recovery from schizophrenia often mention "the voices" as one of the most frightening aspects of the disorder.
- Thought insertion or withdrawal. These terms refer to the notion that other beings or forces (God, aliens from outer space, the CIA, etc.) can put thoughts or ideas into one's mind or remove them.

Other positive symptoms of schizophrenia include:

- Disorganized speech and thinking. A person with schizophrenia may ramble from one topic to another (derailment or loose associations); may give unrelated answers to questions (tangentiality); or may say things that cannot be understood because there is no grammatical structure to the language ("word salad" or incoherence).
- Disorganized behavior. This symptom includes such behaviors as agitation; age-inappropriate silliness; inability to maintain personal hygiene; dressing inappropriately for the weather; sexual self-stimulation in public; shouting at people, etc. In one case study, the patient played his flute for hours on end while standing on top of the family car.
- Catatonic behavior. Catatonic behaviors have been described with regard to the catatonic subtype of schizophrenia. This particular symptom is sometimes found in other mental disorders.

NEGATIVE SYMPTOMS. The negative symptoms of schizophrenia include:

- Blunted or flattened affect. This term refers to loss of emotional expressiveness. The person's face may be unresponsive or expressionless, and speech may lack vitality or warmth.
- Alogia. Alogia is sometimes called poverty of speech. The person has little to say and is not able to expand on their statements. A doctor examining the patient must be able to distinguish between alogia and unwillingness to speak.
- Avolition. The person is unable to begin or stay with goal-directed activities. They may sit in one location for long periods of time or show little interest in joining group activities.
- Anhedonia. Anhedonia refers to the loss of one's capacity for enjoyment or pleasure.

OTHER SYMPTOMS AND CHARACTERISTICS. Although the following symptoms and features are not diagnostic criteria of schizophrenia, most patients with the disorder have one or more:

- Dissociative symptoms, particularly **depersonalization** and derealization.
- Anosognosia. This term originally referred to the inability of **stroke** patients to recognize their physical disabilities, but is sometimes used to refer to lack of insight in patients with schizophrenia. Anosognosia is associated with higher rates of noncompliance with treatment, a higher risk of repeated psychotic episodes, and a poorer prognosis for recovery.
- High rates of substance abuse disorders. About 50% of patients diagnosed with schizophrenia meet criteria for substance abuse or dependence. While substance abuse does not cause schizophrenia, it can worsen the symptoms of the disorder. Patients may have particularly bad reactions to **amphetamines**, cocaine, PCP ("angel dust") or marijuana. It is thought that patients with schizophrenia are attracted to drugs of abuse as self-medication for some of their symptoms. The most common substance abused by patients with schizophrenia is tobacco; 90% of patients are heavy cigarette smokers, compared to 25%–30% in the general adult population. Smoking is a serious problem for people with schizophrenia because it interferes with the effectiveness of their antipsychotic medications as well as increasing their risk of lung cancer and other respiratory diseases.
- High risk of **suicide**. About 40% of patients with schizophrenia attempt suicide at least once, and 10% eventually complete the act.
- High rates of **obsessive-compulsive disorder** and panic disorder.
- Downward drift. Downward drift is a sociological term that refers to having lower levels of educational achievement and/or employment than one's parents.

VIOLENT BEHAVIOR. The connection between schizophrenia and personal assault or violence deserves mention because it is a major factor in the reactions of family members and the general public to the diagnosis. Researchers in both the United Kingdom and the United States have found that schizophrenia carries a heavier **stigma** than most other mental disorders, largely because of the mass media's fascination with bizarre murders, dismemberment of animals, or other gruesome acts committed by people with schizophrenia. Many patients report that the popular image of a schizophrenic as "a time bomb waiting to explode" is a source of considerable emotional stress.

Risk factors for violence in a patient diagnosed with schizophrenia include male sex, age below 30, prediagnosis history of violence, paranoid subtype, nonadherence to medication regimen, and heavy substance abuse. On the other hand, it should be noted that most crimes of violence are committed by people without a diagnosis of schizophrenia. In addition, a study of patients with schizophrenia living in the community found that "... individuals in this sample were at least 14 times more likely to be victims of a violent crime than to be arrested for one."

Demographics

In the United States, Canada, and Western Europe, the sex ratio in schizophrenia is 1.2:1, with males being affected slightly more often than females. There is a significant gender difference in average age at onset, however; the average for males is between ages 18 and 25, whereas for women there are two peaks, one between ages 25 and 35, and a second rise in incidence after age 45. About 15% of all women who develop schizophrenia are diagnosed after age 35. In some women, the first symptoms of the disorder appear postpartum (after giving birth). Many women with schizophrenia are initially misdiagnosed as having depression or **bipolar disorder**, because women with schizophrenia are likely to have more difficulties with emotional regulation than men with the disorder. In general, however, females have higher levels of functioning prior to symptom onset than males.

The incidence of schizophrenia in the United States appears to be uniform across racial and ethnic groups, with the exception of minority groups in urban neighborhoods in which they are a small proportion of the total population. A recent study done in the United Kingdom replicated American findings: there are significantly higher rates of schizophrenia among racial minorities living in large cities. The rates of schizophrenia are highest in areas in which these minority groups form the smallest proportion of the local population. The British study included Africans, Caribbeans of African descent, and Asians.

The incidence of schizophrenia in most developed countries appears to be higher among people born in cities than among those born in rural areas. In addition, there appears to be a small historical/generational factor, with the incidence of schizophrenia gradually declining in later-born groups.

Schizophrenia is a leading cause of disability, not only in the United States, but in other developed countries around the world. In 1997, the World Health Organization (WHO) listed schizophrenia as the world's ninth leading cause of disability. According to the National Institute of Mental Health (NIMH), 2.2 million American adults, or 1.1% of the population over age 18, suffer from schizophrenia. Other estimates run as high as 1.5% of the population.

Schizophrenia is disproportionately costly to society for reasons that go beyond the sheer number of people affected by the disorder. Although patients with schizophrenia are little more than 1% of the population, they account for 2.5% of all health care costs—$40 billion per year in the United States, $2.35 billion in Canada (in Canadian dollars), and 2.6 billion pounds sterling (about $7.28 billion in US dollars) in Great Britain. In the United States, patients with schizophrenia fill 25% of all hospital beds and account for about 20% of all Social Security disability days.

In addition, the onset of the disorder typically occurs during a young person's last years of high school or their first years in college or the workforce; thus it often destroys their long-term plans for their future. According to the federal Agency for Healthcare Research and Quality, 70%–80% of people diagnosed with schizophrenia are either unemployed or underemployed (working in jobs well below their actual capabilities). Ten percent of Americans with permanent disabilities have schizophrenia, as well as 20%–30% of the homeless population.

Diagnosis

There are no symptoms that are unique to schizophrenia and no single symptom that is a diagnostic hallmark of the disorder. In addition, as of 2002 there are no laboratory tests or **imaging studies** that can establish or confirm a diagnosis of schizophrenia. The diagnosis is based on a constellation or group of related symptoms that are, according to *DSM-IV-TR,* "associated with impaired occupational or social functioning."

As part of the process of diagnosis, the doctor will take a careful medical history and order laboratory tests of the patient's blood or urine in order to rule out general

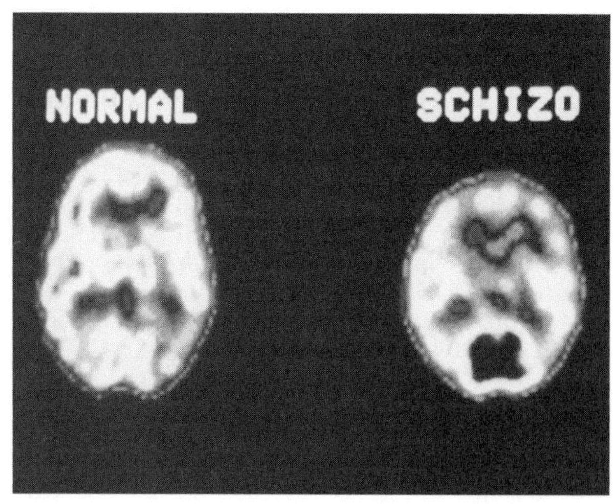

Colored positron emission tomography (PET) scans comparing normal brain (left) with the brain of a person with schizophrenia (right). *(Photo Researchers, Inc. Reproduced by permission.) See color insert for color version of photo.*

medical conditions or substance abuse disorders that may be accompanied by disturbed behavior. X rays or other imaging studies of the head may also be ordered. Medical conditions to be ruled out include epilepsy, head trauma, brain tumor, Cushing's syndrome, Wilson's disease, Huntington's disease, and encephalitis. Drugs of abuse that may cause symptoms resembling schizophrenia include amphetamines ("speed"), cocaine, and phencyclidine (PCP). In older patients, **dementia** and **delirium** must be ruled out. If the patient has held jobs involving exposure to mercury, polychlorinated biphenyls (PCBs), or other toxic substances, environmental poisoning must also be considered in the differential diagnosis.

The doctor must then rule out other mental disorders that may be accompanied by psychotic symptoms, such as mood disorders; brief psychotic disorders; dissociative disorder not otherwise specified or **dissociative identity disorder**; **delusional disorder**; schizotypal, schizoid, or paranoid **personality disorders**; and **pervasive developmental disorders**. In children, childhood-onset schizophrenia must be distinguished from communication disorders with disorganized speech and from **attention-deficit/hyperactivity disorder**.

After the doctor has ruled out other organic and mental disorders, he or she must then determine whether the patient meets the following criteria, as specified by *DSM-IV-TR*:

- Presence of positive and negative symptoms. The patient must have two (or more) of the following symptoms during a one-month period: delusions; hallucinations; disorganized speech; disorganized or catatonic behavior; negative symptoms.

- Decline in social, interpersonal, or occupational functioning, including personal hygiene or self-care.
- Duration. The symptomatic behavior must last for at least six months.

Treatments

Current treatment of schizophrenia focuses on symptom reduction and relapse prevention, since the causes of the disorder have not yet been clearly identified. Unfortunately, not all patients with schizophrenia receive adequate treatment. In 2000, the NIMH released the results of a large-scale community study, which indicated that fewer than half of patients with schizophrenia receive correct dosages of their medications or adequate psychosocial treatment.

Medications

Medications are the mainstay of treatment for schizophrenia. Drug therapy for the disorder, however, is complicated by several factors: the unpredictability of a given patient's response to specific medications, the number of potentially troublesome side effects, the high rate of substance abuse among patients with schizophrenia, and the possibility of drug interactions between antipsychotic medications and antidepressants or other medications that may be prescribed for the patient.

NEUROLEPTICS. The first antipsychotic medications for schizophrenia were introduced in the 1950s, and known as dopamine antagonists, or DAs. They are sometimes called neuroleptics, and include **haloperidol** (Haldol), **chlorpromazine** (Thorazine), **perphenazine** (Trilafon), and **fluphenazine** (Prolixin). About 40% of patients, however, fail to respond to treatment with these medications. Neuroleptics can control most of the positive symptoms of schizophrenia as well as reduce the frequency and severity of relapses but they have little effect on negative symptoms. In addition, these medications have problematic side effects, ranging from dry mouth, blurry vision, and restlessness (akathisia) to such long-term side effects as **tardive dyskinesia** (TD). TD is a disorder characterized by involuntary movements of the mouth, lips, arms, or legs; it affects about 15%–20% of patients who have been receiving neuroleptic medications over a period of years. Discomfort related to these side effects is one reason why 40% of patients treated with the older antipsychotics do not adhere to their medication regimens.

ATYPICAL ANTIPSYCHOTICS. The atypical antipsychotics are newer medications introduced in the 1990s. They are sometimes called serotonin dopamine antagonists, or SDAs. These medications include **clozapine** (Clozaril), **risperidone** (Risperdal), **quetiapine** (Seroquel), **ziprasidone** (Geodon), and **olanzapine** (Zyprexa). These newer drugs are more effective in treating the negative symptoms of schizophrenia and have fewer side effects than the older antipsychotics. Clozapine has been reported to be effective in patients who do not respond to neuroleptics, and to reduce the risk of suicide attempts. The atypical antipsychotics, however, do have weight gain as a side effect; and patients taking clozapine must have their blood monitored periodically for signs of agranulocytosis, or a drop in the number of white blood cells. These drugs are now considered first-line treatments for patients having their first psychotic episode.

OTHER PRESCRIPTION MEDICATIONS. Patients with schizophrenia have a lifetime prevalence of 80% for major depression; others suffer from phobias or other anxiety disorders. The doctor may prescribe antidepressants or a short course of benzodiazepines along with antipsychotic medications.

Inpatient treatment

Patients with schizophrenia are usually hospitalized during acute psychotic episodes, to prevent harm to themselves or to others, and to begin treatment with antipsychotic medications. A patient having a first psychotic episode is usually given a **computed tomography** (CT) or **magnetic resonance imaging** (MRI) scan to rule out structural brain disease.

Outpatient treatment

In recent years, patients with schizophrenia who have been stabilized on antipsychotic medications have been given psychosocial therapies of various types to assist them with motivation, self-care, and forming relationships with others. In addition, because many patients have had their education or vocational training interrupted by the onset of the disorder, they may be helped by therapies directed toward improving their social functioning and work skills.

Specific outpatient treatments that have been used with patients with schizophrenia include:

- Rehabilitation programs. These programs may offer vocational counseling, job training, problem-solving and money management skills, use of public transportation, and **social skills training**.
- **Cognitive-behavioral therapy** and supportive **psychotherapy**.
- **Family psychoeducation**. This approach is intended to help family members understand the patient's illness, cope with the problems it creates for other family members, and minimize stresses that may increase the patient's risk of relapse.

- **Self-help groups**. These groups provide mutual support for family members as well as patients. They can also serve as advocacy groups for better research and treatment, and to protest social stigma and employment discrimination.

Alternative and complementary therapies

Alternative and complementary therapies that are being investigated for the treatment of schizophrenia include **gingko biloba**, an Asian shrub, and vitamin therapy. One Chinese study reported that a group of patients who had not responded to conventional antipsychotic medications benefited from a thirteen-week trial of gingko extract, with significantly fewer side effects. Vitamin therapy is recommended by naturopathic practitioners on the grounds that many hospitalized patients with schizophrenia suffer from nutritional deficiencies. The supplements recommended include folic acid, niacin, vitamin B_6, and vitamin C.

Prognosis

The prognosis for patients diagnosed with schizophrenia varies. About 20% recover their previous level of functioning, while another 10% achieve significant and lasting improvement. About 30%–35% show some improvement with intermittent relapses and some disabilities, while the remainder are severely and permanently incapacitated. Factors associated with a good prognosis include relatively good functioning prior to the first psychotic episode; a late or sudden onset of illness; female sex; treatment with antipsychotic medications shortly after onset; good **compliance** with treatment; a family history of mood disorders rather than schizophrenia; minimal cognitive impairment; and a diagnosis of paranoid or nondeficit subtype. Factors associated with a poor prognosis include early age of onset; a low level of prior functioning; delayed treatment; heavy substance abuse; noncompliance with treatment; a family history of schizophrenia; and a diagnosis of disorganized or deficit subtype with many negative symptoms.

Prevention

The multifactorial and polygenic etiology (origins or causes) of schizophrenia complicates the search for preventive measures against the disorder. It is possible that the complete mapping of the human genome will identify a finite number of genes that contribute to susceptibility to schizophrenia. The NIMH has presently compiled the world's largest registry of families affected by schizophrenia in order to pinpoint specific genes for further study. The NIMH also sponsors a Prevention Research Initiative to identify points in the development of schizophrenia at which patients could benefit from the application of preventive efforts.

See also Medication-induced movement disorders

Resources

BOOKS

American Psychiatric Association. *Diagnostic and Statistical Manual of Mental Disorders.* 4th edition, text revised. Washington, DC: American Psychiatric Association, 2000.

Friedrich, Otto. *Going Crazy: An Inquiry Into Madness in Our Time.* New York: Avon Books, 1977.

Martin, John H., PhD. *Neuroanatomy: Text and Atlas.* Second edition. Norwalk, CT: Appleton and Lange, 1996.

North, Carol S., MD. *Welcome Silence: My Triumph Over Schizophrenia.* New York: Simon and Schuster, Inc., 1989.

Pelletier, Kenneth R., MD. "CAM Therapies for Specific Conditions: Schizophrenia." In *The Best Alternative Medicine*, Part II. New York: Simon and Schuster, 2002.

"Schizophrenia and Related Disorders." Section 15, Chapter 193 in *The Merck Manual of Diagnosis and Therapy,* edited by Mark H. Beers, MD, and Robert Berkow, MD. Whitehouse Station, NJ: Merck Research Laboratories, 2001.

Wahl, Otto F. *Telling Is Risky Business: Mental Health Consumers Confront Stigma.* New Brunswick, NJ: Rutgers University Press, 1999.

PERIODICALS

AACAP Council. "Practice Parameter for the Assessment and Treatment of Children and Adolescents with Schizophrenia." *Journal of the American Academy of Child and Adolescent Psychiatry* 40 (July 2001 Supplement): 4S–23S.

Barrowclough, Christine, Gillian Haddock, Nicholas Tarrier, and others. "Randomized Controlled Trial of Motivational Interviewing, Cognitive Behavior Therapy, and Family Intervention for Patients with Comorbid Schizophrenia and Substance Use Disorders." *American Journal of Psychiatry* 158 (October 2001): 1706–1713.

Bassett, A. S., S. O'Neill, J. Murphy, and others. "Expression of Schizophrenic Symptoms in 22q Deletion Syndrome." *American Journal of Human Genetics* 69 (October 2001): 287.

Bower, Bruce. "Back from the Brink (Therapies for Schizophrenia)." *Science News* 159 (April 28, 2001): 268.

Boydell, J., J. van Os, K. McKenzie, and others. "Incidence of Schizophrenia in Ethnic Minorities in London: Ecological Study Into Interactions With the Environment." *British Medical Journal* 323 (December 8, 2001): 1336–1338.

Brekke, John S. "Risks for Individuals with Schizophrenia Who Are Living in the Community." *Journal of the American Medical Association* 286 (December 19, 2001): 2922.

Camp, Nicola J., Susan L. Neuhausen, Josepha Tiobech, and others. "Genomewide Multipoint Linkage Analysis of Seven Extended Palauan Pedigrees with Schizophrenia, by a Markov-Chain Monte Carlo Method." *American Journal of Human Genetics* 69 (December 2001): 1278–1289.

"Consider Clozapine for Reducing Suicide Risk in Schizophrenia." *Clinical Psychiatry News* 29 (November 2001): 22.

Cormac, I., C. Jones, C. Campbell. "Cognitive Behaviour Therapy for Schizophrenia (Cochrane Review)." *Cochrane Database Systems Review* (2002): CD000524.

Fisher, Daniel B. "Recovering from Schizophrenia." (Guest Editorial). *Clinical Psychiatry News* 29 (November 2001): 30.

Frangou, Sophia. "How to Manage the First Episode of Schizophrenia: Early Diagnosis and Treatment May Prevent Social Disability Later." *British Medical Journal* 321 (September 2, 2000): 522.

Jancin, Bruce. "Women Often Defy Schizophrenia's Classic Course." *Clinical Psychiatry News* 29 (October 2001): 30.

Lehman, A. F., R. Goldberg, L. B. Dixon, and others. "Improving Employment Outcomes for Persons with Severe Mental Illness." *Archives of General Psychiatry* 59 (February 2002): 165–172.

McGrath, John. "Treatment of Schizophrenia." *British Medical Journal* 319 (October 16, 1999): 1045–1083.

"MRI Reveals Brain Changes Associated with Schizophrenia." *Mental Health Weekly* 11 (October 1, 2001): 8.

Myin-Germeys I., L. Krabbendam, J. Jolles, and others. "Are Cognitive Impairments Associated with Sensitivity to Stress in Schizophrenia? An Experience Sampling Study." *American Journal of Psychiatry* 159 (March 2002): 443–449.

Nakaya, M., K. Kusumoto, K. Ohmori. "Subjective Experiences of Japanese Inpatients with Chronic Schizophrenia." *Journal of Nervous and Mental Disorders* 190 (February 2002): 80–85.

"Old Fathers and Schizophrenia." *Harvard Mental Health Letter* 18 (October 2001).

Ross, Brendan. "Novel Antipsychotic Drugs in the Management of Schizophrenia." *Drug Topics* (May 7, 2001): 72–84.

"Schizophrenia May Be Linked to Brain Protein Deficiency." *Mental Health Weekly* 11 (November 19, 2001): 7.

Swofford, Cheryl D. "Double Jeopardy: Schizophrenia and Substance Abuse." *American Journal of Drug and Alcohol Abuse* 26 (August 2000): 343.

Weiser, Mark, Avraham Reichenberg, Jonathan Rabinowitz, and others. "Association Between Nonpsychotic Psychiatric Diagnoses in Adolescent Males and Subsequent Onset of Schizophrenia." *Archives of General Psychiatry* 58 (October 2001): 959–964.

Werbach, Melvyn R. "Vitamins for Treating Schizophrenia." *Townsend Letter for Doctors and Patients* (April 2001): 55–60.

ORGANIZATIONS

American Academy of Child and Adolescent Psychiatry. 3615 Wisconsin Avenue, NW, Washington, DC 20016-3007. (202) 966-7300. Fax: (202) 966-2891. <www.aacap.org>.

The National Alliance for the Mentally Ill (NAMI). 200 North Glebe Road, Suite 1015, Arlington, VA 22203-3754. (800) 950-NAMI or (703) 524-7600. <www.nami.org>.

National Alliance for Research on Schizophrenia and Depression (NARSAD). 60 Cutter Mill Road, Suite 404, Great Neck, NY 11021. (516) 829-0091. <www.mhsource.com>.

National Institute of Mental Health. 6001 Executive Boulevard, Room 8184, MSC 9663, Bethesda, MD 20892-9663. (301) 443-4513. <www.nimh.nih.gov>.

National Mental Health Association (NMHA). 1021 Prince Street, Alexandria, VA 22314-2971. (800) 969-6942 or (703) 684-7722. <www.nmha.org>.

OTHER

National Institute of Mental Health (NIMH). *The Numbers Count.* NIH Publication No. 01-4584 (2000). <www.nimh.nih.gov/publicat/numbers.cfm>.

National Institutes of Health (NIH). News Release, January 28, 2002. "Scans Link 2 Key Pieces of Schizophrenia Puzzle." <www.nih.gov/news/pr/jan2002/nimh-28.htm>.

Rebecca J. Frey, Ph.D.

Schizophreniform disorder

Definition

Schizophreniform disorder (SFD) is a time-limited illness wherein the sufferer has experienced at least two of the major symptoms of **psychosis** for longer than one month but fewer than six months. **Hallucinations**, **delusions**, and strange bodily movements or lack of movements (catatonic behavior) are all symptoms that may be observed. Additionally, minimal or peculiar speech, lack of drive to act on one's own behalf, bizarre behavior, a wooden quality to one's emotions or near-absent emotionality are all typical psychotic symptoms that may occur in SFD.

Part of defining SFD involves examining possible biological influences on the development of the individual's psychotic symptoms. When the psychotic features result from a physical disease, a reaction to medication, or intoxication with drugs or alcohol, then these symptoms are not considered SFD. Also, if hallucinations, delusions or other psychotic symptoms are experienced solely during episodes of clinical depression or mania, then SFD is not diagnosed. Instead, a mood disorder **diagnosis** is given.

The ***Diagnostic and Statistical Manual of Mental Disorders*** Fourth Edition Text Revision, or *DSM-IV-TR*, produced by the American Psychiatric Association in 2000, outlines the diagnostic criteria for SFD.

Description

The person experiencing SFD shows at least two psychotic symptoms, which may be either "positive" or "negative" psychotic symptoms. The terms "positive" and "negative" are not used in their usual meanings of positive being good and negative being bad. In discussing psychosis, positive and negative are used with a more formal medical connotation. Medically, "positive" refers to a factor being present that does not normally occur, or to an excess of some factor or behavior. **Positive symptoms** of psychosis include hallucinations, delusions, strange bodily movements or frozen movement (catatonic behavior), peculiar speech and bizarre or primitive (socially inappropriate) behavior. Negative, when used in medical fashion, refers to an absence or deficiency of a factor that is usually at a reasonable level during normal functioning. Various deficiencies in behavior, emotionality or speech constitute the **negative symptoms** of psychosis which are observed in some cases of SFD. Negative symptoms of psychosis include *avolition*, *affective flattening* and *alogia*.

Avolition is a lack of effort to act on one's own behalf or to engage in behaviors directed at accomplishing a purpose. Affective flattening or blunted **affect** refers to a decrease or low level of emotion, shown as a wooden quality to one's emotions or a near absence of emotionality. Alogia derives from the Greek root term for speech or thought, and the "a" that begins the word indicates an absence. Thus, alogia refers to a disruption in thought process reflected in the person's speech. One form of alogia is *poverty of speech*. Impoverished speech is brief, limited, terse and generally emerges only in response to questions or prompts rather than flowing spontaneously. An impairment termed *poverty of content* occurs when the information or concepts that the individual is attempting to convey cannot be understood because of limitations in the method of communicating. The meaning behind the phrases is obscured or missing. Typically, in poverty of content, the person's speech, while comprehensible in terms of its orderliness of grammar and vocabulary, does not convey substantial meaning because the phrasing is overly concrete and literal or overly abstract and fanciful.

KEY TERMS

Erotomanic delusions—Erotomanic delusions involve the mistaken conviction that someone is in love with the delusional person. Often, the love object is a public figure of some prominence, such as an actress, rock star, or political figure. David Letterman and Jodie Foster are celebrities who have both been victimized by persons with erotomanic delusions.

Grandiose delusions—Grandiose delusions magnify the person's importance; the delusional person may believe himself or herself to be a famous person, to have magical superpowers, or to be someone in a position of enormous power (such as being the King or President).

Hallucinations—False sensory perceptions. A person experiencing a hallucination may "hear" sounds or "see" people or objects that are not really present. Hallucinations can also affect the senses of smell, touch, and taste.

Psychosis—Severe state that is characterized by loss of contact with reality and deterioration in normal social functioning; examples are schizophrenia and paranoia. Psychosis is usually one feature of an over-arching disorder, not a disorder in itself. (Plural: psychoses)

Somatic—Somatic comes from *soma*, the Greek word for body; thus, somatic hallucinations are bodily experienced hallucinations. Somatic delusions are strongly held but erroneous ideas about the characteristics or functioning of one's body. An example is a mental health client who refuses to eat because of a belief that there is a hole in the stomach that will spill anything consumed into the body cavity, when such is not actually the case.

Among the various positive symptoms of psychosis that can be a part of SFD, delusions are a fairly common psychotic feature. Delusions are strongly held irrational and unrealistic beliefs that are highly resistant to alteration. Even when the person encounters evidence that would invalidate the delusion, the unjustified and improbable belief remains a conviction. Often, delusions are paranoid or persecutory in tone. In these types of delusions, the person is excessively suspicious and continually feels at the mercy of conspirators believed to be determined to cause harm to the sufferer. However, delusions can also take on other overtones. Some delusions are grandiose, or involve elaborate love fantasies (erotomanic delusions). Delusions may involve somatic content, or may revolve around extreme and irrational jealousy.

Peculiar or disorganized speech, catatonic behavior and bizarre or primitive behavior are all additional positive psychotic symptoms that may occur in SFD. Disorganized speech is seen in some cases of SFD. Speech disorganization can involve words blended together into incomprehensible statements, also known as "word salad." In some persons disorganized speech takes the form of echolalia, which is the repetition of another person's exact spoken words, restated either immediately after the initial speaker or after a delay of minutes to hours. Catatonic behavior or **catatonia** involves the presence of one of the possible extremes related to movement. Catalepsy is the motionless end of the catatonic spectrum; in catalepsy, a person may remain unmoving in one fixed position for long periods. The opposite end of the catatonia phenomenon is demonstrated in rapid or persistently repeated movements, recurrent grimacing and odd facial expressions, and contorted or strange gestures. Bizarre or primitive behavior in SFD ranges from child-like behaviors in unsuitable circumstances to unusual practices such as hoarding refuse items perceived by the sufferer to be valuable, caching food all over the home, or wandering purposelessly through the streets.

Only rarely would all these various psychotic symptoms be observed simultaneously in one person with SFD. Instead, each individual with SFD has a constellation of symptoms, practices and thought processes that is unique to that person. However, frequent occurrence of at least two of these psychotic symptoms persisting for one month to six months is considered to be SFD. A different diagnosis, which includes the presence of psychotic symptoms, is given if the symptoms have been present for longer than six months. Also, if there is some other psychiatric syndrome that better explains the behaviors, or if there are biological causes (such as a physical illness, like a **brain** tumor) that caused the symptoms to appear, another diagnosis is utilized.

Unlike any other diagnoses offered in *DSM-IV-TR*, the SFD diagnosis always includes an indication of the patient's *prognosis*. Prognosis refers to the potential outcome for an individual with a particular illness, based on the features already observed and the usual course of the illness. If an individual with SFD has several positive prognostic factors, then there is a much higher likelihood of complete recovery without relapse into psychosis. Positive prognostic factors in SFD include: prominent confusion during the illness, rapid (rather than gradual) development of symptoms during a four-week period, good previous interpersonal and goal-oriented functioning, and lack of negative symptoms of psychosis.

Causes and symptoms

Causes

Several views regarding the causes of the disorder have been put forth by researchers and clinicians.

AN EARLY PHASE OF ANOTHER PSYCHIATRIC DISORDER. A number of follow-up studies have examined the relationship between SFD and other disorders such as **schizophrenia**, **schizoaffective disorder** and **bipolar disorder**. The majority of these studies have found that between 50% and 75% of persons with SFD eventually develop schizophrenia. Of those persons with a history of SFD who do not subsequently receive a schizophrenia diagnosis, only a small portion have no further psychiatric disturbance. The other diagnoses that may be observed in persons formerly diagnosed with SFD are schizoaffective disorder or bipolar disorder (the Type I form). The most common subsequent diagnosis is schizophrenia, with the next most common being schizoaffective disorder. Because of the high rate of later schizophrenia in SFD sufferers, many clinicians have come to think of SFD as being an initial phase of schizophrenia. It is impossible to identify, during an episode of SFD, whether any one particular case will improve without any relapse into psychotic symptoms, or if the mental health client is actually in the early phase of schizophrenia or schizoaffective disorder. Follow-up studies indicate that being frequently confused during a period of SFD is often associated with gradual complete recovery.

LENGTHY POSTPARTUM PSYCHOSIS. Intense hormonal changes occurring in childbirth and immediately afterward can result in a short-term psychotic disorder often referred to as *postpartum psychosis*. When the psychotic symptoms in this condition persist for longer than one month but fewer than six months, the SFD diagnosis may be given.

DIATHESIS X STRESS. *Diathesis* is a medical term meaning that some element of one's physiology makes one particularly prone to develop an illness if exposed to the right conditions. Diathesis is another way of saying there is a personal predisposition to develop a disorder; the predisposition is biologically based and is genetically acquired (inherited in the person's genes). Temporary psychotic reactions may occur in persons who have the diathesis for psychosis, when the individual is placed under marked **stress**. The stress may result from typical life transition experiences such as moving away from home the first time, being widowed or getting divorced. In some cases, the stressor is more intense or unusual, such as surviving a natural disaster, wartime service, being taken hostage or surviving a terrorist attack. When the psychotic responses last less than a month, then this reaction is labeled "**brief psychotic disorder**." Highly susceptible persons may show psychotic symptoms for greater than one month and might be given the SFD diagnosis. If the psychotic symptoms are purely reactive, when the stressor ceases or more support is available, the individual is likely to return to a non-psychotic mode of functioning. In persons with a strong diathesis or predisposition, the initial psychotic reaction may "tip over" from the category of a brief reaction into a longer-term, persistent psychiatric disorder. The diathesis x stress model is applied not only to SFD, but also to schizophrenia, schizoaffective disorder and the most severe forms of mood disorders.

CULTURALLY DEFINED DISORDERS. Many cultures have forms of mental disorder, unique to that culture, that would meet criteria for SFD. In culturally defined disorders, a consistent set of features and presumed causes of the syndrome are localized to that community. Such disorders are termed "culture-bound." Examples of culture-bound syndromes that might meet SFD criteria are *amok* (Malaysia), or *locura* (Latino Americans). Amok is a syndrome characterized by brooding, persecutory delusions and aggressive actions. Locura involves incoherence, agitation, social dysfunction, erratic behavior, and hallucinations.

Symptoms

DSM-IV-TR provides three major criteria for SFD:

AT LEAST TWO PERSISTENT POSITIVE OR NEGATIVE SYMPTOMS OF PSYCHOSIS.

- delusions
- disorganized speech which is strange, peculiar, difficult to comprehend
- disorganized (bizarre or child-like) behavior
- catatonic behavior
- hallucinations
- negative symptoms (affective flattening, alogia, avolition)

LIMITED DURATION.

- The psychotic symptoms have occurred for at least one month but less than six months.

CAUSE. The symptoms cannot:

- occur as part of a mood disorder
- occur as part of schizoaffective disorder or schizophrenia
- be due to intoxication with drugs or alcohol
- be an adverse reaction to a medication
- be caused by a physical injury or medical illness

Demographics

The actual rate of SFD is unknown, mainly because SFD is difficult to measure except in retrospect. In the first few weeks of symptoms, SFD cannot be differentiated from brief psychotic disorder. Once the symptoms persist past one month and are identified as SFD, six months or more must pass before one can determine if a mental health consumer had "classic" SFD or was in the early phase of a more chronic mental disorder. Given that a majority of SFD sufferers go on to be diagnosed with schizophrenia, the best inferences about demographics and gender differences in SFD would be drawn from similar information available regarding schizophrenia.

Diagnosis

Despite the clarity of the *DSM-IV-TR* criteria, identification of SFD is less than clear-cut. The emphasis on the length of time that symptoms have been evident and the presence or absence of good prognostic factors make SFD one of the most unusually defined of the *DSM-IV-TR* disorders. While duration of symptoms is the major distinction among brief psychotic disorder, SFD and schizophrenia, it can be difficult to clearly determine the length of time symptoms have existed. An additional complication is that the cultural context in which the "psychotic symptoms" are experienced determines whether the behaviors are viewed as pathological or acceptable. When psychotic-like behaviors are expected to occur normally as part of the person's culture or religion, and when the behaviors occur in a culturally positive context such as a religious service, SFD would not be diagnosed.

Information about current and past experiences is collected in an interview with the client, and possibly in discussion with the client's family. Psychological assessment instruments, such as the **Rorschach technique**, the **Minnesota Multiphasic Personality Inventory**, and mood disorder questionnaires or structured diagnostic interviews may also be used to aid in the diagnosis.

Treatments

The main line of treatment for SFD is antipsychotic medication. These medications are often very effective in treating SFD. Mood-stabilizing drugs similar to those used in bipolar disorder may be used if there is little response to other interventions. Postpartum psychosis is also treated with antipsychotics and possibly, hormones. Supportive therapy and education about mental illness is often valuable. The most useful interventions in culture-bound syndromes are those that are societally prescribed; for example, a sacred ceremony to ease the rest-

of deceased ancestors might be a usual
nding the psychotic-like state, in that partic-

Prognosis

Given the large number of mental health consumers with SFD who go on to be diagnosed with a more chronic form of mental illness, the prognosis is fairly poor. As noted earlier, prominent confusion during the illness, rapid (rather than gradual) development of symptoms during a four-week period, good previous interpersonal and goal-oriented functioning and lack of negative symptoms of psychosis suggest a better outcome.

Prevention

If the SFD is a persistent postpartum psychosis, a prevention option is to avoid having additional children. The physician may anticipate the postpartum problem and prescribe an antipsychotic medication regimen to begin immediately after delivery as a preventive measure. Although prevention of psychotic disorders is difficult to accomplish, the earlier treatment begins, the better the outcome. Therefore, efforts are more generally focused on early identification of SFD and other psychotic-spectrum disorders.

See also Delusional disorder; Dementia; Schizotypal personality disorder

Resources

BOOKS

American Psychiatric Association. *Diagnostic and Statistical Manual of Mental Disorders.* 4th edition, text revised. Washington, DC: American Psychiatric Association, 2000.

PERIODICALS

Ferfel D. "Rationale and guidelines for the inpatient treatment of acute psychosis." *Journal of Clinical Psychiatry* 61, Suppl 14 (2000): 27–32.

Iancu, I, P. V. Dannon, R. Ziv, and E. Lepkifker. "A follow-up study of patients with DSM-IV schizophreniform disorder." *Canadian Journal of Psychiatry* 47, no. 1 (2000): 56–60.

Kulhara, P., S. Chakrabarti. "Culture, schizophrenia and psychotic disorder." *Psychiatric Clinics of North America* 24, no. 3 (2001): 449–464.

Stocky A, J. Lynch. "Acute psychiatric disturbance in pregnancy and the puerperium." *Baillere's Best Practices and Research in Obstetrics and Gynaecology* 14, no. 1 (2000): 73–87.

Deborah Rosch Eifert, Ph.D.

Schizotypal personality disorder

Definition

Schizotypal personality disorder is characterized by an ongoing pattern in which the affected person distances him- or herself from social and interpersonal relationships. Affected people typically have an acute discomfort when put in circumstances where they must relate to others. These individuals are also prone to cognitive and perceptual distortions and a display a variety of eccentric behaviors that others often find confusing.

Description

People with schizotypal personality disorder are more comfortable turning inward, away from others, than learning to have meaningful interpersonal relationships. This preferred isolation contributes to distorted perceptions about how interpersonal relationships are supposed to happen. These individuals remain on the periphery of life and often drift from one aimless activity to another with few, if any, meaningful relationships.

A person with schizotypal personality disorder has odd behaviors and thoughts that would typically be viewed by others as eccentric, erratic, and bizarre. They are known on occasion to have brief periods of psychotic episodes. Their speech, while coherent, is marked by a focus on trivial detail. Thought processes of schizotypals include magical thinking, suspiciousness, and illusions. These thought patterns are believed to be the schizotypal's unconscious way of coping with social anxiety. To some extent, these behaviors stem from being socially isolated and having a distorted view of appropriate interpersonal relations.

Causes and symptoms

Causes

Schizotypal personality disorder is believed to stem from the affected person's original family, or family of origin. Usually the parents of the affected person were emotionally distant, formal, and displayed confusing parental communication. This **modeling** of remote, unaffectionate relationships is then reenacted in the social relationships encountered in the developing years. The social development of people with schizotypal personality disorder shows that many were also regularly humiliated by their parents, siblings, and peers resulting in significant relational mistrust. Many display low self-esteem, self-criticism and self-deprecating behavior. This further contributes to a sense that they are socially incapable of having meaningful interpersonal relationships.

Symptoms

The *Diagnostic and Statistical Manual of Mental Disorders*, a professional manual, specifies nine diagnostic criteria for schizotypal personality disorder:

- Incorrect interpretations of events. Individuals with schizotypal personality disorder often have difficulty seeing the correct cause and effect of situations and how they affect others. For instance, the schizotypal may misread a simple non-verbal communication cue, such as a frown, as someone being displeased with them, when in reality it may have nothing to do with them. Their perceptions are often distortions of what is really happening externally, but they tend to believe their perceptions more than what others might say or do.
- Odd beliefs or magical thinking. These individuals may be superstitious or preoccupied with the paranormal. They often engage in these behaviors as a desperate means to find some emotional connection with the world they live in. This behavior is seen as a coping mechanism to add meaning in a world devoid of much meaning because of the social isolation these individuals experience.
- Unusual perceptual experiences. These might include having illusions, or attributing a particular event to some mysterious force or person who is not present. Affected people may also feel they have special powers to influence events or predict an event before it happens.
- Odd thinking and speech. People with schizotypal personality disorder may have speech patterns that appear strange in their structure and phrasing. Their ideas are often loosely associated, prone to tangents, or vague in description. Some may verbalize responses by being overly concrete or abstract and insert words that serve to confuse rather than clarify a particular situation, yet make sense to them. They are typically unable to have ongoing conversation and tend to talk only about matters that need immediate attention.
- Suspicious or paranoid thoughts. Individuals with schizotypal personality disorder are often suspicious of others and display paranoid tendencies.
- Emotionally inexpressive. Their general social demeanor is to appear aloof and isolated, behaving in a way that communicates they derive little joy from life. Most have an intense fear of being humiliated or rejected, yet repress most of these feelings for protective reasons.
- Eccentric behavior. People with schizotypal personality disorder are often viewed as odd or eccentric due to their unusual mannerisms or unconventional clothing choices. Their personal appearance may look unkempt—clothing choices that do not "fit together," clothes may be too small or large, or clothes may be noticeably unclean.

KEY TERMS

Millon Clinical Multiaxial Inventory (MCMI-II)—A self-report instrument designed to help the clinician assess DSM-IV-related personality disorders and clinical syndromes. It provides insight into 14 personality disorders and 10 clinical syndromes.

Minnesota Multiphasic Personality Inventory (MMPI-2)—A comprehensive assessment tool widely used to diagnose personality disorders.

Rorschach Psychodiagnostic Test—This series of 10 "ink blot" images allows the patient to project their interpretations which can be used to diagnose particular disorders.

Thematic Apperception Test (TAT)—A projective test using stories and descriptions of pictures to reveal some of the dominant drives, emotions, sentiments, conflicts, and complexes of a personality.

- Lack of close friends. Because they lack the skills and confidence to develop meaningful interpersonal relationships, they prefer privacy and isolation. As they withdraw from relationships, they increasingly turn inward to avoid possible social rejection or ridicule. If they do have any ongoing social contact, it is usually restricted to immediate family members.
- Socially anxious. Schizotypals are noticeably anxious in social situations, especially with those they are not familiar with. They can interact with people when necessary, but prefer to avoid as much interaction as possible because their self-perception is that they do not "fit in." Even when exposed to the same group of people over time, their social anxiety does not seem to lessen. In fact, it may progress into distorted perceptions of **paranoia** involving the people with whom they are in social contact.

Demographics

Schizotypal personality disorder appears to occur more frequently in individuals who have an immediate family member with **schizophrenia**. The prevalence of schizotypal personality disorder is approximately 3% of the general population and is believed to occur slightly more often in males.

Symptoms that characterize a typical **diagnosis** of schizotypal personality disorder should be evaluated in the context of the individual's cultural situation, particularly those regarding superstitious or religious beliefs and practices. (Some behaviors that Western cultures may view as psychotic are viewed within the range of normal behavior in other cultures.)

Diagnosis

The symptoms of schizotypal personality disorder may begin in childhood or adolescence showing as a tendency toward solitary pursuit of activities, poor peer relationships, pronounced social anxiety, and underachievement in school. Other symptoms that may be present during the developmental years are hypersensitivity to criticism or correction, unusual use of language, odd thoughts, or bizarre fantasies. Children with these tendencies appear socially out-of-step with peers and often become the object of malicious teasing by their peers, which increases the feelings of isolation and social ineptness they feel. For a diagnosis of schizotypal personality disorder to be accurately made, there must also be the presence of at least four of the above-mentioned symptoms.

The symptoms of schizotypal personality disorder can sometimes be confused with the symptoms seen in schizophrenia. The bizarre thinking associated with schizotypal personality disorder can be perceived as a psychotic episode and misdiagnosed. While brief psychotic episodes can occur in the patient with schizotypal personality disorder, the **psychosis** is not as pronounced, frequent, or as intense as in schizophrenia. For an accurate diagnosis of schizotypal personality disorder, the symptoms for schizotypal cannot occur exclusively during the course of schizophrenia or other mood disorder that has psychotic features.

Another common difficulty in diagnosing schizotypal personality disorder is distinguishing it from other the schizoid, avoidant, and paranoid **personality disorders**. Some researchers believe that schizotypal personality disorder is essentially the same disorder as schizoid, but many feel there are distinguishing characteristics. Schizoids are deficient in their ability to experience emotion, while schizotypals are more pronounced in their inability to understand human motivation and communication. While **avoidant personality disorder** has many of the same symptoms as schizotypal personality disorder, the distinguishing symptom in schizotypal is the presence of behavior that is noticeably eccentric. The schizotypal differs from the paranoid by tangential thinking and eccentric behavior.

The diagnosis of schizotypal personality disorder is based on a clinical interview to assess symptomatic behavior. Other assessment tools helpful in confirming the diagnosis of schizotypal personality disorder include:

- **Minnesota Multiphasic Personality Inventory** (MMPI-2)
- Millon Clinical Multiaxial Inventory (MCMI-II)
- Rorschach Psychodiagnostic Test
- **Thematic Apperception Test** (TAT)

Treatments

The patient with schizotypal personality disorder finds it difficult to engage and remain in treatment. For those higher-functioning individuals who seek treatment, the goal will be to help them function more effectively in relationships rather than restructuring their personality.

Psychodynamically oriented therapies

A psychodynamic approach would typically seek to build a therapeutically trusting relationship that attempts to counter the mistrust most people with this disorder intrinsically hold. The hope is that some degree of attachment in a therapeutic relationship could be generalized to other relationships. Offering interpretations about the patient's behavior will not typically be helpful. More highly functioning schizotypals who have some capacity for empathy and emotional warmth tend to have better outcomes in psychodynamic approaches to treatment.

Cognitive-behavioral therapy

Cognitive approaches will most likely focus on attempting to identify and alter the content of the schizotypal's thoughts. Distortions that occur in both perception and thought processes would be addressed. An important foundation for this work would be the establishment of a trusting therapeutic relationship. This would relax some of the social anxiety felt in most interpersonal relationships and allow for some exploration of the thought processes. Constructive ways of accomplishing this might include communication skills training, the use of videotape feedback to help the affected person perceive his or her behavior and appearance objectively, and practical suggestions about personal hygiene, employment, among others.

Interpersonal therapy

Treatment using an interpersonal approach would allow the individual with schizotypal personality disorder to remain relationally distant while he or she "warms up" to the therapist. Gradually the therapist would hope to engage the patient after becoming "safe" through lack of coercion. The goal would be to develop trust in order to help the patient gain insight into the distorted and magical thinking that dominates. New self-talk can be introduced to help orient the individual to reality-based experience. The therapist can mirror this objectivity to the patient.

Group therapy

Group therapy may provide the patient with a socializing experience that exposes them to feedback from others in a safe, controlled environment. It is typically recommended only for schizotypals who do not display severe eccentric or paranoid behavior. Most group members would be uncomfortable with these behavioral displays and it would likely prove destructive to the group dynamic.

Family and marital therapy

It is unlikely that a person with **schizoid personality disorder** will seek family or marital therapy. Many schizoid types do not marry and end up living with and being dependent upon first-degree family members. If they do marry they often have problems centered on insensitivity to their partner's feelings or behavior. Marital therapy (**couples therapy**) may focus on helping the couple to become more involved in each other's lives or improve communication patterns.

Medications

There is considerable research on the use of medications for the treatment of schizotypal personality disorder due to its close symptomatic relationship with schizophrenia. Among the most helpful medications are the antipsychotics that have been shown to control symptoms such as illusions and phobic anxiety, among others. **Amoxapine** (trade name Asendin), is a tricyclic antidepressant with antipsychotic properties, and has been effective in improving schizophrenic-like and depressive symptoms in schizotypal patients. Other antidepressants such as **fluoxetine** (Prozac) have also been used successfully to reduce symptoms of anxiety, paranoid thinking, and depression.

Prognosis

The prognosis for the individual with schizotypal personality disorder is poor due to the ingrained nature of the coping mechanisms already in place. Schizotypals who depend heavily on family members or others are likely to regress into a state of **apathy** and further isolation. While some measurable gains can be made with mildly affected individuals, most are not able to alter their ingrained ways of perceiving or interpreting reality. When combined with poor social support structure, most will not enter any type of treatment.

Prevention

Since schizotypal personality disorder originates in the patient's family of origin, the only known preventative measure is a nurturing, emotionally stimulating and expressive caretaking environment.

Resources

BOOKS

American Psychiatric Association. *Diagnostic and Statistical Manual of Mental Disorders.* Fourth edition, text revision. Washington, DC: American Psychiatric Association, 2000.

Beers, Mark H., M.D., and Robert Berkow, M.D., eds. *The Merck Manual of Diagnosis and Therapy.* 17th edition. Whitehouse Station, NJ: Merck Research Laboratories, 1999.

Millon, Theodore, Ph.D., D.Sc. *Disorders of Personality: DSM IV and Beyond.* New York: John Wiley and Sons, Inc., 1996.

Sperry, Len, M.D., Ph.D. *Handbook of Diagnosis and Treatment of DSM-IV Personality Disoders.* New York: Brunner/Mazel, Inc., 1995.

PERIODICALS

International Society for the Study of Personality Disorders. *Journal of Personality Disorders.* Guilford Publications, 72 Spring St., New York, NY 10012. <http://www.guilford.com>. (800) 365-7006.

ORGANIZATIONS

American Psychiatric Association. 1400 K Street NW, Washington D.C. 20005. <http://www.psych.org>.

Gary Gilles, M.A.

Seasonal affective disorder

Definition

Seasonal affective disorder, often abbreviated as SAD, is a type of mood disorder that follows an annual pattern consistent with the seasons. The most common course for SAD includes an onset of depressive symptoms late in the fall, continuation of symptoms throughout winter, and remission of symptoms in the spring.

Description

According to the handbook used by mental health professionals to diagnose mental disorders, the ***Diagnostic and Statistical Manual of Mental Disorders*** fourth edition text revised, or *DSM-IV-TR*, SAD is not considered a disorder or syndrome on its own. Instead, SAD is considered a pattern specifier, or subtype, of another mood disorder **diagnosis**. For example, an individual may be diagnosed as having a major depressive episode with a seasonal pattern.

The most common type of seasonal pattern is one in which an individual first experiences symptoms in the late fall, has continued and heightened symptoms in winter, and then experiences a remission of symptoms in the spring. However, other patterns are possible. For example, a person may become depressed in the summer and then become less depressed when the weather becomes colder.

Causes and symptoms

Causes

Lack of sunlight, normally associated with winter, is considered to be the primary cause of SAD. Although winter temperature may also have an impact, especially in colder areas, the lack of light is most important. This is supported by the effectiveness of therapy in which individuals are exposed to high-intensity light (**light therapy**). The causes of rarer types of seasonal symptoms, such as those experienced by individuals who become depressed in summer, are more difficult to determine.

Symptoms

The symptoms experienced by people with SAD are similar to some of those experienced by depressed people in general: change in appetite, weight gain or loss, **fatigue**, reduced energy, irritability, and avoidance of social situations. To meet the diagnostic criteria for the disorder as indicated in the *DSM-IV-TR,* these symptoms must be present during the season the individual is depressed and must lessen or abate when that season is over.

Demographics

Some studies have shown that up to 6% of people experience some depressive symptoms in winter. SAD is a more common phenomenon in women than men. According to the *DSM-IV-TR*, women make up 60–90% of people with the seasonal pattern of depression. SAD primarily affects adults, although it is possible for children and adolescents to suffer from it. Research indicates that SAD is much more common in countries and regions where there are distinct seasonal changes. In countries near the equator, where changes in climate and light are mild, SAD generally does not occur.

Diagnosis

SAD is diagnosed through a clinical interview with the patient and careful history-taking by the physician. For the seasonal pattern specifier to be applied to a *DSM-IV-TR* mood disorder diagnosis, the following criteria must be met: there is a relationship between the onset of the depressive episode and a particular time of year; the depressive symptoms are in remission at a particular time of year; the onset and remissions have occurred at these times for the past two years; and seasonal depressive episodes outnumber non-seasonal depressive episodes over the person's lifetime. Also, the seasonal pattern specifier must not be given when depressive symptoms are due to seasonally linked stressors, such as the beginning of school or an employment schedule.

An individual with seasonal depression must be distinguished from one with who has depressive symptoms all year long.

Treatments

Light therapy, in which the person experiencing SAD is exposed to high-intensity light, is often used—usually for one to two hours per day. Sometimes, briefer periods of exposure to higher-intensity light can be used. The exposure to light may be facilitated through the use of a box which emits the prescribed light or through the use of a light visor the patient wears on his or her head. Tanning beds should not be used for light therapy. Light therapy has been found to be the most effective treatment for people correctly diagnosed with seasonal symptoms in the winter. It does not appear to have serious side effects.

Prognosis

Light therapy is considered to be a safe and effective treatment. However, it is time consuming and people do not always stay on the prescribed course of treatment. Also, SAD can be a persistent problem; even if light therapy is effective one year, symptoms may return the following year.

See also Bipolar disorders; Depressive disorders

Resources

BOOKS

American Psychiatric Association. *Diagnostic and Statistical Manual of Mental Disorders.* 4th edition, text revision. Washington, DC: American Psychiatric Association, 2000.

Salkovskis, Paul. *Comprehensive Clinical Psychology Volume 6: Adults: Clinical Formulation and Treatment.* Amsterdam: Elsevier, 1998.

ORGANIZATIONS

Depression and Related Affective Disorders Association. 600 N. Wolfe St., Baltimore, MD, 21287. <http://www.drada.org>.

Seasonal Affective Disorder Association. PO Box 989, Steyning BN44 3HG, England. <http://www.sada.org.uk>.

Ali Fahmy, Ph.D.

Sedatives and related disorders

Definition

Sedatives are compounds that cause physiological and mental slowing of the body. They have many legitimate medical uses. However, people who use them improperly may develop symptoms of abuse, dependence, and withdrawal. Several other classes of compounds, including sleep-promoting drugs (hypnotics) and some anti-anxiety (anxiolytic) drugs produce effects and disorders similar to those of sedatives. Sedatives are often referred to as tranquilizers, and the similar classes of sedatives and hypnotics are sometimes thought of as one group: the sedative-hypnotics.

Description

Sedatives and similar drugs are available by prescription and have many medical uses. They are used in conjunction with surgery and are prescribed to treat pain, anxiety, panic attacks, **insomnia**, and in some cases, convulsions. Most people who take prescription sedatives take them responsibly and benefit from their use. Some people misuse these drugs. They may do so unintentionally by increasing their prescribed dose without medical advice. Intentional abusers buy these drugs off the street for recreational use or get them from friends or family members who have prescriptions. Sedatives are not popular street drugs, and when they are used recreationally, it is usually in conjunction with other illicit drugs or alcohol. When taken exactly as prescribed, sedatives rarely create major health risks.

A chemically diverse group of drugs are discussed together in this entry because they all appear to work in the body the same way and produce similar problems of abuse, dependence, intoxication, and withdrawal. These drugs work in the **brain** by increasing the amount of the neurotransmitter gamma-aminobutyric acid (GABA). **Neurotransmitters** help to regulate the speed at which nerve impulses travel. When the amount of GABA increases, the speed of nerve transmissions decreases. Thus these drugs depress the nervous system and cause reduced pain, sleepiness, reduced anxiety, and muscle relaxation.

The most widely prescribed and best-studied sedatives belong to a group called benzodiazepines. Prescription benzodiazepines and their relatives include **alprazolam** (Xanax), **chlordiazepoxide** (Librium), **clonazepam** (Klonopin), **clorazepate** (Tranxene), **diazepam** (Valium), **estazolam** (ProSom), **flurazepam** (Dalmane), halazepam (Paxipam), **lorazepam**, (Ativan), **oxazepam** (Serax), prazepam (Centrax), **quazepam** (Doral), **temazepam** (Restoril), **triazolam** (Halcion). Other drugs that act in a similar manner include the **barbiturates** amobarbital (Amytal), aprobarbital (Alurate), butabarbital (Butisol), phenobarbitol, (Nebutal), and secobarbital, (Seconal). In addition, **chloral hydrate** (Notec), ethchlorvynol (Placidyl), glutehimide (Doriden), meprobamate (Miltown, Equanil, Equagesic, Deprol) and **zolpidem** (Ambien) have similar actions.

KEY TERMS

Neurotransmitter—A chemical in the brain that transmits messages between neurons, or nerve cells.

Tolerance—Progressive decrease in the effectiveness of a drug with long-term use.

Withdrawal—Symptoms experienced by a person who has become physically dependent on a drug, experienced when the drug use is discontinued.

Causes and symptoms

Sedatives and other drugs in this class are physically and sometimes psychologically addicting. People taking sedatives rapidly develop tolerance for the drugs. Tolerance occurs when a larger and larger dose must be taken to produce the same effect. Because sedatives are physically addicting, people with sedative dependence experience physical withdrawal symptoms when these drugs are discontinued.

Sedative abuse occurs when people misuse these drugs but are not addicted to them. Many people who abuse sedatives also use other illicit drugs. They may use sedatives to come down off a cocaine high or to enhance the effect of **methadone**, a heroin substitute.

Sedative dependence occurs when there is a physical **addiction**, when a person actively seeks sedatives (for example, by going to several doctors and getting multiple prescriptions) and when a person continues to use these drugs despite the fact that they cause interpersonal problems and difficulties meeting the responsibilities of daily life.

Sedative intoxication

Sedative intoxication occurs when a person has recently used one of these drugs and shows certain psychosocial symptoms such as hostility or aggression, swings in mood, poor judgment, inability to function in social settings or at work, or inappropriate sexual behavior. Because sedatives depress the central nervous system, physical symptoms include slurred speech, lack of coordination, inattention, impaired memory or "blackouts" and extreme sluggishness, stupor, or coma. Sedative intoxication can appear very similar to alcohol intoxication in its symptoms. Overdoses can be fatal.

Sedative withdrawal

Physical addiction is the main problem with sedative dependence. Sedative withdrawal is similar to alcohol withdrawal. Symptoms of sedative withdrawal are almost the reverse of the symptoms of sedative intoxication. They include:

- increased heart rate
- faster breathing
- elevated blood pressure
- increased body temperature
- sweating
- shaky hands
- inability to sleep
- anxiety
- nausea
- restlessness

About one-quarter of people undergoing sedative withdrawal have **seizures**. If withdrawal is severe, they may also have visual or auditory **hallucinations** (sedative withdrawal **delirium**). Often people who experience these more severe symptoms are using other drugs and not just sedatives.

The timeframe for withdrawal symptoms to appear varies depending on the chemical structure of the drug being taken. Withdrawal symptoms can occur hours or days after stopping use. For example, people withdrawing from Valium may not develop withdrawal symptoms for a week, and may not have peak symptoms until the second week. Low-level symptoms may linger even longer. Generally the longer a person takes a drug and the higher the dose, the more severe the withdrawal symptoms. It is possible to have withdrawal symptoms when a therapeutically prescribed dose is taken for a long time.

Sedative dependence is thought to be able to induce other mental health disorders, although there is some disagreement in the mental health community about how these disorders are defined and classified. Other disorders that may result from sedative dependence and withdrawal include:

- sedative-induced persisting dementia
- sedative-induced persisting amnestic disorder
- sedative-induced psychotic disorder (with or without hallucinations)
- sedative-induced mood disorder
- sedative-induced anxiety disorder
- sedative-induced sexually dysfunction
- sedative-induced sleep disorder

Demographics

Many people, including about 90% of those who are hospitalized, are given some type of prescription sedative. Of the people who use sedatives, only a few become dependent. People who become dependent usually fall into three categories. Some are drug addicts who use sedatives along with other street drugs. These are usually young people between the ages of 15 and 25. Others are alcoholics who use sedatives to treat chronic anxiety or sleep problems associated with their alcohol dependence. Still others use sedatives under the direction of a doctor to treat long-term pain, anxiety, or sleeplessness. These people may become dependent by increasing the amount of sedative they take as tolerance develops without telling their doctor.

Sedative abuse is not a major addiction problem with street drug users. Many people who are dependent on sedatives are middle-age and middle-class people who start taking the drug for a legitimate medical reason. Women may be more at risk than men for developing sedative dependence. Sedative dependence is the most common type of drug addiction among the elderly. Older people do not clear the drug from their bodies as efficiently as younger people, and thus may become dependent on lower, therapeutic doses.

Diagnosis

Diagnosis of sedative intoxication is made based on recent use of the drug, presence of the symptoms listed above, and presence of the drug in a blood or urine sample. Without a blood or urine test, sedative intoxication can be difficult to distinguish from alcohol intoxication except for the absence of the odor of alcohol. People experiencing sedative intoxication usually remain grounded in reality. However, if they lose touch with reality they may be diagnosed as having sedative intoxication delirium.

Diagnosis of sedative withdrawal is based on the symptoms listed above. It can be difficult to distinguish from alcohol withdrawal. Withdrawal may occur with or without hallucinations and delirium. Diagnosis depends on whether a person remains grounded in reality during withdrawal.

Diagnosis of other mental disorders induced by sedative dependence requires that the symptoms be in excess of those usually found with sedative intoxication or withdrawal. They cannot be accounted for by other substance abuse or another mental or physical disorder.

Treatments

Treatment depends on how large a dose of sedative the patient is taking, the length of time it has been used, and the patient's individual psychological and physical state.

Physiological treatment

Successful treatment of sedative dependence is based on the idea of gradually decreasing the amount of drug the patient uses in order to keep withdrawal symptoms to a manageable level. This is called a drug taper. The rate of taper depends on the dependency dose of the drug, the length of time the drug has been taken, a person's individual mental and physical response to drug withdrawal, and any complicating factors such as other substance abuse or other physical or mental illness.

For people dependent on a low dose of sedatives, the current level of use is determined, then the amount of drug is then reduced by 10 to 25 percent. If withdrawal symptoms are manageable, reduction is continued on a weekly basis. If withdrawal symptoms are too severe, the patient is stabilized at the lowest dose with manageable symptoms until tapering can be re-started. This gradual reduction of use may take weeks, and the rate must be adjusted to the response of each patient individually.

People dependent on high doses of sedatives are usually hospitalized because of the possibility of life-threatening withdrawal symptoms. A blood or urine test is used to determine the current level of usage. The patient is often switched to an equivalent dose of a different sedative or phenobarbitol (a barbiturate) to aid in withdrawal while controlling withdrawal symptoms. The tapering process begins, but more gradually than with low-dose dependency. Often other drugs are given to combat some of the withdrawal symptoms.

Psychological treatment

Cognitive-behavioral therapy may be used in conjunction with drug tapering. This type of **talk therapy** aims at two things: to educate patients to recognize and cope with the symptoms of anxiety associated with withdrawal, and to help patients change their behavior in ways that promote coping with **stress**. Patients are taught to mentally talk their way through their anxiety and stress. Some people find **support groups** and journal keeping to be helpful in their recovery. Recovering from dependency is a slow process, best achieved when a person has a good social support system, patience, and persistence.

Prognosis

The people who have the best chance of becoming sedative-free are those who became dependent through taking long-term therapeutic doses. Although stopping any addiction takes time and work, with a properly managed course of treatment, chances of success are good.

People who abuse multiple street drugs must receive treatment for their multiple drug dependencies. Sedative abuse is low on their list of problems, and the chances of their becoming drug-free are low. Alcoholics also have a difficult time withdrawing from sedatives.

Prevention

The best way to prevent sedative-related disorders is to take these drugs only for the exact length of time and in the exact amount prescribed by a doctor.

Resources

BOOKS

American Psychiatric Association. *Diagnostic and Statistical Manual of Mental Disorders.* 4th ed. text revision. Washington DC: American Psychiatric Association, 2000.

Galanter, Marc and Herbert D. Kleber, eds. *Textbook of Substance Abuse Treatment.* 2nd ed. Washington DC: American Psychiatric Press, Inc., 1999.

Giannini, James. *Drug Abuse: A Family Guide to Detection, Treatment and Education.* Los Angeles: Health Information Press, 1999.

Sadock, Benjamin J. and Virginia A. Sadock, eds. *Comprehensive Textbook of Psychiatry.* 7th ed. Vol. 1. Philadelphia: Lippincott Williams and Wilkins, 2000.

ORGANIZATIONS

National Clearinghouse for Alcohol and Drug Information. P. O. Box 2345, Rockville, MD 20852. (800) 729-6686. <http://www.health.org>.

National Institute on Drug Abuse. 5600 Fishers Lane, Room 10 A-39, Rockville, MD 20857. 1-888-644-6432<http://niad.nih.gov>.

OTHER

Benzodiazepine Recovery. <www.benzodiazepine.org>. This site offers chat and support groups for people recovering from sedative dependence and has links to many sources of information on these drugs.

Tish Davidson, A.M.

Seizures

Definition

A seizure is a sudden change in behavior characterized by changes in sensory perception (sense of feeling) or motor activity (movement) due to an abnormal firing of nerve cells in the **brain**. Epilepsy is a condition characterized by recurrent seizures that may include repetitive muscle jerking called convulsions.

Description

Seizure disorders and their classification date back to the earliest medical literature accounts in history. In 1964, the Commission on Classification and Terminology of the International League Against Epilepsy (ILAE) devised the first official classification of seizures, which was revised again in 1981. This classification is accepted worldwide and is based on electroencephalographic (EEG) studies. Based on this system, seizures can be classified as either focal or generalized. Each of these categories can also be further subdivided.

Focal seizures

A focal (partial) seizure develops when a limited, confined population of nerve cells fire their impulses abnormally on one hemisphere of the brain. (The brain has two portions or cerebral hemispheres—the right and left hemispheres.) Focal seizures are divided into simple or complex based on the level of consciousness (wakefulness) during an attack. Simple partial seizures occur in patients who are conscious, whereas complex partial seizures demonstrate impaired levels of consciousness.

Generalized seizures

A generalized seizure results from initial abnormal firing of brain nerve cells throughout both left and right hemispheres. Generalized seizures can be classified as follows:

- Tonic-clonic seizures: This is the most common type among all age groups and is categorized into several phases beginning with vague symptoms hours or days before an attack. These seizures are sometimes called grand mal seizures.
- Tonic seizures: These are typically characterized by a sustained nonvibratory contraction of muscles in the legs and arms. Consciousness is also impaired during these episodes.
- Atonic seizures (also called "drop attacks"): These are characterized by sudden, limp posture and a brief period of unconsciousness and last for one to two seconds.
- Clonic seizures: These are characterized by a rapid loss of consciousness with loss of muscle tone, tonic spasm, and jerks. The muscles become rigid for about 30 seconds during the tonic phase of the seizure and alternately contract and relax during the clonic phase, which lasts 30–60 seconds.
- Absence seizures: These are subdivided into typical and atypical forms based on duration of attack and level of consciousness. Absence (petit mal) seizures generally begin at about the age of four and stop by the time the child becomes an adolescent. They usually begin with a brief loss of consciousness and last between one and 10 seconds. People having a petit mal seizure become very quiet and may blink, stare blankly, roll their eyes, or move their lips. A petit mal seizure lasts 15–20 seconds. When it ends, the individual resumes whatever he or she was doing before the seizure began, will not remember the seizure, and may not realize that anything unusual happened. Untreated, petit mal seizures can recur as many as 100 times a day and may progress to grand mal seizures.
- Myoclonic seizures: These are characterized by rapid muscular contractions accompanied with jerks in facial and pelvic muscles.

Subcategories are commonly diagnosed based on EEG results. Terminology for classification in infants and newborns is still controversial.

Causes and symptoms

Causes

Simple partial seizures can be caused by congenital abnormalities (abnormalities present at birth), tumor growths, head trauma, **stroke**, and infections in the brain or nearby structures. Generalized tonic-clonic seizures are associated with drug and alcohol abuse, and low levels of blood glucose (blood sugar) and sodium. Certain psychiatric medications, antihistamines, and even antibiotics can precipitate tonic-clonic seizures. Absence seizures are implicated with an abnormal imbalance of certain chemicals in the brain that modulate nerve cell activity (one of these **neurotransmitters** is called GABA, which functions as an inhibitor). Myoclonic seizures are commonly diagnosed in newborns and children.

Symptoms

Symptoms for the different types of seizures are specific.

Partial seizures

SIMPLE PARTIAL SEIZURES. Multiple signs and symptoms may be present during a single simple partial seizure. These symptoms include specific muscles tensing and then alternately contracting and relaxing, speech arrest, vocalizations, and involuntary turning of the eyes or head. There could be changes in vision, hearing, balance, taste, and smell. Additionally, patients with simple partial seizures may have a sensation in the abdomen, sweating, paleness, flushing, hair follicles standing up (piloerection), and dilated pupils (the dark center in the eye enlarges). Seizures with psychological symptoms include thinking disturbances and **hallucinations**, or illusions of memory, sound, sight, time, and self-image.

COMPLEX PARTIAL SEIZURES. Complex partial seizures often begin with a motionless stare or arrest of activity; this is followed by a series of involuntary movements, speech disturbances, and eye movements.

Generalized seizures

Generalized seizures have a more complex set of signs and symptoms.

TONIC-CLONIC SEIZURES. Tonic-clonic seizures usually have vague prodromal (pre-attack) symptoms that can start hours or days before a seizure. These symptoms include anxiety, mood changes, irritability, weakness, dizziness, lightheadedness, and changes in appetite. The tonic phases may be preceded with brief (lasting only a few seconds in duration) muscle contractions on both sides of affected muscle groups. The tonic phase typically begins with a brief flexing of trunk muscles, upward movement of the eyes, and pupil dilation. Patients usually emit a characteristic vocalization. This sound is caused by contraction of trunk muscles that forces air from the lungs across spasmodic (abnormally tensed) throat muscles. This is followed by a very short period (10–15 seconds) of general muscle relaxation. The clonic phase consists of muscular contractions with alternating periods of no movements (muscle atonia) of gradually increasing duration until abnormal muscular contractions stop. Tonic-clonic seizures end in a final generalized spasm. The affected person can lose consciousness during tonic and clonic phases of seizure.

Tonic-clonic seizures can also produce chemical changes in the body. Patients commonly experience lowered carbon dioxide (hypocarbia) due to breathing alterations, increased blood glucose (blood sugar), and elevated level of a hormone called prolactin. Once the affected person regains consciousness, he or she is usually weak, and has headache and muscle pain. Tonic-clonic seizures can cause serious medical problems such as trauma to the head and mouth, fractures in the spinal column, pulmonary edema (water in the lungs), aspiration pneumonia (a pneumonia caused by a foreign body being lodged in the lungs), and sudden death. Attacks are generally one minute in duration.

TONIC SEIZURES. Tonic and atonic seizures have distinct differences but are often present in the same patient. Tonic seizures are characterized by nonvibratory muscle contractions, usually involving flexing of arms and relaxing or flexing of legs. The seizure usually lasts less than 10 seconds but may be as long as one minute. Tonic seizures are usually abrupt and patients lose consciousness. Tonic seizures commonly occur during nonrapid eye movement (nonREM) sleep and drowsiness. Tonic seizures that occur during wakeful states commonly produce physical injuries due to abrupt, unexpected falls.

ATONIC SEIZURES. Atonic seizures, also called "drop attacks," are abrupt, with loss of muscle tone lasting one to two seconds, but with rapid recovery. Consciousness is usually impaired. The rapid loss of muscular tone could

KEY TERMS

Electroencephalograph—(EEG) An instrument that measures the electrical activity of the brain. The EEG traces the electrical activity in the form of wave pattens onto recording paper. Wave patterns that have sudden spikes or sharp waves strongly suggest seizures. An EEG with a seizure-type wave pattern is called an epileptiform EEG.

Hallucination—False sensory perceptions. A person experiencing a hallucination may "hear" sounds or "see" people or objects that are not really present. Hallucinations can also affect the senses of smell, touch, and taste.

Illusion—A misperception or misinterpretation in the presence of a real external stimulus.

be limited to head and neck muscles, resulting in head drop, or it may be more extensive involving muscles for balance, causing unexpected falls with physical injury.

CLONIC SEIZURES. Generalized clonic seizures are rare and seen typically in children with elevated fever. These seizures are characterized by a rapid loss of consciousness, decreased muscle tone, and generalized spasm that is followed by jerky movements.

ABSENCE SEIZURES. Absence seizures are classified as either typical or atypical. The typical absence seizure is characterized by unresponsiveness and behavioral arrest, abnormal muscular movements of the face and eyelids, and lasts less than 10 seconds. In atypical absence seizures, the affected person is generally more conscious, the seizures begin and end more gradually, and do not exceed 10 seconds in duration.

MYOCLONIC SEIZURES. Myoclonic seizures commonly exhibit rapid muscular contractions. Myoclonic seizures are seen in newborns and children who have either symptomatic or idiopathic (cause is unknown) epilepsy.

Demographics

Approximately 1.5 million persons in the United States suffer from a type of seizure disorder. The annual incidence (number of new cases) for all types of seizures is 1.2 per 1,000 and, for recurrent seizures, is 0.54 per 1,000. Isolated seizures may occur in up to 10% of the general population. Approximately 10–20% of all patients have intractable epilepsy (epilepsy that is difficult to manage or treat). It is estimated that 45 million people in the world are affected by seizures. Seizures affect males and females equally and can occur among all age groups. There seems to be a strong genetic correlation, since seizures are three times more prevalent among close relatives than they are in the general population.

Children delivered in the breech position have increased prevalence (3.8%) of seizures when compared to infants delivered in the normal delivery position (2.2%). Seizures caused by fever have a recurrence rate of 51% if the attack occurred in the first year of life, whereas recurrence rate is decreased to 25% if the seizure took place during the second year. Approximately 88% of children who experience seizures caused by fever in the first two years experience recurrence.

Approximately 45 million people worldwide are affected by epilepsy. The incidence is highest among young children and the elderly. High-risk groups include persons with a previous history of brain injury or lesions.

Diagnosis

Patients seeking help for seizures should first undergo an EEG that records brain-wave patterns emitted between nerve cells. Electrodes are placed on the head, sometimes for 24 hours, to monitor brain-wave activity and detect both normal and abnormal impulses. **Imaging studies** such as **magnetic resonance imaging** (MRI) and computed axial tomography (CAT)—that take still "pictures"—are useful in detecting abnormalities in the temporal lobes (parts of the brain associated with hearing) or for helping diagnose tonic-clonic seizures. A complete blood count (CBC) can be helpful in determining whether a seizure is caused by a neurological infection, which is typically accompanied by high fever. If drugs or toxins in the blood are suspected to be the cause of the seizure(s), blood and urine screening tests for these compounds may be necessary.

Antiseizure medication can be altered by many commonly used medications such as sulfa drugs, erythromycin, warfarin, and cimetidine. Pregnancy may also decrease serum concentration of antiseizure medications; therefore, frequent monitoring and dose adjustments are vital to maintain appropriate blood concentrations of the antiseizure medication—known as the therapeutic blood concentration. **Diagnosis** requires a detailed and accurate history, and a physical examination is important since this may help identify neurological or systemic causes. In cases in which a central nervous system (CNS) infection (i.e., meningitis or encephalitis) is suspected, a lumbar puncture (or spinal tap) can help detect an increase in immune cells (white blood cells) that develop to fight the specific infection. (A lumbar puncture is removing from the spinal chord, by syringe, of a small amount of cerebrospinal fluid—the fluid that bathes and nourishes the brain and spinal cord.)

Treatments

Treatment is targeted primarily to:

- assist the patient in adjusting psychologically to the diagnosis and in maintaining as normal a lifestyle as possible
- reduce or eliminate seizure occurrence
- avoid side effects of long-term drug treatment

Simple and complex partial seizures respond to drugs such as **carbamazepine**, **valproic acid** (valproate), phenytoin, **gabapentin**, tiagabine, **lamotrigine**, and topiramate. Tonic-clonic seizures tend to respond to valproate, carbamazepine, phenytoin, and lamotrigine. Absence seizures seem to be sensitive to ethosuximide, valproate, and lamotrigine. Myoclonic seizures can be treated with valproate and **clonazepam**. Tonic seizures seem to respond favorably to valproate, felbamate, and clonazepam.

People treated with a class of medications called **barbiturates** (Mysoline, Mebral, phenobarbital) have adverse cognitive (thinking) effects. These cognitive effects can include decreased general intelligence, attention, memory, problem solving, motor speed, and visual motor functions. The drug phenytoin (Dilantin) can adversely affect speed of response, memory, and attention. Other medications used for treatment of seizures do not have substantial cognitive impairment.

Surgical treatment may be considered when medications fail. Advances in medical sciences and techniques have improved methods of identifying the parts of the brain that generate abnormal discharge of nerve impulses. Surgical treatment now accounts for about 5,000 procedures annually. The most common type of surgery is the focal cortical resection. In this procedure, a small part of the brain responsible for causing the seizures is removed. Surgical **intervention** may be considered a feasible treatment option if:

- the site of seizures is identifiable and localized
- surgery can remove the seizure-generating (epileptogenic) area
- surgical procedure will not cause damage to nearby areas

Prognosis

About 30% of patients with severe seizures (starting in early childhood), continue to have attacks and usually never achieve a remission state. In the United States, the prevalence of treatment-resistant seizures is about one to two per 1,000 persons. About 60–70% of persons achieve a five-year remission within 10 years of initial diagnosis. Approximately half of these patients become seizure-free. Usually the prognosis is better if seizures can be controlled by one medication, the frequency of seizures decreases, and there is a normal EEG and neurological examination prior to medication cessation.

People affected by seizure have increased death rates compared with the general population. Patients who have seizures of unknown cause have an increased chance of dying due to accidents (primarily drowning). Other causes of seizure-associated death include abnormal heart rhythms, water in the lungs, or heart attack.

Prevention

There are no gold standard recommendations for prevention, since seizures can be caused by genetic factors, blood abnormalities, many medications, illicit drugs, infection, neurologic conditions, and other systemic diseases. If a person has had a previous attack or has a genetic propensity, care is advised when receiving medical treatment or if diagnosed with an illness correlated with possible seizure development.

See also Computed tomography (CAT); Electroencephalography (EEG); Magnetic resonance imaging (MRI); Substance abuse and related disorders

Resources

BOOKS

Goldman, Lee, and others. *Cecil Textbook of Medicine.* 21st edition. Philadelphia: W. B. Saunders Company, 2000.

Goroll, Allan H. *Primary Care Medicine.* 4th edition. Philadelphia: Lippincott Williams and Wilkins, 2000.

Goetz, Christopher G . *Textbook of Clinical Neurology.* 1st edition. Philadelphia: W. B. Saunders Company, 1999.

PERIODICALS

Dodrill, C. R., C. G. Matthew. "The role of Neuropsychology in the Assessment and Treatment of Persons with Epilepsy." *American Psychologist* September 1992.

ORGANIZATIONS

Epilepsy Foundation. 4351 Garden City Drive, Landover, MD 20785-7223. Phone: (800) 332-1000. Web site: <http://www.efa.org/>.

Laith Farid Gulli, M.D.
Alfredo Mori, M.D., FACEM

Selective mutism

Definition

Selective mutism is a childhood disorder in which a child does not speak in some social situations although he or she is able to talk normally at other times.

Description

Selective mutism was first described in the 1870s, at which time it was called "aphasia voluntaria." This name shows that the absence of speech was considered to be under the control of the child's will. In 1934 the disorder began to be called selective mutism, a name that still implied purposefulness on the part of the silent child. In the 1994 edition of the ***Diagnostic and Statistical Manual of Mental Disorders*** (*DSM-IV*) the disorder was renamed selective mutism. This name is considered preferable because it suggests that the child is mute only

KEY TERMS

Stimulus fading—A form of behavior modification used to treat children with selective mutism, in which goals of gradually increasing difficulty are set for the child.

in certain situations, without the implication that the child remains silent on purpose.

Selective mutism is characterized by a child's inability to speak in one or more types of social situation, although the child is developmentally advanced to the point that speech is possible. The child speaks proficiently in at least one setting, most often at home with one or both parents, and sometimes with siblings or extended family members. Some children also speak to certain friends or to adults that are not related to them, but this variant of selective mutism is somewhat less common.

The most common place for children to exhibit mute behavior is in the classroom, so that the disorder is often first noticed by teachers. Because of this characteristic, selective mutism is most frequently diagnosed in children of preschool age through second grade. As the expectation of speech becomes more evident, selective mutism can have more pronounced negative effects on academic performance. Children who do not talk in classroom settings or other social situations because the language of instruction is not their first tongue are not considered to have the disorder of selective mutism.

Causes and symptoms

The symptoms of selective mutism are fairly obvious. The child does not talk in one or more social situations in which speech is commonly expected and would facilitate understanding. Some children with selective mutism do not communicate in any way in certain settings, and act generally shy and withdrawn. The disorder is also often associated with crying, clinging to the parent, and other signs of social anxiety. Other children with the disorder, however, may smile, gesture, nod, and even giggle, although they do not talk.

Consensus regarding the most common causes of selective mutism has changed significantly over time. When the disorder was first studied, and for many years thereafter, it was thought to be caused by severe trauma in early childhood. Some of these causative traumas were thought to include rape, molestation, incest, severe physical or emotional **abuse**, and similar experiences. In addition, many researchers attributed selective mutism to family dynamics that included an overprotective mother and an abnormally strict or very distant father. As of 2002, these factors have not been completely eliminated as causes of selective mutism in most cases, but it is generally agreed that they are not the most common causes.

Instead, selective mutism is frequently attributed at present to high levels of social anxiety in children and not to traumatic events in their early years. Children with selective mutism have been found to be more timid and shy than most children in social situations, and to exhibit signs of depression, **obsessive-compulsive disorder**, and anxiety disorders. Some children have been reported to dislike speaking because they are uncomfortable with the sound of their own voice or because they think their voice sounds abnormal.

Many links have also been found between selective mutism and speech development problems. Language reception problems have also been documented in selectively mute children. Although there is no evidence indicating that selective mutism is the direct result of any of these difficulties in language development, possible connections are being explored.

Demographics

Selective mutism is generally considered a rare disorder. It is found in about 1% of patients in mental health settings, but it occurs in only about 0.01% of the general United States population. Some researchers maintain, however, that selective mutism occurs more frequently than these data suggest. There may be many unreported cases of selective mutism that resolve with time and require no **intervention**.

In terms of age grouping, selective mutism may appear at the very beginning of a child's social experience or may begin in later childhood. Some cases have been recorded in which selective mutism does not begin until high school. Onset in late adolescence is unusual, however; the most common age of onset for the disorder is the early elementary school years.

Selective mutism is often associated with **social phobia** in adult life. Children with selective mutism disorder may be more likely as adults to have a high level of social anxiety even if they do not meet the diagnostic criteria for social phobia. The disorder appears to run in families. Children whose parents are anxious in social settings, were exceptionally timid as children, or suffered from selective mutism themselves in childhood, are at greater risk for developing selective mutism.

Diagnosis

The criteria for diagnosing selective mutism disorder given by the reference manual, the *Diagnostic and Statistical Manual of Mental Disorders*, fourth edition, text revision (*DSM-IV-TR*) include the failure to speak in some social situations even though the child may talk at other times. This criterion is not met if the child does not speak at all in any situation.

The child's inability to talk must interfere with the achievement of such relevant goals as schoolwork, play with friends, or communication of needs. In addition, the lack of speech must persist for at least one month. The first month of school should not be included in this measurement because many children are shy and unwilling to talk freely until they feel comfortable with their new teacher, classmates, and surroundings.

Furthermore, the child's lack of speech cannot be attributed to unfamiliarity with the language they must use in school or social settings. The **diagnosis** of selective mutism does not apply to children from immigrant families who may not feel comfortable conversing in a second language. Moreover, the child's inability to talk cannot be attributed to **stuttering** or similar speech disorders, which may make the child uncomfortable because they are aware that their speech sounds different from the speech of their peers. The lack of speech also must not be attributable to **schizophrenia**, **autism**, or other mental health disorders.

The disorder of selective mutism is usually noticed first by parents or teachers of affected children. It is often hard for doctors to diagnose selective mutism because it is unlikely that the child in question will talk to them. Therefore it may be difficult for a general practitioner to assess the existence of any underlying language or developmental problems that may be either causing or exacerbating the disorder. Tests that evaluate mental development without verbal responses from the patient may be used successfully to evaluate children with selective mutism.

There are also ways to test the child's speech development in the situations in which he or she does talk. One method involves interviews with the parents or whomever the child does speak to on a regular basis. This method can be fairly subjective, however. It is more useful for the doctor to obtain a tape or video recording of the child talking in a situation in which he or she feels comfortable. The child's hearing should be checked, as speech problems are often related to hearing disorders. Observing the child at play activities or asking him or her to draw pictures offer other effective ways to determine the child's reactions in social situations.

Treatments

A number of different approaches have been used in attempts to treat selective mutism. Recent opinion has moved away from the idea that it is caused by a trauma, and attempts to treat it have followed accordingly. The factors that are most intensively studied at present are underlying anxiety problems. In the few cases in which an underlying trauma is discovered to be the source of the problem, counseling to help treat the underlying problems is recommended. Treatments of any kind are generally found to be more effective when the family of the child is involved in decisions about his or her treatment.

Behavior modification

Selective mutism can be treated by using a **reinforcement** approach. This method gives positive rewards to the child in the form of praise, treats, privileges, or anything else that the child values. In general rewards are given for speech, and withheld for silence. The use of punishments alongside the rewards is not generally recommended because it would place more **stress** on children who are already severely anxious. The positive reinforcement technique is generally found to be at least partially successful in most cases.

Another technique for modifying behavior in children with selective mutism is known as stimulus fading. This technique sets goals of increasing difficulty for the child to meet. For example, the child might be encouraged to start talking by whispering, then work up gradually to talking at full volume. Alternately, the child could start by talking to one person who is not a family member and gradually add names until he or she feels comfortable talking to more than one person at a time. Stimulus fading has been found to be particularly effective when it is used in conjunction with positive reinforcement techniques.

Treatment with medications

In some cases, selective mutism is treatable with medication. **Fluoxetine** (Prozac), which is one of the selective serotonin reuptake inhibitors (SSRIs) is the drug that has been studied most often as a treatment for selective mutism. Treatment with medication is more successful in younger children. Overall, fluoxetine has been found to reduce the symptoms of selective mutism in about three-fourths of children. Other drugs used to treat anxiety and social phobia disorders may also be effective in certain cases.

Prognosis

Selective mutism is frequently treatable, in that many cases of the disorder are thought to resolve on their own. Sometimes reported cases do resolve with time, although treatment can be very effective. There is little information about the long-term outcome of selective mutism. Researchers have noted that while many children with the disorder do show improvement in speech, their anxiety in social situations persists.

Resources

BOOKS

American Psychiatric Association. *Diagnostic and Statistical Manual of Mental Disorders.* 4th edition, text revised. Washington DC: American Psychiatric Association, 2000.

Sadock, Benjamin J. and Virginia A. Sadock, eds. *Comprehensive Textbook of Psychiatry.* 7th edition, vol. 2. Philadelphia: Lippincott Williams and Wilkins, 2000.

PERIODICALS

Dow, Sara P., and others. "Practical Guidelines for the Assessment and Treatment of Selective Mutism." *Journal of the American Academy of Child and Adolescent Psychiatry* 34 no. 7 (July 1995): 836-847.

Dummit, Steven E. III, and others. "Fluoxetine treatment of children with selective mutism: an open trial." *Journal of the American Academy of Child and Adolescent Psychiatry* 35 no. 5 (May 1996): 615-622.

Joseph, Paul R. "Selective Mutism—The Child Who Doesn't Speak at School." *Pediatrics* 104, no. 2 (August 1999): 308.

Stein, Martin T., Isabelle Rapin, and Diane Yapko. "Selective Mutism." *Journal of Developmental & Behavioral Pediatrics* 22, no. 2 (April 2001): S123.

ORGANIZATIONS

Selective Mutism Group—A Division of Childhood Anxiety Network Inc. <www.selectivemutsim.org>.

Tish Davidson, A.M.

Self-control strategies

Definition

Self-control strategies are cognitive and behavioral skills used by individuals to maintain self-motivation and achieve personal goals. Initially the skills may be learned from a therapist, text, or self-help book. However, the individual is responsible for using these skills in real-life situations to produce the desired changes.

There are many varieties of self-control strategies. Other terms for self-control strategies are behavioral self-control training, cognitive self-regulation, and self-management techniques. In recent years, the term "self-management" has replaced "self-control," because self-control implies changing behavior through sheer willpower. Self-management, on the other hand, involves becoming aware of the natural processes that affect a particular behavior and consciously altering those processes, resulting in the desired behavior change.

Purpose

Most people who decide to use self-control strategies are dissatisfied with a certain aspect of their lives. For example, they may feel they smoke too much, exercise too little, or have difficulty controlling anger. Self-control strategies are useful for a wide range of concerns, including medical (such as diabetes, chronic pain, asthma, arthritis, incontinence, or **obesity**), addictions (such as drug and alcohol abuse, smoking, gambling, or eating disorders), occupational (such as study habits, organizational skills, or job productivity), and psychological (such as **stress**, anxiety, depression, excessive anger, hyperactivity, or shyness). If symptoms are severe, self-control strategies may be used in conjunction with other therapies, but should not be the only form of treatment.

The goal of self-control strategies is to reduce behavioral deficiencies or behavioral excesses. Behavioral deficiencies occur when an individual does not engage in a positive, desirable behavior frequently enough. The result is a missed future benefit. For example, a student who rarely studies may not graduate. Behavioral excesses occur when an individual engages in negative, undesirable behavior too often. This results in a negative future consequence. For example, a person who smokes may develop lung cancer.

In the case of behavioral deficiencies, one may fail to engage in a desirable behavior because it does not provide immediate gratification. With behavioral excesses, there is usually some type of immediate gratification and no immediate negative consequence. Self-control strategies help individuals to become aware of their own patterns of behavior and to alter those patterns (usually by creating artificial rewards or punishments) so that the behavior will be more or less likely to occur.

Description

Theoretical bases for self-control strategies

Self-control strategies are based primarily on the social cognitive theory of Albert Bandura. According to Bandura, one's behavior is influenced by a variety of fac-

KEY TERMS

Antecedents—Events that occur immediately before the target behavior.

Behavioral deficiency—Failure to engage in a positive, desirable behavior frequently enough.

Behavioral excess—Engaging in negative, undesirable behavior too often.

Competing behaviors—Behaviors that interfere with the target behavior because they are preferred by the individual.

Consequences—Events that occur immediately after the target behavior.

Contingencies—Naturally occurring or artificially designated reinforcers or punishers that follow a behavior.

Controlled behavior—The behavior to be changed by self-control strategies; also known as the target behavior.

Controlling behaviors—Self-control strategies used to change the controlled or target behavior.

Feedback loop—A naturally occurring process whereby individuals control their behavior by self-monitoring, self-evaluation, and self-reinforcement.

Outcome expectancies—What one believes will happen as a result of engaging in a certain behavior.

Punisher—Anything that causes a decrease of a particular behavior.

Reinforcer—Anything that causes an increase of a particular behavior.

Self-efficacy—One's belief about how well he or she can perform a given task, regardless of that person's actual ability.

Self-instructional training—Teaches individuals to become aware of their self-statements, evaluate whether these self-statements are helpful or hindering, and replace maladaptive self-statements with adaptive ones.

Short-circuiting of contingencies—The proper reinforcer or punisher for a given behavior is not administered.

Social cognitive theory—The theory that behavior is determined by an interaction between cognitive, behavioral, and environmental factors.

Target behavior—The specific behavior to be increased or decreased during treatment

tors, including one's own thoughts and beliefs, and elements in the environment. Bandura proposed that certain beliefs, self-efficacy and outcome expectancies, are important factors in determining which behaviors an individual will attempt, and how motivated the individual will be when engaging in those behaviors. Self-efficacy is one's belief about how well he or she can perform a given task, regardless of that person's actual ability. Outcome expectancies are what the person believes will happen as a result of engaging in a certain behavior. If self-efficacy and outcome expectancies are inaccurate, the individual may experience behavioral deficits or excesses.

Donald Meichenbaum developed the idea of self-instructional training, which is a major part of self-control strategies. Meichenbaum believed that learning to control behavior begins in childhood, based on parental instruction. Children eventually control their own behavior by mentally repeating the instructions of their parents. These internal instructions may be positive or negative. Self-instructional training teaches individuals to become aware of their self-statements, evaluate whether these self-statements are helpful or hindering, and replace maladaptive self-statements with adaptive ones.

Frederick Kanfer suggested that individuals achieve self-control by using a feedback loop consisting of continuous monitoring, evaluating, and reinforcing of their own behavior. This loop occurs naturally in everyone. However, the loop can be maladaptive if (a) only negative factors are noticed and positive factors are ignored during the monitoring phase, (b) standards are unrealistic during the evaluation phase, or (c) responsibility is accepted for negative behaviors but not for positive behaviors during the **reinforcement** phase. Self-control strategies help individuals to be aware of these phases and to make the appropriate changes in monitoring, evaluation, and reinforcement.

Development of a self-control program

Self-control strategies are often taught in treatment centers, group or individual therapies, schools, or vocational settings. However, self-control programs may also be designed without the help of a professional, especially if the problem being addressed is not severe. The use of professionals, at least initially, may increase the likelihood that the program will succeed. Following are the necessary steps for creating a self-control program:

- Making a commitment. A plan cannot succeed unless one is committed to following through. Ways of increasing commitment level include listing the benefits of adhering to the program, telling others about one's intentions, posting written reminders of commitments around one's home, putting a significant amount of time and energy into designing the program, and planning ways to deal with obstacles ahead of time.
- Identifying the problem. The behavior in need of change is referred to as the target behavior or the controlled behavior. A precise definition of the target behavior is a crucial first step. This is usually done by keeping detailed records about when, where, and how the behavior occurs for one to two weeks. The record-keeping should also focus on other competing behaviors that may be interfering with the target behavior. For example, for a person who is trying to cut down on calorie consumption, a competing behavior would be eating high-calorie snack foods. It is important to note the antecedents and consequences of the target and competing behaviors; in other words, what typically occurs immediately before (antecedents) and after (consequences) these behaviors? The antecedents and consequences are factors that influence the occurrence of the behavior. Sometimes just the process of record-keeping alters the target behavior by increasing the individual's awareness of what he or she is doing.
- Setting a goal. Once the target behavior has been defined, the individual must decide in what way that behavior should be changed. The goal should be specific so that future progress can be measured. This may entail listing circumstances or behaviors that must be present, as well as to what degree they must be present, in order for a goal to be achieved. For example, a goal to "reduce hyperactivity" in a grade-school student is vague. "Remaining in seat for seven out of fourteen half-hour periods daily" is much more specific. Indicating a time frame in which the goal can realistically be achieved is also recommended. Goals should be realistic. It is better to set a small goal and progress to bigger goals than to set a big goal and become quickly discouraged.
- Applying self-control strategies. The self-control strategies are known as controlling behaviors. Choice of strategies will depend on the target behavior. Types of strategies are discussed later.
- Self-monitoring. While using the self-control strategies, one should continue to keep records regarding the occurrence of the target behavior. Keeping written records is essential for determining if the strategies are effective. If one is gradually meeting the goal requirements, the strategies can be assumed effective. If little progress towards the goal is evident, either the strategies are being used incorrectly, or the strategies are ineffective and should be changed. Self-monitoring can be done informally (for instance, by making notes on an index card) or formally (by using pre-designed data sheets). In any case, self-monitoring should gather the necessary information, but should not become too lengthy or complex. The individual will lose motivation to continue monitoring if the procedures are overly time-consuming or inconvenient.
- Making revisions as necessary. Based on the information gathered during self-monitoring, the individual decides if changes in the plan are necessary. One advantage of self-control programs is that the individual chooses the strategies that will work best for him or her. This freedom of choice increases the likelihood that the individual will adhere to the program. Therefore, self-control programs should always be flexible and adaptable.

Types of self-control strategies

Self-control strategies can be grouped into three broad categories:

ENVIRONMENTAL STRATEGIES. Environmental strategies involve changing times, places, or situations where one experiences problematic behavior. Examples include:

- changing the group of people with whom one socializes
- avoiding situations or settings where an undesirable behavior is more likely to occur
- changing the time of day for participating in a desirable behavior to a time when one will be more productive or successful

BEHAVIORAL STRATEGIES. Behavioral strategies involve changing the antecedents or consequences of a behavior. Examples include:

- increasing social support by asking others to work towards the same or a similar goal
- placing visual cues or reminders about one's goal in one's daily environment
- developing reinforcers (rewards) for engaging in desirable behaviors or punishers for engaging in undesirable behaviors
- eliminating naturally occurring reinforcers for undesirable behavior
- engaging in alternative, positive behaviors when one is inclined to engage in an undesirable behavior

- creating ways to make a desirable behavior more enjoyable or convenient
- scheduling a specific time to engage in a desirable behavior
- writing a behavioral contract to hold oneself accountable for carrying out the self-control program

COGNITIVE STRATEGIES. Cognitive strategies involve changing one's thoughts or beliefs about a particular behavior. Examples include:

- using self-instructions to cue oneself about what to do and how to do it
- using self-praise to commend oneself for engaging in a desirable behavior
- thinking about the benefits of reaching one's goal
- imagining oneself successfully achieving a goal or using imagery to distract oneself from engaging in an undesirable behavior
- substituting positive self-statements for unproductive, negative self-statements

In a therapeutic setting, self-control strategies are usually taught in weekly group sessions over a period of several weeks. The sessions typically include an educational lecture regarding a specific strategy, group discussion of how the strategy should be applied and how to cope with potential obstacles (relapse prevention), role-plays or rehearsal of the strategy, a review of the session, and a homework assignment for further practice. Sessions usually focus on one type of strategy at a time. Preferably, an individual should master one strategy before attempting another. After the series of training sessions are complete, the individual is responsible for implementing the strategies in daily life.

Aftercare

Relapse is a concern in any therapeutic situation. Current research suggests that individuals are more likely to continue using newly learned self-control strategies if they have periodic follow-up contact with a professional or other designated person. The contact serves at least three purposes: (1) a source of accountability, (2) review of strategy use to ensure proper application, and (3) discussion of problematic situations and development of plans to overcome these situations.

Risks

Self-control strategies are especially prone to short-circuiting of contingencies. This refers to the tendency for individuals to partake of reinforcers at inappropriate occasions, or to avoid punishers designated in their plan. If contingencies are short-circuited, the desired behavior change is unlikely to occur.

Relapse is another risk involved in self-control strategies. Causes of relapse include: (a) a poorly defined target behavior (progress cannot be recognized); (b) unrealistic or long-term goals without immediate sources of reinforcement; (c) failure to anticipate and plan for obstacles to goal-achievement; (d) overreaction to occasional setbacks; (e) negative self-talk, especially when one feels goals are not being satisfactorily met; (f) failure to use desirable or frequent reinforcers; (g) ineffective consequences for undesirable behavior; and (h) an inaccurate or unnecessarily complex monitoring system.

Normal results

Ideally individuals will use self-control strategies independently in their everyday surroundings to meet their designated goal. They will decrease behavioral deficiencies and excesses, engaging in desirable behaviors more often, or engaging in undesirable behaviors less frequently or not at all.

Abnormal results

If the self-control strategies are ineffective or used improperly, individuals may show no changes or increases in behavioral deficiencies or excesses.

See also Behavior modification; Bibliotherapy; Cognitive retraining techniques; Cognitive-behavioral therapy; Guided imagery therapy; Rational emotive therapy; Social skills training

Resources

BOOKS

Dobson, Keith S., ed. *Handbook of Cognitive-Behavioral Therapies.* 2nd ed. New York: Guilford Press, 2001.

Martin, Garry. *Behavior Modification: What It Is and How to Do It.* 6th ed. Upper Saddle River, New Jersey: Prentice-Hall, 1999.

Miltenberger, Raymond G. *Behavior Modification: Principles and Procedures.* 2nd ed. Belmont, California: Wadsworth/Thomson Learning, 2001.

PERIODICALS

Davies, Susan, and Raymond Witte. "Self-Management and Peer-Monitoring Within a Group Contingency to Decrease Uncontrolled Verbalizations of Children with Attention-Deficit/Hyperactivity Disorder." *Psychology in the Schools* 37, no. 2 (2000): 135-147.

Frayne, Colette A., and J. Michael Geringer. "Self-Management Training for Improving Job Performance: A Field Experiment Involving Salespeople." *Journal of Applied Psychology* 85, no. 1 (2000): 361-372.

Rokke, Paul D., Judith A. Tomhave, and Zelijko Jocic. "Self-Management Therapy and Educational Group Therapy for Depressed Elders." *Cognitive Therapy and Research* 24, no. 1 (2000): 99-119.

Saelens, Brian E., Christine A. Gehrman, James F. Sallis, Karen J. Calfas, Julie A. Sarkin, and Susan Caparosa. "Use of Self-Management Strategies in a 2-Year Cognitive Behavioral Intervention to Promote Physical Activity." *Behavior Therapy* 31 (2000): 365-379.

ORGANIZATIONS

Association for Behavioral Analysis. 213 West Hall, Western Michigan University, 1903 W. Michigan Avenue, Kalamazoo, Michigan 49008-5301. (616) 387-8341; (616) 384-8342. <http://www.wmich.edu/aba>.

Beck Institute for Cognitive Therapy. GSB Building, City Line and Belmont Avenues, Suite 700, Bala Cynwyd, Pennsylvania 19004-1610. (610) 664-3020. <http://www.beckinstitute.org>.

Cambridge Center for Behavioral Studies. 336 Baker Avenue, Concord, Massachusetts 01742-2107. (978) 369-2227. <http://www.behavior.org>.

Cognitive-Behavioral Therapy Institute. 211 East 43rd Street, Suite 1500, New York, New York 10017. (212) 490-3590. <http://www.cbtinstitute.com>.

Sandra L. Friedrich, M.A.

Self-help groups

Introduction

Self-help groups—also called mutual help or mutual aid groups—are composed of peers who share a similar mental, emotional, or physical problem, or who are interested in a focal issue, such as education or parenting. Historically, people banded together to improve their chances for survival by pooling their social and economic resources; however, contemporary groups are more likely to organize around a theme or problem.

Most self-help groups are voluntary, non-profit associations open to anyone with a similar need or interest; however, spin-off groups also exist to meet the needs of particular types of people; for example, the elderly, women, or Hispanics. Usually, groups are led by peers, have an informal structure, and are free (except for small donations to cover meeting expenses). However, professionals of various kinds lead some self-help groups.

In the past thirty years, the number of self-help organizations and groups operating in communities throughout the U.S. has dramatically risen; some organizations operate in several countries, primarily in the developed world. One of the reasons for the rapid proliferation of groups focusing on health problems may be the advent of managed health care. For individuals with insurance plans offering limited mental health coverage, self-help groups are an economical way to find emotional and social support.

Self-help groups and therapy

Because of the peer-led, informal, and democratic (as opposed to hierarchical and medical) structure, health professionals consider self-help groups for mental or emotional problems to be an adjunct to therapy. While there are therapeutic aspects associated with participation—principally, intimacy as a result of self-disclosure, personal growth in response to others' role modeling, and erosion of **denial** as a result of social confrontation—the primary value of contemporary groups is in the mutual aid offered by members to one another. Though the nature of self-help groups is outside of the medical realm, doctors and therapists see participation as a way to improve the outcome related to either ongoing or future formal treatment.

Another issue arguing against considering self-help groups as a type of therapy is that the variety of groups is extensive; groups available may include advocacy groups with a focus on legal or social remedies, groups organized around housing or employment needs, and groups focusing on racial or gender issues. Additionally, the self-help movement shares some characteristics with volunteerism and consumerism. In general, members who persevere have experience with other voluntary organizations and believe in the value of donating time and service; also, members may be thought of as consumers who participate in their own care and who have experience and knowledge of relevant goods and services.

Types of self-help groups

Twelve-step groups

The most popular type of self-help group is based on the Twelve Steps and Twelve Traditions of Alcoholics Anonymous (AA), founded in 1935. The Twelve Steps are a guide to recovery from alcoholism or **addiction**, whereas the Twelve Traditions are a code of ethics. AA and other 12-step programs are based on the spiritual premise that turning one's life and will over to a personally meaningful "higher power," such as God or Spirit, is the key to recovery. Another essential idea is that sobriety or recovery (not cure) depends on the admission of powerlessness with respect to alcohol or the substance(s) abused. This idea is offensive to critics of 12-step groups, but others believe that this admission accurately reflects the contemporary view of addiction as a disease. Furthermore, people with a familial, genetic vulnerability to addiction are particularly at risk. While some studies suggest that 20% of people suffering from alcoholism will experience remission without benefit of therapy or a 12-step group, most will suffer deteriorating health and dysfunctional, if not ruined, social relationships. In other words, most alcoholics need formal therapy or an informal self-help program to recover. While the dropout rate for AA groups during the first three months is high, alcoholics who persevere have a good chance of attaining and maintaining sobriety or abstinence. This is especially true if the person regularly attends a home group (90 meetings in the first 90 days, slowly diminishing to two or three times per week for years thereafter) and finds an experienced and sympathetic sponsor who also is in recovery.

In addition to AA and its sister organizations, Narcotics Anonymous (NA) and Cocaine Anonymous (CA), a number of 12-step organizations exist for a variety of disorders, such as Gambler's Anonymous (GA), Schizophrenics Anonymous (SA), Emotions Anonymous (EA), and Overeaters Anonymous (OA).

Other groups for health problems and diseases

Self-help organizations also provide support for individuals who are ill or have health problems. For example, support exists for people coping with weight management, HIV/AIDS, multiple sclerosis, muscular dystrophy, cancer, incontinence, and for the families of individuals who suffer from these conditions. Also, support exists for people who share interests or circumstances, such as groups for women who breast-feed (LaLeche League), singles, older adults, and new parents.

Self-help groups for family members are available since illness, addiction, and distress affect the entire family. Family members may unwittingly reinforce illness or addictive behaviors, or may need help coping with the person in distress. Al-Anon, an organization for friends and families of alcoholics, is a companion organization to AA, as is Alateen, a program for teenagers who have been hurt by the alcoholism of significant people in their lives. **Support groups** for caregivers of individuals with life-threatening or terminal illnesses, such as cancer, often meet at treatment centers and hospitals. One popular club for people with cancer, as well as for their friends and family, is Gilda's Club, founded by the actor/comedian Gene Wilder, Gilda Radner's husband. Gilda Radner, the well-known comedienne from Saturday Night Live, died at age 40 from ovarian cancer. Gilda's Clubs can be found in at least a half-dozen cities in the U.S., Canada, and London.

KEY TERMS

Clearinghouse—A centralized organization that is a repository of information and that facilitates access to information.

Cognitive restructuring—An approach to psychotherapy that focuses on helping the patient examine distorted patterns of perceiving and thinking in order to change their emotional responses to people and situations.

Experiential knowledge—Knowledge gained from experience, often practical, in contrast with theoretical or professional knowledge.

Online groups and clearinghouses

A growing trend in the self-help movement is the online support communities, as well as online resource centers and clearinghouses. Chat rooms, bulletin boards, and electronic mailing lists all provide convenient, around-the-clock access to peer support. Many large-scale, consumer health care web sites provide forums for discussions on numerous diseases and disorders, and major online commercial services, such as America Online (AOL), provide sites for health care and patient support. In some cases, professionals moderate online groups, although many are exclusively organized and populated by peers. There are self-help groups, such as LaLeche League, that hold some meetings online, often at their own web sites.

Features of self-help groups

Accessibility

Accessibility and economy are appealing features of self-help groups. Since the groups are free, organizations such as AA and NA are very cost-effective. In addition, meetings are easy to locate through local newspaper announcements, hospitals, health care centers, churches, school counselors, and community agencies. For AA and sister organizations that encourage frequent attendance, hundreds of meetings may be held each week in large metropolitan areas. Furthermore, with the proliferation of online support communities and growth of connectivity to the Internet, self-help groups are becoming as accessible for individuals in rural areas as they are for those in large cities.

Anonymity

An important characteristic of 12-step groups is the preservation of anonymity by revealing first names only and by maintaining strict confidentiality of stories shared during meetings. Online self-help groups offer even more anonymity since the exchanges are not face to face. The virtual anonymity of online experience helps to reduce social discomfort and discrimination, or stereotyping otherwise associated with real-life perceptions of age, disabilities, race, gender, or culture.

Social support and mutual aid

Self-help groups provide an intact community and a sense of belonging. The social support and mutual aid available in a group may be critical to recovery, rehabilitation, or healthy coping. This is especially true for socially isolated people or people from dysfunctional families, who may have little or no emotional support. Participating in a social network of peers reduces social and emotional isolation and supports healthy behavior. Group members can offer unconditional support and, collectively, are a repository of helpful experiential knowledge.

Self-esteem and self-efficacy

Self-help groups promote self-esteem or self-respect by encouraging reciprocal caring; the concept of self-efficacy, or the belief that one is capable, is promoted by reinforcing appropriate behavior and beliefs and by sharing relevant information regarding the disease or condition. For example, there may be an exchange of information regarding how to cope with failed or disrupted relationships, about what is reasonable to expect from health care professionals, about how to manage pain or public embarrassment, about where to go and to whom for a variety of needs. In groups such as AA, self-efficacy also is promoted by sponsors who act as mentors and role models, and by encouraging rotating leadership roles.

Introspection and insight

Introspection, or contemplation, is another fundamental feature of many self-help groups, particularly for groups that follow a 12-step program of recovery. For example, the fourth step of AA states that members make "a searching and fearless moral inventory" of themselves, and the tenth step states that members continue "to take personal inventory" and admit wrongdoing. Introspection is particularly beneficial to individuals who are not entirely aware of the moral repercussions of and motivation for their behavior. In a sense, working through some of the 12 steps resembles the cognitive restructuring learned in **cognitive-behavioral therapy** (CBT), as maladaptive ideas and behaviors are transformed.

Spiritual recovery

The final step in a 12-step program recognizes that recovery entails a spiritual awakening; furthermore, recovering addicts are enjoined to spread the message to others suffering from addiction. Recovery depends on giving up both injurious self-will and denial of maladaptive behavior, and turning to a higher power. Members are urged to seek guidance or inspiration from this higher power. For many addicts, the key to recovery is a spiritually guided movement away from self-centeredness or self-absorption, and a turning towards the "Power greater than ourselves" through prayer and **meditation**.

Advocacy

Some self-help groups meet to advocate or promote social and legislative remedies with respect to the issue of concern. For example, HIV/AIDS groups have lobbied for improved access to prescription drugs. Groups lobby for reforms by identifying key legislators and policy makers; they submit papers or suggestions for more equitable laws and policies to these key people. They also conduct public education programs (including programs meant to redress the harm of stigmatization). There are groups that advocate for more funds for research and for improved services for people who suffer from one of many diseases or mental disorders. The most important grass roots organization of families and consumers of psychiatric services (former or current patients) is the National Alliance for the Mentally Ill (NAMI). This organization was founded in 1979, and blends self-help with advocacy efforts for the improvement of research, services, and public awareness of major mental illnesses. Their advocacy efforts target both the federal and state levels.

Limitations

Advocacy vs. mutual aid

In some organizations, there is a growing overlap between self-help efforts and community development. Critics maintain that focusing on issues such as crime prevention, affordable housing, and economic development drains time and effort from social support and mutual aid. Nevertheless, some organizations continue to develop both advocacy and support.

Lack of professional involvement

The absence of professional guidance may mean that a member in need of formal **psychotherapy** or treatment may be discouraged from seeking professional help. On the other hand, too much professional involvement in the group may compromise the quality of mutual aid.

The " thirteenth step"

There is a well-known risk associated with attending 12-step groups termed the "thirteenth step." Women new to the groups, especially young women, are at their most vulnerable in the early stages of recovery. Male sexual predators who attend meetings take advantage of the atmosphere of intimacy and mutual trust. To cope with the possibility of sexual exploitation, young females are encouraged to attend meetings with a family member or a trusted adult, and all women are encouraged to find a same-sex sponsor.

Substituting addictions

The early months of a 12-step program are especially difficult. Typically, an addict in early recovery either replaces an addictive substance with a new one, or intensifies his/her concurrent use of another substance.

It is not uncommon for people who are chemically dependent to also have an addictive sexual disorder. (When someone is addicted to sex, there is an intense desire to gratify sexual urges and fantasies or to behave in ways that cause clinically significant distress; sexual indulgence, often compulsive, is a major disruptive force with respect to social relationships.) In one four-year study of a treatment program, 33% of the chemically addicted patients also were sexually compulsive. Some physicians believe that the predatory "thirteenth step" is evidence of turning from one addiction to another—in this case, addictive sexual disorder.

An Alcoholics Anonymous meeting in progress. *(Larry Mulvehill. Photo Researchers, Inc. Reproduced by permission.)*

Members at varying stages of recovery

Another common risk is associated with the varying levels of recovery in a self-help group—that of being actively involved in the abuse of alcohol and/or drugs. Newcomers need to realize that not all members are interested in supporting their recovery, and that people in later stages of recovery may be more reliable. Furthermore, some members are required to attend by disciplinary entities, such as employers or correctional authorities.

Ongoing meetings

One criticism of self-help groups, especially 12-step groups, is that in the eyes of families and friends, members who persevere and faithfully attend the seemingly endless number of meetings only to become "addicted" to the program. However, physicians who support self-help groups point out that since addiction is a disease, addicts are particularly vulnerable to relapse, and that ongoing involvement with a self-help community surely is better than suffering the recurring misery associated with active addiction.

Rational alternatives to 12-step groups

For addicts who find the spirituality of 12-step groups offensive and irrational, and who believe that public proclamation of powerlessness at group meetings is demoralizing, alternative groups exist. For example, a well-known organization, Rational Recovery (RR), is based on the cognitive-behavioral principles of Albert Ellis. RR emphasizes self-reliance, rational thinking as a result of cognitive restructuring, and the development of a new repertoire of behaviors to respond effectively to events that trigger relapse.

Conclusion

Worldwide, self-help groups are becoming increasingly popular. They are effective in providing mutual support and are good resources for finding needed information. However, when searching for an appropriate group, prospective members should ask their friends, physicians, and counselors for references, and then visit a few groups before deciding on which one to attend. Also, information clearinghouses on the Internet are a good first step.

See also Depression and depressive disorders; Disease concept of chemical dependency; Dual diagnosis; Group therapy; Pathological gambling; Poly-substance abuse; Sedatives and related disorders; Support groups

Resources

BOOKS

American Self-Help Clearinghouse. *Self-Help Sourcebook Online*. Mental Help Net, 1993–2002.

Borkman, Thomasina Jo. *Understanding Self-Help/Mutual Aid: Experiential Learning in the Commons*. New Brunswick, NJ: Rutgers University Press, 1999.

DuPont, Robert L. *The Selfish Brain: Learning from Addiction.* Washington, DC: American Psychiatric Press, Inc., 1997.

Galanter, Marc, Ricardo Castañeda, and Hugo Franco. "Group Therapy, Self-Help Groups, and Network Therapy." In *Clinical Textbook of Addictive Disorders,*, edited by Richard J. Frances and Sheldon I. Miller. 2nd ed. New York: Guilford Press, 1998.

Hyndman, Brian. *Does Self-Help Help? A Review of the Literature on the Effectiveness of Self-Help Programs.* Evaluation in Health Promotion Series: Canadian and International Perspectives, no. 7. Toronto: Center for Health Promotion, University of Toronto, 1997.

Lefley, Harriet P. "Advocacy, Self-help, and Consumer-Operated Services." In *Psychiatry,* edited by Allan Tasman, Jerald Kay, and Jeffrey A. Lieberman. Philadelphia: W. B. Saunders Company, 1997.

Miller, Norman S., ed. *The Principles and Practice of Addictions in Psychiatry.* Philadelphia: W. B. Saunders Company, 1997.

ORGANIZATIONS

Aloholics Anonymous. Grand Central Station, PO Box 459, New York, NY 10163. <www.alcoholicsanonymous.org>.

Gilda's Club Worldwide. 322 Eighth Avenue, Suite 1402, New York, NY 10001. (888) GILDA-4-U. <http://www.gildasclub.org/>.

Narcotics Anonyomous World Service Office. PO Box 9999, Van Nuys, California 91409. Telephone: (818) 773-9999. Fax (818) 700-0700. <http://www.na.org/>.

National Self-Help Clearinghouse. Graduate School and University Center of The City University of New York, 365 5th Avenue, Suite 3300, New York, NY 10016. (212) 817-1822. <http://www.selfhelpweb.org>.

Tanja Bekhuis, Ph.D.
Paula Ford-Martin, M.A.

Separation anxiety disorder

Definition

Like many childhood concerns, separation anxiety is normal at certain developmental stages. For example, when a child between the ages of eight and 14 months is separated from her mother or other primary caretaker, she may experience distress. This is normal. However, separation anxiety that occurs at later ages is considered a disorder because it is outside of normal developmental expectations, and because of the intensity of the child's emotional response. Separation anxiety disorder occurs most frequently from the ages of five to seven and from 11 to 14.

Environmental stimuli and internal cues from the child himself interact in the presentation of separation anxiety disorder. Separation anxiety disorder is defined by the primary expression of excessive anxiety that occurs upon the actual or anticipated separation of the child from adult caregivers—most often the parents. Significant problems in daily functioning for the child and parents can result from the disorder. Common fears observed in the presentation of separation anxiety include concerns about the parents' health or well-being (less frequently the child's own health), general catastrophes, natural disasters, or the child becoming lost/separated from the parents. Disrupted sleep, difficulty falling asleep alone, fear of monsters, or nightmares are also commonly experienced by children with separation anxiety disorder.

Family routines, parents' work schedules, and siblings' activities may all be negatively affected by the excessive anxiety and demands of the child with separation anxiety disorder. Family life is often disrupted by efforts to soothe the child. Parents can become stressed themselves as they try to maintain their daily routines and obligations, while attempting to manage their child's anxiety. The family's adjustment is often made more difficult due to the sudden appearance of symptoms.

Description

Children experiencing separation anxiety disorder display significant distress upon separation from the parent or other primary caregiver. Separation anxiety disorder often becomes problematic for families during elementary school, although it can also occur in older or younger children. The child appears fearful because he or she thinks something horrible will happen to the child or parent while they are apart. The child's responses to separation may include crying or becoming angry with the adult in an attempt to manipulate the situation. When thwarted by the adult's appropriate boundaries, expectations, and structure (the child must attend school, for example), the child's distress may become displaced into other maladaptive or negative behaviors. The child may begin to exhibit behavioral problems at school or at home when there has been no previous history of such problems. The child may seek out a new, negative peer group in order to gain attention or avoid separation.

Many children are unable to describe their specific fear. The feelings may seem more general and engulfing, especially to the younger child, making description more difficult and the feelings more overpowering. Children, and even adolescents, may experience difficulty describing their internal thoughts and feelings, which is normal. The ability to self-monitor, or observe one's own behavior or decision-making process, does not develop until late in adolescence for some individuals. When caregivers press the child experiencing separation anxiety for explanations, the feelings of anxiety can actually become more overwhelming. The intensity of the child's emotional response, accompanied by a lack of explanation, can become very frustrating for parents. Children or adolescents with an angry or frustrated parent may create a reasonable explanation for their fears to appease caregivers, and to keep them from leaving. Lying to take the emphasis off their strong feelings may be one of the early behavioral changes that can accompany separation anxiety.

Although exposure to a specific stressor is not required for the development of separation anxiety disorder, in many cases, a specific incident may precipitate the onset of the disorder (the traumatic events of September 11, 2001, for example). Another common precipitant is the holiday or summer break from school. Some children experience significant difficulty returning to school after a relatively short break, but certainly after summer and holidays.

Causes and symptoms

Causes

- Environmental change. Separation anxiety disorder is often precipitated by change or **stress** in the child's life and daily routine, such as a move, death or illness of a close relative or pet, starting a new school, a traumatic event, or even a return to school after summer vacation.
- Genetic influence. Evidence suggests a genetic link between separation anxiety disorders in children and a history of **panic disorder**, anxiety, or depression in their parents. Infants with anxious temperaments may have a predisposition toward later development of anxiety disorders.

KEY TERMS

Neurotransmitter—A chemical in the brain that transmits messages between neurons, or nerve cells.

- Parent/child attachment. Quality of attachment between children and their parents has also been identified as a factor in separation anxiety disorder. If the child senses emotional distance, the behaviors may be an attempt to draw the parent in more closely. The problematic behaviors can also draw the attention and care of others as well.
- Developmental considerations. Children develop at different rates when compared to each other (boys mature slower than girls, for example). Furthermore, the rate of development within the same person can vary across different types of functioning (for example, a gifted child is advanced intellectually but may be behind developmental expectations for social and emotional areas of functioning). A slower rate of development in the intellectual, social, emotional, or physical arena can foster anxiety within the child, making the separation more difficult.
- Cognitive factors. Children repeatedly worry about what they are afraid of (getting lost or a parent getting hurt, for example). The thought patterns are repeated within the child's mind until his emotions are beyond his control. The child may feel he is unable to think about anything else other than his fears, which contributes to his anxiety and irrational behaviors.
- Behavioral factors. The child or adolescent's crying and clinging behaviors may be developed by the child to cope with the feelings of anxiety associated with certain people, environment, or situations, such as attending school. The behaviors serve to distract attention away from the child's negative feelings, while nurturing the anxiety and fear into a greater part of the child's daily experience. For children, the behavioral component often becomes the mode of expression for the anxiety. The behavior may appear manipulative at times, due to the quick disappearance of symptoms once the threat of separation passes.
- Stress factors and influence. Symptoms of separation anxiety disorder may be exacerbated by a change in routine, illness, lack of adequate rest, a family move, or change in family structure (such as death, divorce, parent illness, birth of a sibling). The child's symptoms may also be affected by a change in caregivers or changes in parents' response to the child in terms of

discipline, availability, or daily routine. Even if changes are positive or exciting, the change may feel uncomfortable and precipitate an anxious response in the child.

Symptoms

The *Diagnostic and Statistical Manual of Mental Disorders (DSM-IV-TR)*, a handbook for mental health professionals that aids in **diagnosis**, lists the following criteria for separation anxiety disorder.

- Recurrent excessive distress upon separation. The child may become focused on the separation long before the actual event, or simply at the time of the anticipated separation. The recurrent behavioral pattern does not respond to **intervention**. The child experiences extreme distress, a highly charged emotional response that is repeated when the child anticipates separation from the caregiver. The child's fears trigger more anxiety and the emotional response intensifies.
- Persistent and excessive worry. The content of the worry may include some type of harm occurring to the child himself or toward the parents, or it may focus on becoming lost or separated indefinitely from the parent or caregiver.
- Repetitive nightmares. The child may experience repeated nightmares with themes of being chased, harmed, or separated from her family. Some fears are age-appropriate, but in separation anxiety disorder, the intensity of the fears becomes overwhelming to the child, leaving little opportunity for the child to control her emotions or behaviors. Although dreams are often a way of exploring and making sense of daily life, children with separation anxiety disorder report nightmares that represent their irrational fears or preoccupation with disaster.
- Complaints of physical symptoms. The child may feign illness (headaches, stomachaches, etc.) to avoid separation, or the child may actually experience nausea upon separation. If allowed to continue, the child may develop psychosomatic symptoms (physical symptoms with a psychological origin) that prevent the child from attending or fully participating in school activities. In these cases, the separation anxiety may develop into a more serious hypochondriacal state in which the child complains of chronic pain, which results in the child getting what she wants (i.e., not attending school).
- Persistent reluctance or refusal to engage in age-appropriate activities. The child may refuse to attend school because of preoccupation about separation from the parent. The child may also experience reluctance to be alone at home or at school without another adult being immediately available. The child may resist sleep without an adult present. The disorder causes significant disruption in the child's daily routine and may decrease the ability to perform previously mastered tasks. The child may appear to have reverted to behaviors from a younger age. The intensity of her emotions blocks the child's ability to communicate her feelings in ways other than through behaviors. Examples include tantrums, hitting, or clinging. Crying is one of the primary behaviors associated with separation anxiety disorder. The crying can become quite intense, making it difficult for the child to regain composure.
- Enmeshment or unusual interest in parents' schedules. The child wants to know all the details of the daily routine, a behavior which minimizes the anxiety the child is feeling.
- Quick resolution of symptoms (upon meeting child's demands). It may be hard for parents to accept the reality of the disorder because the symptoms often disappear quickly when separation does not occur. It is this component that can feel manipulative to those in the child's life.

Demographics

Prevalence estimates of separation anxiety disorder are 4–5% of the population. Gender differences have not been observed, although girls do present more often with anxiety disorders in general. Of those diagnosed with separation anxiety disorder, approximately 75% experience school refusal. The most frequently observed ages for occurrence of separation anxiety disorder are in children ages five to seven years and again from ages 11 to 14 years. It is at these times the children may feel more challenged by the developmental tasks of entering school or beginning puberty.

Diagnosis

The mental health professional will usually make the diagnosis of separation anxiety disorder based on information gathered during an interview process involving the parent(s) and the child. It is usually preferable for the interviews with the parent and child to occur separately; however that may not be possible because of the child's intense anxiety about separation.

Separation anxiety disorder is generally diagnosed by history, including parental report; however, a few measures of general anxiety exist that can be used to supplement the history. These include Pediatric Anxiety Rating Scale, Children's Global Assessment Scale, Children's Anxiety Scale, Screen for Child Anxiety Related Emotional Disorders (SCARED-R), Multi-

Dimensional Anxiety Scale for Children, and Achenbach's Child Behavior Checklist.

Duration of disturbance prior to diagnosis is a minimum of four weeks, occurring prior to the age of 18 years.

The disorder is described as "early onset" prior to the age of six years, and is generally not diagnosed after the age of 18. However, some researchers are describing another type of separation anxiety experienced by parents when their adolescents leave home. Readers may recognize this stage of life as the "empty nest syndrome"; however, no such formal diagnosis exists for a parental form of separation anxiety.

Treatments

The most effective treatments for separation anxiety disorder involve parents, as well as school personnel when appropriate. Giving the child a sense of safety and security is key to successful treatment. Current treatment methods combine some form of group or individual cognitive behavioral intervention. A number of treatment options are discussed below.

Cognitive-behavioral therapy

Cognitive-behavioral therapy is a treatment approach designed to alter a person's thoughts, beliefs, and images as a way of changing behavior. In treating a child with separation anxiety disorder, the goal is to help the child label her fears and identify the irrational beliefs and assumptions underlying her fears. By confronting and correcting her false beliefs, a parent can help his or her child become less anxious about separation.

Imagery

With imagery, a child uses his imagination to see himself being successful in a stressful situation. For example, before heading off to school, a child could imagine how he will handle separation from mom. Instead of crying, he sees himself calmly saying goodbye to his mom. The use of positive mental pictures may help diminish some of the child's anxiety and fear before separation actually occurs.

Modeling

Parents and teachers can be helpful in **modeling** appropriate behaviors and coping mechanisms at home and at school. For example, parents can model being relaxed when saying goodbye to their children and other people.

Systematic desensitization

Systematic desensitization is a **behavior modification** technique in which a person is gradually exposed to an anxiety-provoking or fearful object or situation while learning to be relaxed. A child with separation anxiety disorder may be taught relaxation techniques for managing her anxiety, and, as a result, can spend longer and longer periods of time at school without a caregiver present by teaching her.

Positive role models

Using positive role models, whether in real life or in books, can also be helpful for children. Reading books about other children successfully separating from their caregiver can give the anxious child the confidence that he can do it, too. Watching his friends calmly separate from their caregivers can also empower the child to do the same.

Behavior modification

Behavior modification uses a system of rewards and reinforcements to change behavior. This method has been shown to be effective in a majority of cases involving children and separation anxiety disorder, even at one-year follow-up.

Reminders

Small items that remind the child of his bond with his parents can sometimes be helpful in managing the child's anxiety. Typical objects could include a smooth stone in the child's pocket, a picture of the family in the child's notebook, or a friendship bracelet. Allowing phone calls or contact throughout the day is generally not effective, as it provides a more direct reminder of the caregiver's absence.

Distraction and altruism

Distraction and altruism is another strategy that can be useful in treating separation anxiety disorder. Helping the child focus on things outside himself can provide a healthy distraction. For instance, the child may be asked to take care of a pet at school. Such distractions from the child's internal thoughts and feelings coupled with a "fun" responsibility can help the child move away from his internal state of anxiety.

Medication management

Medication is helpful in certain cases where the anxiety is so debilitating that the child is unable to participate in other forms of treatment, or go about his daily routine. Medication management most often involves some type of anti-anxiety or anti-depressive drug. The newest classes include the SSRIs or selective serotonin re-uptake inhibitors that influence **neurotransmitters** in the **brain** to regulate emotional response. Before any medication is given, however, it is essential that a careful medical and psychiatric evaluation be performed by a trained health professional.

Prognosis

Over 60% of children participating with their parents in cognitive-behavioral treatment are successful in managing their symptoms without medication. Symptoms generally do not re-appear in exactly the same way as the initial presentation; however, the child may have a heightened sensitivity to normal life transitions, such as changing schools. Families can help children cope with these transitions by visiting the new school, meeting teachers, and getting to know some students.

Separation anxiety disorder has a poorer prognosis in environments where threat of physical harm or separation actually exist.

Existence of other conditions, such as **autism**, decrease the likelihood of a positive prognosis. Presence of separation anxiety disorder in childhood is sometimes associated with early onset panic disorder in adults.

Studies indicate a lower prevalence of alcohol use and suicidal ideation in children or adolescents who experience separation anxiety disorder. Depression is commonly associated with anxiety disorders. Developing social skills can also be negatively affected by separation anxiety disorder.

Prevention

Prevention can be enhanced through parent effectiveness training that emphasizes the child's positive and successful coping strategies when dealing with separation. Overly anxious parents may need to develop their own support mechanisms and systems to manage their feelings and avoid influencing their children negatively.

Resources

BOOKS

American Psychiatric Association. *Diagnostic and Statistical Manual of Mental Disorders.* 4th edition, text revised. Washington, DC: American Psychiatric Association, 2000.

Silverman, W. K. and P. D. Treffers, Eds. *Anxiety Disorders in Children and Adolescents: Research, Assessment and Intervention.* New York, NY: Cambridge University Press, 2001.

PERIODICALS

Burke, P., R. C. Baker. "Is Fluvoxamine Safe and Effective for Treating Anxiety Disorders in Children?" *Journal of Family Practice* 50, no. 8 (2001): 719.

Goodwin, R., J. D. Lipsitz, T. F. Chapman, S. Mannuzza, and A. J. Fyer. "Obsessive-compulsive Disorder and Separation Anxiety Co-morbidity in Early Onset Panic Disorder" *Psychological Medicine* 31, no. 7 (October 2001): 1307-1310.

Kaplow, J. B., P. J. Curran, A. Angold, E. J. Costello.; "The Prospective Relation between Dimensions of Anxiety and the Initiation of Adolescent Alcohol Use." *Journal of Clinical Child Psychology* 30, no. 3 (2001): 316-326.

Kendall, P.C., E. V. Brady, T. Verduin. "Comorbidity in Childhood Anxiety Disorders and Treatment Outcome." *Journal of the American Academy of Child & Adolescent Psychiatry* 40, no. 7 (2001): 787.

Muris, P., B. Mayer, E. Bartelds, S. Tierney, and N. Bogie. "The Revised Version of the Screen for Child Anxiety Related Emotional Disorders (SCARED:R)." *British Journal of Clinical Psychology* 40 (2001): 323-336.

Shortt, A. L., P. M. Barrett, T. L. Fox. "Evaluating the FRIENDS Program: A Cognitive-Behavioral Group Treatment for Anxious Children and Their Parents." *Journal of Clinical Child Psychology* 30, no. 4 (2001): 525-535.

Southam-Gerow, M. A., P. C. Kendall, V. R. Weersing. "Examining Outcome Variability: Correlates of Treatment Response in a Child and Adolescent Anxiety Clinic." *Journal of Clinical Child Psychology* 30, no. 3 (2001): 422-436.

Walkup, J. T., M. J. Labellarte, M. A. Riddle, Daniel S. Pine, L. Greenhill, R. Kelin, M. Davies, M. Sweeney, H. Abikoff, S. Hack, B. Klee, J. McCracken, L. Bergman, J. Piacentini, J. March, S. Compton, J. Robinson, T. O'Hara, S. Baker, B. Vitiello, L. A. Ritz, M. Roper. "Fluvoxamine for the Treatment of Anxiety Disorders in Children and Adolescents." *The New England Journal of Medicine* 344, no. 17 (2001): 1279.

ORGANIZATIONS

American Academy of Child & Adolescent Psychiatry. <www.aacap.org>.

Anxiety Disorders Association of America. 11900 Parklawn Drive, Suite 100, Rockville, MD 20852. Phone: (301) 231-9350. Web site: <www.adaa.org>.

OTHER

Brandt, Amy, Eida de la Vega, and Janice Lee Porter. *Benjamin Comes Back.* Saint Paul: Redleaf Press, 2000.

Penn, Audrey, Ruth E. Harper, Nancy M. Leak. *The Kissing Hand.* Washington: Child Welfare League of America, Incorporated, 1993.

Deanna Pledge, Ph.D.

Serax *see* **Oxazepam**

Serentil *see* **Mesoridazine**
Seroquel *see* **Quetiapine**
Serotonin *see* **Neurotransmitters**

Sertraline

Definition

Sertraline is an antidepressant that belongs to the class of drugs called selective serotonin reuptake inhibitors (SSRIs). In the in United States it is sold under the brand name Zoloft.

Purpose

Sertraline is used to treat depression, **obsessive-compulsive disorder**, **panic disorder**, and **post-traumatic stress disorder**.

Description

Serotonin, one of the **neurotransmitters**, is a **brain** chemical that carries nerve impulses from one nerve cell to another. Researchers think that depression and certain other mental disorders may be caused, in part, because there is not enough serotonin being released and transmitted in the brain. Like the other SSRI antidepressants, **fluvoxamine** (Luvox), **fluoxetine** (Prozac), and **paroxetine** (Paxil), sertraline increases the level of brain serotonin (also known as 5-HT). Increased serotonin levels in the brain may be beneficial in patients with obsessive-compulsive disorder, alcoholism, certain types of headaches, post-traumatic stress disorder (PTSD), pre-menstrual tension and mood swings, and panic disorder. Sertraline is not more or less effective than the other SSRI drugs although selected characteristics of each drug in this class may offer greater benefits in some patients. Fewer drug interactions have been reported with sertraline, however, than with other medications in the same class.

The benefits of sertraline develop slowly over a period of up to four weeks. Patients should be aware of this and continue to take the drug as directed, even if they feel no immediate improvement.

Sertraline is available in 25-mg, 50-mg and 100-mg tablets, or as a 20-mg per ml solution.

Recommended dosage

The recommended dosage of sertraline depends on the disorder being treated. The initial recommended dosage for depression and obsessive-compulsive disorder is 50 mg daily. This may be increased at intervals of at least one week to the maximum recommended dosage of 200 mg daily. For the treatment of panic disorder and post-traumatic stress disorder, the initial dose is 25 mg once daily. This dosage is increased to 50 mg daily after one week. If there is no therapeutic response, the dosage may be increased to the maximum of 200 mg daily at intervals of at least one week. These dosages may need to be reduced in elderly patients (over age 65) or in people with liver disease.

For the treatment of obsessive-compulsive disorder in the pediatric population, treatment should be initiated at a dose of 25 mg per day in children six to 12 years of age and 50 mg per day in children 13 to 17 years of age. Doses may be increased at one-week intervals to a total daily dose of 200 mg.

Precautions

A group of serious side effects, called serotonin syndrome, have resulted from the combination of antidepressants such as sertraline and members of another class of antidepressants known as monoamine oxidase (MAO)

KEY TERMS

Obsessive-compulsive disorder—Disorder in which the affected individual has an obsession (such as a fear of contamination, or thoughts he or she doesn't like to have and can't control) and feels compelled to perform a certain act to neutralize the obsession (such as repeated handwashing).

Panic disorder—An anxiety disorder in which an individual experiences sudden, debilitating attacks of intense fear.

Post-traumatic stress disorder—A disorder caused by an extremely stressful or traumatic event (such as rape, act of war, or natural disaster) in which the trauma victim is haunted by flashbacks. In the flashbacks, the event is re-experienced in the present. Other symptoms include nightmares and feelings of anxiety.

Serotonin syndrome—A condition characterized by at least three of the following symptoms: diarrhea, fever, extreme perspiration, mood or behavior changes, overactive reflexes, fast heart rate, restlessness, shivering or shaking. It is a result of too much serotonin in the body.

inhibitors. Serotonin syndrome usually consists of at least three of the following symptoms: diarrhea, fever, sweatiness, mood or behavior changes, overactive reflexes, fast heart rate, restlessness, shivering or shaking. Because of this, sertraline should never be taken in combination with MAO inhibitors. Patient taking any MAO inhibitors, for example Nardil (**phenelzine** sulfate) or Parmate (**tranylcypromine** sulfate), should stop the MAO inhibitor then wait at least 14 days before starting sertraline or any other antidepressant. The same holds true when discontinuing sertraline and starting an MAO inhibitor. Also, people should not take sertraline oral concentrate while using **disulfiram** (Antabuse). Sertraline should never be taken by people who are any other SSRI antidepressants.

Sertraline should be used with cautiously and with close physician supervision by people with a prior history of **seizures**, people who are at an increased risk of bleeding, and those for whom weight loss is undesirable. Sertraline may precipitate a shift to mania in patients with bipolar (formerly manic-depressive) disease.

Side effects

More than 5% of patients experience **insomnia**, dizziness, and headache. About 14% of men report delayed ejaculation while 6% report decreased sex drive while taking this drug. In order to reduce these sexual side effects, patients can wait for tolerance to develop (this may take up to 12 weeks), reduce the dose, have drug holidays (where the weekend dose is either decreased or skipped), or discus with their physician using a different antidepressant.

More than 10% of patients report nausea and diarrhea while taking sertraline. Other possible side effects include agitation, anxiety, rash, constipation, vomiting, tremors, or visual difficulty. Although most side effects eventually subside, it may take up to four weeks for people to adjust to the drug.

Interactions

Sertraline interacts with **St. John's Wort**, an herbal remedy for depression. The risk of seizures is increased in patients using tramadol and sertraline. Taking sertraline with MAO inhibitors may result in the serious side effects discussed above. Erythromycin, an antibiotic, may inhibit the breakdown of sertraline in the liver and cause increased central nervous system effects such as drowsiness and decreasing of mental alertness. Other antidepressants should not be taken by people using sertraline except in rare cases when prescribed by a physician. If a combination of antidepressants is considered beneficial, a low dose of tricyclic antidepressants (10–25 mg daily) should be used.

Sertraline should not be taken with grapefruit juice as the combination may increase sertraline levels in the body.

Resources

BOOKS

Kay, Jerald. *Psychiatry: Behavioral Science and Clinical Essentials*. Philadelphia: W. B. Saunders Company, 2000.

Pfizer Inc. Staff. Product Information for Zoloft-Sertraline. New York: Pfizer Inc. Revised 9/2000, reviewed 3/2001.

PERIODICALS

Edwards, Guy. "Systemic Review and Guide to Selection of Selective Serotonin Reuptake Inhibitors." *Drugs*. 57 (1999): 507-33.

Hirschfeld, Robert. "Management of Sexual Side Effects of Antidepressant Therapy." *Journal of Clinical Psychiatry*. 60 (1999): 27-30.

Ajna Hamidovic, Pharm.D.

Serzone *see* **Nefazodone**

Sexual abuse *see* **Abuse**

Sexual aversion disorder

Definition

Sexual aversion disorder is a disorder characterized by disgust, fear, revulsion, or lack of desire in consensual relationships involving genital contact.

Normal loss of desire

To understand sexual aversion disorder, one should first understand that there are circumstances in which it is normal for people to lose interest in sexual activity. The reader can then compare these situations to the loss of desire associated with serious sexual disorders, including sexual aversion disorder.

There are a number of reasons that people lose interest in sexual intercourse. It is normal to experience a loss of desire during menopause; directly after the birth of a child; before or during menstruation; during recovery from an illness or surgery; and during such major or stressful life changes as death of a loved one, job loss, retirement, or divorce. These are considered normal causes for fluctuations in sexual desire and are generally temporary. Changing roles, such as becoming a parent for the first time or making a career change have also been found to cause loss of desire. Not having enough time for oneself or to be alone with one's partner may also contribute to normal and naturally reversible loss of desire. Loss of privacy resulting from moving a dependent elderly parent into one's home is a common cause of loss of desire in middle-aged couples. Depression, **fatigue**, or **stress** also contribute to lessening of sexual interest.

Description

Sexual aversion disorder represents a much stronger dislike of and active avoidance of sexual activity than the normal ups and downs in desire described above. Sexual aversion disorder is characterized not only by a lack of desire, but also by fear, revulsion, disgust, or similar emotions when the person with the disorder engages in genital contact with a partner. The aversion may take a number of different forms; it may be related to specific aspects of sexual intercourse, such as the sight of the partner's genitals or the smell of his or her body secretions, but it may include kissing, hugging, and petting as well as intercourse itself. In some cases the person with sexual aversion disorder avoids any form of sexual contact; others, however, are not upset by kissing and caressing, and are able to proceed normally until genital contact occurs.

There are several subclassifications of sexual aversion disorder. It may be lifelong (always present) or acquired after a traumatic experience; situational (with a specific partner or in a specific set of circumstances) or generalized (occurring with any partner and in all situations). Sexual aversion may be caused by psychological factors or by a combination of physical and psychological factors.

Causes and symptoms

There are a number of causes of sexual aversion disorder. The most common causes are interpersonal problems and traumatic experiences. Interpersonal problems generally cause situation-specific sexual aversion disorder, in which the symptoms occur only with a specific partner or under certain conditions. In such cases, underlying tension or discontent with the relationship is often the cause. Reasons for unhappiness with the relationship may include the discovery of marital infidelity; major disagreements over children, money, and family roles; domestic violence; lack of personal hygiene on the partner's side; or similar problems. Interpersonal problems are often the cause if intercourse was once enjoyed but is no longer desired.

Traumatic experiences have also been found to cause sexual aversion disorder, often of the generalized variety. Some possible traumas include rape, incest, molestation, or other forms of sexual **abuse**. The patient then associates intercourse with a painful experience or memory, possibly one that he or she is trying to forget. Sexual aversion disorder may also be caused by religious or cultural teachings that associate sexual activity with excessive feelings of guilt.

The symptoms of sexual aversion disorder can range from mild to severe. Mild symptoms include lack of interest and mild disgust. Severe symptoms can include panic attacks with all the symptoms of such an attack, including dizziness, shortness of breath, intense fear, and rapid heartbeat. People suffering from sexual aversion disorder often go out of their way to avoid situations that could end in sexual contact through any means they can think of, including going to bed at different times from the spouse, spending extra time at work, or trying to make themselves less sexually attractive.

KEY TERMS

Coitus—Sexual intercourse.

Demographics

Both men and women can experience sexual aversion disorder. It is thought to be more common in women than in men, possibly because women are more likely than men to be victims of rape and other forms of sexual assault. There are relatively few statistics on the number of people with sexual aversion disorder because it is often confused with other disorders, or with the normal fluctuations in desire associated with life stress. Also, many people find sex a difficult subject to discuss even with a physician, so that the number of people who seek help are probably fewer than the number of people with the disorder overall.

Diagnosis

A **diagnosis** of sexual aversion disorder is usually made when the affected person or his or her partner mentions the problem itself or their dissatisfaction with the relationship to their family physician, gynecologist, or psychotherapist. An important first step in diagnosis is a thorough physical examination, preferably of both partners, to rule out physical causes of the disorder in the affected person, and to rule out a sexually transmitted disease, physical deformity, or lack of personal cleanliness in the partner that may contribute to the affected person's avoidance of sex.

According to the mental health professional's ***Diagnostic and Statistical Manual of Mental Disorders*** (*DSM-IV-TR*) of the American Psychiatric Association, to meet criteria for a diagnosis of sexual aversion disorder the patient must not only avoid nearly all genital contact with his or her partner, but have strong negative feelings about such contact or its possibility. In addition, the problem must be causing serious difficulties and unhappiness either for the patient or for his or her partner. In addition, there must not be any underlying physical causes, such as certain disorders of the circulatory system, skin diseases, medication side effects, or similar problems that could cause a loss of desire. To be diagnosed with sexual aversion disorder, the affected person does not have to avoid all sexual contact, but must indicate that he or she is actively avoiding genital contact.

Many other sexual disorders have signs and symptoms similar to those of sexual aversion disorder, which complicates the diagnosis. Sexual aversion disorder is often found in conjunction with other sexual disorders; in some cases several diagnoses are appropriate for one patient.

One disorder similar in many aspects to sexual aversion disorder is hypoactive sexual disorder. Many of the signs, such as avoiding sexual contact in a variety of ways, are similar. The primary difference between the two disorders is that a patient with hypoactive sexual disorder is not interested in sex at all and does not have sexual fantasies of any variety. A patient with sexual aversion disorder, by comparison, may have normal sexual fantasies, and even function normally with some partners, although not with a specific partner. Also, a patient with hyposexual disorder will not enjoy or desire any anticipation in sexual activities including kissing and caressing. Some, though not all, people with sexual aversion disorder do enjoy sexual foreplay until the point of genital contact.

Sexual aversion disorder and hypoactive sexual disorder are both considered to be caused mainly by psychological factors and to manifest psychological symptoms. Another disorder that can have some similar symptoms is **female sexual arousal disorder** (FSAD). FSAD refers to a woman's recurrent inability to achieve or maintain an adequate lubrication-swelling response during sexual activity. Lack of lubrication is a physical problem that may have either physical or psychological causes. Women with FSAD find intercourse uncomfortable or even painful. As a result of the physical discomfort, the woman often will avoid intercourse and sexual activity with her partner that may lead to intercourse. Although FSAD is a disorder with physical symptoms as well as psychological ones, it is easily confused with sexual aversion disorder because it may manifest as a problem of interest or desire.

Treatments

Sexual aversion disorder is not thought to have any commonplace underlying physiological causes. The usual treatment is a course of **psychotherapy** for the psychological condition(s) that may be causing the problem. Marriage counseling, or **couples counseling**, is often appropriate if the disorder concerns a spouse. Medications can be used to treat some symptoms that may be associated with sexual aversion disorder, such as panic attacks, if they are severe enough to be causing additional distress.

Prognosis

When sexual aversion disorder is addressed as a psychological disorder, treatment can be very successful. Psychotherapy to treat the underlying psychological problems can be successful as long as the patient is willing to attend counseling sessions regularly. For sexual aversion disorder that is situational or acquired, psychotherapy for both the patient and his or her partner may help to resolve interpersonal conflicts that may be contributing to the disorder. Panic attacks caused by or associated with the disorder can be treated successfully by medication if the doctor considers this form of treatment necessary.

If sexual aversion disorder is not diagnosed, discussed, or treated, the result may be infidelity, divorce, or chronic unhappiness in the relationship or marriage.

Resources

BOOKS

American Psychiatric Association. *Diagnostic and Statistical Manual of Mental Disorders.* 4th ed., text revised. Washington DC: American Psychiatric Association, 2000.

Sadock, Benjamin J., and Virginia A. Sadock, eds. *Comprehensive Textbook of Psychiatry.* 7th ed. Vol. 2. Philadelphia: Lippincott Williams and Wilkins, 2000.

PERIODICALS

Butcher, Josie. "Female Sexual Problems: Loss of Desire." *Western Journal of Medicine* 171 no. 1 (July 1999): 41.

Everard, Walter, and Ellen Laan. "Drug Treatments for Women's Sexual Disorders." *The Journal of Sex Research* 37 no. 3 (August 2000): 195.

OTHER

Duffy, Jim. "Sexual Healing." *Hopkins Medical News* Winter 1999 (cited 21 March 2002). <www.hopkinsmedicine.org/hmn/W99/top.htm;>.

Tish Davidson, A.M.

Sexual deviance *see* **Paraphilias**

Sexual dysfunctions

Definition

Sexual dysfunction disorders are problems that interfere with the initiation, consummation, or satisfaction with sex. They occur in both men and women and are independent of sexual orientation.

Description

Probably nowhere in human health do the body and mind interact more than during sex. There are four generally recognized phases of sexual activity, involving both mental and physical responses and are applicable to both men and women. These phases are in sequence:

- desire or appetite—fantasies or thoughts about sex.
- excitement—physical changes to prepare the body for intercourse and accompanying sense of sexual pleasure
- orgasm—physical response that leads to the peak of physical pleasure and release of sexual tension
- resolution—physical relaxation accompanied by a feeling of well-being and satisfaction

Sexual dysfunction disorders can occur in any of these four phases. Their cause may be physiological or psychological. More than one sexual dysfunction disorder may appear simultaneously. The ***Diagnostic and Statistical Manual of Mental Disorders***, (*DSM-IV-TR*), produced by the American Psychiatric Association and used by most mental health professionals in North America and Europe to diagnose mental disorders, recognizes nine specific sexual dysfunctions:

- Disorders of desire: These interfere with the initiation of sex and include **hypoactive sexual desire disorder** (low interest in sex) and **sexual aversion disorder** (objections to having the genitals touched).
- Disorders of excitement or sexual arousal: These are **female sexual arousal disorder** (when a woman fails to have physiological responses associated with arousal), and male erectile disorder (when a man fails to get an adequate erection, also referred to as "**erectile dysfunction**").
- Disorders of the orgasm phase: These are **female orgasmic disorder** (when a woman fails to reach orgasm); and **male orgasmic disorder** (when a man fails to reach orgasm) and **premature ejaculation** (when a man reaches orgasm too soon).
- Sexual pain disorders (associated with intercourse and orgasm): These disorders are **vaginismus** (the outer part of a woman's vagina spasms causing pain) and **dyspareunia** (pain during intercourse in either men or women).

In addition, medications or illicit drugs may cause substance-induced sexual dysfunction and sexual dysfunction may be caused by a general medical condition such as diabetes or nerve damage. If the sexual dysfunction falls into none of the above areas, it is classified as sexual dysfunction not otherwise specified.

The causes of sexual dysfunction disorders are varied, as are their symptoms. In general, symptoms either prevent the initiation of sex or the completion of the sex act, or they interfere with satisfaction derived from sex. Almost everyone has some problem with sexual functioning or fulfillment at some point in their lives, but not all problems are considered sexual dysfunction disorders. Sexual satisfaction is very personal and individual, so that what may be an annoyance for one couple may be a serious problem for another. However, estimates suggest that roughly one-fourth of the adult population may have a sexual dysfunction disorder. More women than men report having sexual dysfunction disorders, but the difference may be that women are more open and active about seeking help with sexual problems than are men.

Diagnosis begins with a sexual and medical history, and often a physical examination and laboratory tests. Treatment must be individualized based on the cause and the specific dysfunction and includes physiological treatment, **psychotherapy**, and education and communication counseling. Most people can be helped to resolve their problems and improve their sex life. Generally, the sooner the person receives help, the easier the problem is to resolve. Support of a partner is often critical to successful resolution of the problem.

Resources

BOOKS

American Psychiatric Association. *Diagnostic and Statistical Manual of Mental Disorders.* 4th ed. text revised. Washington DC: American Psychiatric Association, 2000.

Berman, Jennifer, M.D., and Laura Berman, Ph. D. *For Women Only: A Revolutionary Guide to Overcoming Sexual Dysfunction and Reclaiming Your Sex Life.* New York: Henry Holt, 2001.

Hales, Robert E., Stuart C. Yudofsky, and John A. Talbot. *The American Psychiatric Press Textbook of Psychiatry.* 3rd ed. Washington, DC: American Psychiatric Press, 2000.

Sadock, Benjamin J. and Virginia A. Sadock, eds. *Comprehensive Textbook of Psychiatry.* 7th ed. Vol. 2. Philadelphia: Lippincott Williams and Wilkins, 2000.

ORGANIZATIONS

American Association of Sex Educators, Counselors, and Therapists (AASECT). P. O. Box 238, Mount Vernon, IA 53214-0238. (319) 895-8407. <www.aasect.org>.

Sexual Information and Education Council of the United States (SIECUS). West 42 Street, Suite 350, New York, NY 10036-7802. <www.siecus.org>.

Tish Davidson, A.M.

Sexual masochism

Definition

The essential feature of sexual masochism is the feeling of sexual arousal or excitement resulting from receiving pain, suffering, or humiliation. The pain, suffering, or humiliation is real and not imagined and can be physical or psychological in nature. A person with a **diagnosis** of sexual masochism is sometimes called a masochist.

The ***Diagnostic and Statistical Manual of Mental Disorders***, also known as the *DSM*, is used by mental health professionals to diagnose specific mental disorders. In the 2000 edition of this manual (the Fourth Edition Text Revision also known as *DSM-IV-TR*) sexual masochism is one of several **paraphilias**. Paraphilias are intense and recurrent sexually arousing urges, fantasies, or behaviors.

Description

In addition to the sexual pleasure or excitement derived from receiving pain and humiliation, an individual with sexual masochism often experiences significant impairment or distress in functioning due to masochistic behaviors or fantasies.

With regard to actual masochistic behavior, the person may be receiving the pain, suffering, or humiliation at the hands of another person. This partner may have a diagnosis of **sexual sadism** but this is not necessarily the case. Such behavior involving a partner is sometimes referred to as sadomasochism.

Masochistic acts include being physically restrained through the use of handcuffs, cages, chains, and ropes. Other acts and fantasies related to sexual masochism include receiving punishment or pain by means of paddling, spanking, whipping, burning, beating, electrical shocks, cutting, rape, and mutilation. Psychological humiliation and degradation can also be involved.

Masochistic behavior can also occur in the context of a role-playing fantasy. For example, a sadist can play the role of teacher or master and a masochist can play the role of student or slave.

The person with sexual masochism may also be inflicting the pain or suffering on himself or herself. This can be done through self-mutilation, cutting, or burning.

The masochistic acts experienced or fantasized by the person sometimes reflect a sexual or psychological submission on the part of the masochist. These acts can range from relatively safe behaviors to very physically and psychologically dangerous behavior.

The *DSM* lists one particularly dangerous and deadly form of sexual masochism called hypoxyphilia. People with hypoxyphilia experience sexual arousal by being deprived of oxygen. The deprivation can be caused by chest compression, noose, plastic bag, mask, or other means and can be administered by another person or be self-inflicted.

Causes and symptoms

Causes

There is no universally accepted cause or theory explaining the origin of sexual masochism, or sadomasochism in general. However, there are some theories that attempt to explain the presence of sexual paraphilias in general. One theory is based on learning theory that paraphilias originate because inappropriate sexual fantasies are suppressed. Because they are not acted upon initially, the urge to carry out the fantasies increases and when they are finally acted upon, a person is in a state of considerable distress and/or arousal. In the case of sexual masochism, masochistic behavior becomes associated with and inextricably linked to sexual behavior.

There is also a belief that masochistic individuals truly want to be in the dominating role. This causes them to become conflicted and thus submissive to others.

Another theory suggests that people seek out sadomasochistic behavior as a means of escape. They get to act out fantasies and become new and different people.

Symptoms

Individuals with sexual masochism experience sexual excitement from physically or psychologically receiving pain, suffering, and/or humiliation. They may be receiving the pain, suffering, or humiliation at the hands of another person, who may or may not be a sadist, or they may be administering the pain, suffering, or humiliation themselves.

They experience distressed or impaired functioning because of the masochistic behaviors, urges, and fantasies. This distress or impairment can impact functioning in social, occupational, or other contexts.

Demographics

Although masochistic sexual fantasies often begin in childhood, the onset of sexual masochism typically occurs during early adulthood. When actual masochistic behavior begins, it will often continue on a chronic course for people with this disorder, especially when no treatment is sought.

Sadomasochism involving consenting partners is not considered rare or unusual in the United States. It often occurs outside of the realm of a mental disorder. More people consider themselves masochistic than sadistic.

Sexual masochism is slightly more prevalent in males than in females.

Death due to hypoxyphilia is a relatively rare phenomenon. Data indicate that less than two people per million in the United States and other countries die from hypoxyphilia.

Diagnosis

The *DSM* criteria for sexual masochism include recurrent intense sexual fantasies, urges, or behaviors involving real acts in which the individual with the disorder is receiving psychological or physical suffering, pain, and humiliation. The suffering, pain, and humiliation cause the person with sexual masochism to be sexually aroused. The fantasies, urges, or behaviors must be present for at least six months.

The diagnostic criteria also require that the person has experienced significant distress or impairment because of these behaviors, urges, or fantasies. The distress and impairment can be present in social, occupational, or other functioning.

Sexual masochism must be differentiated from normal sexual arousal, behavior, and experimentation. It should also be differentiated from sadomasochistic behavior involving mild pain and/or the simulation of more dangerous pain. When this is the case, a diagnosis of sexual masochism is not necessarily warranted.

Sexual masochism must also be differentiated from self-defeating or self-mutilating behavior that is performed for reasons other than sexual arousal.

Individuals with sexual masochism often have other sexual disorders or paraphilias. Some individuals, especially males, have diagnoses of both sexual sadism and sexual masochism.

Treatments

Behavior therapy is often used to treat paraphilias. This can include management and conditioning of arousal patterns and masturbation. Therapies involving cognitive restructuring and **social skills training** are also utilized.

Medication is also used to reduce fantasies and behavior relating to paraphilias. This is especially true of people who exhibit severely dangerous masochistic behaviors.

Treatment can also be complicated by health problems relating to sexual behavior. Sexually transmitted diseases and other medical problems, especially when the sadomasochistic behavior involves the release of blood, can be present. Also, people participating in hypoxyphilia and other dangerous behaviors can suffer extreme pain and even death.

Prognosis

Because of the chronic course of sexual masochism and the uncertainty of its causes, treatment is often difficult. The fact that many masochistic fantasies are socially unacceptable or unusual leads some people who may have the disorder not to seek or continue treatment.

Treating a paraphilia is often a sensitive subject for many mental health professionals. Severe or difficult cases of sexual masochism should be referred to professionals who have experience treating such cases.

Prevention

Because it is sometimes unclear whether sadomasochistic behavior is within the realm of normal experimentation or indicative of a diagnosis of sexual masochism, prevention is a tricky issue. Often, prevention refers to managing sadomasochistic behavior so it primarily involves only the simulation of severe pain and it always involves consenting partners familiar with each other's limitations.

Also, because fantasies and urges originating in childhood or adolescence may form the basis for sadomasochistic behavior in adulthood, prevention is made difficult. People may be very unwilling to divulge their urges and discuss their sadistic fantasies as part of treatment.

Resources

BOOKS

American Psychiatric Association. *Diagnostic and Statistical Manual of Mental Disorders.* 4th edition, text revised. Washington, DC: American Psychiatric Association, 2000.

Andreasen, Nancy C., M.D., Ph.D., and Donald W. Black, M.D. *Introductory Textbook of Psychiatry.* Third edition. Washington, DC: American Psychiatric Publishing, Inc., 2000.

Baxter, Lewis R., Jr., M.D. and Robert O. Friedel, M.D., eds. *Current Psychiatric Diagnosis & Treatment.* Philadelphia: Current Medicine, 1999.

Ebert, Michael H., Peter T. Loosen, and Barry Nurcombe, eds. *Current Diagnosis & Treatment in Psychiatry.* New York: Lange Medical Books, 2000.

Ali Fahmy, Ph.D.

Sexual sadism

Definition

The essential feature of sexual sadism is a feeling of sexual excitement resulting from administering pain, suffering, or humiliation to another person. The pain, suffering, or humiliation inflicted on the other is real; it is not imagined and may be either physical or psychological in nature. A person with a **diagnosis** of sexual sadism is sometimes called a sadist. The name of the disorder is derived from the proper name of the Marquis Donatien de Sade (1740-1814), a French aristocrat who became notorious for writing novels around the theme of inflicting pain as a source of sexual pleasure.

The ***Diagnostic and Statistical Manual of Mental Disorders***, also known as the *DSM*, is used by mental health professionals to give diagnoses of specific mental disorders. In the 2000 edition of this manual— the Fourth Edition, Text Revision, also known as *DSM-IV-TR*— sexual sadism is listed as one of several **paraphilias**. The paraphilias are a group of mental disorders characterized by **obsession** with unusual sexual practices or with sexual activity involving nonconsenting or inappropriate partners (such as children or animals). The paraphilias may include recurrent sexually arousing urges or fantasies as well as actual behaviors.

Description

In addition to the sexual pleasure or excitement derived from inflicting pain and humiliation on another, a person diagnosed with sexual sadism often experiences significant impairment or distress in functioning due to actual sadistic behaviors or sadistic fantasies.

With regard to actual sadistic behavior, the person receiving the pain, suffering, or humiliation may or may not be a willing partner. Whether or not the partner is consenting, it is the very real suffering they are experiencing that is arousing to the sadist. When the sexual activity is consensual, the behavior is sometimes referred to as sadomasochism. The consenting partner may be given a diagnosis of **sexual masochism**. Like sadism, masochism is a term derived from a proper name; in this instance, from Leopold von Sacher-Masoch (1836-1895), an Austrian novelist who described the disorder in his books.

The sadistic acts performed or fantasized by a person with sadism often reflect a desire for sexual or psychological domination of another person. These acts range from behavior that is not physically harmful although it may be humiliating to the other person (such as being urinated upon), to criminal and potentially deadly behavior. Acts of domination may include restraining or imprisoning the partner through the use of handcuffs, cages, chains, or ropes. Other acts and fantasies related to sexual sadism include paddling, spanking, whipping, burning, beating, administering electrical shocks, biting, urinating or defecating on the other person, cutting, rape, murder, and mutilation.

In extreme cases, sexual sadism can lead to serious injury or death for the other person. According to the *DSM* these catastrophic results are more likely when the paraphilia is diagnosed as severe, and when it is associated with **antisocial personality disorder**, a personality disorder that may include psychotic symptoms.

Causes and symptoms

Causes

There is no universally accepted cause or theory explaining the origin of sexual sadism, or of sadomasochism. Some researchers attempt to explain the presence of sexual paraphilias in general as the result of biological factors. Evidence for this viewpoint comes from abnormal findings from neuropsychological and neurological tests of sex offenders.

Some researchers believe that paraphilias are related to such other problems as **brain** injury, **schizophrenia**, or another mental disorder. Often, people with sexual disorders or symptoms of paraphilia are diagnosed with other mental disorders.

Another theory about paraphilias is derived from learning theory. It suggests that paraphilias develop because the person is required to suppress, or squelch, inappropriate sexual fantasies. Because the fantasies are not acted out initially, the urge to carry them out increases. When the person finally acts upon the fantasies, they are in a state of considerable distress and/or arousal. This theory is not accepted by forensic experts at the Federal Bureau of Investigation (FBI) and other researchers who study sexual offenses. Rather than suppressing fantasies, most people who are eventually arrested for crimes involving sexual sadism begin with milder forms of acting on them and progressing to more harmful ways of acting out. For example, the FBI's database indicates that these people— almost always males— start out by collecting pornographic materials that depict sadistic acts, or they may draw ropes and chains on the photographs of models in swimsuit or lingerie advertisements. They then typically progress to following women at a distance, to hiring a prostitute in order to act out the fantasy, and to asking a girlfriend or other willing partner to cooperate with their fantasy. In other words, the severity of sadistic acts tends to increase over time.

Symptoms

Individuals with sexual sadism derive sexual excitement from physically or psychologically administering pain, suffering, and/or humiliation to another person, who may or may not be a consenting partner.

They may experience distressed or impaired functioning because of the sadistic behaviors or fantasies. This distress or impairment may be due to the fact that the partner is not consenting.

Demographics

Although sadistic sexual fantasies often begin in the person's childhood, the onset of active sexual sadism typically occurs during early adult life. When actual sadistic behavior begins, it will often continue on a chronic course for people with this disorder, especially if they do not seek help.

Sexual sadism with consenting partners is much more common than with nonconsensual partners. When consenting partners are involved, the sadist and the masochist may be either male or female. When non-consenting partners are involved, the sadist is almost always a male.

Sadomasochism involving consenting partners is not considered rare or unusual in the United States. It often occurs outside of the realm of a mental disorder. Fewer people consider themselves sadistic than masochistic.

Diagnosis

The diagnosis of sexual sadism is complicated by several factors, beginning with the fact that most persons with the disorder do not enter therapy voluntarily. Some are referred to treatment by a court order. Some are motivated by fear of discovery by employers or family members, and a minority enter therapy because their wife or girl friend is distressed by the disorder. The diagnosis of sexual sadism is based on the results of a psychiatrist's interview with the patient. In some cases, a person with sexual sadism may be referred to a specialized clinic for the treatment of sexual disorders. In the clinic, he will be given questionnaires intended to measure the presence and extent of cognitive distortions regarding rape and other forms of coercion, aggression, and impulsivity.

DSM-IV-TR criteria for sexual sadism include recurrent intense sexual fantasies, urges, or behaviors involving real acts in which another person is suffering psychological or physical suffering, pain, and humiliation. The victim's suffering, pain, and humiliation cause the person with sexual sadism to become aroused. The fantasies, urges, or behaviors must be present for at least six months.

The diagnostic criteria also require either that the person has acted on these urges or fantasies with a nonconsenting person, or that the person has experienced noticeable distress or interpersonal problems because of these urges or fantasies.

Sexual sadism must be differentiated from normal sexual arousal, behavior, and experimentation. Some forms of mild aggression, such as "love bites" or scratching, are within the range of normal behavior during sexual intercourse. Sadism should also be differentiated

KEY TERMS

Forensic—Pertaining to courtroom procedure or evidence used in courts of law.

Masochism—A mental disorder in which a person obtains sexual satisfaction through pain or humiliation inflicted by the self or by another person. The term is sometimes used more generally to refer to a tendency to find pleasure in submissiveness or self-denial.

Medroxyprogesterone acetate (MPA)—A female hormone that may be prescribed for male patients with sexual sadism or other paraphilias. MPA helps to control sexual urges in men by speeding up the clearance of testosterone from the bloodstream.

Paraphilias—A group of mental disorders that is characterized by recurrent intense sexual urges and sexually arousing fantasies generally involving (1) non-human objects, (2) the suffering or humiliation of oneself or one's partner (not merely simulated), or (3) children or other non-consenting persons.

Sadism—A mental disorder in which sexual arousal and gratification are obtained by inflicting pain or humiliation on another person.

from sadomasochistic behavior that involves only mild pain and/or the simulation of more dangerous pain. When these factors are present, a diagnosis of sexual sadism is not necessarily warranted.

Other mental disorders, such as the psychotic disorders, may include elements of sadism or other paraphilias. For example, patients with psychotic symptoms may perform sadistic acts for reasons other than sexual excitement. In these cases, an additional diagnosis of sexual sadism is not warranted.

Persons diagnosed with sexual sadism may have other sexual disorders or paraphilias. Some individuals, especially males, have diagnoses of both sexual sadism and sexual masochism.

Treatments

Behavior therapy is often used to treat paraphilias. This approach to treatment may include the management and conditioning of arousal patterns and masturbation. Therapies involving cognitive restructuring and **social skills training** are also often utilized.

Medication may be used to reduce fantasies and behavior relating to paraphilias. This form of treatment is especially recommended for people who exhibit sadistic behaviors that are dangerous to others. The medications that may be used include female hormones (most commonly medroxyprogesterone acetate, or MPA), which speed up the clearance of testosterone from the bloodstream; antiandrogen medications, which block the body's uptake of testosterone; and the selective serotonin reuptake inhibitors, or SSRIs.

Nonconsensual sadistic behavior often leads to problems with the criminal justice system. Issues related to legal problems may impair or delay the patient's treatment. Persons with sexual sadism may be reluctant to seek or continue treatment because they fear being reported to the police or being named in a lawsuit by an unwilling partner.

Treatment of sexual sadism may also be complicated by health problems related to sexual behavior. Sexually transmitted diseases and other medical problems may be present, especially when the sadistic behavior involves the release of blood or other body fluids.

Prognosis

Because of the chronic course of sexual sadism and the uncertainty of its causes, treatment is often difficult. The fact that many sadistic fantasies are socially unacceptable or unusual leads many people who may have the disorder to avoid or drop out of treatment. Treating a paraphilia is often a sensitive subject for many mental health professionals. Severe or difficult cases of sexual sadism should be referred to a specialized clinic for the treatment of sexual disorders or to professionals with experience in treating such cases.

As was noted previously, acts of sexual sadism tend to grow more violent or bizarre over time. As males with the disorder grow older, however, their ability to commit such acts begins to decrease. Sexual sadism is rarely diagnosed in men over 50.

Prevention

Because it is sometimes unclear whether sadomasochistic behavior is within the realm of normal experimentation or indicative of a diagnosis of sexual sadism, prevention is a tricky issue. Often, prevention refers to managing sadistic behavior so it never involves non-consenting individuals and it primarily involves the simulation of pain and not real pain.

Also, because fantasies and urges originating in childhood or adolescence may form the basis for sadomasochistic behavior in adulthood, prevention is made difficult. People may be very unwilling to divulge their urges and discuss their sadistic fantasies.

See also Cognitive-behavioral therapy; Sexual masochism; Sexual Violence Risk-20

Resources

BOOKS

American Psychiatric Association. *Diagnostic and Statistical Manual of Mental Disorders.* 4th edition, text revised. Washington, DC: American Psychiatric Association, 2000.

Andreasen, Nancy C., M.D., Ph.D., and Donald W. Black, M.D. *Introductory Textbook of Psychiatry.* Third edition. Washington, DC: American Psychiatric Publishing, Inc., 2000.

Baxter, Lewis R., Jr., M.D. and Robert O. Friedel, M.D., eds. *Current Psychiatric Diagnosis & Treatment.* Philadelphia: Current Medicine, 1999.

Douglas, John, and Mark Olshaker. *Mindhunter: Inside the FBI's Elite Serial Crime Unit.* New York: Simon and Schuster, 1995.

Ebert, Michael H., Peter T. Loosen, and Barry Nurcombe, eds. *Current Diagnosis & Treatment in Psychiatry.* New York: Lange Medical Books, 2000.

Ali Fahmy, Ph.D.

Sexual Violence Risk-20

Definition

The Sexual Violence Risk-20, also called the SVR-20, is an assessment instrument used by mental health professionals.

Purpose

The SVR-20 provides a structure for reviewing information important in characterizing an individual's risk of committing sexual violence and for targeting plans to manage that risk. The instrument's authors define sexual violence as, "Actual, attempted or threatened sexual contact with a person who is non-consenting or unable to give consent."

KEY TERMS

High-density sex offenses—Several offenses within a short period of time.

Risk assessment—The process of gathering and interpreting data useful in estimating the probability that an individual will demonstrate sexual violence.

Risk management—Using the results of a risk assessment to tailor intervention strategies intended to reduce the likelihood that an individual will demonstrate sexual violence.

Sexual violence—Actual, attempted or threatened sexual contact with a person who is non-consenting or unable to give consent.

Precautions

SVR-20 results should be finalized and interpreted by a professional who is familiar with the scientific literature on sexual violence, and who is experienced in conducting individual assessments on sexual and violent offenders. The instrument is not capable of providing new information about past behavior or of profiling an examinee as a sexually violent offender. Rather, it helps provide a structure to follow in estimating risk of sexual violence under certain circumstances. The instrument should not be used as a stand-alone measure, and predictions derived from its use should be subject to critical review. It is especially important to place results in the contexts of the examinee's personal style, likely environmental conditions, and base rates of sexual violence in other offenders with similar characteristics.

Description

The SVR-20 is a tool that helps guide a professional in conducting a minimally comprehensive assessment of sexual violence risk. The assessment process is based on six principles:

- It is important to gather a depth of information about the examinee's personal, social, occupational, mental health, illegal, and other relevant behavior.
- Information should be gathered using a variety of sources and methods, including (and not limited to) record reviews, interviews, and psychological, physiological, and medical techniques.
- Information should be gathered from the examinee, his or her relatives and acquaintances, the victim(s), professionals who have interacted with the examinee, and any other sources likely to yield useful information.
- The examinee's history and future exposure to risk factors should be considered.
- The examiner should critically weigh the accuracy, credibility and applicability of the data that has been gathered.
- The risk assessment process should be ongoing, with regular re-assessments for many examinees.

The content of the SVR-20 was developed following a comprehensive review of similar instruments and of the scientific literature on risk for sexual violence and re-offense. The SVR-20 materials consist of a reference manual and protocol sheets that are filled out by the examiner. The instrument includes three major sections: Psychosocial Adjustment, Sexual Offenses, and Future Plans. The SVR-20 items are coded based on presence (Yes or No) and if present, whether there has been a recent change in status regarding that factor (Exacerbation, No Change, Amelioration).

The Psychosocial Adjustment section includes 11 risk factors: sexual deviation, victim of child **abuse**, psychopathy, major mental illness, substance use problems, suicidal/homicidal ideation (ideas), relationship problems, employment problems, past non-sexual violent offenses, past non-violent offenses, and past supervision failure.

The Sexual Offenses section includes seven risk factors: high-density sex offenses, multiple sex offense types, physical harm to victim(s) in sex offenses, escalation in frequency and severity of sex offenses, extreme minimization or **denial** of sex offenses, and attitudes that support or condone sex offenses.

The Future Plans section includes two factors: lacks realistic plans, and negative attitude toward **intervention**. Aside from factors related to the examinee's thinking and personality, items found in the first and second sections reference fixed or relatively stable characteristics.

The first and third sections are relevant not only to sexual violence, but also to violence in general. There is also an unstructured supplementary section entitled "Other Considerations," that can be used to describe unique factors relevant to an examinee's probability of risk.

Results

The SVR-20 does not allow for the definite prediction of sexual violence. Prediction of risk is summarized using a rating of low, moderate or high. Although the instrument's authors did not provide decision-making guidelines for determining the appropriate rating, they did recommend five questions to consider in communicating a "Risk Message" derived from the results:

- What is the likelihood that the individual will engage in sexual violence, if no efforts are made to manage the risk?
- What is the probable nature, frequency, and severity of any future sexual violence?
- Who are the likely victims of any future sexual violence?
- What steps could be taken to manage the individual's risk for sexual violence?
- What circumstances might exacerbate the individual's risk for sexual violence?

Typically, answers to these and other questions are fashioned in the form of a report for those responsible for making decisions about the examinee.

Resources

BOOKS

Boer, D., S. Hart, P. Kropp, and C. Webster. *Manual for the Sexual Violence Risk-20.* Burnaby, British Columbia, Canada: The British Columbia Institute Against Family Violence, co-published with the Mental Health, Law, and Policy Institute at Simon Fraser University, 1997.

Laws, D., and W. O'Donohue. (Eds.) *Sexual deviance: Theory, assessment and treatment.* New York: Guilford, 1997.

Marshall, W., D. Laws, and H. Barbaree. (Eds.) *Handbook of Sexual Assault: Issues, theories, and treatment of the offender.* New York: Plenum Press, 1990.

PERIODICALS

Menzies, R., and C. Webster. "Construction and validation of risk assessments in a six-year follow-up of forensic patients: A tridimensional analysis." *Journal of Consulting and Clinical Psychology* 63 (1995): 766-778.

Monahan, J. "Mental disorder and violent behavior." *American Psychologist* 47 (1992): 511-521.

ORGANIZATIONS

American Psychological Association. 750 First Street, NE, Washington, DC 20002-4242. Telephone: (800) 374-2721. <www.apa.org>.

Association for the Treatment of Sexual Offenders. 4900 S.W. Griffith Drive, Suite 274, Beaverton, Oregon 97005. Telephone: (503) 643-1023. <http://www.atsa.com>.

British Columbia Institute Against Family Violence, 409 Granville Street, Suite 551, Vancouver, BC V6C 1T2. Telephone: (604) 669-7055 or Toll free (Canada): (877) 755-7055. <http://www.bcifv.org>.

Geoffrey G. Grimm, Ph.D., LPC

Shared psychotic disorder

Definition

Shared psychotic disorder, a rare and atypical psychotic disorder, occurs when an otherwise healthy person (secondary partner) begins believing the **delusions** of someone with whom they have a close relationship (primary partner) who is already suffering from a psychotic disorder with prominent delusions. This disorder is also referred to as "folie á deux."

Description

In cases of shared psychotic disorder, the primary partner is most often in a position of strong influence over the other person. This allows them, over time, to erode the defenses of the secondary partner, forcing their strange belief upon them. In the beginning, the secondary partner is probably healthy, but has such a passive or dependent relationship with the primary partner that imposition of the delusional system is but a matter of time. Most of the time, this disorder occurs in a nuclear family. In fact, more than 95% of the cases reported involved people in the same family. Without regard to the number of persons within the family, shared delusions generally involve two people. There is the primary, most often the dominant person, and the secondary or submissive person. This becomes fertile ground for the primary (dominant) partner to press for understanding and belief by others in the family.

Shared psychotic disorder has also been referred to by other names such as **psychosis** of association, contagious insanity, infectious insanity, double insanity, and communicated insanity. There have been cases involving multiple persons, the most significant being a case involving an entire family of 12 people (folie á douze).

Causes and symptoms

Causes

Given the fact that the preponderance of cases occur within the same family, the theory about the origins of the disorder come from a psychosocial perspective. Approximately 55% of secondary cases of the disorder have first-degree relatives with psychiatric disorders, not including the primary partner. This is not true of individuals with the primary **diagnosis**, as they showed a roughly 35% incidence.

There are several variables which have great influence on the creation of shared psychotic disorder. For example, family isolation, closeness of the relationship to the person with the primary diagnosis, the length of time the relationship has existed, and the existence of a dominant-submissive factor within the relationship. The submissive partner in the relationship may be predisposed to have a mental disorder. Often the submissive partner meets the criteria for **dependent personality disorder**. Nearly 75% of the delusions are of the persecutory type.

An example of shared psychotic disorder involving the delusion of persecution, is that of a 52-year-old married female and her 48-year-old husband with multiple sclerosis, who believed that they were being harassed and watched by the Irish Republican Army (IRA). They were hospitalized and both became stable after two weeks on an antipsychotic medication. However, an interesting point in this case is that they were separated for that two-week period. The general consensus has been that, once separated, the submissive partner will let go of the delusion, that it would resolve itself simply due to separation. That did not happen in this case. Both partners had to be treated with proper medications before the delusion resolved.

In a case involving a middle-aged mother and an adolescent daughter, the delusions were multifaceted. The mother held the persecutory belief that someone in her neighborhood was manufacturing illegal drugs of some sort, and that they were periodically spraying something odorless, tasteless, and invisible into the air. The sprayed substance made her and her teen-aged daughter "act crazy." Oddly enough, the effects of the spraying began shortly after the husband left for work in the morning, and resolved shortly before he returned in the afternoon. The family raised ducks at their home, and the mother and daughter believed that the men making the illegal drugs were using the family ducks "as a food source" in order to stay near their hideout and avoid detection by police. Finally, mother and daughter also believed that occasional gunshots in their countryside landscape were meant as warnings to prevent anyone from learning about the misdeeds of the drug makers. This case was revealed when the daughter ran away from home, fearing that men with guns were coming to kill them. She was subsequently placed in the care of a child protective services agency, and the bizarre stories began to unfold. Both mother and daughter received psychiatric care.

KEY TERMS

Delusion—A false belief that is resistant to reason or contrary to actual fact.

Schizophrenia—A severe mental illness in which a person has difficulty distinguishing what is real from what is not real. It is often characterized by hallucinations, delusions, language and communication disturbances, and withdrawal from people and social activities.

Symptoms

The principal feature of shared psychotic disorder is the unwavering belief by the secondary partner in the dominant partner's delusion. The delusions experienced by both primary partners in shared psychotic disorder are far less bizarre than those found in schizophrenic patients; they are, therefore, believable. Since these delusions are often within the realm of possibility, it is easier for the dominant partner to impose his/her idea upon the submissive, secondary partner.

Demographics

Little data is available to determine the prevalence of shared psychotic disorder. While it has been argued that some cases go undiagnosed, it is nevertheless a rare finding in clinical settings.

Diagnosis

A clinical interview is required to diagnose shared psychotic disorder. There are basically three symptoms required for the determination of the existence of this disorder:

- An otherwise healthy person, in a close relationship with someone who already has an established delusion, develops a delusion himself/herself.

- The content of the shared delusion follows exactly or closely resembles that of the established delusion.
- Some other psychotic disorder, such as **schizophrenia**, is not in place and cannot better account for the delusion manifested by the secondary partner.

Treatments

The treatment approach most recommended is to separate the secondary partner from the source of the delusion. If symptoms have not dissipated within one to two weeks, antipsychotic medications may be in order.

Once stabilized, **psychotherapy** should be undertaken with the secondary partner, with an eye toward integrating the dominant partner, once he/she has also received medical treatment and is stable.

Prognosis

If the secondary partner is removed from the source of the delusion and proper medical and psychotherapeutic treatment are rendered, the prognosis is good. However, as stated above, the separation alone may not be successful. The secondary partner may require antipsychotic medication. Even after treatment, since this shared psychotic disorder is primarily found in families, the family members tend to reunite following treatment and release. If family dynamics return to pretreatment modes, a relapse could occur. Periodic monitoring by a social services agency is advised for as long as a year following treatment.

Prevention

In an effort to prevent relapse, **family therapy** should also be considered to re-establish the nuclear family and to provide social support to modify old family dynamics. The family cannot continue in isolation as it did in the past, and will require support from community agencies.

Resources

BOOKS

American Psychiatric Association. *Diagnostic and Statistical Manual of Mental Disorders.* 4th edition, text revised. Washington, DC: American Psychiatric Association, 2000.

Kaplan, Harold and Benjamin Sadock. *Synopsis of Psychiatry* 8th edition. New York: Lippincott, Williams and Wilkins, 1997.

PERIODICALS

Lai, Tony T. S, W. C. Chan, David M. C. Lai, S. W. Li. "Folie á deux in the aged: A case report." *Clinical Gerontologist* 22 (2001): 113-117.

Malik, Mansoor A. and Serena Condon. "Induced psychosis (folie á deux) associated with multiple sclerosis." *Irish Journal of Psychological Medicine* 17 (2000): 73-77.

Jack H. Booth, Psy.D.

Simple phobia *see* **Specific phobias**

Sinequan *see* **Doxepin**

Single photon emission computed tomography

Definition

Single photon emission **computed tomography** (SPECT) is an imaging study that uses radioactive materials injected through a vein that will pass into the **brain** generating a high-resolution brain image.

Description

SPECT is used to diagnose head trauma, epilepsy, **dementia**, and cerebrovascular disease. Development of a radiotracer called Tc99m label has increased the resolution of brain images generated from SPECT. The images yield very accurate spatial and contrast resolutions. The resulting sharp images enable the clinician to visualize very small structures within the brain. The accuracy of SPECT brain images makes it a very useful clinical and research tool.

Clinically, SPECT is useful for diagnosing the following disease states:

- Cerebrovascular disease or **stroke**: SPECT is useful to detect ischemia (reduced blood flow), determination of stroke causes, evaluate transient ischemia, determine prognosis, and monitor treatment.
- Dementia such as in Alzheimer's disease: SPECT studies can be used effectively to rule out other medical causes of dementia.
- Head trauma: Evidence suggests that SPECT is useful to detect greater number of lesions following the period after head trauma. It seems that the high resolution and accurate brain images of SPECT can detect lesions in the brain that are not possible to visualize using other techniques such as **positron emission tomography**

(PET) scanning. SPECT images can give clinicians important information concerning prognosis (also sometimes called outcome) and treatment of persons affected with head injury.

- Epilepsy: The radioactive material injected before SPECT imaging concentrates at the seizure locus (the region that contains nerve cells that generate an abnormal impulse). This can help identify the location of **seizures** and assist clinicians concerning management and outcomes.
- SPECT allows clinicians to visualize a specific area of the brain called the striatum, which contains a neurotransmitter (a chemical that communicates nerve impulse from one nerve cell to another) called dopamine. Circuitry in the striatum and interaction with dopamine can help provide valuable information concerning **movement disorders**, **schizophrenia**, mood disorders, and hormone diseases (since hormones require control and regulation from the brain in structures called the pituitary gland and hypothalamus).

As a research tool, SPECT imaging seems to be sensitive tool to measure blood flow through the brain (cerebral blood flow), in persons who have psychological disorder such as **obsessive-compulsive disorder** (higher blood flow) and alcoholism (lower blood flow).

Other dianostic indications and procedures are similar to other **imaging studies** such as computed tomography, **magnetic resonance imaging**, and PET.

Resources

PERIODICALS

Busatto, Geraldo, F. "Regional cerebral blood flow abnormalities in early-onset obsessive-compulsive disorder: an exploratory SPECT study." *Journal of the American Academy of Child and Adolescent Psychiatry* 43, no. 3. (March 2001): 347.

Gansler, David A. "Hypoperfusion of inferior frontal brain regions in abstinent alcoholics: a pilot SPECT study." *Journal of Studies on Alcohol* 61, no. 1 (January 2000): 32.

Van Heertum, R. "Single photon emission, CT, and positron emission tomography in the evaluation of neurologic disease." *Radiologic Clinics of North America* 39, no. 5 (September 2001).

Laith Farid Gulli, M.D.
Alfredo Mori, M.D.
Jean Suvan, B.Sc., R.D.H.

Skills training *see* **Social skills training**

Sleep disorders

Definition

Sleep disorders are chronic disturbances in the quantity or quality of sleep that interfere with a person's ability to function normally.

Description

An estimated 15% of Americans have chronic sleep problems, while about 10% have occasional trouble sleeping. Sleep disorders are listed among the clinical syndromes in Axis I of the American Psychiatric Association's ***Diagnostic and Statistical Manual of Mental Disorders***, also known as the *DSM*. They may be either primary (unrelated to any other disorder—medical or psychological) or secondary (the result of physical illness, psychological disorders, or drug or alcohol use).

In the revised fourth edition of the *DSM* (*DSM-IV-TR*), the primary sleep disorders are categorized as either dyssomnias or parasomnias. Dyssomnias pertain to the amount, quality, or timing of sleep, whereas parasomnias pertain to abnormal behavioral or physiological events that occur while sleeping. Dyssomnias include:

- Primary insomnia—difficulty getting to sleep or staying asleep. Sleep loss is so severe that it interferes with daytime functioning and well-being. Three types of **insomnia** have been identified (although a single person can have more than one): sleep-onset insomnia (difficulty falling asleep); sleep-maintenance insomnia (difficulty staying asleep); and terminal insomnia (waking early and not being able to go back to sleep). While insomnia can occur at any stage of life, it becomes increasingly common as people get older.
- Primary **hypersomnia**—excessive sleepiness either at night or during the day.
- **Narcolepsy**—sudden attacks of REM sleep during waking hours. Many narcoleptics experience additional symptoms including cataplexy (a sudden loss of muscle tone while in a conscious state), **hallucinations** and other unusual perceptual phenomena, and sleep paralysis, an inability to move for several minutes upon awakening. The disorder is caused by a physiological **brain** dysfunction that can be inherited or develop after trauma to the brain from disease or injury.
- **Breathing-related sleep disorder**—abnormalities in breathing cause sleep disruptions. Sleep apnea consists of disrupted breathing which wakens a person repeatedly during the night. Though unaware of the problem while it is occurring, people with sleep apnea are unable to get a good night's sleep and feel tired and

sleepy during the day. The condition is generally caused either by a physical obstruction of the upper airway or an impairment of the brain's respiration control centers.

- **Circadian rhythm sleep disorder**—environmental disruptions to an individual's internal 24-hour-clock affect his or her sleep patterns. This disorder has four subtypes: delayed sleep phase type, jet lag type, shift work type, and unspecified type.

Parasomnias include:

- **Nightmare disorder**—nightmares repeatedly awaken the affected individual.
- **Sleep terror disorder**—affected individual is repeatedly awakened from sleep and remains awake and frightened for a short period of time (about 10 minutes or so, usually less), and during that time, the individual is difficult to awaken or comfort. No dream is recalled, and the person often does not remember the event the following day.
- **Sleepwalking disorder**—repeated episodes of motor activity during sleep, including getting out of bed and walking around.

Other features of parasomnias not listed in the *DSM-IV-TR* include bruxism (teeth grinding) and **enuresis** (bed-wetting). Both are often stress-related, although enuresis may also be caused by genitourinary disorders, neurological disturbances, or toilet training problems. A parasomnia only identified in the late twenieth century is REM sleep behavior disorder. Those affected by this condition—usually middle-aged or older men—engage in vigorous and bizarre physical activities during REM sleep in response to dreams, which are generally of a violent, intense nature. As their actions may injure themselves or their sleeping partners, this disorder, thought to be neurological in nature, has been treated with hypnosis and medications, including **clonazepam** and **carbamazepine**.

Resources

BOOKS

American Psychiatric Association. *Diagnostic and Statistical Manual of Mental Disorders.* Fourth edition, text revised. Washington DC: American Psychiatric Association, 2000.

Buchman, Dian Duncin. *The Complete Guide to Natural Sleep.* Collingdale: DIANE Publishing Company, 1999.

Mottolova, Jamin K. *Sleep-deficiency, Deprivations, Disturbances and Disorders: Index of New Information and Guide-Book for Consumers, Reference and Research.* Washington DC: Annandale, 2002.

Reite, Martin, John Ruddy, and Kim Nagel. *Concise Guide to Evaluation and Management of Sleep Disorders.* Washington DC: American Psychiatric Publishing Group, Inc., 2002.

ORGANIZATIONS

The American Academy of Sleep Medicine (formerly the American Sleep Disorders Association), and the Sleep Medicine Education and Research Foundation. 6301 Bandel Road, Suite 101, Rochester, MN 55901. Telephone: (507) 287-6006. Web site: <http://www.aasmnet.org>.

Sleep terror disorder

Definition

Sleep terror disorder is defined as repeated temporary arousal from sleep, during which the affected person appears and acts extremely frightened.

Description

Sleep terror disorder is sometimes referred to as *pavor nocturnus* when it occurs in children, and *incubus* when it occurs in adults. Sleep terrors are also sometimes called night terrors, though sleep terror is the preferred term, as episodes can occur during daytime naps as well as at night. Sleep terror is a disorder that primarily affects children, although a small number of adults are affected as well.

Causes and symptoms

Causes

The causes of sleep terror are for the most part unknown. Some researchers suggest that sleep terrors are caused by a delay in the maturation of the child's central nervous system. Such factors as sleep deprivation, psychological **stress**, and fever may also trigger episodes of sleep terror.

Symptoms

The symptoms of sleep terror are very similar to the physical symptoms of extreme fear. These include rapid heartbeat, sweating, and rapid breathing (hyperventilation). The heart rate can increase up to two to four times the person's regular rate. Sleep terrors cause people to be jolted into motion, often sitting up suddenly in bed. People sometimes scream or cry. The person's facial expression may be fearful.

People experiencing sleep terror disorder sometimes get out of bed and act as if they are fighting or fleeing something. During this time injuries can occur. Cases have been reported of people falling out of windows or falling down stairs during episodes of sleep terror.

People experiencing sleep terror are not fully awake. They are nearly impossible to bring to consciousness or comfort, and sometimes respond violently to attempts to console or restrain them. In many cases, once the episode is over the person returns to sleep without ever waking fully. People often do not have any recollection of the episode after later awaking normally, although they may recall a sense of fear.

Episodes of sleep terror usually occur during the first third of a person's night sleep, although they can occur even during naps taken in the daytime. The average sleep terror episode lasts less than 15 minutes. Usually only one episode occurs per night, but in some cases terror episodes occur in clusters. It is unusual for a person to have many episodes in a single night, although upwards of 40 have been reported. Most persons with the disorder have only one occurrence per week, or just a few per month.

Demographics

Sleep terror disorder is much more common in children than it is in adults. It is estimated that approximately 1%–6% of children in the United States experience sleep terror at some point in their childhood. For most children, sleep terrors begin between the ages of four and 12. The problem usually disappears during adolescence. Sleep terror disorder appears to be more common in boys than in girls; some studies have reported that preadolescent boys are the group most commonly affected. No figures are available for the rates of the disorder in different racial or ethnic groups. Sleep terrors in children are not associated with any psychological disorders.

Fewer than 1% of adults have sleep terror disorder. For most adults, sleep terrors begin in their 20s or 30s, although it is possible for someone to suffer from episodes of sleep terror from childhood onward. In the adult population, sleep terrors affect both sexes equally. They are, however, often associated with psychological disorders, most commonly anxiety, personality, or post-traumatic disorders. People who have a family history of sleep terrors or **sleepwalking disorder** are about 10 times more likely to develop sleep terror disorder than those who do not.

Diagnosis

Sleep terror is diagnosed most often in children when parents express concern to the child's pediatrician. A fact sheet from the American Academy of Child and Adolescent Psychiatry suggests that parents consult a child **psychiatrist** if the child has several episodes of sleep terror each night, if the episodes occur every night for weeks at a time, or if they interfere with the child's daytime activities. The **diagnosis** is usually made on the basis of the child's and parents' description of the symptoms. There are no laboratory tests for sleep terror disorder. In adults, the disorder is usually self-reported to the patient's family doctor. Again, the diagnosis is usually based on the patient's description of the symptoms.

Sleep terror is characterized by an abrupt arousal from sleep followed by symptoms of extreme fear. The symptoms often include screams, rapid heartbeat, heavy breathing, and sweating, as well as a subjective feeling of terror. According to the ***Diagnostic and Statistical Manual of Mental Disorders***, fourth edition, text revision (*DSM-IV-TR*), which is the standard reference work used by mental health professionals to diagnose mental disorders, people with sleep terror disorder do not respond to attempts to comfort or awaken them. In order to meet criteria for the diagnosis, the patients must not be able to recall their dreams, and they must not remember the episode itself. In addition, the episodes may not be attributed to a medical condition or drug use.

Sleep terror disorder is frequently confused with **nightmare disorder**. The two are similar in the sense that both are related to bad dreams. Nightmare disorder, however, involves a significantly smaller amount of physical movement than does sleep terror. Normally, people experiencing nightmare disorder do not get out of bed.

Moreover, people experiencing nightmare disorder often have problems going back to sleep because of the nature of their dream. Most people experiencing sleep terrors, however, go back to deep sleep without ever having fully awakened. People experiencing nightmares can generally remember their dreams and some of the events in the dream leading up to their awakening. People often awake from nightmares just as they are about to experience the most frightening part of a disturbing dream. People experiencing sleep terrors, however, can sometimes recall a sense of profound fear, but often do not remember the episode at all.

Treatments

If sleep terror episodes are infrequent, then treatment may not be necessary as long as the episodes are not

KEY TERMS

Hypnotic—A type of medication that induces sleep.

Pavor nocturnus—The Latin medical term for sleep terror disorder.

interfering significantly with the person's life. Some people may want to rearrange their bedroom furniture to minimize the possibility of hurting themselves or others if they get out of bed during a sleep terror episode. To keep children from becoming overly worried about their sleep terrors, experts suggest that parents avoid placing unnecessary emphasis on the episodes. **Psychotherapy** is often helpful for adults concerned about the specific triggers of sleep terror episodes.

Several different medications have been used to treat sleep terror disorder, with varying degrees of success. One of the most common is **diazepam** (Valium). Diazepam is a hypnotic (sleep-inducing medication), and is thought to be useful in the prevention of sleep terror episodes because it acts as a nervous system depressant. There are many different types of hypnotics, and choosing one for a patient depends on other drugs that the patient may be taking, any medical or psychological conditions, and other health factors. Most studies of medications as treatments for sleep terror disorder have been done on adult patients; there is little information available on the use of medications to treat the disorder in children.

Prognosis

In most children, sleep terror disorder resolves before or during adolescence without any treatment. Adults often respond well to diazepam or another hypnotic. Psychotherapy and avoidance of stressors that may precipitate terror episodes may be helpful as well. Episodes of sleep terrors often decrease with age. This decrease is due to the fact that the amount of slow-wave sleep, which is the sleep phase during which terror episodes usually occur, declines with age.

Resources

BOOKS

Aldrich, Michael S. *Sleep Medicines.* New York: Oxford University Press,1999.

American Psychiatric Association. *Diagnostic and Statistical Manual of Mental Disorders.* 4th ed. text revised. Washington DC: American Psychiatric Association, 2000.

Chokroverty, Susan, ed. *Sleep Disorders Medicine: Basic Science, Technical Considerations, and Clinical Aspects.* 2nd ed. Boston: Butterworth-Heinemann, 1999.

Sadock, Benjamin J. and Virginia A. Sadock, eds. *Comprehensive Textbook of Psychiatry.* 7th ed. Vol. 2. Philadelphia: Lippincott Williams and Wilkins, 2000.

Thorpy, Michael J, ed. *Handbook of Sleep Disorders.* New York: Marcel Dekker Inc., 1990.

PERIODICALS

Owens, Judith A., Richard P. Millman, Anthony Spirito. "Sleep Terrors in a 5-Year-Old Girl." *Pediatrics & Adolescent Medicine* 153, no. 3 (March 1999).

ORGANIZATIONS

American Academy of Child and Adolescent Psychiatry. 3615 Wisconsin Avenue NW, Washington, DC 20016-3007. (202) 966-7300. Fax: (202) 966-2891. <www.aacap.org>.

American Academy of Sleep Medicine. 6301 Bandel Road NW, Suite 101, Rochester, MN 55901. (507) 287-6006. <www.asda.org>.

OTHER

American Academy of Child & Adolescent Psychiatry (AACAP). "Children's Sleep Problems." AACAP Facts For Families Pamphlet #34. Washington, DC: American Academy of Child & Adolescent Psychiatry, 2000.

Tish Davidson, A.M.

Sleepwalking disorder

Definition

Sleepwalking disorder, also called somnambulism, is characterized by repeating episodes of motor activity during sleep such as sitting up in bed, rising, and walking around, among others. The person appears to be awake because their eyes are usually open and they can maneuver around objects, but is considered asleep.

Sleepwalking disorder is one of several **sleep disorders** listed in the ***Diagnostic and Statistical Manual of Mental Disorders***, often called *DSM-IV-TR*, produced by the American Psychiatric Association and used by most mental health professionals in North America and Europe to diagnose mental disorders.

Description

Sleepwalking episodes usually occur during the first third of the night during the deepest phase of sleep. The episodes can last anywhere from a few minutes up to one hour, with five to 15 minutes being average. Sleepwalkers appear to be awake but are typically unresponsive to individuals who attempt to communicate with them. Persons who sleepwalk typically have no memory or awareness of their actions or movement upon waking.

Causes and symptoms

Causes

There appears to be a genetic component for individuals who sleepwalk. The condition is 10 times more likely to occur in close relatives of known sleepwalkers than in the general public. These families also tend to be deep sleepers.

Sleepwalking may also be triggered by fever, which directly affects the nervous system, general illness, alcohol use, sleep deprivation, and emotional **stress**. Hormonal changes that occur during adolescence, menstruation, and pregnancy can be also be triggers for sleepwalking. Sleepwalking episodes are more likely during times of physiological or psychological stress.

Certain classes of medication have also been shown to precipitate sleepwalking episodes in some individuals. These include: Anti-anxiety or sleep-inducing drugs, antiseizure medications, stimulants, antihistamines, and anti-arrhythmic heart drugs.

Symptoms

The *DSM-IV-TR* specifies six diagnostic criteria for sleepwalking disorder:

- Repeated episodes of rising from bed during sleep: These episodes may include sitting up in bed, looking around, and walking, and usually occur during the first third of the night.
- Is unresponsive to attempts at communication: During sleepwalking, the person typically has eyes open, dilated pupils, a blank stare, and does not respond to another's attempts at communication. Affected persons typically are only awakened with great difficulty.
- No recollection of the sleepwalking incident: Upon waking, the person typically has no memory of the sleepwalking events. If the individual does awaken from the sleepwalking episode, they may have a vague memory of the incident. Often, sleepwalkers will return to bed, or fall asleep in another place with no recall as to how they got there.
- No impairment of mental activity upon waking: If an individual awakens during a sleepwalking episode, there may be a short period of confusion or disorientation, but there is no impairment of mental activity or behavior.
- Causes significant distress to life situations: Sleepwalking causes significant disruption of social and occupational situations, or affects other abilities to function.
- Not due to substance use or abuse: Sleepwalking disorder is not diagnosed if the cause is related to drug abuse, medication, or a general medical condition.

Demographics

Sleepwalking can occur at any age but is most common in children, with the first episodes usually between the ages of four and eight years. The peak of sleepwalking behavior occurs at about 12 years of age. Between 10 and 30% of children have had at least one episode of sleepwalking. Sleepwalking disorder is seen in only 1–5% of children and occurs more frequently in boys. Adults who sleepwalk typically have a history of sleepwalking that stems back to childhood. Sleepwalking events occur in approximately 1–7% of adults while sleepwalking disorder occurs in about 0.5%.

Diagnosis

The line that separates periodic sleepwalking from sleepwalking disorder is not clearly defined. Individuals or families most often seek professional help when the episodes of sleepwalking are violent, pose a risk for injury, or impair the person's ability to function. For a **diagnosis** of sleepwalking disorder to be made, the person must experience a significant amount of social, occupational, or other impairment related to the sleepwalking problem. Episodes that have a long history extending from childhood through adolescence and especially into adulthood are more likely to be diagnosed with sleepwalking disorder.

Since the individual cannot recall the sleepwalking activity, diagnosis by means of interview is of little benefit, unless it involves someone who has witnessed the sleepwalking behavior. The preferred method for accurate diagnosis is through **polysomnography**. This technique involves hooking electrodes to different locations on the affected person's body to monitor **brain** wave activity, heart rate, breathing, and other vital signs while the individual sleeps. Monitoring brain-wave patterns and physiologic responses during sleep can usually give sleep specialists an accurate diagnosis of the condition and determine the effective means of treatment, if any.

Sleepwalking disorder can be difficult to distinguish from **sleep terror disorder**. In both cases, the individual has motor movement, is difficult to awaken, and does not remember the incident. The primary difference is that sleep terror disorder typically has an initial scream and signs of intense fear and panic associated with the other behaviors.

Treatments

Treatment for sleepwalking is often unnecessary, especially if episodes are infrequent and pose no hazard to the sleepwalker or others. If sleepwalking is recurrent, or daytime **fatigue** is suspected to result from disturbed sleep patterns, polysomnography may be recommended to determine whether some form of treatment may be helpful. If stress appears to trigger sleepwalking events in adults, stress management, **biofeedback** training, or relaxation techniques can be beneficial. Hypnosis has been used help sleepwalkers awaken once their feet touch the floor. **Psychotherapy** may help individuals who have underlying psychological issues that could be contributing to sleep problems.

Medications are sometimes used in the more severe cases with adults. Benzodiazepines—anti-anxiety drugs—such as **diazepam** (Valium) or **alprazolam** (Xanax) can be used to help relax muscles, although these may not result in fewer episodes of sleepwalking. When medications are used, they are typically prescribed in the lowest dose necessary and only for a limited period.

Prognosis

Most cases of sleepwalking subside over time. Sleepwalking in childhood usually disappears without treatment by age 15. If sleepwalking episodes persist into early adulthood, treatment is recommended. With an accurate diagnosis and appropriate treatment, episodes of sleepwalking can be greatly reduced and, in some cases, eliminated.

Prevention

In children, sleepwalking is relatively common and is not cause for concern. The major risk associated with sleepwalking is accidental injury. Parents should take precautions to block stairways, lock windows, keep floors cleared of harmful objects, etc.

If taking certain medications, a medical condition, or exposure to significant stressors are suspected triggers of sleepwalking episodes, a doctor should be consulted for a complete assessment.

Resources

BOOKS

American Psychiatric Association. *Diagnostic and Statistical Manual of Mental Disorders.* 4th edition, text revised. Washington, DC: American Psychiatric Association, 2000.

Beers, Mark H., M.D., and Robert Berkow, M.D., eds. *The Merck Manual of Diagnosis and Therapy.* 17th edition. Whitehouse Station, NJ: Merck Research Laboratories, 1999.

Hales, Diane., Robert E. Hales, M.D. *Caring for the Mind: The Comprehensive Guide to Mental Health.* New York: Bantam Books, 1995.

ORGANIZATIONS

American Academy of Sleep Medicine. 6301 Bandel Road NW, Suite 101, Rochester, MN 55901, (507) 287-6006 <http://www.assmnet.org/>.

American Psychiatric Association. 1400 K Street NW, Washington D.C. 20005. <http://www.psych.org>.

Better Sleep Council. 501 Wythe Street, Alexandria, VA 22314. (703) 683-8371. <http://www.bettersleep.org/>.

Health Communications.com. *Sleep Channel.* <http://www.sleepdisorderchannel.net/sleepwalking/index.shtml>.

Gary Gilles, M.A.

Smoking *see* **Nicotine and related disorders**

Social phobia

Definition

Social phobia is defined by *DSM-IV-TR* as an anxiety disorder characterized by a strong and persistent fear of social or performance situations in which the patient might feel embarrassment or humiliation. Generalized social phobia refers to a fear of most social interactions combined with fear of most performance situations, such as speaking in public or eating in a restaurant. Persons who are afraid of only one type of performance situation or afraid of only a few rather than most social situations may be described as having nongeneralized, circumscribed, or specific social phobia.

Social phobia, which is also known as social anxiety disorder, is a serious mental health problem in the United States. In any given year, social phobia affects 3.7% of the American population between the ages of 18 and 54, or about 5.3 million people. It is the third most common psychiatric condition after depression and alcoholism. Patients diagnosed with social phobia have the highest risk of alcohol abuse of all patients with anxiety disorders; in addition, they suffer from worse impairment than patients with major medical illnesses, including congestive heart failure and diabetes.

KEY TERMS

Amygdala—An almond-shaped brain structure in the limbic system that is activated in acute stress situations to trigger the emotion of fear. Some studies suggest that social phobia may be related to changes in or overfunctioning of the amygdala.

Behavioral inhibition—A set of behaviors that appear in early infancy that are displayed when the child is confronted with a new situation or unfamiliar people. These behaviors include moving around, crying, and general irritability, followed by withdrawing, and seeking comfort from a familiar person. These behaviors are associated with an increased risk of social phobia and panic disorder in later life. Behavioral inhibition in children appears to be linked to anxiety and mood disorders in their parents.

Cognitive restructuring—An approach to psychotherapy that focuses on helping the patient examine distorted patterns of perceiving and thinking in order to change their emotional responses to people and situations.

Exposure therapy—A form of cognitive-behavioral therapy in which patients suffering from phobias are exposed to their feared objects or situations while accompanied by the therapist. The length of exposure is gradually increased until the association between the feared situation and the patient's experienced panic symptoms is no longer present.

Limbic system—A group of structures in the brain that includes the amygdala, hippocampus, olfactory bulbs, and hypothalamus. The limbic system is associated with homeostasis and the regulation and arousal of emotions.

Mutism—Inability to speak due to conscious refusal or psychogenic inhibition. Mutism is a common symptom of social phobia in children.

Performance anxiety—A subcategory of circumscribed social phobia in which the patient's fear is limited to performing certain activities or tasks in public. Common areas of performance anxiety include public speaking, acting on stage, solo singing, and playing instrumental solos.

Phobia—Irrational fear of places, things, or situations that lead to avoidance.

Social modeling—A process of learning behavioral and emotional response patterns from observing one's parents or other adults. Some researchers think that social modeling plays a part in the development of social phobia.

Temperament—A person's natural disposition or inborn combination of mental and emotional traits. Children with a shy or withdrawn temperament are at increased risk of developing social phobia in adolescence.

Description

Social phobia varies in its development and initial presentation. In some young people, the disorder grows out of a long-term history of shyness or social inhibition. In others, social phobia becomes apparent following a move to a new school or similar developmental challenge. In adults, circumscribed social phobia may be associated with a change of occupation or job promotion, the most common example being the emergence of the disorder with regard to public speaking in a person whose previous jobs did not require them to make presentations or speeches in front of others. The onset of social phobia may be insidious, which means that it gets worse by slow degrees. About half of all patients, however, experience a sudden onset of social phobia following a particularly humiliating or frightening experience. For example, in one British case study the patient's social phobia developed abruptly after her father's sudden death. The patient had had an argument with him one morning and he was killed in an accident later in the day. The onset of social phobia almost always occurs in childhood or the mid-teens; onset after age 25 is unusual. The disorder is often a lifelong problem, although its severity may diminish in adult life.

Adults and adolescents with social phobia, as well as many children with the disorder, have sufficient insight to recognize that their fears are excessive or unwarranted. This factor often adds to their distress and feelings of inferiority.

Social phobia is of major concern to society as a whole for two reasons. One reason is the disorder's very high rate of comorbidity with such other mental health problems as major depression and substance abuse. In comparison with patients diagnosed with other anxiety disorders, patients with social phobia have higher averages of concurrent anxiety disorders (1.21 versus 0.45); comorbid depression or other disorders (2.05 versus 1.19); and lifetime disorders (3.11 versus 2.05). The most common comorbid disorders diagnosed in patients with social phobia are major depression (43%); **panic disorder** (33%); **generalized anxiety disorder** (19%); PTSD (36%); alcohol or substance abuse disorder (18%); and attempted **suicide** (23%).

The second reason is the loss to the larger society of the gifts and talents that these patients possess. Social phobia can have a devastating effect on young people's intellectual life and choice of career, causing them to abandon their educations, stay stuck in dead-end jobs, refuse promotions involving travel or relocation, and make similar self-defeating choices because of their fear of classroom participation, job interviews, and other social interactions in educational and workplace settings. One sample of patients diagnosed with social phobia found that almost half had failed to finish high school; 70% were in the bottom two quartiles of socioeconomic status (SES); and 22% were on welfare. In addition to their academic and employment-related difficulties, people with social phobia have limited or nonexistent social support networks. They are less likely to marry and start families of their own because of their fear of interpersonal relationships. Many continue to live at home with their parents even as adults, or remain in unfulfilling relationships.

Causes and symptoms

Causes

The causes of social phobia appear to be a combination of physical and environmental factors.

NEUROBIOLOGICAL FACTORS. There is some evidence as of 2002 that social phobia can be inherited. A group of researchers at Yale has identified a genetic locus on human chromosome 3 that is linked to **agoraphobia** and two genetic loci on chromosomes 1 and 11q linked to panic disorder. Because social phobia shares some traits with panic disorder, it is likely that there are also genes that govern a person's susceptibility to social phobia. In addition, researchers at the National Institute of Mental Health (NIMH) have identified a gene in mice that appears to govern fearfulness.

Positron emission tomography (PET) scans of patients diagnosed with social phobia indicate that blood flow is increased in a region of the **brain** (the amygdala) associated with fear responses when the patients are asked to speak in public. In contrast, PET scans of control subjects without social phobia show that blood flow during the public speaking exercise is increased in the cerebral cortex, an area of the brain associated with thinking and evaluation rather than emotional arousal. The researchers have concluded that patients with social phobia have a different neurochemical response to certain social situations or challenges that activates the limbic system rather than the cerebral cortex.

TEMPERAMENT. A number of researchers have pointed to inborn temperament (natural predisposition) as a broad vulnerability factor in the development of anxiety and mood disorders, including social phobia. More specifically, children who manifest what is known as behavioral inhibition in early infancy are at increased risk for developing more than one anxiety disorder in adult life, particularly if the inhibition remains over time. Behavioral inhibition refers to a group of behaviors that are displayed when the child is confronted with a new situation or unfamiliar people. These behaviors include moving around, crying, and general irritability, followed by withdrawing, seeking comfort from a familiar person, and stopping what one is doing when one notices the new person or situation. Children of depressed or anxious parents are more likely to develop behavioral inhibition. One study of preadolescent children diagnosed with social phobia reported that many of these children had been identified as behaviorally inhibited in early childhood.

PSYCHOSOCIAL FACTORS. The development of social phobia is also influenced by parent-child interactions in a patient's family of origin. Several studies have found that the children of parents with major depression, whether or not it is comorbid with panic disorder, are at increased risk of developing social phobia. Children of parents with major depression and comorbid panic disorder are at increased risk of developing more than one anxiety disorder. A family pattern of social phobia, however, is stronger for the generalized than for the specific or circumscribed subtype.

It is highly likely that the children of depressed parents may acquire certain attitudes and behaviors from their parents that make them more susceptible to developing social phobia. One study of children with social phobia found that their cognitive assessment of ambiguous situations was strongly negative, not only with regard to the dangerousness of the situation but also in terms of their ability to cope with it. In other words, these children tend to overestimate the threats and dangers in life and to underestimate their strength, intelligence, and other resources for coping. This process of learning from observing the behavior of one's parents or other adults is called social **modeling**.

Still another psychosocial factor related to the development of social phobia in children and adolescents is the general disintegration in the social fabric of the developed countries since World War II. A number of social theorists as well as physicians and therapists have noted that children are exposed more frequently to both real-life and media depictions of aggressive behavior and abrasive language than earlier generations. Children also learn about frightening or unpleasant social realities at earlier and earlier ages. The increased rate of social phobia and school refusal among adolescent girls has been linked to the greater crudity of teasing from boys in junior high and high school. The American Association of University Women released a study in 1998 that reported that 70% of girls experience verbal sexual harassment in high school and 50%, unwanted sexual touching. In addition, the fortress mentality reflected in the architecture of high-rise apartment buildings and gated communities for those who can afford them also sends children the message that other people are to be feared. While trends in the larger society may not directly cause social phobia (or other mental disorders), they are nonetheless important indirect influences.

Symptoms

The symptoms of social phobia are somewhat different in children and adults, in that the early onset of social phobia typically means that children with the disorder fail to achieve at their predicted level, whereas adults and adolescents show declines from previously achieved levels of functioning.

SYMPTOMS IN CHILDREN. Symptoms of social phobia in children frequently include tantrums, crying, "freezing," clinging to parents or other familiar people, and inhibiting interactions to the point of refusing to talk to others (mutism).

SYMPTOMS IN ADULTS. The symptoms of social phobia in adults include a range of physical signs of anxiety as well as attitudes and behaviors.

- blushing, sweating, nausea, diarrhea, dry mouth, tremors, and other physical indications of anxiety
- difficulties with self-assertion
- extreme sensitivity to criticism, rejection, or negative evaluations
- intense preoccupation with the reactions and responses of others
- heightened fears of being embarrassed or humiliated
- avoidance of the feared situation(s) and anticipatory anxiety

In adults, there is often a "vicious circle" quality to the symptoms, in that the anxiety and symptoms lead to actual or perceived poor performances, which in turn increase the anxiety and avoidance. A common example is performance anxiety related to musical instruments; the person who is afraid of having to play the piano in a

Social phobia is an anxiety disorder characterized by a strong and persistent fear of social or performance situations in which the patient might feel embarrassment or humiliation. Performance situations are those such as speaking in front of an audience. *(Bill Varie/CORBIS. Photo reproduced by permission.)*

recital, for example, may become so anxious that the muscles in the hands become tense, thus producing frequent mistakes in fingering and sound production during the recital performance.

Not all adults with social phobia appear shy or outwardly nervous to other people. Some adults are able to force themselves to attend social events, give public presentations, or interact with others by self-medicating with alcohol or limiting the time period of their interactions. These strategies, however, prevent the underlying fears and disabilities from being addressed.

Demographics

The prevalence of social phobia in the general United States population is difficult to evaluate because researchers differ in their estimation of the threshold of "significant interference" with the person's occupational or educational functioning. In addition, different studies have focused on different subtypes of social phobia. One study found that about 20% of the adults surveyed reported high levels of anxiety related to public speaking or other types of public performance, but only 2% indicated sufficient distress to meet the diagnostic criteria of social phobia. Because of these differences in measurement, epidemiological and community-based studies give figures for a lifetime prevalence of social phobia that fall between 3% and 13%.

The types of situations associated with social phobia are different in the general population as contrasted with clinical populations. Surveys of adults in the general population indicate that most people diagnosed with social phobia are afraid of public speaking; only 45% report being afraid of meeting new people or having to talk to strangers. Fears related to eating, drinking, or writing in public, or using a public restroom, are much less common in this group of patients. By contrast, people being treated for social phobia in outpatient clinics are more likely to be afraid of a range of social situations rather than just one. Social phobia accounts for 10%–20% of the anxiety disorders diagnosed in patients in outpatient clinics, but it is rarely the reason for hospitalizing a patient.

The same difference between general and clinical populations affects the sex ratios given for social phobia. Community-based studies suggest that social phobia is more common in women, but in most samples of clinical patients, the sex ratio is either 1:1 or males are in the majority. A study of social phobia in prepubertal children found that girls were more likely to verbalize anxiety than boys, but the researchers who observed the children interact with adults and with one another did not observe any behavioral differences between boys and girls. The researchers concluded that the apparently higher rates of social phobia in women may simply reflect women's greater openness about their feelings.

With regard to race, the same study found no statistically significant difference in the incidence of social phobia between Caucasian and African American children. This finding was consistent with a 1995 study that failed to find differences based on race in lists of children's top 10 fears. Further research, however, is necessary in order to determine whether social phobia has different symptom patterns or rates of development in different racial or ethnic groups.

The demographics of social phobia in young children are particularly difficult to determine because of changes in diagnostic categories and criteria in successive editions of *DSM*. Social phobia was introduced as a diagnostic category in *DSM-III*, which was published in 1980. Neither *DSM-III* nor its 1987 revision restricted social phobia to adults, but the disorder was rarely diagnosed in children—most likely because *DSM-III* and *DSM-III-R* listed two diagnoses for children, overanxious disorder and avoidant disorder of childhood, whose symptoms overlapped with those of social phobia. Statistics based on *DSM-III-R*'s criteria for social phobia placed the prevalence of the disorder in children in the general population at about 1%. The revisions of the diagnostic criteria in *DSM-IV*, however, have led to an apparent dramatic increase in the prevalence of social phobia in children. One study done in 1997 reported that 18% of the children in a clinical sample met *DSM-III-R* criteria for social phobia, but that 40% of the children in the same sample had social phobia according to *DSM-IV* criteria.

Diagnosis

The **diagnosis** of social phobia is usually made on the basis of the patient's history and reported symptoms. The doctor may also decide to administer diagnostic questionnaires intended to rule out other phobias, other anxiety disorders, and major depression. In diagnosing a child, the doctor will usually ask the child's parents, teachers, or others who know the child well for their observations.

Children and adolescents

A doctor who is evaluating a child for social phobia must take into account that children do not have the freedom that adults usually have to avoid the situations that frighten them. As a result, they may not be able to explain why they are anxious. It is important to evaluate the child's capacity for social relationships with people that he or she knows; and to assess his or her interactions with peers for indications of social phobia, not only his or her behavior around adults.

A semi-structured interview that a doctor can use to assess social phobia in children is the Anxiety Disorders Interview Schedule for Children, or ADIS-C. A newer clinician-administered test is the Liebowitz Social Anxiety Scale for Children and Adolescents, or LSAS-CA. Self-report inventories for children include the **Child Depression Inventory**, or CDI, and the Social Phobia and Anxiety Inventory for Children, or SPAI-C. Parents can be asked to complete the Child Behavior Checklist (CBL), and teachers may be given the Teacher's Report Form (TRF).

Adults

Diagnostic instruments for assessing social phobia in adults are more problematic. Some general screeners that are used in primary care settings, such as the Structured Clinical Interview for DSM-IV-Screen (SCID-Screen), do include questions related to social phobia but can take as long as 25 minutes to administer. Others, such as the Primary Care Evaluation of Mental Disorders, or Prime-MD, are not specific for social phobia. Instruments designed to measure social phobia by itself, such as the Fear of Negative Evaluation Scale and the Social Avoidance and Distress Scale, are lengthy and generally more useful for monitoring the progress of therapy. Another clinician-administered interview for social phobia in adults, the Liebowitz Social Anxiety Scale (LSAS), is not yet in widespread use.

Many physicians, however, have found that the addition of a few selected questions to a general screener for mental disorders is helpful in detecting social phobia. One study found that giving patients three specific statements with yes/no answers detected 89% of cases of social phobia:

- Being embarrassed or looking stupid are among my worst fears.
- Fear of embarrassment causes me to avoid doing things or speaking to people.
- I avoid activities in which I am the center of attention.

As of 2002 there are no laboratory tests or brain imaging techniques that can help to diagnose social phobia in adults.

Treatments

Social phobia responds well to proper treatment; however, patients with social phobia have a distinctive set of barriers to treatment. Unlike persons with some other types of mental disorders, they are unlikely to deny that they have a problem. What researchers have found is that in comparison to persons suffering from other disorders, persons with social phobia are significantly more likely to say that financial problems, uncertainty over where to go for help, and fear of what others might think prevent them from seeking treatment. The researchers concluded that providing better information about community services as well as easing the psychological and financial burdens of patients with social phobia would significantly improve their chances of recovery. Left untreated, social phobia can become a chronic, disabling disorder that increases the patient's risk of suicide.

Medications

About 53% of patients diagnosed with social phobia are treated with medications. Drug treatment has proven beneficial to patients with this disorder; however, no one type of medication appears to be clearly superior to others. Selection of a medication depends on the subtype of the patient's social phobia; the presence of other mental disorders; and the patient's occupation and personal preferences.

Specific medications that are used to treat social phobia include:

- Benzodiazepine tranquilizers. These are often prescribed for patients who need immediate relief from anxiety. They have two major drawbacks, however; they are habit-forming, and they are unsuitable for patients with comorbid alcohol or substance abuse disorders. Benzodiazepines are, however, sometimes prescribed for patients who have a low risk for substance abuse and have not responded to other medications.
- Monoamine oxidase inhibitors (MAOIs). About two-thirds of patients with social phobia show significant improvement when treated with these drugs. MAOIs, however, have the disadvantage of requiring patients to stick to a low-tyramine diet that excludes many popular foods, and requiring them to avoid many over-the-counter cold and cough preparations.
- Selective serotonin reuptake inhibitors (SSRIs). About 50%–75% of patients with social phobia benefit from treatment with SSRIs. The SSRIs appear to work best in patients with comorbid major depression or panic disorder. **Sertraline** (Zoloft) has been recommended for patients with generalized social phobia.
- Newer drugs. A recent placebo-controlled study indicates that **gabapentin** (Neurontin) shows promise as a treatment for social phobia.
- **Beta blockers**. These medications, which include **propranolol** (Inderal), are given to patients with mild to moderate circumscribed performance anxiety. The patient takes the medication on an as-needed basis rather than a standing dosage. Beta-blockers do not appear to be helpful for patients with generalized social phobia.

Psychotherapy

The type of **psychotherapy** most commonly recommended for treatment of social phobia is **cognitive-behavioral therapy** (CBT). Mild to moderate cases of social phobia often show considerable improvement with CBT alone; patients with more severe social phobia benefit from a combination of CBT and an appropriate medication. Cognitive-behavioral treatment of adults diagnosed with social phobia usually combines exposure therapy with cognitive restructuring techniques. In exposure therapy, the patient is exposed to small "doses" of the feared situation that are gradually lengthened in time. The chief drawback to exposure therapy for social phobia is that some feared situations are easier to replicate for purposes of treatment than others. Patients who are afraid of public speaking or musical performance can practice performing in front of any group of people that can be collected to help; but it is not so easy to arrange exposure sessions for a patient who is afraid of interactions with a specific teacher, employer, or supervisor. The other aspect of CBT that is used in treating social phobia in adults is cognitive restructuring. This approach challenges the patient to reconsider and then replace the biased cognitions that have led him or her to overestimate the dangers in social situations and to underestimate his or her own resources for coping with them.

Several trial programs of CBT **group therapy** have been used with adolescents with social phobia. One pilot program situated the group meetings in the school rather than in a clinic, on the grounds that most of the fears of adolescents with social phobia revolve around school activities. Another CBT group for adolescents was conducted in a clinical setting. Both programs included **social skills training** alongside exposure therapy and cognitive restructuring, and both were reported to be moderately successful at one-year follow-up.

Other

Other approaches that have been used to treat social phobia include **family therapy** and relaxation techniques.

Prognosis

The prognosis for recovery from social phobia is good, given early diagnosis and appropriate treatment. The prognosis for persons with untreated social phobia, however, is poor. In most cases, these individuals become long-term underachievers, at high risk for alcoholism, major depression, and suicide.

Prevention

Given that some of the factors implicated in social phobia are neurobiological or genetic, the best preventive strategy as of 2002 is early identification of children with behavioral inhibition and developing techniques for assisting their social development.

See also Child Depression Inventory; Exposure Treatment

Resources

BOOKS

American Psychiatric Association. *Diagnostic and Statistical Manual of Mental Disorders.* 4th edition, text revised. Washington, DC: American Psychiatric Association, 2000.

"Phobic Disorders," Section 15, Chapter 187 in*The Merck Manual of Diagnosis and Therapy*, edited by Mark H. Beers, MD, and Robert Berkow, MD. Whitehouse Station, NJ: Merck Research Laboratories, 2001.

Rowe, Dorothy. *Beyond Fear.* London, UK: Fontana/ Collins, 1987.

PERIODICALS

Beidel, Deborah C., and others. "Psychopathology of Childhood Social Phobia." *Journal of the American Academy of Child and Adolescent Psychiatry* 38 (June 1999): 643.

Biederman, Joseph, Stephen V. Faraone, Dina R. Hirshfeld-Becker, and others. "Patterns of Psychopathology and Dysfunction in High-Risk Children of Parents with Panic Disorder and Major Depression." *American Journal of Psychiatry* 158 (January 2001): 49-57.

Bogels, Susan M., and Denise Zigterman. "Dysfunctional Cognitions in Children with Social Phobia, Separation Anxiety Disorder, and Generalized Anxiety Disorder." *Journal of Abnormal Child Psychology* 28 (April 2000): 205.

Bruce, Timothy J., PhD, and Sy A. Saeed, MD. "Social Anxiety Disorder: A Common, Underrecognized Mental Disorder." *American Family Physician* 60 (November 15, 1999): 2311-2322.

Hayward, C., and others. "Cognitive-Behavioral Group Therapy for Social Phobia in Female Adolescents: Results of a Pilot Study." *Journal of the American Academy of Child and Adolescent Psychiatry* 39 (June 2000): 721-726.

Kubetin, Sally Koch. "Social Phobia Dx Missed." *OB/GYN News* 36 (September 15, 2001): 23.

McHugh, Paul R., MD. "How Psychiatry Lost Its Way." *Commentary* 108 (December 1999): 32.

Masia, Carrie L., and others. "School-Based Behavioral Treatment for Social Anxiety Disorder in Adolescents: Results of a Pilot Study." *Journal of the American Academy of Child and Adolescent Psychiatry* 40 (July 2001): 780-786.

Olfson, Mark, Mary Guardino, Elmer Struening, and others. "Barriers to the Treatment of Social Anxiety." *American Journal of Psychiatry* 157 (April 2001): 521-527.

Pande, A. C., J. R. T. Davidson, J. W. Jefferson, and others. "Treatment of Social Phobia with Gabapentin: A Placebo-Controlled Study." *Journal of Clinical Psychopharmacology* 19 (1999): 341-348.

Stein, Murray B. "Social Anxiety Disorder and the Risk of Depression: A Prospective Community Study of Adolescents and Young Adults." *Journal of the American Medical Association* 285 (June 13, 2001): 2839.

Tillfors, Maria, Tomas Furmark, Ina Marteinsdottir, and others. "Cerebral Blood Flow in Subjects with Social Phobia During Stressful Speaking Tasks: A PET Study." *American Journal of Psychiatry* 158 (August 2001): 1220-1226.

Van Ameringen, M. A., R. M. Lane, R. C. Bowen, and others. "Sertraline Treatment of Generalized Social Phobia: A 20-Week, Double-Blind, Placebo-Controlled Study." *American Journal of Psychiatry* 158 (2001): 275-281.

Zoler, Mitchel L. "Drug Update: SSRIs in Social Phobia." *Family Practice News* 31 (February 1, 2001): 28.

ORGANIZATIONS

Anxiety Disorders Association of America. 11900 Parklawn Drive, Suite 100, Rockville, MD 20852-2624. (301) 231-9350. <www.adaa.org>.

Anxiety Disorders Education Program, National Institute of Mental Health. 6001 Executive Blvd., Room 8184, MSC 9663, Bethesda, MD 20892-9663. (301) 443-4513. <www.nimh.nih.gov>.

OTHER

National Institute of Mental Health (NIMH). *Facts About Social Phobia.* NIH publication OM-99 4171, revised edition (2000). <www.nimh.nih.gov/anxiety/phobiafacts.cfm>.

Rebecca J. Frey, Ph.D.

Social skills training

Definition

Social skills training (SST) is a form of behavior therapy used by teachers, therapists, and trainers to help persons who have difficulties relating to other people.

Purpose

Goals

A major goal of social skills training is teaching persons who may or may not have emotional problems about the verbal as well as nonverbal behaviors involved in social interactions. There are many people who have never been taught such interpersonal skills as making "small talk" in social settings, or the importance of good eye contact during a conversation. In addition, many people have not learned to "read" the many subtle cues contained in social interactions, such as how to tell when someone wants to change the topic of conversation or shift to another activity. Social skills training helps patients to learn to interpret these and other social signals, so that they can determine how to act appropriately in the company of other people in a variety of different situations. SST proceeds on the assumption that when people improve their social skills or change selected behaviors, they will raise their self-esteem and increase the likelihood that others will respond favorably to them. Trainees learn to change their social behavior patterns by practicing selected behaviors in individual or **group therapy** sessions. Another goal of social skills training is improving a patient's ability to function in everyday social situations. Social skills training can help patients to work on specific issues—for example, improving one's telephone manners—that interfere with their jobs or daily lives.

Treatment of specific disorders

A person who lacks certain social skills may have great difficulty building a network of supportive friends and acquaintances as he or she grows older, and may become socially isolated. Moreover, one of the consequences of loneliness is an increased risk of developing emotional problems or mental disorders. Social skills training has been shown to be effective in treating patients with a broad range of emotional problems and diagnoses. Some of the disorders treated by social skills trainers include shyness; adjustment disorders; marital and family conflicts, anxiety disorders, **attention-deficit/hyperactivity disorder**, **social phobia**, alcohol dependence; depression; **bipolar disorder**; **schizophrenia**; developmental disabilities; **avoidant personality disorder**; **paranoid personality disorder**; **obsessive-compulsive disorder**; and **schizotypal personality disorder**.

A specific example of the ways in which social skills training can be helpful includes its application to alcohol dependence. In treating patients with alcohol dependence, a therapist who is using social skills training focuses on teaching the patients ways to avoid drinking when they go to parties where alcohol is served, or when they find themselves in other situations in which others may pressure them to drink.

KEY TERMS

Cue—Any behavior or event in a person's environment that serves to stimulate a particular response. For example, the smell of liquor may be a cue for some people to pour themselves a drink. In social skills training, the term is usually used to refer to social signals, whether spoken or unspoken.

Feedback—A reaction or response from others to a particular behavior or activity.

Generalization—A person's ongoing use of new behaviors that were previously modeled for him or her. Generalization is also called transfer of training or maintenance.

Modeling—A type of teaching method used in social skills training. Therapists who use this method may offer positive and negative examples of the behaviors that make up a social skill.

Psychoeducation—An approach to treatment that combines instruction with various therapeutic techniques.

Reinforcement—In social skills training, responding to a client's changed behavior in ways that will make the client want to perform the behavior again.

Role-playing—A technique used in social skills training and therapy in which participants act out roles relevant to real-life situations in order to change their attitudes and behaviors.

Shaping—A technique used in teaching social skills by prompting and reinforcing behaviors that come close to the desired behavior.

Social perspective-taking—A skill that involves a person's capacity to perceive or recognize other people's thoughts and feelings.

Another example is the application of social skills training to social phobia or shyness. People who suffer from social phobia or shyness are not ignorant of social cues, but they tend to avoid specific situations in which their limitations might cause them embarrassment. Social skills training can help these patients to improve their communication and social skills so that they will be able to mingle with others or go to job interviews with greater ease and self-confidence. Some studies indicate that the social skills training given to patients with shyness and social phobia can be applied to those with avoidant personality disorder, but more research is needed to differentiate among the particular types of social skills that benefit specific groups of patients, rather than treating social skills as a single entity. When trainers apply social skills training to the treatment of other **personality disorders**, they focus on the specific skills required to handle the issues that emerge with each disorder. For example, in the treatment of **obsessive-compulsive personality disorder** (OCD), social skills trainers focus on helping patients with OCD to deal with heavy responsibilities and **stress**.

People with disabilities in any age group can benefit from social skills training. Several studies demonstrate that children with developmental disabilities can acquire positive social skills with training. Extensive research on the effects of social skills training on children with attention-deficit/hyperactivity disorder shows that SST programs are effective in reducing these children's experiences of school failure or rejection as well as the aggressiveness and isolation that often develop in them because they have problems relating to others.

SST can be adapted to the treatment of depression with a focus on **assertiveness training**. Depressed patients often benefit from learning to set limits to others, to obtain satisfaction for their own needs, and to feel more self-confident in social interactions. Research suggests that patients who are depressed because they tend to withdraw from others can benefit from social skills training by learning to increase positive social interactions with others instead of pulling back.

There has been extensive research on the effective use of social skills training for the treatment of schizophrenia, in outpatient clinics as well as inpatient units. SST can be used to help patients with schizophrenia make better eye contact with other people, increase assertiveness, and improve their general conversational skills.

Social skills training in combination with other therapies

Social skills training is often used in combination with other therapies in the treatment of mental disorders. For example, in the treatment of individuals with alcohol dependence, social skills training has been used together with cognitive restructuring and coping skills training. Social skills training has also been integrated with exposure therapy, cognitive restructuring, and medication in the treatment of social phobia. Social skills training has been used within **family therapy** itself in the treatment of marital and family conflicts. Moreover, SST works well together with medication for the treatment of depression. For the treatment of schizophrenia, social skills training has often been combined with pharmacotherapy, family therapy, and assertive **case management**.

Precautions

Social skills training should rest on an objective assessment of the patient's actual problems in relating to other people.

It is important for therapists who are using SST to move slowly so that the patient is not overwhelmed by trying to change too many behaviors at one time. In addition, social skill trainers should be careful not to intensify the patient's feelings of social incompetence. This caution is particularly important in treating patients with social phobia, who are already worried about others' opinions of them.

An additional precaution is related to the transfer of social skills from the therapy setting to real-life situations. This transfer is called generalization or maintenance. Generalization takes place more readily when the social skills training has a clear focus and the patient is highly motivated to reach a realistic goal. In addition, social skills trainers should be sure that the new skills being taught are suitable for the specific patients involved.

Description

Techniques in social skills training

Therapists who use social skills training begin by breaking down complex social behaviors into smaller portions. Next, they arrange these smaller parts in order of difficulty, and gradually introduce them to the patients. For example, a therapist who is helping a patient learn to feel more comfortable at parties might make a list of specific behaviors that belong to the complex behavior called "acting appropriately at a party," such as introducing oneself to others; making conversation with several people at the party rather than just one other guest; keeping one's conversation pleasant and interesting; thanking the host or hostess before leaving; and so on. The patient would then work on one specific behavior at a time rather than trying to learn them all at once.

Such specific techniques as instruction, **modeling**, role-playing, shaping, feedback, and **reinforcement** of positive interactions may be used in SST. For example, instruction may be used to convey the differences among assertive, passive, and aggressive styles of communication. The technique of monitoring may be used to ask patients to increase their eye contact during a conversation. In role-playing exercises, group members have the opportunity to offer feedback to one another about their performances in simulated situations. For example, two members of the group may role-play a situation in which a customer is trying to return a defective purchase to a store. The others can then give feedback about the "customer's" assertiveness or the "clerk's" responses.

Content of social skills training

SST may be used to teach people specific sets of social competencies. A common focus of SST programs is communication skills. A program designed to improve people's skills in this area might include helping them with nonverbal and assertive communication and with making conversation. It might also include conversational skills that are needed in different specific situations, for example job interviews, informal parties, and dating. The skills might be divided further into such subjects as beginning, holding, and ending conversations, or expressing feelings in appropriate ways.

Another common focus of SST programs involves improving a patient's ability to perceive and act on social cues. Many people have problems communicating with others because they fail to notice or do not understand other people's cues, whether verbal or nonverbal. For example, some children become unpopular with their peers because they force their way into small play groups, when a child who has learned to read social signals would know that the children in the small group do not want someone else to join them, at least not at that moment. Learning to understand another person's spoken or unspoken messages is as important as learning conversational skills. A social skills program may include skills related to the perceptual processing of the conversation of other individuals.

Scheduling

Social skills training may be given as an individual or as a group treatment once or twice a week, or more often depending upon the severity of a patient's disorder and the level of his or her social skills. Generally speaking, children appear to gain more from SST in a peer group setting than in individual therapy. Social skill training groups usually consist of approximately 10 patients, a therapist, and a co-therapist.

Culture and gender issues

Social skills training programs may be modified somewhat to allow for cultural and gender differences. For example, eye contact is a frequently targeted behavior to be taught during social skills training. In some cultures, however, downcast eyes are a sign of respect rather than an indication of social anxiety or shyness. In addition, girls or women in some cultures may be considered immodest if they look at others, particularly adult males, too directly. These modifications can usually be made without changing the basic format of the SST program.

Generalization or transfer of skills

Current trends in social skills training are aimed at developing training programs that meet the demands of specific roles or situations. This need developed from studies that found that social skills acquired in one setting or situation are not easily generalized or transferred to another setting or situation. To assist patients in using their new skills in real-life situations, trainers use role-playing, teaching, modeling, and practice.

Preparation

Preparation for social skills training requires tact on the therapist's part, as patients with such disorders as social phobia or paranoid personality disorder may be discouraged or upset by being told that they need help with their social skills. One possible approach is through reading. The social skills therapist may recommend some self-help books on social skills in preparation for the treatment. Second, the therapist can ease the patient's self-consciousness or embarrassment by explaining that no one has perfect social skills. An additional consideration before starting treatment is the possibility of interference from medication side effects. The therapist will usually ask the patient for a list of all medications that he or she takes regularly.

One of the most critical tasks in preparation for social skills training is the selection of suitable target behaviors. It is often more helpful for the therapist to ask the patient to identify behaviors that he or she would like to change, rather than pointing to problem areas that the therapist has identified. The treatment should consider the patient's particular needs and interests. Whereas social skills training for some patients may include learning assertiveness on the job, training for others may include learning strategies for dating. Therapists can prepare patients for homework by explaining that the homework is the practice of new skills in other settings; and that it is as relevant as the therapy session itself.

Aftercare

Some studies strongly suggest the need for follow-up support after an initial course of social skills training. One study showed that follow-up support doubled the rate of employment for a group of patients with schizophrenia, compared to a group that had no follow-up.

Normal results

Outcome studies indicate that social skills training has moderate short-term effects, but limited long-term effects. SST programs that include social perspective-taking may have greater long-term effects than traditional SST programs based on cognitive-behavioral models. In general, social skills training tends to generalize or transfer to similar contexts rather than to contexts that are not similar to the training. SST programs for patients with developmental disabilities should include programming for generalization, so that the patients can transfer their newly acquired skills more effectively to real-life settings. One approach to improving generalization is to situate the training exercises within the patient's work, living, or social environment.

The benefits of social skills training programs include flexibility. The treatment can take place either as individual or group therapy, and new trainers can learn the techniques of SST fairly quickly. An additional advantage of SST is that it focuses on teaching skills that can be learned rather than emphasizing the internal or biological determinants of social adequacy. Future research should explore the integration of social skills training with the needs of families from different cultural backgrounds; the relationship between social skills training and different categories of mental disorders; the transfer of skills from therapeutic contexts to daily life; and improving patients' long-term gains from SST.

See also Assertiveness training; Bibliotherapy; Cognitive problem-solving skills training; Conduct disorder; Modeling; Peer groups

Resources

BOOKS

Antony, Martin, M., Ph.D., and Richard P. Swinson, M.D. *Phobic Disorders and Panic in Adults: A Guide to Assessment and Treatment.* Washington, DC: American Psychological Association, 2000.

Bellack, Alan S., and Michel Hersen, eds. *Research and Practice in Social Skills Training.* New York: Plenum Press: 1979.

Carter, Jane. "Social Skills Training." In *Beyond Behavior Modification: A Cognitive-Behavioral Approach to Behavior Management in the School,* edited by Joseph S. Kaplan, Jane Carter, and Nancy Cross. 3rd edition. Austin, Texas: Pro-Ed, 1998.

McKay, Matthew, Martha Davis, and Patrick Fanning. *Messages: The Communication Skills Book.* 2nd edition. Oakland, CA: New Harbinger, 1995.

Millon, Theodore, Ph.D. *Personality-Guided Therapy.* 3rd edition. New York: Wiley, 1999.

PERIODICALS

Bellack, Alan S., Robert W. Buchanan, James M. Gold. "The American Psychiatric Association Practice Guidelines for Schizophrenia: Scientific Base and Relevance for Behavior Therapy." *Behavior Therapy* 32 (2001): 283-308.

DeRubeis, Robert J., and Paul Crits-Christoph. "Empirically Supported Individual and Group Psychological Treatments for Adult Mental Disorders." *Journal of Consulting and Clinical Psychology* 66, no. 1 (1998): 37-52.

Griffiths, Dorothy, Maurice A. Feldman, and Susan Tough. "Programming Generalization of Social Skills in Adults With Developmental Disabilities: Effects on Generalization and Social Validity." *Behavior Therapy* 28 (1997): 253-269.

Grizenko, Natalie, M.D., Michael Zappitelli, M.D., Jean-Phillipe Langevin, Sophie Hrychko, M.D., Amira El-Messidi, David Kaminester, M.D., Nicole Pawliuk, M.A., and Marina Ter Stepanian, B.A. "Effectiveness of a Social Skills Training Program Using Self/Other Perspective-Taking: A Nine-Month Follow-Up." *American Journal of Orthopsychiatry* 70, no. 4 (October 2000): 501-509.

Heinssen, Robert K., Robert P. Liberman, and Alex Kopelowicz. "Psychosocial Skills Training for Schizophrenia: Lessons From the Laboratory." *Schizophrenia Bulletin* 26, no. 1 (2000): 21-46.

Ison, Mirta S. "Training in Social Skills: An Alternative Technique for Handling Disruptive Child Behavior." *Psychological Reports* 88 (2001): 903-911.

Pfiffner, Linda, J., and Keith McBurnett. "Social Skills Training With Parent Generalization: Treatment Effects for Children With Attention Deficit Disorder." *Journal of Consulting and Clinical Psychology* 65, no. 5 (1997): 749-757.

Tsang, Hector W.-H., and Veronica Pearson. "Work-Related Social Skills Training for People With Schizophrenia in Hong Kong." *Schizophrenia Bulletin* 27, no. 1 (2001): 139-148.

ORGANIZATIONS

American Psychological Association, 750 First Street, NE, Washington, D.C. 20002-4242. (202) 336-5500. <http://www.apa.org>.

Judy Koenigsberg, Ph.D.

Social workers

Definition

A social worker is a helping professional who is distinguished from other human service professionals by a focus on both the individual and his or her environment. Generally, social workers have at least a bachelor's degree from an accredited education program and in most states they must be licensed, certified, or registered. A Master's in Social Work is required for those who provide **psychotherapy** or work in specific settings such as hospitals or nursing homes.

Description

Social workers comprise a profession that had its beginnings in 1889 when Jane Addams founded Hull House and the American settlement house movement in Chicago's West Side. The ethics and values that informed her work became the basis for the social work profession. They include respect for the dignity of human beings, especially those who are vulnerable, an understanding that people are influenced by their environment, and a desire to work for social change that rectifies gross or unjust differences.

The social work profession is broader than most disciplines with regard to the range and types of problems addressed, the settings in which the work takes place, the levels of practice, interventions used, and populations served. It has been observed that social work is defined in its own place in the larger social environment, continuously evolving to respond to and address a changing world. Although several definitions of social work have been provided throughout its history, common to all definitions is the focus on both the individual and the environment, distinguishing it from other helping professions.

Social workers may be engaged in a variety of occupations ranging from hospitals, schools, clinics, police departments, public agencies, court systems to private practices or businesses. They provide the majority of mental health care to persons of all ages in this country, and in rural areas they are often the sole providers of services. In general, they assist people to obtain tangible services, help communities or groups provide or improve social and health services, provide counseling and psychotherapy with individuals, families, and groups, and participate in policy change through legislative processes. The practice of social work requires knowledge of human development and behavior, of social, economic and cultural institutions, and of the interaction of all these factors.

Resources

PERIODICALS

Gibelman, Margaret. "The Search for Identity: Defining Social Work—Past, Present, Future." *Social Work* 44, no. 4. (1999).

ORGANIZATIONS

National Association of Social Workers. 750 First St. NE, Washington, D.C. 20002-4241. <http://www.naswdc.org>.

OTHER

National Association of Social Workers. *Choices: Careers in Social Work.* (2002). <http://www.naswdc.org/pubs/choices/choices.htm>.

National Association of Social Workers. *Professional Social Work Centennial: 1898–1998, Addams' Work Laid the Foundation.* 1998 (2002). <http://www.naswdc.org/nasw/centennial/addams.htm>.

Judy Leaver, M.A.

Sodium amobarbital *see* **Barbiturates**

Sodium pentobarbital *see* **Barbiturates**

Somatization and somatoform disorders

Definition

Somatization is a term that describes the expression of psychological or mental difficulties through physical symptoms. Somatization takes a number of forms, ranging from preoccupation with potential or genuine but mild physical problems to the development of actual physical pain, discomfort, or dysfunction. The *Diagnostic and Statistical Manual of Mental Disorders (DSM-IV-TR)*, the professional handbook clinicians use to diagnose mental disorders, describes seven disorders under the category of somatoform disorders. These disorders are **somatization disorder**, **undifferentiated somatoform disorder**, **conversion disorder**, **pain disorder**, **hypochondriasis**, **body dysmorphic disorder**, and somatoform disorder not otherwise specified. Somatization appears to be fairly common, and a somatoform disorder **diagnosis** is not warranted unless symptoms cause significant distress or disability.

Description

Somatization disorder is characterized by a history of multiple unexplained medical problems or physical

KEY TERMS

Dysmorphic—Malformed.

Somatization—The expression of mental or psychological experiences through physical symptoms.

Somatoform—Referring to physical symptoms with a psychological origin.

complaints beginning prior to age 30. In the nineteenth and early twentieth centuries, somatization disorder was known as Briquet's syndrome or hysteria—a more generic term for such a condition. People with somatization disorder report symptoms affecting multiple organ systems or physical functions, including pain, gastrointestinal distress, sexual problems, and symptoms that mimic neurological disorders. Although medical explanations for their symptoms cannot be identified, individuals with somatization disorder experience genuine physical discomfort and distress. Review of their medical histories will usually reveal visits to a number of medical specialists, and many patients take numerous medications prescribed by different doctors, running the risk of dangerous drug interactions.

Undifferentiated somatoform disorder is similar to somatization disorder, but may involve fewer symptoms, have a shorter duration or begin after the age of 30. Common symptoms include chronic **fatigue**, loss of appetite, gastrointestinal distress or problems involving the genitals or urinary tract. This diagnosis is appropriate for patients with symptoms of somatization disorder who do not meet all diagnostic criteria.

Conversion disorder is marked by unexplained sensory or motor symptoms that resemble those of a neurological or medical illness or injury. Common symptoms include paralysis, loss of sensation, double vision, **seizures**, inability to speak or swallow and problems with coordination and balance. Symptoms often reflect a naive understanding of the nervous system, and physicians often detect conversion disorder when symptoms do not make sense anatomically. For instance, a patient may report loss of both touch and pain sensation on one side of the body, when, in fact, a genuine lesion would result in loss of touch and pain sense on opposite sides of the body. The name conversion disorder reflects a theoretical understanding of the disorder as a symbolic conversion of a psychological conflict into a concrete physical representation. Interestingly, patients with conversion disorder may not express the level of distress one would expect from someone with a disabling neurological condition. This phenomenon is traditionally called *la belle indifference*.

The primary feature of pain disorder is physical pain that causes significant distress or disability or leads an individual to seek medical attention. Pain may be medically unexplained, or it may be associated with an identifiable medical condition but far more severe than the condition would warrant. Common symptoms include headache, backache and generalized pain in muscles and joints. Pain disorder can be severely disabling, causing immobility that prevents patients from working, fulfilling family responsibilities or engaging in social activities. Like patients with somatization disorder, people with pain disorder often have a history of consultations with numerous physicians.

Hypochondriasis is diagnosed when a person is excessively concerned by fears of having a physical disease or injury. Individuals with hypochondriasis usually do not complain of disabling or painful symptoms. Instead, they tend to overreact to minor physical symptoms or sensations, like rapid heartbeat, sweating, small sores or fatigue. Many people with hypochondriasis develop fears in response to the illness or death of a friend or family member or after reading about a condition or seeing a feature on television. Hypochondriacal fears can be confined to a single disease or may involve a number of different physical concerns. Individuals with hypochondriasis seek frequent reassurance by consulting physicians or talking about their fears, yet these efforts provide only temporary relief from their fears. Although hypochondriasis is usually not as disabling as somatoform disorders involving the development of actual physical symptoms, it can put **stress** on relationships or reduce work productivity through time lost to frequent medical appointments and tests.

Body dysmorphic disorder is characterized by preoccupation with a defect in physical appearance. Often the defect of concern is not apparent to other observers, or if there is a genuine defect it is far less disfiguring than the patient imagines. Common preoccupations include concerns about the size or shape of the nose, skin blemishes, body or facial hair, hair loss, or "ugly" hands or feet. Individuals with body dysmorphic disorder may be extremely self-conscious, avoiding social situations because they fear others will notice their physical defects or even make fun of them. They may spend hours examining the imagined defect or avoid mirrors altogether. Time-consuming efforts to hide the defect, such as application of cosmetics or adjustments of clothing or hair, are common. Many people with body dysmorphic disorder undergo procedures like plastic surgery or cosmetic dentistry, but are seldom satisfied with the results.

Somatoform disorder, not otherwise specified, is diagnosed when somatoform symptoms are present but criteria for another somatoform disorder are not met. *DSM-IV-TR* includes several examples of symptoms that could merit this diagnosis, including false pregnancy, and hypochondriacal fears or unexplained physical symptoms of recent onset or short duration.

There is some disagreement among researchers about the *DSM-IV-TR* somatoform disorders category. Some have argued that hypochondriasis and body dysmorphic disorder are more similar to **obsessive-compulsive disorder** than to other somatoform disorders, while others think hypochondriasis may be more appropriately classified with the anxiety disorders.

Resources

BOOKS

American Psychiatric Association. *Diagnostic and Statistical Manual of Mental Disorders.* 4th edition, text revised. Washington, DC: American Psychiatric Association, 2000.

Phillips, Katherine A. *The Broken Mirror: Understanding and Treating Body Dysmorphic Disorder.* New York: Oxford University Press, 1996.

Pilowsky, Issy. *Abnormal Illness Behavior.* Chichester, UK: John Wiley and Sons, 1997.

PERIODICALS

Neziroglu, Fugen, Dean McKay, and Jose A. Yaryura-Tobias. "Overlapping and distinctive features of hypochondriasis and obsessive-compulsive disorder." *Journal of Anxiety Disorders* 14, no. 6 (2000): 603–614.

Danielle Barry, M.S.

Somatization disorder

Definition

Somatization disorder is a psychiatric condition marked by multiple medically unexplained physical, or somatic, symptoms. In order to qualify for the **diagnosis** of somatization disorder, somatic complaints must be serious enough to interfere significantly with a person's ability to perform important activities, such as work, school or family and social responsibilities, or lead the person experiencing the symptoms to seek medical treatment.

Somatization disorder has long been recognized by psychiatrists and psychologists, and was originally called Briquet's syndrome in honor of Paul Briquet, a French physician who first described the disorder in the nineteenth century. It is included in the category of somatoform disorders in the *Diagnostic and Statistical Manual of Mental Disorders (DSM-IV-TR),* the professional handbook that aids clinicians in diagnosing patients' mental disorders. The term "somatoform" means that the physical symptoms have a psychological origin.

KEY TERMS

Somatization—Conversion of mental experiences into physical symptoms.

Description

Individuals with somatization disorder suffer from a number of vague physical symptoms, involving at least four different physical functions or parts of the body. The physical symptoms that characterize somatization disorder cannot be attributed to medical conditions or to the use of drugs, and individuals with somatization disorder often undergo numerous medical tests (with negative results) before the psychological cause of their distress is identified. They often use impressionistic and colorful language to describe their symptoms, describing burning sensations, pains that move from place to place, strange tastes on the tongue, tingling, or tremors. While many symptoms resemble those associated with genuine diseases, some of the symptoms reported by people with somatization disorder are not. The individual usually visits many different physicians, but the information they provide about the patient's symptoms can be inconsistent. It is important to note that while the physical symptoms of somatization disorder frequently lack medical explanations, they are not intentionally fabricated. The typical person with somatization disorder has suffered from physical pain, discomfort, and dysfunction for an extended period of time and consulted several doctors; they are hopeful that they one can be found who can identify the cause of their illness and provide relief.

Somatization disorder can be dangerous, since patients may end up taking several different medications, thereby risking harmful drug interactions.

Causes and symptoms

Causes

DEFENSE AGAINST PSYCHOLOGICAL DISTRESS. One of the oldest theories about the cause of somatization disorder suggests that it is a way of avoiding psychological distress. Rather than experiencing depression or anxiety, some individuals will develop physical symptoms.

According to this model, somatization disorder is a defense against psychological pain that allows some people to avoid the **stigma** of a psychiatric diagnosis. While getting the care and nurturing they need from doctors and others who are responsive to their apparent medical illnesses, many patients are encouraged to continue their manipulative behavior.

Many patients described by Sigmund Freud would be diagnosed today with somatization disorder. His patients were usually young women who complained of numerous physical symptoms. In the process of speaking with Freud, they would often recall a number of distressing memories; discussing these memories frequently led to the relief of physical symptoms. These cases formed the foundation of Freud's psychoanalytic treatment. Although this theory offers a plausible explanation for somatization disorder, research indicates that people with multiple physical symptoms are actually more likely to report psychiatric symptoms than those with few physical problems. These findings appear to support a connection between psychological and physical distress, but are inconsistent with the idea that physical symptoms offer a defense against overt psychiatric symptoms.

HEIGHTENED SENSITIVITY TO PHYSICAL SENSATIONS. An alternative theory suggests that somatization disorder arises from a heightened sensitivity to internal sensations. People with somatization disorder may be keenly aware of the minor pains and discomforts that most people simply ignore. A similar theory has been offered to account for **panic disorder**. Studies have shown that people with panic disorder are particularly sensitive to internal sensations like breathing rate and heartbeats, which may lead them to react with intense fear to minor internal changes. The physiological or psychological origins of this hypersensitivity to internal sensations and their relevance to somatization disorder are still not well understood.

CATASTROPHIC THINKING ABOUT PHYSICAL SENSATIONS. According to these thoughts, somatization disorder results from negative beliefs and exaggerated fears about the significance of physical sensations. Individuals with somatization disorder are thus more likely to believe that vague physical symptoms are indicators of serious disease and to seek treatment for them. For instance, someone with somatization disorder may fear that a headache signals a **brain** tumor, or that shortness of breath indicates the onset of asthma. When their doctors can find no medical explanation for the symptoms, the patients may fear that they have a rare disease; they frantically look for specialists who can provide a diagnosis. Anxiety causes them to focus even more intensely on their symptoms, which in turn become more disabling. Many people with somatization disorder reduce or eliminate many activities out of fear that exertion will worsen their symptoms. With fewer activities to distract them from their symptoms, they spend more time worrying about physical problems, resulting in greater distress and disability.

Symptoms

Gastrointestinal (GI) complaints, such as nausea, bloating, diarrhea, and sensitivities to certain foods are common, and at least two different GI symptoms are required for the diagnosis. Sexual or reproductive symptoms, including pain during intercourse, menstrual problems, and **erectile dysfunction** are also necessary features for a diagnosis for somatization disorder. Other frequent symptoms are headaches, pain in the back or joints, difficulty swallowing or speaking, and urinary retention. To qualify for the diagnosis, at least one symptom must resemble a neurological disorder, such as **seizures**, problems with coordination or balance, or paralysis.

Demographics

According to the *DSM-IV-TR*, somatization disorder is rare in males in the United States, although higher rates are seen among males from some cultural and ethnic groups. The *DSM-IV-TR* estimates that between 0.2% and 2% of women, and less than 0.2% of men, suffer from somatization disorder in the U.S. Sex ratios may arise from different rates of seeking treatment. However, studies of unexplained somatic symptoms in the general population find less striking differences in rates between men and women. Specific symptoms may vary across cultures. For example, the *DSM-IV-TR* notes that the sensation of worms in the head or ants crawling under the skin are sometimes reported in African and South Asian countries, but rarely seen in North American patients.

Diagnosis

To receive a diagnosis of somatization disorder, the individual must have a history of multiple physical complaints that began before age 30 and that continued for several years (*DSM-IV-TR*). These symptoms must cause significant impairment to social, occupational or other areas of functioning—or lead the patient to seek medical treatment.

Each of the following four criteria must be met.

- The individual must report a history of pain affecting at least four different parts or functions of the body. Examples include headaches, back, joint, chest or abdominal pain, or pain during menstruation or sexual intercourse.

- A history of at least two gastrointestinal symptoms, such as nausea, bloating, vomiting, diarrhea, or food intolerance must be reported.
- There must be a history of at least one sexual or reproductive symptom, such as lack of interest in sex, problems achieving erection or ejaculation, irregular menstrual periods, excessive menstrual bleeding, or vomiting throughout pregnancy.
- One symptom must mimic a neurological condition. Examples include weakness, paralysis, problems with balance or coordination, seizures, **hallucinations**, loss of sensations such as touch, seeing, hearing, tasting, smelling—or difficulty swallowing or speaking, or **amnesia** and loss of consciousness. Pseudo-neurologic symptoms like these are the primary characteristics of another somatoform disorder known as "conversion disorder."

If a thorough medical evaluation reveals no evidence of an underlying medical- or drug- or medication-induced condition, the diagnosis of somatization disorder is likely. People with genuine medical conditions can qualify for the diagnosis if the level of functional impairment reported is more than would be expected based on medical findings. The symptoms must not be intentionally produced. If the patient is feigning symptoms, a diagnosis of **factitious disorder** or **malingering** would most likely be considered.

Treatments

Cognitive behavior therapy

Cognitive-behavioral therapy (CBT) for somatization disorder focuses on changing negative patterns of thoughts, feelings, and behavior that contribute to somatic symptoms. The cognitive component of the treatment focuses on helping patients identify dysfunctional thinking about physical sensations. With practice, patients learn to recognize catastrophic thinking and develop more rational explanations for their feelings. The behavioral component aims to increase activity. Patients with somatization disorder have usually reduced their activity levels as a result of discomfort or out of fear that activity will worsen symptoms. CBT patients are instructed to increase activity gradually while avoiding overexertion that could reinforce fears. Other important types of treatment include relaxation training, sleep hygiene, and communication skills training. Preliminary findings suggest that CBT may help reduce distress and discomfort associated with somatic symptoms; however, it has not yet been systematically compared with other forms of therapy.

Medications

Antidepressant medications may help to alleviate symptoms of somatization disorder. According to one study, patients with somatization disorder who took the antidepressant **nefazodone** (Serzone) showed reductions in physical symptoms, increased activity levels, and lower levels of anxiety and depression at the end of treatment.

Prognosis

Untreated somatization disorder is usually a chronic condition, though specific symptoms can come and go and overall severity may fluctuate over time. Somatization disorder poses a serious problem for society, since many who suffer from it become functionally disabled and unable to work. In addition, patients with unexplained physical symptoms strain already overburdened health care resources. Unexplained physical symptoms are extremely common among patients visiting general practitioners, with some estimates suggesting that over two-thirds of general medical patients have symptoms that cannot be explained by medical tests. Fortunately, there is preliminary evidence that **psychotherapy** and medication can effectively reduce symptoms and disability.

Prevention

Greater awareness of somatization disorder, particularly among physicians, can help them identify individuals with somatization disorder, and help these patients get appropriate psychological or psychiatric treatment.

Resources

BOOKS

American Psychiatric Association. *Diagnostic and Statistical Manual of Mental Disorders.* 4th edition, text revised. Washington, DC: American Psychiatric Association, 2000.

Breuer, Josef and Sigmund Freud. *Studies on Hysteria.* New York: Basic Books, 2000.

Butcher, James N. and Carolyn L. Williams. *Essentials of MMPI2 and MMPIA Interpretation.* 2nd edition. Minneapolis: University of Minnesota Press, 2000.

PERIODICALS

Allen, Lesley A., Robert L. Woolfolk, Paul M. Lehrer, Michael A. Gara, Javier I. Escobar. "Cognitive behavior therapy for somatization disorder: A preliminary investigation." *Journal of Behaviour Therapy and Experimental Psychiatry* 32 (2001): 53-62.

Cameron, Oliver G. " Interoception: The inside story—A model for psychosomatic process." *Psychosomatic Medicine* 63 (2001): 697-710.

Hotopf, Matthew, Michael Wadsworth, and Simon Wessely. "Is 'somatisation' a defense against the acknowledgement of psychiatric disorder?" *Journal of Psychosomatic Research* 50 (2001): 119-124.

Menza, Matthew, Marc Lauritano, Lesley Allen, Melissa Warman, Frank Ostella, Robert M. Hmaer, and Javier Escobar. "Treatment of somatization disorder with nefazodone: A prospective, open-label study." *Annals of Clinical Psychiatry* 13, no. 3 (Sep 2001): 153-158.

Nimnuan, Chaichana, Matthew Hotopf, and Simon Wessely. "Medically unexplained symptoms: An epidemiological study in seven specialties." *Journal of Psychosomatic Research* 51 (2001): 361-367.

Rief, Winifred, Aike Hessel, and Elmar Braehler. "Somatization symptoms and hypochondriacal features in the general population." *Psychosomatic Medicine* 63: 595-602.

Danielle Barry, M.S.

Somnambulism *see* **Sleepwalking disorder**

Somnote *see* **Chloral hydrate**

Sonata *see* **Zaleplon**

Specific phobias

Definition

Specific phobia is a type of disorder in which the affected individual displays a marked and enduring fear of specific situations or objects. Individuals with specific phobias experience extreme fear as soon as they encounter a defined situation or object, a phobic stimulus. For example, an individual with a specific phobia of dogs will become anxious when coerced to confront a dog. The specific phobia triggers a lot of distress or significantly impairs an affected individual.

Mental health professionals use the ***Diagnostic and Statistical Manual of Mental Disorders*** (the *DSM*) to diagnose mental disorders. The 2000 edition of this manual (the Fourth Edition Text Revision, also called the *DSM-IV-TR*) classifies specific phobia as a type of anxiety disorder. Formerly, specific phobia was known as simple phobia. In the last few years, mental health professionals have paid more attention to specific phobias.

Description

Specific phobia has a unique position among the anxiety disorders in that individuals with this disorder do not experience pervasive anxiety nor do they seek treatment as readily as individuals with other anxiety disorders. Unlike individuals with other anxiety disorders, the fear of individuals with specific phobias is limited to defined situations or objects. Individuals with specific phobias experience impairment or a significant amount of anguish. They may lead restricted lifestyles depending upon the phobia type. Adults and adolescents with specific phobias recognize that their fear is unreasonable. Children, on the other hand, may not recognize that their fear of the phobic stimulus is unreasonable or extreme.

The types of specific phobias include situational, object, and other. The situational type is diagnosed if an individual's fear is cued by a defined situation. Examples include situations such as flying, enclosed places, tunnels, driving, bridges, elevators, or public transportation. Object types include animal, natural environment, and blood-injection-injury types. Animal type is diagnosed if an individual's fear is cued by animals or insects. Natural environment type is diagnosed if an individual's fear is cued by storms, water, or heights. Blood-injection-injury type is diagnosed if an individual's fear is cued by seeing an injury or blood or by an injection or other invasive medical treatment. Other type is diagnosed if an individual's fear is cued by other stimuli such as fears of vomiting, choking, becoming ill, and falling down if far from a means of physical support, and a child's fears of loud noises or characters in costumes.

Researchers have found that the frequency of type for adults in clinical settings, from least to most frequent, is: animal, blood-injection-injury, natural environment, and situational. The most common phobias for community samples, however, include phobias of heights, mice, spiders, and insects.

Causes and symptoms

Causes

The development of a specific phobia may be determined by a variety of factors. Behavioral, cognitive, and social theories of learning and conditioning, psychodynamic models such as the psychoanalytic theory of Freud, physiological studies of the **brain**, family background and genetic predisposition, variations in sociocultural themes, and theories on trauma can influence the development of specific phobia disorder. Some theorists propose that biological researchers have ignored specific phobias because pharmacological treatment is not the treatment of choice for this disorder.

LEARNING AND CONDITIONING CAUSES. As of 2002, research on phobias focuses on information-processing, learning, and conditioning themes. Learning to experience fear is the core of a conditioning perspective. Informational and instructional factors can result in the formation of fears. For example, an individual who frequently hears of plane crashes in the news may develop a specific phobia of flying. Research shows that individuals with specific phobias pay more attention to information about danger than do individuals who do not have specific phobias. Vicarious acquisition occurs when an individual witnesses a traumatic event or sees another individual behave with fear when confronting a phobic stimulus. Direct conditioning occurs when an individual is frightened by a phobic stimulus.

A major determinant of specific phobias is conditioning. Association and avoidance are types of conditioning. In association conditioning, a stimulus that was initially neutral begins to trigger an anxiety response. For example, if an individual was driving one day and experienced a strong anxiety response, an association may form between driving and anxiety. Individuals do not learn to become phobic until they begin to avoid. In avoidance conditioning, individuals learn to avoid a stimulus that triggers anxiety. Every time individuals avoid the phobic stimulus—driving, for example—they are rewarded by the relief from anxiety.

TRAUMATIC CAUSES. A determinant of specific phobias includes traumas. For example, individuals who have been attacked by a dog may develop a specific phobia disorder and become conditioned to fear dogs. Individuals who observe others experiencing a trauma (the others are "modeling" behavior for the individual who will be affected) may become predisposed to developing specific phobia disorder. For example, individuals who witness people falling from a building may develop a specific phobia disorder. Phobias with a traumatic origin may develop acutely, or, in other words, have a more sudden onset than other phobias that develop more gradually.

PSYCHODYNAMIC CAUSES. Psychodynamic theorists explain that phobias emerge because individuals have impulses that are unacceptable, and they repress these impulses. More specifically, Freud proposed that phobias emerge because of an unresolved oedipal conflict. According to Freud's theory, an oedipal conflict is a developmental conflict that emerges during the third (or oedipal) stage of Freud's psychosexual development stages. During this stage, a conflict emerges with regard to the triad of father, mother, and child. The conflict concerns the sexual impulses that the child has toward the parent of the opposite gender and the hostile impulses that the child has towards the parent of the same gender. During this stage, the developmental conflict concerns a resolution of oedipal issues. Psychoanalysts propose that when repression does not work, individuals with phobias displace their anxiety connected to the unresolved oedipal conflict upon a situation or object that is less relevant. The feared situation or object symbolizes the source of the conflict. For example, a specific phobia may be connected to an individual's conflict about aggressive or sexual thoughts and feelings. In one sense, a phobia protects individuals from realizing their emotional issues.

KEY TERMS

Axis I—Axis I offers mental health professionals a diagnostic coding domain for listing disorders or conditions that are not classified as personality disorders and mental retardation.

Oedipal conflict—A developmental conflict that emerges during the third or oedipal stage of Freud's psychosexual development stages. During this stage, a conflict emerges with regard to the triad of father, mother, and child. The conflict concerns the sexual impulses that the child has toward the parent of the opposite gender and the hostile impulses that the child has towards the parent of the same gender. During this stage, the developmental conflict concerns a resolution of oedipal issues.

The case of Hans, a boy with a horse phobia, is Freud's paradigm example of a phobia. Freud attributed Hans' fear of horses to an oedipal conflict that was not resolved, and he explained that Hans repressed his sexual feelings for his mother and his wish that his father would die. Freud proposed that Hans feared that his father would discover his wish, repressed his wish to attack his father, and displaced his fear of his father's aggression onto horses. The young boy resolved the conflict of loving and hating his father by hating horses rather than admitting that he had aggressive feelings towards his father. Hans was better able to avoid the feared horses than his father. Thus, the phobia in the case of Hans represents a compromise of intrapsychic movement.

PHYSIOLOGICAL CAUSES. Some research has suggested that the high activation of brain pathways that correspond to the cognitive and emotional constituents of anxiety biologically predispose individuals to specific phobias.

GENETIC AND FAMILY CAUSES. Although specific phobia is frequently attributed to environmental issues such as **modeling**, learning by association, and negative **reinforcement**, genetic predisposition can influence this disorder. An individual who has a family member with a specific phobia is at an increased risk for developing this disorder. Some research indicates that the pattern of types are similar within families. For example, a first-degree biological relative of individuals with a situational type is likely to have phobias of situations. Studies indicate that the blood and injury phobias have strong familial patterns.

SOCIOCULTURAL CAUSES. There is a paucity of information about cultural differences in specific phobias. Phobia content may vary by culture. Fear of a phobic stimulus such as magic or spirits, present in several cultures, is diagnosed as a specific phobia only if the fear is excessive for a particular culture and if the fear triggers major distress or interferes with functioning. Some research indicates that African Americans are more likely than whites to report specific phobias. Some studies show that specific phobias are less common among whites born in the U.S. or immigrant Mexican-Americans than among Mexican-Americans born in the U.S. Research suggests mixed data with regard to socioeconomic level, with some data associating specific phobia disorder with a lower socioeconomic level.

PERSONAL VARIABLES. Studies suggest a relationship between age and specific phobia. Research indicates some connections between the age of individuals with specific phobias and insight into the extreme quality of their fears. Insight increases with age. Children, unlike adults and adolescents, often do not report feelings of distress about having phobias. Insight into the unreasonable nature of the fear is not required for a **diagnosis** of specific phobia in children. The animal and natural environment types of specific phobia are common and generally transitory in children. Some studies indicate a connection between gender and specific phobia. Research shows that specific phobias from the animal type are more common among women. Some studies suggest that women are more likely to report specific phobias and to seek treatment than men.

Symptoms

DSM-IV-TR delineates seven diagnostic criteria for specific phobia:

- Significant and enduring fear of phobic stimulus: Patients with specific phobia display marked and enduring fear when they encounter a defined situation or object, the phobic stimulus.
- Anxiety response to phobic stimulus: Patients with specific phobia display anxiety as soon as they confront the phobic stimulus. When they confront the phobic stimulus, a defined situation or object, patients with specific phobia may experience a **panic attack** related to the specific situation. Children may cry, cling, freeze, or display tantrums when they express their anxiety in the face of the phobic stimulus.
- Recognition: Although adolescents and adults realize that their fear is unreasonable and disproportionate to the situation, children may not recognize that their fear is excessive.
- Avoidance: Individuals with specific phobia avoid the phobic stimulus or endure it with deep distress and anxiety.
- Impairment and distress: Individuals with specific phobia display avoidance, distress, and anxious anticipation when they encounter the phobic stimulus. Their avoidance reactions interfere with their daily functioning, or they express significant distress about having a phobia.
- Duration: To diagnose specific phobia in a patient who is under 18 years of age, the duration of the disorder needs to be at least six months.
- Not accounted for by another disorder: A diagnosis of specific phobia is assigned if the phobic avoidance, panic attacks, or anxiety related to the defined situation or object are not better accounted for by other disorders.

Demographics

General United States population

Specific phobias are common. The prevalence rates of specific phobia in community samples range from 4% to 8%. Over the course of a lifetime, the prevalence estimates in community samples range from 7.2% to 11.3%.

High-risk populations

Individuals whose family members have specific phobia are at a higher risk for developing this disorder.

Cross-cultural issues

Prior to assigning a diagnosis of specific phobia, clinicians need to consider whether a patient's fear is extreme in the context of a particular culture and whether the phobia causes difficulties in daily functioning or triggers a lot of distress. Further research is needed on the effects of culture upon the symptoms of specific phobia.

Gender issues

There are twice as many women with specific phobia than there are men with this disorder. The gender ratio variable varies depending upon the type of specific phobia. Approximately 75%–90% of people with the animal, situational, and natural environment types are female.

Approximately 55%–70% of people with the blood-injection-injury subtype are female. For height phobias, there are fewer women than men than for other specific phobia types; however, illness phobias are more common in men.

Diagnosis

The diagnosis of specific phobia is complicated by factors such as degree of impairment and differential diagnosis. Although fears of specified situations or objects are common, a diagnosis of specific phobia relies on the degree of sufficient impairment.

With regard to differentiating specific phobia types, factors such as the focus of fear and the predictability and timing of the reaction to the phobic stimulus across the specific phobia types can assist clinicians to differentiate. With regard to differentiating specific phobia from other disorders, there are several disorders with similar symptoms. They include **panic disorder** with **agoraphobia**, **social phobia**, **post-traumatic stress disorder**, **obsessive-compulsive disorder**, **hypochondriasis**, **schizophrenia**, delusional, and other psychotic disorders. Generally, a diagnosis of specific phobia rather than panic disorder is made when there are no spontaneous panic attacks and no fear of panic attacks. It is often difficult to differentiate specific phobia, situational type, from panic disorder with agoraphobia. Specific phobia, situational type, is commonly diagnosed when an individual displays situational avoidance without unexpected and recurrent panic attacks. On the other hand, panic disorder with agoraphobia is diagnosed if an individual experiences an initial onset of panic attacks that are not anticipated and subsequently experiences avoidance of several situations considered triggers of panic attacks. Although individuals with specific phobia, unlike individuals with panic disorder with agoraphobia, do not display enduring anxiety, anxious anticipation may occur when confrontation with a phobic stimulus is more likely to occur. *DSM-IV-TR* outlines differentiating factors as the type and number of panic attacks, the number of avoided contexts, and the focus of the fear. At times, both diagnoses, specific phobia and panic disorder with agoraphobia, need to be assigned.

Psychological measures

Measures used to diagnose specific phobia include behavioral observation, clinical interviews, physiological evaluation, and self-report measures. The Behavioral Avoidance Task (BAT) is a common behavioral observation method used to assess specific phobia. Often, the diagnosis of specific phobia is made on the basis of an individual's responses to semistructured interviews such as the Anxiety Disorders Interview Schedule for *DSM-IV* (ADIS-IV) and the Structured Clinical Interview for *DSM-IV* Axis I Disorders (SCID-IV). To assist in differential diagnosis between specific phobias and other disorders with similar characteristics, clinicians use the Anxiety Disorders Interview Schedule for *DSM-IV* (ADIS-IV). Physiological evaluations usually include heart rate monitors. Self-report questionnaires include measures such as the SUDS (subjective units of discomfort/distress scale), the most frequently used self-report measure, the Fear Survey Schedule (FSS-III), and the Mutilation Questionnaire, specifically for measuring fear of the blood type of specific phobia.

This woman suffers from claustrophobia— the fear of enclosed spaces. *(Nathan Benn/CORBIS. Photo reproduced by permission.)*

Time of onset/symptom duration

Generally, the initial symptoms of specific phobia occur when an individual is a child or a young adolescent. The type of phobia determines the age of onset. The blood, animal, and natural environment types begin when an individual is a child; however, many new cases of the natural environment type occur when an individual is a young adult. The onset for the height type begins in adolescence. The onset age for the situational type occurs in childhood, but peaks again in the mid-twenties. There is no specific onset age for phobias with a traumatic origin.

Individual variations in specific phobia

Classification systems distinguish between individuals with different types of specific phobias. The types of specific phobia, situation, object, and other, relate to particular features such as the age, gender, and culture of an individual. Some researchers propose that to distinguish individual differences in treatment planning, it is more helpful to simply name the specific phobia rather than to use the type classification system. For example, researchers have found that for the animal type, some animals such as a tiger or a bear did not trigger disgust for tiger-phobic or bear-phobic individuals, but other animals such as a spider triggered disgust for some spider phobic individuals, but did not trigger disgust for other spider phobic individuals.

Dual diagnoses

Specific phobia often occurs with other disorders of mood and anxiety, and with substance-related disorders. When specific phobias occur with other disorders in clinical contexts, the primary diagnosis is associated with greater distress than is the specific phobia. The blood-injury-injection type of specific phobia may occur with physical symptoms such as vasovagal fainting. The vasovagal fainting response is characterized by a short heart rate acceleration and blood pressure elevation. Then, the heart rate decelerates and the blood pressure drops. Research shows that individuals who have one specific phobia type are more likely to have other phobias of the same type.

Treatments

Specific phobias are highly treatable. They are most effectively treated by psychological rather than biological treatments. The primary goal of most treatments of specific phobias is to reduce fear, phobic avoidance, impairment, and distress. Approximately 12%–30% seek treatment for specific phobias.

Cognitive-behavioral therapy

Cognitive-behavioral therapy has been effective in treating specific phobias. There has not been much research on the effects of cognitive therapy alone on specific phobias. Cognitive therapists challenge fearful thoughts and replace them with more positive thoughts. Although some studies show benefits in that cognitive therapy may assist patients to decrease anxiety related to their exposure exercises, research indicates that cognitive therapy alone is probably not an effective treatment for specific phobia. Researchers suggest adding panic management strategies such as cognitive restructuring to assist with behavioral treatments.

Several studies indicate that real-life (in vivo) desensitization or exposure is the most effective and long-lasting treatment for a broad range of specific phobias. **Systematic desensitization** includes a process by which individuals unlearn the association between the phobic stimulus and anxiety. Incremental exposure involves the patient's gradual facing of the phobic stimulus through a series of graded steps. Wolpe's imagery desensitization is suggested so that patients with specific phobias can face the fear in imagery prior to attempting in vivo exposure. Unlike many of the other treatments, the treatment gains of in vivo exposure are maintained upon follow-up. Some desensitization treatments employ flooding as a useful strategy. When flooding is used, patients maintain a high anxiety level without retreating. Similar to desensitization, flooding can be used both in imagination and in vivo. Flooding is not suggested for most individuals because it can trigger a higher level of sensitization and fear reinforcement. For in vivo treatment, a patient needs to be highly motivated because the treatment may lead to temporary discomfort. The primary reasons for poor **compliance** with cognitive-behavioral treatment include lack of time, anxiety, and low motivation.

Psychodynamic therapy

Psychodynamic psychotherapy, or insight-oriented therapy assists patients to become more aware of the symbolic nature of their anxiety and to explore traumatic past events. Insight-oriented therapy is a psychodynamic therapy that aims to expose and reduce patients' unconscious conflicts, increase patients' understanding of their underlying thoughts, and assist patients to gain conscious control over their psychological conflicts. In psychodynamic therapy, for example, patients may discover that their anxiety may be connected to aggressive or sexual feelings and thoughts.

Group therapy

There is little research on **group therapy** for specific phobia disorder. Some studies suggest that group treatment has been effective for dental and spider phobias.

Medications

There has been a paucity of research on the relationship between medication and specific phobia. Generally, pharmacotherapy has not been considered to be a treatment of choice for individuals with specific phobias. Benzodiazepines, however, (medications that slow the central nervous system to ease nervousness and tension) may decrease anticipatory anxiety prior to an individual's entrance into a phobic situation. A low dose of a benzodiazepine such as **clonazepam** (Klonopin) or **alprazolam** (Xanax) is indicated to decrease some fear arousal prior to in vivo exposure. The reduction of symptoms, however, may interfere with the treatment. Prior to beginning in vivo exposure, an antidepressant such as **sertraline** (Zoloft) or **paroxetine** (Paxil) is suggested to increase motivation for undertaking an uncomfortable treatment. **Beta blockers** can assist individuals to confront the specific phobia.

Alternative therapies

Research shows some benefits for specific phobias with applied relaxation. Relaxation training includes abdominal breathing and muscle relaxation on a regular basis. Studies have indicated that applied muscle tension has been highly effective for individuals with blood type phobias who faint in that the treatment triggers an early response. When using applied tension, therapists request that patients tense their muscles several times. The repeated muscle tensing results in a temporary increase in blood pressure and prevents fainting when patients see blood. Similar to in vivo exposure, the gains from applied tension are maintained upon follow-up. Some alternative therapies include immersive virtual reality, **hypnotherapy**, eye-movement desensitization and reprocessing (EMDR), and energy balance approaches such as massage and **acupuncture**.

Prognosis

If specific phobias exist in adolescence, they have a greater chance of persisting in early adulthood. Specific phobias that continue into adulthood generally become chronic if they are not treated. Furthermore, there is a greater chance for an individual diagnosed with specific phobia to develop new phobias as a young adult. Phobias contracted during childhood or adolescence that continue when individuals become young adults remit approximately 20% of the time. Individuals with specific phobias do not often seek treatment. For those who seek treatment, research suggests that compared to individuals with specific phobias whose fear diminishes slowly during exposure, individuals with specific phobias whose fear diminishes more rapidly have a better prognosis for recovery.

A consideration of prognosis takes into account the distinction between fear onset and phobia onset. Studies indicate that individuals with specific phobias of animal, blood, heights, and driving had a fear onset nine years earlier than their phobia onset. Some studies have shown that generalized anxiety level, severity of symptoms, and prior experience with the phobic stimulus are factors that have been associated with treatment outcome.

Although most mental health professionals consider specific phobia that begins in childhood to be a benign disorder, it can last for years if left untreated. Some studies indicate, however, that specific phobia does not become worse and usually diminishes as an individual ages. Without treatment, the prognosis is poor for an individual who has several phobias.

Prevention

Early detection is a key to assisting individuals with mild cases of specific phobia to seek treatment to prevent the development of full-blown cases of the disorder. Individuals who are at risk for developing specific phobia as well as individuals who already have been diagnosed with specific phobia need to avoid caffeine because caffeine can increase arousal. Further research is needed to discover variables that predict the reason that only certain individuals will develop specific phobias after conditioning or acquiring information that leads to fear.

See also Anxiety-reduction techniques; Generalized anxiety disorder; Exposure treatment

Resources

BOOKS

American Psychiatric Association. *Diagnostic and Statistical Manual of Mental Disorders.* 4th edition, text revised. Washington, DC: American Psychiatric Association, 2000.

Antony, Martin, M., Ph.D., and David H. Barlow, Ph.D. "Social Phobia, Specific Phobia." In *Psychiatry.* Volume 2. Edited by Allan Tasman, M.D., Jerald Kay, M.D., and Jeffrey A. Lieberman, M.D. Philadelphia: W. B. Saunders Company, 1997.

Antony, Martin, M., Ph.D., and Richard P. Swinson. *Phobic Disorders and Panic in Adults: A Guide to Assessment and Treatment.* Washington, DC: American Psychological Association, 2000.

Bourne, Edmund J., Ph.D. *The Anxiety and Phobia Workbook.* 3rd Edition. Oakland, CA: New Harbinger Publications, 2001.

Bourne, Edmund J., Ph.D. *Beyond Anxiety and Phobia: A Step-by-Step Guide to Lifetime Recovery.* Oakland, CA: New Harbinger Publications, 2001.

Donahue, Brad, and James Johnston. "Specific Phobia." In *Diagnosis, Conceptualization, and Treatment Planning for Adults: A Step-by-Step Guide,* edited by Michel Hersen and Linda K. Porzelius. Mahwah, New Jersey: Lawrence Erlbaum Associates, Publishers, 2002.

Elkin, David, M.D., and Cameron S. Carter, M.D. "Anxiety Disorders." In *Introduction to Clinical Psychiatry,* edited by G. David Elkin, M.D. 1st edition. Stamford, Connecticut: Appleton and Lange, 1999.

PERIODICALS

Mager, Ralph, Alex H. Bullinger, Franz Mueller-Spahn, Marcus F. Kuntze, and Robert Stoermer. "Real-Time Monitoring of Brain Activity in Patients with Specific Phobia during Exposure Therapy, Employing a Stereoscopic Virtual Environment." *CyberPsychology and Behavior* 4, no. 4 (2001): 465–469.

ORGANIZATIONS

American Psychological Association. 750 First Street NE, Washington, D.C. 20002-4242. (202) 336-5500. <http://www.apa.org>.

Anxiety Disorders Association of America (ADAA). 11900 Parklawn Drive, Suite 100, Rockville, MD. 20852-2624. (301) 231-9350. <http://www.adaa.org>.

Phobics Anonymous. P.O. Box 1180, Palm Springs, CA. 92213. (760) 322-COPE.

Judy Koenigsberg, Ph.D.

SPECT *see* **Single photon emission computed tomography**

Speech therapy *see* **Speech-language pathology**

Speech-language pathology

Definition

Speech-language pathology is the treatment for the improvement or cure of communication disorders, including speech, language, and swallowing disorders. The term used to describe professionals in this discipline is speech and language pathologist (SLP).

Description

The discipline of speech-language pathology includes professionals that are trained in the techniques, strategies, and interventions designed to improve or correct communication disorders. Communication disorders include disorders of speech, language, and swallowing.

In 2000, there were nearly 88,000 speech-language pathologists in the United States certified by the American Speech-Language-Hearing Association (ASHA), and an additional 13,000 audiologists, who often work with speech pathologists to diagnose disorders. Speech disorders treated by speech-language pathologists include voice disorders (abnormalities in pitch, volume, vocal quality, or resonance or duration of sounds), articulation disorders (problems producing speech sounds), and fluency disorders (impairment in speech fluency, such as **stuttering**). Language disorders include developmental or acquired conditions that lead to difficulties in understanding or producing language. Speech-language pathologists participate in the screening, assessment, and treatment of patients who experience one or a combination of these disorders.

A young girl repeats sounds after the speech pathologist. *(Photo Researchers, Inc. Reproduced by permission.)*

Persons with isolated speech sound disorders are often helped by articulation therapy, in which they practice repeating specific sounds, words, phrases, and sentences. For individuals experiencing voice disorders, a combination of medical and behavioral treatments are often helpful. For stuttering and other fluency disorders, treatment approaches usually help individuals develop techniques to both reduce the severity of stuttering and allow the individual to produce more fluent speech. For all of these therapies, individuals are taught to cope more effectively with their speech in progressively difficult situations, starting with speaking alone to the pathologist and ending with speaking to a group of people. In treating children with developmental language disorders, treatment often focusses on **modeling** and stimulation of correct productions of language. This type of approach may also be useful for adults with language disorders, secondary to a **stroke** or degenerative neurological disorder. For people with severe communication disorders, those due to either a speech or language problem, speech pathologists can assist with alternate means of communication, such as manual signing and computer-synthesized speech. Finally, speech-language pathologists have become increasingly involved with the assessment and treatment of individuals with swallowing disorders, or dysphagia.

The majority of speech-language pathologists work in public schools. They are also found at both residential health care facilities and outpatient clinics that specialize in communication disorders. Finally, speech-language pathologists are often employed at hospitals and universities. Professional training programs in speech-language pathology are offered at both the undergraduate and graduate levels. Undergraduate training may include classes in biology, anatomy, psychology, linguistics, education, and special education. Graduate training, at both the masters and doctoral level, provides much deeper opportunities to study communication disorders and their treatment. To receive the Certificate of Clinical Competence (CCC) in speech-language pathology, individuals must hold a master's degree in communications sciences and disorders from a program accredited by the ASHA and complete their Clinical Fellowship Year (CFY).

Resources

ORGANIZATIONS

American Academy of Private Practice in Speech-Language Pathology and Audiology. 7349 Topanga Canyon Boulevard, Canoga Park, CA 91303.

American Speech-Language-Hearing Association. 10801 Rockville Pike, Rockville, MD 20785.

National Black Association for Speech, Language and Hearing. 3542 Gentry Ridge Court, Silver Spring, MD 20904.

Rodney Gabel, Ph.D.

KEY TERMS

Immunosuppressant—Medications that suppress or lower the body's immune system, primarily used to help the body accept a transplanted organ.

Monoamine oxidase inhibitors—A group of antidepressant drugs that decrease the activity of monoamine oxidase, a neurotransmitter found in the brain that affects mood.

Reserpine—Medication to treat high blood pressure. Brand names include Serpalan, Novoreserpine, and Reserfia.

Theophylline—A medication used to treat asthma. Sold under many brand names, including Aerolate Sr, Respbid, and Theolair.

Warfarin—A medication that helps to prevent the formation of clots in the blood vessels. Sold as Coumadin in the U.S.

Split personality disorder *see* **Dissociative identity disorder**

St. John's wort

Definition

St. John's wort is a perennial, yellow-flowering plant that grows in the wild throughout Europe and is now found also in North America. The plant tends to be in blossom in the month of June, around the day considered to be the birthday of John the Baptist; hence its popular name. The plant's Latin name is *Hypericum perforatum.*

St. John's wort has been used as a popular herbal folk remedy for centuries. More recently, practitioners of conventional Western medicine have been exploring its utility for treating depression and anxiety.

Purpose

Writings since the Middle Ages have described using St. John's wort as treatment for inflammation, injuries, burns, muscle pain, anxiety, high blood pressure, stomach problems, fluid retention, **insomnia**, hemorrhoids, cancer, and depression. Research conducted over the 1990s in Europe studied the efficacy of St. John's wort for the treatment of depression and anxiety. Research protocols have been developed in the United States to study the same issues, to determine appropriate dosages, to develop standard formulations, and to define whether it can be used for all forms of depression or only for more mild forms of the condition.

Description

Research has yet to completely explain how St. John's wort affects the **brain** in depression. It is, however, thought to change the balance of chemicals in the brain in much the same way as selective serotonin reuptake inhibitors (SSRIs) such as **fluoxetine** (Prozac), and monoamine oxidase inhibitors (MAOIs). The active ingredients are thought to be compounds called hypericin and pseudohypericin, although researchers are attempting to identify other chemicals that may be involved in the herb's effectiveness.

The leaves and flowers of St. John's wort are both used. St. John's wort is available as pills, capsules, extracts, dried herbs for tea, and oil infusions for skin applications.

Recommended dosage

Because dosages of herbal preparations are not always standardized, it is important to discuss with a knowledgeable practitioner the most reliable form of St. John's wort. Recommendations call for 300–500 mg (of a standardized 0.3% hypericin extract) three times daily. It can take four to six weeks to notice the antidepressant effects of this preparation.

Alternatively, one to two teaspoons of dried St. John's wort can be put into a cup of boiling water and

St. John's wort flowers. *(Photo Researchers, Inc. Reproduced by permission.) See color insert for color version of photo.*

steeped for 10 minutes to make tea. The recommended dosage of tea is one to two cups daily. Again, four to six weeks may be necessary in order to notice improvement in symptoms of depression.

Precautions

The following precautions should be considered and discussed with a knowledgeable practitioner before St. John's wort is taken:

- Some people may become more sensitive to the sun.
- Patients taking MAOIs must carefully avoid taking St. John's wort due to serious adverse effects of combining the two.
- Because the effects of St. John's wort are still being studied, pregnant and breast-feeding women should avoid its use.
- Depression can be a serious, even life-threatening, condition; therefore, it is imperative that depressed patients using St. John's wort are carefully monitored.

Side effects

People taking St. John's wort may develop one or all of the following side effects:

- skin rash due to sun sensitivity—the most common side effect
- headache, dizziness, dry mouth, constipation
- abdominal pain, confusion, sleep problems, and high blood pressure are less frequently experienced

Interactions

Again, a knowledgeable professional should be consulted before St. John's wort is taken to determine the appropriateness of its use and avoid serious interactions. Interactions include:

- Possible decrease in effectiveness of reserpine, warfarin, theophylline, immunosuppressant medications such as cyclosporine, and antiviral drugs such as indinavir.
- Dangerous interactions when used with other antidepressant medicines (especially MAOIs), digoxin, and loperamide.
- Interactions with oral birth control pills. St. John's wort may interfere with the effectiveness of birth control pills, increasing the risk of pregnancy; an alternative form of birth control should be considered while taking St. John's wort. In addition, women taking both birth control pills and St. John's wort may notice bleeding between menstrual periods.

See also Depression and depressive disorders

Resources

BOOKS

Blumenthal, Mark and others, eds. *The Complete German Commission E Monographs: Therapeutic Guide to Herbal Medicines.* Austin: American Botanical Council, 1998.

PERIODICALS

Zink, Therese and Jody Chaffin. "Herbal 'Health' Products: What Family Physicians Need to Know." *American Family Physician* 58 (October 1, 1998): 1133.

Rosalyn Carson-DeWitt, M.D.

Stanford-Binet Intelligence Scale

Definition

The Stanford-Binet Intelligence Scale: Fourth Edition (SB: FE) is a standardized test that measures intelligence and cognitive abilities in children and adults, from age two through mature adulthood.

Purpose

The Stanford-Binet Intelligence Scale was originally developed to help place children in appropriate educational settings. It can help determine the level of intellectual and cognitive functioning in preschoolers, children, adolescents and adults, and assist in the **diagnosis** of a learning disability, developmental delay, **mental retardation**, or giftedness. It is used to provide educational planning and placement, neuropsychological assessment, and research. The Stanford-Binet Intelligence Scale is generally administered in a school or clinical setting.

Precautions

The Stanford-Binet Intelligence Scale is considered to be one of the best and most widely used **intelligence tests** available. It is especially useful in providing intellectual assessment in young children, adolescents, and young adults. The test has been criticized for not being comparable for all age ranges. This is because different age ranges are administered different subtests. Additionally, for very young preschoolers, it is not uncommon to receive a score of zero due to test difficulty or the child's unwillingness to cooperate. Consequently, it is difficult to discriminate abilities in this age group among the lower scorers.

Administration and interpretation of results of the Stanford-Binet Intelligence Scale requires a competent examiner who is trained in psychology and individual intellectual assessment, preferably a **psychologist**.

Description

The Stanford-Binet Intelligence Scale has a rich history. It is a descendant of the Binet-Simon scale which was developed in 1905 and became the first intelligence test. The Stanford-Binet Intelligence Scale was developed in 1916 and was revised in 1937, 1960, and 1986. The present edition was published in 1986. The Stanford Binet Intelligence Scale is currently being revised and the Fifth Edition is expected to be available in the spring of 2003.

Administration of the Stanford-Binet Intelligence Scale typically takes between 45 to 90 minutes, but can take as long as two hours, 30 minutes. The older the child and the more subtests administered, the longer the test generally takes to complete. The Stanford-Binet Intelligence Scale is comprised of four cognitive area scores which together determine the composite score and factor scores. These area scores include: Verbal Reasoning, Abstract/Visual Reasoning, Quantitative Reasoning, and Short-Term Memory. The composite score is considered to be what the authors call the best estimate of "g" or "general reasoning ability" and is the sum of all of subtest scores. General reasoning ability or "g" is considered to represent a person's ability to solve novel problems. The composite score is a global estimate of a person's intellectual functioning.

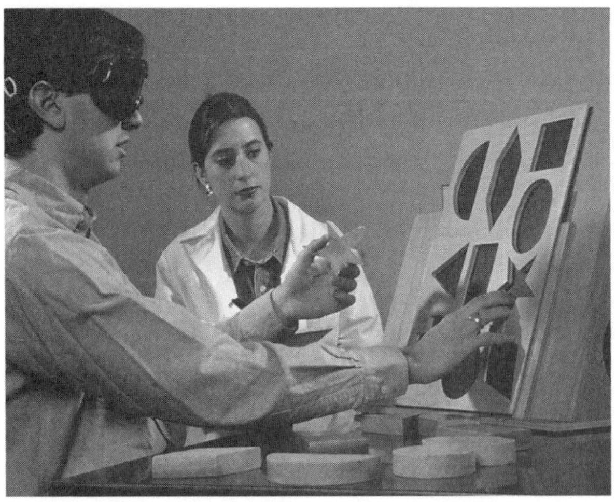

Abstract and visual reasoning are analyzed in Stanford-Binet intelligence tests. This blindfolded subject is matching shapes by touch. *(Richard Nowitz. Photo Researchers, Inc. Reproduced by permission.)*

The test consists of 15 subtests, which are grouped into the four area scores. Not all subtests are administered to each age group; but six subtests are administered to all age levels. These subtests are: Vocabulary, Comprehension, Pattern Analysis, Quantitative, Bead Memory, and Memory for Sentences. The number of tests administered and general test difficulty is adjusted based on the test taker's age and performance on the subtest that measures word knowledge. The subtest measuring word knowledge is given to all test takers and is the first subtest administered.

The following is a review of the specific cognitive abilities that the four area scores measure. The Verbal Reasoning area score measures verbal knowledge and understanding obtained from the school and home learning environment and reflects the ability to apply verbal skills to new situations. Examples of subtests comprising this factor measure skills which include: word knowledge, social judgment and awareness, ability to isolate the inappropriate feature in visual material and social intelligence, and the ability to differentiate essential from non-essential detail.

The Abstract/Visual Reasoning area score examines the ability to interpret and perform mathematic operations, the ability to visualize patterns, visual/motor skills, and problem-solving skills through the use of reasoning.

An example of a subtest which determines the Abstract/Visual Reasoning score is a timed test that involves tasks such as completing a basic puzzle and replicating black and white cube designs.

The Quantitative Reasoning area score measures: numerical reasoning, concentration, and knowledge and application of numerical concepts. The Quantitative Reasoning area is combined with the Abstract/Visual Reasoning area score to create an Abstract/Visual Reasoning Factor Score.

The Short-Term Memory score measures concentration skills, short-term memory, and sequencing skills. Subtests comprising this area score measure visual short-term memory and auditory short term memory involving both sentences and number sequences. In one subtest that measures visual short-term memory, the participant is presented with pictures of a bead design, and asked to replicate it from memory.

Results

The Stanford-Binet Intelligence Scale is a standardized test, which means that a large sample of children and adults were administered the exam as a means of developing test norms. The population in the sample was representative of the population of the United States based on age, gender, race or ethnic group, geographic region, community size, parental education, educational placement (normal versus special classes), etc. From this sample, norms were established. Norms are the performance of a comparison group of subjects—that nature of the group should be specified, and this usually constitutes a normal group so that the performance of the tested individual can be compared to this group and thus evaluated.

The numbers of correct responses on the given subtests are converted to a SAS score or Standard Age Score which is based on the chronological age of the test subject. This score is similar to an I.Q. score. Based on these norms, the Area Scores and Test Composite on the Stanford-Binet Intelligence Scale each have a mean or average score of 100 and a standard deviation of 16. For this test, as with most measures of intelligence, a score of 100 is in the normal or average range. The standard deviation indicates how above or below the norm a child's score is. For example, a score of 84 is one standard deviation below the norm score of 100. Based on the number of correct responses on a given subtest, an age-equivalent is available to help interpret the person's level of functioning.

Test scores provide an estimate of the level at which a child is functioning based on a combination of many different subtests or measures of skills. A trained psychologist is needed to evaluate and interpret the results, determine strengths and weaknesses, and make overall recommendations based on the findings and observed behavioral observations.

Resources

BOOKS

Sattler, Jerome. *Assessment of Children.* 3rd Edition. San Diego, CA, Jerome Sattler, Publisher Inc. 1992.

PERIODICALS

Caruso, J. "Reliable Component Analysis of the Stanford-Binet: Fourth Edition for 2–6-Year Olds." *Psychological Assessment* 13, no. 2. (2001): 827–840.

Grunau, R., M. Whitfield, and J. Petrie. "Predicting IQ of Biologically 'At Risk' Children from Age 3 to School Entry." *Developmental and Behavioral Pediatrics* 21, no. 6 (2000): 401–407.

ORGANIZATIONS

The American Psychological Association. 750 First St., NE, Washington, DC 20002-4242. (202) 336-5500 <www.apa.org>.

The National Association of School Psychologists. 4340 East West Highway, Suite 402, Bethesda, MD 20814. (301) 657-0270. <www.nasponline.com>.

Jenifer P. Marom, Ph.D.

Stelazine *see* **Trifluoperazine**

Stereotypic movement disorder

Definition

Stereotypic movement disorder is a disorder characterized by repeated, rhythmic, purposeless movements or activities such as head banging, nail biting, or body rocking. These movements either cause self-injury or severely interfere with normal activities. Until 1994, the American Psychiatric Association referred to stereotypic movement disorder as stereotypy/habit disorder.

Description

Stereotypic movements were first described as a psychiatric symptom in the early 1900s. Since then, they have been recognized as a symptom of both psychotic and neurological disorders. They may also arise from unexplained causes. These movements may include:

- head banging
- nail biting

- playing with hair (but not hair pulling, which is considered the separate disorder of **trichotillomania**)
- thumb sucking
- hand flapping
- nose picking
- whirling
- body rocking
- picking at the body
- self-biting
- object biting
- self-hitting
- compulsive scratching
- eye gouging
- teeth grinding (bruxism)
- breath holding
- stereotyped sound production

The precise definition of stereotypic movement disorder has changed over the past 20 years. Today, it limits the disorder to repetitive movements that cause physical harm or severely interfere with normal activities. These movements cannot be better described by another psychiatric condition such as anxiety disorder, a general medical condition such as Huntington's disease, or as the side effect of a medication or illicit drug (for example, cocaine use).

Stereotypic movements occur in people of any age, including the very young, but they are most prevalent in adolescence. People may exhibit only one particular stereotyped movement or several. The movements may be slow and gentle, fast and frenetic, or varied in intensity. They seem to increase with boredom, tension, or frustration, and it appears that the movements are self-stimulatory and sometimes pleasurable. The root causes are unknown.

Stereotypic movements are common in infants and toddlers. Some estimates suggest that 15–20 percent of children under age three exhibit some kind of rhythmic, repetitive movements. Certainly thumb sucking and body rocking are common self-comforting mechanisms in the very young. This type of repeated movement is temporary, and usually ends by age three or four. It is not the same as stereotypic movement disorder.

Causes and symptoms

Causes

Stereotypic movements can be caused by:

- sensory deprivation (blindness or deafness)
- drug use (cocaine, amphetamines)
- brain disease (**seizures**, infection)
- major psychiatric disorders (anxiety disorder, **obsessive-compulsive disorder**, **autism**)
- **mental retardation**

It has also been suggested that inadequate caregiving may cause the disorder. Although many situations can give rise to stereotypic movements, the root cause of stereotypic movement disorder is unknown. Different theories propose that the causes are behavioral, neurological, and/or genetic. Although there are many theories to account for this disorder, no hard evidence clearly supports one line of reasoning or specific cause.

Symptoms

Symptoms of stereotypic movement disorder include all the activities listed above. It should be noted that many of these activities are normal in infants. They usually begin between five and 11 months, and disappear on their own by age three. In fact, about 55% of infants grind their teeth. These passing phases of repetitive movement in infants are not the same as stereotypic movement disorder. They do not cause harm, and often serve the purpose of self-comforting or helping the child learn a new motor skill.

People with stereotypic movement disorder often hurt themselves. They may pick their nail cuticles or skin until they bleed. They may repeatedly gouge their eyes, bite or hit themselves causing bleeding, bruising, and sometimes, as in the case of eye gouging or head banging, even more severe damage. Some people develop behaviors such as keeping their hands in their pockets, to prevent these movements. In other cases those who hurt themselves appear to welcome, rather than fight, physical restraints that keep them safe. However when these restraints are removed, they return to their harmful behaviors.

Demographics

Stereotypic movement disorder is most strongly associated with severe or profound mental retardation, especially among people who are institutionalized and perhaps deprived of adequate sensory stimulation. It is estimated that 2–3% of people with mental retardation living in the community have stereotypic movement disorder. About 25% of all people with mental retardation who are institutionalized have the disorder. Among those with severe or profound retardation, the rate is about 60%, with 15% showing behavior that causes self-injury.

Stereotypic movements are common among children with **pervasive developmental disorders** such as autism, childhood degenerative disorder, and **Asperger's disorder**. These movements can also be seen in people with Tourette's disorder or with tics. Head banging is estimated to affect about 5% of children, with boys outnumbering girls three to one, although other stereotypic behaviors appear to be distributed equally between males and females. Despite its association with psychiatric disorders, there are some people with normal intelligence and adequate caregiving who still develop stereotypic movement disorder.

Diagnosis

Stereotypic movements are diagnosed by the presence of the activities mentioned above. Young children rarely try to hide these movements, although older children may, and the first sign of them may be the physical harm they cause (bleeding skin, chewed nails). Often parents mention these repetitive movements when the physician takes a history of the child.

The difficulty in diagnosing stereotypic movement disorder comes from distinguishing it from other disorders where rhythmic, repetitive movements occur. To be diagnosed with stereotypic movement disorder, the following conditions must be met:

- The patient must show repeated, purposeless motor behavior.
- The patient must experience physical harm from this behavior or it must seriously interfere with activities.
- If the patient is mentally retarded, the behavior must be serious enough to need treatment.
- The behavior must not be a symptom of another psychiatric disorder.
- The behavior must not be a side effect of medicinal or illicit substance use.
- The behavior must not be caused by a diagnosed medical condition.
- The behavior must last at least four weeks. The disorder may be classified as either with self-injurious behavior or without self-harm.

This definition of stereotypic movement disorder rules out many people who show repetitive movement because of autism or other pervasive developmental disorders. It also rules out those with obsessive-compulsive disorder, where movements are apt to be ritualistic and follow rigid rules or patterns. In addition, specific disorders such as trichotillomania (hair pulling) do not fall under the **diagnosis** of stereotypic movement disorder, nor do developmentally appropriate self-stimulatory behavior among young children, such as thumb sucking, rocking or transient pediatric head banging.

Treatments

There are few successful treatments for stereotypic movement disorder. When the patient harms himself, physical restraints may be required. In less severe situations, behavioral modifications using both rewards and punishments may help decrease the intensity of the behavior. Drugs that have been used with some success to treat stereotypic movement disorder include **clomipramine** (Anafranil), **desipramine** (Norpramin), **haloperidol** (Haldol) and **chlorpromazine** (Thorazine).

Prognosis

Stereotypic movements peak in adolescence, then decline, and sometimes disappear. Although **behavior modification** may reduce the intensity of the stereotypic movements, rarely does it completely eliminate them. **Stress** and physical pain may bring on these movements, (which may come and go for years), especially among those patients with severe mental retardation.

Prevention

Stereotypic movement disorder cannot be prevented. Interventions should be done to prevent self-injury.

Resources

BOOKS

American Psychiatric Association. *Diagnostic and Statistical Manual of Mental Disorders.* 4th ed. text revised. Washington DC: American Psychiatric Association, 2000.

Hales, Robert E., Stuart C. Yudofsky, and John A. Talbot. *The American Psychiatric Press Textbook of Psychiatry.* 3rd ed. Washington, DC: American Psychiatric Press, 2000.

Sadock, Benjamin J. and Virginia A. Sadock, eds. *Comprehensive Textbook of Psychiatry.* 7th ed. Vol. 2. Philadelphia: Lippincott Williams and Wilkins, 2000.

Tish Davidson, A.M.

Stigma

Definitions

The 1999 report on mental health by the Surgeon General of the United States was regarded as a landmark document in the United Kingdom, as well as the United States. This was because of its straightforward identification of the stigma associated with mental illness as the chief obstacle to effective treatment of persons with mental disorders. *Stigma* (plural, stigmata) is a Greek word that in its origins referred to a kind of tattoo mark that was cut or burned into the skin of criminals, slaves, or traitors in order to visibly identify them as blemished or morally polluted persons. These individuals were to be avoided or shunned, particularly in public places. The word was later applied to other personal attributes that are considered shameful or discrediting.

Social psychologists have distinguished three large classes, or categories, of stigma:

- Physical deformities. These include extremes of height and weight and such conditions as albinism and facial disfigurements or missing limbs. In the developed countries, this category also includes such signs of aging as gray hair, wrinkles, and stooped posture.
- Weaknesses or defects of individual character. This category includes biographical data that are held to indicate personal moral defect, such as a criminal record, **addiction**, divorce, treatment for mental illness, unemployment, **suicide** attempts, etc.
- Tribal stigma. This type of stigma refers to a person's membership in a race, ethnic group, religion, or (for women) gender that is thought to disqualify all members of the group.

The nature of stigma

Origins

One explanation for the origin of stigmata is that its roots in the human being's concern for group survival at earlier times in their evolutionary journey. According to this theory, stigmatizing people who were perceived as unable to contribute to the group's survival, or who were seen as threats to its well-being, were stigmatized in order to justify being forced out or being isolated.

The group survival theory is also thought to explain why certain human attributes seem to be universally regarded as stigmata, while others are specific to certain cultures or periods of history. Mental illness appears to be a characteristic that has nearly always led to the stigmatization and exclusion of its victims. The primary influences on Western culture, the classical philosophical tradition of Greece and Rome, and the religious traditions of Judaism and Christianity indicate that mental illness was a feared affliction that carried a heavy stigma. The classical philosopher's definition of a human being as a "rational animal" excluded him or her who had lost the use of reason and was no longer regarded as fully human; most likely he or she was under a divine curse. This attitude was summarized in the well-known saying of Lucretius, "Whom the gods wish to destroy, they first make mad."

In the Bible, both the Old and the New Testaments reflect the same fear of mental illness. In 1 Samuel 21, there is an account of David's pretending to be insane in order to get away from the king of a neighboring territory. "He changed his behavior before [the king's servants]; he pretended to be mad in their presence. He scratched marks on the doors of the gate, and let his spittle run down his beard." The king, who was taken in by an act that certainly fits the ***Diagnostic and Statistical Manual of Mental Disorders*** criteria for **malingering**, quickly sent David on his way. In the New Testament, one of Jesus' most famous miracles of healing (Mark 5:1-20) is the restoration of sanity to a man so stigmatized by his village that he was hunkered down in the graveyard (itself a stigmatized place) outside the village when Jesus met him. Mark's account also notes that the villagers had tried at different times to chain or handcuff the man because they were so afraid of him. One important positive contribution of Biblical heritage, however, is a sense of religious obligation toward the mentally ill. Among Christians, the New Testament's account of Jesus' openness to all kinds of stigmatized people—tax collectors, prostitutes, and physically deformed people, as well as the mentally ill—became the basis for the establishment of the first shelters and hospitals for the mentally ill.

Contemporary contexts

The core feature of stigma in the modern world is defined by social psychologists as the possession of an attribute "that conveys a devalued social identity within a particular context." Context is important in assessing the nature and severity of **stress** that a person suffers with regard to stigma. Certain attributes, such as race or sex, affect an individual's interactions with other people in so many different situations that they have been termed "master status" attributes. These have become the classic identifying characteristic of the person who possesses them. Dorothy Sayers' essay, "Are Women Human?" is not only a witty satire on the way men used to describe a woman's job or occupation (with constant reference to feminine qualities), but a keen social analysis of the problems created by master status attributes for persons who are stigmatized.

KEY TERMS

Stigma—A mark or characteristic trait of a disease or defect; by extension, a cause for reproach or a stain on one's reputation.

Other forms of devalued social identity are relative to specific cultures or subcultures. In one social context, a person who is stigmatized for an attribute devalued by a particular group may find acceptance in another group that values the particular attribute. A common example is that of an artistically or athletically talented child who grows up in a family that values only intellectual accomplishment. When the youngster is old enough to leave the family of origin, he or she can find a school or program for other students who share the same interest. A less marked contrast, but one that is relevant to the treatment of mental illness, is the cultural differences with regard to the degree of response to certain symptoms of mental illness. A study conducted in the early 21st century assessed the reaction of family members to elderly people who were diagnosed with **Alzheimer's disease** (AD). Findings pointed to considerable variation across racial and ethnic groups. Asian Americans were most affected by feelings of shame and social stigma relative to the memory loss of a family member, while African Americans were the least affected.

One additional complicating feature of stigma is the issue of overlapping stigmata. Many people belong to several stigmatized groups or categories, and it is not always easy to determine which category triggers the unkind or discriminatory treatment encountered. For example, one study of the inadequate medical treatment that is offered to most HIV-positive Native Americans noted that the stigma of Acquired Immune Deficiency Syndrome (AIDS) provides a strong motivation for not seeking treatment. The study protocol, however, did not seek to investigate whether young Native American men are afraid of being stigmatized for their sexual orientation, their race, their low socioeconomic status, or all three.

Stigma and mental illness

Stigma and specific disorders

The stigma that is still attached to mental illness in the developed countries does not represent a simple or straightforward problem. Public health experts who have studied the stigmatization of mental illness in recent years have noted that the general public's perception of mental illness varies, depending on the nature of the disorder. While in general the stigma of mental illness in contemporary society is primarily associated with the second of the three categories of stigma listed above,—supposed character failings—it also spills over into the first category. Mental disorders that affect a person's physical appearance—particularly weight gain—are more heavily stigmatized than those that do not.

The stigma related to certain types of mental disorders has declined since the 1950s, most notably in regard to depression and the anxiety disorders. It is thought that the reason for this change is that people are more likely nowadays to attribute these disorders to stress, with which most people can identify. On the other hand, the stigma associated with psychotic disorders appears to be worse than it was in the 1950s. Changes in public attitude are also reflected in age-group patterns in seeking or dropping out of treatment for mental disorders. One study demonstrated that older adults being treated for depression were more likely than younger adults to drop out of treatment because they felt stigmatized. The difference in behavior is related to public attitudes toward mental illness that were widespread when the older adults were adolescents.

In 2002, the types of mental disorders that carry the heaviest stigma fall into the following categories:

- Disorders associated in the popular mind with violence and/or illegal activity. These include **schizophrenia**, mental problems associated with HIV infection, and substance abuse disorders.
- Disorders in which the patient's behavior in public may embarrass family members. These include **dementia** in the elderly, **borderline personality disorder** in adults, and the autistic spectrum disorders in children.
- Disorders treated with medications that cause weight gain or other visible side effects.

The role of the media

The role of the media in perpetuating the stigmatization of mental illness has received increasing attention from public health researchers, particularly in Great Britain. In 1998, the Royal College of Psychiatrists launched a five-year campaign intended to educate the general public about the nature and treatment of mental illness. Surveys conducted among present and former mental patients found that they considered media coverage of their disorders to be strongly biased toward the sensational and the negative. One-third of patients said that they felt more depressed or anxious as a result of news stories about the mentally ill, and 22% felt more withdrawn. The main complaint from mental health professionals, as well as patients, is that the media presented mentally ill people as "dangerous time bombs waiting to explode" when in fact 95% of murders in the United Kingdom are committed by people with no mental illness. The proportion of homicides committed by the mentally ill has decreased by 3% per year since 1957, but this statistic goes unreported. Much the same story of unfair stigmatization in the media could be told in the United States, as the Surgeon General's report indicates.

Physicians' attitudes toward mental illness

Physicians' attitudes toward the mentally ill are also increasingly recognized as part of the problem of stigmatization. The patronizing attitude of moral superiority toward the mentally ill in the early 1960s, specifically in mental hospitals, has not disappeared. This was reported by Erving Goffman in his classic study. A Canadian insurance executive told a conference of physicians in May 2000 that they should look in the mirror for a picture of the ongoing stigmatization of the mentally ill. The executive was quoted as saying, "Stigma among physicians deters the detection of mental disorders, defers or pre-empts correct **diagnosis** and proper treatment and, by definition, prolongs suffering." An American physician who specializes in the treatment of substance addicts cites three reasons for the persistence of stigmatizing attitudes among his colleagues: their tendency to see substance abuse as a social issue, rather than a health issue; their lack of training in detecting substance abuse; and their mistaken belief that no effective treatments exist. A similar lack of information about effective treatments characterizes many psychiatrists' attitudes toward borderline personality disorder.

Stigma as cause of mental illness

It is significant that researchers in the field of social psychology have moved in recent years to analyzing stigma in terms of stress. Newer studies in this field now refer to membership in a stigmatized group as a stressor that increases a person's risk of developing a mental illness. The physiological and psychological effects of stress caused by racist behavior, for example, have been documented in African Americans. Similar studies of obese people have found that the stigmatization of **obesity** is the single most important factor in the psychological problems of these patients. To give still another example, the high rates of depression among post-menopausal women have been attributed to the fact that aging is a much heavier stigma for women than for men in contemporary society.

Stigma has a secondary effect on rates of mental illness in that members of stigmatized groups have less access to educational opportunities, well-paying jobs, and adequate health care. They are therefore exposed to more environmental stressors in addition to the stigma itself.

Stigma as effect

Stigma resulting from mental illness has been shown to increase the likelihood of a patient's relapse. Since a mental disorder is not as immediately apparent as race, sex, or physical handicaps, many people with mental disorders undergo considerable strain trying to conceal their condition from strangers or casual acquaintances. More seriously, the stigma causes problems in the job market, leading to stress that is related to lying to a potential employer and fears of being found out. Erving Goffman reported in the 1960s that a common way around the dilemma involved taking a job for about six months after discharge from a mental institution, then quitting that job and applying for another with a recommendation from the first employer that did not mention the history of mental illness.

The stigmatization of the patient with mental illness extends to family members, partly because they are often seen as the source of the patient's disorder. A recent editorial in the *Journal of the American Medical Association* tells the story of two sets of parents coping with the stress caused by other people's reactions to their children's mental illness, and the different responses they received when the children's disorders were thought to be a physical problem. The writer also tells of the problems encountered by the parents of an autistic child. The writer stated that family excursions were difficult, and continued, "My friend's wife was reprimanded by strangers for not being able to control her son. The boy was stared at and ridiculed. The inventive parent, fed up with the situation, bought a wheelchair to take the child out. The family was now asked about their child's disability. They were praised for their tolerance of his physical hardship and for their courage; the son was commended for his bravery. Same parents, same child, different view."

The results of stigma

The stigmatization of mental disorders has a number of consequences for the larger society. Patients' refusal to seek treatment, noncompliance with treatment, and inability to find work has a high price tag. Disability related to mental illness accounts for fully 15% of the economic burden caused by *all* diseases in developed countries.

Seeking treatment

Stigmatization of mental illness is an important factor in preventing persons with mental disorders from asking for help. This factor affects even mental health services on university campuses; interviews with Harvard students following a 1995 murder in which a depressed student killed a classmate, found that students hesitated to consult mental health professionals because many of their concerns were treated as disciplinary infractions, rather than illnesses. The tendency to stigmatize mental disorders as character faults is as prevalent among educators as among medical professionals. In addition, studies of large corporations indicate that employees frequently hesitate to seek treatment for depression and other stress-related disorders for fear of receiving negative evaluations of job performance and possible termination. These fears are especially acute during economic downturns and periods of corporate downsizing.

Compliance with treatment

Another connection between mental disorders and stigma is the low rates of treatment **compliance** among patients. To a large extent, patient compliance is a direct reflection of the quality of the doctor-patient relationship. One British study found that patients with mental disorders were likely to prefer the form of treatment recommended by psychiatrists with whom they had good relationships, even if the treatment itself was painful or difficult. Some patients preferred **electroconvulsive therapy** (ECT) to tranquilizers for depression because they had built up trusting relationships with the doctors who used ECT, and perceived the doctors who recommended medications as bullying and condescending. Other reasons for low compliance with treatment regimens are related to stigmatized side effects. Many patients, particularly women, discontinue medications that cause weight gain because of the social stigma attached to obesity in females.

Social and economic consequences

As already mentioned, persons with a history of treatment for mental disorders frequently encounter prejudice in the job market and the likelihood of long periods of unemployment; this can result in lower socioeconomic status, as well as loss of self-esteem. These problems are not limited to North America. A recent study of mental health patients in Norway, which is generally considered a progressive nation, found that the patients had difficulty finding housing as well as jobs, and were frequently harassed on the street as well as being socially isolated. In 1990, the Congress of the U.S. included mental disorders (with a few exceptions for disorders related to substance abuse and compulsive sexual behaviors) in the anti-discriminatory provisions of the Americans with Disabilities Act (ADA). As of 2002, mental disorders constitute the third-largest category of discrimination claims against employers.

Stigmatization of mental disorders also affects funding for research into the causes and treatment of mental disorders. Records of recent Congressional debates indicate that money for mental health research is still grudgingly apportioned as of 2002.

Future prospects

The stigma of mental illness will not disappear overnight. Slow changes in attitudes toward other social issues have occurred in the past three decades, giving hope to the lessening of stigma toward people with mental illness. However, limitations on indefinite economic expansion are an reason for concern. As the economic "pie" has to be divided among a larger number of groups, causing competition for public funding, persons with mental disorders will need skilled and committed advocates if their many serious needs are to receive adequate attention and help.

See also Stress

Resources

BOOKS

Goffman, Erving. *Asylums: Essays on the Social Situation of Mental Patients and Other Inmates.* New York: Anchor Books, 1961.

Goffman, Erving. *Stigma: Notes on the Management of Spoiled Identity.* New York: Simon and Schuster, Inc., 1963.

PERIODICALS

"AIDS Treatment Eludes Many Indians." *AIDS Weekly* (December 17, 2001): 10.

Britten, Nicky. "Psychiatry, Stigma, and Resistance: Psychiatrists Need to Concentrate on Understanding, Not Simply Compliance." *British Medical Journal* 317 (October 10, 1998): 763-764.

Corner, L., and J. Bond. "Insight and Perceptions of Risk in Dementia." *The Gerontologist* (October 15, 2001): 76.

Farriman, Annabel. "The Stigma of Schizophrenia" *British Medical Journal* 320 (February 19, 2000): 601.

Leshner, Alan I. "Taking the Stigma Out of Addiction." *Family Practice News* 30 (August 15, 2000): 30.

Lyons, Declan, and Declan M. McLoughlin. "Psychiatry (Recent Advances)." *British Medical Journal* 323 (November 24, 2001): 1228-1231.

Maher, Tracy. "Tackling the Stigma of Schizophrenia." *Practice Nurse* 20 (November 2000): 466-470.

Mahoney, D. "Understanding Racial/Ethnic Variations in Family's Response to Dementia." *The Gerontologist* (October 15, 2001): 120.

Myers, A., and J. C. Rosen. "Obesity Stigmatization and Coping: Relation to Mental Health Symptoms, Body Image, and Self-Esteem." *International Journal of Obesity and Related Metabolic Disorders* 23 (March 1999): 221-230.

Neil, Janice A. "The Stigma Scale: Measuring Body Image and the Skin." *Plastic Surgical Nursing* 21 (Summer 2001): 79.

Parker, Gordon, Gemma Gladstone, Kuan Tsee Chee. "Depression in the Planet's Largest Ethnic Group: The Chinese." *American Journal of Psychiatry* 158 (June 2001): 857.

Perlick, D. A., R. A. Rosenheck, J. F. Clarkin, and others. "Stigma as a Barrier to Recovery: Adverse Effects of Perceived Stigma on Social Adaptation of Persons

Diagnosed with Bipolar Affective Disorder." *Psychiatric Services* 52 (December 2001): 1627-1632.

"Reducing the Stigma of Mental Illness." *Lancet* 357 (April 7, 2001): 1055.

Russell, J. M., and J. A. Mackell. "Bodyweight Gain Associated with Atypical Antipsychotics: Epidemiology and Therapeutic Implications." *CNS Drugs* 15 (July 2001): 537-551.

Sirey, Jo Anne, Martha L. Bruce, George S. Alexopoulos, and others. "Perceived Stigma as a Predictor of Treatment Discontinuation in Young and Older Outpatients with Depression." *American Journal of Psychiatry* 158 (March 2001): 479-481.

Smart, L., and D. M. Wegner. "Covering Up What Can't Be Seen: Concealable Stigma and Mental Control." *Journal of Personal and Social Psychology* 77 (September 1999): 474-486.

Thesen, J. "Being a Psychiatric Patient in the Community—Reclassified as the Stigmatized 'Other.'" *Scandinavian Journal of Public Health* 29 (December 2001): 248-255.

Weissman, Myrna M. "Stigma." *Journal of the American Medical Association* 285 (January 17, 2001): 261.

Wojcik, Joanne. "Campaign Seeks to Remove Stigma of Mental Illness." *Business Insurance* 36 (January 21, 2002): 1.

Yanos, Philip T., Sarah Rosenfeld, Allan V. Horwitz. "Negative and Supportive Social Interactions and Quality of Life Among Persons Diagnosed with Severe Mental Illness." *Community Mental Health Journal* 37 (October 2001): 405.

ORGANIZATIONS

National Alliance for the Mentally Ill (NAMI). Colonial Place Three, 2107 Wilson Blvd., Suite 300, Arlington, VA 22201. (800) 950-6264. <www.nami.org>.

OTHER

National Institute of Mental Health (NIMH). *The Impact of Mental Illness on Society.* NIH Publication No. 01-4586. <www.nimh.nih.gov/publicat/burden.cfm>.

Office of the Surgeon General. *Mental Health: A Report of the Surgeon General.* Washington, D.C.: Government Printing Office, 1999. A copy of the report may be ordered by faxing the Superintendent of Documents at (202) 512-2250.

Rebecca J. Frey, Ph.D.

Stress

Definitions

Stress is a term that refers to the sum of the physical, mental, and emotional strains or tensions on a person. Feelings of stress in humans result from interactions between persons and their environment that are perceived as straining or exceeding their adaptive capacities and threatening their well-being. The element of perception indicates that human stress responses reflect differences in personality as well as differences in physical strength or health.

A stressor is defined as a stimulus or event that provokes a stress response in an organism. Stressors can be categorized as acute or chronic, and as external or internal to the organism. The ***Diagnostic and Statistical Manual of Mental Disorders*** (*DSM-IV-TR*) defines a psychosocial stressor as "any life event or life change that may be associated temporally (and perhaps causally) with the onset, occurrence, or exacerbation [worsening] of a mental disorder."

Stress affects the lives of most adults in developed countries in many ways. It is a major factor in rising health care costs; one public health expert maintains that 90% of all diseases and disorders in the United States are stress-related. Stress plays a part in many social problems such as child and elder **abuse**, workplace violence, juvenile crime, **suicide**, substance **addiction**, "road rage," and the general decline of courtesy and good manners. Stress also affects the productivity of businesses and industries. One nationwide survey found that 53% of American workers name their job as the single greatest source of stress in their lives. Furthermore, the overall cost of medical care, time lost from work, and workplace accidents in the United States comes to over $150 million per year.

The neurobiology of stress

One way to understand stress as a contemporary health problem is to look at the human stress response as a biologically conditioned set of reactions that was a necessary adaptation at earlier points in human evolution, but is less adaptive under the circumstances of modern life. Hans Selye (1907-1982), a Canadian researcher, was a pioneer in studying stress. Selye defined stress, in essence, as the rate of wear and tear on the body. He observed that an increasing number of people, particularly in the developed countries, die of so-called diseases of civilization, or degenerative diseases, which are primarily caused by stress. Selye also observed that stress in humans depends partly on people's evaluation of a situation and their emotional reaction to it; thus, an experience that one person finds stimulating and exciting—for example, bungee jumping—would produce harmful stress in another.

The stress response

In humans, the biochemical response to acute stress is known as the "fight-or-flight" reaction. It begins with

KEY TERMS

Adjustment disorder—A disorder defined by the development of significant emotional or behavioral symptoms in response to a stressful event or series of events. Symptoms may include depressed mood, anxiety, and impairment of social and occupational functioning.

Adrenaline—Another name for epinephrine, the hormone released by the adrenal glands in response to stress. It is the principal blood-pressure raising hormone and a bronchial and intestinal smooth muscles relaxant.

Allostasis—The process of an organism's adaptation to acute stress.

Amygdala—An almond-shaped brain structure in the limbic system that is activated in acute stress situations to trigger the emotion of fear.

Burnout—An emotional condition that interferes with job performance, marked by fatigue, loss of interest, or frustration; usually regarded as the result of prolonged stress.

Catecholamine—A group of neurotransmitters synthesized from the amino acid tyrosine and released by the hypothalamic-pituitary-adrenal system in the brain in response to acute stress. The catecholamines include dopamine, serotonin, norepinephrine, and epinephrine.

Coping—In psychology, a term that refers to a person's patterns of response to stress.

Cortisol—A steroid hormone released by the cortex (outer portion) of the adrenal gland when a person is under stress.

Dissociation—A reaction to trauma in which the mind splits off certain aspects of the traumatic event from conscious awareness. Dissociation can affect the patient's memory, sense of reality, and sense of identity.

Eustress—A term that is sometimes used to refer to positive stress.

Flashback—The re-emergence of a traumatic memory as a vivid recollection of sounds, images, and sensations associated with the trauma. The person having the flashback typically feels as if he or she is reliving the event.

Hippocampus—A part of the brain that is involved in memory formation and learning. The hippocampus is shaped like a curved ridge and belongs to an organ system called the limbic system.

Homeostasis—The tendency of the physiological system in humans and other mammals to maintain its internal stability by means of a coordinated response to any stimulus that disturbs its normal condition.

Limbic system—A group of structures in the brain that includes the amygdala, hippocampus, olfactory bulbs, and hypothalamus. The limbic system is associated with homeostasis and the regulation and arousal of emotions.

Relaxation response—The body's inactivation of stress responses and return of stress hormone levels to normal after a threat has passed.

Stress management—A set of techniques and programs intended to help people deal more effectively with stress in their lives by analyzing the specific stressors and taking positive actions to minimize their effects. Most stress management programs deal with job stress and workplace issues.

Stressor—A stimulus or event that provokes a stress response in an organism. Stressors can be categorized as acute or chronic, and as external or internal to the organism.

the activation of a section of the **brain** called the hypothalamic-pituitary-adrenal system, or HPA. This system first activates the release of steroid hormones, which are also known as glucocorticoids. These hormones include cortisol, the primary stress hormone in humans.

The HPA system then releases a set of **neurotransmitters** known as catecholamines, which include dopamine, norepinephrine, and epinephrine (also known as adrenaline). Catecholamines have three important effects:

- They activate the amygdala, an almond-shaped structure in the limbic system that triggers an emotional response of fear.
- They signal the hippocampus, another part of the limbic system, to store the emotional experience in long-term memory.
- They suppress activity in parts of the brain associated with short-term memory, concentration, and rational thinking. This suppression allows a human to react

quickly to a stressful situation, but it also lowers ability to deal with complex social or intellectual tasks that may be part of the situation.

In reaction to stress, heart rate and blood pressure rise, and the person breathes more rapidly, which allows the lungs to take in more oxygen. Blood flow to the muscles, lungs, and brain may increase by 300–400%. The spleen releases more blood cells into the circulation, which increases the blood's ability to transport oxygen. The immune system redirects white blood cells to the skin, bone marrow, and lymph nodes; these are areas where injury or infection is most likely.

At the same time, nonessential body systems shut down. The skin becomes cool and sweaty as blood is drawn away from it toward the heart and muscles. The mouth becomes dry, and the digestive system slows down.

The relaxation response

After the crisis passes, the levels of stress hormones drop and the body's various organ systems return to normal. This return is called the relaxation response. Some people are more vulnerable to stress than others because their hormone levels do not return to normal after a stressful event. An absent or incomplete relaxation response is most likely to occur in professional athletes and in people with a history of depression.

Physical effects of chronic stress

In chronic stress, the organ systems of the body do not have the opportunity to return fully to normal levels. Different organs become under- or overactivated on a long-term basis. In time, these abnormal levels of activity can damage an organ or organ system.

Cardiovascular system

Stress has a number of negative effects on the heart and circulatory system. Sudden stress increases heart rate, but also causes the arteries to narrow, which may block the flow of blood to the heart. The emotional effects of stress can alter the rhythm of the heart. In addition, stress causes the release of extra clotting factors into the blood, which increases the risk of a clot forming and blocking an artery. Stress also triggers the release of fat into the bloodstream, which temporarily raises blood cholesterol levels. Lastly, it is thought that people who regularly have sudden increases in blood pressure due to mental stress may over time suffer injuries to the inner lining of their blood vessels.

Gastrointestinal system

The effects of chronic stress on the gastrointestinal system include diarrhea, constipation, bloating, and irritable bowel syndrome. Although stress is not the direct cause of either peptic ulcers or inflammatory bowel disease, it may predispose people to develop ulcers and worsen flareups of inflammatory bowel disease.

Stress is the cause of abnormal weight loss in some people and of weight gain in others, largely from stress-related eating. It is thought that stress related to the physical and emotional changes of puberty is a major factor in the development of eating disorders.

Reproductive system

Stress affects sexual desire in both men and women and can cause impotence in men. It appears to worsen the symptoms of premenstrual syndrome (PMS) in women. Stress affects fertility, in that high levels of cortisol in the blood can affect the hypothalamus, which produces hormones related to reproduction. Very high levels of cortisol can cause amenorrhea, or cessation of menstrual periods.

Stress during pregnancy is associated with a 50% higher risk of miscarriage. High stress levels on the mother during pregnancy are also related to higher rates of premature births and babies of lower than average birth weight; both are risk factors for infant mortality.

Musculoskeletal system

Stress intensifies the chronic pain of arthritis and other joint disorders. It also produces tension-type headaches, caused by the tightening of the muscles in the neck and scalp. Research indicates that people who have frequent tension headaches have a biological predisposition for converting emotional stress into muscle contraction.

Brain

The physical effects of stress hormones on the brain include interference with memory and learning. Acute stress interferes with short-term memory, although this effect goes away after the stress is resolved. People who are under severe stress become unable to concentrate; they may become physically inefficient, clumsy, and accident-prone. In children, however, the brain's biochemical responses to stress clearly hamper the ability to learn.

Chronic stress appears to be a more important factor than aging in the loss of memory in older adults. Older people with low levels of stress hormones perform as well as younger people in tests of cognitive (knowledge-related) skills, but those with high levels of stress hormones test between 20% and 50% lower than the younger test subjects.

Immune system

Chronic stress affects the human immune system and increases a person's risk of getting an infectious illness. Several research studies have shown that people under chronic stress have lower than normal white blood cell counts and are more vulnerable to colds and influenza. Men with HIV infection and high stress levels progress more rapidly to AIDS than infected men with lower stress levels.

Stress and mental disorders

DSM-IV-TR specifies two major categories of mental disorders directly related to stress—the post-traumatic syndromes and adjustment disorders. Stress is, however, also closely associated with depression, and can worsen the symptoms of most other disorders.

Post-traumatic disorders

Post-traumatic stress disorder (PTSD) and **acute stress disorder** (ASD) are defined by their temporal connection to a traumatic event in the individual's life. The post-traumatic disorders are characterized by a cluster of anxiety and dissociative symptoms, and by their interference with the patient's normal level of functioning. **Magnetic resonance imaging** (MRI) studies have shown that the high levels of sustained stress in some PTSD patients cause demonstrable damage to the hippocampus. Excessive amounts of stress hormones in brain tissue cause the nerve cells, or neurons, in parts of the hippocampus to wither and eventually die. One group of Vietnam veterans with PTSD had lost as much as 8% of the tissue in the hippocampus.

Substance abuse disorders

Stress is related to substance abuse disorders in that chronic stress frequently leads people to self-medicate with drugs of abuse or alcohol. Substance abuse disorders are associated with a specific type of strategy for dealing with stress called emotion-focused coping. Emotion-focused coping strategies concentrate on regulating painful emotions related to stress, as distinct from problem-focused coping strategies, which involve efforts to change or eliminate the impact of a stressful event. Persons who handle stress from a problem-oriented perspective are less likely to turn to mood-altering substances when they are under stress.

Adjustment disorders

DSM-IV-TR defines adjustment disorders as psychological responses to stressors that are excessive given the nature of the stressor; or result in impairment of the person's academic, occupational, or social functioning. The most important difference between the post-traumatic disorders and adjustment disorders is that most people would not necessarily regard those stressors involved in the latter disorder as traumatic. **Adjustment disorder** appear to be most common following natural disasters, divorce, becoming a parent, and retirement from work.

Causes of stress

The causes of stress may include any event or situation that a person considers a threat to his or her resources or coping strategies. A certain amount of stress is a normal part of life; it represents a person's response to inevitable changes in his or her physical or social environment. Moreover, positive events can generate stress as well as negative events. Graduating from college, for example, is accompanied by stress related to employment or possible geographical relocation and the stress of saying good-bye to friends and family, as well as feelings of positive accomplishment. Some researchers refer to stress associated with positive events as eustress.

Acute stress is defined as a reaction to something perceived as an immediate threat. Acute stress reactions can occur to a falsely perceived danger as well as to a genuine threat; they can also occur in response to memories. For example, a war veteran who hears a car backfire may drop to the ground because the noise triggers vivid memories, called flashbacks, of combat experience. Common acute stressors include loud, sudden noises being in a crowded space such as an elevator, being cut off in heavy traffic; and dangerous weather. Chronic stress is a reaction to a situation that is stressful but ongoing, such as financial worries or caring for an elderly parent. Modern life is stressful because changes in various areas of life have increased the number of acute and chronic stressors in most people's lives at the same time that they have weakened certain buffers or protections against stress.

Social changes

Social changes that have increased the stress level of modern life include increased population mobility and the sprawling size of modern cities. It is not unusual for adults to live hundreds of miles away from parents and siblings; and it is hard to make and keep friendships when people move every few years. In most large cities, many people live in apartment buildings where they do not know their neighbors. Social isolation and loneliness can produce chronic stress. A study done in Norway between 1987 and 1993 found that social support networks made a significant difference in lowering the impact of both acute and chronic stress on mental health.

Social scientists have observed that the increased isolation of married couples from extended families and friendship networks increases strains on the marriage. The rising divorce rate in the United States has been attributed in part to the loss of social supports that once helped to keep married couples together. The experience of divorce then adds to the stress level on the former spouses and the children, if any. A long-term study at the University of Pittsburgh has found that divorce is associated with a higher rate of premature death in men.

Economic changes

The rapid pace of change in manufacturing and other businesses means that few people will work at the same job for their entire career. In addition, corporate mergers and downsizing have weakened job security, thus producing chronic anxiety about unemployment in the minds of many employees. Many people work two jobs in order to make ends meet; and even those who work only one job often have to commute by car or train to their workplace. In many large American cities, traffic jams, cost of gasoline, and other problems related to commuting are a major factor in job-related stress. Another stress factor is sleep deprivation. Many people get only six or less hours of sleep each night even though the National Sleep Foundation estimates that most adults need 8–8-1/2 hours per night for good health. **Fatigue** due to sleep deprivation causes additional stress.

Lastly, economic trends have produced a "winner-take-all" economy in which the gap between the well-off and the average family is constantly widening. Socioeconomic status (SES) affects health in a number of ways. Persons of higher SES can afford better health care, are less likely to suffer from exposure to environmental toxins, and generally lead healthier lifestyles. In addition, chronic stress associated with low SES appears to increase morbidity and mortality among persons in these income groups.

Technological changes

Technology has proved to be a source of stress as well as a solution to some kinds of stress. Machines that help workers to be more productive also make their jobs more complicated and raise the level of demands on them. An office clerk in 2002 can produce many more letters per day than one in 1952, but is often expected to produce more elaborate, professional-looking documents as well as a higher number of them.

One specific technological development that has been singled out as a major stressor in modern life is the evolution of news reporting. For most of human history, people had to wait several days or even weeks to hear about the outcome of an election, a battle, or some other important event. Moreover, they usually heard only the news that affected their region or their country. Today, however, news is reported as soon as it happens, it is broadcast 24 hours a day, and it covers events around the world. This "communications overload," as it has been termed, is a source of genuine stress to many people, particularly when the newscast emphasizes upsetting or frightening events. It is not surprising that a common recommendation for lowering one's stress level is to cut down on watching television news programs. A team of physicians conducted telephone interviews following the events of September 11, 2001, in order to assess stress reactions in the general American population. The team found that the single most important factor was not geographical location relative to the attacks or educational level, but the amount of time spent watching televised reports of the attacks. The interviewers discovered that 49% of the adults had watched at least eight hours of television on September 11, and also that "extensive television viewing was associated with a substantial stress reaction."

Environmental changes

One significant source of stress in modern life is the cumulative effect of various toxic waste products on the environment. Studies of the aftermath of such environmental disasters as Three Mile Island and Chernobyl found that not only evacuees and people living in the contaminated area had high levels of emotional distress, but also cleanup workers and people living in nearby noncontaminated areas. In the case of Chernobyl, Russian physicians have reported a psychoneurological syndrome with several unexplained symptoms, including fatigue, impaired memory, muscle or joint pain, and sleep disturbances. The syndrome appears to be due to chronic emotional stress rather than radiation exposure.

Changes in beliefs and attitudes

Changes in beliefs that influence stress levels include the contemporary emphasis on individualism and a corresponding change in attitudes toward trauma. A number of observers have remarked that Western culture has moved away from its traditional high valuation of the family and community toward an increased focus on the individual. Some have called this trend the "Me First!" society—it emphasizes personal rights and entitlements rather than duties and responsibilities to others. It has, in the view of some physicians, encouraged people to dwell on trauma and its effects on them as individuals rather than to live up to more traditional ideals of composure and resilience in the face of distress.

Risk factors

Research indicates that some categories of people have a higher risk of stress-related illnesses and disorders:

- Children have very little control over their environments. In addition, they are often unable to communicate their feelings accurately.
- In elderly adults, aging appears to affect the body's response to stress, so that the relaxation response following a stressful event is slower and less complete. In addition, the elderly are often affected by such major stressors as health problems, the death of a spouse or close friends, and financial worries.
- Caregivers of mentally or physically disabled family members.
- Women in general.
- People with less education.
- People who belong to racial or ethnic groups that suffer discrimination.
- People who live in cities.
- People who are anger-prone. Chronic anger is associated with narrowing of the arteries, a factor in heart disease.
- People who lack family or friends.
- People who are biologically predisposed to an inadequate relaxation response.

Coping with stress

Coping is defined as a person's patterns of response to stress. Many clinicians think that differences in attitudes toward and approaches to stressful events are the single most important factor in assessing a person's vulnerability to stress-related illnesses. A person's ability to cope with stress depends in part on his or her interpretation of the event. One person may regard a stressful event as a challenge that can be surmounted while another views it as a problem with no solution. The person's resources, previous physical and psychological health, and previous life experience affect interpretation of the event. Someone who has had good experiences of overcoming hardships is more likely to develop a positive interpretation of stressful events than someone who has been repeatedly beaten down by abuse and later traumas.

Coping styles

The ways in which people cope with stress can be categorized according to two different sets of distinctions. One is the distinction between emotion-focused and problem-focused styles of coping, which was described earlier in connection with substance abuse. Problem-focused coping is believed to lower the impact of stress on health; people who use problem-focused coping have fewer illnesses, are less likely to become emotionally exhausted, and report higher levels of satisfaction in their work and feelings of personal accomplishment. Emotion-focused coping, on the other hand, is associated with higher levels of interpersonal problems, depression, and social isolation. Although some studies reported that men are more likely to use problem-focused coping and women to use emotion-focused coping, other research done in the last decade has found no significant gender differences in coping styles.

The second set of categories distinguishes between control-related and escape-related coping styles. Control-related coping styles include direct action, behavior that can be done alone; help-seeking, behavior that involves social support; and positive thinking, a cognitive style that involves giving oneself pep talks. Escape-related coping styles include avoidance/resignation, as in distancing oneself from the stressful event, and alcohol use. There appears to be no relationship between gender and a preference for control-related or escape-related coping.

Stress management

Stress management refers to a set of programs or techniques intended to help people deal more effectively with stress. Many of these programs are oriented toward job- or workplace-related stress in that burnout is a frequent result of long-term occupational stress. Most stress management programs ask participants to analyze or identify the specific aspects of their job that they find stressful, and then plan a course of positive action to minimize the stress. In general, the severity of job-related stress appears to be related to two factors: the magnitude of the demands being made on the worker, and the degree of control that she or he has in dealing with the demands. The workers who are most vulnerable to stress-related heart disease are those who are subjected to high demands but have little control over the way they do their job. In many cases, stress management recommendations include giving an employee more decision-making power.

Treatments for stress

There are a number of allopathic and alternative/complementary treatments that are effective in relieving the symptoms of stress-related disorders:

- Medications may include drugs to control anxiety and depression as well as drugs that treat such physical symptoms of stress as indigestion or high blood pressure.
- Psychotherapy, including insight-oriented and cognitive/behavioral approaches, is effective in helping people understand how they learned to overreact to stressors, and in helping them reframe their perceptions and

interpretations of stressful events. Anger management techniques are recommended for people who have stress-related symptoms due to chronic anger.

- Relaxation techniques, **anxiety reduction techniques**, breathing exercises, **yoga**, and other physical exercise programs that improve the body's relaxation response.
- Therapeutic massage, hydrotherapy, and **bodywork** are forms of treatment that are particularly helpful for people who tend to carry stress in their muscles and joints.
- **Aromatherapy**, pet therapy, humor therapy, music therapy, and other approaches that emphasize sensory pleasure are suggested for severely stressed people who lose their capacity to enjoy life; sensory-based therapies can counteract this tendency.
- Naturopathic recommendations regarding diet, exercise, and adequate sleep, and the holistic approach of naturopathic medicine can help persons with stress-related disorders to recognize and activate the body's own capacities for self-healing.

Resources

BOOKS

American Psychiatric Association. *Diagnostic and Statistical Manual of Mental Disorders.* 4th edition, text revised. Washington, DC: American Psychiatric Association, 2000.

Gleick, James. *Faster: The Acceleration of Just About Everything.* New York: Pantheon Books, 1999.

Herman, Judith, MD. *Trauma and Recovery.* 2nd ed., revised. New York: Basic Books, 1997.

"Psychosomatic Medicine (Biopsychosocial Medicine)." Section 15, Chapter 185 in *The Merck Manual of Diagnosis and Therapy*, edited by Mark H. Beers, MD, and Robert Berkow, MD. Whitehouse Station, NJ: Merck Research Laboratories, 2000.

Selye, Hans. *The Stress of Life.* Revised edition. New York: McGraw-Hill Book Company, Inc., 1976.

PERIODICALS

Adler, N. E., and K. Newman. "Socioeconomic Disparities in Health: Pathways and Policies. Inequality in Education, Income, and Occupation Exacerbates the Gaps Between the Health 'Haves' and 'Have-Nots.'" *Health Affairs (Millwood)* 21 (March-April 2002): 60-76.

Evans, O., and A. Steptoe. "The Contribution of Gender-Role Orientation, Work Factors and Home Stressors to Psychological Well-Being and Sickness Absence in Male- and Female-Dominated Occupational Groups." *Social Science in Medicine* 54 (February 2002): 481-492.

Levenstein, Susan. "Stress and Peptic Ulcer: Life Beyond Helicobacter." *British Medical Journal* 316 (February 1998): 538-541.

Lombroso, Paul J. "Stress and Brain Development, Part 1." *Journal of the American Academy of Child and Adolescent Psychiatry* 37 (December 1998).

McEwen, Bruce. "Stress and Brain Development, Part 2." *Journal of the American Academy of Child and Adolescent Psychiatry* 38 (January 1999).

Matthews, K. A., and B. B. Gump. "Chronic Work Stress and Marital Dissolution Increase Risk of Posttrial Mortality in Men from the Multiple Risk Factor Intervention Trial." *Archives of Internal Medicine* 162 (February 2002): 309-315.

Mayer, Merry. "Breaking Point (Job Stress and Problem Employees)." *HR Magazine* 46 (October 2001): 79-85.

Olstad, R., H. Sexton, and A. J. Sogaard. "The Finnmark Study: A Prospective Population Study of the Social Support Buffer Hypothesis, Specific Stressors and Mental Distress." *Social Psychiatry and Psychiatric Epidemiology* 36 (December 2001): 582-589.

Pastel, R. H. "Radiophobia: Long-Term Psychological Consequences of Chernobyl." *Military Medicine* 167 (February 2002): 134-136.

Schuster, Mark A., Bradley D. Stein, Lisa H. Jaycox, and others. "A National Survey of Stress Reactions After the September 11, 2001, Terrorist Attacks." *New England Journal of Medicine* 345 (November 15, 2001): 1507-1512.

Summerfield, Derek. "The Invention of Post-Traumatic Stress Disorder and the Social Usefulness of a Psychiatric Category." *British Medical Journal* 322 (January 13, 2001): 95-98.

van der Kolk, Bessel. "The Body Keeps the Score: Memory and the Evolving Psychobiology of PTSD." *Harvard Review of Psychiatry* 1 (1994): 253-265.

ORGANIZATIONS

The American Institute of Stress. 124 Park Avenue, Yonkers, NY 10703. (914) 963-1200. Fax: (914) 965-6267. <www.stress.org.>.

Anxiety Disorders Association of America. 11900 Parklawn Drive, Suite 100, Rockville, MD 20852-2624. (301) 231-9350. <www.adaa.org>.

Stress and Anxiety Research Society (STAR). <www.star-society.org>.

See also Creative therapies; Diets; Nutrition and mental health

Rebecca J. Frey, Ph.D.

Stroke

Definition

A stroke, also called a cerebral vascular accident (CVA), is the sudden death of cells in a specific area of the **brain** due to inadequate blood flow.

KEY TERMS

Aneurysm—A symptomless bulging of a weak arterial wall that can rupture, leading to stroke.

Angiography—A procedure in which a contrast medium is injected into the bloodstream (through an artery in the neck) and its progress through the brain is tracked. This illustrates where a blockage or hemorrhage has occurred.

Anticoagulant—A medication (such as warfarin, Coumadin, or Heparin) that decreases the blood's clotting ability preventing the formation of new clots. Although anticoagulants will not dissolve existing clots, they can stop them from getting larger. These drugs are commonly called blood thinners.

Atrial fibrillation—A disorder in which the upper chambers (atria) of the heart do not completely empty with each contraction (heartbeat). This can allow blood clots to form and is associated with a higher risk of stroke.

Electrocardiogram—(EKG) A test that measures the electrical activity of the heart as it beats. An abnormal EKG can indicate possible cardiac disease.

Electroencephalogram—(EEG) A test that measures the electrical activity of the brain by means of electrodes placed on the scalp or on or in the brain itself. It may be used to determine whether or not a stroke victim has had a seizure.

Hypertension—High blood pressure, often brought on by smoking, obesity, or other causes; one of the major causes of strokes.

Pressure ulcers—Also known as pressure sores or bed sores, these can develop in stroke patients who are unable to move. If not treated properly, they can become infected.

Tissue plasminogen activator (tPA)—A drug that is sometimes given to patients within three hours of a stroke to dissolve blood clots within the brain; also used to treat heart attack victims.

Ultrasound—A noninvasive test in which high-frequency sound waves are reflected off a patient's internal organs allowing them to be viewed. In stroke victims, a cardiac ultrasound, or echocardiogram, allows the beating heart to be examined.

Description

A stroke occurs when blood flow is interrupted to a part of the brain, either when an artery bursts or becomes closed when a blood clot lodges in it. Blood circulation to the area of the brain served by that artery stops at the point of disturbance, and the brain tissue beyond that is damaged or dies. (Brain cells need blood to supply oxygen and nutrients and to remove waste products.) Depending on the region of the brain affected, a stroke can cause paralysis, loss of vision, speech impairment, memory loss and reasoning ability, coma, or death. The effects of a stroke are determined by how much damage occurs, and which portion of the brain is affected.

About a third of all strokes are preceded by transient ischemic attacks (TIAs), or mini-strokes, that temporarily interrupt blood flow to the brain. While TIAs cause similar symptoms (such as sudden vision loss or temporary weakness in a limb), they abate much more quickly than full-fledged strokes, usually within a few hours—sometimes as quickly as a few minutes.

Stroke is a medical emergency requiring immediate treatment. Prompt treatment improves the chances of survival and increases the degree of recovery that may be expected. A person who may have suffered a stroke should be seen in a hospital emergency room without delay. Treatment to break up a blood clot, the major cause of stroke, must begin within three hours of the stroke to be most effective. Improved medical treatment of all types of stroke has resulted in a dramatic decline in death rates in recent decades. In 1950 nine in ten stroke victims died, compared to slightly less than one in three today.

Causes and symptoms

Causes

There are four main types of stroke: cerebral thrombosis, cerebral embolism, subarachnoid hemorrhage, and intracerebral hemorrhage. *Cerebral thrombosis* and *cerebral embolism,* known as *ischemic strokes,* are caused by blood clots that block an artery supplying the brain, either in the brain itself or in the neck. They account for 70–80% of all strokes. *Subarachnoid hemorrhage* and *intracerebral hemorrhage* are *hemorrhagic strokes* that occur when a blood vessel bursts around or in the brain, either from trauma or excess internal pressure. Hypertension (high blood pressure) and atherosclerosis are usually contributing factors in these types of strokes.

CEREBRAL THROMBOSIS. Cerebral thrombosis, the most common type of stroke, occurs when a blood clot, or thrombus, forms within the brain itself, blocking blood flow through the affected vessel. This is usually due to atherosclerosis (hardening) of brain arteries, caused by a buildup of fatty deposits inside the blood vessels. Cerebral thrombosis occurs most often at night or early in the morning, and is often preceded by a TIA. Recognizing the occurrence of a TIA, and seeking immediate treatment, is an important step in stroke prevention.

CEREBRAL EMBOLISM. Cerebral embolism occurs when a blood clot from elsewhere in the circulatory system breaks free. If it becomes lodged in an artery supplying the brain, either in the brain or in the neck, it can cause a stroke. The most common cause of cerebral embolism is atrial fibrillation, which occurs when the upper chambers (atria) of the heart beat weakly and rapidly, instead of slowly and steadily. Blood within the atria does not empty completely, and may form clots that can then break off and enter the circulation. Atrial fibrillation is a factor in about 15% of all strokes, but this risk can be dramatically reduced with daily use of anticoagulant medication (such as Heparin or Coumadin).

SUBARACHNOID HEMORRHAGE. In this type of stroke, blood spills into the subarachnoid space between the brain and cranium. As fluid builds up, pressure on the brain increases, impairing its function. Hypertension is a frequent cause of these types of stroke, but vessels with preexisting defects, such as an aneurysm, are also at risk for rupture. Aneurysms are most likely to burst when blood pressure is highest, and controlling blood pressure is an important preventive strategy. Subarachnoid hemorrhages account for about 7% of all strokes.

INTRACEREBRAL HEMORRHAGE. Representing about 10% of all strokes, intracerebral hemorrhage affects vessels and tissue within the brain itself. As with subarachnoid hemorrhage, bleeding deprives affected tissues of blood supply, and the accumulation of fluid within the inflexible skull creates pressure on the brain that can quickly become fatal. Despite this, recovery may be more complete for a person who survives hemorrhage than for one who survives a clot, because the effects of blood deprivation are usually not as severe.

Risk factors

Risk factors for stroke involve:

- *Age and sex*—the risk of stroke increases with age, doubling for each decade after age 55. Men are more likely to have a stroke than women.
- *Heredity*—People with a family history of stroke have an increased risk of stroke themselves. In addition, African-Americans, Asians, and Hispanics all have higher rates of stroke than whites, related partly to higher blood pressure.
- *Diseases*—People with diabetes, heart disease (especially atrial fibrillation), high blood pressure, or prior stroke are at greater risk for stroke. Patients with one or more TIAs have ten times the risk.
- *Other medical conditions*—Stroke risk increases with **obesity**, high blood cholesterol, or high red blood cell count.
- *Lifestyle choices*—Stroke risk increases with cigarette smoking (especially if combined with the use of oral contraceptives), a sedentary lifestyle, alcohol consumption above two drinks per day, and/or the use of cocaine or intravenous drugs.

Symptoms

Knowing the symptoms of stroke is as important as knowing those of a heart attack. Patients with stroke symptoms should seek emergency treatment without delay, which may mean dialing 911 rather than their family physician. Specific symptoms of a stroke depend on the type, but all types share some characteristics in common.

An embolic stroke usually comes on quite suddenly and is intense right from the start, while symptoms of a thrombotic stroke come on more gradually. Symptoms for these ischemic strokes may include:

- blurring or decreased vision in one or both eyes
- severe headache, often described as "the worst headache of my life"
- weakness, numbness, or paralysis of the face, arm, or leg, usually confined to one side of the body
- dizziness, loss of balance or coordination, especially when combined with other symptoms

Hemorrhagic strokes are somewhat different. An intracranial hemorrhage exhibits any or all of the following symptoms:

- loss of consciousness
- altered mental state
- seizure
- vomiting or severe nausea
- extreme hypertension
- weakness, numbness, or paralysis, especially on one side of the body
- sudden, severe headache

Symptoms of a subarachnoid hemorrhage include:

- severe headache that begins suddenly

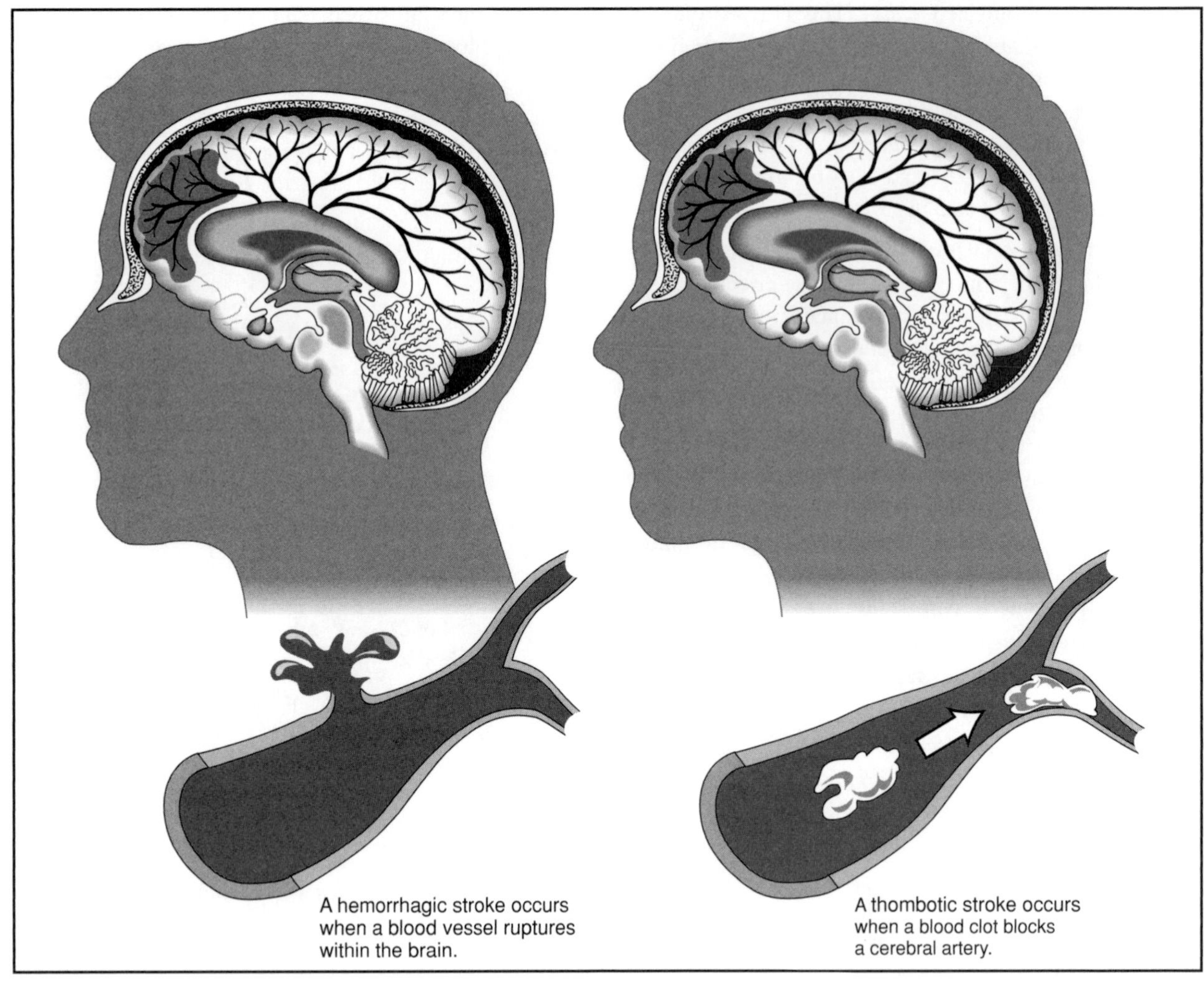

A hemorrhagic stroke (left) compared to a thrombotic stroke (right). *(Illustration by Hans & Cassady, Inc.)*

- nausea or vomiting
- stiff neck
- light intolerance
- loss of consciousness

Demographics

Each year, more than half a million people in the United States have a stroke. It is the third leading cause of death, killing about a third of its victims—approximately 150,000 Americans each year. For those that survive, stroke is the leading cause of disability. Two-thirds of all strokes occur in people over age 65, with men more affected than women, although women are more likely to die from a stroke. African-Americans suffer strokes more often than whites, and are more likely to be die from them as well. This may be because African-Americans tend to suffer from hypertension more frequently than other groups.

Diagnosis

Diagnosing a stroke begins with a careful medical history, especially concerning the onset and distribution of symptoms, presence of risk factors; in this way other possible causes are excluded. A brief neurological exam is performed to identify the degree and location of any deficits, such as weakness, lack of coordination, or vision loss.

Once stroke is suspected, imaging technology is used to determine what type the patient has suffered—a critical distinction that guides therapy. A noncontrast **computed tomography** scan (CT scan) can reliably identify hemorrhagic strokes, caused by uncontrolled bleeding in the brain. **Magnetic resonance imaging** (MRI), on the other hand, particularly diffusion-weighted imaging, can detect ischemic strokes, caused by blood clots, earlier and more reliably than CT scanning.

Blood and urine tests are also run to look for possible abnormalities. Other investigations that may be performed to guide treatment include electrocardiogram, angiography, ultrasound, and electroencephalogram.

Treatment

When brain cells die during a stroke, they release toxic chemicals that can trigger a chain reaction that can injure or kill other nearby cells. Damage from stroke may be significantly reduced by emergency treatment, and is a significant factor in how fully a patient will recover.

Emergency treatment

Emergency treatment of an ischemic stroke attempts to dissolve the clot. This "thrombolytic therapy" is performed most often with tissue plasminogen activator (t-PA), which must be administered within three hours of the stroke event. (Patients who awaken with stroke symptoms are ineligible for this type of therapy, since the time of onset cannot be reliably determined.) t-PA therapy has been shown to improve recovery and decrease long-term disability in patients. It carries a 6.4% risk of inducing a cerebral hemorrhage, however, and is not appropriate for patients with bleeding disorders, very high blood pressure, known aneurysms, any evidence of intracranial hemorrhage, or incidence of stroke, head trauma, or intracranial surgery within the past three months. Patients with clot-related stroke who are ineligible for t-PA treatment may be treated with heparin or other blood thinners, or with aspirin or other anticlotting agents in some cases.

Emergency treatment of hemorrhagic stroke is aimed at controlling intracranial pressure that accompanies these types of strokes. New surgical techniques can effectively relieve the pressure, especially when begun soon after the stroke event occurs. Surgery for hemorrhage due to aneurysm may be performed if the aneurysm is close enough to the cranial surface to allow access. Ruptured vessels are closed off to prevent rebleeding. For aneurysms that are difficult to reach surgically, endovascular treatment, in which a catheter is guided from a larger artery up into the brain to reach the aneurysm, may be effective. Small coils of wire are discharged into the aneurysm, which plug it up and block off blood flow from the main artery.

Rehabilitation

Rehabilitation refers to a comprehensive program designed to regain as much function as possible and compensate for permanent losses. Approximately 10% of stroke survivors are without any significant disability and able to function independently. Another 10% are so severely affected that they must remain institutionalized for severe disability. The remaining 80% can return home with appropriate therapy, training, support, and care.

Rehabilitation is coordinated by a team of medical professionals and may include the services of a neurologist, a physician who specializes in rehabilitation medicine, a physical therapist, an occupational therapist, a speech-language pathologist, a nutritionist, a mental health professional, and a social worker. Rehabilitation services may be provided in an acute care hospital, rehabilitation hospital, long-term care facility, outpatient clinic, or at home.

The rehabilitation program is based on the patient's individual deficits and strengths. Strokes on the left side of the brain primarily affect the right half of the body, and vice versa. In addition, in left brain-dominant people, who constitute a significant majority of the population, left-brain strokes usually lead to speech and language deficits, while right-brain strokes may affect spatial perception. Patients with right-brain strokes may also deny their illness, neglect the affected side of their body, and behave impulsively.

Rehabilitation may be complicated by cognitive losses, including diminished ability to understand and follow directions. Poor results are more likely in patients whose strokes left them with significant or prolonged cognitive changes, sensory losses, language deficits, or incontinence.

PREVENTING COMPLICATIONS. Rehabilitation begins with prevention of medical complications, including stroke recurrence, using many of the same measures used to prevent stroke, such as smoking cessation and getting hypertension under control.

One of the most common medical complications following stroke is deep venous thrombosis, in which a clot forms within a limb immobilized by paralysis. Clots can also become lodged in an artery feeding the lungs, a condition called pulmonary embolism, that is a common cause of death in the weeks following a stroke. Resuming activity within a day or two after the stroke is an important preventive measure, along with use of elastic stockings on the lower limbs. Drugs that prevent clotting may also be given, including intravenous heparin and oral warfarin.

Weakness and loss of coordination of the swallowing muscles may impair swallowing (dysphagia), and allow food to enter the lower airway. This may lead to aspiration pneumonia, another common cause of death shortly after a stroke. Dysphagia may be treated with retraining exercises and temporary use of pureed foods.

Other medical complications include urinary tract infections, pressure ulcers, falls, and **seizures**. Not surprisingly, depression occurs in 30–60% of stroke patients; its severity is usually related to the level of permanent functional impairment It can be treated with antidepressants and **psychotherapy**.

TYPES OF REHABILITATIVE THERAPY. Brain tissue that dies in a stroke cannot regenerate. In some cases, however, rehabilitation training can help other brain regions perform the same functions of that tissue. In other cases, compensatory actions may be developed to replace lost abilities.

Physical therapy is used to maintain and restore range of motion and strength in affected limbs, and to maximize mobility in walking, wheelchair use, and transferring (from wheelchair to toilet or from standing to sitting, for instance). The physical therapist advises patients on mobility aids such as wheelchairs, braces, and canes. In the recovery period, a stroke patient may develop muscle spasticity and contractures (abnormal muscle contractions) that can be treated with a combination of stretching and splinting.

Occupational therapy improves self-care skills such as feeding, bathing, and dressing, and helps develop effective compensatory strategies and devices for activities of daily living. A speech-language pathologist focuses on communication and swallowing skills. When dysphagia is a problem, a nutritionist can advise alternative meals that provide adequate nutrition.

Psychological therapy can help treat depression or loss of thinking (cognitive) skills. A social worker may help coordinate services and ease the transition out of the hospital back into the home. Both **social workers** and mental health professionals help counsel the patient and family during the difficult rehabilitation period. Caring for a person affected with stroke requires a new set of skills and adaptation to new demands and limitations. Home caregivers may develop **stress**, anxiety, and depression—caring for the caregiver is an important part of the overall stroke treatment program. **Support groups** can provide an important source of information, advice, and comfort for stroke patients and caregivers; joining one can be an important step in the rehabilitation process.

Prognosis

Stroke is fatal for about 27% of white males, 52% of African-American males, 23% of white females, and 40% of African-American females. Stroke survivors may be left with significant deficits. Emergency treatment and comprehensive rehabilitation can significantly improve both survival and recovery.

Prevention

The risk of stroke can be reduced through lifestyle changes:

- stop smoking
- control blood pressure
- get regular exercise
- maintain a healthy weight
- avoid excessive alcohol consumption
- get regular checkups and follow the doctor's advice regarding diet and medicines

Use of high-estrogen dose oral contraceptives increase the chances for developing stroke, particularly in women who smoke and/or who are over 35. Currently, there are low-estrogen dose oral contraceptives, for which a clear relationship with stroke development is unclear.

Treatment of atrial fibrillation may also significantly reduce the risk of stroke. Preventive anticoagulant therapy may benefit those with untreated atrial fibrillation. Warfarin (Coumadin) has proven to be more effective than aspirin for those with higher risk.

Screening for aneurysms may be an effective preventive measure in those with a family history of aneurysms or autosomal polycystic kidney disease, which tends to be associated with aneurysms.

Resources

BOOKS

Caplan, L. R., M. L. Dyken, and J. D. Easton. *American Heart Association Family Guide to Stroke Treatment, Recovery, and Prevention.* New York: Times Books, 1996.

Duthie, Edmund H., Jr. *Practice of Geriatrics.* 3rd Edition. Philadelphia: W. B. Saunders, 1998: 328-335.

Goetz, Christopher G., and others. *Textbook of Clinical Neurology.* 1st edition. Philadelphia: W. B. Saunders, 1999: 909-911.

Warlow, C. P., and others. *Stroke: A Practical Guide to Management.* Boston: Blackwell Science, 1996.

PERIODICALS

Krishnan, K. Ranga Rama. "Depression as a contributing factor in cerebrovascular disease." *American Heart Journal* 140 (October 2000): 563.

ORGANIZATIONS

American Heart Association and American Stroke Association. 7272 Greenville Ave. Dallas, TX 75231. (214) 373-6300. <http://www.americanheart.org>.

National Stroke Association. 9707 E. Easter Lane, Englewood, Co. 80112. (800) 787-6537. <http://www.stroke.org>.

Laith Farid Gulli, M.D.
Bilal Nasser, M.D.

Stuttering

Definition

There is no standard definition of stuttering, but most attempt to define stuttering as the blockages, discoordination, or fragmentations of the forward flow of speech (fluency). These stoppages, referred to as disfluencies, are often excessive and characterized by specific types of disfluency. These types of disfluencies include repetitions of sounds and syllables, prolongation of sounds, and blockages of airflow. Individuals who stutter are often aware of their stuttering and feel a loss of control when they are disfluent. Both children and adults stutterers expend an excessive amount of physical and mental energy when speaking. Older children and adults who stutter show myriad negative reactive behaviors, feelings, and attitudes. These behaviors, referred to as "secondary behaviors," make the disorder more severe and difficult.

Description

Stuttering is a confusing and often misunderstood developmental speech and language disorder. Before discussing stuttering, it is important to understand the concepts of speech fluency and disfluency. Fluency is generally described as the forward flow of speech. For most speakers, fluent speech is easy and effortless. Fluent speech is free of any interruptions, blockages, or fragmentations. Disfluency is defined as a breakdown or blockage in the forward flow of speech, or fluency. For all speakers, some occurrence of disfluency is normal. For example, people may insert short sounds or words, referred to as "interjections," when speaking; examples of such are "um," "like," or "uh." Also, speakers might repeat phrases, revise words or phrases, or sometimes repeat whole words for the purpose of clarification. For young children, disfluency is a part of the normal development of speech and language, especially during the preschool years (between the ages of two and five years).

The occurrence of disfluency is not the same as stuttering, though stuttered speech is characterized by an excessive amount of disfluency. The disfluencies produced by people who stutter will often be similar to those in the speech of individuals who do not stutter; however, certain types of disfluent behavior are likely to appear only in the speech of people who stutter. These disfluencies are sound and syllable repetitions (i.e., ca-ca-ca-cat), sound prolongations ("sssss-salad," "ffffff-fish"), and complete blockages of airflow. These behaviors, often referred to as stuttering type disfluencies, distinguish stuttered speech from nonstuttered speech.

KEY TERMS

Disfluency—Disruptions, breakage, or blockages in the forward flow of speech.

Secondary behaviors—Negative behavioral, emotional, or cognitive reactions to stuttering.

Speech-language pathologist—Specialists trained in assessment and diagnosis of communication disorders.

Unlike speakers who do not stutter, most people who stutter react negatively to their disfluencies. A person may develop a number of physical reactions, including tension of the muscles involved in speech (tongue, jaw, lips, or chest, for example) and tension in muscles not related to speech (such as shoulders, limbs, and forehead). In addition to these physiological reactions, people who stutter will often have negative emotional reactions to the disorder. Among the emotions that people who stutter report are embarrassment, guilt, and frustration.

Finally, many people who stutter will develop a number of negative attitudes and beliefs regarding themselves and speaking—because of their stuttering. These may be negative attitudes and beliefs in certain speaking situations, with people with whom they interact, and in their own abilities. These physiological, emotional, and attitudinal (cognitive) reactions to stuttering, described as secondary stuttering behaviors, are often very disruptive to the communication process and the person's life.

Stuttering behaviors can develop and vary throughout the life span. Sometimes, children will experience periods when the stuttering appears to "go away," only to return in a more severe pattern. Many children, (estimates range between 50 and 80%) will develop normal fluency after periods of stuttering. For those who continue to stutter during late childhood, adolescence, and into adulthood, stuttering can become a chronic problem. Lifelong efforts will be needed to cope successfully with the behavior.

Due to the effect that stuttering has on communication, the person who stutters may experience certain difficulties in various parts of his/her life. These problems might be secondary to factors inside the person (symptoms of stuttering) and outside the person (society's attitudes toward stuttering and other barriers). For example, many people who stutter report difficulties in social settings. Children who stutter often experience teasing and other social penalties. Adolescents and adults also report a variety of social problems. Academic settings may be difficult for children who stutter because of the emphasis schools place on verbal performance.

Finally, there appears to be some evidence that people who stutter might confront barriers in employment. These barriers might take the form of inability to do certain tasks easily (talking on the phone, for example), limitations in job choices, and discrimination in the hiring and promotion processes.

Causes and symptoms

Though research has not identified a single cause, there appears to be several factors that are viewed as being important to the onset and development of stuttering. Therefore, stuttering is often described as being related to multiple factors and having possibly multiple causes. First, there is a genetic predisposition to stutter, as evidenced by studies of families and twins. A second important factor in the onset of stuttering is the physiological makeup of people who stutter. Research suggests that the brains of people who stutter may function abnormally during speech production. These differences in functioning may lead to breakdowns in speech production and to the development of disfluent speech.

Third, there is some evidence that speech and language development is an important issue in understanding the development of stuttering. Studies have found some evidence that children who are showing stuttering type behaviors may also have other difficulties with speech-language. Additionally, children with speech-language delays will often show stuttering type behaviors. Finally, environmental issues have a significant impact on the development of stuttering behaviors. An environment that is overly stressful or demanding, may cause children to have difficulties developing fluent speech. Though the environment, in particular parental behaviors, does not cause stuttering, it is an important factor that might adversely affect a child who is operating at a reduced capacity for developing fluent speech.

There is no evidence that stuttering is secondary to a psychological disturbance. It is reasonable to assume that stuttering might have some effect on psychological adjustment and a person's ability to cope with speaking situations. People who stutter might experience a lower self-esteem and some might report feeling depressed. These feelings and difficulties with coping are most likely the result and not the cause of stuttering. In addition, several research studies have reported that many people who stutter report high levels of anxiety and **stress** when they are talking and stuttering. These feelings, psychological states, and difficulties with coping are most likely the result and not the cause of stuttering.

Generally, children begin to stutter between the ages of two and five years. Nevertheless, there are instances when individuals begin to show stuttering type behaviors in late childhood or as adults. These instances are often related to specific causes such as a **stroke** or a degenerative neurological disease. This type of stuttering, stuttering secondary to a specific neurological process, is referred to as neurogenic stuttering. In other cases, stuttering may be secondary to a psychological **conversion disorder** due to a psychologically traumatic event. When stuttering has abrupt onset secondary to a psychological trauma, it is described as psychogenic stuttering.

As stated earlier, the primary symptoms of stuttering include excessive disfluency, both stuttering and normal types (core behaviors), as well as physical, emotional, and cognitive reactions to the problem. These behaviors will vary in severity across people who stutter from very mild to very severe. Additionally, the behaviors will vary considerably across different speaking situations. There are specific situations when people tend to experience more stuttering (such as talking on the phone or with an authority figure) or less stuttering (speaking with a pet or to themselves, for example). It is likely that this variability might even extend to people having periods (days and even weeks) when they can maintain normally fluent or nonstuttered speech.

Demographics

Stuttering is a relatively low-prevalence disorder. Across all cultures, roughly 1% of people currently has a stuttering disorder. This differs from incidence, or number of individuals who have been diagnosed with stuttering at some point in their lives. Research suggests that roughly 5% of the population has ever been diagnosed with a stuttering disorder. This difference suggests that a significant number of individuals who stutter will someday develop through or “”grow out of” the problem. Research suggests that roughly 50-80% of all children who begin to stutter will stop stuttering. In addition, approximately three times as many men stutter as women. This ratio seems to be lower early in childhood, with a similar number of girls and boys stuttering. The ratio of boys to girls appears to get larger as children become older. This phenomenon suggests that males are more likely to continue to stutter than females.

Diagnosis

Speech-language pathologists are responsible for making the **diagnosis** and managing the treatment of adults and children who stutter. Preferably, a board-certified speech-language pathologist board should be sought for direct **intervention** or consulting. Diagnosis of stuttering, or identifying children at risk for stuttering, is difficult because most children will show excessive disfluencies in their speech. With children, diagnostic procedures include the collection and analysis of speech and disfluent behaviors in a variety of situations. In addition, the child's general speech-language abilities will be evaluated.

Finally, the speech-language pathologist will interview parents and teachers regarding the child's general developmental, speech-language development, and their perceptions of the child's stuttering behaviors. For adults and older children, the diagnostic procedures will also include gathering and analyzing speech samples from a variety of settings. In addition, the speech-language pathologist will conduct a lengthy interview with the person about their stuttering and history of their stuttering problem. Finally, the person who stutters might be asked to report his/her attitudes and feelings related to stuttering, either while being interviewed or by completing a series of questionnaires.

Treatments

General considerations

It is generally accepted that conducting interventions with children and families early in childhood (preschool) is the most effective means of total recovery from stuttering. The chances for a person to fully recover from stuttering by obtaining near-normal fluency are reduced as the person ages. This is why early intervention is critical. For older children and adults for which stuttering has become a chronic disorder, the focus of therapy is on developing positive coping mechanisms for dealing with the problem. This therapy varies in success based on the individual.

Treatment options for young children

Treatment of young children generally follows one of two basic approaches. These approaches may also be combined into a single treatment program. The first type of approach, often referred to as indirect therapy, focuses on altering the environment to allow the child opportunities to develop fluent speech. With this approach, counseling parents regarding the alteration of behaviors that affect fluency is the focus. For example, parents may be taught to reduce the amount of household stress or in the level of speech-language demands being placed on the child. In addition, parents may be advised to change characteristics of their speech, such as their speech rate and turn-taking style; this is done to help their children develop more fluent speech.

The other basic approach in treatment with young children targets the development of fluent speech. This type of approach, often referred to as direct therapy, teaches children to use skills that will help them improve fluency and they are sometimes given verbal rewards for producing fluent speech.

Treatment options for older children and adults

Treatment approaches for older children and adults usually take one of two forms. These approaches target either helping the person to modify his/her stuttering or modify his/her fluency. Approaches that focus on modifying stuttering will usually teach individuals to reduce the severity of their stuttering behaviors by identifying and eliminating all of the secondary or reactive behaviors. Individuals will also work to reduce the amount of emotional reaction toward stuttering.

Finally, the speech-language pathologist will help the individual to learn techniques that allow them to stutter in an easier manner. Therapy does not focus on helping the individual to speak fluently, though most individuals will attain higher levels of fluency if this approach is successful. The other groups of approaches will focus on assisting adults and children who stutter to speak more fluently. This type of therapy, which focuses less on changing secondary and emotional reactions, helps the person to modify their speech movements in a specific manner that allows for fluent sounding speech. These procedures require the individual to focus on developing new speech patterns. This often requires a significant amount of practice and skill. The successful outcome of these approaches is nonstuttered, fluent sounding speech. Many therapists will integrate stuttering modification and fluency shaping approaches into more complete treatment programs. In addition, psychological counseling may be used to supplement traditional speech therapy.

Prognosis

Complete alleviation of recovery from stuttering is most likely possible when children and their families receive treatment close to the time of onset. Thus, early identification and treatment of stuttering is critical. For older children and adults, stuttering becomes a chronic problem that requires a lifetime of formal and self-directed therapy. For individuals who show this more chronic form of the disorder, internal motivation for change and support from significant others is an important part of recovery.

Resources

BOOKS

Bloodstein, O. *A Handbook on Stuttering.* 5th ed., revised. San Diego, CA. Singular Publishing, 1995.

Guitar, B. *Stuttering: An Integrated Approach to Its Nature and treatment.* 2nd edition, text revision. Baltimore, MD: Lippincott Williams and Willkins, 1998.

Manning, W. H. *Clinical Decision Making in Fluency Disorders*. 2nd. ed., revised. San Diego, CA. Singular Publishing, 2001.

ORGANIZATIONS

National Stuttering Association. 5100 East La Palma, Suite #208, Anaheim Hills, CA 92807. <http://www.nsastutter.org>.

Stuttering Foundation of America. 3100 Walnut Grove Road, Suite 603, P.O. Box 11749, Memphis, TN 38111-0749. <http://www.stuttersfa.org>.

See also Speech-language pathology

Rodney Gabel, Ph.D.

Substance abuse and related disorders

Definition

Substance-related disorders are disorders of intoxication, dependence, abuse, and substance withdrawal caused by various substances, both legal and illegal. These substances include: alcohol, **amphetamines**, caffeine, inhalants, nicotine, prescription medications that may be abused (such as sedatives), opioids (morphine, heroin), marijuana (cannabis), cocaine, hallucinogens, and phencyclidine (PCP).

Description

According to the mental health clinician's handbook, ***Diagnostic and Statistical Manual of Mental Disorders*** (the *DSM*), fourth edition text revised (*DSM-IV-TR*), all of the substances listed above, with the exceptions of nicotine and caffeine, have disorders of two types: substance use disorders and substance-induced disorders. Substance use disorders include abuse and dependence. Substance-induced disorders include intoxication, withdrawal, and various mental states (**dementia**, **psychosis**, anxiety, mood disorder, etc.) that the substance induces when it is used.

Substance dependence is characterized by continued use of a substance even after the user has experienced serious substance-related problems. The dependent user desires the substance ("craving") and needs more of the substance to achieve the effect that a lesser amount of the substance induced in the past. This phenomenon is known as tolerance. The dependent user also experiences withdrawal symptoms when the substance is not used. Withdrawal symptoms vary with the substance, but some symptoms may include increased heart rate, shaking, **insomnia**, **fatigue**, and irritability.

Substance abuse is continued use of a substance in spite of school- or work-related or interpersonal problems, but the user has not gotten dependent on the substance. The individual who abuses a substance may experience legal problems and may have problems fulfilling responsibilities, such as caring for a child.

Intoxication is the direct effect of the substance after an individual has used or has been exposed to the substance. Different substances affect individuals in various ways, but some of the effects seen in intoxication might include impaired judgment, emotional instability, increase or decrease in appetite, or changed sleep patterns.

The *DSM-IV-TR* does not recognize caffeine abuse or dependence, but does recognize the caffeine-induced disorders caffeine intoxication (restlessness, nervousness, excitement, etc. after caffeine consumption), caffeine-induced anxiety disorder (feelings of anxiety or panic attacks after caffeine consumption), and caffeine-induced sleep disorder (usually insomnia, but some may experience excessive sleepiness when caffeine is not consumed). As for nicotine, the *DSM-IV-TR* recognizes nicotine dependence and nicotine withdrawal.

The *DSM-IV-TR* lists disorders in the following categories:

- alcohol-related disorders
- amphetamine-related disorders
- caffeine-related disorders
- cannabis-related disorders
- cocaine-related disorders
- hallucinogen-related disorders
- inhalant-related disorders
- nicotine-related disorders
- opioid-related disorders
- phencyclidine-related disorders
- sedative-, hypnotic-, or anxiolytic-related disorders
- polysubstance dependence

See also Addiction; Alcohol and related disorders; Amnestic disorders; Amphetamines and related disorders; Antianxiety drugs and abuse-related disorders; Caffeine and related disorders; Cannabis and related disorders; Cocaine and related disorders; Denial; Disease concept of chemical dependency; Hallucinogens and related disorders; Inhalants and related disorders; Nicotine and related disorders; Opioids and related disorders; Phencyclidine and related disorders; Polysubstance dependence; Sedatives and related disorders; Substance Abuse Subtle

KEY TERMS

Amphetamines—A group of powerful and highly addictive substances that stimulate the central nervous system. May be prescribed for various medical conditions, but are often purchased illicitly and abused.

Anxiety—A feeling of apprehension and fear characterized by physical symptoms (heart palpitations, sweating, and feelings of stress, for example).

Anxiolytic—A preparation or substance given to relieve anxiety; a tranquilizer.

Dementia—A group of symptoms (syndrome) associated with a progressive loss of memory and other intellectual functions that is serious enough to interfere with a person's ability to perform the tasks of daily life. Dementia impairs memory, alters personality, leads to deterioration in personal grooming, impairs reasoning ability, and causes disorientation.

Hallucinogens—Substances that cause hallucinations.

Hypnotic—A type of medication that induces sleep.

Inhalants—A class of drugs that are inhaled in order for the user to experience a temporary "high." These chemicals include volatile solvents (liquids that vaporize at room temperature) and aerosols (sprays that contain solvents and propellants), and include glue, gasoline, paint thinner, hair spray, and others. They are dangerous because they can cause hallucinations, delusions, difficulty breathing, headache, nausea, vomiting, and even "sudden sniffing death." Inhalants can also cause permanent damage to the brain, lung, kidney, muscle, and heart.

Opioids—Substances that reduce pain and may induce sleep. Some opioids are endogenous, which means that they are produced within the human body. Other opioids are produced by plants or formulated synthetically in the laboratory.

Phencyclidine—The full name of the drug commonly called PCP that is often abused to induce hallucinations.

Psychosis—Severe state that is characterized by loss of contact with reality and deterioration in normal social functioning; examples are schizophrenia and paranoia. Psychosis is usually one feature of an over-arching disorder, not a disorder in itself. (Plural: psychoses)

Sedative—A medication that induces relaxation and sleep.

Screening Inventory; Substance-induced anxiety disorder; Substance-induced psychotic disorder; Urine drug screening; Wernicke-Korsakoff syndrome

Resources

BOOKS

American Psychiatric Association. *Diagnostic and Statistical Manual of Mental Disorders.* Fourth edition, text revised. Washington DC: American Psychiatric Association, 2000.

Substance Abuse Subtle Screening Inventory

Definition

The Substance Abuse Subtle Screening Inventory is also referred to as the SASSI. Dr. Glenn A. Miller developed the SASSI as a screening questionnaire for identifying people with a high probability of having a substance dependence disorder.

Purpose

The SASSI is intended for gathering information, organizing it, and using it to help make decisions about the likelihood of an individual having a substance dependence disorder, even if the individual does not acknowledge symptoms of the disorder or misuse of substances. Guidelines are available for professionals to flag individuals with a potential substance abuse disorder for further evaluation. Interpreting the results of the SASSI helps professionals understand their clients better and plan their treatment.

Precautions

When used by trained professionals, the SASSI can be an important tool in the assessment of substance use disorders. The SASSI is not intended to prove or diagnose an individual as an alcoholic or addict; it is intended to screen for a person who has a "high probability of having a substance dependence disorder." It should be kept in mind that a thorough assessment integrates other available information, such as self-report and family history, and is done by a skilled professional. This comprehensive assessment is required to determine if an individual meets the accepted standards in the mental health professional's handbook, ***Diagnostic and Statistical Manual of Mental Disorders***, for a clinical **diagnosis** of a substance-related disorder.

The accuracy rate of the SASSI is 94%. Although that is very high, this means that there is a 6% probability that an individual will be misclassified based on SASSI scores. While the SASSI is a popular and widely used screening questionnaire, independent research on it has been limited. Some researchers have questions about the SASSI regarding the extent to which subscales measure what they are intended to measure and the accuracy of classification based on direct versus indirect scales. In addition, the SASSI is not to be used to discriminate against individuals, including disqualifying job applicants. It would be a violation of the Americans With Disabilities Act to eliminate a job applicant based on SASSI scores.

Description

The SASSI is a simple, brief one-page paper-and-pencil questionnaire that can be answered in 10 to 15 minutes. The SASSI is easy to administer, to individuals or groups, and can be objectively scored by hand and interpreted, based on objective decision rules, in a minute or two. Optical scanning equipment is available for mass scoring and interpretation. The SASSI does not require a high level of reading ability. The SASSI may be used by a variety of programs and professionals, including school counselors, student assistance programs, employee assistance programs, vocational counselors, psychotherapists, medical personnel, criminal justice programs, and other human service providers.

The SASSI went through rigorous scientific development over a 16-year period before it was first published in 1988. Two new scales were added, and the SASSI-2 was published in 1994. In 1997 the SASSI-3 was published with a new scale and increased accuracy. Items on the SASSI were selected based on established research methods and statistical analysis. Items were included that identified individuals with substance dependence disorders. The selected items were consistently answered differently by individuals with a substance dependence disorder compared to individuals without a substance dependence disorder.

In 1996, a Spanish version was made available. In addition to the paper and pencil format, computer versions of the SASSI, in several formats, are available.

Some questions on the SASSI ask how frequently clients have had certain experiences directly related to alcohol and other drugs. These are answered on a four-point scale, ranging from never to repeatedly. Some items that may appear to be unrelated to substance use (indirect or subtle items) are in a true/false format. Overall, the items make up 10 subscales. The results are reported on a profile form that is discussed with the client. There are separate profile forms for males and females. The objective scoring system results in a yes or no answer about whether the client has a high probability of having a substance dependence disorder. The SASSI-3 has been empirically tested and can identify substance dependence disorder with an overall accuracy of 94%. More specifically, the SASSI identifies individuals with a substance dependence disorder with 94% accuracy, and it identifies those without a substance dependence disorder with 94% accuracy. The accuracy of the SASSI is not significantly affected by gender, age, socioeconomic status, ethnicity, occupational status, marital status, educational level, drug of choice, and general level of functioning. Research is ongoing to improve the accuracy and usefulness of the SASSI.

Since 1990 an adolescent version of the SASSI has been available. The second version of the Adolescent SASSI (SASSI-A2) has a 94% overall accuracy of identifying an adolescent with a substance dependence disorder, including both substance abuse and substance dependence. The SASSI-A2 is designed to screen individuals who are 12 to 18 years old. The accuracy of the SASSI-A2 is not affected by the respondent's gender, age, ethnicity, education, employment status, living situation, prior legal history, or general level of functioning.

Results

A profile of the SASSI results will be reviewed with the client. The actual scores are plotted on a profile graph in comparison to a sample of people who were not being evaluated or treated for addictions or other clinical problems (also called a normative sample). Feedback is then given in terms of whether the individual has a high or low probability of having a substance dependence disorder. Individual scale scores may be used to come up with ideas or hypotheses for further evaluation and treatment. This information is based on clinical experience with the SASSI. The results may indicate issues that are important for treatment (such as difficulty acknowledging personal shortcomings, or primarily focusing on others' needs while unaware of one's own needs). The results may suggest an approach to take with the client (such as increasing awareness, or acknowledging and validating their feelings). The results may suggest a treatment plan that the client may respond to (such as addiction self-help groups or an education-focused program). Finally, the results may indicate appropriate treatment goals for the client (anger management and/ or social skills, for example). The goal of providing feedback about SASSI results is to have a two-way sharing and understanding of information that is descriptive and not judgmental.

See also Substance abuse and related disorders

Resources

BOOKS

Miller, Franklin G., Ph.D., and others. *SASSI-3 User's Guide: A Quick Reference for Administration and Scoring.* Bloomington: Baugh Enterprises, 1997.

The SASSI Institute. *The Reliability and Validity of the SASSI-3.* Springville: The SASSI Institute, 1998.

The SASSI Institute. *Summary of the Consistency and Accuracy of the Adolescent SASSI-A2 for Non-Statisticians.* Springville: The SASSI Institute, 2001.

PERIODICALS

Gray, B. Thomas. "A Factor Analytic Study of the Substance Abuse Subtle Screening Inventory (SASSI)." *Educational and Psychological Measurement* 61 (2001): 102–118.

Joneis Thomas, Ph.D.

KEY TERMS

Anticholinergic agents—Medicines that include atropine, belladonna, hyoscyamine, scopolamine, and related products; used to relieve cramps or spasms of the stomach, intestines, and bladder.

Delirium—A disturbance of consciousness marked by confusion, difficulty paying attention, delusions, hallucinations, or restlessness.

Dementia—A group of symptoms (syndrome) associated with a progressive loss of memory and other intellectual functions that is serious enough to interfere with a person's ability to perform the tasks of daily life. Dementia impairs memory, alters personality, leads to deterioration in personal grooming, impairs reasoning ability, and causes disorientation.

Obsessive-compulsive—Characterized by obsessive and compulsive behaviors.

Phobia—Irrational fear of places, things, or situations that lead to avoidance.

Psychoactive substance—A drug that produces mood changes and distorted perceptions; mind-altering drug.

Sympathomimetics—Drugs that mimic the effects of impulses conveyed by adrenergic postganglionic fibres of the sympathetic nervous system.

Substance-induced anxiety disorder

Definition

Prominent anxiety symptoms (i.e., generalized anxiety, panic attacks, obsessive-compulsive symptoms, or phobia symptoms) determined to be caused by the effects of a psychoactive substance is the primary feature of a **substance-induced psychotic disorder**. A substance may induce psychotic symptoms during intoxication (i.e., while the individual is under the influence of the drug) or during withdrawal (i.e., after an individual stops using the drug).

Description

A substance-induced anxiety disorder is subtyped or categorized based on whether the prominent feature is generalized anxiety, panic attacks, obsessive-compulsive symptoms, or phobia symptoms. In addition, the disorder is subtyped based on whether it began during intoxication on a substance or during withdrawal from a substance. A substance-induced anxiety disorder that begins during substance use can last as long as the drug is used. A substance-induced anxiety disorder that begins during withdrawal may first manifest up to four weeks after an individual stops using the substance.

Causes and symptoms

Causes

A substance-induced anxiety disorder, by definition, is directly caused by the effects of drugs—including alcohol, medications, and toxins. Anxiety symptoms can result from intoxication on alcohol, **amphetamines** (and related substances), caffeine, cannabis (marijuana), cocaine, hallucinogens, inhalants, phencyclidine (PCP) and related substances, and other or unknown substances. Anxiety symptoms can also result from withdrawal from alcohol, sedatives, hypnotics, and anxiolytics, cocaine, and other or unknown substances. Some of the medications which may induce anxiety symptoms include anesthetics and analgesics, sympathomimetics (epinephrine or norepinephrine, for example) or other bronchodilators, anticholinergic agents, anticonvulsants, antihistamines, insulin, thyroid preparations, oral contraceptives, antihypertensive and cardiovascular medications, antiparkinsonian medications, corticosteroids, antidepressant medications, **lithium carbonate**, and antipsychotic medications. Heavy metals and toxins, such as volatile substances like fuel and paint, organophosphate insecticides, nerve gases, carbon monoxide, and carbon dioxide may also induce anxiety.

Symptoms

The ***Diagnostic and Statistical Manual of Mental Disorders***, (*DSM-IV-TR*)—produced by the American Psychiatric Association and used by most mental health professionals in North America and Europe to diagnose mental disorders—notes that a **diagnosis** is made only when the anxiety symptoms are above and beyond what would be expected during intoxication or withdrawal and when severe. The following list is the criteria necessary for the diagnosis of a substance-induced anxiety disorder as listed in the *DSM-IV-TR*:

- Prominent anxiety, panic attacks, or obsessions or compulsions.
- Symptoms develop during, or within one month, of intoxication or withdrawal from a substance or medication known to cause anxiety symptoms.
- Symptoms are not actually part of another anxiety disorder (such as **generalized anxiety disorder**, phobias, **panic disorder**, or **obsessive-compulsive personality disorder**) that is not substance induced. For instance, if the anxiety symptoms began prior to substance or medication use, then another anxiety disorder is likely.
- Symptoms do not occur only during **delirium**.
- Symptoms cause significant distress or impairment in functioning.

Demographics

Little is known regarding the demographics of substance-induced anxiety disorders. However, it is clear that they occur more commonly in individuals who abuse alcohol or other drugs.

Diagnosis

Diagnosis of a substance-induced anxiety disorder must be differentiated from an anxiety disorder due to a general medical condition. There are some medical conditions (such as hyperthyroidism, hypothyroidism, or hypoglycemia) that can produce anxiety symptoms, and since individuals are likely to be taking medications for these conditions, it can be difficult to determine the cause of the anxiety symptoms. If the symptoms are determined to be due to the medical condition, then a diagnosis of an anxiety disorder due to a general medical condition is warranted. Substance-induced anxiety disorders also need to be distinguished from delirium, **dementia**, primary psychotic disorders, and substance intoxication and withdrawal.

Clinical history and physical examination are the best methods to help diagnose anxiety disorders in general; however, appropriate laboratory testing will most likely be necessary to specifically identify substance-induced anxiety disorder. Lab tests may include:

- complete blood count (CBC)
- chemistry panels
- serum and/or urine screens for drugs

Treatments

The underlying cause of the anxiety symptoms, as well as the specific type of symptoms, determine course of treatment and is often similar to treatment for a primary anxiety disorder such as generalized anxiety disorder, phobias, panic disorder, or **obsessive-compulsive disorder**. Appropriate treatment usually includes medication (antianxiety or antidepressant medication, for example).

Prognosis

Anxiety symptoms induced by substance intoxication usually subside once the substance responsible is eliminated. Symptoms persist depending on the half-life of the substances (i.e., how long it takes the before the substance is no longer present in an individual's system). Symptoms, therefore, can persist for hours, days, or weeks after a substance is last used. Obsessive-compulsive symptoms induced by substances sometimes do not disappear, even although the substance inducing them has been eliminated. More intensive treatment for the obsessive-compulsive symptoms would be necessary and should include a combination of medication and behavioral therapy.

Prevention

Little is documented regarding the prevention of substance-induced anxiety disorder. However, abstaining from drugs and alcohol, or using these substances only in moderation, would clearly reduce the risk of developing this disorder. In addition, taking medication under the supervision of an appropriately trained physician should reduce the likelihood of a medication-induced anxiety disorder. Finally, reducing one's exposure to toxins and heavy metals would reduce the risk of toxin-induced anxiety disorder.

See also Alcohol and related disorders; Amphetamines and related disorders; Anti-anxiety drugs and abuse-related disorders; Anxiety and anxiety disorders; Caffeine and related disorders; Cannabis and related disorders; Cocaine and related disorders; Hallucinogens and related disorders; Inhalants and related disorders; Phencyclidine and related disorders; Psychosis; Sedatives and related disorders; Substance abuse and related disorders; Substance-induced psychotic disorder

Resources

BOOKS

American Psychiatric Association. *Diagnostic and Statistical Manual of Mental Disorders*. 4th edition, text revised. Washington, DC: American Psychiatric Association, 2000.

Kaplan, Harold I.,M.D., and Benjamin J. Sadock, M.D. *Kaplan and Sadock's Synopsis of Psychiatry: Behavioral Sciences, Clinical Psychiatry.* 8th edition. Baltimore: Williams and Wilkins.

Jennifer Hahn, Ph.D.

Substance-induced persisting amnestic disorder *see* **Amnestic disorders; Wernicke-Korsakoff syndrome**

KEY TERMS

Anticholinergic agents—Medicines that include atropine, belladonna, hyoscyamine, scopolamine, and related products; used to relieve cramps or spasms of the stomach, intestines, and bladder.

Delirium—A disturbance of consciousness marked by confusion, difficulty paying attention, delusions, hallucinations, or restlessness.

Delusion—A false belief that is resistant to reason or contrary to actual fact.

Dementia—A group of symptoms (syndrome) associated with a progressive loss of memory and other intellectual functions that is serious enough to interfere with a person's ability to perform the tasks of daily life. Dementia impairs memory, alters personality, leads to deterioration in personal grooming, impairs reasoning ability, and causes disorientation.

Hallucinations—False sensory perceptions. A person experiencing a hallucination may "hear" sounds or "see" people or objects that are not really present. Hallucinations can also affect the senses of smell, touch, and taste.

Persecutory delusions—Unrealistic conviction of being harassed, tormented, and persecuted.

Psychotic/psychosis—Episodes of inability to accurately perceive reality, think logically, and speak or behave normally. Hallucinations and delusions are symptoms of psychosis.

Substance-induced psychotic disorder

Definition

Prominent psychotic symptoms (i.e., **hallucinations** and/or **delusions**) determined to be caused by the effects of a psychoactive substance is the primary feature of a substance-induced psychotic disorder. A substance may induce psychotic symptoms during intoxication (while the individual is under the influence of the drug) or during withdrawal (after an individual stops using the drug).

Description

A substance-induced psychotic disorder is subtyped or categorized based on whether the prominent feature is delusions or hallucinations. Delusions are fixed, false beliefs. Hallucinations are seeing, hearing, feeling, tasting, or smelling things that are not there. In addition, the disorder is subtyped based on whether it began during intoxication on a substance or during withdrawal from a substance. A substance-induced psychotic disorder that begins during substance use can last as long as the drug is used. A substance-induced psychotic disorder that begins during withdrawal may first manifest up to four weeks after an individual stops using the substance.

Causes and symptoms

Causes

A substance-induced psychotic disorder, by definition, is directly caused by the effects of drugs including alcohol, medications, and toxins. Psychotic symptoms can result from intoxication on alcohol, **amphetamines** (and related substances), cannabis (marijuana), cocaine, hallucinogens, inhalants, opioids, phencyclidine (PCP) and related substances, sedatives, hypnotics, anxiolytics, and other or unknown substances. Psychotic symptoms can also result from withdrawal from alcohol, sedatives, hypnotics, anxiolytics, and other or unknown substances.

Some medications that may induce psychotic symptoms include anesthetics and analgesics, anticholinergic agents, anticonvulsants, antihistamines, antihypertensive and cardiovascular medications, antimicrobial medications, antiparkinsonian medications, chemotherapeutic agents, corticosteroids, gastrointestinal medications, muscle relaxants, nonsteroidal anti-inflammatory medications, other over-the-counter medications, antidepressant medications, and **disulfiram**. Toxins that may induce psychotic symptoms include anticholinesterase, organophosphate insecticides, nerve gases, carbon monoxide, carbon dioxide, and volatile substances (such as fuel or paint).

The speed of onset of psychotic symptoms varies depending on the type of substance. For example, using a lot of cocaine can produce psychotic symptoms within minutes. On the other hand, psychotic symptoms may result from alcohol use only after days or weeks of intensive use.

The type of psychotic symptoms also tends to vary according to the type of substance. For instance, auditory hallucinations (specifically, hearing voices), visual hallucinations, and tactile hallucinations are most common in an alcohol-induced psychotic disorder, whereas persecutory delusions and tactile hallucinations (especially formication) are commonly seen in a cocaine- or amphetamine-induced psychotic disorder.

Symptoms

The ***Diagnostic and Statistical Manual of Mental Disorders*** (*DSM-IV-TR*) notes that a **diagnosis** is made only when the psychotic symptoms are above and beyond what would be expected during intoxication or withdrawal and when the psychotic symptoms are severe. Following are criteria necessary for diagnosis of a substance-induced psychotic disorder as listed in the *DSM-IV-TR*:

- Presence of prominent hallucinations or delusions.
- Hallucinations and/or delusions develop during, or within one month of, intoxication or withdrawal from a substance or medication known to cause psychotic symptoms.
- Psychotic symptoms are not actually part of another psychotic disorder (such as **schizophrenia**, **schizophreniform disorder**, **schizoaffective disorder**) that is not substance induced. For instance, if the psychotic symptoms began prior to substance or medication use, then another psychotic disorder is likely.
- Psychotic symptoms do not only occur during **delirium**.

Demographics

Little is known regarding the demographics of substance-induced **psychosis**. However, it is clear that substance-induced psychotic disorders occur more commonly in individuals who abuse alcohol or other drugs.

Diagnosis

Diagnosis of a substance-induced psychotic disorder must be differentiated from a psychotic disorder due to a general medical condition. Some medical conditions (such as temporal lobe epilepsy or Huntington's chorea) can produce psychotic symptoms, and, since individuals are likely to be taking medications for these conditions, it can be difficult to determine the cause of the psychotic symptoms. If the symptoms are determined to be due to the medical condition, then a diagnosis of a psychotic disorder due to a general medical condition is warranted.

Substance-induced psychotic disorder also needs to be distinguished from delirium, **dementia**, primary psychotic disorders, and substance intoxication and withdrawal. While there are no absolute means of determining substance use as a cause, a good patient history that includes careful assessment of onset and course of symptoms, along with that of substance use, is imperative. Often, the patient's testimony is unreliable, necessitating the gathering of information from family, friends, coworkers, employment records, medical records, and the like. Differentiating between substance-induced disorder and a psychiatric disorder may be aided by the following:

- Time of onset: If symptoms began prior to substance use, it is most likely a psychiatric disorder.
- Substance use patterns: If symptoms persist for three months or longer after substance is discontinued, a psychiatric disorder is probable.
- Consistency of symptoms: Symptoms more exaggerated than one would expect with a particular substance type and dose most likely amounts to a psychiatric disorder.
- Family history: A family history of mental illness may indicate a psychiatric disorder.
- Response to substance abuse treatment: Clients with both psychiatric and substance use disorders often have serious difficulty with traditional substance abuse treatment programs and relapse during or shortly after treatment cessation.
- Client's stated reason for substance use: Those with a primary psychiatric diagnosis and secondary substance use disorder will often indicate they "medicate symptoms," for example, drink to dispel auditory hallucina-

tions, use stimulants to combat depression, use depressants to reduce anxiety or soothe a manic phase. While such substance use most often exacerbates the psychotic condition, it does not necessarily mean it is a substance-induced psychotic disorder.

Unfortunately, psychological tests are not always helpful in determining if a psychotic disorder is caused by substance use or is being exacerbated by it. However, evaluations, such as the MMPI-2 MAC-R scale or the Wechsler Memory Scale—Revised, can be useful in making a differential diagnosis.

Treatments

Treatment is determined by the underlying cause and severity of psychotic symptoms. However, treatment of a substance-induced psychotic disorder is often similar to treatment for a primary psychotic disorder such as schizophrenia. Appropriate treatments may include psychiatric **hospitalization** and antipsychotic medication.

Prognosis

Psychotic symptoms induced by substance intoxication usually subside once the substance is eliminated. Symptoms persist depending on the half-life of the substances (i.e., how long it takes the before the substance is no longer present in an individual's system). Symptoms, therefore, can persist for hours, days, or weeks after a substance is last used.

Prevention

There is very little documented regarding prevention of substance-induced psychotic disorder. However, abstaining from drugs and alcohol or using these substances only in moderation would clearly reduce the risk of developing this disorder. In addition, taking medication under the supervision of an appropriately trained physician should reduce the likelihood of a medication-induced psychotic disorder. Finally, reducing one's exposure to toxins would reduce the risk of toxin-induced psychotic disorder.

See also Alcohol and related disorders; Amphetamines and related disorders; Antianxiety drugs and abuse-related disorders; Cannabis and related disorders; Cocaine and related disorders; Hallucinogens and related disorders; Inhalants and related disorders; Opioids and related disorders; Phencyclidine and related disorders; Psychosis; Sedatives and related disorders; Substance abuse and related disorders; Substance-induced anxiety disorders

Resources

BOOKS

American Psychiatric Association. *Diagnostic and Statistical Manual of Mental Disorders.* 4th edition, text revised. Washington, DC: American Psychiatric Association, 2000.

Kaplan, Harold I., M.D., and Benjamin J. Sadock, M.D. *Kaplan and Sadock's Synopsis of Psychiatry: Behavioral Sciences, Clinical Psychiatry.* 8th edition. Baltimore: Williams and Wilkins, 2002.

Jennifer Hahn, Ph.D.

Suicide

Definition

Suicide is defined as the intentional taking of one's own life. In some European languages, the word for suicide translates into English as "self-murder " Until the end of the twentieth century, approximately, suicide was considered a criminal act; legal terminology used the Latin phrase *felo-de-se*, which means "a crime against the self." Much of the social **stigma** that is still associated with suicide derives from its former connection with legal judgment, as well as with religious condemnation.

In the social climate of 2002, suicidal behavior is most commonly regarded— and responded to— as a psychiatric emergency.

Demographics of suicide

In the United States, the rate of suicide has continued to rise since the 1950s. More people die from suicide than from homicide in North America. Suicide is the eighth leading cause of death in the U.S., and the third leading cause of death for people aged 15 to 24. There are over 30,000 suicides per year in the U.S., or about 86 per day; each day about 1,500 people attempt suicide.

The demographics of suicide vary considerably from state to state. Some states, like Pennsylvania, have suicide rates that are very close to the national average; others, such as Connecticut, have significantly lower rates. However, other states have much higher rates than the national average. These variations are due in part to differences among age groups and racial groups, and between men and women. Males are three to five times more likely to succeed in their suicide attempts than females, but females are more likely to attempt suicide. Most suicides occur in persons below the age of 40; how-

KEY TERMS

Assisted suicide—A form of self-inflicted death in which a person voluntarily brings about his or her own death with the help of another, usually a physician, relative, or friend.

Cortisol—A steroid hormone released by the cortex (outer portion) of the adrenal gland when a person is under stress. Cortisol levels are now considered a biological marker of suicide risk.

Diathesis—The medical term for predisposition. The stress/diathesis model is a diagram that is used to explain why some people are at greater risk of suicidal behavior than others.

Euthanasia—The act of putting a person or animal to death painlessly or allowing them to die by withholding medical services, usually because of a painful and incurable disease. Mercy killing is another term for euthanasia.

Frontal cortex—The part of the human brain associated with aggressiveness and impulse control. Abnormalities in the frontal cortex are associated with an increased risk of suicide.

Serotonin—A widely distributed neurotransmitter that is found in blood platelets, the lining of the digestive tract, and the brain, and that works in combination with norepinephrine. It causes very powerful contractions of smooth muscle, and is associated with mood, attention, emotions, and sleep. Low levels of serotonin are associated with depression.

Slow suicide—A term used to refer to lifestyle behaviors known to shorten life expectancy, such as smoking, drinking heavily, having unsafe sex, etc.

Suicide gesture—Attempted suicide characterized by a low-lethality method, low level of intent or planning, and little physical damage. Pseudocide is another term for a suicide gesture.

ever, elderly Caucasians are the sector of the population with the highest suicide rate.

Race is also a factor in the demographics of suicide. Between 1979 and 1992, the suicide rate of Native Americans was 1.5 times the national average, with young males between the ages of 15 and 24 accounted for 64% of Native American deaths by suicide. Asian-American women have the highest suicide rate among all women over the age of 65. Further, between 1980 and 1996 the suicide rate more than doubled for African-American males between the ages of 15 and 19.

High-risk factors

Research indicates that the following factors increase a person's risk of suicide:

- Male sex.
- Age over 75.
- A family history of suicide.
- A history of suicide attempts.
- A history of **abuse** in childhood.
- Traumatic experiences after childhood
- Recent stressful events, such as separation or divorce, job loss, or death of spouse.
- Chronic medical illness. Patients with AIDS have a rate of suicide 20 times that of the general population.
- Access to a gun. Death by firearms is now the fastest-growing method of suicide among men and women. Nearly 57% of deaths caused by guns in the U.S. are suicides.
- Alcohol or substance abuse. While mood-altering substances do not cause a person to kill himself/herself, they weaken impulse control.
- High blood cholesterol levels.
- Presence of a psychiatric illness. Over 90% of Americans who commit suicide have a mental illness. Major depression accounts for 60% of suicides, followed by **schizophrenia**, alcoholism, substance abuse, **borderline personality disorder**, Huntington's disease, and epilepsy. The lifetime mortality due to suicide in psychiatric patients is 15% for major depression; 20% for **bipolar disorder**; 18% for alcoholism; 10% for schizophrenia; and 5–10% for borderline and certain other personality disorders.

Low-risk factors

Factors that lower a person's risk of suicide include:

- a significant friendship network outside the workplace
- religious faith and practice
- a stable marriage
- a close-knit extended family
- a strong interest in or commitment to a project or cause that brings people together, including community service, environmental concerns, neighborhood associations, animal rescue groups, etc.

Suicide in other countries

Suicide has become a major social and medical problem around the world. The World Health Organization (WHO) reported that one million people worldwide died from suicide in the year 2000. That is a global mortality rate of 16:100,000—or one death by suicide every 40 seconds. Since the mid-1950s, suicide rates around the world have risen by 60%. Rates among young people have risen even faster, to the point where they are now the age group at highest risk in 35% of the world's countries.

The specific demographics, however, vary from country to country. China's pattern, for example, is very different from that of most other countries. China has a suicide mortality rate of 23:100,000, with a total of 287,000 deaths by suicide each year. The rate for women is 25% higher than that for men, and rates in rural areas are three times higher than in cities. The means also vary; In China, Sri Lanka, and Turkey the primary means of suicide is ingestion of pesticides, rather than using guns.

Suicide in children and adolescents

The suicide rate among children and adolescents in the U.S. has risen faster than that of the world population as a whole. The suicide rate for Caucasian males aged 15 to 24 years has tripled since 1950; and it has more than doubled for Caucasian females in the same age bracket. In 1999, a survey of high school students found that 20% had seriously considered suicide or attempted it in the previous year. Of adolescents who do commit suicide, 90% have at least one diagnosable psychiatric disorder at the time of their death. Most frequently it is major depression, substance abuse disorder, or **conduct disorder**. Adolescents are particularly susceptible to dramatic or glamorized portrayals of suicide in the mass media.

Causes

Suicide is an act that represents the end result of a combination of factors in any individual. One model that has been used by clinicians to explain why people suffering under the same life stresses respond differently is known as the stress/diathesis model. Diathesis is a medical term for a predisposition that makes some people more vulnerable to thoughts of suicide. Components of a person's diathesis may include:

Neurobiological and genetic factors

Post-mortem studies of the brains of suicide victims indicate that the part of the brain associated with controlling agression and other impulsive behaviors (the frontal cortex) has a significantly lower level of serotonin, a neurotransmitter associated with mood disorders. Low serotonin levels are correlated with major depression. In addition, suicide victims have higher than normal levels of cortisol, a hormone produced in stressful situations, in the tissues of their central nervous system. Studies of the levels of other neurotransmitters in brain tissue are underway.

Other research has indicated that abuse in childhood may have permanent effects on the level of serotonin in the brain, possibly "resetting" the level abnormally low. In addition, twin studies have suggested that there may be genetic susceptibility in males to both suicidal ideation and suicide attempts which cannot be explained by inheritance of common psychiatric disorders. No twin studies of susceptibility to suicide in women have yet been reported.

History and lifestyle

Other components of a diathesis include:

- Chronic illness
- Traumatic experiences after childhood
- Alcohol or substance abuse
- High blood cholesterol levels.

Factors in the wider society

In addition to factors at the individual level, factors in the wider society have been identified as contributing to the rising rate of suicide in the United States:

- Stresses on the nuclear family, including divorce and economic hardship.
- The loss of a set of moral values held in common by the entire society.
- The weakening of churches, synagogues, and other mid-range social groups outside the family. In the past, these institutions often provided a sense of belonging for people from troubled or emotionally distant families.
- Frequent geographical moves, which makes it hard for people to make and keep long-term friendships outside their immediate family.
- Sensationalized treatment of suicide in the mass media. A number of research studies have shown that there is a definite risk of "contagion" suicides from irresponsible reporting, particularly among impressionable adolescents.
- The development over the past century of medications that allow relatively painless suicide. For most of human history, the available means of suicide were uncertain, painful, or both.
- The easy availability of firearms in the United States.

Treatment of attempted suicide

Researchers estimate that 8–25 people attempt suicide for every person who completes the act. Suicide attempts can be broadly categorized along a continuum that ranges from seriously planned attempts involving a highly lethal method that fail by good fortune, to impulsive or poorly planned attempts using a less lethal method. Suicide attempts at the lower end of the spectrum are sometimes referred to as suicide gestures or pseudocide.

A suicide attempt of any kind, however, is treated as a psychiatric emergency by rescue personnel. Treatment in a hospital emergency room includes a complete psychiatric evaluation, a mental status examination, and a detailed assessment of the circumstances surrounding the attempt. The physician will interview relatives or anyone else who accompanied the patient in order to obtain as much information as possible. As a rule, suicide attempts requiring advance planning, including precautions taken against discovery, and the use of violent or highly lethal methods are regarded as the most serious. The patient will be kept under observation while decisions are made about the need for **hospitalization**.

A person who has attempted suicide and who is considered a serious danger to him- or herself or to others can be hospitalized against their will. The doctor will base the decision on the severity of the patient's depression or agitation; availability of friends, relatives, or other social support; and the presence of other suicide risk factors, including a history of previous suicide attempts, substance abuse, recent stressful events, and symptoms of **psychosis**. If the attempt is judged to be a nonlethal suicide gesture, the patient may be released after the psychiatric assessment is completed.

Related issues

Survivors of suicide

One group of people that is often overlooked in discussions of suicide is the friends and family bereaved by the suicide. It is estimated that each person who kills him- or herself leaves six survivors to deal with the aftermath. On the basis of this figure, there are at least 4.5 million survivors of suicide in the United States. In addition to the **grief** that ordinarily accompanies death, survivors of suicide often struggle with feelings of guilt and shame as well. In spite of a general liberalization of social attitudes since World War II, suicide is still stigmatized in many parts of Europe and the United States. Survivors often benefit from group or individual **psychotherapy** in order to work through such issues as wondering whether they could have prevented the suicide or whether they are likely to commit suicide themselves. Increasing numbers of clergy as well as mental health professionals are taking advanced training in counseling survivors of suicide.

Assisted suicide

One question that has been raised in developed countries as the average life expectancy increases is the legalization of assisted suicide for persons suffering from a painful terminal illness. Physician-assisted suicide has become a topic of concern since it was legalized by recent legislation in the Netherlands (in April 2001) and in the state of Oregon. It is important to distinguish between physician-assisted suicide and euthanasia, or "mercy killing." Assisted suicide, which is often called "self-deliverance" in Britain, refers to a person's bringing about his or her own death with the help of another person. Because the other person is often a physician, the act is often called "doctor-assisted suicide." Euthanasia strictly speaking means that the physician or other person is the one who performs the last act that causes death. For example, if a physician injects a patient with a lethal overdose of a pain-killing medication, he or she is performing euthanasia. If the physician leaves the patient with a loaded syringe and the patient injects himself or herself with it, the act is an assisted suicide. As of 2002, assisted suicide is illegal everywhere in the United States except for Oregon, and euthanasia is illegal in all fifty states.

Media treatment of suicide

In 1989, the Centers for Disease Control (CDC) sponsored a national workshop to address the issue of the connection between sensationalized media treatments of suicide and the rising rate of suicide among American youth. The CDC and the American Association of Suicidology subsequently adopted a set of guidelines for media coverage of suicide intended to reduce the risk of suicide by contagion.

The CDC guidelines point out that the following types of reporting may increase the risk of "copycat" suicides:

- Presenting oversimplified explanations of suicide, when in fact many factors usually contribute to it. One example concerns the suicide of the widow of a man who was killed in the collapse of the World Trade Center on September 11, 2001. Most newspapers that covered the story described her death as due solely to the act of terrorism, even though she had a history of depressive illness.

- Excessive, ongoing, or repetitive coverage of the suicide.
- Sensationalizing the suicide by inclusion of morbid details or dramatic photographs. Some news accounts of the suicide of an Enron executive in January 2002 are examples of this problem.
- Giving "how-to" descriptions of the method of suicide.
- Referring to suicide as an effective coping strategy or as a way to achieve certain goals.
- Glorifying the act of suicide or the person who commits suicide.
- Focusing on the person's positive traits without mentioning his or her problems.

Prevention

Brain research is an important aspect of suicide prevention as of 2002. Since major depression is the single most common **diagnosis** in suicidal people, earlier and more effective recognition of depression is a necessary preventive measure. Known biological markers for an increased risk of suicide can now be correlated with personality profiles linked to suicidal behavior under **stress** to help identify individuals at risk. In addition, brain **imaging studies** using **positron emission tomography** (PET) are presently in use to detect abnormal patterns of serotonin uptake in specific regions of the brain. Genetic studies are also yielding new information about inherited predispositions to suicide.

A second major preventive measure is education of clinicians, media people, and the general public. Public health studies carried out in Sweden have shown that seminars for primary care physicians in the recognition and treatment of depression resulted in a rise in the number of prescriptions for antidepressants and a drop in suicide rates. Education of the general public includes a growing number of CDC, NIMH, and other web sites posting information about suicide, tips for identifying symptoms of depressed and suicidal thinking, and advice about helping friends or loved ones who may be at risk. Many of these web sites have direct connections to suicide hotlines.

An additional preventive strategy is restricting access to firearms in the developed countries and to pesticides and other poisons in countries where these are the preferred method of suicide.

Resources

BOOKS

American Psychiatric Association. *Diagnostic and Statistical Manual of Mental Disorders.* 4th edition, text revised. Washington, DC: American Psychiatric Association, 2000.

Eisendrath, Stuart J., MD, and Jonathan E. Lichtmacher, MD. "Psychiatric Disorders." In *Current Medical Diagnosis & Treatment 2001*, edited by L. M. Tierney, Jr., MD, and others. 40th edition. New York: Lange Medical Books/McGraw-Hill, 2001.

"Psychiatric Emergencies." Section 15, Chapter 194 in *The Merck Manual of Diagnosis and Therapy*, edited by Mark H. Beers, MD, and Robert Berkow, MD. Whitehouse Station, NJ: Merck Research Laboratories, 2001.

"Suicidal Behavior." Section 15, Chapter 190 in *The Merck Manual of Diagnosis and Therapy*, edited by Mark H. Beers, MD, and Robert Berkow, MD. Whitehouse Station, NJ: Merck Research Laboratories, 2001.

"Suicide in Children and Adolescents." Section 19, Chapter 264 in *The Merck Manual of Diagnosis and Therapy*, edited by Mark H. Beers, MD, and Robert Berkow, MD. Whitehouse Station, NJ: Merck Research Laboratories, 1999.

PERIODICALS

Byard, R. W., and J. D. Gilbert. "Cervical Fracture, Decapitation, and Vehicle-Assisted Suicide." *Journal of Forensic Science* 47 (March 2002): 392-394.

Fu, Q., A. C. Heath, K. K. Bucholz, and others. "A Twin Study of Genetic and Environmental Influences on Suicidality in Men." *Psychology in Medicine* 32 (January 2002): 11-24.

Gibb, Brandon E., Lauren B. Alloy, Lyn Y. Abramson, and others. "Childhood Maltreatment and College Students' Current Suicidal Ideation: A Test of the Hopelessness Theory." *Suicide and Life-Threatening Behavior* 31 (2001): 405-415.

Kara, I. H., and others. "Sociodemographic, Clinical, and Laboratory Features of Cases of Organic Phosphorus Intoxication in the Southeast Anatolian Region of Turkey." *Environmental Research* 88 (February 2002): 82-88.

Mancinelli, Iginia, MD, and others. "Mass Suicide: Historical and Psychodynamic Considerations." *Suicide and Life-Threatening Behavior* 32 (2002): 91-100.

Phillips, M. R., X Li, and Y. Zhang. "Suicide Rates in China, 1995-99." *Lancet* 359 (March 9, 2002): 835-840.

Plunkett, A., B. O'Toole, H. Swanston, and others. "Suicide Risk Following Child Sexual Abuse." *Ambulatory Pediatrics* 1 (September-October 2001): 262-266.

Vieta, E., F. Colom, B. Corbella, and others. "Clinical Correlates of Psychiatric Comorbidity in Bipolar I Patients." *Bipolar Disorders* 3 (October 2001): 253-258.

ORGANIZATIONS

American Academy of Child and Adolescent Psychiatry. 3615 Wisconsin Avenue, NW, Washington, DC 20016-3007. (202) 966-7300. Fax: (202) 966-2891. <www.aacap.org>.

American Association of Suicidology. Suite 310, 4201 Connecticut Avenue, NW, Washington, DC 20008. (202) 237-2280. Fax: (202) 237-2282. <www.suicidology.org>.

National Institutes of Mental Health (NIMH). NIMH Public Inquiries: (800) 421-4211. <www.nimh.nih.gov>.

OTHER

Befrienders International. <www.befrienders.org>.

Centers for Disease Control and Prevention, National Center for Injury Prevention and Control. *Programs for the Prevention of Suicide Among Adolescents and Young Adults; and Suicide Contagion and the Reporting of Suicide: Recommendations from a National Workshop.* MMWR 1994; 43 (No. RR-6). <www.cdc.gov/ncipc>.

Mann, J. John, MD. "The Neurobiology of Suicide." Mental Health Clinical Research Center for the Study of Suicidal Behavior, Columbia-Presbyterian Medical Center, New York. <www.afsp.org>.

National Suicide Hotline: (800) SUICIDE (800-784-2433).

Rebecca J. Frey, Ph.D.

Support groups

Definition

Support groups are an informal resource that attempts to provide healing components to a variety of problems and challenges. An informal support outside of family, friends, or professionals often provides greater understanding, more similarity (from individuals experiencing similar life events), an opportunity for empathy and altruism, and a sense of identity for participants. Learning new ways to handle challenges, cope with changes, and maintain new behaviors are all important aspects of the support group experience.

A characteristic unique to support groups is the mutual support members are able to provide one another. This support and validation from other group members help facilitate personal growth and change in a way that individual therapy cannot. Although experts and professionals can provide support and positive direction, the mutual exchange of information between group members is a powerful experience that often induces lasting change.

Description

Most support groups are facilitated or led by lay persons, often in conjunction with existing organizations (such as NAMI, the National Alliance for the Mentally Ill, or AA, Alcoholics Anonymous). Support groups usually have a set meeting time (generally weekly or monthly), and an open format. Open format means that the groups are ongoing, and members have the option of attending when it is convenient for them. This is in contrast to other types of structured treatment or psycho-educational groups that may meet for a certain number of sessions, with the expectation that participants attend every meeting. The open format allows members to feel some degree of anonymity, and to participate as they are comfortable. For some people, simply attending meetings and listening to the experiences of others can be helpful.

The healing power of groups is well documented, and support groups offer many of the same therapeutic characteristics as more structured groups. These factors include: altruism (chance to help others), belongingness, universality (there are others who struggle with similar challenges), interpersonal learning, guidance, catharsis, identification, self-understanding, instillation of hope, and existential factors (such as the search for larger meaning in life). Each of these factors is directly related to the mutual support that members provide one another.

Support groups are generally less structured than psycho-educational groups or therapy groups; however, each group usually sets its own norms, rules, and schedules. Some groups, such as AA, traditionally reserve time for individual members to discuss their own challenges and progress in front of the group. Others bring in speakers periodically to provide information about disorders or specific coping skills. However, the strength of support groups lies in its members, and their willingness to share their own experiences, challenges, and solutions in the context of the group.

In addition to these traditional, face-to-face support groups, technology has had an impact on the functioning and availability of support groups. There are many listserves, e-mail groups, and chat groups that provide information about specific life problems (adoption of children outside the United States, for example), certain types of mental illness, and specific health problems. While there is always the risk of communicating with others who are not honest, many people benefit from these Internet interactions. Some individuals are actually more comfortable participating in Internet support groups due to the greater anonymity they offer.

There are a variety of problems and challenges that are addressed in support groups. Generally speaking, the severity of the symptom, as well as the phase of the illness or disorder, will determine whether participation in a support group is appropriate. For more severe types of mental illness, such as **schizophrenia**, or depression with psychotic episodes, a support group is probably not the optimal **intervention**, particularly at initial onset. After stabilization through therapy and medication (as appropriate), a support group may offer an important addition to more formal treatment. In these cases, the socialization, interpersonal relationships, and social support that can be gained through the group may not be available elsewhere, and as such, it can be a very positive experience for the participant. In a group situation, a participant can learn how to express feelings in a healthy and positive way, practice assertive communication, receive feedback about appropriate and inappropriate content for conversation, receive feedback about nonverbal communication, learn new ways to ask for help from others, be able to help others, learn how to form friendships, and learn new coping skills and behaviors.

Types of support groups

Various types of support groups exist. Some groups provide support for very specific types of loss, illness, or life adjustment. A representative sample is listed below.

BEREAVEMENT/GRIEF COUNSELING GROUPS. Bereavement and **grief counseling** groups provide support to people who have experienced a loss. There are groups for people who have lost a spouse or partner, parents, children, or pets. There are specific groups for people who have lost a loved one due to homicide, **suicide**, SIDS, cancer, or miscarriage. These groups help individuals adjust to the death of a family member or friend, learn how to accept the loss, honor the memory of their loved one, and adjust to life after the loss.

MEDICAL SUPPORT GROUPS. Medical support groups may be more short-term than other types of support groups, depending on the specific disorder. Some groups are formed to help patients adjust to specific treatments, such as chemotherapy or radiation, while others focus on longer-term adjustment and recovery issues, such as a breast cancer support group. These groups may have a stronger educational component to help members understand physical changes they may be experiencing as a result of their medical procedures.

WEIGHT LOSS GROUPS. Although these groups are very specific in their focus, their individual structures can vary greatly. Some weight loss support groups are actively involved in the process of losing weight, and may include monitoring of diet and exercise, while others focus on maintaining weight loss, and, therefore, may focus more on social support.

MENTAL HEALTH/ILLNESS SUPPORT GROUPS. These groups usually focus on specific disorders, such as bipolar or eating disorders. Members of these support groups are often at different phases in dealing with their illnesses, and, therefore, the needs and contributions of individual members may vary greatly from meeting to meeting.

Most support groups are facilitated by lay persons, and usually have a set meeting time (generally weekly or monthly), and an open format. The open format allows members to feel some degree of anonymity, and to participate as they are comfortable. For some people, simply attending meetings and listening to the experiences of others can be helpful. *(Richard T. Nowitz/ CORBIS. Photo reproduced by permission.)*

FAMILY SUPPORT GROUPS. Family support groups, such as CHADD for parents of children with ADD, or NAMI for families with members who struggle with any type of mental illness, provide support from other parents and children who may be feeling the same level of frustration and exasperation. Meeting others who truly understand one's experience has a very powerful effect. For many parents, participation in a support group is the first opportunity to learn that there are other parents who are experiencing the same challenges and frustrations.

LIFE TRANSITIONS GROUPS. Life transitions groups include divorce and aging support groups. Support groups for children of divorce also exist in many communities and schools.

ADDICTIONS SUPPORT GROUPS. Traditional **addiction** support groups include Alcoholics Anonymous (AA), Narcotics Anonymous (NA), and Gambler's Anonymous (GA). Many of these groups follow the traditional "12-step" program of working through various aspects of the addiction, and, as such, are more structured than many other types of support groups.

Support group locations

Support groups meet in many different locations within a community. Hospitals and medical centers may provide meeting locations for medical support groups. **Community mental health** centers, inpatient psychiatric programs, and residential treatment centers are common locations for mental health and mental illness-related support groups. Life transition groups are often provided through schools, senior centers, and daycare centers. Bereavement groups and addiction support groups often meet in churches, community meeting rooms of local businesses, and mental health agencies.

Structure of support groups

Support groups are most successful when composed of persons close in age who are experiencing similar life challenges. Support groups are usually led by members of the group, such as the chapter president or another member of the organizing group. Some support groups may be led by paraprofessionals if they are offered as part of an aftercare program associated with a treatment facility.

Support groups usually have explicit norms and expectations for member participation, such as respecting members' feelings and opinions, and coming to meetings free from drugs or alcohol. Due to the open nature of most support groups, members typically feel free to miss a session here or there, which is usually not acceptable in a treatment or therapy group.

Conclusion

Group experiences can be very powerful in changing behavior and maintaining that change. The support group becomes part of the individual's daily life, and promotes healthy functioning by providing reminders about change and support when he or she is feeling down or is drawn toward old patterns. It also provides opportunities to own one's change by helping others. These factors contribute to the positive prognosis for most who participate in a group experience. However, a person could be harmed by a group experience as well. Much of this risk is dependent on the characteristics of individual members, particularly in support groups that operate without professional guidance. For example, if certain individuals dominate the group with their own agenda, perhaps at the expense of other group members, then the experience may have a negative impact on more vulnerable individuals.

See also Grief counseling and therapy

Resources

BOOKS

Giuseppe, R. and Galimberti, C., eds. *Towards cyberpsychology: Mind, cognition and society in the internet age* Amsterdam, Netherlands IOS Press, 2001.

Kaduson, H.G. and Schaefer, C. E., eds. *Short-term play therapy for children.* New York: The Guilford Press, 2000.

Yalom, I. D. *The theory and practice of group psychotherapy.* 3rd edition. New York: Basic Books, Inc., 1985.

PERIODICALS

Evans, J., J. Jones, I. Mansell. " Supporting siblings: Evaluation of support groups for brothers and sisters of children with learning disabilities and challenging behavior." *Journal of Learning Disabilities* 5, no. 1 (Mar 2001): 69-78.

Gottlieb, B. H. "Self-help, mutual aid, and support groups among older adults." *Canadian Journal on Aging* 19, Suppl 1 (Sum 2000): 58-74

Martin, D. J., D. Riopelle, J. Steckart, N. Geshke, and S. Lin. "Support group participation, HIV viral lead and sexual risk behavior " *American Journal of Health Behavior* 25, no. 6 (Nov-Dec 2001): 513-527.

Montazeri, A., and others. " Anxiety and depression in breast cancer patients before and after participation in a cancer support group." *Patient Education & Counseling* 45, no. 3 (Dec 2001): 195-198.

Sansone, R. A. "Patient-to-patient e-mail: Support for clinical practices." *Eating Disorders: the Journal of Treatment and Prevention* 9, no. 4 (Win 2001): 373-375.

ORGANIZATIONS

Children and Adults with Attention Deficit/Hyperactivity Disorder (CHADD) <www.chadd.org>.

National Alliance for the Mentally Ill (NAMI). <www.nami.org>.

Deanna Pledge, Ph.D.

Surmontil *see* **Trimipramine**

SVR-20 *see* **Sexual Violence Risk-20**

Symmetrel *see* **Amantadine**

Systematic desensitization

Definition

Systematic desensitization is a technique used to treat phobias and other extreme or erroneous fears based on principles of **behavior modification**.

Purpose

Systematic desensitization is used to help the client cope with phobias and other fears, and to induce relaxation. In progressive relaxation, one first tightens and then relaxes various muscle groups in the body. During the alternating clenching and relaxing, the client should be focusing on the contrast between the initial tension and the subsequent feelings of relaxation and softening that develop once the tightened muscles are released. After discovering how muscles feel when they are deeply relaxed, repeated practice enables a person to recreate the relaxed sensation intentionally in a variety of situations.

After learning relaxation skills, the client and therapist create an "anxiety hierarchy." The hierarchy is a catalogue of anxiety-provoking situations or stimuli arranged in order from least to most distressing. For a person who is frightened by snakes, the anxiety hierarchy might start with seeing a picture of a snake, eventually move to viewing a caged snake from a distance, and culminate in actually handling a snake. With the therapist's support and assistance, the client proceeds through the anxiety hierarchy, responding to the presentation of each fearful image or act by producing the state of relaxation. The person undergoing treatment stays with each step until a relaxed state is reliably produced when faced with each item. As tolerance develops for each identified item in the series, the client moves on to the next. In facing more menacing situations progressively, and developing a consistent pairing of relaxation with the feared object, relaxation rather than anxiety becomes associated with the source of their anxiety. Thus, a gradual desensitization occurs, with relaxation replacing alarm. Several means of confronting the feared situations can be used. In the pre-computer era, the exposure occurred either through imagination and visualization (imagining a plane flight) or through actual real-life — or so-called *in vivo* — encounters with the feared situation (going on an actual plane flight). More recently, during the 1990s, virtual reality or computer simulated exposure has come to be utilized in lieu of *in vivo* exposure. Research findings indicate that mental imagery is the least effective means of exposure; *in vivo* and virtual reality exposure appear to be indistinguishable in terms of effectiveness.

Description

Systematic desensitization is a therapeutic **intervention** that reduces the learned link between anxiety and objects or situations that are typically fear-producing. The aim of systematic desensitization is to reduce or eliminate fears or phobias that sufferers find are distressing or that impair their ability to manage daily life. By substituting a new response to a feared situation — a trained contradictory response of relaxation which is irreconcilable with an anxious response — phobic reactions are diminished or eradicated.

This behavior modification technique, which is founded on the principles of classical conditioning, was developed by Joseph Wolpe in the 1950s. Some of the most common fears treated with desensitization include fear of public speaking, fear of flying, stage fright, elevator phobias, driving phobias and animal phobias. Relaxation responses are trained to occur through *progressive relaxation training*, a technique initially perfected by Edmund Jacobson during the 1930s.

KEY TERMS

Behavior modification—An approach to therapy based on the principles of operant conditioning. Behavior modification seeks to replace undesirable behaviors with preferable behaviors through the use of positive or negative reinforcement.

Classical conditioning—In psychology, a process in which a previously neutral stimulus eventually produces a specific response by being paired repeatedly with another stimulus that produces that response. The best-known example of classical conditioning is Pavlov's dogs, who were conditioned to salivate when they heard a bell ring (the previously neutral stimulus) because the sound had been paired repeatedly with their feeding time.

Precautions

Because of the potential for extreme panic reactions to occur, which can increase the phobia, this technique should only be conducted by a well-qualified, trained professional. Also, the relaxation response should be thoroughly learned before confronting the anxiety-provoking hierarchy.

Normal results

Desensitization is an effective form of therapy. Individuals who have a positive response are enabled to resume daily activities that were previously avoided. The majority of persons undergoing this treatment show symptom reduction.

See also Anxiety disorders

Resources

BOOKS

Craighead, W. Edward. *Behavior Modification: Principles, Issues, and Applications.* New York: Houghton Mifflin, 1976.

Wolpe, Joseph. *The Practice of Behavior Therapy.* Tarrytown, NY: Pergamon Press, 1990.

PERIODICALS

North, M. M., S. M. North, and J. R. Coble. "Virtual reality therapy: An effective treatment for psychological disorders." *Student Health Technology and Information* 44 (1997), 59–70.

Rothbaum, B., L. Hodges, S. Smith, J. H. Lee and L. Price. "A controlled study of virtual reality exposure therapy for the fear of flying."*Journal of Consulting and Clinical Psychology* 68, number 6 (2000), 1020–1026.

Deborah Rosch Eifert, Ph.D.

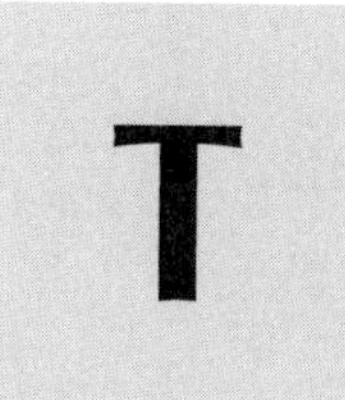

Tacrine

Definition

Tacrine is a drug used to treat **dementia** associated with **Alzheimer's disease**. In the United States tacrine is sold under the brand name drug Cognex. It is also sometimes called tetrahydroaminoacridine or THA.

Purpose

Tacrine is used to treat symptoms of Alzheimer's disease in people with mild to moderate illness. The drug may result in mild improvements in thinking for a short period. Tacrine does not cure or stop the progression of Alzheimer's disease.

Description

The Food and Drug Administration approved tacrine in 1993 for treating Alzheimer's disease. In Alzheimer's disease, some cells in specific regions of the **brain** die. Because of this cell death, these brain cells lose their ability to transmit nerve impulses. Brain cells normally transmit nerve impulses another by secreting various chemicals known as **neurotransmitters**.

Brain cells that make and secrete a neurotransmitter called acetylcholine are affected early in the course of Alzheimer's disease. Tacrine helps prevent the breakdown of acetylcholine in the brain, thus temporarily increasing its concentration. In doing so, tacrine may improve the thinking process by facilitating nerve impulse transmission within the brain.

Tacrine is available as capsules in several different strengths. Tacrine is broken down by the liver.

Recommended dosage

The dose of tacrine will be different for different people. An initial dosage of tacrine is usually 10 mg taken four times per day. This dose should be continued for four weeks while liver function is monitored. If no adverse liver effects are detected, the dosage should be increased to 20 mg taken four times per day. Higher dosages such as 30-40 mg given four times per day may also be used. Liver function must be monitored every other week during the first 16 weeks of treatment. After 16 weeks of tacrine therapy, liver function can be assessed every three months. Dosage increases should not occur more often than every four weeks. Tacrine should be taken on an empty stomach between meals, but if stomach upset occurs, it may be taken with food.

If problems in liver function arise, tacrine may be stopped, or the dosage reduced, until liver function returns to normal. Very specific guidelines should be followed by physicians with regard to dosage adjustments based upon the severity of liver effects. Newer drugs that work in the same manner as tacrine are not as toxic to the liver and may be preferred for patients just beginning therapy for Alzheimer's-type dementia.

Precautions

Tacrine may cause liver damage. It may not be the best drug to treat symptoms of Alzeheimer's disease in people with known liver damage. If these individuals take tacrine, their liver function should be closely monitored. Tacrine may also slow heart rates, increase acid secretion in the stomach, make urination difficult, cause breathing difficulties, or contribute to **seizures**. As a result, it should be used carefully in people with certain heart conditions, those who are prone to stomach ulcers, people with bladder obstruction, individuals with asthma, and those with a history of seizure disorders.

People should not stop taking tacrine suddenly because this could cause behavioral disturbances. The drug may be stopped slowly if improvements are not noted by caregivers or physicians.

KEY TERMS

Acetylcholine—A naturally occurring chemical in the body that transmits nerve impulses from cell to cell. Generally, it has opposite effects from dopamine and norepinephrine; it causes blood vessels to dilate, lowers blood pressure, and slows the heartbeat. Central nervous system well-being is dependent on a balance among acetylcholine, dopamine, serotonin, and norepinephrine.

Dementia—A group of symptoms (syndrome) associated with a progressive loss of memory and other intellectual functions that is serious enough to interfere with a person's ability to perform the tasks of daily life. Dementia impairs memory, alters personality, leads to deterioration in personal grooming, impairs reasoning ability, and causes disorientation.

Milligram (mg)—One-thousandth of a gram. A gram is the metric measure that equals about 0.035 ounces.

Neurotransmitter—A chemical in the brain that transmits messages between neurons, or nerve cells.

Placebo—An inactive substance or preparation used as a control in experiments with human subjects to test the effectiveness of a drug or herbal preparation. Some patients may experience a medicinal response or experience side effects to a placebo simply because they have faith in its powers even though it contains no medicine.

Side effects

The most common side effect of tacrine is impaired liver function. This causes 8% of people to stop taking the drug. Other common side effects occurring in at least 5% of people and at twice the rate of placebo are stomach upset (nausea, vomiting, diarrhea, indigestion, or anorexia), muscle aches, and difficulty walking. Side effects affecting the stomach appear to be more severe at higher dosages.

Side effects that occur less often are behavioral disturbances, abnormal thinking, hostility, tremor, inability to sleep, slow heart rates, changes in blood pressure, urinary difficulties, rash, flushing, aggravation of asthma, or cold-like symptoms.

Health care providers should be informed immediately if nausea, vomiting, loose stools, or diarrhea occur soon after the dose of tacrine is increased or if rash, jaundice (yellow tinge to eyes or skin), or changes in stool color occur at any time.

Interactions

Many drugs can alter the effects of tacrine. Some drugs such as dicyclomine may lessen the effects of tacrine. Other drugs such as **propranolol**, cimetidine, ciprofloxacin, **fluoxetine**, **fluvoxamine**, neostigmine, or bethanechol may increase some of tacrine's side effects. **Rivastigmine** may interact with some of the drugs used to relax muscles during surgery. The interaction increases the effects of both drugs.

Tacrine may also diminish the effects of levodopa and increase the side effects of theophylline. Smoking cigarettes may reduce the effectiveness of tacrine.

Resources

BOOKS

Ellsworth, Allan J., and others, eds. *Mosby's Medical Drug Reference*. St. Louis, MO: Mosby, Inc, 1999.

Facts and Comparisons Staff. *Drug Facts and Comparisons*. 6th Edition. St. Louis, MO: Facts and Comparisons, 2002.

Medical Economics Co. Staff. *Physician's Desk Reference*. 56th edition Montvale, NJ: Medical Economics Company, 2002.

Kelly Karpa, RPh, Ph.D.

T'ai chi *see* **Bodywork therapies**

Talk therapy

Definition

Talk therapy is an alternate name for the various forms of **psychotherapy** that emphasize the importance of the client or patient speaking to the therapist as the main means of expressing and resolving issues.

Description

Psychoanalysis, the first modern form of psychotherapy, was called the "talking cure," and the many varieties of therapy practiced today are still characterized by their common dependence on a verbal exchange between the counselor or therapist and the person seeking help. Some of these therapies that are characterized by the verbal exchange include: **cognitive-behavioral therapy**, behavior therapy, **couples therapy**, **family therapy**, **grief counseling** and therapy, **group therapy**, **interpersonal therapy**, **person-centered therapy**, **psychodynamic psychotherapy**, and **rational emotive therapy**. Both **self-help groups** and **support groups** also rely on the discussion of an issue as a main part of the cure.

KEY TERMS

Akathisia—An uncontrollable feeling of restlessness.

Dystonia—A neurological disorder characterized by involuntary muscle spasms. The spasms can cause a painful twisting of the body and difficulty walking or moving.

Tardive dyskinesia

Definition

Tardive dyskinesia is a neurological disorder consisting of abnormal, involuntary body movements caused by certain medicines. It is usually associated with long-term use of medicines for treating **schizophrenia** and other psychotic disorders.

Description

Tardive means "late" and dyskinesia means "abnormal movements." It refers to abnormal body movements that occur after a person has been taking a certain medicine for a long period of time. It sometimes starts after the medicine has been discontinued. In the early stages, the movements may be so subtle that neither the person nor the people around him or her notice them. For instance, the person may blink rapidly or lick their lips often. In later stages, the movements become noticeable and may affect the person's physical abilities.

Other types of tardive dyskinesia can occur. In tardive dystonia, there are abnormal contractions of the neck and shoulder muscles. In tardive akathisia, the person feels restless all the time.

Causes and symptoms

Causes

It is not altogether certain what causes tardive dyskinesia. The medicines that cause it affect how nerve impulses are transmitted across gaps between nerve cells (synapses). They do this in part by blocking a chemical made by the body called dopamine. After a while, the nerves seem to become hypersensitive to dopamine. Stimulation by even a little bit of dopamine may cause the abnormal movements.

The medicines most commonly associated with tardive dyskinesia include:

- Antipsychotic medicines used to treat schizophrenia and other psychoses. These are also known as neuroleptic medicines.
- Levodopa or L-dopa, which is used to treat Parkinson's disease (although high doses of L-dopa may actually help control tardive dyskinesia).
- Antiemetic medicines used to control nausea and vomiting.
- Tricyclic antidepressants used to treat depression and other mood disorders.
- Other medicines that block dopamine.

Symptoms

Symptoms of tardive dyskinesia include:

- involuntary movements of the face, including frowning, blinking, smiling, lip licking, mouth puckering, biting or chewing, clenching the jaw, sticking out the tongue, or rolling the tongue around in the mouth
- involuntary movements of the hands, arms, feet, or legs, such as twitching the hands or tapping the feet
- trunk movements, such as rocking, twisting, or squirming
- grunting or trouble speaking because of involuntary movements of the diaphragm

Movements may be rapid or slow and complicated. They are usually irregular and do not follow a pattern.

Demographics

Tardive dyskinesia develops in about a third of all people who take antipsychotic medicines for several years. The risk is higher in older patients. Approximately 5% of young adults taking antipsychotic medicines will develop tardive dyskinesia after a year of treatment, compared with a rate of 30% in elderly patients.

Treatments

Each case is treated differently. In some cases, the medicine causing the problem can be stopped. However, most people taking antipsychotic medicine cannot stop taking the medicine because of the high risk that their **psychosis** will return. Some newer antipsychotic medicines such as **clozapine** (Clozaril) do not seem to cause tardive dyskinesia. It may be possible to switch to a newer antipsychotic medication. If not, it may be possible to lower the dose to a level that does not cause the movements. There is controversy about whether or not "drug holidays" reduce the likelihood of developing tardive dyskinesia. "Drug holidays" are planned periods of time in which the person goes off the medicine, then resumes it.

Vitamin E has been shown to be helpful in patients, especially those who have had the problem for less than five years. L-dopa and some other medicines are sometimes helpful.

Prognosis

The earlier the problem is noticed and treatment begun, the better chance there is that the abnormal movements will go away. Most patients have a noticeable improvement in their symptoms within a year and a half. However, some abnormal movements may remain. People who are over 60 have a greater chance of having the problem go away on its own.

See also Medication-induced movement disorders

Resources

BOOKS

Hales Robert E., Yudofsky Stuart C., Talbott John A., eds. *The American Psychiatric Press Textbook of Psychiatry.* 3rd ed. Washington DC: American Psychiatric Press, 1999.

ORGANIZATIONS

National Alliance for the Mentally Ill. Colonial Place Three, 2107 Wilson Blvd., Suite 300, Arlington, VA 22201. Telephone: (703) 524-7600. NAMI HelpLine: (800) 950-NAMI. < www.nami.org>.

National Institute of Neurological Disorders and Stroke. Part of the National Institutes of Health (NIH), Bethesda, Maryland 20892.<www.ninds.nih.gov>.

Jody Bower, M.S.W

TAT *see* **Thematic Apperception Test**

Tegretol *see* **Carbamazepine**

Temazepam

Definition

Temazepam is a drug that belongs to a family of drugs known as benzodiazepines. Temazepam is sold under the brand name Restoril in the United States. Temazepam is also available as a generic.

Purpose

Temazepam is given to patients with sleeping problems (**insomnia**). It is often prescribed for insomnia characterized by frequent awakening during the night or by awakening early in the morning.

Description

Temazepam is one of several drugs in the class known as benzodiazepines. These drugs produce a variety of effects, but most cause some degree of drowsiness (sedation). Temazepam is used almost exclusively as a hypnotic, or drug given to help people fall asleep. It is nearly always taken just before bedtime. This drug produces its effects in the body by slowing down certain impulses in the **brain**, allowing the patient to fall asleep.

Recommended dosage

The typical dose starting for adults is 7.5–15 mg taken *just before* bedtime. The maximum recommended dose is 30 mg. Elderly patients and those in a weakened condition may need only 7.5 mg. The doctor should determine the dose in children 18 years of age and younger on an individual basis.

Precautions

The doctor should monitor any patient taking this drug to ensure that significant side effects do not develop. Insomnia that lasts longer than seven to 10 days may point to a significant medical problem that should be thoroughly evaluated. Temazepam should not be combined with alcohol or other drugs that lower the level of activity in the central nervous system. Examples of such drugs include prescription pain medications, antihistamines, **barbiturates**, and muscle relaxants. Some people may develop dizziness, lightheadedness, and clumsiness after taking temazepam. These side effects are especially common in the elderly.

Those with a history of anemia, liver disease, kidney disease, drug abuse, serious psychological disorders, and **suicide** attempts should be given temazepam only after being thoroughly evaluated by their physician. This caution also applies to persons with a history of lung disease, seizure disorders, and narrow-angle glaucoma.

People who are taking temazepam should not stop taking it abruptly. Instead, the dose should be reduced gradually. Withdrawal symptoms, including depressed mood, sweating, abdominal cramps, muscle cramps, vomiting, **seizures**, and shakiness can develop if the medication is stopped suddenly.

Although patients are instructed to take temazepam in the evening before bedtime, they often experience side effects the next day, particularly drowsiness and loss of coordination or clumsiness. Pregnant women should not use this drug because it increases the risk of birth defects in the baby. Nursing mothers should not be given temazepam because it can make their babies drowsy and unable to nurse properly. Patients should not operate heavy machinery or drive a car while they are taking temazepam or any other benzodiazepine.

Side effects

Temazepam is a relatively safe drug, safer than most of the benzodiazepines. Its less serious but more common side effects include clumsiness or unsteady behavior, dizziness, drowsiness, and slurred speech. Some patients taking temazepam experience abdominal cramps, dry mouth, constipation, diarrhea, headache, nausea, vomiting, a giddy sense of well-being, and changes in sexual drive.

A small number of patients taking temazepam have experienced anger outbursts, confusion, mental depression, unusually low blood pressure, memory difficulties, nervousness, irritability, and muscle weakness. As they can with many prescription drugs, people can overdose on temazepam. Symptoms of a temazepam overdose include extreme drowsiness, significant confusion, breathing difficulties, a very slow heartbeat, and staggering.

Rebound insomnia is one of the more common side effects of tapering a patient's dose of temazepam. Rebound insomnia is a reaction characterized by the reemergence of the symptom that the drug was originally given to suppress, namely problems with falling or staying asleep. When a person takes a medication for sleep on a regular basis, the body adjusts to the presence of the drug. It tries to counteract the effects of the medication. As a result, when the person stops taking the sleeping medication, the body will take a few nights to return to its normal condition. During this period of readjustment, the person may experience a few sleepless hours each night. In addition, people often mistake the rebound insomnia for the ordinary variety, and consider it a good reason to continue taking the temazepam.

KEY TERMS

Antihistamine—A medication used to alleviate allergy or cold symptoms such as runny nose, itching, hives, watering eyes, or sneezing.

Barbiturates—A class of medications (including Seconal and Nembutal) that causes sedation and drowsiness. They may be prescribed legally, but may also be used as drugs of abuse.

Generic—A term that refers to a medication that is not protected by a registered trademark.

Hypnotic—A type of medication that induces sleep.

Insomnia—A chronic inability to sleep or to remain asleep throughout the night.

Narrow-angle glaucoma—An eye disorder caused by a buildup of fluid pressure inside the eyeball due to an abnormally small angle between the iris (the colored portion of the eye) and the cornea (the transparent front part of the eye).

Rebound effect—A physical reaction to stopping a medication characterized by the reappearance of the symptom(s) that the medication was given to suppress. For example, people who stop taking temazepam may experience rebound excitability and sleeping problems.

Sedation—A state of emotional or physical relaxation. The term is usually used to refer to this condition when it is produced by a medication.

Withdrawal—Symptoms experienced by a person who has become physically dependent on a drug, experienced when the drug use is discontinued.

People can also develop withdrawal symptoms even when they are gradually decreasing their dose of temazepam, particularly if the original dose was high. The more common withdrawal symptoms include sleeping difficulties, irritability, and nervousness. Less common withdrawal side effects include abdominal cramps, confusion, sweating, nausea, trembling, increased heart rate, and mental depression.

Interactions

Patients should always inform any health care provider that they see—doctors, dentists, nurses, and others—about all the medications they are taking, including temazepam. This information is important because temazepam interacts with certain other drugs, including cimetidine (an antihistamine); **disulfiram** (a drug given to help patients control cravings for alcohol); or **clozapine** (an antipsychotic medication). Rifampin, which is an antibiotic, may decrease the effectiveness of the temazepam if the two are taken together. The most important warning, however, is that the patient should avoid drinking alcohol or taking other medications that cause drowsiness (such as antihistamines) while taking temazepam, because these substances will intensify its effects. Heavy smoking, however, interferes with the effectiveness of temazepam.

See also Sleep disorders

Resources

BOOKS

Consumer Reports Staff, eds. *Consumer Reports Complete Drug Reference.* 2002 ed. Denver, CO: Micromedex Thomson Healthcare, 2001.

Ellsworth, Allan J. and others. *Mosby's Medical Drug Reference.* 2001-2002. St. Louis, MO: Mosby, 2001.

Hardman, Joel G., Lee E. Limbird, eds. *Goodman & Gilman's The Pharmacological Basis of Therapeutics.* 10th ed. New York, NY: McGraw-Hill, 2001

Mosby's GenRx staff. *Mosby's GenRx.* 9th ed. St. Louis, MO: Mosby, 1999.

Venes, Donald, and others, eds. *Taber's Cyclopedic Medical Dictionary.* 19th ed. Philadelphia: F. A. Davis, 2001.

Mark Mitchell, M.D.

Thematic Apperception Test

Definition

The Thematic Apperception Test, or TAT, is a projective measure intended to evaluate a person's patterns of thought, attitudes, observational capacity, and emotional responses to ambiguous test materials. In the case of the TAT, the ambiguous materials consist of a set of cards that portray human figures in a variety of settings and situations. The subject is asked to tell the examiner a story about each card that includes the following elements: the event shown in the picture; what has led up to it; what the characters in the picture are feeling and thinking; and the outcome of the event.

Because the TAT is an example of a *projective* instrument— that is, it asks the subject to project his or her habitual patterns of thought and emotional responses onto the pictures on the cards— many psychologists prefer not to call it a "test," because it implies that there are "right" and "wrong" answers to the questions. They consider the term "technique" to be a more accurate description of the TAT and other projective assessments.

Purpose

Individual assessments

The TAT is often administered to individuals as part of a battery, or group, of tests intended to evaluate personality. It is considered to be effective in eliciting information about a person's view of the world and his or her attitudes toward the self and others. As people taking the TAT proceed through the various story cards and tell stories about the pictures, they reveal their expectations of relationships with peers, parents or other authority figures, subordinates, and possible romantic partners. In addition to assessing the content of the stories that the subject is telling, the examiner evaluates the subject's manner, vocal tone, posture, hesitations, and other signs of an emotional response to a particular story picture. For example, a person who is made anxious by a certain picture may make comments about the artistic style of the picture, or remark that he or she does not like the picture; this is a way of avoiding telling a story about it.

The TAT is often used in individual assessments of candidates for employment in fields requiring a high degree of skill in dealing with other people and/or ability to cope with high levels of psychological stress— such as law enforcement, military leadership positions, religious ministry, education, diplomatic service, etc. Although the TAT should not be used in the differential **diagnosis** of mental disorders, it is often administered to individuals who have already received a diagnosis in order to match them with the type of **psychotherapy** best suited to their personalities. Lastly, the TAT is sometimes used for forensic purposes in evaluating the motivations and general attitudes of persons accused of violent crimes. For example, the TAT was recently administered to a 24-year-old man in prison for a series of sexual murders. The results indicated that his attitudes toward other people are not only outside normal limits but are similar to those of other persons found guilty of the same type of crime.

The TAT can be given repeatedly to an individual as a way of measuring progress in psychotherapy or, in some cases, to help the therapist understand why the treatment seems to be stalled or blocked.

Research

In addition to its application in individual assessments, the TAT is frequently used for research into specific aspects of human personality, most often needs for achievement, fears of failure, hostility and aggression, and interpersonal object relations. "Object relations" is a phrase used in psychiatry and psychology to refer to the ways people internalize their relationships with others and the emotional tone of their relationships. Research into object relations using the TAT investigates a variety of different topics, including the extent to which people are emotionally involved in relationships with others; their ability to understand the complexities of human relationships; their ability to distinguish between their viewpoint on a situation and the perspectives of others involved; their ability to control aggressive impulses; self-esteem issues; and issues of personal identity. For example, one recent study compared responses to the TAT from a group of psychiatric inpatients diagnosed with dissociative disorders with responses from a group of non-dissociative inpatients, in order to investigate some of the controversies about **dissociative identity disorder** (formerly called multiple personality disorder).

Precautions

Students in medicine, psychology, or other fields who are learning to administer and interpret the TAT receive detailed instructions about the number of factors that can influence a person's responses to the story cards. In general, they are advised to be conservative in their interpretations, and to err "on the side of health" rather than of psychopathology when evaluating a subject's responses. In addition, the 1992 Code of Ethics of the American Psychological Association requires examiners to be knowledgeable about cultural and social differences, and to be responsible in interpreting test results with regard to these differences.

Experts in the use of the TAT recommend obtaining a personal and medical history from the subject before giving the TAT, in order to have some context for evaluating what might otherwise appear to be abnormal or unusual responses. For example, frequent references to death or **grief** in the stories would not be particularly surprising from a subject who had recently been bereaved. In addition, the TAT should not be used as the sole examination in evaluating an individual; it should be combined with other interviews and tests.

Cultural, gender, and class issues

The large number of research studies that have used the TAT have indicated that cultural, gender, and class issues must be taken into account when determining whether a specific response to a story card is "abnormal" strictly speaking, or whether it may be a normal response from a person in a particular group. For example, the card labeled 6GF shows a younger woman who is seated turning toward a somewhat older man who is standing behind her and smoking a pipe. Most male subjects do not react to this picture as implying aggressiveness, but most female subjects regard it as a very aggressive picture, with unpleasant overtones of intrusiveness and danger. Many researchers consider the gender difference in responses to this card as a reflection of the general imbalance in power between men and women in the larger society.

KEY TERMS

Apperception—The process of understanding through linkage with previous experience. The term was coined by one of the authors of the TAT to underscore the fact that people don't "perceive" the story cards in a vacuum; rather, they construct their stories on the basis of past experiences as well as present personality traits.

Battery—A number of separate items (such as tests) used together. In psychology, a group or series of tests given with a common purpose, such as personality assessment or measurement of intelligence.

Forensic—Pertaining to courtroom procedure or evidence used in courts of law.

Idiographic—An approach to interpreting the results of a projective test within the context of the individual subject's record.

Nomothetic—An approach to interpreting the results of a projective test in which the subject's answers are measured against a normative comparison sample.

Object relations—In psychology, a phrase that refers to the way in which a subject describes relationships with other people in their environment, and the ways in which he or she has internalized interpersonal relationships.

Projective test or projective measure—A type of psychological evaluation that assesses a person's thinking patterns, observational ability, feelings, and attitudes on the basis of responses to ambiguous test materials. Projective measures are not intended to diagnose psychiatric disorders, although they are often used in outcome studies to compare the effectiveness of different forms of psychotherapy.

Rorschach test—A commonly administered projective measure in which subjects are asked to describe a series of black or colored inkblots.

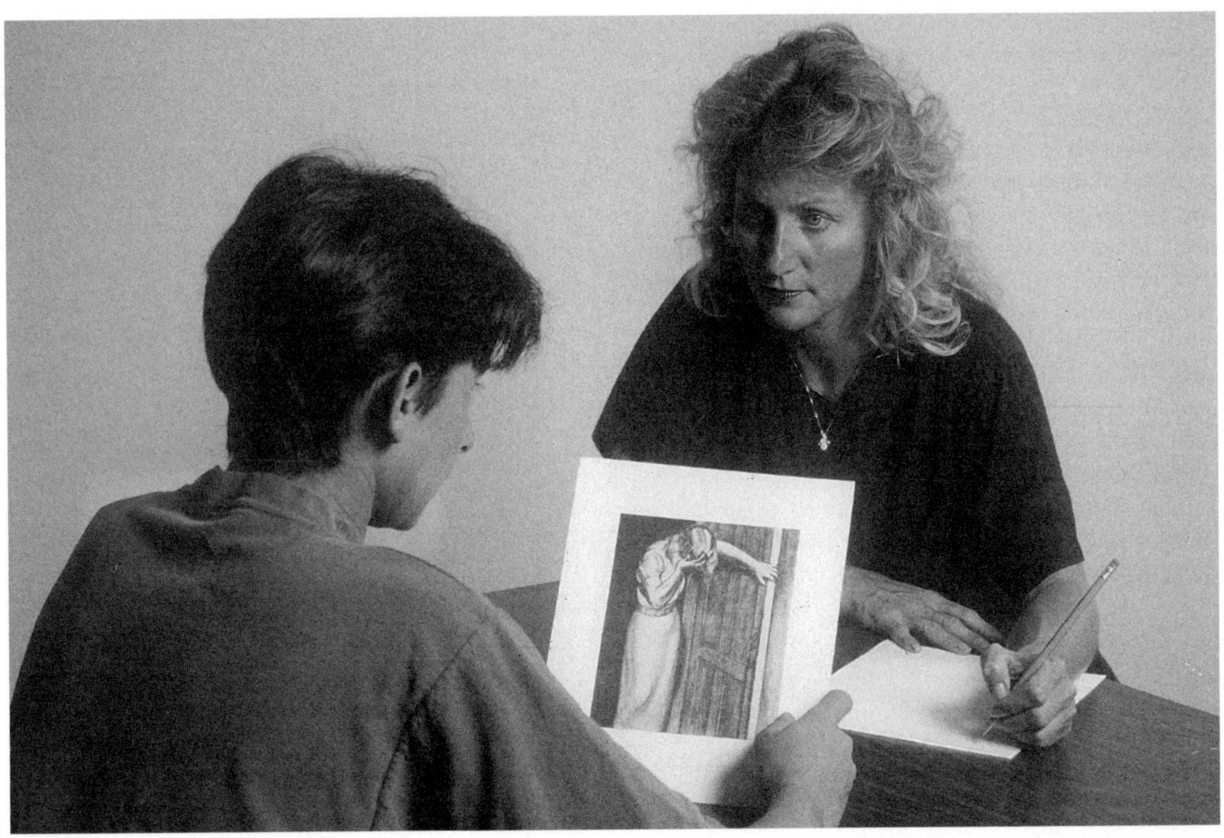

In the TAT, the test subject (the boy shown here) examines a set of cards that portray human figures in a variety of settings and situations, and is asked to tell a story about each card. The story includes the event shown in the picture, preceding events, emotions and thoughts of those portrayed, and the outcome of the event shown. The story content and structure are thought to reveal the subject's attitudes, inner conflicts, and views. *(Lew Merrim/ Science Source. Photo Researchers, Inc. Reproduced by permission.)*

Race is another issue related to the TAT story cards. The original story cards, which were created in 1935, all involved Caucasian figures. As early as 1949, researchers who were administering the TAT to African Americans asked whether the race of the figures in the cards would influence the subjects' responses. Newer sets of TAT story cards have introduced figures representing a wider variety of races and ethnic groups. As of 2002, however, it is not clear whether a subject's ability to identify with the race of the figures in the story cards improves the results of a TAT assessment.

Multiplicity of scoring systems

One precaution required in general assessment of the TAT is the absence of a normative scoring system for responses. The original scoring system devised in 1943 by Henry Murray, one of the authors of the TAT, attempted to account for every variable that it measures. Murray's scoring system is time-consuming and unwieldy, and as a result has been little used by later interpreters. Other scoring systems have since been introduced that focus on one or two specific variables—for example, hostility or depression. While these systems are more practical for clinical use, they lack comprehensiveness. No single system presently used for scoring the TAT has achieved widespread acceptance. The basic drawback of any scoring system in evaluating responses to the TAT story cards is that information that is not relevant to that particular system is simply lost.

Computer scoring

A recent subject of controversy in TAT interpretation concerns the use of computers to evaluate responses. While computers were used initially only to score tests with simple yes/no answers, they were soon applied to interpretation of projective measures. A computerized system for interpreting the Rorschach was devised as early as 1964. As of 2002, there are no computerized systems for evaluating responses to the TAT; however, users of the TAT should be aware of the controversies in this field. Computers have two basic limitations for use with the TAT: the first is that they cannot observe and record the subject's vocal tone, eye contact, and other aspects of behavior that a human examiner can note. Second, computers are not adequate for the interpretation of unusual subject profiles.

Description

The TAT is one of the oldest projective measures in continuous use. It has become the most popular projective technique among English-speaking psychiatrists and psychologists, and is better accepted among clinicians than the Rorschach.

History of the TAT

The TAT was first developed in 1935 by Henry Murray, Christiana Morgan, and their colleagues at the Harvard Psychological Clinic. The early versions of the TAT listed Morgan as the first author, but later versions dropped her name. One of the controversies surrounding the history of the TAT concerns the long and conflict-ridden extramarital relationship between Morgan and Murray, and its reinforcement of the prejudices that existed in the 1930s against women in academic psychology and psychiatry.

It is generally agreed, however, that the basic idea behind the TAT came from one of Murray's undergraduate students. The student mentioned that her son had spent his time recuperating from an illness by cutting pictures out of magazines and making up stories about them. The student wondered whether similar pictures could be used in therapy to tap into the nature of a patient's fantasies.

Administration

The TAT is usually administered to individuals in a quiet room free from interruptions or distractions. The subject sits at the edge of a table or desk next to the examiner. The examiner shows the subject a series of story cards taken from the full set of 31 TAT cards. The usual number of cards shown to the subject is between 10 and 14, although Murray recommended the use of 20 cards, administered in two separate one-hour sessions with the subject. The original 31 cards were divided into three categories, for use with men only, with women only, or for use with subjects of either sex. Recent practice has moved away from the use of separate sets of cards for men and women.

The subject is then instructed to tell a story about the picture on each card, with specific instructions to include a description of the event in the picture, the developments that led up to the event, the thoughts and feelings of the people in the picture, and the outcome of the story. The examiner keeps the cards in a pile face down in front of him or her, gives them to the subject one at a time, and asks the subject to place each card face down as its story is completed. Administration of the TAT usually takes about an hour.

Recording

Murray's original practice was to take notes by hand on the subject's responses, including his or her nonverbal behaviors. Research has indicated, however, that a great deal of significant material is lost when notes are recorded in this way. As a result, some examiners now use a tape recorder to record subjects' answers. Another option involves asking the subject to write down his or her answers.

Interpretation

There are two basic approaches to interpreting responses to the TAT, called *nomothetic* and *idiographic* respectively. Nomothetic interpretation refers to the practice of establishing norms for answers from subjects in specific age, gender, racial, or educational level groups and then measuring a given subject's responses against those norms. Idiographic interpretation refers to evaluating the unique features of the subject's view of the world and relationships. Most psychologists would classify the TAT as better suited to idiographic than nomothetic interpretation.

In interpreting responses to the TAT, examiners typically focus their attention on one of three areas: the content of the stories that the subject tells; the feeling or tone of the stories; or the subject's behaviors apart from responses. These behaviors may include verbal remarks (for example, comments about feeling stressed by the situation or not being a good storyteller) as well as nonverbal actions or signs (blushing, stammering, fidgeting in the chair, difficulties making eye contact with the examiner, etc.) The story content usually reveals the subject's attitudes, fantasies, wishes, inner conflicts, and view of the outside world. The story structure typically reflects the subject's feelings, assumptions about the world, and an underlying attitude of optimism or pessimism.

Results

The results of the TAT must be interpreted in the context of the subject's personal history, age, sex, level of education, occupation, racial or ethnic identification, first language, and other characteristics that may be important. "Normal" results are difficult to define in a complex multicultural society like the contemporary United States.

Resources

BOOKS

Aronow, Edward, Kim Altman Weiss, and Marvin Reznikoff. *A Practical Guide to the Thematic Apperception Test: The TAT in Clinical Practice.* Philadelphia, PA: Taylor and Francis, 2001.

Dana, Richard H. "Thematic Apperception Test." In *International Encyclopedia of Psychiatry, Psychology, Psychoanalysis, & Neurology*, vol. 11, edited by Benjamin B. Wolman. New York: Aesculapius Publishers, Inc., 1977.

Douglas, Claire. *Translate This Darkness: The Life of Christiana Morgan.* New York: Simon and Schuster, 1993.

Geiser, Lon, and Morris I. Stein. *Evocative Images: The Thematic Apperception Test and the Art of Projection.* Washington, DC: American Psychological Association, 1999.

Sweetland, R. C., PhD, and D. J. Keyser, PhD, eds. *Tests: A Comprehensive Reference for Assessments in Psychology, Education, and Business.* 2nd edition. Kansas City, KS: Test Corporation of America, 1986.

PERIODICALS

Pica, M., and others. "The Responses of Dissociative Patients on the Thematic Apperception Test." *Journal of Clinical Psychology* 57 (July 2001): 847-864.

Porcerelli, J. H. and others. "Object Relations and Defense Mechanisms of a Psychopathic Serial Sexual Homicide Perpetrator: A TAT Analysis." *Journal of Personality Assessment* 77 (August 2001): 87-104.

Schultheiss, O. C., and J. C. Brunstein. "Assessment of Implicit Motives with a Research Version of the TAT: Picture Profiles, Gender Differences, and Relations to Other Personality Measures." *Journal of Personality Assessment* 77 (August 2001): 71-86.

ORGANIZATIONS

American Psychological Association. 750 First Street, NE, Washington, DC 20002. (800) 374-2721. Web site: <http://www.apa.org>.

Rebecca J. Frey, Ph.D.

Thioridazine

Definition

Thioridazine is a potent antianxiety and antipsychotic agent. It is a member of the phenothiazine family of compounds. In the United States, thioridazine is sold as under the brand name of Mellaril and is also available under its generic name.

Purpose

Thioridazine is used to manage psychotic disorders. It reduces excitement, abnormal levels of energy, excessive movements (hypermotility), and agitation. The drug is also useful in the short-term treatment of depression that accompanies anxiety, sleep disturbances, agitation, and tension. Thioridazine is used in short-term treatment of children who display seriously inappropriate responses to exciting stimuli.

Description

Thioridazine is used in treating anxiety and **psychosis**. When used for the treatment of **schizophrenia**, thioridazine reduces symptoms of emotional withdrawal, anxiety, tension, **hallucinations**, and suspiciousness. Compared to other phenothiazine drugs, it is less likely to cause vomiting and Parkinson-like symptoms.

It is often successfully used to treat children who have impulsive conduct, difficulty in maintaining attention, or show high levels of aggression or have poor tolerance for frustration when other drugs have failed.

Recommended dosage

The dosage of thioridazine must be adjusted to each individual for whom it is prescribed to achieve maximum therapeutic effects and to minimize side effects. The usual initial dosage for adults is 50 to 100 mg three times a day. This may be gradually increased to a maximum of 800 mg per day. Once the desired therapeutic effect has been achieved, the dosage should be stabilized. A typical maintenance dosage is 200 to 800 mg per day, given in three to four doses.

The usual initial dosage for adults being treated for symptoms of anxiety is 25 mg three times per day. After reaching equilibrium and controlling undesired symptoms, the typical maintenance dosage is 20 to 200 mg per day divided into three or four doses.

For children between the ages of two and 12, the usual daily dosage of thioridazine is 0.5 to 3.0 mg per kg of body weight. Severely psychotic children who are hospitalized may receive 25 mg twice each day.

Precautions

It is dangerous to give thioridazine to persons in a comatose state. **Seizures** due to thioridazine therapy have been reported but are unusual. A sudden decrease in blood pressure due to a change in body position (orthostatic hypotension) with accompanying lightheadedness, may occur in people who have taken the drug. This is more common among women than among men.

Thioridazine increases the level of prolactin, a hormone that stimulates the mammary glands in the breast, in the blood. This is a potential problem for persons with a personal or family history of breast cancer and may increase the risk of breast cancer. For this reason, the benefits and risks of the drug must be carefully evaluated before it is administered.

Long-term use of thioridazine increases the probability of developing **tardive dyskinesia** (See below). Because of potentially serious side effects, the risks and benefits of thioridazine must be carefully explained and understood before the drug is started.

Side effects

A common side effect of thioridazine is drowsiness and lack of physical and mental alertness. This side effect is especially noticeable early in therapy. Patients taking it should refrain from performing hazardous activities requiring mental alertness or coordination. Other common side effects include greater sensitivity to the sun and increased risk of serious sunburn, dry mouth, constipation, and urinary retention. Urinary retention (difficulty starting a urine flow or passing urine,) is a particular problem in men with enlarged prostates.

Thioridazine use may lead to the development of symptoms that resemble Parkinson's disease, but that are not caused by Parkinson's. These symptoms may include a taut or mask-like expression on the face, drooling, tremors, pill-rolling motions in the hands, cogwheel rigidity (abnormal rigidity in muscles, characterized by jerky movements when the muscle is passively stretched), and a shuffling gait. Taking anti-Parkinson drugs **benztropine** mesylate or **trihexyphenidyl** hydrochloride along with **trifluoperazine** usually readily controls these symptoms.

Thioridazine has the potential to produce a serious side effect called tardive dyskinesia. This syndrome consists of involuntary, uncoordinated movements that may not disappear or may only partially improve after the drug is stopped. Tardive dyskinesia involves involuntary movements of the tongue, jaw, mouth or face or other groups of skeletal muscles. The incidence of tardive dyskinesia increases with increasing age and with increasing dosage of thioridazine. It may also appear after thioridazine use has been discontinued. Women are at greater risk than men for developing tardive dyskinesia. There is no known effective treatment for tardive dyskinesia, although gradual (but rarely complete) improvement may occur over a long period.

KEY TERMS

Akathisia—Agitated or restless movement, usually affecting the legs. Movement is accompanied by a sense of discomfort and an inability to sit, stand still, or remain inactive for periods of time. Akathisia is a common side effect of some neuroleptic (antipsychotic) medications.

Dystonia—A neurological disorder characterized by involuntary muscle spasms. The spasms can cause a painful twisting of the body and difficulty walking or moving.

Orthostatic hypotension—A sudden decrease in blood pressure due to a change in body position, as when moving from a sitting to standing position.

Prolactin—A hormone that stimulates milk production and breast development.

Schizophrenia—A severe mental illness in which a person has difficulty distinguishing what is real from what is not real. It is often characterized by hallucinations, delusions, language and communication disturbances, and withdrawal from people and social activities.

Tardive dyskinesia—A condition that involves involuntary movements of the tongue, jaw, mouth or face or other groups of skeletal muscles that usually occurs either late in antipsychotic therapy or even after the therapy is discontinued. It may be irreversible.

An occasionally reported side effect of thioridazine is neuroleptic malignant syndrome. This is a complicated and potentially fatal condition characterized by muscle rigidity, high fever, alterations in mental status, and cardiac symptoms such as irregular pulse or blood pressure, sweating, tachycardia (fast heartbeat), and arrhythmias (irregular heartbeat). People who think they may be experiencing any side effects from this or any other medication should talk to their physician promptly.

Interactions

Thioridazine increases the effect of drugs and substances that depress the central nervous system. This class of drugs includes anesthetics, opiates, **barbiturates**, atropine, and alcohol. These substances should be avoided or used sparingly by people taking thioridazine.

Propranolol increases the concentration of thioridazine. Concurrent administration of pindolol also increases the concentration of thioridazine. The reverse effect also occurs: thioridazine increases the concentration of pindolol in the body. Thioridazine may interact with other drugs used to treat mental disorders. People planning to take this drug should review the other medications they are taking with their doctor and pharmacist before starting the drug.

Resources

BOOKS

Adams, Michael and Norman Holland. *Core Concepts in Pharmacology.* Philadelphia: Lippincott-Raven, 1998.

Foreman, John C. and Torben Johansen. *Textbook of Receptor Pharmacology.* 2nd ed. Boca Raton, FL: CRC Press, 2002.

Page, Clive P., and Michael Murphy. *Integrated Pharmacology.* St. Louis: Mosby-Year Book, 2002.

Von Boxtel, Chris J., Budiono Santoso, and I. Ralph Edwards. *Drug Benefits and Risks: International Textbook of Clinical Pharmacology.* New York: John Wiley and Sons, 2001.

PERIODICALS

Dallaire S. "Thioridazine (Mellaril) and mesoridazine (Serentil): prolongation of the QTc interval." *Canadian Medical Association Journal* 164, no 1 (2001): 91-95.

Nelson J. C. "Diagnosing and treating depression in the elderly." *Journal of Clinical Psychiatry* 62, Supplement 24 (2001): 18-22.

Pisani F., G. Oteri, C. Costa, G. Di Raimondo, and R. Di Perri. "Effects of psychotropic drugs on seizure threshold." *Drug Safety* 25, no. 2 (2002): 91-110.

Ray W. A., S. Meredith, P. B. Thapa, K. G. Meador, K. Hall, and K. T. Murray. "Antipsychotics and the risk of sudden cardiac death." *Archives of General Psychiatry* 58, no. 12 (2001): 1161-1167.

Varvel A., E. Vann, E. Wise, D. Philibin, and H. Porter. "Effects of antipsychotic drugs on operant responding after acute and repeated administration." *Psychopharmacology (Berlin)* 160, no. 2 (2002): 182-191.

OTHER

American Academy of Clinical Toxicology. 777 East Park Drive, PO Box 8820, Harrisburg, PA 17105-8820. Telephone: (717) 558-7750. Fax: (717) 558-7845. Web site: <http://www.clintox.org/index.html>.

American Academy of Family Physicians. 11400 Tomahawk Creek Parkway, Leawood, KS 66211-2672. Telephone: (913) 906-6000. Web site: <http://www.aafp.org/>.

American Medical Association. 515 N. State Street, Chicago, IL 60610. Telephone: (312) 464-5000. Web site: <http://www.ama-assn.org/>.

American Psychiatric Association. 1400 K Street NW, Washington, DC 20005. Telephone: (888) 357-7924. Fax: (202) 682-6850. Web site: <http://www.psych.org/>.

American Society for Clinical Pharmacology and Therapeutics. 528 North Washington Street, Alexandria, VA 22314. Telephone: (703) 836-6981. Fax: (703) 836-5223.

American Society for Pharmacology and Experimental Therapeutics. 9650 Rockville Pike, Bethesda, MD 20814-3995. Telephone: (301) 530-7060. Fax: (301) 530-7061. Web site: <http://www.aspet.org/>.

L. Fleming Fallon, Jr., M.D., Dr.P.H.

Thiothixene

Definition

Thiothixene is in a class of drugs called antipsychotics. It is available with a prescription under the generic name of thiothixene or the brand name Navane.

Purpose

Thiothixene is a drug used to treat symptoms of **schizophrenia**. It is also sometimes used to calm severely agitated people.

Description

Thiothixene has been used in the United States for many years as a treatment for schizophrenia. It is believed to modify the balance of naturally occurring chemicals in the **brain** called **neurotransmitters** that regulate the transmission of nerve impulses from cell to cell. The proper balance between neurotransmitters is responsible, in part, for maintaining mental well-being. Thiothixene is thought to alter the balance among neurotransmitters in a way that improves symptoms of schizophrenia.

Thiothixene is available in several different strengths as capsules, as an injection, and as a concentrated liquid form taken by mouth. It is broken down by the liver and eliminated from the body by the kidneys.

Recommended dosage

The dosage of thiothixene varies widely from one individual to another. Initially, 2 mg of thiothixene taken by mouth three times daily is used in milder cases. This dosage may be increased slowly. Fifteen to 30 mg per day is often an effective range.

For more severe cases, 5 mg taken by mouth twice per day is a common starting dosage, with slow increases to 20–30 mg per day. Up to 60 mg of thiothixene may be taken daily. Doses greater than 60 mg per day usually do not provide any additional benefit, but may increase side effects.

Precautions

Thiothixene may alter the rhythm of the heart. As a result, it should not be used by people with a history of irregular or prolonged heart rhythms (long QT syndrome), those with heart failure, or people who have recently had a heart attack. People with other heart conditions should discuss with their physician whether thiothixene is the right antipsychotic drug for them.

Thiothixene may increase the tendency to have **seizures**. People who have had seizures in the past, including alcohol or drug-induced seizures, should take thiothixene only after discussing the risks and benefits with their physician. People taking thiothixene should call their doctor immediately if they experience any abnormal, involuntary muscle movements, because this adverse effect may be permanent. The risk of abnormal, involuntary muscle movements is believed to increase with long-term use of thiothixene and high dosages.

Thiothixene may increase body temperatures to dangerously high levels. People who exercise strenuously, those exposed to extreme heat, individuals taking drugs with anticholinergic effects (this includes many common antidepressants), and those prone to dehydration, should be alert to increased body temperatures and dehydration-related side effects. Fevers, difficulty moving muscles, irregular heartbeats, rapid heartbeats, or excessive sweating are warning signs of possible overheating that should be addressed by a physician immediately.

People taking thiothixene should have regular eye examinations, since use of thiothixene has been associated with abnormalities of the retina, the light-sensitive layer of the eye. Thiothixene may also alter reproductive hormone levels causing irregular menstrual periods, difficulty getting pregnant, enlarged breasts, and breast milk production. Thiothixene can cause enlarged breasts and breast milk secretion in men as well as women. People who have had breast cancer should not take thiothixene unless the benefits of this drug substantially outweigh the risks.

Thiothixene may cause drowsiness. People should not perform hazardous tasks that require mental alertness until they see how the drug affects them. This side effect usually diminishes with continued use of the drug. Thiothixene may make it more difficult to make a patient vomit after a drug overdose or accidental poisoning. Because there is a high incidence of **suicide** in all patients with psychotic illnesses, people using thiothixene should be observed carefully for signs of suicidal behavior. Women who are pregnant or breast-feeding should not take thiothixene.

KEY TERMS

Anticholinergic—Related to the ability of a drug to block the nervous system chemical acetylcholine. When acetylcholine is blocked, patients often experience dry mouth and skin, increased heart rate, blurred vision, and difficulty in urinating. In severe cases, blocking acetylcholine may cloud thinking and cause delirium.

Antihistamine—A medication used to alleviate allergy or cold symptoms such as runny nose, itching, hives, watering eyes, or sneezing.

Antipsychotic—A medication used to treat psychotic symptoms of schizophrenia such as hallucinations, delusions and delirium. May be used to treat symptoms in other disorders, as well.

Milligram (mg)—One-thousandth of a gram. A gram is the metric measure that equals about 0.035 ounces.

Neurotransmitter—A chemical in the brain that transmits messages between neurons, or nerve cells.

Schizophrenia—A severe mental illness in which a person has difficulty distinguishing what is real from what is not real. It is often characterized by hallucinations, delusions, language and communication disturbances, and withdrawal from people and social activities.

Side effects

Common side effects associated with the use of thiothixene are abnormal muscle movements and muscle stiffness, muscle tremors, weight gain, sleepiness, dry mouth, dry eyes, difficulty urinating, constipation, and sudden decreases in blood pressure that cause dizziness when standing up suddenly.

Other side effects that may occur when using thiothixene are headaches, seizures, high blood pressure, rapid heartbeats, blurred vision, liver changes, irregular menstrual periods, abnormal blood cell counts, difficulty breathing, and rash.

Uncommon and serious side effects include neuroleptic malignant syndrome and **tardive dyskinesia**. Neuroleptic malignant syndrome is an unusual but potentially life-threatening condition. The person with this syndrome becomes extremely rigid, has a high fever, rapid heart rate, and abnormalities on blood tests. The affected person also may have a difficult time breathing and may sweat, and will be admitted to the hospital. Tardive dyskinesia (TD) is a condition that may occur after a long period of using antipsychotic medications. TD is characterized by involuntary movements of the facial muscles and tongue, and may also involve muscles in the trunk or hands or feet. TD may disappear as soon as the medication is stopped, but it may not; if it does not, it is difficult to treat. These potential side effects should be discussed with the patient's doctor.

Interactions

When thiothixene is used with drugs such as bethanechol, **propranolol**, levodopa, and some antidepressants, some of the side effects associated with thiothixene may increase. Use of narcotic drugs with thiothixene may cause blood pressure to fall to dangerously low levels. If thiothixene is used with levodopa, the actions of levodopa may be diminished.

When thiothixene is used with **barbiturates** or lithium, thiothixene may be less effective. Because thiothixene may cause sleepiness, it should not be used with other drugs that also cause drowsiness, such as antidepressants, antihistamines, some pain relievers, and alcohol.

Resources

BOOKS

Ellsworth, Allan J., and others. *Mosby's Medical Drug Reference.* St. Louis, MO: Mosby, Inc, 1999.

Facts and Comparisons Staff. *Drug Facts and Comparisons.* 6th Edition. St. Louis, MO: Facts and Comparisons, 2002.

Mylan Staff. *Thiothixene Package Insert.* Morgantown, WV: Mylan Pharmaceuticals, Inc, 1998.

Kelly Karpa, RPh, Ph.D.

Thorazine *see* **Chlorpromazine**

Tic disorders

Definition

Tic disorders are characterized by the persistent presence of tics, which are abrupt, repetitive involuntary movements and sounds that have been described as caricatures of normal physical acts. The best known of these disorders is Tourette's disorder, or Tourette's syndrome.

Description

Tics are sudden, painless, nonrhythmic behaviors that are either motor (related to movement) or vocal and that appear out of context— for example, knee bends in science class. They are fairly common in childhood; in the vast majority of cases, they are temporary conditions that resolve on their own. In some children, however, the tics persist over time, becoming more complex and severe.

Tics may be simple (using only a few muscles or simple sounds) or complex (using many muscle groups or full words and sentences). Simple motor tics are brief, meaningless movements like eye blinking, facial grimacing, head jerks or shoulder shrugs. They usually last less than one second. Complex motor tics involve slower, longer, and more purposeful movements like sustained looks, facial gestures, biting, banging, whirling or twisting around, or copropraxia (obscene gestures).

Simple phonic tics are meaningless sounds or noises like throat clearing, coughing, sniffling, barking, or hissing. Complex phonic tics include syllables, words, phrases, and such statements as "Shut up!" or "Now you've done it!" The child's speech may be abnormal, with unusual rhythms, tones, accents or intensities. The echo phenomenon is a tic characterized by the immediate repetition of one's own or another's words. Coprolalia is a tic made up of obscene, inappropriate or aggressive words and statements. It occurs in fewer than 10% of people with tic disorders.

Children under the age of 10 with simple tics find them to be difficult to suppress, or control. Many older patients and children with complex tics describe feeling strong sensory urges in their joints, muscles and bones that are relieved by the performance of a motor tic in that particular body part. These patients also report inner conflict over whether and when to yield to these urges. A sensation of relief and reduction of anxiety frequently follows the performance of a tic. Unless the tic disorder is very severe, most people with tics can suppress them for varying periods of time.

Motor and vocal tics may be worsened by anxiety, **stress**, boredom, **fatigue**, or excitement. Some people have reported that tics are intensified by premenstrual syndrome, additives in food, and stimulants. The symptoms of tic disorders may be lessened while the patient is asleep. Cannabis (marijuana), alcohol, relaxation, playing a sport, or concentrating on an enjoyable task are also reported to reduce the severity and frequency of symptoms.

Tics are the core symptom shared by transient tic disorder, chronic motor or vocal tic disorder, and Tourette's disorder. It is the severity and course that distinguishes these disorders from one another. The age of onset for these disorders is between two and 15 years. In 75% of Tourette's disorder patients, the symptoms appear by age 11.

Causes and symptoms

Causes

Emotional factors were once viewed as the cause of tics, but this explanation has been largely discounted. The search for causes now focuses on biological, chemical and environmental factors. As of 2002, however, no definitive cause of tics has been discovered.

There appear to be both functional and structural abnormalities in the brains of people with tic disorders. While the exact neurochemical cause is unknown, it is believed that abnormal **neurotransmitters** (chemical messengers within the **brain**) contribute to the disorders. The affected neurotransmitters are dopamine, serotonin, and cyclic AMP. Researchers have also found changes within the brain itself, specifically in the basal ganglia (an area of the brain concerned with movement) and the anterior cingulate cortex. Functional imaging using **positron emission tomography** (PET) and **single photon emission computerized tomography** (SPECT) has highlighted abnormal patterns of blood flow and metabolism in the basal ganglia, thalamus, and frontal and temporal cortical areas of the brain. [The reader may wish to consult the "Brain" entry for a diagram of the brain's structures.]

Vulnerability to tic disorders appears to be genetic, or transmitted within families. Genetic factors are present in 75% of cases, although no single gene has been found to cause tic disorders. Researchers have not found a pattern suggesting that certain types of parenting or childhood experiences lead to the development of tic disorders, although some think that there is an interaction between genetic and environmental factors. Researchers are paying close attention to prenatal factors, which are thought to influence the development of the disorders.

In some cases, tic disorders appear to be caused or worsened by recreational drugs or prescription medications. The drugs most commonly involved are such psychomotor stimulants as **methylphenidate** (Ritalin); **pemoline** (Cylert); **amphetamines**; and cocaine. It is not clear whether tics would have developed anyway if stimulants had not been used. In a smaller percentage of cases, antihistamines, tricyclic antidepressants, antiseizure medications, and opioids have been shown to worsen tics.

Some forms of tic may be triggered by the environment. A cough that began during an upper respiratory infection may continue as an involuntary vocal tic. New tics may also begin as imitations of normally occurring events, such as mimicking a dog barking. How these particular triggers come to form enduring symptoms is a matter for further study.

In some cases, neuropsychiatric disorders, such as tic disorders and **obsessive-compulsive disorder**, have been shown to develop after streptococcal infection. No precise mechanism for this connection has been determined, although it appears to be related to the autoimmune system. There are other illness-related causes of tics, though they appear to be rare. These include the development of tics after head trauma, viral encephalitis or **stroke**.

Symptoms

The diagnostic criteria of all tic disorders specify that the symptoms must appear before the age of 18, and that they cannot result from ingestion of such substances as stimulants, or from such general medical conditions as Huntington's disease. Tic disorders can be seen as occurring along a continuum of least to most severe in terms of disruption and impairment, with transient tic disorder at one end and Tourette's disorder at the other.

Tics increase in frequency when a person is under any form of mental or physical stress, even if it is of a positive nature (excitement about an upcoming holiday, for example). Some people's tics are most obvious when the person is in a relaxed situation, such as quietly watching television. Tics tend to diminish when the person is placed in a new or highly structured situation, such as a doctor's office— a factor that can complicate **diagnosis**. When the symptoms of a tic are present over long time periods, they do not remain constant but will wax and wane in their severity.

Transient tic disorder occurs in approximately 4%–24% of schoolchildren. It is the mildest form of tic disorder, and may be underreported because of its temporary nature. In transient tic disorder, there may be single or multiple motor and/or vocal tics that occur many times a day nearly every day for at least four weeks, but not for longer than one year. If the criteria have been met at one time for Tourette's disorder or for chronic motor or vocal tic disorder, transient tic disorder may not be diagnosed.

Chronic motor or vocal tic disorder is characterized by either motor tics or vocal tics, but not both. The tics occur many times a day nearly every day, or intermittently for a period of more than one year. During that

KEY TERMS

Atypical antipsychotics—A group of newer medications for the treatment of psychotic symptoms that were introduced in the 1990s. The atypical antipsychotics include clozapine, risperidone, quetiapine, ziprasidone, and olanzapine. They are sometimes called serotonin dopamine antagonists, or SDAs.

Basal ganglia—A group of masses of gray matter located in the cerebral hemispheres of the brain that control movement as well as some aspects of emotion and cognition.

Behavioral therapy—An approach to treatment that focuses on extinguishing undesirable behavior and replacing it with desired behavior.

Benzodiazepines—A group of central nervous system depressants used to relieve anxiety or to induce sleep.

Cognitive-behavioral therapy—An approach to psychotherapy that emphasizes the correction of distorted thinking patterns and changing one's behaviors accordingly.

Comorbidity—Association or presence of two or more mental disorders in the same patient. A disorder that is said to have a high degree of comorbidity is likely to occur in patients diagnosed with other disorders that may share or reinforce some of its symptoms.

Compulsion—A strong impulse to perform an act, particularly one that is irrational or contrary to one's will.

Coprolalia—A vocal tic characterized by uttering obscene, hostile, or inappropriate words. A motor tic characterized by obscene gestures is called copropraxia.

Cyclic AMP—A small molecule of adenosine monophosphate (AMP) that activates enzymes and increases the effects of hormones and other neurotransmitters.

Dopamine—A chemical in brain tissue that serves to transmit nerve impulses (is a neurotransmitter) and helps to regulate movement and emotions.

Holistic—A treatment approach that is comprehensive and respectful of a person's emotional, social, cognitive, and interpersonal needs.

Neuroleptic—Another name for the older antipsychotic medications, such as haloperidol (Haldol) and chlorpromazine (Thorazine).

Neurotransmitter—A chemical in the brain that transmits messages between neurons, or nerve cells.

Obsession—A persistent image, idea, or desire that dominates a person's thoughts or feelings.

Onset—The point in time at which the symptoms of a disorder first became apparent.

Phenothiazines—A class of drugs widely used in the treatment of psychosis.

Remission—In the course of an illness or disorder, a period of time when symptoms are absent.

Serotonin—A widely distributed neurotransmitter that is found in blood platelets, the lining of the digestive tract, and the brain, and that works in combination with norepinephrine. It causes very powerful contractions of smooth muscle, and is associated with mood, attention, emotions, and sleep. Low levels of serotonin are associated with depression.

Stigma—A mark or characteristic trait of a disease or defect; by extension, a cause for reproach or a stain on one's reputation. Tic disorders are sometimes regarded as a stigma by the patient's family.

Tardive dyskinesia—A condition that involves involuntary movements of the tongue, jaw, mouth or face or other groups of skeletal muscles that usually occurs either late in antipsychotic therapy or even after the therapy is discontinued. It may be irreversible.

Thalamus—The middle part of the diencephalon (a part of the human forebrain), responsible for transmitting and integrating information from the senses.

Tic—A sudden involuntary behavior that is difficult or impossible for the person to suppress. Tics may be either motor (related to movement) or vocal, and may become more pronounced under stress.

time, the patient is never without symptoms for more than three consecutive months. The severity of the symptoms and functional impairment is usually much less than for patients with Tourette's disorder.

For a diagnosis of Tourette's disorder, a patient must have experienced both multiple motor and one or more vocal tics at some time during the illness, though they do not have to occur at the same time. The tics occur many times a day, usually in bouts, nearly every day or intermittently for a period of more than one year. The patient is never symptom-free for more than three months at a time.

Children and adolescents with Tourette's disorder frequently experience additional problems including aggressiveness, self-harming behaviors, emotional immaturity, social withdrawal, physical complaints, conduct disorders, affective disorders, anxiety, panic attacks, **stuttering**, **sleep disorders**, migraine headaches, and inappropriate sexual behaviors.

Tics seem to worsen during the patient's adolescence, although some clinicians think that the symptoms become more problematic rather than more severe, because the patient experiences them as more embarrassing than previously. The symptoms do become more unpredictable from day to day during adolescence. Many teenagers may refuse to go to school when their tics are severe. Coprolalia often appears first in adolescence; this symptom causes considerable distress for individuals and their families.

Behavioral problems also become more prominent in adolescence. There is some evidence that temper tantrums, aggressiveness, and explosive behavior appear in preadolescence, intensify in adolescence, and gradually diminish by early adulthood. Interestingly, aggression appears to increase at approximately the same time that the tics decrease in severity.

Demographics

Tourette's disorder is three to four times more common in males than females. Tic disorders have been reported in people of all races, ethnic groups, and socioeconomic classes. Tic disorders appear to occur more frequently in Caucasians than African Americans.

Diagnosis

There are no diagnostic laboratory tests to screen for tic disorders. Except for the tics, the results of the patient's physical and neurological examinations are normal. The doctor takes a complete medical history including a detailed account of prenatal events, birth history, head injuries, episodes of encephalitis or meningitis, poisonings, and medication or drug use. The patient's developmental, behavioral, and academic histories are also important.

There is an average delay of five to 12 years between the initial symptoms of a tic disorder and the correct diagnosis. This delay is largely related to the misperception that tics are caused by anxiety and should be treated by **psychotherapy**. This misperception in turn is fueled by the fact that tics tend to increase in severity when the affected person is angry, anxious, excited or fatigued. It is also common for the patient to manifest fewer tics in a doctor's office than at home, leaving parents feeling frustrated and undermined and physicians confused. In addition, children quickly learn to mask their symptoms by converting them to more socially acceptable movements and sounds. The diagnosis of a tic disorder can be aided in some cases by directly observing, videotaping or audiotaping the patient in a more natural setting.

Clinicians can also become confused by such additional symptoms of tic disorders as touching, hitting, jumping, smelling hands or objects, stomping, twirling and doing deep knee bends. They disagree, however, as to whether such symptoms should be classified as tics or compulsions. There appears to be a significant overlap between the symptoms of tic disorders and those of obsessive-compulsive disorder (OCD).

Abnormal obsessive-compulsive behavior has been found in 40% of patients with Tourette's disorder between the ages of six and 10 years. Obsessions are persistent ideas, thoughts, impulses, or images that are experienced as intrusive, inappropriate, senseless, and repetitive. Compulsions are defined as repetitive behaviors performed to reduce the anxiety or distress caused by the obsessions. For those diagnosed with OCD, common obsessions have to do with dirt, germs, and contamination. Patients with Tourette's disorder often have obsessions that involve violent scenes, sexual thoughts, and counting; their compulsions are often related to symmetry (lining things up and getting them "just right," for example). OCD symptoms occur considerably later than tics, and appear to worsen with age. Some theorists have suggested that obsessive thoughts are cognitive tics.

Tic disorders can be differentiated from **movement disorders** by the following characteristics: they are suppressible; they tend to persist during sleep; they are preceded by sensory symptoms; they have both phonic and motor components; and they wax and wane.

Dual diagnoses

Children and adults with tic disorders are at increased risk for depression and other mood disorders, as well as anxiety disorders. This comorbidity may be due to the burden of dealing with a chronic, disruptive, and often stigmatizing disorder. The energy and watchfulness required to suppress tic symptoms may contribute to social anxiety, social withdrawal, self-preoccupation, and fatigue. Low self-esteem and feelings of hopelessness are common in patients diagnosed with tic disorders.

While OCD behaviors have been noted in as many as 80% of individuals with tic disorders, only 30% meet the full criteria for OCD. Distinguishing complex tics from simple compulsions can be difficult. Touching compulsions appear to be characteristic of the tic-related type of OCD. Compared to obsessive-compulsive disorder in persons without a history of tics, there will likely be an earlier age of onset, a greater proportion of males, a more frequent family history of chronic tics, and a poorer therapeutic response to selective serotonin reuptake inhibitors (SSRIs)— although the addition of a neuroleptic to the treatment regimen sometimes brings about improvement.

As many as 50%–80% of children with Tourette's disorder have some symptoms of **attention-deficit/hyperactivity disorder** (ADHD), including a short attention span, restlessness, poor concentration, and diminished impulse control. On average, ADHD will manifest two and a half years before the tics appear. A **dual diagnosis** of ADHD and tic disorder is associated with more severe tics and greater social impairment than for tic disorder by itself. Over time, the problems caused by the inattention, impulsivity, motor overactivity and the resultant underachievement in school associated with ADHD are often more disabling than the tics themselves.

Children with tic disorders are five times as likely as other children to require special education programs. The tics may be disruptive and mistakenly interpreted by teachers as intended to disturb the class. Often, children with tic disorders have underlying learning disabilities as well. While there does not appear to be any impairment in general intellectual functioning, researchers have identified patterns of specific learning problems in children with tic disorders. These problems include abnormal visual-perceptual performance, reduced visual-motor skills, and discrepancies between verbal and performance IQ. Many of these learning difficulties are also commonly found in children with ADHD.

Increasing numbers of children with tic disorders are also diagnosed with a **conduct disorder**. Children with conduct disorder show inappropriate and sometimes severe aggression toward people and animals. They may also act out other destructive impulses. Unfortunately, some of these children grow up to develop a personality disorder.

Treatments

A holistic approach is recommended for the treatment of tic disorders. A multidisciplinary team should work together with the affected child's parents and teachers to put together a comprehensive treatment plan. Treatment should include the following:

- Educating the patient and family about the course of the disorder in a reassuring manner.
- Completion of necessary diagnostic tests, including self-reports (by child and parents); clinician-administered ratings; and direct observational methods.
- Comprehensive assessment, including the child's cognitive abilities, perception, motor skills, behavior and adaptive functioning.
- Collaboration with school personnel to create a learning environment conducive to academic success.
- Therapy, most often behavioral or cognitive-behavioral, though other modalities may be appropriate.
- If necessary, evaluation for medication.

Behavioral and cognitive-behavioral therapy

Massed negative practice has been one of the most frequently used behavioral therapy techniques in the treatment of children with tic disorder. The patient is asked to deliberately perform the tic movement for specified periods of time interspersed with brief periods of rest. Patients have shown some decrease in tic frequency, but the long-term benefits of massed negative practice are unclear.

Contingency management is another behavioral treatment. It is based on positive **reinforcement**, usually administered by parents. Children are praised and rewarded for not performing tics and for replacing them with alternative behaviors. Contingency management, however, appears to be of limited use outside of such controlled settings as schools or institutions.

Self-monitoring consists of having the patient record tics by using a wrist counter or small notebook. It is fairly effective in reducing some tics by increasing the child's awareness.

Habit reversal is the most commonly used technique, combining relaxation exercises, awareness training, and contingency management for positive reinforcement. This method shows a 64%–100% success rate.

Adding a cognitive component to habit reversal involves the introduction of flexibility into rigid thinking, and confronting the child's irrational expectations and unrealistic anticipations. It has not been shown as of 2002 to increase treatment effectiveness. The specific cognitive technique of distraction, however, has been shown to help patients resist sensory urges and to restore the patient's sense of control over the tic.

Medications

Medication is the main treatment for motor and vocal tics. Patients and their families, however, should be evaluated fully and use other treatment methods in conjunction with medication. Because the symptoms of tic disorders overlap those of OCD and ADHD, it is essential to determine which symptoms are causing the greatest concern and impairment, and treat the patient according to the single diagnostic category that best fits him or her, whether it is a tic disorder, OCD, or ADHD.

Medications prescribed for patients with tic disorders include:

- Typical neuroleptics (antipsychotic medications), including **haloperidol** (Haldol) and **pimozide** (Orap). Neuroleptics can have significant side effects, which include concentration problems, cognitive blunting, and rarely, **tardive dyskinesia** (a movement disorder that consists of lip, mouth, and tongue movements). Such side effects as stiffness, rigidity, tremor, sedation, and depression are common with haloperidol, but are less so with pimozide.
- Alpha-adrenergic receptor agonists, including **clonidine** (Catapres) and guanfacine (Tenex). Clonidine has fewer and milder side effects than the neuroleptics in general, with the most common being sedation. Sedation occurs in 10%–20% of cases and can often be controlled through adjusting the dosage.
- The phenothiazines may be used when haloperidol or pimozide has proven ineffective.
- Atypical antipsychotics and other agents that block dopamine receptors include **risperidone** (Risperdal) and **clozapine** (Clozaril).
- Tetrabenazine is a promising new medication with fewer side effects than other typical neuroleptics. It can be used in combination with the older antipsychotic medications, allowing for lower doses of both medications with substantial relief.
- Selective serotonin reuptake inhibitors (SSRIs), which include such medications as **fluoxetine** (Prozac) and **sertraline** (Zoloft), can be used to treat the obsessive-compulsive behaviors associated with Tourette's disorder. They can also be helpful with depression and impulse control difficulties, though they must be given at higher dosages for OCD than for depression. The SSRIs, however, can cause gastric upset and nausea.
- Benzodiazepines are used in some cases to lower the patient's anxiety level, but are often avoided because they can cause dependence and tolerance.
- Nicotine chewing gum appears to reduce tics when added to ongoing treatment with haloperidol, but is in need of further study.

Alternative therapies

There is growing interest in dietary changes and nutritional supplements to prevent and manage the symptoms of tic disorders, although formal studies have not yet been conducted in this area. Some theorists have suggested that hidden food and chemical allergies or nutritional deficiencies may influence the development and maintenance of tic disorders. Recommendations include eating organic food and avoiding pesticides; taking antioxidants; increasing intake of folic acid and the B vitamins; eating foods high in zinc and magnesium; eliminating caffeine from the diet; and avoiding artificial sweeteners, colors and dyes.

Prognosis

There is presently no cure for tic disorders, and there is no evidence that early treatment alters prognosis. When a child is first evaluated, it is not possible to determine whether the tics will be chronic or transient, mild or severe.

As recently as twenty years ago, tic disorders were considered to be lifelong conditions, with remissions believed to be rare. There is now a general consensus that if a tic disorder is the only diagnosis, the prognosis is favorable. Up to 73% of patients report that their tics decreased markedly or disappeared as they entered the later years of adolescence or early adulthood.

In a small number of patients, the most severe and debilitating forms of a tic disorder occur in adult life. In addition, stress in later life can cause tics to re-emerge. In rare cases, the tics may be new developments in adulthood, though this phenomenon may be more common than previously thought. Remission rates for tic disorders are difficult to pinpoint among this seldom-studied population, but appear to be extremely low.

While the tics themselves may decline, however, the associated problems often continue into adult life. Obsessive-compulsive symptoms and other behavioral problems, as well as learning disabilities, may grow worse. Obsessive-compulsive behaviors become most pronounced at age 15 and remain at that level. Panic attacks, depression, **agoraphobia** and alcoholism are most significant in the early adult years, while a tendency toward **obesity** increases steadily with age, particularly in women.

In adulthood, a patient's repertoire of tics is reduced and becomes predictable during periods of fatigue and heightened emotionality. Some studies suggest remission rates, with the complete cessation of symptoms, to be as high as 50%. Cases of total remission appear to be related to the family's treatment of the patient when he or she was a child. Persons who were punished, misunderstood and stigmatized experience greater functional impairment as adults than those who were supported and understood as children.

Prevention

There are few preventive strategies for tic disorders. There is some evidence that maternal emotional stress during pregnancy and severe nausea and vomiting during the first trimester may affect tic severity. Attempting to minimize prenatal stress may possibly serve a limited preventive function.

Similarly, because people with tic disorders are sensitive to stress, attempting to maintain a low-stress environment can help minimize the number or severity of tics (reducing the number of social gatherings, which can be anxiety-provoking, for example). This approach cannot prevent tics altogether, and must be undertaken with an awareness that it is neither healthful nor advisable to attempt to eliminate all stressful events in life.

See also Abnormal Involuntary Movement Scale; Neuropsychological testing; Stereotypic movement disorder

Resources

BOOKS

American Psychiatric Association. *Diagnostic and Statistical Manual of Mental Disorders.* 4th edition, text revision. Washington, DC: American Psychiatric Association, 2000.

Kurlan, Roger, ed. *Handbook of Tourette's Syndrome and Related Tic and Behavioral Disorders.* New York: Marcel Dekker, Inc., 1993.

Leckman, James. F., and Donald J. Cohen. *Tourette's Syndrome Tics, Obsessions, Compulsions: Developmental Psychopathology and Clinical Care.* New York: John Wiley and Sons, Inc., 1999.

Robertson, Mary M., and Simon Baron-Cohen. *Tourette Syndrome: The Facts.* New York: Oxford University Press, 1998.

PERIODICALS

Chouinard, Sylvain, and Blair Ford. "Adult onset tic disorders." *Journal of Neurology, Neurosurgery, & Psychiatry* (June, 2000): 68.

Evidente, Virgilio G. H., M.D. "Is it a tic or Tourette's?: Clues for differentiating simple from more complex tic disorders." *Postgraduate Medicine* (October, 2000): 108.

Kurlan, R., M.D., and others. "Prevalence of tics in schoolchildren and association with placement in special education." *Neurology* (October, 2001): 57.

Marcus, David, M.D., and Roger Kurlan, M.D. "Tic and its disorders." *Movement Disorders* (August, 2001): 19.

O'Connor, K. P., and others. "Evaluation of a cognitive-behavioural program for the management of chronic tic and habit disorders." *Behaviour Research and Therapy* (June, 2001): 39.

O'Connor, Kieran P. "Clinical and psychological features distinguishing obsessive-compulsive and chronic tic disorders" *Clinical Psychology Review* (June, 2001): 21.

ORGANIZATIONS

Association for Comprehensive Neurotherapy. 1128 Royal Palm Beach Boulevard #283, Royal Palm Beach, FL 33411. <http://www.latitudes.org>.

National Institutes of Health/National Institute of Neurological Diseases and Stroke (NINDS). P.O. Box 5801, Bethesda, MD 20824. <http://www.ninds.nih.gov>.

The Tourette Syndrome Association, Inc. 42-40 Bell Boulevard, Bayside, NY 11361-2861 <http://www.tsa-usa.org>.

OTHER

Nutritional Supplements and Tourette's Syndrome <www.latitudes.org>.

Holly Scherstuhl, M.Ed.

Tofranil *see* **Imipramine**

Token economy system

Definition

A token economy is a form of **behavior modification** designed to increase desirable behavior and decrease undesirable behavior with the use of tokens. Individuals receive tokens immediately after displaying desirable behavior. The tokens are collected and later exchanged for a meaningful object or privilege.

Purpose

The primary goal of a token economy is to increase desirable behavior and decrease undesirable behavior. Often token economies are used in institutional settings (such as psychiatric hospitals or correctional facilities) to manage the behavior of individuals who may be aggressive or unpredictable. However, the larger goal of token economies is to teach appropriate behavior and social skills that can be used in one's natural environment. Special education (for children with developmental or learning disabilities, hyperactivity, attention deficit, or behavioral disorders), regular education, colleges, various types of **group homes**, military divisions, nursing homes, **addiction** treatment programs, occupational settings, family homes (for marital or parenting difficulties), and hospitals may also use token economies. Token economies can be used individually or in groups.

Description

Several elements are necessary in every token economy:

- Tokens: Anything that is visible and countable can be used as a token. Tokens should preferably be attractive, easy to carry and dispense, and difficult to counterfeit. Commonly used items include poker chips, stickers, point tallies, or play money. When an individual displays desirable behavior, he or she is immediately given a designated number of tokens. Tokens have no value of their own. They are collected and later exchanged for meaningful objects, privileges or activities. Individuals can also lose tokens (response cost) for displaying undesirable behavior.
- A clearly defined target behavior: Individuals participating in a token economy need to know exactly what they must do in order to receive tokens. Desirable and undesirable behavior is explained ahead of time in simple, specific terms. The number of tokens awarded or lost for each particular behavior is also specified.
- Back-up reinforcers: Back-up reinforcers are the meaningful objects, privileges, or activities that individuals receive in exchange for their tokens. Examples include food items, toys, extra free time, or outings. The success of a token economy depends on the appeal of the back-up reinforcers. Individuals will only be motivated to earn tokens if they anticipate the future reward represented by the tokens. A well-designed token economy will use back-up reinforcers chosen by individuals in treatment rather than by staff.
- A system for exchanging tokens: A time and place for purchasing back-up reinforcers is necessary. The token value of each back-up reinforcer is pre-determined based on monetary value, demand, or therapeutic value. For example, if the reinforcer is expensive or highly attractive, the token value should be higher. If possession of or participation in the reinforcer would aid in the individual's acquisition of skills, the token value should be lower. If the token value is set too low, individuals will be less motivated to earn tokens. Conversely, if the value is set too high, individuals may become easily discouraged. It is important that each individual can earn at least some tokens.

KEY TERMS

Back-up reinforcer—A desirable item, privilege, or activity that is purchased with tokens and serves as a delayed reward and subsequent motivation for target (desired) behavior.

Baseline data—Information regarding the frequency and severity of behavior, gathered before treatment begins.

Behavior modification—An approach to therapy based on the principles of operant conditioning. Behavior modification seeks to replace undesirable behaviors with preferable behaviors through the use of positive or negative reinforcement.

Fading—Gradually decreasing the amount or frequency of a reinforcer so that the target behavior will begin to occur independent of any rewards.

Reinforcement schedule—The frequency and amount of reinforcers administered.

Reinforcer—Anything that causes an increase of a particular behavior.

Response cost—A behavioral technique that involves removing a stimulus from an individual's environment so that the response that directly precedes the removal is weakened. In a token economy system, response cost is a form of punishment involving loss of tokens due to inappropriate behavior, which consequently results in decreased ability to purchase back-up reinforcers.

Target behavior—The specific behavior to be increased or decreased during treatment.

Therapeutic value—The potential benefit of an object or situation, in terms of its ability to enhance functioning (social, emotional, intellectual, occupational, etc.) in an individual.

Token—Any item that can be seen and collected (such as stickers or points in a point tally) that has no value of its own, but is used as an immediate reward for desirable behavior that is later exchanged for back-up reinforcers.

- A system for recording data: Before treatment begins, information (baseline data) is gathered about each individual's current behavior. Changes in behavior are then recorded on daily data sheets. This information is used to measure individual progress, as well as the effectiveness of the token economy. Information regarding the exchange of tokens also needs to be recorded.

- Consistent implementation of the token economy by staff: In order for a token economy to succeed, all involved staff members must reward the same behaviors, use the appropriate amount of tokens, avoid dispensing back-up reinforcers for free, and prevent tokens from being counterfeited, stolen, or otherwise unjustly obtained. Staff responsibilities and the rules of the token economy should be described in a written manual. Staff members should also be evaluated periodically and given the opportunity to raise questions or concerns.

Initially tokens are awarded frequently and in higher amounts, but as individuals learn the desirable behavior, opportunities to earn tokens decrease. (The amount and frequency of token dispensing is called a **reinforcement** schedule.) For example, in a classroom, each student may earn 25 to 75 tokens the first day, so that they quickly learn the value of the tokens. Later, students may earn 15 to 30 tokens per day. By gradually decreasing the availability of tokens (fading), students should learn to display the desirable behavior independently, without the unnatural use of tokens. Reinforcers that individuals would normally encounter in society, such as verbal praise, should accompany the awarding of tokens to aid in the fading process.

Advantages of token economies are that behaviors can be rewarded immediately, rewards are the same for all members of a group, use of punishment (response cost) is less restrictive than other forms of punishment, and individuals can learn skills related to planning for the future. Disadvantages include considerable cost, effort, and extensive staff training and management. Some professionals find token economies to be time-consuming and impractical.

Risks

Risks involved in token economies are similar to those in other forms of behavior modification. Staff members implementing the therapy may intentionally or unintentionally neglect the rights of individuals receiving treatment. Token economies should never deprive individuals of their basic needs, such as sufficient food, comfortable bedding, or reasonable opportunities for leisure. If staff members are inadequately trained or there is a shortage of staff, desirable behaviors may not be rewarded or undesirable behaviors may be inadvertently rewarded, resulting in an increase of negative behavior. Controversy exists regarding placing individuals in treatment against their will (such as in a psychiatric hospital), and deciding which behaviors should be considered desirable and which should be considered undesirable.

Normal results

Ideally, individuals will use the skills learned in a token economy in their everyday surroundings. They will display the undesirable behavior less frequently or not at all. They will also engage in positive, adaptive behaviors more often.

Abnormal results

If the token economy was ineffective, or time spent in the token economy was limited, individuals may show no changes or increases in the undesirable behavior.

Resources

BOOKS

Ayllon, Teodoro. *How to Use Token Economy and Point Systems.* 2nd ed. Austin, Texas: Pro-Ed, 1999.

Higgins, Stephen T. and Kenneth Silverman. *Motivating Change Among Illicit Drug Abusers: Research on Contingency Management Interventions.* Washington, DC: American Psychological Association, 1999.

Martin, Garry. *Behavior Modification: What It Is and How to Do It.* 6th ed. Upper Saddle River, New Jersey: Prentice-Hall, 1999.

Miltenberger, Raymond G. *Behavior Modification: Principles and Procedures.* 2nd ed. Belmont, California: Wadsworth/Thomson Learning, 2001.

PERIODICALS

Moore, James W., Daniel H. Tingstrom, R. Anthony Doggett, and William D. Carlyon. "Restructuring an Existing Token Economy in a Psychiatric Facility for Children." *Child & Family Behavior Therapy* 23, no. 3 (2001): 53–59.

ORGANIZATIONS

Association for Behavioral Analysis. 213 West Hall, Western Michigan University, 1903 W. Michigan Avenue, Kalamazoo, Michigan 49008-5301. (616) 387-8341; (616) 384-8342. <http://www.wmich.edu/aba>.

Cambridge Center for Behavioral Studies. 336 Baker Avenue, Concord, Massachusetts 01742-2107. (978) 369-2227. <www.behavior.org>.

Sandra L. Friedrich, M.A.

Tourette's disorder *see* **Tic disorders**

Tranquilizers *see* **Anti-anxiety drugs and abuse**

Transient tic disorder *see* **Tic disorders**

Transsexualism *see* **Gender identity disorder**

Transvestic fetishism

Definition

Transvestic **fetishism** is defined by the mental health professional's handbook, the ***Diagnostic and Statistical Manual of Mental Disorders***, fourth edition, text revision (2000), which is also called *DSM-IV-TR*, as one of the **paraphilias**. The paraphilias are a group of mental disorders characterized by **obsession** with unusual sexual practices or with sexual activity involving nonconsenting or inappropriate partners (such as children or animals). The essential feature of transvestic fetishism is recurrent intense sexual urges and sexually arousing fantasies involving dressing in clothing associated with members of the opposite sex. Another term for tranvestic fetishism is cross-dressing; people who frequently engage in cross-dressing are sometimes called transvestites. A **diagnosis** of transvestic fetishism is made only if an individual has acted on these urges or is markedly distressed by them. In other systems of psychiatric classification, transvestic fetishism is considered a sexual deviation.

For some people who are diagnosed with transvestic fetishism, fantasies or stimuli associated with cross-dressing may always be necessary for erotic arousal and are always included in sexual activity, if not actually acted out alone or with a partner. In other patients, cross-dressing may occur only episodically, for example, during periods of **stress**. At other times the person is able to function sexually without the transvestic fetish or related stimuli.

Description

A person with a transvestic fetish derives sexual gratification from dressing in clothing appropriate for a member of the opposite sex. Almost all patients diagnosed with transvestic fetishism, however, are men dressing as women. This lopsided gender ratio may be partly due to the fact that contemporary Western societies allow women to dress in a wide range of clothing styles influenced by menswear, whereas the reverse is not the case. While it is not at all unusual to see women wearing jeans, tailored trousers, Western-style boots, or even tuxedos in some circumstances, men wearing dresses or high-heeled shoes look distinctly out of place.

A person's participation in transvestism is usually gradual. Over time, a person with a transvestic fetish assumes the role and appearance of a member of the opposite gender. It is important to note that this activity is closely associated with achieving sexual gratification. Persons who have had extensive experience with a transvestic fetish may be difficult to distinguish from members of the opposite sex. A so-called mature transvestic fetish involves adopting all of the mannerisms, clothing, materials and other items associated with persons of the opposite sex.

KEY TERMS

Cross-dressing—Wearing clothing and other attire appropriate to the opposite sex.

Fetishism—A paraphilia in which a person requires a nonliving object (or occasionally a non-genital part of the body, such as the partner's feet) in order to achieve sexual arousal and satisfaction.

Gender dysphoria—A state of persistent discomfort or depression associated with one's gender role or biological sex.

Paraphilias—A group of mental disorders that is characterized by recurrent intense sexual urges and sexually arousing fantasies generally involving (1) non-human objects, (2) the suffering or humiliation of oneself or one's partner (not merely simulated), or (3) children or other non-consenting persons.

Transvestite—A person who derives sexual pleasure or gratification from dressing in clothing of the opposite sex.

Causes and symptoms

Causes

The basis for a transvestic fetish is obtaining sexual gratification by dressing in clothing appropriate for the opposite sex. The cause may be adolescent curiosity. A person with a transvestic fetish may not be aware of its roots. Transvestic fetishism sometimes begins when a young boy dresses up in the clothes of an older sister or his mother. The activity is continued because it is enjoyable but the reasons for the enjoyment remain unconscious. In other cases a boy's mother may initiate the cross-dressing by dressing him as if he were a girl. This behavior is sometimes related to the mother's anger at men or to a preference for having daughters rather than sons.

Persons with transvestic fetishes should not be assumed to be homosexual. According to *DSM-IV-TR*, most men who practice cross-dressing are basically heterosexual in their orientation. Some, however, have occasional sexual encounters with other men.

Symptoms

Early symptoms of transvestic fetishism involve touching or wearing items of clothing that are considered typically feminine. This initial interest may progress to wearing undergarments or other items that can be hidden from the view of others while providing arousal to the wearer. Over time, the extent of dressing in women's clothing expands, sometimes to the point of dressing as a woman on a regular basis. A developed transvestic fetish often involves feminine hair styling and the use of women's cosmetics and accessories.

In some persons diagnosed with transvestic fetishism, the motivation for cross-dressing may change over time from a search for sexual excitement to simple relief from stress, depression, or anxiety.

In some cases, persons with a transvestic fetish discover that they are unhappy with their biological sex, a condition known as gender dysphoria. They may elect to have hormonal and surgical procedures to change their bodies. Some may choose to have gender reassignment surgery. The incidence of gender dysphoria and subsequent gender reassignment among persons diagnosed with transvestic fetishism is not known.

Demographics

Except for **sexual masochism**, in which the gender ratio is estimated to be 20 males for each female, paraphilias such as transvestic fetishism are practically never diagnosed in females, although a few cases have been reported. Virtually no information is available on family patterns of the disorder.

Diagnosis

Persons with transvestic fetishism may or may not seek **psychotherapy** on their own account. In some instances, the patient has agreed to consult a **psychiatrist** because his wife or girlfriend is distressed by the cross-dressing. The actual diagnosis of transvestic fetishism is most commonly made by taking a history or by direct observation. The diagnosis is made only if the patient has been markedly distressed by inability to dress in such a manner or if the disorder is interfering with his education, occupation, or social life. Dressing in women's clothing for such occasions as Halloween or a costume party is not sufficient for a diagnosis of transvestic fetishism.

Treatments

In the earliest period of behavior therapy, transvestic fetishes were narrowly viewed as inappropriate behavior that was confined to a limited range of situations, and were sometimes treated with **aversion therapy**, usually with electric shocks. This approach was largely unsuccessful. Persons with fetishes have also been treated by using a form of behavioral therapy known as orgasmic reorientation, which attempts to help people learn to respond sexually to culturally appropriate stimuli. This treatment also has had limited success.

Most persons who have a transvestic fetish never seek treatment from professionals. Most are capable of achieving sexual gratification in culturally appropriate situations. Their preoccupation with cross-dressing is viewed as essentially harmless to other persons, since transvestism is not associated with criminal activities or forcing one's sexual preferences on others. As of 2002, American society has developed tolerance for transvestites, thus further reducing the demand for professional treatment.

Prognosis

The prognosis for treatment of transvestic fetishism is poor, as most persons with this disorder do not desire to change. Most cases in which treatment was demanded by a spouse as a condition of continuing in a marriage have not been successful. The prognosis for personal adjustment is good, however, as a person with a transvestic fetish and his related activities do not usually disturb others.

Prevention

Most experts agree that providing gender-appropriate guidance in a culturally appropriate situation will prevent the formation of a transvestic fetish. The origin of some cases of transvestism may be a random association between clothing inappropriate for one's own gender and sexual gratification. There is no reliable way to predict the formation of such associations. Supervision during childhood and adolescence, combined with acceptance of a child's biological sex, may be the best deterrent that parents can provide.

See also Aversion therapy; Gender identity disorder; Gender issues in mental health

Resources

BOOKS

Gelder, Michael, Richard Mayou, and Philip Cowen. *Shorter Oxford Textbook of Psychiatry.* 4th ed. New York: Oxford University Press, 2001.

Kohut, John J., Roland Sweet. *Real Sex: Titillating but True Tales of Bizarre Fetishes, Strange Compulsions, and Just Plain Weird Stuff.* New York: Plume, 2000.

Wilson, Josephine F. *Biological Foundations of Human Behavior.* New York: Harcourt, 2002.

PERIODICALS

Dessens, A. B., P. T. Cohen-Kettenis, G. J. Mellenbergh, G. J. Koppe, and K. Boer. "Prenatal exposure to anticonvulsants and psychosexual development." *Archives of Sexual Behavior* 28, no. 1 (1999): 31-44.

Docter, R. F., J. S. Fleming. "Measures of transgender behavior." *Archives of Sexual Behavior* 30, no. 3 (2001): 255-271.

Green, R. "Family co-occurrence of 'gender dysphoria': ten sibling or parent-child pairs." *Archives of Sexual Behavior* 29, no. 5 (2000): 499-507.

ORGANIZATIONS

American Academy of Family Physicians. 11400 Tomahawk Creek Parkway, Leawood, KS 66211-2672. Telephone: (913) 906-6000. Web site: <http://www.aafp.org>.

American Academy of Pediatrics. 141 Northwest Point Boulevard, Elk Grove Village, IL 60007-1098. Telephone: (847) 434-4000. Fax: (847) 434-8000. Web site: <http://www.aap.org/default.htm>.

American College of Physicians. 190 N Independence Mall West, Philadelphia, PA 19106-1572. Telephone: (800) 523-1546, x 2600 or (215) 351-2600. Web site: <http://www.acponline.org>.

American Medical Association. 515 N. State Street, Chicago, IL 60610. Telephone: (312) 464-5000. Web site: <http://www.ama-assn.org>.

American Psychiatric Association. 1400 K Street NW, Washington, DC 20005. Telephone: (888) 357-7924. Fax (202) 682-6850.

American Psychological Association. 750 First Street NW, Washington, DC, 20002-4242. Telephone: (800) 374-2721 or (202) 336-5500. Web site: <http://www.apa.org>.

American Public Health Association. 800 I Street, NW, Washington, DC 20001-3710. Telephone: (202) 777-2742. Fax: (202) 777-2534. Web site: <http://www.apha.org>.

L. Fleming Fallon, Jr., M.D., Dr.P.H.

Tranxene *see* **Clorazepate**

Tranylcypromine

Definition

Tranylcypromine is classified as a monoamine oxidase (MAO) inhibitor. It is used to treat serious depression. In the United States, tranylcypromine is sold under the brand name Parnate. As of 2002, there were no generic forms of tranylcypromine available in the United States.

KEY TERMS

Agoraphobia—People with this condition worry that they will not be able to get help or flee a place if they have a panic attack; or refusal to go to places that might trigger a panic attack.

Bulimia—An eating disorder characterized by binges in which large amounts of food are consumed, followed by forced vomiting.

Congestive heart failure—Condition characterized by abdominal pain, swelling in the lower extremities, and weakness caused by a reduced output of blood from the left side of the heart.

Diabetes mellitus—A chronic disease affecting the metabolism of carbohydrates that is caused by insufficient production of insulin in the body.

Panic disorder—An anxiety disorder in which an individual experiences sudden, debilitating attacks of intense fear.

Schizophrenia—A severe mental illness in which a person has difficulty distinguishing what is real from what is not real. It is often characterized by hallucinations, delusions, language and communication disturbances, and withdrawal from people and social activities.

Tyramine—Intermediate product between the chemicals tyrosine and epinephrine in the body and a substance normally found in many foods. Found especially in protein-rich foods that have been aged or fermented, pickled, or bacterially contaminated, such as cheese, beer, yeast, wine, and chicken liver.

Purpose

Tranylcypromine is used primarily to treat depression that does not respond to other types of drug therapy. It is also used occasionally to treat **panic disorder**, **agoraphobia**, and **bulimia nervosa**.

Description

Trancyclopromine is a member of a class of drugs called monoamine oxidase inhibitors. Monoamine oxidase, or MAO, is an enzyme found throughout the body. In the **brain**, MAO breaks down norepinephrine and serotonin, two naturally occurring chemicals that are important for maintaining mental well-being preventing depression. Monoamine oxidase inhibitors, such as tranylcypromine, reduce the activity of MAO. Less norepinephrine and serotonin are broken down, so their levels rise. This helps to lift depression.

Tranylcypromine is effective for treating depression, especially complicated types of depression that have not responded to more traditional antidepressants. However, tranylcypromine also affects the MAO enzyme in many other areas of the body. This accounts for the large number of serious side effects and drug interactions it causes.

Recommended dosage

The typical starting dosage of tranylcypromine in adults is 10 mg taken twice per day. This dosage is sometimes increased to 30 mg per day after a two-week period. The maximum recommended amount is 60 mg per day. The elderly (over age 60) are usually started on a dose of 2.5 mg per day. After this, their doctor will make an individualized decision about increasing the dosage. Older adults typically take smaller doses and do not take more than 45 mg per day. A doctor must make an individual determination of whether to give tranylcypromine to youths under the age of 18 years, because guidelines for this age group have not been developed.

The benefits of this drug may not become apparent for several weeks. Patients should be aware of this and continue taking the drug as directed, even if they do not see an immediate improvement.

Precautions

People taking tranylcypromine should not eat foods rich in tyramine. These foods include yeast or meat extracts, fermented sausage, overripe fruit, sauerkraut, cheese, and fava beans. Alcohol should not be consumed, and the same holds true for alcohol-free beer and wine. Large amounts of caffeine-containing food and beverages, such as chocolate, tea, coffee, and cola should be avoided. The treating doctor needs to approve the use of any drug, including prescription, over-the-counter drugs, and herbal treatments, that the patient takes while taking tranylcypromine.

Tranylcypromine should be used with great caution in pregnant and nursing women only after the risks and benefits of treatment have been assessed. Likewise, this drug may not be appropriate for people with a history of **seizures**, children under age 18 years, people at risk for **suicide**, those with severe depression, a history of **schizophrenia**, or diabetes mellitus. People with these conditions should discuss the risks and benefits of this drug with their physician, and a decision to treat should be made on an individual basis. People should not stop taking tranylcypromine suddenly. Instead, the dose should be gradually reduced, then discontinued.

People with a history of high blood pressure, congestive heart failure, severe liver disease, severe kidney disease, severe heart disease, and blood vessel problems in the brain should not take tranylcypromine.

Side effects

The enzyme monoamine oxidase regulates functions throughout the body. Phenelzine decreases the activity of monoamine oxidase in all the areas of the body where it exists, not just in the brain. This is why tranylcypromine is capable of causing a wide variety of side effects in many different organ systems.

Tranylcypromine should be stopped if symptoms of unusually high blood pressure develop. These symptoms include severe chest pain, severe headache, nausea, vomiting, stiff or sore neck, enlarged pupils, and significant changes in heart rate. If these symptoms develop, it should be considered an emergency, and the affected person should get medical help immediately. Generally, these serious side effects are rare.

More common but less serious side effects include lightheadedness or dizziness when arising from a sitting position. These symptoms need to be reported to a doctor but are not considered an emergency. Less common symptoms that should be reported include pounding heartbeat, swelling of the lower extremities, nervousness, and diarrhea. Rare but reportable symptoms include fever, skin rash, dark urine, slurred speech, yellowing of the eyes or skin, and staggering when walking. Common but not serious side effects include decreased sexual performance, increased appetite, muscle twitching, trembling, blurred vision, and reduced urine output.

Overdose symptoms include confusion, seizures, severe dizziness, **hallucinations**, severe headache, severe drowsiness, significant changes in blood pressure, difficulty in sleeping, breathing difficulties, and increased irritability.

Interactions

Tranylcypromine interacts with a long list of drugs. Some of these interactions can cause death. This section is not a complete list of interactions, but it includes the most serious ones. Patients must make sure every health care professional who takes care of them (for example, doctors, dentists, podiatrists, optometrists, pharmacists, nurses) knows that they take tranylcypromine, as well as all of the other prescription, nonprescription, and herbal drugs that they take.

The combination of tranylcypromine with any type of stimulant can increase the risk of developing serious increases in blood pressure. Tranylcypromine when taken with antidiabetic drugs can reduce blood sugar levels to far below normal. The combination of tranylcypromine with **barbiturates** can prolong the effects of the barbiturate drug.

Tranylcypromine should never be combined with other antidepressant drugs, especially the selective serotonin reuptake inhibitors (SSRIs), because of potentially severe or fatal reactions, including increased risk of dangerously high blood pressure. Patients taking tranylcypromine should stop the drug, then wait at least 14 days before starting any other antidepressant. The same holds true when discontinuing another antidepressant and starting tranylcypromine.

Alcohol combined with tranylcypromine can lead to significantly increased blood pressure. Tranylcypromine combined with the blood pressure drug guanethidine (Ismelin) can reduce the beneficial effects of the guanethidine. When tranylcypromine is combined with levodopa (Dopar, Larodopa), a drug used to treat Parkinson disease, severely increased blood pressure can develop. Tranylcypromine combined with lithium can cause fever. Meperidine (Demerol), when combined with tranylcypromine, can cause fever, seizures, increased blood pressure, and agitation. Tranylcypromine combined with norepinephrine can cause increased response to norepinephrine. Tranylcypromine combined with reserpine (Serpalan, Serpasil) can produce greatly increased blood pressure. When tranylcypromine is combined with the migraine drug sumatriptan (Imitrex), significantly increased concentrations of the latter drug develop that can produce potentially toxic effects.

Resources

BOOKS

Consumer Reports Staff. *Consumer Reports Complete Drug Reference.* 2002 ed. Denver: Micromedex Thomson Healthcare, 2001.

Ellsworth, Allan J. and others. *Mosby's Medical Drug Reference.* 2001-2002. St. Louis: Mosby, 2001.

Hardman, Joel G., Lee E. Limbird,ed.*Goodman & Gilman's The Pharmacological Basis of Therapeutics.* 10th ed. New York: McGraw-Hill, 2001.

Mosby's GenRx Staff. *Mosby's GenRx.* 9th ed. St. Louis: Mosby, 1999.

Venes, Donald, and others, eds. *Taber's Cyclopedic Medical Dictionary.* 19th ed. Philadelphia: F. A. Davis, 2001.

Mark Mitchell, M.D.

Trazodone

Definition

Trazodone is an oral antidepressant. It is sold in the United States under the brand name Desyrel and is also available under its generic name.

Purpose

Trazodone is used to treat depression and to treat the combination of symptoms of anxiety and depression. Like most antidepressants, trazodone has also been used in limited numbers of patients to treat **panic disorder**, **obsessive-compulsive disorder**, **attention-deficit/hyperactivity disorder**, **enuresis** (bed-wetting), eating disorders such as **bulimia nervosa**, cocaine dependency, and the depressive phase of bipolar (manic-depressive) disorder. It should be noted, however, that trazodone has not received official approval from the United States Food and Drug Administration (FDA) for these secondary uses.

Description

Trazodone acts to change the balance of naturally occurring chemicals in the **brain** that regulate the transmission of nerve impulses between cells. Its action primarily increases the concentration of norepinephrine and serotonin (both chemicals that stimulate nerve cells) and, to a lesser extent, blocks the action of another brain chemical, acetylcholine. Trazodone is classified as an atypical antidepressant, but it shares many of the properties of tricyclic antidepressants (**amitriptyline**, **clomipramine**, **desipramine**, **doxepin**, **imipramine**, **nortriptyline**, **protriptyline**, and **trimipramine**). It also shares some of the properties of selective serotonin reuptake inhibitor antidepressants (**fluoxetine**, **paroxetine**, and **sertraline**). Trazodone is the most sedating, and least anticholinergic, of all the currently marketed antidepressants.

The therapeutic effects of trazodone, like other antidepressants, appear slowly. Maximum benefit is often not evident for at least two weeks after starting the drug. People taking trazodone should be aware of this and continue taking the drug as directed even if they do not see immediate improvement.

Recommended dosage

As with any antidepressant, trazodone must be carefully adjusted by the physician to produce the desired therapeutic effect. Trazodone is available as 50-mg, 100-mg, and 150-mg film-coated tablets that cannot be divid-

KEY TERMS

Acetylcholine—A naturally occurring chemical in the body that generally produces effects that are the opposite of those produced by dopamine and norepinephrine. Central nervous system well-being is dependent on a balance between acetylcholine, serotonin, dopamine and norepinephrine.

Anticholinergic—Related to the ability of a drug to block the nervous system chemical, acetylcholine. When acetylcholine is blocked, patients often experience dry mouth and skin, increased heart rate, blurred vision, and difficulty urinating. In severe cases, blocking acetylcholine may cloud thinking and cause delirium.

Benign prostate hypertrophy—Enlargement of the prostate gland.

Norepinephrine—A neurotransmitter in the brain that acts to constrict blood vessels and raise blood pressure. It works in combination with serotonin.

Serotonin—A widely distributed neurotransmitter that is found in blood platelets, the lining of the digestive tract, and the brain, and that works in combination with norepinephrine. It causes very powerful contractions of smooth muscle, and is associated with mood, attention, emotions, and sleep. Low levels of serotonin are associated with depression.

ed, and 150-mg and 300-mg oral tablets that can be split. Therapy is usually started at a total of 150 mg per day divided into two or three doses. This dose is increased by 50 mg every three or four days until the desired effects are seen. Daily doses may be increased to a maximum of 400 mg per day in outpatients and up to 600 mg per day in hospitalized patients. In cases of extreme depression, daily doses of up to 800 mg have been used in hospitalized patients. To minimize daytime drowsiness, a major portion of the daily dose can be given at bedtime.

Precautions

The most common problem with trazodone is sedation (drowsiness, lack of mental and physical alertness). This side effect is especially noticeable early in therapy. In most patients, sedation decreases or disappears entirely with time, but until then patients taking trazodone should not perform hazardous activities requiring mental alertness or coordination, including driving and similar activities. The sedative effect is increased when trazodone is taken with other central nervous system depressants, such as alcoholic beverages, sleeping medications, other sedatives, or antihistamines. It may be dangerous to take trazodone in combination with these substances.

Although lower in anticholinergic side effects than tricyclic antidepressants, trazodone should be used cautiously and with close physician supervision in people, especially the elderly, who have benign prostatic hypertrophy, urinary retention, and glaucoma, especially angle-closure glaucoma (the most severe form). Before starting treatment, people with these conditions should discuss the relative risks and benefits of treatment with their doctors to help determine if protriptyline is the right antidepressant for them.

Trazodone may increase heart rate and stress on the heart. It may be dangerous for people with cardiovascular disease, especially those who have recently had a heart attack, to take this drug. In rare cases where patients with cardiovascular disease must take trazodone, they should be monitored closely for cardiac rhythm disturbances and signs of cardiac stress or damage.

Side effects

Trazodone shares side effects common to many antidepressants. The most frequent of these are dry mouth, constipation, and urinary retention, though these are less common than with tricyclic antidepressants. Increased heart rate, sedation, irritability, dizziness, and decreased coordination can also occur. As with most side effects associated with antidepressants, the intensity is highest at the beginning of therapy and tends to decrease with continued use.

Dry mouth, if severe to the point of causing difficulty in speaking or swallowing, may be managed by dosage reduction or temporary discontinuation of the drug. Patients may also chew sugarless gum or suck on sugarless candy in order to increase the flow of saliva. Some artificial saliva products may give temporary relief.

Men with prostate enlargement who take trazodone may be especially likely to have problems with urinary retention. Symptoms include having difficulty starting a urine flow and more difficulty than usual passing urine. In most cases, urinary retention is managed with dose reduction or by switching to another type of antidepressant. In extreme cases, patients may require treatment with bethanechol, a drug that reverses this particular side effect. In rare cases, trazodone has also been known to cause priapism, a prolonged and painful penile erection. People who think they may be experiencing any side effects from this or any other medication should tell their physicians.

Interactions

Because both trazodone and members of the class of antidepressants known as monoamine oxidase (MAO) inhibitors may increase serotonin levels in the brain, the combination of these drugs can lead to a condition known as serotonin syndrome. Symptoms of serotonin syndrome include a prolonged rapid heart rate, hypertension (high blood pressure), flushing of the skin, **hallucinations**, tremors, and hyperthermia (increased body temperature). Because of this, it can be dangerous to take trazodone in combination with MAO inhibitors such as Nardil (**phenelzine** sulfate) or Parmate (**tranylcypromine** sulfate). The same holds true when combining trazodone with a selective serotonin uptake inhibitor (SSRI) antidepressant such as Prozac (fluoxetine), paroxetine, or sertraline.

Trazodone may increase the blood pressure–lowering effects in patients who are taking antihypertensive medications. Patients who take these drugs together should have their blood pressure monitored regularly so that their antihypertensive medications can be adjusted if their blood pressure becomes too low.

The sedative effects of trazodone are increased by other central nervous system depressants such as alcohol, sedatives, sleeping medications, or medications used for other mental disorders such as **schizophrenia**. The anticholinergic effects of trazodone may be additive with other anticholinergic drugs such as **benztropine**, **biperiden**, **trihexyphenidyl**, and antihistamines.

See also Neurotransmitters

Resources

BOOKS

American Society of Health-System Pharmacists. *AHFS Drug Information 2002.* Bethesda: American Society of Health-System Pharmacists, 2002.

DeVane, C. Lindsay, Pharm.D. "Drug Therapy for Mood Disorders." In *Fundamentals of Monitoring Psychoactive Drug Therapy.* Baltimore: Williams & Wilkins, 1990.

Jack Raber, Pharm.D.

Triazolam

Definition

Triazolam is a hypnotic drug. It is a member of the benzodiazepine family of drugs. In the United States, it is sold under the brand name Halcion as well as under its generic name.

KEY TERMS

Amnesia—A general medical term for loss of memory that is not due to ordinary forgetfulness. Amnesia can be caused by head injuries, brain disease, or epilepsy as well as by dissociation.

Euphoria—A feeling or state of well-being or elation.

Hypnotic—A type of medication that induces sleep.

Insomnia—A chronic inability to sleep or to remain asleep throughout the night.

Tachycardia—A pulse rate above 100 beats per minute.

Purpose

Triazolam is used for the short-term (generally seven to 10 days) treatment of **insomnia**. Continued usage for more than two to three weeks requires a complete reevaluation of the person receiving the drug.

Description

Triazolam increases the speed with which people achieve sleep, it increases the duration of sleep, and decreases the likelihood of being awakened during sleep. The effect of triazolam decreases after 14 days of continuous use. Often, sleep patterns return to those experienced prior to beginning use of triazolam or worse. This is called rebound insomnia.

Recommended dosage

The recommended dose of triazolam is 0.25 mg before going to bed. Persons with smaller body masses and older individuals can receive a comparable effect with 0.125 mg of triazolam. The lowest effective dosage of drug should be used to minimize adverse reactions.

Precautions

Because of problems with rebound insomnia, patients should not receive triazolam for more than seven consecutive days. Accompanying rebound insomnia may be daytime anxiety.

Triazolam can cause serious birth defects. Women should not take this medicine if they are pregnant, think they may be pregnant, or are trying to get pregnant.

The drug may cause daytime anxiety after as few as 10 days of continuous usage. If this occurs, triazolam use should be discontinued.

Persons using triazolam should exercise caution when driving or using power tools or machinery.

People who use **temazepam** to reduce jet lag on long flights should be aware of a condition sometimes called "traveler's amnesia." This is a condition where the traveler completes the flight and carries on with normal activities but has no memory of these activities. The period of **amnesia** may last for a few minutes to a few hours. Traveler's amnesia is most common when the traveler has had too little sleep or has been drinking alcohol.

Side effects

Triazolam has relatively few side effects. Those that have been reported include drowsiness, headache, dizziness, nervousness, a feeling of being light-headed, problems with coordination, nausea and vomiting.

Less frequent side effects include euphoria, tachycardia, **fatigue**, confusion, impaired memory, muscle cramping and pain and depression.

Interactions

Triazolam increases the effect of drugs and substances that depress the central nervous system. This class of drugs includes anesthetics, narcotics, sedatives and other sleeping pills, atropine and alcohol.

Some drugs and foods increase the effects of triazolam. They may also increase the chances of having side effects. These include cimetidine, isoniazid, oral contraceptives, and grapefruit juice.

Resources

BOOKS

Adams, Michael and Norman Holland. *Core Concepts in Pharmacology.* Philadelphia: Lippincott-Raven, 1998.

Foreman, John C. and Torben Johansen. *Textbook of Receptor Pharmacology.* 2nd ed. Boca Raton, FL: CRC Press, 2002.

Page, Clive P., and Michael Murphy. *Integrated Pharmacology.* St. Louis: Mosby-Year Book, 2002.

Von Boxtel, Chris J., Budiono Santoso, and I. Ralph Edwards. *Drug Benefits and Risks: International Textbook of Clinical Pharmacology.* New York: John Wiley and Sons, 2001.

PERIODICALS

Fillmore M. T., C. R. Rush, T. H. Kelly, and L. Hays. "Triazolam impairs inhibitory control of behavior in humans." *Experimental Clinical Psychopharmacology* 9, no. 4 (2001): 363-371.

Mintzer, M. Z., R. R. Griffiths, C. Contoreggi, A. S. Kimes, E. D. London, and M. Ernst. "Effects of triazolam on brain activity during episodic memory encoding: a PET study." *Neuropsychopharmacology* 25, no. 5 (2001): 744-756.

Nelson, J. C. "Diagnosing and treating depression in the elderly." *Journal of Clinical Psychiatry* 62, Supplement 24 (2001): 18-22.

ORGANIZATIONS

American Academy of Clinical Toxicology. 777 East Park Drive, PO Box 8820, Harrisburg, PA 17105-8820. Telephone: (717) 558-7750. Fax: (717) 558-7845. Web site: <http://www.clintox.org/index.html>.

American Academy of Family Physicians. 11400 Tomahawk Creek Parkway, Leawood, KS 66211-2672. Telephone: (913) 906-6000. Web site: <http://www.aafp.org/>.

American Medical Association. 515 N. State Street, Chicago, IL 60610. Telephone: (312) 464-5000. Web site: <http://www.ama-assn.org/>.

American Psychiatric Association. 1400 K Street NW, Washington, DC 20005. Telephone: (888) 357-7924. Fax (202) 682-6850. Web site: <http://www.psych.org/>.

American Society for Clinical Pharmacology and Therapeutics. 528 North Washington Street, Alexandria, VA 22314. Telephone: (703) 836-6981. Fax: (703) 836-5223.

American Society for Pharmacology and Experimental Therapeutics. 9650 Rockville Pike, Bethesda, MD 20814-3995. Telephone: (301) 530-7060. Fax: (301) 530-7061. Web site: <http://www.aspet.org/>.

L. Fleming Fallon, Jr., M.D., Dr.P.H.

Trichotillomania

Definition

Individuals with trichotillomania repetitively pull out their own hair. Trichotillomania as an impulse-control disorder. Some researchers view it as a type of affective or **obsessive-compulsive disorder**. Nail-biting, skin-picking, and thumb-sucking are considered to be related conditions.

Description

Trichotillomania involves hair-pulling episodes that result in noticeable hair loss. Although any area of the body can be a target, the most common areas are the scalp, followed by the eyelashes, eyebrows, and pubic region. Hair-pulling can occur without the individual's awareness, but is frequently preceded by a sense of increasing tension and followed by a sense of relief or gratification. The resulting hair loss can be a source of embarrassment or shame. Because of a tendency to hide symptoms, and because professionals are relatively unfamiliar with the disorder, individuals either may not seek, or are offered treatment. Untreated trichotillomania can result in impaired social functioning and medical complications.

Causes and symptoms

Causes

Scientific research regarding trichotillomania has been conducted primarily in the past 10 years and causes are only theoretical. Psychoanalytic theories suggest that the behavior is a way of dealing with unconscious conflicts or childhood trauma (such as sexual **abuse**). Biological theories look for a genetic basis. For instance, people with trichotillomania often have a first-degree relative with an obsessive-compulsive spectrum disorder. Researchers are also evaluating similarities between trichotillomania and Tourette's disorder. Behavioral theories assume that symptoms are learned, that a child may imitate a parent who engages in hair-pulling. The behavior may also be learned independently if it serves a purpose. For example, hair-pulling may begin as a response to **stress** and then develop into a habit.

Symptoms

According to the ***Diagnostic and Statistical Manual of Mental Disorders***, (*DSM-IV-TR*), produced by the American Psychiatric Association and used by most mental health professionals in North America and Europe to diagnose mental disorders, the following conditions must be present for a **diagnosis** of trichotillomania:

- noticeable hair loss (alopecia) due to recurrent hair-pulling
- tension immediately before hair-pulling, or when attempting to resist hair-pulling
- reduction of tension, or a feeling of pleasure or gratification, immediately following hair-pulling
- significant distress or impairment in social, occupational, or other important areas of functioning

In addition, the *DSM-IV-TR* requires that hair-pulling not be due to another medical or mental disorder. The tension-release requirement is controversial because 17% of people who otherwise qualify for this diagnosis do not experience this.

Symptoms usually emerge in early adolescence. Episodes may last a few minutes or a few hours during periods of stress or relaxation. Hairs with unique textures or qualities may be preferred. The pulling may include rituals, such as twirling hair off or examining the root. Half of those individuals with trichotillomania engage in oral behaviors—running hair across the lips or through the teeth, biting off the root (trichophagy), or eating hair (trichophagia). The usually try to control their behavior in the presence of others and may hide the affected areas. Symptoms may come and go for weeks, months, or years at a time.

KEY TERMS

Alopecia—Hair loss (also, loss of feathers or wool in animals).

Selective serotonin reuptake inhibitors—Commonly prescribed drugs for treating depression. SSRIs affect the chemicals that nerves in the brain use to send messages to one another. These chemical messengers (neurotransmitters) are released by one nerve cell and taken up by others. Neurotransmitters not taken up by other nerve cells are taken up by the same cells that released them. This process is termed "reuptake". SSRIs work by inhibiting the reuptake of serotonin, an action which allows more serotonin to be taken up by other nerve cells.

Serotonergic—Containing, activating, or otherwise involving serotonin, which is a chemical that aids in the transmission of nerve impulses.

Trichobezoar—A hairball that results from a buildup of swallowed hairs becoming lodged in the digestive system.

Trichophagia—Eating hair.

Trichophagy—Biting hair.

Demographics

Once regarded as rare, trichotillomania is now considered more common, affecting 1–4% of people in the general population. When the tension-release requirement is excluded, trichotillomania occurs in adult females (3.4%) more often than adult males (1.5%). Among children, both genders are affected equally.

Diagnosis

Other possible causes of symptoms must first be ruled out. Hair loss may have a medical cause, such as a dermatological condition. Hair-pulling may have another

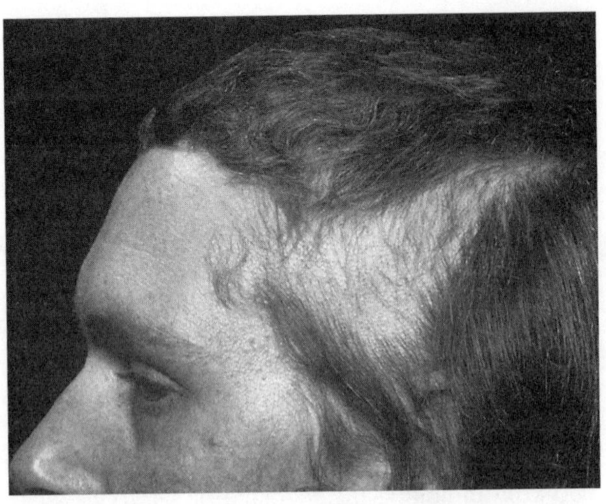

Left side of a man's scalp showing the effects of trichotillomania. *(Custom Medical Stock Photo. Reproduced by permission.)*

psychological cause, such as a delusion or hallucination in **schizophrenia**.

Severity of symptoms is also important. Twisting or playing with hair when nervous does not qualify as trichotillomania. If symptoms are minor or undetectable, a diagnosis should be given only if the individual expresses significant distress. Children should be given the diagnosis only if symptoms persist because hair-pulling may be a temporary phase, much like thumb-sucking.

If individuals deny symptoms, hair-pulling behavior can be assessed by objective measures such as the presence of short, broken hairs or damaged follicles. Some psychological assessment instruments are also available.

Treatments

Treatment usually starts by determining the current frequency and severity of symptoms. This information, which serves as a measure of progress, is gathered by (a) self-report; (b) reports from significant others; (c) objective measures, such as saving pulled hairs, videotapes, or measuring areas of hair loss; or (d) a combination of these methods.

Primarily, three categories of therapy have been used in the treatment of trichotillomania:

- **Psychoanalysis** focuses on childhood experiences and unresolved conflicts during early development.
- Medications. Those typically used are antidepressants with serotonergic properties (also used with obsessive-compulsive disorders). **Clomipramine** (Anafranil) has proven most effective. The selective serotonin reuptake inhibitors (SSRIs) have had mixed results. Some researchers recommend low doses of antipsychotic drugs (neuroleptics) in conjunction with SSRIs. Medications are usually combined with behavior therapy.
- Behavior therapy. This includes a number of different approaches: Punishment procedures such as electric shock, topical cream to enhance pain, or mittens placed on the person's hands, are effective but controversial. They are intrusive and are often used with individuals who may be unable to consent, such as children or people with developmental disabilities. Habit-reversal training is the most accepted approach. It teaches individuals to monitor their hair-pulling and substitute it for more healthy behaviors. Alternative forms of behavior therapy include **biofeedback** and hypnosis.

Prognosis

The effects of trichotillomania can be very serious: Associated feelings of shame may result in avoidance of social situations; chewing hair can result in dental erosion; eating hair may result in hairballs (trichobezoars) becoming lodged in the stomach or large intestine, which can lead to anemia, abdominal pain, nausea and vomiting, hematemesis (vomiting blood), or bowel obstruction or perforation.

Studies show low success rates with medications and traditional psychoanalysis. Behavioral therapy has reported long-term success rates of 90% or better. Follow-up sessions are encouraged to prevent relapse. A major issue in prognosis is whether an individual receives treatment. Professionals may not recognize or know how to treat trichotillomania effectively. Conversely, individuals with the disorder may be too embarrassed to address their symptoms.

Prevention

Because scientific research is lacking, no specific information is available regarding prevention.

See also Anxiety and anxiety disorders; Cognitive-behavioral therapy; Tic disorders

Resources

BOOKS

American Psychiatric Association. *Diagnostic and Statistical Manual of Mental Disorders.* 4th edition, text revised. Washington, DC: American Psychiatric Association, 2000.

Keuthen, Nancy J., Dan J. Stein, and Gary A. Christenson. *Help for Hair Pullers: Understanding and Coping with Trichotillomania.* Oakland, CA: New Harbinger Publications, 2001.

Stein, Dan J., Gary A. Christenson, and Eric Hollander, eds. *Trichotillomania*. Washington, D.C.: American Psychiatric Press, Inc., 1999.

PERIODICALS

Diefenbach, Gretchen J., David Reitman, and Donald A. Williamson. "Trichotillomania: A Challenge to Research and Practice." *Clinical Psychology Review* 20, no. 3 (2000): 289-309.

Elliot, Amy J. and R. Wayne Fuqua. "Trichotillomania: Conceptualization, Measurement, and Treatment." *Behavior Therapy* 31 (2000): 529-545.

ORGANIZATIONS

Trichotillomania Learning Center, Inc. 303 Potrero #51, Santa Cruz, CA 95060. (831) 457-1004. <http://www.trich.org>.

Sandra L. Friedrich, M.A.

Trifluoperazine

Definition

Trifluoperazine is a phenothiazine antipsychotic agent. In the United States, this drug is sold under the brand name Stelazine.

Purpose

Trifluoperazine is a drug used to treat psychotic disorders, agitation, and **dementia**.

Description

Trifluoperazine is an effective agent in treating symptoms of psychotic behavior. When used for the treatment of **schizophrenia**, trifluoperazine reduces symptoms of emotional withdrawal, anxiety, tension, **hallucinations**, and suspiciousness.

KEY TERMS

Akathisia—Agitated or restless movement, usually affecting the legs. Movement is accompanied by a sense of discomfort and an inability to sit, stand still, or remain inactive for periods of time. Akathisia is a common side effect of some neuroleptic (antipsychotic) medications.

Amenorrhea—Absence of menstrual periods.

Anorexia—Loss of appetite or unwillingness to eat. Can be caused by medications, depression, or many other factors.

Cogwheel rigidity—An abnormal rigidity in muscles, characterized by jerky movements when the muscle is passively stretched.

Dystonia—A neurological disorder characterized by involuntary muscle spasms. The spasms can cause a painful twisting of the body and difficulty walking or moving.

Orthostatic hypotension—A sudden decrease in blood pressure due to a change in body position, as when moving from a sitting to standing position.

Schizophrenia—A severe mental illness in which a person has difficulty distinguishing what is real from what is not real. It is often characterized by hallucinations, delusions, language and communication disturbances, and withdrawal from people and social activities.

Tardive dyskinesia—A condition that involves involuntary movements of the tongue, jaw, mouth or face or other groups of skeletal muscles that usually occurs either late in antipsychotic therapy or even after the therapy is discontinued. It may be irreversible.

Recommended dosage

The dosage of trifluoperazine should be adjusted to the lowest level needed to control symptoms. The drug may be given orally or by intramuscular injection (a shot).

A useful initial dosage of trifluoperazine for psychotic adults is 2 to 5 mg two times each day. A common total dosage is 15 to 20 mg per day. Some persons may require up to 40 or more mg per day. When using deep intramuscular injection, 1 to 2 mg every four to six hours is usually sufficient to control symptoms within 24 hours. Total intramuscular trifluoperazine should not exceed 10 mg per day.

Control of psychotic symptoms in children between the ages of six and 12 can usually be achieved with 1 to 2 mg per day, given in 1-mg increments. Trifluoperazine is not recommended for use in children younger than six.

Precautions

Trifluoperazine increases the level of prolactin, a hormone that stimulates the mammary glands in the breast, in the blood. This is a potential problem for persons with a personal or family history of breast cancer and may increase the risk of breast cancer. For this reason, the benefits and risks of the drug must be carefully evaluated before it is administered.

Side effects

Relatively common side effects that accompany trifluoperazine include drowsiness, dizziness, rash, dry mouth, **insomnia**, **fatigue**, muscular weakness, anorexia, blurred vision, some loss of muscular control, and amenorrhea (lack of menstruation)in women.

Dystonia (difficulty walking or moving) may occur with trifluoperazine use. This condition may subside in 24 to 48 hours even when the person continues taking the drug and usually disappears when trifluoperazine is discontinued.

Trifluoperazine use may lead to the development of symptoms that resemble Parkinson's disease. These symptoms may include a tight or mask-like expression on the face, drooling, tremors, pill-rolling motions in the hands, cogwheel rigidity (abnormal rigidity in muscles characterized by jerky movements when the muscle is passively stretched), and a shuffling gait. Taking anti-Parkinson drugs **benztropine** mesylate or **trihexyphenidyl** hydrochloride along with the trifluoperazine usually controls these symptoms.

Trifluoperazine has the potential to produce a serious side effect called **tardive dyskinesia**. This syndrome consists of involuntary, uncoordinated movements that may appear late in therapy and may not disappear even after the drug is stopped. Tardive dyskinesia involves involuntary movements of the tongue, jaw, mouth or face or other groups of skeletal muscles. The incidence of tardive dyskinesia increases with increasing age and with increasing dosage of trifluoperazine. Women are at greater risk than men for developing tardive dyskinesia. There is no known effective treatment for tardive dyskinesia, although gradual (but rarely complete) improvement may occur over a long period.

An occasionally reported side effect of trifluoperazine is neuroleptic malignant syndrome. This is a complicated and potentially fatal condition characterized by muscle rigidity, high fever, alterations in mental status, and cardiac symptoms such as irregular pulse or blood pressure, sweating, tachycardia (fast heartbeat), and arrhythmias (irregular heartbeat). People who think they may be experiencing any side effects from this or any other medication should talk to their physician promptly.

Interactions

Trifluoperazine may reduce the effectiveness of oral anticoagulant (blood thinning) drugs.

Trifluoperazine increases the effect of drugs and substances that depress the central nervous system and. These drugs include anesthetics, opiates, **barbiturates**, atropine, and alcohol. These substances should be avoided or used sparingly by people taking trifluoperazine.

Propranolol increases the concentration of trifluoperazine. The blood pressure-lowering effects of guanethidine may be diminished by trifluoperazine. The use of diuretics with trifluoperazine may cause a sudden decrease in blood pressure often accompanied by dizziness due to a change in body position (known as orthostatic hypotension).

The blood concentration of phenytoin is increased by trifluoperazine. This may lead to phenytoin toxicity.

Resources

BOOKS

Adams, Michael and Norman Holland. *Core Concepts in Pharmacology.* Philadelphia: Lippincott-Raven, 1998.

Foreman, John C. and Torben Johansen. *Textbook of Receptor Pharmacology.* 2nd ed. Boca Raton, FL: CRC Press, 2002.

Page, Clive P., and Michael Murphy. *Integrated Pharmacology.* St. Louis: Mosby-Year Book, 2002.

Von Boxtel, Chris J., Budiono Santoso, and I. Ralph Edwards. *Drug Benefits and Risks: International Textbook of Clinical Pharmacology.* New York: John Wiley and Sons, 2001.

PERIODICALS

Nelson J. C. "Diagnosing and treating depression in the elderly." *Journal of Clinical Psychiatry* 62, Supplement 24 (2001): 18-22.

Pisani F., G. Oteri, C. Costa, G. Di Raimondo, and R. Di Perri. "Effects of psychotropic drugs on seizure threshold." *Drug Safety* 25, no. 2 (2002): 91-110.

Varvel A., E. Vann, E. Wise, D. Philibin, and H. Porter. "Effects of antipsychotic drugs on operant responding after acute and repeated administration." *Psychopharmacology (Berlin)* 160, no. 2 (2002): 182-191.

ORGANIZATIONS

American Academy of Clinical Toxicology. 777 East Park Drive, PO Box 8820, Harrisburg, PA 17105-8820. Telephone: (717) 558-7750. Fax: (717) 558-7845. Web site: <http://www.clintox.org/index.html>.

American Academy of Family Physicians, 11400 Tomahawk Creek Parkway, Leawood, KS 66211-2672. Telephone: (913) 906-6000. Web site: <http://www.aafp.org/>.

American Medical Association. 515 N. State Street, Chicago, IL 60610. Telephone: (312) 464-5000. Web site: <http://www.ama-assn.org/>.

American Psychiatric Association. 1400 K Street NW, Washington, DC 20005. Telephone: (888) 357-7924. Fax: (202) 682-6850. Web site: <http://www.psych.org/>.

American Society for Clinical Pharmacology and Therapeutics. 528 North Washington Street, Alexandria, VA 22314. Telephone: (703) 836-6981. Fax: (703) 836-5223.

American Society for Pharmacology and Experimental Therapeutics. 9650 Rockville Pike, Bethesda, MD 20814-3995. Telephone: (301) 530-7060. Fax: (301) 530-7061. Web site: <http://www.aspet.org/>.

L. Fleming Fallon, Jr., M.D., Dr.P.H.

Trihexyphenidyl

Definition

Trihexyphenidyl is classified as an antiparkinsonian agent. It is sold in the United States under the brand name Artane and is also available under its generic name.

Purpose

Trihexyphenidyl is used to treat a group of side effects (called parkinsonian side effects) that include tremors, difficulty walking, and slack muscle tone. These side effects may occur in patients who are taking antipsychotic medications used to treat mental disorders such as **schizophrenia**.

Description

Some medicines, called antipsychotic drugs, that are used to treat schizophrenia and other mental disorders can cause side effects that are similar to the symptoms of Parkinson's disease. The patient does not have Parkinson's disease, but he or she may experience shaking in muscles while at rest, difficulty with voluntary movements, and poor muscle tone. These symptoms are similar to the symptoms of Parkinson's disease.

One way to eliminate these undesirable side effects is to stop taking the antipsychotic medicine. Unfortunately, the symptoms of the original mental disorder usually come back, so in most cases simply stopping the antipsychotic medication is not a reasonable option. Some drugs such as trihexyphenidyl that control the symptoms of Parkinson's disease also control the parkinsonian side effects of antipsychotic medicines.

KEY TERMS

Acetylcholine—A naturally occurring chemical in the body that transmits nerve impulses from cell to cell. Generally, it has opposite effects from dopamine and norepinephrine; it causes blood vessels to dilate, lowers blood pressure, and slows the heartbeat. Central nervous system well-being is dependent on a balance among acetylcholine, dopamine, serotonin, and norepinephrine.

Anticholinergic—Related to the ability of a drug to block the nervous system chemical acetylcholine. When acetylcholine is blocked, patients often experience dry mouth and skin, increased heart rate, blurred vision, and difficulty in urinating. In severe cases, blocking acetylcholine may cloud thinking and cause delirium.

Catheterization—Placing a tube in the bladder so that it can be emptied of urine.

Dopamine—A chemical in brain tissue that serves to transmit nerve impulses (is a neurotransmitter) and helps to regulate movement and emotions.

Neurotransmitter—A chemical involved in the transmission of nervous impulses from cell to cell.

Parkinsonian—Related to symptoms associated with Parkinson's disease, a nervous system disorder characterized by abnormal muscle movement of the tongue, face, and neck, inability to walk or move quickly, walking in a shuffling manner, restlessness, and/or tremors.

Trihexyphenidyl works by restoring the chemical balance between dopamine and acetylcholine, two neurotransmitter chemicals in the **brain**. Taking trihexyphenidyl along with the antipsychotic medicine helps to control symptoms of the mental disorder, while reducing parkinsonian side effects. Trihexyphenidyl is in the same family of drugs (commonly known as anticholinergic drugs) as **biperiden** and **benztropine**.

Recommended dosage

Trihexyphenidyl is available in 2-mg and 5-mg tablets and an elixir containing 2 mg per teaspoonful. For the treatment of tremor, poor muscle tone, and similar side effects, trihexyphenidyl should be started at a dose of 1 to 2 mg orally two to three times daily or as needed, to a maximum daily dose of 15 mg per day. Parkinson-like side effects caused by antipsychotic drugs may come and go, so trihexyphenidyl may not be needed on a regular basis. Trihexyphenidyl may also be prescribed to prevent these side effects before they actually occur. This is called prophylactic (preventative) therapy.

Precautions

Trihexyphenidyl should never be used in children under age three. It should be used cautiously and with close physician supervision in older children and in people over age 60. Trihexyphenidyl, like all anticholinergic drugs, decreases sweating and the body's ability to cool itself. People who are unaccustomed to being outside in hot weather should take care to stay as cool as possible and drink extra fluids. People who are chronically ill, have a central nervous system disease, or who work outside during hot weather may need to avoid taking trihexyphenidyl.

People who have the following medical problems may experience increased negative side effects when taking trihexyphenidyl. Anyone with these problems should discuss their condition with their physician before starting the drug:

- glaucoma, especially closed-angle glaucoma
- intestinal obstruction
- prostate enlargement
- urinary bladder obstruction

Although rare, some patients experience euphoria while taking trihexyphenidyl and may abuse it for this reason. Euphoria can occur at doses only two to four times the normal daily dose. Patients with a history of drug abuse should be observed carefully for trihexyphenidyl abuse.

Side effects

Although trihexyphenidyl helps to control the side effects of antipsychotic drugs, it can produce side effects of its own. A person taking trihexyphenidyl may have some of the following reactions, which may vary in intensity:

- dry mouth
- dry skin
- blurred vision
- nausea or vomiting
- constipation
- disorientation
- drowsiness
- irritability
- increased heart rate
- urinary retention

Dry mouth, if severe to the point of causing difficulty speaking or swallowing, may be managed by reducing or temporarily discontinuing trihexyphenidyl. Chewing sugarless gum or sucking on sugarless candy may also help to increase the flow of saliva. Some artificial saliva products may give temporary relief.

Men with prostate enlargement may be especially prone to urinary retention. Symptoms of this problem include having difficulty starting a urine flow and more difficulty passing urine than usual. This side effect may be severe and require discontinuation of the drug. Urinary retention may require catheterization. People who think they may be experiencing any side effects from this or any other medication should tell their physicians.

Patients who take an overdose of trihexyphenidyl are treated with forced vomiting, removal of stomach contents and stomach washing, activated charcoal, and respiratory support if needed. They are also given physostigmine, an antidote for anticholinergic drug poisoning.

Interactions

When drugs such as trihexyphenidyl are taken with antidepressants such as **amitriptyline**, **imipramine**, **trimipramine**, **desipramine**, **nortriptyline**, **protriptyline**, **amoxapine**, and **doxepin** or with many antihistamines that also have anticholinergic properties, the effects and side effects of trihexyphenidyl are usually intensified.

Drugs such as trihexyphenidyl decrease the speed with which food moves through the stomach and intestines. Because of this, the absorption of other drugs being taken may be enhanced by trihexyphenidyl. Patients receiving trihexyphenidyl should be alert to unusual responses to other drugs they might be taking and report any changes to their physician.

Resources

BOOKS

American Society of Health-System Pharmacists. *AHFS Drug Information 2002.* Bethesda: American Society of Health-System Pharmacists, 2002.

DeVane, C. Lindsay, Pharm.D. "Drug Therapy for Psychoses." In *Fundamentals of Monitoring Psychoactive Drug Therapy.* Baltimore: Williams and Wilkins, 1990.

Jack Raber, Pharm.D.

Trilafon *see* **Perphenazine**

Trimipramine

Definition

Trimipramine is an oral tricyclic antidepressant. It is sold in the United States under the brand name Surmontil.

Purpose

Trimipramine is used primarily to treat depression and to treat the combination of symptoms of anxiety and depression. Like most antidepressants of this chemical and pharmacological class, trimipramine has also been used in limited numbers of patients to treat **panic disorder**, **obsessive-compulsive disorder**, **attention-deficit/hyperactivity disorder**, **enuresis** (bed-wetting), eating disorders such as **bulimia nervosa**, cocaine dependency, and the depressive phase of bipolar (manic-depressive) disorder.

Description

Tricyclic antidepressants act to change the balance of naturally occurring chemicals in the **brain** that regulate the transmission of nerve impulses between cells. Trimipramine acts primarily to increase the concentration of norepinephrine and serotonin (both chemicals that stimulate nerve cells) and, to a lesser extent, to block the action of another brain chemical, acetylcholine. Trimipramine shares most of the properties of other tricyclic antidepressants, such as **amitriptyline**, **amoxapine**, **clomipramine**, **desipramine**, **imipramine**, **nortriptyline**, and **protriptyline**. Studies comparing trimipramine with these other drugs have shown that trimipramine is no more or less effective than other antidepressants of its type. Its choice for treatment is as much a function of physician preference as any other factor.

The therapeutic effects of trimipramine, like other antidepressants, appear slowly. Maximum benefit is often not evident for at least two weeks after starting the drug. People taking trimipramine should be aware of this and continue taking the drug as directed even if they do not see immediate improvement.

Recommended dosage

As with any antidepressant, trimipramine must be carefully adjusted by a physician to produce the desired therapeutic effect. Trimipramine is available as 25-mg, 50-mg, and 100-mg oral capsules. Therapy is usually started at 75 to 100 mg per day and gradually increased up to 200 mg daily as needed. Hospitalized patients with more severe depression may require 300 mg per day.

KEY TERMS

Acetylcholine—A naturally occurring chemical in the body that transmits nerve impulses from cell to cell. Generally, it has opposite effects from dopamine and norepinephrine; it causes blood vessels to dilate, lowers blood pressure, and slows the heartbeat. Central nervous system well-being is dependent on a balance among acetylcholine, dopamine, serotonin, and norepinephrine.

Anticholinergic—Related to the ability of a drug to block the nervous system chemical acetylcholine. When acetylcholine is blocked, patients often experience dry mouth and skin, increased heart rate, blurred vision, and difficulty urinating. In severe cases, blocking acetylcholine may cloud thinking and cause delirium.

Benign prostate hypertrophy—Enlargement of the prostate gland.

Norepinephrine—A neurotransmitter in the brain that acts to constrict blood vessels and raise blood pressure. It works in combination with serotonin.

Serotonin—A widely distributed neurotransmitter that is found in blood platelets, the lining of the digestive tract, and the brain, and that works in combination with norepinephrine. It causes very powerful contractions of smooth muscle, and is associated with mood, attention, emotions, and sleep. Low levels of serotonin are associated with depression.

Amounts up to 200 mg may be given as a single dose. In people over age 60 and in adolescents, the therapeutic dose should start at 50 mg per day and is rarely increased beyond 100 mg per day.

Precautions

Like all tricyclic antidepressants, trimipramine should be used cautiously and with close physician supervision in people, especially the elderly, who have benign prostatic hypertrophy, urinary retention, and glaucoma, especially angle-closure glaucoma (the most severe form). Before starting treatment, people with these conditions should discuss the relative risks and benefits of treatment with their doctors to help determine if trimipramine is the right antidepressant for them.

A common problem with tricyclic antidepressants is sedation (drowsiness, lack of physical and mental alertness). This side effect is especially noticeable early in therapy. In most patients, sedation decreases or disappears entirely with time, but until then patients taking trimipramine should not perform hazardous activities requiring mental alertness or coordination. The sedative effect is increased when trimipramine is taken with other central nervous system depressants, such as alcoholic beverages, sleeping medications, other sedatives, or antihistamines. It may be dangerous to take trimipramine in combination with these substances. Trimipramine may increase the possibility of having **seizures**. Patients should tell their physician if they have a history of seizures, including seizures brought on by the abuse of drugs or alcohol. These people should use trimipramine only with caution and be closely monitored by their physician.

Trimipramine may increase heart rate and **stress** on the heart. It may be dangerous for people with cardiovascular disease, especially those who have recently had a heart attack, to take this drug or other antidepressants in the same pharmacological class. In rare cases where patients with cardiovascular disease must receive trimipramine, they should be monitored closely for cardiac rhythm disturbances and signs of cardiac stress or damage.

Side effects

Trimipramine shares side effects common to all tricyclic antidepressants. The most frequent of these are dry mouth, constipation, urinary retention, increased heart rate, sedation, irritability, dizziness, and decreased coordination. As with most side effects associated with tricyclic antidepressants, the intensity is highest at the beginning of therapy and tends to decrease with continued use.

Dry mouth, if severe to the point of causing difficulty speaking or swallowing, may be managed by dosage reduction or temporary discontinuation of the drug. Patients may also chew sugarless gum or suck on sugarless candy in order to increase the flow of saliva. Some artificial saliva products may give temporary relief.

Men with prostate enlargement who take trimipramine may be especially likely to have problems with urinary retention. Symptoms include having difficulty starting a urine flow and more difficulty than usual passing urine. In most cases, urinary retention is managed with dose reduction or by switching to another type of antidepressant. In extreme cases, patients may require treatment with bethanechol, a drug that reverses this particular side effect. People who think they may be experiencing any side effects from this or any other medication should tell their physicians.

Interactions

Dangerously high blood pressure has resulted from the combination of tricyclic antidepressants, such as trimipramine, and members of another class of antidepressants known as monoamine oxidase (MAO) inhibitors. Because of this, trimipramine should never be taken in combination with MAO inhibitors. Patient taking any MAO inhibitors, for example Nardil (**phenelzine** sulfate) or Parmate (**tranylcypromine** sulfate), should stop the MAO inhibitor then wait at least 14 days before starting trimipramine or any other tricyclic antidepressant. The same holds true when discontinuing trimipramine and starting an MAO inhibitor.

Trimipramine may decrease the blood pressure–lowering effects of **clonidine**. Patients who take both drugs should be monitored for loss of blood-pressure control and the dose of clonidine increased as needed.

The sedative effects of trimipramine are increased by other central nervous system depressants such as alcohol, sedatives, sleeping medications, or medications used for other mental disorders such as **schizophrenia**. The anticholinergic effects of trimipramine are additive with other anticholinergic drugs such as **benztropine**, **biperiden**, **trihexyphenidyl**, and antihistamines.

See also Neurotransmitters

Resources

BOOKS

American Society of Health-System Pharmacists. *AHFS Drug Information 2002*. Bethesda: American Society of Health-System Pharmacists, 2002.

DeVane, C. Lindsay, Pharm.D. "Drug Therapy for Mood Disorders." In *Fundamentals of Monitoring Psychoactive Drug Therapy*. Baltimore: Williams and Wilkins, 1990.

Jack Raber, Pharm.D.

Undifferentiated somatoform disorder

Definition

Undifferentiated somatoform disorder occurs when a person has physical complaints for more than six months that cannot be attributed to a medical condition. If there is a medical condition present, the complaints must be far more severe than can be accounted for by the presence of the medical problem.

Description

The physical complaints that are expressed by people with undifferentiated somatoform disorder are many and varied. The similarity between all physical complaints associated with undifferentiated somatoform disorder is an absence of medical evidence for the symptoms or for their severity.

The physical complaints usually begin or worsen when the patient is under **stress**. People with undifferentiated somatoform disorder experience problems functioning in their daily lives due to the physical symptoms that they experience. Seeing multiple doctors in an effort to find a physical cause for the reported symptoms is typical of people with this disorder. Undifferentiated somatoform disorder is also sometimes referred to as somatization syndrome.

Causes and symptoms

The symptoms of undifferentiated somatoform disorder vary widely from person to person. Some of the most common physical complaints are pain, **fatigue**, appetite loss, and various gastrointestinal problems. The physical complaints generally last for long periods. Patients with undifferentiated somatoform disorder tend to complain of many different physical problems over time.

No matter what symptoms a person complains about, the overarching characteristic of the complaints is that no physical reason can be found for them. Laboratory tests and thorough examinations by doctors will reveal no medical reason for the pains or problems the person is having. The physical problems, however, persist after the person has been told no explanation can be found.

The causes of undifferentiated somatoform disorder are not clear. Some experts believe that problems in the family when the affected person was a child may be related to the development of this disorder. Depression and stress are thought to be other possible causes. Other possible causes, especially in people who overreact to even minor medical conditions, include paying obsessive attention to any minor changes or sensations that their bodies experience. They give the feelings undue weight and worry unnecessarily about them.

Demographics

Undifferentiated somatoform disorder is relatively common. It is estimated that between 4% and 11% of the population experience the disorder at some time in their lives. Women are more likely than men to have undifferentiated somatoform disorder, as are the elderly and people of lower socioeconomic backgrounds. Young women who have low socioeconomic status are the most likely group to have undifferentiated somatoform disorder. Fifty percent of the people with this disorder have other psychological or psychiatric disorders as well, such as anxiety or depression.

Diagnosis

A person with undifferentiated somatoform disorder usually begins by visiting physicians looking for treatments for physical complaints. Later, he or she may be referred to a mental health professional. Referring physicians may continue to see the patient, however, so that a trusting relationship can be established, and the patient does not continue to bounce from doctor to doctor.

Mental health professionals use the handbook called the ***Diagnostic and Statistical Manual of Mental Disorders*** to diagnose mental disorders. The book lists diagnostic criteria, and requires that the following conditions be met in order for the clinician to diagnose this disorder:

- There must be no underlying medical cause evident that could explain the patient's physical complaints. If there is a medical condition that could be related to the complaints, the symptoms reported must be far worse than any that could be explained by the existing medical problems.
- The unexplained physical symptoms must persist for at least six months.
- The symptoms must cause problems in the patient's daily life or relationships or interfere with the patient achieving his or her goals.
- There cannot be another mental disorder that accounts for the complaints.
- The patient cannot knowingly make false complaints of physical distress.

Somatization disorder

Somatization disorder is very similar to undifferentiated somatoform disorder and the two can be easily confused. The symptoms are the same, but the diagnostic criteria are much more specific for somatization disorder. To be diagnosed with somatization disorder, the patient must have four different pain symptoms, two gastrointestinal symptoms, one sexual symptom, and one pseudoneurological symptom. These symptoms can occur at different times. The symptoms must be present for several years and must have begun before the patient was thirty years old. Just as with undifferentiated somatoform disorder, the complaints must not be traceable to any medical cause.

Hypochondriasis

Hypochondriasis is also similar in many ways to undifferentiated somatoform disorder. Patients with hypochondriasis are convinced that the physical symptoms they are experiencing are the signs of a major illness. Alternately, they may simply have an obsessive fear of contracting or developing a major illness. These patients often have a specific **diagnosis** in mind when they visit a doctor, unlike most patients with undifferentiated somatoform disorder who have complaints but do not have a cause in mind.

Treatments

Most treatments of undifferentiated somatoform disorder focus on treating any underlying psychological problems or stresses that may be causing the disorder. When the disorder occurs in conjunction with another mental health problem such as depression, treating that problem often helps to resolve or lessen the symptoms of undifferentiated somatoform disorder. Some studies indicate that antidepressants are effective in treating this disorder. Patients also may benefit from programs intended to teach them how to manage stress and to understand the correlation between psychological stressors and physiological symptoms. These programs also teach people how to cope with criticism and how to stop negative behavior patterns.

Prognosis

For many people, undifferentiated somatoform disorder is a life-long disorder. Often, the physical complaints increase or decrease in relation to stressors in the affected person's life. Many people with this disorder are eventually diagnosed with another mental disorder or with a legitimate medical problem. For some people, treatment can be successful at lessening or completely resolving symptoms.

Prevention

There are no known ways to prevent undifferentiated somatoform disorder; it is possible, however, for people who appear to be developing the disorder to enroll in programs designed to teach them coping strategies and about the relationship between psychological factors and physical symptoms.

Resources

BOOKS

American Psychiatric Association. *Diagnostic and Statistical Manual of Mental Disorders.* 4th ed., text revised. Washington DC: American Psychiatric Association, 2000.

Sadock, Benjamin J. and Virginia A. Sadock, eds. *Comprehensive Textbook of Psychiatry.* 7th ed. Philadelphia: Lippincott Williams and Wilkins, 2000.

PERIODICALS

Ford, Charles V., Wayne J. Katon, Mack Lipkin Jr. "Managing Somatization and Hypochondriasis." *Patient Care* 27 no. 2 (January 30, 1993): 31-41.

"Illness Without Disease." *Harvard Mental Health Letter* 16, no. 3 (September 1999).

Locke, Steven E. "Treating Somatzation: an Update." *Behavioral Health Management* 17, no. 4 (July 1997): 22.

Tish Davidson, A.M.

Urine drug screening

Definition

Urine drug screening, or toxicological screening, is a process of chemical analysis designed to test patients for drug abuse, or to insure that a patient is substance-free before undergoing a medical procedure.

Description

Urine drug screening can be used to evaluate possible accidental or intentional overdose or poisoning, to assess the type and amount of prescribed and/or illicit drugs used by a person, or to determine the cause of acute drug toxicity. It is also used to monitor drug dependency or to determine the presence of drugs in the body for medical and legal purposes.

In many occupations, urine drug screening has become a required condition of employment. Nearly all workers in certain occupations, such as law enforcement and transportation, must submit to periodic, random, and post-incident drug screening. Federal laws mandate the administration of drug screens to workers in the transportation industry, including bus drivers, truckers, airline employees, and railroad workers. Federally required testing must be conducted by a laboratory certified by the Substance Abuse and Mental Health Services Administration. Other industries must follow state regulations, which vary considerably.

Urine screening tests are able to detect general classes of compounds, such as **amphetamines**, **barbiturates**, benzodiazepines, and opiates. Drug screening can also detect cocaine, marijuana, and phencyclidine (PCP). The screening tests themselves are unable to distinguish between illicit and prescription drugs within the same class. A patient taking prescribed codeine pills and an individual using heroin would both show positive urine screening tests for opiates. It is also possible for some over-the-counter medications to cause a positive drug screen in someone who has taken neither illegal nor prescription drugs. These incorrect reactions are known as "false-positives."

Urine drug screens can detect the use of several drugs. Some of these drugs are as follows:

- cocaine
- amphetamines
- heroin
- morphine
- phencyclidine (PCP)
- benzodiazepines
- alcohol
- hydromorphone

KEY TERMS

Amphetamines—A group of powerful and highly addictive substances that stimulate the central nervous system. May be prescribed for various medical conditions, but are often purchased illicitly and abused.

Barbiturate—A class of medications (including Seconal and Nembutal) that causes sedation and drowsiness. They may be prescribed legally, but may also be used as drugs of abuse.

Benzodiazepines—A group of central nervous system depressants used to relieve anxiety or to induce sleep.

Cocaine—An illegal drug that increases energy and induces euphoria. It is addictive and is often abused.

Codeine—A medication that may be prescribed but also may be purchased illegally and is used to reduce pain.

False-positive—A test result that is positive for a specific condition or disorder, but this result is inaccurate.

Gas chromatography/mass spectrometry (GC/MS)—A definitive method of testing for specific drugs, used to confirm immunoassay results indicating drug use. GC/MS separates the substances present in the urine sample, then breaks them into unique molecular fragments, which are matched against a database of known substances.

Hydromorphone—A prescribed opiate (Dilaudid) used to treat severe pain; also abused illegally.

Immunoassay—The method used in routine or preliminary urine drug screening.

Methadone—A drug often prescribed legally as a replacement for heroin. It induces a slight high but blocks heroin from producing a more powerful euphoric effect. It may be used in heroin detoxification to ease the process, or it may be used daily after detoxification as maintenance therapy. Methadone maintenance therapy is controversial.

Tetrahydracannabinol (THC)—The active substance in marijuana.

- tetrahydrocannabinol (THC)
- propoxyphene
- methadone
- codeine
- barbituates

Certain foods, such as poppy seeds, may result in a positive urine screen for opiates, since poppy seeds are derived from opium poppies. Preliminary urine screening results, when positive, should be confirmed by a more accurate method that can distinguish between poppy seed ingestion and use of heroin or other opiates. Poppy seeds and opiates produce different chemicals, known as metabolic breakdown products or metabolites, as they travel through the body, allowing them to be distinguished from one another.

Sample collection

The method of collecting a urine sample for drug screening can be important. Some illicit drug users may attempt to substitute another person's urine, or chemically alter their own specimen. If the urine drug screen is being used for an important decision, such as employment or legal action, procedures to minimize chances of an adulterated or substituted sample may be necessary. These include measuring the temperature or pH of the sample immediately after it is procured, and using tamper-proof containers. Supervised specimen collection may be conducted to ensure that the urine indeed comes from the person being screened.

The most commonly used method for urine drug screening is immunoassay, a rapid and accurate test that uses antibodies embedded on test strips to reveal drug use. Antibodies react only in the presence of very specific substances—in this case, drugs present in urine. When a sufficient concentration of a drug (or drugs) are present, the test strip will indicate which substances have been detected. A control band on each strip confirms that the test was done correctly.

Positive screening results should always be confirmed by a more sensitive method. The most widely accepted corroborative test for all drugs is gas chromatography/mass spectrometry (GC/MS), which can determine the specific substances in the body by recognizing not only the molecular structure of the original compound, but also its metabolite, a chemical created when the drug is metabolized.

See also Addiction; Amphetamines and related disorders; Anti-anxiety drugs and abuse-related disorders; Barbiturates; Cannabis and related disorders; Cocaine and related disorders; Disease concept of chemical dependency; Methadone; Opioids and related disorders; Sedatives and related disorders

Resources

BOOKS

Kaplan, Harold, MD, and Benjamin J. Sadock, MD. *Synopsis of Psychiatry.* 8th edition. Philadelphia: Lippincott Williams and Wilkins, 1998.

PERIODICALS

Persoon, Thomas, MS. "Virtual Hospital: Clinical Laboratory Improvement Act: Therapeutic Drug Monitoring and Drug Abuse Screening, IV." *Screening for Drugs of Abuse.* The University of Iowa, 1999.

Policy Statement: Drug and Alcohol Screening. American Academy of child and Adolescent Psychiatry, Approved by Council, October 1990.

Barbara S. Sternberg, Ph.D.

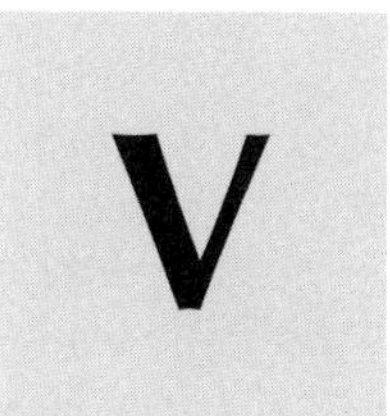

Vaginismus

Definition

Vaginismus occurs when the muscles around the outer third of the vagina contract involuntarily when vaginal penetration is attempted during sexual intercourse.

Description

Vaginismus is a sexual disorder that is characterized by the outer third of the vaginal muscles tightening, often painfully. A woman with vaginismus does not willfully or intentionally contract her vaginal muscles. However, when the vagina is going to be penetrated, the muscles tighten spontaneously due to psychological or other reasons.

Vaginismus can occur under different circumstances. It can begin the first time vaginal penetration is attempted. This is known as "lifelong vaginismus." Alternately, vaginismus can begin after a period of normal sexual functioning. This is known as "acquired-type vaginismus." For some women, vaginal tightening occurs in all situations where vaginal penetration is attempted (generalized type). For other women, it occurs in only one or a few situations, such as during a gynecological examination at the doctor's office, or with a specific sex partner (situational type). According to the professional's handbook, the *Diagnostic and Statistical Manual of Mental Disorders (DSM-IV-TR)*, in order for a condition to be diagnosed as vaginismus, the response must be due to psychological factors or a combination of psychological and medical factors, but not to medical factors alone. Because of this *DSM-IV-TR* criterion, this entry focuses on the psychological causes and treatments of vaginismus.

Causes and symptoms

Causes

There are many possible causes of vaginismus. One example is an upbringing in which sex was considered wrong or sinful—as in the case of some strict religious backgrounds. This is common among women with this disorder. Concern that penetration is going to be painful, such as during a first sexual experience, is another possible cause. It is also thought that women who feel threatened or powerless in their relationship may subconsciously use this tightening of the vaginal muscles as a defense or silent objection to the relationship. A traumatic childhood experience, such as sexual molestation, is thought to be a possible cause of vaginismus. Acquired-type vaginismus is often the result of sexual assault or rape.

Symptoms

Vaginismus can occur when any kind of penetration of the vagina is attempted. This includes attempted penetration by a penis, speculum, tampon, or other objects. The outer third of the vaginal muscles contract severely. This either prevents penetration completely, or makes it difficult and painful. The woman may truly believe that she wants to have sexual intercourse or allow the penetration. She may find that her subconscious desires or decisions do not allow her to relax the vaginal muscles.

Diagnosis

Diagnosing sexual disorders, including vaginismus, can often be very difficult. This is mainly due to lack of comfort many people feel in discussing sexual relations, even with their physicians. Often, cultural norms and taboos deter women from seeking assistance when they are experiencing such problems. When a physician or gynecologist is consulted, involuntary spasm during pelvic examination can confirm the **diagnosis** of vaginismus, and the physician will rule out any physiological causes for the condition. When psychological causes are suspected, referral should be made to a **psychologist** or **psychiatrist**.

According to the *DSM-IV-TR*, the first criterion for the diagnosis of vaginismus is the spasm of the muscles in the outer third of the vagina that are involuntary and recur-

KEY TERMS

Coitus—Sexual intercourse.

ring or persistent. The symptoms must cause physical or emotional distress, or, in particular, problems with relationships. The symptoms cannot occur during the course of another mental disorder that can account for them—they must exist on their own. As mentioned, the muscle spasm cannot be the direct result of any sort of physical or medical condition for vaginismus to be diagnosed.

Demographics

Although many women experience sexual disorders, it is hard to gather accurate data regarding the frequency of specific problems. Many cases go unreported. Vaginismus is thought to occur most often in women who are highly educated and of high socioeconomic status.

Treatment

There are many different treatments of vaginismus, as there is a multitude of ways to treat most sexual disorders. Therapists can use behavioral, hypnotic, psychological, educational, or **group therapy** techniques. Multiple techniques are often used simultaneously for the same patient. Much treatment is aimed at reducing the anxiety associated with penetration.

Psychotherapy

There are three settings in which psychological treatment can occur. These are in individual, couple, or group settings. During individual therapy, the treatment focuses on identifying and resolving any underlying psychological problems that could be causing the disorder. Problems stemming from issues such as childhood trauma or rape are often resolved this way. Revealing insecurities or fears about sex resulting from such things as parents' attitudes about it, or a religious upbringing, can often be discussed successfully if the affected woman can trust her therapist.

Couples therapy has been referred to as "dual-sex therapy." The idea behind couples therapy is that any sexual problem should be treated as a problem for the couple as a whole, and not just addressed as a problem for one person. Because this view is taken, the therapist interacts with the patients both separately and as a couple. The therapist addresses both the couple's sexual history and any other problems that may be occurring in the relationship. Confronting these problems may help to resolve the cause of the vaginismus. Working with a therapist on relationship problems can be very effective—perhaps especially so if the vaginismus is caused by a subconscious use of vaginal muscle spasms as a nonverbal form of protest about one or more aspects of the relationship. The couple is educated about vaginismus disorder and given advice on the kind of activities that can be engaged in at home that may be helpful in overcoming the disorder.

Group therapy, which can be very effective, is another form of therapy for vaginismus. In this form of therapy, couples or individuals who have the same or similar sexual disorders are brought together. For people who are embarrassed or ashamed of their disorder, this setting can provide comfort and strength. It is often very beneficial to witness another person discussing sex and sexual problems in an open and honest forum. It can also help to inspire patients to become more open and honest themselves.

Another positive feature of group therapy is that it provides a certain amount of pressure. Pressure to open up can help to provide a needed "push." Also the group's expectations for each other can provide positive pressure and encouragement for the group members. For example, the therapist may recommend "homework" outside the therapy sessions, including masturbation or certain kinds of foreplay. The group members will expect each other to complete the homework, and that expectation may help individual couples overcome their aversions to completing the activities.

Hypnotherapy

Hypnotherapy is also effective for some patients. In general, hypnotherapy tends to focus on overcoming the vaginismus itself, as opposed to resolving any causes or conflicts behind it. The therapist will determine if hypnotherapy is appropriate for a particular patient. There are often a number of sessions, during which the patient and therapist work to define the goals of the hypnotherapy. When the actual hypnosis occurs, the suggestions made are intended to resolve underlying fears or concerns, and to alleviate symptoms. For example, the patient may be told that she can have coitus without it being a painful experience, and that she will be able to overcome the muscle spasm.

During hypnosis, the problems causing the vaginismus may be explored, or an attempt may even be made to reverse feelings or fears that could be causing the disorder. Exploring causal relationships, as well as suggesting to the woman she can overcome her vaginal muscle spasms, can be very effective for certain patients.

Other treatments

Behavioral therapy is also used to treat vaginismus. When behavioral therapy is chosen, it is assumed that the vaginismus is a learned behavior that can be unlearned. Behavioral therapy generally involves desensitization. Patients are exposed to situations that they find create a mild sense of psychological discomfort or anxiety. Once these situations are conquered, the patient is exposed to sexual situations that they find more threatening, until coitus is eventually achieved without difficulty.

Another type of treatment for vaginismus involves desensitization over a period of time using systematic vaginal dilation. In the beginning of the treatment, the woman inserts a small object into her vagina. Over time, she inserts larger and larger vaginal dilators. Eventually, a dilator the size of a penis can be inserted comfortably and sexual intercourse can be achieved. There is some debate about this procedure, as it treats the symptoms and not the underlying causes of the vaginismus disorder.

Prognosis

Vaginismus is generally considered to be the most treatable sexual disorder. Successful treatment has been reported to be 63% or higher. For different people, the possibility of success using different treatments varies, because different cases of vaginismus disorder have varying causes. Generally, a treatment plan combining two or more therapeutic techniques is recommended.

Prevention

There is no known way to successfully prevent vaginismus; however, maintaining open marital communication may help to prevent the disorder, or to encourage seeking help if it does arise.

See also Cognitive-behavioral therapy; Systematic desensitization

Resources

BOOKS

American Psychiatric Association. *Diagnostic and Statistical Manual of Mental Disorders.* 4th ed., text revised. Washington DC: American Psychiatric Association, 2000.

Sadock, Benjamin J. and Virginia A. Sadock, eds. *Comprehensive Textbook of Psychiatry.* 7th ed. Philadelphia: Lippincott Williams and Wilkins, 2000.

PERIODICALS

Kleinplatz, Peggy J. "Sex Therapy for Vaginismus: a Review, Critique, and Humanistic Alternative." *The Journal of Humanistic Psychology* 38 no. 2 (Spring 1998): 51- 82.

Sadovsky, Richard. "Management of Dyspareunia and Vaginismus." *American Family Physician* 61 no. 8 (April 15, 2000): 2511.

ORGANIZATIONS

American Psychological Association. 750 First Street NE, Washington, D.C. 20002-4242, 800-374-2721;<www.apa.org>.

Tish Davidson, A.M.

Valerian

Definition

Valerian is an herbal remedy derived from the dried roots of the valerian plant, *Valeriana officinalis.* The plant belongs to the Valerianaceae family. It has been used for over a thousand years as a mild sedative and hypnotic (a preparation that brings on sleep). Valerian is native to Europe and parts of Asia; it has since been introduced in the United States, placed under cultivation and now growing in the wild, as well. It is often cultivated for its pinkish white or lavender flowers as well as for its medicinal uses. The name "valerian" is thought to derive from the Latin verb *valere*, which means "to be well." It is also sometimes said to derive from Valeria, the province of the Roman Empire where the plant may have originated.

According to one marketing research firm, valerian is the fastest-growing herbal remedy in the United States; its sales more than doubled between 2000 and 2001.

Purpose

Valerian is most commonly used to relieve mild cases of anxiety and **insomnia**. It was given during World War I to soldiers suffering from battle shock. It has also been recommended for the relief of menstrual cramps and as a carminative, or preparation that relieves gas in the stomach and intestines. Lotions made with valerian extract are said to soothe skin rashes and swollen joints.

Description

The valerian plant prefers the damp lime-rich soil near streams or rivers, where it may grow as tall as 5 ft (1.5 m). It can, however, be grown in drier soil at higher elevations, where it may grow only 2 ft (.67 m) tall. Some herbalists consider the drier-climate variety of valerian to have greater medicinal potency.

KEY TERMS

Carminative—A substance or preparation that relieves digestive gas.

Hypnotic—A type of medication that induces sleep.

Neurotransmitter—A chemical in the brain that transmits messages between neurons, or nerve cells.

Placebo—An inactive substance or preparation used as a control in experiments with human subjects to test the effectiveness of a drug or herbal preparation. Some patients may experience a medicinal response or experience side effects to a placebo simply because they have faith in its powers even though it contains no medicine.

Rhizome—The fleshy underground horizontal root of certain plants. Valerian preparations are made from dried rhizomes as well as from roots of the valerian plant.

Tincture—An alcohol-based herbal extract prepared by soaking parts of the plant in a mixture of alcohol and water. Established ratios and dilutions are followed.

Valerenic acid—The primary medicinal component in valerian preparations.

The parts of the plant that are used for medicinal purposes are the roots and rhizomes (horizontal underground stems), which are typically yellowish-brown in color. The roots and rhizomes are harvested in the autumn of the plant's second year. They can be freeze-dried and used to prepare tablets or capsules containing the ground herb. Juice can be pressed from the fresh root, or the root may be mixed with alcohol to become a fluid extract or tincture of valerian. When valerian is used to relieve tension or induce sleep, it is frequently combined with either **passionflower** (*Passiflora incarnata*), lemon balm (*Melissa officinalis*) or skullcap (*Scutellaria laterifolia*). Because valerian tea has a somewhat bitter taste, flavorings are often added, including peppermint or fruit flavor, to make a more pleasant-tasting drink.

Although not all the compounds in valerian that have medicinal value have been identified, two compounds in its essential oil—valerenic acid and bornyl— appear to be the most important. Like most prescription tranquilizers, valerian appears to affect a neurotransmitter (GABA) in the central nervous system.

There is some disagreement among researchers about the efficacy of valerian as a tranquilizer and aid to sleep. While a team of Swiss researchers found a valerian/lemon balm combination to be significantly more effective than a placebo in inducing sleep, another group in the United States concluded that valerian is overrated as a sedative. Further research may help to settle the question, but multiple studies that are currently available are inconclusive. It appears to have mild sedative properties.

Recommended dosage

Experts in herbal preparations recommend that valerian products should be standardized to contain 0.8% valerenic or valeric acid.

Adults may use the following amounts of valerian to reduce nervousness or relieve menstrual cramps:

- 2–3 g dried root in tea, up to several times daily
- 1/4–1/2 tsp (1–3 mL) valerian tincture, up to several times daily
- 1/4 tsp (1–2 mL) fluid extract
- 150–300 mg valerian extract, standardized to contain 0.8% valerenic acid

To relieve insomnia, one of the above dosages may be taken 30–45 min before bedtime. It may take one to two weeks of regular use before the herbal preparation takes effect.

When giving valerian to children, recommended adult dosages should be adjusted in proportion to the child's weight. Most dosages of herbal products are calculated for an adult weighing 150 lb (70 kg). A child weighing 75 lb (35 kg) should therefore receive 1/2 the adult dose.

Precautions

Persons who take valerian should consult an experienced herbalist about dosage and about reliable sources of the herb. Because herbal preparations are not regulated by the U. S. Food and Drug Administration, consumers cannot be certain of the freshness and potency of commercial herbal products. In July 2001, an independent laboratory published the results of its tests of 17 valerian products; only nine contained the amount of valerian that their labels claimed. Of the remaining eight products, four contained only half the amount of valerian that they should have, and the other four contained none at all.

Although valerian has a good reputation for safety when used as directed, it should not be used in high doses or taken continuously for longer than two to three weeks.

Side effects

Some people taking valerian may experience a paradoxical effect; that is, they may feel agitated or jittery instead of relaxed or sleepy. This side effect is not dangerous, but it should be reported to the patient's health care provider. If the dosage is too high, an individual could experience longer sleep than usual, and wake up not feeling well-rested.

Prolonged use of valerian results in tolerance, and increasing the dose may have serious side effects. According to some researchers, long-term use of valerian may cause psychological depression, damage to the liver, or damage to the central nervous system.

High short-term doses of valerian have been reported to cause headaches, muscle spasms, dizziness, digestive upsets, insomnia, and confusion.

Interactions

Although valerian has been regarded as a relatively safe herb because few interactions with prescription medications have been reported, newer research indicates that it should be used cautiously following surgery. Like **St. John's wort**, valerian can interact with anesthetics and other medications given to patients after surgery. Because valerian has a mild sedative effect, it should not be taken together with alcoholic beverages, benzodiazepines, **barbiturates**, or antihistamines. Some components of valerian are metabolized in the liver. This herb has the potential to interact with liver metabolizaed prescription medicines.

Resources

BOOKS

Medical Economics Staff. *PDR for Herbal Medicines.* Montvale, NJ: Medical Economics Company, 1998.

Tyler, Varro E., Ph.D. *The Honest Herbal.* New York: Pharmaceutical Products Press, 1993.

PERIODICALS

Ang-Lee, Michael, and others. " Herbal Medicines and Perioperative Care." *Journal of the American Medical Association* 286 (July 11, 2001): 208.

Cerny, A., and K. Schmid. "Tolerability and efficacy of valerian/lemon balm in healthy volunteers (a double-blind, placebo-controlled, multicentre study)." *Fitoterapia* 70 (1999): 221–228.

"Valerian for Insomnia: Jury Still Out." *Consumer Reports on Health* 13 (December 2001): 10.

Wallace, Phil. " Valerian Products Found to Lack Key Ingredient." *Food Chemical News* 43 (July, 2001): 12.

Rebecca J. Frey, Ph.D.

Valium *see* **Diazepam**

Valproic acid

Definition

Valproic acid is an anticonvulsant (anti-seizure) drug. In the United States, valproic acid is also known as valproate, and is sold under the brand name Depakene.

Purpose

The United States Food and Drug Administration (FDA) recognizes valproic acid for the treatment of epilepsy and for mania that occurs with **bipolar disorder** (previously called manic-depressive disorder). Valproic acid is also approved for the prevention of migraine headaches.

Description

Valproic acid's properties in preventing **seizures** were first discovered in Europe in 1963. The medication was first used clinically in the United Stated in 1978.

Valproic acid is effective in treating a variety of seizure types, which include simple and complex absence seizures, partial seizures, and clonic-tonic seizures (grand mal seizures). Valproic acid is effective in treating the manic episodes of patients with bipolar disorder. Patients who have bipolar disorder resulting from a head injury and patients who do not respond to or who cannot tolerate conventional lithium therapy (normally the therapy of choice for bipolar disorder) can be treated with valproic acid. In addition, valproic acid provides a 50% or greater reduction in the frequency of migraine headaches. Valproic acid is also safe and effective in preventing headaches that arise as a side effect of taking a class of drugs known as selective serotonin reuptake inhibitors (SSRI). These drugs include **sertraline** (Zoloft), **paroxetine** (Paxil), **fluoxetine** (Prozac), **fluvoxamine** (Luvox), and **citalopram** (Celexa).

Valproic acid comes in 250-mg gelatin capsule and in 250 mg/5ml-syrup.

Recommended dosage

The dosage of valproic acid used to treat epilepsy depends on the type of seizures the patient has. The doses are determined based on the patient's weight and never based on the patient's age.

KEY TERMS

Absence seizure—Absence (petit mal) seizures usually begin with a brief loss of consciousness and last between one and 10 seconds. People having a petit mal seizure become very quiet and may blink, stare blankly, roll their eyes, or move their lips. A petit mal seizure lasts 15–20 seconds. When it ends, the individual resumes whatever he or she was doing before the seizure began, and may not realize that anything unusual happened.

Clonic-tonic seizure—This is the most common type of seizure among all age groups and is categorized into several phases beginning with vague symptoms hours or days before an attack. These seizures are sometimes called grand mal seizures.

The initial dose of valproic acid used to treat mania is 750 mg daily. This dose is then reduced to the lowest dose that will achieve the desired effects. Another dosage strategy is based on patient weight. The starting dose is 30 mg per kilogram of body weight on days one and two followed by 20 mg per kg of body weight taken daily on days three through ten.

For prevention of migraine headaches, a dose of 250 mg twice daily is beneficial. It may take up to 1,000 mg of valproic acid to control migraine attacks.

Precautions

Patients who have liver disease should not take valproic acid. Pregnant women should not take valproic acid, because it can harm the developing fetus. Patients who are allergic to valproic acid should not take it.

When it is necessary for children under age two and patients who have pancreatitis to take valproic acid, the drug should be used cautiously and with close physician monitoring.

Side effects

Valproic acid can cause liver damage. Before starting valproic acid therapy, every patient should have a blood test to assess his or her liver function. The risk of valproic acid causing liver damage is greatest during the first six months of treatment. Liver function tests should be done once a month during the first three months, then every three to six months for as long as the patient continues to take the drug. Vomiting, lethargy, anorexia, and jaundice (yellowing of the skin) may precede signs of liver damage. If a patient develops severe or unusual abdominal pain, this may be a sign of pancreatitis (inflammation of the pancreas). Pancreatitis can occur in both children and adults. It can develop shortly after valproic acid is started or after several years of use.

Other side effects of valproic acid may include nausea, vomiting, indigestion, and either diarrhea or constipation. Headaches, dizziness, lack of coordination, confusion, **fatigue**, tremor, drowsiness, and seizures have also been associated with the use of valproic acid. Behavioral changes associated with the drug including irritability, longer and deeper sleep, hyperactivity, increased sociability, increased sadness, happiness or aggression, are seen more often in children than in adults taking valproic acid.

Fewer than 1% of patients experience appetite changes. These changes may include either diminished or increased appetite. Skin rash, photosensitivity (acute sensitivity to the sun), hair loss, and other hair changes have also been reported in people using valproic acid.

Interactions

Using valproic acid with other anticonvulsant drugs, such as phenobarbital, **clonazepam**, and **lamotrigine** may cause excessive sedation (drowsiness and lack of physical and mental alertness). Valproic acid may diminish the benefits of phenytoin which is another commonly used anticonvulsant.

Taking aspirin during valproic acid therapy may cause valproic acid levels to increase to toxic (poisonous) levels. Other medications that may cause valproic acid toxicity are erythromycin, an antibiotic, and the antidepressant **amitriptyline**. Drugs that can decrease the effectiveness of valproic acid include **carbamazepine** and cholestyramine. **Ginkgo biloba**, an herbal supplement commonly available in the United States, may be prepared with a chemical called 4'-O-methylpyridoxine. If this chemical remains in the herbal preparation, it can cause seizures, and reduce the effectiveness of valproic acid. Severe central nervous depression has been reported with the use of valproic acid and another anticonvulsant called primidone.

Resources

BOOKS

Kaplan, Harold. *Comprehensive Textbook of Psychiatry.* Williams and Wilkins, 1995.

Lacy, Charles F. *Drug Information Handbook.* Lexi-Comp, Inc. 2002.

PERIODICALS

Hirschfeld, Robert. "Safety and Tolerability of Oral Loading Divalproex Sodium in Acutely Manic Bipolar Patients." *Journal of Clinical Psychiatry.* 60 (1999): 815-818.

Ajna Hamidovic, Pharm.D.

Vascular dementia

Definition

Dementia is a decline in a person's mental capacities and intellectual abilities that is great enough to affect the person's normal daily functioning. Vascular dementia is dementia that is caused by disease of the blood vessels of the **brain** (cerebrovascular disease).

Description

Vascular dementia is caused by cerebrovascular disease that occurs almost entirely in the elderly. People with vascular dementia generally experience a decline in thought processes (cognitive function) that follows specific steps. This decline is often punctuated by small strokes—ruptures of tiny blood vessels in the brain. People experiencing vascular dementia often have problems with memory, abstract thinking, object identification or recognition, speech creation, speech comprehension, and motor activities.

Causes and symptoms

The signs of dementia often begin with impaired memory function. Sometimes a person has difficulty learning new things or remembering new events, and sometimes the person has difficulty recalling events or things that he or she used to know. Other signs of dementia include impairment in other areas of thought processing. Sometimes a person with vascular dementia may have difficulty producing coherent speech, or may have other language impairments, such as problems understanding spoken or written language. The signs of vascular dementia are similar to those of Alzheimer's disease (AD).

Difficulty with motor activities is a problem for some people with vascular dementia. Things that require hand-eye coordination, such as tying shoes or undoing buttons, are examples of motor activities that may be impaired. People with vascular dementia may also have difficulty recognizing familiar objects, or may be unable to name them. Problems organizing things, putting events in sequence, or problems performing other types of abstract thinking may be present.

KEY TERMS

Cerebrovascular—Blood flow in the brain.

Delirium—A disturbance of consciousness marked by confusion, difficulty paying attention, delusions, hallucinations, or restlessness.

Vascular—Pertaining to the bloodstream (arteries, veins, and blood vessels).

Some people with vascular dementia exhibit neurological signs that indicate the presence of cerebrovascular disease. They may have weakness of the arms or legs, abnormal reflexes, or abnormalities in the way they walk. Some people also exhibit behavioral disturbances related to the dementia. A person can be violent or aggressive towards others—often his or her caretaker. The person may act impulsively and irritably, and sometimes scream.

Vascular dementia is thought to be caused by small strokes that interfere with blood flow to the brain. Usually, vascular dementia is caused by many small strokes over time, rather than one large **stroke**. Sometimes this is referred to as multi-infarct dementia (MID). If the vascular dementia is caused by one large stroke, or develops in less than three months, then it is called "acute onset vascular dementia." Acute onset vascular dementia is rare.

Demographics

In most countries, vascular dementia is a much less common form of dementia than AD. This is true in North America and Europe, but is not so in Japan, where it is more common than AD. Overall, vascular dementia is the second most common form of dementia, after AD. About 10–20% of patients who experience dementia have the vascular form of the disorder. The difference in prevalence in different countries may result from different lifestyle factors rooted in the culture.

Vascular dementia is more common in men than in women, which may be because men are more likely than women to suffer from strokes. Vascular dementia becomes increasingly prevalent as people grow older. The number of people affected by vascular dementia rises dramatically during and after the sixth decade. Vascular dementia usually occurs at a younger age than AD.

Diagnosis

The first step in the **diagnosis** of vascular dementia is to verify that dementia is present. The *DSM* indicates that impairments to memory must be present for a diagnosis of vascular dementia. Memory problems can include difficulties in learning and retaining new information, problems remembering past events, or things that were learned before dementia took root.

In addition to memory impairment, the *DSM* also specifies that one or more other impairments must be present. These impairments can include language problems that encompass not being able to form speech and/or not being able to understand language, either spoken or written. The patient may have problems performing activities that require hand-eye coordination such as tying shoes, even though motor function is normal. Another possible impairment is a problem recognizing or identifying objects, although the person is able to use his or her sense organs fully. Also, problems doing tasks such as organizing things, planning events, putting things into sequence, or problems thinking abstractly may exist.

If the patient has memory problems and one or more other impairments, For a diagnosis of vascular dementia to be made, these impairments must cause problems for the patient's functioning in important parts of his or her daily life. Also, the patient must be significantly less able to function than during a previous time. In addition, the problems cannot occur during the course of an event that is categorized as a **delirium**. There must be evidence that the problem is a result of cerebrovascular disease.

If the dementia occurs without any other significant signs or symptoms, then it is classified as uncomplicated. There are three other possible classifications as given by the *DSM*. These are based on the predominant feature of the dementia. They are: vascular dementia with delirium, vascular dementia with **delusions**, and vascular dementia with depressed mood. If there are significant behavioral disturbances occurring as a result of the dementia, then that is specified.

Vascular dementia and AD are similar in many ways, and can be confused. The most significant difference between the two is that vascular dementia can be diagnosed using physiological evidence of cerebrovascular disease. Also, AD generally occurs first as a slow loss of memory function, and then as a gradual decline into eventual dementia. Vascular dementia, however, generally occurs suddenly. The patient often declines in a stepwise fashion, with each step occurring after a stroke.

Treatments

The treatments for vascular dementia focus on attempts to slow or halt the progression of the disorder and alleviate some of the symptoms. The disorder cannot be cured or reversed. The most common way to treat vascular dementia is to try to prevent further strokes. Treatments include diet and drug treatment for hypertension (high blood pressure), aspirin therapy, smoking cessation, avoidance of heavy alcohol use, and **stress** reduction. Some drugs that are used to treat mild AD are being studied for their effectiveness in treating vascular dementia.

Prognosis

Vascular dementia is a disorder that cannot be reversed. The progression of the disorder can, however, be slowed. Using drugs, along with lifestyle changes to prevent more strokes from occurring, can be effective at slowing the progression of vascular dementia.

Prevention

Vascular dementia is generally associated with a series of strokes causing increasing mental impairment. Measures generally recommended by physicians may prevent strokes and may be effective in helping to prevent vascular dementia. These measures include such things as quitting smoking, decreasing cholesterol levels, treating hypertension by reducing sodium (salt) intake, decreasing alcohol consumption, quitting smoking, and other lifestyle changes. One study illustrated that consuming a small amount of red wine regularly reduces the risk of all forms of dementia.

See also Alzheimer's disease

Resources

BOOKS

American Psychiatric Association. *Diagnostic and Statistical Manual of Mental Disorders.* 4th ed., text revised. Washington DC: American Psychiatric Association, 2000.

Sadock, Benjamin J. and Virginia A. Sadock, eds. *Comprehensive Textbook of Psychiatry.* 7th ed. Vol. 2. Philadelphia: Lippincott Williams and Wilkins, 2000.

PERIODICALS

Anonymous. "New Alzheimer's Drug is First Therapy to Show Efficacy in Vascular Dementia." *Formulary* 36 no. 8 (August 2001): 596.

Buchalter, Eric N., Melinda S. Lantz. "Treatment of Impulsivity and Aggression in a Patient with Vascular Dementia." *Geriatrics* 56 no. 2 (February 2001): 53.

Gross, Joel S., Joshua R. Shua-Haim. "Multi-infaract Dementia: a Common Form of Dementia Associated with

Cerebrovascular Disease." *Geriatrics* 52 no. 5 (May 1997): 95.

Jagust, William. "Untangling Vascular Dementia." *The Lancet* 358, no. 9299 (December 22 2001): 2097.

Larson, Eric B. "Illness Causing Dementia in the Very Elderly." *The New England Journal of Medicine* 328, no. 3 (January 21 1993): 203-2055.

ORGANIZATIONS

National Institute on Aging. Building 31, Room 5C27 31 Center Drive, MSC 2292 Bethesda, MD 20892. Telephone: (301) 496-1752. Web site: <www.nia.nih.gov>.

Tish Davidson, A.M.

Venlafaxine

Definition

Venlafaxine is an antidepressant available in the United States under the trade name of Effexor or Effexor XR.

Purpose

Venlafaxine is used to treat depression and **generalized anxiety disorder**. It has also been used to treat **obsessive-compulsive disorder** and irritable bowel syndrome.

Description

Venlafaxine is an antidepressant. It has actions common to both the cyclic antidepressants such as **imipramine** (Tofranil) and **amitriptyline** (Elavil,) and the selective serotonin reuptake inhibitors (SSRIs) such as fluoxetine (Prozac), **sertraline** (Zoloft), and **paroxetine** (Paxil). It is believed to derive its actions by increasing levels of both norepinephrine and serotonin in the **brain**.

The therapeutic effects of venlafaxine, like other antidepressants, appear slowly. Maximum benefit is often not evident for at least two weeks after starting the drug. People taking venlafaxine should be aware of this and continue taking the drug as directed even if they do not see immediate improvement.

Venlafaxine is broken down by the liver and eliminated from the body by the kidneys. As a result, the dose of venlafaxine must be lowered in people with liver or kidney disease.

KEY TERMS

Antihistamine—A medication used to alleviate allergy or cold symptoms such as runny nose, itching, hives, watering eyes, or sneezing.

Antipsychotic—A medication used to treat psychotic symptoms of schizophrenia such as hallucinations, delusions and delirium. May be used to treat symptoms in other disorders, as well.

Depression—A mental state characterized by excessive sadness. Other symptoms include altered sleep patterns, thoughts of suicide, difficulty concentrating, agitation, lack of energy, and loss of enjoyment in activities that are usually pleasurable.

Generalized anxiety disorder—A general form of fear that can dominate a person's life.

Mania—An elevated or euphoric mood or irritable state that is characteristic of bipolar I disorder. This state is characterized by mental and physical hyperactivity, disorganization of behavior, and inappropriate elevation of mood.

Neurotransmitter—A chemical in the brain that transmits messages between neurons, or nerve cells.

Obsessive-compulsive disorder—Disorder in which the affected individual has an obsession (such as a fear of contamination, or thoughts he or she doesn't like to have and can't control) and feels compelled to perform a certain act to neutralize the obsession (such as repeated handwashing).

Serotonin syndrome—A condition characterized by at least three of the following symptoms: diarrhea, fever, extreme perspiration, mood or behavior changes, overactive reflexes, fast heart rate, restlessness, shivering or shaking. It is a result of too much serotonin in the body.

Venlafaxine is available in 25-mg, 37.5-mg, 50-mg, 75-mg, and 100-mg rapid-release tablets and 75-mg and 150-mg extended-action capsules.

Recommended dosage

The recommended initial dose of venlafaxine is 75 mg daily taken as two or three equal doses. The dose may be increased in 75-mg increments every four days as needed until symptoms of depression or anxiety resolve. Most commonly, dosages range between 150 mg to 225 mg daily. although in severe situations, 375 mg per day may be needed. Once patients are stabilized using the rapid-acting tablets, they may be converted over to the appropriate dose of extended-release capsules.

In people with liver disease, the daily dosage of venlafaxine should be cut in half. In patients with kidney disease, the daily dosage of venlafaxine should be reduced 25–50%, depending upon the extent of kidney damage. When stopping venlafaxine, the dosage should be reduced gradually over a period of at least two weeks before the drug is totally stopped.

Precautions

Patients taking venlafaxine should be monitored closely for **insomnia**, anxiety, mania, significant weight loss, **seizures**, and thoughts of **suicide**.

Caution should also be exercised when prescribing venlafaxine to patients with impaired liver or kidney function, the elderly (over age 60) children, individuals with known manic-depressive disorder or a history of seizures, people with diabetes, and individuals expressing ideas of committing suicide.

Individuals should not take MAO inhibitors such as Nardil during venlafaxine therapy, for two weeks prior to beginning venlafaxine therapy, and for five weeks after stopping venlafaxine therapy.

Care should be taken to weigh the risks and benefit of this drug in women who are, or wish to become, pregnant, as well as in breast-feeding mothers.

People with diabetes should monitor their blood or urine sugar more carefully, since venlafaxine may affect blood sugar.

Until an individual understands the effects that venlafaxine may have, he or she should avoid driving, operating dangerous machinery, or participating in hazardous activities. Alcohol should not be used while taking venlafaxine.

Side effects

More common side effects include decreased sexual drive, restlessness, difficulty sitting still, skin rash, hives, and itching.

Less common side effects include fever and/or chills, and pain in joints or muscles.

Rare side effects include pain or enlargement of breasts and/or abnormal milk production in women, seizures, fast heart rate, irregular heartbeats, red or purple spots on the skin, low blood sugar and its symptoms (anxiety, chills, cold sweats, confusion, difficulty concentrating, drowsiness, excess hunger, rapid heart rate, headache, shakiness or unsteadiness, severe **fatigue**), low blood sodium and its symptoms (including confusion, seizures, drowsiness, dry mouth, severe thirst, decreased energy), serotonin syndrome (usually at least three of the following: diarrhea, fever, sweatiness, mood or behavior changes, overactive reflexes, fast heart rate, restlessness, shivering or shaking), excitability, agitation, irritability, pressured talking, difficulty breathing, and odd body or facial movements.

Interactions

Venlafaxine interacts with a long list of other medications. Anyone starting this drug should review the other medications they are taking with their physician and pharmacist for possible interactions. Patients should always inform all their health care providers, including dentists, that they are taking venlafaxine.

Dangerously high blood pressure, rapid changes in heart rate, high fever, muscle stiffness, and sudden muscle spasms have resulted from the combination of antidepressants, such as venlafaxine, and members of another class of antidepressants known as monoamine oxidase (MAO) inhibitors. Because of these serious adverse reactions, venlafaxine should never be taken in combination with MAO inhibitors. Patient taking any MAO inhibitors, for example Nardil (**phenelzine** sulfate) or Parmate (**tranylcypromine** sulfate), should stop the MAO inhibitor then wait at least 14 days before starting venlafaxine or a tricyclic antidepressant. The same holds true when discontinuing venlafaxine and starting an MAO inhibitor.

Some other drugs such as **trazodone** (Desyrel), sibutramine (Meridia), and sumatriptan (Imitrex) also interact with venlafaxine and cause a syndrome known as neuroleptic malignant syndrome, characterized by irritability, muscle stiffness, shivering, muscle spasms, and altered consciousness.

The sedative effects (drowsiness, lack of mental clarity) of venlafaxine are increased by other central nervous system depressants such as alcohol, sedatives, sleeping medications, or other medications used for mental disorders such as **schizophrenia**.

Resources

BOOKS

Facts and Comparisons Staff. *Drug Facts and Comparisons.* 6th Edition. St. Louis, MO: Facts and Comparisons, 2002.

Mosby Staff. *Mosby's Medical Drug Reference.* St. Louis, MO: Mosby, Inc, 1999.

Wyeth Laboratories Staff. *Effexor Package Insert.* Philadelphia, PA: Wyeth Laboratories, 2001.

Kelly Karpa, RPh, Ph.D.

Vivactil *see* **Protriptyline**

Vocal tic *see* **Tic disorders**

Vocational rehabilitation

Definition

Vocational rehabilitation (VR) is a set of services offered to individuals with mental or physical disabilities. These services are designed to enable participants to attain skills, resources, attitudes, and expectations needed to compete in the interview process, get a job, and keep a job. Services offered may also help an individual retrain for employment after an injury or mental disorder has disrupted previous employment.

Purpose

Vocational rehabilitation services prepare qualified applicants to achieve a lifestyle of independence and integration within their workplace, family and local community. This transition is achieved through work evaluation and job readiness services, job counseling services, and medical and therapeutic services. For individuals with psychiatric disabilities, situational assessments are generally used to evaluate vocational skills and potential.

Precautions

Vocational rehabilitation as operated by state agencies is not an entitlement program. Only individuals considered eligible can receive VR services. Eligibility criteria require that an individual be at least 16 years old, unemployed or under-employed, and have a physical or mental disability that results in a substantial barrier to employment, such as psychotic disorders, alcohol and other drug abuse dependence, mental and emotional disorders, attention deficit disorders, specific learning disabilities, and physical and sensory disabilities. In addition, the individual must be able to benefit from VR services. An individual must also need help to prepare for, find, and succeed in paid employment. When resources are limited, individuals with the most significant disabilities must be served first.

KEY TERMS

IEP (Individualized Education Plan)—Under federal law governing special education, every child in public schools who is determined through assessment to have special mental disability needs has an IEP. An IEP is typically developed by a team of professionals that may include special education teachers, physical, occupational and speech therapists, psychologists, parents or guardians, and others who may be called on to provide expertise. The team meets at least once a year to set goals for the next school year and to assess progress on already established goals. Parents who are not satisfied with school-based assessments have the right to ask for independent assessments that must be paid for by the school system.

Integrated setting—Placing individuals in usual employment situations rather than making placements into sheltered workshops or other segregated settings.

Natural supports—Using a person's already existing support network to help the person reach a goal, such as the employment of their choice.

Person-centered planning—A technique in which a plan for a person's future is developed by a team consisting of the person, family members, service providers and friends (natural supports). The team develops a practical plan based on the person's wishes and dreams. Each team member agrees to perform certain tasks identified in the plan to help the person reach goals.

Section 504—This section of the Rehabilitation Act of 1973 provides that no person may be discriminated against because of a physical disability. For instance, a child who uses a wheelchair. If a science class is on the second floor and the building has no elevator, the school must find a way to ensure that children in wheelchairs have access to that science class. An educational plan for a child who has both cognitive and physical disabilities is developed under an IEP.

Description

Vocational rehabilitation services are based on individual needs and defined as any goods or services an individual might need to be employable, such as assistive technology devices and services. For instance, a person who is blind would need screen reading software to access a computer and people with a cognitive or mental disability might need a talking electronic reminder device programmed to prompt them when it is time to perform certain tasks.

Vocational rehabilitation can be provided by private organizations, but is not typically funded under **managed care** arrangements. Thus, most people apply to state vocational rehabilitation agencies that are funded through federal and state monies. Typically, state agencies have offices in their state's major cities and towns. State VR agencies do not necessarily offer the same services or deliver services in the same way in every state, so individuals seeking services must learn how to access the VR program in their own state. The federal VR component is administered by the U.S. Department of Education Rehabilitation Services Administration and authorized by the Rehabilitation Act of 1973 as amended in the 1988 reauthorization.

Most vocational rehabilitation services are free for eligible applicants; however, applicants may be asked to use other benefits, such as: insurance, Pell grants or other financial aid for training or higher education, to pay part of program costs.

Best practices in vocational rehabilitation include individual choice, person-centered planning, integrated setting, natural supports, rapid placement, and career development. The term *integrated setting* refers to placing individuals in usual employment situations rather than making placements into sheltered workshops or other segregated settings. Natural supports are the person's already existing support network, including family members, service providers, and friends, who can help the person reach a goal, such as the employment of their choice. Person-centered planning is a technique in which a plan for a person's future is developed by a team consisting of the person and his or her natural supports, and the team develops a practical plan based on the person's wishes and dreams. Each teammember agrees to perform certain tasks identified in the plan to help the person reach goals. Unfortunately, not all VR programs incorporate all of these best practices.

Preparation

Vocational rehabilitation transition planning services are required for all public and private education students aged 16 and over, who have Individualized Education Plans (IEPs) or Rehabilitation Act Section 504 Plans. Transition services help students make the transition from school to employment, training or higher education. Older individuals who have acquired disabilities and are applying for VR services must undergo medical and psychological assessments at their local VR office to determine the extent of their disabilities, except for individuals receiving SSDI or SSI who are presumed eligible without assessments. Applicants may receive treatment and counseling, if needed, before training and employment. All VR services are described in an applicant's Individualized Plan for Employment (IPE). Applicants may design the IPE either on their own or with the assistance of their assigned VR counselor, usually a person with a master's degree in rehabilitation counseling.

Aftercare

A vocational rehabilitation counselor will assist an applicant gain access to an employment agency to help locate a job. Counselors may provide support (supported employment programs) if applicants need support to keep a job. This support may include job coaching, which includes working with the person in the workplace until the person is comfortable with the work. The counselors also act as resources if a job does not work out by assessing what happened and counseling the person on how to improve performance or change habits that were not perceived favorably in the workplace.

Risks

Applicants may not be satisfied with the pace of progress toward their employment goal through VR or they may not believe their wishes or talents and skills are being taken seriously. Applicants wanting to start their own businesses or engage in telecommuting may not be successful in receiving vocational rehabilitation assistance. Applicants may find that VR counselors tend to recommend low-level and low-paying jobs traditionally recommended for VR applicants, such as food service and janitorial work. Applicants may also be turned away by VR counselors because the counselors decide the applicant's disability is too severe for the person to benefit from VR services. An additional risk for individuals with mental disorders is a usual lack of coordination between VR and mental health systems.

To address these problems in the VR system, the United States Congress passed the Ticket To Work Act. Under this Act, persons with mental or physical disabilities will receive a ticket worth a certain amount of money. They may take this ticket to any private or public entity that provides job training and placement, including state VR programs. The entities providing the employment-related services will be able to redeem the tickets only after the person is gainfully employed for a certain period of time. States are on a staggered schedule to begin implementing the program; persons in the first states started receiving tickets in 2001. All states will be instituting the Ticket to Work Act by 2004.

Normal results

Individuals with mental or physical disabilities will receive the assessments, counseling, training, placement, accommodations and long-term supports needed to allow them to engage in the gainful employment of their choice.

Abnormal results

Individuals with mental or physical disabilities remain unemployed or under employed. More than 70% of people with disabilities are unemployed; for people with mental disorders, that percentage ranges from 70-90%.

Resources

BOOKS

Fischler, Gary and Nan Booth. *Vocational Impact of Psychiatric Disorders: A Guide for Rehabilitation Professionals.* Austin: PRO-ED, Incorporated, 1999.

PERIODICALS

Cook, Judith A. "Research-Based Principles of Vocational Rehabilitation for Psychiatric Disability." International Association of Psychosocial Rehabilitation Services newsletter *Connection* issue 4 (September 1999). Also available on the Veterans Industry web site: <www.va.gov/vetind/page.cfm?pg=6>.

Harding, Courtney. "Some Things We've Learned about Vocational Rehabilitation of the Seriously and Persistently Mentally Ill." Western Interstate Commission for Higher Education newsletter *West Link: Western Health Development in the United States* vol. 18, no 2 (1997). Also available at <http://www.wiche.edu/mentalhealth/westlink/>.

Lehman, Anthony F. "Vocational Rehabilitation in Schizophrenia." In *Schizophrenia Bulletin* 21, no. 4 (1995): 24-36.

MacDonald-Wilson, K. "Unique Issues in Assessing Work Function Among Individuals with Psychiatric Disabilities." *Journal of Occupational Rehabilitation* 11, no. 3 (2001): 217-232.

Maronne, J., C. Gandolfo, M. Gold, and D. Hoff. "If You Think Work Is Bad for People with Mental Illness, Then Try Poverty, Unemployment, and Social Isolation." *Psychiatric Rehabilitation Journal* 23, no. 2 (2000): 187-193.

ORGANIZATIONS

Association for Persons in Supported Employment (APSE) provides a nationwide supported employment network through its national program and state chapters. APSE works to increase supported employment opportunities, educate consumers regarding their rights in supported employment activities and train professionals to create quality supported employment services. APSE, 1627 Monument Avenue, Richmond, VA 23220. Phone: (804) 278-9187. Fax: (804) 278-9377. <http://www.apse.org/>.

The Office of Special Education and Rehabilitative Services' Rehabilitation Services Administration (RSA) web site describes the programs offered, federal law and regulations governing VR programs, and includes a link to all state VR programs and agencies. <http://www.ed.gov/offices/OSERS/RSA/>.

State Rehabilitation Councils. These councils advise and assist state VR programs in preparing state plans for vocational services to promote employment for persons with disabilities and ensure a link between citizen participation and the legislative process. Persons with disabilities or their family members must make up 60% or more of a Council's membership. The Pennsylvania Rehabilitation Council has a web site with links to various state rehabilitation councils at <http://www.parac.org/>. The Pennsylvania Rehabilitation Council can be reached at: Rehabilitation Council Support Project, 1902 Market Street, Camp Hill, PA 17011. Telephone: (717) 975-2004, or toll free: (888) 250-5175. TTY: (877) 827-9974. Fax: (888) 524-9282.

Geoffrey Grimm, Ph.D., LPC

Voyeurism

Definition

Voyeurism is a psychosexual disorder in which a person derives sexual pleasure and gratification from looking at the naked bodies and genital organs or observing the sexual acts of others. The voyeur is usually hidden from view of others. Voyeurism is a form of paraphilia.

A variant form of voyeurism involves listening to erotic conversations. This is commonly referred to as telephone sex, although it is usually considered voyeurism primarily in the instance of listening to unsuspecting persons.

Description

The object of voyeurism is to observe unsuspecting individuals who are naked, in the process of undressing or engaging in sexual acts. The person being observed is usually a stranger to the observer. The act of looking or peeping is undertaken for the purpose of achieving sexual excitement. The observer generally does not seek to have sexual contact or activity with the person being observed.

If orgasm is sought, it is usually achieved through masturbation. This may occur during the act of observation or later, relying on the memory of the act that was observed.

KEY TERMS

Paraphilia—A disorder that is characterized by recurrent intense sexual urges and sexually arousing fantasies generally involving (1) non-human objects, (2) the suffering or humiliation of oneself or one's partner (not merely simulated), or (3) children or other non-consenting persons.

Voyeur—A person who engages in the behavior of voyeurism.

Frequently, a voyeur may have a fantasy of engaging in sexual activity with the person being observed. In reality, this fantasy is rarely consummated.

A number of states have statutes that render voyeurism a crime. Such statutes vary widely regarding definitions of voyeurism. Most states specifically prohibit anyone from photographing or videotaping another person, without consent, while observing that person in the privacy of his home or some other private place.

Causes and symptoms

Causes

There is no scientific consensus concerning the basis for voyeurism. Most experts attribute the behavior to an initially random or accidental observation of an unsuspecting person who is naked, in the process of disrobing, or engaging in sexual activity. Successive repetitions of the act tend to reinforce and perpetuate the voyeuristic behavior.

Symptoms

The act of voyeurism is the observation of an unsuspecting person who is naked, in the process of disrobing, or engaging in sexual activity that provides sexual arousal. To be clinically diagnosed, the symptoms must include the following elements:

- recurrent, intense or sexually arousing fantasies, sexual urges, or behaviors
- fantasies, urges, or behaviors that cause significant distress to an individual or are disruptive of his or her everyday functioning.

Demographics

Voyeurism is apparently more common in men, but does occasionally occur in women. However, the prevalence of voyeurism is not known. Contemporary U.S. society is increasingly voyeuristic (as in the example of "real" television); however **diagnosis** is made only when this is a preferred or exclusive means of sexual gratification.

The onset of voyeuristic activity is usually prior to the age of 15 years. There are no reliable statistics pertaining to the incidence of voyeurism in adulthood.

Diagnosis

According to the mental health professional's handbook, ***Diagnostic and Statistical Manual of Mental Disorders***, two criteria are required to make a diagnosis of voyeurism:

- Over a period of at least six months, an individual must experience recurrent, intense, sexually arousing fantasies, sexual urges, or behaviors that involve the act of observing an unsuspecting person who is naked, in the process of disrobing, or engaging in sexual activity.
- The fantasies, sexual urges, or behaviors must cause clinically significant distress or impairment in social, occupational, or other important areas of functioning.

In order for a condition to be labeled "voyeurism," the fantasies, urges, or behaviors to watch other persons must cause significant distress in the individual or be disruptive to his or her everyday functioning.

Treatments

For treatment to be successful, a voyeur must want to modify existing patterns of behavior. This initial step is difficult for most voyeurs to admit and then take. Most must be compelled to accept treatment. This may often be the result of a court order.

Behavioral therapy is commonly used to try to treat voyeurism. The voyeur must learn to control the impulse to watch non-consenting victims, and just as importanly to acquire more acceptable means of sexual gratification. Outcomes of behavioral therapy are not known. There are no direct drug treatments for voyeurism.

Voyeurism is a criminal act in many jurisdictions. It is usually classified as a misdemeanor. As a result, legal penalties are often minor. The possibility of exposure and embarrassment may deter some voyeurs. It is also not easy to prosecute voyeurs as intent to watch is difficult to prove. In their defense statements, they usually claim that the observation was accidental.

Prognosis

Once voyeuristic activity is undertaken, it commonly does not stop. Over time, it may become the main form of sexual gratification for the voyeur. Its course tends to be chronic.

The prognosis for eliminating voyeurism is poor because most voyeurs have no desire to change their pattern of behavior. Since voyeurism involves non-consenting partners and is against the law in many jurisdictions, the possibility of embarrassment may deter some individuals.

Prevention

Most experts agree that providing guidance regarding behavior that is culturally acceptable will prevent the development of a paraphilia such as voyeurism. The origin of some instances of voyeurism may be accidental observation with subsequent sexual gratification. There is no way to predict when such an event and association will occur.

Members of society at large can reduce the incidence of voyeurism by drawing curtains, dropping blinds or closing window curtains. Reducing opportunities for voyeurism may reduce the practice.

See also Paraphilia; Exhibitionism

Resources

BOOKS

American Psychiatric Association. *Diagnostic and Statistical Manual of Mental Disorders.* Fourth edition, text revised. Washington DC: American Psychiatric Association, 2000.

Gelder, Michael, Richard Mayou, and Philip Cowen. *Shorter Oxford Textbook of Psychiatry.* 4th ed. New York: Oxford University Press, 2001.

Kohut, John J., Roland Sweet. *Real Sex: Titillating but True Tales of Bizarre Fetishes, Strange Compulsions, and Just Plain Weird Stuff.* New York: Plume, 2000.

Wilson, Josephine F. *Biological Foundations of Human Behavior.* New York: Harcourt, 2002.

PERIODICALS

Abouesh, A., and A. Clayton. "Compulsive voyeurism and exhibitionism: a clinical response to paroxetine." *Archives of Sexual Behavior* 28, no. 1 (1999): 23–30.

Furnham, A., and E. Haraldsen. "Lay theories of etiology and 'cure' for four types of paraphilia: fetishism; pedophilia; sexual sadism; and voyeurism." *Journal of Clinical Psychology* 54, no. 5 (1998): 689–700.

Rosler, A., and E. Witztum. "Pharmacotherapy of paraphilias in the next millennium." *Behavioral Science Law* 18, no. 1 (2000): 43–56.

Simon, R. I. "Video voyeurs and the covert videotaping of unsuspecting victims: psychological and legal consequences." *Journal of Forensic Science* 42, no. 5 (1997): 884-889.

ORGANIZATIONS

American Medical Association. 515 N. State Street, Chicago, IL 60610. Telephone: (312) 464-5000. Web site: <http://www.ama-assn.org/>.

American Psychiatric Association. 1400 K Street NW, Washington, DC 20005. Telephone: (888) 357-7924. Fax: (202) 682-6850. Web site: <http://www.psych.org/>.

American Psychological Association. 750 First Street NW, Washington, DC, 20002-4242. Telephone: (800) 374-2721 or (202) 336-5500. Web site: <http://www.apa.org/>.

L. Fleming Fallon, Jr., M.D., Dr.P.H.

WAIS *see* **Wechsler Adult Intelligence Scale**

Wechsler adult intelligence scale

Definition

The Wechsler adult intelligence scale (WAIS) is an individually administered measure of intelligence, intended for adults aged 16–89.

Purpose

The WAIS is intended to measure human intelligence reflected in both verbal and performance abilities. Dr. David Wechsler, a clinical **psychologist**, believed that intelligence is a global construct, reflecting a variety of measurable skills and should be considered in the context of the overall personality. The WAIS is also administered as part of a test battery to make inferences about personality and pathology, both through the content of specific answers and patterns of subtest scores.

Besides being utilized as an intelligence assessment, the WAIS is used in neuropsychological evaluation, specifically with regard to **brain** dysfunction. Large differences in verbal and nonverbal intelligence may indicate specific types of brain damage.

The WAIS is also administered for diagnostic purposes. Intelligence quotient (IQ) scores reported by the WAIS can be used as part of the diagnostic criteria for **mental retardation**, specific learning disabilities, and **attention-deficit/hyperactivity disorder** (ADHD).

Precautions

The Wechsler intelligence scales are not considered adequate measures of extremely high and low intelligence (IQ scores below 40 and above 160). The nature of the scoring process does not allow for scores outside of this range for test takers at particular ages. Wechsler himself was even more conservative, stressing that his scales were not appropriate for people with an IQ below 70 or above 130. Also, when administering the WAIS to people at extreme ends of the age range (below 20 years of age or above 70), caution should be used when interpreting scores. The age range for the WAIS overlaps with that of the **Wechsler Intelligence Scale for Children** (WISC) for people between 16 and 17 years of age, and it is suggested that the WISC provides a better measure for this age range.

Administration and scoring of the WAIS require an active test administrator who must interact with the test taker and must know test protocol and specifications. WAIS administrators must receive proper training and be aware of all test guidelines.

Description

The Wechsler **intelligence tests**, which include the WAIS, the WISC, and the WPPSI (Wechsler preschool and primary scale of intelligence), are the most widely used intelligence assessments and among the most widely used neuropsychological assessments. Wechsler published the first version of the WAIS in 1939, initially called the Wechsler-Bellevue. The newest version is the WAIS-III (the third edition, most recently updated in 1997). Since Wechsler's death in 1981, the Wechsler tests have been revised by the publisher, the Psychological Corporation.

The theoretical basis for the WAIS and the other Wechlser scales came from Wechsler's belief that intelligence is a complex ability involving a variety of skills. Because intelligence is multifaceted, Wechsler believed, a test measuring intelligence must reflect this multitude of skills. After dividing intelligence into two major types of skills—verbal and performance—Wechsler utilized the statistical technique of factor analysis to determine specific skills within these two major domains. These more specific factors formed the basis of the Wechsler subtests.

KEY TERMS

Factor Analysis—A statistical method for summarizing relationships between variables. With the WAIS, items that correlated highly with each other were considered to be part of certain factors underlying intelligence. These factors are the basis for the 14 WAIS subtests.

Indices—Scores based on performance in more than one area. On the WAIS, there are four index scores, each based on an individual's performance in more than one subtest.

Mean—The mathematical average of all scores in a set of scores. The WAIS has been standardized to have a mean of 100.

Percentile rank—The point at which a given percentage of people fall at or below the individual's test score being calculated. For example, if a person's test score was at the 60th percentile, 40% of other test takers received a higher score, while 60% received a score that was at or below that of the test taker.

Standard deviation—A measure of variability in a set of scores. The WAIS has been standardized to have a standard deviation of 15.

Standardization—The administration of a test to a sample group of people for the purpose of establishing scoring norms. Prior to the publication of each version of the WAIS, it is standardized.

The WAIS-III consists of 14 subtests and takes about 60–75 minutes to complete. The test is taken individually, with a test administrator present to give instructions. Each subtest is given separately, and proceeds from very easy items to very difficult ones. There is some flexibility in the administration of the WAIS—the administrator may end some subtests early if test takers seem to reach the limit of their capacity. Tasks on the WAIS include questions of general knowledge, traditional arithmetic problems, a test of vocabulary, completion of pictures with missing elements, arrangements of blocks and pictures, and assembly of objects.

The WAIS is considered to be a valid and reliable measure of general intelligence. When undergoing reliability and validity studies, other intelligence tests are often compared to the Wechsler scales. It is regularly used by researchers in many areas of psychology as a measure of intelligence. Research has demonstrated correlations between WAIS IQ scores and a variety of socioeconomic, physiological, and environmental characteristics.

The WAIS has also been found to be a good measure of both fluid and crystallized intelligence. Fluid intelligence refers to inductive and deductive reasoning, skills considered to be largely influenced by neurological and biological factors. In the WAIS, fluid intelligence is reflected in the performance subtests. Crystallized intelligence refers to knowledge and skills that are primarily influenced by environmental and sociocultural factors. In the WAIS, crystallized intelligence is reflected in the verbal subtests. Wechsler himself did not divide overall intelligence into these two types. However, the consideration of fluid and crystallized intelligence as two major categories of cognitive ability has been a focus for many intelligence theorists.

The Wechshler scales were originally developed and later revised using standardization samples. The samples were meant to be demographically representative of the United States population at the time of the standardization.

Results

The WAIS elicits three intelligence quotient scores, based on an average of 100, as well as subtest and index scores. WAIS subtests measure specific verbal abilities and specific performance abilities.

The WAIS elicits an overall intelligence quotient, called the full-scale IQ, as well as a verbal IQ and a performance IQ. The three IQ scores are standardized in such a way that the scores have a mean of 100 and a standard deviation of 15. Wechsler pioneered the use of deviation IQ scores, allowing test takers to be compared to others of different as well as the same age. WAIS scores are sometimes converted into percentile ranks. The verbal and performance IQ scores are based on scores on the 14 subtests. The 14 subtest scores have a mean of 10 and a standard deviation of three. The WAIS also elicits four indices, each based on a different set of subtests: verbal comprehension, perceptual organization, working memory, and processing speed.

The full-scale IQ is based on scores on all of the subtests and is a reflection of both verbal IQ and performance IQ. It is considered the single most reliable and valid score elicited by the WAIS. However, when an examinee's verbal and performance IQ scores differ significantly, the full-scale IQ should be interpreted cautiously.

The verbal IQ

The verbal IQ is derived from scores on seven of the subtests: information, digit span, vocabulary, arithmetic, comprehension, similarities, and letter-number sequencing. Letter-number sequencing is a new subtest added to the most recent edition of the WAIS (WAIS-III).

The information subtest is a test of general knowledge, including questions about geography and literature. The digit span subtest requires test takers to repeat strings of digits. The vocabulary and arithmetic subtests are general measures of a person's vocabulary and arithmetic skills. The comprehension subtest requires test takers to solve practical problems and explain the meaning of proverbs. The similarities subtest requires test takers to indicate the similarities between pairs of things. The letter-number sequencing subtest involves ordering numbers and letters presented in an unordered sequence. Scores on the verbal subtests are based primarily on correct answers.

The performance IQ

The performance IQ is derived from scores on the remaining seven subtests: picture completion, picture arrangement, block design, object assembly, digit symbol, matrix reasoning, and symbol search. Matrix reasoning and symbol search are new subtests and were added to the most recent edition of the WAIS (WAIS-III).

In the picture completion subtest, the test taker is required to complete pictures with missing elements. The picture arrangement subtest entails arranging pictures in order to tell a story. The block design subtest requires test takers to use blocks to make specific designs. The object assembly subtest requires people to assemble pieces in such a way that a whole object is built. In the digit symbol subtest, digits and symbols are presented as pairs and test takers then must pair additional digits and symbols. The matrix reasoning subtest requires test takers to identify geometric shapes. The symbol search subtest requires examinees to match symbols appearing in different groups. Scores on the performance subtests are based on both response speed and correct answers.

See also Stanford-Binet intelligence scales

Resources

BOOKS

Groth-Marnat, Gary. *Handbook of Psychological Assessment,* 3rd edition. New York: John Wiley and Sons, 1997.

Kline, Paul. *The Handbook of Psychological Testing.* New York: Routledge, 1999.

McGrew, Kevin S., and Dawn P. Flanagan. *The Intelligence Test Desk Reference.* Needham Heights, MA: Allyn and Bacon, 1998.

Ali Fahmy, Ph.D.

Tasks on the WAIS include questions of general knowledge, traditional arithmetic problems, a test of vocabulary, completion of pictures with missing elements, arrangements of blocks and pictures, and assembly of objects. The picture arrangement subtest (shown above) entails arranging pictures in order to tell a story. *(Laura Dwight/ CORBIS. Photo reproduced by permission.)*

Wechsler Intelligence Scale for Children

Definition

The Wechsler Intelligence Scale for Children, often abbreviated as WISC, is an individually administered measure of intelligence intended for children aged six years to 16 years and 11 months.

Purpose

The WISC is designed to measure human intelligence as reflected in both verbal and nonverbal (performance) abilities. David Wechsler, the author of the test, believed that intelligence has a global quality that reflects a variety of measurable skills. He also thought that it should be considered in the context of the person's overall personality.

The WISC is used in schools as part of placement evaluations for programs for gifted children and for children who are developmentally disabled.

In addition to its uses in intelligence assessment, the WISC is used in neuropsychological evaluation, specifically with regard to **brain** dysfunction. Large differences in verbal and nonverbal intelligence may indicate specific types of brain damage.

The WISC is also used for other diagnostic purposes. IQ scores reported by the WISC can be used as part

KEY TERMS

Crystallized intelligence—A type of intelligence that reflects knowledge and skills influenced by a person's sociocultural environment.

Factor analysis—A statistical method for summarizing relationships between variables.

Fluid intelligence—A type of intelligence that involves inductive and deductive reasoning ability.

Intelligence quotient (IQ)—A measurement of intelligence obtained by dividing a person's mental age (determined by level of performance on an age-graded test) by his or her chronological age and multiplying by 100. For example, a ten-year-old with a mental age of thirteen would have an IQ of 130.

Standardization—The administration of a test to a sample group of people for the purpose of establishing scoring norms.

of the diagnostic criteria for **mental retardation** and specific learning disabilities. The test may also serve to better evaluate children with **attention-deficit/hyperactivity disorder** (ADHD) and other behavior disorders.

Precautions

The Wechsler intelligence scales are not considered adequate measures of extreme intelligence (IQ scores below 40 and above 160). The scoring process does not allow for scores outside this range for test takers at particular ages. Wechsler himself was even more conservative, stressing that his scales were not appropriate for people with IQs below 70 or above 130. Despite this restriction, many people use the WISC as a measure of the intelligence of gifted children, who typically score above 130. The age range for the WISC overlaps with that of the **Wechsler Adult Intelligence Scale** (WAIS) for people between 16 and 17 years of age, but experts suggest that the WISC provides a better measure for people in this age range.

Administration and scoring of the WISC require a competent administrator who must be able to interact and communicate with children of different ages and must know test protocol and specifications. WISC administrators must receive training in the proper use of the instrument and demonstrate awareness of all test guidelines.

Description

The Wechsler **intelligence tests**, which include the WISC, the WAIS, and the WPPSI (Wechsler Preschool and Primary Scale of Intelligence), are the most widely used intelligence and neuropsychological assessments. The first version of the WISC was written in 1949 by David Wechsler. The newest version of the WISC is the WISC-III (Wechsler Intelligence Scale for Children-Third Edition, most recently updated in 1991). Since Wechsler's death in 1981, the tests have been revised by their publisher, the Psychological Corporation.

The theoretical basis for the WISC and the other Wechsler scales is Wechsler's belief that human intelligence is a complex ability involving a variety of skills. Because intelligence is multifaceted, Wechsler believed, a test measuring intelligence must reflect this diversity. After dividing intelligence into two major types of skills—verbal and performance—Wechsler used a statistical technique called factor analysis to determine which specific skills fit within these two major domains.

The current version of the WISC (the WISC-III) consists of 13 subtests and takes between 50 and 75 minutes to complete. The test is taken individually, with an administrator present to give instructions. Each subtest is given separately. There is some flexibility in the administration of the WISC—the administrator may end some subtests early if the test taker appears to have reached the limit of his or her capacity. Tasks on the WISC include questions of general knowledge, traditional arithmetic problems, English vocabulary, completion of mazes, and arrangements of blocks and pictures.

Children who take the WISC are scored by comparing their performance to other test takers of the same age. The WISC yields three IQ (intelligence quotient) scores, based on an average of 100, as well as subtest and index scores. WISC subtests measure specific verbal and performance abilities. The Wecshler scales were originally developed and later revised using standardization samples. The samples were meant to be representative of the United States population at the time of standardization.

The WISC is considered to be a valid and reliable measure of general intelligence in children. It is regularly used by researchers in many areas of psychology and child development as a general measure of intelligence. It has also been found to be a good measure of both fluid and crystallized intelligence. Fluid intelligence refers to inductive and deductive reasoning, skills that are thought to be largely influenced by neurological and biological factors. Fluid intelligence is measured by the performance subtests of the WISC. Crystallized intelligence refers to knowledge and skills that are primarily influenced by environmental and sociocultural factors. It is measured by the verbal subtests of the WISC. Wechsler himself did not divide overall intelligence into these two types. The definition of fluid and crystallized intelligence as two major categories of cognitive ability, however, has been a focus of research for many intelligence theorists.

Verbal IQ

The child's verbal IQ score is derived from scores on six of the subtests: information, digit span, vocabulary, arithmetic, comprehension, and similarities.

The information subtest is a test of general knowledge, including questions about geography and literature. The digit span subtest requires the child to repeat strings of digits recited by the examiner. The vocabulary and arithmetic subtests are general measures of the child's vocabulary and arithmetic skills. The comprehension subtest asks the child to solve practical problems and explain the meaning of simple proverbs. The similarities subtest asks the child to describe the similarities between pairs of items, for example that apples and oranges are both fruits.

Performance IQ

The child's performance IQ is derived from scores on the remaining seven subtests: picture completion, picture arrangement, block design, object assembly, coding, mazes, and symbol search.

In the picture completion subtest, the child is asked to complete pictures with missing elements. The picture arrangement subtest entails arranging pictures in order to tell a story. The block design subtest requires the child to use blocks to make specific designs. The object assembly subtest asks the child to put together pieces in such a way as to construct an entire object. In the coding subtest, the child makes pairs from a series of shapes or numbers. The mazes subtest asks the child to solve maze puzzles of increasing difficulty. The symbol search subtest requires the child to match symbols that appear in different groups. Scores on the performance subtests are based on both the speed of response and the number of correct answers.

Results

WISC scores yield an overall intelligence quotient, called the full scale IQ, as well as a verbal IQ and a performance IQ. The three IQ scores are standardized in such a way that a score of 100 is considered average and serves as a benchmark for higher and lower scores. Verbal and performance IQ scores are based on scores on the 13 subtests.

The full scale IQ is derived from the child's scores on all of the subtests. It reflects both verbal IQ and performance IQ and is considered the single most reliable and valid score obtained by the WISC. When a child's verbal and performance IQ scores are far apart, however, the full scale IQ should be interpreted cautiously.

A child taking the picture arrangement portion of the WISC. *(Lew Merrim/ Science Source/ Photo Researchers, Inc. Photo reproduced by permission.)*

See also Stanford-Binet intelligence scales

Resources

BOOKS

Groth-Marnat, Gary. *Handbook of Psychological Assessment.* 3rd edition. New York: John Wiley and Sons, 1997.

Kline, Paul. *The Handbook of Psychological Testing.* New York: Routledge, 1999.

McGrew, Kevin S., and Dawn P. Flanagan. *The Intelligence Test Desk Reference.* Needham Heights, MA: Allyn and Bacon, 1998.

Ali Fahmy, Ph.D.

Wellbutrin *see* **Bupropion**

Wernicke-Korsakoff syndrome

Definition

Wernicke-Korsakoff syndrome is a severe memory disorder usually associated with chronic excessive alcohol consumption, although the direct cause is a deficiency in the B vitamin thiamin.

KEY TERMS

Anterograde amnesia—Amnesia for events that occurred after a physical injury or emotional trauma but before the present moment.

Apathy—Lack of feelings or emotions.

Cognitive—Pertaining to the mental processes of memory, perception, judgment, and reasoning.

Encephalopathy—Brain disease that causes damage or degeneration.

Explicit memory—Consciously recalled memory for facts or events.

Implicit memory—Unconsciously recalled memory for skills, procedures, or associations.

Neurons—Nerve cells in the brain that produce nerve impulses.

Neurotransmitter—A chemical in the brain that transmits messages between neurons, or nerve cells.

Retrograde amnesia—Amnesia for events that occurred before a traumatic injury.

Serotonin—A widely distributed neurotransmitter that is found in blood platelets, the lining of the digestive tract, and the brain, and that works in combination with norepinephrine. It causes very powerful contractions of smooth muscle, and is associated with mood, attention, emotions, and sleep. Low levels of serotonin are associated with depression.

Syndrome—A group of symptoms that together characterize a disease or disorder.

The *Diagnostic and Statistical Manual of Mental Disorders (DSM-IV-TR)*, the professional handbook that aids clinicians in diagnosing patients' mental disorders, refers to Korsakoff syndrome as alcohol-induced persisting amnestic disorder and includes it under the category of substance-induced persisting **amnestic disorders**.

Description

The disorder was first identified in the late nineteenth century. The first phase of the condition, called Wernicke's encephalopathy, was described by German neurologist and **psychiatrist** Karl Wernicke in 1881. He noted three key symptoms in three patients—two with alcoholism and one who had swallowed sulfuric acid. These patients suffered from mental confusion, eye **movement disorders**, and ataxia (poor motor coordination). A few years later, S. S. Korsakoff, a Russian psychiatrist, began publishing reports describing a syndrome of anterograde amnesia—an inability to form new memories—and confabulation in individuals with severe alcoholism or certain medical illnesses. (Confabulation refers to the practice of filling in gaps in memory by fabrication.) By 1900, researchers and clinicians studying alcoholism recognized a connection between the two conditions. The typical syndrome begins with acute Wernicke's encephalopathy, with Korsakoff syndrome emerging when the acute phase resolves. The symptoms of Wernicke's encephalopathy appear suddenly. The most prominent symptom initially is mental confusion including memory problems. On examination, patients have difficulty moving their eyes to follow a visual stimulus due to paralysis of the muscles controlling eye movements. For instance, a patient may have trouble looking upward or to the side with one or both eyes. Problems maintaining balance while standing or walking, a condition known as ataxia, are frequently observed as well. If left untreated, most of these symptoms may resolve spontaneously, but the severe memory disorder characteristic of Korsakoff syndrome remains.

The typical person with Korsakoff syndrome appears fairly normal on first impression. Intelligence is intact, and individuals with the syndrome can carry on a conversation quite naturally. They are usually able to recall and talk about incidents that took place before the onset of the disorder and recognize family members and old friends without much difficulty. The ability to form new memories is nearly absent, however. In the course of conversation, people with Korsakoff syndrome may repeat comments or questions several times. They will fail to recognize people they met minutes before or greet a friend with excitement and surprise after a brief trip to another room. These are the characteristics of anterograde **amnesia**. Research shows that anterograde amnesia results from a failure of memory formation and storage. New information is processed normally, but almost immediately forgotten, never making it into the regions of the **brain** where memories of the past are stored. People with Korsakoff syndrome thus have no memories of events that happened after the onset of the illness. Many previously stored memories are still available, however, explaining why individuals with Korsakoff syndrome can usually remember the distant past quite well.

Causes and symptoms

Causes

Wernicke-Korsakoff syndrome is caused by thiamin deficiency. It is most commonly observed in people with alcoholism since heavy drinkers often eat poorly, and alcoholism interferes with absorption of nutrients from the digestive system. It can also occur in people who are malnourished for other reasons. Thiamin helps produce energy needed to make neurons function properly. Insufficient thiamin can lead to damage or death of neurons.

Thiamin deficiency damages regions of the brain, particularly the thalamus and the mammillary bodies. The thalamus is a structure deep within the brain that serves many important functions. It is often called the major relay station of the brain, and many neurons make connections in the thalamus. The mammillary bodies are part of the hypothalamus, located just below the thalamus. The mammillary bodies receive many neural connections from another part of the brain called the hippocampus, which appears to be the primary part of the brain involved in the formation of memories. Neurons in the mammillary bodies make connections with the thalamus, which in turn makes connections with the cortex of the brain, where long-term memories are stored. This may explain why damage to the mammillary bodies and thalamus can lead to anterograde amnesia. Memories formed in the hippocampus are never stored since connections between hippocampus and cortex are disrupted.

Eye movement disorders observed in the acute phase of the condition are probably due to damage to other nearby brain regions that make connections to the nerves controlling eye muscles. These nerves emerge from the brainstem located right below the thalamus and mammillary bodies. Nerves involved in balance also make connections with other nerves in the brainstem, but a separate part of the brain called the cerebellum may also contribute to ataxia. Reasons why some regions of the brain are selectively affected by thiamin deficiency are not yet fully understood, but selective vulnerability of certain **neurotransmitters** is suspected.

Symptoms

Mental confusion, eye movement disturbances, and ataxia are the primary symptoms of Wernicke's encephalopathy—the first, acute stage of Wernicke-Korsakoff syndrome. At first glance, confusion and ataxia may resemble the effects of severe alcohol intoxication, but they persist after intoxication wears off. Some patients with Wernicke's encephalopathy will recover completely without residual memory deficits, particularly if they are treated quickly with thiamin.

The chronic stage of Wernicke-Korsakoff syndrome, sometimes called Korsakoff **psychosis**, is distinguished by anterograde amnesia, and most untreated patients with Wernicke's encephalopathy will develop this severe memory disorder, which prevents them from forming lasting memories of events or information encountered after the onset of the initial symptoms. Symptoms of Korsakoff syndrome may also develop spontaneously in many patients who never show signs of Wernicke's encephalopathy. Once patients develop Korsakoff's amnesia, recovery is unlikely.

Loss of memory for past events is called retrograde amnesia. Many people with Korsakoff syndrome have some retrograde amnesia in addition to anterograde amnesia, particularly for events that occurred shortly before the onset of illness, but most can recall the distant past without difficulty.

Immediate memory is not affected. For instance, an individual with Korsakoff syndrome could repeat a sentence or string of numbers immediately after hearing them, although this information would likely be forgotten within half a minute. Preservation of immediate memory allows individuals with Korsakoff syndrome to interact with others and respond to questions. Implicit memory is also preserved, so people with Korsakoff syndrome can learn new motor skills or develop conditioned reactions to stimuli. For example, individuals who play computer games can show improved performance each time they play, even if they cannot explicitly remember having played the game before.

Confabulation is another striking feature of Korsakoff syndrome, although it is not always observed. Confabulation refers to falsification of memory. The individual appears to be making up stories to cover up for inability to remember. Confabulation often seems to involve a confusion of the past and present. For example, if patients with Korsakoff syndrome are asked why they are in the hospital, they may say they just had a baby, are recovering from pneumonia, undergoing medical tests, or even applying for a job.

Patients with Wernicke-Korsakoff syndrome may also show signs of **apathy** and a lack of spontaneous behavior. Emotional expression may be lacking as well.

Interestingly, autopsies often reveal brain lesions characteristic of Wernicke-Koraskoff syndrome in alcoholic patients who showed general cognitive problems like those seen in **dementia**, but who never developed anterograde amnesia. These findings suggest that onset may be gradual in some patients.

Demographics

When **diagnosis** is based on postmortem findings, the estimated prevalence of Wernicke-Korsakoff syndrome is between 1 and 2% of the population. The classic presentation with acute onset of Wernicke's encephalopathy is fairly rare, about 0.05% of all hospital admissions, although this does not account for patients who do not seek medical attention. Wernicke-Korsakoff syndrome usually follows many years of chronic alcoholism or malnutrition and is seldom seen among people under 20. Most patients are 40 years of age or older. The disorder is apparently more common in alcoholic individuals who are particularly vulnerable to malnutrition such as indigent or homeless people.

Diagnosis

Wernicke's encephalopathy is diagnosed when patients seek medical attention and have the classic trio of signs: mental confusion, eye movement disorders, and ataxia. The diagnosis of Korsakoff syndrome is given when anterograde amnesia is present in an individual with a history of chronic, heavy drinking or malnutrition. When Korsakoff syndrome follows Wernicke's encephalopathy, the entire Wernicke-Korsakoff syndrome diagnosis is appropriate. The diagnosis is supported by neuroimaging or autopsy findings showing degeneration of the thalamus and mammillary bodies and loss of brain volume in the area surrounding the fourth ventricle—a fluid-filled cavity near the brainstem.

Although *DSM-IV-TR* criteria for alcohol-induced persisting amnestic disorder apply to most people with Wernicke-Korsakoff syndrome, there are some differences between the two diagnoses. Despite research findings suggesting that severe amnesia is not a necessary symptom of Wernicke-Korsakoff syndrome, the *DSM-IV-TR* requires the presence of either anterograde or retrograde amnesia for a diagnosis of alcohol-induced persisting amnestic disorder. One additional cognitive symptom is also required. Symptoms listed in the *DSM-IV-TR* include language disturbance (aphasia), inability to carry out motor activities (apraxia), inability to recognize objects (agnosia), or deficits in planning, initiation, organization and abstraction (executive functions). Individuals with Wernicke-Korsakoff syndrome frequently demonstrate problems with executive functions that contribute to the symptoms of confabulation and apathy. Aphasia, apraxia, and agnosia are not common signs of Wernicke-Korsakoff syndrome.

The *DSM-IV-TR* also requires that memory impairment must significantly impair a person's ability to perform normal activities and functions, and it must represent a decline from a previous level of functioning. Amnesia cannot occur exclusively during states of **delirium**, alcohol intoxication, or withdrawal, or be exclusively associated with a dementia. Both of the these requirements are consistent with the usual presentation of Wernicke-Korsakoff syndrome.

Finally, the *DSM-IV-TR* requires evidence that amnesia is caused by use of alcohol. Such evidence can include an extensive history of heavy drinking; or physical examination or laboratory findings revealing other signs of heavy alcohol use, such as abnormal liver function tests. Despite this *DSM-IV-TR* requirement, Wernicke-Korsakoff's syndrome can occur in the absence of heavy alcohol use. Emergence of the disorder in people without alcoholism is much less common today than it was in the past, however, since vitamins are now added to many foods. In practice, most people who show the hallmark symptoms of Wernicke-Korsakoff syndrome also qualify for the *DSM-IV-TR* diagnosis.

Treatments

Nutritional

Individuals with signs of Wernicke's encephalopathy should be treated with thiamin immediately. In many cases, prompt administration of thiamin reverses the symptoms and prevents amnesia from developing. Thiamin can be administered intravenously or directly into the digestive system. Unfortunately, thiamin is less effective in the chronic phase of the condition. Based on autopsy findings suggesting the presence of Wernicke-Korsakoff syndrome in people with milder cognitive problems who do not show the classic signs of the disorder, researchers have examined the usefulness of thiamin treatment in people with alcohol dependence who are at risk of developing the syndrome. Results suggest that thiamin treatment improves performance on memory tests in this group, and that higher thiamin doses are associated with better performance. These findings suggest that thiamin treatment can help prevent Wernicke-Korsakoff syndrome in heavy drinkers.

Medication

Recent reports suggest that **donepezil** and **rivastigmine**, drugs used to treat **Alzheimer's disease**, may improve memory in patients with Wernicke-Korsakoff syndrome. Both drugs prevent the breakdown of the neurotransmitter acetylcholine, which is important for the formation of memories. Patients treated with these drugs showed improvements on memory tests and were more able to recognize hospital staff and family members. Although improvements appear to be rather modest, these drugs may be useful for patients who do not respond to thiamin. Antidepressants that increase levels of serotonin may also be helpful, although the reasons why are not clear since these drugs are not effective with other memory disorders.

Conditioning

The fact that implicit memory is not affected by Wernicke-Korsakoff syndrome has led some researchers to explore the use of classical conditioning procedures in helping patients to remember specific people. In classical conditioning, animals and people learn to associate a stimulus with an outcome. The most famous example is the pairing of a ringing bell with food. Dogs naturally salivate when given food. In a famous experiment, Ivan Pavlov rang a bell immediately before serving food to dogs. After doing this repeatedly, Pavlov found that the dogs salivated upon hearing the bell ring even when the food was not presented. This form of learning does not rely on the hippocampus and cortex but appears to involve neurons in other parts of the brain. Patients with Wernicke-Korsakoff syndrome who are given specific rewards for correctly choosing a picture of a face that matches a face they have seen previously are more able to choose the correct face than those who do not receive the rewards. Although these individuals do not explicitly remember the face they saw previously, they are still able to make the correct choice. Training patients in this way could enable them to recognize familiar people and differentiate them from strangers.

Prognosis

The prognosis for full recovery from Wernicke-Korsakoff syndrome is poor. Once chronic Korsakoff's amnesia ensues, approximately 80% of patients will never fully recover the ability to learn and remember new information. Because they cannot learn from experience, individuals with Wernicke-Korsakoff syndrome almost always require some form of custodial care. They are usually unable to work, although some can perform simple tasks they learned prior to onset of the condition if closely supervised.

Prevention

Wernicke-Korsakoff syndrome can be prevented with a nutritious diet containing sufficient thiamin. Because severe chronic alcoholism is the most common cause of thiamin deficiency, treatment of alcohol dependence is extremely important. In order to prevent Wernicke-Korsakoff syndrome among people who are unable to stop drinking or among particularly vulnerable individuals like homeless drinkers, some researchers and clinicians have advocated supplementing alcoholic beverages with thiamin.

See also Alcohol and related disorders; Amnestic disorders; Brain; Dementia; Executive function

Resources

BOOKS

American Psychiatric Association. *Diagnostic and Statistical Manual of Mental Disorders.* 4th edition, text revised. Washington, DC: American Psychiatric Association, 2000.

Hochhalter, Angela K., Whitney A. Sweeney, Lisa M. Savage, Bruce L. Bakke, and J. Bruce Overmier. "Using animal models to address the memory deficits of Wernicke-Korsakoff syndrome." In *Animal Research in Human Health: Advancing Human Welfare Through Behavioral Science,* edited by Marilyn E. Carroll and J. Bruce Overmier. Washington, DC: American Psychological Association, 2001.

Mesulam, M.-Marsel. *Principles of Behavioral and Cognitive Neurology.* 2nd edition. Oxford: Oxford University Press, 2000.

Nolte, John. *The Human Brain: An Introduction to Its Functional Anatomy.* 5th edition. St. Louis: Mosby, 2002.

Walsh, Kevin and David Darby. *Neuropsychology: A Clinical Approach.* 4th edition. Edinburgh: Churchill Livingstone, 1999.

PERIODICALS

Ambrose, Margaret L., Stephen C. Bowden, and Greg Whelen. "Thiamin treatment and working memory function of alcohol-dependent people: Preliminary findings." *Alcoholism: Clinical and Experimental Research* 25, no. 1 (2001): 112-116.

Angunawela, Indira I. and Andrew Barker. "Anticholinesterase drugs for alcoholic Korsakoff syndrome." *International Journal of Geriatric Psychiatry* 16 (2001): 338-339.

Harding, Antony, Glenda Halliday, Diana Caine, and Jillian Kril. "Degeneration of anterior thalamic nuclei differentiates alcoholics with amnesia." *Brain* 123 (2000): 141-154.

Iga, Jun-Ichi, Makoto Araki, Yasuhito Ishimoto, and Tetsuro Ohmori. "A case of Korsakoff's syndrome improved by high doses of donepezil." *Alcohol and Alcoholism* 36, no. 6 (2001): 553-555.

ORGANIZATIONS

Family Caregiver Alliance. 690 Market Street, Suite 600, San Francisco, CA 94104. <http://www.caregiver.org/>.

Medical Council on Alcohol. 3 St. Andrew's Place, Regent's Park, London, UK NW1 4LB. <http://www.medicouncilalcol.demon.co.uk>.

National Institute on Alcohol Abuse and Alcoholism (NIAAA). Willco Building, 6000 Executive Boulevard, Bethesda, MD 20892. <http://www.niaaa.nih.gov>.

OTHER

Memory Loss and the Brain Newsletter, Memory Disorders Project, Rutgers University, 197 University Avenue, Newark, NJ 07102 <http://www.memorylossonline.com/>.

Danielle Barry, M.S.

Wide Range Achievement Test

Definition

Wide Range Achievement Test, 3rd ed. or WRAT-3 is a screening test that can be administered to determine if a more comprehensive achievement test is needed. Achievement tests refer to skills that individuals learn through direct instruction or **intervention**.

Purpose

The WRAT-3 measures basic skills in reading, arithmetic, and spelling. The test covers ages from five to 75 years old and takes approximately 30 minutes to administer.

Precautions

Although screening instruments may save time, these instruments can sometimes have misleading results. For instance, the scores may overestimate or underestimate a person's skills or the test does not measure other important achievement abilities. To obtain a more in-depth result of an examinee's abilities, a more comprehensive achievement test must be administered. For example, the WRAT-3 has no assessment of fundamental skills such as reading comprehension, writing abilities, and applying mathematical concepts to real-life situations. Finally, psychometric testing requires a clinically trained examiner. Therefore, the test should only be administered and interpreted by a trained examiner.

Description

The WRAT-3 has two alternative testing forms (tan and blue). One form is administered with the second form available if needed. Both testing forms (both the tan and blue forms) can be administered. When this is done, a combined scored is obtained. Each testing form consists of one reading test, one arithmetic test, and one spelling test. The reading test is administered individually, but the other two tests may be given in groups of up to five people. The reading test consists of 15 letters and 42 individual words that the examinee is asked to name or pronounce. The spelling test consists of writing one's name, 13 letters, and up to 40 words dictated to the examinee and used in a sentence. The spelling items increase with difficulty. Finally, the arithmetic test consists of two parts. Part I requires counting, reading number symbols, and solving simple arithmetic problems that are verbally presented to the examinee. Part II consists of using paper and a pencil to calculate up to 40 arithmetic problems within 15 minutes. These arithmetic problems are presented in a test booklet.

KEY TERMS

Normal curve equivalents—Standard scores with an average of 100. The normal curve equivalents divide the normal or bell-shaped curve into 100 equal parts. As a result, those scores can be used for statistical analysis because they can be added, subtracted, multiplied and divided.

Percentile ranks—The point at which a given percentage of people fall at or below the individual's test score being calculated. For example, if a person's test score was at the 60th percentile, 40% of other test takers received a higher score, while 60% received a score that was at or below that of the test taker.

Psychometric—Pertaining to testing and measurement of mental or psychological abilities. Psychometric tests convert an individual's psychological traits and attributes into a numerical estimation or evaluation.

Results

Scoring consists of a 1 for a correct answer and a 0 for an incorrect answer. The raw scores are converted to standard scores. These are scores that allow the examiner to compare the individual's score to other people who have taken the test. Additionally, by converting raw scores to standard scores the examiner has uniform scores and can more easily compare an individual's performance on one test with the individual's performance on another test. The average score for each test of the WRAT-3 is 100. An examiner can also obtain grade-equivalent scores, percentile ranks, and normal curve equivalents. A poor performance in any of the three areas assessed by this instrument can indicate the need for further testing.

Resources

BOOKS

Kaufman, Alan, S., and Elizabeth O. Lichtenberger. *Assessing Adolescent and Adult Intelligence*. Boston: Allyn and Bacon, 2001.

Sattler, Jerome M. "Assessment of Academic Achievement." In *Assessment of Children: Behavioral and Clinical Applications*. 4th ed. San Diego: Jerome M. Sattler, Publisher, Inc., 2002.

Wilkinson, G. S. *Wide Range Achievement Test–Revision 3*. Wilmington, DE: Jastak Association, 1993.

Keith Beard, Psy.D.

WISC *see* **Wechsler Intelligence Scale for Children**

Xanax *see* **Alprazolam**

Yoga

Definition

Yoga is an ancient system of breathing practices, physical exercises and postures, and **meditation** intended to integrate the practitioner's body, mind, and spirit. It originated in India several thousand years ago, and its principles were first written down by a scholar named Patanjali in the second century B.C. The word *yoga* comes from a Sanskrit word, *yukti*, and means "union" or "yoke." The various physical and mental disciplines of yoga were seen as a method for individuals to attain union with the divine.

In the contemporary West, however, yoga is more often regarded as a beneficial form of physical exercise than as a philosophy or total way of life. As of 2002, more than six million people in the United States were practicing some form of yoga, with 1.7 million claiming to practice it regularly.

Purpose

Yoga has been recommended as an adjunct to **psychotherapy** and standard medical treatments for a number of reasons. Its integration of the mental, physical, and spiritual dimensions of human life is helpful to patients struggling with distorted cognitions or pain syndromes. The stretching, bending, and balancing involved in the asanas (physical postures that are part of a yoga practice) help to align the head and spinal column; stimulate the circulatory system, endocrine glands, and other organs; and keep muscles and joints strong and flexible. Yoga programs have been shown to reduce the risk of heart disease by lowering blood pressure and anxiety levels. The breath control exercises, known as *pranayama*, emphasize slow and deep abdominal breathing. They benefit the respiratory system, help to induce a sense of relaxation, and are useful in pain management. The meditation that is an integral part of classical yoga practice has been shown to strengthen the human immune system. Although Western medical researchers have been studying yoga only since the 1970s, clinical trials in the United States have demonstrated its effectiveness in treating asthma, osteoarthritis, heart disease, stress-related illnesses, high blood pressure, anxiety, and mood disorders. Other reports indicate that yoga merits further research in the treatment of **obsessive-compulsive disorder** (OCD) and substance abuse. Studies done in Germany have focused on the psychological benefits of yoga. One clinical trial done in 1994 at the University of Wurzburg found that the volunteer subjects who had practiced yoga scored higher in life satisfaction, with lower levels of irritability and pychosomatic complaints, than the control group.

One of the advantages of yoga as a complementary therapy is its adaptability to patients with a wide variety of physical and psychiatric conditions. There are a number of different schools of yoga—over 40, according to one expert in the field—and even within a particular school or tradition, the asanas and breathing exercises can be tailored to the patient's needs. One can find special yoga courses for children; for people over 50; for people with fibromyalgia, arthritis, or back problems; for cancer patients; and for people struggling with weight. Although most people who take up yoga attend classes, it is possible to learn the basic postures and breathing techniques at home from beginners' manuals or videotapes. Patients who feel self-conscious about exercising in the presence of others may find yoga appealing for this reason. The American Yoga Association has produced a manual and videotape for beginners, as well as a book called *The American Yoga Association's Easy Does It Yoga* for persons wih physical limitations. In addition, yoga does not require expensive equipment or special courts, tracks, or playing fields. An area of floor space about 6 ft by 8 ft, a so-called "sticky mat" to keep the feet from slipping, and loose clothing that allows the wearer to move freely are all that is needed.

KEY TERMS

Asana—The Indian term for the poses or postures that are done in sequence during hatha yoga practice.

Hatha yoga—The form of yoga most familiar to Westerners; often practiced as a form of physical therapy.

Pranayama—The breathing exercises that accompany the asanas in hatha yoga.

Yogi (feminine, yogini)—A person who is a respected expert in or teacher of yoga.

Woman in child's pose, a hatha yoga position. *(Photo Researchers, Inc. Reproduced by permission.)*

Precautions

Patients with a history of heart disease, severe back injuries, inner ear problems or other difficulties with balance, or recent surgery should consult a physician before beginning yoga. Pregnant women are usually advised to modify their yoga practice during the first trimester.

People diagnosed with a dissociative disorder should not attempt advanced forms of pranayama (yogic breathing) without the supervision of an experienced teacher. Some yogic breathing exercises may trigger symptoms of derealization or **depersonalization** in these patients.

Yoga should not be practiced on a full stomach. It is best to wait at least two hours after a meal before beginning one's yoga practice. In addition, while yoga can be practiced outdoors, it should not be done in direct sunlight.

One additional precaution is often necessary for Westerners. Yoga is not a competitive sport, and a "good" practice is defined as whatever one's body and mind are capable of giving on a specific day. Westerners are, however, accustomed to pushing themselves hard, comparing their performances to those of others, and assuming that exercise is not beneficial unless it hurts—an attitude summed up in the phrase "no pain, no gain." Yoga teaches a gentle and accepting attitude toward one's body rather than a punishing or perfectionistic approach. A person should go into the stretches and poses gradually, not forcibly or violently. Stretching should not be done past the point of mild discomfort, which is normal for beginners; frank pain is a warning that the body is not properly aligned in the pose or that the joints are being overstressed. Most people beginning yoga will experience measurable progress in their strength and flexibility after a week or two of daily practice.

Description

There are six major branches of yoga: hatha, raja, karma, bhakti, jnana, and tantra yoga. Hatha yoga, the type most familiar to Westerners, will be discussed more fully in the following paragraph. Raja yoga is a spiritual path of self-renunciation and simplicity; karma yoga emphasizes selfless work as a service to others. Bhakti yoga is the path of cultivating an open heart and single-minded love of God. Jnana yoga is the sage or philosopher's approach; it cultivates wisdom and discernment, and is considered the most difficult type of yoga. Tantra yoga emphasizes transcending the self through religious rituals, including sacred sexuality.

Hatha yoga is the best-known form of yoga in the West because it is often taught as a form of physical therapy. A typical hatha yoga practice consists of a sequence of asanas, or physical poses, designed to exercise all parts of the body in the course of the practice. The asanas incorporate three basic types of movement: forward bends, backward bends, and twists. Practitioners of hatha yoga have over 200 asanas to choose from in creating a sequence for practice. The postures have traditional Indian names, such as Eagle Pose, Half Moon Pose, or Mountain Pose. There are steps for entering and leaving the pose, and the student is taught to concentrate on proper form and alignment. The pose is held for a period of time (usually 10–20 seconds), during which the practitioner concentrates on breathing correctly. Mental focus and discipline is necessary in order to maintain one's poise and balance in the asana. At the close of the practice, most students of yoga rest in a position that allows for a period of meditation. Most yoga practices take about an hour, although some are as short as 20 minutes.

There are a number of different styles of hatha yoga taught in the United States, the best known being Iyengar,

Demonstrations of the tree, cobra, and lotus yoga poses. The tree and triangle are good for balance and coordination. The cobra stretches the pelvic muscles and strengthens the back. Lotus is a meditative pose. *(Illustration by Electronic Illustrators Group.)*

Bikram, Kripalu, and ashtanga yoga. Iyengar yoga, which was developed by B.K.S. Iyengar, emphasizes attention to the details of a pose and the use of such props as blocks and belts to help students gain flexibility. Bikram yoga, taught on the West Coast by Bikram Choudhury, is practiced in heated rooms intended to make participants sweat freely as they warm and stretch their joints and muscles. Kripalu yoga, sometimes called the yoga of consciousness, emphasizes breathing exercises and the proper coordination of breath and movement. It also teaches awareness of one's psychological and emotional reactions to the various poses and movements of the body. Ashtanga yoga, developed by K. Pattabhi Jois, is the basis of so-called power yoga. Ashtanga yoga is a physically demanding workout that is not suitable for beginners.

Preparation

Good preparation for yoga requires spiritual and mental readiness as well as appropriate clothing and a suitable space. Many practitioners of yoga begin their practice with simple breathing exercises and stretches intended to clear the mind as well as open up the lungs.

Clothing should be comfortable and allow free movement. Some women prefer to practice in a dancer's leotard or similar garment made of stretchy fabric, but a simple tunic or beach cover-up worn over a pair of running shorts works just as well. Brassieres should not be worn during practice because they tend to restrict breathing. Men often practice in swim trunks or running shorts. Both men and women can use an oversize men's cotton T-shirt as a practice garment— these are inexpensive, easy to wash, and nonbinding. The feet are bare.

Aftercare

As was mentioned earlier, traditional hatha yoga practice ends the sequence of asanas with a pose in which meditation is possible, either sitting or lying flat on the back. Other than quiet resting, no particular aftercare is necessary.

Risks

Most reported injuries in yoga result from lack of concentration or attempts to perform difficult poses without working up to them. People who have consulted a physician before starting yoga and practice under the supervision of an experienced teacher are unlikely to suffer serious injury.

Normal results

Normal results following yoga practice are improved posture, lowered blood pressure, increased flexibility in the joints, higher energy levels, and a sense of relaxation.

Abnormal results

Abnormal physical results would include serious injuries to joints or muscles; abnormal psychological results would include dissociative episodes.

Resources

BOOKS

Choudhury, Bikram, with Bonnie Jones Reynolds. *Bikram's Beginning Yoga Class*. New York: Jeremy P. Tarcher/Perigee, 1978.

Feuerstein, Georg, and Stephan Bodian, eds. *Living Yoga: A Comprehensive Guide for Daily Life*. New York: Jeremy P. Tarcher/Perigee, 1993.

Pelletier, Kenneth R., MD. "Ayurvedic Medicine and Yoga: From Buddha to the Millennium." Chapter 10 in *The Best Alternative Medicine*. New York: Simon and Schuster, 2002.

PERIODICALS

Janakiramaiah, N., B. N. Gangadhar, P. J. Naga Venkatesha Murthy, and others. "Antidepressant Efficacy of Sudarshan Kriya Yoga (SKY) in Melancholia: A Randomized Comparison with Electroconvulsive Therapy (ECT) and Imipramine." *Journal of Affective Disorders* 57 (January-March 2000): 255–259.

Shaffer, H. J., T. A. LaSalvia, and J. P. Stein. "Comparing Hatha Yoga with Dynamic Group Psychotherapy for Enhancing Methadone Maintenance Treatment: A Randomized Clinical Trial." *Alternative Therapies in Health and Medicine* 3 (July 1997): 57–66.

Shannahoff-Khalsa, D. S., and L. R. Beckett. "Clinical Case Report: Efficacy of Yogic Techniques in the Treatment of Obsessive-Compulsive Disorders." *International Journal of Neuroscience* 85 (March 1996): 1–17.

ORGANIZATIONS

American Yoga Association. <www.americanyoga association.org>.

International Association of Yoga Therapists (IAYT). 4150 Tivoli Avenue, Los Angeles, CA 90066.

Yoga Research and Education Center (YREC). 2400A County Center Drive, Santa Rosa, CA 95403. (707) 566-0000. <www.yrec.org>.

Rebecca J. Frey, Ph.D.

Z

Zaleplon

Definition

Zaleplon is classified as a hypnotic drug. These drugs help people sleep. Zaleplon is available in the United States as the brand name drug Sonata.

Purpose

Zaleplon is a drug that is used to treat short-term **insomnia**, and it can be habit-forming.

Description

The United States Food and Drug Administration approved Zaleplon in 1999 to treat short-term problems sleeping. Zaleplon is thought to act by mimicking a chemical in the **brain** that helps to facilitate sleep. It is different from other sleeping pills, because it begins to work almost immediately and its effects are rather short-lived (a few hours). These properties make it beneficial both for people who have troubling falling asleep at bedtime and for people who awaken in the middle of the night and have trouble falling back to sleep. Zaleplon may be taken in the middle of the night so long as the person can sleep at least four more hours before having to awaken.

Zaleplon is available as capsules. The drug is broken down by the liver. It is a controlled substance and can be habit-forming.

Recommended dosage

The usual dose of zaleplon for adults is 5–20 mg. For healthy adults, 10 mg is a common dosage. However, people over age 65, small adults with low body weight, and people with serious health problems (especially liver disease) should take a dose at the low end of this range (usually 5 mg). Zaleplon is taken immediately before bedtime. It usually takes only about 30 minutes for the sleep-inducing actions of zaleplon to be felt, and sleep-facilitating effects appear to last only a few hours. If zaleplon is taken with a meal, it will take longer to work. For the fastest sleep onset, it should be taken on an empty stomach. The maximum dose for one day is 20 mg. Under no circumstances should a person take more than 20 mg in one day.

Precautions

Zaleplon can be habit-forming and should be taken exactly as directed by a physician. A person who forgets a dose of zaleplon should skip the dose and take the next dose at the regularly scheduled time.

Because zaleplon is used to help people fall asleep, it should not be used with other drugs (over-the-counter or prescription) that also cause drowsiness. Zaleplon should be used only with close physician supervision in people with liver disease and in the elderly, because these individuals are especially sensitive to the sedative properties of zaleplon. Zaleplon should not be used before driving, operating machinery, or performing activities that require mental alertness. People with a history of drug abuse, psychiatric disorders, or depression should be carefully monitored when using zaleplon since zaleplon may worsen symptoms of some psychiatric disorders and can become a drug of abuse.

If zaleplon is needed for more than seven to ten days, patients should be re-evaluated by a physician to determine if another disorder is causing their difficulty sleeping. When zaleplon or other sleeping pills are used every night for more than a few weeks, they begin to lose their effectiveness and/or people may become dependent upon them to fall asleep. Zaleplon can be addictive. People using zaleplon should not stop taking the drug suddenly because withdrawal symptoms, including sleep disturbances, may occur even if zaleplon has been used only for a short time.

KEY TERMS

Amnesia—A general medical term for loss of memory that is not due to ordinary forgetfulness. Amnesia can be caused by head injuries, brain disease, or epilepsy as well as by dissociation.

Antidepressant—A medication used to treat the symptoms of depression.

Antihistamine—A medication used to alleviate allergy or cold symptoms such as runny nose, itching, hives, watering eyes, or sneezing.

Antipsychotic—A medication used to treat psychotic symptoms of schizophrenia such as hallucinations, delusions and delirium. May be used to treat symptoms in other disorders, as well.

Hypnotic—A type of medication that induces sleep.

Milligram (mg)—One-thousandth of a gram. A gram is the metric measure that equals approximately 0.035 ounces.

Tuberculosis—An infection caused by the bacteria *Mycobacterium tuberculosis* that usually affects the lungs. Individuals with tuberculosis may have nighttime sweating, fever, weight loss, cough, and may spit up blood and mucus.

Side effects

Some sleeping pills such as zaleplon can cause aggressiveness, agitation, **hallucinations**, and **amnesia** (memory problems). A patient experiencing these side effects should call a physician immediately. A physician should also be called immediately if a person taking zaleplon develops a fast or irregular heartbeat, chest pains, skin rash, or itching.

The most common side effects of zaleplon are less serious and include dizziness, drowsiness, impaired coordination, upset stomach, nausea, headache, dry mouth, and muscle aches. Other side effects that may occur include: fever, amnesia, tremor, or eye pain. Many side effects appear worse at higher doses, so it is important to use the lowest dose that will induce sleep.

Interactions

Any drug that causes drowsiness may lead to substantially decreased mental alertness and impaired motor skills when taken with zaleplon. Some examples include alcohol, antidepressants such as **imipramine** or **paroxetine**, antipsychotics like **thioridazine**, and some antihistamines.

Because zaleplon is broken down by the liver, it may interact with other drugs broken down by the liver. For example, the drug rifampin, which is used to treat tuberculosis, may cause zaleplon to be less effective. Alternatively, cimetidine (Tagamet), a drug commonly used to treat heartburn, may cause people to be more sensitive to zaleplon.

Resources

BOOKS

Facts and Comparisons Staff. *Drug Facts and Comparisons.* 6th Edition. St. Louis: A Wolter Kluwer Company, 2002.

Wyeth Laboratories Staff. *Sonata Package Insert.* Philadelphia: A Wyeth-Ayerst Company, 1999.

Kelly Karpa, RPh, PhD

Ziprasidone

Definition

Ziprasidone is a drug used to treat **schizophrenia**. It is available with a prescription under the brand name Geodan.

Purpose

Ziprasidone is in a class of drugs called antipsychotics. It is used to control symptoms of schizophrenia.

Description

The United States Food and Drug Administration approved ziprasidone for treatment of schizophrenia in 2001. Mental well-being is partially related to maintaining a balance between naturally occurring chemicals in the **brain** called **neurotransmitters**. Ziprasidone is thought to modify the actions of several neurotransmitters and in this way restore appropriate function to chemical systems in the brain that are out of balance in people with schizophrenia.

Recommended dosage

The dosage of ziprasidone varies widely from one individual to another. A common initially dosage is 20 mg of ziprasidone taken twice daily. The dosage is gradually increased until symptoms of schizophrenia subside.

Dosages of up to 100 mg may be taken twice daily. Ziprasidone should be taken with food.

Precautions

Ziprasidone may alter the rhythm of the heart. Because of the risk of irregular heartbeats or even death, it should not be taken by people with a history of irregular or prolonged heart rhythms (long QT syndrome), those with heart failure, or individuals who have recently had a heart attack. People with a history of heart disease should discuss the risks and benefits of treatment with their doctor before starting ziprasidone. Ziprasidone may lower blood pressure to dangerously low levels, causing people to faint. It should not be taken by people who have slow heartbeats and those with low levels of potassium or magnesium in their blood.

Individuals with a history of seizure, even seizure brought on by drug or alcohol abuse, should use ziprasidone cautiously and with close physician supervision, because it may increase the tendency to have **seizures**.

Ziprasidone may increase body temperatures to dangerously high levels. People who exercise strenuously, those exposed to extreme heat, individuals taking drugs with anticholinergic effects (this includes many common antidepressants), and persons prone to dehydration, should use the drug cautiously and be alert to dehydration-related side effects. Elderly persons with increased risk of developing pneumonia should be carefully monitored while taking ziprasidone. Because there is a high incidence of **suicide** in all patients with psychotic illnesses, people using ziprasidone should be observed carefully for signs of suicidal behavior. Women who are pregnant or breast-feeding should not take ziprasidone.

Side effects

The most common reason that ziprasidone is stopped is due to development of a rash. Another common side effect is drowsiness. This side effect is usually worse when starting the drug and becomes less severe with continued use. People performing tasks that require mental alertness such as driving or operating machinery should refrain from doing so until they see how the drug affects them. Other side effects that may occur are abnormal, involuntary twitching (5%), and respiratory disorders (8%). Nausea, constipation, indigestion, and dizziness due to low blood pressure occur in more than 5% of people taking ziprasidone.

Other, less common, side effects are rapid heartbeats, low blood pressure, agitation, tremor, confusion, **amnesia**, dry mouth, increased salivation, joint pains, and abnormal vision.

The incidence of some adverse effects such as low blood pressure, anorexia, abnormal involuntary movements, sleepiness, tremor, cold symptoms, rash, abnormal vision, dry mouth or increased salivation appears to increase at higher dosages.

People taking ziprasidone should alert their health care provider immediately if they develop a rash or hives since this could indicate a potentially serious adverse reaction. Patients should also notify their health care provider immediately if they experience any abnormal involuntary muscle movements. People who think they may be experiencing any side effects from this or any other medication should talk to their physicians.

Interactions

Ziprasidone interacts with many other drugs. It is a good idea to review all medications being taken with a physician or pharmacist before starting this drug. Since ziprasidone may alter the rhythm of the heart, people who are also taking drugs such as quinidine, dofetilide, **pimozide**, sotalol, erythromycin, **thioridazine**, moxifloxacin, and sparfloxacin should not take it. These drugs may also affect properties of the heart and taken with ziprasidone increase the risk of irregular heart rhythms

KEY TERMS

Anticholinergic—Related to the ability of a drug to block the nervous system chemical acetylcholine. When acetylcholine is blocked, patients often experience dry mouth and skin, increased heart rate, blurred vision, and difficulty in urinating. In severe cases, blocking acetylcholine may cloud thinking and cause delirium.

Milligram (mg)—One-thousandth of a gram. A gram is the metric measure that equals about 0.035 ounces.

Neurotransmitter—A chemical in the brain that transmits messages between neurons, or nerve cells.

Schizophrenia—A severe mental illness in which a person has difficulty distinguishing what is real from what is not real. It is often characterized by hallucinations, delusions, language and communication disturbances, and withdrawal from people and social activities.

and other cardiac problems. Because ziprasidone causes sleepiness, it should be used sparingly and with care with other drugs that also have a tendency to make people drowsy such as antidepressants, antihistamines, some pain relievers, and alcohol. Ziprasidone may lower blood pressure to the point at which people feel dizzy or faint. People taking medication to regulate their blood pressure should have their blood pressure monitored and treatment modified as needed. Ziprasidone may also decrease the effects of drugs used to treat Parkinson's disease such as levodopa.

Other drugs taken in combination with ziprasidone may alter the effects of ziprasidone. For example, drugs such as **carbamazepine**, used to treat seizures, increases liver metabolism and may cause ziprasidone to be less effective. Alternatively, drugs such as ketoconazole slow liver metabolism and may increase negative side effects associated with ziprasidone.

Resources

BOOKS

Facts and Comparisons Staff. *Drug Facts and Comparisons.* 6th Edition. St. Louis: Facts and Comparisons, 2002.

Pfizer Staff. *Geodan Package Insert.* New York, New York: Pfizer Inc, 2001.

Kelly Karpa, RPh, Ph.D.

Zoloft *see* **Sertraline**

Zolpidem

Definition

Zolpidem is classified as a hypnotic drug. These drugs help people sleep. In the United States, zolpidem is available as tablets under the brand name of Ambien.

Purpose

Zolpidem is a drug that is used to treat **insomnia**. Zolpidem is especially helpful for people who have trouble falling asleep. However, once individuals have fallen asleep, zolpidem also helps them continue to sleep restfully. Zolpidem should be used only for short periods, approximately seven to ten days. If sleeping pills are needed for a long period, an evaluation by a physician is recommended to determine if another medical condition is responsible for the insomnia.

Description

Although the way zolpidem helps people sleep is not entirely understood, it is believed to mimic a chemical in the **brain** called gamma-aminobutyric acid (GABA) that naturally helps to facilitate sleep. Zolpidem is a central nervous system depressant. This means that it slows down the nervous system. Unlike some sleeping pills, zolpidem does not interfere with the quality of sleep or usually leave the user feeling sedated in the morning. As a result, most people using zolpidem usually awake feeling refreshed in the morning.

Recommended dosage

The usual dose of zolpidem in adults is 5–10 mg. For healthy adults, 10 mg is commonly recommended. However, people taking other drugs that cause drowsiness, people who have severe health problems, especially liver disease, and older people (over age 65) should take a lower dose, usually 5 mg. Zolpidem should be taken immediately before bedtime and only if the person can count on getting seven or eight hours of uninterrupted sleep. It usually takes only about 30 minutes for the sleep-inducing actions of zolpidem to be felt. Unlike some sleeping pills, the sleep-facilitating effects appear to last six to eight hours.

If zolpidem is taken with a meal, it will take longer to work. For the fastest sleep onset, it should be taken on an empty stomach. The maximum dose for one day is 10 mg. People who miss a dose of zolpidem should skip the missed dose, and take the next dose at the regularly scheduled time. Under no circumstances should a person take more than 10 mg in one day. Zolpidem should be taken exactly as directed by the prescribing physician.

Precautions

Because zolpidem is used to help people fall asleep, it should not be used with other drugs (either over-the-counter, herbal, or prescription) that also cause drowsiness (for example, antihistamines or alcohol). Zolpidem should be used only with close physician supervision in people with liver disease and in the elderly, because these individuals are especially sensitive to the sedative properties of zolpidem. Zolpidem should not be used before driving, operating machinery, or performing activities that require mental alertness. People with a history of drug abuse, psychiatric disorders, or depression should be carefully monitored when using zolpidem since zolpidem may worsen symptoms of some psychiatric disorders.

If zolpidem is needed for more than seven to ten days, patients should be re-evaluated by a physician to determine if another disorder is causing their difficulty

KEY TERMS

Amnesia—A general medical term for loss of memory that is not due to ordinary forgetfulness. Amnesia can be caused by head injuries, brain disease, or epilepsy as well as by dissociation.

Antidepressant—A medication used to treat the symptoms of depression.

Antihistamine—A medication used to alleviate allergy or cold symptoms such as runny nose, itching, hives, watering eyes, or sneezing.

Antipsychotic—A medication used to treat psychotic symptoms of schizophrenia such as hallucinations, delusions and delirium. May be used to treat symptoms in other disorders, as well.

Milligram (mg)—One-thousandth of a gram. A gram is the metric measure that equals approximately 0.035 ounces.

Tuberculosis—An infection caused by the bacteria *Mycobacterium tuberculosis* that usually affects the lungs. Individuals with tuberculosis may have nighttime sweating, fever, weight loss, cough, and may spit up blood and mucus.

sleeping. When zolpidem or other sleeping pills are used every night for more than a few weeks, they begin to lose their effectiveness and/or people may become dependent upon them to fall asleep. Zolpidem can be habit-forming when taken over a long period. People using zolpidem should not stop taking the drug suddenly, but gradually reduce the dose over a few days before quitting, even if zolpidem has been used only a for short time.

Side effects

Some sleeping pills such as zolpidem can cause aggressiveness, agitation, **hallucinations**, and **amnesia** (memory problems), rapid, racing heartbeat, and chest pains. These side effects are rare, but the patient should call a physician immediately if they occur.

Side effects that occur in more than 5% of patients are headache, nausea, muscle aches, and drowsiness. Although drowsiness is desired when trying to fall asleep, a few people continue to be drowsy the next day. Daytime drowsiness may cause people, especially the elderly, to be less coordinated and more susceptible to falls. Other less common side effects are anxiety, confusion, dizziness, and stomach upset.

Interactions

Any drug that causes drowsiness may lead to substantially decreased mental alertness and impaired motor skills when taken with zolpidem. Some examples include alcohol, antidepressants such as **imipramine** or **paroxetine**, antipsychotics such as **thioridazine**, and antihistamines (commonly found in allergy and cold medications).

The effectiveness of zolpidem may be reduced if taken with rifampin, an antibiotic that is commonly used to treat tuberculosis infections.

Resources

BOOKS

Ellsworth, Allan J., and others. *Mosby's Medical Drug Reference*. St. Louis, MO: Mosby, Inc, 1999.

Facts and Comparisons Staff. *Drug Facts and Comparisons*. 6th Edition. St. Louis, MO: Facts and Comparisons, 2002.

Medical Economics Co. Staff. *Physician's Desk Reference*. 56th edition. Montvale, NJ: Medical Economics Company, 2002.

Kelly Karpa, RPh, Ph.D.

Zyprexa *see* **Olanzapine**

SYMPTOMS LIST

The following list of symptoms is intended *not* for diagnosis, but to reveal patterns in symptoms and disorders and to provide a starting point for research or discussion with a health care provider. Not every symptom with all of its accompanying disorders could be included.

A

Admiration, need for
- narcissistic personality disorder

Aggression
- Alzheimer's disease
- antisocial personality disorder
- borderline personality disorder
- conduct disorder
- intermittent explosive disorder
- may occur with tic disorders
- may occur with vascular dementia
- oppositional defiant disorder
- paranoid personality disorder
- substance intoxication

Agitation
- Alzheimer's disease
- major depressive disorder
- substance use, abuse, or dependence

Agoraphobia
- may occur with panic disorder

Amenorrhea (loss of menstrual periods)
- anorexia nervosa
- bulimia nervosa

Amnesia (memory loss)
- acute stress disorder
- Alzheimer's disease
- dissociative amnesia
- dissociative fugue
- dissociative identity disorder
- post-traumatic stress disorder
- vascular dementia
- Wernicke-Korsakoff syndrome

Anxiety
- acute stress disorder
- adjustment disorder
- agoraphobia
- borderline personality disorder
- generalized anxiety disorder
- may occur with tic disorders
- nightmare disorder
- pain disorder
- panic disorder
- schizotypal personality disorder
- separation anxiety disorder
- sleep terror disorder
- social phobia
- specific phobias
- substance abuse
- substance intoxication

Apathy
- dysthymic disorder
- feeding disorder of infancy or early childhood
- Internet addiction
- major depressive disorder
- may occur with Wernicke-Korsakoff syndrome
- schizoaffective disorder
- schizoid personality disorder
- schizophrenia
- schizotypal personality disorder

Appetite, loss of
- major depressive disorder
- postpartum depression
- seasonal affective disorder
- substance dependence
- undifferentiated somatoform disorder

Arousal, sexual
- from receiving pain: sexual masochism
- from administering pain: sexual sadism

Attention difficulties
- attention-deficit/hyperactivity disorder
- major depressive disorder
- nightmare disorder
- post-traumatic stress disorder

Attention-seeking behavior
- histrionic personality disorder
- narcissistic personality disorder

Aversion to sex
- hypoactive sexual desire disorder
- sexual aversion disorder

Avoidance
- acute stress disorder
- agoraphobia
- of conflict or disagreement: dependent personality disorder
- of pleasure: schizoid personality disorder; schizotypal personality disorder
- of relationships: schizoid personality disorder; schizotypal personality disorder
- of sex: hypoactive sexual desire disorder; schizoid personality disorder; sexual aversion disorder
- of social situations: avoidant personality disorder; seasonal affective disorder; separation anxiety disorder; may occur with tic disorders
- of specific feared situations: social phobia
- of specific feared situations or objects: specific phobias

B

Binge eating, followed by purging
- bulimia nervosa

Bizarre behavior
- brief psychotic disorder
- delusional disorder
- schizoaffective disorder
- schizophrenia
- schizophreniform disorder

- schizotypal personality disorder
- Blood pressure changes
  - substance abuse
  - substance intoxication
- Body image issues
  - anorexia nervosa
  - bulimia nervosa
- Body temperature, raised
  - sleep terror disorder
  - substance abuse
  - substance intoxication
- Bowel movements, in inappropriate places
  - encopresis

C

- Calculations, difficulty performing
  - mathematical disorder
- Cataplexy
  - narcolepsy
- Catatonia
  - brief psychotic disorder
  - major depressive disorder
  - schizophrenia
  - schizophreniform disorder
- Cold hands and feet
  - anorexia nervosa
- Communication. *See* language difficulties
- Compulsions
  - obsessive-compulsive disorder
  - *See also* urge.
- Control, need to
  - obsessive-compulsive personality disorder
- Coordination impairment (motor skills)
  - Asperger's disorder
  - childhood disintegrative disorder
  - developmental coordination disorder
  - Rett's disorder
  - somatization disorder
  - substance intoxication
  - vascular dementia
- Criminal activity
  - antisocial personality disorder
- Cross-dressing
  - gender identity disorder
  - transvestic fetishism
- Crying, intense
  - separation anxiety disorder

D

- Daily activities difficulties
  - Alzheimer's disease
  - childhood disintegrative disorder
- Decision-making difficulties
  - dependent personality disorder
  - major depressive disorder
- Defiance
  - oppositional defiant disorder
- Delusions
  - Alzheimer's disease
  - brief psychotic disorder
  - delusional disorder
  - schizoaffective disorder
  - schizophrenia
  - schizophreniform disorder
  - shared psychotic disorder
  - substance abuse
- Dementia
  - Alzheimer's disease
- Denial
  - Internet addiction
  - subtance dependence
- Dependence on others
  - dependent personality disorder
- Depersonalization
  - acute stress disorder
  - borderline personality disorder
  - depersonalization disorder
  - dissociative identity disorder
  - panic disorder
  - post-traumatic stress disorder
- Depression
  - Alzheimer's disease
  - bipolar disorder
  - borderline personality disorder
  - cyclothymic disorder
  - dysthymic disorder
  - major depressive disorder
  - may occur with pyromania
  - may occur with sexual dysfunctions
  - pain disorder
  - postpartum depression
  - seasonal affective disorder
  - substance abuse
  - substance dependence
- Derealization
  - dissociative identity disorder
- Desire. *See* urge.
- Destruction of property
  - conduct disorder
- Developmental delays
  - feeding disorder of infancy or early childhood
- Diarrhea
  - somatization disorder
- Discomfort with one's anatomic sex and gender
  - gender identity disorder
- Dissociation
  - acute stress disorder
  - borderline personality disorder
- Dissociative amnesia
  - acute stress disorder
- Distress upon separation
  - separation anxiety disorder
- Dizziness
  - substance intoxication
- Dramatic behaviors
  - histrionic personality disorder
- Dry skin
  - anorexia nervosa

E

- Eating inedible items (like hair)
  - pica
- Emotions. *See* instability, emotional
- Empathy, lack of
  - narcissistic personality disorder
  - schizophrenia
- Erectile dysfunction
  - male erectile disorder
  - somatization disorder

F

- Fatigue
  - agoraphobia
  - anorexia nervosa
  - bipolar disorder
  - breathing-related sleep disorder
  - circadian rhythm sleep disorder
  - generalized anxiety disorder
  - hypersomnia
  - insomnia
  - Internet addiction
  - major depressive disorder
  - narcolepsy
  - pain disorder
  - postpartum depression
  - seasonal affective disorder
  - undifferentiated somatoform disorder

Fear of being alone
- dependent personality disorder

Fear of embarrassment or humiliation
- social phobia

Fear of specific object or situation
- specific phobias

Feigning symptoms
- malingering

Flashbacks
- acute stress disorder
- post-traumatic stress disorder

Food, fear/avoidance of
- anorexia nervosa

G

Gastrointestinal complaints
- somatization disorder
- undifferentiated somatoform disorder

Grandiose fantasies or behavior
- narcissistic personality disorder

H

Hair loss
- anorexia nervosa

Hair pulling
- trichotillomania

Hallucinations
- Alzheimer's disease
- brief psychotic disorder
- may occur with postpartum depression
- narcolepsy
- schizoaffective disorder
- schizophrenia
- schizophreniform disorder
- substance intoxication

Headache
- anorexia nervosa

Head growth, slowed
- Rett's disorder

Heart palpitations
- agoraphobia
- sleep terror disorder
- substance intoxication

Hospital admissions, multiple
- factitious disorder
- Munchausen syndrome by proxy

Hostility
- oppositional defiant disorder

Hyperactivity
- attention-deficit/hyperactivity disorder
- bipolar disorder

Hypomanic episode
- bipolar disorder
- cyclothymic disorder

I

Identity disturbances
- dissociative identity disorder

Impulsivity
- attention-deficit/hyperactivity disorder
- bipolar disorder
- borderline personality disorder
- substance intoxication

Inactivity
- pain disorder

Inflexibility (temperament, not physical attribute)
- autism
- obsessive-compulsive personality disorder

Insomnia
- acute stress disorder
- circadian rhythm sleep disorder
- major depressive disorder
- nightmare disorder
- pain disorder
- postpartum depression
- post-traumatic stress disorder
- Rett's disorder
- substance abuse

Instability, emotional
- borderline personality disorder
- histrionic personality disorder

Internet use, excessive
- Internet addiction

Interpersonal problems
- borderline personality disorder
- generalized anxiety disorder
- Internet addiction
- may occur with sexual dysfunctions
- pain disorder
- paranoid personality disorder
- pathological gambling
- may occur with pyromania
- substance abuse
- substance dependence

Irritability
- anorexia nervosa
- bipolar disorder
- borderline personality disorder
- cyclothymic disorder
- feeding disorder of infancy or early childhood
- generalized anxiety disorder
- Internet addiction
- may occur with vascular dementia
- nightmare disorder
- postpartum depression
- Rett's disorder
- seasonal affective disorder
- substance abuse or dependence

L

Lack of interest
- in activities normally enjoyable:
  - major depressive disorder
- in sex: hypoactive sexual desire disorder

Language difficulties
- Alzheimer's disease
- Asperger's disorder
- autism
- brief psychotic disorder
- childhood disintegrative disorder
- expressive language disorder
- mixed receptive-expressive language disorder
- phonological disorder
- schizoaffective disorder
- schizophrenia
- schizophreniform disorder
- schizotypal personality disorder
- substance intoxication
- vascular dementia

Learning difficulties
- Asperger's disorder
- learning disorders

Legal problems
- pathological gambling
- substance abuse

Listening difficulties
- attention-deficit/hyperactivity disorder

Loss of skills
- childhood disintegrative disorder
- Rett's disorder

Lying
- antisocial personality disorder
- conduct disorder

M

Manic episode
  bipolar disorder
Math, difficulties with
  mathematical disorder
Medical history, vague or inconsistent
  factitious disorder
Memory impairment
  substance abuse
  substance dependence
  substance intoxication
  See also amnesia
Mental clarity. *See* thinking impairments
Misinterpretation of events on regular basis
  schizotypal personality disorder
Mixed episode
  bipolar disorder
  cyclothymic disorder
Mood, abrupt changes in
  cyclothymic disorder
Movement difficulties
  Alzheimer's disease
  developmental coordination disorder
  slowed movements: major depressive disorder
  See also coordination impairment
Movement, involuntary
  medication-induced movement disorder
  tardive dyskinesia
  tic disorders
  vaginismus
Muscle, loss of control
  narcolepsy

N

Nausea
  agoraphobia
  bulimia nervosa
  social phobia
  somatization disorder
  substance intoxication
Nightmares
  nightmare disorder
  post-traumatic stress disorder
  separation anxiety disorder
Normal development, then loss of skills
  childhood disintegrative disorder
Numbers, difficulty with
  mathematical disorder

O

Object needed for sexual arousal
  fetishism
Obsessions
  obsessive-compulsive disorder
Odd beliefs
  schizotypal personality disorder
Orgasm difficulties
  female orgasmic disorder
  male orgasmic disorder

P

Pain
  administering: sexual sadism
  during sexual intercourse: dyspareunia; female sexual arousal disorder; somatization disorder; vaginismus
  pain disorder
  receiving: sexual masochism
  undifferentiated somatoform disorder
Panic attacks
  may occur with tic disorders
  panic disorder
  substance use; substance abuse
Paranoia
  borderline personality disorder
  paranoid personality disorder
  schizotypal personality disorder
  substance abuse
Perfectionism
  obsessive-compulsive personality disorder
Personal care difficulties
  Alzheimer's disease
Preoccupation with fears of serious physical illness or injury
  hypochondriasis
Preoccupation with others' reactions
  social phobia
Preoccupation with particular body part
  body dysmorphic disorder
Preoccupation with seeking and using substance
  Substance dependence
Preoccupation with weight/ body image
  anorexia nervosa
  bulimia nervosa
Producing symptoms deliberately
  malingering

R

Reading difficulties
  reading disorder
Recognition difficulties
  Alzheimer's disease
  vascular dementia
Regurgitation
  rumination disorder
Relationship problems. *See* interpersonal problems
Repetitive movements
  autism
  childhood disintegrative disorder
  Rett's disorder
  stereotypic movement disorder
Responsibilities, failure to live up to
  pathological gambling
  substance abuse
  substance dependence
Restlessness
  attention-deficit/hyperactivity disorder
  generalized anxiety disorder
Rigidity, muscular
  medication-induced movement disorder
  Rett's disorder
  See also inflexibility
Risk-taking behaviors
  substance abuse
Rule violations
  conduct disorder

S

Sadness. *See* depression
Scars, multiple
  from surgery: factitious disorder
  on hand from self-induced vomiting: bulimia nervosa
Seductive behavior

histrionic personality disorder
Seizures
  Rett's disorder
  substance intoxication
Self-esteem problems
  dependent personality disorder
  major depressive disorder
Sensitivity to criticism
  social phobia
Separation distress
  separation anxiety disorder
Sexual dysfunctions
  substance abuse
  substance dependence
  substance intoxication
Shaking. *See* trembling
Sitting up suddenly in bed
  sleep terror disorder
  sleepwalking disorder
Sleep attacks
  narcolepsy
Sleep cycle disturbances
  circadian rhythm sleep disorder
Sleep, disturbed nighttime
  insomnia
  may occur with tic disorders
  narcolepsy
  nightmare disorder
  post-traumatic stress disorder
  Rett's disorder
  sleep terror disorder
  sleepwalking disorder
Sleep paralysis
  narcolepsy
Sleepiness, excessive daytime
  hypersomnia
  insomnia
  Internet addiction
  nightmare disorder
Sleepwalking
  sleepwalking disorder
Snoring, sometimes followed by periods of silence
  breathing-related sleep disorder
Social skills impairment
  acute stress disorder
  adjustment disorder
  Asperger's disorder
  autism
  avoidant personality disorder
  childhood disintegrative disorder
  reactive attachment disorder of infancy or early childhood
Spasms, muscular
  medication-induced movement disorder
  tardive dyskinesia
  vaginismus
Speak, refusal to
  selective mutism
Speech. *See* language difficulties
Stealing, repeated and uncontrollable
  kleptomania
Stressful event, or stressor
  adjustment disorder
Substance use despite legal and interpersonal problems
  substance abuse
  substance dependence
Suicidal threats or behavior
  borderline personality disorder
  major depressive disorder
  may occur with schizophrenia

T

Thinking impairment
  Alzheimer's disease
  anorexia nervosa
  insomnia
  major depressive disorder
  schizophrenia
  substance intoxication
  vascular dementia
Tics
  tic disorders
Time, excessive amounts
  spent on the Internet: Internet addiction
Tolerance to a substance
  substance dependence
Trauma
  acute stress disorder
  post-traumatic stress disorder
Travel, unexpected
  dissociative fugue
Trembling
  agoraphobia
  developmental coordination disorder
  medication-induced movement disorder
  Rett's disorder

U

Unsteadiness
  developmental coordination disorder
  Rett's disorder
Urge for sexual activity with a child
  pedophilia
Urge to expose oneself
  exhibitionism
Urge to rub against a non-consenting person
  frotteurism
Urge to set fires
  pyromania
Urge to watch others when they are unaware
  voyeurism
Urination, in inappropriate places
  enuresis

V

Visual problems
  developmental coordination disorder

W

Wandering
  Alzheimer's disease
Weight, fear of gaining and refusal to maintain at normal level
  anorexia nervosa
Withdrawal symptoms (actual symptoms vary with substance)
  substance dependence
Writing difficulties
  disorder of written expression

GLOSSARY

A

ABSENCE SEIZURE. An epileptic seizure characterized by a sudden, momentary loss of consciousness, occasionally accompanied by some minor, jerky movements in the neck or upper arms, a twitching of the face, or a loss of muscle tone.

ABSTINENCE. Refraining from sexual intercourse for a period of time; may also refer to refraining from use of a substance, such as alcohol.

ABSTRACTION. Ability to think about concepts or ideas separate from specific examples.

ABUSE. Substance abuse is a milder form of addiction than substance dependence. Generally, people who have been diagnosed with substance abuse don't experience the tolerance or withdrawal symptoms—the signs of physiological dependence—that people dependent on a substance experience.

ACETYLCHOLINE. A naturally occurring chemical in the body that transmits nerve impulses from cell to cell. Generally, it has opposite effects from dopamine and norepinephrine; it causes blood vessels to dilate, lowers blood pressure, and slows the heartbeat. Central nervous system well-being is dependent on a balance among acetylcholine, dopamine, serotonin, and norepinephrine.

ACETYLCHOLINESTERASE. The chemical responsible for the breakdown of acetylcholine.

ACTIVE COPING STRATEGIES. Ways of handling stress that affect the problem or situation in some way.

ACUTE PSYCHOSIS. A severe mental disorder marked by delusions, hallucinations, and other symptoms that indicate that the patient is not in contact with reality.

ACUTE STRESS DISORDER. Symptoms occuring in an individual following a traumatic event to oneself or surrounding environment. Symptoms include a continued response of intense fear, helplessness, or terror within four weeks of the event, extreme nervousness, sleep disorders, increased anxiety, poor concentration, absence of emotional response to surroundings, and sometimes a dissociative amnesia—not recalling the significance of the trauma. Symptoms last a minimum of two days and maximum of four weeks. Can become post-traumatic stress disorder.

ADAPTOGEN. A remedy that helps the body adapt to change, and thus lowers the risk of stress-related illnesses.

ADDICTION. A compulsive need for, and use of, a habit-forming substance or behavior.

ADDICTIVE DISORDER. A disorder involving repetitive participation in a certain activity, in spite of negative consequences and despite attempts to stop the behavior. Alcohol abuse is an example.

ADDISON'S DISEASE. Disease caused by malfunctioning adrenal glands that can be treated with cortisol replacement therapy. Symptoms include anemia, low blood pressure, digestive complaints, and diarrhea.

ADENOSINE. A compound that serves to modulate the activities of nerve cells (neurons) and to produce a mild sedative effect when it activates certain types of adenosine receptors. Caffeine is thought to produce its stimulating effect by competing with adenosine for activation of these receptors.

ADJUNCT. A form of treatment that is not strictly necessary to a therapy regimen but is helpful.

ADJUSTMENT DISORDER. A disorder defined by the development of significant emotional or behavioral symptoms in response to a stressful event or series of events. Symptoms may include depressed mood, anxiety, and impairment of social and occupational functioning.

ADRENAL GLAND. A small organ located above each kidney that produces hormones related to the sex drive.

ADRENALINE. Another name for epinephrine, the hormone released by the adrenal glands in response to stress. It is the principal blood pressure-raising hormone and a bronchial and intestinal smooth muscles relaxant.

AEROSOL. A liquid substance sealed in a metal container under pressure with an inert gas that propels the liquid as a spray or foam through a nozzle.

AFFECT. The expression of emotion displayed to others through facial expressions, hand gestures, tone of voice, etc. Types of affect include: flat (inanimate, no expression), blunted (minimally responsive), inappropriate (incongruous expressions of emotion relative to the content of a conversation), and labile (sudden and abrupt changes in type and intensity of emotion).

AFFECTIVE DISORDER. A disorder involving extreme emotional experience that is not congruent with the environmental circumstances (for example, feeling sad when there is no easily identifiable reason, as in depression).

AGE-ASSOCIATED MEMORY IMPAIRMENT (AAMI). A condition in which an older person suffers some memory loss and takes longer to learn new information. AAMI is distinguished from dementia in that it is not progressive and does not represent a serious decline from the person's previous level of functioning. Benign senescent forgetfulness is another term for AAMI.

AGITATION. Excessive restlessness or emotional disturbance often associated with anxiety or psychosis. Agitation may be associated with middle-stage Alzheimer's disease.

AGNOSIA. Loss of the ability to recognize familiar people, places, and objects.

AGONIST. A chemical that reproduces the mechanism of action of a neurotransmitter.

AGORAPHOBIA. People with this condition worry that they will not be able to get help or flee a place if they have a panic attack and may refuse to go to places that might trigger a panic attack.

AGRANULOCYTOSIS. A blood disorder characterized by a reduction in the number of circulating white blood cells (granulocytes). White blood cells defend the body against infections. Agranulocytosis is a potential side effect of some of the newer antipsychotic medications used to treat schizophrenia.

AKATHISIA. Agitated or restless movement, usually affecting the legs. Movement is accompanied by a sense of discomfort and an inability to sit, stand still, or remain inactive for periods of time. Akathisia is a common side effect of some neuroleptic (antipsychotic) medications.

AKINESIA. Absence of physical movement.

ALBUMIN. A simple protein that is widely distributed in human blood.

ALLOSTASIS. The process of an organism's adaptation to acute stress.

ALOPECIA. Hair loss (also, loss of feathers or wool in animals).

ALTER. An alternate or secondary personality in a person with dissociative identity disorder. Each alter has a unique way of looking at and interacting with the world.

ALVEOLAR. Pertaining to alveoli, which are tiny air sacs at the ends of the small air passages in the lungs.

ALZHEIMER'S DISEASE. An incurable dementia marked by the loss of cognitive ability and memory over a period of 10–15 years. Usually affects elderly people.

AMBULATION. Ability to walk.

AMENORRHEA. Absence of menstrual periods.

AMINO ACID. A building block of protein.

AMNESIA. A general medical term for loss of memory that is not due to ordinary forgetfulness. Amnesia can be caused by head injuries, brain disease, or epilepsy, as well as by dissociation.

AMNIOCENTESIS. A test usually done between 16 and 20 weeks of pregnancy to detect any abnormalities in the development of the fetus. A small amount of the fluid surrounding the fetus (amniotic fluid) is drawn out through a needle inserted into the mother's womb. Laboratory analysis of this fluid can detect various genetic defects, such as Down syndrome, or neural tube defects.

AMOTIVATIONAL SYNDROME. Loss of ambition associated with chronic cannabis (marijuana) use.

AMPHETAMINE ABUSE. An amphetamine problem in which the user experiences negative consequences from the use, but has not reached the point of dependence.

AMPHETAMINE DEPENDENCE. The most serious type of amphetamine problem.

AMPHETAMINE INTOXICATION. The effects on the body that develop during or shortly after amphetamine use.

AMPHETAMINE WITHDRAWAL. Symptoms that develop shortly after reducing or stopping heavy amphetamine use.

AMPHETAMINES. A group of powerful and highly addictive substances that stimulate the central nervous system. May be prescribed for various medical conditions, but are often purchased illicitly and abused.

AMYGDALA. An almond-shaped brain structure in the limbic system that is activated in stressful situations to trigger the emotion of fear. It is thought that the emotional overreactions in Alzheimer's patients are related to the destruction of neurons in the amygdala.

AMYLOID. A waxy translucent substance composed mostly of protein, that forms plaques (abnormal deposits) in the brain during the progression of Alzheimer's disease.

ANALEPTIC. A substance that acts as a stimulant of the central nervous system. Caffeine is classified as an analeptic.

ANALGESIC. A substance that provides relief from pain.

ANANDAMIDE. One type of endocannabinoid that appears to help regulate early pregnancy.

ANANKASTIC PERSONALITY DISORDER. The European term for obsessive-compulsive personality disorder.

ANDROGYNY. A way of behaving that includes high levels of both masculinity and femininity.

ANEMIA. Condition that results when there is a deficiency of oxygen in the blood. Can cause fatigue and impair mental functions.

ANEURYSM. A symptomless bulging of a weak arterial wall that can rupture, leading to stroke.

ANGINA. Severe pain and a feeling of constriction around the heart.

ANGIOGRAPHY. A procedure in which a contrast medium is injected into the bloodstream (through an artery in the neck) and its progress through the brain is tracked. This illustrates where a blockage or hemorrhage has occurred.

ANHEDONIA. Loss of the capacity to experience pleasure. Anhedonia is one of the so-called negative symptoms of schizophrenia, and is also a symptom of major depression.

ANOREXIA. Loss of appetite or unwillingness to eat. Can be caused by medications, depression, or many other factors.

ANOREXIA NERVOSA. An eating disorder characterized by an intense fear of weight gain accompanied by a distorted perception of one's own underweight body.

ANOSOGNOSIA. Lack of awareness of the nature of one's illness. The term is usually applied to stroke patients, but is sometimes used to refer to lack of insight on the part of patients with schizophrenia. Anosognosia appears to be caused by the illness itself; it does not appear to be a form of denial or inappropriate coping mechanism. It is, however, a factor in nonadherence to treatment regimens and the increased risk of relapse.

ANOXIA. Lack of oxygen.

ANTI-ANXIETY AGENT. A medication that is used to treat symptoms of generalized fear that dominates a person's life.

ANTAGONIST. A substance whose actions counteract the effects of or work in the opposite way from another chemical or drug.

ANTECEDENTS. Events that occur immediately before the target behavior.

ANTEROGRADE AMNESIA. Amnesia for events that occurred after a physical injury or emotional trauma but before the present moment.

ANTHELMINTHIC. A type of medication given to expel or eliminate intestinal worms.

ANTICHOLINERGIC. Related to the ability of a drug to block the nervous system chemical acetylcholine. When acetylcholine is blocked, patients often experience dry mouth and skin, increased heart rate, blurred vision, and difficulty in urinating. In severe cases, blocking acetylcholine may cloud thinking and cause delirium.

ANTICHOLINERGIC TOXICITY. A poisonous effect brought about by ingestion of medications or other toxins that block acetylcholine receptors. When these receptors are blocked, the person taking the medication may find that he or she gets overheated, has dry mouth, has blurry vision, and his or her body may retain urine.

ANTICIPATION. In medicine, a phenomenon in which certain diseases manifest at earlier ages or in more severe phenotypes in each successive generation of an affected family.

ANTICOAGULANT. A medication (such as warfarin, Coumadin, or Heparin) that decreases the blood's clotting ability, preventing the formation of new clots. Although anticoagulants will not dissolve existing clots, they can stop them from getting larger. These drugs are commonly called blood thinners.

ANTICONVULSANT MEDICATION. A medication that prevents convulsions or seizures; often prescribed in the treatment of epilepsy. Several anticonvulsant medications have been found effective in the treatment of bipolar disorder.

ANTIDEPRESSANT. A medication used to treat the symptoms of depression.

ANTIHISTAMINE. A medication used to alleviate allergy or cold symptoms such as runny nose, itching, hives, watering eyes, or sneezing.

ANTIHYPERTENSIVE. An agent used in the treatment of hypertension (high blood pressure).

ANTIOXIDANT. Substance that protects the body from damaging reactive oxygen molecules in the body. These reactive oxygen molecules can come from inside the body or from environmental pollution and are thought to play a role in the aging process and the development of degenerative disease.

ANTIPSYCHOTIC MEDICATION. A medication used to treat psychotic symptoms of schizophrenia such as hallucinations, delusions, and delirium. May be used to treat symptoms in other disorders, as well.

ANTISOCIAL BEHAVIOR. Behavior characterized by high levels of anger, aggression, manipulation, or violence.

ANTISOCIAL PERSONALITY DISORDER. Disorder characterized by behavior pattern of disregard for others' rights. People with this disorder often deceive and manipulate, or their behavior might include aggression to people or animals or property destruction, for example. This disorder has also been called sociopathy or psychopathy.

ANTISPASMODIC. A medication or preparation given to relieve muscle or digestive cramps.

ANXIETY. A feeling of apprehension and fear characterized by physical symptoms (heart palpitations, sweating, and feelings of stress, for example).

ANXIETY AND ANXIETY DISORDERS. Chronic conditions that can be characterized by an excessive and regular sense of apprehension, with physical symptoms such as sweating, palpitations, and feelings of stress. Anxiety disorders can be caused by biological and environmental events.

ANXIETY-REDUCTION TECHNIQUES. Skills taught by a therapist to help an individual overcome anxiety, stress, and tension, and can include relaxation, visualization and imagery, diaphragmatic breathing, stress inoculation, and meditation.

ANXIOLYTIC. A preparation or substance given to relieve anxiety; a tranquilizer.

APATHY. Lack of feelings or emotions.

APHASIA. Loss of language abilities.

APHONIA. Inability to speak caused by a functional disturbance of the voice box or vocal cords.

APHRODISIAC. A medication or preparation given to stimulate sexual desire.

APLASTIC ANEMIA. A form of anemia in which the bone marrow does not produce adequate amounts of peripheral blood components such as red cells, white cells, and platelets.

APNEA. A brief suspension or interruption of breathing.

APOLIPOPROTEIN E. A protein that transports cholesterol through the body. One form of this protein, apoE4, is associated with a 60% risk of late-onset Alzheimer's disease.

APPERCEPTION. The process of understanding through linkage with previous experience. The term was coined by one of the authors of the Thematic Apperception Test to underscore the fact that people don't "perceive" the story cards in a vacuum; rather, they construct their stories on the basis of past experiences as well as present personality traits.

APPETITE SUPPRESSANTS. Medications that assist in weight loss by reducing appetite or increasing the sensation of fullness.

APRAXIA. Inability to perform purposeful movements that is not caused by paralysis or loss of feeling.

ARRHYTHMIA. Any disturbance in the normal rhythm of the heartbeat.

ARSON. The deliberate setting of fires for criminal purposes, usually to collect insurance money or to cover up evidence of another crime. It is distinguished from pyromania by its connection with planning and forethought rather than failure of impulse control.

ARTERIOSCLEROSIS. A thickening, hardening, and loss of elasticity of the walls of the arteries.

ASANA. The Indian term for the poses or postures that are done in sequence during hatha yoga practice.

ASPERGER'S DISORDER. A condition in which young children experience impaired social interactions and develop limited repetitive patterns of behavior.

ASSAULTIVE. An act with intent of causing harm.

ASSERTIVE. Confidently self-assured; able to express oneself constructively and directly.

ASSESSMENT. In the context of psychological assessment (a structured interview), assessment is information-gathering to diagnose a mental disorder.

ASSISTED SUICIDE. A form of self-inflicted death in which a person voluntarily brings about his or her own death with the help of another, usually a physician, relative, or friend.

ASSOCIATIONISM. A theory about human learning that explains complex psychological phenomena in terms of coincidental relationships. For example, a person with agoraphobia who is afraid of riding in a car may have had a panic attack in a car on one occasion and has learned to associate cars with the physical symptoms of a panic attack.

ASTRINGENT. A substance or compound that causes contraction or constriction of soft tissue.

ATAQUE DE NERVIOS. A culture-specific anxiety syndrome found among some Latino groups in the United States and in Latin America. It resembles panic disorder in some respects but also includes dissociative symptoms, and frequently occurs in response to a stressful event.

ATHEORETICAL. Unrelated to any specific theoretical approach or conceptual framework. The classification system of *DSM-IV-TR* is atheoretical.

ATHEROSCLEROSIS. Clogging of the arteries, creating a risk factor for stroke.

ATRIAL FIBRILLATION. A disorder in which the upper chambers (atria) of the heart do not completely empty with each contraction (heartbeat). This can allow blood clots to form and is associated with a higher risk of stroke.

ATTENTION DEFICIT DISORDER. A condition that mostly affects children and involves the inability to concentrate on various tasks.

ATTENTION-DEFICIT/HYPERACTIVITY DISORDER (ADHD). A learning and behavioral disorder characterized by difficulty in sustaining attention, impulsive behavior, and excessive activity.

ATYPICAL ANTIPSYCHOTICS. A group of newer medications for the treatment of psychotic symptoms that were introduced in the 1990s. The atypical antipsychotics include clozapine, risperidone, quetiapine, ziprasidone, and olanzapine. They are sometimes called serotonin dopamine antagonists, or SDAs.

AUDITORY. Pertaining to the sense of hearing.

AURA. An energy field that is thought to emanate from the human body and to be visible to people with special psychic or spiritual powers.

AUTISM. A developmental disability that appears early in life, in which normal brain development is disrupted and social and communication skills are retarded, sometimes severely.

AUTISTIC PSYCHOPATHY. Hans Asperger's original name for the condition now known as Asperger's disorder. It is still used occasionally as a synonym for the disorder.

AUTONOMIC NERVOUS SYSTEM. The part of the nervous system that governs the heart, involuntary muscles, and glands.

AVERSION. A strong feeling of dislike or disgust. Aversion therapy makes use of this feeling to reduce or eliminate an undesirable behavior.

AVERSION THERAPY. An approach to treatment in which an unpleasant or painful stimulus is linked to an undesirable behavior in order to condition the patient to dislike or avoid the behavior. Chemicals or medications used to produce unpleasant effects are called aversants.

AVOIDANT COPING STRATEGIES. Ways of coping with stress that do not alter the problem in any way, but instead provide temporary relief or distraction.

AYURVEDIC MEDICINE. The traditional medical system of India. Ayurvedic treatments include diet, exercises, herbal treatments, meditation, massage, breathing techniques, and exposure to sunlight.

B

BACK-UP REINFORCER. A desirable item, privilege, or activity that is purchased with tokens and serves as a delayed reward and subsequent motivation for desired behavior.

BARBITURATES. A class of medications (including Seconal and Nembutal) that causes sedation and drowsiness. They may be prescribed legally but may also be used as drugs of abuse.

BASAL GANGLIA. A group of masses of gray matter located in the cerebral hemispheres of the brain that control movement as well as some aspects of emotion and cognition.

BASELINE DATA. Information regarding the frequency and severity of behavior, gathered before treatment begins.

BATTERY. A number of separate items (such as tests) used together. In psychology, a group or series of tests given with a common purpose, such as personality assessment or measurement of intelligence.

BEHAVIOR. A stereotyped motor response to an internal or external stimulus.

BEHAVIOR DISORDERS. Disorders characterized by disruptive behaviors such as conduct disorder, oppositional defiant disorder, and attention-deficit/hyperactivity disorder.

BEHAVIOR MODIFICATION. An approach to therapy based on the principles of operant conditioning. Behavior modification seeks to replace undesirable behaviors with preferable behaviors through the use of positive or negative reinforcement.

BEHAVIOR THERAPIES. Numerous techniques all having their roots in principles of learning.

BEHAVIORAL CONTRACTS. A behavioral contract is a written agreement that defines the behaviors to be performed and the consequences of the specified behaviors.

BEHAVIORAL DEFICIENCY. Failure to engage in a positive, desirable behavior frequently enough.

BEHAVIORAL EXCESS. Engaging in negative, undesirable behavior too often.

BEHAVIORAL INHIBITION. A set of behaviors that appear in early infancy that are displayed when the child is confronted with a new situation or unfamiliar people. These behaviors include moving around, crying, and general irritability, followed by withdrawing and seeking comfort from a familiar person. These behaviors are associated with an increased risk of social phobia and panic disorder in later life. Behavioral inhibition in children appears to be linked to anxiety and mood disorders in their parents.

BEHAVIORAL PHENOTYPE. A term that refers to the greater likelihood that people with a specific genetic syndrome will have certain behavioral or developmental characteristics, compared to people who do not have the syndrome.

BEHAVIORAL THERAPY. An approach to treatment that focuses on extinguishing undesirable behavior and replacing it with desired behavior.

BENIGN PROSTATE HYPERTROPHY. Enlargement of the prostate gland.

BENZODIAZEPINES. A group of central nervous system depressants used to relieve anxiety or to induce sleep.

BEREAVEMENT. The emotional experience of loss after the death of a friend or relative.

BETA AMYLOID PROTEIN. A starchy substance that builds up in the brains of people with Alzheimer's disease to form the plaques that are characteristic of the disease. Beta amyloid is formed when amyloid precursor protein, or APP, is not broken down properly by the body.

BETA BLOCKER. Drugs that block beta-adrenergic receptors on neurons in the central nervous system. When these sites are blocked, heart rate, blood pressure, and anxiety levels decrease.

BEZOAR. A hard ball of hair or vegetable fiber that may develop in the stomach of humans as the result of ingesting nonfood items.

BINGE. An excessive amount of food consumed in a short period of time. Usually, while a person binge-eats, he or she feels disconnected from reality, and feels unable to stop. The bingeing may temporarily relieve depression or anxiety, but after the binge, the person usually feels guilty and depressed.

BINGEING. An excessive amount of food consumed in a short period of time. Usually, while a person binge-eats, he or she feels disconnected from reality, and feels unable to stop. The bingeing may temporarily relieve depression or anxiety, but after the binge, the person usually feels guilty and depressed.

BIOAVAILABILITY. Medication that is available in the body. If the bioavailability of a drug is increased, more is available to the body for use, and if it is decreased, less is available for use.

BIOCHEMICAL. Chemical reactions occurring in living systems.

BIOFEEDBACK. Biofeedback is a technique that uses monitoring instruments to measure and feed back information about muscle tension, heart rate, sweat responses, skin temperature, or brain activity.

BIOFIELD THERAPIES. A subgroup of energy therapies that make use of energy fields (biofields) thought to exist within or emanate from the human body. Biofield therapies include such approaches as Reiki, therapeutic touch, qigong, and polarity balancing.

BIOLOGICAL MARKER. An indicator or characteristic trait of a disease that facilitates differential diagnosis (the process of distinguishing one disorder from other, similar disorders).

BIOPSYCHOSOCIAL HISTORY. A history of significant past and current experiences that influence client behaviors, including medical, educational, employment, and interpersonal experiences. Alcohol or drug use and involvement with the legal system are also assessed in a biopsychosocial history.

BIOPSYCHOSOCIAL MODEL. A hypothetical explanation for why something occurs that includes biological, psychological, and social causes or correlates.

BIOSOCIAL. A biosocial model in psychology asserts that social and biological factors contribute toward the development of personality.

BIPOLAR AFFECTIVE DISORDER. A disorder in which a person alternates manic and depressive episodes.

BIPOLAR DISORDER (FORMERLY MANIC-DEPRESSIVE DISORDER). A mental disorder characterized by dramatic and sometimes rapid mood swings, resulting in both manic and depressive episodes.

BIPOLAR DISORDER NOT OTHERWISE SPECIFIED. Disorder of mood involving mood swings that do not meet criteria for other disorders specified above.

BIPOLAR DISORDERS. Disorders characterized by wide fluctuations in mood.

BIPOLAR I DISORDER. A major mood disorder characterized by full-blown manic episodes, often interspersed with episodes of major depression.

BIPOLAR II DISORDER. Disorder with major depressive episodes and mild manic episodes known as hypomania.

BLACKOUT. A period of loss of consciousness or memory.

BLENDED FAMILY. A family formed by the remarriage of a divorced or widowed parent. It includes the new husband and wife, plus some or all of their children from previous marriages.

BLEOMYCIN HYDROLASE. An enzyme involved in the body's processing of amyloid precursor protein. If the gene that governs production of BH mutates, the APP accumulates, producing the plaques in the brains of patients with Alzheimer's disease.

BLUNTED AFFECT. A term that refers to the loss of emotional expressiveness sometimes found in patients with schizophrenia. It is sometimes called flattened affect.

BODY IMAGE. A term that refers to a person's inner picture of his or her outward appearance. It has two components: perceptions of the appearance of one's body, and emotional responses to those perceptions.

BODY MASS. The quantity of matter in the body (measured by dividing weight by acceleration due to gravity).

BODY MASS INDEX, OR BMI. A measure of body fat, calculated as weight in kilograms over the square of height in meters.

BODYWORK. Any technique involving hands-on massage or manipulation of the body.

BORDERLINE PERSONALITY DISORDER. A severe and usually life-long mental disorder characterized by violent mood swings and severe difficulties in sustaining interpersonal relationships.

BRACHYCARDIA. Slow heartbeat, defined as a rate of less than 60 beats per minute.

BRAIN STEM. The part of the brain that is continuous with the spinal cord and controls most basic life functions. It is the last part of the brain that is destroyed by Alzheimer's disease.

BREEMA. An alternative therapy that originated in California in the 1980s. Breema combines biofield therapy with certain elements of chiropractics and bodywork.

BRUXISM. Habitual, often unconscious, grinding of the teeth.

BULIMIA NERVOSA. An eating disorder characterized by binges in which large amounts of food are consumed, followed by forced vomiting.

BUPRENORPHINE. A medication that blocks some of the withdrawal effects during heroin detoxification.

BURDEN. First described by Treudley in 1946, this term generally refers to the consequences for the family of close contact with a person who is severely mentally ill.

BURNOUT. An emotional condition that interferes with job performance, marked by fatigue, loss of interest, or frustration; usually regarded as the result of prolonged stress.

C

CAFFEINISM. A disorder caused by ingesting very high doses of caffeine (10g or more per day) and characterized by seizures and respiratory failure.

CALORIE. The quantity of heat necessary to raise the temperature of 1kg of water 1°C.

CANCER SCREENING. A procedure designed to detect cancer even though a person has no symptoms, usually performed using an imaging technique.

CANNABIS. The collective name for several varieties of Indian hemp plant. Also known as marijuana.

CANNABIS ABUSE. Periodic use of cannabis, less serious than dependence, but still capable of causing problems for the user.

CANNABIS DEPENDENCE. The compulsive need to use cannabis, leading to problems.

CANNABIS INTOXICATION. The direct effects of acute cannabis use and the reactions that accompany those effects.

CAPITATED PAYMENT SYSTEM. A contract between managed care organizations and health care providers involving a prepaid amount for blocks of services.

CARDIAC TAMPONADE. A condition in which blood leaking into the membrane surrounding the heart puts pressure on the heart muscle, preventing complete filling of the heart's chambers and normal heartbeat.

CARMINATIVE. A substance or preparation that relieves digestive gas.

CARPAL TUNNEL SYNDROME. A disorder of the hand and wrist characterized by pain, weakness, or numbness in the thumb and other fingers. It is caused by pressure on a nerve in the wrist. Carpal tunnel syndrome is frequently associated with heavy use of a computer, typewriter, or musical keyboard.

CARRIER. A vegetable oil such as safflower, olive, grapeseed, or wheatgerm oil used to dilute essential oils for massage.

CARVE-OUT PLANS. Managed care plans that make provision for mental health services by creating subcontracts involving different terms of payment and utilization review from those used for general health care.

CASE MANAGER. A professional who designs and monitors implementation of comprehensive care plans (i.e., services addressing medical, financial, housing, psychiatric, vocational, social needs) for individuals seeking mental health or social services.

CASE RATE. A type of contract between managed care organizations and health care providers involving a prepaid amount for services on a case-by-case basis.

CASTRATION. Desexing a person or animal by surgical removal of the testes (in males) or ovaries (in females). Castration is sometimes offered as a treatment option to violent rapists and pedophiles who are repeat offenders.

CATALEPSY. An abnormal condition characterized by postural rigidity and mental stupor, associated with certain mental disorders.

CATAPLEXY. A symptom of narcolepsy marked by a sudden episode of muscle weakness triggered by strong emotions. The muscle weakness may cause the person's knees to buckle, or the head to drop. In severe cases, the patient may become paralyzed for a few seconds to minutes.

CATATONIC BEHAVIOR OR CATATONIA. Term that describes both possible extremes related to movement. Catalepsy is the motionless aspect of catatonia—a person with catalepsy may remain fixed in the same position for hours on end. Rapid or persistently repeated movements, frequent grimacing and strange facial expressions, and unusual gestures are the opposite end of the catatonia phenomenon, involving an excess or distorted extreme of movement.

CATATONIC DISORDER. A severe disturbance of motor behavior characterized by either extreme immobility or stupor, or by random and purposeless activity.

CATATONIC SCHIZOPHRENIA. A subtype of a severe mental disorder that affects thinking, feeling, and behavior, and that is also characterized by catatonic behaviors—either extreme stupor or random, purposeless activity.

CATCHMENT. In mental health, a term that refers to a particular geographical area served by a particular mental health agency.

CATECHOLAMINE. A group of neurotransmitters synthesized from the amino acid tyrosine and released by the hypothalamic-pituitary-adrenal system in the brain in response to acute stress. The catecholamines include dopamine, serotonin, norepinephrine, and epinephrine.

CATHARSIS. A powerful emotional release followed by a feeling of great relief.

CATHETERIZATION. Placing a tube in the bladder so that it can be emptied of urine.

CENTRAL NERVOUS SYSTEM DEPRESSANT. Any drug that lowers the level of stimulation or excitement in the central nervous system.

CENTRAL NERVOUS SYSTEM STIMULANT. Any drug that raises the level of activity in the central nervous system.

CEREBRAL ATERIOGRAPHY. A procudure that allows a wire to be inserted in blood vessels in the brain, which generates an image of diseases in these arteries.

CEREBROVASCULAR. Blood flow in the brain.

CERVIX. The neck or narrow lower end of a woman's uterus.

CHAKRA. One of the seven major energy centers in the body, according to traditional Indian yoga.

CHASING. Betting larger and larger sums of money, or taking greater risks, in order to make up for money previously lost in gambling.

CHELATION. A method of treating lead or mercury poisoning by giving medications that remove heavy metals from the bloodstream. The medications that are used are called chelating agents.

CHOLINESTERASE INHIBITORS. A group of medications given to slow the progression of Alzheimer's disease.

CHOREATHETOID MOVEMENTS. Repetitive dance-like movements that have no rhythm.

CHROMATHERAPY. An alternative form of light therapy in which colored light is directed toward a specific chakra or part of the body in order to heal or correct energy imbalances. Practitioners of chromatherapy are sometimes called chromapaths.

CHRONIC OBSTRUCTIVE PULMONARY DISEASE. Disorder characterized by the decreasing ability of the lungs to ventilate adequately.

CHRYSIN. A flavonoid found in passionflower that may be the source of its anxiolytic properties.

CLASSICAL CONDITIONING. In psychology, a process in which a previously neutral stimulus eventually produces a specific response by being paired repeatedly with another stimulus that produces that response. The best-known example of classical conditioning is Pavlov's dogs, who were conditioned to salivate when they heard a bell ring (the previously neutral stimulus) because the sound had been paired repeatedly with their feeding time.

CLEARINGHOUSE. A centralized organization that is a repository of information and that facilitates access to information.

CLITORIS. The most sensitive area of the female external genitals. Stimulation of the clitoris causes most women to reach orgasm.

CLONIC-TONIC SEIZURE. This is the most common type of seizure among all age groups and is categorized into several phases beginning with vague symptoms hours or days before an attack. These seizures are sometimes called grand mal seizures.

CLOZAPINE. A newer antipsychotic medication that is often given to patients who are developing signs of tardive dyskinesia.

CLUSTER SUICIDE. Refers to the phenomenon of additional suicides being attempted or completed after one suicide has occurred within a small community, such as a group of high school students.

COCA PLANT. The plant that is the source of cocaine.

COCAINE. An illegal drug that increases energy and induces euphoria. It is addictive and is often abused.

CODEINE. A medication that may be prescribed but also may be purchased illegally and is used to reduce pain.

CODON. A three-member nucleotide sequence in messenger RNA that codes for a specific amino acid in synthesizing protein molecules.

COGNITION. The act or process of knowing or perceiving.

COGNITIVE. Pertaining to the mental processes of memory, perception, judgment, and reasoning.

COGNITIVE RESTRUCTURING. An approach to psychotherapy that focuses on helping the patient examine distorted patterns of perceiving and thinking in order to change their emotional responses to people and situations.

COGNITIVE STYLE. A way in which an individual works with and performs cognitive tasks such as reasoning, learning, thinking, understanding, making decisions, and using memory.

COGNITIVE THERAPY. Psychological treatment aimed at changing a person's way of thinking in order to change his or her behavior and emotional state.

COGNITIVE-BEHAVIORAL THERAPY (CBT). An approach to psychotherapy that emphasizes the correction of distorted thinking patterns and changing one's behaviors accordingly.

COGWHEEL RIGIDITY. An abnormal rigidity in muscles, characterized by jerky movements when the muscle is passively stretched.

COITUS. Sexual intercourse.

COLD TURKEY. A slang term for stopping the use of nicotine (or any other addictive drug) suddenly and completely.

COMA. Unconsciousness.

COMMUNITY MENTAL HEALTH CENTERS. Organizations that manage and deliver a comprehensive range of mental health services, education, and outreach to residents of a given community.

COMMUNITY MENTAL HEALTH CENTERS ACT OF 1963. Federal legislation providing grants for the operation of community mental health centers and related services.

COMORBID. Having another disorder or condition simultaneously.

COMORBID PSYCHOPATHOLOGY. The presence of other mental disorders in a patient together with the disorder that is the immediate focus of therapy.

COMORBIDITY. Association or presence of two or more mental disorders in the same patient. A disorder that is said to have a high degree of comorbidity is likely to occur in patients diagnosed with other disorders that may share or reinforce some of its symptoms.

COMPENSATORY. Counterbalancing or offsetting. A compensatory strategy is one that makes up for or balances a weakness in some area of functioning.

COMPETING BEHAVIORS. Behaviors that interfere with the target behavior because they are preferred by the individual.

COMPLEX ABSENCE SEIZURE. Absence (petit mal) seizures usually begin with a brief loss of consciousness and last between one and 10 seconds. People having a petit mal seizure become very quiet and may blink, stare blankly, roll their eyes, or move their lips. A petit mal seizure lasts 15–20 seconds. When it ends, the individual resumes whatever he or she was doing before the seizure began, and may not realize that anything unusual happened.

COMPLEX SEIZURE. In complex seizures, the person experiences impaired consciousness.

COMPLIANCE. In medicine or psychiatry, cooperation with a treatment plan or schedule of medications.

COMPULSION. A strong impulse to perform an act, particularly one that is irrational or contrary to one's will.

CONDUCT DISORDER. A behavioral and emotional disorder of childhood and adolescence in which children display physical aggression and infringe on or violate the rights of others. Youths diagnosed with conduct disorder may set fires, exhibit cruelty toward animals or other children, sexually assault others, or lie and steal for personal gain.

CONFABULATION. In psychiatry, the filling-in of gaps in memory with false information that the patient believes to be true. It is not deliberate telling of lies.

CONGENITAL. Present at birth.

CONGESTIVE HEART FAILURE. Condition characterized by abdominal pain, swelling in the lower extremities, and weakness caused by a reduced output of blood from the left side of the heart.

CONGRUENCE. A quality of the client-centered therapist, consisting of openness to the client.

CONSEQUENCES. Events that occur immediately after the target behavior.

CONSTIPATION. Difficult bowel movements caused by the infrequent production of hard stools.

CONTINGENCIES. Naturally occurring or artificially designated reinforcers or punishers that follow a behavior.

CONTRAST AGENT, or MEDIUM. A substance injected into the body that illuminates certain structures that would otherwise be hard to see on the radiograph (film).

CONTROLLED BEHAVIOR. The behavior to be changed by self-control strategies; also known as the target behavior.

CONTROLLING BEHAVIORS. Self-control strategies used to change the controlled or target behavior.

CONVERSION. In psychiatry, a process in which a repressed feeling, impulse, thought, or memory emerges in the form of a bodily symptom.

CONVERSION DISORDER. A type of somatoform disorder in which unconscious psychological conflicts or other factors take the form of physical symptoms that are produced unintentionally.

CONVULSION. A violent, involuntary contraction or series of contractions of muscles.

COPING. In psychology, a term that refers to a person's patterns of response to stress.

COPROLALIA. A vocal tic characterized by uttering obscene, hostile, or inappropriate words. A motor tic characterized by obscene gestures is called copropraxia.

CORONARY OCCLUSION. Blockage of the arteries supplying the blood to the heart.

CORPUS CALLOSUM. (plural, corpora callosa) A thick bundle of nerve fibers lying deep in the brain that connects the two cerebral hemispheres and coordinates their functions.

CORTEX. Region in the brain where sensation and perception are processed and integrated into thoughts, memories, and abilities; also where actions are planned and initiated.

CORTICOSTEROIDS. Any one of a number of hormonal steroid compounds that are derived from the adrenal gland.

CORTISOL. A steroid hormone released by the cortex (outer portion) of the adrenal gland when a person is under stress.

COVERT. Concealed, hidden, or disguised.

CRACK. A slang term for a form of cocaine that is smokable.

CREUTZFELDT-JAKOB DISEASE. A degenerative disease of the central nervous system caused by a prion, or "slow virus."

CRITICAL INCIDENT. Also known as a crisis event. An event that is stressful enough to overwhelm the coping skills of a person or group.

CROSS-DRESSING. Wearing clothing and other attire appropriate to the opposite sex.

CRYSTALLIZED INTELLIGENCE. A type of intelligence that reflects knowledge and skills influenced by a person's sociocultural environment.

CT SCAN. An imaging technique that uses a computer to combine multiple x-ray images into a two-dimensional cross-sectional image. The full name is *computed tomography*.

CUE. Any behavior or event in a person's environment that serves to stimulate a particular response. For example, the smell of liquor may be a cue for some people to pour themselves a drink.

CUTOFF SCORES. In psychological testing, scores that indicate the borderline between normal and impaired functioning.

CYCLIC AMP. A small molecule of adenosine monophosphate (AMP) that activates enzymes and increases the effects of hormones and other neurotransmitters.

CYCLOTHYMIA. An alternate name for cyclothymic disorder.

CYCLOTHYMIC DISORDER. A relatively mild mood disorder characterized by mood swings between mild depression to mild mania.

CYTOGENETICS. The branch of biology that combines the study of genetic inheritance with the study of cell structure.

D

DAWN SIMULATION. A form of light therapy in which the patient is exposed while asleep to gradually brightening white light over a period of an hour and a half.

DECISION-MAKERS. In some mental health contexts, the term refers to prison or court officials, treatment facility administrators, or family members.

DECONDITIONING. Loss of physical strength or stamina resulting from bed rest or lack of exercise.

DEDUCTIBLE. The amount of money that must be paid out of pocket by health care consumers before the insurance provider will make payments.

DEFENSE. An unconscious mental process that protects the conscious mind from unacceptable or painful thoughts, impulses, or desires. Examples of defenses include denial, rationalization, projection, and repression. Some defenses are considered to represent lower levels of maturation than others; thus, identifying a child's defenses may be helpful in evaluating his or her level of psychological maturity.

DEFENSE MECHANISMS. Indirect strategies used to reduce anxiety rather than directly facing the issues causing the anxiety.

DEINSTITUTIONALIZATION. The process of moving people out of mental hospitals into treatment programs or halfway houses in local communities. With this movement, the responsibility for care shifted from large (often governmental) agencies to families and community organizations.

DELIRIUM. A disturbance of consciousness marked by confusion, difficulty paying attention, delusions, hallucinations, or restlessness. It can be distinguished from dementia by its relatively sudden onset and variation in the severity of the symptoms.

DELIRIUM TREMENS. Serious alcohol withdrawal symptoms that must be treated in a hospital and that may include shaking, delirium, and hallucinations.

DELTA-9-TETRAHYDROCANNABINOL(THC). The primary active ingredient in marijuana.

DELUSION. A false belief that is resistant to reason or contrary to actual fact. A patient may be convinced, for example, that someone is trying to poison him or her, or that he or she has a fatal illness despite evidence to the contrary.

DELUSIONAL DISORDER OF THE PERSECUTORY TYPE. A psychotic disorder characterized by a patient's belief that others are conspiring against him or her.

DEMENTIA. A group of symptoms (syndrome) associated with a progressive loss of memory and other intellectual functions that is serious enough to interfere with a person's ability to perform the tasks of daily life. Dementia impairs memory, alters personality, leads to deterioration in personal grooming, impairs reasoning ability, and causes disorientation.

DEMENTIA INFANTILIS. Another term for childhood disintegrative disorder, used more frequently in the European medical literature. The Latin name literally means "early childhood dementia."

DEMENTIA PRAECOX. A late nineteenth-century term for schizophrenia.

DENIAL. A psychological defense mechanism that reduces anxiety by excluding recognition of an addiction or similar problem from the conscious mind.

DEPENDENCE. The adaptation of neurons and other physical processes to the use of a drug, followed by withdrawal symptoms when the drug is removed; physiological and/or psychological addiction.

DEPENDENT PERSONALITY DISORDER. Personality disorder characterized by a constant, unhealthy need to be liked and appreciated by others at all costs.

DEPERSONALIZATION. A dissociative symptom in which the patient feels that his or her body is unreal, changing, or dissolving.

DEPERSONALIZATION NEUROSIS. Another name for depersonalization disorder.

DEPRESSANT. Something that slows down functioning.

DEPRESSION. A mental state characterized by excessive sadness. Other symptoms include altered sleep patterns, thoughts of suicide, difficulty concentrating, agitation, lack of energy, and loss of enjoyment in activities that are usually pleasurable.

DEREALIZATION. A dissociative symptom in which the external environment is perceived as unreal or dreamlike.

DERVISH. A person who belongs to one of the various mystical and ascetic Muslim orders, such as the Sufis. A whirling dervish meditates by whirling or spinning in an ecstatic dance.

DESENSITIZATION. The reduction or elimination of an overly intense reaction to a cue by controlled, repeated exposures to the cue.

DESIGNER AMPHETAMINES. Substances close in chemical structure to classic amphetamines that provide both stimulant and hallucinogenic effects.

DETOXIFICATION. A process in which the body is allowed to free itself of a drug while the symptoms of withdrawal are treated. It is the primary step in any treatment program for drug or alcohol abuse.

DEVELOPMENTAL DELAY. The failure to meet certain developmental milestones, such as sitting, walking, and talking, at the average age. Developmental delay may indicate a problem in development of the central nervous system.

DEVELOPMENTAL DISABILITIES. Disabilities that are present from birth and delay or prevent normal development, such as mental retardation or autism.

DEXFENFLURAMINE (REDUX). A prescription appetite suppressant for weight loss that was withdrawn from the market due to unacceptable health risks.

DIABETES MELLITUS. A chronic disease affecting the metabolism of carbohydrates that is caused by insufficient production of insulin in the body.

DIABETIC NEUROPATHY. A condition in which the nerve endings, particularly in the legs and feet, become less sensitive. Minor injuries, such as blisters or callouses, are not felt and can thus become infected and become more serious problems.

DIAGNOSTIC AND STATISTICAL MANUAL OF MENTAL DISORDERS. A handbook for mental health professionals that includes lists of symptoms that indicate diagnoses of mental disorders.

DIATHESIS. The medical term for predisposition. The stress/diathesis model is a diagram that is used to explain why some people are at greater risk of suicidal behavior than others.

DIETHYLPROPION (TENUATE, TENUATE DOSPAN). A prescription appetite suppressant currently on the market for weight loss.

DIFFERENTIAL DIAGNOSIS. The process of distinguishing one disorder from other, similar disorders.

DIFFERENTIATION. The ability to retain one's identity within a family system while maintaining emotional connections with the other members.

DIGRAPH. A pair of letters that represents a single speech sound. In English, the *th* in "thumb" and the *ei* in "vein" are examples of digraphs.

DIPLOPIA. A disorder of vision in which a single object appears double. Diplopia is sometimes called double vision.

DISFLUENCY. Disruptions, breakage, or blockages in the forward flow of speech.

DISPLACEMENT. A psychological process in which feelings originating from one source are expressed outwardly in terms of concern or preoccupation with an issue or problem that the patient considers more acceptable. In some patients with body dysmorphic disorder, obsession about the body includes displaced feelings, often related to a history of childhood abuse.

DISSOCIATED. Feelings of experiencing an altered state of reality, similar to a trance state. During the period of dissociation, the affected person may feel as if he or she is an observer instead of a participant in events, and may feel as if surroundings are unreal or distorted.

DISSOCIATION. A reaction to trauma in which the mind splits off certain aspects of the traumatic event from conscious awareness. Dissociation can affect the patient's memory, sense of reality, and sense of identity.

DISSOCIATIVE AMNESIA. A dissociative disorder characterized by loss of memory for a period or periods of time in the patient's life. May occur as a result of a traumatic event.

DISSOCIATIVE DISORDERS. A group of disorders marked by the separation (dissociation) of perception, memory, personal identity, and consciousness. Depersonalization disorder is one of five dissociative disorders defined by *DSM-IV-TR*.

DISSOCIATIVE IDENTITY DISORDER (DID). Term that replaced *multiple personality disorder*. A condition in which two or more distinctive identities or personality states alternate in controlling a person's consciousness and behavior.

DISTENSION. The condition of being stretched or expanded, as the abdomen of a pregnant woman.

DISULFIRAM. A medication helps reinforce abstinence from alcohol in people who are recovering from alcohol abuse. If a person taking disulfiram drinks even a small amount of alcohol, he or she experiences facial flushing, headache, nausea, and vomiting.

DIURETIC. A medication or substance given to increase the amount of urine excreted.

DIZYGOTIC. Developed from two fertilized ova. Dizygotic twins are sometimes called fraternal twins.

DOMINANT HAND. The hand that one prefers to use when performing various tasks such as writing or throwing an object.

DOPAMINE. A chemical in brain tissue that serves to transmit nerve impulses (is a neurotransmitter) and helps to regulate movement and emotions.

DOUBLE ANXIETY. Acute anxiety from a recent stressful event combined with underlying persistent anxiety associated with generalized anxiety disorder.

DOUBLE-BLIND PLACEBO-CONTROLLED STUDY. A study in which patients are divided into two groups—those who will recive a medication, and those who will receive a placebo (a pill that looks like the medication but has no active ingredients). Neither the patients nor their physicians know which pill any specific patient is receiving.

DOUCHE. A jet or current of water, often with a medication or cleansing agent dissolved in it, applied to a body cavity for medicinal or hygienic purposes.

DOWN SYNDROME. A genetic disorder characterized by an extra chromosome 21 (trisomy 21), mental retardation, and susceptibility to early-onset Alzheimer's disease.

DREAM ANXIETY DISORDER. Another name for nightmare disorder.

DSM. Abbreviation for the *Diagnostic and Statistical Manual of Mental Disorders,* a handbook for mental health professionals that includes lists of symptoms that indicate specific diagnoses. The text is periodically revised, and the latest version was published in 2000 and is called *DSM-IV-TR*, for Fourth Edition, Text Revised.

DUE PROCESS. A term referring to the regular administration of a system of laws that conform to fundamental legal principles and are applied without favor or prejudice to all citizens. In the context of involuntary commitment or hospitalization, due process means that people diagnosed with a mental illness cannot be deprived of equal protection under the laws of the United States on the basis of their diagnosis.

DYSARTHRIA. A group of speech disorders caused by disturbances in the strength or coordination of the muscles of the speech mechanism as a result of damage to the brain or nerves. Difficulty talking and speaking.

DYSKINESIA. Difficulty in performing voluntary muscular movements.

DYSLEXIA. A type of reading disorder.

DYSMORPHIC. Malformed.

DYSPAREUNIA. Painful sexual intercourse.

DYSPRAXIA. Developmental dyspraxia is an impairment or immaturity of the organization of movement. It is a defect in the way the brain processes information, resulting in messages not being correctly or fully transmitted. The term dyspraxia comes from the word "praxis," meaning "doing" or "acting." Dyspraxia is associated with problems of perception, language, and thought.

DYSSOMNIA. A type of sleep disorder characterized by a problem with the amount, quality, or timing of the patient's sleep.

DYSTHYMIA. Depression of low intensity.

DYSTHYMIC DISORDER. A mood disorder that is less severe than depression but usually more chronic.

DYSTONIA. A neurological disorder characterized by involuntary muscle spasms. The spasms can cause a painful twisting of the body and difficulty walking or moving. Some medications can cause dystonia.

E

ECHOLALIA. Meaningless repetition of words or phrases spoken by another.

ECHOPRAXIA. Imitation of another person's physical movements in a repetitious or senseless manner.

ECSTASY. Best known of the so-called designer amphetamines, also known as MDMA. It produces both stimulant and hallucinogenic effects.

ECT. Electroconvulsive therapy is sometimes used to treat depression or mania when pharmaceutical treatment fails.

ECZEMA. An inflammation of the skin characterized by itching and oozing of a clear fluid.

EDEMA. Abnormal accumulation of fluid in the interstitial spaces of bodily tissue.

EGO. In Freudian psychology, the conscious, rational part of the mind that experiences and reacts to the outside world.

EGOCENTRICITY. Self-centeredness.

EJACULATION. The discharge of semen by the male reproductive organs.

ELECTROACUPUNCTURE. A variation of acupuncture in which the practitioner stimulates the traditional acupuncture points electronically.

ELECTROCARDIOGRAM. (EKG) A test that measures the electrical activity of the heart as it beats. An abnormal EKG can indicate possible cardiac disease.

ELECTROCONVULSIVE THERAPY. Medical treatment that uses electrical currents to cause seizures; sometimes used to treat depression.

ELECTROENCEPHALOGRAM. (EEG) A test that measures the electrical activity of the brain by means of electrodes placed on the scalp or on or in the brain itself.

ELECTROENCEPHALOGRAPH. (EEG) An instrument that measures the normal and abnormal electrical activity in the brain.

ELECTROENCEPHALOGRAPHY. The measurement and recording of the brain's electrical activity.

ELECTROLYTES. Substances or elements that dissociate into electrically charged particles (ions) when dissolved in the blood. The electrolytes in human blood include potassium, magnesium, and chloride.

ELECTRON. One of the small particles that make up an atom. An electron has the same mass and amount of charge as a positron, but the electron has a negative charge.

ELIMINATION. The medical term for expelling wastes from the body.

EMETIC. A medication intended to cause vomiting. Emetics are sometimes used in aversion therapy in place of electric shock. Their most common use in mainstream medicine is in treating accidental poisoning.

EMPATHY. A quality of the client-centered therapist, characterized by the therapist's conveying appreciation and understanding of the client's point of view.

EMPIRICAL. Verified by actual experience or by scientific experimentation.

ENCEPHALITIS. Inflammation of the brain.

ENCEPHALOPATHY. Brain disease that causes damage or degeneration.

ENCOUNTER GROUPS. A term coined by Carl Rogers for therapist-run groups that focus on personal exploration, experiencing in the here-and-now (that is, feelings and interpersonal exchanges occurring in the group setting), and genuine concern and honesty among the members.

ENDOCANNABINOIDS. Cannabis-like compounds produced naturally in the human body.

ENDOGENOUS DEPRESSION. Depression arising from causes within a person, such as chemical or hormonal imbalances.

ENDORPHINS. A group of peptide compounds released by the body in response to stress or traumatic injury. Endorphins react with opiate receptors in the brain to reduce or relieve pain.

ENERGY. The capability of producing force, performing work, or generating heat.

ENFLEURAGE. A technique for extracting essential oils from flower petals by placing them on a layer of purified fat.

ENURESIS. The inability to control urination; bed-wetting.

EPHEBOPHILIA. Sexual desire on the part of an adult for youths in the early stages of puberty, as distinct from prepubertal children.

EPHEDRINE. An amphetamine-like substance used as a nasal decongestant.

EPIDEMIOLOGY. The study of the causes, incidence, transmission, and control of diseases.

EPILEPSY. A neurological disorder characterized by the onset of seizures. Seizures are caused by a disturbance in the electrical activity in the brain and can cause loss of consciousness, muscle spasms, rhythmic movements, abnormal sensory experiences, or altered mental states.

EPINEPHRINE (ADRENALINE). The principal blood-pressure raising hormone secreted by the adrenal glands in response to stress; a bronchial and intestinal smooth muscles relaxant.

EPISODIC DYSCONTROL. Another term for intermittent explosive disorder.

EROTOMANIC DELUSIONS. Erotomanic delusions involve the mistaken conviction that someone is in love with the delusional person. Often, the love object is a public figure of some prominence, such as an actress, rock star, or political figure. David Letterman and Jodie Foster are celebrities who have both been victimized by persons with erotomanic delusions.

ESSENTIAL FATTY ACIDS (EFAS). a group of polyunsaturated fats that are essential to life and growth but cannot be produced by the body.

ESSENTIAL OIL. The product of special ducts or cells in the tissues of aromatic plants (or the sap of certain trees) that gives the plant its characteristic aroma and therapeutic properties. Essential oils are sometimes called volatile oils because they evaporate readily at room temperature.

ETIOLOGY. The cause or origin of a disease or disorder. The word is also used to refer to the study of the causes of disease.

EUPHORIA. A feeling or state of well-being or elation.

EUSTRESS. A term that is sometimes used to refer to positive stress.

EUTHANASIA. The act of putting a person or animal to death painlessly or allowing them to die by withholding medical services, usually because of a painful and incurable disease. Mercy killing is another term for euthanasia.

EXECUTIVE. Pertaining to supervision, planning, and carrying out duties or actions.

EXECUTIVE FUNCTIONS. A set of cognitive abilities that control and regulate other abilities and behaviors. Necessary for goal-directed behavior, they include the ability to initiate and stop actions, to monitor and change behavior as needed, and to plan future behavior when faced with novel tasks and situations.

EXISTENTIAL FACTORS. Realities of life including death, isolation, freedom, and meaninglessness that must be faced by all individuals.

EXON. A segment of DNA that is transcribed to RNA and encodes information about the protein sequence.

EXPANSION MUTATION. A genetic mutation caused by additional repetitions of a triplet, or trinucleotide sequence, during the process of genetic transmission. In Huntington's disease, the expansion mutation produces more of a toxic gene product.

EXPERIENTIAL KNOWLEDGE. Knowledge gained from experience, often practical, in contrast with theoretical or professional knowledge.

EXPERIENTIAL THERAPY. An approach to therapy that focuses on experiencing inner feelings, rather than talking about problems in a disconnected, intellectual way. Although it is based on person-centered therapy, experiential therapy is more directive because it uses techniques from a variety of therapeutic approaches to draw out a person's inner experiences.

EXPLICIT MEMORY. Consciously recalled memory for facts or events.

EXPOSURE THERAPY. A form of cognitive-behavioral therapy in which patients suffering from phobias are exposed to their feared objects or situations while accompanied by the therapist. The length of exposure is gradually increased until the association between the feared situation and the patient's experienced panic symptoms is no longer present.

EXPRESSIVE THERAPY. An approach to psychotherapy that seeks to relieve the patient's symptoms through exploration of previously unconscious material, leading to greater insight and more adaptive behaviors.

EXTENDED FAMILY FIELD. A person's family of origin plus grandparents, in-laws, and other relatives.

EXTENSIVE SUPPORT. Ongoing daily support required to assist an individual in a specific adaptive area, such as daily help with preparing meals.

EXTERNALIZING DISORDERS. Mental disorders with primary symptoms that involve outward behavior as opposed to inner emotions.

EXTINCTION. The elimination or removal of a person's reaction to a cue as a result of exposure treatment.

EXTRAPYRAMIDAL. Brain structures located outside the pyramidal tracts of the central nervous system.

EXTRAPYRAMIDAL MOVEMENT DISORDERS. Involuntary movements that occur as a side effect of some psychiatric medications.

EXTRAPYRAMIDAL SIDE EFFECTS. A group of neurological side effects including muscle spasms, involuntary movements, and symptoms that resemble Parkinson's disease (also called drug-induced Parkinsonism).

F

FACTITIOUS DISORDER. A type of mental disturbance in which patients intentionally act physically or mentally ill without obvious benefits. It is distinguished from malingering by the absence of an obvious motive, and from conversion disorder by intentional production of symptoms.

FACTOR ANALYSIS. A statistical method for summarizing relationships between variables. For the HAS, factor analysis was utilized to determine the specific sets of symptoms relating to overall anxiety, somatic anxiety, and psychic anxiety.

FADING. Gradually decreasing the amount or frequency of a reinforcer so that the target behavior will begin to occur independent of any rewards.

FAIR HOUSING ACT OF 1968. Federal legislation regarding access to housing that prohibits discrimination based on race, color, national origin, sex, religion, disability, or familial status.

FALSE-POSITIVE. A test result that is positive for a specific condition or disorder, but this result is inaccurate.

FAMILY SYSTEMS THEORY. An approach to treatment that emphasizes the interdependency of family members rather than focusing on individuals in isolation from the family. This theory underlies the most influential forms of contemporary family therapy.

FARADIC. A type of discontinuous alternating electric current sometimes used in aversion therapy. It is named for Michael Faraday, an eminent British physicist.

FASCIA (PLURAL, FASCIAE). A band or sheath of connective tissue that covers, supports, or connects the muscles and the internal organs.

FECES. Waste products eliminated from the large intestine; excrement.

FEEDBACK. A reaction or response from others to a particular behavior or activity.

FEEDBACK LOOP. A naturally occurring process whereby individuals control their behavior by self-monitoring, self-evaluation, and self-reinforcement.

FEEDBACK LOOPS. Chains of biochemical reactions in which the products of reactions limit or enhance the subsequent reactions, and in which the chain ends up back at the first reaction, either limiting or enhancing it.

FEMININITY. Prescribed behavior for females, characterized by interpersonal warmth, passivity, and lack of aggression.

FENFLURAMINE (PONDIMIN). A prescription appetite suppressant for weight loss that was withdrawn from the market due to unacceptable health risks.

FETISHISM. A paraphilia in which a person requires a nonliving object (or occasionally a nongenital part of the body, such as the partner's feet) in order to achieve sexual arousal and satisfaction.

FIRST-RANK SYMPTOMS. A list of symptoms that have been considered to be diagnostic of schizophrenia. They include, delusions, somatic hallucinations, hearing voices commenting on one's behavior, and thought insertion or withdrawal. First-rank symptoms are sometimes called Schneiderian symptoms, after the name of Kurt Schneider, the German psychiatrist who listed them in 1959.

FLASHBACK. The re-emergence of a traumatic memory as a vivid recollection of sounds, images, and sensations associated with the trauma. The person having the flashback typically feels as if he or she is reliving the event.

FLAVONOIDS. Plant pigments that have a variety of effects on human physiology. Some of these pigments have anti-inflammatory, anti-carcinogenic, and antioxidant effects, for example.

FLOODING. A type of exposure treatment in which the patient is exposed to an anxiety-provoking or feared situation all at once and kept in it until the anxiety and fear subside.

FLUID INTELLIGENCE. A type of intelligence that involves inductive and deductive reasoning ability.

FOLIC ACID. An essential B-vitamin that humans obtain through diet.

FOOD FREQUENCY QUESTIONNAIRE. A listing of how often a person consumes foods from certain food groups in a given period of time.

FORENSIC. Pertaining to courtroom procedure or evidence used in courts of law.

FORMICATION. The sensation of bugs creeping on the skin.

FREE-FLOATING. A term used in psychiatry to describe anxiety that is unfocused or lacking an apparent cause or object.

FREQUENCY DISTRIBUTION. In statistics, the correspondence between a set of frequencies and the set of categories used to classify the group being tested.

FRONTAL CORTEX. The part of the human brain associated with aggressiveness and impulse control. Abnormalities in the frontal cortex are associated with an increased risk of suicide.

FRONTAL LOBE DEMENTIA. Dementia caused by a disorder, usually genetic, that affects the front portion of the brain.

FRONTAL LOBES. A region of the brain that influences higher mental functions often associated with intelligence, such as the ability to foresee the consequences of actions, planning, comprehension, and mood.

FROTTAGE. The act of touching or rubbing against the body or genitals of a non-consenting individual.

FUGUE. A dissociative experience during which a person travels away from home, has amnesia for their past, and may be confused about their identity but otherwise appears normal.

FUGUE STATE. A form of amnesia in which the person appears to be conscious and to make rational decisions, but upon recovery, the period is not remembered. Fugue states represent one type of reaction to traumatic experiences.

G

GABA. Gamma-aminobutyric acid, an inhibitory neurotransmitter in the brain.

GADOLINIUM. A very rare metallic element useful for its sensitivity to electromagnetic resonance, among other things. Traces of it can be injected into the body to enhance MRI pictures.

GALACTORRHEA. Lactation occurring in the absence of pregnancy.

GAMMA RAY. A high-energy photon emitted by radioactive substances.

GAMMA-AMINOBUTYRIC ACID (GABA). A neurotransmitter that helps to lower or reduce the level of excitement in the nerves, leading to muscle relaxation, calmness, sleep, and prevention of seizures.

GANSER SYNDROME. A rare subtype of factitious disorder accompanied by dissociative symptoms. It is most often seen in male patients under severe stress in prison or courtroom settings.

GANTRY. A name for the couch or table used in a CT scan. The patient lies on the gantry while it slides into the x-ray scanner.

GAS CHROMATOGRAPHY/MASS SPECTROMETRY (GC/MS). A definitive method of testing for specific drugs, used to confirm immunoassay results indicating drug use. GC/MS separates the substances present in the urine sample, then breaks them into unique molecular fragments, which are matched against a database of known substances.

GASTRITIS. Inflammation of the lining of the stomach.

GATEWAY DRUG. A mood-altering drug or substance, typically used by younger or new drug users, that may lead to the use of more dangerous drugs.

GENDER DYSPHORIA. A state of persistent discomfort or depression associated with one's gender role or biological sex.

GENDER ROLE CONFLICT OR STRESS. A negative psychological state resulting from a discrepancy between gender role expectations and how one actually thinks, feels, or behaves.

GENDER ROLES. Stereotypical expectations regarding how one should think, behave, and feel depending on whether one is male or female.

GENERALIZATION. A person's ongoing use of new behaviors that were previously modeled for him or her. Generalization is also called transfer of training or maintenance.

GENERALIZED ANXIETY DISORDER. A general form of fear that can dominate a person's life.

GENERIC. A term that refers to a medication that is not protected by a registered trademark.

GENETIC POOL. The genetic material of an entire population.

GENOGRAM. A family tree diagram that represents the names, birth order, sex, and relationships of the members of a family. Therapists use genograms to detect recurrent patterns in the family history and to help the members understand their problem(s).

GENOME. The total genetic makeup of a cell or organism. The human genome is the complete genetic constitution of a human being.

GENOMIC IMPRINTING. The process in which specific genes or DNA segments are modified during the development of sperm or egg cells in a parent-specific fashion. The modification is reversible and appears to include the addition or removal of methyl groups to specific areas within the DNA sequence.

GENOTYPE. The genetic makeup of an organism or a set of organisms.

GESTALT. A German word that means "form" or "structure." The Gestalt Closure subtest on the K-SNAP measures a person's ability to identify a whole object from a partially completed drawing of its form.

GESTALT THERAPY. A therapeutic approach that focuses on increasing awareness of feelings and impulses in the present.

GHB. GHB, or gamma hydroxybutyrate, is a central nervous system depressant that has been abused in the United States for euphoric, sedative, body-building, and date-rape purposes.

GILLBERG'S CRITERIA. A six-item checklist for AS developed by Christopher Gillberg, a Swedish researcher. It is widely used in Europe as a diagnostic tool.

GINGKO BILOBA. A shade tree native to China with fan-shaped leaves and fleshy seeds with edible kernels. Gingko extract is being studied as a possible complementary or adjunctive treatment for Alzheimer's.

GINSENG ABUSE SYNDROME. A group of symptoms recognized by Chinese physicians as the result of excessive use of ginseng. The symptoms include dizziness, high blood pressure, restlessness, nausea, possible bleeding from the digestive tract, and skin rashes.

GLANS. The tip of the penis.

GLAUCOMA. A group of eye diseases characterized by increased pressure within the eye significant enough to damage eye tissue and structures. If untreated, glaucoma results in blindness.

GRAND MAL SEIZURE. A seizure characterized by a sudden loss of consciousness that is immediately followed by generalized convulsions. Such a seizure is usually preceded by a sensory experience, called an aura, which provides a warning as to an impending convulsion.

GRANDIOSE. Having an exaggerated belief in one's importance or status. In some people, grandiosity may be so extreme as to be delusional.

GRANDIOSE DELUSIONS. Grandiose delusions magnify the person's importance; the delusional person may believe himself or herself to be a famous person, to have magical superpowers, or to be someone in a position of enormous power (such as being the Prime Minister or President).

GRANDIOSITY. Exaggerated and unrealistic self-importance; inflated self-assessment. Grandiosity is considered one of the core characteristics of persons diagnosed with narcissistic personality disorder.

GRIDIRON ABDOMEN. An abdomen with a network of parallel scars from repeated surgical operations.

GROUP COHESIVENESS. The degree to which a group functions well in its assigned task.

GROUP PSYCHOTHERAPY; GROUP THERAPY. A form of therapy in which a small, carefully selected group of individuals meets regularly with a therapist to assist each individual in emotional growth and personal problem-solving. The group provides support and correction through feedback, constructive criticism, and a forum for consultation and reference.

GUANETHIDINE. A medication used to treat high blood pressure.

GUIDED IMAGERY. Techniques in which individuals actively imagine themselves in a scene (usually a different location, such as a relaxing beach, or a trigger situation where one handles the situation successfully), typically guided by another person describing the scene.

H

HABITUATION. The reduction of a person's emotional or behavioral reaction to a cue by repeated or prolonged exposure.

HALF-LIFE. The time required for half of the atoms in a radioactive substance to disintegrate.

HALLUCINATIONS. False sensory perceptions. A person experiencing a hallucination may "hear" sounds or "see" people or objects that are not really present.

Hallucinations can also affect the senses of smell, touch, and taste.

HALLUCINOGENS. Substances that cause hallucinations.

HASHISH. The dark, blackish resinous material that exudes from the leaves of the Indian hemp plant.

HATHA YOGA. The form of yoga most familiar to Westerners; often practiced as a form of physical therapy.

HEALTH MAINTENANCE ORGANIZATION (HMO). A type of managed care system that involves payment contracts with a group or panel of health care providers.

HEALTH MAINTENANCE ORGANIZATION ACT OF 1973. Federal legislation that provided aid to develop HMOs.

HEBEPHRENIC SCHIZOPHRENIA. An older term for what is now known as the disorganized subtype of schizophrenia.

HEMATEMESIS. Vomiting blood. Hematemesis is a symptom that sometimes occurs with gastrointestinal ulcers made worse by high levels of caffeine consumption.

HEMATOMA. An accumulation of blood, often clotted, in a body tissue or organ, usually caused by a break or tear in a blood vessel.

HEMISPHERE. One side of the brain, right or left.

HEPATITIS. An inflammation of the liver that can be caused by a variety of factors.

HIB DISEASE. An infection caused by *Haemophilus influenza*, type b (Hib). This disease mainly affects children under the age of five. In that age group, it is the leading cause of bacterial meningitis, pneumonia, joint and bone infections, and throat inflammations.

HIERARCHY. In exposure therapy, a list of feared items or situations, ranked from least fearsome to most fearsome.

HIGH-DENSITY SEX OFFENSES. Several offenses within a short period of time.

HIGH-FUNCTIONING AUTISM (HFA). A subcategory of autistic disorder consisting of children diagnosed with IQs of 70 or higher.

HIPPOCAMPUS. A part of the brain that is involved in memory formation and learning. The hippocampus is shaped like a curved ridge and belongs to an organ system called the limbic system.

HISTAMINE. Substance released during allergic reactions.

HISTRIONIC. Theatrical.

HOLDING THERAPY. A controversial treatment for autism, reactive attachment disorder, and other problems of children in which an adult holds a child despite any resistance from the child until the child submits and experiences an emotional release.

HOLISTIC. An approach to health care that emphasizes the totality of an individual's spiritual, psychological, and physical, well-being, and that situates a disease or disorder within that totality.

HOMEOSTASIS. The tendency of a family system to maintain internal stability and resist change.

HOMOCYSTEINE. A chemical that builds up in the blood when methionine is not properly processed. High blood levels of homocysteine increase risk of heart disease and stroke.

HOST. The dominant or main alter in a person with dissociative identity disorder.

HUMAN POTENTIAL MOVEMENT. A movement dating back to the beginning of the 1900s that reflected an altered perspective of human nature from inherently corrupt to inherently good.

HUMANISTIC AND EXISTENTIAL THERAPIES. Therapies that focus on achieving one's full potential, guided by subjective experience.

HUMOR. In ancient medicine, one of four body fluids (blood, phlegm, yellow bile, and black bile) that were thought to determine a person's basic constitution and personality.

HUMORAL. A term describing a hormonal substance secreted by an endocrine gland (such as the thyroid).

HUNTINGTON'S DISEASE. A hereditary disorder that appears in middle age and is characterized by gradual brain deterioration, progressive dementia, and loss of voluntary movement. It is sometimes called Huntington's chorea.

HYDRATED. Combining a substance with water.

HYDROCEPHALUS. The accumulation of cerebrospinal fluid (CSF) in the ventricles of the brain.

HYDROGEN. The simplest, most common element known in the universe. It is composed of a single electron (negatively charged particle). It is the nuclear proton of hydrogen that makes MRI possible by reacting resonantly to radio waves while aligned in a magnetic field.

HYDROMORPHONE. A prescribed opiate (Dilaudid) used to treat severe pain; also abused illegally.

HYPERACTIVE. Behavior disturbances, usually in children and adolescents, that involves impulsiveness, low levels of concentration, and distractibility.

HYPERAROUSAL. A symptom of traumatic stress characterized by abnormally intense reactions to stimuli. A heightened startle response is one sign of hyperarousal.

HYPEREMESIS GRAVIDARUM. Uncontrollable nausea and vomiting associated with pregnancy. Acupuncture appears to be an effective treatment for this condition.

HYPERPHAGIA. An abnormally large appetite for food. Hyperphagia is one of the symptoms of Prader-Willi syndrome.

HYPERSENSITIVE INTERNAL SUFFOCATION ALARM. A sensitive alarm goes off and the affected person's brain sends the body false signals that not enough oxygen is being received, which causes an increase in their breathing rate.

HYPERTENSION. High blood pressure, often brought on by smoking, obesity, or other causes; one of the major causes of strokes.

HYPERTHERMIA. Elevated body temperature resulting from ingestion of amphetamines.

HYPERTHYROIDISM. Condition resulting from the thyroid glands secreting excessive thyroid hormone, causing increased basal metabolic rate, and causing an increased need for food to meet the demand of the metabolic activity; generally, however, weight loss results.

HYPERVENTILATION. A pattern of rapid, shallow breathing that is frequently found in patients with Rett's disorder.

HYPERVIGILANCE. A state of abnormally intense wariness or watchfulness that is found in survivors of trauma or long-term abuse. Hypervigilance is sometimes described as "being on red alert all the time."

HYPERVIGILANT. Extreme attention to both internal and external stimuli.

HYPNAGOGIC HALLUCINATIONS. Dream-like auditory or visual hallucinations that occur while a person is falling asleep.

HYPNOSIS. The means by which a state of extreme relaxation and suggestibility is induced; used to treat amnesia and identity disturbances that occur in dissociative disorders.

HYPNOTHERAPY. The use of an induced trance state, or hypnosis, as a therapy.

HYPNOTIC. A type of medication that induces sleep.

HYPOCHONDRIASIS. A mental condition in which the affected person perceives illness or symptoms of illness when none exist.

HYPOGONADISM. Abnormally decreased gonad function with retardation of sexual development.

HYPOKALEMIA. Abnormally low levels of potassium in the blood. Hypokalemia is a potential medical emergency, as it can lead to disturbances of the heart rhythm. Muscle cramps and pain are a common symptom of hypokalemia in bulimic patients.

HYPOKINESIA. A condition of abnormally diminished motor activity.

HYPOMANIA. A milder form of mania which is characteristic of bipolar II disorder.

HYPONATREMIA. A condition characterized by an abnormally low concentration of sodium in the blood.

HYPOPNEA. Breathing that is too shallow to maintain adequate levels of oxygen in the blood.

HYPOTENSION. Low blood pressure.

HYPOTHALAMIC-PITUITARY-ADRENAL (HPA) SYSTEM. A part of the brain involved in the human stress response. The HPA system releases cortisol, the primary human stress hormone, and neurotransmitters that activate other brain structures associated with the "fight-or-flight" reaction. The HPA system appears to function in abnormal ways in patients diagnosed with depersonalization disorder. It is sometimes called the HPA axis.

HYPOTHALAMUS. A part of the forebrain that controls heartbeat, body temperature, thirst, hunger, blood pressure, blood sugar levels, and other functions.

HYPOTHESIS. An assumption, proposition, or educated guess that can be tested empirically.

HYPOTHYROIDISM. Thyroid gland that is abnormally low-functioning. A lowered metabolic rate results.

HYPOVENTILATION. An abnormally low level of blood oxygenation in the lungs.

HYSTERIA. In nineteenth-century psychiatric use, a neurotic disorder characterized by violent emotional outbursts and disturbances of the sensory and motor (movement-related) functions. The term "hysterical neurosis" is still used by some psychiatrists as a synonym for conversion disorder.

I

ID. A construct in Freudian psycho dynamic theory that represents the irrational, self-centered aspects of human thought.

IDEAL WEIGHT. A range of body weights recommended for generally healthy adults.

IDENTIFIED PATIENT (IP). The family member in whom the family's symptom has emerged or is most obvious.

IDENTITY DIFFUSION. A character formation that is scattered or spread around rather than an identity that becomes solidified or consolidated.

IDIOGRAPHIC. An approach to interpreting the results of a projective test within the context of the individual subject's record.

IEP. *See* Individualized Education Plan

ILLUSION. A misperception or misinterpretation in the presence of a real external stimulus.

IMITATIVE BEHAVIOR. Behaviors of a therapist or group member that are imitated, consciously or unconsciously, by other group members.

IMMUNOASSAY. The method used in routine or preliminary urine drug screening.

IMMUNOSUPPRESSANT. Medications that suppress or lower the body's immune system, primarily used to help the body accept a transplanted organ.

IMPLICIT. Implied or suggested without being clearly stated. Some critics of *DSM-IV-TR* maintain that its contributors based the criteria sets for certain disorders on an implicit notion of a mentally healthy human being.

IMPLICIT MEMORY. Unconsciously recalled memory for skills, procedures, or associations.

IMPULSE CONTROL DISORDERS. Group of disorders characterized by impulsive behavior, such as stealing.

IN VIVO. A Latin phrase that means "in life." In modeling and exposure therapies, it refers to practicing new behaviors in a real setting, as distinct from using imagery or imagined settings.

INBORN ERROR OF METABOLISM. A rare enzyme deficiency; children with inborn errors of metabolism do not have certain enzymes that the body requires to maintain organ functions. Inborn errors of metabolism can cause brain damage and mental retardation if left untreated. Phenylketonuria is an inborn error of metabolism.

INCEST. Unlawful sexual contact between persons who are biologically related. Many therapists, however, use the term to refer to inappropriate sexual contact between any members of a family, including stepparents and stepsiblings.

INCISORS. The four teeth in the front of each jaw in humans. The incisors of patients with bulimia frequently show signs of erosion from stomach acid.

INCONTINENCE. Inability to control the release of urine or feces.

INDEMNITY INSURANCE. Insurance plans that pay on a fee-for-service basis in the event of illness or injury.

INDICES. Scores based on performance in more than one area. On the WAIS, there are four index scores, each based on an individual's performance in more than one subtest.

INDIVIDUALIZED EDUCATION PLAN (IEP). A plan of instruction drawn up for an individual student who is having specific difficulties with mathematics, reading, or other skills necessary to progress beyond elementary school.

INDIVIDUAL PSYCHOTHERAPY. A relationship between therapist and patient designed to foster the patient's emotional growth and personal problem-solving skills.

INFORMATION GIVING. Imparting of information about a disease or condition as part of the therapeutic process.

INFORMED CONSENT. A person's agreement to undergo a medical or surgical procedure, or to participate in a clinical study, after being properly advised of the medical facts related to the procedure or study and the risks involved.

INFUSION. The most potent form of extraction of an herb into water. Infusions are steeped for a longer period of time than teas.

INHALANTS. A class of drugs that are inhaled in order for the user to experience a temporary "high." These chemicals include volatile solvents (liquids that vaporize at room temperature) and aerosols (sprays that contain solvents and propellants), and include glue, gasoline, paint thinner, hair spray, and others. They are dangerous because they can cause hallucinations, delusions, difficulty breathing, headache, nausea, vomiting, and even "sudden sniffing death." Inhalants can also cause permanent damage to the brain, lung, kidney, muscle, and heart.

INSIDIOUS. Proceeding gradually and inconspicuously but with serious effect.

INSOMNIA. A chronic inability to sleep or to remain asleep throughout the night.

INSULIN RESISTANCE. The body's inability to utilize blood sugar, at times leading to diabetes.

INSULT. In medicine, an injury or trauma to the brain or other part of the body.

INTEGRATED SETTING. Placing individuals in typical employment situations rather than making placements into sheltered workshops or other segregated settings.

INTELLIGENCE QUOTIENT (IQ). A measurement of intelligence obtained by dividing a person's mental age (determined by level of performance on an age-graded test) by his or her chronological age and multiplying by 100. For example, a ten-year-old with a mental age of thirteen would have an IQ of 130.

INTER-RATER RELIABILITY. The degree to which judgments about a person are consistent among raters or diagnosticians.

INTERMEDIATE CARE FACILITY. An inpatient facility that provides periodic nursing care.

INTERNALIZING DISORDERS. Mental disorders with primary symptoms that involve inner emotions as opposed to outward behavior.

INTEROCEPTIVE. Referring to stimuli or sensations that arise inside the body. In interoceptive exposure treatment, the patient is asked to exercise or perform other actions that produce feared internal physical sensations.

INTERPERSONAL LEARNING. Learning that takes place via feedback from others.

INTERPERSONAL THERAPY. An approach that includes psychoeducation about the sick role, and emphasis on the present and improving interpersonal dynamics and relationships. Interpersonal therapy is effective in treating adjustment disorders related to physical illness.

INTOXICATION. The condition of being drunk.

INTRAMUSCULAR. An injection that is given into a muscle.

INTRAPSYCHIC. Occurring inside a person's mind or psyche.

INTRON. A segment of DNA that interrupts an exon and that does not encode any information about the protein sequence.

IONIZING RADIATION. Electromagnetic radiation that can damage living tissue by disrupting and destroying individual cells. All types of nuclear decay radiation (including x rays) are potentially ionizing. Radio waves do not damage organic tissues they pass through.

IPECAC. The dried root of *Caephalis ipecacuanha*, a South American plant. Given in syrup form, ipecac is most commonly used to induce vomiting in cases of accidental poisoning.

IRRITABLE BOWEL SYNDROME (IBS). A condition affecting the small and large intestine, usually associated with emotional stress. There may be complaints of diarrhea and pain in the lower abdomen.

ISCHEMIA. Localized anemia of tissues due to obstructed inflow of blood.

J

JAUNDICE. A yellowing of the skin caused by excess bilirubin in the blood; a liver disorder.

JOURNALING. Involves writing out thoughts and feelings in an unstructured format. A "stream of consciousness" approach (writing whatever comes to mind) is suggested for greatest effectiveness.

K

KAVALACTONES. Medically active compounds in kava root that act as local anesthetics in the mouth and as minor tranquilizers.

KAVAPYRONES. Compounds in kava root that act as muscle relaxants and anticonvulsants.

KETAMINE. An anesthetic, used predominantly by veterinarians to treat animals, that can be used as a date-rape drug.

KI. The Japanese spelling of qi, the traditional Chinese term for vital energy or the life force.

KILOGRAM. A metric unit of weight. It equals 2.2 lb.

KLEPTOMANIA. A disorder of impulse control characterized by repeated stealing or shoplifting of items that the person does not need.

KLINEFELTER'S SYNDROME. A genetic disorder in males characterized by the presence of an extra X chromosome in addition to the normal XY. Most men with Klinefelter's syndrome have learning problems, are sterile, and have a shortened life expectancy.

KORSAKOFF'S SYNDROME. A disorder of the central nervous system resulting from long-term thiamine deficiency. It is characterized by amnesia, confusion, confabulation, and unsteady gait, and is most commonly seen in alcoholics.

KUNDALINI. In Indian yoga, a vital force or energy at the base of the spine that is activated or released by certain yoga postures or breathing techniques. This release is called the "awakening" of the kundalini. Some Westerners have had kundalini experiences that were diagnosed as psychotic episodes or symptoms of schizophrenia.

L

(LA) BELLE INDIFFÉRENCE. A psychiatric symptom sometimes found in patients with conversion disorder, in which the patient shows a surprising lack of concern about the nature or implications of his/her physical symptom.

LABIA. The outside folds of tissue that surround the clitoris and the opening of the urethra in women.

LABILE. Subject to frequent change, particularly in reference to mood.

LANUGO. Downy hair, usually associated with infants, that sometimes develops on the face and back of people affected by anorexia nervosa.

LAPSE. A single, isolated occurrence of a symptom or negative behavior.

LARYNGOSPASM. Spasms that close the vocal apparatus of the larynx (the organ of voice production).

LATERALIZATION. The control of specific neurological functions by one side of the brain or the other; for example, in most right-handed people, language functions are controlled by the left side of the brain and spatial and visual functions are controlled by the right side of the brain.

LAXATIVE. Substance or medication that encourages a bowel movement.

LEAST RESTRICTIVE ENVIRONMENT. Refers to care options that involve the least amount of restraint and the greatest degree of independence possible, while still meeting the individual's needs and maintaining safety.

LEUCOTOMY OR LEUKOTOMY. White matter cutting—severing the white matter of the frontal lobe of the brain.

LEUKODYSTROPHY. A disturbance of the white matter of the brain.

LEWY BODIES. Areas of injury found on damaged nerve cells in certain parts of the brain associated with dementia. Lewy body dementia was first ecognized in the 1980s and is now distinguished from Alzheimer's disease.

LEWY-BODY DISEASE. A type of dementia that resembles Alzheimer's disease, but progresses more rapidly. Common symptoms include fluctuations in confusion and recurring visual hallucinations. In this disease, abnormal brain cells are distributed throughout the brain.

LIBIDO. Psychic energy or instinctual drive associated with sexual desire, pleasure, or creativity.

LIMBIC SYSTEM. A group of structures in the brain that includes the amygdala, hippocampus, olfactory bulbs, and hypothalamus. The limbic system is associated with homeostasis and the regulation and arousal of emotions.

LIMITED SUPPORT. A predetermined period of assistance required to deal with a specific event, such as training for a new job.

LOBOTOMY. A surgical procedure involving the cutting of nerve fiber bundles in the brain.

LOCALIZATION. The control of specific neurological functions by specific areas in the brain.

LOCUS CERULEUS. A part of the brain where the neurotransmitter causes excitation.

LOFEXIDINE. A medication approved for use in England to aid the opioid detoxification process.

LOW AFFECT. Severe lack of interest and emotions; emotional numbness.

LUX. The International System unit for measuring illumination, equal to one lumen per square meter.

M

MACERATION. A technique for extracting essential oils from plant leaves and stems by crushing the plant parts and soaking them in warm vegetable oil.

MACHISMO. The exaggerated image of extreme masculinity that includes such qualities as concern for personal honor, virility, physical strength, heavy drinking, toughness, aggression, risk taking, authoritarianism, and self-centeredness.

MACROSOCIAL. Pertaining to the wider society, as distinct from such smaller social groupings as families, neighborhoods, etc.

MAGNETIC FIELD. The three-dimensional area surrounding a magnet, in which its force is active. During

MRI, the patient's body is permeated by the force field of a superconducting magnet.

MAINTENANCE TREATMENT. The period of treatment beginning after the initial introduction of the treatment medication. During this period, the dose of medication can be either increased or decreased, depending on the program and needs of the patient.

MALADROITNESS. Another word for awkwardness or clumsiness.

MALAISE. The medical term for a general condition of unease, discomfort, or weakness.

MALINGERING. Knowingly pretending to be physically or mentally ill to avoid some unpleasant duty or responsibility, or for economic benefit.

MANIA. An elevated or euphoric mood or irritable state that is characteristic of bipolar I disorder. This state is characterized by mental and physical hyperactivity, disorganization of behavior, and inappropriate elevation of mood.

MANIC. Referring to mania.

MANTRA. Originally, a sacred word or phrase repeated over and over to help focus the mind during meditation; in the Western world, this may refer to any repeated syllable, word, or phrase used to meditate.

MAO INHIBITORS. A group of antidepressant drugs that decrease the activity of monoamine oxidase, a neurotransmitter found in the brain that affects mood.

MARIJUANA. The dried and shredded or chopped leaves of the Indian hemp plant.

MASCULINITY. Prescribed behavior for males, characterized by independence, strength, control, and avoidance of emotional expressiveness.

MASOCHISM. A mental disorder in which a person obtains sexual satisfaction through pain or humiliation inflicted by the self or by another person. The term is sometimes used more generally to refer to a tendency to find pleasure in submissiveness or self-denial.

MASOCHISTIC TENDENCIES. Tendencies to direct harm or hatred toward oneself.

MAZINDOL (SANOREX, MAZANOR). A prescription medication for weight loss currently on the market.

MEAN. The mathematical average of all scores in a set of scores.

MEDICAID. A program jointly funded by state and federal governments that reimburses hospitals and physicians for the care of individuals who cannot pay for their own medical expenses. These individuals may be in low-income households or may have chronic disabilities.

MEDICAID HOME AND COMMUNITY-BASED WAIVER. Legislation regarding the use of Medicaid funds for care services; allows certain federal requirements to be bypassed so that states can use the funds more flexibly for accessing home- and community-based services rather than using hospitals or intermediate-care facilities.

MEDICAL MODEL. The basic conceptual framework in the West since the nineteenth century for understanding, researching, and classifying mental disorders.

MEDICARE. A federally funded health insurance program for individuals age 65 and older or certain categories of younger persons with disabilities.

MEDROXYPROGESTERONE. A progestin, a female hormone.

MEDROXYPROGESTERONE ACETATE (MPA). A female hormone that may be prescribed for male patients with sexual sadism or other paraphilias. MPA helps to control sexual urges in men by speeding up the clearance of testosterone from the bloodstream.

MELANCHOLIA. A form of severe depression characterized by weight loss, insomnia, and an inability to experience pleasure.

MENINGES. A membrane covering the brain and spinal cord that consists of three layers: the *pia mater,* the innermost layer; the *arachnoid,* in the middle; and the *dura mater,* the outermost layer.

MENOPAUSE. A period of decreasing hormonal activity in women, when ovulation stops and conception is no longer possible.

MERIDIANS. In traditional Chinese medicine, a network of pathways or channels that convey qi (also sometimes spelled "ki"), or vital energy, through the body.

MERYCISM. Another name for rumination disorder.

META-ANALYSIS. The statistical analysis of a large collection of analyses from individual studies for the purpose of integrating the findings.

METABOLISM. The group of biochemical processes within the body that release energy in support of life.

METHADONE. A drug often prescribed legally as a replacement for heroin. It induces a slight high but blocks heroin from producing a more powerful euphoric effect. It may be used in heroin detoxification to ease the process, or it may be used daily after detoxification as maintenance therapy. Methadone maintenance therapy is controversial.

METHAMPHETAMINE. The most common illegally produced amphetamine.

METHIONINE. An amino acid that, when not metabolized properly, allows homocysteine to build up in the blood. Folic acid aids methionine metabolism.

METHYLPHENIDATE. A mild central nervous system stimulant that is used to treat hyperactivity.

MIDDLE NOTE. A term used in perfumery and aromatherapy to designate essential oils whose odors emerge later than top notes but evaporate more rapidly than bottom notes. Chamomile is considered a middle note in aromatherapy.

MILD COGNITIVE IMPAIRMENT (MCI). A transitional phase of memory loss in older people that precedes dementia or Alzheimer's disease.

MILLIGRAM (MG). One-thousandth of a gram. A gram is the metric measure that equals about 0.035 ounces.

MILLON CLINICAL MULTIAXIAL INVENTORY (MCMI-II). A self-report instrument designed to help the clinician assess DSM-IV-related personality disorders and clinical syndromes. It provides insight into 14 personality disorders and 10 clinical syndromes.

MINNESOTA MULTIPHASIC PERSONALITY INVENTORY (MMPI-2). A comprehensive assessment tool widely used to diagnosed personality disorders.

MIXED MANIA/MIXED STATE. A mental state in which symptoms of both depression and mania occur simultaneously.

MODALITY. One of the primary forms of sensation, such as vision, touch, or hearing.

MODELING. A type of teaching method used in social skills training. Therapists who use this method may offer positive and negative examples of the behaviors that make up a social skill.

MONOAMINE OXIDASE INHIBITORS (MAOIS). A group of antidepressant drugs that decrease the activity of monoamine oxidase, a neurotransmitter found in the brain that affects mood.

MONOGENIC. Determined or controlled by a single gene. Huntington's disease is one of the few psychiatric disorders that is monogenic.

MONOMANIA. A nineteenth-century term for a pathological obsession with one idea or one social cause. Nineteenth-century psychiatrists often associated explosive behavior with monomania. The word is no longer used as a technical term.

MONOZYGOTIC. Developed from a single fertilized ovum. Monozygotic twins are sometimes called identical twins.

MORBIDITY. The unhealthiness or disease characteristics associated with a mental disorder.

MOSAICISM. A genetic condition in which some cells in an organism have one set of chromosomes and other cells have a different set.

MOTIVATIONAL ENHANCEMENT THERAPY. Therapy that focuses on increasing motivation for change by empathically comparing and contrasting the consequences and benefits of changing or not changing.

MOTOR. Involving muscle movement.

MOTOR SKILLS. Skills pertaining to or involving muscular movement.

MOVEMENT EDUCATION. A term that refers to the active phase of bodywork, in which clients learn to move with greater freedom and to maintain the proper alignment of their bodies.

MOXIBUSTION. A technique in traditional Chinese medicine that involves burning a *Moxa*, or cone of dried wormwood leaves, close to the skin to relieve pain. When used with acupuncture, the cone is placed on top of the needle at an acupuncture point and burned.

MRI. Magnetic resonance imaging. A special imaging technique used to image internal parts of the body, especially soft tissues.

MULTI-INFARCT DEMENTIA. Dementia caused by damage to brain tissue resulting from a series of blood clots or clogs in the blood vessels. It is also called vascular dementia.

MULTIAXIAL. Refers to a type of classification system that involves numeric measurement along more than one dimension and is not based on assignment to mutually exclusive categories.

MULTIMODAL. Involving several types of therapeutic interventions such as heat or ice packs, electrical stimulation, and ultrasound; sometimes refers to a mix of physical and psychological therapies.

MULTIPLE PERSONALITY DISORDER (MPD). An older term for dissociative identity disorder (DID).

MULTIPLE SCLEROSIS. A disease characterized by patches of hardened tissue in the brain or spinal cord, paralysis, and/or muscle tremors.

MUSCLE DYSMORPHIA. A subtype of BDD, described as excessive preoccupation with muscularity and bodybuilding to the point of interference with social, educational, or occupational functioning.

MUTATION. A spontaneous change in the sequence of nucleotides in a chromosome or gene. Mutations may affect the number and structure of chromosomes or cause deletions of part of a chromosome. Rett's disorder is caused by a mutation on the long arm of the X chromosome.

MUTISM. Inability to speak due to conscious refusal or psychological inhibition.

MYASTHENIA GRAVIS. A disease characterized by weakness of the muscles caused by an autoimmune reaction.

MYELIN SHEATHS. A fatty layer around nerve cells that aids the transmission of nerve impulses.

MYOCARDIAL DISEASE. Disease of the muscular layer of the heart wall.

MYOCLONUS. An abrupt spasm or twitching in a muscle or group of muscles. It is more common in early-onset AD than in late-onset Alzheimer's.

N

NARCISSISTIC PERSONALITY DISORDER. Personality characterized by continually exaggerating one's own positive qualities and refusing to recognize personal defects or flaws.

NARCISSISTIC PERSONALITY INVENTORY (NPI). The most widely used English-language diagnostic instrument for narcissistic personality disorder. Based on the *DSM-III* criteria for NPD, the NPI is frequently used in research studies as well as patient assessment.

NARCOLEPSY. A disorder characterized by frequent and uncontrollable attacks of deep sleep.

NARCOTHERAPY. A form of psychotherapy that involves the administration of a drug that makes the patient drowsy.

NALOXONE. A drug that combines competitively with opiate receptors on the nerve cells and blocks or reverses the action of narcotic analgesics.

NARROW-ANGLE GLAUCOMA. An eye disorder caused by a buildup of fluid pressure inside the eyeball due to an abnormally small angle between the iris (the colored portion of the eye) and the cornea (the transparent front part of the eye).

NATURAL SUPPORTS. Using a person's already existing support network to help the person reach a goal, such as the employment of their choice.

NEGATIVE SYMPTOMS. Symptoms of schizophrenia that represent a loss or reduction of normal functioning.

NEPHRITIS. Inflammation of the kidney.

NERVOUS TIC. A repetitive, involuntary action, such as the twitching of a muscle or repeated blinking.

NEUROFIBRILLARY TANGLES. Accumulations of twisted protein fragments found inside the nerve cells in the brains of Alzheimer's patients.

NEUROLEPTIC. Another name for the older antipsychotic medications, such as haloperidol (Haldol) and chlorpromazine (Thorazine).

NEUROLEPTIC MALIGNANT SYNDROME (NMS). An unusual but potentially serious complication that develops in some patients who have been treated with antipsychotic medications. NMS is characterized by changes in blood pressure, altered states of consciousness, rigid muscles, and fever. Untreated NMS can result in coma and death.

NEUROLEPTIC-INDUCED ACUTE DYSTONIA. A severe form of dystonia, a neurological movement disorder, caused by the use of neuroleptic drugs.

NEUROLEPTIC-INDUCED AKATHISIA. Refers to the disorder characterized by a physical restlessness (the inability to sit still, for example), and excessive voluntary movements, as a result of the use of neuroleptic drugs; research indicates it is likely the most common of neuroleptic-induced movement disorders.

NEUROLEPTIC-INDUCED PARKINSONISM. Symptoms similar to Parkinson's disease that may appear in people taking neuroleptic (antipsychotic) medications. These symptoms include tremors in muscles and a shuffling gait.

NEUROLEPTIC-INDUCED TARDIVE DYSKINESIA. A potentially irreversible neurological disorder caused by the use of antipsychotic/neuroleptic medications, with symptoms involving uncontrollable movement of various body parts. Some of these movements include involuntary movements of the tongue and mouth, grimacing, and lip-smacking.

NEUROLOGIC. Pertaining to the nervous system (brain and nerve cells).

NEURONS. Nerve cells in the brain that produce nerve impulses.

NEUROPATHIC. Relating to neural damage.

NEUROPSYCHOLOGICAL FUNCTIONING. The ability of the nervous system and brain to process and interpret information received through the senses.

NEUROTRANMISSION. The conduction of a nerve impulse along a chain of nerve cells, which occurs when a cell in the chain secretes a chemical substance, called a neurotransmitter, onto a subsequent cell.

NEUROTRANSMITTER. A chemical in the brain that transmits messages between neurons, or nerve cells.

NEUROTRANSMITTERS. Chemicals that carry nerve impulses from one nerve cell to another. Alzheimer's disease causes a drop in the production of several important neurotransmitters.

NIMBY PHENOMENON. Acronym for Not In My Backyard, describing the common opposition displayed by citizens toward the placement of group homes or other social service facilities in their neighborhoods.

NOMOTHETIC. An approach to interpreting the results of a projective test in which the subject's answers are measured against a normative comparison sample.

NON-AMBULATORY. Unable to walk.

NON-DOMINANT HAND. The hand that one does not typically use when performing various tasks, such as writing or throwing an object.

NONDIRECTIVE THERAPY. An approach to therapy in which the therapist actively attempts to avoid giving advice, making interpretations, or otherwise influencing the focus of the individual's thoughts or statements.

NONENDOGENOUS. A factor that arises or is produced outside of the organism.

NORADRENERGIC. Acts similarly to norepinephrine or noradrenaline.

NOREPINEPHRINE. A neurotransmitter in the brain that acts to constrict blood vessels and raise blood pressure. It works in combination with serotonin.

NOREPINEPHRINE (NORADRENALINE). A hormone with similar stimulatory effects to epinephrine but, in contrast to epinephrine, has little effect on cardiac (heart) output and in relaxing smooth muscles.

NORMAL CURVE EQUIVALENTS. Standard scores with an average of 100. The normal curve equivalents divide the normal or bell-shaped curve into 100 equal parts. As a result, those scores can be used for statistical analysis because they can be added, subtracted, multiplied, and divided.

NORMED. Describes a process used in the developmental stages of a test instrument. The new test is first given to a cross-section of a population for which it is designed. The scores, placements, rankings, etc., of these persons then become the source for all future comparisons (norm group). When a new subject takes the test, his/her score, placement, ranking, etc., is determined based upon comparison with or deviation from the norm group.

NOSOLOGY. The branch of medicine that deals with the systematic classification of diseases and disorders.

NUCLEAR FAMILY. The basic family unit, consisting of father, mother, and their biological children.

NUCLEOTIDE. One of the molecules that form the building blocks of DNA or RNA. The nucleotides of DNA include a phosphate group, four chemical bases (adenine, cytosine, guanine, and thymine), and a sugar containing five carbon atoms. In RNA, the thymine base is replaced by uracil.

NYSTAGMUS. A persistent involuntary movement of the eyes from side to side. It is one of the symptoms of inhalant intoxication syndrome.

O

OBJECT RELATIONS. In psychology, a phrase that refers to the way in which a subject describes relationships with other people in their environment, and the ways in which he or she has internalized interpersonal relationships.

OBJECT-RELATIONS THEORY. An approach to psychological development that includes Nancy Chodorow's stating that children develop according to interactions with their primary caregivers.

OBSESSION. A persistent image, idea, or desire that dominates a person's thoughts or feelings.

OBSESSIVE-COMPULSIVE. Characterized by obsessive and compulsive behaviors.

OBSESSIVE-COMPULSIVE DISORDER. Disorder in which the affected individual has an obsession (such as a fear of contamination, or thoughts he or she doesn't like to have and can't control) and feels compelled to perform a certain act to neutralize the obsession (such as repeated handwashing).

OCCIPITAL. The occipital bone forms the back part of the skull.

OEDIPAL CONFLICT. A developmental conflict that emerges during the third or oedipal stage of Freud's psychosexual development stages. During this stage, a conflict emerges with regard to the triad of father, mother, and child. The conflict concerns the sexual impulses that the child has toward the parent of the opposite gender and the hostile impulses that the child has towards the parent of the same gender. During this stage, the developmental conflict concerns a resolution of oedipal issues.

OLFACTORY NERVE. The cranial nerve that regulates the sense of smell.

ONSET. The point in time at which the symptoms of a disorder first became apparent.

OPERANT. Conditioning in which the desired response is reinforced by an introduced stimulus.

OPIATES. A class of drugs that is either derived from opium (i.e. morphine, hydromorphone, oxymorphone, heroin, codeine, hydrocodone, oxycodone) or resembles these opium derivatives (such as meperidine) and is commonly referred to as narcotics.

OPIOIDS. Substances that reduce pain and may induce sleep. Some opioids are endogenous, which means that they are produced within the human body. Other opioids are produced by plants or formulated synthetically in the laboratory.

OPPOSITIONAL DEFIANT DISORDER. An emotional and behavioral problem of children and adolescents characterized by defiant, hostile, or disobedient behavior that has lasted for longer than six months.

ORAL PHASE. The first of Freud's psychosexual stages of development in which satisfaction is focused on the mouth and lips. During this stage sucking and eating are the primary means of gratification.

ORGANIC BRAIN SYNDROME. A class of disorders characterized by progressive deterioration of mental processes caused by temporary brain dysfunction or permanent brain damage. Symptoms include delusions, dementia, amnesia, and delirium that are not caused by drugs, alcohol, or as a side effect of medication.

ORGASM. Another word for sexual climax.

ORIENTATION. In psychiatry, the ability to locate oneself in one's environment with respect to time, place and people.

ORLISTAT (XENICAL). A prescription medication for weight loss currently on the market.

ORTHOSTATIC HYPOTENSION. A sudden decrease in blood pressure due to a change in body position, as when moving from a sitting to standing position.

OSTEOPOROSIS. A loss of bone minerals.

OUTCOME EXPECTANCIES. What one believes will happen as a result of engaging in a certain behavior.

OVERCOMPENSATION. An attempt to overcome or correct a behavior by going too far in the opposite direction.

OVERVALUED IDEA. An unreasonable, sustained belief that is held with less than delusional intensity (i.e., the person can acknowledge, to some degree, that the belief may be false). The belief is not accounted for by the individual's cultural or religious background.

OXIMETRY. The measurement of blood oxygen levels.

P

PAIN DISORDER. One of several somatoform disorders described in the revised, fourth edition of the mental health professional's handbook, the *Diagnostic and Statistical Manual of Mental Disorders*. The term "somatoform" means that symptoms are physical but are not entirely understood as a consequence of a general medical condition or as a direct effect of a substance, such as a drug.

PAINSTATES. Refers to the four-way classification of pain disorder as being (1) acute with psychological factors, (2) acute with psychological factors and a general medical condition, (3) chronic with psychological factors, and (4) chronic with psychological factors and a general medical condition.

PANACEA. A medicine or other substance regarded as a cure for all ills.

PANIC ATTACK. Specific periods of time when a person has a feeling that s/he is dying or having a heart attack with chest pain, a feeling as though s/he could pass out, and fear that s/he is going insane.

PANIC DISORDER. An anxiety disorder in which an individual experiences sudden, debilitating attacks of intense fear.

PANIC DISORDER WITH AGORAPHOBIA. Repeated panic attacks in which the patient is worried about the attacks enough that the worry restricts their activity.

PANIC DISORDER WITHOUT AGORAPHOBIA. Repeated panic attacks without symptoms of agoraphobia.

PARAMETER. A characteristic or factor that is measured during a test of a complex process or activity like sleep.

PARANOIA. A mental disorder characterized by baseless suspicions or distrust of others, often delusional in intensity.

PARANOID. A mental attitude characterized by unjustified or excessive distrust of other people, usually combined with anger.

PARANOID PERSONALITY. A personality disorder characterized by unwarranted suspicion, jealousy, hypersensitivity, social isolation and a tendency to detect malicious intent in the words and actions of others.

PARAPHILIAS. A group of mental disorders that is characterized by recurrent intense sexual urges and sexually arousing fantasies generally involving (1) nonhuman objects, (2) the suffering or humiliation of oneself or one's partner (not merely simulated), or (3) children or other non-consenting persons.

PARASOMNIA. A type of sleep disorder characterized by abnormal changes in behavior or body functions during sleep, specific stages of sleep, or the transition between sleeping and waking.

PARESTHESIAS. Abnormal sensations of tingling or "pins and needles." Paresthesias are a common panic-like symptom associated with agoraphobia.

PARKINSON'S DISEASE. A disease of the nervous system most common in people over 60, characterized by a shuffling gait, trembling of the fingers and hands, and muscle stiffness. It may be related in some way to Lewy body dementia.

PARKINSONIAN. Related to symptoms associated with Parkinson's disease. These symptoms may be induced by certain medications, and, in these cases, the person does not have Parkinson's disease—they have Parkinson-like or Parkinsonian symptoms.

PASSIVE-AGGRESSIVE BEHAVIORS. Behaviors that represent covert expressions of hostile or negative feelings that the person is unable or unwilling to express directly.

PATHOGNOMONIC. Describing symptoms characteristic of a particular disease.

PATIENT CARE EPISODES. A specific measure of the volume of care provided by an organization or system. It begins with a treatment visit to a health care facility (a hospital or residential treatment center, for example) and ends when a person leaves the facility, so it may vary by patient and visit. Over time, the volume of patient care episodes indicates the degree to which a population uses certain health care capacities. Other measures that may be used to measure volume of care include number of beds or bed-days, total number of patients served, and also more specific measures like patient-contact hours.

PAVOR NOCTURNUS. The Latin medical term for sleep terror disorder.

PELVIS. The basin-like cavity in the human body below the abdomen, enclosed by a framework of four bones.

PENETRANCE. In genetics, the frequency with which a specific gene produces its effects in a group of people or other organisms. Penetrance is expressed as a percentage.

PENIS. The external male sex organ.

PERCENTILE RANK. The point at which a given percentage of people fall at or below the individual's test score being calculated. For example, if a person's test score was at the 60th percentile, 40% of other test takers received a higher score, while 60% received a score that was at or below that of the test taker.

PERFORMANCE ANXIETY. A subcategory of circumscribed social phobia in which the patient's fear is limited to performing certain activities or tasks in public. Common areas of performance anxiety include public speaking, acting on stage, solo singing, and playing instrumental solos.

PERINEAL. An anatomical area located between the external genitals and the anus.

PERIPHERAL NERVE. A nerve in a distant location from the brain that receives information in the form of an impulse from the brain and spinal cord.

PERSECUTORY DELUSIONS. Unrealistic conviction of being harassed, tormented, and persecuted.

PERSON-CENTERED PLANNING. A technique in which a plan for a person's future is developed by a team consisting of the person, family members, service providers and friends (natural supports). The team develops a practical plan based on the person's wishes and dreams. Each team member agrees to perform certain tasks identified in the plan to help the person reach goals.

PERSON-CENTERED THERAPY. A therapeutic approach that believes the client's own drive towards growth and development is the most important factor in healing.

PERSONALITY DISORDER. A personality disorder is a maladaptive pattern of behavior, affect, and/or cognitive style displayed in a broad range of settings. The pattern deviates from the accepted norms of the individual's culture and can occur over a lifetime.

PERSONALITY INVENTORY. A type of psychological test that is designed to assess a client's major personality traits, behavioral patterns, coping styles, and similar characteristics. The Minnesota Multiphasic Personality Inventory is an example of a personality inventory.

PERSONALIZATION. The tendency to refer large-scale events or general patterns of events to the self in inappropriate ways. For example, a person who regards the loss of a friend or relative in an accident as punishment for having quarreled with them before the accident is said to be personalizing the event. Personalization increases a person's risk of developing acute stress disorder or post-traumatic stress disorder after a traumatic event.

PERVASIVE DEVELOPMENTAL DISORDERS (PDDS). A category of childhood disorders that includes Asperger's syndrome and Rett's disorder. The PDDs are sometimes referred to collectively as autistic spectrum disorders.

PET. Abbreviation for positron emission tomography, a highly specialized imaging technique using radioactive substances to identify active tumors, as well as nuerological disease progression.

PETECHIAE. Pinpoint-sized hemorrhages in the skin or a mucous membrane. In bulimia, petechiae may appear in the skin around the eyes as a result of increased pressure in the capillaries caused by vomiting.

PHENCYCLIDINE. The full name of the drug commonly called PCP that is often abused to induce hallucinations.

PHENOL. A white crystalline water-soluble substance used chiefly as an antiseptic and disinfectant.

PHENOMENOLOGICAL THERAPY. A therapeutic approach that focuses on the interpretations individuals place on their experiences.

PHENOTHIAZINES. A class of drugs widely used in the treatment of psychosis.

PHENOTYPE. The observable signs, symptoms, and other aspects of the makeup of an organism. The term is also used sometimes to refer to the appearance of an organism resulting from the interaction between its genotype and its environment.

PHENYLKETONURIA. (PKU) An inherited disease in which the body cannot metabolize the amino acid phenylalanine properly. If untreated, phenylketonuria can cause mental retardation.

PHOBIA. Irrational fear of places, things, or situations that leads to avoidance.

PHONICS. A method of teaching reading and spelling based on the phonetic interpretation of ordinary spelling.

PHONOLOGICAL DISORDER. A developmental disorder of childhood in which the child fails to use speech sounds that are appropriate for his or her age level and native language or dialect.

PHOTON. A light particle.

PHOTOTHERAPY. Another name for light therapy in mainstream medical practice.

PHYSICAL DEPENDENCE. A maladaptive behavior that over a three-month period has caused the individual to experience tolerance and withdrawal symptoms.

PHYSIOLOGY. The branch of medicine concerned with biological processes or functions in the human body or any of its parts.

PHYSOSTIGMINE. A short-acting drug that enhances levels of a substance (acetylcholine) between neurons in the brain.

PICK'S DISEASE. A rare type of primary dementia that affects the frontal lobes of the brain. It is characterized by a progressive loss of social skills, language, and memory, leading to personality changes and sometimes loss of moral judgment.

PLACEBO. An inactive substance or preparation used as a control in experiments with human subjects to test the effectiveness of a drug or herbal preparation. Some patients may experience a medicinal response or experience side effects to a placebo simply because they have faith in its powers even though it contains no medicine.

PLAQUE. A sticky cholesterol-containing substance that builds up on the walls of blood vessels, reducing or blocking blood flow.

PLAQUES. Clumps or clusters of beta amyloid fragments, dead or dying nerve cells, and other cellular debris, found in the brains of patients with Alzheimer's disease.

PLAY THERAPY. A type of psychotherapy for young children involving the use of toys and games to build a therapeutic relationship and encourage the child's self-expression.

PNEUMOTHORAX. A condition in which air or gas is present in the chest cavity.

POLARITY THERAPY. A form of energy therapy influenced by Ayurvedic medicine that integrates bodywork with diet, home exercises, and self-awareness techniques. It is sometimes called polarity balancing.

POLYGENIC. A trait or disorder that is determined by a group of genes acting together. Most human characteristics, including height, weight, and general body build, are polygenic. Schizophrenia and late-onset Alzheimer's disease are considered polygenic disorders.

POLYSOMNOGRAM. A machine that is used to diagnose sleep disorders by measuring and recording a variety of body functions related to sleep, including heart rate, eye movements, brain waves, muscle activity, breathing, changes in blood oxygen concentration, and body position.

PORPHYRIA. A group of disorders that arise from changes in the metabolism of porphyrin, a naturally occurring compound in the body. The disorders are characterized by acute abdominal pain and neurological problems.

PORPHYRIN. Any iron- or magnesium-free pyrrole derivative occurring in many plant or animal tissues.

POSITIVE AFFIRMATION STATEMENTS. Statements repeated to oneself, either aloud or mentally, that reflect attitudes of self-worth.

POSITIVE REINFORCEMENT. A procedure or response that rewards a desired behavior.

POSITIVE SYMPTOMS. Symptoms of schizphrenia that represent excesses or distortions of normal mental functions.

POSITRON. One of the small particles that make up an atom. A positron has the same mass and amount of charge as an electron, but the positron has a positive charge.

POST MORTEM. After death. The definitive diagnosis of Alzheimer's disease can be made only after the patient's death.

POST-TRAUMATIC STRESS DISORDER. A disorder caused by an extremely stressful or traumatic event (such as rape, act of war, or natural disaster) in which the trauma victim is haunted by flashbacks. In the flashbacks, the event is re-experienced in the present. Other symptoms include nightmares and feelings of anxiety.

POSTURAL TREMOR. A continuous quiver that affects body posture and movement.

PRADER-WILLI SYNDROME. A developmental disorder of childhood characterized by mental retardation, poor muscle tone, delayed growth and sexual maturation, and childhood onset of an abnormally large appetite for food.

PRANA. The Sanskrit word for vital energy, roughly equivalent to qi in traditional Chinese medicine.

PRANAYAMA. The breathing exercises that accompany the asanas in hatha yoga.

PRE-MENSTRUAL SYNDROME. A severe change in mood that occurs in women immediately prior to, and during, their menstrual period.

PREECLAMPSIA. A complication of pregnancy characterized by high blood pressure, fluid retention, and protein in the urine. If the patient develops convulsions, the condition is called eclampsia.

PREFERRED PROVIDER ORGANIZATION (PPO). A type of managed care system involving payment contracts with a group or panel of health care providers.

PREMIUM. The cost of enrollment in a health insurance plan. Premiums are usually paid on a monthly basis.

PRESENILE DEMENTIA. An older name for Alzheimer's disease.

PRESSURE ULCERS. Also known as pressure sores or bed sores, these can develop in stroke patients who are unable to move. If not treated properly, they can become infected.

PREVALENCE. Occurence in a population.

PRIAPISM. Persistent abnormal erection of the penis, usually without sexual desire, and accompanied by pain and tenderness.

PRIMARY ENURESIS. Bed-wetting in a child who has not yet developed bladder control.

PRIMARY GAIN. In psychiatry, the principal psychological reason for the development of a patient's symptoms. In conversion disorder, the primary gain from the symptom is the reduction of anxiety and the exclusion of an inner conflict from conscious awareness.

PRIMARY NARCISSISM. Sigmund Freud's term for a normal phase in early childhood development in which the infant has not yet learned to distinguish between itself and its world, and sees other people and things in its environment as extensions of itself.

PRIMARY PERSONALITY. The core personality of a patient with dissociative identity disorder. In women, the primary personality is often timid and passive, and may be diagnosed as depressed.

PRIMARY PULMONARY HYPERTENSION (PPH). A rare but potentially fatal disorder that affects the blood vessels in the lungs.

PRION. A protein particle that lacks nucleic acid.

PROCESS ADDICTION. An addiction to a mood-altering behavior or series of behaviors rather than a substance.

PROCESS-EXPERIENTIAL THERAPIES. A group of therapies based on a person-centered approach that incorporates elements of cognitive and Gestalt therapies.

PRODROMAL. Premonitory; having the character of a warning. The first psychotic episode in schizophrenia is often preceded by a prodromal phase.

PROGRESSIVE RELAXATION. A technique for managing stress in which the person relaxes major muscle groups in a fixed sequence, often beginning with the feet and moving towards the head.

PROJECTION. A psychological process in which a person unconsciously attributes unacceptable feelings to someone else. Narcissists often project their envy onto other people, claiming that the person in question is envious of them.

PROJECTIVE TEST. A psychological test in which the test taker responds to or provides ambiguous, abstract, or unstructured stimuli, often in the form of pictures or drawings. A projective test may assess a person's thinking patterns, observational ability, feelings, and attitudes.

PROLACTIN. A hormone that stimulates milk production and breast development.

PROSTAGLANDINS. A group of unsaturated fatty acids involved in the contraction of smooth muscle, control of inflammation, and many other body processes.

PROSTATE GLAND. The gland at the base of a male's urethra that produces a component of semen.

PROTOCOL. A plan for carrying out a scientific study or a patient's course of treatment.

PSEUDODEMENTIA. A term for a depression with symptoms resembling those of dementia. The term "dementia of depression" is now preferred.

PSEUDOSEIZURE. An attack that resembles an epileptic seizure but is not associated with abnormal electrical discharges in the patient's brain.

PSYCHIATRIC EPIDEMIOLOGY. A field of research for establishing the incidence, distribution or prevalence, and control of mental disorders in a population, including the sum of the factors controlling the presence of mental disorders.

PSYCHIC NUMBING. An inability to respond emotionally with normal intensity to people or situations; this affects positive emotions as well as fear or anger.

PSYCHOACTIVE SUBSTANCE. A drug that produces mood changes and distorted perceptions; a mind-altering drug.

PSYCHOANALYTIC THEORY. A psychological theory proposed by Sigmund Freud involving unconscious conflicts and specific stages of development; central themes include sexuality and male superiority.

PSYCHODRAMA. A specific form of role play that focuses on acting out "scripts" of unresolved issues within the family, or helping family members adopt new approaches and understanding of one another.

PSYCHODYNAMIC. Referring to the motivational forces, unconscious as well as conscious, that form human attitudes and behavior.

PSYCHODYNAMIC GROUPS. Psychotherapy groups that utilize the principles of unconscious needs and motivations developed by Sigmund Freud.

PSYCHODYNAMIC THEORISTS. Therapists who believe that the origins of mental problems lie in a person's internal conflicts and complexes.

PSYCHOEDUCATION. An approach to treatment that combines instruction with various therapeutic techniques.

PSYCHOGENIC. Originating in the mind, or in a mental process or condition. The term "psychogenic" is sometimes used as a synonym for "conversion."

PSYCHOLOGICAL ASSESSMENT. A process of gathering and synthesizing information about a person's psychological makeup and history for a specific purpose, which may be educational, diagnostic, or forensic.

PSYCHOMETRIC. Pertaining to testing and measurement of mental or psychological abilities. Psychometric tests convert an individual's psychological traits and attributes into a numerical estimation or evaluation.

PSYCHOMOTOR. Referring to a response or reaction that involves both the brain and muscular movements.

PSYCHOMOTOR RETARDATION. Slowed mental and physical processes characteristic of a bipolar depressive episode.

PSYCHOMOTOR SEIZURE. A seizure characterized by electrical activity that is characterized by variable degrees of loss of consciousness and often accompanied by bizarre behavior.

PSYCHONEUROTIC. Pertaining to a neurosis or disorder of the brain; emotionally unstable.

PSYCHOPATH. A person who ruthlessly preys on others, using charm, deceit, violence or other methods that allows him or her to get what they want. Another word that is sometimes used for psychopath is sociopath.

PSYCHOPATHY. A psychological syndrome that includes lack of a conscience or sense of guilt, lack of empathy, egocentricity, pathological lying, repeated violations of social norms, disregard of the law, shallow emotions, and a history of victimizing others.

PSYCHOSEXUAL CONFLICTS. In Freudian categories, internal conflicts related to problems at a particular stage of childhood development. Freud associated each developmental stage with a particular part of the human body, such as the mouth or the phallus.

PSYCHOSIS. (Plural: psychoses) Severe state that is characterized by loss of contact with reality and deterioration in normal social functioning; examples are schizophrenia and paranoia. Psychosis is usually one feature of an overarching disorder, not a disorder in itself. Psychotic symptoms include delusions and hallucinations.

PSYCHOSOCIAL. A term that refers to the emotional and social aspects of psychological disorders.

PSYCHOSOMATIC. Physical disorder originating in, or aggravated by, the psychic or emotional processes of the individual.

PSYCHOTIC. Mental disorder characterized by disturbances of personality and a loss of normal association with reality.

PSYCHOTROPIC. Having an effect on the mind, brain, behavior, perceptions, or emotions. Psychotropic medications are used to treat mental illnesses because they affect a patient's moods and perceptions.

PTOSIS. Drooping of the upper eyelid.

PUNISHER. Anything that causes a decrease of a particular behavior.

PUNITIVE. Concerned with, or directed toward, punishment.

PURGING. Inappropriate actions taken to prevent weight gain, often after bingeing, including self-induced vomiting or the misuse of laxatives, diuretics, enemas, or other medications.

Q

QI. The Chinese term for energy, life force, or vital force.

QIGONG. A traditional form of Chinese energy therapy that includes physical exercises, breathing techniques, postures, and mental discipline. Internal qigong refers to exercises practiced to maintain one's own health and vitality; external qigong refers to the transfer of energy from a qigong master to another person for healing purposes. External qigong is also known as medical qigong.

QUICKENING. A term that refers to the movements or other signs of life of a fetus in the womb.

R

RADIO WAVES. Electromagnetic energy of the frequency range corresponding to that used in radio communications, usually 10,000 cycles per second to 300 billion cycles per second. Radio waves are the same as visible light, x rays, and all other types of electromagnetic radiation, but are of a higher frequency.

RADIOLOGIST. A medical doctor specially trained in radiology (x ray) interpretation and its use in the diagnosis of disease and injury.

RAPID EYE MOVEMENT (REM) SLEEP. A type of sleep during which the person's eyes move back and forth rapidly underneath their closed eyelids. REM sleep is associated with dreaming.

RAPPORT. A relation of empathy and trust between a therapist and patient.

RATIONAL EMOTIVE THERAPY. A form of psychotherapy developed by Albert Ellis and other psychotherapists based on the theory that emotional response is based on the subjective interpretation of events, not on the events themselves.

RAYNAUD'S SYNDROME. A disorder of the circulatory or vascular system characterized by abnormally cold hands and feet because of constricted blood vessels in these areas.

REALITY TESTING. A phrase that refers to a person's ability to distinguish between subjective feelings and objective reality. A person who knows that their body is real even though they may be experiencing it as unreal, for example, is said to have intact reality testing.

REBOUND EFFECT. A physical reaction to stopping a medication characterized by the reappearance of the symptom that the medication was given to suppress. For example, people who stop taking a sedative may experience rebound insomnia.

RECIDIVISM. A tendency to return to a previously treated activity, or repeated relapse into criminal or deviant behavior.

REFERENTIAL. A type of delusion in which the person misinterprets items, minor occurrences, or other people's behavior as referring to them. Misinterpretations of this sort that are not as resistant to reality as a delusion are sometimes called ideas of reference.

REFOCUSING TECHNIQUES. Techniques that direct one's attention away from overwhelming, negative thoughts and emotions by focusing on inner peace and managing one issue at a time.

REGIMEN. A regulated course of treatment for a medical or mental disorder.

REGISTERED DIETITIAN. A person who has met certain education and experience standards and is well-qualified to provide nutrition counseling.

REGURGITATION. The return of partly digested food from the stomach to the mouth. Regurgitation may be either an intentional act or an involuntary physical reaction.

REHABILITATAIVE. To restore; to put back into good condition.

REIKI. A form of energy therapy that originated in Japan. Reiki practitioners hold their hands on or slightly above specific points on the patient's body in order to convey universal life energy to that area for healing.

REINFORCEMENT. Praise or criticism (or, in substance use, physical consequences) that make a behavior more or less likely in the future. Positive reinforcement (like praise or rewards) increase the likelihood of the behavior, and negative reinforcement (such as criticism or withholding of rewards) decrease the likelihood of the behavior.

REINFORCEMENT SCHEDULE. The frequency and amount of reinforcers administered.

REINFORCER. Anything that causes an increase of a particular behavior.

RELAPSE. A person experiences a relapse when he or she re-engages in a behavior that is harmful and that he or she was trying to change or eliminate. Relapse is a common occurrence after treatment for many disorders, including addictions and eating disorders.

RELAXATION RESPONSE. The body's inactivation of stress responses and return of stress hormone levels to normal after a threat has passed.

RELIABILITY. The ability of a test to yield consistent, repeatable results.

REMISSION. In the course of an illness or disorder, a period of time when symptoms are absent.

REPETITIVE STRESS INJURY (RSI). A type of injury to the musculoskeletal and nervous systems associated with occupational strain or overuse of a specific part of the body.

RESPIRATORY DEPRESSION. Significant impairment of the respiratory system.

RESPONSE COST. A behavioral technique that involves removing a stimulus from an individual's environment so that the response that directly precedes the removal is weakened. In a token economy system, response cost is a form of punishment involving loss of tokens due to inappropriate behavior, which consequently results in decreased ability to purchase back-up reinforcers.

RESPONSE-CONTINGENT. An approach to treatment in which rewards or punishments are given in response to a particular behavior to be encouraged or corrected.

RESPONSE-CONTINGENT LEARNING. A principle that posits that the consequences of a behavior determine whether it will increase or decrease in frequency. Behaviors that bring about desired responses tend to increase, while those that either remove the chance to obtain a desirable outcome, or those that cause some unpleasant or painful consequence, tend to decrease.

RETROGRADE AMNESIA. Amnesia for events that occurred before a traumatic injury.

RETROPERITONEAL. The anatomical area between the peritoneum (lining of the abdominal cavity) and the muscular and connective tissues of the abdominal wall.

RHIZOME. The fleshy underground horizontal root of certain plants. Valerian preparations are made from dried rhizomes as well as from roots of the valerian plant.

RISK ASSESSMENT. The process of gathering and interpreting data useful in estimating the probability that an individual will demonstrate violence.

RISK MANAGEMENT PLAN. Using the results of a risk assessment to tailor intervention strategies intended to reduce the probability that an individual will demonstrate violence.

ROLE. The set of customary or expected behavior patterns associated with a particular position or function in society. For example, a person's role as mother is associated with one set of expected behaviors, and her role as a worker with a very different set.

ROLE TRANSITION. Life changes that require an alteration in one's social or occupational status or self-image.

ROLE-PLAYING. A technique used in assertiveness training and other forms of therapy in which participants act out roles relevant to real-life situations in order to change their attitudes and behaviors.

RORSCHACH TEST. Also known as the Rorschach Psychodiagnostic Test. A commonly administered projective measure in which subjects are asked to describe a series of black or colored inkblots. The inkblots allow the patient to project his or her interpretations, which can be used to diagnose particular disorders.

RUMINATE. To chew or rechew regurgitated food.

RUMINATION. A tendency to dwell on certain thoughts, particularly negative ones, repeatedly or obsessively.

RUSH. The initial intensely pleasurable sensation experienced from injecting a narcotic or stimulant drug. The term has also been applied to the feeling of excitement experienced from the behaviors involved in process addictions.

S

SADISM. A mental disorder in which sexual arousal and gratification are obtained by inflicting pain or humiliation on another person.

SCALE. A subset of test items from a multi-item test.

SCAPEGOATING. the emergence of behavioral problems in one family member, usually the identified patient, who is often punished for problems within the entire family.

SCHILDER'S DISEASE. A disturbance of the white matter of the brain that causes blindness, deafness, and mental deterioration

SCHIZOAFFECTIVE DISORDER. A mental disorder that shows a combination of symptoms of mania and schizophrenia.

SCHIZOPHRENIA. A severe mental illness in which a person has difficulty distinguishing what is real from what is not real. It is often characterized by hallucinations, delusions, language and communication disturbances, and withdrawal from people and social activities.

SCHNEIDERIAN SYMPTOMS. Another name for first-rank symptoms of schizophrenia.

SCOLIOSIS. An abnormal lateral (sidewise) curvature of the spine.

SCREENING TEST. A test given as a preliminary tool, that helps to later target a more thorough analysis.

SEASONAL AFFECTIVE DISORDER (SAD). A mood disorder characterized by depression, weight gain, and sleepiness during the winter months. An estimated 4–6% of the population of Canada and the northern United States suffers from SAD.

SECONDARY BEHAVIORS. Negative behavioral, emotional, or cognitive reactions to stuttering.

SECONDARY ENURESIS. Bed-wetting in a child who has established bladder control but has begun to wet the bed again, usually as the result of emotional stress.

SECONDARY GAIN. A term that refers to other benefits that a patient obtains from a conversion symptom. For example, a patient's loss of function in an arm might require other family members to do the patient's share of household chores; or they might give the patient more attention and sympathy than he or she usually receives.

SECTION 504. This section of the Rehabilitation Act of 1973 provides that no person may be discriminated against because of a physical disability.

SEDATION. A state of emotional or physical relaxation. The term is usually used to refer to this condition when it is produced by a medication.

SEDATIVE. A medication that induces relaxation and sleep.

SELECTIVE SEROTONIN REUPTAKE INHIBITORS (SSRIS). Commonly prescribed drugs for treating depression. SSRIs affect the chemicals that nerves in the brain use to send messages to one another. These chemical messengers (neurotransmitters) are released by one nerve cell and taken up by others. Neurotransmitters not taken up by other nerve cells are taken up by the same cells that released them. This process is termed "reuptake." SSRIs work by inhibiting the reuptake of serotonin, an action which allows more serotonin to be taken up by other nerve cells.

SELF-ACTUALIZATION. The belief that all human beings have an inborn tendency toward growth and self-improvement.

SELF-CONCEPT. Attitudes about oneself.

SELF-EFFICACY. One's belief about how well he or she can perform a given task, regardless of that person's actual ability.

SELF-HELP GROUPS. Groups that fall outside the realm of psychotherapy groups, but that offer help to individuals around a particular problem or concern. These groups typically are not professionally led.

SELF-INSTRUCTIONAL TRAINING. Teaches individuals to become aware of their self-statements, evaluate whether these self-statements are helpful or hindering, and replace maladaptive self-statements with adaptive ones.

SELF-RATED. A term in psychological testing that means that the person taking the test is the one who decides whether a question applies to them and records the answer, as distinct from an examiner's evaluating and recording answers.

SEMANTIC-PRAGMATIC DISORDER. A term that refers to the difficulty that some children with pervasive developmental disorders have with pragmatic language skills. Pragmatic language skills include knowing the proper tone of voice for a given context, using humor appropriately, making eye contact with a conversation partner, maintaining the appropriate volume of one's voice, etc.

SEMEN. A thick whitish fluid containing sperm, produced by the male reproductive organs.

SEMINAL VESICLES. Sac-like structures bordering the male urethra and serving as storage depots for seminal fluid.

SENSITIVITY TRAINING. Training conducted in T-groups to reduce tensions and racial prejudice among the public.

SENSITIZATION. To make sensitive or susceptible.

SENSORY INTEGRATION THERAPY. A treatment that was originally designed for children with autism. Sensory integration therapy is often performed by occupational or physical therapists; its goal is to help the child with autism process information acquired through the senses (hearing, touch, taste, and smell as well as sight) more effectively.

SEQUELA (PLURAL, SEQUELAE). An abnormal condition resulting from a previous disease or disorder. An episode of depression is a common sequela of acute stress disorder.

SEROTONERGIC. Containing, activating, or otherwise involving serotonin, which is a chemical that aids in the transmission of nerve impulses.

SEROTONIN. A widely distributed neurotransmitter that is found in blood platelets, the lining of the digestive tract, and the brain, and that works in combination with norepinephrine. It causes very powerful contractions of smooth muscle, and is associated with mood, attention, emotions, and sleep. Low levels of serotonin are associated with depression.

SEROTONIN SYNDROME. A condition characterized by at least three of the following symptoms: diarrhea, fever, extreme perspiration, mood or behavior changes, overactive reflexes, fast heart rate, restlessness, shivering or shaking. It is a result of too much serotonin in the body.

SEXUAL VIOLENCE. Actual, attempted or threatened sexual contact with a person who is non-consenting or unable to give consent.

SHAMAN. In certain indigenous tribes or groups, a person who acts as an intermediary between the natural and supernatural worlds. Shamans are regarded as having the power or ability to cure illnesses.

SHAPING. A technique used in teaching social skills by prompting and reinforcing behaviors that come close to the desired behavior.

SHIFT. The transition of control from one alter to another in a person with dissociative identity disorder. Usually shifts occur rapidly, within seconds but in some cases a more gradual change over is observed. Also referred to as a switch.

SHORT-CIRCUITING OF CONTINGENCIES. The proper reinforcer or punisher for a given behavior is not administered.

SIBLING RIVALRY. Competition among brothers and sisters in a nuclear family. It is considered to be an important influence in shaping the personalities of children who grow up in middle-class Western societies but less relevant in traditional African and Asian cultures.

SIMPLE PHOBIA. An older term for specific phobia.

SKILLED NURSING FACILITY. An inpatient facility that provides 24-hour nursing services to individuals in need of extended care.

SLE (SYSTEMIC LUPUS ERYTHEMATOSUS). An autoimmune disease that leads to inflammation and damage to various body tissues and parts, including joints, skin, kidneys, heart, lungs, blood vessels, and brain.

SLEEP APNEA. Short periods in which a person stops breathing during sleep. Breathing re-starts spontaneously; however, this condition can lead a lack of oxygen in the body.

SLEEP PARALYSIS. An abnormal episode of sleep in which the patient cannot move for a few minutes, usually occurring while falling asleep or waking up. Sleep paralysis is often found in patients with narcolepsy.

SLEEP TERROR DISORDER. A sleep disorder that is distinguished from nightmare disorder by the intensity of associated anxiety symptoms, the absence of complete wakefulness, and the person's difficulty recalling the episode.

SLOW SUICIDE. A term used to refer to lifestyle behaviors known to shorten life expectancy, such as smoking, drinking heavily, having unsafe sex, etc.

SOCIAL COGNITIVE THEORY. The theory that behavior is determined by an interaction between cognitive, behavioral, and environmental factors.

SOCIAL LEARNING. Learning by observing others' responses and acquiring those responses through imitation of the role model(s).

SOCIAL LEARNING THEORY. A subset of learning theories based on the concept that human behavior originates in and is affected by the interplay among the person's learned experiences, previous behaviors, and environmental influences.

SOCIAL MODELING. A process of learning behavioral and emotional response patterns from observing one's parents or other adults. Some researchers think that social modeling plays a part in the development of conversion disorder in children.

SOCIAL PERSPECTIVE-TAKING. A skill that involves a person's capacity to perceive or recognize other people's thoughts and feelings.

SOCIALIZATION. An ongoing process in which a person learns and internalizes the values and behavior patterns of his or her culture and social group.

SOLUTION-FOCUSED THERAPY. A type of therapy that involves concrete goals and an emphasis on future direction rather than past experiences.

SOMATIC. Relating to the body or to the physical.

SOMATIC CONCERN. Excessive concern about the body, particularly in relation to illness.

SOMATIC EDUCATION. A term used in both Hellerwork and the Feldenkrais method to describe the integration of bodywork with self-awareness, intelligence, and imagination.

SOMATIZATION. When mental or emotional distress is expressed physically in a way that disrupts body function.

SOMATIZATION DISORDER. A type of mental disorder in which the patient suffers from physical complaints that serve as coping strategies for emotional distress.

SOMATOFORM. Referring to physical symptoms with a psychological origin.

SOMATOFORM DISORDERS. A group of psychiatric disorders that are characterized by external physical symptoms or complaints.

SPECIFIC PHOBIA. A type of phobia in which the object or situation that arouses fear is clearly identifiable and limited. An older term for specific phobia is simple phobia.

SPECT. Abbreviation for single photon emission computerized tomography, a highly specialized imaging technique using radioactive substances used in research, and to identify neurological disorder/disease progression.

SPEECH-LANGUAGE PATHOLOGIST. Specialist trained in assessment and diagnosis of communication disorders.

SPIRAL CT. Also referred to as helical CT, this method allows for continuous 360-degree x-ray image capture.

SPLITTING. A psychological process that occurs during the childhood of a person with NPD, in which the child separates aspects of him- or herself that the parents value from those that they disregard.

SPONTANEOUS REMISSION. Recovery from a disease or disorder that cannot be attributed to medical or psychiatric treatments.

STALKING. The intentional pursuit or surveillance of another person, usually with the intent of forcing that person into a dating or marriage relationship. Stalking is now punishable as a crime in all 50 states.

STANDARD DEVIATION. A measure of variability in a set of scores. The standard deviations are based on a comparison to others in the same age group.

STANDARDIZATION. The administration of a test to a sample group of people for the purpose of establishing test norms.

STANDARDIZED TEST. A test that follows a regimented structure, and each individual's scores may be compared with those of groups of people.

STIGMA. A mark or characteristic trait of a disease or defect; by extension, a cause for reproach or a stain on one's reputation. Such sexually transmitted diseases as HIV infection carry a severe social stigma.

STIMULUS. Something that incites or moves a person to thought, emotion, or action. In mainstream psychotherapy, a stimulus can be anything from a certain picture or image to a smell, a sound, or a word or idea. In aversion therapy, the stimulus is typically a mild electric shock or a medication that produces unpleasant results.

STIMULUS FADING. A form of behavior modification used to treat children with selective mutism, in which goals of gradually increasing difficulty are set for the child.

STOOLS. Feces, bowel movements.

STREPTOCOCCUS (PLURAL, STREPTOCOCCI). A type of bacterium that is spherical in shape and occurs in chains or pairs. Some diseases that are caused by streptococci appear to be related to obsessive-compulsive disorder.

STRESS. A physical and psychological response that results from being exposed to a demand or pressure.

STRESS MANAGEMENT. A set of techniques and programs intended to help people cope more effectively with stress in their lives by analyzing the specific stressors and taking positive actions to minimize their effects. Most stress management programs deal with job stress and workplace issues.

STRESSOR. A stimulus or event that provokes a stress response in an organism. Stressors can be categorized as acute or chronic, and as external or internal to the organism.

STRIATUM. A part of the basal ganglia, a deep structure in the cerebral hemisphere of the brain. Abnormally high levels of dopamine in the striatum are thought to be related to the delusions and hallucinations of schizophrenia.

STRUCTURAL INTEGRATION. The term used to describe the method and philosophy of life associated with Rolfing. Its fundamental concept is the vertical line.

STUPOR. A trance-like state that causes a person to appear numb to their environment.

SUBDURAL HEMATOMA. Active bleeding or a blood clot inside the dura (leathery covering of the brain). This bleeding or clot causes swelling of the brain, and, untreated, the condition can cause death.

SUBJECTIVE. Referring to a person's unique internal thoughts and feelings, as distinct from the objects of those thoughts and feelings in the eternal world.

SUBJECTIVE UNITS OF DISTRESS (SUDS) SCALE. A scale used by patients during exposure treatment to rate their levels of fear and anxiety with numbers from zero to 100.

SUBSTANCE ABUSE DISORDER. Disorder that is characterized by: an individual's need for more of a drug or alcohol than intended, an inability to stop using by choice, and an ongoing difficulty in recovering from the effects of the substance.

SUBSTANTIA NIGRA. Dark-colored matter located in a section of the crus cerebri area of the brain.

SUDDEN SNIFFING DEATH. Death resulting from heart failure caused by heavy use of inhalants in a single lengthy session.

SUICIDE GESTURE. Attempted suicide characterized by a low-lethality method, low level of intent or planning, and little physical damage. Pseudocide is another term for a suicide gesture.

SUPEREGO. According to Freud, the part of the mind that represents traditional parental and societal values. The superego is the source of guilt feelings.

SUPPLEMENTAL SECURITY INCOME. A federal program that provides cash to meet basic needs for food, shelter and clothing for aged, blind, and disabled individuals who have little or no income.

SUPPORT GROUP. A group whose primary purpose is the provision of empathy and emotional support for its members. Support groups are less formal and less goal-directed than group therapy.

SUPPORTIVE THERAPY. An approach to psychotherapy that seeks to encourage the patient or offer emotional support to him or her, as distinct from insight-oriented or educational approaches to treatment.

SURVIVOR'S GUILT. A psychological reaction in trauma survivors that takes the form of guilt feelings for having survived or escaped a trauma without serious injury when others did not.

SYDENHAM'S CHOREA. A serious manifestation of acute rheumatic fever that commonly occurs in children ages seven through 14, peaking at age eight. This disease of the central nervous system is characterized by emotional instability, purposeless movements, and muscular weakness. At its peak in the 1950s it occured in nearly 50% of the acute rheumatic fever cases, but by 2002 had subsided to a degree of less than 10% of the acute cases.

SYNAPTIC CLEFT. An area between nerve cells that can contain neurotransmitters.

SYNCOPE. A brief lapse of consciousness caused by a temporarily insufficient flow of blood to the brain.

SYNDROME. A group of symptoms that together characterize a disease or disorder.

SYSTOLIC. Referring to the rhythmic contraction of the heart (systole), when the blood in the chambers of the heart is forced out. Systolic blood pressure is blood pressure measured during this phase.

T

T-GROUPS. Short for "basic skills training groups" that are focused on education and discussion regarding social issues, personal problems experienced outside the group setting, and problems from one's past.

TACHYCARDIA. A pulse rate above 100 beats per minute.

TACTILE/TACTUAL. Perceptible by touch.

TANNIN. An astringent compound found in chamomile, oak bark, and certain other plants. Tannin in large quantities can interfere with iron absorption.

TARDIVE DYSKINESIA. A condition that involves involuntary movements of the tongue, jaw, mouth or face or other groups of skeletal muscles that usually occurs late in antipsychotic therapy or even after the therapy is discontinued. It may be irreversible.

TARGET BEHAVIOR. The specific behavior to be increased or decreased during treatment.

TAU PROTEIN. A protein that is involved in maintaining the internal structure of nerve cells. The tau protein is damaged in Alzheimer's disease and ends up forming the neurofibrillary tangles.

TEMPERAMENT. A person's natural disposition or inborn combination of mental and emotional traits.

TEMPORAL LOBE. Large lobe of each side of the brain that contains a sensory area associated with hearing.

TEMPOROMANDIBULAR JOINT DISORDER (TMJ). Inflammation, irritation, pain, limited range of motion, and clicking sounds in the jaw caused by improper opening and closing of the joint.

TEMPOROMANDIBULAR JOINT DYSFUNCTION. Condition resulting in pain in the head, face, and jaw. Muscle tension or abnormalities of the bones in the area of the hinged joint (the temporomandibular joint) between the lower jaw and the temporal bone are usually the cause.

TERMINATION. The important process of ending a therapy group.

TETRAHYDRACANNABINOL (THC). The active substance in marijuana.

THALAMUS. The middle part of the diencephalon (a part of the human forebrain), responsible for transmitting and integrating information from the senses.

THEMATIC APPERCEPTION TEST (TAT). A projective test using stories and descriptions of pictures to reveal some of the dominant drives, emotions, sentiments, conflicts, and complexes of a personality.

THEMATIC DREAM MATERIAL. Psychoanalysts use the technique of dream interpretation to offer patients insight into their unconscious conflicts. The dreams of patients include themes, notions, or underlying ideas about specific objects, situations, or issues. When patients begin to understand the content or themes of their dreams, they may gain insight into their unconscious motives.

THERAPEUTIC ALLIANCE. The technical term for the cooperative relationship between therapist and patient that is considered essential for successful psychotherapy.

THERAPEUTIC DYAD. A term that refers to the two people involved in a psychotherapeutic relationship, namely the therapist and the person seeking treatment.

THERAPEUTIC LETTER. A letter written to the deceased in order to help the survivors express feelings and thoughts they may not have been able to before the loss.

THERAPEUTIC TOUCH (TT). An American form of energy therapy based on the ancient tradition of the laying-on of hands. TT is thought to work by removing energy blockages or disturbances from the patient's aura.

THERAPEUTIC VALUE. The potential benefit of an object or situation, in terms of its ability to enhance functioning (social, emotional, intellectual, occupational, etc.) in an individual.

THERAPEUTIC WRITING. A treatment technique in which patients are asked to set down in writing an account of the traumatic event and their emotional responses to it.

THERMISTOR. An electrical device whose resistance decreases with rises in temperature.

THIAMIN. A B-vitamin that is essential to normal metabolism and nerve function, and whose absorption is affected by alcoholism.

THORACIC. Refers to the chest area. The thorax runs between the abdomen and neck and is encased in the ribs.

THOUGHT INSERTION/WITHDRAWAL. The notion that an outside force (space aliens, evil people, etc.) can put thoughts or ideas into one's mind or remove them. It is considered one of the first-rank symptoms of schizophrenia.

THROMBOCYTOPENIA. A condition involving abnormally low numbers of platelets (blood-clotting agents) in the blood; usually associated with hemorrhaging (bleeding).

THYROID. A gland in the neck that produces the hormone thyroxin, which is responsible for regulating metabolic activity in the body. Supplemental synthetic thyroid hormone is available as pills taken daily when the thyroid fails to produce enough hormone.

THYROID HORMONE. A complex hormone that regulates metabolic rate of all cells.

THYROTOXICOSIS. A disease characterized by an enlarged thyroid gland and speeded-up body metabolism caused by excessive thyroid secretion. It is also known as Graves' disease.

TIC. A sudden involuntary behavior that is difficult or impossible for the person to suppress. Tics may be either motor (related to movement) or vocal, and may become more pronounced under stress.

TINCTURE. An alcohol-based herbal extract prepared by soaking parts of the plant in a mixture of alcohol and water. Established ratios and dilutions are followed.

TISSUE PLASMINOGEN ACTIVATOR (TPA). A drug that is sometimes given to patients within three hours of a stroke to dissolve blood clots within the brain; also used to treat heart attack victims.

TOKEN. Any item that can be seen and collected (such as stickers or points in a point tally) that has no value of its own, but is used as an immediate reward for desirable behavior that is later exchanged for back-up reinforcers.

TOLERANCE. Progressive decrease in the effectiveness of a drug with long-term use.

TONIC-CLONIC (GRAND MAL) SEIZURE. This is the most common type of seizure and is categorized into several phases beginning with vague symptoms hours or days before an attack. During the seizure, there is abnormal muscle contraction and relaxation and the individual may lose consciousness.

TOPICAL. A type of medication or preparation intended for use on the skin or external surface of the body.

TORPOR. Sluggishness or inactivity.

TOURETTE SYNDROME. Neurological disorder characterized by multiple involuntary movements and uncontrollable vocalizations called tics that come and go over years, usually beginning in childhood and becoming chronic. Sometimes the tics include inappropriate language.

TOURNIQUET. A rubber tube or length of cloth that is used to compress a blood vessel in order to stop bleeding or to shut off circulation in a part of the body. The tourniquet is wrapped around the arm (or other limb) and tightened by twisting.

TOXICOLOGY SCREEN. A blood or urine test that detects the presence of toxic chemicals, alcohol, or drugs in body fluids.

TOXOCARIASIS. Infection with roundworm larvae, commonly transmitted by the feces of dogs and cats.

TOXOPLASMOSIS. A parasitic infection caused by the intracellular protozoan *Toxoplasmosis gondii*. Humans are most commonly infected by swallowing the oocyte form of the parasite in soil (or kitty litter) contaminated by feces from an infected cat; or by swallowing the cyst form of the parasite in raw or undercooked meat.

TRACE MINERAL. An element essential to nutrition or bodily processes that is found in minute quantities.

TRACHEOSTOMY. A surgical procedure in which an artificial opening is made in the patient's windpipe to relieve airway obstruction.

TRAIT ANXIETY. A type of persistent anxiety found in some patients with generalized anxiety disorder. Trait anxiety is regarded as a feature (trait) of a person's temperament.

TRANQUILIZER. A medication that induces a feeling of calm and relaxation.

TRANSCENDENTAL MEDITATION (TM). A meditation technique based on Hindu practices that involves the repetition of a mantra.

TRANSSEXUAL. A person whose gender identity is opposite his or her biologic sex.

TRANSVESTITE. A person who derives sexual pleasure or gratification from dressing in clothing of the opposite sex.

TRAUMA. A disastrous or life-threatening event that can cause severe emotional distress, including dissociative symptoms and disorders.

TREMOR. Involuntary shaking of the hands and arms.

TREPANATION OR TREPANNING. Surgical removal of a piece of the skull to expose the brain.

TRIANGLING. A process in which two family members diminish the tension between them by drawing in a third member.

TRICHOBEZOAR. A hairball that results from a buildup of swallowed hairs becoming lodged in the digestive system.

TRICHOPHAGIA. Eating hair.

TRICHOPHAGY. Biting hair.

TRICHOTILLOMANIA. A disorder marked by repeated pulling and tugging of one's hair, usually resulting in noticeable hair loss on the scalp or elsewhere on the body.

TRICHURIASIS. Infection with the larvae of roundworms. These parasites may live for 10–20 years in humans.

TRICYCLIC ANTIDEPRESSANTS (TCAS). Antidepressant medications that have the common characteristic of a three-ring nucleus in their chemical structure. Imipramine and amitriptyline are examples of tricyclic antidepressants.

TRIGGER. Any situation (people, places, times, events, etc.) that causes one to experience a negative emotional reaction, which is often accompanied by a display of symptoms or problematic behavior.

TRIGLYCERIDES. Fats in the blood.

TRISOMY. An abnormality in chromosomal development. Chromosomes are the structures within a cell that carry its genetic information. They are organized in pairs. Humans have 23 pairs of chromosomes. In a trisomy syndrome, an extra chromosome is present so that the individual has three of a particular chromosome instead of the normal pair. An extra chromosome 18 (trisomy 18) causes mental retardation.

TRYPTOPHAN. An essential amino acid released from proteins during the process of digestion. Tryptophan is an important ingredient in the body's production of serotonin.

TSUBO. In shiatsu, a center of high energy located along one of the body's meridians. Stimulation of the tsubos during a shiatsu treatment is thought to rebalance the flow of vital energy in the body.

TUBERCULOSIS. An infection caused by the bacteria *Mycobacterium tuberculosis* that usually affects the lungs. Individuals with tuberculosis may have nighttime sweating, fever, weight loss, cough, and may spit up blood and mucus.

TYPE II DIABETES. Resistance to the effects of insulin in the presence of normal or elevated insulin levels, resulting in failure of glucose to enter cells and in a cascade of other abnormal physiologic reactions.

TYRAMINE. Intermediate product between the chemicals tyrosine and epinephrine in the body and a substance normally found in many foods. Found especially in protein-rich foods that have been aged or fermented, pickled, or bacterially contaminated, such as cheese, beer, yeast, wine, and chicken liver.

U

ULTRASONOGRAPHY. A process that uses the reflection of high-frequency sound waves to make an image of structures deep within the body. Ultrasonography is routinely used to detect fetal abnormalities. In stroke victims, a cardiac ultrasound, or echocardiogram, allows the beating heart to be examined.

UNCONDITIONAL POSITIVE REGARD. A quality of the client-centered therapist, characterized by the therapist's acceptance of the client without judgment.

UNIVERSALITY. The feeling of being isolated, unique, and separate from others, often experienced by therapy group members.

URETHRA. The tubular passage conducting urine from the bladder to the exterior. In the male, the urethra traverses the penis.

URETHRITIS. Inflammation of the urethra, which is the duct that carries urine and (in males) semen to the outside of the body.

URINARY INCONTINENCE. A term that is sometimes used for enuresis in adults. Urinary incontinence is often found in patients with late-stage Alzheimer's disease or other adult-onset dementias.

URINARY RETENTION. Excessive storage of urine in the body.

URINARY SYSTEM. The kidney, urethra, bladder, and associated organs that process urine and eliminate it from the body.

UTERUS. The hollow muscular sac in which a fetus develops; sometimes called the womb.

UTILIZATION REVIEW. A process used by managed care organizations involving scrutiny of service care delivery to determine whether services are necessary.

V

VAGINA. The part of the female reproductive system that opens to the exterior of the body and into which the penis is inserted during sexual intercourse.

VAGINISMUS. An involuntary tightening of the vaginal muscles that makes sexual intercourse painful, difficult, or impossible.

VALERENIC ACID. The primary medicinal component in valerian preparations.

VALIDITY. The ability of a test to measure accurately what it claims to measure.

VASCULAR. Pertaining to the bloodstream (arteries, veins, and blood vessels).

VETERAN'S ADMINISTRATION HOSPITALS. Medical facilities operated by the federal government explicitly for veterans of the United States military.

VICARIOUS. Acquired through imagined participation in the experience of others. Modeling is a form of vicarious learning.

VIRTUAL REALITY. A realistic simulation of an environment, produced by a computer system using interactive hardware and software.

VOLATILE SOLVENT. A solvent (substance that will dissolve another substance) that evaporates at room temperature.

VOYEUR. A person who engages in the behavior of voyeurism.

VOYEURISM. A paraphilia that involves watching unsuspecting people, usually strangers, undress or engage in sexual activity.

VULVAR VESTIBULITIS SYNDROME (VVS). Vulvar vestibulitis syndrome is thought to be the most frequent cause of dyspareunia in premenopausal women. A chronic, persistent clinical syndrome, vulvar vestibulitis is characterized by severe pain on vestibular touch or attempted vaginal entry.

W

WAXY FLEXIBILITY. A condition in which a person can be molded into a strange position and hold that position for a long period of time.

WERNICKE'S SYNDROME. A group of symptoms that appears in some people who are dependent on alcohol. Due to low levels of thiamin, the syndrome results in disordered eye movements, very poor balance and difficulty walking.

WERNICKE-KORSAKOFF SYNDROME. Group of symptoms that appears in people who are dependent on alcohol. The syndrome is due to a thiamin deficiency, and severely affects one's memory, preventing new learning from taking place.

WITHDRAWAL. Symptoms experienced by a person who has become physically dependent on a drug, experienced when the drug use is discontinued.

WRAPAROUND. A relatively new form of mental health service delivery that strives to accommodate all family members based on self-defined needs, flexibly incorporating both formal and informal community services.

X

XANTHINE. A class of crystalline nitrogenous compounds that includes caffeine.

Y

YIN AND YANG. In traditional Chinese medicine and philosophy, a pair of opposing forces whose harmonious balance in the body is necessary to good health.

YOGA. A system of exercises for achieving bodily or mental control and well-being.

YOGI (FEMININE, YOGINI). A person who is a respected expert in or teacher of yoga.

GENERAL INDEX

References to individual volumes are listed before colons; numbers following a colon refer to page numbers. A **boldface** page number indicates the main essay for a topic. An *italicized* page number refers to a photo or illustration.

A

B

C

D

F

G

H

I

J

K

L

M

O

P

Q

R

S

T

U

V

W

X

Y

Z

DATE DUE

R
616.89
GAL

Gale encyclopedia of mental
disorders V.2

Paul Lawrence Dunbar High School
Price: $275.00/Set
Date of Purchase: 11/27/02